The Marketing Book

Fifth Edition

Edited by
MICHAEL J. BAKER

OXFORD AMSTERDAM BOSTON LONDON NEW YORK PARIS
SAN DIEGO SAN FRANCISCO SINGAPORE SYDNEY TOKYO

Butterworth-Heinemann
An imprint of Elsevier Science
Linacre House, Jordan Hill, Oxford OX2 8DP
200 Wheeler Road, Burlington MA 01803

First published 1987
Reprinted 1987, 1990 (twice)
Second edition, 1991
Reprinted 1992, 1993
Third edition, 1994
Reprinted 1995, 1997
Fourth edition 1999
Reprinted 2000, 2001
Fifth edition, 2003

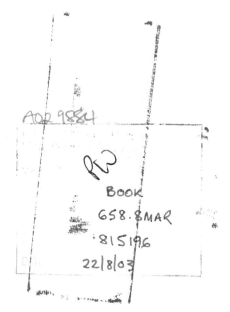

British Library Cataloguing in Publication Data
A catalogue record for this book is available from the British Library

Library of Congress Cataloguing in Publication Data
A catalogue record for this book is available from the Library of Congress

ISBN 0 7506 5536 4

For information on all Butterworth-Heinemann publications visit
our website at: www.bh.com

Composition by Genesis Typesetting, Rochester, Kent
Printed and bound in Great Britain

Contents

Illustrations

Tables

Contributors

Sue Adkins is the director and founder of the Cause Related Marketing Campaign at Business in the Community. Sue's responsibility has been to define Cause Related Marketing and put it on the map in the UK. Sue and the Business in the Community Cause Related Marketing Campaign is acknowledged for having been fundamental in raising the awareness and understanding of Cause Related Marketing leading to its development in the UK. Sue is recognised as an international expert in this area and has spoken around the world at events ranging from national and international conferences, to sharing platforms with Government ministers and lecturing at universities and business schools, whilst acting as consultant to a variety of companies. She is the author of *Cause Related Marketing: Who Cares Wins* (Butterworth-Heinemann, 1999) and has contributed to numerous books and written hundreds of articles on the subject.

Before joining Business in the Community, Sue worked for Sampson Tyrrell (now Enterprise IG), part of the WPP Group, and prior to this Sue was in marketing for InterCity, responsible for its business products portfolio, and worked for Boots plc in both buying and marketing.

In her spare time, Sue is a school governor, the trustee of a charity and an obsessive Milliner.

Michael J. Baker, TD, BA, BSc(Econ), Cert ITP, DBA, Hon. LL.D., DipM, FCIM, FCAM, FRSA, FSCOTVEC, FRSE, FAM is Emeritus Professor of Marketing at the University of Strathclyde where he founded the Department of Marketing in 1971. He served as Dean of the Strathclyde Business School from 1978 to 1984, Deputy Principal of the University from 1984 to 1991 and Senior Adviser to the Principal 1991–1994. He has served as Chairman of SCOTBEC, the Chartered Institute of Marketing and the Marketing Education Group, as a Governor of the CAM Foundation and Member of the ESRC and UGC. He is the author/editor of more than twenty books of which the best known are *Marketing* (Macmillan, 6th edition, 1996), *Dictionary of Marketing and Advertising* (Macmillan, 3rd edition, 1998), and *Marketing Strategy and Management* (Macmillan, 3rd edition, 1999). A member of numerous editorial boards he was also the Founding Editor of the *Journal of Marketing Management*. He has extensive international experience and has held Visiting Professorships in Australia, Canada, Egypt, France, Hong Kong, New Zealand and Qatar as well as acting as a consultant to numerous international companies.

Stephen Brown is Professor of Marketing Research at the University of Ulster. Best known for *Postmodern Marketing* (1995), he has written or co-edited twelve other books, including *Marketing Apocalypse* (1996), *Postmodern Marketing Two* (1998) and *Marketing – The Retro Revolution* (2001). His articles have been published in the *Journal of Marketing*, *Harvard Business Review*, *Journal of Advertising*, *Business Horizons*, *Journal of Retailing*, *European Management Journal* and many more.

David Carson is Professor of Marketing at the University of Ulster, Northern Ireland. His research interests lie in marketing for SMEs and quality of marketing in service industries. He has published widely in both of these areas. He has wide business experience both in consultancy and directorship roles. He is joint editor of the *European Journal of Marketing*, a category one international academic journal with a world-wide circulation. He is Vice President of the Academy of Marketing UK, the foremost representative body of marketing academics in the UK and Ireland. He is also a Fellow of the Chartered Institute of Marketing (CIM) and a member of the CIM Academic Senate. He has been a Visiting Professor at numerous universities in Australia, New Zealand, Hong Kong and Bahrain.

Dave Chaffey, BSc, PhD, MCIM has been course director for Chartered Institute of Marketing seminars in e-marketing since 1997 and has delivered over 50 seminars on all aspects of e-marketing. He is Director of Marketing Insights Limited (www.marketing-insights.co.uk), a consultancy and training company offering the WebInsights™ service for evaluation and recommendation of organizations' e-marketing strategy and execution. Between 1988 and 1995, he worked in industry as a business analyst/project manager, developing marketing solutions for companies such as Ford Europe, WH Smith and the Halifax. Between 1995 and 2001, he was Senior Lecturer in the Business School at the University of Derby, where his research specialism was approaches to measuring and improving e-marketing performance. He was involved in the development of the BA (Hons) Internet Marketing and MSc in Electronic Commerce, and also taught on the MBA and MA Marketing Management Programmes. He continues to lecture on e-marketing at universities including Cranfield, Derby, Leeds and Warwick. He was involved in the development of the Chartered Institute of Marketing e-marketing professional development award, for which he is an examiner. He also writes the *E-marketing Insights* column for the monthly CIM Newsletter *What's New in Marketing* (www.wnim.com). He is author of five successful business books, including *Internet Marketing: Strategy, Implementation and Practice*; *E-business and E-commerce Management* and *eMarketing eXcellence* (with PR Smith). He has compiled a regularly updated website of Internet marketing resources at www.marketing-online.co.uk to support the seminars and books.

Martin Charter is the Director and Visiting Professor of Sustainable Product Design at The Centre for Sustainable Design at the Surrey Institute of Art & Design, University College. Since 1988, he has worked at director level in 'business and environment' issues in consultancy, leisure, publishing, training, events and research. Prior to this he held a range of management positions in strategy, research and marketing in gardening, construction, trade exhibitions, financial services and consultancy, including being a launch Director of Greenleaf Publishing and Marketing Director at the Earth Centre.

   Martin is the former co-ordinator of one of the UK's first green business clubs for SMEs and presently also directs a regional network focused on 'producer responsibility' issues. Martin is presently editor of the *Journal of Sustainable Product Design* and was the previous editor of *The Green Management Letter* and *Greener Management International* (where he retains Editorial Board involvement). Other responsibilities include a member of the Judging Panels of Design Sense and ACCA's corporate environmental reporting awards, member of ISO and BSI groups on 'Integrating Environmental Aspects into Product Development' (ISO14062) and member of international advisory board of CARE electronics network. He is the author, editor and joint editor of various books and publications including *Greener Marketing* (1992 and 1999), *The Green Management Gurus* (1996) (e-book), *Managing Eco-design* (1997), *Sustainable Solutions* (2001) and *Sustainable Value* (2002). Martin has an MBA from Aston Business School in the UK, and has academic and business interests in sustainable product design, eco-product development, e-publishing, and creativity and innovation.

Martin Christopher is Professor of Marketing and Logistics at Cranfield School of Management, where he is Head of the Marketing and Logistics Faculty and Chairman of the Cranfield Centre for Logistics and Transportation. In addition, he is Deputy Director of the School of Management responsible for Executive Development Programmes. His interests in marketing and logistics strategy are reflected in his consultancy and management development activities. In this connection he has worked for major international companies in North America, Europe, the Far East and Australasia. In addition, he is a non-executive director of a number of companies. As an author, he has written numerous books and articles and is on the editorial advisory board of a number of professional journals in the marketing and logistics area. He is co-editor of *The International Journal of Logistics Management* and his recent books have focused upon relationship marketing, customer service and logistics strategy. He has held appointments as Visiting Professor at the University of British Columbia, Canada, the University of New South Wales, Australia and the University of South Florida, USA. Professor Christopher is a Fellow of the Chartered Institute of Marketing and of the Institute of Logistics Management, on whose Council he sits. In 1987 he was awarded the Sir Robert Lawrence medal of the Institute of Logistics and Distribution Management for his contribution to the development of logistics education in Great Britain.

Keith Crosier, BSc, MSc, DipCAM is Honorary Research Fellow in the Department of Marketing at the University of Strathclyde, where he was previously Director of the Honours Programme and Director of Teaching. After a degree in earth sciences, he unaccountably embarked on a career in marketing communications, starting as a copywriter in the in-house promotional unit of a multinational pharmaceutical company. After seven years with various responsibilities for advertising, publicity and sales promotion with Olivetti in London and New York, he came home to spend two years as executive assistant to the managing director of a small, family-owned electronic engineering firm. A mid-career master's degree in management studies at Durham University Business School converted him to academe, first as Director of the Diploma in Management Studies at what is now Teesside University. Moving to Strathclyde as a Research Fellow, studying the consumer movement, he stayed on to lecture in his managerial specialism. Periodic consultancy and four years as a monthly columnist for a Scottish professional magazine kept him in touch with developments in the marketing communications business. During the early nineties, he experienced as a regular visiting lecturer the excitement and challenges attending the emergence of organized management education in Poland. He was until 1998 Vice Chairman of the Marketing Education Group, now the Academy of Marketing. He is Assistant Editor of *Marketing Intelligence and Planning*.

Leslie de Chernatony, BSc, PhD, FCIM, FMRS is Professor of Brand Marketing and Director of the Centre for Research in Brand Marketing at the Birmingham Business School, The University of Birmingham. After a career in the marketing departments of a few blue chip organizations he completed his doctorate in brand marketing which laid the foundations for his research focus. With a substantial number of publications on brand management in American and European journals, Leslie is a regular presenter at international conferences. His papers have won best paper awards in journals and at conferences. He has several books on brand management, the two most recent being *Creating Powerful Brands* and *From Brand Vision to Brand Evaluation*, both published by Butterworth–Heinemann. Winning several major research grants has helped support his research into factors associated with high performance brands and also strategies for succeeding with services brands. Leslie was Visiting Professor at Madrid Business School and is currently Visiting Professor at Thammasat University, Bangkok and Lugano University, Switzerland. He sits on the editorial boards of several scholarly journals. A firm believer of the importance of research having applied value, he acts as an international consultant to organizations seeking more effective brand strategies and has run numerous acclaimed branding seminars throughout Europe, Asia, the Far East and North America.

Adamantios Diamantopoulos, BA, MSc, PhD, FCIM, FBAM, MMRS is Professor of Marketing and Business Research at Loughborough University Business School. He was previously Professor of International Marketing at the European Business Management School, University of Wales Swansea, where he headed the Marketing Group. Other past academic posts include full-time appointments at the University of Edinburgh and the University of Strathclyde, and Visiting Professorships at the University of Miami, Vienna University of Economics and Business, Université Robert Schuman (Strasbourg), Lund University and Dortmund University. His main research interests are in pricing, sales forecasting, marketing research and international marketing and he is the author of some 180 publications in these areas. His work has appeared, among others, in the *Journal of Marketing Research*, *Journal of Business Research*, *Journal of International Business Studies*, *International Journal of Research in Marketing*, *Journal of International Marketing* and *International Journal of Forecasting*. He has presented his research at more than 70 international conferences and has been the recipient of several Best Paper Awards. He sits on the editorial review boards of eight marketing journals, is a founder member of the Consortium for International Marketing Research (CIMaR), Associate Editor of the *International Journal of Research in Marketing* and *International Journal of Forecasting*, and a referee for several academic journals, professional associations and funding bodies.

Bill Donaldson, BA, PhD, MCIM is Senior Lecturer in Marketing at the Strathclyde Graduate Business School. He had more than ten years' experience in marketing positions, with three different companies, before joining Strathclyde in December 1983 and was awarded his PhD in 1993 for his thesis: 'An inquiry into the relative importance of customer service in the marketing of industrial products.' Author of *Sales and Management: Theory and Practice* (Macmillan, 2nd edition, 1998) and *Strategic Marketing Relationships* (Wiley, 2001), he also has several publications on customer service and the characteristics of customer-driven organizations. His current research interests continue in the area of sales operations, customer service and relationship marketing. He has taught sales operations at undergraduate level and a specialist class in managing customer relations. In addition to undergraduate and MBA teaching he has experience in training and consultancy with a number of leading companies. He is currently a Chartered Marketer and senior examiner for the Institute of Professional Sales.

Peter Doyle is Professor of Marketing and Strategic Management at the University of Warwick. Previously he has taught at the London Business School, INSEAD, and Bradford University. He has also been Visiting Professor at Stanford, University of Hawaii and the University of South Carolina. He graduated with a first in economics from Manchester University and took a PhD in industrial administration from Carnegie-Mellon University, USA. His research interests are in marketing modelling and strategic planning. Publications include six books and numerous articles in leading journals, including *Journal of Marketing Research*, *Management Science*, *Journal of Business*, *Journal of Marketing*, *Journal of the Operational Research Society* and the *Economic Journal*. He is on the editorial boards of the *European Journal of Marketing*, *Journal of Business Research*, *International Journal of Advertising*, *International Journal of Research in Marketing* and the *Journal of Marketing Management* and he is a member of the Industry and Employment and International Activities Committees of the ESRC. He also acts as a consultant on international marketing and strategy with a number of companies including IBM, Shell, ICI, Unilever, 3M, Hewlett Packard, British Telecom and Marks and Spencer.

Martin Evans, BA, MA, MIDM, MMRS, FCIM is Senior Teaching Fellow at Cardiff Business School. He previously held professional posts at the Universities of Portsmouth, Glamorgan and West of England. His industrial experience was with Hawker Siddeley and then as a consultant to a variety of organizations over 25 years. He has co-authored six books and has over 100 other publications, appearing in a range of journals including *Journal of Marketing Management*, *European Journal of Marketing*, *International Journal of Advertising* and *Journal of Marketing Communications*. He is on the Editorial Board of eight academic journals and is Managing Editor of *Journal of Consumer Behaviour: An International Research Review*. He is an academic prize winner at the International Marketing Communications Conference and the Academy of Marketing.

Gordon R. Foxall is Distinguished Research Professor at Cardiff University. He has a first degree from the University of Salford, where he won the Final Year Course Prize for Social Science. His master's degree, in management, is from the same university. He is also a graduate of the University of Birmingham (PhD in industrial economics and business studies) and of the University of Strathclyde (PhD in psychology), and holds a higher doctorate of the University of Birmingham (DSocSc). He is the author of some 16 books on consumer behaviour and related themes, including the monograph *Marketing Psychology: The Paradigm in the Wings* (Macmillan, 1997) and the best-selling text *Consumer Psychology for Marketing*, co-authored with Ron Goldsmith and Stephen Brown (Thomson, 1998). He has just edited *Consumer Behaviour Analysis: Critical Perspectives* (Routledge, 2002). In addition, he has authored numerous refereed articles, chapters and papers on consumer behaviour and marketing. His other professorial appointments were at the Universities of Strathclyde, Birmingham and Keele, and he has also held posts at Cranfield University and the University of Newcastle-upon-Tyne. He has held visiting appointments at the Universities of Michigan, Guelph, South Australia and UMIST, and is currently a visiting professor at De Montfort and Keele Universities. A Fellow of both the British Psychological Society and the British Academy of Management, he was recently elected an Academician of the Academy of Learned Societies for the Social Sciences. Professor Foxall's research interests lie in marketing theory and consumer psychology.

Susan Hart, is a Professor of Marketing and Head of the Department of Marketing at the University of Strathclyde. After working in industry in France and the UK, she joined the University of Strathclyde as a researcher. She completed her PhD on the subject of product management and has published widely on subjects such as the contribution of marketing to competitive success, and product design and development in the manufacturing industry. Current research interests are in the development of new products and innovation, the contribution of marketing to company success, loyalty marketing, and accounting for marketing performance.

Gerard Hastings is Professor of Social Marketing in the Department of Marketing at the University of Strathclyde. His research interests are in social marketing, and he is the founder and Director of the Centre for Social Marketing (CSM). CSM is a self-funded research unit which investigates the applicability of marketing ideas to the solution of health and social problems, as well as monitoring the potentially harmful effects of commercial marketing. Current funders include the World Health Organization, the Home Office and the Robert Wood Johnson Foundation. Professor Hastings is also the Director of the Cancer Research UK-funded Centre for Tobacco Control Research, which investigates the effectiveness of different models of tobacco control. Professor Hastings has published widely in journals such as the *British Medical Journal*, the *British Dental Journal*, the *Journal of Advertising* and the *European Journal of Marketing*. He has served as a non-executive director of Forth Valley Health Board and SACRO, was a member of the OECD Expert Committee on Social Marketing, and a consultant to the Home Office Drugs Prevention Initiative, the EU and WHO. He is currently on the Editorial Boards of *Health Promotion International*, the *Health Education Journal* and *Social Marketing Quarterly*.

Sheena Leek is a Research Associate at Birmingham Business School. She is currently working with Peter W. Turnbull on an international business-to-business marketing project examining how changes in the environment have affected business relationships. In particular, she is interested in the effect of information technology on interactions between companies.

Lynn MacFadyen is Senior Researcher in the Cancer Research UK-Funded Centre for Tobacco Control Research at the University of Strathclyde. Her PhD examined the influence of tobacco marketing communications on young people's smoking behaviour. Her main research interests are social marketing and societal marketing issues, particularly the marketing activities of the tobacco industry. She is also interested in tobacco control and smoking cessation and prevention initiatives, and has published widely in tobacco control journals.

Graeme McCorkell has introduced direct marketing to many organizations, including Abbey National, Volvo and P&O, as well as assisting past masters such as the AA, American Express, the Consumers Association, GUS and *Newsweek*. Until 1995, Graeme was the Chariman of the Institute of Direct Marketing. He is an independent direct marketing consultant and is the author of *Advertising that Pulls Response* (McGraw-Hill, 1990) and *Direct and Database Marketing* (Kogan Page, 1997).

Malcolm McDonald, MA(Oxon), MSc, PhD, DLitt, FCIM, FRSA is Professor of Marketing and Deputy Director of the Cranfield School of Management. He is a graduate in English Language and Literature from Oxford University, in Business Studies from Bradford University Management Centre, has a PhD from Cranfield University and an honorary Doctorate of Letters from Bradford University. He has extensive industrial experience, including a number of years as Marketing Director of Canada Dry. During the past twenty years he has run seminars and workshops on marketing planning in the UK, Europe, India, the Far East, Australasia and the USA. He has written thirty-seven books, including the best-seller *Marketing Plans: How to Prepare Them, How to Use Them* (Butterworth-Heinemann, fifth edition, 2002) and many of his papers have been published. His current interests centre around IT in marketing, the development of expert systems in marketing, and key account management.

Peter J. McGoldrick is the Professor of Retailing in the Manchester School of Management at UMIST. He has authored, edited or co-edited over 200 books, chapters and articles on aspects of retail strategy or consumer behaviour. He is the UMIST Director of the International Centre for Retail Studies. A major research interest has been the area of retail pricing with grants from the ESRC and the Office of Fair Trading. An extension of this work has been the measurement of how shoppers judge value, supported by a series of grants from the Department of Trade and Industry. Another major theme is electronic service delivery systems, work funded by EPSRC, DTI, BA, BT and Microsoft. He is Director of the Manchester Retail Research Forum, comprising senior executives or directors from 16 blue chip companies – they help establish the research agenda for the Centre, as well as sponsoring and facilitating a range of studies into key areas of retailing strategy.

Arthur Meidan, BSc(Econ), MBA, PhD, FCIM was Professor of Marketing at the School of Management, University of Sheffield. He has spent over twenty-five years in management teaching, instructing, consulting and researching. He is the author of many articles, monographs and textbooks including *The Appraisal of Managerial Performance* (American Marketing Association,

1981), *Marketing Applications of Operational Research Techniques* (MCB University Press, 1981), *Bank Marketing Management* (Macmillan, 1984), *Industrial Salesforce Management* (Croom Helm, 1986) and *Cases in Marketing of Services* (with L. Moutinho, Addison-Wesley, 1994). His research interests are in marketing of financial services and tourism. Professor Meidan has published over seventy refereed academic journals and conference proceedings in Britain and elsewhere and has consulted and taught post-experience courses, particularly on marketing of financial services and tourism, in Europe, Asia, America and Australia.

Luiz Moutinho, BA, MA, PhD, FCIM is Professor of Marketing, University of Glasgow Business School. He completed his PhD at the University of Sheffield in 1982 and held posts at Cardiff Business School, University of Wales College of Cardiff, Cleveland State University, Ohio, USA, Northern Arizona University, USA and California State University, USA, as well as visiting Professorship positions in New Zealand and Brazil. Between 1987 and 1989 he was the Director of the Doctoral Programmes at the Confederation of Scottish Business Schools and at the Cardiff Business School between 1993 and 1996. He is currently the Director of the Doctoral Programme at the University of Glasgow Department of Business and Management. In addition to publishing seventeen books and presenting papers at many international conferences, he also has had a vast number of articles published in international journals. He is also a member of the Editorial Board of several international academic journals. He has been a full Professor of Marketing since 1989 and was appointed in 1996 to the Foundation Chair of Marketing at the University of Glasgow.

Lisa O'Malley, PhD is a Lecturer in Marketing at the University of Limerick. Lisa's main teaching and research interests are in the areas of marketing theory, direct marketing and relationship marketing. She has published widely on relationship marketing including articles in the *Journal of Marketing Management*, the *European Journal of Marketing*, *Service Industries Journal*, *Journal of Business Research* and *Interactive Marketing*. These include critical works on RM in mass consumer markets as well as investigations on the role of relationships in professional services.

Stanley J. Paliwoda, BA, MSc, PhD, FCIM, FCMI, MIEx, ILT.M is Head of the Marketing Group and Head of the Department of Commerce of the Birmingham Business School, The University of Birmingham. He was previously Professor and Chair of Marketing at the University of Calgary, Alberta, Canada. He continues to be Visiting Professor in Marketing at the Warsaw School of Economics, Poland. He has a master's degree from Bradford University, a PhD from Cranfield and was previously with the University of Manchester Institute of Science and Technology. His interests are primarily in international marketing focusing on market entry strategy, business-to-business marketing strategy and marketing relationship management. He is a Fellow of the Chartered Management Institute, a Fellow of the Chartered Institute of Marketing, a chartered marketer, a professional member of the Institute of Export and a former examiner for their International Marketing professional examinations. He is the author of seventeen books, some of which have been translated into Spanish and Chinese. Books include *International Marketing*, now in its third edition with Butterworth-Heinemann, 1998; *Investing in Eastern Europe*, Addison-Wesley/EIU Books, 1995; and *The International Marketing Reader*, Routledge, 1995 (with John K. Ryans Jr). He is founding author of *The Journal of East–West Business* published by Haworth Press, New York; Canadian editor of the *Journal of Marketing Management* and is on the editorial board of eleven other journals including: *International Marketing Review*; *Asia-Pacific International Journal of Marketing*; *Journal of Global Marketing*; *Journal of Euromarketing*; *International Business Review*; *Journal of Qualitative Market Research*.

Adrian Palmer is Professor of Marketing at the University of Gloucestershire. Before joining academia he held marketing management positions within the travel industry. In recent years he has published extensively on the subject of relationship marketing and customer loyalty in publications which include *European Journal of Marketing*, *Journal of Marketing Management*, *Journal of Services Marketing*, *International Business Review* and *Annals of Tourism Research*. He is a member of the editorial review board for *Journal of Marketing Management*, *European Journal of Marketing* and *Journal of Vacation Marketing*. He is a Fellow of the Chartered Institute of Marketing and a Chartered Marketer. During his academic career he has spent time teaching abroad and giving guest lectures in a number of countries, including the United States, Australia, the Far East, India and Eastern Europe.

Adrian Payne, PhD, MSc, MEd, FRMIT, FCIM is Professor of Services and Relationship Marketing and Director of the Centre for Customer Relationship Management at the Cranfield School of Management, Cranfield University. He has practical experience in marketing, market research, corporate planning and general management. His previous appointments include positions as chief executive for a manufacturing company and he has also held senior appointments in corporate planning and marketing. He is an author of six books on relationship marketing and customer relationship management. His research interests are in customer retention economics; the impact of IT on CRM and marketing strategy and planning in service businesses. Adrian is a frequent keynote speaker at public and in-company seminars and conferences around the world. He also acts as a consultant and educator to many service organizations, professional service firms and manufacturing companies.

Ken Peattie is a Professor of Marketing and Strategy at Cardiff Business School, which he joined in 1986. Before becoming an academic, he worked in marketing and systems analysis for an American paper multinational, and as a strategic planner within the UK electronics industry. He has been researching into the business implications of environmentalism for almost fifteen years, and is the author of *Environmental Marketing Management: Meeting the Green Challenge* (Pitman, 1995) and *Green Marketing* (Pitman, 1992). He has also written a range of journal articles and book chapters on the implications of environmentally related issues for corporate and marketing strategies, and on the greening of management education. His books have been translated into languages included Japanese, Swedish and Chinese. In 2001 he became Director of the ESRC Research Centre for Business Relationships, Accountability, Sustainability and Society (BRASS), a joint venture between Cardiff's Schools of Business and of Law, and its Department of City and Regional Planning. His other research interests include innovations in sales promotion, social marketing, and corporate social responsibility.

Sue Peattie, BA, MA, PGCE(FE), PhD is a Lecturer in Marketing at Cardiff Business School. She has taught a variety of undergraduate and postgraduate courses in both marketing and statistics since 1986, after completing a masters degree in economics at Simon Fraser University in Vancouver. Her research interests and publications concentrate on the application of sales promotions in different sectors, and the use of social marketing in promoting both health and environmental causes.

Nigel F. Piercy BA, MA, PhD, DipM, FInstM is Professor of Strategic Marketing and Director of the Strategic Sales Research Consortium at Cranfield School of Management, Cranfield University. In addition, he has held visiting professor positions at: Texas Christian University; the Fuqua School of Business, Duke University; and the Columbia Graduate School of Business, New York. He was for several years the Sir Julian Hodge Chair in Marketing and Strategy at Cardiff University. Prior to an academic career, he worked in retail management and in business planning. He is an active consultant and management workshop speaker, and has worked with executives in many organizations in the UK, the USA, Europe, Ireland, Greece, Hong Kong, Malaysia, South Africa and Zimbabwe. He has published widely on marketing and management topics, including papers in the *Journal of Marketing*, the *Journal of the Academy of Marketing Science*, the *Journal of World Business*, the *Journal of Personal Selling and Sales Management*, and many others. His work has focused mainly on process issues in developing and implementing market strategies, and he is currently engaged in research into the effectiveness of the sales/marketing interface and the modern transformation of the sales organization. His best-known managerial books are: *Market-Led Strategic Change: A Guide to Transforming the Process of Going To Market*, 3rd edn (Butterworth-Heinemann, 2002) and *Tales From the Marketplace: Stories of Revolution, Reinvention and Renewal* (Butterworth-Heinemann, 1999). Forthcoming books include: David W. Cravens and Nigel F. Piercy, *Strategic Marketing*, 7th edn (Irwin/McGraw-Hill, 2002), and James M. Hulbert, Noel Capon and Nigel F. Piercy *Total Integrated Marketing* (Free Press, 2003).

Martine Stead is Senior Researcher at the Centre for Social Marketing (CSM) at the University of Strathclyde, having joined in 1992 with a BA (Hons) in English and a background in health promotion and the media. Her research interests include social marketing theory and practice, health communication, development and evaluation of mass media interventions, health inequalities, smoking cessation and health inequalities. She has recently conducted with colleagues a major Home Office evaluation of a 3-year drugs prevention intervention in the north-east of England. She has published in the *British Medical Journal, Health Education Research* and the *Health Education Journal* and is on the editorial board of *Social Marketing Quarterly*.

Peter W. Turnbull is Professor of Marketing and a member of the marketing faculty in the University of Birmingham Business School. He is a well-known researcher and writer in the field of industrial and international marketing. His books include *International Marketing and Purchasing* (Macmillan, 1981), *Strategies for International Industrial Marketing* (John Wiley, 1986), *Research Developments in International Marketing* (Croom Helm, 1996) and *Managing Business Relationships* (Wiley, 1998). Additionally, he has written numerous articles for scholarly management journals. He has lectured widely in Western Europe and North America and has acted as consultant to a number of national and international companies.

Caroline Tynan is Professor of Marketing and Head of the Marketing Division at Nottingham University Business School, Chair of the Academy of Marketing, a member of the Academic Senate of the Chartered Institute of Marketing, and a Visiting Professor of Marketing at the University of Ljubljana, Slovenia. Her research interests include relationship marketing, particularly regarding issues related to its application within business-to-consumer and cross-cultural contexts, services marketing and marketing in transition economies. She has published in a number of journals, including *Journal of Business Research, European Journal of Marketing, Journal of Marketing Management*, and *Journal of Strategic Marketing*, and she currently edits *The Marketing Review*.

Keith Ward is Visiting Professor of Financial Strategy at Cranfield School of Management. He studied economics at Cambridge and then qualified as both a chartered accountant and a cost and management accountant. He has worked both in the City and abroad as a consultant and held senior financial positions in manufacturing and trading companies (the last being as Group

Financial Director of Sterling International). He then joined Cranfield School of Management and progressed to Head of the Finance and Accounting Group and Director of the Research Centre in Competitive Performance. His research interests are primarily in the fields of financial strategy, strategic management accounting and accounting for marketing activities. He is the author of *Corporate Financial Strategy*, *Strategic Management Accounting*, *Financial Management for Service Companies* and *Financial Aspects of Marketing*, as well as co-authoring *Management Accounting for Financial Decisions*. He has also published numerous articles and contributed to several other books, including as editor.

John Webb is currently the Director of the MSc in Marketing at Strathclyde University. After a first degree in optics, and research into visual psychophysics, he was an arts administrator in the UK and the USA for seven years. He read for an MBA in 1981 and was a freelance business consultant for two years before joining the Department of Marketing at Strathclyde University as a Teaching Company Associate. He was awarded his PhD in 1987 and appointed to a lectureship in the same year. His research interests concern the role of technology in business administration, marketing and the arts, and international marketing research. He has taught in Singapore, Hong Kong, Malaysia, the Czech Republic, the People's Republic of China, and France. He is the author of *Understanding and Designing Marketing Research*.

Robin Wensley is Professor of Strategic Management and Marketing and Deputy Dean at Warwick Business School. He was Chair of the School from 1989 to 1994 and Chair of the Faculty of Social Studies from 1997 to 1999. He was previously with RHM Foods, Tube Investments and London Business School, and was visiting professor twice at UCLA and once at the University of Florida. He is a Council member of the ESRC, having been a member of the Research Grants Board from 1991 to 1995. He is also Chair of the Council of the Tavistock Institute of Human Relations. His research interests include the long-term evolution of competitive markets and structures, the process of strategic decision making and the nature of sustainable advantages, and he has published a number of books, most recently the *Handbook of Marketing*, and articles in the *Harvard Business Review*, the *Journal of Marketing* and the *Strategic Management Journal*, and has worked closely with other academics both in Europe and the USA. He is joint editor of the *Journal of Management Studies* and has twice won the annual Alpha Kappa Psi Award for the most influential article in the US *Journal of Marketing*, as well as the *Journal of Marketing Management* Millennium Article award.

Tony Yeshin, BSc(Econ), MCIM, is currently Senior Lecturer in Marketing at the University of Greenwich, where he is also Programme Leader for the BA in Marketing Communications. Prior to joining the University, his entire career was spent in the field of marketing communications, predominantly within advertising and Sales Promotion. In 1972, with a colleague, he started a company – The Above and Below Group – specifically designed to create integrated marketing communications programmes for its diverse clients. Having worked on a wide range of both domestic and international accounts, his practical experience of developing and implementing marketing communications programmes is now combined with a solid academic background. He is the author of several books. His first, *Inside Advertising*, was published by the professional body, the Institute of Practitioners in Advertising. He is the co-author of the *Chartered Institute of Marketing Postgraduate Coursebook on Integrated Marketing Communications*, and the author of the text *Integrated Marketing Communications: The Holistic Approach* (Butterworth-Heinemann, 1998). He is currently developing a series of titles covering individual areas of marketing communications activities.

Preface to the fifth edition

The fifth edition of *The Marketing Book* is a testimony to both the continuing demand for an authoritative overview of the marketing discipline and the constantly changing nature of its subject matter. First published in 1987 to coincide with the Editor's appointment as the first academic National Chairman of the Institute of Marketing, the original concept was:

> To produce an authoritative handbook setting out the scope and nature of the marketing function, its managerial applications and its contribution to corporate success.

To implement this concept, contributing authors were advised: '*The Marketing Book* should serve as first point of reference for experienced practitioners and managers from other functions, and as an introduction to those embarking on a career in marketing. In short, the kind of book which every member and student of the Chartered Institute of Marketing will find relevant and useful.'

The fact that the book has been continuously in print for 15 years and is now in its fifth edition is clear evidence that there is a continuing need for such a publication.

While it is unlikely anyone other than the Editor and Publisher would wish to make an analysis of the content of successive editions, such a review would reveal that while some contributions have changed very little others have been extensively updated, a few topics have been dropped and a significant number of new ones added. In parallel, the list of contributing authors has also changed markedly over the years. However, the present roll of contributors shares a common feature with all the preceding editions – the authors are all leading experts in their fields. All have published widely on the topics for which they are responsible and many of them have written one or more definitive and widely used textbooks on the subject of their contribution. Another distinctive feature is that all the authors, both academics and practitioners, are based in Britain, so that the current collection reflects a British view of what is important and relevant in the theory and practice of marketing. Obviously, this view recognizes and reflects international perspectives but, in a subject where so much published work is written from a purely American point of view, I consider it important that an alternative, albeit similar, interpretation be available.

Six chapters have been dropped from the last edition and eight new ones added. The chapters that had to be left out from this new edition were 'Environmental scanning' by Douglas Brownlie, 'The evolution and use of communication and information technology' by Keith Fletcher, 'Developing marketing information capabilities' by Nigel Piercy and Martin Evans, 'Organizational marketing' by Dale Littler, 'Marketing for non-profit organizations' by Keith Blois, and 'The Internet: the direct route to growth and development' by Jim Hamill and Sean Ennis. In every case the reason for omitting these chapters is that their content is covered by other entries. Some of these are completely new and are evidence of the way in which the subject of marketing is developing, while others mirror the incorporation of what were emerging areas into mainstream marketing. All these chapters are, of course, still available in the fourth edition.

A number of chapters remain much the same as they appeared in the fourth edition. These are:

Chapter 1   'One more time – what is marketing?' by Michael J. Baker
Chapter 4   'The basics of marketing strategy' by Robin Wensley
Chapter 5   'Strategic marketing planning: theory and practice' by Malcolm McDonald
Chapter 6   'Consumer decision making: process, level and style' by Gordon R. Foxall
Chapter 8   'Marketing research' by John Webb
Chapter 12   'New product development' by Susan Hart
Chapter 13   'Pricing' by Adamantios Diamantopoulos
Chapter 14   'Selling and sales management' by Bill Donaldson
Chapter 18   'Sales promotion' by Sue and Ken Peattie
Chapter 20   'Controlling marketing and the measurement of marketing effectiveness' by Keith Ward
Chapter 23   'The marketing of services' by Adrian Palmer
Chapter 24   'International marketing – the issues' by Stanley J. Paliwoda
Chapter 27   'Social marketing' by Lynn MacFadyen, Martine Stead and Gerard Hastings
Chapter 28   'Green marketing' by Ken Peattie and Martin Charter
Chapter 29   'Marketing for small-to-medium enterprises' by David Carson
Chapter 30   'Retailing' by Peter J. McGoldrick

All these chapters have been updated with some new material, some quite radically, and more recent references where appropriate. They all meet the criteria that they give a clear and authoritative overview of their subject matter.

Given the strictures of my good friend and Publisher Tim Goodfellow not to exceed the limit of 450 000 words for this edition, I shall confine my comments on the content of this edition mainly to the new contributions or to those chapters that have been radically rewritten. That said, I should explain why my own first chapter has been changed very little from earlier editions.

Chapter 1 is intended to provide an overview of the evolution of the modern marketing concept as a foundation for the detailed examination of the more important topics associated with the theory and practice of the discipline covered in the succeeding chapters. As it stands, the content is little changed from earlier editions. Some might claim, with justification, that it represents a conservative and conventional treatment of the subject. In my defence, I would argue that it still provides essential background to a question – What is marketing? – that many marketers, both academics and practitioners, regard as rhetorical. In doing so, and by failing to define clearly and explicitly what are the origins, scope, nature and boundaries of our discipline, we then express surprise when others claim ownership of theories and practices that marketers consider their own. Obviously, the remainder of the book provides a detailed response to the question, but some kind of general introduction is still seen as necessary.

Chapter 2 – 'Postmodern marketing' by Stephen Brown – is new to this edition and identifies an important new trend in marketing thought. Since the Enlightenment of the eighteenth century, the dominant model for research has been positivistic. The defining characteristic of positivism has been a belief in the existence of an objective reality that can be defined, explained and understood through the application of scientific methods. In turn, this belief has given rise to 'modern' society, of which mass production, mass consumption and modern marketing are major manifestations. It would seem, therefore, that 'postmodern' must refer to the nature of society that has or is likely to evolve out of the 'modern' state. To establish if this is or is not the case, I invited one of the most widely published and cited authorities on the subject – Stephen Brown – to contribute a chapter on the subject. Its positioning immediately after my own attempts to define modern marketing is deliberate.

It would be facile to try and summarize Stephen's chapter. However, in my view it provides one of the clearest expositions of what postmodern marketing is or is perceived to be. (It is also written in his own distinctive and entertaining style.) Whether or not you are converted to this perspective of marketing, it is important that you are aware of its defining characteristics as with the more traditional views contained in Chapter 1.

Chapter 3 is also new and deals with a topic – relationship marketing – that has been widely referred to in earlier editions (and in this edition). Several pages were given to the topic in my own introductory chapter in the fourth edition and are retained in this edition. However, relationship marketing (RM) has evolved to become the dominant paradigm in marketing and it is now deserving of an entry of its own.

While there are many distinguished authors that might have been approached to contribute this chapter, the choice of Lisa O'Malley and Caroline Tynan was an obvious one. In 2001, I had the good fortune to act as an external examiner for Lisa's doctoral thesis, supervised by Caroline. The other examiner, Christian Gronroos, is recognized internationally as one of the founding fathers of relationship marketing. Both of us were very impressed with Lisa's review of the RM literature and the new chapter is based on this.

As the authors make clear, relationship marketing has evolved over the past 25 years or so as a reconceptualization of the *transactional* model of marketing, based upon the application of the marketing mix to the marketing of mass-produced products to large, homogeneous consumer markets. This model was seen to be inappropriate in industrial or business-to-business markets, and also to the marketing of services, and a new approach based on the creation and maintenance of relationships began to emerge. Accordingly, 'The purpose of this chapter is to begin to describe how the rich body of knowledge that is relationship marketing has come into being, what its major underpinning theories are, what defining moments occurred, and what might shape its future'.

In my view, it accomplishes this in a clear and scholarly way. Plainly, having evolved from a number of different, albeit complementary, research traditions, relationship marketing is not a single monolithic concept – 'Indeed, relationship marketing is less a coherent body of knowledge and more a collection of loosely aligned understandings'. To know what these are, how they have developed and how they might be applied in practice, this chapter is 'must' reading. And, for those wishing to dig deeper, the References are an invaluable resource in their own right.

A new section and author have been added to Chapter 7 – 'Business-to-business marketing: organizational buying behaviour, relationships and networks'. The new author is Sheena Leek of Birmingham Business School and the new section is entitled 'Relationship management and networks'. The latter addresses the sets of relationships that have come to be termed the 'network approach'. Issues of relationship portfolio analysis are also examined, although it is acknowledged that practitioners will need to use insight and judgement in selecting from a growing number of theoretical models. Several additions have also been made to the recommended reading list for those wishing to pursue these issues further.

Chapter 10 – 'Market segmentation' – first appeared in the third edition. As the author, Martin Evans, points out in his introduction, while many aspects of segmentation have remained constant there have been significant changes in practice. Information technology and new techniques have now made it possible to target individual customers with pinpoint accuracy, leading to more personalized and often one-to-one communications (see Chapter 22 for more on this).

The chapter has been extensively revised to take account of these developments. In addition to reviewing the more traditional methods for segmentation and targeting based upon demographics, psychographics and geodemographics, Evans explores the fusion of personalized data which permits biographical segmentation. Of particular value is consideration of the differences between segmenting a 'cold' market from scratch and the application of the new methodologies to current customer databases.

The use of segmentation data in the development of customer relationship management (CRM) and relationship marketing is explored and should be considered in association with Chapters 3 and 19, which deal with these topics in greater detail.

Peter Doyle has completely rewritten his chapter (11) on 'Managing the marketing mix' to show how the adoption of value-based approaches to management may transform what traditionally has been a craft-based activity into a professional practice. In the past, marketing has lacked influence in the boardroom due to its inability to justify its contribution to the overall success of an organization – a failing epitomized by Lord Leverhume's comment that 'I know half my advertising expenditure is wasted, the problem is I don't know which half'. In a rigorous, analytical, clinical but easily accessible way, Doyle explains how the concept of shareholder value and the application of financial analysis techniques can be used to manage each of the elements of the marketing mix effectively.

As he states in his summary: 'Finally, shareholder value provides the vehicle for the marketing professional to have an increasing impact in the boardroom. In the past, senior managers have often discounted the recommendations of their marketing teams because the marketing mix and strategies for investment have lacked a rational goal. Marketers have not had the framework for translating marketing strategies into what counts for today's top executives – maximizing shareholder value. Value-based provides the tools for optimizing the marketing mix.'

This is a *tour de force* from one of the UK's leading marketing academics and consultants that will undoubtedly encourage many readers to access the extended treatment to be found in his widely acclaimed book *Value-based Marketing: Marketing Strategies for Corporate Growth and Shareholder Value* (Wiley, 2000).

While the subject of branding has appeared in every edition of the *Marketing Book*, Chapter 15 is completely new as a result of a change in authorship. For this edition Leslie de Chernatony has taken over from Peter Doyle. Leslie is the author of a number of best-selling texts on branding, and was an obvious choice to provide a comprehensive overview of current thinking and practice on the subject.

In markets distinguished by hypercompetition it is becoming increasingly difficult to sustain a competitive advantage through product differentiation. As a consequence, marketing communications have assumed an even more important role in enabling sellers to position themselves effectively against competitors. To meet this challenge more traditional approaches emphasizing a particular communication approach and techniques have given way to a more strategic method in which a variety of communication disciplines are coordinated into an integrated procedure. This is identified as integrated marketing communications (IMC) and is the subject of an entirely new Chapter 16 by Tony Yeshin – an expert in the field.

As Yeshin points out: 'If all other things are equal – or at least more or less so – then it is what people think, feel and believe about a product and its competitors which will be important. Since products in many areas will achieve parity or comparability in purely functional terms, it will be the perceptual differences which consumers will use to discriminate between rival brands. Only through the use of sustained and integrated marketing communication campaigns will manufacturers be able to achieve the differentiation they require.'

Having defined the nature and origins of IMC in some detail, Yeshin reviews the factors that have precipitated the growing interest in the subject. The impact and benefits of IMC are then spelled out followed by a detailed review of the organizational issues involved in developing an integrated approach. Finally, the potential barriers to achieving IMC are discussed, as are the international implications.

Chapter 17 – 'Promotion' by Keith Crosier – has appeared in every edition of the *Marketing Book*. For many of the reasons identified in the preceding chapter by Tony Yeshin, it is a subject in what appears to the less knowledgeable to be in a state of constant flux. To cope with this, Keith has to undertake substantially more revision than most of his fellow contributors. This he has done.

In revising the chapter, Keith has taken the opportunity to correct what he perceived to be an imbalance towards advertising and sizeable chunks of certain sections have been deleted, particularly the long description of the commission system. However, this is still covered well through cross-referencing. There are numerous new references and the latest available statistics at the time of going to press.

In previous editions Martin Christopher has contributed a chapter on the subject of 'Customer service and logistics strategy'. In this edition Martin is joined by his Cranfield colleague Adrian Payne to offer an extensively reworked chapter entitled 'Integrating customer relationship management and supply chain management'. As the title implies, the focus is on the critical link between customer relationship management (CRM) and supply chain management (SCM). Both concepts are described in some detail prior to an analysis of how the two may be combined to improve customer service and develop integrated market-driven strategies. The chapter builds upon earlier contributions and demonstrates how marketing practice is evolving to meet the challenge of new competitive forces.

Many of the changes identified by Martin Evans in his chapter on 'Market segmentation' pointed to the need for a new chapter dealing with direct marketing. Such a chapter has also been anticipated in other chapters in which the emphasis upon relationships, interaction, information technology and the Internet have highlighted the opportunity for direct contact between buyer and seller. Who better to write such a chapter than Graeme McCorkell, past Chairman of the Institute of Direct Marketing, author of a best-selling book on the subject and a consultant who has introduced direct marketing into numerous leading organizations.

Attributing its origins to mail order as an alternative method of distribution, McCorkell explains how the lessons learned from the direct distribution experience have enabled the principles to be applied to every kind of business. Drawing on his extensive experience, and citing numerous examples, McCorkell covers all aspects of direct marketing and then compares this with interactive marketing, which he defines as direct marketing through new media. Clearly, these media have created both threats and opportunities – both are clearly explained.

Whatever the medium, success in direct marketing depends upon the management of information systems, and especially the components of response, measurement and continuity that underpin the creation of databases. It is the database that lies at the heart of all effective direct marketing systems, and data mining and data warehousing are discussed as contributors to the database and the development of CRM systems. Finally, the importance of looking beyond the customer information system, which only records actual customers, to the larger market from which they are drawn is emphasized.

McCorkell's chapter on direct and interactive marketing provides a natural introduction to another new chapter by Dave Chaffey on e-marketing. Given the spectacular failure of a number of dotcom companies in recent years, there is a need for a critical appraisal of the potential of e-marketing. This is provided by this chapter.

Opening with a set of clear definitions of various aspects of e-marketing, Chaffey then identifies the key communications characteristics of digital media as the basis for determining how these may be used to best effect. Once these are understood it is possible to develop an e-marketing plan and Chaffey proposes using his SOSTAC framework which embraces Situation analysis, Objectives and Strategy, Tactics, Action and Control. This structure is broadly consistent with other models of strategic marketing planning, as described by Malcolm McDonald in Chapter 5. Each of these elements is discussed in detail.

Chaffey concludes that while a minority of businesses have converted extensively to the use of the Internet, for most it simply represents another channel to the market. This chapter, and Dave Chaffey's textbooks from which it has been developed, provide comprehensive advice on how best to incorporate the Internet into more effective marketing practice.

Finally, Chapter 26 by Sue Adkins is a completely new addition to *The Marketing Book*. Earlier editions contained a chapter on 'Marketing for non-profit organizations' by Keith Blois and this contains much useful advice of relevance for such organizations. For this edition it was decided to take a more focused look at the application of marketing to specific causes and the result is 'Cause-related marketing: who cares wins'. Unfortunately, space limitations meant that the more broadly based chapter had to be dropped but, of course, it is still available in the earlier editions.

As Adkins points out: 'Around the world we are witnessing a drawing back of the state and the process of deregulation, trade liberalization and the rapid internationalizing of markets. As state funding reduces across the globe, a gap is developing between society's needs and the government's or the state's ability to provide for them.' One means of filling this gap is through cause-related marketing. Cause-related marketing is defined by Business in the Community as 'a commercial activity by which businesses and charities or good causes form a partnership with each other to market an image, product or service for mutual benefit'. Drawing on her extensive experience and using a variety of case studies, Sue Adkins explains clearly what cause-related marketing is, what are some of the critical success factors in developing effective programmes, and specific advice on how readers may develop their own strategies and programmes.

Compiling a contributed book of this kind is not without its challenges. While it is true that if you want to get something done you should ask a busy person, it is also true that busy people have many compelling calls on their time and writing a chapter for a book may not be their top priority! That said, I am greatly indebted to all the contributors who have, with great good humour, responded to my pleas to meet pressing deadlines. I am also greatly indebted to my daughter Anne Foy who, in addition to running Westburn Publishers, found the time to collate the chapters as they came in and forward them to me as I travelled around the world, while giving nearly everyone the impression that I was firmly anchored to my desk in Scotland. (Nearly everyone – she told Robin Wensley I was on a beach in Fiji.)

Finally, I would like to thank my friends in the Department of Marketing, Monash University, for allowing me to spend a Scottish winter with them and compile what I consider to be a distillation of the best in British marketing. For any faults I accept total responsibility.

Michael J. Baker
Monash University
February 2002

Part One
Organization and Planning for Marketing

CHAPTER 1

One more time – what is marketing?

MICHAEL J. BAKER

The enigma of marketing is that it is one of man's oldest activities and yet it is regarded as the most recent of the business disciplines.
Michael J. Baker, *Marketing: Theory and Practice*, 1st Edn, Macmillan, 1976

Introduction

As a discipline, marketing is in the process of transition from an art which is practised to a profession with strong theoretical foundations. In doing so it is following closely the precedents set by professions such as medicine, architecture and engineering, all of which have also been practised for thousands of years and have built up a wealth of descriptive information concerning the art which has both chronicled and advanced its evolution. At some juncture, however, continued progress demands a transition from description to analysis, such as that initiated by Harvey's discovery of the circulation of the blood. If marketing is to develop it, too, must make the transition from art to applied science and develop sound theoretical foundations, mastery of which should become an essential qualification for practice.

Adoption of this proposition is as threatening to many of today's marketers as the establishment of the British Medical Association

was to the surgeon-barber. But, today, you would not dream of going to a barber for medical advice.

Of course, first aid will still be practised, books on healthy living will feature on the best-sellers list and harmless potions will be bought over the counter in drug stores and pharmacies. This is an amateur activity akin to much of what passes for marketing in British industry. While there was no threat of the cancer of competition it might have sufficed, but once the Japanese, Germans and others invade your markets you are going to need much stronger medicine if you are to survive. To do so you must have the courage to face up to the reality that aggressive competition can prove fatal, quickly; have the necessary determination to resist rather than succumb, and seek the best possible professional advice and treatment to assist you. Unfortunately, many people are unwilling to face up to reality. Even more unfortunate, many of the best minds and abilities are concentrated on activities which support the essential functions of an economy, by which we all survive, but have come to believe that these can exist by themselves independent of the manufacturing heart. Bankers, financiers, politicians and civil servants all fall into this category. As John Harvey-Jones pointed out so eloquently in the 1986 David Dimbleby lecture, much of our wealth is created by manufacturing industry and much of the output of service industries is dependent upon manufactured products for its continued existence. To assume service industries can replace manufacturing as the heart and engine of economic growth is naive, to say the least.

But merely to increase the size of manufacturing industry will not solve any of our current problems. Indeed, the contraction and decline of our manufacturing industry is not directly attributable to government and the City – it is largely due to the incompetence of industry itself. Those that survive will undoubtedly be the fittest and all will testify to the importance of marketing as an essential requirement for continued success.

However, none of this preamble addresses the central question 'What is marketing?' save perhaps to suggest that it is a newly emerging discipline inextricably linked with manufacturing. But this latter link is of extreme importance because in the evangelical excess of its original statement in the early 1960s, marketing and production were caricatured as antithetically opposed to one another. Forty years later most marketers have developed sufficient self-confidence not to feel it necessary to 'knock' another function to emphasize the importance and relevance of their own. So, what is marketing?

Marketing is both a managerial orientation – some would claim a business philosophy – and a business function. To understand marketing it is essential to distinguish clearly between the two.

Marketing as a managerial orientation

> Management ... the technique, practice, or science of managing or controlling; the skilful or resourceful use of materials, time, etc.
> *Collins Concise English Dictionary*

Ever since people have lived and worked together in groups there have been managers

concerned with solving the central economic problem of maximizing satisfaction through the utilization of scarce resources. If we trace the course of economic development we find that periods of rapid growth have followed changes in the manner in which work is organized, usually accompanied by changes in technology. Thus from simple collecting and nomadic communities we have progressed to hybrid agricultural and collecting communities accompanied by the concept of the division of labour. The division of labour increases output and creates a need for exchange and enhances the standard of living. Improved standards of living result in more people and further increases in output accompanied by simple mechanization which culminates in a breakthrough when the potential of the division of labour is enhanced through task specialization. Task specialization leads to the development of teams of workers and to more sophisticated and efficient mechanical devices and, with the discovery of steam power, results in an industrial revolution. A major feature of our own industrial revolution (and that of most which emulated it in the nineteenth century) is that production becomes increasingly concentrated in areas of natural advantage, that larger production units develop and that specialization increases as the potential for economies of scale and efficiency are exploited.

At least two consequences deserve special mention. First, economic growth fuels itself as improvements in living standards result in population growth which increases demand and lends impetus to increases in output and productivity. Second, concentration and specialization result in producer and consumer becoming increasingly distant from one another (both physically and psychologically) and require the development of new channels of distribution and communication to bridge this gap.

What of the managers responsible for the direction and control of this enormous diversity of human effort? By and large, it seems safe to assume that they were (and are) motivated essentially by (an occasionally enlightened) self-interest. Given the enormity and self-evident nature of unsatisfied demand and the distribution of purchasing power, it is unsurprising that most managers concentrated on making more for less and that to do so they pursued vigorously policies of standardization and mass production. Thus the first half of the twentieth century was characterized in the advanced industrialized economies of the West by mass production and mass consumption – usually described as a production orientation and a consumer society. But changes were occurring in both.

On the supply side the enormous concentration of wealth and power in super-corporations had led to legislation to limit the influence of cartels and monopolies. An obvious consequence of this was to encourage diversification. Second, the accelerating pace of technological and organizational innovation began to catch up with and even overtake the natural growth in demand due to population increases. Faced with stagnant markets and the spectre of price competition, producers sought to stimulate demand through increased selling efforts. To succeed, however, one must be able to offer some tangible benefit which will distinguish one supplier's product from another's. If all products are perceived as being the same then price becomes the distinguishing feature and the supplier becomes a price taker, thus having to relinquish the important managerial function of exercising control. Faced with such an impasse the real manager recognizes that salvation (and control) will be achieved through a policy of *product differentiation*. Preferably this will be achieved through the manufacture of a product which is physically different in some objective way from competitive offerings but, if this is not possible, then subjective benefits must be created through service, advertising and promotional efforts.

With the growth of product differentiation and promotional activity social commentators began to complain about the materialistic nature of society and question its value. Perhaps the

earliest manifestation of the consumerist movement of the 1950s and 1960s is to be found in Edwin Chamberlin and Joan Robinson's articulation of the concept of imperfect competition in the 1930s. Hitherto, economists had argued that economic welfare would be maximized through perfect competition in which supply and demand would be brought into equilibrium through the price mechanism. Clearly, as producers struggled to avoid becoming virtually passive pawns of market forces they declined to accept the 'rules' of perfect competition and it was this behaviour which was described by Chamberlin and Robinson under the pejorative title of 'imperfect' competition. Shades of the 'hidden persuaders' and 'waste makers' to come.

The outbreak of war and the reconstruction which followed delayed the first clear statement of the managerial approach which was to displace the production orientation. It was not to be selling and a sales orientation, for these can only be a temporary and transitional strategy in which one buys time in which to disengage from past practices, reform and regroup and then move on to the offensive again. The Americans appreciated this in the 1950s, the West Germans and Japanese in the 1960s, the British, belatedly in the late 1970s (until the mid-1970s nearly all our commercial heroes were sales people, not marketers – hence their problems – Stokes, Bloom, Laker). The real solution is marketing.

Marketing myopia – a watershed

If one had to pick a single event which marked the watershed between the production/sales approach to business and the emergence of a marketing orientation then most marketing scholars would probably choose the publication of Theodore Levitt's article entitled 'Marketing myopia' in the July–August 1960 issue of the *Harvard Business Review*.

Building upon the trenchant statement 'The history of every dead and dying "growth" industry shows a self-deceiving cycle of bountiful expansion and undetected decay', Levitt proposed the thesis that declining or defunct industries got into such a state because they were product orientated rather than customer orientated. As a result, the concept of their business was defined too narrowly. Thus the railroads failed to perceive that they were and are in the *transportation* business, and so allowed new forms of transport to woo their customers away from them. Similarly, the Hollywood movie moguls ignored the threat of television until it was almost too late because they saw themselves as being in the cinema industry rather than the *entertainment* business.

Levitt proposes four factors which make such a cycle inevitable:

1 A belief in growth as a natural consequence of an expanding and increasingly affluent population.
2 A belief that there is no competitive substitute for the industry's major product.
3 A pursuit of the economies of scale through mass production in the belief that lower unit cost will automatically lead to higher consumption and bigger overall profits.
4 Preoccupation with the potential of research and development (R&D) to the neglect of market needs (i.e. a technology push rather than market pull approach).

Belief number two has never been true but, until very recently, there was good reason to subscribe to the other three propositions. Despite Malthus's gloomy prognostications in the eighteenth century the world's population has continued to grow exponentially; most of the world's most successful corporations see the pursuit of market share as their primary goal, and most radical innovations are the result of basic R&D rather than product engineering to meet consumer needs. Certainly the dead and dying industries which Levitt referred to in his analysis were entitled to consider these three factors as reasonable assumptions on which to develop a strategy.

In this, then, Levitt was anticipating rather than analysing but, in doing so, he was building upon perhaps the most widely known yet most misunderstood theoretical construct in marketing – the concept of the product life cycle (PLC).

The PLC concept draws an analogy between biological life cycles and the pattern of sales growth exhibited by successful products. In doing so it distinguishes four basic stages in the life of the product: introduction; growth; maturity; and decline (see Figure 1.1).

Thus at birth or first introduction to the market a new product initially makes slow progress as people have to be made aware of its existence and only the bold and innovative will seek to try it as a substitute for the established product which the new one is seeking to improve on or displace. Clearly, there will be a strong relationship between how much better the new product is, and how easy it is for users to accept this and the speed at which it will be taken up. But, as a generalization, progress is slow.

However, as people take up the new product they will talk about it and make it more visible to non-users and reduce the perceived

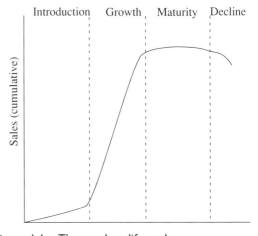

Figure 1.1 The product life cycle

risk seen in any innovation. As a consequence, a contagion or bandwagon effect will be initiated as consumers seek to obtain supplies of the new product and producers, recognizing the trend, switch over to making the new product in place of the old. The result is exponential growth.

Ultimately, however, all markets are finite and sales will level off as the market becomes saturated. Thereafter sales will settle down at a level which reflects new entrants to the market plus replacement/repeat purchase sales which constitutes the mature phase of the PLC. It is this phase which Levitt rightly characterizes as self-deceiving. Following the pangs of birth and introduction and the frenetic competitive struggle when demand took off, is it surprising that producers relax and perhaps become complacent when they are the established leaders in mature and profitable markets? But consumers, like producers, are motivated by self-interest rather than loyalty and will be quite willing to switch their allegiance if another new product comes along which offers advantages not present in the existing offering. Recognition of this represents a market opportunity for other innovators and entrepreneurs which they will seek to exploit by introducing their own new product and so initiating another new PLC while bringing to an end that of the product to be displaced.

The import of the PLC is quite simple, but frequently forgotten – *change is inevitable*. Its misunderstanding and misuse arise from the fact that people try to use it as a specific predictive device. Clearly, this is as misconceived as trying to guess the identity of a biological organism from the representation of a life cycle curve which applies equally to gnats and elephants.

Life cycles and evolution

As noted earlier, the PLC concept is based upon biological life cycles and this raises the question as to whether one can further extend the analogy from the specific level of the growth of organisms and products to the general case of the evolution of species and economies. At a conceptual level this seems both possible and worthwhile.

Consider the case of a very simple organism which reproduces by cell division placed into a bounded environment – a sealed test tube containing nutrients necessary for the cell's existence. As the cell divides the population will grow exponentially, even allowing for the fact that some cells will die for whatever reason, up to the point when the colony reaches a ceiling to further growth imposed by its bounded environment. What happens next closely parallels what happens in product life cycles, industry life cycles and overall economic cycles – a strong reaction sets in. Discussing this in a biological context, Derek de Solla Price cites a number of ways in which an exponentially growing phenomenon will seek to avoid a reduction in growth as it nears its ceiling. Two of these, 'escalation', and 'loss of definition', seem particularly relevant in an economic context.

In the case of escalation, modification of the original takes place at or near the point of inflection and '. . . a new logistic curve rises phoenix-like on the ashes of the old'. In other words, the cell modifies itself so that it can prosper and survive despite the constraints which had impeded its immediate predecessor. In marketing, such a phenomenon is apparent in a strategy of product rejuvenation in which either new uses or new customers are found to revitalize demand.

In many cases, however, it is not possible to 'raise the ceiling' through modification and the cell, or whatever, will begin to oscillate wildly in an attempt to avoid the inevitable (the 'hausse' in the economic cycle which precedes crisis and depression). As a result of these oscillations the phenomenon may become so changed as to be unrecognizable, i.e. it mutates or diversifies and recommences life in an entirely new guise. Alternatively, the phenomenon may accept the inevitable, smoothing out the oscillations and settling in equilibrium at a stable limit or, under different circumstances, slowly decline to nothing.

Over time, therefore, civilizations (and economies) rise and fall but the overall progression is upwards and characterized by periods of rapid development and/or stability when conditions are favourable and of decline when they are not. Observation would also seem to suggest that not only is change inevitable but that its pace is accelerating.

While it is often difficult to analyse the major causes and likely effect of major structural change when one is living in the midst of it, it seems likely that future historians will regard the 1960s and 1970s as a period of hausse in our economic and social evolution. Certainly economic forecasters are inclined in this direction through their interest in 'the long wave' or Kondratieff cycle in economic development. Similarly, management writers of the standing of Drucker talk of 'turbulence' while Toffler speaks of the third wave which will bring about Galbraith's post-industrial society.

And what has this to do with marketing? Quite simply, everything. For the past two hundred years the advanced industrial economies have prospered because the nature of demand has been basic and obvious and entrepreneurs have been able to devote their energies to producing as much as possible for as little as possible. But, in a materialistic society, basic demand for standardized and undifferentiated products has become saturated and the ability to off-load surpluses onto Third World developing economies is limited by their inability to pay for these surpluses. Product differentiation and an emphasis upon selling provide temporary respite from the imbalance but the accelerating pace of technological change rapidly outruns these. Indeed, in the short run the substitution of technology for unskilled and semi-skilled labour has resulted in a rich working population, with much higher discretionary purchasing power than ever before, and a poor, unemployed and aging sector with limited or no discretionary purchasing power at all.

All the indications would seem to point to the fact that we are in an age of transition from one order to another. In terms of personal aspirations many people are growing out of materialism and want, in Maslow's terminology, to 'self-actualize' or 'do their own thing'. As a consequence we are moving towards a post-industrial, post-mass consumption society which is concerned with quality not quantity and the individual rather than the mass. To cope with this we need a complete rethink of our attitudes to production, distribution and consumption and it is this which marketing offers.

Marketing starts with the market and the consumer. It recognizes that in a consumer democracy money votes are cast daily and that to win those votes you need to offer either a better product at the same price or the same product at a lower price than your competitors. Price is objective and tangible but what is 'a better product'? Only one person can tell you – the consumer. It follows, therefore, that a marketing orientation starts and ends with consumers and requires one to make what one can sell rather than struggle to sell what one can make. But marketing is not a philanthropic exercise in which producers give away their goods. Indeed, the long-run interest of the consumer requires that they do not, for otherwise as with eating the seed corn, we will eventually finish up with nothing at all. Producers are entitled to profits and the more value they add and the greater the satisfaction they deliver, the more the customer will be prepared to pay for this greater satisfaction. Marketing therefore is all about mutually satisfying exchange relationships for which the catalyst is the producer's attempt to define and satisfy the customer's need better.

Marketing misunderstood

The emphasis thus far, and of the chapter as a whole, has been upon the need for a new approach to managing production and distribution in response to major environmental changes. The solution proposed is the adoption of a marketing orientation which puts the customer at the beginning rather than the end of the production–consumption cycle. To do so requires a fundamental shift of attitude on the part of all those concerned with production and consumption. Unfortunately, while this concept seems both simple and obvious to those who have subscribed to it there is ample evidence that it is widely misunderstood and hence misapplied.

In 1970, Charles Ames drew attention to this in an article in the *Harvard Business Review* entitled 'Trappings versus substance in industrial marketing'. The thesis of this was that industrial companies that complained marketing was not working for them as it appeared to do so for the consumer good companies had only themselves to blame as they had not understood the substance of the marketing concept but had merely adopted some of its superficial trappings. At worst, they had merely changed the name of their personnel from 'sales' to 'marketing'.

More recently in the *Journal of Marketing Management* (1985), Stephen King diagnosed at least four different misinterpretations of marketing in the UK as follows:

1   *Thrust marketing* – this occurs when the sales managers change their name to marketing managers. But the emphasis is still upon selling what we can make with an emphasis upon price and cost cutting but little attention to fitness for purpose, quality and value for money. In other words, it ignores what the customer really wants.
2   *Marketing department marketing* – indicated by the establishment of a bolt-on specialized department intended to remedy the lack of customer understanding. Some improvement followed in markets where change was slow and gradual but it did not address the critical areas where radical innovation was called for. A sort of 'fine tuning' of the customer service

function but based on existing products and customers.
3   *Accountants marketing* – prevalent where chief executive officers have no direct experience of selling or marketing and concentrate upon short-term returns to the neglect of long-run survival. This approach was pungently criticized by Hayes and Abernathy in their 1980 *Harvard Business Review* article 'Managing our way to economic decline', which has been echoed many times since. Accountants marketing neglects investment in R&D, manufacturing and marketing and leads to a vicious downward spiral.
4   *Formula marketing* – in which control is seen as more important than innovation. This emphasizes sticking to the tried and true and reflects a risk-averse strategy. It appears professional (many MBAs) and concentrates on managing facts and information but its consumer research bias tends to tell you more about the past than the future.

Failure of these approaches suggests that *real* marketing has four essential features:

1   Start with the customer.
2   A long-run perspective.
3   Full use of *all* the company's resources.
4   Innovation.

The marketing function

From the foregoing it is clear that without commitment to the concept there is little likelihood that the marketing *function* will be executed effectively. It is also clear that the size and nature of the marketing function will vary enormously according to the nature of the company or organization and the markets which it serves.

Basically, the marketing function is responsible for the management of the marketing mix which, at its simplest, is summarized by the four Ps of product, price, place and promotion.

While much more elaborate formulations containing a dozen or more elements are to be found in the marketing textbooks such fine distinctions are not central to the present inquiry into the nature of marketing. As a function marketing has as many quirks and mysteries as research and development, finance and production but the important point to establish here is that the adoption of a marketing orientation does not mean nor require that the marketing function should be seen as the largest or the most important. In fact, in a truly marketing-orientated organization the need for a specialized marketing function is probably far less than it is in a sales- or production-dominated company. Appreciation of this fact would do much to disarm the resistance of other functional specialists who equate the adoption of a marketing orientation with a diminution in their own organizational status and influence.

Ideally, of course, such functional divisions would not exist. Perhaps, if everyone were marketing orientated would they disappear to our continuing competitive advantage?

During the late 1980s and early 1990s there was considerable evidence to suggest that the marketing orientation had become so widely accepted that commentators were beginning to question the need for a separate marketing function to assume responsibility for it. Marketing's 'mid-life crisis' caused more than a frisson of anxiety amongst marketing academics and practitioners alike!

In retrospect it seems that the collapse of communism in the late 1980s had a significant effect on managerial perceptions of marketing and highlighted the need to reconsider its role and function. During the years following World War II, politics and economics were dominated by the 'super powers' – the USA and the Soviet Union – each of which represented a quite different ideology and approach to economic organization – capitalism and communism. An essential difference between the two is that the former believes in and encourages competition in free markets while the latter is founded on

central control and an absence of competition in the marketplace.

The fall of the Berlin Wall and the disintegration of the Soviet Union which followed it would seem to confirm the view that competition is necessary to encourage change and progress. But the collapse of communism created the kind of dilemma addressed by Chamberlin and Robinson in the 1930s which led to the articulation of the theory of imperfect competition. Prior to this economists had focused analysis on the polar opposites of monopoly (no competition) and perfect competition with only limited attention given to intermediate conditions such as oligopoly. Clearly, there are many degrees of competition in the real world which lie between the polar extremes and it was these that came to be designated as imperfect.

The analogy may be extended if one considers communism to represent monopoly and the 'free' market as perfect competition. It was against this background that the dominant model of competition post-1950 was modelled on the United States and gave rise to what we now distinguish as the marketing management paradigm immortalized in Levitt's (1960) article, 'Marketing myopia', McCarthy's 4Ps and Kotler's seminal (1967) *Marketing Management: Analysis, Planning and Control*. Because of its primacy few gave much attention to free markets subject to varying degrees of regulation despite the fact that these probably, like imperfect competition, represented the majority. All that was to change in 1989!

In a penetrating analysis entitled *Capitalisme contre Capitalisme* Michel Albert (1991) pointed out that there is no single, monolithic definition of capitalism just as there is no single model of competition. Dussart (1994) elaborated on this and contrasted the American, Friedmanite model of unfettered competition practised in the USA and UK (Anglo-Saxon competition) with a modified form to be found in many social democracies in which a degree of market control is exercised by the state to moderate the excesses of big business. This Alpine/Germanic model of competition is strongly associated with most West European economies, and also with Japan and the 'tiger' economies of South East Asia, most of which have achieved a consistently better economic performance than the USA and UK since 1950.

The essential difference between the Anglo-Saxon/marketing management approach and the Alpine/Germanic style of competition is that the former takes a short-term, zero-sum adversarial view based on one-off transactions while the later adopts a long-term perspective which promotes win–win relationships.

Relationship marketing

According to Möller and Halinen-Kaila (1997) relationship marketing or RM was the 'hot topic' of the marketing discipline during the 1990s, but 'the rhetoric is often characterized more by elegance than by rigorous examination of the actual contents' (p. 2/3). The debate raises at least four critical questions:

1 Will RM replace the traditional marketing management school?
2 Will RM make marketing management theory obsolete?
3 Is RM a completely new theory, or does it derive from older traditions?
4 Do we need different theories of RM depending on the type of exchange relationships?

Möller and Halinen-Kaila seek to answer these questions. In doing so they stress the need to look back as well as forward and link new ideas with existing knowledge. They see the current interest in RM as deriving from four basic sources – marketing channels, business-to-business marketing (interorganizational marketing), services marketing and direct and database marketing (consumer marketing).

The dominant marketing management paradigm founded on the manipulation of the mix began to be questioned in the 1970s as it provided an inadequate explanation of the marketing of services. Such a challenge was unsurprising given that services had become the largest sector in the advanced industrial economies. Specifically, services marketing calls for recognition of both buyer and seller in the exchange process. Developments in information technology during the 1980s made it possible to both model and operationalize individual relationships through the use of databases.

However, the different research approaches are derived from different perspectives and conceptual frames of reference and provide only partial explanations which have yet to be synthesized and integrated into a holistic metatheory. Metatheory is derived from meta analysis which follows one of two closely related approaches – profiling or typology development. The latter tends to be abstract, the former descriptive, and it is this procedure which is followed by Möller and Halinen-Kaila who develop a detailed comparison matrix in which they examine the four traditions specified earlier across a number of dimensions, as illustrated in Table 1.1. While the authors acknowledge that such a matrix glosses over many details, none the less it provides useful generalization of the ways in which the different research traditions handle exchange relationships. To reduce the complexity of their comparison matrix with its four traditions, the authors collapse these into two categories – consumer and interorganizational relationships – and summarize their salient characteristics as in Table 1.1.

Although relationships are recognized as existing on a continuum in terms of closeness/involvement of the parties, the definition of the two categories is seen as helpful in 'anchoring' the ends of this continuum. This distinction is reinforced when one considers the different viewpoint or perspective taken in terms of the underlying assumptions on which consumer and interorganizational relationships have been evaluated – the former

Table 1.1 Comparison matrix of research approaches to marketing exchange relationships

Research tradition / Characteristics	Database and direct consumer marketing	Services marketing	Channel relationships	Interaction and networks
Basic goals	Enhance marketing efficiency through better targeting of marketing activities, especially marketing communications – channels and messages. Strong managerial emphasis, integrated marketing communications (IMC) an important agenda.	Explain and understand services marketing relationships and services management. Managerial goal: enhance the efficiency of managing customer encounters and customer relationships through managing the perceived quality of the service offer and relationship.	Theoretical goal: explain governance structures and dyadic behaviour in the channel context. Normative goal: determine efficient relational forms between channel members.	Three interrelated sets of goals: (i) Understand and explain interorganizational exchange behaviour and relationship development at a dyadic level in a network context: (ii) understand how nets of relationships between actors evolve, and (iii) understand how markets function and evolve from a network perspective. Managerial goal: gain a more valid view of reality through network theory.
View of relationship	Organization-personal customer relationships, often distant and generally comprising discrete transactions over time, handled through customized mass communication.	Personal customer relationships attended by service personnel and influenced through other marketing activities. Earlier a strong focus on the service encounter, later expanded to include the life cycle of relationships.	Interorganizational business relationships characterized by economic exchange and use of power. Actors are dependent on each other and behave reciprocally.	Relationships exist between different types of actors: firms, government and research agencies, individual actors. Not only goods, but all kinds of resources are exchanged through relationships. Relationships are seen as vehicles for accessing and controlling resources, and creating new resources.
Questions asked	How to provide value for the customer, how to develop loyal customers, how to adapt marketing activities along the customer's life cycle, how to retain customers?	How to provide value and perceived quality for the customer, how to manage service encounters, how to create and manage customer relationships?	What forms of governance are efficient for what types of channel relationships? How is the use of power related to relationship efficiency? How can the more dependent party safeguard against the dominant party? In what way is the dyadic relationship contingent on the larger channel context?	How are relationships created and managed; how do nets of relationships evolve, how can an actor manage these relationships and create a position in a net?
Disciplinary background	No disciplinary background; driven by information technology, marketing communication applications, and consultants.	No clear disciplinary background early phase a response to 'traditional marketing management', later consumer behaviour perspective and general management outlook. Empirically – and theory-driven with heavy managerial orientation.	Primarily theory-driven, attempts to combine the economic and political aspects (power, dependency) of channels. The tradition relies on transaction cost theory, relational law, social exchange theory, political economy, power and conflict in organizational sociology.	Both empirically- and theory driven; earlier influenced by channels research, organizational buying behaviour, resource dependency theory, social exchange theory and institutional economics; later by institutional theory, dynamic industrial economics, organizational sociology and resource-based theory.
World view and assumptions about relationships	Pragmatic – no explicit assumptions; implicitly assumes competitive markets of customers; S-O-R view with	Primarily the management perspective; dyadic interactive relationship but customers often seen as objects; i.e., the marketer is	Both parties can be active and reciprocally interdependent; the basic interest is in economic exchange and its efficiency. The	Depending on the research goals, the relationship perspective can be dyadic, focal firm or network type. Any actor can be active, actors are generally

	feedback the marketer is active, plans the offers and communications on the basis of customer status (profile) and feedback. Relatively weak dependency between buyer and seller, as the goods exchanged are relatively substitutable and many buyers and sellers exist.	generally the active party. Interdependence between the seller and the customer varies from weak to relatively strong. The basic service is often relatively substitutable, but the service relationship can be differentiated and individualized	relationship is unique, its substitutability depends on the availability of alternative buyers and sellers and the amount of switching costs related to relationship-specific investments.	seen as subjects. There is often relatively strong interdependency between actors, caused by heterogeneity of resources which makes substitution difficult.
Topics/concepts important for RM	Customer retention, share of customer, database as a device for managing direct communications, integrated use of channels.	Service encounters, experience & expectations, service & relationship quality, life-time value of the customer, internal marketing, empowerment of personnel.	Bases of power, uses of power and conflict behaviour, interdependence, goal congruity, decision domains, environmental influence on dyadic behaviour, transaction-specific investments, switching costs, dyadic governance, dyad outcomes: efficiency, satisfaction, relational norms.	Interaction processes, adaptation and investments into relationships, phases of relationships, actor bonds, resource ties, activity chains and relationship outcomes; nets and networks of relationships; network dynamics and embeddedness.
Level/unit of analysis and contextuality	Individual consumer, a group of consumers (segment); in applications customers are practically always aggregated into groups (segments). No conscious assumptions about the contextuality of the customer relationships; the competitive situation is the general contextuality perspective.	Individual customer, group or segment, service provider–client relationship. Little emphasis on contextuality, sometimes the history of a relationship is emphasized – generally handled through 'experience'; generally implicit assumption about the market as the dominant environmental form.	Firm, dyadic relationship in the channel context. Contingency perspective: dyadic behaviour and efficient forms of governance are dependent on the channel context. Well developed 'environment' theory.	Actor (organization, person), dyadic relationship, net of relationships. Transactions are episodes in the long-term relationship. The emphasis is on the embeddedness of relationships in nets and networks, and their history – no understanding of the present situation without history.
Time orientation, focus on structure vs. process	Rhetoric emphasizes the long-term view, no published tools for handling long-term issues of relationships. The focus is on the content of a customer profile, little emphasis/ conceptual effort on tackling the dynamism of customer development.	Earlier emphasis on short-term encounters, now shifting to a more enduring relational perspective. The process aspect is evident, but empirical research is primarily on the content of relationship characteristics.	Emphasis on efficient forms of channel relationships ranging from market-like transactions to long-term reciprocal relationships. Theoretically dynamic, but the majority of empirical research is static; the focus is on structure not process.	Time is an essential phenomenon. Dynamic perspective, focus on both structure (content) and processes (how dyads, nets, and networks evolve).
Methodological orientation	No conscious methodology, primarily cross-sectional analysis of survey data and customer databases.	Divided methodology: North American emphasis on explanation through hypothesis testing by multivariate analysis; Nordic emphasis on understanding through qualitative research.	Hypothetical – deductive reasoning, explanation through hypothesis testing by multivariate analysis.	Divided methodology, European emphasis (IMP Group) on understanding through historical case analysis; North American emphasis on explanation through hypothesis testing by multivariate analysis (this is primarily limited to dyads).

Source: Möller and Halinen-Kaila (1997, p. 10).

following a market perspective, the latter a network/systemic perspective.

In identifying two distinct streams of thought within the RM literature Möller and Halinen-Kaila recognize that they may be 'swimming against the fashionable stream of RM as the general marketing theory rhetoric!' (p. 16). If so, they are not alone as Mattsson (1997) is clearly of a similar opinion as is the author for, otherwise, he would have promoted an alternative perspective. That said, by adopting the Möller and Halinen-Kaila approach and identifying the key characteristics of the different schools of thought, it becomes possible to recognize both similarities and differences in much the same way that the concepts of pure competition and monopoly enabled the emergence of a theory of imperfect competition which reflects messy reality rather than theoretical purity. As Möller and Halinen-Kaila point out, the key managerial challenge in both forms of RM is how to manage a portfolio of exchange relationships. Within the domain of consumer or 'limited' relationship marketing, numerous approaches and techniques have evolved which are highly relevant to addressing this problem. Indeed, with the developments in information technology in recent years many of these have become of practical rather than theoretical interest. We should not lightly discard these methods.

In the domain of interorganizational relationships their complexity is likely to limit the extent to which 'packaged' solutions may be applied. While useful generalizations will have an important role to play, the situation-specific nature of most problems will continue to require decision-makers to use experience and judgement in coming up with effective solutions.

Summary

In this introductory chapter we have attempted to trace the evolution of exchange relationships

and provide at least a partial answer to the question 'What is marketing?' In the process we have established that exchange is at the very heart of human development in both economic and social terms. Until recently, however, the desirability of enhancing consumer satisfaction through the provision of more and better goods and services has been so self-evident that little consideration has been given as to how to define 'more' and 'better', or the processes by which such evaluations are made. As Adam Smith observed in his *Wealth of Nations* (1776), 'Consumption is the sole end and purpose of production'. Having stated the obvious the remainder of his great work is devoted wholly to issues of improving supply with no consideration of demand *per se*.

As we have seen, it is only with the stabilization of populations in advanced economies, and the continuous and accelerating improvements in productivity attributable to technological innovation, that a preoccupation with supply side problems has given way to demand side considerations. Modern marketing, dating from the 1950s, reflects this transition. But, as we have attempted to show, the marketing management model which emerged was itself a purely transitional response to managing the changing balance between sellers and buyers. Initially, the marketing management model was concerned with what sellers needed to do to retain control over the transaction, with consumers seen as passive participants in the process. With the evolution of service dominated economies, so the balance of power changed and supply was now seen to be subservient to demand and consumer sovereignty.

As we noted in the last edition prepared in 1998, the problem with the change in emphasis is that it still sees exchange as a zero-sum game. While buyers are winners, sellers are losers! As predicted then, the dangers of this adversarial approach to exchange are readily apparent, especially in the manufacturing sector, where the greatest potential for growth and added value exist. Thus, the outsourcing of manufacturing by the wealthier economies to the newly industrializing countries has tended to exaggerate rather than reduce the unequal distribution of wealth between these economies. But, at the same time, it has led to unemployment in these wealthier economies, stagnating demand and recession – a recession that is global in its impact.

This gloomy scenario is compounded when one recognizes that the concentration of much of the world's wealth in the hands of a minority of the world's population was undoubtedly a factor in the horrific events of September 11th. 2001. While it would be overly simplistic to attribute these events solely to envy and resentment of the disproportionate consumption of resources by the American people, it is clear that Americans, and others, are having difficulty in adjusting to the fact that such win–lose situations engender such feelings among the 'losers'.

What is needed is a proper appreciation of the true marketing concept of exchange based on *mutually satisfying relationships* in which both parties get what they want – a true win–win situation. Such a concept reflects the 'Golden Rule' central to most religious ideologies – 'Do unto others as you would be done by'. While it would be unrealistic to expect those enjoying high standards of living to reduce these radically overnight, it should not be impossible to promote a more equitable global society by encouraging the win–win outcomes advocated by the marketing concept and its emphasis on mutually satisfying relationships.

In our view, implementation of this concept/orientation demands the existence of a marketing function and the management of the marketing mix. The remainder of *The Marketing Book* draws on the expertise of leading thinkers and practitioners to see how we might achieve this desired state.

References

Albert, M. (1991) *Capitalisme contre Capitalisme*, Seuil, L'Historie Immédiate, Paris.

Ames, C. (1970) Trappings versus substance in industrial marketing, *Harvard Business Review*, July–August, 93–103.

Dussart, C. (1994) 'Capitalism versus Capitalism', in Baker, M. J. (ed.) *Perspectives on Marketing Management*, Vol. 4, John Wiley & Sons, Chichester.

Hayes, R. and Abernathy, W. (1980) Managing our way to economic decline, *Harvard Business Review*, July–August, 67–77.

King, S. (1985) Has marketing failed or was it never really tried?, *Journal of Marketing Management*, **1**(1), Summer, 1–19.

Kotler, P. (1967) *Marketing Management: Analysis, Planning and Control*, Prentice-Hall, Englewood Cliffs, NJ.

Levitt, T. (1960) Marketing myopia, *Harvard Business Review*, July–August, 45–60.

Mattsson, L.-G. (1997) 'Relationship marketing' and the 'markets-as-networks approach' – a comparative analysis of two evolving streams of research, *Journal of Marketing Management*, **13**, 447–61.

Möller, K. and Halinen-Kaila, A., (1997) 'Relationship Marketing: Its Disciplinary Roots and Future Directions', Helsinki School of Economics and Business Administration, Helsinki: *Working Papers*, W-194.

Further reading

Baker, M. J. (2000) 'Marketing – Philosophy or Function?', Chapter 1 in Baker, M. J. (ed.) *Encyclopedia of Marketing*, 2nd edn, ITP, London.

CHAPTER 2

Postmodern marketing: everything must go!

STEPHEN BROWN

Grand opening offer

What on earth does 'postmodern' mean? A very good question, and one that is not easily answered, because the word, many believe, is as meaningless as it is ubiquitous. It is a word that has been applied to everything from making love (over the Internet, by means of teledildonic body suits) to making war (as in the Gulf or Kosovo, where virtual attacks are mounted and western casualties avoided at all costs). What's worse, the word has attracted the anoraks of this world, like legendary moths to a proverbial flame, all determined to define the indefinable.

The inevitable upshot of this mission to explain the postmodern is a massive, rapidly growing and almost unreadable mound of books, articles and anthologies. The shelves of our libraries and bookshops literally groan under the weight of texts with 'postmodern' in the title; the A to Z of academic disciplines – from accountancy to zoology – has been infiltrated by postmodern fanatics, and many academic careers have been made, or unmade, on the back of this infuriating intellectual beast (Appignanesi and Garratt, 1995; Best and Kellner, 2001; Calás and Smircich, 1997; Crews, 2001; Ward, 1997).

Indeed, so pervasive is the discourse on the postmodern (and so pervasive is the discourse on the discourse . . .), that postmodernism has become one of the dominant organizing concepts – if it is a concept – across the social and human sciences. Granted, comparatively few people in each academic discipline espouse a postmodernist position, albeit many more are involved in the wider pro/con debate. Some subject areas, moreover, are further down the postmodern road than others (in org. studies, for instance, it is fairly well established, whereas in marketing and consumer research it remains the preserve of the fighting few). Be that as it may, the very omnipresence of postmodernism is deeply ironic, since it is opposed to universal modes of thought and sets great store by difference, diversity, singularity and so on. For postmodernists, however, this ubiquity of the unique is not a major problem, because contradiction, inconsistency and paradox are themselves characteristic features of the postmodern. They are to be celebrated not condemned, flaunted not faulted, encouraged not excoriated.

The *real* irony of the postmodern is much, much closer to home, insofar as many sociologists, anthropologists, literary theorists and cultural studies specialists consider marketing and consumption to be central to the post-modern condition (e.g. Bocock, 1993; Falk and Campbell, 1997; Featherstone, 1991; Warde, 2002). Consumer behaviour, global brands, advertising campaigns, department stores, regional malls, positioning strategies and the entire apparatus of marketing are widely considered to be part and parcel of the post-modern. Yet postmodern perspectives remain comparatively rare within the academic marketing community. Indeed, the ultimate irony is that the analyses of marketing artefacts undertaken by non-marketers are often superior, more insightful and much more in keeping with our paradoxical postmodern times than those which derive from the positivistic, model-building, law-abiding, information-processing, truth-seeking marketing scientists who continue to hold sway in our field (Brown, 1996, 2002).

No down payment

Perhaps the best way of getting to grips with the postmodern is to recognize that the very word is multifaceted. It is a signifier with many signifieds, a portmanteau or umbrella term, an ever-expanding linguistic universe, if you will. However, for the synoptic purposes of the present chapter, four forms of the formulation can be set forth (see Brown 1995, 1998a).

Postmodernism

For many commentators, postmodernism is primarily an aesthetic movement, a revolt against the once shocking, subsequently tamed 'modern' movement of the early- to mid-twentieth century. (In fact, some reserve the term 'postmodernism' for developments in the cultural sphere.) To cite but three examples: in architecture, PoMo is characterized by the eschewal of the austere, unembellished, 'glass box' International Style of Le Corbusier and Mies van der Rohe, and a return to inviting, ornamented, mix 'n' matched, vernacular or pseudo-vernacular forms, as found in the work of Venturi, Portman and Jencks. In literature, likewise, the spare, experimental, and, as often as not, inaccessible writings of the giants of high modernism – Joyce, Proust, Eliot etc. – have given way to the parodic, reader-friendly vulgarities of Martin Amis, Will Self and Bret Easton Ellis. In popular music, moreover, the 'modern' era of The Beatles, Rolling Stones, Beach Boys and Bob Dylan (albeit there is some debate over the existence of modernist pop/rock), has sundered into a multiplicity of modalities – house, jungle, techno, rap, roots, world, drum 'n' bass, speed garage and the like – many of which are parasitic upon (sampling, scratch), pastiches of (the tribute group phenomenon) or cross-pollinated with extant musical forms (alt.county, nü-metal, neo-disco etc.).

Postmodernity

A second thread in the tangled postmodern skein is drawn from the economic base, as opposed to the aesthetic superstructure. The world, according to this viewpoint, has entered a whole new, qualitatively different, historical epoch; an epoch of multinational, globalized, ever-more rapacious capitalism, where traditional ways of working, producing, consumption and exchange have changed, and changed utterly. Frequently described by the epithet 'postmodernity', this is the world of the world wide web, 24/7 day-trading, satellite television, soundbitten and spin-doctored politics, mobile phoneophilia, pick 'n' mix lifestyles, serial monogamy and relentless McDonaldization. It is a world of ephemerality, instability, proliferation, hallucination and, above all, chaos. It is a world where the beating of a butterfly's wings in South America can cause a stock market crash in Hong Kong or swerve the ball into the net at Old Trafford. It is a world of unexpected, unpredictable, uncontrollable, unremitting, some would say unnecessary, upheaval.

The postmodern condition

Paralleling the transformations that are taking place in the aesthetic and economic spheres, a postmodern turn in the nature of knowledge and thought has transpired. The so-called Enlightenment Project, which commenced in western Europe during the eighteenth century and comprised a systematic, rigorous, supposedly dispassionate search for objective knowledge, universal laws, meaningful generalizations and absolute truths, has run slowly but irreversibly into the sand. Its replacement, to some extent at least, is a low-key postmodern worldview, which emphasizes the boundedness of knowledge, the limits to generalization, the lack of universal laws, the prevalence of disorder over order, irrationality rather than rationality, subjectivity instead of objectivity, and passionate participation as an alternative to dispassionate spectatorship. Thus, the 'grand narratives' of the project of modernity – progress, freedom, profit, utopia, liberalism, truth, science etc. – have been superseded by an awareness of the lack of progress, the absence of freedom, the price of profit, the dystopia that is utopia, the illiberalism of liberalism, the fiction that is truth and the artistry of science.

Postmodern apocalypse

Another, and in certain respects the most straightforward, way of grasping the postmodern is to eschew the idea that it is an 'it'. Its 'itness', after all, assumes a referential model of language (i.e. that there are 'things' out there in the world that the word 'postmodern' refers to), which is something card-carrying postmodernists are loath to concede (assuming, of course, that there are things out there called postmodernists). Postmodernism, rather, is better regarded as an attitude, a feeling, a mood, a sensibility, an orientation, a way of looking at the world – a way of looking askance at the world. A pose, if you prefer. Irony, parody, playfulness, irreverence, insolence, couldn't-care-less cynicism and absolute unwillingness

to accept the accepted are postmodernism's distinguishing features. Hence, the progressive, optimistic, forward-looking, ever-onward-ever-upward worldview of the modern era has been replaced by a pessimistic, almost apocalyptic, sense of apprehension, anxiety, apathy and anomie. The postmodern, then, is suffused with an air of exhaustion, ending, crisis and (calamitous) change. Its characteristic attitude is a 'mixture of worldweariness and cleverness, an attempt to make you think that I'm half-kidding, though you're not quite sure about what' (Apple, 1984, p. 39).

Money back guarantee

Now, it doesn't take a great deal of cleverness, let alone world-weariness, to recognize that many of these purported postmodern traits are discernible in today's marketing and consumer environment. Consider shopping centres. The archetypal Arndale developments of the 1960s – all reinforced concrete, flat roofs, straight lines, low ceilings and oozing mastic – have been eclipsed by postmodern shopping malls, which are bright, airy, eclectic, ornamented, extravagantly themed, unashamedly ersatz and invariably welcoming. Instead of a glowering, intimidating, brutalist bulk, a blot on the cityscape that seemed to say, 'enter if you dare, go about your business and get out as quickly as possible', postmodern centres suggest that shopping is a pleasure not a chore. They say, in effect, 'enjoy yourself, call again, bring the family, fulfil your fantasies, relive your childhood, imagine yourself in another world or another part of the world, or both' (Goss, 1993; Maclaran and Brown, 2001; Shields, 1992).

In advertising, likewise, the straightforward marketing pitch of tradition – 'this product is good, buy it' – is almost unheard of these days (except when it's used ironically). Contemporary commercials are invariably sly, subtle, allusive, indirect, clever, parodic, insouciant, self-referential (ads about ads), cross-referential (ads that cite other cultural forms – soap operas, movies etc.) and made with staggeringly expensive, semi-cinematic production values. They not only presuppose a highly sophisticated, advertising- and marketing-literate audience, but work on the basic premise that advertising-inculcated images (cool, sexy, smart and the like) are the essence of the product offer. Products, in fact, are little more than the campaign's tie-in merchandise, along with the videos, CDs, PR hoop-la and media coverage of the agency's self-aggrandizing endeavours (Berger, 2001; Davidson, 1992; Goldman and Papson, 1996).

Consumers, too, are changing. As Chapter 6 explains, the certainties, uniformities and unambiguities of the modern era – where mass production produced mass marketing which produced mass consumption which produced mass production – are being trumped by the individualities, instabilities and fluidities of the postmodern epoch. Postmodernity is a place where there are no rules only choices, no fashion only fashions, the Joneses are kept well away from and anything not only goes but it has already left the building. It is a place where 'one listens to reggae, watches a western, eats McDonald's food for lunch and local cuisine for dinner, wears Paris perfume in Tokyo and retro clothes in Hong Kong' (Lyotard, 1984, p. 76). It is a place where 'we have literally shopped 'til we dropped into our slumped, channel surfing, couch-potatoed position, with the remote control in one hand, a slice of pizza in the other and a six-pack of Australian lager between our prematurely swollen ankles' (Brown *et al.*, 1997). It is a place where the world is no longer contained in William Blake's grain of sand but stocked, bar-coded, date-stamped and on special offer at your local Sainsbury's superstore or friendly neighbourhood category killer. It is a place, as the irascible novelist Will Self notes, where anti-capitalist, anti-globalization, anti-marketing protesters 'take global airlines so that they can put on Gap clothes to throw rocks at Gap shops' (Dugdale, 2001, p. 37).

Batteries not included

At a time when consumption is all the academic rage – as demonstrated by the outpouring of books by non-consumer researchers (e.g. Corrigan, 1997; Edwards, 2000; Howes, 1996; Lury, 1996; Miles *et al.*, 2002; Miller, 1995; Nava *et al.*, 1997; Ritzer, 1999) – it is difficult to 'step outside' and comment meaningfully upon this marketing maelstrom. The most cogent attempt to do so has been made by two prophets of the postmodern turn: A. Fuat Firat and Alladi Venkatesh (1995). In a lengthy article on the 're-enchantment of consumption', they contend that postmodern marketing is characterized by five main themes: *hyperreality, fragmentation, reversed production and consumption, decentred subjects* and the *juxtaposition of opposites* (Table 2.1).

Hyperreality

Exemplified by the virtual worlds of cyberspace and the pseudo worlds of theme parks, hotels and heritage centres, hyperreality involves the creation of marketing environments that are 'more real than real'. The distinction between reality and fantasy is momentarily blurred, as in the back lot tour of 'working' movie studios in Universal City, Los Angeles. In certain respects, indeed, hyperreality is *superior* to everyday mundane reality, since the aversive side of authentic consumption experiences – anti-tourist terrorism in Egypt, muggings in New York, dysentery in Delhi – magically disappears when such destinations are recreated in Las Vegas, Busch Gardens, Walt Disney World or the manifold variations on the theme park theme. Ironically, however, the perceived superiority of the fake is predicated upon an (often) unwarranted stereotype of reality, and the reality of the fake – e.g. the queues in Disneyland – may be much worse than anything the average visitor would actually experience in Egypt, New York, Delhi or wherever. But such is the cultural logic of postmodern marketing.

Table 2.1 Postmodern conditions and their main themes				
Hyperreality	*Fragmentation*	*Reversal of production and consumption*	*Decentred subject*	*Juxtaposition of opposites*
Reality as part of symbolic world and constructed rather than given	Consumption experiences are multiple, disjointed	Postmodernism is basically a culture of consumption, while modernism represents a culture of production	The following modernist notions of the subject are called into question:	Pastiche as the underlying principle of juxtaposition
Signifier/signified (structure) replaced by the notion of endless signifiers	Human subject has a divided self		Human subject as a self-knowing, independent agent	Consumption experiences are not meant to reconcile differences and paradoxes, but to allow them to exist freely
The emergence of symbolic and the spectacle as the basis of reality	Terms such as 'authentic self' and 'centered connections' are questionable	Abandonment of the notion that production creates value while consumption destroys it	Human subject as a cognitive subject	
The idea that marketing is constantly involved in the creation of *more* real than real	Lack of commitment to any (central) theme	Sign value replaces exchange value as the basis of consumption	Human subject as a unified subject	Acknowledges that fragmentation, rather than unification, is the basis of consumption
The blurring of the distinction between real and non-real	Abandonment of history, origin, and context		Postmodernist notions of human subject: Human subject is historically and culturally constructed	
	Marketing is an activity that fragments consumption signs and environments and reconfigures them through style and fashion	Consumer paradox: Consumers are active producers of symbols and signs of consumption, as marketers are	Language, not cognition, is the basis for subjectivity	
	Fragmentation as the basis for the creation of body culture	Consumers are also objects in the marketing process, while products become active agents	Instead of a cognitive subject, we have a communicative subject	
			Authentic self is displaced by made-up self	
			Rejection of modernist subject as a male subject	

Source: adapted from Firat and Venkatesh (1995).

Fragmentation

Consumption in postmodernity is unfailingly fast, furious, frenetic, frenzied, fleeting, hyperactive. It is akin to zapping from channel to channel, or flicking through the pages of the glossies, in search of something worth watching, reading or buying. Shopping on Speed. This disjointedness is partly attributable to the activities of marketers with their ceaseless proliferation of brands, ever-burgeoning channels of distribution, increasingly condensed commercial breaks and apparent preparedness to press every available surface into advertising service (sidewalks, urinals, communications satellites, 1950s sitcoms and so forth). It is also due to the disconnected postmodern lifestyles, behaviours, moods, whims and vagaries of contemporary consumers. A product of profusion with a profusion of products, the postmodern consumer performs a host of roles – wife and mother, career woman, sports enthusiast, fashion victim, DIY enthusiast, culture vulture, hapless holidaymaker, websurfing Internet avatar and many more – each with its appropriate brand name array. These identities or selves, furthermore, are neither sequential nor stable, but fluid, mutable and, not least, negotiable. Pick 'n' mix personae are proliferating. Off-the-shelf selves are available in every conceivable size, style, colour, fit and price point. Made to measure selves cost extra.

Reversed production and consumption

This fragmented, hyperrealized, postmodern consumer, it must also be stressed, is not the unwitting dupe of legend, who responds rat-like to environmental stimuli of Skinnerian caprice. Nor is the postmodern consumer transfixed, rabbit-like, in the headlights of multinational capital. Nor, for that matter, is he or she likely to be seduced by the sexual textual embeds of subliminal advertisers, though (s)he might pretend to be. On the contrary, the very idea that consumers have something 'done' to them by marketers and advertisers no longer passes muster. Postmodern consumers, in fact, *do* things with advertising; they are active in the production of meaning, of marketing, of consumption. As Firat and Venkatesh (1995, p. 251) rightly observe:

> It is not to brands that consumers will be loyal, but to images and symbols, especially to images and symbols that *they* produce while they consume. Because symbols keep shifting, consumer loyalties cannot be fixed. In such a case a modernist might argue that the consumers are fickle – which perhaps says more about the modernist intolerance of uncertainty – while the postmodernist interpretation would be that consumers respond strategically by making themselves unpredictable. The consumer finds his/her liberatory potential in subverting the market rather than being seduced by it.

Decentred subjects

This idea of a multiphrenic, fragmented, knowing consumer is further developed in Firat and Venkatesh's notion of decentred subjectivity. The centredness that is characteristic of modernity, where individuals are unambiguously defined by their occupation, social class, demographics, postcode, personalities and so on, has been ripped asunder in postmodernity. Traditional segmentation criteria *may* be applied to such people, and marketing strategies formulated, but it is increasingly accepted that these fleetingly capture, or freeze-frame at most, a constantly moving target market. Even the much-vaunted 'markets of one', in which marketing technologies are supposedly adapted to the specific needs of individual consumers, is doomed to fail in postmodernity, since each consumer comprises a multiplicity of shopping homunculi, so to speak. The harder marketers try to pin down the decentred consuming subject, the less successful they'll be. Today's consumers are always just beyond the reach of marketing scientists, marketing strategists, marketing tacticians, marketing technologists, marketing taxonomists and all the rest. In the words of leading marketing authority, Alan Mitchell (2001, p. 60):

> There is nothing wrong with trying to be scientific about marketing; in trying to understand cause and effect. And stimulus–response marketing has chalked up many successes. Nevertheless, it now faces rapidly diminishing returns. Consumers are becoming 'marketing literate'. They know they are being stimulated and are developing a resistance to these stimuli, even learning to turn the tables. Consumers increasingly refuse to buy at full price, for example, knowing that a sale is just around the corner. They have fun 'deconstructing' advertisements. The observed has started playing games with the observer. Buyers are starting to use the system for their own purposes, just as marketers attempted to use it for theirs.

Juxtaposition of opposites

Although it is well-nigh impossible to 'target' or 'capture' the inscrutable, amorphous, unpindownable entity that is the postmodern consumer, it is still possible to engage with, appeal to, or successfully attract them. The key to this quasi-conversation is not ever more precise segmentation and positioning, but the exact opposite. An open, untargeted, ill-defined, imprecise approach, which leaves scope for imaginative consumer participation (e.g. ironic advertising treatments where the purpose, pitch or indeed 'product' is unclear), is typical of postmodern marketing. This sense of fluidity and porosity is achieved by pastiche, by bricolage, by radical juxtaposition, by the mixing and matching of opposites, by combinations of contradictory styles, motifs and allusions, whether it be in the shimmering surfaces of pseudo-rococo postmodern buildings or the ceaseless cavalcade of contrasting images that are regularly encountered in commercial breaks, shop windows or roadside billboards. Occasionally, these succeed in exceeding the sum of their parts and combine to produce a sublime whole, an ephemeral spectacular, a fleeting moment of postmodern transcendence,

as in *Riverdance*, *Shrek* or *Kotler on Marketing*. Well, okay, two out of three ain't bad . . .

Limited time only

While few would deny that Firat and Venkatesh have done much to explain the postmodern marketing condition, their analysis is not without its weaknesses. Many commentators would contest their inventory of overarching themes and, indeed, the very idea itself of identifiable overarching themes. Little is accomplished by reciting such shortcomings. It is sufficient to note that all manner of alternative takes on postmodern marketing are now available and all sorts of signature 'themes' have been suggested. Cova (1996), for example, considers it to be about the 'co-creation of meaning'. Thompson (2000) regards 'reflexivity' as the be all and end all. O'Donohoe (1997) draws attention to the importance of 'intertextuality'. And Sherry (1998) sets great store by PoMo's preoccupation with 'place'. The important point, however, is not that any of these readings is 'right' or 'wrong', but that postmodern marketing is itself plurivalent and open to multiple, highly personal, often irreconcilable interpretations.

For my own part, I reckon that *retrospection* is the defining feature of the present postmodern epoch and acerbic comedian George Carlin concurs (Table 2.2). The merest glance across the marketing landscape reveals that retro goods and services are all around. Old-fashioned brands, such as Atari, Airstream and Action Man, have been adroitly revived and successfully relaunched. Ostensibly extinct trade characters, like Mr Whipple, Morris the Cat and Charlie the Tuna, are cavorting on the supermarket shelves once more. Ancient commercials are being rebroadcast (Ovaltine, Alka-Seltzer); time-worn slogans are being resuscitated (Britney Spears sings 'Come Alive' for Pepsi); and long-established products are being repackaged in their original, eye-catching liveries (Blue Nun, Sun Maid raisins). Even motor cars and washing

Table 2.2   Anything but the present
America has no now. We're reluctant to acknowledge the present. It's too embarrassing. Instead, we reach into the past. Our culture is composed of sequels, reruns, remakes, revivals, reissues, re-releases, re-creations, re-enactments, adaptations, anniversaries, memorabilia, oldies radio, and nostalgia record collections. World War Two has been refought on television so many times, the Germans and Japanese are now drawing residuals. Of course, being essentially full of shit, we sometimes feel the need to dress up this past-preoccupation, as with pathetic references to reruns as 'encore presentations'. Even instant replay is a form of token nostalgia: a brief visit to the immediate past for re-examination, before slapping it onto a highlight video for further review and re-review on into the indefinite future. Our 'yestermania' includes fantasy baseball camps, where ageing sad sacks pay money to catch baseballs thrown by men who were once their heroes. It is part of the fascination with sports memorabilia, a 'memory industry' so lucrative it has attracted counterfeiters. In this the Age of Hyphens, we are truly retro-Americans.
Source: Carlin (1997, p. 110).

powder, long the apotheosis of marketing's new-and-improved, whiter-than-white, we-have-the-technology worldview, are getting in on the retrospective act, as the success of the BMW Mini Cooper and Colour Protection Persil daily remind us (Hedberg and Singh, 2001).

The service sector, similarly, is adopting a time-was ethos. Retro casinos, retro restaurants, retro retail stores, retro holiday resorts, retro home pages and retro roller-coasters are two a penny. The movie business is replete with sequels, remakes and sequels of prequels, such as *Star Wars: The Attack of the Clones*, to say nothing of historical spectaculars and post-modern period pieces like *Moulin Rouge* and *Gladiator*. *The Producers, Kiss Me Kate, Rocky Horror* and analogous revivals are keeping the theatrical flag flying; meanwhile, television programming is so retro that reruns of classic weather reports can't be far away. The music business, what is more, is retro a go-go. Michael Jackson makes an invincible comeback.

Madonna goes on tour again, after an eight-year hiatus. The artist formerly known as Prince is known as Prince, like before. Bruce Springsteen reconvenes the E-Street Band. Simple Minds are promising another miracle. Robbie Williams sings Sinatra. And U2 reclaim their title as the best U2 tribute band in the world. It's a beautiful payday.

Above and beyond the practices of retro marketing, this back-to-the-future propensity has significant implications for established marketing principles. As Brown (2001a, b) explains (after a fashion), it involves abandoning modern marketing's 'new and improved' mindset and returning to the retro ethic of 'as good as always'. It spurns the dispassionate, white-coated, wonder-working laboratories of marketing science in favour of the extravagant, over-the-top hyperbole of pre-modern marketers like P. T. Barnum (consider the postmodern publicity stunts of retro CEO, Richard Branson). It eschews the chimera of customer-orientation for a marketing philosophy predicated on imagination, creativity and rule breaking. It refuses to truck with the guru du jour and goes back to the marketing giants of yesteryear – Wroe Alderson, Ralph Breyer, Melvin Copeland and all the rest. It not only ignores the latest marketing best-seller but seeks inspiration instead in anthologies of recycled, reheated and rehashed articles by scholarly back-scratchers (two plugs and a gratuitous insult in one paragraph; must be a record!).

One careful owner

The retro marketing revolution is all very well, but the postmodern paradigm of which it is part poses a very important question for marketing and consumer researchers. Namely, how is it possible to understand, represent or describe postmodern marketing phenomena, when postmodernism challenges the very premises of conventional research? The logic, order, rationality and model-building modalities of the modernist research tradition seem singularly inappropriate when addressing postmodern concerns. Now, this is not to suggest that established tools and techniques *cannot* be applied to postmodern artefacts and occurrences. There are any number of essentially modernist portrayals of the postmodern marketing condition (what is it?, what are its principal characteristics?, what can we 'do' with it?). Yet the relevance of such approaches remains moot. Is it *really* possible to capture the exuberance, the flamboyance, the incongruity, the energy, the playfulness of postmodern consumption in a standard, all-too-standard research report?

On the surface, this may seem like a comparatively trivial matter – if we jazz up our reports and use expressive language, everything will be okay – but it goes to the very heart of why we do what we do, how we do it and who we do it for. The decision facing marketing, as it has faced other academic disciplines grappling with postmodern incursions, is whether we should strive to be postmodern marketing researchers or researchers of postmodern marketing. The former implies that the modalities of postmodernism should be imported into marketing research, that we should endeavour to 'walk the talk', to *be* postmodern in our publications, presentations and what have you. The latter intimates that researchers should confine themselves to applying proven tools and techniques to the brave old world of postmodern marketing. Just because the market has changed, or is supposed to have changed, it does not necessarily follow that tried and trusted methods of marketing research must change as well.

Although this choice is nothing if not clear-cut, a moment's reflection reveals it to be deeply divisive at best and potentially ruinous at worst. After all, if one group of marketing researchers works in a postmodern mode, a mode that is unlike anything that has gone before, it is fated to 'fail' when conventional standards of assessment are applied. Postmodern marketing research *cannot* meet the criteria – rigour, reliability, trustworthiness and so on – that are accepted, indeed *expected*, by champions of established methods and used to judge the worth, the contribution, the success or otherwise of a particular piece of work. For many commentators, then, postmodern marketing research does not constitute 'research' as such (other terms, invariably pejorative, are usually applied). However, as academic careers depend upon the publication of research findings, the potential for internecine conflict is self-evident. True, the etiquette of intellectual discourse emphasizes mutual tolerance, openness to opposing points of view, the community of scholars and suchlike, but the practicalities of academic politics belie this placid facade. Insurgence, in-fighting and intolerance are the order of the day. Hell, they'll be criticizing Shelby Hunt next!

It would be excessive to imply that this latter-day postmodern dalliance has precipitated a civil war in the marketing academy – albeit 'civil', in the sense of maintaining a semblance of scholarly decorum whilst slugging it out, describes the situation very well – but the PoMo fandango undoubtedly carries connotations of crisis, of uncertainty, of catastrophe, of intellectual meltdown. Indeed, almost every commentator on the postmodern condition refers to this oppressive atmosphere of 'crisis'. Denzin (1997), for instance, describes three contemporary crises facing the citadels of cerebration:

- *crisis of representation*, where established modes of depicting 'reality' (e.g. theories, metaphors, textual genres) are inadequate to the task;
- *crisis of legitimacy*, where conventional criteria for assessing research output (validity, reliability, objectivity etc.) leave a lot to be desired; and
- *crisis of praxis*, where academic contributions signally fail to contribute to the resolution, or even clarification, of practical problems.

Although formulated with regard to the human sciences generally, these concerns are highly relevant to the state of late-twentieth-century marketing and consumer research. Our models are outmoded, our theories undertheorized, our laws lawless. Reliability is increasingly unreliable, the pursuit of reason unreasonable, and there are mounting objections to objectivity. Practitioners often fail to see the point of scholarly endeavour, despite the enormous amount of energy it absorbs, and get absolutely nothing of worth from the principal journals. Except, of course, when postmodernists publish therein.

This way up

The picture, however, is not completely bleak. The postmodern manoeuvre in marketing and consumer research, which has been in train for more than a decade, has brought benefits as well as costs. Scholarly conflict, remember, is not necessarily a 'bad thing'. On the contrary, a host of thinkers, from Nietzsche to Feyerabend, has observed that conflict can be a force for the good, since it helps avoid intellectual disintegration, dilapidation and decline (Brown, 1998b; Collins, 1992).

Be that as it may, perhaps the greatest benefit of this postmodern pirouette is that it led to dramatic changes in the methodology, domain and source material of marketing research (see Belk, 1991, 1995; Hirschman and Holbrook, 1992; Sherry, 1991). Methodologically, it opened the door to an array of qualitative/interpretive research procedures predicated on hermeneutics, semiotics, phenomenology, ethnography and personal introspection, to name but the most prominent. In terms of domain, it focused attention on issues previously considered marginal to the managerial mainstream of brand choice and shopper behaviour (e.g. gift giving, compulsive consumption, obsessive collecting, grooming rituals, the meaning of personal possessions) and which has further encouraged researchers' interest in the tangential, peripheral or hitherto ignored (homelessness, drug addiction, prostitution, consumer resistance, conspicuous consumption in the developing world etc.). With regard to source material, moreover, it has given rise to the realization that meaningful insights into marketing and consumption can be obtained from 'unorthodox' sources like novels, movies, plays, poetry, newspaper columns, comedy routines and so forth. Few would deny that restaurant critic Jonathan Meades' portrayal of the Hamburger Hades, colloquially known as Planet Hollywood, is just as good, if not better, than anything currently available in the academic literature (Table 2.3).

The outcome of the postmodern schism is summarized in Table 2.4, though it is important to reiterate that this rupture is not as clear-cut as the columns suggest. Truth to tell, modernist approaches remain very much in the academic ascendant, notwithstanding postmodernists' brazen appropriation of the 'cutting edge'

Table 2.3 Hurray for Planet Hollywood

The genius of Planet Hollywood is that it is a restaurant which replicates the way tracksuit bottoms eat at home. It gives a new meaning to home cooking. You can come here and eat couch-potato-style grot whilst gaping at a screen. Just the way you do at home. And you don't even have to button-punch. Your minimal attention span is addressed by the commensurate brevity of the clips. Planet Hollywood is ill named. Planet MTV would be apter. Planet Trash would be aptest. One wonders if the whole tawdry show is not some elaborate experiment being conducted by a disciple of the loopy behaviourist B. F. Skinner. The Hollywood it celebrates is not that of Welles or Siodmark or Sirk or Coppola, but that of aesthetic midgets with big budgets.

You fight your way (with no great enthusiasm) past merchandising 'opportunities' up a staircase to a world of operatives with clipboards – keen, smiley people who may or may not be victims of EST. They are frighteningly keen, alarmingly smiley. Our waiter, or customer chum, or whatever, was called Mike. He cared. He really cared about whether we were enjoying the whole experience. He kept asking. The pity of it is that he probably did care – he was so hyped up by the Planetary geist that he sought salvation through kiddy approbation.

He offered a trip of the premises. Politely declined. Close inspection is not liable to improve them. Over there is the sci-fi section within zoomorphic megagirders. Look that way and you've got the James Bond room, whose entrance apes the camera shutter device those mostly tiresome films used to use in their titles. Above us slung from the ceiling was a motorbike apparently used in a film I'd not even seen. It looked dangerous and I kept thinking that there would be no more pathetic way to die than by being crushed in so dreadful a place.

Source: Meades (1997, p. 33).

Table 2.4 Modern and postmodern research approaches

Modern	*Postmodern*
Positivist	Non-positivist
Experiments/Surveys	Ethnographies
Quantitative	Qualitative
A priori theory	Emergent theory
Economic/Psychological	Sociological/Anthropological
Micro/Managerial	Macro/Cultural
Focus on buying	Focus on consuming
Emphasis on cognitions	Emphasis on emotions
American	Multicultural

Source: Belk (1995).

mantle. Similarly, the preferred stance of postmodern marketing researchers is by no means consistent or devoid of internal discord. Although the postmodern/post-positivist/ interpretive/qualitative perspective (the terms themselves are indicative of intra-paradigmatic wrangling) is often depicted in a monolithic manner, albeit largely for political purposes of the 'us against them' variety, postmodernism itself is unreservedly pluralist. It is a veritable monolith of pluralism.

Some 'postmodern' marketing researchers, for example, employ qualitative methods that are overwhelmingly 'scientific' in tenor (e.g. grounded theory), whereas others utilize procedures that hail from the liberal wing of the liberal arts (personal introspection). Some surmise that such research should be evaluated according to conventional, if adapted, assessment criteria (trustworthiness, reliability etc.), while others contend that entirely different measures (such as verisimilitude, defamiliarization or resonance) are rather more appropriate. Some say that the vaguely voguish term 'postmodern' has been usurped by non-postmodern, self-serving marketing researchers, although all such attempts to palisade the unpalisadable are themselves contrary to the unconditional postmodern spirit. Some, indeed, say it is impossible to 'do' postmodern research, since the attendant crisis of representation renders all theoretical, methodological and textual representations untenable. The 'purpose' of postmodernism is simply to expose the shortcomings of modernist marketing research, not offer an actionable alternative (see Brown, 1998a).

Open other side

Irrespective of internal debates, it is not unreasonable to conclude that the postmodern fissure has opened up a significant intellectual space within the field of marketing scholarship. Perhaps the most obvious manifestation of this 'space' is the manner in which marketing scholarship is communicated. Traditional research reports and academic articles have been supplemented with works of poetry, drama, photoessays, videography, netnography, musical performances and many more (Stern, 1998). Conventional modes of academic discourse – unadorned, passive voiced, third personed, painfully pseudo-scientific prose – are being joined by exercises in 'experimental' writing, where exaggeration, alliteration and flights of rhetorical fancy are the order of the day. The success of such experiments is moot, admittedly, and many mainstream marketing scholars are understandably appalled by such egregious exhibitions of self-indulgence. If nothing else, however, they *do* draw attention to the fact that writing in a 'scientific' manner isn't the only way of writing about marketing. There is no law that says marketing discourse must be as dry as dust, though a perusal of the principal academic journals might lead one to think otherwise.

The postmodernists, then, are few in number. But they have challenged the conventions of marketing scholarship and, while this might not seem like much, it is having a significant impact on mainstream marketing. Consider *Market-Led Strategic Change*, Nigel Piercy's mega-selling, CIM-certified, every-home-should-have-one textbook. The first edition was written in a very conventional, straight-down-the-middle manner (Piercy, 1992). However, the reflexive, insouciant, self-referential tone of the second edition clearly shows the influence of postmodern modalities, as does the recently published third. True, Piercy goes out of his way to disparage postmodern precepts – alleging that the libel laws, no less, prevent the venting of his scholarly spleen – nevertheless there is no question that his text has taken a postmodern turn, some would say for the worse (but not me, your honour).

Pointing Piercy at the post is quite an achievement, most marketers would surely agree. Unfortunately, there's a long line ahead of him. In this regard, perhaps the most striking thing about marketing's postmodern apocalypse is the fact that it resonates with what a raft of management commentators are saying. The business sections of high street bookstores may not be heaving with 'postmodern' titles, but they are replete with works that challenge the received marketing wisdom and contend that it is time for a change. As with the postmodernists, this emerging school of marketing thought is highly variegated and somewhat contradictory. However, the principal contributions can be quickly summarized under the following Eight Es:

- *Experiential* – ecstasy, emotion, extraordinary experience (e.g. Schmitt, 1999).
- *Environmental* – space, place and *genius loci* (Sherry, 1998).
- *Esthetic* – beauty, art, design (Dickinson and Svensen, 2000).
- *Entertainment* – every business is show business (Wolf, 1999).
- *Evanescence* – fads, buzz, the wonderful word of mouth (Rosen, 2000).
- *Evangelical* – spirituality, meaning, transcendence (Finan, 1998).
- *Ethical* – buy a lippy, save the world (Roddick, 2001).
- *Effrontery* – shock sells, who bares wins, gross is good (Ridderstrale and Nordstrom, 2000).

E-type marketing is many and varied, yet its espousers and enthusiasts share the belief that marketing *must* change. Nowhere is this ebullient ethos better illustrated than in John Grant's *New Marketing Manifesto*. 'New Marketing', he argues, is predicated on creativity; it treats brands as living ideas; it is incorrigibly entrepreneurial; it favours change over conservatism; it is driven by insight not analysis; and it is humanist in spirit rather than 'scientific'. Granted, Grant's final chapter reveals that New Marketing isn't so new after all (retro rides again) and at no point does he align his precepts with postmodernism (be thankful, as they say, for small mercies), but the fact of the matter is that he's singing from the postmodern marketing hymnbook (Grant, 1999, p. 182):

New Marketing is a challenge to the pseudo-scientific age of business. It is a great human, subjective enterprise. It is an art. New Marketing needs New Market Research. Old market research was largely there to objectify and to justify – to support conventions. New Marketing is here to challenge and seek the unconventional.

Thus spake postmodernism. I think . . .

Closing down sale

For many, 'postmodern' is the latest in a long line of pseudo-intellectual buzz-words that attain prominence for a moment, only to pass swiftly into merciful obscurity. However, postmodernism's fifteen minutes of Warholesque fame seems to be dragging on a bit. Postmodern intrusions are evident across the entire spectrum of scholarly subject areas, marketing and consumer research among them. Indeed, the flotsam, jetsam and general detritus of consumer society are widely regarded, by non-business academics especially, as the very epitome of postmodernity.

'Postmodern', admittedly, is an umbrella term which shelters a number of closely related positions. These range from latter-day developments in the aesthetic sphere, most notably the blurring of hitherto sacrosanct boundaries between high culture and low, to the re-emergence of counter-Enlightenment proclivities among para-intellectuals and academicians.

The multifaceted character of postmodernity is equally apparent in marketing milieux. The phenomenon known as the postmodern consumer, which comprises gendered subject positions indulging in playful combinations of contrasting identities, roles and characters (each with its requisite regalia of consumables), is now an accepted, if under-investigated, socio-cultural artefact, as is the so-called 'post-shopper'. The latter shops in a knowing, cynical, been-there-done-that-didn't-buy-the-souvenirs manner or loiters in the mall looking at other consumers looking at them. For Firat and Venkatesh, indeed, the essential character of postmodern marketing is captured in five main themes – *hyperreality, fragmentation, reversed production and consumption, decentred subjects* and *juxtaposition of opposites* – though these categories are not clear-cut and other commentators see things differently.

Above and beyond empirical manifestations of the postmodern impulse, the field of marketing and consumer research has been infiltrated by postmodern methodologies, epistemologies, axiologies, ontologies, eschatologies (any ologies you can think of, really). Although there is some debate over what actually constitutes postmodern marketing research, it is frequently associated with the qualitative or interpretive turn that was precipitated by the Consumer Odyssey of the mid-1980s and academics' attendant interest in non-managerial concerns. Perhaps the clearest sign of 'postmodernists at work', however, is the convoluted, hyperbolic and utterly incomprehensible language in which their arguments are couched, albeit their apparently boundless self-absorption is another distinctive textual trait. Does my brand look big in this?

In fairness, the postmodernists' linguistic excesses and apparent self-preoccupation serve a very important purpose. Their language mangling draws attention to the fact that 'academic' styles of writing are conventions not commandments, decided upon not decreed, an option not an order. But, hey, don't take my word for it; check out the further reading below.

References

Appignanesi, R. and Garratt, C. (1995) *Postmodernism for Beginners*, Icon, Trumpington.

Apple, M. (1984) *Free Agents*, Harper & Row, New York. Reprinted in McHale, B. (1992) *Constructing Postmodernism*, Routledge, London, pp. 38–41.

Belk, R. W. (ed.) (1991) *Highways and Buyways: Naturalistic Research from the Consumer Behavior Odyssey*, Association for Consumer Research, Provo.

Belk, R. W. (1995) Studies in the new consumer behaviour, in Miller, D. (ed.), *Acknowledging Consumption*, Routledge, London, pp. 58–95.

Berger, W. (2001) *Advertising Today*, Phaidon, London.

Best, S. and Kellner, D. (2001) *The Postmodern Adventure*, Guilford, New York.

Bocock, R. (1993) *Consumption*, Routledge, London.

Brown, S. (1995) *Postmodern Marketing*, Routledge, London.

Brown, S. (1996) Art or science?: fifty years of marketing debate, *Journal of Marketing Management*, **12**(4), 243–267.

Brown, S. (1998a) *Postmodern Marketing Two: Telling Tales*, ITBP, London.

Brown, S. (1998b) Slacker scholarship and the well wrought turn, in Stern, B. B. (ed.), *Representing Consumers*, Routledge, London, pp. 365–383.

Brown, S. (2001a) *Marketing – The Retro Revolution*, Sage, London.

Brown, S. (2001b) Torment your customers (they'll love it), *Harvard Business Review*, **79**(9), 82–88.

Brown, S. (2002) Art or science?: postmodern postscript, *The Marketing Review*, in press.

Brown, S., Bell, J. and Carson, D. (1996) Apocaholics anoymous: looking back on the end of marketing, in Brown, S. *et al.* (eds), *Marketing Apocalypse: Eschatology, Escapology and the Illusion of the End*, Routledge, London, pp. 1–20.

Brown, S., Bell, J. and Smithee, A. (1997) From genesis to revelation – introduction to the special issue, *European Journal of Marketing*, **31**(9/10), 632–638.

Calás, M. B. and Smircich, L. (eds) (1997) *Postmodern Management Theory*, Ashgate, Dartmouth.

Carlin, G. (1997) *Brain Droppings*, Hyperion, New York.

Collins, R. (1992) On the sociology of intellectual stagnation: the late twentieth century in perspective, in Featherstone, M. (ed.), *Cultural Theory and Cultural Change*, Sage, London, pp. 73–96.

Cova, B. (1996) What postmodernism means to marketing managers, *European Management Journal*, **14**(5), 494–499.

Corrigan, P. (1997) *The Sociology of Consumption*, Sage, London.

Crews, F. (2001) *Postmodern Pooh*, North Point, New York.

Davidson, M. (1992) *The Consumerist Manifesto: Advertising in Postmodern Times*, Routledge, London.

Denzin, N. K. (1997) *Interpretive Ethnography: Ethnographic Practices for the 21st Century*, Sage, Thousand Oaks.

Dickinson, P. and Svensen, N. (2000) *Beautiful Corporations: Corporate Style in Action*, Pearson, London.

Dugdale, J. (2001) Diary, *The Sunday Times*, Culture, 28 January, p. 37.

Edwards, T. (2000) *Contradictions of Consumption: Concepts, Practices and Politics in Consumer Society*, Open University, Buckingham.

Falk, P. and Campbell, C. (eds) (1997) *The Shopping Experience*, Sage, London.

Featherstone, M. (1991) *Consumer Culture and Postmodernism*, Sage, London.

Finan, A. (1998) *Corporate Christ*, Management Books, Chalford.

Firat, A. F. and Venkatesh, A. (1995) Liberatory postmodernism and the reenchantment of consumption, *Journal of Consumer Research*, **22** (December), 239–267.

Goldman, R. and Papson, S. (1996) *Sign Wars: The Cluttered Landscape of Advertising*, Guilford, New York.

Goss, J. (1993) The magic of the mall: an analysis of form, function and meaning in the contemporary retail built environment, *Annals of the Association of American Geographers*, **83**(1), 18–47.

Grant, J. (1999) *The New Marketing Manifesto*, Orion, London.

Hedberg, A. and Singh, S. (2001) Retro chic or cheap relics?, *Marketing Week*, **18** October, pp. 24–27.

Hirschman, E. C. and Holbrook, M. B. (1992) *Postmodern Consumer Research: The Study of Consumption as Text*, Sage, Newbury Park.

Howes, D. (1996) *Cross-Cultural Consumption: Global Markets, Local Realities*, Routledge, London.

Lury, C. (1996) *Consumer Culture*, Polity, Cambridge.

Lyotard, J.-F. (1984 [1979]), *The Postmodern Condition: A Report on Knowledge*, Bennington, G. and Massumi, B. (trans.), Manchester University Press, Manchester.

Maclaran, P. and Brown, S. (2001) The future perfect declined: utopian studies and consumer research, *Journal of Marketing Management*, **17**(3/4), 367–390.

Meades, J. (1997) Eating out, *The Times Magazine*, Saturday 20 December, p. 33.

Miles, S., Anderson, A. and Meethan, K. (eds) (2002) *The Changing Consumer: Markets and Meanings*, Routledge, London.

Miller, D. (ed.) (1995) *Acknowledging Consumption: A Review of New Studies*, Routledge, London.

Mitchell, A. (2001) *Right Side Up: Building Brands in the Age of the Organized Consumer*, HarperCollins, London.

Nava, M., Blake, A., MacRury, I. and Richards, B. (eds) (1997) *Buy this Book: Studies in Advertising and Consumption*, Routledge, London.

O'Donohoe, S. (1997) Raiding the pantry: advertising intertextuality and the young adult audience, *European Journal of Marketing*, **31**(3/4), 234–253.

Piercy, N. (1992, 1997, 2002) *Market-Led Strategic Change*, Butterworth-Heinemann, Oxford.

Ridderstrale, J. and Nordstrom, K. (2000) *Funky Business: Talent Makes Capital Dance*, FTCom, London.

Ritzer, G. (1999) *Enchanting a Disenchanted World: Revolutionizing the Means of Consumption*, Pine Forge, Thousand Oaks.

Roddick, A. (2001) *Business as Unusual: The Triumph of Anita Roddick*, Thorsons, London.

Rosen, E. (2000) *The Anatomy of Buzz*, Harper-Collins, London.

Schmitt, B. (1999) *Experential Marketing*, Free Press, New York.

Sherry, J. F. (1991) Postmodern alternatives: the interpretive turn in consumer research, in Robertson, T. S. and Kassarjian, H. H. (eds), *Handbook of Consumer Research*, Prentice-Hall, Englewood Cliffs, NJ, pp. 548–591.

Sherry, J. F. (ed.) (1998) *Servicescapes: The Concept of Place in Contemporary Markets*, NTC Books, Chicago.

Shields, R. (ed.) (1992) *Lifestyle Shopping: The Subject of Consumption*, Routledge, London.

Stern, B. B. (ed.) (1998) *Representing Consumers: Voices, Views and Visions*, Routledge, London.

Thompson, C. J. (2000) Postmodern consumer goals made easy!!!', in Ratneshwar, S., Mick, D. G. and Huffman, C. (eds), *The Why of Consumption: Contemporary Perspectives on Consumer Motives, Goals and Desires*, Routledge, London, pp. 120–139.

Ward, G. (1997) *Teach Yourself Postmodernism*, Hodder Headline, London.

Warde, A. (2002) Setting the scene: changing conceptions of consumption, in Miles, S., Anderson, A. and Meethan, K. (eds), *The Changing Consumer: Markets and Meanings*, Routledge, London, pp. 10–24.

Wolf, M. J. (1999) *The Entertainment Economy*, Penguin, London.

Further reading

Modesty forbids, you understand, but you might find the following of interest:

Brown, S. (1995) *Postmodern Marketing*, Routledge, London. Summarizes the major strands of postmodern thought, coupled with a critique of 'modern' marketing theory.

Brown, S. (1998) *Postmodern Marketing Two: Telling Tales*, International Thomson, London. Extends the first book by arguing that art, aesthetics, storytelling etc. offer a possible way forward for twenty-first century marketing scholarship.

Brown, S. (2001) *Marketing – The Retro Revolution*, Sage, London. Rummages through the dustbin of marketing history and comes up with an alternative to the 'modern' marketing paradigm.

CHAPTER 3

Relationship marketing

LISA O'MALLEY and CAROLINE TYNAN

Introduction

Marketing as a body of knowledge and an academic discipline owes a great deal to what Bartels (1976) calls the period of re-conceptualization, where the marketing concept and the mix management paradigm (4Ps), introduced in the 1950s and 1960s, defined the nature and content of marketing management. This approach focused predominantly on the marketing of products to large homogeneous consumer markets (as existed in the USA). Underpinning this approach are assumptions from micro-economics that markets are efficient, buyers and sellers are anonymous, previous and future transactions are irrelevant, and that the price and quality function contains all of the information needed for consumers to make a rational decision (Easton and Araujo, 1994). However, even within this *transactional* approach to marketing, it is obvious that these assumptions are questionable given the increasing importance of marketing communications, branding and relationships in consumers' decision making in the last 50 years.

The mix management approach focuses on the sale of products to consumers. However, a great deal of marketing occurs in situations other than this, for example when the object of

exchange is a service rather than a product and when the buyer is a company rather than an individual consumer. The mix management paradigm had very little to offer in situations other than mass consumer product markets, and therefore new approaches sensitive to specific contexts and cultures needed to be developed (see Shostack, 1977; Håkansson, 1982; Gummesson, 1987). This resulted in a new approach to marketing, based on the creation and maintenance of relationships, becoming popular. This approach, known as relationship marketing, is the focus of this chapter.

The purpose of this chapter then is to begin to describe how the rich body of knowledge that is relationship marketing has come into being, what its major underpinning theories are, what defining moments occurred, and what might shape its future. The chapter begins by defining what is commonly understood by relationship marketing. Next, a brief review is offered of the development of relationship marketing in the key areas of services marketing, business-to-business and consumer marketing. In a chapter such as this, only a brief overview of the field can be offered and, thus, readers are directed towards the seminal works in each area. Because implementation is considered to be a particularly problematic aspect of relationship marketing, specific attention is paid to processual models of relationship development and the key aspects of relationships on which there is general agreement. Finally, some possible research opportunities are identified as a basis for further work in this rich and exciting area.

Relationship marketing defined

There are numerous definitions of relationship marketing and interested readers are directed toward Harker (1998) for a thorough review. Some of those most commonly used are the definitions offered by particularly influential authors, which are outlined below:

> [Marketing is] the process of identifying and establishing, maintaining, enhancing and when necessary terminating relationships with customers and other stakeholders, at a profit, so that the objectives of all parties involved are met, where this is done by a mutual giving and fulfilment of promises.
>
> (Grönroos, 1997, p. 407)

> All marketing efforts directed towards establishing, developing and maintaining successful relational exchanges.
>
> (Morgan and Hunt, 1994, p. 23)

> Relationship marketing is about understanding, creating, and managing exchange relationships between economic partners; manufacturers, service providers, various channel members, and final consumers.
>
> (Möller and Wilson, 1995, p. 1)

> Marketing seen as relationships, networks and interaction.
>
> (Gummesson, 1994, p. 12)

The definitions offered above derive from different research perspectives and variously emphasize different things. For example, Morgan and Hunt in their definition identify the focus of relationship marketing in practice, while others emphasize its purpose (Grönroos) and the processes by which it might be enacted

(e.g. Möller and Wilson). Gummesson (1994) takes a much broader view, and simply suggests that interaction, relationships and networks become the focus of attention when a relational lens is adopted. Which definition one chooses is likely to be influenced by the choice of empirical context, the focus of the study (e.g. practical, processual or philosophical), as well as the research stream to which the author belongs. However, irrespective of this diversity in the definitions offered above, the following basic issues are generally agreed upon.

- Relationship marketing refers to commercial relationships between economic partners, service providers and customers at various levels of the marketing channel and the broader business environment.
- This recognition results in a focus on the creation, maintenance and termination of these commercial relationships in order that parties to the relationship achieve their objectives (mutual benefit).
- Profit remains an underlying business concern and relational objectives are achieved through the fulfilment of promises.
- Trust is essential to this process of relationship development and centres upon the keeping of promises.

Although some writers have bemoaned the lack of common understanding (e.g. Buttle, 1996), it is obvious that a single definition of relationship marketing is unlikely to be possible because, as already stated, each of the definitions above are influenced by the different research traditions and different assumptions that influenced their authors. Indeed, relationship marketing is less a coherent body of knowledge and more a collection of loosely aligned understandings. These understandings have, in turn, different conceptual underpinnings and are strongly affected by the problems and issues that dominate the empirical situation. Thus, most definitions of relationship marketing are context specific, reflecting their respective research perspectives (e.g. Ford,

1980; Berry, 1983; Jackson, 1985; Webster, 1992), and therefore are not definitive. Later in the chapter we will explore the conceptual underpinnings of relationship marketing in greater detail in order to highlight the richness and diversity of the various research streams.

History of relationship marketing

One of the most interesting things about the body of knowledge that has come to be known as relationship marketing is that it emerged at the end of the 1970s in different research areas and in several different countries independently. What is particularly surprising about this is that it was not until some time later that we begin to see any discussion emerge between these various schools of thought. In other words, relationship marketing was discussed, defined and explored in different research 'silos' with very little consideration of what was taking place elsewhere. This section will briefly review the motivation, contribution and important concepts to emerge in services and business-to-business research. For a more detailed review of the history, interested readers are directed to Möller and Halinen (2000).

The relational paradigm has a relatively long history within the management literature (Levine and White, 1961; Evan, 1966; Van de Ven, 1976). In marketing, this approach to understanding business markets became popular among the IMP group in Europe in the mid-1970s with their network or interaction approach, and received some attention in North America within the marketing channels literature (Anderson and Narus, 1984) and later in the buyer–seller literature (Dwyer *et al.*, 1987). Since the late 1980s, the issue of inter-firm relationships has become more strategic (Wilson, 1995) because of the increasing emphasis on networks (Thorelli, 1986) for securing sustainable competitive advantage (Jarillo, 1988). The focus on relationships is still relevant, because

networks are seen to be formed by 'webs of relationships' (Andersson and Söderlund, 1988; Möller and Wilson, 1995). Thus, by the mid-1990s, the literature on interorganizational marketing relationships was characterized by a dual emphasis on single dyadic relationships (the relational paradigm) and on relationships within the context of networks (the network paradigm). Through a review of the contributions from each sector, it becomes obvious how 'interaction, relationships and networks' have come to dominate contemporary understandings of marketing.

Contributions from services marketing

The 1970s saw the emergence of services marketing as a distinct aspect of marketing. Early attempts to apply marketing techniques were dismissed as being essentially product focused and failing to deal with the unique characteristics of services (see Shostack, 1977). Essentially, the unique characteristics of services – inseparability, intangibility, heterogeneity and perishability (Zeithaml *et al.*, 1985) – highlight the importance of people in the service experience. Although one hopeful contribution to the services literature in terms of extending the marketing mix to 7Ps was offered by Booms and Bitner (1981), this proved to be less compelling than a focus on the service encounter (Solomon *et al.*, 1985) and on interaction (Grönroos, 1983). The recognition that customer retention was central to service marketing focused attention on the notion of creating service relationships (Grönroos, 1983, 1989, 1994; Gummesson, 1987) and led Berry (1983) to coin the term relationship marketing. To ensure that service delivery personnel were fully trained and motivated to build and maintain service relationships, internal marketing was developed. It rested on the recognition that 'a service must be successfully marketed to the personnel so that the employees accept the service offering and thoroughly engage in performing their marketing duties' (Grönroos, 1978, p. 594).

Contributions to the relational paradigm from services marketing include the development and understanding of service encounters (Solomon *et al.*, 1985), internal marketing (George, 1977; Grönroos, 1978; Berry, 1983; Gummesson, 1987), service design (Shostack, 1984) and service quality (Parasuraman *et al.*, 1985). Although viewed as distinct research streams within services marketing (Fisk *et al.*, 1993), they share many common themes. In particular, there is an emphasis on the interaction process (relationship marketing, service encounter and service design), and on creating and understanding quality from the point of view of the customer (service quality and internal marketing). Specific contributions from research in services marketing which develop our understanding of relationship marketing include the following conclusions:

- Service provision can be customized to suit the specific requirements of the buyer (Lovelock, 1983).
- The development of formal, ongoing relationships is a viable strategy in attempting to engender and build customer loyalty (Lovelock, 1983).
- The nature of services forces the buyer into intimate contact with the seller (Grönroos, 1978).
- The service encounter (interaction) has an important impact on customers' perceptions of, and satisfaction with, the service (Grönroos, 1983, 1994).
- Service encounters facilitate the development of social bonds (Crosby and Stephens, 1987; Berry and Parasuraman, 1991).
- The SERVQUAL gap model emerged as a useful managerial tool that distinguishes between *actual quality* and *customer-perceived quality* (Parasuraman *et al.*, 1985, 1988).
- Customers assess services on the basis of both *technical* quality (the quality of the service itself) and *functional* quality (the quality of the service delivery process) (Gummesson, 1987; Grönroos, 1990).

- The importance of *part-time marketers* (i.e. those individuals who are service providers but probably not marketing personnel) was recognized and highlighted (Gummesson, 1987).
- Internal marketing using a marketing approach within the business to target employees was recognized as an important tool in ensuring service quality (Gummesson, 1987; Grönroos, 1994; Berry, 1995) and was posited as integral to relationship management.
- Not all service encounters are necessarily relational, only those which are extended, emotive or intimate (Crosby *et al.*, 1990; Price *et al.*, 1995).

Contributions from business-to-business marketing

The major contribution in this area comes from the IMP research in Europe. Researchers within the IMP fail to agree on the exact meaning of the acronym, with some suggesting that it is the Industrial Marketing and Purchasing Group and others referring to the International Marketing and Purchasing Group (see Ford, 1997). The problem occurs because industrial (or business-to-business) marketing in Europe is, by definition, international. IMP researchers relied primarily on qualitative methodologies (observation, interviewing managers and archive data) within a number of case studies in order to explore interorganizational exchange. This work resulted in the recognition that relationships are important to the facilitation of interorganizational exchange (often more important than price) and that the *interaction* between buyer and seller organizations was integral to the formation and maintenance of relationships. A detailed review of the Interaction Approach was published in a very influential book (Håkansson, 1982). Indeed, this view of interaction and relationships is integral to the subsequent development of the relational paradigm. The major contribution of the Interaction Paradigm was the recognition (in contrast to the mix management paradigm) that buyers and sellers could be equally active in pursuing exchange. Equally, the work identified the influence of the business environment and atmosphere on both short-term exchange episodes and long-term relationships affecting cooperation, adaptation and institutionalization (Håkansson, 1982). Although the Interaction Approach was commended for advancing understanding of exchange in a business-to-business context, it was also criticized for (a) taking a single actor (buyer or seller) perspective (see Ford, 1997) and (b) being too difficult to operationalize (see Wilson, 1995). Whilst the latter problem has not been overcome, the early focus on dyadic interaction (one buyer and seller pair) was later superseded by the network approach, which looks at webs of linked relationships (see Andersson and Söderlund, 1988; Ford, 1997).

The major contributions of the interaction approach to our present understanding of relationship marketing include the following issues:

- Both buyers and sellers have similar roles in forming, developing and operating relationships (Håkansson, 1982; Ford, 1990).
- The match between supplier capability and customer need is accomplished by interaction between the two parties, and adaptation by one or both of them (Håkansson, 1982).
- Personal contacts are frequently used as a mechanism for initiating, developing and maintaining relationships (Turnbull, 1979; Cunningham and Homse, 1986).
- Interaction with other companies is the force that unifies the company and gives it the capability to perform its activities (Ford, 1990).
- Each party to a relationship may take the initiative in seeking a partner, and either party may attempt to specify, manipulate or control the transaction process. Thus, 'this process is not one of action and reaction: it is one of interaction' (Ford, 1997, p. xi).
- The relationship between buyer and seller is frequently long-term, close and involves complex patterns of interactions.

- The links between buyer and seller often become institutionalized into a set of roles that each party expects the other to perform.
- Both parties are likely to be involved in adaptations of their own processes or product technologies to accommodate the other, and neither party is likely to make unilateral changes to its activities without consultation or at least consideration of the reaction of their opposite number in the relationship.

In the USA, research was also underway on business-to-business exchange, although, initially at least, this remained within the dominant mix management and adversarial paradigm. Earlier research had demonstrated the importance of power and conflict, particularly in channel research (El-Ansary and Stern, 1972; Wilkinson, 1973, 1979; Etgar, 1976), and in the early 1980s there was the beginning of a recognition that co-operation might prove to be a more important explanatory variable. In the latter part of the 1980s, two significant events occurred. Firstly, within the business environment generally, the impact of Japanese business systems, particularly 'just-in-time', was having an important impact on the competitiveness of US and European companies (see Speckman, 1988; Webster, 1992). One of the major sources of competitive advantage enjoyed by the Japanese was assumed to be the strength of business relationships and the nature of their distribution systems, where a major Japanese company would 'sit in a web of strong permanent relationships with its major creditors, suppliers, key customers and other important stakeholders ... bound together by complex and evolving ties of mutual benefit and commercial interest' (Doyle, 2002, p. 14). This propelled an interest in relationships generally (Webster, 1992; Möller and Wilson, 1995). Secondly, Dwyer *et al.* (1987) wrote a seminal paper that employed social exchange theory to offer insights into the motivation and process of relationship formation. The major contribution of this paper was the suggestion that, like business markets, consumer markets might also benefit from attention to the conditions that foster relational bonds. Thus, this important paper legitimized relationship marketing in business markets and opened up the possibility that it might be an appropriate vehicle to engender customer retention in mass consumer markets.

The major contributions of US researchers include:

- Interaction between organizations must be understood in terms of economic, behavioural and political influences (Stern and Reve, 1980).
- Explicit consideration of social exchange theory (SET) in conceptualizing relationship development (Anderson and Narus, 1984, 1990; Dwyer *et al.*, 1987).
- Creation of models of relationship development explained in terms of increasing commitment and trust (Anderson and Narus, 1984, 1990; Dwyer *et al.*, 1987). This work underpinned the later work of Morgan and Hunt (1984).
- The recognition that co-operation and communication lead to trust, which in turn leads to greater levels of co-operation (Anderson and Narus, 1984, 1990).

Relationship marketing in consumer markets

Relationship marketing developed in industrial and service marketing contexts as a reaction against the limitations of mainstream (transactional) marketing. Initially eschewed by manufacturers interested in mass consumer markets because of the efficiency of the mix management paradigm, changes in the competitive climate in the latter part of the 1980s and early 1990s propelled the interest in relationship marketing in mass consumer markets. Indeed, it may be useful to conceptualize considerations of relationship marketing in mass consumer markets in terms of four phases: obscurity, discovery, acceptance and popularity (see O'Malley and Tynan, 2000). Prior to the mid-1980s (obscurity) there was little

consideration of the need for customer retention (cf. Rosenberg and Czepiel, 1984). In the latter part of the 1980s, technology developments fuelled the growth of direct and database marketing (Fletcher *et al.*, 1991; Evans *et al.*, 1996), which Dwyer *et al.* (1987) argued could usefully form the basis of relationship marketing in mass consumer markets. This, together with other academic considerations of direct and database marketing, marked the period of discovery for relationship marketing (O'Malley and Tynan, 2000). Essentially, the recognition that customer retention is far less costly and significantly more profitable than a focus on customer acquisition (Rosenberg and Czepiel, 1984; Reichheld and Sasser, 1990) cemented the business argument justifying a new approach. Acceptance is largely attributed to the work of Sheth and Parvatiyar (1995), who not only argued the benefits of relationship marketing in a consumer context but, more importantly, reframed relationship marketing within the extant consumer behaviour literature. Thus, although there were some suggestions that relationship marketing might not be appropriate in a consumer context (e.g. Grönroos, 1994; Barnes, 1994, 1995), marketing practitioners were already doing relationship marketing – often in the form of loyalty or retention programmes. Relationship marketing became increasingly popular throughout the latter part of the 1990s and is still hugely popular today.

Whilst some argue that relationships have always been important to consumers (e.g. Sheth and Parvatiyar, 1995) and that these relationships can be facilitated by recourse to technology (Dwyer *et al.*, 1987; Blattberg and Deighton, 1991), others argue that this is a convenient repackaging of direct marketing within the philosophy of relationship marketing (see O'Malley and Tynan, 1999, 2000). Notwithstanding the conceptual debate, relationship marketing is greatly facilitated by advances in technology and, in particular, the database. Whilst this is largely viewed as unproblematic, there have been suggestions that the overt emphasis on technology actually undermines relationship-building efforts (see O'Malley *et al.*, 1997; Fournier *et al.*, 1998). In spite of these fears, the emphasis on technology as a solution has continued (for an interesting review, see Sisodia and Wolf, 2000). Indeed, such is the contribution of database marketing that Coviello *et al.* (1997) suggest that database marketing is actually a type of relationship marketing.

Recently, this focus on consumer markets has evolved into CRM, which is variously understood as Customer Relationship Marketing and/or Customer Relationship Management. Although philosophically in line with relationship marketing, the focus in CRM is on the technology, particularly that technology which attempts to manage all customer touch points and facilitate the integration of various database systems to provide a single picture of the customer (Peppers and Rogers, 1995; Ryals and Knox, 2001). This picture encompasses the customer's needs, preferences, buying behaviour and price sensitivity, and allows the CRM business to focus on building customer retention and profitability. However, underpinning both approaches is that CRM is a technology tool which facilitates interaction between different databases and different interaction media in order to facilitate segmentation and communication (see Ryals and Knox, 2001).

Thus, the 1990s marked a turbulent time for marketing, with two apparently competing paradigms vying for attention and supremacy. Despite its centrality to the theory and practice of marketing, the mix management paradigm (4Ps) began to be seriously questioned (Kent, 1986; van Waterschoot and van den Bulte, 1992; Grönroos, 1994; O'Malley and Patterson, 1998). Now, in the early years of the new millennium, it appears that the debates that emerged throughout the 1980s and 1990s have been quieted (if not resolved) and that relationship marketing is synonymous with marketing. As such, it is difficult to conceive a marketing problem or issue that does not have the notion of building, maintaining or dissolving relationships at its core. Indeed, within contemporary

conceptualizations, to do relationship marketing well is simply to do traditional marketing better.

Thus far, this chapter has addressed the history of relationship marketing in several disparate schools and considered some of the most commonly used definitions. The previous section should go some way to explaining why it is difficult to find a single, readily agreed upon definition, because each research stream has emphasized different elements and is itself influenced by diverse underpinning theories. These are identified in Figure 3.1.

Essentially, what is obvious from the above is the number of different empirical contexts in which relationship marketing research was initially considered. These have been explored earlier in the chapter and include services marketing, buyer–seller and channel theory in the USA (Anderson and Narus, 1984, 1990) and in Europe (Ford, 1980; Håkansson 1982; Turnbull and Valla, 1985). Each have been influenced to a greater or lesser degree by a number of underpinning theories. Although it is not possible to consider these in detail, readers are directed to research within particular traditions. For example, when considering resource dependence theory and micro-economic theory, useful discussions are provided by Gattora (1978), Arndt (1983), and Easton and Araujo (1994). Similarly, for institutional economics and Transaction Cost Analysis, consult Gattora (1978), Williamson (1975, 1985), and Weitz and Jap (1995). Macneil (1980) explained the basis for contractual relations (usefully employed by Dwyer *et al.*, 1987), and Stern and Reve (1980), Arndt (1983), and Möller (1994) provide interesting discussions of the Political Economy Paradigm (PEP). Social Exchange Theory (SET) is considered to be the most influential, particularly in terms of the ideology of relationship marketing (see O'Malley and Tynan, 1999), and is based on the work of Homans (1950), Blau (1964), and Thibaut and Kelley (1959). This diversity in underpinning theories is the basis for the rich tapestry that relationship marketing has become and it has helped to define particular research traditions.

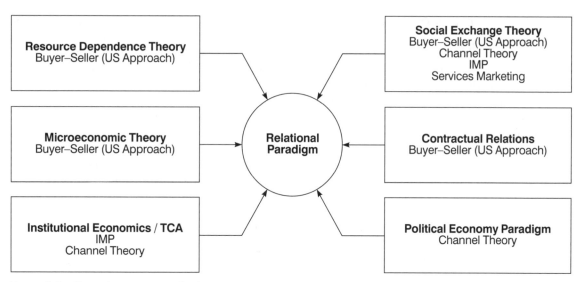

Figure 3.1   Disciplinary roots of relationship marketing

However, this diversity inhibits any possibility of creating a commonly understood definition of relationship marketing and, more importantly for practitioners, any commonly agreed approach to implementation.

Having accepted that relationship marketing is not a single, internally consistent school of thought – but rather a loose collection of shared research themes – we need to consider (a) in which contexts relationship marketing is appropriate and (b) what are the most useful concepts to explore. Here again, we have little agreement, with some considering that relationship marketing spans every conceivable business relationship (see, for example, Gummesson, 1999) and others considering a more limited range of relationship categories (Morgan and Hunt, 1994). These issues are considered in the next section.

Focal relationships

The relational paradigm drives an organization to focus on relationships (Gummesson, 1987; Håkansson, 1982; Czepiel, 1990). Strategically,

this involves identifying which relationships are to be pursued and how they are to be managed (Morgan and Hunt, 1994; Gummesson, 1994). In terms of the first issue, identifying marketing relationships, there are a number of competing views. One essentially suggests that relationships are not chosen, rather relationships exist and the choice is whether to manage them explicitly or not. Within this perspective, Gummesson's 30R approach considers thirty important relationships and identifies a broad organizational remit for the firm which gives customer relationships and environmental relationships (by definition) equal importance (Gummesson, 1999). Morgan and Hunt (1994) limit their definition of relationships more precisely within the conventional business domain. Of particular importance here is to recognize that a firm is constrained by its environment and cannot be involved in every possible relationship. Equally, it is important to consider how each relationship should be managed, i.e. should all customers be treated equally, what resources should be invested in each relationship, how should the portfolio of relationships be managed? These issues are encapsulated into what Håkansson (1982) refers to as handling problems and limitation problems.

Gummesson (1987) argues that, because of their importance, relationships must become central to strategic planning both at corporate and marketing levels. This suggests that there are relationships that are of concern to corporate planners and relationships that are the sole concern of marketing. Despite this, Morgan and Hunt (1994) and Gummesson (1994) identify a range of relationships in which a company is likely to be involved, and thus, by implication, within the domain of marketing. Morgan and Hunt's (1994) conceptualization is presented in Figure 3.2. It suggests four broad categories of relationships: supplier partnerships, lateral partnerships, customer partnerships and internal partnerships. Within each of these categories, the authors further specify a number of particular relationships. These include supplier relationships (with goods and service suppliers), internal relationships (with employees etc.), lateral relationships (with government, competitors etc.) and buyer relationships (with immediate and ultimate customers).

Gummesson (1994) takes a much broader view of the number of marketing relationships a company is likely to be concerned with than Morgan and Hunt (1994). He specifies 30Rs – or thirty different relationships that span his conceptualization of different levels of relationship. However, marketing cannot, and indeed may not, wish to be involved in all relationships. While some authors consider that marketers should focus only on the consumer, others argue that marketers should adopt a more strategic role in the organization and take responsibility for any relationship that influences the ultimate sale. Berry (1995, p. 242) defines relationship marketing in terms of a means–end equation: 'in effect, companies must establish relationships with non-customer groups (the means) in order to establish relationships with customers (the end)'. This definition effectively re-focuses marketing in terms of end-customer relationships. This position is consistent with other definitions that assume that the aim of marketing is the development of customer relationships (cf. Ford, 1980; Berry, 1983; Jackson, 1985). Grönroos' (1994) definition does mention customers, but also acknowledges the importance of 'other partners'. However, this position identifies a very broad domain for marketing.

Having identified the range of relationships that a firm must establish, maintain and where necessary terminate, the next issue to be addressed is how relationships can be formed, maintained, enhanced and terminated. It is also important to consider the factors that influence these processes and the outcomes that are sought by companies. The next section explores models of relationship development and considers these issues.

Models of relationship development

Relationship marketing represents an incredibly broad area of marketing thought and has been strongly influenced by empirical evidence from several business sectors, as well as by theories and concepts from diverse disciplines. Indeed, concepts such as retention, loyalty, commitment, trust, mutuality, reciprocity, structural bonds and attraction are central to understanding relationships. These concepts have their origins in economics, sociology, social exchange theory, small group behaviour, psychology and elsewhere, and have been borrowed, refined and moulded by contemporary understandings of service relationships, business relationships and consumer behaviour. Add to this understandings of market-related behaviours influenced by contemporary understandings of postmodernism, critical theory, branding, consumer literacy and organizational networks, and we begin to understand how this intricate and influential body of thought has been woven, such that it is difficult to divide new from old marketing theory, and marketing from other

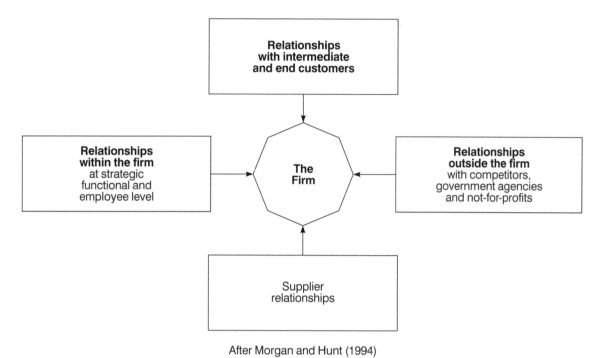

After Morgan and Hunt (1994)

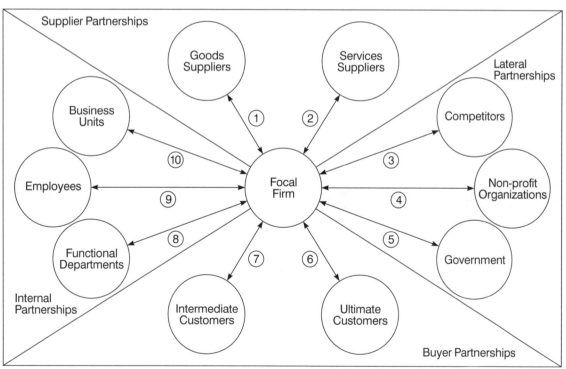

Figure 3.2   The relational exchanges in marketing relationships

aspects of management which consider business structures and business networks as aspects of its core.

A key issue within the relationship marketing literature is the conceptualization of relationship development (Wilson, 1995). All of the models offered (see Table 3.1) implicitly adopt a life cycle approach, suggesting that relationships are created, develop and ultimately end. Within this conceptualization, relationship formation is envisaged as a series of exchanges that lead to increasing commitment. Of these, the Ford (1980) model is interesting in terms of the managerial implications delineated at each phase, while the Dwyer *et al.* model (1987) specifically considers the move from transactions to relationships and suggests that this is an equally appropriate conceptualization for relationships in consumer markets as it is in other empirical contexts.

In the *pre-relationship stage* a potential new supplier is evaluated. The distance between the firm and the new supplier has five dimensions, namely:

- Social distance or unfamiliarity in working methods.
- Cultural distance concerning differing norms and values.
- Technological distance between product and process technologies.

- Time distance between contact and product or service transfer.
- Geographical distance between the two companies.

In the *early stage*, where initial contact and trial orders occur, there will be much uncertainty and little evidence to judge the commitment of a relationship partner. In the *development stage*, the firms become more used to dealing with each other and the frequency of orders and communication increase. Both the distance and uncertainty that characterize the earlier stages decrease. By the time the *long-term stage* is reached, formal contracts are likely to have been established and the firms are mutually dependent. Uncertainty is further reduced and the firms work so closely together that their relationship may become institutionalized and unquestioned within either business. Commitment to working with the partner firm will be demonstrated by adaptations. In the *final stage*, which is reached over the long term in stable markets, relationships are close and institutionalization continues to the extent that attempts to change may be met with sanctions by the partner firm.

Importantly, Dwyer and colleagues cite Levitt's (1983, p. iii) marriage metaphor as their point of departure in developing their conceptual model:

Table 3.1   Process models of relationship development

Ford (1980)	Frazier (1983)	Dwyer et al. (1987)	Borys and Jemison (1989)	Wilson (1995)
Pre-Relationship Stage	Review	Awareness		Search and selection
Early Stage		Exploration	Defining purpose	Defining purpose
Development Stage	Implementation	Expansion	Setting boundaries	Setting boundaries
Long-Term Stage	Outcomes	Commitment	Value creation	Value creation
Final Stage			Hybrid stability	Hybrid stability
		Dissolution		

... the sale merely consummates the courtship. Then the marriage begins. How good the marriage is depends on how well the relationship is managed by the seller.

As a result of the marriage metaphor, Dwyer *et al.* (1987) employ the extant marriage literature in making sense of buyer–seller relationships (Tynan, 1999). Although Levitt is credited as being the first to make this comparison, it is interesting to note that Guillet de Monthaux (1975) offered an earlier review of relationship development in terms of courtship, marriage and divorce.

The influence of social exchange theory is particularly obvious when we consider the concepts that we use to describe and explain relationship development and, indeed, the relationship success variables. In a useful and very thorough literature review, Wilson (1995) attempts to identify those concepts that are most widely used. These are identified in Table 3.2.

Depending on the specific context, these variables are likely to be more or less important. However, it is worth noting that, of these, trust, commitment, co-operation and mutual benefit have attracted the most empirical attention, and are considered fundamental to understanding and creating commercial relationships

Table 3.2 Summary of variables of relationship success models

Commitment	Social bonds
Trust	Structural bonds
Co-operation	Summative constructs
Mutual goals	Shared technology
Interdependence/ power imbalance	Non-retrievable investments
Performance satisfaction	Comparison level of alternatives
Adaptation	

Source: Wilson (1995).

(Dwyer *et al.*, 1987; Anderson and Narus, 1990; Crosby *et al.*, 1990; Czepiel, 1990; Grönroos, 1990; Heide and John, 1990; Moorman *et al.*, 1992; Rusbult and Buunk, 1993; Barnes, 1994; Morgan and Hunt, 1994).

Håkansson (1982) suggests that relationships are developed to reduce uncertainty and/ or add value. In terms of reducing uncertainty, Håkansson (1982) highlights improvements in the firm's forecasting abilities. In contrast, Möller and Wilson (1995, p. 40) take a broader perspective, and argue that 'firms generally develop business relationships for multiple reasons that are not based on any singular dimension'. They suggest that relationship development can be motivated by the need for economic gains, the quest for stability or predictability; the search for reciprocity; the quest for efficient and effective operations, to establish legitimacy; or because the firm lacks resources, or wishes to utilize an asymmetrical power base (Möller and Wilson, 1995). In services marketing, the organization seeks relationships with customers in order to enhance loyalty. Within this context, consumers are believed to seek relationships in order to minimize risk (Berry, 1995).

It is acknowledged that not all customers are profitable as relationship customers (Ford, 1980; Håkansson, 1982; Reichheld and Sasser, 1990; Berry, 1995). Thus, a first stage of relationship management must clearly be the identification of relationship potential. Even then, not all customers will necessarily be interested in, or merit, the same level of investment, and thus a relationship specification phase must be included. This specification phase may occur before, after or simultaneous to the relationship initiation phase. Furthermore, while some definitions incorporate enhancing and maintaining relationships as distinct stages, this is an unnecessary distinction. Some relationships will require continual enhancement in order to be maintained, whereas others will not. Thus, it is argued that it is implicit in the relationship maintenance concept that relationship investments, enhancements and communication are likely to be required. Equally, the nature of the relationship may change, and a reduction in resources or a redefinition (re-specification) of the norms of the relationship may be most appropriate. Finally, there may come a time when the relationship is no longer appropriate at all, and thus there is clearly a phase of relationship dissolution. The phases that have just been described clearly need more refinement. However, it is recognized that they are dynamic and ongoing, and are unlikely to reflect a linear process. Therefore, a matrix or building block approach to defining relationship development stages seems most appropriate. This process is therefore seen to include: identification of relationship potential; specification of relationship format; relationship initiation; relationship maintenance, and relationship dissolution.

Critique and emerging issues

Conceptually, relationship marketing continues to be understood in different and often very interesting ways. Whilst this provides richness and diversity to the literature, it is difficult to share research findings between different empirical contexts and conceptual frameworks. For new researchers entering the field, attention to the original works will offer particular insights and understanding, which will in turn inform their understanding and critique of current developments. Thus, for a review of the history and development of relationship marketing, a number of treatments are essential reading. These include Sheth and Parvatiyar (1995), Möller and Halinen (2000), Grönroos (1994), and Aijo (1996). Furthermore, a special issue of the *Journal of the Academy of Marketing Science* (Cravens, 1995) provides a series of insightful commentaries on relationship marketing in different empirical contexts. Added to this, the relational perspective as discussed by the IMP group (Håkansson, 1982; Turnbull and Valla, 1985; Ford, 1997) and services researchers

(Grönroos, 1978; Berry, 1983; Shostack, 1984; Parasuraman *et al.*, 1985; Solomon *et al.*, 1985; Gummesson, 1987) are equally important.

The richness and conceptual diversity of relationship marketing results in a lack of understanding and agreement as to how relationship marketing should be implemented. Thus, a number of issues require further conceptual and empirical work. The following is not an exhaustive list of such issues, but merely serves to highlight the numerous gaps in our knowledge.

Identification and assessment of relational partners

Definitions of relationship marketing suggest that marketing is concerned with developing relationships with key customers and other parties (Grönroos, 1994; Möller and Wilson, 1995; O'Malley *et al.*, 1997), indeed that relationship marketing 'refers to all marketing activities directed towards establishing, developing, and maintaining successful relational exchanges' (Morgan and Hunt, 1994, p. 23). However, little attention has been paid to how potentially successful relational partners might be identified. This is important, given the limitation problems that exist for organizations in terms of the portfolio of relationships with which they can be involved (Håkansson, 1982). It is also recognized that there is an opportunity cost associated with each relationship, and thus great care must be taken in selecting relational partners. Within consumer markets the concept of lifetime value is being used. However, this approach focuses only on the potential dyad, and ignores the network, the limitation problems and opportunity costs involved. Clearly, further research is required in this area.

The continued utility of the mix management paradigm

What is the continued role of product, price, place and promotion in terms of implementing relationship marketing? This question has already been addressed in this chapter. It has been suggested that there are fundamental differences between both approaches (Grönroos, 1991; Johanson and Mattsson, 1994), and yet there is still a lack of consensus within the literature as to whether the paradigms are competing or complementary. This question needs to be addressed because it has important implications for developing a framework for implementing the new paradigm. Is it acceptable for relational and transactional approaches to marketing to coexist, and in some cases to be merged?

Training for relationship marketing managers

What management training is required to facilitate the implementation of relationship marketing? Wilson (1995) suggests that relationships are now more difficult to develop and manage given that the race for relationship partners has accelerated. In consumer markets there is often the simplistic assumption that all that is required is a database and direct communications. However, it is likely that more attention needs to be paid to developing relational skills in customer-facing staff. Services marketers may be more advanced than others in terms of managing interaction (SERVQUAL; the gap model; critical incident technique), and as a result may provide some useful guidelines. In any case, it is unlikely that a relationship strategy can be simply tagged on to the prevailing mix management strategy. As such, practising marketers need to embrace 'the full extent of the paradigm shift implicit in Relationship Marketing' (O'Malley *et al.*, 1997, p. 554), and they clearly require appropriate guidelines. Thus, research investigating the training needs of practising marketers would be particularly useful.

Relationship policy

How should organizations devise relationship policies? Relationship policy refers to the management of a portfolio of relationships. As such, it is concerned with both handling and limitation problems (Håkansson, 1982), and with positioning strategies within the network (Andersson and Söderlund, 1988). Research is required to address issues such as relationship investments and adaptation, how individual relationships should be managed, and how the integral elements of relationships can be fostered with exchange partners (O'Malley *et al.*, 1997).

Relationship dissolution

How do organizations dissolve relationships? Relationship dissolution has not received a great deal of attention within the literature (cf. Dwyer *et al.*, 1987; Stewart, 1998). It is clearly an important part of relationship policy, and should be incorporated within training issues. Dissolution is particularly important given the emphasis on deepening trust and commitment within commercial relationships. Despite this, there are likely to be situations when firms wish to dissolve relationships, especially given the dynamic and competitive nature of today's global marketplace. Thus, research addressing how and why relationships can be dissolved would be particularly beneficial.

Relationship seeking

In what circumstances, or situations, do customers want relationships? There is currently a tendency to assume that relationships are seen as desirable, and are sought by customers (Sheth and Parvatiyar, 1995). Christy *et al.* (1996) deal with this issue to some extent in consumer markets. Other literature in consumer markets implicitly questions this assumption (Barnes, 1995; Fournier *et al.*, 1998; Tynan, 1997; O'Malley and Tynan, 1999, 2000). It may well be the case that relationships are desirable, but research that supports this is clearly needed. In particular, it should identify the types of situations or circumstances when relationships are especially sought.

If marketing is now about managing relationships, but this job is too important to remain in the marketing department, what is the current function of marketing? This is another particularly problematic issue that has yet to be resolved. The literature suggests that 'the traditional ways of organising the marketing function, and of thinking about marketing activity must be re-examined' (Wilson, 1995, p. 10). The problem revolves around the broad gamut of relationship partners that have been identified (Gummesson, 1994; Morgan and Hunt, 1994). This range of relationships tends to fall outside the existing domain of marketing and, as a result, it has been argued by IMP researchers that many of these are organizational strategy rather than marketing issues. The problem is exacerbated when the interface between the company and its customers is primarily through part-time marketers (Gummesson, 1987). As a result, the role of marketing must be identified within the relational paradigm, as this has important implications for developing a framework for implementation, for devising relationship policy, and for dealing with training requirements.

Exploring relationship variables

What are the antecedents of trust, commitment etc.? The integral elements of successful relationships have been identified (Wilson, 1995) and discussed. However, further research investigating the antecedents of these elements is clearly desirable. Taking greater account of the contextual elements surrounding dyadic relationships would substantially enhance this. Thus, the incorporation of broader underpinning theory, other than just social exchange theory, would be useful here.

Do bonds create relationships or do relationships create bonds? Andersson and Söderlund (1988, p. 65) suggest that 'relationships can create bonds of technical, planning, knowledge, social and legal content'. Since much of the other literature suggests that bonds, in fact, create relationships, research illuminating the direction of causality would be beneficial. Understanding of causal direction would also be particularly relevant as an input into managerial training. Alternatively, it may be that causal directions cannot be identified as a result of the integrative and interactive nature of relationship variables, the context in which the research occurs, and the expectations of the parties concerned.

Domain of relationship marketing

There are many questions over the domain of relationship marketing (Saren and Tzokas, 1998). Relationship marketing has not been subjected to sufficient critical scrutiny and has been indiscriminately applied to any issue where traditional marketing has proved useful. As discussed in an earlier section, the theoretical roots of relationship marketing are firmly grounded in business-to-business and services marketing. However, its wholesale extension into business-to-consumer markets and not-for-profit contexts has been of questionable value. The issues of power and conflict, which have been so carefully explored in other contexts, are ignored in business-to-consumer marketing (see Fitchett and McDonagh, 2000; Smith and Higgins, 2000). Can a single, individual consumer really have a relationship with a huge, multinational company? If the customer does recognize a relationship in such a situation, is the relationship with the service delivery employee not with the firm itself? Does not the sheer size and marketing budget of the firm make the possibility of a mutually beneficial relationship unlikely, if not impossible? For the consumer there are likely to be only a few possible providers of a particular offer, whereas for the firm there are likely to be millions of potential customers for their offer, so there is no equity in the issue of power or importance.

Technology and relationship marketing (CRM)

The interface between marketing and CRM is another field where there is substantial need for research. CRM is based upon sound marketing principles, through identifying customer needs, segmentation, offering superior customer value and customer retention, all of which are enabled by the application of sophisticated technology. However, the processes by which this is specified and managed and whether that is controlled by technologists or marketers is as yet an issue of some debate and little empirical knowledge (Sisodia and Wolf, 2000). Issues relating to consumer privacy are likely to be exacerbated within this new environment and may ultimately undermine consumer trust (O'Malley *et al.*, 1997). Moreover, there needs to be greater consideration of how consumer information should be acquired and used. Ultimately, it must be remembered that the objective is to build relationships, not databases. This is achieved through dialogue (see Grönroos, 2000) and not one-way communication.

Relationship marketing in cross-cultural contexts

Relationship marketing is frequently applied in cross-cultural contexts, but the theoretical and empirical work upon which it is grounded has been largely conducted in Scandinavia, Britain and North America. Unfortunately, these regions share many cultural similarities, exhibiting high power distance, low individualism and low context communication scores (Hall, 1960, Hofstede, 1991). So it is more than possible that our understandings of relationship marketing will not be relevant to cultures that are less hierarchical, more collectivist, and where understanding communication is highly dependent upon the context in which it takes place. Some initial work has been conducted on these issues, largely from the perspective of the Chinese system of Guanxi (Ambler, 1995; Ambler and

Styles, 2000), but much remains to be done on a wider geographical basis.

Operationalizing relationship marketing

It is surprising how little research has been conducted which sheds light upon suitable approaches to operationalizing relationship marketing. It is impossible to support or refute particular approaches to developing a relationship marketing strategy, implementing it or assessing its performance. The processes by which relational partners should be identified, the appropriate levels of investment in the relationship established, the portfolio of simultaneous relationships appropriately managed, or the termination of an unprofitable relationship achieved without rancour, are all unknown. As yet we have no metrics by which the success or failure of relationship marketing approaches can be evaluated. There is much research and theorizing to be done before we can make strategic use of relationship marketing.

Staff retention and empowerment

Additionally, our understanding of issues concerning staff retention and empowerment have largely been developed in the field of services marketing and to some extent small business maketing. There is little research available on the importance of employees in the relationship, their training and retention, which had been specifically conducted in the context of a relational view of marketing. Whether this will prove to be an important issue cannot be established until more research has been conducted.

Conclusion

This chapter has reviewed the history, definition and core concepts that are part of the emerging understanding of relationship marketing. Central to this is the recognition that, although there is some shared understanding, relationship marketing is also shaded by the empirical context and by the nature of the parties in the relationship. It is clear that understandings which emerge from services marketing research differ from that which has emerged in a business-to-business context, for example. Relationship marketing is also influenced by underpinning theories such that integration can never be possible. So, although there will never be one agreed definition, one common approach, one single understanding, there is much to learn from these many and various strands of research on the topic. For example, insights can be gained into why firms need to develop a relational approach, what is the range of relationships they focus on, what are the success variables and how the interaction process is managed. We can also learn, from the many models of relationship development, what might promote and what might impede relationship formation, development and maintenance.

There is much to understand about this innovative and developing paradigm. This paper has drawn attention to the many unknowns in this field, to the questions, the gaps and the under-researched issues. As such, it offers some suggestions for new researchers as to possible topics and issues for research. May we hope that you will join us in exploring this interesting and exciting topic.

References

Aijo, T. S. (1996) The Theoretical and Philosophical Underpinnings of Relationship Marketing: Environmental Factors Behind the Changing Marketing Paradigm, *European Journal of Marketing*, **30**(2), 8–18.

Ambler, T. (1995) Reflections in China: Reorienting Images of Marketing, *Global Marketing*, **4**(1), 22–30.

Ambler, T. and Styles, C. (2000) The Future of Relational Research in International Marketing: Constructs and Conduits, *International Marketing Review*, **17**(6), 492–508.

Anderson, J. C. and Narus, J. A. (1984) A Model of the Distributor's Perspective of Distributor–Manufacturer Working Relationships, *Journal of Marketing*, **48** (Fall), 62–74.

Anderson, J. C. and Narus, J. A. (1990) A Model of Distributor Firm and Manufacturer Firm Working Partnerships, *Journal of Marketing*, **54** (January), 42–45.

Andersson, P. and Söderlund, M. (1988) The Network Approach to Marketing, *Irish Marketing Review*, **3**, 63–68.

Arndt, J. (1983) The Political Economy Paradigm: Foundations for Theory Building in Marketing, *Journal of Marketing*, **47** (Fall), 44–54.

Barnes, J. G. (1994) Close to the Customer: But is it Really a Relationship?, *Journal of Marketing Management*, **10**, 561–570.

Barnes, J. G. (1995) Establishing Relationships – Getting Closer to the Customer may be more Difficult than you Think, *Irish Marketing Review*, **8**, 107–116.

Bartels, R. (1976) *The History of Marketing Thought*, GRID, Columbus, OH.

Berry, L. L. (1983) Relationship Marketing, in Berry, L. L., Shostack, G. L. and Upah, G. D. (eds), *Perspectives on Services Marketing*, American Marketing Association, Chicago, pp. 25–28.

Berry, L. L. (1995) Relationship Marketing of Services – Growing Interest, Emerging Perspectives, *Journal of the Academy of Marketing Science*, 23(4), 236–245.

Berry, L. L. and Parasuraman, A. (1991) *Marketing Services – Competition Through Quality*, Free Press, New York.

Blattberg, R. C. and Deighton, J. (1991) Interactive Marketing: Exploiting the Age of Addressability, *Sloan Management Review*, Fall, 5–14.

Blau, P. M. (1964) *Exchange and Power in Social Life*, John Wiley, New York.

Booms, B. H. and Bitner, M. J. (1981) Marketing Strategies and Organisational Structures for Service Firms, in Donnelly, J. H. and George, W. R. (eds), *Marketing of Services*, American Marketing Association, Chicago.

Borys, B. and Jemison, D. B. (1989) Hybrid Arrangements As Strategic: Theoretical Issues in Organisational Combinations, *Academy of Management Review*, **14**(2), 234–240.

Buttle, F. (1996) *Relationship Marketing, Theory and Practice*, Paul Chapman, London.

Christopher, M., Payne, A. and Ballantyne, D. (1991) *Relationship Marketing: Bringing Quality, Customer Service and Marketing Together*, Butterworth-Heinemann, Oxford.

Christy, R., Oliver, G. and Penn, J. (1996) Relationship Marketing in Consumer Markets, *Journal of Marketing Management*, **12**, 175–187.

Coviello, N. E., Brodie, R. J. and Munro, H. J. (1997) Understanding Contemporary Marketing: Development of a Classification Scheme, *Journal of Marketing Management*, **13**, 501–552.

Cravens, D. W. (1995) Special Issue on Relationship Marketing, *Journal of the Academy of Marketing Science*, **23**(4).

Crosby, L. A. and Stephens, N. (1987) Effects of Relationship Marketing on Satisfaction, Retention, and Prices in the Life Insurance Industry, *Journal of Marketing Research*, **24** (November), 404–411.

Crosby, L. A., Evans, K. R. and Cowles, D. (1990) Relationship Quality in Services Selling: An Interpersonal Influence Perspective, *Journal of Marketing*, **54** (July), 68–81.

Cunningham, M. T. and Homse, E. (1986) Controlling the Marketing–Purchasing Interface: Resource Development and Organisational Implications, *Industrial Marketing and Purchasing*, **1**(2), 3–27.

Czepiel, J. A. (1990) Service Encounters and Service Relationships: Implications for Research, *Journal of Business Research*, **20**, 13–21.

Doyle, P. (2002) *Marketing Manaegement and Strategy*, 3rd edn, Financial Times-Prentice Hall, Harlow, UK.

Dwyer, R. F., Schurr, P. H. and Oh, S. (1987) Developing Buyer–Seller Relationships, *Journal of Marketing*, **51** (April), 11–27.

Easton, G. and Araujo, L. (1994) Market Exchange, Social Structures and Time, *European Journal of Marketing*, **28**(3), 72–81.

El-Ansary, A. I. and Stern, L. W. (1972) Power Measurement in the Distribution Channel, *Journal of Marketing*, **38**(1), 47–52.

Etgar, M. (1976) Channel Domination and Countervailing Power in Distributive Channels, *Journal of Marketing Research*, **13** (August), 254–262.

Evan, W. (1966) The Organisational Set: Toward a Theory of Inter-Organisational Relations, in Thomson, J. (ed.), *Approaches to Organisation Design*, Free Press, New York.

Evans, M., O'Malley, L. and Patterson, M. (1996) Direct Marketing Communications in the UK: A Study of Growth, Past, Present and Future, *Journal of Marketing Communications*, **2**, 51–65.

Fisk, R. P., Brown, S. W. and Bitner, M. J. (1993) Tracking the Evolution of the Services Marketing Literature, *Journal of Retailing*, **69**(1), 61–94.

Fitchett, J. A. and McDonagh, P. (2000) A Citizen's Critique of Relationship Marketing in Risk Society, *Journal of Marketing Strategy*, **8**(2), 209–222.

Fletcher, K., Wheeler, C. and Wright, J. (1991) Database Marketing: A Channel, A Medium, or a Strategic Approach, *Marketing Intelligence and Planning*, **10**(6), 18–23.

Ford, D. (1980) The Development of Buyer–Seller Relationships in Industrial Markets, *European Journal of Marketing*, **14**(5/6), 339–354.

Ford, D. (1990) *Understanding Business Markets: Interaction, Relationships, Networks*, Academic Press, Harcourt Brace, London.

Ford, D. (1997) *Understanding Business Markets: Interaction, Relationships, Networks*, 2nd edn, Academic Press, Harcourt Brace, London.

Fournier, S., Dobscha, S. and Glen Mick, D. (1998) Preventing the Premature Death of Relationship Marketing, *Harvard Business Review*, January–February, 42–51.

Frazier, G. L. (1983) Inter-organisational Exchange Behaviour In Marketing Channels: A Broadened Perspective, *Journal of Marketing*, **47** (Fall), 68–71.

Gattora, J. (1978) Channels of Distribution, *European Journal of Marketing*, **12**(7), 452–471.

George, W. R. (1977) The Retailing of Services: A Challenging Future, *Journal of Retailing*, **53**(3), 85–98.

Grönroos, C. (1978) A Service-Orientated Approach to Marketing of Services, *European Journal of Marketing*, **12**(8), 588–601.

Grönroos, C. (1983) *Strategic Management and Marketing in the Service Sector*, Marketing Science Institute, Cambridge, MA.

Grönroos, C. (1989) Defining Marketing: A Market-Orientated Approach, *European Journal of Marketing*, **23**(1), 52–60.

Grönroos, C. (1990) Relationship Approach to Marketing in Service Contexts: The Marketing and Organisational Behaviour Interface, *Journal of Business Research*, **20** (January), 3–11.

Grönroos, C. (1991) The Marketing Strategy Continuum: Towards a Marketing Concept for the 1990s, *Management Decision*, **29**(1), 7–13.

Grönroos, C. (1994) From Marketing Mix to Relationship Marketing: Towards a Paradigm Shift in Marketing, *Management Decision*, **32**(2), 4–20.

Grönroos, C. (1997) Value-driven Relational Marketing: From Products to Resources and Competencies, *Journal of Marketing Management*, **13**, 407–19.

Grönroos, C. (2000) Creating A Relationship Dialogue: Communication, Interaction and Value, *The Marketing Review*, **1**(1), 5–14.

Guillet de Monthaux, P. B. L. (1975) Organizational Mating and Industrial Marketing Theory – Some Reasons Why Industrial Marketing Managers Resist Marketing Theory, *Industrial Marketing Management*, **4**, 25–36.

Gummesson, E. (1987) The New Marketing – Developing Long-Term Interactive Relationships, *Long Range Planning*, **20**, 10–20.

Gummesson, E. (1994) Making Relationship Marketing Operational, *International Journal of Service Industry Management*, **5**(5), 5–20.

Gummesson, E. (1996) Relationship Marketing and the Imaginary Organisation: A Synthesis, *European Journal of Marketing*, **30**(2), 31–44.

Gummesson, E. (1999) *Total Relationship Marketing*, Butterworth-Heinemann/The Chartered Institute of Marketing, Oxford, UK.

Håkansson, H. (1982) *International Marketing and Purchasing of Industrial Goods*, John Wiley, New York.

Hall, E. T. (1960) The Silent Language of Overseas Business, *Harvard Business Review*, May–June, 87–96.

Harker, M. J. (1998) Relationship Marketing Defined?, *Marketing Intelligence and Planning*, **17**(1), 13–20.

Heide, J. B. and John, G. (1990) Alliances in Industrial Purchasing: The Determinants of Joint Action in Buyer–Seller Relationships, *Journal of Marketing Research*, **27** (February), 24–36.

Hofstede, G. (1991) *Culture in Organisations: Software of the Mind*. McGraw-Hill, London.

Homans, G. C. (1950). *The Human Group*, Harcourt Brace, New York.

Jackson, B. B. (1985) Build Customer Relationships That Last, *Harvard Business Review*, November–December, 120–128.

Jarillo, J. C. (1988) On Strategic Networks, *Strategic Management Journal*, **9**, 31–41.

Johanson, J. and Mattsson, L.-G. (1994) The Markets-as-Networks Tradition in Sweden, in Laurent, G., Lilian, G. L. and Pras, B. (eds), *Research Traditions in Marketing*, Kluwer Academic, London, pp. 321–342.

Kent, R. A. (1986) Faith in Four P's: An Alternative, *Journal of Marketing Management*, **2**(2), 145–154.

Levine, S. and White, P. E. (1961) Exchange as a Conceptual Framework for the Study of Inter-Organisational Relationships, *Administrative Science Quarterly*, **5**, 583–601.

Levitt, T. (1983) *The Marketing Imagination*, Free Press, New York.

Lovelock, C. H. (1983) Classifying Services to Gain Strategic Marketing Insights, *Journal of Marketing*, **47** (Summer), 9–20.

Macneil, I. R. (1980) *The New Social Contract: An Inquiry into Modern Contractual Relations*, Yale University Press, New Haven, CT.

Möller, K. (1994) Inter-organisational Marketing Exchange: Metatheoretical Analysis of Current Research Approaches, in Laurent, G., Lilian G. L. and Pras, B. (eds), *Research Traditions in Marketing*, Kluwer Academic, London, pp. 347–372.

Möller, K. and Halinen, A. (2000) Relationship Marketing Theory: Its Roots and Direction, *Journal of Marketing Management*, **16**, 29–54.

Möller, K. and Wilson, D. T. (eds) (1995) *Business Marketing: An Interaction and Network Perspective*, Kluwer Academic, Norwell, MA.

Moorman, C., Zaltman, G. and Deshpande, R. (1992) Relationships Between Providers and Users of Market Research; The Dynamics of Trust Within and Between Organisations, *Journal of Marketing Research*, **29** (August), 314–329.

Morgan, R. M. and Hunt, S. D. (1994) The Commitment–Trust Theory of Relationship Marketing, *Journal of Marketing*, **58** (July), 20–38.

O'Malley, L. and Patterson, M. (1998) Vanishing Point: The Mix Management Paradigm Re-Viewed, *Journal of Marketing Management*, **14**(8), 829–852.

O'Malley, L. and Tynan, A. C. (1999) The Utility of the Relationship Metaphor in Consumer Markets: A Critical Evaluation, *Journal of Marketing Management*, **15**, 487–602.

O'Malley, L. and Tynan, A. C. (2000) Relationship Marketing in Consumer Markets: Rhetoric or Reality?, *European Journal of Marketing*, **34**(7), 797–815.

O'Malley, L. and Tynan, A. C. (2001) Reframing Relationship Marketing for Consumer Markets, *Interactive Marketing*, **2**(3), 240–246.

O'Malley, L., Patterson, M. and Evans, M. J. (1997) Intimacy or Intrusion: The Privacy Dilemma for Relationship Marketing in Consumer Markets, *Journal of Marketing Management*, **13**(6), 541–560.

Parasuraman, A., Zeithaml, V. A. and Berry, L. L. (1985) A Conceptual Model of Service Quality and Its Implications for Further Research, *Journal of Marketing*, **49** (Fall), 41–50.

Parasuraman, A., Zeithaml, V. A. and Berry, L. L. (1988) SERVQUAL: A Multiple-Item Scale for Measuring Consumer Perceptions of Service Quality, *Journal of Retailing*, **64**(1), 12–40.

Peppers, D. and Rogers, M. (1995) A New Marketing Paradigm, *Planning Review*, **23**(2), 14–18.

Price, L. L., Arnould, E. J. and Tierney, P. (1995) Going to Extremes: Managing Service Encounters and Assessing Provider Performance, *Journal of Marketing*, **59** (April), 83–97.

Reichheld, F. F. and Sasser, E. W. Jr. (1990) Zero Defections: Quality Comes to Services, *Harvard Business Review*, **69** (September–October), 105–111.

Rosenberg, L. J. and Czepiel, J. (1984) A Marketing Approach for Customer Retention, *Journal of Consumer Marketing*, **1** (Spring), 45–51.

Rusbult, C. E. and Buunk, B. P. (1993) Commitment Processes in Close Relationships: An Interdependent Analysis, *Journal of Social and Personal Relationships*, **10**, 175–204.

Ryals, L. and Knox, S. (2001) Cross-Functional Issues in The Implementation of Relationship Marketing Through Customer Relationship Management, *European Management Journal*, **19**(5), October, 534–542.

Saren, M. J. and Tzokas, N. X. (1998) Some Dangerous Axioms of Relationship Marketing, *Journal of Strategic Marketing*, **6**, 187–196.

Sheth, J. N. and Parvatiyar, A. (1995) Relationship Marketing in Consumer Markets: Antecedents and Consequences, *Journal of the Academy of Marketing Science*, **23**(4), 255–271.

Shostack, L. G. (1977) Breaking Free From Product Marketing, *Journal of Marketing*, **45** (April), 73–80.

Shostack, L. G. (1984) Designing Services That Deliver, *Harvard Business Review*, **62** (January–February), 133–139.

Sisodia, R. S. and Wolf, D. B. (2000) Information Technology, in Sheth, J. N. and Parvatiyar, A. (eds), *Handbook of Relationship Marketing*, Sage Publications: Thousand Oaks, CA, pp. 525–563.

Smith, W. and Higgins, M. (2000) Reconsidering the Relationship Analogy, *Journal of Marketing Management*, **16**, 81–94.

Solomon, M. R., Suprenant, C., Czepiel, J. A. and Gutman, E. G. (1985) A Role Theory Perspective on Dyadic Interactions: The Service Encounter, *Journal of Marketing*, **49** (Winter), 99–111.

Speckman, R. E. (1988) Strategic Supplier Selection: Understanding Long-Term Buyer Relationships, *Business Horizons*, **31**(4), 75–81.

Stern, L. W. and Reve, T. (1980) Distribution Channels as Political Economies: A Framework For Comparative Analysis, *Journal of Marketing*, **44** (Summer), 52–64.

Stewart, K. (1998) An Exploration of Customer Exit in Retail Banking, *International Journal of Bank Marketing*, **16**(1), 6–14.

Thibaut, J. W. and Kelley, H. (1959) *The Social Psychology of Groups*, John Wiley & Sons, New York.

Thorelli, H. B. (1986) Networks: Between Markets and Hierarchies, *Strategic Management Journal*, **7**, 37–51.

Turnbull, P. (1979) Roles of Personal Contacts in Industrial Export Marketing, *Scandinavian Journal of Management*, **7**, 325–339.

Turnbull, P. and Valla, J. P. (eds) (1985) *Strategies for International Industrial Marketing*, Croom Helm, London.

Tynan, A. C. (1997) A Review of the Marriage Analogy in Relationship Marketing, *Journal of Marketing Management*, **13**, 695–703.

Tynan, A. C. (1999) Metaphor, Marketing and Marriage, *Irish Marketing Review*, **12**(1), 17–26.

Van de Ven, A. (1976) On the Nature, Formation, and Maintenance of Relations Among Organisations, *Academy of Management Review*, October, 24–36.

van Waterschoot, W. and van den Bulte, C. (1992) The 4P Classification of the Marketing Mix Revisited, *Journal of Marketing*, **56** (October), 83–93.

Webster, F. E. (1992) The Changing Role of Marketing in the Corporation, *Journal of Marketing*, **56** (October), 1–17.

Weitz, B. A. and Jap, S. D. (1995) Relationship Marketing and Distribution Channels, *Journal of the Academy of Marketing Science*, **23**(4), 305–320.

Wilkinson, I. F. (1973) Power and Influence Structures in Distribution Channels, *European Journal of Marketing*, **7**(2), 119–129.

Wilkinson, I. F. (1979) Power and Satisfaction in Channels of Distribution, *Journal of Retailing*, **55** (Summer), 79–94.

Williamson, O. E. (1975) *Markets and Hierarchies: Analysis and Antitrust Implications*, Free Press, New York.

Williamson, O. E. (1985) *The Economic Institutions of Capitalism: Firms, Markets, Relational Contracting*, Free Press, New York.

Wilson, D. T. (1995) An Integrated Model of Buyer–Seller Relationships, *Journal of the Academy of Marketing Science*, **23**(4), 335–345.

Zeithaml, V. H., Parasuraman, A. and Berry, L. L. (1985) Problems and Strategies in Services Marketing, *Journal of Marketing*, **49**, 33–46.

CHAPTER 4

The basics of marketing strategy

ROBIN WENSLEY

Marketing strategy sometimes claims to provide an answer to one of the most difficult questions in our understanding of competitive markets: how to recognize and achieve an economic advantage which endures. In attempting to do so, marketing strategy, as with the field of strategy itself, has had to address the continual dialectic between analysis and action, or in more common managerial terms between strategy formulation and strategic implementation. At the same time, it has also had to address a perhaps more fundamental question: how far, at least from a demand or market perspective, can we ever develop general rules for achieving enduring economic advantage.

Strategy: from formulation to implementation

From the late 1960s to the mid-1980s at least, management strategy seemed to be inevitably linked to issues of product-market selection and hence to marketing strategy. Perhaps ironically this was not primarily or mainly as a result of the contribution of marketing scholars or indeed practitioners. The most significant initial contributors, such as Bruce Henderson

and Michael Porter, were both to be found at or closely linked to the Harvard Business School, but were really informed more by particular aspects of economic analysis: neo-marginal economics and Industrial Organizational Economics respectively. Labelling the intellectual pedigree for Bruce Henderson and the Boston Consulting Group is rather more difficult than for Michael Porter. This is partly because much of the approach developed out of consulting practice (cf. Morrison and Wensley, 1991) in the context of a broad rather than focus notion of economic analysis. Some of the intellectual pedigree for the approach can be found in Henderson, who was at Harvard also, and Quant (1958), but some basic ideas such as dynamic economies of scale have a much longer pedigree (see, for instance, Jones, 1926). However, in various institutions the marketing academics were not slow to recognize what was going on and also to see that the centrality of product-market choice linked well with the importance attached to marketing. This expansion of the teaching domain had a much less significant impact on the research agenda and activity within marketing itself, where the focus continued to underplay the emerging importance of the competitive dimension (Day and Wensley, 1983). Hence the relatively atheoretical development continued into the process of codification of this new area, most obviously in the first key text by Abell and Hammond (1979), which was based on a, by then, well-established second year MBA option at Harvard. The book itself is clearly influenced by the work related to the Profit Impact of Market Strategy (PIMS) project, as well as work in management consultancies such as McKinsey, ADL and, perhaps most importantly, Boston Consulting Group, whose founder, Bruce Henderson, had close links with Derek Abell. The MBA course itself started in 1975 with a broad notion of 'filling the gap' between what was seen then as the marketing domain and the much broader area of Business Policy, so encompassing issues relating to Research and Development, Distribution and Competitive Costs. The course itself was a second year elective and rapidly expanded to four sections with a major commitment on development and case writing in 1976 and 1977. For a more historical analysis of the ways in which the case method has been used to incorporate new issues in management whilst avoiding some central concerns about the nature of power and influence, see Contardo and Wensley (2002).

In retrospect, this period was the high point for the uncontested impact of competitive market-related analysis on strategic management practice. With the advantage of hindsight, it is clear that a serious alternative perspective was also developing, most obviously signalled by Peters and Waterman (1982), which was to have a very substantial impact on what was taught in strategic management courses and what was marketed by consultancies. It was also a significant book in the sense that, although not widely recognized as so doing, it also attempted to integrate, at least to some degree, earlier work by other relevant academics such as Mintzberg (1973), Pettigrew (1973), and Weick (1976).

As the decade progressed, it was inevitable that, at least to some degree, each side recognized the other as a key protagonist. Perhaps one of the most noteworthy comments is that in which Robert Waterman challenged the value

of a Michael Porter-based analysis of competition. Waterman (1988) argued that the Porter approach does not work because 'people get stuck in trying to carry out his ideas'[1] for three reasons: the lack of a single competitor, the actual nature of interfirm co-operation as well as competition and, finally, the fact that competitors were neither 'dumb nor superhuman'. This is a particular, and rather colourful, way of representing the notion of 'rational expectations' (Muth, 1961; Simon, 1979) in economics, to which we will return later in this chapter.

Equally, the economists have not taken such attacks lying down: somewhat more recently, Kay (1993) attempted to wrest back the intellectual dominance in matters of corporate strategy and Porter (1990) extended his domain to the nation state itself.

The story, of course, has also become complicated in other ways, many of which are outside the scope of this chapter. In terms of key perspectives, Tom Peters has become more and more polemical about the nature of success (indeed, to the extent of arguing in one interview that innovative behaviour now depends on ignoring rather than exploiting market evidence), C. K. Prahalad has refined his original notion of dominant logic to reflect in general terms the importance of transferable capabilities and technological interdependencies in the development of strategic advantage (for instance, see Bettis and Prahalad, 1995; Prahalad and Hamel, 1990; Prahalad and Bettis, 1989), whist Gary Hamel, who started his work with C. K. Prahalad on Strategic Intent (1989), has moved on to espousing radical and revolutionary change (2000) and, of course, Peter Senge (1992) reiterated the importance of information structures, and Hammer and Champy (1993) introduced a 'new' approach labelled business process analysis.

In terms of the disciplinary debate, what was originally broadly a debate between economists and sociologists now also involves

[1] It is noteworthy that the very representation of the five-forces diagram, for instance, is one which emphasizes that the firm is under pressure from all sides.

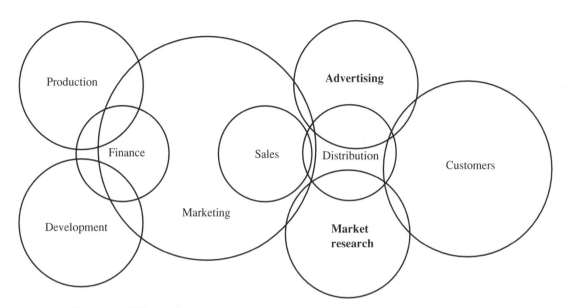

Figure 4.1 The early 1970s perspective on the marketing context

psychologists, social anthropologists and, if they are a distinct discipline, systems theorists.

However, the key change in emphasis has been the one from analysis to process, from formulation to implementation. Perhaps the single most important contributor to this change has been Henry Mintzberg, who has developed over the period an extensive critique of what he calls the 'Design School' in Strategic Management, culminating in his 1994 book. In this he even challenges the notion of planning in strategy:

> Thus we arrive at the planning school's grand fallacy: because analysis is not synthesis, strategic planning is not strategy formation. Analysis may precede and support synthesis, by defining the parts that can be combined into wholes. Analysis may follow and elaborate synthesis, by decomposing and formalising its consequences. But analysis cannot substitute for synthesis. No amount of elaboration will ever enable formal procedures to forecast discontinuities, to inform managers who are detached from their operations, to create novel strategies. Ultimately the term 'strategic planning' has proved to be an oxymoron.
>
> (p. 321)

Whilst his approach and indeed critique of strategy analysis is itself rather polemical and overstated,[2] there is little doubt that the general emphasis in strategic management has shifted significantly towards implementation and away from formulation and planning.

The nature of the competitive market environment

As our analysis of marketing strategy has developed over the last 30 years, so our representation of the marketing context has also changed.

As an example, Figure 4.1 is an overhead which the author used 30 years ago in describing the nature of the marketing context. A number of major omissions are clear. In particular, there is no recognition of competitors and

[2] In fact, Mintzberg himself goes on to argue three roles for 'corporate planning': (1) a more refined approach in traditional contexts; (2) a focus on techniques which emphasize the uncertain and emergent nature of strategic phenomena; and/or (3) a more creative and intuitive form of strategic planning (see Wensley, 1996a).

distribution is clearly seen as a solely logistical function. On top of this, customers are very much represented as 'at a distance'.

More recently, marketing has recognized much more explicitly this further range of issues, including the key role of competition and the importance of a longer term so-called relationship perspective, particularly in the context of customers. On top of this, various entities in the distribution chain are now clearly seen as very active intermediaries rather than just passive logistics agents.

However, the development of this more complex dynamic representation of the competitive market, which can be seen broadly in the marketing strategy triangle of the 3Cs (see Figure 4.2) – customers, competitors and channels – also implies a more fluid and complex context for systematic modelling purposes.

Customers, competitors and channels

The early, more static model of the nature of the competitive market, which informed many of the still current and useful tools of analysis, was both positional and non-interactive. It was assumed that the market backcloth, often referred to as the product-market space, remained relatively stable and static so that, at

least in terms of first order effects, strategies could be defined in positional terms. Similarly, the general perspective, strongly reinforced by representations such as that in Figure 4.1, was that actions by the firm would generally not create equivalent reactions from the relatively passive 'consumers'. This perspective on the nature of marketing, which might be fairly labelled the 'patient' perspective (Wensley, 1990), is to be found rather widely in marketing texts and commentaries, despite the continued espousal of slogans such as 'the customer is king'.

With the adoption of the more interactive and dynamic perspective implied in the 3Cs approach, the nature of market-based strategy becomes much more complex. At the same time, we must be wary of the temptation to continue to apply the old tools and concepts without considering critically whether they are appropriate in new situations. They represent in general a special or limiting case, which quite often requires us to distort the nature of environment that we are attempting to characterize. The key question as to how far this distortion is, as our legal colleagues would say, material is another but frequently unresolved matter. This notion of materiality is really linked to impact on actions rather than just understanding and the degree to which, in practice, particular forms of marketing strategy

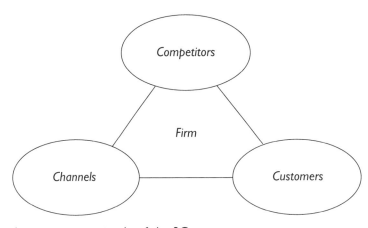

Figure 4.2   The marketing strategy triangle of the 3Cs

analysis encourage actions which are either sub-optimal or indeed dysfunctional.

Lacking further experimental or research evidence on this question, this chapter is mainly written around the assumption that we need to recognize, in using these simplifying approaches, that (i) the degree to which they actually explain the outcomes of interest will be limited, particularly when it is a direct measure of individual competitive performance, and (ii) the ways in which the underlying assumptions can cause unintentional biases.

The evolution of analysis, interpretation and modelling in marketing strategy from customers to competitors to channels

Given that the underlying representation of the competitive market environment has changed so, not surprisingly, have our processes of analysis, interpretation and modelling. Initially, the key focus was on customer-based positioning studies, in a particular product-market space. Such work remains a key component in the analysis of much market research data, but from the marketing strategy perspective, we need to recognize that the dimensionality of the analytical space has often been rather low, indeed in some situations little more than a single price dimension, which has been seen as highly correlated with an equivalent quality dimension. There are undoubtedly good reasons for adopting such a low dimensionality approach in the name of either stability, which is clearly a critical issue if strategic choices are going to be made in this context, and/or a hierarchy of effects in which strategic choices at this level dominate later, more complex choices in a higher dimension perceptual space, but it is often doubtful whether either or both of these rationales are based on firm empirical evidence in many situations.

The increased emphasis on the analysis of competitors has also required us to make certain compromises. One, of course, relates to the balance between what might be termed public information, legitimate inference and private information. The other to the fact that our colleagues in business strategy now give emphasis to two rather different perspectives on the nature of competitive firms, one essentially based on similarities (strategic groups: McGee and Thomas, 1986), the other on differences (resource-based perspective: Wernerfeld, 1984, 1995a). Sound competitor analysis should at least enable us to avoid making inconsistent assumptions, particularly in the context of public data, like, for instance, assuming that we will be able to exploit an opportunity which is known to all, without a significant amount of competitive reaction.

Finally, there is the question of channels or, in more general terms, supply chains. The issue of retailers in particular as independent and significant economic intermediaries rather than just logistical channels to the final consumer has been an important consideration in consumer marketing, at least since the 1970s. Similarly, in industrial markets the issue of the supply chain and the central importance of some form of organization and co-ordination of the various independent entities within the chain has been seen as an increasingly important strategic issue. Both these developments have meant that any strategic marketing analysis needs to find ways to evaluate the likely impact of such independent strategies pursued by intermediaries, although in many cases our tools and techniques for doing this remain rather limited and often ¹ʸ on no more than an attempt to speculate ·¹ght be their preferred strategic acti⟨

Beyond this the⟨ attempt to introduce⟨ as relationship mark⟨ of this chapter to ⟨ from a strategic v⟨ tant issues that n⟨ is that a recog⟨ pattern of the⟨ particularly ⟨ described a⟨

spective, is not necessarily the same as a more prescriptive notion of the need to manage such relationships. Mattsson (1997) provides a very useful comparison and evaluation of the similarities and differences between the two approaches, which we will discuss later. The second is that whilst the relationship perspective rightly moves our attention away from individual transactions towards patterns of interaction over longer time periods, it often seems to assume that the motivations of each party are symmetric. In practice, in both consumer (Fournier *et al.*, 1998) and industrial markets (Faria and Wensley, 2002), this may prove to be a very problematic assumption.

The codification of marketing strategy analysis in terms of three strategies, four boxes and five forces

What can now be regarded as 'traditional' marketing strategy analysis was developed primarily in the 1970s. It was codified in various ways, including the strategic triangle developed by Ohmae (1982) as reproduced in Figure 4.3, but perhaps more memorably, the most significant elements in the analysis can be defined in terms of the three generic strategies, the four boxes (or perhaps more appropriately strategic contexts) and the five forces.

These particular frameworks also represent the substantial debt that marketing strategy owes to economic analysis; the three strategies and the five forces are directly taken from Michael Porter's influential work, which derived from his earlier work in Industrial Organization Economics. The four contexts were initially popularized by the Boston Consulting Group under Bruce Henderson, again [?] influenced by micro-economic analy[sis?] each of these approaches remains a [?]mponent in much marketing [?](see Morrison and Wensley,

1991), we also need to recognize some of the key considerations and assumptions which need to be considered in any critical application.

The three strategies

It could reasonably be argued that Porter really reintroduced the standard economic notion of scale to the distinction between cost and differentiation to arrive at the three generic strategies of focus, cost and differentiation. Indeed, in his later formulation of the three strategies they really became four in that he suggested, rightly, that the choice between an emphasis on competition via cost or differentiation can be made at various scales of operation.

With further consideration it is clear that both of these dimensions are themselves not only continuous, but also likely to be the aggregate of a number of relatively independent elements or dimensions. Hence scale is in many contexts not just a single measure of volume of finished output, but also of relative volumes of sub-assemblies and activities which may well be shared. Even more so in the case of 'differentiation', where we can expect that there are various different ways in which any supplier attempts to differentiate their offerings. On top of this, a number of other commentators, most particularly John Kay (1993), have noted that not only may the cost differentiation scale be continuous rather than dichotomous, but it also might not be seen as a real dimension at all. At some point this could become a semantic squabble, but there clearly is an important point that many successful strategies are built around a notion of good value for money rather than a pure emphasis on cost or differentiation at any price. Michael Porter (1980) might describe this as a 'middle' strategy, but rather crucially he has consistently claimed that there is a severe danger of getting 'caught in the middle'. In fact, it might be reasonable to assume that in many cases being in the middle is the best place to be: after all, Porter

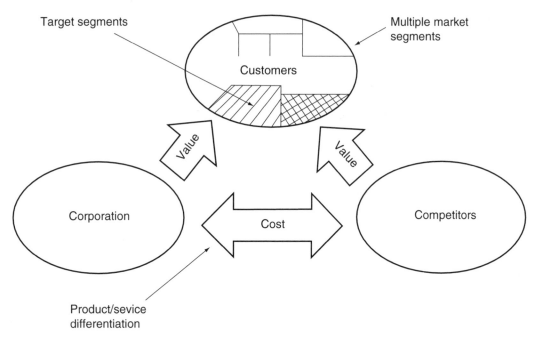

Figure 4.3　The strategic triangle
Source: Ohmae (1982, p. 92)

has never presented significant systematic evidence to support his own assertion (cf. Wensley, 1994).

The four contexts

The four boxes (contexts) relate to the market share/market growth matrix originally developed by the Boston Consulting Group (BCG) under Bruce Henderson. Although there have inevitably been a whole range of different matrix frameworks which have emerged since the early days, the BCG one remains an outstanding exemplar not only because of its widespread popularity and impact (nowadays even University vice-chancellors have been heard to use terms such as 'cash cow'), but because there was an underlying basic economic logic in its development. Many other similar frameworks just adopted the rather tautologous proposition that one should invest in domains which were both attractive and where one had comparative advantage!

The market growth/market share matrix, however, still involved a set of key assumptions which were certainly contestable. In particular, alongside the relatively uncontroversial one that in general the growth rate in markets tends to decline, there were the assumptions that it was in some sense both easier to gain market share in higher growth rate markets, and also that the returns to such gains were likely to be of longer duration.

This issue can be seen as assumptions about first the cost and then the benefit of investment in market share, and has been discussed and debated widely in marketing over the last 20 years (see Jacobson and Aaker, 1985; Jacobson, 1994). The general conclusions would appear to be that:

(i)　market share as an investment is not on average under-priced, and may well be over-priced;

(ii)　the cost of gaining market share is less related to the market growth rate and much more to the relationship between actual growth rates and competitors' expectations;

(iii)   much of the benefit attributed to market share is probably better interpreted as the result of competitive advantages generated by more specific resources and choices in marketing or other corporate areas.

On this basis, it would seem that the bias implied in the BCG matrix towards investment in market share at the early stages of market growth is not really justified, particularly when one takes into account that at this stage in market development many investments are likely to be somewhat more risky as well. We do, however, need to be clear between the simple trade-off between risk and return and the undoubted fact that, in more risky situations, it may be more advisable to make optional invetsments, that is to look at what are termed 'real options' (see Dixit and Pindyck, 1995). However, companies can benefit from a focus on market share position when it encourages them to place greater emphasis on the marketing fundamentals for a particular business.

More generally, the matrix as an analytical device suffers from some of the problems which we illustrated for the three strategies approach: an analysis which is essentially based on extreme points when in practice many of the portfolio choices are actually around the centre of the diagram. This implies that any discrimination between business units needs to be on the basis of much more specific analysis rather than broad general characteristics.

The five forces

The five forces analysis was originally introduced by Michael Porter to emphasize the extent to which the overall basis of competition was much wider than just the rivalries between established competitors in a particular market. Whilst not exactly novel as an insight, particularly to suggest that firms also face competition from new entrants and substitutes, it was

presented in a very effective manner and served to emphasize not only the specific and increasing importance of competition as we discussed, but also the extent to which competition should be seen as a much wider activity within the value chain as Porter termed it, although it might now be more likely to be seen as the supply chain. Actually, of course, the situation is a little more complex than this.

Porter used the term value chain when in essence he was concentrating more on the chain of actual costs. More recent commentators such as McGee (2002) maintain a distinction between the value chain, which represents those activities undertaken by a firm, and the supply chain, of which the value chain is a subset, which refers to all the activities leading up to the final product for the consumer. Whilst ex post from an economic point-of-view, there is no difference between value and cost, it is indeed the process of both competition and collaboration between various firms and intermediaries which finally results in the attribution of value throughout the relevant network. In this sense, as others have recognized, a supply chain is an intermediate organization form where there is a higher degree of co-operation between the firms within the chain and a greater degree of competition between the firms within different chains. In this context, Porter's analysis has tended to focus much more clearly on the issue of competition rather than co-operation. Indeed, at least in its representational form, it has tended to go further than this and focus attention on the nature of the competitive pressures on the firm itself rather than interaction between the firm and other organizations in the marketplace.

The search for generic rules for success amidst diversity

As we have suggested above, the codification of marketing strategy was based on three essential schemata. This structure, while it was based on some valid theoretical concepts, did not really provide a systematic approach to the central question: the nature of sustained economic performance in the competitive marketplace. Whilst such an objective was clearly recognized in the so-called search for Sustainable Competitive Advantage (Day and Wensley, 1988), there remained some central concerns as to whether such a notion was realistic given the dynamic and uncertain nature of the competitive marketplace (Dickinson, 1992).

Indeed, not only is it dynamic and uncertain, but it is also diverse: firms are heterogeneous and so is the nature of demand.

A useful way of looking at demand side heterogeneity is from the user perspective directly. Again, I will avoid terms such as customer or consumer and focus attention on defining the individual or group concerned purely in terms of product or service usage. Arguably from its relatively early origins marketing, or at least the more functional focused study of marketing management, has been concerned with managerial effective ways of responding to this heterogeneity, particularly in terms of market segmentation. Indeed, it would be reasonable to suggest that without a substantial level of demand heterogeneity, there would be little need for marketing approaches as they are found in most of our textbooks. Whilst there remains a substantial debate about the degree to which this market-based heterogeneity is indeed 'manageable' from a marketing perspective (cf. Wensley, 1995; Saunders, 1995), to which we will partly return later in this chapter, our concern at the moment is merely to recognize the substantial degree of heterogeneity and consider the degree to which such diversity on both the supply and demand side facilitates or negates the possibility of developing robust 'rules for success'.

To address this question, we need to consider the most useful way of characterizing the competitive market process. This is clearly a substantial topic in its own right, with proponents of various analogies or metaphors along a spectrum including game theory, sports games and military strategy.

To illustrate this issue, let us consider the field of ecology, where we observe wide diversity in terms of both species and habitat. There are two critical aspects which must inform any attempt to transfer this analogy into the field of strategy. The first is the interactive relationship between any species and its habitat, nicely encapsulated in the title of the book by Levins and Leowontin (1985): *The Dialectical Biologist*. Particularly in the context of strategy, it is important to recognize that the habitat (for which read market domain) evolves and develops at least as fast as the species (for which, rather more problematically, read the individual firm). For a much more developed discussion of the application of such notions as species to competitive strategy at the firm level, see McKelvey (1982).

The second aspect addresses directly our question of 'rules for success'. How far can we identify, particularly through the historical record, whether there are any reliable rules for success for particular species characteristics. Of course, it is very difficult to address this question without being strongly influenced by hindsight and most observations are seen as contentious. However, Stephen Jay Gould (1987, 1990) has perhaps most directly considered this issue in his various writings, particularly the analysis of the Burgess Shale, and come to the uncompromising conclusion that it is difficult if not impossible to recognize any species features or characteristics that provided a reliable ex ante rule for success.

It would seem that we should at least be very cautious in any search for rules for success amidst a world of interactive diversity. Hence we should hardly be surprised that marketing strategy analysis does not provide for consistent and sustainable individual success in the competitive marketplace. However, we do have a set of theoretical frameworks and practical tools which at least allow us to represent some of the key dynamics of both customer and competitive behaviour in a way which ensures we avoid errors of inconsistency or simple naivety.

As we have discussed above, most analysis in marketing strategy is informed by what are essentially economic frameworks and so tend to focus attention on situations in which both the competitive structure of the market and the nature of consumer preferences are relatively well established. As we move our attention to more novel situations, these structures tend to be at best indeterminate and therefore the analytical frameworks are less appropriate. We encounter the first of many ironies in the nature of marketing strategy analysis. It is often least applicable in the very situations in which there is a real opportunity for a new source of economic advantage based on a restructuring of either or both the competitive environment and consumer preferences. However, recent detailed work on customer perceptions of market structure actually suggests that in even relatively stable contexts such as autos and motor cycles, the structures may be quite dynamic (Rosa *et al.*, 1999; Rosa and Porac, 2002).

Models of competition: game theory versus evolutionary ecology

To develop a formal approach to the modelling of competitive behaviour we need to define:

1 The nature of the arena in which the competitive activity takes place.
2 The structure or rules which govern the behaviour of the participants.
3 The options available in terms of competitor behaviour (when these consist of a sequence of actions through time, or over a number of 'plays', then they are often referred to in game theory as strategies).

In this section, however, we particularly wish to contrast game theory approaches, which in many ways link directly to the economic analysis to which we have already referred, and

analogies from evolutionary biology, which raise difficult questions about the inherent feasibility of any systematic model building at the level of the individual firm.

Game theory models of competition

A game theory model is characterized by a set of rules which described: (1) the number of firms competing against each other; (2) the set of actions that each firm can take at each point in time; (3) the profits that each firm will realize for each set of competitive actions; (4) the time pattern of actions – whether they occur simultaneously or one firm moves first; and (5) the nature of information about competitive activity – who knows what, when? The notion of rationality also plays a particularly important role in models of competitive behaviour. Rationality implies a link between actions and intentions but not common intentions between competitors. A wider and comprehensive review of the application of game theory to marketing situations can be found in Moorthy (1985).

Models describing competitive activity are designed to understand the behaviour of 'free' economic agents. Thus, these models start with an assumption of 'weak' rationality – the agents will take actions that are consistent with their longer-term objectives. The models also assume a stronger form of rationality – the intentions of the agents can be expressed in terms of a number of economic measures of outcome states, such as profit, sales, growth, or market share objectives.

Do the results of the game theory model indicate how firms should act in competitive situations? Do the models describe the evolution of competitive interactions in the real world? These questions have spawned a lively debate among management scientists concerning the usefulness of game theory models. Kadane and Larkey (1982) suggested that game theory models are conditionally normative and conditionally descriptive. The results indicate how firms should behave given a set of assumptions about the alternatives, the payoffs, and the properties of an 'optimal' solution (the equilibrium). Similarly, game theory results describe the evolution of competitive strategy, but only given a specific set of assumptions.

The seemingly unrealistic and simplistic nature of the competitive reactions incorporated in game theory models and the nature of the equilibrium concept led some marketers to question the managerial relevance of these models (Dolan, 1981). However, all models involve simplifying assumptions and game theory models,[3] whilst often highly structured, underpin most attempts to apply economic analysis to issues of competition among a limited number of firms. Indeed, as Goeree and Holt (2001) observe:

> Game theory has finally gained the central role . . . in some areas of economics (e.g. industrial organization) virtually all recent developments are applications of game theory.
>
> (p. 1402)

As discussed above, Industrial Organization (IO) economics provides one way of extending basic game theory approaches by examining the nature of competitive behaviour when assumptions about homogeneous firms and customers are relaxed. IO economists, especially Richard Caves (1980) and Michael Porter (1981), directed the development of IO theory to strategic management issues. The concepts of strategic groups and mobility barriers are key elements in this new IO perspective. As Richard Caves (1984) indicates: 'The concepts of strategic groups and mobility barriers do not add up to a tight formal model. Rather, they serve to organize predictions that come from

tight models and assist in confronting them with empirical evidence – a dynamised add-on to the traditional structure–conduct–performance paradigm.'

Evolutionary ecological analogies

Evolutionary ecology has also emerged as a popular analogy for understanding the types of market-based strategies pursued by companies (Coyle, 1986; Lambkin and Day, 1989). These analogies have been previously used to describe both the nature of the competitive process itself (Henderson, 1983) as well as the notion of 'niche' strategy (Hofer and Schendel, 1977). Organizational theorists and sociologists have adopted an ecological model, describing the growth of a specie in an ecology, to describe the types of firms in an environment.

r- and k-Strategies

From an ecological perspective, there is an upper limit on the population of a species in a resource environment. When the population of a species is small, the effects of the carrying capacity are minimal and the growth is an exponential function of the natural growth rate. The carrying capacity only becomes important when the population size is large relative to the carrying capacity. The parameters of the standard growth model have been used to describe two alternative strategies: r-strategies and k-strategies. r-Strategists enter a new resource space (product-market space) at an early stage when few other organizations are present, while k-strategists join later when there are a larger number of organizations in the environment. Once a particular type of organization has established itself in an environment, it resists change due to the development of vested interest within the organization. The number of firms in an environment at one point in time, referred to as the population density, is a proxy for the intensity of competition.

Based on this perspective, the initial entrants into an environment are usually

---

[3] A good coverage of game theory approaches is to be found in Kreps (1990), but as indeed Goeree and Holt (2001) note, there remain some significant problems with the predictive power of game theory models when they are compared with actual behaviour, most obviously in asymmetric pay-off situations, which raises questions about the underlying notion of rationality.

r-strategist-small, new firms that are quick to move and not constrained by the inherent inertia confronting firms established in other environments. While r-strategists are flexible, they are also inefficient due to their lack of experience. After several r-strategists have entered a new environment, established organizations, k-strategists, overcome their inertia, enter the environment, and exploit their advantage of greater efficiency based on extensive experience. The characteristics of the environment and particularly the viable niches that emerge determine whether these successive entrants can coexist.

A niche is defined as the specific combination of resources that is needed to support a species or type of organization. Niche width indicates whether this combination of resource is available over a broad range of the resource source space or whether it is only available in a narrow range of the space. A generalist is able to operate in a broad range while a specialist is restricted to a narrow range. The nature of a particular environment favours either generalists or specialists.

Environments are described by two dimensions: variability and frequency of environmental change. In a highly variable environment, changes are dramatic, and fundamentally different strategic responses are required for survival. In contrast, strategic alterations are not required to cope with an environment of low variability. A specialist strategy in which high performance occurs in a narrow portion of the environment is surprisingly more appropriate when environmental changes are dramatic and frequent. Under these conditions, it is unlikely that a generalist would have sufficient flexibility to cope with the wide range of environmental conditions it would face, whilst the specialist can at least outperform it in a specific environment. For a more detailed discussion of this analysis, see Lambkin and Day (1989), as well as an introduction to more complex strategy options involving polymorphism and portfolios. Achrol (1991) also develops this approach further with some useful examples. A generalist strategist is most appropriate in an environment characterized by infrequent, minor changes, because this environment allows the generalist to exploit its large-scale efficiencies.

Comparing the key elements in different models of competition

In this analysis we have left out two other generic types of competitive analogy which are commonly used: sports games and military conflict. Whilst in general these can both be illuminating and informative, they represent in many ways intermediate categories between game theory and evolutionary ecology.

The sports game approach focuses on the relationship between prior planning and the action in the game itself (including the degree of co-ordination between the various individual players), the interaction between competitive response within different time periods (play, game, season), the multiple routes to success but the general evidence that it is necessary to compete on more than one dimension, and that success rapidly encourages imitation. Within the sports game analogy, we recognize the key role of 'rules' and particularly changes in rules as a means of influencing competitive strategies.

The military analogies raise the related issue of what happens in competitive situations when the rules themselves are neither well codified nor necessarily fully accepted, combined with the fact that there is no analogy to the referee in the sports game context. Perhaps most useful from the point of view of competitive strategy is the focus on the balance between clarity and confusion in one's intentions and the general notion of signalling. It is important to avoid becoming over-committed to a particular approach because one's intentions can be read unambiguously by the enemy; on the other hand, a sense of direction is required to maintain internal cohesion and morale. The military perspective also reinforces the multiple time periods of the sports game competitive analogy. In most military conflicts it is assumed that the problems can be overcome with enough resources and effort, but then this degree of commitment could prove too much from a wider perspective, and hence the old adage of winning the battle but not the war.

In terms of limitations sports game analogies, or at least the ones with most common currency, which tend to be games of position such as American football rather than games of flow such as soccer, focus on a simple territorial logic and a well-defined and unchanging set of rules (Kierstead, 1972). They also presume a high degree of control over the activities of individual players. Conversely, military analogies inevitably focus on conflict, and again, in their most popular manifestations, direct and immediate conflict. The physical terrain often occupies a critical role in the analysis of competitive dispositions and there is a focus on the nature of external factors, as opposed to internal organization and control, and supply logistics.

The strategic groups and mobility barriers in the Industrial Organization economics approach recognize the critical asymmetries between competing firms. This approach identifies three methods by which firms can isolate themselves from competition – (1) differentiation, (2) cost efficiency and (3) collusion – although the latter issue has tended to be ignored. The developments within the IO paradigm have therefore tended to usefully focus on the nature and significance of various mechanisms for isolating the firm from its competition. The evolutionary ecological analogy, on the other hand, focuses on the notion of scope with the general distinction between specialists and generalists. The ecological approach also raises interesting questions about the form, level and type of 'organization' that we are considering. In particular, we need to recognize most markets as forms of organization in their own right, as those who have argued the 'markets as networks' approach have done, and question how far we can justify an exclusive focus on the firm as the key organization unit. Finally, the ana[...] more directly the concern about the in[...] between various different units (specie[...] their evolving habitat. The marketplace, like [...] habitat, can become relatively unstable and s[...] both affect and be affected by the strategies of the individual firms.

As we have suggested, any analogy is far from perfect, as we would expect. The limitations are as critical as the issues that are raised because they give us some sense of the bounds within which the analogy itself is likely to be useful. Extending it outside these bounds is likely to be counter-productive and misleading.

The Organization Economics approach in practice tends to neglect the interaction between cost and quality. We have already suggested that while the notion 'focus' within this analogy is an attempt to recognize this problem, it is only partially successful because it subsumes a characteristic of any successful competitive strategy into one generic category. We must further consider the extent to which we can reasonably reliably distinguish between the various forms of mixed strategies over time and the extent to which the strategic groups themselves remain stable.

The limitations of analogies from evolutionary ecology are more in terms of the questions that are not answered than those where the answers are misleading. The nature of 'competition' is both unclear and complex, there is confusion as to the level and appropriate unit of analysis, and the notion of 'niche' which has become so current in much strategy writing overlooks the fact that, by definition, every species has one anyway.

Frequently, business commentators link the concept of a niche to a competitive exclusion principle that no two species (identical organisms or companies) can occupy the same niche (compete in the same manner). Ecologists are quite critical of this concept of a niche:

> A niche, then, in either meaning is a description of the ecology of the species and there is absolutely no justification for supposing that

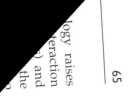

of pigeon-holes into
until the community
e result of using the
the minds of readers
s occupy exclusive
ties and, therefore,
placement because
ecies in one niche.
mpetition does not
...placement in a number of representative examples.

(Pontin, 1982)

Characterizing marketing strategy in terms of evolving differentiation in time and space

Central to any notion of competition from a
marketing strategy viewpoint is the issue of
differentiation in time and space. What makes a
real market interesting is that (i) the market
demand is heterogeneous, (ii) the suppliers are
differentiated, and (iii) there are processes of
feedback and change through time. Clearly,
these three elements interact significantly, yet in
most cases we find that to reduce the complexity
in our analysis and understanding we treat each
item relatively independently. For instance, in
most current treatments of these issues in
marketing strategy we would use some form of
market segmentation schema to map heterogeneous demand, some notion of the *resource-based
view* of the firm to reflect the differentiation
amongst suppliers, and some model of market
evolution such as the *product life cycle* to reflect
the nature of the time dynamic.

Such an approach has two major limitations which may act to remove any benefit from
the undoubted reduction of analytical complexity. First, it assumes implicitly that this decomposition is reasonably first order correct: that
the impact of the individual elements is more
important than their interaction terms. To
examine this assumption critically we need
some alternative form of analysis and representation, such as modelling the phenomena of

interest as the co-evolution of firms and customers in a dynamic phase space, which allows
for the fact that time and space interact.

Second, it assumes that the ways of representing the individual elements that we use, in
particular market segmentation and product
life cycle concepts, are in fact robust representations of the underlying phenomena. In terms of
the adequacy of each element in its own terms,
we need to look more closely at the ways in
which individual improvements may be achieved and finally we might wish to consider
whether it would be better to model partial
interactions, say, between two elements only
rather than the complete system.

Differentiation in space: issues of market segmentation

The analysis of spatial competition has, of
course, a long history back at least to the classical
Hotelling model of linear competition, such as
that faced by the two ice-cream sellers on the sea
front. The basic Hotelling model, however, did
capture the two critical issues in spatial competition: the notion of a space dimension which
separated the various competitive suppliers, as
well as the fact that these suppliers themselves
would have some degree of mobility. In traditional economic terms Hotelling was interested
in establishing the equilibrium solution under
these two considerations, whereas in marketing
we are often more concerned with the impact
and likelihood of particular spatial moves,
although some notion of the stable long-term
equilibrium, if it exists, is obviously important.
The Hotelling model provides us with the basic
structure of spatial competition: a definition of
the space domain, some model of the relationship between the positioning of the relevant
suppliers within this space, and their relative
demands.

In marketing, the competitive space is
generally characterized in terms of market
segmentation. Market segmentation has, of
course, received considerable attention in both

marketing research and practice. There is by now a very large body of empirical work in the general field of market segmentation, but even so there remain some critical problems. In particular:

1   We have evidence that the cross-elasticities with respect to different marketing mix elements are likely to be not only of different orders, but actually imply different structures of relationship between individual product offerings.
2   Competitive behaviour patterns, which after all in a strict sense, determine the nature of the experiment from which the elasticities can be derived, seem to be, to use a term coined by Leeflang and Wittick (1993), 'out of balance' with the cross-elasticity data.[4]

Beyond this, the topic of market segmentation is covered in much greater depth elsewhere in this book. For the purposes of this chapter we wish to concentrate on the specific question as to how far segmentation provides us with an appropriate definition of the space within which competition evolves. In this sense, the key questions are, as we discussed above, about the dimensionality of the space concerned, the stability of the demand function and the degree of mobility for individual firms (or more correctly individual offerings) in terms of repositioning.

---

[4] This, of course, raises questions about the nature and causes of this imbalance. Leeflang and Wittick, in their original approach, were particularly interested in the notion that forms of conjoint analysis could be used to determine the underlying customer trade-off matrix which is, of course, only partly revealed in the empirical customer elasticities (because individual customers can only respond to the actual offerings that are available) and which is 'assumed' (with some degree of bias and error) by individual competitors in determining their competitive actions and reactions. More recently, they have argued that much of the managerial behaviour they observe could be explained by the imbalance in incentive structures in that management will rarely get criticized for reacting to competitive moves! Similarly, Clark and Montgomery (1995) have argued that such over-reaction, or as they term it 'paranoia', may actually not result in lower performance.

These are, in practice, very difficult questions to deal with for two critical reasons:

(i)   The nature of the choice process is such that, for many offerings, individual consumers choose from a portfolio of items rather than merely make exclusive choices and, hence, in principle it is difficult to isolate the impact of one offering from the others in the portfolio.
(ii) The dimensions of the choice space are often inferred from the responses to current offerings, and therefore it is difficult to distinguish between the effects of current offerings and some notion of an underlying set of preference structures.

Segmentation and positioning

In principle, we can describe the nature of spatial competition in a market either in demand terms or in supply terms. Market segmentation represents the demand perspective on structure, whilst competitive positioning represents the supply perspective.

Market segmentation takes as its starting point assumptions about the differing requirements that individual customers have with respect to bundles of benefits, in particular use situations. Most obviously in this context it is an 'ideal' approach in that it is effectively assumed that each customer can/does specify their own ideal benefit bundle and their purchase choice in the relevant use situation is based on proximity to this ideal point. In consumer psychology this is equivalent to an assumption that individuals have strong and stable preferences.

The competitive positioning approach uses consumer judgements, normally on an aggregate basis, to the similarities and differences between specific competitive offerings. In principle, this provides an analytical output roughly equivalent to the spatial distribution in the Hotelling model. Such an analysis can also be used to provide an estimate of the dimensionality of the discriminant space, but in many situations for ease of presentation the results are presented in a constrained 2D format. Equally, benefit segmentation studies can be used along with techniques such as factor analysis to try and arrive at an estimate of the dimensionality of the demand side.

We can be reasonably certain that the attitude space for customers in any particular market is generally, say, $N > 3$: factor analytical studies might suggest at least four or five in general and that of competitive offerings is of at least a similar order. Indeed, in the latter case, if we considered the resource-based view of the firm very seriously we might go for a dimensionality as high as the number of competitors.

Of more interest from a strategy point-of-view is how we represent what happens in terms of actual purchase behaviour in a competitive market through time. Although there is relatively little high quality empirical and indeed theoretical work in this area, so far there are intriguing results to suggest that the dimensionality of the market space for this purpose can be much reduced, although we may still then have problems with some second order effects in terms of market evolution. There have been a number of attempts to apply segmentation analysis to behavioural data with much less information as to attitudes or intention. In one of the more detailed of such studies, Chintagunta (1994) suggested that the dimensionality of the revealed competitive space was two-dimensional but even this might be really an over-estimate. In his own interpretation of the results he focuses on the degree to which the data analysis reveals interesting differences in terms of brand position revealed by individual purchase patterns through time. In fact, on closer inspection it is clear that we can achieve a high level of discrimination with the one-dimensional map where there are two distinct groupings, and one intermediate brand and one 'outlier' brand. It is significant that these groupings are not either brand or pack-sized based, but a mixture. In fact, the only result in moving from the one-dimensional to the two-dimensional analysis is that one brand has

become less discriminated (see Wensley, 1996b). Hence it would appear that we can rather surprisingly reduce the effective competitive space to a single dimension, with the possibility of only some second order anomalies.

In terms of second order anomalies, we can also consider some of the issues raised by the so-called 'compromise effect' in choice situations where the choice between two alternatives depends on other, less attractive, alternatives. In an intriguing paper, Wernerfeld (1995b) argues that this effect can be systematically explained by the notion that consumers draw inferences about their own personal valuations from the portfolio of offerings. However, it may be that a compromise effect could also be seen as the result of mapping an $N > 1$ attribute and preference space on to an $N = 1$ set of purchase decisions. The classical Victorian monograph 'Flatland' (Abbott, 1884; 1992) provided an early illustration of many perceptual problems of moving between space of different dimensions.

A simple model of spatial competition might therefore be one in which a considerable amount of competition can be seen as along a single dimension, in circumstances in which multiple offerings are possible, and where there is no reason to believe *a priori* that individual offerings will be grouped either by common brand or specification, with a fixed entry cost for each item and a distribution of demand which is multi-modal. To this extent it may actually be true that the very simplifications that many criticize in the Porter 'three generic strategies' approach may be reasonably appropriate in building a first order model of competitive market evolution (see Campbell-Hunt, 2000). In the short term, following the notion of 'clout' and 'vulnerability' (Cooper and Nakanishi, 1988), we might also expect changes in position in this competitive dimension could be a function of a whole range of what might often be seen as tactical as well as strategic marketing actions.

Cooper has more recently (see Cooper and Inoue, 1996) extended his own approach to understanding market structures by marrying two different data types – switching probabilities and attribute ratings. Despite the fact that the models developed appear to perform well against the appropriate statistical test, there remain basic issues which link to the issue of the time dynamic evolution of the market or demand space. When the model is applied to the well-established dataset on car purchase switching behaviour (Harshman *et al.*, 1982), it is clear that it provides an interesting and informative analysis of the ways in which various customer 'segments' have evolved over time both in terms of their size and attribute preferences. However, given the nature of the data and the form of analysis, the dynamic process whereby customer desires change in response to both new competitive offerings and other endogenous and exogenous factors can only be seen in terms of changes in attributes and specific switching decisions. We must now consider, however, particularly in the context of understanding the time-based nature of market strategies, how we might incorporate in more detail a longer-term time dimension with a stronger customer focus.

Differentiation in time: beyond the product life cycle – characterizing the nature of competitive market evolution

Few management concepts have been so widely accepted or thoroughly criticized as the product life cycle.

(Lambkin and Day, 1989, p. 4)

The product life cycle has the advantage that it represents the most simple form of path development for any product (introduction, growth, maturity, decline) but, as has been widely recognized, this remains a highly stylized representation of the product sales pattern for most products during their lifetime. Whilst it is reasonably clear that it is difficult if not impossible to propose a better single generic

time pattern, any such pattern is subject to considerable distortion as a result of interactions with changes in technology, as well as both customer and competitor behaviour.

Lambkin and Day (1989) suggested that an understanding of the process of product-market evolution required a more explicit distinction between issues of the demand system, the supply system and the resource environment. However, they chose to emphasize the nature of the demand evolution primarily in terms of diffusion processes. This approach tends to underestimate the extent to which demand side evolution is as much about the way(s) in which the structure of the demand space is changing as the more aggregate issue of the total demand itself. Lambkin and Day (1989) themselves treat these two issues at different levels of analysis, with 'segmentation' as an issue in market evolution which is defined as the resource environment within which the process of the product life cycle takes place.

Beyond this, more recent research, on the process of market evolution, partly building on some of the ideas developed by Lambkin and Day (1989), has attempted to incorporate some insights from, amongst other areas, evolutionary ecology. In particular, work on the extensive disk-drive database, which gives quarterly data on all disk-drive manufacturers, has allowed Christensen (1997) and Freeman (1997) to look at the ways in which, at the early stages in the market development, the existence of competitive offerings seems to encourage market growth, whereas at later stages the likelihood of firm exit increases with firm density. Other computer-related industries have also provided the opportunity for empirical work on some of the issues relating to both the impact of standardization, modularization and the nature of generation effects (Sanchez, 1995), although in the latter case it must be admitted that the effects themselves can sometimes be seen as a result of marketing actions in their own right.

Much of the market shift towards standardization as it evolves can be seen as analogous to more recent work on the mathematics of chaos, and particular questions of the nature of boundaries between domains of chaos and those of order: often labelled the phenomena of complexity (Cohen and Stewart, 1995). Whether we can use such models to provide a better understanding of the nature of market evolution beyond the basic analogy remains an important question for empirical research.

More recent attempts to apply spatial competition models which demonstrate some level of chaotic or complexity characteristics either to competitive behaviour in a retailing context (Krider and Weinberg, 1997), or in the case of both multi-brand category competition (Rungie, 1998) and competition between audit service providers (Chan *et al.*, 1999), show that such models may be able to give us significant new insights as to the nature of competitive market evolution.

Research in marketing strategy: fallacies of free lunches and the nature of answerable research questions

Distinguishing between information about means, variances and outliers

As we indicated at the start of this chapter, much research in marketing strategy attempts to address what is in some senses an impossible question: what is the basic nature of a successful competitive marketing strategy. Such a question presumes the equivalent of a free lunch: we research to find the equivalent of a universal money machine. Before we explore this issue further we need to establish a few basic principles. The competitive process is such that:

(i)   Average performance can only produce average results, which in the general nature of a competitive system means that success

is related to above average and sometimes even outlier levels of performance.

(ii)   The basic principle of rational expectations is that we can expect our competitors to be able, on average, to interpret any public data to reveal profitable opportunities as well as we can. In more direct terms it means that, on average, competitors are as clever or as stupid as we are. A combination of public information and the impact of basic rational expectations approaches therefore means that the route to success cannot lie in simply exploiting public information in an effective manner, although such a strategy may enable a firm to improve its own performance.

(iii)   As we have discussed above, the basis of individual firm or unit performance is a complex mix of firm, competitor and market factors. We therefore can expect that any attempt to explain performance will be subject to considerable error given that it is difficult or not impossible to identify an adequate range of variables which cover both the specifics of the firm's own situation and the details of the market and competitor behaviour.

For these reasons research in marketing strategy, as in the strategy field as a whole, has almost always tended to be in one of the two categories:

1   Database, quantitative analysis that has relied on statistical and econometric approaches to produce results which indicate certain independent variables that, on average, correlate with performance. As McCloskey and Ziliak (1996) indicated, more generally in econometric work, there is a danger that we often confuse statistical significance with what they term economic significance. This notion of economic significance can, from a managerial perspective, be decomposed into two elements: first, the extent to which the relationship identified actually relates to a significant proportion of the variation in the

dependent variable and, second, the extent to which even if it does this regularity actually enables one to produce a clear prescription for managerial action.

2 Case study-based research on selected firms, often based on the notion of some form of outliers, such as those that perform particularly well. Here the problems are the extent to which the story that is told about the particular nature of the success concerned can be used to guide action in other organizations. In practice this often results in managerial prescriptions that are rather tautological and at the same time non-discriminating.

We will now consider examples of both types of this research.

Market share and ROI: the 10 per cent rule in practice

One of the most famous results from the PIMS database was that first reported by Bob Buzzell,

Brad Gale and Ralph Sultan in the *Harvard Business Review* in 1975 under the title 'Market Share – A Key to Profitability'. They reported on the relationship between ROI and market share on a cross-sectional basis within the then current PIMS database. Although, over the years, estimates of the R^2 of this relationship have varied, it generally shows a value of around 10 per cent up to a maximum of 15 per cent. We can start by simulating the original data that were used (Figure 4.4).

Figure 4.4 is a scatter plot of 500 datapoints (notional observations) where the relationship between the two implied variables is actually the equivalent of an R^2 of 0.12 or 12 per cent. Because of the statistical nature of the data distribution in the PIMS database, the fact that it is not strictly normal, it is only possible to simulate a dataset which has either the right range or the right slope within the correct proportion of variance explained. This simulation is based on the right range of values, so that the extreme points are estimated correctly. As a result, however, the actual slope is underestimated (see Wensley 1997a, b; Roberts,

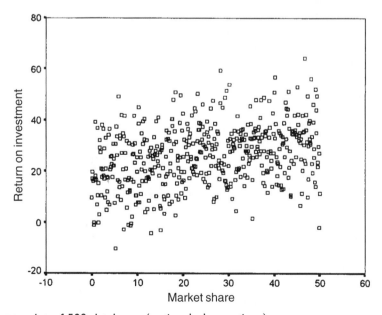

Figure 4.4   A scatter plot of 500 databases (notional observations)

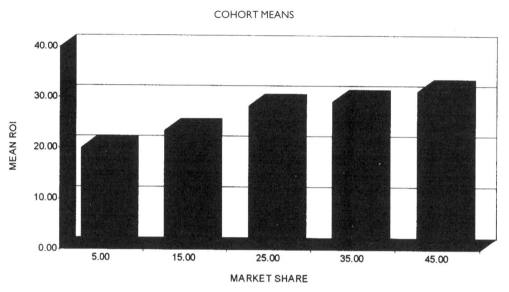

Figure 4.5   Cohort means

1997). In their original article, Buzzell *et al.* 'removed' much of the variation by calculating cohort means. We can do the same and also use more typical modern computer-generated graphics to represent the results (Figure 4.5).

The cohort mean approach, although now not commonly used in strategy research of this sort, will show, as above, some deviations from the straight line trend at sample sizes such as 500, but as samples get even larger the deviations become, on average, even smaller: indeed, some textbook representations of the results go as far as merely illustrating the trend with no deviations at all. Hence, in the process of producing a clearer message from the data, we have nearly eliminated nine tenths of the variability in our performance variable. This is much like the 'trick' used by many speakers (including, of course, University Professors) of allocating the last five minutes of a one-hour talk to 'other factors', or 'limitations with this approach', or some such heading. All very well provided that the issues covered in the last five minutes do not really dominate those which were explored in much greater detail in the first 55 minutes!

How does one explain the 'unexplained' 90 per cent?

If we return to the scatter diagram and treat it as if it represented the current performance of 500 business units within a single corporate portfolio in terms of the relationship between return on investment (ROI) and market share, then we can see some of the problems that arise when we try and make managerial evaluations. The first set of problems relates to the nature of the data and the way in the which the axes are measured. In most analyses of this sort, and in the PIMS data as we discussed above, the data are essentially cross-sectional, i.e. either annual or averaged out over a longer fixed period. Any lead or lag effects are therefore excluded and any particular one-off effects are compensated for only to the extent that they are already discounted from the input data, which are normally based on management accounts. The nature of the axes in a standard market share/ ROI analysis is a problem in that they are both ratios. There are very considerable advantages that accrue from using ratios in this situation – most obviously the fact that it is possible to plot on the same graph units of very different absolute sizes – but we do then have the problem of measurement errors in both the numerator and denominator for both axes.

Finally, the basic data are also inevitably limited in the extent to which they can measure the specifics of any particular business unit situation. Using basic financial and accounting data, we cannot take into account issues such as managerial effectiveness as well as the degree of integration to achieve scale economies and efficiencies in terms of marketing and other activities.

However, we must also put this overall critique of 'market share/return' analysis in context. We should not underestimate the original impact of the 'market share' discovery. Even if it only 'explains' around 10 per cent of financial performance, this is still a considerable achievement. The problem is that, as we have seen, even at this level we face difficult interpretation problems. In the end, one perhaps concludes that its greatest impact was merely that it legitimized debate and discussion about key competitive market assumptions in any strategy dialogue.

Getting to management action: the additional problem of economics

Even if we can identify the source of a particular success or indeed the cause of a particular failure, it is a big jump to assuming that suitable action can be taken at no cost or even at a cost which is justified by the subsequent benefits.

We therefore need to overlay our notion of practical significance with one of economic significance: a factor or set of factors which explain a significant proportion of success can also be used as a decision rule for subsequent successful management action. This is a big jump. To return to the market share/ROI relationship, even if we conclude that there is a significant correlation between market share and profitability, we have to make two further assumptions to justify an economic rule of 'investing' in market share. First, we have to move from the more general notion of 'correlation' or 'explanation' to the much more specific one of 'causation'. Second, we have to assume that whatever its benefits, market share is somehow underpriced. If our first assumption is correct then broadly it can only be underpriced if either our competitors, both current and potential, have a different view or, for some unspecified reason, happen to value the asset (market share) significantly lower then we do. In fact, in specific situations this latter assumption may be rather less unlikely than it at first appears: our competitors could indeed value the benefits differently given their differing portfolio of assets and market positions, but it all depends on the specifics and the details of the individual situation rather than the general.

In the end, it is likely that the continued search for general rules for strategic success via statistical analysis and large databases will prove illusory. This does not make the research effort worthless, we merely have to be realistic about what can and cannot be achieved. After all, the in-depth case study narrative approach, which we will consider shortly, often results in another type of economic rule: the truth which is virtually impossible to apply. Perhaps the best example is to be found in Peters and Waterman's original work. Amongst many memorable criteria for success to be found in *In Search of Excellence* was that undeniable one: the achievement of simultaneous 'loose-tight' linkages. To those who thought that this might seem contradictory, Peters and Waterman (1982) provided the helpful observation that:

> These are the apparent contradictions that turn out in practice not to be contradictions at all.
> (p. 320)

The Honda case: interpreting success

One of the best known examples of a case history which has been interpreted to generate a number of marketing strategy lessons is the case of Honda and their entry into the American motor cycle market. The various interpretations and a set of comparative commentaries are to be found in a set of articles in the *California Management Review* (Mintzberg, 1996a).

In summary, the original consultancy study conducted for the UK government by the Boston Consulting Group interpreted the success that Honda enjoyed in the USA particularly at the expense of the UK imports as the result of substantial economies of scale for their small bikes based on the Cub model, along with a market entry strategy to identify and exploit a new segment and set of customers. Richard Pascale, on the other hand, interviewed rather later a number of the key executives who had worked for American Honda at the time and they told a story which suggested the whole operation was very much on a shoestring and the final success was down to a number of lucky breaks, including a buyer from Sears persuading them to let him sell their small model bikes when they were really trying, and failing, to break into the big bike market.

The debate recorded in the *California Management Review* certainly illustrated how the same story can be interpreted in very different ways. It also emphasizes the problem that learning from the undoubted final success that Honda achieved can be very problematic: even perhaps for Honda itself. It would seem that in many ways one of the underlying dilemmas for Honda, as indeed for any new market entrant, was that if they took the existing market structure as fixed and given then the possibilities for them were remote; on the other hand, market knowledge could only really hint at possibilities for new market structures.

In the end, Michael Goold (1996), who worked for BCG at the time, concluded that:

> The (BCG) report does not dwell on how the Honda strategy was evolved and on the learning that took place. However, the report was commissioned for industry in crisis, with a brief of identifying commercially viable alternatives. The perspective required was managerial, not

historical. And for most executives concerned with strategic management the primary interest will always be what should we do now?

Presumably the (Mintzberg) recommendation would be 'try something, see if it works and learn from your experience'; indeed there is some suggestion that one should specifically try probable non-starters. For the manager such advice would be unhelpful even irritating. 'Of course we should learn from experience,' he will say, 'but we have neither the time nor the money to experiment with endless fruitless non-starters.' Where the manager needs help is in what he should try to make work. This surely is exactly where strategic management thinking should endeavour to be useful.

Whilst, Mintzberg (1996b) comments:

> How then did BCG's clients actually learn from this report? And what lessons did BCG itself take from this particular bit of history? Did it take a good look at its own performance – do some analysis about the impact of its own analysis?
>
> The British motorcycle and parts exports to the United States collapsed to 10 million dollars in 1976, the year after the report was published. So much for the result of this practical managerial perspective. I believe that managers who have neither the time nor the money to experiment are destined to go to the road of the British motorcycle industry. How in the world can anyone identify those endless, fruitless non-starters in advance? To assume such an ability is simply arrogance, and would, in fact, have eliminated many, if not most, of the really innovative products we have come to know.

In the terms of our previous analysis we could argue that Goold is focusing attention on the 10 per cent that can be explained analytically, whilst Mintzberg is arguing not only that the 90 per cent is much more important but, much more importantly, that a realization of specific causes of success can be achieved more effectively through processes such as learning. This is, in practice, a strong assertion about the efficacy of learning processes in organizations that others might dispute, perhaps most obviously James March, who in a number of contributions has argued that notions such as forgetting and foolishness are in fact much more important.

In a further and more recent commentary on the whole debate about the Honda study, Mair (1999) argues that:

> The weaker hypothesis is therefore that Honda seeks ways to make apparent contradictory polarities in strategic management concepts mutually compatible. A strong hypothesis is that Honda has found ways to make the polarities mutually supportive, so that they are in fact positively rather than negatively correlated.
>
> This suggest that . . . an appropriate paradigm under which the strategy industry could learn from Honda would be to analyse and reconstruct how Honda does not choose between the polar positions of the dichotomies of strategic management but synthesizes them in its strategy making. This . . . would of course include analysis of the problems that arise when Honda fails to implement such an approach, notably the apparent over-domination of the product led aspects of strategy as revealed by the crisis in the 1990s.

The recourse to processes, people and purpose in marketing as well as strategy as a whole

More recently in marketing strategy, as in strategy as a whole, there has been a move away from analysis based on real substantive recommendations for management action towards a concern more for processes, people and purposes rather than structure, strategies and systems. This change in emphasis was particularly introduced by Bartlett and Ghoshal (1995) in their influential *Harvard Business Review* article.

Whilst this shift can be seen as a reasonable response to our lack of substantive generalizable knowledge about the nature of successful marketing strategies in a competitive marketplace, as we have discussed above, it

should also be seen as one which itself has rather limited evidence to support it. In marketing strategy in particular, two areas can be identified where this trend has been very evident and we will look critically at both of these: the shift towards a focus on networks and relationship marketing, and the increased emphasis on marketing processes within the firm.

Markets as networks

It is clear, as Easton (1990) has indicated, that actual firm relationships must be seen on a spectrum between outright competition at one end and collusion at the other. At the very least, such a self-evident observation raises the issue of the firm (or business unit) as the basic, and often only, unit of analysis: in certain circumstances we might more appropriately consider an informal coalition of such firms as the key unit:

> Earlier, the border of the company was seen as the dividing line between co-operation and conflict – co-operation within the company and conflict in relation to all external units. The corresponding means for co-ordination are hierarchy and the market mechanism. The existence of relationships makes this picture much more diffuse. There are great opportunities for co-operation with a lot of external units forming, for example, coalitions. Thus, it is often more fruitful to see the company as a part of a network instead of a free and independent actor in an atomistic market.
>
> (Hakansson, 1987, p. 13)

However, the recognition that there is a network of relationships is merely the first step. Approaches need to be developed for the analysis of the network. Hakansson has, for instance, suggested that the key elements of any network are actors, activities and resources. He also suggests that the overall network is bound together by a number of forces, including functional interdependence, as well as power, knowledge and time-related structure.

There is a danger in confusing a detailed descriptive model with a simple but robust predictive one, let alone one which aids the diagnostic process. The basic micro-economic framework which underlies the 'competitive advantage' approach, central to much marketing strategy analysis, should not be seen as an adequate description of the analytical and processual complexities in specific situations. It is a framework for predicting the key impacts of a series of market-mediated transactions: at the very least outcomes are the joint effect of decisions themselves and the selection process. In this sense the only valid criticism of the application of such a model is that either the needs of the situation are not met by the inherent nature of the model or that the model fails to perform within its own terms.

Relationship marketing

Equally, we may wonder how far the new found concern for relationship marketing is indeed new at all. The recognition that customers faced switching costs and that therefore the retention of existing customers was clearly an effective economic strategy is certainly not new. One can therefore sympathize with Baker (1993) when he commented:

> For example, the propositions that companies need to understand the industry infrastructure and/or that working closely with customers is likely to improve product development success rates have been known and accepted many years now and are embedded in the curricula of most business schools.
>
> (p. 88)

on the book by Regis McKenna (1992), *Relationship Marketing*.

More recently, Mattsson (1997) has considered much more critically the relationship between the underlying approaches in the 'markets as networks' and relationship marketing perspectives. He rightly observed that much of the problem lay in the various different approaches claiming to represent relationship marketing:

My conclusion is that if we take the limited view of relationship marketing, we come close to the first extreme position stated in the beginning of this article: relationship marketing and the network perspective have very little in common. Some relationship marketing aspects are even contradictory to basic views in the network perspective. Relationship marketing in its limited interpretation is just a marketing strategy aimed to increase customer loyalty, customer satisfaction and customer retention. Relationship marketing is aided by modern information technology that makes it possible to individualize communication with customers in a mass market. In that sense relationship marketing is just a basic application of the marketing management thinking.

However, let us consider the extended view that the relationship marketing means true interaction between the parties over time, a relatively high mutual dependency between seller and buyer and a major concern for how individual relationships are interconnected in nets and networks. Then we will come much closer to my second initial position that relationship marketing and the network perspective have much to gain from more research interaction and mutual awareness than what is presently the case. Relationship marketing research would benefit from the following aspects of network perspective research: more focus on embeddedness of actors and relationships, more consideration of the buyer's point of view, more descriptive studies on interaction and relationships over time, more concern at the meso and macro levels in the governance structure, more use of longitudinal research methods, including case studies. Obviously, both relationship marketing and the network perspective must become increasingly aware of, and contribute to, research developments in a broader social science framework where the focus is on the function of relationships between economic actors.

It may well be that the relationship marketing movement will have a rather similar impact on marketing to that of the market share in the 1970s and early 1980s. As such, the renewed emphasis on the nature of the customer relationship, which is self-evidently important in industrial markets, will encourage retail marketers to take their customers more seriously, even to regard them as intelligent and rational agents.[5] To do so, however, would also mean to recognize severe scepticism about the various developments in relationship marketing, such as 'loyalty' cards and one-to-one targeting.

However, it may also be true that the relationship and network perspectives will, in the longer term, change our perception of the critical strategic questions faced by firms as they and their 'markets' evolve and develop. Easton *et al.* (1993), for instance, suggest that the notion of competition and markets is really only appropriate at specific stages in the life cycle of the firm or business unit. Indeed, their approach could be taken further to suggest that, at the time when there is significant indeterminacy in terms of competitor and customer choice, this way of characterizing strategic choice is, of itself, of limited either theoretical or practical value. Almost by definition, the product technology and market structure needs to be relatively stable for such strategic choices to be formulated, yet by this stage the feasible choice set itself may be very restricted. The argument is, of course, rather more complicated than this and relates to the previous debate between Child (1972) and Aldrich (1979) on the more general issue of strategic choice.

Emergent or enacted environments

The notion of emergent phenomena has itself emerged as a key concept in organizational strategy. Much of the credit for this must go to Mintzberg (1994), but ironically his analysis of

the concept itself has been rather limited. Indeed, he has tended to define the nature of emergent phenomena in a rather idiosyncratic manner:

> Much as planners can study and interpret patterns in the organization's own behavior to identify its emergent strategies, so too can they study and interpret patterns in the external environment to identify possible opportunities and threats (including, as already noted, the patterns of competitors actions in order to identify their strategies).
>
> (p. 375)

This implies that emergent phenomena are such that they can ex post be related to intentions or actions through time of the individual actors. However, a more common use of the term emergence incorporates some notion of interpretation at different levels of aggregation. After all, for instance, as a number of authors have previously commented, markets themselves are emergent phenomena. It was originally Adam Smith's insight that each actor in a market following their own interest could under certain conditions create an overall situation of welfare maximization: in this sense the invisible hand was much more effective than any attempts at local or even global optimization.

Others have paid much greater attention to the nature of emergent properties, but we also need to recognize a further distinction between what have been termed emergent and enacted environments. In a number of relevant areas, such as information systems, there is no overall agreement on the nature of the differences (see Mingers, 1995), but in the absolute an emergent environment is one in which there are a set of rules but they are generally undetermining of the outcome states, or at least the only way in which an outcome state can be predicted is by a process of simulation, whereas an enacted environment is one in which the nature of the environment is itself defined by the cognitive patterns of the constituents.

[5] To emphasize this perspective, the ESRC for National Science Week 2002 organized a meeting entitled 'The Confident Consumer', which introduced both Richard Scase's new book *Living in the Corporate Zoo* (Capstone Publishing, 2002) as well as the ESRC cultures of consumption research programme (see http://www.esrc.ac.uk/esrccontent/researchfunding/cultures_of_consumption.asp).

This distinction is particularly important when we consider the notion of 'markets as networks' as a perspective to understand the nature of competitive market phenomena. If we understand the nature of the phenomena we are trying to understand as essentially emergent, then there remains considerable value in attempting to model the relevant structure of rules or relationships that characterize the environment.[6] If, on the other hand, we are more inclined to an enactive view of the relationship between organizations and their environment, we need to consider the degree to which the structure of the network is not more than a surface phenomenon, itself resulting from other deeper processes: in this analysis we need to consider the phenomena that Giddens (1979) identifies in terms of 'structuration'. In this process agents and organizations are simultaneously both creators of structures, but also have their action constrained by these structures.

However, even if we are willing to give a relatively privileged ontological status to the detailed network structure in a particular context, we may still face insurmountable problems in developing high-level regularities from a more detailed analysis. As Cohen and Stewart (1995) assert:

> We've argued that emergence is the rule rather than the exception, and that there are at least two distinct ways for high-level rules to emerge from low-level rules – simplexity and

complicity.[7] Can we write down the equations for emergence? The short answer is no ... Essentially what is needed is a mathematical justification for the belief that simple high-level rules not only can, but usually do, emerge from complex interactions of low-level rules. By 'emerge' we mean that a detailed derivation of the high-level rules from the low-level ones would be so complicated that it could never be written down in full let alone understood.

> (p. 436)

It seems that whilst Cohen and Stewart warn convincingly about the dangers of drowning in the detail of low-level rules, they give only limited useful advice as to the practical nature of the alternatives. There has recently been a spate of interest in mathematical approaches under the general title of 'Complexity'. In the context of the economics of forms of market organization, perhaps the most obvious is that due to Kaufmann (1995):

> Organizations around the globe were becoming less hierarchical, flatter, more decentralized, and were doing so in the hopes of increased flexibility and overall competitive advantage. Was there much coherent theory about how to decentralize, I wondered. For I was just in the process of finding surprising new phenomena, that hinted at the possibility of a deeper understanding of how and why flatter, more decentralized organizations – business, political or otherwise – might actually be more flexible and carry an overall competitive adavantage.

> (pp. 245–246)

With a fine, if unintentional, sense of irony, the chapter in Kauffman's book which addresses

---

[6] Actually, even this statement incorporates another critical assumption. As Mingers notes in commenting on assumptions about the nature of social systems and the degree to which they can be seen as self-producing (autopoietic), even those who develop such an analysis define the nature of the organizations and their environment in unexpected ways:

> Luhmann ... in conceptualizing societies as autopoietic ... (sees them) as constituted not by people but by communications. Societies and their component subsystems are networks of communicative events, each communication being triggered by a previous one and leading in turn to another ... People are not part of society but part of its environment.

> (p. 211)

[7] Cohen and Stewart use specific meanings for both 'simplexity' and 'complicity' which roughly describe phenomena where in the former case similar low-level rules create high-level similar structures, whereas in the latter case 'totally different rules converge to produce similar features and so exhibit the same large scale structural patterns' (p. 414). As they emphasize, in the case of complicity one of the critical effects is the way in which 'this kind of system ... *enlarges the space of the possible*' (original emphasis).

these questions has the same title as the infamous Peters and Waterman classic, 'In Search of Excellence'. Interestingly, however, Kauffman is drawing a distinction between the 'lesser' criteria of 'excellence' compared with 'optimality'! Kaufmann goes on to discuss the logic of what he calls a 'patch' structure in which at various levels the form of organization involves a series of relatively autonomous subunits, which under certain conditions are more effective at achieving a system-wide performance maxima compared with the more extreme options which he terms, rather controversially, the fully integrated 'Stalinist' system, or the fully autonomous 'Italian leftist' system!

However, despite the fact that some of these general notions are now to be seen in the mainstream of strategic management thought (see Stacey, 1995), we should remain cautious. Horgan (1997) suggests that we should be cautious of the likely advances to be made in the field that he has dubbed 'chaoplexity':

> So far, chaoplexologists have created some potent metaphors, the butterfly effect, fractals, artificial life, the edge of chaos, self-organized criticality. But they had not told us anything about the world that is both concrete and truly surprising, either in a negative, or in a positive sense. They have slightly extended the borders of our knowledge in certain areas, and they have more sharply delineated the boundaries of knowledge elsewhere.
>
> (p. 226)

Marketing processes

Not surprisingly, the 1990s saw a renewed interest in the marketing process and particularly in the nature of the processes which support the development of a marketing orientation. This approach has been encouraged by the renewed attempts to model the nature of marketing orientation due to both Narver and Slater (1990) and Kohli and Jaworski (1990). In essence, the shift is one that Herb Simon (1979) recognized in his original distinction between substantive and procedural rationality, in which he suggested that it was an appropriate response to the problem of bounded rationality to focus attention more on the appropriate process for arriving at a particular choice rather than developing a general analytical approach to make that choice in any particular situation.

Much empirical research, in particular that based on key informant surveys, has been undertaken to establish the extent to which various operational measures of marketing orientation are correlated with commercial success. On top of this, there has been work to establish some of the possible antecedents for such orientation, including measures related to the accumulation and organizational dispersion of market research data. The results remain somewhat contradictory, but it seems likely that some level of association will finally emerge, although whether it will achieve the minimum 10 per cent target which we considered earlier is rather another question. It is worth noting that, even for samples of only 50, we can roughly speaking achieve a significant result, using the 'normal' $p < 0.05$ criterion, and yet only have about 5 per cent of the variability 'explained'.

On top of this, we need to address more fundamental questions about the underlying logic of procedural rationality in this context. As we have suggested above, it is reasonable to argue that some consideration in any marketing context of each element in the 3Cs (customers, competitors and channels) must surely be seen as sensible. How far such a process should be routinized within a particular planning or decision making schema is another matter. Much of the writing in the area of marketing orientation suggests that the appropriate mechanisms and procedures are unproblematic, yet everyday experience in organizations suggests that achieving an effective response to the market is difficult and indeed may not be susceptible to programmed responses.

The new analytics: resource advantage, co-evolution and agent-based modelling

Earlier on in this chapter we identified a number of key characteristics of a competitive market which determine the effectiveness of any specific strategic analysis, in particular: the heterogenity of demand; the interaction between customer choices and producer offerings; and the degree to which both producers and customers are active agents in this process. More recently, various new analytical approaches have given us new and different ways to address these central issues.

First, Hunt (2000a) has argued that the traditional resource-based view of the firm is so dominated by a supply side perspective that a more comprehensive theoretical approach, which he labels 'resource advantage', is required.

There are some concerns, however, as to whether Hunt's framework actually provides the most effective way of incorporating heterogeneity of demand (Wensley, 2002a), particularly in the context of the evolution of marketing structure. For instance, one of the most established issues in the nature of a market structure is what Wroe Alderson referred to as the sequential processes of 'sorting' between supplier offerings in order to 'match' specific portfolios to customer demands, yet Hunt (2000b) himself observes that so far he is unclear how this might be incorporated within his framework.

At best, therefore, it remains an open question how far the developments proposed by Hunt will help us to understand not only a static view of market demand, but even more a dynamic and evolving one, although it does provide a very useful perspective on the nature of strategic choices for the individual firm or business unit.

Second, there have also been interesting developments in empirical studies of co-evolution, but unfortunately most of these so far have focused on process between organizations, as Lewin and Volberda (1999) note:

> However, studies of simultaneous evolution or co-evolution of organizations and their environments are still rare. We define co-evolution as the joint outcome of managerial intentionality, environment, and institutional effects. Co-evolution assumes that change may occur in all interacting populations of organizations. Change can be driven by direct interactions and feedback from the rest of the system. In other words, change can be recursive and need not be an outcome of either managerial adaptation or environmental selection but rather the joint outcome of managerial intentionality and environmental effects.

As an exception they also note the Galunic and Eisenhardt (1996) study on selection and adaptation at the intra-corporate level of analysis, which used charter changes to align and realign the competencies of various divisions with co-evolving markets and opportunities. However, the model adopted for the process of market evolution remained a simple three-stage life cycle one: start-up, growth and maturity. They found that, broadly speaking, the process of charter changes, which equate with the agreed domain of any division's activity, could be seen as one which was based on selecting the successes from a portfolio of start-ups, the reinforcing focus and finally requiring disposals as the particular market opportunity went through the three stages.

From a market strategy perspective, however, it is noteworthy that even those few studies which attempt to model the nature of market evolution specifically, rather than treat it more as a backcloth upon which other sociological and economic processes take place, tend to represent the actual process in very limited ways. Only in the resource partitioning approach (Carroll and Swaminathan, 1992) do we perhaps see the direct opportunities for a more complex model of market development which represents both its continuity, in the sense that one reasonably expects cycles of competitive imitation followed by the emergence of new forms and market positions for competition, and its indeterminacy, in that various new 'realized niches' could emerge. Even here, however, the implicit emphasis is on the individual firms as the motivating force rather than the collective of customers in the various markets.

Third, advances in agent-based modelling promise new ways of simulating more complex interactive processes of spatial competition (Tesfatsion, 2001; Ishibuchi *et al.*, 2001). Agent-based modelling essentially depends on allowing a simulation to evolve with individual 'agents' making choices within an underming but defined rule structure. It may well provide us with a better understanding of the patterns of market-based evolution and the nature of some of the key contingencies.

Conclusions: the limits of relevance and the problems of application

The study and application of marketing strategy therefore reflects a basic dilemma. The key demand in terms of application is to address the causes of an individual firm or unit success in the competitive marketplace, yet we can be reasonably confident from a theoretical perspective that such knowledge is not systematically available because of the nature of the competitive process itself. In this way, the academic study of marketing strategy remains open to the challenge that it is not relevant to marketing practice. Yet to represent the problem solely in this way is to privilege one particular notion of the nature and use of academic research in marketing as well as the relationship between research and practice. The issue of the relationship between theory and practice and the notion of relevance as the intermediary construct between the two is of course itself both problematic in general (Wensley, 1997c; Brownlie, 1998), as well as open to a range of further critical questions, particularly with respect to the institutional structures that have been developed and sustained on the assumption of the divide itself

(Wensley, 2002b), and therefore at some level represent interest in maintaining the divide but in the name of bridging it! Recognizing the limits to our knowledge in marketing strategy may also help in a constructive way to define what can and cannot be achieved by more investigation and research.

There are a number of areas in which we can both improve our level of knowledge and provide some guidance and assistance in the development of strategy. First, we can identify some of the generic patterns in the process of market evolution which give some guidance as to how we might think about and frame appropriate questions to be asked in the development of marketing strategy. Such questions would be added to those we are used to using in any marketing management context, such as the nature of the (economic) value added to the customer based on market research evidence and analysis. It has been suggested in strategy by writers such as Dickinson (1992) that such additional questions are most usefully framed not around questions of imitation and sustainability that assume sustainability is a serious option, but rather around the more general patterns of market evolution: standardization, maturity of technology, and the stability of current networks. Of course, such a view about sustainability is also very much in tune with both Schumpeterian views about the nature of economic innovation and the general Austrian view about the nature of the economic system (Wensley, 1982; Jacobson, 1992).

When it comes to the generics of success, we face an even greater problem. By definition, any approach which really depends on analysis of means or averages leaves us with a further dilemma: not only does any relative 'usable' explanation only provide us with a very partial picture where there are many unexplained outcomes, but also the very notion of a publicly available 'rule for success' in a competitive market is itself contradictory, except in the context of a possible temporary advantage. Indeed, it would appear that in very rapid response markets such as currency markets this temporal advantage is itself measured only in seconds: it is reasonable to assume it is somewhat longer in product and service markets! We can try and resolve the problem by looking at the behaviour of what might be called successful outliers, but here we face a severe issue of interpretation. As we have seen, as we might expect the interpretations of such success are themselves ambiguous and often tautological: we often end up really asserting either that to be successful one needs to be successful or that the route to success is some ill-defined combination of innovation, effectiveness and good organization.

It may well be that the best we can do with such analysis is to map the ways in which the variances of performance change in different market contexts: just like our finance colleagues we can do little more than identify the conditions under which variances in performance are likely to be greater and therefore through economic logic the average performance will increase to compensate for the higher risks.

Finally, we may need to recognize that the comfortable distinction between marketing management, which has often been framed in terms of the more tactical side of marketing, and marketing strategy is not really sustainable. At one level all marketing actions are strategic: we have little knowledge as to how even specific brand choices at the detailed level impact or not on the broad development of a particular market, so we are hardly in a position to label some choices as strategic in this sense and others as not. On the other hand, the knowledge that we already have and are likely to develop in the context of the longer-term evolutionary patterns for competitive markets will not enable us to engage directly with marketing managerial actions and choices at the level of the firm: the units of both analysis and description are likely to be different. In our search for a middle way which can inform individual practice, it may well be that some of the thinking tools and analogies that we have already developed will prove useful, but very much as means to an end rather than solutions in their own right.

References and further reading

Abbot, E.A.(1992) _Flatland: A Romance of Many Dimensions_, Mineola, NY, Dover Publications (first published by Seeley and Co Ltd, London, 1884).

Abell, D. and Hammond, J. (1979) _Strategic Marketing Planning: Problems and Analytical Approaches_, Prentice-Hall, Englewood Cliffs, NJ.

Achrol, R. S. (1991) Evolution of the Marketing Organisation: New Forms for Turbulent Environments, _Journal of Marketing_, **55**(4), 77–93.

Aldrich, H. E. (1979) _Organizations and Environments_, Prentice-Hall, Englewood Cliffs, NJ.

Baker, M. (1993) Book Review, _Journal of Marketing Management_, **9**, 97–98.

Bartlett, C. A. and Ghoshal, S. (1995) Changing the Role of Top Management: Beyond Systems to People, _Harvard Business Review_, **73**(3), May–June, 132–142.

Bettis, R. A. and Prahalad, C. K. (1995) The Dominant Logic: Retrospective and Extension, _Strategic Management Journal_, **16**, 5–14.

Bogner, W. and Thomas, H. (1994) Core Competence and Competitive Advantage: A Model and Illustrative Evidence from the Pharmaceutical Industry, in Hamel, G. and Heene, A. (eds), _Competence Based Competition_, Wiley, Chichester.

Brownlie, D. (1998) Marketing Disequilibrium: On Redress and Restoration, in Brownlie, D., Saren, M., Wensley, R. and Whittington, R. (eds), _Rethinking Marketing_, Sage, London.

Buzzell, R. D., Gale, B. T. and Sultan, R. G. M. (1975) Market Share – A Key to Profitability, _Harvard Business Review_, **53**, Jan–Feb, 97–106.

Campbell-Hunt, Colin (2000) What Have We Learned about Generic Competitive Strategy? A Meta-analysis, _Strategic Management Journal_, **21**(2), 127–54.

Carroll, Glenn R. and Swaminathan, Anand (1992) The Organizational Ecology of Strategic Groups in the American Brewing Industry from 1975 to 1990, _Industrial and Corporate Change_, **1**, 65–97.

Caves, R. E. (1980) Industrial Organization, Corporate Strategy and Structure, *Journal of Economic Literature*, **43**, March, 64–92.

Caves, R. E. (1984) Economic Analysis and The Quest for Competitive Advantage, *American Economic Association Papers and Proceedings*, May, 130.

Caves, R. E. and Porter, M. E. (1977) From Entry Barriers to Mobility Barriers: Conjectural Decisions and Contrived Deterrence to New Competition, *Quarterly Journal of Economics*, **91**, May, 241–262.

Chan, Derek K., Feltham, Gerald A. and Simunic, Dan A. (1999) A Spatial Analysis of Competition in the Market for Audit Services, August (available at http://www.ecom. unimelb. edu.au/accwww/seminars/ Papers 99/paper30.pdf).

Child, J. (1972) Organisational Structure, Environment and Performance: The Role of Strategic Choice, *Sociology*, **6**, 1–22.

Chintagunta, P. (1994) Heterogeneous Logit Model Implications for Brand Positioning, *Journal of Marketing Research*, **XXXI**, May, 304–311.

Christensen, C. M. (1997) *The Innovator's Dilemma*, Harvard Business School Press, Boston.

Clark, B. H. and Montgomery, D. B. (1995) Perceiving Competitive Reactions: the Value of Accuracy (and Paranoia), Stanford GSB Research Paper, 1335R.

Cohen, J. and Stewart, I. (1995) *The Collapse of Chaos*, Penguin Books, USA.

Contardo, I. and Wensley, R. (2002) The Harvard Business School Story: Avoiding Knowledge by being Relevant, *Organization* (forthcoming).

Cooper, L. G. and Inoue, A. (1996) Building Market Structures from Consumer Preferences, *Journal of Marketing Research*, **33** (August), 293–306.

Cooper, L. and Nakanishi, M. (1988) *Market Share Analysis: Evaluating Competitive Marketing Effectiveness*, Kluwer Academic Press, Boston.

Coyle, M. L. (1986) Competition in Developing Markets: The Impact of Order of Entry, Faculty of Management Studies Paper, University of Toronto, June.

Day, G. S. and Wensley, R. (1983) Marketing Theory with a Strategic Orientation, *Journal of Marketing*, Fall, 79–89.

Day, G. S. and Wensley, R. (1988) Assessing Advantage: A Framework for Diagnosing Competitive Superiority, *Journal of Marketing*, **52**, April, 1–20.

Dickinson, P. R. (1992) Toward a General Theory of Competitive Rationality, *Journal of Marketing*, **56**(1), January, 68–83.

Dixit, A.K. and Pindyck R.S. (1995) The Options Approach to Capital Investment, *Harvard Business Review*, **73**(3), 105–15.

Dolan, R. J. (1981) Models of Competition: a Review of Theory and Empirical Findings, *Review of Marketing 1981*, B.M. Enis and K.J. Roering (eds), Chicago, American Marketing Association, pp. 224–34.

Easton, G. (1990) Relationship Between Competitors, in Day, G. S., Weitz, B. and Wensley, R. (eds), *The Interface of Marketing and Strategy*, JAI Press, Connecticut.

Easton, G., Burell G., Rothschild, R. and Shearman, C. (1993) *Managers and Competition*, Blackwell, Oxford.

Ehrenberg, A. S. C. (1972) *Repeat Buying: Theory and Applications*, North-Holland, London.

Ehrenberg, A. S. C. and Uncles, M. (1995) Dirichlet-Type Markets: A Review, Working Paper, November.

Faria, A. and Wensley, R. (2002) In Search of 'Inter-Firm Management' in Supply Chains: Recognising Contradictions of Language and Power by Listening, *Journal of Business Research*, **55**(7), 603–10.

Fournier, S., Dobscha, S. and Mick, D. G. (1998) Preventing the Premature Death of Relationship Marketing, *Harvard Business Review*, Jan–Feb, 42–50.

Freeman, J. (1997) Dynamics of Market Evolution, *European Marketing Academy. Proceedings of the 26th Annual Conference*, May.

Galunic, D.C. and Eisenhardt, K.M. (1996) The Evolution of Intracorporate Domains: Divisional Charter Losses in High-technology,

Multidivisional Corporations, *Organizational Science*, **7**(3), 255–82.

Giddens, A. (1979) *Central Problems in Social Theory: Action, Structure and Contradiction in Social Analysis*, Macmillan, London.

Goeree, J. K. and Holt, C. A. (2001) Ten Little Treasures of Game Theory and Ten Intuitive Contradictions, *American Economic Review*, **91**(5), 1402–22.

Goold, M. (1996) Learning, Planning and Strategy: Extra Time, *California Management Review*, **38**(4), 100–102.

Gould, S. J. (1987) *Time's Arrow, Time's Cycle: Myth and Metaphor in the Discovery of Geological Time*, Harvard University Press, Cambridge, MA.

Gould, S. J. (1990) *Wonderful Life: the Burgess Shale and the Nature of History*, Hutchinson Radius, London.

Hakansson, H. (1987) *Industrial Technological Development: A Network Approach*, Croom Helm, London.

Hammer, M. and Champy, J. (1993) *Reengineering the Corporation: A Manifesto for Business Revolution*, Brealey, London.

Hannan, M. T. and Freeman, J. (1977) The Population Ecology of Organizations, *American Journal of Sociology*, **82**(5), 929–963.

Harland, C. and Wensley, R. (1997) Strategising Networks or Playing with Power: Understanding Interdependence in Both Industrial and Academic Networks, Working paper presented at Lancaster/Warwick Conference on New Forms of Organization, Warwick, April.

Harshman, R.A., Green, P.E., Wind, Y. and Lundy, M.E. (1982) A Model for the Analysis of Asymmetric Data in Marketing Research, *Marketing Science*, **1**(Spring), 205–42.

Henderson, B. (1980) Strategic and Natural Competition, *BCG Perspectives*, 231.

Henderson, B. D. (1983) The Anatomy of Competition, *Journal of Marketing*, **2**, 7–11.

Henderson, J. M. and Quant, R. E. (1958) *Microeconomic Theory: A Mathematical Approach*, McGraw-Hill, New York.

Hofer, C. W. and Schendel, D. (1977) *Strategy Formulation: Analytical Concepts*, West Publishing, St Paul, MN.

Horgan, J. (1997) *The End of Science*, Broadway Books, New York.

Hunt, M. S. (1972) Competition in the Major Home Appliance Industry, 1960–1970. Unpublished doctoral dissertation, Harvard University.

Hunt Shelby, D. (2000a) *A General Theory of Competition: Resources, Competences, Productivity and Economic Growth*, Thousand Oaks, CA, Sage Publishing.

Hunt Shelby, D. (2000b) A General Theory of Competition: Too Eclectic or Not Eclectic Enough? Too Incremental or Not Incremental Enough? Too Neoclassical or Not Neoclassical Enough?, *Journal of Macromarketing*, **20**(1), 77–81.

Ishibuchi, Hisao, Sakamoto, Ryoji and Nakashima, Tomoharu (2001) Evolution of Unplanned Coordination in a Market Selection Game, *IEEE Transactions on Evolutionary Computation*, 5, 5.

Jacobson, R. (1992) The 'Austrian' School of Strategy, *Academy of Management Review* (October).

Jacobson, R. (1994) The Cost of the Market Share Quest, Working Paper, University of Washington, Seattle.

Jacobson, R. and Aaker, D. (1985) Is Market Share All That It's Cracked Up To Be?, *Journal of Marketing*, **49**(4), Fall, 11–22.

Jones, H. J. (1926) *The Economics of Private Enterprise*, Pitman, London.

Kadane, J.B. and Larkey, P.D. (1982) Subjective Probability and the Theory of Games, *Management Science*, 28 (February), 1982, 113–20.

Kaufmann, S. (1995) *At Home in the Universe*, Oxford University Press, New York.

Kay, J. (1993) *Foundations of Corporate Success*. Oxford University Press, Oxford.

Kierstead, B. S. (1972) Decision Taking and the Theory of Games, in Carter, C. F. and Ford, J. L. (eds), *Uncertainty and Expectation in Economics: Essays in Honour of G. L. Shackle*, Blackwell, Oxford.

Kohli, A. K. and Jaworski, B. J. (1990) Market Orientation: The Construct, Research Propositions and Managerial Implications, *Journal of Marketing*, **54**(2), April, 1–18.

Kotler, P. (1991) Philip Kotler Explores the New Marketing Paradigm, *Marketing Science Institute Review*, Spring.

Kreps, David M. (1990) *Game Theory and Economic Modeling*, Oxford, Clarendon Press.

Krider, R.E. and Weinberg, C.B. (1997) Spatial Competition and Bounded Rationality: Retailing at the Edge of Chaos, *Geographical Analysis*, **29**(1), January, 17–34.

Lambkin, M. and Day, G. (1989) Evolutionary Processes in Competitive Markets: Beyond the Product Life Cycle, *Journal of Marketing*, **53**(3), July, 4–20.

Leeflang, P. S. H. and Wittick, D. (1993) Diagnosing Competition: Developments and Findings, in Laurent, G., Lillien, G. L. and Pras, B. (eds), *Research Traditions in Marketing*, Kluwer Academic, Norwell, MA.

Levins, R. and Leowontin, R. (1985) *The Dialectical Biologist*, Harvard University Press, Cambridge, MA.

Lewin, Arie Y. and Volberda, Henk W. (1999) Prolegomena on Coevolution: A Framework for Research on Strategy and New Organizational Forms, *Organizational Science*, **10**(5), 519–34.

Mair, A. (1999) The Business of Knowledge: Honda and the Strategy Industry, *Journal of Management Studies* (forthcoming).

Mattsson, L.-G. (1997) 'Relationship Marketing' and the 'Markets-as-Networks Approach' – A Comparative Analysis of Two Evolving Streams of Research, *Journal of Marketing Management*, **13**, 447–461.

McCloskey, D. N. and Ziliak, S. T. (1996) The Standard Error of Regressions, *Journal of Economic Literature*, **XXXIV**, March, 97–114.

McGee, J. (2002) Strategy as Knowledge, in S. Cummings and D. Wilson (eds), *Images of Strategy*, Oxford, Blackwells.

McGee, J. and Thomas, H. (1986) Strategic Groups: Theory, Research and Taxonomy, *Strategic Management Journal*, **7**, 141–160.

McKelvey, B. (1982) *Organisational Systematics: Taxonomy, Evolution, Classification*, University of California Press, Berkeley, CA.

McKenna, R. (1992) *Relationship Marketing*, Century Business.

Mingers, J. (1995) *Self-Producing Systems*, Plenum Press, New York.

Mintzberg, H. (1973) *The Nature of Managerial Work*, Harper & Row, New York.

Mintzberg, H. (1994) *The Rise and Fall of Strategic Planning*, Prentice-Hall, Englewood Cliffs, NJ.

Mintzberg, H. (1996a) CMR Forum: the Honda Effect Revisited, *California Management Review*, **38**(4), 78–79.

Mintzberg, H. (1996b) Reply to Michael Goold, *California Management Review*, **38**(4), 96–99.

Moorthy, J. S. (1985) Using Game Theory to Model Competition, *Journal of Marketing Research*, **22**, August, 262–282.

Morrison, A. and Wensley, R. (1991) A Short History of the Growth/Share Matrix: Boxed Up or Boxed In?, *Journal of Marketing Management*, **7**(2), April, 105–129.

Muth, J. F. (1961) Rational Expectations and the Theory of Price Movements, *Econometrica*, 29 July.

Narver, J. C. and Slater, S. F. (1990) The Effect of Market Orientation on Business Profitability, *Journal of Marketing*, **54**(4), October, 20–35.

Ohmae, K. (1982) *The Mind of the Strategist*, McGraw-Hill, London.

Peters, T. J. and Waterman, R. H. (1982) *In Search of Excellence*, Harper & Row, New York.

Pettigrew, A. M. (1973) *The Politics of Organisational Decision Making*, Tavistock, London.

Pontin, A. J. (1982) *Competition and Coexistence*, Pitman-Longman, London.

Porter, M. E. (1979) The Structure Within Industries and Companies' Performance, *Review of Economics & Statistics*, **61**, May, 214–227.

Porter, M. E. (1980) *Competitive Strategy*, Free Press, New York.

Porter, M. E. (1981) The Contribution of Industrial Organization to Strategic Management, *Academy of Management Review*, **6**, 609–620.

Porter, M. E. (1985) *Competitive Advantage*, Free Press, New York.

Porter, M. E. (1990) *The Competitive Advantage of Nations*, Free Press, New York.

Prahalad, C. K. and Bettis, R. A. (1989) The Dominant Logic: A New Linkage Between Diversity and Performance, *Strategic Management Journal*, **10**(6), 523–552.

Prahalad, C. K. and Hamel, G. (1990) The Core Competence of the Corporation, *Harvard Business Review*, May–June, 79–91.

Roberts, K. (1997) Explaining Success – Hard Work not Illusion, *Business Strategy Review*, **8**(2), 75–77.

Rosa, J. A. and Porac, J. F. (2002) Category Dynamics in Mature Consumer Markets through a Socio-Cognitive Lens, *Journal of Management Studies* (forthcoming).

Rosa, J. A., Porac, J. F., Runser-Spanjol, J. and Saxon, M. S. (1999) Sociocognitive Dynamics in a Product Market, *Journal of Marketing*, **63** (special issue), 64–77.

Rumelt, R. P. (1996) The Many Faces of Honda, *Californian Management Review*, **38**(4), 103–111.

Rungie, C. (1998) Measuring the Impact of Horizontal Differentiation on Market Share, Working Paper, Marketing Science Centre, University of South Australia, November.

Sanchez, R. (1995) Strategic Flexibility in Product Competition, *Strategic Management Journal*, **16** (special issue), 135–159.

Saunders, J. (1995) Invited Response to Wensley, *British Journal of Management*, **6** (Special Issue).

Scase, R. (2002) *Britain in 2010*, Oxford, Capstone Publishing.

Senge, P. (1992) *The Fifth Discipline: The Art and Practice of the Learning Organization*, Century Business, London.

Simon, H. A. (1979) Rational Decision Making in Business Organizations, *American Economic Review*, September.

Stacey, R. D. (1995) The Science of Complexity: An Alternative Perspective for Strategic Change Processes, *Strategic Management Journal*, **16**(6), September.

Tesfatsion, L. (2001) Guest Editorial: Agent-Based Modelling of Evolutionary Economic Systems, *IEEE Transactions on Evolutionary Computation*, 5, 5.

Waterman, R. H. (1988) *The Renewal Factor*, Bantam Books, London.

Weick, K. E. (1976) Educational Organizations as Loosely Coupled Systems, *Administrative Science Quarterly*, **21**, 1–19.

Wensley, R. (1982) PIMS and BCG: New Horizon or False Dawn, *Strategic Management Journal*, **3**, 147–153.

Wensley, R. (1990) 'The Voice of the Consumer?': Speculations on the Limits to the Marketing Analogy, *European Journal of Marketing*, **24**(7), 49–60.

Wensley, R. (1994) Strategic Marketing: A Review, in Baker, M. (ed.), *The Marketing Book*, Butterworth-Heinemann, London, pp. 33–53.

Wensley, R. (1995) A Critical Review of Research in Marketing, *British Journal of Management*, **6** (Special Issue), December, S63–S82.

Wensley, R. (1996a) Book Review: Henry Mintzberg and Kevin Kelly, *BAM Newsletter*, Spring, 4–7.

Wensley, R. (1996b) Forms of Segmentation: Definitions and Empirical Evidence, MEG Conference Proceedings (CD Version) Session G Track 8, Department of Marketing, University of Strathclyde, July 9–12, 1996, pp. 1–11.

Wensley, R. (1997a) Explaining Success: the Rule of Ten Percent and the Example of Market Share, *Business Strategy Review*, **8**(1), Spring, 63–70.

Wensley, R. (1997b) Rejoinder to ' Hard Work, not Illusions', *Business Strategy Review*, **8**(2), Summer, 77.

Wensley, R. (1997c) Two Marketing Cultures in Search of the Chimera of Relevance, Keynote address at joint AMA and AM Seminar 'Marketing Without Borders', Manchester, 7 July.

Wensley, R. (2002a) Marketing for the New Century: Issues of Practice and Consumption, *Journal of Marketing Management*, **18**(1/2), 229–38.

Wensley, R. (2002b) Strategy as Intention and Anticipation, in S. Cummings and D. Wilson (eds), *Images of Strategy*, Oxford, Blackwells.

Wernerfeld, B. (1984) A Resource-based View of the Firm, *Strategic Management Journal*, **5**(2), 171–180.

Wernerfeld, B. (1995a) The Resource-based View of the Firm: Ten Years After, *Strategic Management Journal*, **16**, 171–174.

Wernerfeld, B. (1995b) A Rational Reconstruction of the Compromise Effect, *Journal of Consumer Research*, **21**, March, 627–633.

CHAPTER 5

Strategic marketing planning: theory and practice

MALCOLM McDONALD

Summary

In order to explore the complexities of developing a strategic marketing plan, this chapter is written in three sections.

The first describes the strategic marketing planning process itself and the key steps within it.

The second section provides guidelines for the marketer which will ensure that the input to the marketing plan is customer focused and considers the strategic dimension of all of the relationships the organization has with its business environment.

The final section looks at the barriers which prevent organizations from reaping the benefits which stem from a well-considered strategic marketing plan.

Introduction

Although it can bring many hidden benefits, like the better coordination of company activities, a strategic marketing plan is mainly concerned with competitive advantage – that is to say, establishing, building, defending and maintaining it.

In order to be realistic, it must take into account the organizations' existing competitive position, where it wants to be in the future, its capabilities and the competitive environment it faces. This means that the marketing planner must learn to use the various available processes and techniques which help to make sense of external trends, and to understand the organization's traditional ways of responding to these.

However, this poses the problem regarding which are the most relevant and useful tools and techniques, for each has strengths and weaknesses and no individual concept or technique can satisfactorily describe and illuminate the whole picture. As with a jigsaw puzzle, a sense of unity only emerges as the various pieces are connected together.

The links between strategy and performance have been the subject of detailed statistical analysis by the Strategic Planning Institute. The PIMS (Profit Impact of Market Strategy) project identified from 2600 businesses, six major links (Buzzell, 1987). From this analysis, principles have been derived for the selection of different strategies according to industry type, market conditions and the competitive position of the company.

However, not all observers are prepared to take these conclusions at face value. Like strategy consultants Lubatkin and Pitts (1985), who believe that all businesses are unique, they are suspicious that something as critical as competitive advantage can be the outcome of a few specific formulae. For them, the PIMS perspective is too mechanistic and glosses over the complex managerial and organizational problems which beset most businesses.

What is agreed, however, is that strategic marketing planning presents a useful process by which an organization formulates its strategies, *providing it is adapted* to the organization and its environment.

Let us first, however, position strategic marketing planning firmly within the context of marketing itself.

As can be deduced from Chapter 1, marketing is a process for:

- defining markets
- quantifying the needs of the customer groups (segments) within these markets
- determining the value propositions to meet these needs
- communicating these value propositions to all those people in the organization responsible

for delivering them and getting their buy-in to their role
- playing an appropriate part in delivering these value propositions to the chosen market segments
- monitoring the value actually delivered.

For this process to be effective, we have also seen that organizations need to be consumer/customer-driven.

A map of this process is shown below.

This process is clearly cyclical, in that monitoring the value delivered will update the organization's understanding of the value that is required by its customers. The cycle is predominantly an annual one, with a marketing plan documenting the output from the 'understand value' and 'determine value proposition' processes, but equally changes throughout the year may involve fast iterations around the cycle to respond to particular opportunities or problems.

It is well known that not all of the value proposition delivering processes will be under the control of the marketing department, whose role varies considerably between organizations.

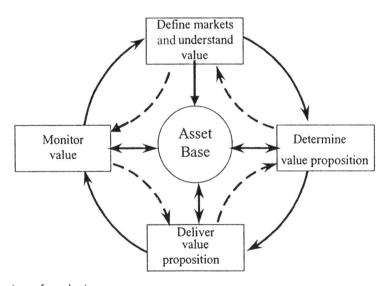

Figure 5.1   Overview of marketing

The marketing department is likely to be responsible for the first two processes, 'Understand value' and 'Determine value proposition', although even these need to involve numerous functions, albeit co-ordinated by specialist marketing personnel. The 'Deliver value' process is the role of the whole company, including, for example, product development, manufacturing, purchasing, sales promotion, direct mail, distribution, sales and customer service. The marketing department will also be responsible for monitoring the effectiveness of the value delivered.

The various choices made during this marketing process are constrained and informed not just by the outside world, but also by the organization's asset base. Whereas an efficient new factory with much spare capacity might underpin a growth strategy in a particular market, a factory running at full capacity would cause more reflection on whether price should be used to control demand, unless the potential demand warranted further capital investment. As well as physical assets, choices may be influenced by financial, human resources, brand and information technology assets, to name just a few.

Thus, it can be seen that the first two boxes are concerned with strategic marketing planning processes (in other words, developing market strategies), whilst the third and fourth boxes are concerned with the actual delivery in the market of what was planned and then measuring the effect.

Input to this process will commonly include:

- The corporate mission and objectives, which will determine which particular markets are of interest;
- External data such as market research;
- Internal data which flow from ongoing operations.

Also, it is necessary to define the markets the organization is in, or wishes to be in, and how these divide into segments of customers with similar needs. The choice of markets will be influenced by the corporate objectives as well as the asset base. Information will be collected about the markets, such as the market's size and growth, with estimates for the future.

The map is inherently cross-functional. 'Deliver value proposition', for example, involves every aspect of the organization, from new product development through inbound logistics and production to outbound logistics and customer service.

The map represents best practice, not common practice. Many aspects of the map are not explicitly addressed by well-embedded processes, even in sophisticated companies.

Also, the map is changing. One-to-one communications and principles of relationship marketing demand a radically different sales process from that traditionally practised. Hence exploiting new media such as the Internet requires a substantial shift in thinking, not just changes to IT and hard processes. An example is illuminating. Marketing managers at one company related to us their early experience with a website which was enabling them to reach new customers considerably more cost-effectively than their traditional sales force. When the website was first launched, potential customers were finding the company on the Web, deciding the products were appropriate on the basis of the website, and sending an e-mail to ask to buy. So far so good. But stuck in a traditional model of the sales process, the company would allocate the 'lead' to a salesperson, who would phone up and make an appointment perhaps three weeks' hence. The customer would by now probably have moved on to another on-line supplier who could sell the product today, but those that remained were subjected to a sales pitch which was totally unnecessary, the customer having already decided to buy. Those that were not put off would proceed to be registered as able to buy over the Web, but the company had lost the opportunity to improve its margins by using the sales force more judiciously. In time the company realised its mistake: unlike those prospects which the company identified and contacted, which might indeed need 'selling' to, many new Web customers were initiating the dialogue themselves, and simply required the company to respond effectively and rapidly. The sales force was increasingly freed up to concentrate on major clients and on relationship building.

Having put marketing planning into the context of marketing and other corporate functions, we can now turn specifically to the marketing planning process, how it should be done and what the barriers are to doing it effectively. We are, of course, referring specifically to the second box in Figure 5.1. See Chapters 10 and 27 for more detail on market segmentation.

1 The marketing planning process

Most managers accept that some kind of procedure for marketing planning is necessary. Accordingly they need a system which will help them to think in a structured way and also make explicit their intuitive economic models of the business. Unfortunately, very few companies have planning systems which possess these characteristics. However, those that do tend to follow a similar pattern of steps.

Figure 5.2 illustrates the several stages that have to be gone through in order to arrive at a marketing plan. This illustrates the difference between the process of marketing planning and the actual plan itself, which is the output of the process.

Experience has shown that a marketing plan should contain:

- A mission statement.
- A financial summary.
- A brief market overview.
- A summary of all the principal external factors which affected the company's marketing performance during the previous year, together with a statement of the company's strengths

and weaknesses vis-à-vis the competition. This is what we call SWOT (strengths, weaknesses, opportunities, threats) analyses.
- Some assumptions about the key determinants of marketing success and failure.
- Overall marketing objectives and strategies.
- Programmes containing details of timing, responsibilities and costs, with sales forecasts and budgets.

Each of the stages illustrated in Figure 5.2 will be discussed in more detail later in this chapter. The dotted lines joining up stages 5–8 are meant to indicate the reality of the planning process, in that it is likely that each of these steps will have to be gone through more than once before final programmes can be written.

Although research has shown these marketing planning steps to be universally applicable, the degree to which each of the separate steps in the diagram needs to be formalized depends to a large extent on the size and nature of the company. For example, an undiversified company generally uses less formalized procedures, since top management tends to have greater functional knowledge and expertise than subordinates, and because the lack of diversity of operations enables direct control to be exercised over most of the key determinants of success. Thus, situation reviews, the setting of marketing objectives, and so on, are not always made explicit in writing, although these steps have to be gone through.

In contrast, in a diversified company, it is usually not possible for top management to have greater functional knowledge and expertise than subordinate management, hence planning tends to be more formalized in order to provide a consistent discipline for those who have to make the decisions throughout the organization.

Either way, there is now a substantial body of evidence to show that formalized planning procedures generally result in greater profitability and stability in the long term and also help to reduce friction and operational difficulties within organizations.

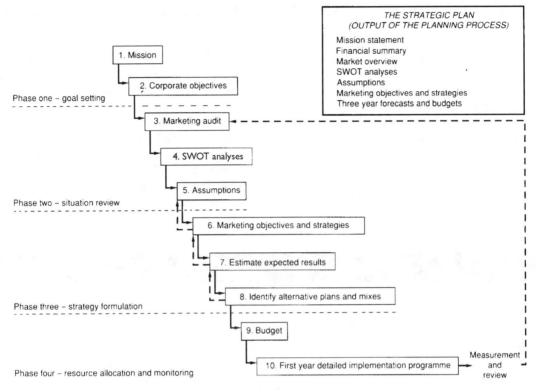

Figure 5.2   The ten steps of the strategic marketing planning process

Where marketing planning has failed, it has generally been because companies have placed too much emphasis on the procedures themselves and the resulting paperwork, rather than on generating information useful to and consumable by management. But more about reasons for failure later. For now, let us look at the marketing planning process in more detail, starting with the marketing audit.

What is a marketing audit?

Any plan will only be as good as the information on which it is based, and the marketing audit is the means by which information for planning is organized. There is no reason why marketing cannot be audited in the same way as accounts, in spite of its more innovative, subjective nature. A marketing audit is a systematic appraisal of all the external and internal factors that have affected a company's commercial performance over a defined period.

Given the growing turbulence of the business environment and the shorter product life cycles that have resulted, no one would deny the need to stop at least once a year at a particular point in the planning cycle to try to form a reasoned view of how all the many external and internal factors have influenced performance.

Sometimes, of course, a company will conduct a marketing audit because it is in financial trouble. At times like these, management often attempts to treat the wrong symptoms, most frequently by reorganizing the company. But such measures are unlikely to be effective if there are more fundamental problems which have not been identified. Of course, if the company survived for long enough, it might eventually solve its problems through a process of elimination. Essentially, though, the argument is that the problems have first to be properly defined. The audit is a means of helping to define them.

Two kinds of variable

Any company carrying out an audit will be faced with two kinds of variable. There is the kind over which the company has no direct control, for example economic and market factors. Second, there are those over which the company has complete control, the operational variables, which are usually the firm's internal resources. This division suggests that the best way to structure an audit is in two parts, external and internal. Table 5.1 shows areas which should be investigated under both headings. Each should be examined with a view to building up an information base relevant to the company's performance.

Many people mistakenly believe that the marketing audit should be some kind of final

Table 5.1 Conducting an audit	
External audit	*Internal audit*
Business and economic environment Economic political, fiscal, legal, social, cultural Technological Intra-company	Own company Sales (total, by geographical location, by industrial type, by customer, by product) Market shares Profit margins, costs
The market Total market, size, growth and trends (value volume) Market characteristics, developments and trends; products, prices, physical distribution, channels, customers, consumers, communication, industry practices	Marketing information research Marketing mix variables: product management, price, distribution, promotion, operations and resources Key strengths and weaknesses
Competition Major competitors Size Market share coverage Market standing and reputation Production capabilities Distribution policies Marketing methods Extent of diversification Personnel issues International links Profitability	

attempt to define a company's marketing problems, or, at best, something done by an independent body from time to time to ensure that a company is on the right track. However, many highly successful companies, as well as using normal information and control procedures and marketing research throughout the year, start their planning cycle each year with a formal, audit-type process, of everything that has had an important influence on marketing activities. Certainly, in many leading consumer goods companies, the annual self-audit approach is a tried and tested discipline.

Occasionally, it may be justified for outside consultants to carry out the audit in order to check that the company is getting the most out of its resources. However, it seems an unnecessary expense to have this done every year.

Objections to line managers doing their own audits usually centre around the problem of time and objectivity. In practice, a disciplined approach and thorough training will help. But the discipline must be applied from the highest to the lowest levels of management if the tunnel vision that often results from a lack of critical appraisal is to be avoided.

Where relevant, the marketing audit should contain life cycles for major products and for market segments, for which the future shape will be predicted using the audit information. Also, major products and markets should be plotted on some kind of matrix to show their current competitive position.

The next question is: what happens to the results of the audit? Some companies consume valuable resources carrying out audits that produce very little in the way of results. The audit is simply a database, and the task remains of turning it into intelligence, that is, information essential to decision making.

It is often helpful to adopt a regular format for the major findings. One way of doing this is in the form of a SWOT analysis. This is a summary of the audit under the headings of internal strengths and weaknesses as they relate to external opportunities and threats. There will be a number of SWOT analyses for each major product for market to be included in the marketing plan.

The section containing SWOT analyses should, if possible, contain no more than four or five pages of commentary, focusing only on key factors. It should highlight internal strengths and weaknesses measured against the competition's, and key external opportunities and threats. A summary of reasons for good or bad performance should be included. It should be interesting to read, contain concise statements, include only relevant and important data and give greater emphasis to creative analysis.

It is important to remember at this stage that we are merely describing the process of marketing planning as outlined in Figure 5.2. The format of the strategic marketing plan itself (i.e. what should actually appear in the written plan) is given in Table 5.2 (p. 96).

Having completed the marketing audit and SWOT analyses, fundamental assumptions on future conditions have to be made. It would be no good receiving plans from two product managers, one of whom believed the market was going to increase by 10 per cent and the other who believed it was going to decline by 10 per cent.

An example of a written assumption might be: 'With respect to the company's industrial climate, it is assumed that over-capacity will increase from 105 per cent to 115 per cent as new industrial plants come into operation, price competition will force price levels down by 10 per cent across the board; a new product will be introduced by our major competitor before the end of the second quarter.' Assumptions should be few in number. If a plan is possible irrespective of the assumptions made, then the assumptions are unnecessary.

Setting marketing objectives and strategies

The next step is the writing of marketing objectives and strategies. This is the key to the whole process and undoubtedly the most important and difficult of all stages. If this is not done properly, everything that follows is of little value.

It is an obvious activity to follow on with, since a thorough review, particularly of its markets, should enable the company to determine whether it will be able to meet the long range financial targets with its current range of products. Any projected gap has to be filled by new product development or market extension.

The important point to make is that this is the stage in the planning cycle at which a compromise has to be reached between what is wanted by various departments and what is practicable, given all the constraints upon the company. At this stage, objectives and strategies should be set for three years ahead, or for whatever the planning horizon is.

An objective is what you want to achieve, a strategy is how you plan to achieve it. Thus, there can be objectives and strategies at all levels in marketing, such as for service levels, for advertising, for pricing, and so on.

The important point to remember about marketing objectives is that they are concerned solely with products and markets. Common sense will confirm that it is only by selling something to someone that the company's financial goals can be achieved; pricing and service levels are the means by which the goals are achieved. Thus, pricing, sales promotion and advertising objectives should not be confused with marketing objectives.

The latter are concerned with one or more of the following:

- Existing products in existing markets.
- New products for existing markets.
- Existing products for new markets.
- New products for new markets.

They should be capable of measurement, otherwise they are not worthwhile. Directional terms, such as 'maximize', 'minimize', 'penetrate' and 'increase', are only acceptable if quantitative measurement can be attached to

them. Measurement should be in terms of sales volume, value, market share, percentage penetration of outlet and so on.

Marketing strategies, the means by which the objectives will be achieved, are generally concerned with the 'four Ps':

1 *Product*: deletions, modifications, additions, designs, packaging, etc.
2 *Price*: policies to be followed for product groups in market segments.
3 *Place*: distribution channels and customer service levels.
4 *Promotion*: communicating with customers under the relevant headings, i.e. advertising, sales force, sales promotion, public relations, exhibitions, direct mail, etc.

There is some debate about whether or not the four Ps are adequate to describe the marketing mix. Some academics advocate that people, procedures and almost anything else beginning with 'P' should be included. However, we believe that these 'new' factors are already subsumed in the existing four Ps.

Estimate expected results, identify alternative plans and mixes

Having completed this major planning task, it is normal at this stage to employ judgement, experience, field tests and so on to test out the feasibility of the objectives and strategies in terms of market share, sales, costs and profits. It is also at this stage that alternative plans and mixes are normally considered.

General marketing strategies should now be reduced to specific objectives, each supported by more detailed strategy and action statements. A company organized according to functions might have an advertising plan, a sales promotion plan and a pricing plan. A product-based company might have a product plan, with objectives, strategies and tactics for price, place and promotion, as required. A market or geographically based company might have a market plan, with objectives, strategies and tactics for the four Ps, as required. Likewise, a company with a few major customers might have a customer plan. Any combination of the above might be suitable, depending on circumstances.

There is a clear distinction between strategy and detailed implementation of tactics. Marketing strategy reflects the company's best opinion as to how it can most profitably apply its skills and resources to the marketplace. It is inevitably broad in scope. The plan which stems from it will spell out action and timings and will contain the detailed contribution expected from each department.

There is a similarity between strategy in business and the development of military strategy. One looks at the enemy, the terrain, the resources under command, and then decides whether to attack the whole front, an area of enemy weakness, to feint in one direction while attacking in another, or to attempt an encirclement of the enemy's position. The policy and mix, the type of tactics to be used, and the criteria for judging success, all come under the heading of strategy. The action steps are tactics.

Similarly, in marketing, the same commitment, mix and type of resources as well as tactical guidelines and criteria that must be met, all come under the heading of strategy. For example, the decision to use distributors in all but the three largest market areas, in which company sales people will be used, is a strategic decision. The selection of particular distributors is a tactical decision.

The following list of marketing strategies (in summary form) cover the majority of options open under the headings of the four Ps:

1 Product:
   - Expand the line.
   - Change performance, quality or features.
   - Consolidate the line.
   - Standardize design.
   - Positioning.
   - Change the mix.
   - Branding.

2 Price:
   - Change price, terms or conditions.
   - Skimming policies.
   - Penetration policies.

3 Promotion:
   - Change advertising or promotion.
   - Change selling.

4 Place:
   - Change delivery or distribution.
   - Change service.
   - Change channels.
   - Change the degree of forward integration.

Formulating marketing strategies is one of the most critical and difficult parts of the entire marketing process. It sets the limit of success. Communicated to all management levels, it indicates what strengths are to be developed, what weaknesses are to be remedied, and in what manner. Marketing strategies enable operating decisions to bring the company into the right relationship with the emerging pattern of market opportunities which previous analysis has shown to offer the highest prospect of success.

The budget

This is merely the cost of implementing the strategies over the planning period and will obviously be deducted from the net revenue, giving a marketing contribution. There may be a number of iterations of this stage.

The first year detailed implementation programme

The first year of the strategic marketing plan is now converted into a detailed scheduling and costing out of the specific actions required to achieve the first year's budget.

What should appear in a strategic marketing plan?

A written marketing plan is the back-drop against which operational decisions are taken.

Table 5.2   What should appear in a strategic marketing plan

1. Start with a mission statement.
2. Here, include a financial summary which illustrates graphically revenue and profit for the full planning period.
3. Now do a market overview:
    Has the market declined or grown?
    How does it break down into segments?
    What is your share of each?
    Keep it simple. If you do not have the facts, make estimates. Use life cycles, bar charts and pie charts to make it all crystal clear.
4. Now identify the key segments and do a SWOT analysis for each one:
    Outline the major external influences and their impact on each segment.
    List the key factors for success. These should be less than five.
    Give an assessment of the company's differential strengths and weaknesses compared with those of it competitors. Score yourself and your competitors out of 10 and then multiply each score by a weighting factor for each critical success factor (e.g. CSF 1 = 60, CSF 2 = 25, CSF 3 = 10, CSF 4 = 5).
5. Make a brief statement about the key issues that have to be addressed in the planning period.
6. Summarize the SWOTs using a portfolio matrix in order to illustrate the important relationships between your key products and markets.
7. List your assumptions.
8. Set objectives and strategies.
9. Summarize your resource requirements for the planning period in the form of a budget.

Consequently, too much detail should be avoided. Its major function is to determine where the company is, where it wants to go and how it can get there. It lies at the heart of a company's revenue-generating activities, such as the timing of the cash flow and the size and character of the labour force. What should actually appear in a written strategic marketing plan is shown in Table 5.2. This strategic marketing plan should be distributed only to those who need it, but it can only be an aid to effective management. It cannot be a substitute for it.

It will be obvious from Table 5.2 that not only does budget setting become much easier and more realistic, but the resulting budgets are more likely to reflect what the whole company wants to achieve, rather than just one department.

The problem of designing a dynamic system for setting budgets is a major challenge to the marketing and financial directors of all companies. The most satisfactory approach would be for a marketing director to justify all marketing expenditure from a zero base each year against the tasks to be accomplished. If these procedures are followed, a hierarchy of objectives is built in such a way that every item of budgeted expenditure can be related directly back to the initial financial objectives.

For example, if sales promotion is a major means of achieving an objective, when a sales promotion item appears in the programme, it has a specific purpose which can be related back to a major objective. Thus every item of expenditure is fully accounted for.

Marketing expense can be considered to be all costs that are incurred after the product leaves the 'factory', apart from those involved in physical distribution. When it comes to pricing, any form of discounting that reduces the expected gross income – such as promotional or quantity discounts, overriders, sales commission and unpaid invoices – should be given the most careful attention as marketing expenses. Most obvious marketing expenses will occur, however, under the heading of promotion, in the form of advertising, sales salaries and expenses, sales promotion and direct mail costs.

The important point about the measurable effects of marketing activity is that anticipated levels should result from careful analysis of what is required to take the company towards its goals, while the most careful attention should be paid to gathering all items of expenditure under appropriate headings. The healthiest way of treating these issues is through zero-based budgeting.

We have just described the strategic marketing plan and what it should contain. The tactical marketing plan layout and content should be similar, but the detail is much greater, as it is for one year only.

Marketing planning systems design and implementation

While the actual process of marketing planning is simple in outline, a number of contextual issues have to be considered that make marketing planning one of the most baffling of all management problems. The following are some of those issues:

- When should it be done, how often, by whom, and how?
- Is it different in a large and a small company?
- Is it different in a diversified and an undiversified company?
- What is the role of the chief executive?
- What is the role of the planning department?
- Should marketing planning be top-down or bottom-up?

- What is the relationship between operational (one year) and strategic (longer-term) planning?

Requisite strategic marketing planning

Many companies with financial difficulties have recognized the need for a more structured approach to planning their marketing and have opted for the kind of standardized, formalized procedures written about so much in textbooks. Yet, these rarely bring any benefits and often bring marketing planning itself into disrepute.

It is quite clear that any attempt at the introduction of formalized marketing planning requires a change in a company's approach to managing its business. It is also clear that unless a company recognizes these implications, and plans to seek ways of coping with them, formalized strategic planning will be ineffective.

Research has shown that the implications are principally as follows:

1 Any closed-loop planning system (but especially one that is essentially a forecasting and budgeting system) will lead to dull and ineffective marketing. Therefore, there has to be some mechanism for preventing inertia from setting in through the over-bureaucratization of the system.
2 Planning undertaken at the functional level of marketing, in the absence of a means of integration with other functional areas of the business at general management level, will be largely ineffective.
3 The separation of responsibility for operational and strategic planning will lead to a divergence of the short-term thrust of a business at the operational level from the long-term objectives of the enterprise as a whole. This will encourage preoccupation with short-term results at operational level, which normally makes the firm less effective in the longer term.

4 Unless the chief executive understands and takes an active role in strategic marketing planning, it will never be an effective system.

5 A period of up to three years is necessary (especially in large firms) for the successful introduction of an effective strategic marketing planning system.

Let us be dogmatic about requisite planning levels. First, in a large diversified group, irrespective of such organizational issues, anything other than a systematic approach approximating to a formalized marketing planning system is unlikely to enable the necessary control to be exercised over the corporate identity. Second, unnecessary planning, or overplanning, could easily result from an inadequate or indiscriminate consideration of the real planning needs at the different levels in the hierarchical chain. Third, as size and diversity grow, so the degree of formalization of the marketing planning process must also increase. This can be simplified in the form of a matrix, Figure 5.3.

It has been found that the degree of formalization increases with the evolving size and diversity of operations (see Figure 5.3). However, while the degree of formalization

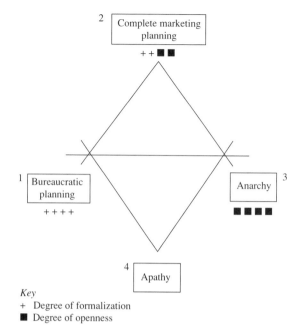

Key
+ Degree of formalization
■ Degree of openness

Figure 5.4   Four key outcomes

will change, the need for an effective marketing planning system does not. The problems that companies suffer, then, are a function of either the degree to which they have a requisite marketing planning system or the degree to which the formalization of their system grows with the situational complexities attendant upon the size and diversity of operations.

Figure 5.4 shows four key outcomes that marketing planning can evoke. It can be seen that systems 1, 3 and 4 (i.e. where the individual is totally subordinate to a formalized system, or where there is neither system nor creativity), are less successful than system 2, in which the individual is allowed to be entrepreneurial within a total system. System 2, then, will be an effective marketing planning system, but one in which the degree of formalization will be a function of company size and diversity.

One of the most encouraging findings to emerge from research is that the theory of marketing planning is universally applicable. While the planning task is less complicated in

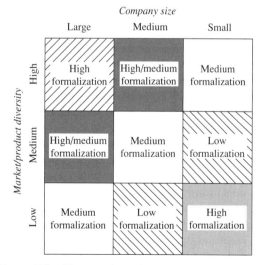

Figure 5.3   Planning formalization

small, undiversified companies and there is less need for formalized procedures than in large, diversified companies, the fact is that exactly the same framework should be used in all circumstances, and that this approach brings similar benefits to all.

How far ahead should we plan?

It is clear that one and three year planning periods are by far the most common. Lead time for the initiation of major new product innovations, the length of time necessary to recover capital investment costs, the continuing availability of customers and raw materials and the size and usefulness of existing plant and buildings are the most frequently mentioned reasons for having a three year planning horizon.

Many companies, however, do not give sufficient thought to what represents a sensible planning horizon for their particular circumstances. A five year time span is clearly too long for some companies, particularly those with highly versatile machinery operating in volatile fashion-conscious markets. The effect of this is to rob strategic plans of reality.

The conclusion to be reached is that there is a natural point of focus into the future beyond which it is pointless to look. This point of focus is a function of the relative size of a company. Small companies, because of their size and the way they are managed, tend to be comparatively flexible in the way in which they can react to environmental turbulence in the short term. Large companies, on the other hand, need a much longer lead time in which to make changes in direction. Consequently, they tend to need to look further into the future and to use formalized systems for this purpose so that managers throughout the organization have a common means of communication.

How the marketing planning process works

As a basic principle, strategic marketing planning should take place as near to the marketplace as possible in the first instance, but such plans should then be reviewed at higher levels within an organization to see what issues may have been overlooked.

It has been suggested that each manager in the organization should complete an audit and SWOT analysis on his or her own area of responsibility. The only way that this can work in practice is by means of a hierarchy of audits. The principle is simply demonstrated in Figure 5.5. This figure illustrates the principle of auditing at different levels within an organization. The marketing audit format will be universally applicable. It is only the detail that varies from level to level and from company to company within the same group.

Figure 5.6 illustrates the total corporate strategic and planning process. This time, however, a time element is added, and the relationship between strategic planning briefings, long-term corporate plans and short-term operational plans is clarified. It is important to note that there are two 'open-loop' points on this last diagram. These are the key times in the planning process when a subordinate's views and findings should be subjected to the closest examination by his or her superior. It is by taking these opportunities that marketing planning can be transformed into the critical and creative process it is supposed to be rather than the dull, repetitive ritual it so often turns out to be.

Since in anything but the smallest of undiversified companies it is not possible for top management to set detailed objectives for operating units, it is suggested that at this stage in the planning process strategic guidelines should be issued. One way of doing this is in the form of a strategic planning letter. Another is by means of a personal briefing by the chief executive at 'kick-off' meetings. As in the case of the audit, these guidelines would proceed from the broad to the specific, and would become more detailed as they progressed through the company towards operating units.

These guidelines would be under the headings of financial, manpower and organization, operations and, of course, marketing.

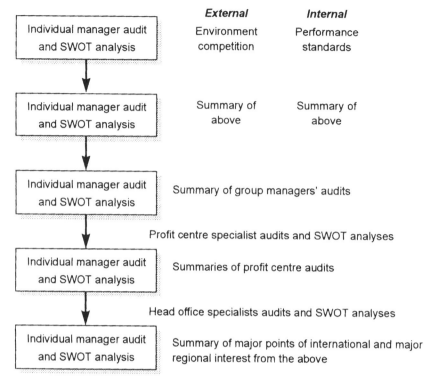

Figure 5.5   Hierarchy of audits

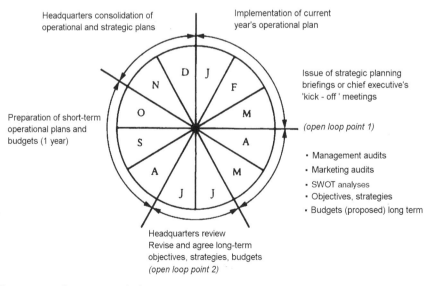

Figure 5.6   Strategic and operational planning

Under marketing, for example, at the highest level in a large group, top management may ask for particular attention to be paid to issues such as the technical impact of microprocessors on electromechanical component equipment, leadership and innovation strategies, vulnerability to attack from the flood of Japanese, Korean and Third World products, and so on. At operating company level, it is possible to be more explicit about target markets, product development, and the like.

Part I conclusions

In concluding this section, we must stress that there can be no such thing as an off-the-peg marketing planning system and anyone who offers one must be viewed with great suspicion. In the end, strategic marketing planning success comes from an endless willingness to learn and to adapt the system to the people and the circumstances of the firm. It also comes from a deep understanding about the nature of marketing planning, which is something that, in the final analysis, cannot be taught.

However, strategic marketing planning demands that the organization recognizes the challenges that face it and their effect on its potential for future success. It must learn to focus on customers and their needs at all times and explore every avenue which may provide it with a differential advantage over its competitors.

The next section looks at some guidelines which lead to effective marketing planning.

2 Guidelines for effective marketing planning

Although innovation remains a major ingredient in commercial success, there are nevertheless other challenges which companies must overcome if they wish to become competitive marketers. While their impact may vary from company to company, challenges such as the pace of change, the maturity of markets and the implications of globalization need to be given serious consideration. Some of the more obvious challenges are shown in Table 5.3.

To overcome these challenges the following guidelines are recommended to help the marketer to focus on effective marketing strategies.

Twelve guidelines for effective marketing

1 *Understanding the sources of competitive advantage*

Guideline 1 (p. 64) shows a universally recognized list of sources of competitive advantage. For small firms, they are more likely to be the ones listed on the left. It is clearly possible to focus on highly individual niches with specialized skills and to develop customer-focused relationships to an extent not possible for large organizations. Flexibility is also a potential source of competitive advantage.

Wherever possible, all organizations should seek to avoid competing with an undifferentiated product or service in too broad a market.

The author frequently has to emphasize to those who seek his advice that without something different to offer (required by the market, of course!), they will continue to struggle and will have to rely on the crumbs that fall from the tables of others. This leads on to the second point.

2 *Understanding differentiation*

Guideline 2 takes this point a little further and spells out the main sources of differentiation. One in particular, superior service, has increasingly become a source of competitive advantage. Companies should work relentlessly toward the differential advantage that these will bring. Points 1 and 2 have been confirmed by results from a 1994 survey of over 8000 small and medium sized enterprises (SMEs).

Table 5.3   Change and the challenge to marketing

Nature of change	*Marketing challenges*
Pace of change	
• Compressed time horizons	• Ability to exploit markets more rapidly
• Shorter product life cycles	• More effective new product development
• Transient customer preferences	• Flexibility in approach to markets
	• Accuracy in demand forecasting
	• Ability to optimize price-setting
Process thinking	
• Move to flexible manufacturing and control systems	• Dealing with micro-segmentation
• Materials substitution	• Finding ways to shift from single transaction focus to the forging of long-term relationships
• Developments in microelectronics and robotization	• Creating greater customer commitment
• Quality focus	
Market maturity	
• Over-capacity	• Adding value leading to differentiation
• Low margins	• New market creation and stimulation
• Lack of growth	
• Stronger competition	
• Trading down	
• Cost-cutting	
Customer's expertise and power	
• More demanding	• Finding ways of getting closer to the customer
• Higher expectations	• Managing the complexities of multiple market channels
• More knowledgeable	
• Concentration of buying power	
• More sophisticated buyer behaviour	
Internationalization of business	
• More competitors	• Restructuring of domestic operations to compete internationally
• Stronger competition	• Becoming customer-focused in larger and more disparate markets
• Lower margins	
• More customer choice	
• Larger markets	
• More disparate customer needs	

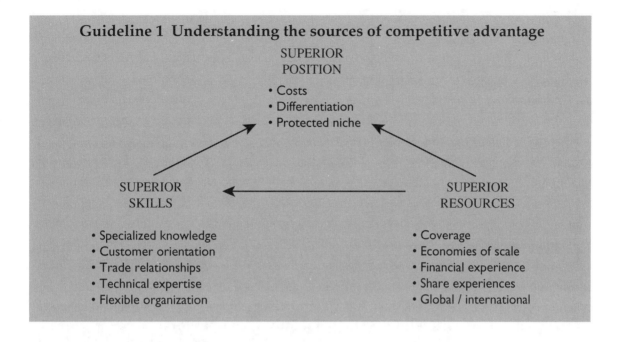

Guideline 1 Understanding the sources of competitive advantage

SUPERIOR
POSITION

• Costs
• Differentiation
• Protected niche

SUPERIOR
SKILLS

• Specialized knowledge
• Customer orientation
• Trade relationships
• Technical expertise
• Flexible organization

SUPERIOR
RESOURCES

• Coverage
• Economies of scale
• Financial experience
• Share experiences
• Global / international

Guideline 2   Understanding differentiation

• Superior product quality
• Innovative product features
• Unique product or service
• Strong brand name
• Superior service (speed, responsiveness, ability to solve problems)
• Wide distribution coverage

Continuously strive to serve customer needs more effectively

3   *Understanding the environment*

Guideline 3 spells out what is meant by the term environment in the context of companies. There is now an overwhelming body of evidence to show that it is failure to monitor the hostile environmental changes that is the biggest cause of failure in both large and small companies. Had anyone predicted that IBM would lose billions of dollars during the last decade, they would have been derided. Yet it was the failure of IBM to respond sufficiently quickly to the changes taking place around them that caused their recent problems.

Clearly, marketing has a key role to play in the process. For all organizations, this means devoting at least some of the key executives' time and resources to monitoring formally the changes taking place about them. Guidelines 3, 4 and 5 comprise the research necessary to complete a marketing audit. This leads on naturally to the next point.

Guideline 3   Understanding the environment
(opportunities and threats)

1   MACRO ENVIRONMENT
  • Political/regulatory
  • Economic
  • Technological
  • Societal
2   MARKET/INDUSTRY ENVIRONMENT
  • Market size and potential
  • Customer behaviour
  • Segmentation
  • Suppliers
  • Channels
  • Industry practices
  • Industry profitability

Carry out a formal marketing audit.

Guideline 4   Understanding competitors

  • Direct competitors
  • Potential competitors
  • Substitute products
  • Forward integration by suppliers
  • Backward integration by customers
  • Competitors' profitability
  • Competitors' strengths and weaknesses

Develop a structured competitor monitoring process. Include the results in the marketing audit.

Guideline 5   Understanding strengths and weaknesses

Carry out a formal position audit of your own product/market position in each segment in which you compete, particularly of your own ability to:

  • Conceive/design
  • Buy
  • Produce
  • Distribute
  • Market
  • Service
  • Finance
  • Manage
  • Look for market opportunities where you can utilize your strengths

Include the results in the marketing audit.

Guideline 6   Understanding market segmentation

- Not all customers in a broadly-defined market have the same needs.
- Positioning is easy. Market segmentation is difficult. Positioning problems stem from poor segmentation.
- Select a segment and serve it. Do not straddle segments and sit between them.

    1 Understand how your market works (market structure)
    2 List what is bought (including where, when, how, applications)
    3 List who buys (demographics; psychographics)
    4 List why they buy (needs, benefits sought)
    5 Search for groups with similar needs.

Guideline 7   Understanding the dynamics of product/market evolution

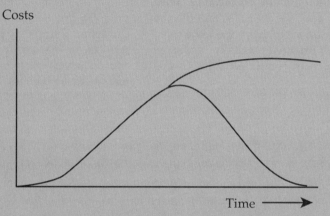

The biological analogy of birth, growth, maturity and decline is apt. Corporate behaviour, particularly in respect of the marketing mix, must evolve with the market.
Share-building in mature markets is difficult and often results in lower prices.
Those with lower costs have an advantage at the stage of maturity.
Life cycles will be different between segments.

4   Understanding competitors

Guideline 4 is merely an extension of the marketing audit. Suffice it to say that if any organization, big or small, does not know as much about its close competitors as it knows about itself, it should not be surprised if it fails to stay ahead.

5   Understanding strengths and weaknesses

Guideline 5 sets out potential sources of differentiation for an organization. It represents a fairly comprehensive audit of the asset base. Together with written summaries of the other two sections of the marketing audit (Guidelines 3 and 4), there should be a written summary of all the conclusions.

If the sources of the company's own competitive advantage cannot be summarized on a couple of sheets of paper, the audit has not been done properly. If this is the case, the chances are that the organization is relying on luck. Alas, luck has a habit of being somewhat fickle!

6   Understanding marketing segmentation

Guideline 6 looks somewhat technical and even esoteric, at first sight. None the less, market segmentation is one of the key sources of commercial success and needs to be taken seriously by all organizations, as the days of the easy marketability of products and services have long since disappeared for all but a lucky few.

The ability to recognize groups of customers who share the same, or similar, needs has always come much easier to SMEs than to large organizations. The secret of success, of course, is to change the offer in accordance with changing needs and not to offer exactly the same product or service to everyone – the most frequent product-oriented mistake of large organizations. Closely connected with this is the next point.

7   Understanding the dynamics of product/market evolution

Although at first sight Guideline 7 looks as if it applies principally to large companies, few will need reminding of the short-lived nature of many retailing concepts, such as the boutiques of the late 1980s. Those who clung doggedly onto a concept that had had its day lived to regret it.

Few organizations today will need to be reminded of the transitory nature of their business success.

8   Understanding a portfolio of products and markets

Guideline 8 suggests plotting either products/ services, or markets (or, in some cases, customers) on a vertical axis in descending order of market attractiveness. (The potential of each for

---

Guideline 8   Understanding a portfolio of products and markets

You cannot be all things to all people. A deep understanding of portfolio analysis will enable you to set appropriate objectives and allocate resources effectively. Portfolio logic arrays competitive position against market attractiveness in a matrix form.

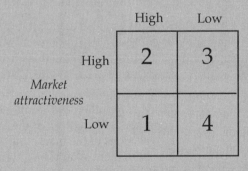

Box 1   Maintain and manage for sustained earnings
Box 2   Invest and build for growth
Box 3   Selectively invest
Box 4   Manage for cash

the achievement of organizational and commercial aims and objectives should be used as a criterion as, clearly, they cannot all be equal.) The organization will obviously have a greater or lesser strength in serving each of these 'markets', and this will determine their competitive position. For each location on the graph, a circle, representing the size of current sales, should be drawn.

The graph is divided into a four-box matrix, and each box assessed by management as suggested in the figure. This will give a reasonably accurate 'picture' of the business at a glance and will indicate whether or not it is a well-balanced portfolio. Too much business in any one box should be regarded as dangerous.

9 *Setting clear strategic priorities and sticking to them*

Guideline 9 suggests writing down the results in the form of a strategic marketing plan with all those benefits outlined in Part 1 of this chapter.

Commercial history has demonstrated that any fool can spell out the financial results they wish to achieve. But it takes intellect to spell out how they are to be achieved. This implies setting clear strategic priorities and sticking to them.

10 *Understanding customer orientation*

Guideline 10 will be familiar to all successful companies. Quality standards, such as ISO 9001

Guideline 9   Setting clear strategic priorities and sticking to them

- Focus your best resources on the best opportunities for achieving continuous growth in sales and profits.
- This means having a written strategic marketing plan for three years containing:
  - A mission statement
  - A financial summary
  - A market overview
  - A SWOT on key segments
  - A portfolio summary
  - Assumptions
  - Marketing objectives and strategies
  - A budget
- This strategic plan can then be converted into a detailed one year plan.
- To do this, an agreed marketing planning process will be necessary.
- Focus on key performance indicators with an unrelenting discipline.

Guideline 10   Understanding customer orientation

- Develop customer orientation in all functions. Ensure that every function understands that they are there to serve the customer, not their own narrow functional interests.
- This must be driven from the board downwards.
- Where possible, organize in cross-functional teams around customer groups and core processes.
- Make customers the arbiter of quality.

and the like, although useful for those with operations such as production processes, have, in the past, had little to do with real quality, which, of course, can only be seen through the eyes of the customer. (It is obvious that making something perfectly is something of a pointless exercise if no one buys it.)

It is imperative today to monitor customer satisfaction, so this should be done continuously, for it is clearly the only real arbiter of quality.

11   *Being professional*

Guideline 11 sets out some of the marketing skills essential to continuous success. Professional management skills, particularly in marketing, are becoming the hallmark of com-

mercial success in the late 1990s and the early twenty-first century. There are countless professional development skills courses available today. Alas, many directors consider themselves too busy to attend, which is an extremely short-sighted attitude. Entrepreneurial skills, combined with hard-edged management skills, will see any company through the turbulence of today's markets.

12   *Giving leadership*

Guideline 12 sets out the final factor of success in the 1990s – leadership. Charismatic leadership, however, without the eleven other pillars of success, will be to no avail. Few will need reminding of the charisma of Maxwell, Halpern, Saunders and countless others during the

---

Guideline 11   Being professional

Particularly in marketing, it is essential to have professional marketing skills, which implies formal training in the underlying concepts, tools and techniques of marketing. In particular, the following are core:

- Market research
- Gap analysis
- Market segmentation/positioning
- Product life cycle analysis
- Portfolio management
- Database management
- The four Ps
  - Product management
  - Pricing
  - Place (customer service, channel management)
  - Promotion (selling, sales force management, advertising, sales promotion)

Guideline 12   Giving leadership

- Do not let doom and gloom pervade your thinking.
- The hostile environment offers many opportunities for companies with toughness and insight.
- Lead your team strongly.
- Do not accept poor performance in the most critical positions.

past decade. Charisma, without something to sell that the market values, will ultimately be pointless. It is, however, still an important ingredient in success.

Part 2 conclusions

Lest readers should think that these twelve guidelines for success are a figment of the imagination, there is much recent research to suggest otherwise. The four ingredients listed in Figure 5.7 are common to all commercially successful organizations, irrespective of their national origin.

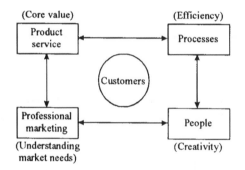

Figure 5.7   Business success

From this it can be seen, first, that the core product or service on offer has to be excellent.

Secondly, operations have to be efficient and, preferably, state-of-the-art.

Thirdly, research stresses the need for creativity in leadership and personnel, something frequently discouraged by excessive bureaucracy in large organizations.

Finally, excellent companies do professional marketing. This means that the organization continuously monitors the environment, the market, competitors and its own performance against customer-driven standards and produces a strategic marketing plan which sets out the value that everyone in the organization has to deliver.

3 Barriers to marketing planning

As we have seen, the marketing planning process is quite rational and proposes nothing which, on the surface at least, is risky or outrageous. Similarly, the guidelines for marketing competitiveness are built on current good practice and common sense. It is extremely surprising, therefore, that when confronted by an unfriendly economic environment, a majority of business people perpetuate an essentially parochial and short-term strategy as a coping mechanism.

By their own admission 80 per cent of companies in recent research studies did not produce anything approximating to an integrated, co-ordinated and internally consistent plan for their marketing activities.

Marketing's contribution to business success lies in its commitment to detailed analysis of future opportunities to meet customer needs. In other words, identifying what products or services go to which customers. It rewards those managers with a sense of vision who realize that there is no place for 'rear view mirror' planning, i.e. extrapolations from past results. Of course, it is wise to learn from history, but fatal for businesses to attempt to relive it.

It is clear that any attempt to introduce formalized marketing planning systems will have profound implications for the business in terms of its organization and behaviour. Until these implications are recognized and addressed, it is unlikely that strategic marketing planning will be effective. Moreover, the task of designing and implementing sensible planning systems and procedures becomes progressively more complex as the size and diversity of the company grows.

The author's research has identified the items in Table 5.4 as the most frequently encountered barriers to successful marketing planning.

This final section will discuss each of these design and implementation problems.

Table 5.4   Barriers to the integration of strategic marketing planning

1. Weak support from the chief executive and top management.
2. Lack of a plan for planning.
3. Lack of line management support due to any of the following, either singly or in combination:
   - hostility
   - lack of skills
   - lack of information
   - lack of resources
   - inadequate organizational structure.
4. Confusion over planning terms.
5. Numbers in lieu of written objectives and strategies.
6. Too much detail, too far ahead.
7. Once-a-year ritual.
8. Separation of operational planning from strategic planning.
9. Failure to integrate marketing planning into total corporate planning system.
10. Delegation of planning to a planner.

Weak support from chief executive and top management

Since the chief executive and top management are the key influences in the company, without their active support and participation any formalized marketing planning system is unlikely to work. This fact emerged very clearly from the author's research. Their indifference very quickly destroyed any credibility that the emerging plans might have had, led to the demise of the procedures, and to serious levels of frustration throughout the organization.

There is a depressing preponderance of directors who live by the rule of 'the bottom line' and who apply universal financial criteria indiscriminately to all products and markets, irrespective of the long-term consequences. There is a similar preponderance of engineers who see marketing as an unworthy activity and who think of their products only in terms of their technical features and functional characteristics, in spite of the overwhelming body of evidence that exists that these are only a part of what a customer buys. Not surprisingly, in companies headed by people like this, market-

ing planning is either non-existent, or where it is tried, it fails. This is the most frequently encountered barrier to effective marketing planning.

Lack of a plan for planning

The next most common cause of the failure or partial failure of marketing planning systems is the belief that, once a system is designed, it can be implemented immediately. One company achieved virtually no improvement in the quality of the plans coming into headquarters from the operating companies over a year after the introduction of a very sophisticated system. The evidence indicates that a period of around three years is required in a major company before a complete marketing planning system can be implemented according to its design.

Failure, or partial failure, then, is often the result of not developing a timetable for introducing a new system, to take account of the following:

1   The need to communicate why a marketing planning system is necessary.

2 The need to recruit top management support and participation.

3 The need to test the system out on a limited basis to demonstrate its effectiveness and value.

4 The need for training programmes, or workshops, to train line management in its use.

5 Lack of data and information in some parts of the world.

6 Shortage of resources in some parts of the world.

Above all, a resolute sense of purpose and dedication is required, tempered by patience and a willingness to appreciate the inevitable problems which will be encountered in its implementation.

This problem is closely linked with the third major reason for planning system failure, which is lack of line management support.

Lack of line management support

Hostility, lack of skills, lack of data and information, lack of resources, and an inadequate organizational structure, all add up to a failure to obtain the willing participation of operational managers.

Hostility on the part of line managers is by far the most common reaction to the introduction of new marketing planning systems. The reasons for this are not hard to find, and are related to the system initiators' lack of a plan for planning.

New systems inevitably require considerable explanation of the procedures involved and are usually accompanied by pro formas, flow charts and the like. Often these devices are most conveniently presented in the form of a manual. When such a document arrives on the desk of a busy line manager, unheralded by previous explanation or discussion, the immediate reaction often appears to be fear of their possible inability to understand it and to comply with it, followed by anger, and finally rejection. They begin to picture headquarters as

a remote 'ivory tower', totally divorced from the reality of the marketplace.

This is often exacerbated by their absorption in the current operating and reward system, which is geared to the achievement of current results, while the new system is geared to the future. Also, because of the trend in recent years towards the frequent movement of executives around organizations, there is less interest in planning for future business gains from which someone else is likely to benefit.

Allied to this is the fact that many line managers are ignorant of basic marketing principles, have never been used to breaking up their markets into strategically relevant segments, nor of collecting meaningful information about them.

This lack of skill is compounded by the fact that the are many countries in the world which cannot match the wealth of useful information and data available in the USA and Europe. This applies particularly to rapidly-growing economies, where the limited aggregate statistics are not only unreliable and incomplete, but also quickly out of date. The problem of lack of reliable data and information can only be solved by devoting time and money to its solution, and where available resources are scarce, it is unlikely that the information demands of headquarters can be met.

In medium sized and large companies, particularly those that are divisionalized, there is rarely any provision at board level for marketing as a discipline. Sometimes there is a commercial director, with line management responsibility for the operating divisions, but apart from sales managers at divisional level, or a marketing manager at head office level, marketing as a function is not particularly well catered for. Where there is a marketing manager, he tends to be somewhat isolated from the mainstream activities.

The most successful organizations are those with a fully integrated marketing function, whether it is line management responsible for sales, or a staff function, with operating units being a microcosm of the head office organization. Without a suitable organizational structure, any attempt to implement a marketing planning system which requires the collection, analysis and synthesis of market-related information is unlikely to be successful.

Confusion over planning terms

Confusion over planning terms is another reason for the failure of marketing planning systems. The initiators of these systems, often highly qualified, frequently use a form of planning terminology that is perceived by operational managers as meaningless jargon.

Those companies with successful planning systems try to use terminology which will be familiar to operational management, and where terms such as 'objectives' and 'strategies' are used, these are clearly defined, with examples given of their practical use.

Numbers in lieu of written objectives and strategies

Most managers in operating units are accustomed to completing sales forecasts, together with the associated financial implications. They are not accustomed to considering underlying causal factors for past performance or expected results, nor of highlighting opportunities, emphasizing key issues, and so on. Their outlook is essentially parochial, with a marked tendency to extrapolate numbers and to project the current business unchanged into the next fiscal year.

Thus, when a marketing planning system suddenly requires that they should make explicit their understanding of the business, they cannot do it. So, instead of finding words to express the logic of their objectives and strategies, they repeat their past behaviour and fill in the data sheets provided without any narrative.

It is the provision of data sheets, and the emphasis which the system places on the physical counting of things, that encourages the questionnaire-completion mentality and hinders the development of the creative analysis so essential to effective strategic planning.

Those companies with successful marketing planning systems ask only for essential data and place greater emphasis or narrative to explain the underlying thinking behind the objectives and strategies.

Too much detail, too far ahead

Connected with this is the problem of over-planning, usually caused by elaborate systems that demand information and data that headquarters do not need and can never use. Systems that generate vast quantities of paper are generally demotivating for all concerned.

The biggest problem in this connection is undoubtedly the insistence on a detailed and thorough marketing audit. In itself this is not a bad discipline to impose on managers, but to do so without also providing some guidance on how it should be summarized to point up the key issues merely leads to the production of vast quantities of useless information. Its uselessness stems from the fact that it robs the ensuing plans of focus and confuses those who read it by the amount of detail provided.

The trouble is that few managers have the creative or analytical ability to isolate the really key issues, with the result that far more problems and opportunities are identified than the company can ever cope with. Consequently, the truly key strategic issues are buried deep in the detail and do not receive the attention they deserve until it is too late.

Not surprisingly, companies with highly detailed and institutionalized marketing planning systems find it impossible to identify what their major objectives and strategies are. As a result they try to do too many things at once, and extend in too many directions, which makes control over a confusingly heterogeneous portfolio of products and markets extremely difficult.

In companies with successful planning systems, there is system of 'layering'. At each successive level of management throughout the organization, lower-level analyses are synthesized into a form that ensures that only the essential information needed for decision-making and control purpose reaches the next level of management. Thus, there are hierarchies of audits, SWOT analyses, assumptions, objectives, strategies and plans. This means, for example, that at conglomerate headquarters, top management have a clear understanding of the really key macro issues of company-wide significance, while at the lower level of profit responsibility, management also have a clear understanding of the really key macro issues of significance to the unit.

It can be concluded that a good measure of the effectiveness of a company's marketing planning system is the extent to which different managers in the organization can make a clear, lucid and logical statement about the major problems and opportunities they face, how they intend to deal with these, and how what they are doing fits in with some greater overall purpose.

Once-a-year ritual

One of the commonest weaknesses in the marketing planning systems of those companies whose planning systems fail to bring the expected benefits, is the ritualistic nature of the activity. In such cases, operating managers treat the writing of the marketing plan as a thoroughly irksome and unpleasant duty. The pro formas are completed, not always very diligently, and the resulting plans are quickly filed away, never to be referred to again. They are seen as something which is required by headquarters rather than as an essential tool of management. In other words, the production of the marketing plan is seen as a once-a-year ritual, a sort of game of management bluff. It is not surprising that the resulting plans are not used or relegated to a position of secondary importance.

In companies with effective systems, the planning cycle will start in month three or four

and run through to month nine or ten, with the total twelve-month period being used to evaluate the ongoing progress of existing plans by means of the company's marketing intelligence system. Thus, by spreading the planning activity over a longer period, and by means of the active participation of all levels of management at the appropriate moment, planning becomes an accepted and integral part of management behaviour rather than an addition to it which calls for unusual behaviour. There is a much better chance that plans resulting from such a system will be formulated in the sort of form that can be converted into things that people are actually going to do.

Separation of operational planning from strategic planning

Most companies make long-term projections. Unfortunately, in the majority of cases these are totally separate from the short-term planning activity that takes place largely in the form of forecasting and budgeting. The view that they should be separate is supported by many of the writers in this field, who describe strategic planning. Indeed, many stress that failure to understand the essential difference between the two leads to confusion and prevents planning from becoming an integrated part of the company's overall management system. Yet it is precisely this separation between short- and long-term plans which the author's research revealed as being the major cause of the problems experienced today by many of the respondents. It is the failure of long-term plans to determine the difficult choices between the emphasis to be placed on current operations and the development of new business that lead to the failure of operating management to consider any alternatives to what they are currently doing.

The almost total separation of operational or short-term planning from strategic or long-term planning is a feature of many companies whose systems are not very effective. More often than not, the long-term strategic plans tend to be straight-line extrapolations of past trends, and because different people are often involved, such as corporate planners, to the exclusion of some levels of operating management, the resulting plans bear virtually no relationship to the more detailed and immediate short-term plans.

This separation positively discourages operational managers from thinking strategically, with the result that detailed operational plans are completed in a vacuum. The so-called strategic plans do not provide the much-needed cohesion and logic, because they are seen as an ivory tower exercise which contains figures in which no one really believes.

The detailed operational plan should be the first year of the long-term plan, and operational managers should be encouraged to complete their long-term projections at the same time as their short-term projections. The advantage is that it encourages managers to think about what decisions have to be made in the current planning year, in order to achieve the long-term projections.

Failure to integrate marketing planning into a total corporate planning system

It is difficult to initiate an effective marketing planning system in the absence of a parallel corporate planning system. This is yet another facet of the separation of operational planning from strategic planning. For unless similar processes and time scales to those being used in the marketing planning system are also being used by other major functions such as distribution, production, finance and personnel, the sort of trade-offs and compromises that have to be made in any company between what is wanted and what is practicable and affordable, will not take place in a rational way. These trade-offs have to be made on the basis of the fullest possible understanding of the reality of the company's

multifunctional strengths and weaknesses and opportunities and threats.

One of the problems of systems in which there is either a separation of the strategic corporate planning process or in which marketing planning is the only formalized system, is the lack of participation of key functions of the company, such as engineering or production. Where these are key determinants of success, as in capital goods companies, a separate marketing planning system is virtually ineffective.

Where marketing, however, is a major activity, as in fast-moving industrial goods companies, it is possible to initiate a separate marketing planning system. The indications are that when this happens successfully, similar systems for other functional areas of the business quickly follow suit because of the benefits which are observed by the chief executive.

Delegation of planning to a planner

The incidence of this is higher with corporate planning than with marketing planning, although where there is some kind of corporate planning function at headquarters and no organizational function for marketing, whatever strategic marketing planning takes place is done by the corporate planners as part of a system which is divorced from the operational planning mechanism. Not surprisingly, this exacerbates the separation of operational planning from strategic planning and encourages short-term thinking in the operational units.

The literature sees the planner basically as a co-ordinator of the planning, not as an initiator of goals and strategies. It is clear that without the ability and the willingness of operational management to co-operate, a planner becomes little more than a kind of headquarters administrative assistant. In many large companies, where there is a person at headquarters with the specific title of marketing planning manager, they have usually been appointed as a result of the difficulty of controlling businesses that have grown rapidly in size and diversity, and which present a baffling array of new problems to deal with.

Their tasks are essentially those of system design and co-ordination of inputs, although they are also expected to formulate overall objectives and strategies for the board. In all cases, it is lack of line management skills and inadequate organizational structures that frustrates the company's marketing efforts, rather than inadequacies on the part of the planner. This puts the onus on planners themselves to do a lot of the planning, which is, not surprisingly, largely ineffective.

Two particularly interesting facts emerged from the author's research. Firstly, the marketing planning manager, as the designer and initiator of systems for marketing planning, is often in an impossibly delicate political position vis-à-vis both their superior line managers and more junior operational managers. It is clear that not too many chief executives understand the role of planning and have unrealistic expectations of the planner, whereas for their part the planner cannot operate effectively without the full understanding, co-operation and participation of top management, and this rarely happens.

This leads on naturally to a second point. For the inevitable consequence of employing a marketing planning manager is that they will need to initiate changes in management behaviour in order to become effective. Usually these are far reaching in their implications, affecting training, resource allocation, and organizational structures. As the catalyst for such changes, the planner, not surprisingly, comes up against enormous political barriers, the result of which is that they often become frustrated and eventually ineffective. This is without doubt a major issue, particularly in big companies.

The problems which are raised by a marketing planning manager occur directly as a result of the failure of top management to give thought to the formulation of overall strategies. They have not done this in the past because they have not felt the need. However, when market pressures force the emerging problems of diversity and control to the surface, without a total willingness on their part to participate in far-reaching changes, there really is not much that a planner can do.

This raises the question again of the key role of the chief executive in the whole business of marketing planning.

Part 3 conclusions

Consultants have learned that introducing change does not always mean forcing new ideas into an unreceptive client system. Indeed, such an approach invariably meets resistance for the organization's 'anti-bodies' whose sole purpose is to protect the status quo from the germs of innovation.

A quicker and more effective method is to remove or reduce the effect of the barriers which will stop the proposed improvement from becoming effective. Thus, any attempt to introduce systematic strategic marketing planning must pay due concern to all the barriers listed in this section.

Of course, not all of them will be the same for every organization, but without a doubt the most critical barrier remains the degree of support provided by the chief executive and top management. Unless that support is forthcoming, in an overt and genuine way, marketing planning will never be wholly effective.

Summary

Strategic marketing planning, when sensibly institutionalized and driven by an organization's top management, can make a significant contribution to the creation of sustainable competitive advantage. It is, however, important to distinguish between the *process* of marketing planning and the *output*. Indeed, much of the benefit will accrue from the process of analysis and debate amongst relevant managers and directors rather than from the written document itself.

Twelve guidelines were provided which have been shown to be significant contributors to determining an organization's competitiveness.

Finally, there are many human organizational and cultural barriers which prevent an organization deriving the maximum benefit from strategic marketing planning. Being aware of what these are will go some way to helping organizations overcome them.

References

Burns, P. (1994) Growth in the 1990s: winner and losers, Special Report 12, 31 European Enterprise Centre, Cranfield School of Management, UK.

Buzzell, R. D. and Gale, B. T. (1987) *The PIMS Principles: Linking Strategy to Performance*, Free Press, New York.

Lubatkin, M. and Pitts, M. (1985) The PIMS and the Policy Perspective: a Rebuttal, *Journal of Business Strategy*, Summer, 85–92.

McDonald, M. (1994) *Marketing – the Challenge of Change*, Chartered Institute of Marketing study.

Porter, M. (1980) *Competitive Strategy: Techniques for Analysing Industries and Competitors*, Free Press, New York.

Saunders, J. and Wong, V. (1993) Business Orientations and Corporate Success, *Journal of Strategic Marketing*, **1**(1), 20–40.

Further reading

Brown, S. (1996) Art or Science?: Fifty Years of Marketing Debate, *Journal of Marketing Management*, **12**, 243–267. This fascinating and highly readable paper discusses the eternal debate about whether marketing is more art than science. It is recommended here because readers should never lose sight of the need for strategic marketing plans and the process that produces them to be creative as well as diagnostic.

Leppard, J. and McDonald, M. (1987) A Reappraisal of the Role of Marketing Planning, *Journal of Marketing Management*, **3**(2). This paper throws quite a considerable amount of light onto why marketing planning is rarely done. It examines the organization's context in which marketing planning takes place and gives a fascinating insight into how corporate culture and politics often prevent the marketing concept from taking hold.

McDonald, M. (1996) Strategic Marketing Planning: Theory; Practice; and Research Agendas, *Journal of Marketing Management*, **12**(1–3), Jan./Feb./March/April, 5–27. This paper summarizes the whole domain of marketing planning, from its early days to the current debate taking place about its contribution. It also explores forms of marketing planning other than the more rational/scientific one described in this chapter.

McDonald, M. (1999) *Marketing Plans: How to Prepare Them; How to Use Them*, 4th edn, Butterworth-Heinemann, Oxford. This book is the standard text on marketing planning in universities and organizations around the world. It is practical, as well as being based on sound theoretical concepts.

Part Two
The Framework of Marketing

CHAPTER 6

Consumer decision making: process, level and style

GORDON R. FOXALL

Introduction

Consumer decision making is usually depicted as a cognitive process. Consumers become aware of a need or want and a possible means of satisfying it, typically announced in an advertisement for a new brand. They call mentally on the information they have at hand to evaluate the advertiser's claims and, when that proves inadequate, search for further information – perhaps from other manufacturers and from friends. The ensuing deliberation entails a detailed comparison of the probable attributes of the competing brands and the selection of the brand which comes closest to fulfilling the consumer's goals. When the cognitive models of consumer behaviour were first formulated in the 1960s, it did not seem to matter much whether the consumer was buying a brand in a familiar product class such as medicated shampoo or making a first time purchase of a new durable. The assumed pattern of decision making, modelled on the information processing of digital computers, was the same.

Real consumers have a habit of disappointing the theoreticians. Empirical research indicates that, far from going through a detailed decision process and becoming loyal to a single brand as the formal models suggest, many consumers: (1) show little sign of pre-purchase decision making based on the rational processing of information (Olshavsky and Granbois, 1979); (2) use brand trial – rather than pre-purchase deliberation – in order to obtain information about and evaluate brands (Ehrenberg, 1988); (3) show multibrand purchasing within a small repertoire of brands which share attributes (or characteristics) that are common to all members of their product class (Ehrenberg, 1988); and (4) rely substantially on situational pressures and constraints in making brand decisions (Wilkie and Dickson, 1991).

As a result, the conventional understanding of consumer choice needs to be modified in three ways. First, it must take account of the level of involvement consumers show in the decisions they make, their personal interest and engagement in the process. This refinement of consumer decision models is already under way: issues raised by high and low involvement are quickly becoming standard elements in the consumer behaviour texts, though there remains much room for clarification of the concept and its marketing implications. Second, our models of choice need to take account of the style of decision making preferred by various groups of consumers. Some prefer to work in a detailed, conservative and cautious fashion, buying only after long deliberation and evaluation; others prefer a more impulsive approach, buying many products on trial and possibly discarding them quickly in favour of other novelties. The style of consumer decision making has far-reaching potential implications for consumers' awareness, their openness to marketing information and the ways in which they use it, the purchase decisions they make, and the probability that they will become brand or product loyal. Finally, the situational context in which consumer behaviour occurs needs to receive detailed attention.

The modern message of marketing is that the needs of the consumer are paramount and those of the producer contingent. So, before we examine the process, involvement and style of consumer behaviour, let's ask why marketers should be interested in all this. Marketing has been defined in a somewhat basic way as whatever comes between production and consumption, the distribution of products and services to those who buy them. Only subsistence economies, where everything is quickly consumed by the family that produces it, can escape making provision for marketing in this fundamental sense. More structured economies, even if they emphasize barter, must tailor production in some degree to the wants of its recipients. They must also make provision for the storage and physical handling of goods and for informing likely consumers about them. The invention of money made economic exchange easier, though more uncertain, for the wants of consumers had to be anticipated before market transactions occurred, perhaps even before production took place. The affluent market economies with which we are familiar today put even greater stress on understanding the consumer, on supplying what he or she will buy rather than what the manufacturer happens to be able to supply or thinks is good for the customer.

A popular view claims, however, that marketing is largely a matter of persuading or even duping customers into parting with their money for products and services they do not want, let alone need. All the paraphernalia of market research, advertising, retail design and credit provision are seen as manipulating the hapless consumer by removing their discretion and making their decisions for them. Of course, marketing can be a powerful force, communicating ideas and practices to a population that might otherwise remain unaware of them, providing goods that might otherwise be unthought of, 'taking the waiting out of wanting'. No responsible society ought to allow these activities to go unmonitored, nor abuses unchecked, and none does. The network of voluntary and mandatory provisions for the regulation of advertising should be enough to convince us of that.

The influence of marketing is limited in a more fundamental way. Most new consumer products are launched only after the most thorough development process in which they are tested physically, functionally and in terms of their acceptability to consumers. It is true, as the critics allege, that market research, product development and marketing communications are all planned and executed with professional expertise. Yet, even after all the pre-launch testing, test marketing and marketing planning that accompanies most consumer product entries, the majority fail at the stage of customer acceptance. Not because the creation and delivery of these products is poor – we have noted that they are highly sophisticated procedures – but because consumers have choice.

As a result, modern marketing links production and consumption in a particular way, a managerial style known as consumer-orientated management. Unless a firm enjoys a monopoly, its managers have little discretion in the matter of adopting a consumer-orientated approach. Consumer affluence and competition among suppliers give buyers enormous discretion over what they buy, from whom they buy it, and how they pay. They have discretion not only over what they spend their money on, but to whom they listen, by whom they are persuaded. And it has long been known that consumers are far more likely to be influenced by the word-of-mouth evaluations of other consumers than by formal marketing communications. This managerial style is forced on to the firm if it is to survive and prosper. The need to understand consumer behaviour is, therefore, premier if it is to be forecast, anticipated and stimulated by marketing management.

The consumer decision process

This means more than monitoring sales: consumer-orientated marketing needs a far wider definition of consumer behaviour. Engel *et al.* (1991, p. 4) define their subject matter as 'those activities directly involved in obtaining, consuming, and disposing of products and services, including the decision processes that precede and follow these actions'. In addition to making a purchase, therefore, we shall understand consumer behaviour to include any pre-purchase and post-purchase activities that are relevant to marketing management. Pre-purchase activities would include the growing awareness of a want or need, and the search for and evaluation of information about the products and brands that might satisfy it. Post-purchase activities would include the evaluation of the purchased item in use, and any attempt to assuage feelings of anxiety which frequently follow the purchase of an expensive and infrequently bought item such as a car. Each of these influences whether consumers will repurchase a chosen brand, what they will tell other potential buyers, and how amenable they are to marketing communications and the other elements of the marketing mix.

Consumer behaviour, we have seen, can be modelled as a cognitive process, an intellectual sequence of thinking, evaluating and deciding. These information processing activities are believed to shape the more overt aspects of choice: acquiring information from a sales-person, placing an order, using the product selected, and so on. The inputs to the process are the most basic bits of data available to the consumer, stimuli from the environment in the form of marketing messages and conversations with friends and relatives. The processing itself consists of the mental treatment of these data as the consumer stores them, links them with existing ideas and memories, and evaluates their relevance to his or her personal goals. The outputs are the attitudes the consumer forms towards, say, an advertised brand, an intention to buy or postpone buying, and – if attitude and intention are positive – the act of purchase. A similar sequence characterizes the use of the purchased item: it is evaluated again in use and a decision is reached about its suitability for repurchase.

Awareness

Figure 6.1, derived from Foxall *et al.* (1998), summarizes the process of consumer decision making. Consumer awareness is not automatic; it is the endpoint of a highly selective procedure. Every day, consumers are bombarded by thousands of messages that seek to persuade them – from advertising, from political organizations, from religious groups, from employers, and from numerous other sources. There is enormous competition for the attention and understanding of the average citizen to the extent that no one could possibly cope with the cumulative effect on the nervous system of so great a mass of information. Fortunately, most of these social, economic and marketing stimuli in the environment are filtered out by the individual's attentional and perceptual processes, and have no effect on the decision process.

Efficiency in decision making requires that attention and perception be selective; a kind of perceptual defence mechanism screens out all but those messages that are familiar, consistent with our current beliefs and prejudices, motives, expectations and wants. Even so-called subliminal messages – an attempt to

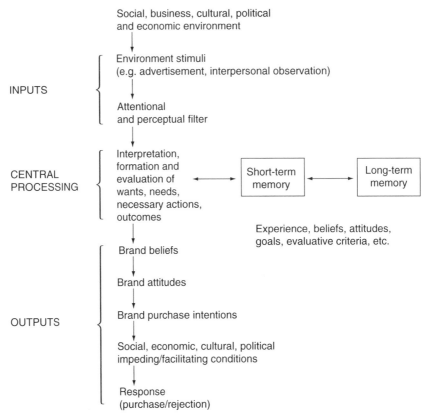

Figure 6.1 Consumer information processing

circumvent this filter by being so weak that they are not recognized by the senses and yet influence our cognitive processes – do not exert an influence on our mental operations. Perception is clearly more than the process in which stimuli impinge on the senses; it is the beginning of information processing, the interpretation of those stimuli to which we pay attention according to our existing mental set-up – attitudes, experience, motivation. Only when an advertising message has got through the filter and had some meaning attached to it in this preliminary processing activity can the consumer be said to be aware of a problem in his or her life (e.g. dandruff), its consequences (possibly for their health and social activity) and the proffered means of overcoming it (the advertised brand of shampoo).

Search and evaluation

Even awareness of a problem does not guarantee that the process of decision making will continue. Only if the problem is important to the consumer and he or she believes that a solution is available will it continue. If a sufficiently high level of involvement or engagement with the problem is present, the consumer is likely to seek further information to evaluate the claims of the advertiser. Internal search takes place within the consumer's memory system; it is an attempt to locate information in the form of pre-existing knowledge, especially beliefs and attitudes about the problem, the likely solutions, and remedies that are already in use. If the problem or the proffered solution is radically new to the customer, this may prove inadequate and an external search may be necessary. External search may be an active seeking of information from neighbours or colleagues, salespersons or other advertisements, newspapers or magazines, *Which?* or *Consumer Reports*.

All of this activity is accompanied by the mental processing of the advertising message in the consumer's short-term and long-term memory stores. We have seen that much information fails to get this far, but even that which is stored in short-term memory is there only briefly. If it is not transferred to the long-term store, where it will be effective in this and subsequent decisions, it is lost within about a minute. Three operations may occur in the consumer's memory to ensure that information can be retained and retrieved:

- rehearsal – the mental repetition of information which links it to information already stored;
- encoding – the symbolic representation of information which permits its long-term association with other stored information; and
- storage – the elaboration of information in which it is organized into structures from which it can be retrieved, i.e. returned from long-term to short-term memory and used in momentary decision making.

The outputs of information processing are the beliefs and attitudes that shape decisions and the intentions that predispose certain actions such as buying, consuming and saving. Beliefs are statements about the product or brand that the consumer assumes to be factual; attitudes are evaluations of the product or brand; and intentions are strong motivations to act in accordance with beliefs and attitudes. Together they form the cognitive (intellectual), affective (evaluative) and conative (action-oriented) components of the consumer's decision activity.

A great disappointment for the information processing approach to consumer decision making was the finding that attitudes, intentions and behaviour often do not correlate well (or at all)

with each other (Foxall, 1997). Measuring attitudes and intentions might not, therefore, be a useful way of predicting behaviour; nor might persuasive attempts to change attitudes be the key to prompting changes in consumers' actual brand selections. The work of Fishbein and Ajzen (1975) has done much to resolve this problem. Rather than measure general attitudes towards an object, as previous researchers had tended to do, these researchers chose very specific measures of an attitude towards a behaviour. By ensuring that the attitude measure corresponded to the measure of behaviour – in terms of the target object, the action or behaviour towards it, the time and the context of the behaviour – they showed that very high correlations could be achieved.

For instance, previous researchers would typically ask how consumers evaluated, say, chocolate bars (a general or 'global' attitude towards this object) and then expect to forecast accurately whether they would buy a particular brand of chocolate on their next shopping trip (a highly specific behavioural criterion). Fishbein and Ajzen showed that by measuring consumers' attitudes towards a specific act, say buying a stated brand of chocolate on their next supermarket trip, much higher correlations between the evaluation and the act were forthcoming (Ajzen and Fishbein, 1980). The attitude measure used was the sum of a respondent's beliefs about the consequences of the act in question, weighted by their evaluations of those consequences.

By taking another measure – of the consumer's subjective norm – Fishbein and Ajzen were able to take into consideration many of the factors other than attitude that determine a consumer's intention to perform a specific behaviour. The subjective norm consists of the respondent's beliefs about the evaluations another person (whom they hold in high regard) would put on the act in question, weighted by their motivation to comply with the other person's evaluations. Attitude and subjective norm correlate with the consumer's behavioural intention, his or her disposition to perform the act in question. And behavioural intentions usually correlate highly with the performance of the behaviour itself.

Fishbein and Ajzen refer to this approach to the prediction of behavioural intentions as the Theory of Reasoned Action. Ajzen (1985) has proposed a second theory, the Theory of Planned Behaviour, which incorporates an additional determinant of intention. This is *perceived behavioural control*, or the individual's belief that he succeeds in the task in hand. Bagozzi and Warshaw (1990) have proposed a Theory of Trying in which past behaviour is taken into consideration as a means of predicting future choice. A full discussion of these approaches is available in Foxall (1997).

Post-decisional evaluation

Another filtering device determines the extent to which consumers quickly put their intentions into practice, shown in Figure 6.1 as 'impeding and facilitating conditions'. These are the situational variables, such as access to funds or credit, availability of compatible products, social acceptability, that determine whether a particular purchase will take place or not. No amount of strong intention will guarantee purchase in the absence of these and a hundred other facilitating conditions. Purchasing also depends on past behaviour. It would be absurd and naive to suppose that a consumer who had just bought a video recorder based on an obsolete system could simply go through the above decision process and make another, more lasting, purchase a week later.

But the consumer decision process does not end when a purchase has been made. Most important of all from a marketing viewpoint is whether the consumer will buy the selected brand again on a later purchase occasion. The first purchase of a brand – or even the first few purchases – can be considered no more than a trial by the consumer. The clearest indication of whether it is worth buying again comes from its evaluation in use (Ehrenberg, 1988). Something that often needs to be resolved in the case of

expensive, infrequently bought items such as consumer durables is the cognitive dissonance or feeling of mental unease that follows their purchase. Cognitive dissonance arises when two contradictory beliefs are held at the same time: 'I have spent so much on this car and my neighbour tells me his gets from 0 to 60 mph a second faster!' People tend to try to reduce dissonance by dropping one or other of the opposing beliefs or by emphasizing one at the expense of the other. The car purchaser might well conclude, therefore, that his car was more prestigious since it had cost more or had a more auspicious marque. Or that his car was guaranteed for longer, or ran unleaded fuel, or needed less frequent services. Some advertising is deliberately geared to the needs of the dissonant consumer who has recently purchased; although they are less obvious than they used to be, ads for cars still sometimes stress the performance characteristics of the advertised and competing makes.

Selectivity

We have seen that a frequent assumption in consumer research has been that consumer decision making must be a uniform process for all consumers. Once the stages outlined above had been identified, it was common for researchers and managers to expect all consumers to pass through them in a similar fashion on each purchase occasion. Yet both common sense and our experience as consumers suggests that not all transactions are preceded by this entire process of cognitive learning. Both personal and situational factors often intervene at one or other stage to throw the procedure off course or to circumvent it totally.

A striking characteristic of consumer decision making is the selectivity it entails. Consumers are not exposed to all of the stimuli that might conceivably influence them; their attentional and perceptual processes are highly selective in what they admit and consider. Memory processes are similarly limited since the encoding of information and its rehearsal are highly selective too. Many factors account for the limited consideration sets (the range of brands actively appraised) consumers' decision processes can encompass and the apparently arbitrary processing they receive. Prior experience, personal circumstances, attitudes and expectations, states of deprivation and motivation, and numerous personality dimensions can all give rise to variation in the manner of information processing (Kardes, 1994). The two summary factors which we consider here are involvement and cognitive style.

Consumers are motivated more or less strongly to participate in the full information processing sequence. Sometimes they feel a need to reduce their uncertainty and risk by seeking a broad spectrum of information and evaluating it thoroughly before making a purchase. On other occasions, they will telescope the procedure, apparently muddling through the decision as they call instantly on accumulated knowledge and experience. More recently, substantial attention has been given to one aspect of the decision sequence which may modify its form from situation to situation: the level of involvement which the consumer feels as he or she approaches the decision making process. We discuss that aspect in this section.

Another factor is the style of decision making shown by consumers. Even when two potential buyers go through all of the decision stages outlined above, they may do so in quite distinct ways, considering different information, a varying range of products, and fundamentally different ways of solving their problems. Far less attention has been paid to consumers' decision styles, though research in the last few years shows how crucial cognitive styles are to understanding the entire decision process.

Levels of consumer involvement

Some products such as high performance cars seem inherently involving because of their complexity, risk and cost, while others such as toothpaste seem uninvolving by comparison because of their familiarity, low risk and low cost (Laaksonen, 1994). In fact, while this is true in a general way, involvement is actually a relationship rather than a property of this or that product or service. It reflects not only the degree of uncertainty experienced by a consumer when he or she is faced with consideration of a product, but also the personal characteristics of the consumer (some people find everything more involving than others) and on the situation in which purchase and consumption take place. Involvement is commonly defined as the consumer's personal interest in buying or using an item from a given product field, an approach which nicely summarizes the individual, experiential and situational components of the relationship. This is not the time to go into the concept in detail (though the sources referenced above will be a helpful starting point for those who can) but to note its influence on the decision making process.

One of the most prominent sources of situational influence on consumer motivation and choice derives from the newness of the product under consideration to the potential buyer (Howard, 1977). Although we speak generally of new products being innovations, such items differ markedly from the radically novel – such as video recorders at the time of their introduction – to the incrementally different – an improved version of an established brand of shampoo. Robertson (1967) categorized innovations in terms of the amount of disruption they caused in existing consumption patterns. Radically new products which had maximal disruptive effect he termed discontinuous innovations. TV aerial dishes, supersonic transatlantic travel and, in its day, television itself all came into this category. Note that the disruption involved is not necessarily a problem to be overcome: in the case of Concorde flights it provided a much improved and superior service for those who both needed it and could afford it. Many new products are not so revolutionary, though they still present additional benefits to the consumer that were not previously available. Electric lawnmowers, for instance, do the same job accomplished by manual versions, but with less effort and more quickly. Their 'disruptiveness' consists of the change they effect in consumers' lifestyles. These moderately novel products which do a known job better are called dynamically continuous innovations. Finally, there are the most familiar 'new' products of all, the improved shampoos, slightly faster cars, third editions of successful textbooks. These are minimally disruptive of established consumption patterns; they allow life to go on much as before but provide the benefits of the most recent developments in technology and thought. They are continuous innovations.

Genuinely discontinuous innovations are few and far between. When such an item is introduced, it is the first brand in a wholly new product class, right at the beginning of the product life cycle (Howard and Moore, 1982). People are often suspicious of such radical innovations. Most prefer to wait and see what happens to the first adopters before they themselves make a purchase. The consumers who do buy at this stage are usually highly involved in the product field. They are heavy users of whatever preceded the innovation – perhaps radio and movies in the case of television, audio cassettes in the case of VCRs, conventional air travel in the case of Concorde. In terms of personality factors, they have an apparent 'need for newness', wanting to be the first to try novel ideas and thereby to communicate them to other, more cautious consumers who buy later, if at all. They are better off than these later adopters, have a higher social status, are upwardly mobile, better educated, and socially integrated with broader horizons.

All of this adds up to a strong personal interest in the product field or what has become known as high involvement. Their decision processes are not necessarily longer or more intensive than those of later adopters; it depends how familiar they are personally with the product field and the new product. In a lot

of cases, because of their heavy use of its precedents, they require very little information processing before quickly adopting the discontinuous innovation (cf. Howard, 1989). In other cases, where their personal innovativeness relies more on having the money to spend and seeking the status of being first, they may need to go through most of the stages in the consumer choice process shown in Figure 6.1 before testing the water. What sets both types of early consumer off from later adopters is the degree of involvement they show in the product, their personal interest (in both senses) in possessing and using it, and in showing it off.

Their decision process is likely to have been formal: they became aware of the innovation through their more accentuated use of the mass media for such items; their search and evaluation procedures will have been deliberative, even though there is limited information to go on. They may have insisted on trying the product before buying if this is feasible and will have been eager to ascertain its compatibility with their present lifestyle and practices, its advantages relative to what they already use, and maybe its conspicuousness in use (since they are often motivated by the thought of being seen with the radically novel). They are likely to minimize the risks and the complexities involved in owning and operating the innovation, while those who do not adopt at this stage will magnify these 'problems'.

New products that survive the introduction stage of the life cycle attract the attention not only of consumers but of other manufacturers. As the product progresses through the growth stage of the cycle, it is likely to be modified by the original marketer and those who are drawn to enter the field by the expectation of high profits. All of these suppliers introduce changes to the product, tailoring it to the needs of successive market segments and incorporating technological changes as they are created. The new versions they market are often dynamically continuous innovations which attract the initially sceptical consumer, who now sees that the early promise of the product has been fulfilled and who is especially attracted by the additional benefits and lower prices offered at this stage. Of course, the first adopters may also be rebuying at this stage and are also pleased to endorse the enhanced brands as they become available. But they are no longer highly involved. Nor are those who now buy for the first time more than moderately involved. This latter group may have had a long decision period prior to buying; since first hearing of the innovation and perhaps dismissing it as some kind of newfangled gadget that is clearly not for them, they will have become gradually accustomed to its merits. It will have begun to be obvious in the homes or garages of their neighbours, in the soaps on television, in the stores and showrooms in which they browse for and buy other products. All these consumers are likely to be only moderately involved in the product field; after all, its familiarity has removed many of the attractions of being first to own it and it has become more of a necessity than a luxury. Their awareness and evaluation of the product will have come about almost unconsciously as it has slowly been legitimated through the positive experience of others. Their decision process appears to be a curtailed version of that shown in Figure 6.1 because they have gradually formed brand attitudes and intentions without being aware of doing so. The first adopters have done this by using the product and judging its performance; the latest adopters have done so vicariously and informally. Neither group has to form detailed conceptualizations of the product and where it fits into the overall repertoire of products among which they choose. They have gradually formed their ideas of what the product is, what it does and how it relates to other products: at most, they have to compare a new brand in this product field in terms of the dimensions that are important to them (see Howard, 1989).

Finally, as the product field enters its maturity stage, many manufacturers have moved in to the market place, introducing numerous variants of the original innovation.

Each of these 'new' versions can be described simply as continuous. The product has become commonplace; its capabilities and limitations are known, its risks are minimal and its price is as low as it is going to get. The least well off members of the community can afford it and there is no special social kudos attached to owning it (indeed, there may even be ridicule for not owning it). Everybody has one. The very ubiquity of the product means that there is no reason for most consumers to show anything but the lowest level of involvement with it. Those who now buy for the first time have acquired a lot of knowledge about the product field, even if they have not studied it in an involved way. But they hardly have a high or even moderate level of involvement with it. Nor do those earlier adopters who now repurchase the item routinely. The routine buying process that is usual at this stage involves no more than an awareness of the brand's identity, its membership of a known product class and, for repeat buying, a favourable evaluation of how well it has served the consumer. Involvement may be high at the product level as particular situations evoke strong feelings of needing the item: as Otker (1990, p. 31) points out, 'Shampoo can be more important to a teenager on a Saturday evening than anything else in the world'. But the brand – as long as it is an acceptable member of the product class – is far less important.

Consumers' decision styles

Consumers bring distinctive personal approaches to problem awareness, search, evaluation, decision and post-decisional activities. These differences have far-reaching implications for such features of marketing management as market segmentation, new product development and marketing communications.

Psychologists use the term *cognitive style* to refer to the manner in which individuals make decisions and solve problems (Guilford, 1980;

McKenna, 1984; Messick, 1984). Cognitive style must be distinguished from cognitive level, which is the extent of intelligence, intellectual complexity or capacity shown by a decision maker. When we speak of consumers' cognitive styles, we are not talking about their intelligence or intellectual level. We simply mean the way in which they accomplish decision making problem solving. No style is inherently superior to any other, though each may come into its own in appropriate circumstances. The theory of adaptive–innovative cognitive styles advanced by Kirton (1994) proposes that everyone can be placed somewhere on a continuum between two extreme styles of decision making. At one extreme, adaptors prefer to make decisions in an orderly and precise manner, and they confine their problem solving endeavours to the frame of reference in which the problem has arisen. They prefer to seek better ways of accomplishing known tasks, coming up with solutions that can be unobtrusively implemented within their everyday routines. The extreme adaptor is preoccupied with the accuracy of details, prudence, soundness, efficiency, and a degree of conformity. The adaptor is happiest working within a well-established pattern of rules and operating procedures.

By contrast, the extreme innovator prefers to think tangentially, challenges rules and procedures, and is uninhibited about breaking with established methods and advocating novel perspectives and solutions. The innovator is easily bored by routine and seeks novelty and stimulating in discontinuous change; he or she tends towards risk-taking, exploration and trial (Kirton, 1994). Innovators' solutions generally transcend the context in which the problem has arisen. They tend to produce different ways of behaving which often entail radical change. This dimension of cognitive style is measured by the Kirton Adaption–Innovation Inventory (KAI).

KAI respondents estimate on 32 five-point ratings how easy or difficult they would find it to sustain particular adaptive and innovative behaviours over long periods of time. The measure is scored in the direction of innovativeness from an adaptive extreme (32) to an innovative extreme (160), and with a theoretical mean suggested by the scale midpoint (96). International general population samples have observed means of 95 ± 0.05, about which scores are approximately normally distributed within the restricted range of 45–146. The KAI shows high levels of internal reliability and validity and suitability for consumer research (Bagozzi and Foxall, 1996). As would be expected of a measure of style, KAI scores do not correlate with measures of cognitive level such as IQ and intellectual capacity (Kirton, 1994).

Interest in using this theory and measure in consumer research derives from the fact that the dimensions of personality shown to be weakly characteristic of *market initiators*, the earliest adopters of new brands and products (Figure 6.2), are also characteristic of those high-KAI scorers whom Kirton calls innovators (Kirton, 1994). This term is used in preference to the more usual 'consumer innovators' to distinguish the first adopters of new products and brands from innovators in the sense defined by Kirton (Foxall, 1995). The early identification of market initiators during the firm's new product development process is strategically important for four reasons (Goldsmith and Flynn, 1992). First, they represent the immediate source of cash flow to the company eager to start retrieving the expenses of new product development: the fact that initiators are usually heavy users of the product class in question means that they play a disproportionate role in recouping developmental costs. Second, they may provide market leadership and help set up barriers to new competition that prevent other firms making a fast entry into the market. Third, they provide important feedback to the company on further new product development. And, fourth, they communicate the innovation to the less active sections of the market, the bulk of the market who will eventually provide the high levels of sales and profits.

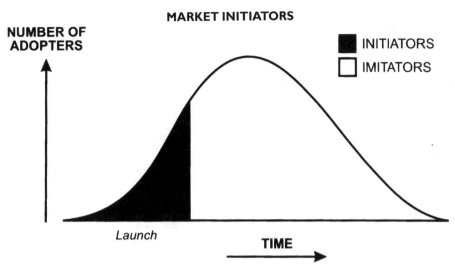

Figure 6.2   Initiators and imitators

Although personality measures have proved generally poor predictors of consumer behaviour, a considerable body of evidence has identified the personality profile of the earliest adopters of innovations. Market initiators emerge as individuals who have a broader perceptual category width than later adopters, i.e. they perceive novel products as more closely related to those already in use than do the later buyers. Market initiators also show greater tolerance of ambiguity, flexibility, self-esteem and tendency towards sensation seeking than do the later adopters. The evidence in each study is somewhat weak, though positive, but the rationale for expecting market initiators to show an innovative cognitive style stems from the fact that these five cognitive-personality factors also correlate highly and consistently with the KAI, indicating that innovators, as defined by Kirton, are more likely to possess these traits than adaptors.

Studies of consumers' food purchasing

However, the results of an investigation of the cognitive styles of initial adopters of general new food brands were enigmatic given the expectation that these market initiators would be innovators (Foxall, 1995). KAI scores of respondents did not correlate with the number of new brands purchased and 40 per cent of the sample were adaptors. Most intriguing of all was the finding that the consumers who bought the largest number of new brands were adaptors. A similar pattern of results was apparent from a second study, this time of 'healthy' food products, those promoted on the basis of their alleged contribution to consumers' health and welfare, such as wholemeal flour, low sodium salt and low calorie meals. At the time of the study, these products were new to supermarkets; prior to that time they had to be obtained from specialist health food stores. Again, the expected correlation did not appear and again 40 per cent of the sample were adaptors. Moreover, purchasers of the very highest level of new products in this class were adaptive (Foxall, 1995).

A possible reason for this unanticipated result emerged from further consideration of adaption–innovation theory. Innovators are likely to purchase novel items impulsively, independently and perhaps haphazardly. By their very nature, they will probably choose a number of innovative products just to try them out. But, while these sensation-seekers are more likely to try many new products, they are also likely to retain few of them in their repertoires (Mittelstaedt *et al.*, 1976). Adaptors, however, will presumably show two patterns of behaviour. Those who are not much interested in the product field will, as we originally thought, be suspicious of new products; in both studies the buyers of fewest brands or products were adaptors. Yet those adaptors who have a high level of personal involvement with a product field will act quite differently. Cognitive style itself does not change much over the lifetime of the individual, but its effects can be accentuated by the degree of engagement the individual feels in the activity at hand. The consumer who displays a very high level of commitment to acquiring a healthier lifestyle, for instance, will continue to act consistently with their underlying cognitive style, but their behaviour may be quite different from that of a less committed consumer whose cognitive style is similar (Chaffee and Roser, 1986). Those adaptors who are fundamentally 'converted' to the pursuit of a healthier way of life and, thereby, to healthier eating, may well seek out not one or two, but as many appropriate items as possible, showing a greater assiduousness in their search and evaluation than other consumers, adaptive or innovative.

This possibility was tested in the third study, which was concerned with new brands within 'healthy' food classes (Foxall, 1995). This time, respondents were asked to indicate their level of personal involvement with 'healthy' foods. The instrument used to measure this construct was the Zaichkowsky (1987) Personal Involvement Inventory, which measures ego involvement or the personal interest shown by individuals in a named product field. Once again, no correlation was found between the number of innovations bought and KAI, and well over half the sample were adaptors. More importantly, the results con-

firmed the hypothesis: the highest level of purchase was shown by more-involved adaptors.

Let us pause a moment to consider the implications of these findings. It appears that the post-launch market for new foods is not a homogeneous collection of innovators whose personalities predispose them to be venturesome, risk-taking, flexible and self-assured – as the textbooks portray initial adopters. Rather, that market consists of three psychographic segments, each with its own personality profile: less-involved adaptors (who buy least), innovators (who buy an intermediate number regardless of their level of involvement) and more-involved adaptors (who buy most). Moreover, each of these segments has its own distinctive style of decision making. Each segment is likely to become aware of new brands/products in a different fashion, to search and evaluate information in its own way, to choose uniquely and to have a distinctive post-decisional reaction. The launch marketing strategy for a new product needs to accommodate all three.

The conventional wisdom, which assumes a uniform process of consumer decision making, must be modified to include considerations not only of level of involvement, but also of consumers' differing cognitive styles. But results for a single product field, even if they are gained from three separate and increasingly sophisticated studies, hardly constitute a court revolution. Replication is required on several dimensions. Foods are often thought of as 'inherently' low-involving items: it would, therefore, be useful to repeat the research using a more 'inherently' involving product. The first three studies have involved the initial stage of the product life cycle: some evidence for or against the presence of differing cognitive styles among consumers of an established product is needed. These three studies have also involved purchasing: what evidence is there of a similar pattern in consumption? And do situational influences, as opposed to cognitive factors, affect the results?

Studies of software consumption

Two further investigations have taken the use of personal computers as their focal interest: the use of a range of software is usually thought to be highly involving, personal computers are well past the introduction stage of their product life cycle, the research involved consumption rather than purchasing, and it allowed situational variables to be examined (Foxall, 1995).

The first of these studies sought a link between KAI and the number of software packages used by home computer owners. Although there was no correlation between the two, a very small group of consumers with high KAI and high PII scores were responsible for the highest level of software applications use. The sample contained both adaptors and innovators once more but, of the two cognitive variables, it was personal involvement with computers and computing that was generally associated with high levels of use initiation (this term is preferred to the more common 'use innovativeness', again to avoid confusion; see Foxall, 1995), i.e. a large number of software applications. However, while personal involvement was the major explanatory cognitive factor, both adaptors and innovators were found in substantial proportions among users. In other words, the market contained four segments: first there were groups of less- and more-involved users, each of which could be subdivided into its adaptive and innovative subsegments. Each of these subsegments can be expected to make decisions in its own characteristic style. Finally, this study drew attention to the importance of situational factors in the multiple use of computers. More important than the cognitive variables were the number of years computing experience the respondents had and the type of computer they owned.

Clearly a more structured study was needed to account in detail for the role of cognitive variables in view of situational factors (Franz and Robey, 1986). The final investigation involved the use of computer software by graduate management students in the Strath-clyde Graduate Business School in Glasgow. Students following three programmes took part (Foxall and Bhate, 1998). Those taking the Business Information Technology Studies (BITS) programme were required by their course to make frequent and extensive use of computers; those taking Marketing received instruction in computer use but had discretion over where and when they used the computer as part of their studies; and the students on the Legal Practice programme received minimal instruction in the use of computers and were under little if any pressure to use computing techniques. Both KAI and PII correlated with the number of software applications used, whether or not the course affiliations were taken into consideration. (A study of computer use by managers in an administrative organization has confirmed several of these findings; see Foxall and Hackett, 1992.) Although situational influences proved stronger than the cognitive factors, two crucial points must be made with respect to the roles of cognitive style and involvement. Yet again, while involvement played a causative role in the amount of product use undertaken, both adaptive and innovative cognitive styles were represented and could be expected to affect the consumption behaviour of the respondents. The same four segments were apparent as in the study on home computing.

Studies of financial services purchase and consumption

Recent studies have investigated consumer behaviour for financial services. Foxall and Pallister (1998) investigated four financial products bearing a maturity value or benefit sometime in the future: (i) pensions; (ii) life assurance; (iii) mortgages; (iv) savings and investment. These products not only contrast with the targets of the earlier research, but are of intrinsic interest in view of the extent of strategic change and product development which characterizes the contemporary financial services industry. The opportunity was taken on this occasion to examine the usefulness of an alternative measure of innovativeness, that proposed by Hurt *et al.* (1977). This scale correlates with the KAI (Kirton, 1994) and so we were confident in assuming that high scorers would possess the characteristics of Kirton's *innovators*, while low scorers would be *adaptive*. Respondents also completed Zaichkowsky's revised PII, revealing their involvement with financial services. The results show a remarkable pattern. Buyers of mortgages were highly-involved adaptors; so were purchasers of pension products. But life assurance purchasers were less-involved adaptors and buyers of savings and investments products were highly-involved innovators. Clearly, even within a broadly defined product category like financial services, consumers vary significantly and each segment requires its own unique marketing approach.

Additional research on financial services has investigated styles of cashless consumption, i.e. consumers' preferred patterns of payment card usage. Szmigin and Foxall (1998) used the KAI to identify adaptive and innovative consumers whose payment method preferences were investigated using qualitative research methods. Four market segments emerged. For *product enthusiasts*, cards have intrinsic value; these consumers enjoy immediate consumption and find the use of payment cards easy. They delay paying, show little control in their purchasing, and are avid obtainers and users of credit facilities. Their self-indulgence often manifests as impulse buying. These consumers tended to be highly-involved adaptors. *Finessers* pay off their account at the end of each month, incurring as little interest as possible. They also use cheques and like debit cards, have many cards and use a wide range of payment methods. They are quick adopters of new payment methods. These consumers were highly-involved innovators. *Controllers* show tight regulation of their financial affairs, prefer credit to debit cards, and pay back what they owe each month. They see little point in store

cards and look for tangible benefits from adopting a payment method. In our research, these consumers were predominantly less-involved adaptors. Finally, *money managers* juggle the use of many cards and seek the best advantage from using each (or cash) in each situation they encounter. They are seeking the security of a system of payment that works efficiently and quickly, and that is functional. These individuals tended to be less-involved innovators.

Once again, financial services consumers showed several styles of consumption, each linked to a unique pattern of cognitive style and involvement, and requiring a special marketing mix.

Implications for marketing management

In order to make sense of these results, let us ask three questions for each of the product classes investigated: (a) Do the innovators actually adopt more innovations? (b) What other variables are involved in early adoption? And (c) What are the marketing implications? Table 6.1 summarizes the responses.

In the case of new foods, adaptors buy most; for software applications, innovators are the most likely to adopt most applications; financial services present a more mixed picture. Involvement is a crucial factor in each case and situational variables in some. Overall, the conventional wisdom is sometimes correct, but unsophisticated, and our conclusion is that the marketing strategies must thus be multifaceted. But how should they be designed and implemented?

One way of trying to make sense of these findings is to assume that the general involvement level engendered by the product is all-important. Foods might be classified as inherently low involvement items, everyday purchases, continuous innovations. Software, by contrast, would be highly involving, since

Table 6.1 Summary of the results				
	Food innovations	Home software applications	Organizational software use	Financial services
Do innovators buy or use more?	No – adaptors do	Yes	No. Involved adaptors and innovators	For some products
What other factors influence behaviour?	Involvement	Involvement, situation	Involvement, situation	Involvement, situation
Principal consumer behaviour(s)	Complex Dissonant/ Variety-seeking [Habitual]	Dissonant Variety-seeking Complex Habitual	Dissonant Complex	Complex
Marketing mix considerations	Dual strategy	Dual strategy	Dual strategy	Tailor to individual product

each application is a discrete, discontinuous use initiation. And financial services might fall between the two: of medium involvement, representing an infrequent but important purchase, a dynamically continuous innovation. Assael (1991/1996) uses similar dimensions of buying situations to classify the consumer behaviours for different types of product (Bhate, 1992). Hence:

Complex buying behaviour occurs when the consumer is highly involved, the product is expensive and risky, and there are perceived differences in the brands available. The consumer in this case goes through a cognitive learning process, i.e. search for information, evaluation of products etc. Assael (1996) claims that it is typical consumer behaviour for appliances and durables such as 'autos, electronics, photography systems'. Consumers actively search for information to evaluate and consider alternative brands by applying specific criteria

such as resolution and portability for a camera, and economy, durability and service for a car.

Dissonant buying behaviour occurs when the consumer is highly involved, sees no significant differences among the brands available and buys the product in a hurry, but once purchase has been made has second thoughts. He or she may go out again and collect information to reduce dissonance. Such behaviour is typical of the purchase of adult cereals and snack foods. There is limited problem solving here, because the consumer is not familiar with the brands. A new line of microwaveable snacks might be introduced; unaware of the product class, the consumer is attracted to the idea of trial to compare with known snackfoods. Limited information search takes place and limited evaluation of brand alternatives.

Habitual buying occurs when there is no significant difference in brands and the consumer is not highly involved in the purchase, e.g. salt. In such a case, there is no learning process. It is characteristic of athletic shoes and adult cereals. Such choice is repetitive: the consumer learns from past experience and with little or no decision making buys a brand that is satisfactory. The purchase is important to the consumer because of involvement in sport in the case of athletic shoes and nutritional needs in the case of cereals. Brand loyalty is probable on the basis of satisfaction with a repertoire of known brands. This does not necessarily reflect active brand commitment; it is just satisfying. Information search and evaluation are limited, if they exist at all. Since most brands in established markets are similar however, a consumer may on occasion try a new brand if it appears to provide the characteristics of the product class.

Variety-seeking behaviour occurs when there is low involvement and significant brand differences. The consumer chooses something new to relieve boredom. This is typical consumer behaviour for canned vegetables and paper towels. Boredom and a search for variety leads to multi-brand purchasing, when risks are minimal and the consumer has less commitment to a particular brand. The decision is not important enough to make pre-planning worthwhile, so the decision is made in the store. There is little to lose by buying a new kind of biscuit on impulse.

The conventional wisdom provides easy prescriptions for managerial action: just focus on market initiators, who can be assumed to be innovators, at each stage of the new product development and marketing process. But the research indicates that there are three problems with that. First, each launch segment has a unique decision making style. Second, each active segment therefore requires its own launch marketing mix, reflecting the decision style and involvement level of its members. Third, post-launch markets – the markets for imitators – are also segmented by decision style and require multifaceted marketing.

The results show that more than one of these patterns of buying behaviour is characteristic of new product purchasing or use for the same product, at the same time. A more sophisticated analysis is suggested in Figure 6.3, which proposes that complex buying is typical of highly-involved adaptors, dissonant buying of highly-involved innovators, habitual buying of low-involved adaptors, and variety-seeking of low-involved innovators.

Complex consumer behaviour occurs when the consumer is highly involved and perceives the product as discontinuous. The consumer goes through a cognitive learning process, i.e. information search, brand evaluation, detailed post-adoption appraisal etc. *Such behaviour is typical of highly involved adaptors.*

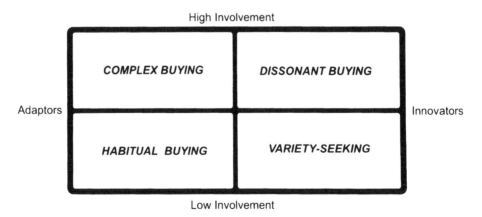

Figure 6.3   Decision styles of market initiators

Dissonant buying behaviour occurs when the consumer is highly involved but sees no significant differences among the brands available and buys the product in a hurry. Such consumers are likely to continue to seek alternative brands that will fulfil their expectations. *It is typical of highly involved innovators.*

Habitual buying occurs when there is no significant difference in brands and the consumer is not highly involved in the purchase, e.g. salt. Extended information processing is unnecessary; experience is the safest guide. *It is typical of low-involved adaptors.*

Variety-seeking behaviour occurs when there is low involvement and brand proliferation. The consumer chooses something new to relieve boredom. *It is typical of low-involved innovators.*

Each active segment has its own decision style and its own level of involvement (see Table 6.2).

For all of the products we have investigated, launch markets are likely to be composed predominantly of involved consumers; the predominant consumer behaviours are therefore complexity and dissonance. However, some less-involved consumers also adopt at this stage: habit and variety-seeking are also likely to be encountered. All four types of consumer behaviour will also be encountered to different extents in post-launch markets. In fact, the market or markets for imitators may be more heterogeneous and require a more dynamic marketing approach.

In general, higher levels of involvement with a product field are considered a sign of greater problem awareness and pre-purchase search and evaluation, a higher level of purchase, and more detailed and informed post-decisional evaluation. If involvement is, after all, principally a measure of personal interest, it follows that positive behaviours of these kinds will be more probable where such involvement is greater. The appropriate strategies of market segmentation and product positioning have attracted much attention (e.g. Tyebjee, 1979). However, the issue of adaptive–innovative cognitive style complicates the prescriptions offered by this marketing approach. Highly-involved adaptors are far more likely to engage in detailed information processing than innovators, but limited decision making may characterize highly-involved innovators.

The market for new 'healthy' foods contains innovators, more-involved adaptors and a significant group of less-involved adaptors. That for new software applications contains more-involved adaptors, more-involved innovators, plus groups of less-active, less-involved adaptors and innovators. Because new product marketing relies on the diffusion sequence over time, none of these can be ignored, even at the launch stage. What consumers absorb about an innovation at that stage may colour their impressions for a long time to come.

Marketing strategies should therefore be sensitive to the coexistence of adaptors and innovators in both the initial and established markets for new products. A marketing strategy directed towards, say, the adaptors is likely to alienate the innovators. Perhaps the failure of

Table 6.2 Decision styles of market segments				
	Dissonant buying	*Complex buying*	*Variety-seeking*	*Habitual buying*
Problem recognition				
Search and evaluation				
Post-purchase evaluation				

marketing campaigns which, following the conventional wisdom and textbook prescriptions have been aimed principally at innovators and ignored the fact that initial adopters and use-initiators may be adaptors, have contributed to the high failure rates of new consumer products. But the crucial question now is the likely implications of adaptive–innovative cognitive styles for future marketing campaigns. The following propositions follow from the evidence presented above and a considerable body of research over three decades on consumers' cognitive styles.

Product considerations

We have noted the importance of a consumer's category width – the extent to which he or she perceives an innovation to differ from the norm established by existing products or practices – in determining his or her framework for decision making. So-called 'broad categorizers' are more willing than 'narrow categorizers' to consider and adopt new brands or products that diverge from the norm. Category width influences the amount of risk the prospective consumer perceives in buying and using an innovation (Venkatesan, 1973). Broad categorizers are also more likely to adopt radical or discontinuous new products, even though they might be dissatisfied with them, and narrow categorizers are more likely to reduce the possibility of making a mistake by confining their attention to incrementally new items. The implication is that adaptors, who are likely to be narrow categorizers, will try to avoid mistakes in their product purchasing even at the cost of losing out on some positive opportunities. They prefer to operate within the structure they have established and are reluctant to change. It seems therefore that, in their decision making, adaptors will usually tend to be conservative, and that they are more likely than innovators to be attracted to continuous new products. Innovators, categorizing widely, are less likely to perceive great differences even in discontinuous new products.

Compared with innovators, adaptors are usually more intolerant of change and disruption, unwilling to accept ambiguity, more dogmatic and inflexible. Unless they are highly involved, therefore, they are less likely to embrace new products. When adaptors lack involvement, their lack of experience of new products further reinforces their unwillingness to explore. By being willing to risk making mistakes, innovators are more eager to take advantage of the potential gains from exploration. As a rule, they will try more new products, apparently oblivious of the risk of buying an unsatisfactory item. In the process of decision making, highly-involved innovators can be expected to use more of the information available to them than do the less involved, whether adaptors or innovators. But, since they perceive products as more alike than do adaptors, they have less chance than they of becoming brand loyal.

Marketing communications

Adaptors and innovators are also likely to react in quite different ways to marketing communications, particularly mass advertising, regardless of their level of involvement. Innovators' broader category width, tendency to become rapidly bored with familiar products and behaviours, and capacity to work within several frames of analysis suggests that they would respond more positively than adaptors to two-sided appeals. That is, innovators may prefer messages based on pro and con arguments and become easily bored with repetitive messages that are consistent with their current beliefs. Yet adaptors are more likely to respond favourably to uncomplicated one-sided messages, consistent with their current attitudes and habits. This is not due to their having a lower level of cognitive ability (adaptors and innovators do not differ in terms of intelligence or cognitive complexity), but simply to their preferred style of decision making and problem solving. Adaptors are also more likely to respond positively to credible sources of information which are intended to modify their attitudes and behaviour. In comparison, innovators can presumably cope with more discrepant information even if the source is not well known. They may cope better with cognitive dissonance and perhaps be motivated by it to broaden their search for information. They are more likely than adaptors, who have strong needs for clarity, to remember incomplete messages. Innovators' tolerance of ambiguity might well make them more susceptible to postmodern advertising.

Since adaptors are more cautious and analytical in their judgements, more reflective and tentative in their decision making, they are open to rational, apparently objective appeals based on reasoned arguments. This style of advertising would, however, appear dogmatic and authoritarian to innovators. The more impulsive innovator would presumably be more open to personalized, affective advertising.

All of these differences are important in view of the apparently intransigent nature of cognitive styles. One possibility is that the less-involved groups might be the targets for social marketing, the communication of an idea rather than a specific product or product type: 'healthy eating' and 'healthy living' in the first instance; 'getting more out of your computer' in the second. But the problem remains of reaching the more active segments with a message designed to encourage even more extensive purchasing or use that both adaptors and innovators must be reached simultaneously. Even where involvement has emerged as the main explanatory factor in consumer behaviour, the presence of both adaptors and innovators within segments defined by relatively high and relatively low levels of involvement makes a multiple marketing mix strategy inevitable.

Further considerations

In the case of new foods, it is apparent that simultaneous appeals must be made to innovators and highly-involved adaptors. Where the new item is part of a coherent product field such as 'healthy' foods, it may be easier to present it as consistent with the needs and prior behaviour of the involved adaptor (who has already experienced a 'paradigm shift' in embracing healthy eating). The new brand or product can be conceptually positioned by advertising as being close to similar existing means of achieving a healthier lifestyle; its physical positioning in supermarkets can emphasize its continuity with the array of foods the consumer is already enjoying, its incremental contribution to their healthier eating practices. It is this adaptive segment that is likely to form the core of brand/product loyal customers who will ensure its communication to other buyers who form the bulk of the market and its eventual complete diffusion. They are therefore to be considered a key primary market.

The innovator segment is far more likely to respond to the more radical presentation of such products as discontinuously new. However, if they were conceptually positioned in this way by advertising, the effect would be to alienate the potentially more important adaptive segment. Perhaps the answer is to use mass advertising as suggested above for the adaptors while restricting appeals to innovators to in-store promotions. The innovators, who are more likely to buy and try on impulse, might acquire some brand awareness from the mass advertising but would receive their greatest motivation to buy from in-store sources of information.

In the case of applications software, the major marketing (as opposed to social marketing) appeals would be to the involved users, both adaptors and innovators. The innovator is more likely to try applications software that is easily available along with other goods, which can be bought on impulse, tried and adopted/rejected with minimal cost in terms of inconvenience, though not necessarily financial cost. The product mix aimed at the innovator segment might therefore concentrate on the dissemination of combined software. The accompanying promotional mix might aim to increase users' awareness of the range of possible applications available. More specialized individualized software for each application could then be offered as experienced innovative users sought more specialized or higher quality applications. It is probable that the adaptor segment would appreciate separate software packages for specific applications, acquired one at a time. These items should be promoted on the basis of their efficiency and reliability. More prestigious outlets, perhaps of a specialized nature, might be appropriate here, and mail order is also likely to appeal. The sales literature should contain detailed specifications and comparisons with other computers which stress the advantages in terms of precision and accuracy, the general acceptability to other users, and the extensively tried and tested application of the advertised brands.

Once again, there may be no need for the campaigns aimed at different segments to be hermetically sealed from one another, so long as each is created and presented with sensitivity to the coexistence of alternative cognitive styles among the recipients. Selective perception makes it entirely possible that adaptors will not notice the advertisements aimed at innovators sufficiently to be alienated by them; innovators may receive no more than initial brand or product awareness from the messages directed towards adaptors.

Summary and conclusion

Our understanding of both consumer behaviour and the capacity of marketing activities to influence it rest on knowledge of the ways in which consumers choose. Three aspects of consumer decision making require careful attention: the decision process itself, differences in the level of consumer involvement that surrounds and shapes decision making, and differences in the style of decision making.

Most research has been concerned with the first of these. Several models describe in detail the stages consumers may pass through in coming to a decision point and the psychological procedures that accompany them. Questions about the influence of involvement on consumer decision making have been addressed only comparatively recently, yet the issues of intellectual level of information processing and the consumer's level of involvement with the process have far-reaching implications for managerial intervention in the marketplace. Finally, the way in which a consumer characteristically processes information has come on to the agenda of consumer researchers very recently indeed. Again, because consumers do not pass homogeneously through a preordained decision sequence but behave at each stage in accordance with their individual cognitive styles, any attempt by marketing managers to influence the process must take account of the manner as well as the matter of decision processes.

This chapter has taken a consumer-orientated approach to the role of consumer behaviour research. Rather than simply theorize about the likely nature of consumer choice, it has shown how actual consumer behaviour differs from that described by the formal models. It has gone on to show that those deviations in involvement and style that mark consumer behaviour in the real world rather than the textbook, interesting as they are in their own right, have direct implications for marketing management, the design and implementation of marketing mixes that reach consumers.

References

Ajzen, M. (1985) From Intentions to Actions: A Theory of Planned Behavior, in Kuhl, J. and Beckman, J. (eds), *Action Control: From Cognition to Behavior*, Springer, Berlin, pp. 11–39.

Ajzen, M. and Fishbein, M. (1980) *Understanding Attitudes and Predicting Social Behavior*, Prentice-Hall, Englewood Cliffs, NJ.

Assael, H. (1996) *Consumer Behavior and Marketing Action*, 5th edn, Southwestern, Cincinnati, OH (4th edn 1991).

Bagozzi, R. P. and Foxall, G. R. (1996) Construct Validation of a Measure of Adaptive–Innovative Cognitive Styles in Consumption, *International Journal of Research in Marketing*, **13**, 201–213.

Bagozzi, R. P. and Warshaw, P. R. (1990) Trying to Consume, *Journal of Consumer Research*, **17**, 127–140.

Bhate, S. (1992) Cognitive Style and Use/Buying Behaviour: A Reappraisal of the Relationship using Involvement as a Mediating Variable. Unpublished PhD thesis, University of Birmingham.

Chaffee, S. H. and Roser, C. (1986) Involvement and the Consistency of Knowledge, Attitudes and Behaviors, *Communication Research*, **13**, 373–399.

Ehrenberg, A. S. C. (1988) *Repeat Buying*, 2nd edn, Griffin, Edinburgh.

Engel, J. F., Blackwell, R. D. and Miniard, P. (1991) *Consumer Behavior*, 7th edn, Dryden, Hindsdale, IL.

Fishbein, M. and Ajzen, I. (1975) *Belief, Attitude, Intention and Behavior: An Introduction to Theory and Research*, Addison-Wesley, Reading, MA.

Foxall, G. R. (1995) Cognitive Styles of Consumer Initiators, *Technovation*, **15**, 269–288.

Foxall, G. R. (1997) *Marketing Psychology: The Paradigm in the Wings*, Macmillan Press, London.

Foxall, G. R. and Bhate, S. (1999) Computer Use-innovativeness: Cognition and Context, *International Journal of Technology Management*, **17**, 157–172.

Foxall, G. R. and Hackett, P. (1992) Cognitive Style and Extent of Computer Use in Organizations: Relevance of Sufficiency of Originality, Efficiency and Rule-conformity, *Perceptual and Motor Skills*, **74**, 491–497.

Foxall, G. R. and Pallister, J. (1998) Measuring purchase decision involvement for financial services: comparison of the Zaichkowsky and Mittal scales, *International Journal of Bank Marketing*, **16**, 180–194.

Foxall, G. R., Goldsmith, R. E. and Brown, S. (1998) *Consumer Psychology for Marketing*, 2nd edn, International Thomson Business Press, London.

Franz, C. R. and Robey, D. (1986) Organizational Context, User Involvement and the Usefulness of Information Systems, *Decision Sciences*, **17**, 329–357.

Goldsmith, R. E. and Flynn, L. R. (1992) Identifying Innovators in Consumer Product Markets, *European Journal of Marketing*, **26**(12), 42–55.

Guilford, J. P. (1980) Cognitive Styles: What Are They?, *Educational and Psychological Measurement*, **40**, 715–735.

Howard, J. A. (1977) *Consumer Behavior: Application of Theory*, McGraw-Hill, New York.

Howard, J. A. (1989) *Consumer Behavior for Marketing Strategy*, Prentice-Hall, Englewood Cliffs, NJ.

Howard, J. A. and Moore, W. L. (1982) Changes in Consumer Behavior over the Product Life Cycle, in Tushman, M. L. and Moore, W. L. (eds), *Readings in the Management of Innovation*, Pitman, Boston, MA, pp. 122–130.

Howard, J. A. and Sheth, J. N. (1969) *The Theory of Buyer Behavior*, Wiley, New York.

Hurt, H. Y., Joseph, K. and Cook, C. D. (1977) Scales for the Measurement of Innovativeness, *Human Communication Research*, **4**, 58–65.

Kardes, F. R. (1994) Consumer Judgment and Decision Processes, in Wyer, R. S. and Srull, T. K. (eds), *Handbook of Social Cognition*, Vol. 2, Erlbaum, Hillsdale, NJ, pp. 399–466.

Kirton, M. J. (1994) A Theory of Cognitive Style, in Kirton, M. J. (ed.), *Adaptors and Innovators: Styles of Creativity and Problem-Solving*, 2nd edn, Routledge, London, pp. 1–36.

Laaksonen, P. (1994) *Consumer Involvement: Concepts and Research*, Routledge, London.

McKenna, F. P. (1984) Measures of Field Dependence: Cognitive Style or Cognitive Ability?, *Journal of Personality and Social Psychology*, **11**, 51–55.

Messick, S. (1984) The Nature of Cognitive Styles, *Educational Psychologist*, **19**, 59–74.

Mittelstaedt, R. A., Grossbart, S. L., Curtis, W. W. and DeVere, S. P. (1976) Optimal Stimulation Level and the Adoption Decision Process, *Journal of Consumer Research*, **3**, 84–94.

Nicosia, J. M. (1966) *Consumer Decision Processes*, Prentice-Hall, Englewood Cliffs, NJ.

Olshavsky, R. W. and Granbois, D. H. (1979) Consumer Decision Making: Fact or Fiction?, *Journal of Consumer Research*, **6**, 93–100.

Otker, T. (1990) The Highly-involved Consumer: A Marketing Myth?, *Marketing and Research Today*, February, pp. 30–36.

Robertson, T. S. (1967) The Process of Innovation and the Diffusion of Innovation, *Journal of Marketing*, **31**, 14–19.

Szmigin, I. and Foxall, G. R. (1998) Styles of Cashless Consumption, *International Review of Retail, Distribution and Consumer Research*, **9**, 349–365.

Tyebjee, T. (1979) Refinement of the Involvement Concept: An Advertising Planning Point of View, in Maloney, J. and Silverman, B. (eds), *Attitude Research Plays for High Stakes*, American Marketing Association, pp. 94–111.

Venkatesan, M. (1973) Cognitive Consistency and Novelty-seeking, in Ward, S. and Robertson, T. S. (eds), *Consumer Behavior: Theoretical Sources*, Prentice-Hall, Englewood Cliffs, NJ, pp. 354–384.

Wilkie, W. L. and Dickson, P. R. (1991) Shopping for Appliances: Consumers' Strategies and Patterns of Information Search, in Kassarjian, H. H. and Robertson, T. S. (eds), *Perspectives in Consumer Behavior*, 3rd edn, Prentice-Hall, Englewood Cliffs, NJ, pp. 1–26.

Zaichkowsky, J. L. (1987) *The Personal Involvement Inventory: Reduction, Revision and Application to Advertising*. Discussion Paper No. 87–08–08, Simon Fraser University, Faculty of Business Administration.

Further reading

Ehrenberg, A. S. C. (1988) *Repeat Buying*, 2nd edn, Griffin, Edinburgh. A landmark monograph which is fundamental to understanding patterns of buyer behaviour over time on the basis of painstaking empirical observation and analysis. A very necessary antidote to the near-ubiquitous and uncritical presentation of cognitive information processing as the sole approach to understanding consumer choice.

Foxall, G. R. (1997) *Marketing Psychology: The Paradigm in the Wings*, Macmillan, London. *Marketing Psychology* portrays the behaviour of consumers as influenced by its environmental consequences and extends this analysis to marketing management by proposing a novel understanding of the marketing firm. The book undertakes a behaviour analysis of consumer choice, based on a critical extension of radical behaviourism to the interpretation of human economic behaviour. This suggests that consumer behaviour is explained by locating it among the environmental contingencies that shape and maintain it. The analysis of the marketing firm construes marketing management as resting on a behaviouristic understanding of consumer choice and of the role of the firm in the attempted prediction and control of consumer behaviour.

Foxall, G. R. (2002) *Consumer Behaviour Analysis: Critical Perspectives in Business and Management*, Routledge, London. These three volumes take further the analysis begun in *Marketing Psychology*, bringing together a large collection of articles that trace the development of consumer behaviour analysis as an alternative paradigm for consumer research and marketing management.

Foxall, G. R., Goldsmith, R. E. and Brown, S. (1998) *Consumer Psychology for Marketing*, 2nd edn, International Thomson Business Press, London. A new edition of this textbook of consumer behaviour which integrates recent thinking and empirical research with the needs of marketing managers to understand their customers and potential customers.

Kardes, F. R. (1994) Consumer Judgment and Decision Processes, in Wyer, R. S. and Srull, T. K. (eds), *Handbook of Social Cognition*, Vol. 2, Erlbaum, Hillsdale, NJ, pp. 399–466. The entire two-volume handbook is essential reading for consumer psychologists and marketing researchers. Kardes' chapter applies the findings of social cognition research to consumer decision making. It is well informed by the concerns of consumer psy-chology and marketing management, and provides a recent assessment of a fast-growing literature.

Laaksonen, P. (1994) *Consumer Involvement: Concepts and Research*, Routledge, London. A valuable source of recent research and thought on consumer involvement.

Lambkin, M., Foxall, G. R., Van Raaij, F. and Heilbrunn, B. (eds) (1998) *European Perspectives on Consumer Behaviour*, Prentice-Hall, London. The definitive collection of European-authored research on consumer behaviour.

CHAPTER 7

Business-to-business marketing: organizational buying behaviour, relationships and networks

PETER W. TURNBULL and SHEENA LEEK

Introduction

In this chapter an attempt is made to trace the development of research and practice in business-to-business marketing. The term 'business-to-business marketing' is increasingly replacing the more traditional 'industrial marketing' and 'organizational marketing' descriptions, and will be used in this chapter to describe those marketing activities of any kind of organization, public or private, which has exchange relationships with other organizations.

The understanding of organizational buyer behaviour can be seen as a process of development over the past 40 years within the wider context of industrial or business-to-business marketing theory. Unfortunately, the study of business-to-business marketing has 'been a poor relation within the broad family of attempts to understand the markets and marketing in general' (Ford, 1990, p. 1). Most early theory was based on a rather simplistic transfer of consumer goods-based knowledge which propounded 'effective' marketing largely as a manipulation of the marketing mix. Unfortunately, this approach largely ignored the realities of business-to-business markets. However, a number of researchers have recognized the difference of organizational buyers and their behaviour, and a number of paradigms have emerged to better understand and explain the complexity facing researchers and managers working in this field. Perhaps the most important of these more recent conceptualizations is that relating to interaction, relationships and networks, originally developed by the IMP (International Marketing and Purchasing) group – (Hakansson, 1982; Turnbull and Cunningham, 1981), which has led to the current interest in relationship marketing.

An understanding of the organizational buying process is fundamental to the development of appropriate business-to-business marketing strategy. The organizational buyer is influenced by a wide variety of factors, both from outside and within the organization. Understanding these factors and their inter-relationships is critical to the competitive positioning of the business, to the development of appropriate market and product development plans, and to the management of the whole marketing task of the business.

Increasingly, companies are recognizing the significant impact which professional procurement can have on profitability, and British manufacturing industry is increasingly buying in components and subassemblies, rather than manufacturing in-house. For example, some telecommunications equipment manufacturers now buy in items accounting for up to 80 per cent of total cost. Thus, even a 2 per cent procurement saving can have a marked effect on profitability or give the company a significant price advantage in the marketplace. Additionally, professional purchasing also helps secure long-term and improved sources of supply.

This growing importance and recognition of purchasing makes it imperative for business-to-business marketers to also increase their professionalism. A crucial element of such professionalism is, as consumer product marketers have so long recognized, the understanding of buying behaviour. However, in business-to-business markets this is more difficult than in consumer markets and requires an understanding of various academic disciplines, which underlie the polyglot area we term organizational buying behaviour. To be effective, marketers must address a number of key questions:

- How is buying behaviour different in business markets?
- Who are the key participants in purchasing?
- What process and procedures are followed in choosing and evaluating competitive offerings?
- What criteria are used in making buying decisions?
- What sources of information and influence are used?
- What organizational rules and policies are important?

- What key relationships exist with other suppliers and buyers?

These and other questions must be considered and answered if the business-to-business marketer is to be truly professional.

This chapter attempts to provide a framework of understanding by which these questions can be addressed. The most important theoretical and research contributions of the last two decades are briefly reviewed to give a comprehensive picture of the current state of the art in the study of organizational buyer behaviour.

Organizations buy a diverse and often highly complex and interrelated range of goods and services as factor inputs to their own product and service portfolio, as indicated in the following list:

- Raw materials.
- Buildings, machinery and other capital equipment.
- Components.
- Consumable materials.
- Professional services.
- Energy.
- Finance.
- Labour.

Clearly the nature and importance of the type of product/service being purchased will have significant consequences to the purchasing structures, process and criteria.

However, it is important to recognize that no company exists in isolation from other players in the industrial milieu. Success, and failure, depends upon the company's ability to co-operate with its suppliers and customers. The actions of competitors, regulators, governments and many others also have important impacts upon the individual firm.

During the past 20 years, a considerable body of knowledge has developed about the structure, dynamics and processes of business relationships and their management. These relationships are at the heart of the reality of business markets and must be understood if we are to manage the complex networks of relationships in which all companies operate.

It will become apparent through the course of this chapter that organizational buying and marketing is a complex process. Attempts to oversimplify this process ultimately result in a loss of understanding of the dynamics of the process and its constituent elements. However, it is worthwhile to begin with the analysis of the realities of business markets.

The realities of business markets

In trying to understand organizational buying behaviour it is essential to clarify the essential features that characterize the markets and market mechanisms of business markets. For example, we need to recognize that markets are often characterized by customization and dynamism: traditional marketing theory, with its roots in consumer product markets, had typified marketing as a process of manipulation of the marketing mix against predetermined consumer preferences derived from market research. The marketer is seen as the active party whilst customers are essentially passive. This view, however, is not even an adequate representation of what happens in consumer markets: the majority of manufacturers of consumer goods, such as foodstuffs, toiletries and clothing, sell to wholesalers and retailers – not directly to consumers. Thus, they are essentially operating within an organization or business market which displays many of the characteristics of the markets for industrial products such as car components, financial services etc.

Thus, a reality of marketing *per se* is that suppliers face concentrated markets where individual customers may be critically important. These customers are not passive but actively search out and interact with selected suppliers, requiring customized products. These markets are characterized by interaction,

mutual dependency and trust. Negotiation is common and business success if often determined by the ability of individuals to manage the supplier–customer relationships over considerable periods of time. These interactions may involve many people from different functions and levels in both supplier and customer companies. Although specific transactions (the focus of much consumer marketing literature) are often important, it is the overall relationship which is critical to success. Thus, relationship marketing becomes the 'new' marketing management challenge.

Organizational buying structures

An organization is a group of people pursuing a common aim through co-ordinated activities. Organizations are characterized by structure, activity and goals. By analysing organizational buying in the light of these three factors, it is possible to highlight the essential elements of organizational buying behaviour. A major characteristic of organizational buying is that it is a group activity. It is comparatively rare that a single individual within an organization will have sole responsibility for making all the decisions involved in the purchasing process, and commonly we find a number of people from different areas of the business and of varying status involved. This group is usually described as the *decision-making unit* or *buying centre*. Thus, a major challenge facing business marketers and sales people is the identification of these key individuals who constitute the buying centre, the roles of these individuals and the various factors that may influence its constitution, and the major goals being pursued.

Composition of the buying centre

Much research has focused upon the size and structure of the buying centre. Alexander *et al.* (1961) found that in 75 per cent of the firms they interviewed, three or more people became involved in the buying process. Anyon (1963) suggested that there was an average of six people involved, whilst Hill and Hillier (1977) point out that in situations where certain expensive products are being purchased for the first time, as many as 40 people may become involved in the purchase decision. While interesting, generalizations such as these are of little practical help. The business marketer will be more concerned to discover who are the influential people in the different types of organizations they deal with at each stage of the decision-making process and their relative degree of influence.

Shankleman (1970), reporting a study of the purchasing of capital equipment, wrote:

> The managing director would agree to the equipment budget for the research department expressed solely in terms of money. The research manager would decide which of the various requests for money should have priority and the section head would decide which of the various items should be bought on the basis of a detailed study of the reports made by his team.

Similarly, in an earlier study, Thain (1959) concluded that top management made the fundamental policy decision whether or not to buy, but the operational staff decided what to buy.

The structure of the buying centre can also be examined in the light of the different roles of the individuals who constitute it. Webster and Wind (1972a) suggest the major roles found in buying centres to be:

- Users.
- Influencers.
- Deciders.
- Gatekeepers.

It is apparent that there may be many sources of influence on the buying decision, both formal and informal. By piecing together the suggestions of the various research studies into the composition of the buying centre, it is possible to draw up the following list of roles that may be performed:

1 Policy makers.
2 Purchasers.
3 Users.
4 Technologists.
5 Influencers.
6 Gatekeepers.
7 Deciders.

Policy makers

A company may adopt certain general policies in its buying which may affect the purchase behaviour of a single item. For example, it may be company policy to only purchase from British suppliers, or suppliers within a range of 50 kilometres, or for certain items to be multiple sourced.

Purchasers

The purchaser is here defined as the person or persons who have formal authority for ordering the product or service. A considerable amount of research has been completed investigating the importance of the purchasing agent in influencing buying decisions. For example, Weigand (1968) pointed out that the purchasing agent may be no more than a clerical officer and his/her influence on the buying decision may consist of nothing more than filling in the necessary forms to complete the order.

Feldman and Cardozo (1968) and Lister (1967) are among many authors who have pointed out that the purchasing agent's role is dependent upon the management's philosophy towards purchasing. Where this is seen as important the purchasing agent will play an influential part in decision making. In recent years, as the procurement function in business has been given increasing and long overdue importance, buyers have equally become more critical determinants of strategic and operational purchasing decisions.

Nevertheless, it is important to identify the individual who will be primarily responsible for the final ordering of the service. Any assessment of the importance of the purchasing agent must consider the organization's attitude towards the purchasing function, together with the level of risk associated with the purchase. In all instances, these considerations are liable to be situation specific and suppliers must therefore become aware of the differences between their customers.

Users

These are those people who actually operate the product or service. In certain instances their role will coincide with that of the technologist. It is likely that users will be primarily concerned with product performance and ease of use. Weigand (1968) suggests that users with expert knowledge may exert sufficient influence to override certain commercial considerations, such as price or delivery times. It is therefore important that suppliers should establish good relations with all members of a firm who have contact with the service they provide, and ensure that a high level of service is maintained across all their operations.

Technologists

These are the people with the specialist knowledge which enables them to differentiate between the performance of the different products or brands. They are primarily concerned with the technical aspects of the various products or services, and these considerations will be of prime importance in their assessment of them. Technologists are likely to be people with professional qualifications and in seeking to influence them suppliers should be aware of the specialized nature of their influence on the buying centre.

An important finding of the International Marketing and Purchasing (IMP) Project Group in studies of purchasing in Western Europe was that purchasing staff and technologists in Ger-

many and Sweden were more highly qualified than their counterparts in Britain. Thus, British suppliers operating in these export markets faced more technologically demanding customers. German customers were very critical of the technical competence of British companies and this created a barrier to entry for British exporters (Turnbull and Cunningham, 1981).

Influencers

Webster and Wind (1972b) define this category as:

> Those who influence the decision process directly or indirectly by providing information and criteria for evaluating buying actions.

Influencers thus include anybody who has an influence on the buying process, both within and outside the organization. As a category this is too wide to be of any functional use, since it can embrace such a wide range of people. However, it does emphasize that there can be substantial inputs from a wide range of different functions into the buying process.

Gatekeepers

The concept of gatekeeper comes from the theory of opinion leadership and communications flow. A gatekeeper is a person who regulates the flow of information and thus plays a major part in determining the attitudes of other members of the buying centre towards a product. It is possible that the role of gatekeeper will be performed by an individual who has another role within the buying centre, for example the purchasing agent.

Deciders

These are the people who have the formal authority for approving the purchase. It is likely that they occupy senior management positions and therefore, as Shankleman (1970) pointed out, be concerned only at the policy-making level.

These categories are useful indicators of the different areas of interest in the buying centre. A production engineer will view a machine purchase in a different way to a finance director. The transport manager will also take a different view to that of the managing director when the purchase of fleet cars is considered. We should note, however, that these roles can overlap and may vary according to the nature of the purchase and the stage of the buying process.

Having discussed basic purchasing structure, it is important to be aware of the factors that will influence that structure. The next section therefore examines the major variables which determine the composition of the buying centre.

Determinants of the buying centre

It has already been pointed out that the role of the purchasing agent is dependent upon the organization's philosophy towards the purchasing function and is therefore situation specific. While it is possible to suggest certain determining characteristics of the composition of the buying centre, it should be emphasized at the outset that the buying centre's composition will depend upon the specific purchase situation. The importance to suppliers of knowing their customers cannot be over-emphasized. In practical marketing terms, such knowledge can only be built up through extensive contact between suppliers and buyers.

Market factors

Wallace (1976) identifies two features relevant to the study of organizational buying. First, those processes which characterize organizations and their members in their purchasing activity and, second, those characteristics which differentiate organizational buying markets from consumer markets. It is these characteristics that are referred to here as market factors.

Products and services are often technologically complex and this, combined with bulk purchasing, leads to many industrial purchases being of high value. Also, business-to-business markets are characterized by derived demand, and marketing thus requires careful evaluation of the secondary markets which influence demand for the primary product. Furthermore, many business markets are highly concentrated and there tend to be greater differences between buyers. Markets can be either geographically concentrated or concentrated through the size of the firms. As a result, communication channels between industrial buyers and sellers tend to be shorter than in consumer markets.

Finally, many business-to-business markets are characterized by reciprocal trading arrangements between firms, which may inhibit buying practice and make it difficult for new suppliers to enter some markets.

Each market will have its own characteristics and the companies that purchase from or within that market will organize their buying departments to meet the particular conditions that prevail. The organization of the buying centre to meet these market characteristics will vary depending upon the size of the company and the service being purchased.

Company factors

Sheth (1973) suggests three major company variables that will influence the composition of the buying centre: company size, degree of specialization and company orientation. It can be expected that as company size increases the greater the number of buying influences. Additionally, we can generally expect a higher degree of purchasing expertise in large organizations.

A study sponsored by *The Financial Times* (1974) concluded that most companies operating several establishments 'claimed to operate a centralized purchasing policy for the products covered by the survey'. However, the research indicated that companies do in fact vary their practice according to convention or convenience, even within the framework of a centralized policy. Sheth (1973) concludes that the greater the degree of centralization, the less likely the company will tend towards joint decision making.

Organizations with several operating subsidiaries, particularly if these are overseas, will have an overall policy regarding centralization. Even where control is highly centralized, subsidiaries may, nevertheless, be given varying degrees of freedom in choosing suppliers of specified product categories. The degree of centralization may therefore be vital to both the composition of the buying centre for these services, and also relevant to the development of a strategy for international marketing.

Finally, Sheth (1973) suggests that the composition of the buying centre will be dependent upon the company orientation. If a company is technology orientated, the buying centre is likely to be dominated by engineering people who will, in essence, make the buying decision.

These various research findings highlight the necessity for a supplier's marketing management to know the policies and buying routines of its customers. By studying both existing and potential customers, suppliers can develop marketing strategies targeted to the important buying influences.

Product factors

The product variable embraces a number of characteristics, including product essentiality, technical complexity, value of the purchase, consequence of failure, novelty of the purchase and frequency of the purchase.

Weigand (1968) defines a product as 'a variety of promises to perform'. Performance will be judged according to the expectations that the individual has of the product, and it is important to remember that different people and organizations will have different perceptions and expectations of the product. As Alexander *et al.* (1961) have pointed out:

> The broad basic differences between types of goods arises not so much from their variations in their physical characteristics as differences in the ways in which and the purposes for which they are bought.

Where a product is central to an organization's operations it is likely that the purchase will be decided upon jointly by all the parties concerned. This is also likely to be true in instances of high capital expenditure. In both of these instances the consequence of failure may be severe and so where the possibility or the consequence of failure are perceived to be higher it is likely that purchase decisions will be shared.

Bauer (1960) coined the term 'perceived risk', and Cyert and March (1963) applied the concept of risk avoidance as one of their basic concepts explaining the behaviour of the firm. They suggest that, in order to avoid uncertainty and failure, organizations avoid the necessity of having to anticipate events in the future by emphasizing short-term feedback, and impose standard operating procedures to ease the burden of decision making.

Hill and Hillier (1977) use the term 'risky shift' to explain how members of a group take decisions involving a higher degree of risk than they would do as individuals. The 'risky shift' concept is central to the composition of the buying centre, and highlights the point that its composition will vary as a result of the characteristics of the product being purchased and particularly in relation to the perceived risk of the buying situation. More recent work by Greatorex *et al.* (1992) has demonstrated the importance of perceived risk in computer systems purchasing.

Buying situation

Product complexity will be situation specific and should not be regarded *per se*, but rather in the way it is related to the purchaser's technical knowledge and expertise. Knowledge and expertise will arise out of previous experience with the product and consequently lead to a reduction in risk perception. It can therefore be logically concluded that a major determinant of the composition of the buying centre will be the organization's previous experience of the product and the supplier.

Prior experience of the product or supplier will be a determining factor in risk perception. Robinson *et al.* (1967) define three 'buy classes' which are dependent on previous experience: new buy, modified re-buy and straight re-buy. These buy classes influence both the composition of the buying centre and the buying process itself.

- *New buy* – In this situation the organization has no previous experience of the product or supplier. Consequently, perceived risk will be high and purchase decisions will be more likely to be made by senior management. Various strategies to reduce risk will be adopted by buyers, such as extended search, asking for referees, detailed specification and contract negotiation, and, where possible, trial purchase.
- *Modified re-buy* – The company already has prior experience of the product but the particular purchase situation demands some degree of novelty. This may arise due to different specifications in a product or through change of supplier.
- *Straight re-buy* – This usually entails the routine reordering of products on the basis of decisions that have been made previously. There will be little risk perception in these instances and the purchase decision will be taken by lower management. In such cases there may not be a discrete decision at all, but only in relation to the establishment of the order routine. It is usually very difficult to break inertia of routine reordering and a 'new' supplier will have to demonstrate strong reasons to the buying organization to justify the extra risk and effort of changing supplier.

Robinson *et al.* link the buy classes to what they term buy phases or stages in the decision-making process. These stages constitute the last

of the variables influencing the composition of the buying centre. The Robinson *et al.* buy classes can be criticized as somewhat simplistic descriptions of the wide variety of buying situations which exist in practice. An alternative analysis of buying situations is proposed by Bunn (1993), who develops a taxonomy of buying situations and patterns. His classification defines six prototypical buying-decision approaches:

1 Casual purchase.
2 Routine low priority.
3 Simple modified re-buy.
4 Judgemental new task.
5 Complex modified re-buy.
6 Strategic new task.

Bunn (1993) relates these approaches to decision processes such as search behaviour, use of analysis techniques and procedural control, and provides a useful review of research in the field.

Stage in the buying process

Organizational buying decisions are not discrete but result from a variety of stages which interact and upon which the final decision depends. As previously noted, the composition of the buying centre will vary as a result of the particular activity taking place. Product users may provide the stimulus for a new purchase. In specifying the characteristics of a new product, technologists and finance people may be involved. The purchasing department may collect information about new products which will then be evaluated by the users, technologists and finance people. In deciding which alternatives should be short-listed, the finance department may become involved again and the final selection may be made at board level, where all the company interests will be represented.

Many researchers have attempted to categorize the stages of the buying process: Fisher (1969) categorizes three stages; Cunningham and White (1974) also suggest three stages which lead to the final patronage decision; Dewey (1960) suggests a five-stage framework; Webster and Wind (1972a) classify four basic stages. The similarity of the stages suggest some universal pattern of organizational buying. Nevertheless, all models assume a discrete and ordered process which is unrealistic in practice. Empirical findings have always shown that stages can occur simultaneously or out of sequence etc., depending on the particular buying situation. However, it is useful to review the principal activity steps which usually take place in new buy or modified rebuy purchasing.

Search

Searching for information is a major way of reducing risk, and the search for alternative products or suppliers is liable to be most extensive when risk perception is high. Cyert and March (1963) suggested that search, like decision making itself, was problem directed. They made three basic assumptions about organizational search. First, that search is motivated by a problem. Second, that search proceeds on the basis of a simple model of causality, until driven to a more complex one. And, third, that the search would be biased by the searcher's perceptions of the environment. The frequency of search is a function of how well present suppliers and products are meeting organizational goals, and one reason for frequent search is 'to keep present suppliers honest' by comparing them with alternatives.

The collection of information usually has a cost, either financial or in terms of effort or time expended. Buckner (1967) found that suppliers usually only examine a limited range of suppliers. Limited search can particularly be ascribed to the cost of information gathering. White (1969), however, indicated that a major reason for limiting search was work simplification or avoidance.

The search process may therefore be governed in many instances by satisficing rather than maximizing behaviour, particularly in purchase situations where risk is not felt to be high. Organizational search is a continuous process of data gathering which may relate specifically to products or generally to economic trends or markets. Search relating specifically to purchase situations may occur simultaneously with other stages in the decision process as a continuous activity or else as a series of sequential steps. Webster's research

Table 7.1	Percentage of respondents finding each source important by stage in the buying process				
	Awareness	*Interest*	*Evaluation*	*Trial*	*Adoption*
Salespeople	84	90	64	70	56
Trade journals	90	38	22	16	8
Buyers in other companies	18	22	28	16	8
Engineers in other companies	26	34	44	20	18
Trade associations	42	24	14	4	8
Trade shows	76	34	16	12	4

Adapted from Webster (1965).

(1965) clearly showed how different sources of information are used at each stage in the adoption process (see Table 7.1). Thus, advertising in trade journals would appear to be the most efficient method of gaining awareness for a product, but salespeople are more efficient in generating interest. The research also demonstrated a decreasing reliance on external sources as people become increasingly aware of the product.

Evaluation

Hill and Hillier (1977) suggested that evaluation may consist of two main stages: first, selecting companies to tender and, second, making the final selection of product and supplier. Weigand (1968) also proposed a two-step evaluation process: the identification of an approved list of suppliers from which the purchasing agent is at liberty to select on the basis of price, delivery and a variety of other negotiable factors, followed by the selection decision.

Evaluation must obviously be made against some predetermined criteria, often relating to both product and supplier. Green *et*

al. (1968) scaled a number of product and supplier attributes or characteristics, and obtained the rankings on a Thurstonian scale shown in Table 7.2.

These findings were borne out by Cunningham and White (1974), who suggested that certain attributes were essential if a supplier was to be even considered, but that other factors would decide which supplier was ultimately selected. The former they termed qualifying factors and the latter determining factors. They also found that a favourable reputation for delivery, reliability and service were important prerequisites for increasing the chance of being seriously considered as a potential supplier. The strongest determinant of a buyer's patronage decision is his/her past experience, which itself relates to the buyer's perception of the supplier's reputation.

Particular product or supplier attributes and their relative importance will obviously vary according to the product and the buying situation. Previous research into product and supplier evaluation seems to indicate that evaluation is a two-step process where products and suppliers are measured against some kind of preconceived set of criteria.

Table 7.2   Importance of different criteria in evaluating products

Performance characteristic (ranked in order of preference)	Scaling value
Quality/price ratio	3.61
Delivery reliability	2.91
Technical ability and knowledge	1.95
Information and market services	1.86
General reputation	1.65
Geographic location	1.63
Technical	1.61
Extent of previous contact	1.44
Importance of client (reciprocity)	0.61
Extent of personal benefits supplied to buyer	–

Source: Green et al. (1968).

This necessarily brief discussion of buying stages underlines several of the models of buying behaviour discussed later in this chapter. Before moving on to this topic, however, it is necessary to consider the last characteristic of organizations – the motivations and objectives of the organizations and their members.

Buying goals

Both Cox (1966) and Campbell (1966) have analysed the buying behaviour as a problem-solving activity and recognize that the whole purchasing process is designed to meet certain aims or objectives on both the organizational level and the individual level. These objectives, it is suggested, can relate either directly or indirectly to the buying task. However, a variety of factors can intervene between the original purchase objectives and the final buying decision. The cost of searching for the product or service that exactly fits the purchase specifications may be prohibitive or, alternatively, such a product or service may not be available. White (1969) indicated that in some instances a major determinant of buying behaviour is the desire for work simplification.

Therefore, in many instances both organizations and individuals may be pursuing 'satisficing' rather than maximizing courses of action in their behaviour, whereby a compromise will be reached between the attainment of the purchasing objectives and the actual purchase.

Models of organizational buying behaviour

The previous discussion of the decision-making unit, purchase situation and buying stages is fundamental to an understanding of the various models of organizational buyer behaviour which have been postulated in the past 30 years. The purpose of modelling buyer behaviour is to clarify the relationships between various inputs, such as selling, previous experience or competitor activities, the purchasing process and the outputs, which are the purchase or rejection of a product or service from a particular source.

Many models have been proposed and an excellent summary of the early work in the field is made by Webster and Wind (1972b) in their book, *Organizational Buyer Behaviour*. The authors define four main categories of model:

1 Task-related.
2 Non-task related.
3 Complex.
4 Multidimensional.

Task-related models

These are based on the view that the desire for rational or optimal outcomes is a fundamental determinant of behaviour. These models focus on concepts such as lowest purchase price, lowest total cost, constrained choice, rational economics, and materials management.

Non-task-related models

With non-task-related models, the perspective shifts from the demands of the task to be accomplished to the personal interests that might be affected by the outcome. Examples of the key concepts used in non-task-related models include:

- Individual desire for ego enhancement or personal gain.
- Desire to avoid risk in decision making (Bauer, 1960; Newall, 1977).
- Gratification of buyer and seller through a dyadic relationship (Evans, 1963; Bonoma and Johnston, 1978).
- Lateral relationships between buyer and colleagues (Tosi, 1966).
- Relationships with significant other persons from within the company, and their effect on transmission and interpretation of information (Webster, 1965).

Complex models

In the late 1960s, several more comprehensive models were postulated, incorporating a large number of variables. For example, the *decision process model* (Wind and Robinson, 1968) depicts decisions as occurring over a considerable period involving segmented stages, i.e. 'problem alternatives' and 'selection'.

The *compact model* (Robinson *et al.*, 1967) attempts to establish general rules that govern the decision process. Three dimensions of influences are proposed: organization structure; elements of the buying process; and the characteristics of individuals. However, in this model no reference is made to the exchanges and negotiation occurring between parties.

We can criticize these models for adopting only a partial approach, and even the more complex models fail to cover many of the important points observed by Webster and Wind. Moreover, many are theoretical rather than realistic. They are of limited practical use to the marketing or purchasing practitioner.

In an attempt to be more realistic, Robinson *et al.* (1967) proposed the *buygrid model*. This is based on empirical observations of buyer behaviour in companies. In Table 7.3, we see that decisions are thought to vary on two dimensions. First, the stage of the decision (or 'buyphase') and, second, the nature of the decision itself (the 'buyclass').

The buygrid model offers certain improvements over earlier models. For example, it recognizes that buying is often repetitive and has a more normative basis for practising managers. However, Ferguson (1979) found that the buygrid model had only a limited capacity to predict outcomes when he applied it to examples of decision making. In most situations he observed that the proposed systematic decision process was often 'short-circuited'. To overcome these objectives, we must turn to the more comprehensive models which incorporate a wider range of variables.

Complex multidisciplinary models

Clearly, the models described previously are inadequate both as descriptive representations of reality and as predictive tools. Several models have been developed which attempt to

Table 7.3   The buygrid model

Buyphases	Buyclasses		
	New task	Modified re-buy	Straight re-buy
Identification of need	X	X	X
Determination of requirement	X	n/a	n/a
Specific description of requirement	X	n/a	n/a
Search for potential sources	X	n/a	n/a
Examination of sources	X	n/a	n/a
Selection of source	X	X	X
Order routine established	X	X	n/a
Evaluation of performance feedback	X	X	X

n/a = not applicable
Source: Robinson *et al.* (1967).

overcome these problems. In an early attempt to integrate various dimensions of consumer buying behaviour, Howard and Sheth (1969) developed a behavioural model based on social, psychological, cultural and economic variables.

Subsequently, Sheth (1973) proposed a complex model specifically for industrial buyer behaviour, which integrates a large number of variables into one comprehensive model, which is briefly described below.

The Sheth model

Sheth's model of organizational buyer behaviour outlined in Figure 7.1 proposes four broad categories of variables.

Psychological world of the decision makers

The decision makers' perception of the product's ability to satisfy both implicit and explicit criteria, such as quality, delivery time, price, reputation etc., will vary in accordance with the individual's role, education, lifestyle, past experience and knowledge of the product and supplier. This background, which constitutes a sort of 'black box', leads to individual perceptual distortions which will influence each person's approach to the buying task.

Product and company variables

Product-specific factors include perceived risk, type of purchase (new or re-buy situation) and

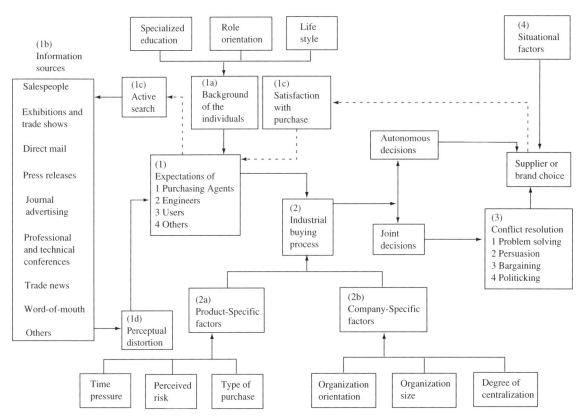

Figure 7.1   The Sheth model of organizational buying behaviour
Source: Sheth, 1973.

time pressure. Perceived risk and purchase situation have been discussed previously. Time pressure refers to the possibility that decisions may need to be made within a time limit. Sheth (1973) suggests that the shorter this time limit, the more likely that the decision will be made autonomously. Company factors include company orientation, company size and centralization, the influence of which has already been discussed.

Structure and methods for problem solving

The decision makers' psychological world and the various product and company variables will lead to the buying task being solved by a particular method. Sheth suggests that these methods can be summed up as either joint or autonomous decision making. Joint decision making often results in conflict between the decision makers, and the third stage of Sheth's (1973) model concentrates on the reasons for and resolution of this conflict. Conflict may stem from:

(a) Disagreement on expectations about the suppliers or their products.
(b) Disagreement about the criteria with which to evaluate suppliers or products.
(c) Fundamental differences in the buying goals or objectives among the members of the buying centre.
(d) Disagreement about the style of decision making.

For each of the bases of conflict the following forms of conflict resolution may apply:

(i) *Problem solving.* Increased search for information and further deliberation about existing information. This additional information is then presented in such a way that conflict is minimized.
(ii) *Persuasion.* An attempt is made to show the dissenting members how their criteria are liable to result in corporate objectives not being fulfilled.

(iii) *Bargaining.* The fundamental differences between the parties are conceded and a decision is arrived at on a 'tit for tat' basis. This will either result in a compromise or else allows an individual to make the decision autonomously in return for some favour or promise of reciprocity in future decision making.
(iv) *Politicking and backstabbing.* These, according to Strauss and Sheth, are common methods of problem solving in industrial buying.

Situational factors

Sheth (1973) argues that organizational buying decisions are often determined by 'ad hoc' situational factors and not by any systematic decision-making process. Thus, specific decisions are a result of certain environmental considerations, such as price controls, the economic environment, strikes, promotional efforts or price changes. These factors can often intervene between the decision-making process and the final decision.

Sheth's model is not intended to be definitive, but offers a framework which draws attention to the dynamics and complexity of organizational buying and presents the relevant factors in a systematic way. The model concentrates on the internal workings of the buying process, does not incorporate external influences and tells us nothing about the relationship between the constituent parts. In discussing the situational factors, Sheth wrote:

> What is needed in these cases is a checklist of empirical observations of the ad hoc events which initiate the neat relationship between the theory or the model and a specific buying situation.

We should note here that a universal buying process does not exist and the model's value lies in its application to particular buying situations or organizations. In this manner it can contribute towards a better understanding of the complexities of organizational buying behaviour.

The Webster and Wind model

Webster and Wind's (1972a) model, outlined in Figure 7.2, stresses the role of the individual as the real decision maker in the organization. Therefore, the individual's motivation, personality, perception, learning and experience are all vital to the actual decision process. This model

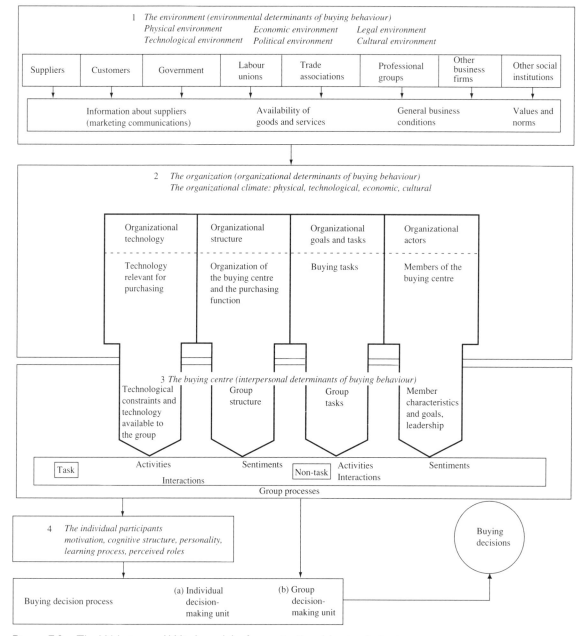

Figure 7.2   The Webster and Wind model of organizational buying behaviour
Source: Webster and Wind, 1972b.

is truly comprehensive, and honours concepts from the fields of individual, organizational and social psychology, economics, management, sociology and politics.

Webster and Wind recognize the existence of a buying centre and argue that organizational buying is a multi-person process subjected to and influenced by the aggregate behaviour of a number of people, and also by the interaction between them. The activities of both individuals and the collective buying centre are influenced by a variety of factors, some of which are related to the buying task (task variables which include rational and economic motivations) and non-task variables (a variety of emotional or non-rational reasons for purchasing decisions).

Webster and Wind suggest that the final buying decision is dependent on influences exerted from four spheres:

1 The general environment
2 The organization
3 Interpersonal influences
4 The influence of the individual

It is possible to identify three key elements of the model and their interplay, as shown in Table 7.4.

Table 7.4 Key factors affecting organizational buying decisions

Level of influence on behaviour	Source of influence	Types of constraints to behaviour that emerge
1. The firm's environment	Physical, legal, economic, technical, political, cultural, suppliers, customers, governments	Information, products and services, business conditions, values, norms
2. The organization	Business climate, physical climate, technological climate, economic climate, cultural climate, structure of work, personnel, organizational goals	Technology relevant for purchasing organization of the buying centre, buying tasks, members of the buying centre
3. The buying team	Technological constraints, buying group structure, buying group tasks, member characteristics, member goals	Task and non-tasks: – activities – interactions – orientations
4. The individual	Motivation, cognition, personality, learning, roles	Buying decision process, individual DM unit, group DM unit ↓ buying decision

Based on Webster and Wind (1972b).

At the most general level we have the firm's environment. This comprises the wide and complex system of institutions that make up the social and industrial infrastructure. By dictating needs, norms and laws, this level of influence affects the practices of the firm and the individual.

Below the firm's environment we encounter the organization's internal environment. Decision making occurs against a background of the firm's technology, the way work is organized, the firm's objectives and goals, and the character of individuals themselves.

The third level of influence proposed is that of the decision-making unit. At this level the roles performed by participants in the decision make a major contribution to the eventual outcome. Thus, the roles of the 'influencer', 'order placer', 'decider', 'gatekeeper' and 'user' may all be present, although we might presume the buying centre to have a common set of expectations and the decision itself may be the outcome of several different collective processes, such as bargaining, consensus negotiation and game strategy. Several writers have commented on tactics used by individuals to promote their own interests. For example, Strauss (1962) suggests that purchasers may avoid or enforce company rules or use political or personal persuasion. Walton and McKenzie (1965) stress the importance of distributive and integrative bargaining plus attitudinal structuring in achieving a 'common front'.

The fourth and lowest level of influence – that of the individual – highlights the fact that all behaviour is ultimately conducted at a personal level. Thus, motivation, cognition, personality, experience and learning may all affect the outcome of the decision process.

Webster and Wind's model focuses our attention on a number of significant features that are particularly relevant in international marketing. Thus, at the most general level, foreign trading partners may well come from very different environments (see Chapter 24). The organizational environments of buying and selling firms may also be different or disjointed. As a result, understanding may be poor and communication difficult.

At the second level, the model accounts for the fact that firms in different cultures may have very different working climates. In addition, the way work is organized could be disparate. At the third level, the model recognizes the possibility of conflicts of interest and the influence of 'significant others'. Perhaps of great interest at the individual level of influence, the model highlights the fact that personal processes and capabilities will affect the outcome of decisions. Thus, training and experience, cognition, personality and motivation will all affect sales and buying performance. Clearly, important differences in personal factors such as these are more likely in different countries.

In essence, Webster and Wind's model is one of the most comprehensive of its kind, and considers a wide range of decision-related factors and variables. However, it is still of limited practical help to the marketer because it does not concentrate on the units of analysis that are fundamental to the real-life processes that are occurring with prospective and ongoing buyer–seller relationships (i.e. the relationship between individuals and the nature of what is exchanged).

Although it covers a multitude of determinant factors, what is lacking is a focus on the processes that are most important in the long- and short-term aspects of a buying decision. No reference is made to the personal relationships and the atmosphere of the relationship that may evolve between buyer and seller. Seeking to resolve this issue, the International Marketing and Purchasing (IMP) group developed a model of business-to-business marketing and purchasing as an iterative process based on long-term relationships.

The interaction approach

The *interaction approach* (Turnbull and Cunningham, 1981; Hakansson, 1982) focuses on the most basic elements of the decision process. It stresses the necessity that marketers are perceptive and flexible in the definition and satisfaction of customer needs. This is done by placing greater emphasis on the processes and relationships which occur between and within buying and selling organizations. The interaction approach to business-to-business marketing is now firmly established and recognized in Europe as an important and realistic conceptualization of the realities of marketing and purchasing behaviour in business markets. More recently, this has been recognized by scholars throughout the world and Webster (1992), in a discussion of the changing role of marketing, recognizes the limitations of previous models and stresses the need for marketers to understand and manage long-term relationships and networks of organizations. Hakansson (1982) emphasizes the following points to distinguish their approach:

- Buyers and sellers are seen as active participants in the transaction. The buyer is thus not limited to a passive role and can seek to influence the nature of the marketing inputs that are offered.
- Buyer–seller relationships are often long term in nature, tend to be based on mutual trust rather than a formal contract, and often start months or even years before money and goods are exchanged.
- Complex patterns of interaction evolve between and within the companies and their different departments.
- Because of the complex nature of relationships, marketers and purchasers may be more involved with supporting and maintaining these than with actually buying and selling.
- The links between buyers and sellers may become institutionalized.

From these observations, industrial purchasing decisions may be seen to vary as a function of four main areas of variables. The interrelationships of these four key areas are illustrated in Figure 7.3.

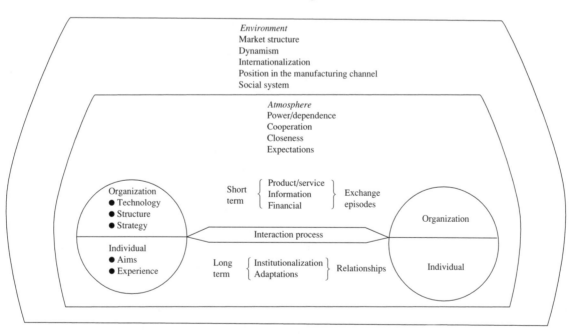

Figure 7.3 The main elements of the interaction model
Source: Hakansson, 1982.

In the brief description of the four areas which follows, we shall emphasize how the interaction model stresses the importance of the individual and the level of his/her interpersonal and intercompany skills.

The interactive process

Relationships between buyers and sellers can be broken into a series of episodes. Each episode contributes to the overall relationship, which will be developed over a greater period of time. These episodes can be considered in terms of elements of exchange. For example, the exchange of the actual product or service, the exchange of information, the exchange of money or social exchanges. The greater the extent of uncertainty concerning these elements, the more likely that increased interaction will take place to resolve these uncertainties and allow the parties to become familiar with each other and develop mutual trust.

The occurrence of episodes over time can lead to the interaction becoming routinized and to preconceptions regarding the role set of both individuals and organizations. Such routine patterns of behaviour may become characteristic of a single relationship or else of a whole industry. Mutual adaptations may occur between buyers and sellers which will result in cost reductions or some other advantage. The existence of such adaptations can serve to bring each party closer together. This can therefore act as a major influence on changing marketing or buying policies.

The participants

Interaction occurs between organizations and individuals, and is dependent on the nature of the organization and its members. Relevant factors may be the firm's technology, size, experience and structure, or the individual's motives, attitudes and perceptions. These factors have already been discussed at some length in previous sections.

The environment

The interaction process takes place in the general prevailing environmental conditions, which will determine certain norms of behaviour and values. Particularly relevant factors may be the market structure, social systems or economic conditions, and the degree of internationalization of the economy and/or the industry.

The atmosphere

The outcome of a relationship is the atmosphere which results from the various exchanges and adaptations. The atmosphere refers specifically to the degree of closeness between the buyer and seller, which will be reflected in the level of conflict or co-operation in their interaction. The nature of the atmosphere can be planned. The development of a close relationship with a 'good atmosphere' may result in advantageous conditions for the buyer and seller. However, in order to avoid power dependence, where one party becomes vulnerable to the power of the other, the 'closeness' of the atmosphere may be regulated and in some circumstances a company may deliberately choose to have a distant, even confrontational, style of relationship.

The interaction model focuses on the relationships between individuals both within and between firms. It portrays dynamic and developing relationships, which approximate to the reality of organizational purchasing, in a way that none of the previous models are able to do. In so doing, it presents a more complex picture of organizational buying and offers a challenge to the researcher to find a universal pattern of relationships from which to build a comprehensive model.

Metcalf *et al.* (1992) have shown how the interaction approach is a valuable paradigm for analysing the relationship development of aircraft engine suppliers and aircraft manufacturing customers, whilst Turnbull and Valla (1986a, b) developed a strategic planning model based on the interaction approach. Hakansson (1989) also demonstrates the robustness of the approach in applying it to innovation and technology transfer.

Relationship management and networks

To fully understand the importance of relationships as an input to, and an outcome of, organizational buying and selling, we need to examine the investments and bonding processes of the relationship partners and other players in the network. Relationships between companies don't just happen, they are the consequences of efforts made by those companies – without such investments the relationships will not develop and will decline. These investments may be relatively trivial, such as a special delivery schedule, or they may be major changes in product design, for example. Both sellers and buyers make such investments, or adaptations, and these define the nature of the relationships – how the companies 'live together'. Relationship management is the process of planning and controlling these efforts in both companies (Turnbull *et al.*, 1996; Ford, 1998).

It is important to note that all companies have relationships with their customers and their suppliers. It is the nature of the relationships which varies – from close, trusting and productive to arms length, conflicting and marginal. The company will have to manage many relationships simultaneously and thus are interconnected. Thus, marketing management is very much to do with the managing of an interconnected portfolio of customer relationships.

Whilst the interaction approach has been acknowledged as an important development in the process of understanding business markets, it has limitations; the approach was originally based on the analysis of bilateral relationships between pairs of organizations. In reality, of course, no relationship exists in isolation but forms part of a connected and interdependent set of relationships. Thus, the way the parties of a relationship will behave will be affected by their connections to other organizations and the interaction occurring. The study of these sets of relationships has come to be termed *the network approach* and can be seen as a logical development of the earlier research on interaction.

It is important to be aware that any one company has a 'network' of different kinds of interconnected relationships. Spencer and Valla (1989) define a network as:

> . . . a set of interconnected relations involving people and organizations called actors, and forming a structured sub-system within a larger system of actors . . . They are involved in a finalized process, with the ultimate purpose of allowing and facilitating the exchange of goods or services between a supplier and a customer, or a set of them.

In a network of relationships it is necessary not only to examine the investments and bonding processes of direct relationship partners, but also other players in the network, the indirect relationships, as they affect buying behaviour. The interconnectedness of direct and indirect business relationships is simply demonstrated in Figure 7.4. It can be observed that the focal company not only has relationships with Customers 1 and 3, but also has a relationship with customer 2, an intermediary, and relationships with Suppliers 1, 2 and 3; it is also necessary to be aware of indirect relationships which may have an impact on the direct relationships. Two of the focal company's customers have relationships with competing suppliers. Customer 2 is also supplied by Competitor 1 and Customer 3 is also supplied by Competitor 2. The focal company's Supplier 2 has relationships with two suppliers. Within a network, the behaviour of organizations in one relationship will influence the companies' behaviour in other relationships. For example, the focal company may provide Customer 2 with a certain level of delivery reliability which Customer 2 may subsequently begin to insist on from its other

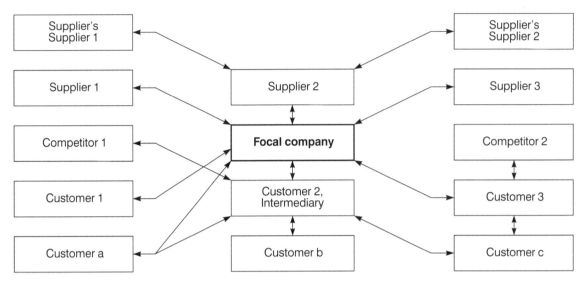

Figure 7.4   Interconnected relationships in a simplified network.

supplier, Competitor 1 in the diagram. Relationships in the network may affect companies
within the network that they have no direct
contact with. For example, Customer 2
becomes concerned when it hears that a close
relationship has developed between companies Customer 3 and Competitor 2 in order to
develop a product to specifically satisfy Customer c. As Customer c is also one of Customer 2's customers, Customer 2 may initiate
collaboration with the focal company to
develop a product specifically for Customer c
to fend off the competition from Customer 3.
Customer 2's collaboration with the focal company may also be beneficial to its other customers, a and b.

Networks are made up of *actors*, the
companies and the individuals within them,
that perform a set of *activities* using sets of
resources (Hakansson and Johanson, 1992;
Hakansson and Snehota, 1995).

- *Actors* – In the process of developing activity
  links and resource ties, the individuals and
  companies interact with each other and actor
  bonds are formed. Strong actor bonds
  between companies will affect other

companies' perceptions; for example, a
supplier who has a strong bond with a big
major customer may be able to use the
relationship to acquire the custom of other
companies.

- *Activities* – The activities refer to the technical,
  administrative, commercial and other activities
  of a company which become connected to the
  other companies as the relationships develop.
  The connection and co-ordination of
  companies' activities has provided the basis of
  'just in time' supply chain management and
  'total quality management' (Hakansson and
  Johanson, 1992; Hakansson and Snehota,
  1995).

- *Resources* – Each company has its own set of
  resources, including manpower, equipment,
  plant, financial means etc., and relationships
  often provide a means of accessing resources
  which may have been unavailable to them
  previously. In addition, companies not only
  bring their own resources to relationships,
  they often invest in each other to create, build
  or acquire resources. New resource
  combinations are likely to arise as the
  companies develop and invest in a relationship,
  leading to new business opportunities.

These three components – actors, activities and resources – are not independent of each other; they are all interconnected. The existence of bonds between actors is necessary in order for any strong activity and resource links to develop. Actors carry out activities and activate resources. Resources may limit the activities which the actors can pursue, but the activities may evolve and change as the abilities of the actors change. Actor bonds, activity and resource links evolve and change, and the three components adjust accordingly, making networks dynamic entities (Hakansson and Snehota, 1992; Michel *et al.*, 2002). Network terminology is generic and all encompassing, it does not specifically address only organizational buying behaviour, but places the focal company within the context of its business environment, taking into account competitors, suppliers, customers, distributors etc.

Implications for marketing management

A company's actor bonds, activity links and resource ties determine its position, strength and reputation within a network. Through examining its position, a company can decide its future strategy, i.e. whether it should enter a new network, leave a network, defend its position in the network or change its position within the network. Johanson and Mattsson (1986) stated that a company's position can be examined from both a micro and a macro perspective. The micro position is characterized by (i) the position of the company in relation to the other company (companies), (ii) its importance to the other company, and (iii) the strength of the relationship with the other company. The macro position is characterized by (i) the identity of the other companies with which the company has direct and indirect relationships in the network, (ii) the role of the company in the network, and (iii) the strength of the relationships with the other companies. Mattsson (1987) believes that implementing any strategic change will lead

to a change in the network position of the company.

The network approach, like the interaction approach from which it has developed, offers a very different perspective from traditional marketing and purchasing behaviour; it integrates the two activities and examines relationships rather than markets. It is useful for determining the focal company's strategy and the allocation of the company's scarce resources. The network approach emphasizes how important it is for companies to consider all of their relationships with their suppliers and buyers, and to develop a rational strategy for managing them (Zolkiewski and Turnbull, 2001).

Relationship portfolio analysis

Companies have become increasingly aware of the importance of managing their network of suppliers and customers. Three major trends have occurred in purchasers' relationships with their suppliers, largely as a result of the move to supply chain management. Buyers have outsourced an increasing number of activities, leaving them to concentrate on their core competencies with the aim of increasing their efficiency and effectiveness. Yet, at the same time, the number of suppliers a purchaser uses has decreased and buyers increasingly want to collaborate in some way with their suppliers. Obviously, implementation of many of these changes is aimed at decreasing the direct and indirect costs of procurement and increasing the ability of the company to generate revenue. In order to achieve these aims, however, it is vital that the company has a thorough knowledge of its suppliers' relationships, including the scope of these relationships (i.e. the extent and importance of buying to the company's overall business), the structure of its supply base (i.e. the number and type of suppliers the company chooses to have) and the posture of its supplier relationships (i.e. how a company handles and deals with its relationships, are the companies close, integrated etc.) (Ford, 1998; Michel *et al.*, 2002).

Suppliers' relationships with their customers cannot be treated in isolation, as they will be increasingly affected by these trends in the supply strategies of customers. Suppliers also need to consider the scope of what they offer, their posture and the structure of their customer relationships. In terms of their offerings to customers, the supplier may have to offer technological innovativeness and competence, adaptations and superior logistics. The posture or type of interaction that occurs between companies will vary from simple transactional relationships to close co-operative relationships (Hakansson and Snehota, 1990). The structure of the customer base is measured by the type and number of relationships the supplier has. These three factors interact and determine how the suppliers allocate their limited resources among their customers.

An understanding of the focal company's position in the network and how the interactions in one relationship may affect the others is necessary for performing relationship portfolio analysis. The aim of relationship portfolio analysis is to provide a framework for analysing current relationships to enable the tactical and strategic management of relationships in the future (Zolkiewsi and Turnbull, 2001). These authors argue that the approach is equally important to both supply and procurement management. This approach highlights:

- existing relationships which need to be developed;
- relationships which should be maintained at the 'status quo';
- relationships which should be terminated;
- areas where new relationships could be developed;
- areas where different elements of the marketing offer should be emphasized.

Essentially, the analysis results in the grouping of similar relationships, whether they are suppliers or buyers, and is a development of segmentation. It allows the characteristics of the different groups of customers and suppliers

to be analysed and is an important aspect of the management of relationships.

A number of relationship portfolio models have been developed over the years: Fiocca (1982), Campbell and Cunningham (1983), Shapiro *et al.* (1987), and Turnbull and Zolkiewski (1997) focus on relationships with customers, whereas Krapfel *et al.* (1991) and Olsen and Ellram (1997) focus on relationships with suppliers (see Zolkiewski and Turnbull, 1999, for a review of the models). These models are quite problematic as they vary considerably in relation to the actual variables used, the number of variables used and the number of steps used to integrate the information. Practitioners need to use their insight and judgement as well as considering carefully the reasons why they are using relationship portfolio analysis when selecting a model. Although all the researchers recognize the major difficulties inherent in the implementation of such an analysis, they agree that, at least conceptually, relationship portfolio analysis, planning and management make an important contribution to effective marketing management.

Key account management is another tool which entails examining relationships from a strategic perspective. It is an approach usually adopted by the supplier who aims to build a portfolio of loyal key accounts by offering them, on a continual basis, a product/service package tailored to their individual needs (McDonald *et al.*, 2000). Once again, an understanding of the focal company's position in the network and its relationships is vital for deciding which relationships should be developed into key accounts. Relationship portfolio analysis could be used to provide a strategic perspective for selecting key accounts (Zolkiewski and Turnbull, 2001). This approach would be an improvement on past approaches put forward by Barrett (1986) and Boles *et al.* (1999), who suggest that key accounts should be large customers relative to the company's typical customer. This is an inadequate strategic approach as it focuses on high volume buyers only. The use of relationship portfolio analysis to identify key accounts would take into consideration such factors as technological capability and the ability to aid entrance to a new market (Wilson and Mummalaneni, 1986). The actual use of relationship portfolio management to support key account management is limited (Zolkiewski and Turnbull, 2001). For the key account to be successful not only does the customer have to be strategically important to the supplier, but the supplier also has to be important to the customer. Therefore, the supplier not only has to offer a tailor made product/service, but also ensure the customer is sufficiently satisfied and valued to encourage them to remain loyal. Berry and Parasuraman (1991) identified three approaches to enhancing customer value:

1 The addition of financial benefits, e.g. improved credit terms.
2 The addition of social benefits.
3 The addition of structural ties, e.g. electronic data interchange, special delivery arrangements.

We would add to this the creation of technological bonds.

Suppliers also need to measure and monitor relationships in order to improve their performance, and be proactive and constantly improving the products/services they are offering. The benefits to be gained from key account management are believed to vary from industry to industry.

It is necessary to have an understanding of organizational buying behaviour as it equips individuals with the capability to obtain what they and other parties want from the process. There is considerable synergy between networks, relationship portfolio management and key account management; they all require an understanding of the decision-making process and the factors which influence it, but they all put it into the context of the business as a whole, and its array of relationships in the network.

We have previously noted in this chapter that the relationship or interaction approach to

business markets can give valuable insights into the marketing of consumer products, given that the majority of such products are sold to organizational buyers or intermediaries. However, it is interesting to note that relationship management has been relatively recently embraced (very enthusiastically in many cases) by companies dealing directly with consumer markets. This has been most obviously manifested in the numerous loyalty card programmes developed by airlines, retailers, car dealers and many others (see Christopher *et al.*, 1991; Buttle, 1996). Relationship marketing is being taken further on the Internet, with companies such as Amazon building one-to-one relationships by placing the customer in their own personalized environment on every contact occasion (Dussart, 2000).

At the heart of this perhaps rather superficial or fashionable management trend is the explicit recognition by those companies involved that strong ties between the supplier and the customer are potentially of huge economic advantage – it is considerably cheaper to keep customers than to gain new ones! It is, of course, critical if these relationship management programmes are to work in the long term that they offer real benefits to the customer as well as the supplier (see Chapter 19 on relationship management).

We should also note that the challenges of managing an array or portfolio of customers in an FMCG market are conceptually similar to those in, for example, the heavy engineering sector. It is the application of the concept where adaptation and flexibility are the core to success.

Conclusion

In reviewing various models of buyer behaviour, an attempt has been made to bring together the various elements of organizational buyer behaviour that were discussed under the heads of organizational structures, activities and goals. No single model adequately explains all the complexities of the organizational buying process and this in itself is a warning against any attempt to construct simplistic models. However, taken together, the complex models provide a framework for empirical research into the buying process, as each of the relevant areas is treated with different emphasis in each model.

The marketer can no longer presume that the company will be a sole or dominant supplier forever. Companies can use theory and tools such as relationship portfolio analysis and key account management to determine their marketing strategy, which existing relationships must be maintained and strengthened to protect against growing competitive pressures. Equally important, to survive in the increasingly international competitive environment of the next decade, suppliers must aggressively seek to establish new relationships both in domestic and foreign markets.

These twin strategies – defending the existing customer base and proactively seeking new accounts – have a common fundamental requirement, the knowledge and understanding of how purchasing takes place in organizations.

Understanding the dynamics of organizational buying behaviour is essential to all major strategic and tactical planning in business-to-business marketing, the identification of profitable segments and motivating those individuals with product and service offerings appropriate to their needs. Thus, every action of the business-to-business marketer is based on the probable response of organizational buyers in relation to adaptations of price, product, distribution, advertising and promotion.

Business-to-business marketing is characterized by complex interaction processes, both within the marketing and purchasing companies and between these companies. High technological and financial dependencies are common to business-to-business markets. These dependencies lead to extensive involvement and interchange over long time periods.

Due to the complex multidisciplinary and multifaceted nature of the buying process, the aim of researchers to develop comprehensive but testable and normative models is still not yet fully achieved.

References

Alexander, M., Cross, T. and Cunningham, S. (1961) *Industrial Marketing*, Richard Irwin, Homewood, IL.

Anyon, G. (1963) *Managing an Integrated Purchasing Process*, Rinehart & Winston, New York.

Barrett, J. (1986) Why Major Account Selling Works, *Industrial Marketing Management*, **15**, 63–73.

Bauer, R. A. (1960) Consumer Behaviour as Risk Taking, in Hancock, R. S. (ed.), *Dynamic Marketing for a Changing World*, Proceedings of 43rd Conference, American Marketing Association.

Berry, L. L. and Parasuraman, A. (1991) *Marketing Services: Competing Through Quality*, Free Press, New York.

Boles, J. S., Johnston, W. and Gardner, A. (1999) The Selection and Organization of National Accounts: A North American Perspective, *Journal of Business and Industrial Marketing*, **14**(4), 264–275.

Bonoma, T. V. and Johnston, W. (1978) The Social Psychology of Industrial Buying and Selling, *Industrial Marketing Management*, **7**(4).

Buckner, H. (1967) *How British Industry Buys*, Hutchinson, London.

Bunn, M. D. (1993) Taxonomy of Buying Decision Approaches, *Journal of Marketing*, **57**, January, 38–56.

Buttle, F. (ed.) (1996) *Relationship Marketing, Theory and Practice*, Paul Chapman, London.

Campbell, N. C. and Cunningham, M. T. (1983) Customer Analysis for Strategy Development in Industrial Markets, *Strategic Management Journal*, **4**, 369–380.

Campbell, R. (1966) A Suggested Paradigm of the Adoption Process, *Rural Sociology*, **31**, December.

Christopher, M., Payne, A. and Ballantyne, D. (1991) *Relationship Marketing*, Butterworth-Heinemann, Oxford.

Cox, D. F. (ed.) (1966) *Risk Taking and Information Handling*, Harvard University Press.

Cunningham, M. and White, R. (1974) The Behaviour of Industrial Buyers in their Search for Suppliers of Machine Tools, *Journal of Management Studies*, May.

Cyert, R. and March, J. (1963) *A Behavioral Theory of the Firm*, Prentice-Hall, Englewood Cliffs, NJ.

Dewey, R. (1960) *How We Think*, D. C. Heath, Lexington, MA.

Dussart, C. (2000) Internet: The One-Plus-Eight 'Re-volutions', *European Management Journal*, **18**(4), 386–397.

Evans, F. B. (1963) Selling as a Dyadic Relationship, *American Behavioral Science*, **6**, May.

Feldman, W. and Cardozo, R. N. (1968) The Industrial Revolution and Models of Buyer Behaviour, *Journal of Purchasing*, **4**, November.

Ferguson, W. (1979) An Evaluation of the Buygrid Analytical Framework, *Industrial Marketing Management*, **8**(1).

The Financial Times (1974), How British Industry Buys, November.

Fiocca, R. (1982) Account Portfolio Analysis for Strategy Development, *Industrial Marketing Management*, **11**, 53–62.

Fisher, L. (1969) *Industrial Marketing*, 2nd edn, Business Books, London.

Ford, D. (ed.) (1990) *Understanding Business Markets*, 1st edn, Dryden Press, London.

Ford, D. (ed.) (1998) *Managing Business Relationships*, Wiley, Chichester.

Greatorex, M., Mitchell, V.-W. and Cunliffe, R. (1992) A Risk Analysis of Industrial Buyers: The Case of Mid-Range Computers, *Journal of Marketing Management*, **8**, 315–333.

Green, P., Robinson, P. and Wind, Y. (1968) The Determinant of Vendor Selection. The Evaluation Function Approach, *Journal of Purchasing*, August.

Hakansson, H. (ed.) (1982) *International Marketing and Purchasing of Industrial Goods*, John Wiley, New York.

Hakansson, H. (1989) *Corporate Technological Behaviour: Cooperation and Networks*, John Wiley, New York.

Hakansson, H. and Johanson, J. (1992), A Model of Industrial Networks, in Ford D. (ed.) (1997), *Understanding Business Markets*, 2nd edn, Dryden Press, London.

Hakansson, H. and Snehota, I. (1990) No Business is an Island: The Network Concept of Business Strategy, in Ford, D. (ed.) (1990), *Understanding Business Markets*, 1st edn, Dryden Press, London.

Hakansson, H. and Snehota, I. (1992) Analysing Business Relationships, in Ford, D. (ed.) (1997), *Understanding Business Markets*, 2nd edn, Dryden Press, London.

Hakansson, H. and Snehota, I. (1995) Analysing Business Relationships, in Ford D. (ed.) (1997), *Understanding Business Markets*, 2nd edn, Dryden Press, London.

Hill, R. and Hillier, F. (1977) *Organisational Buyer Behaviour*, Macmillan, London.

Howard, N. and Sheth, J. (1969) *Consumer Buyer Behaviour*, John Wiley, New York.

Johanson, J. and Mattsson, L. G. (1986) Inter-organisational Relations in Industrial Systems: A Network Approach Compared with a Transaction Cost Approach, Working Paper, University of Uppsala, Sweden.

Krapfel, R. E., Salmond, D. and Spekman, R. (1991) A Strategic Approach to Managing Buyer–Seller Relationships, *European Journal of Marketing*, **25**(9), 72–82.

Lister, P. (1967) Identifying and Evaluating the Purchasing Influence, IMRA, August.

Mattsson, L. G. (1987) Management of Strategic Change in a 'Markets-as-Networks Perspective', in Pettigrew, A. (ed.), *The Management of Strategic Change*, Blackwell, Oxford.

McDonald, M., Rogers, B. and Woodburn, D. (2000), *Key Customers: How to Manage Them Profitably*, Butterworth-Heinemann, Oxford.

Metcalf, L. E., Frear, C. R. and Krishman, R. (1992) Buyer–Seller Relationships: An Application of the IMP Interaction Model, *European Journal of Marketing*, **26**(2), 22–46.

Michel, D., Naudé, P. and Salle, R. (2002) *Business to Business Marketing*. Palgrave Macmillan, London.

Newall, J. (1977) Industrial Buyer Behaviour: A Model of the Implications of Risk Handling Behaviour for Communication Policies in Industrial Marketing, *European Journal of Marketing*, **1**.

Olsen, R. F. and Ellram, L. M. (1997) A Portfolio Approach to Supplier Relationships, *Industrial Marketing Management*, **26**, 101–113.

Robinson, P., Faris, C. and Wind, Y. (1967) *Industrial Buying and Creative Marketing*, Allyn & Bacon, New York.

Shankleman, E. (1970) Study of Industrial Buying Decisions, *New Scientist*, September.

Shapiro, B. P., Rangan, V. K., Moriarty, R. T. and Ross, E. B. (1987) Manage Customers for Profits (Not Just for Sales), *Harvard Business Review*, September/October, 101–108.

Sheth, J. (1973) A Model of Industrial Buyer Behaviour, *Journal of Marketing*, **37**(4), October.

Spencer, R. and Valla, J. P. (1989) The Internationalization of the Firm: An International Development Network Approach, *15th European International Business Association's Annual Conference*, Helsinki, 17–19 December.

Strauss, G. (1962) Tactics of Lateral Relationship – The Purchasing Agent, *Administrative Science Quarterly*, **7**, September.

Thain, D. H. (1959) *How Industry Buys – With Conclusion and Recommendations on Marketing to Industry*, National Industrial Advertisers Association of Canada.

Tosi, H. L. (1966) The Effects of Expectation Level of Role Consensus on the Buyer–Seller Dyad, *Journal of Business*, October.

Turnbull, P. W. and Cunningham, M. T. (1981) *International Marketing and Purchasing*, Macmillan, London.

Turnbull, P. W. and Valla, J. P. (eds) (1986a) *Strategies for International Industrial Marketing*, Croom Helm, London.

Turnbull, P. W. and Valla, J. P. (1986b) Strategic Planning in Industrial Markets – An Interaction Approach, *European Journal of Marketing*, **20**(7).

Turnbull, P. W. and Zolkiewski, J. M. (1997) Profitability in Customer Portfolio Planning, in Ford, D. (ed.) (1997), *Understanding Business Markets*, 2nd edn, Dryden Press, London.

Turnbull, P. W., Ford, D. and Cunningham, M. (1996) Interaction, Relationships and Networks in Business Markets: An Evolving Perspective, *Journal of Business and Industrial Marketing Management*, **11**(3/4), 44–62.

Wallace, A. (1976) A Study of the Buying Process for New Products by Intermediate Marketing Organizations in the Channels of Distribution for Grocery Products, unpublished PhD thesis, UMIST.

Walton, R. E. and McKenzie, R. B. (eds) (1965) *A Behavioral Theory of Labour Negotiations*, McGraw-Hill, New York.

Webster, F. C. (1965) Modelling the Industrial Buying Process, *Journal of Marketing Research*, **2**, November.

Webster, F. E. (1992) The Changing Role of Marketing in the Corporation, *Journal of Marketing*, **56**, October, 1–17.

Webster, F. and Wind, Y. (1972a) A General Model for Understanding Organizational Buyer Behaviour, *Journal of Marketing*, **36**(2), April.

Webster, F. and Wind, Y. (1972b) *Organizational Buyer Behaviour*, Prentice-Hall, Englewood Cliffs, NJ.

Weigand, R. (1968) Why Studying the Purchasing Agent is not Enough, *Journal of Marketing*, **32**(1), January.

White, J. (1969) Some Aspects of the Marketing of Machine Tools in Great Britain, unpublished PhD thesis, UMIST.

Wilson, D. T. and Mummalaneni, V. (1986) Bonding and Commitment in Buyer–Seller Relationships: A Preliminary Conceptualisation, *Journal of Industrial Marketing and Purchasing*, **1**(3), 44–58.

Wind, Y. and Robinson, P. (1968) Generalized Simulation of the Industrial Buying Process,

Marketing Science Institute Working Paper, June 1968.

Zolkiewski, J. and Turnbull, P. W. (1999) A Review of Customer Relationship Planning: Does Customer Profitability and Portfolio Analysis Provide the Key to Successful Relationships, MSM Working Paper Series, Manchester, UK.

Zolkiewski, J. and Turnbull, P. W. (2001) Key Account Management, Customer Portfolios and Networks, Academic Rhetoric or Practitioner Tools?, *Journal of Selling and Major Account Management*, **3**(3), 55–70.

Further reading

Ames, B. C. and Hlavacek, J. D. (1984) *Managerial Marketing for Industrial Firms*, Random House, New York. Shows how modern marketing management concepts and methods can be applied in the realm of industrial marketing.

Chisnall, P. M. (1985) *Strategic Industrial Marketing*, Prentice-Hall, Englewood Cliffs, NJ. A clearly written and practical book by a respected British author. It provides a systematic discussion of the principal strategic factors in the marketing of industrial and organizational goods and services.

Ford, D. (ed.), Hakansson, H. and Turnbull, P. W. (1998) *Managing Business Relationships*, Wiley, Chichester. This book should be essential reading for all business-to-business marketing and relationship marketing courses. It provides a synthesis of interaction and network theory, yet is written in a practical, managerially oriented way.

Ford, I. D. (Editor on behalf of the IMP group) (2001) *Understanding Business Marketing and Purchasing*, 3rd edn, Academic Press, London. This book is aimed at students, instructors, researchers and practitioners who need to understand the complexities of business markets and the management challenges they provide. It brings together the most significant and up-to-the minute work of the IMP group and their research colleagues. The third edition has been extensively revised and includes many new readings. The book provides insights into the *interactions* between business buyers and sellers, and the *relationships* in which business marketing and purchasing take place. The book also sheds light on how business relationships form part of wider networks and provides understanding of the issues facing managers operating in these complex networks.

Ford, I. D. *et al.* (2002) *The Business Marketing Course*, John Wiley, Chichester. This book gives an excellent insight into understanding and managing business marketing. It offers an easily accessible introduction to the reality of business markets and is a useful basis for those taking a course on business marketing on undergraduate or MBA programmes. It should be useful for managers wishing to improve their skills in analysis and strategy development. The book is based on the ideas of the IMP group.

Hakansson, H. (ed.) (1982) *International Marketing & Purchasing of Industrial Goods: An Interaction Approach*, John Wiley, New York. The theoretical base of the interaction approach to industrial marketing is described in detail and then a series of international case studies are presented which show the application potential of the theoretical model.

Hutt, M. D. and Speh, T. W. (2001) *Business Marketing Management: A Strategic View of Industrial and Organizational Markets*, 7th edn, Harcourt College Publishers. Integrates the growing body of literature into an operational treatment of industrial marketing management.

La Placa, P. J. (1984) *Industrial Marketing Management: Cases and Readings*, Random House, New York. An excellent collection of major articles supplemented by a comprehensive selection of case studies. The material is, however, all American based.

Parkinson, S. T. and Baker, M. J. (1986) *Organizational Buying Behaviour*, Macmillan, London. A concise and readable text which uses European case material to develop and enhance the theoretical material.

Robinson, P. J., Faris, C. W. and Wind, Y. (1967) *Industrial Buying and Creative Marketing*, Allyn & Bacon, New York. Still worth reading as one of the early 'classics' in the field of industrial marketing.

Turnbull, P. W. and Valla, J. P. (eds) (1986) *Strategies for International Industrial Marketing*. Croom Helm, London. From the same group of authors as Hakansson, this book provides interesting and unusual insights into industrial marketing strategies.

Turnbull, P. W., Ford, I. D. and Cunningham, M. T. (1996) Interaction, Relationships and Networks in Business Markets: An Evolving Perspective, *Journal of Business and Industrial Marketing Management*, **11**(3/4), 44–62. This article provides a comprehesnive, critical and well-referenced review of the conceptual development of the IMP approach to business-to-business marketing. The evolution of thinking from the initial dyadic approach to relationships to the network concept is explained and the key elements of relationship network management are highlighted. An important review article for both the academic and practitioner audience.

Webster, F. E. Jr. (1992) The Changing Role of Marketing in the Corporation, *Journal of Marketing*, **56**(4), October. An interesting and important review of how, at last, the Americans have begun to recognize interaction and relationships. Perhaps the article should have been titled 'We get there eventually'!

Webster, F. E. and Wind, Y. (1972) *Organizational Buying Behaviour*, Prentice-Hall, Englewood Cliffs, NJ. One of the milestones in published texts on organizational buying behaviour.

CHAPTER 8

Marketing research

JOHN WEBB

In *Marketing Apocalypse* (Brown *et al.*, 1996), Michael Thomas characterized the postmodern environment as one where fragmentation, de-differentiation, hyperreality, pastiche and anti-foundationalism are the new orders of the day – though their theories would appear to be more relevant to industrialized markets than to the whole world.

In earlier days, when barter was the main system by which goods were swapped for money, or other goods, the close physical proximity of the principles facilitated a valid, meaningful and 'noise'-free process of communication. Both parties were satisfied with the result, otherwise it would not have been concluded; goods were accepted by one side at an agreed price, and the other side received an acceptable level of profit which enabled them to remain in business. Such a direct system exchange disappeared many years ago. The Industrial Revolution, which began in the late seventeenth century, and its invention of the factory system of mass manufacture generated a seismic shock, the results of which were to accelerate the rate of separation of those that required goods/services and those who sought to supply them. This distance, both 'psychic' and physical, continues to widen to the present day, as Schlegelmilch and Sinkovics (1998) say: 'The nature of change has changed. It is not evolving in comfortable incremental steps, but it is turbulent, erratic and often rather uncomfortable.'

Factors which have had, and continue to have, a catalytic effect on the parties in the exchange process include:

- an acceleration in the globalization of the provision of goods and services;
- an increasingly rapid rate of technological innovation and implementation;
- the fragmentation of markets into smaller and smaller niches;
- a population of consumers which is becoming better educated, more discriminate in its purchasing habits, and to have higher expectations of goods and services;
- the end of the Cold War, with a resultant increase in the number of independent trading nations;
- individual countries becoming ever more multicultural, with a concomitant rise in the number of specialized goods demanded by each cultural bloc;
- the increasing speed, on a global basis, with which information may be transmitted and goods delivered.

All of these facts, plus many others too numerous to mention, have made it more difficult for producing companies, and, to a certain extent, the middlemen, to fulfil one condition of marketing philosophy, which is that it is an exchange process between parties to their mutual satisfaction. Such a principle demands that producers should place the consumer at the focus of their business strategy.

However, if marketing is accepted as an exchange process – and as Bagozzi (1975) writes, 'in order to satisfy human needs, people and organizations are compelled to engage in social and economic exchange with other people and other organizations . . . they do this by communicating and controlling the media of exchange, which, in turn, comprises the links between one individual and another' – then companies must learn how, not only to communicate with their actual and potential customers, but also to listen to what they are saying. 'Saying' implies the use of language, and the 'language' to be used must be that of the consumer. Organizations must then, in the majority of cases (high technology being somewhat of a case apart), learn consumer-speak, to paraphrase Orwell.

Marketing research is a bundle of techniques which have been developed or annexed from other disciplines that, via the implementation of their new-found linguistic skills, enable companies to generate a stream of valid, timely and apposite information from and about customers concerning their thoughts and ideas about current goods/services and those to which they aspire. As Malo and Marone (2002) note: 'As corporate leaders redefine their priorities and company objectives, in these uncertain times the role that market research can play becomes more important . . . there exists a significant opportunity for marketing research to guide and support strategy development.'

The chapter will be structured as follows: after defining marketing research and detailing the types of research that are available, the process of marketing research will be analysed. The use of secondary data follows, and then the various types of primary quantitative research are described, together with questionnaires and

their design. The various forms of qualitative research are discussed, to be succeeded by a description of the way measurement, in theory and practice, is employed in the research process. The chapter will end with an exposition of the way attitudes are conceptualized and scaled, and how research results should be analysed and presented.

Definitions of the role of marketing research

Marketing research occupies a service function within organizations; its main function is to supply managements with reliable, valid, timely, relevant and current information.

A manager's ability to rely upon their past experience as a guide to the future has been constrained by the factors touched upon in the introduction to this chapter; the amounts of 'danger' in the business environment have increased, and change becomes the only constant. Managers have to take decisions with far-reaching consequences, opportunities must be grasped, threats avoided, markets segmented, target markets selected, control exercised, marketing plans implemented and monitored. But managers do not make decisions in a vacuum – there is an environment, outside their control, of which they must take due note. Marketing research can be viewed as the managerial senses through which managers can view the outside world and then use the imputs from their corporate eyes, ears etc. to moderate those processes over which they do have control, and thus yoke their internal actions with environmental changes.

Managements should learn to act proactively and not reactively; thus, the ability to identify, measure, evaluate and anticipate relevant change is a managerial function which is becoming increasingly critical to the long-term success of organizations. Data should be gathered in such a manner that the end result renders a valid, lifelike representation of the situation under investigation and not some cartoon-like image with distorted features.

There are many definitions of marketing research; here is a sample:

> Marketing research is the function which links the consumer, customer and public to the marketer though information – information used to identify and define market opportunities and problems; generate, refine and evaluate marketing actions; monitor marketing performance; and improve understanding of marketing as a process.
>
> Marketing research specifies the information required to address these issues, designs the method for collecting information; manages and implements the data collection process; analyses the results; and communicates the findings and their implications.
> (The American Marketing Association, 1988, *The Dictionary of Marketing Terms*)

> Marketing research is the systematic and objective approach to the development and provision of information for the marketing decision making process.
> (Kinnear and Taylor, 1996)

> Marketing research is the systematic and objective identification, collection, analysis and dissemination of information for the purpose of assisting management in decision-making related to the identification and solution of problems and opportunities in marketing.
> (Malhotra, 1999)

Through these definitions two key words recur: systematic and objective.

- *Systematic*: the research process should be well planned and organized, with rules set in advance of the project being instigated, to govern the types of data to be collected, the way in which it is to be collected, the system of analysis to be employed etc.
- *Objective*: the research should be conducted in a way that eliminates, as far as possible, bias and the corruption of data by subjectivity/emotion. Marketing research does not take place in a laboratory but it should, at all times, aim for 'scientific' objectivity.

Types of research

Webb (2002) classifies marketing research into three groups:

1 Exploratory research.
2 Conclusive research.
3 Performance monitoring (routine feedback) research.

Each stage in the decision-making process determines the appropriate class of research that should be employed.

Exploratory research

This is usually employed in the initial stages of the research project, when uncertainty/ignorance are at their highest. It is characterized by flexibility, an absence of formal structure and/or the desire to measure. It may be used to define the parameters of the environment in which the problems/opportunities exist, and to uncover those salient variables which are relevant to a full understanding of that environment. Exploratory research may alert the researchers to any temporal/seasonal effects which may have an impact upon the results (Radas and Shugan (1998) say: 'Virtually every product in every industry in every country is seasonal'); it may identify any dialects/jargon which may be the common currency, and it may allow an estimation to be made as to how easy/difficult it will be to carry out any subsequent research. Data sources may include secondary sources of data, observation, mini-surveys, interviews with experts and case histories.

Conclusive research

This can be employed to generate information to evaluate and to select course(s) of action. Conclusive research is formal, objective and systematic; it must include a definition of the objectives of the research, sampling plans, decisions as to what type(s) of survey method to use, possible systems of experimentation, and ways in which the data are to be analysed. The project must always exhibit a valid link between the information that is sought and the possible alternative courses of action under consideration.

Performance-monitoring research

This is a response to an environmental alteration, an opportunity to grasp or a threat to be avoided, which, once implemented, cannot be implemented and then merely ignored; the results of that implementation must be available to management. Monitoring research is the way in which comparisons can be made between what was planned and what actually happened. Not only should marketing mix variables and the salient variables of the environment be subjected to careful evaluation, but also such measures as sales, market share, profit and ROI.

Quantitative and qualitative research methods

These are not mutually exclusive but complementary research methods, each having advantages and disadvantages, which may be used to reduce the negative aspects of one system by the use of the other. The choice(s) of what system, or combination of systems, should be moderated by the specific factors which are found in each research problem and by the project's research objectives. Many research exercises are made up of elements from qualitative and quantitative research schools.

Carson *et al.* (2001) note that: 'The focus of many managerial research problems is on the unfolding of the process rather than the structure; and qualitative methods are particularly suitable as they combine the rational with the

intuitive'. Flick (1998) says that qualitative research is increasingly used because:

> rapid social change and the resulting diversification of life worlds are increasingly confronting social researchers with new social contexts and perspectives. These are so new for them that their traditional deductive methodologies – deriving research questions and hypotheses from theoretical models and testing them against empirical evidence – are failing in the differentiation of objects. Thus research is increasingly forced to make use of inductive strategies.

A comparison of the two methods is shown in Table 8.1.

The process of marketing research

The sequence of steps for marketing research is shown below:

1. Set the objectives of the research programme.
2. Define the research problem.
3. Assess the value of the research.
4. Construct the research proposal.
5. Specify the data collection method(s).
6. Specify the technique(s) of measurement.
7. Select the sample.
8. Data collection.
9. Analysis of the results.
10. Presentation of the final report.

Proctor (1997) says:

> A systematic approach to problem definition can help to direct marketing research staff in their efforts to obtain relevant information. It is also informative to all those people in the organization who will be affected by the findings and recommendations. Problem definition must take into account the situation of the company and its ability to take sound action.

Table 8.1 Comparison of qualitative and quantitative research methods	
Qualitative	*Quantitative*
Open-ended, dynamic, flexible	Statistical and numerical measurement
Depth of understanding	Subgroup sampling or comparisons
Taps consumer creativity	Survey can be repeated in the future and results compared
Database – broader and deeper	Taps individual responses
Penetrates rationalized or superficial responses	Less dependent on research executive skills or orientation
Richer source of ideas for marketing and creative teams	

Source: Gordon and Langmaid (1988).

Poorly thought-out marketing decisions can cause major problems; sometimes with disastrous consequences.

He proceeds to quote Rickards' (1974) goal-oriented approach to problem definition which 'employs identifying needs, obstacles and constraints in the search for an adequate definition of the problem':

1 Write down a description of the problem, then ask:
   (i) What do we need to accomplish (needs)?
   (ii) What are the obstacles?
   (iii) What constraints must we accept to solve the problem?
   (iv) Redefine the problem, bearing the above in mind.

Secondary data

Secondary data, which consist of previously published material, should always be consulted before commencing primary research.

Newsom-Smith (1988) says that secondary data can:

1 Provide a background to primary research; if the research has already been conducted by someone else, why repeat it, if the current research objectives are met? Even if it doesn't fulfil exactly what is needed, it may help determine key variables that any subsequent primary research will have to investigate; it may help determine sampling methods/sample sizes; alert researchers to key personnel in the environment, and illustrate active trends.
2 Act as a substitute for field research; primary research can be very costly and secondary data may help save unnecessary expenditure in that published data may fully meet all the current research objectives. Even if not all questions are answered, then the scope of the primary research may be substantially reduced. A cost–benefit analysis should be made to weigh the cost of further costly primary research against the advantages of less detailed, but cheaper, secondary research.
3 Baker (1991) says that some research may only be carried out realistically by the use of

secondary data, i.e. attempting to establish trends in market behaviour. Longitudinal studies are unrealistic propositions for primary research, engendering a reliance on published, historical data. Much of these data concerning market structures and performance comes from censuses – a method which may provide superior quality data to that gained by sampling a population – the preferred method used in most field studies. Secondary data may also set the boundaries and establish the state of the environment in which primary research will be undertaken.

4   Acquisition studies; acquisition has been a popular strategy for companies to follow in recent years. Predator companies, who do not wish to alert their 'prey', could hardly mount large primary field studies without drawing attention to themselves. Thus, secondary research may be used to gain information on other companies.

But before using secondary data, researchers should ask themselves:

- Are the secondary data relevant?
- What is the cost to acquire these data?
- What is the availability of these data?
- To what extent may the data be biased?
- How accurate are the data?
- Are the data sufficient to meet the current project's research objectives?

Sources of secondary data

Luck and Rubin (1987) state that: '. . . a good rule in all research is parsimony; using only meaningful data' – good advice with the plethora of data which are currently available.

The first place to start a search for 'meaningful data' is within the organization itself. With the increasing use of Management Information Systems, functional departments are now much more likely to have collected and stored data in a form readily accessible to research personnel.

Internal sources of data may be divided as follows:

- *Accounts* – contain information on customers' names and addresses, types and quantities of products purchased, costs of sales, advertising, manufacture, salaries etc., discounts etc.
- *Sales records* – contain information on markets, products, distribution systems.
- *Other reports* – contain information on trade associations and trade fairs, exhibitions, customers' complaint letters, previous marketing research reports, conferences.

If internal sources prove inadequate for the intended task, then external data sources have to be consulted. Where, though, does one start to make sense of the vast amounts of externally published data? Start with the general and then gradually focus on to the specific. Thus, in an unfamiliar research setting, one should start with those guides, either printed or held on computer, which offer suggestions as to the general direction in which to proceed. From such 'directory of directories' publications, e.g. ABI-Inform, Bookbank and Official Publications of the UK, one may begin with, for example, general industry data, and proceed through specific industry data, via market/category information (as given by Retail Intelligence (Mintel)) down to specific company/product data, as in Mintel Market Intelligence Reports.

Trained librarians offer an excellent way of navigating a course through these huge databases, and are especially useful when first consulting computer databases, which can be very complex – as mistakes in their operation can be costly. Then there is the Internet, about which Kumar *et al.* (1999) say: 'The Internet's forte is probably its advantages in researching secondary information'. In its favour, they add, are its very wide scope, coverage and low cost.

But, as Walters (2001) notes, marketing research will only be truly international when literature in languages other than English is evaluated.

Quantitative primary data

Primary data are those which are collected to fulfil the demands of the current research project, and have to be gathered should secondary sources of data fail to provide the information necessary to meet the research objectives.

If individuals hold the data necessary to answer the questions posed by the research objectives, then they may be questioned, observed or invited to become a member of a continuous research panel.

Survey research

Survey research consists of personal interviews, telephone interviews and mail questionnaires. Each have advantages and disadvantages and the optimum choice, or combination of them, is mostly dependent upon matching individual survey methods with the situation-specific demands of the research objectives. Kinnear and Taylor (1996) say that the following are the main factors to be considered when making this choice: available budget, the nature of the problem, the constraints of time, sample control (the ability of the chosen method to reach the stipulated sample), the quantity of data to be collected and the quality of the data to be collected. No author states only one method may be used for a particular research project; in many situations, several, or all, methods may have to be employed.

Survey methods are good for gathering data on: past and present behaviour; attitudes and opinions; respondent variables; knowledge.

Personal interviews

Personal interviews are classified against their degree of structure and directness: structure is the degree of formality/rigidity of the interview schedule; directness refers to the degree to which the respondent is aware of the purpose of the research.

Unstructured–indirect methods are rarely used in marketing research; unstructured–direct and structured–indirect will be covered in the section on qualitative primary research. Structured–direct is the method most often used in research surveys.

Structured–direct survey methods permit the researcher: to reduce respondent anxiety (increasing rapport and, possibly, the response rates); to guide respondents through complex questionnaires; and, within boundaries, to ask for ambiguous answers to be clarified.

Question wording and order are fixed, with answers being recorded in a standard manner, thus reducing possible interviewer bias – potentially troublesome when multiple interviewers are being used. Standardized formats allow for the use of less skilled interviewers, thus reducing costs. Also, pictures, products, signs etc. may be displayed to refresh respondents' memories or to demonstrate some action.

However, personal interviews may be: time consuming, thus the cost per completed interview is high compared with mail questionnaires and telephone interviews; the data gathered may lack depth and richness because of the fixed questionnaire format. Questions are usually closed because of the problems associated with recording the answers to open-ended questions.

Telephone interviews

An administered questionnaire delivered via the telephone. The advantages are: low cost per completed questionnaire; centrally located telephone banks reduce travel times and costs, and permits firm administrative control of interviewers, thus reducing the potential for interviewer bias and error; quicker results may be produced, compared with mail questionnaires and face-to-face interviews; allows for samples to be drawn, easily, from a wide geographical area.

However, there is a problem in establishing rapport with respondents during a call's short duration; this may result in them not being relaxed during the interaction or in allowing them, easily, to terminate the interview. Thus, questions must be short and rapidly able to engage the interest of the interviewee. Respondents may confuse a 'research' call with cold-call telephone sales 'pitch' and terminate the call for fear of being sold something. The sample may not be fully representative of the population, as telephone ownership is not universal (though this reason grows less important as time passes). It is impossible to use visual stimuli to 'jog' respondents' memories or to demonstrate some action.

Mail questionnaires

Mail questionnaires use no interviewer, so that, as a potential source of error, is removed.

Field staff may be reduced to a minimum, resulting in a low cost per completed questionnaire if response rates are high. The relatively anonymous method of data collection may confer on certain respondents sufficient confidence to answer what, to them, are 'embarrassing' questions. They can cover, economically, wide geographical areas. They may gain access to certain areas of the survey's population who refuse to answer personal and telephone interviews. Respondents may fill in the mail questionnaire in their own time, thus reducing some pressure that a few respondents may experience because of the presence of the interviewer; it also allows respondents to consult their files, notes, account records etc.

Its disadvantages are that even though addressed to named individuals, there is no way of knowing who, exactly, filled in the questionnaire. Questions may be read in advance. Therefore, the ability to control the sequence of their presentation is removed; respondents can see exactly where the questions are leading merely by turning to the end of the document. There is no one to explain/interpret complicated/ambiguous questions,

resulting in the possibility that such questions are either omitted or the answer is guessed. Questionnaires which are long, or which are perceived to be long, may either not be answered at all or will have large numbers of questions unanswered. High non-response rates will mean that the cost per completed questionnaire can become prohibitively high.

The e-questionnaire

Questionnaires delivered by e-mail are an increasingly popular research method. The questionnaire is sent, via the Internet, to designated individuals, completed and then returned. Kumar *et al.* (1999) say that their advantages include that questionnaires are delivered (or redelivered, if lost) almost instantaneously, responses and feedback are quick, they are cheaper than mail questionnaires, the messages are read, usually, only by the addressee, and questionnaires can be filled in at the convenience of the reader (unlike telephone interviews). However, they also note that security of e-mail is lower than with more traditional communications, and it is almost impossible to guarantee anonymity because replies will include the name and Internet address of the respondent.

Panel/syndicated research

Data may be gathered from individuals, households, industrial buyers, firms etc. who agree to provide data to research agencies on a regular basis; such data may include information concerning consumer and/or industrial products and store audits. Many panels are computerized; Taylor Nelson AGB uses a sample of 8500 homes who have agreed to provide data on a range of consumer goods. Panellists scan their purchases with a hand-held bar-code reader and the results are sent electronically to the research company for processing and analysis (Crouch and Housden, 1996).

Data sources may be classified into six main groups:

- Consumer data.
- Wholesale data.
- Advertising evaluation data.
- Retail data.
- Industrial data.
- Media/audience data.

Advantages of panel research

Data are generated continuously, so trends such as market share and brand switching etc. may be established, and, as the need to keep generating samples is reduced, the potential effects of sampling error are lessened. Evidence suggests that higher response rates will be enjoyed when compared with rates from ad hoc surveys, and the results are likely to be more accurate as panel members become experienced in recording their purchases. Data may be generated for a comparatively smaller outlay, when compared with the costs of mounting an ad hoc survey. Panels/syndicated research can provide data on competitor activities. Because of its continuous nature, this research method is likely to produce results quicker than with an ad hoc survey.

Disadvantages of panel research

The main disadvantages of panel research rests with the sample itself; once the initial sample has been selected, by whatever means (usually probability-based sampling), selected panellists may refuse to join, thus distorting the representativeness of the sample. Of those panellists that do agree to join, some, over time, may drop out, again 'upsetting' the sample's representativeness, and it may be difficult to find new panel members with equivalent characteristics. Some panel members may have to be replaced when they get too old; age itself is not the problem, but the panel organizers have to maintain a panel that is representative of the general public's

demographics. Panel members *may* alter their purchase patterns as a result of being surveyed, but the effect may be reduced by (i) a reasonable turnover of panel members and/or (ii) disregarding their submissions for the first 2–3 months of membership.

One form of continuous research which is rapidly gaining popularity is that of the 'loyalty card' system operated by large supermarket chains. Customers register with the company by filling in an application form which asks for details such as name, address, post-code, marital status, number of children etc. The members of the scheme are rewarded with bonus points for a set unit of expenditure; the customers are rewarded with discounts or products redeemed by surrendering a certain number of points, and the company gains access to a huge database.

Observation

All members of a society are observers, though usually only on a casual basis – an insufficiently scientific approach for it to be used as a marketing research technique, as it may be subject to large and unreliable amounts of subjectivity and bias on the part of the observer. Therefore, before observation may be used in research, it must be made more objective and rigorous. Observation may not immediately spring to mind as a marketing research method, but there are two situations where it may prove most useful:

1 Where it is the only way of gathering certain types of data, e.g. it might be difficult for respondents to remember their exact journey through a multi-floored department store and the amount of time they spent in each section, but the answer could be obtained by using a trained observer.
2 It may be used to confirm that the results gathered by other methods are valid, though here it may not be thought of as a technique in its own right, rather as half of a two-pronged investigation.

The following three conditions (Tull and Hawkins, 1993) should be met if observation is to be used successfully:

1   The action must be accessible and overt; thus, the measurement of feelings, motivation, attitude etc. is ruled out.
2   Actions should be frequent, repetitive and predictable.
3   Actions should encompass a reasonably short time span.

Modes of observation are classed according to four main factors: naturalness, openness, structure and directness.

Questionnaires and their design

A questionnaire is an ordered set of questions which may be employed in a variety of research situations. They may vary in structure, i.e. the amount of freedom which is allowed to the respondent in answering the questions. Highly structured questionnaires, with set answer formats, are usually easier to administer, answer and analyse; unstructured questionnaires are usually harder to administer, need more thought on the respondent's part and require considerable interpretative skills in their analysis. The situation-specifics of the research context will condition, largely, the type of questionnaire to be employed.

The format of the questions may be dichotomous (a yes/no type answer), multiple-choice (where respondents are invited to select one or a number of responses from a predetermined list) or open-ended (where the respondents reply using their own words). Though these questions are more difficult to interpret, they go some way in eliminating interviewer bias.

When deciding on the questions, Webb (2000) suggests that the following questions be asked:

(i)   Is the question necessary?
(ii)   Will the respondent comprehend the question?

(iii) Is the question sufficient to elicit the required data?
(iv)   Does the respondent have the necessary data to answer the question?
(v)   Is the respondent willing/able to answer the question?

When phrasing the questions, the questionnaire design should ensure that the vocabulary used is appropriate for the respondent being questioned, and that only the clearest and simplest words are used. Also, vague/ambiguous questions should be avoided, as should biased words or questions which might 'lead' the respondent. Those questions which contain estimates or which rest on implicit assumptions may be difficult to analyse, and should only be asked if absolutely necessary. All questionnaires should undergo rigorous pre-testing on a sub-sample of potential respondents before use.

Qualitative research methods

Not all research objectives may be met by the use of a question and answer format, good though these methods are at gathering data concerning knowledge of facts, incidents of past/present behaviour patterns etc.; other areas of human activity do not fall into such convenient and relatively easily accessed categories. Such areas include respondents' attitudes, motivations, opinions, feelings etc., as well as other types of question which might cause respondents to experience heightened levels of anxiety or embarrassment, or where they might feel a difficulty in putting their answers into words.

Qualitative research methods are employed to uncover other ways of gaining access to such types of data; they seek to answer the 'why' and 'how' questions, rather than the 'what happened' or 'how many' types of enquiry.

A comparison between quantitative and qualitative methods has already been given by

Gordon and Langmaid (1988) – where they say that qualitative research is used optimally in situations which will increase understanding, expand knowledge, clarify use, generate hypotheses, identify a range of behaviours, explore/explain motivations and attitudes, highlight distinct behavioural groups, and provide an input into future research. Qualitative research may also be used for basic exploratory studies, new product development, creative development, diagnostic studies and tactical research projects.

The three main techniques are: group discussions, individual depth interviews and projective techniques.

Group discussions

The driving force of this research tool is the dynamic interaction of the members of the group. Group discussions usually last between one and three hours, and employ between six and twelve respondents. Carson *et al.* (2001) say that group discussions may be used for:

1 Interpreting quantitative results obtained previously.
2 Stimulating new ideas and product concepts.
3 Searching for the potential for problems with new programmes, services or products.
4 Generating impressions of products, programmes, services, institutions or other interests.
5 Learning how respondents talk and construct their own understanding of the situation of interest.

Gordon and Langmaid (1988) report that group discussions may be inappropriate under the following circumstances:

(a) in intimate/personal situations;
(b) where there are strong pressures to conform to social norms – peer pressure;
(c) where detailed case histories are required;
(d) where the group is likely to be too heterogeneous with respect to the

idea/product etc. of interest for a meaningful discussion to be able to take place;
(e) where 'complex psychosocial issues' are involved;
(f) where it is difficult to assemble the required sample, e.g. where people are physically widely scattered.

Relaxing, pleasant surroundings are conducive to a free flow of ideas and help to reduce respondents' anxiety. The chair of the discussion (moderator), usually a key member of the research team which has set up the exercise and who will be pivotal in its analysis, should rapidly establish an easygoing but workmanlike rapport with all the respondents.

As group discussions can generate huge amounts of data, which will need lengthy, and consequently expensive, analysis, it is vital that they are carefully planned and administered.

Malhotra (1999) gives the following guide for planning and conducting a group discussion:

1 Set the objectives of the research programme and problem definition.
2 Specify the objectives for the qualitative research.
3 State the objectives to be answered by the group discussion.
4 Write a screening questionnaire to exclude group members who do not fulfil the research requirements.
5 Develop a moderator's outline.
6 Conduct group discussion.
7 Analyse the data.
8 Summarize findings and plan follow-up research or action.

Developing the moderator's outline is a very important step, and will involve detailed debate between the client, the research team and the moderator. This guide will ensure that all the required areas of interest are covered. It will also go some way to improve the reliability of the research method, a problem which may occur if more than one moderator is going to be involved with the project.

Advantages of group discussions

Cost and speed; since a large number of respondents are being 'processed' simultaneously, data collection and analysis are quicker than for individual interviews.

Many individual decisions are made in a social context – groups provide that context. Society's requirements and perspectives are part of the discussion process and not merely an 'optional extra'.

Group discussions allow for the observation, and analysis, of non-verbal communications: this will enable trained moderators to assess the validity of the respondents' statements.

A group of people, in concert, will generate a far wider range of opinions, insights and information, because of stimulation and/or synergism, than they might have done when examined as individuals. Some respondents may feel 'comforted' by the group and less exposed than they would have done in an individual interview; their anxiety being reduced, the method will enable them to produce more valid responses. The unstructured or semi-structured nature of the discussion allows the moderator to probe behind respondents' answers which are incomplete or ambiguous. As many observers can become involved in the collection of the data, apart from the moderator, a higher level of reliability should result from the analysis.

Disadvantages of group discussions

Only a small number of respondents can become involved, therefore the question of unrepresentativeness arises; thus, the ability to 'project' the results onto a population is curtailed. This, however, does not invalidate the method as a research tool, as the method is usually only used, as in exploratory research, where generalizations concerning a population are not required.

Contrary to the 'comfort' factor already mentioned, some respondents may feel over-awed/inhibited by the presence of the other respondents, causing them to act in an atypical manner. Shyer members of the group might be allowed to be 'shouted down' by an ineffective moderator, by those with more dominant personalities; thus, an important role of the moderator is to 'bring out' the shyer members of the group and to restrain the enthusiasm of the more extrovert members. If the group reacts in a negative sense against the moderator, then the chances of generating valid, useful data are much reduced.

Individual depth interviews

Between the poles of structured–direct interviews (the administered questionnaire) and the unstructured–indirect lies the topic of this section – the individual depth interview, that Kahan (1990) calls 'an unstructured personal interview which uses extensive probing to get a single respondent to talk freely and to express detailed beliefs and feelings on a topic ... to discover the more fundamental reasons underlying the respondents' attitudes and behaviour'.

Smith (1998) includes the following categories of depth interviews:

- *Mini-depth interview* – lasts approximately 30 minutes and not as wide ranging as a full in-depth interview.
- *Semi-structured interview* – employs pre-set questions which the interviewer cannot change, but the respondents may reply using their own words.
- *Paired interview* – an interview conducted on two respondents, e.g. the stipulator and user of a product or service.
- *Triangular interview* – three respondents are interviewed, e.g. when investigating leisure, a theatre-goer, member of a gymnasium and amateur cricketer are interviewed.

Group discussions and depth interviews are techniques whose main aim is to seek out, to delve, to try to understand and to explore;

therefore, a flexibility of approach is essential – the interviewer must be able to alter and adapt to changing situations which may arise during the interview.

Depth interviews have been found to be most beneficial where:

1 The discussion topic has the potential to be embarrassing, stressful or of a confidential nature.
2 There is a complex situation, and the need is to uncover attitudes, motivations, beliefs or feelings.
3 Peer pressure may cause respondents to act in an atypical manner (e.g. when they admit to subscribing to certain societal norms when, in reality, they do not).
4 The interviewer needs to ascertain the chronology or a case history of a certain decision process (e.g. when trying to understand complex buying behaviour patterns).
5 The situation is new and/or complex and exploration of a topic, rather than measurement, is the prime objective.

The nature of the relationship between interviewer and subject in an in-depth interview is of prime importance; it is a one-to-one occasion, with no third party to 'protect' either side. Thus, the establishment of a good rapport is an essential interviewer function, and questions aimed at cementing the relationship should come first. Then it is recommended that the general questions gradually give way to the specific, where the heart of the interview lies.

Advantages of individual interviews

Great depth/richness of data, with the ability to attach, directly, an opinion to a single individual, something which may not be so easy in a group discussion.

The lack of peer pressure allows respondents to express unconventional, maybe anti-social, opinions, without fear of sanctions, mockery or embarrassment. Interviewers have

the opportunity to develop close rapport with the subject, creating a level of trust which should encourage a freer flow of valid and useful information.

Disadvantages of individual interviews

They are very costly in terms of time/money, both to conduct the interview and to analyse the results, and because of this high cost, it is usually possible only to work with small samples, thus limiting the ability of the research to generalize about the results.

There may be problems in finding interviewers with the requisite skills.

Because of the highly personal nature of the interchange between the interviewer and the respondent, and because of the unknowable amounts of subjectivity which may 'colour' the proceedings, it may be difficult to compare the information gathered by one interviewer with that from another.

Projective techniques

Appropriated from psychology/psychiatry, projective techniques rely on the principle that the way people organize and respond to relatively ambiguous stimuli will give trained observers an insight into the respondent's perceptions of the outside world and their reactions to it.

Kidder (1981) says that projective techniques are useful in:

> ... encouraging in respondents a state of freedom and spontaneity of expression where there is reason to believe that respondents cannot easily evaluate or describe their motivations or feelings or where topics on which a respondent may hesitate to express their opinions directly for fear of disapproval by the investigator or when respondents are likely to consider direct questions as an unwarranted invasion of privacy or to find them threatening for some reason.

Projective exercises may be classed as structured–indirect research techniques and they receive their name from the way in which respondents 'project' their feelings, attitudes, beliefs etc. onto a third party or object, emotions which might have remained hidden if the chosen research technique had tried to gain access to their ideas/opinion by means of more direct questioning etc. It is not a technique whereby measurements are made, but more one where those emotions which the majority of the population might have difficulty in articulating are uncovered. Piotrowski and Keller (1993) say that they are a popular method of personality assessment, on a worldwide basis, because of the absence of standardized objective tests.

Projective techniques may be used:

(a) to explore and generate hypotheses, which may then subsequently be tested by more quantitative methods;
(b) to expose feelings, beliefs and behaviour patterns which would have remained hidden if a more 'direct' research method of investigation had been used.

There are a great many techniques used in this method of research, but they may be conveniently grouped under the following headings: completion, association, construction, choice ordering and expressive techniques.

Advantages of projective techniques

They are very useful in exploratory studies where emotional guidance, feelings etc. are sought and where inputs to be used in hypothesis generation are required.

They enable researchers to gain access to data which they might have been denied if a more direct, interrogative, technique had been employed.

They may be used to 'break the ice', and help in establishing rapport in the initial stages of qualitative studies.

Disadvantages of projective techniques

They are expensive. To be of use, highly skilled research workers need to be employed; also, it is only possible to employ small samples using these methods, so the ability to generalize about the results is severely restricted.

They are time consuming, both to administer and to analyse the results.

Some respondents may be too shy to take part in the exercises and refuse to join in – therefore, non-response may be a problem.

There are many opportunities for the results to become 'contaminated' by measurement error; the role of the researcher thus becomes of great importance in the reduction of such error.

The research process and measurement

Having chosen the type, or types, of data collection method to be used to meet the research objectives, market researchers now have to choose the system(s) of measurement to be used. Measurement is part of everyday life; food is bought by weight, petroleum/cooking oil/beer is bought by volume, fabric by length – each product being dispensed by using a characteristic (weight, volume, length etc.) by which certain amounts of the object may be isolated.

In marketing research, measurements are also common; for example, the research objectives might stipulate that the project should ascertain the number of people in a certain age group who buy a certain newspaper, or the number of companies using certain distribution systems over a stipulated time period. Such measurements are relatively easy to make as the characteristics of interest are overt, easily accessed, and of a unitary status, i.e. they only have one dimension – number, length, age grouping etc. However, other marketing research projects are not intended to measure such tangible factors; some measurements are far more complicated because of the ambiguous nature of the answer to the question: 'In order to meet the objectives of the research, what is to be measured?'

Torgerson (1958) said measurement is '. . . the assignment of numbers to objects to represent amounts of degrees of a property possessed by all of the objects'. Now while it is a relatively simple process to see how such a definition applies, for example, to age (number of years since birth), weight (number of units of gravitational attraction) etc., it is not such a clear-cut process when it is necessary to measure those factors, important in a social research setting, which are far more covert. For example, there is no universally agreed system for 'the assignment of numbers' to a respondent's attitude towards a certain brand of coffee, or their motivation in purchasing one brand of motor car in preference to another.

In measuring abstract constructs such as beliefs, motivations, feelings, attitudes etc., marketing research may have to express them 'in terms of still other concepts whose meaning is assumed to be more familiar to the inquirer' (Green *et al.*, 1988). To evaluate a research situation, there is a requirement to measure factors/variables, overt and covert, which are relevant, but there is also a need to know *what* to measure. Attitude, for example, can be defined in many ways, some of which have more and some less relevance to a specific situation, because attitude is a multidimensional concept. In making a definition of attitude, some of these components are excluded, thus researchers must note that measurement is never fully able to translate reality into sets of numbers – representation can only ever be incomplete.

Variables are factors relevant to a research situation which vary and in doing so affect the state of that situation. For example, many research studies are concerned with consumer responses to proposed changes in a product's price: thus, the dependent variable is consumer response; the independent variables might include packaging, the price of competing brands/products and brand loyalty. The research objectives will have stipulated what the outcome of interest is – the dependent variable (here, consumer response). There may also have been implicit assumptions as to what the independent variables are, but the implicit needs to be made explicit. One way to accomplish this is to construct a model of the research situation. If there is insufficient information to do this, then some additional research may be required – exploratory, for example. It may also be possible to determine the significant variables by means of a thorough analysis of the literature – secondary data search.

Southern (1988) writes that there are three important components of the measurement process:

1 Measurement is a process; it is controlled and open, not arbitrary or intuitive.
2 Measurement translates qualities into quantities; the numbers may then be manipulated. However, numbers themselves have no meaning, and those who manipulate them must exercise care if the validity of the relationship between number and characteristic is to be preserved.
3 Measurement has formal rules which may vary depending upon the manipulation, but once set, they must be followed consistently if reliability of data is to be guaranteed.

Green *et al.* (1988) say that number systems have:

1 *Order.*
2 *Distance* – differences between numbers are ordered.
3 *Origin* – number systems will have a unique origin indicated by zero.

Scales in marketing research

There are four main levels of measurement – nominal, ordinal, interval and ratio – and each makes different assumptions regarding the way in which the numbers reflect the situation under measurement.

Nominal scales assign numbers to objects, variables or people to show that they belong to some stipulated category, categories which are mutually exhaustive and mutually exclusive.

In this scale, numbers have no mathematical value, they merely show that the people, objects etc. belong to a nominated group. Thus, people who read *The Guardian* might be assigned to the value 7 and those who read *The Times* to the value 456. The only mathematical function which can be undertaken is to count the number of objects inside each category. Bus numbers, bank accounts and football team shirt numbers are all nominal scales.

Ordinal scales rank order objects/people etc. according to the amount of a property which it/they possess. But respondents in a research programme must be able to discriminate between items of interest with respect to an attribute, i.e. they must have the ability to say that this tea, for example, tastes better than that tea. They are saying that this tea, the preferred one, has more of the attribute 'good taste' than the other does – their second choice. Ordinal scales do not enable researchers to know/infer by how much one item is preferred over the others in the same category. Thus, it is not possible to say if the difference between the first and second and between the second and third is the same, more, or less. Students' examination results, first place, second place etc., is an example of an ordinal scale.

Interval scales possess order and distance, but not a unique origin, i.e. their zero point is arbitrary. Thus, meaningful statements about the distance between two objects on a scale may be made. It is permissible to say that the difference between scale points 7 and 8 is the same as the difference between scale points 57 and 58. However, interval scales do not allow researchers to make meaningful statements about the value of a scale point being a multiple of another value on the same scale.

Ratio scales possess order, distance and a unique origin indicated by zero. All mathematical operations are allowed here, so it can be said that a reading of 80 on a scale is four times a reading of 20 on the same scale. Three feet is three times larger than 1 foot and 10 pounds is twice as large as 5 pounds. Measures such as height, weight and volume are examples of ratio scales.

Attitudes and their measurement

Marketing research constantly seeks to measure respondents' attitudes towards, for example, a change in packaging, price, a new product, politicians etc. But attitude measurement can sometimes be a rather difficult concept for such a practical subject as marketing research to come to terms with. How have attitudes been defined?

Two of the most useful and illuminating definitions are as follows:

> . . . an individual's enduring perceptual, knowledge-based, evaluative and action-oriented processes with respect to an object or phenomena.
>
> (Kinnear and Taylor, 1996)

> . . . mental states used by individuals to structure the way they perceive their environment and guide the way they respond to it.
>
> (Aaker *et al.*, 2001)

While there are many definitions other than the above, there is broad agreement that an attitude is a learned mental state of readiness, a way in which individuals construct their own worlds such that when confronted with a certain stimulus they act in a certain manner.

Attitudes are not held to be the only cause of human behaviour, there are many other factors having an impact upon the individual at the moment at which the behaviour under investigation becomes manifest. Attitudes, though internal to the subject, are conditioned through external experience, but experience is not a random or arbitrary process, but one which is organized through a process known as learning.

Components of attitude

Attitudes have three components:

1 *Cognitive* – represents an individual's awareness and knowledge about an object, person etc. They say, 'I have heard about Brand X' or 'I believe that Brand X will carry out this function'.
2 *Affective* – represents an individual's feelings (good/bad etc.) towards an object etc. and is usually expressed as a preference. They say, 'I do not like Brand C' or 'I like Brand D better than Brand F'.
3 *Behavioural* – represents an individual's predisposition to action prior to the actual decision being made, or their expectations of possible future actions towards an object etc.

When researching the link between attitude and behaviour, consultants may try to use the information in one or two ways:

1 By measuring the cognitive and affective components to *predict* future possible behaviour.
2 By altering the cognitive and affective components in order to *influence* future behaviour.

The measurement of attitudes

Cook and Sellitz (1964) put forward, among others methods, the following way in which measured responses may give an indication as to an individual's attitude. They used techniques which rely on a relatively direct style of question which respondents answer in a way which enables an inference to be made as to the strength and direction of the attitude towards the research's object.

Measurement scales may be divided into two groups: rating scales and attitude scales. Rating scales measure a single component of an attitude, a respondent typically indicating their attitude to an object by means of a placement along a continuum of numerical values or of ordered categories. Scales can be labelled with verbal or numerical descriptors, but in using the former, the researcher should be aware that some respondents may not think that there is the same psychological difference between a 'very' and an 'extremely' as does the constructor of the scale; a pre-test should check on this. By allocating a numerical value to the object, depending on the strength with which they hold a given attribute, measurement scales may be used to measure:

1 A respondent's overall attitude towards an object, product, person etc.
2 The degree to which something possesses a certain attribute.
3 A respondent's feeling towards a certain attribute.
4 The importance with which a respondent invests a certain attitude.

Non-comparative rating scales

Respondents are asked to rate, assign a number, to the object of interest in isolation, there being no standard against which measurements are made. Respondents mark their attitude position on a continuum (a graphic scale), or they may chose a response from a limited number of ordered categories (an itemized scale).

For example, the question might be: 'How do you like Brand X of chocolate?'

Comparative rating scales

Respondents make an assessment of the object of interest against a stated standard.

For example, 'How does Brand X of chocolate compare with Brand Y?'

Rank order scales

Respondents are asked to rank order a list of objects/items against a stated criterion, e.g. taste, power etc. Rank order scales are ordinal, thus respondents are only able to show the order of their preferences; the research cannot infer anything about the 'distances' between the items, i.e. it is not possible to say by how much the first item is preferred to the second etc.

Constant sum rating scales

This method overcomes the drawbacks of rank order scales. The respondent is allocated a constant sum (they may be expressed in currency or some other units), usually a round number, 100 units etc., and asked to allocate them between the given items in a way which reflects the object's attributes under investigation. This not only shows the rank order of the items, but also the size of the preference distances.

Attitude scales, which combine many rating scales, are an attempt to overcome the unrepresentativeness that may arise from inferring an individual's overall response to some object etc. by measuring their attitude to only a single aspect of that object etc.; attitude scales try to measure several facets of an individual's attitude to an object, person etc.

Likert or summated scales

Devised in 1932, the Likert or summated scales require that respondents indicate their degree of agreement or disagreement with a number of statements concerning the attitude being measured. Their responses are given a numerical value and/or sign to reflect the strength and direction of the respondent's reaction to the statement. Thus, statements with which the respondent agrees are given positive or high values, while those with which they disagree are given negative or low marks. Scales may run, for example, from 1 to 5, from 5 to 1 or from +2, via zero, to –2. Statements should give the respondent the opportunity to express clear,

unambiguous statements, rather then neutral, ambiguous ones.

Semantic differential scales

These are arguably the most widely used of all attitude scales. Respondents show the position of their attitude to the research object on a seven-point itemized scale, thus revealing both the strength and direction of the attitude. The extremities of the continuum are 'anchored' by a pair of polarized adjectives or adjectival statements.

For example, respondents are asked to record their attitude towards a certain law firm:

Unfriendly	....	Friendly
Modern	....	Old fashioned
Efficient	....	Inefficient
Slow	....	Fast
Pleasant	....	Unpleasant

Osgood *et al.* (1957), who devised the scale, developed some 50 pairs of bipolar adjectives grouped to measure three fundamental components of attitude:

1 *Evaluative* – negative/positive, good/bad.
2 *Activity* – active/passive, fast/slow.
3 *Potency* – weak/strong.

If phrases rather than words are used, then the scale will have more meaning for respondents (Dickson and Albaum, 1977). Luck and Rubin (1987) recommend that no side of the scale should be exclusively reserved for either the positive or the negative aspect of the pairs, as this tends to allow respondents to tick only down one side – the 'halo' effect.

Semantic differential scales may be analysed in two main ways:

- *Aggregate analysis* – where the score is summed for each respondent for all pairs of words/statements, resulting in a numerical value of their attitude. Individual aggregate scores may then be compared with other individuals with respect to the same object, or two or more objects may be compared with respect to the same individual or group of individuals.

- *Profile analysis* – involves calculating the arithmetic median or mean value for each pair of adjectives for an object for each respondent or respondent group. The profile so derived can then be compared with the profile of the object.

The principle disadvantage of semantic differential scales lies in their construction. For valid results, scales need to be made of truly bipolar pairs of adjectives/phrases; the problem arises when some of the pairs/phrases chosen may not be true opposites in the respondents' minds.

The Stapel scale

This is a modified semantic differential scale, and uses a unipolar 10-point verbal rating scale with values from +5 to –5 which measures both the strength and direction of the attitude simultaneously.

For example, respondents are asked to evaluate how well each of the adjectives describes the object under test, e.g. Sheila's apple pie tastes:

+5	+5	+5
+4	+4	+4
+3	+3	+3
+2	+2	+2
+1	+1	+1
Rich	Bitter	Expensive
–1	–1	–1
–2	–2	–2
–3	–3	–3
–4	–4	–4
–5	–5	–5

Stapel scales are easy to administer and require no test that the adjectives are truly in polarity.

Sampling

Without the ability to extract a sample of a population, as opposed to conducting a census, the majority of marketing research projects could not take place. There are four main reasons for this:

1 *Cost* – except where the populations are very small, it is usually cheaper to take a sample rather than conduct a census in the same population.
2 *Time* – a census, compared with a sample for a given population, is always going to be larger (hence it will take longer to collect the results); thus, by the time the results have been collected and analysed, the situation under investigation might have changed. Samples may be extracted and analysed much quicker than a census, for a given population.
3 *Accuracy* – defined as the degree of precision with which a measure of a characteristic in a sample compares with the measure of the same characteristic in the population from which the sample was drawn. In sampling, accuracy is affected by: (1) Sampling error (caused by selecting a probability sample from a population which is not representative of that population); such error can be reduced by increasing the size of the sample. (2) Non-sampling error (all other errors in a marketing research project whose origin is not based in sampling error).
4 *The destructive nature of measurement* – one cannot carry out a census on a bottle of whisky (for quality control) and still have any product for sale. Thus, sampling is the only alternative if quality assurance is required. Some forms of measurement destroy; for example, one can only measure a population's initial reaction to an advertisement once. But, by extracting non-overlapping samples, such an evaluation may be repeated.

Probability sampling techniques

The units which constitute a probability sample are selected randomly, with each unit having a known chance of selection. Thus, before a probability sample can be drawn, the project will need to define a sampling 'frame' for the population. Such a frame will need to ensure that each unit is included only once, and that no unit is excluded; thus, all units have an equal chance of selection. The frame should cover the entire population and be convenient to use.

A probability sample should attempt to be representative of the entire population, but it can never be an exact replica. However, by applying the rule of probability, generalizations concerning the population may be made and calculations made about the degree of confidence with which the results can be viewed.

Sample error, for probability samples, stems from the variability of the sample and/or the size of that sample.

Simple random sampling

Units are chosen at random from the population. Individual units are assigned a number, a sample of these numbers is then selected either by using a 'lottery' system, or by the use of random number tables.

The method is simple to use and it obeys the laws of probability; however, it may produce samples which are not representative of the population.

Stratified random sampling

This method accepts the variability of the population and, by stratifying it before the sample is taken, tries to reduce its potential unrepresentativeness. Stratifiers, which may be geographical, demographic etc., are imposed on the population like a grid, dividing it into groups whose members, inside each 'cell', are as alike as possible with respect to the stratifier. Stratified random sampling adopts the position that each group/stratum is a population in its

own right and then extracts a sample, by simple random means, from each of them.

In *proportionate stratified sampling*, the size of each sub-sample taken from a particular stratum is proportionate to the size of that stratum in the population. Thus, if 25 per cent of the population is aged between 35 and 45, then 25 per cent of the sample should be composed of people in that age group. In *disproportionate stratified sampling*, the proportion of a characteristic, as possessed by the population, is not reflected to the exact extent in the size of the sub-sample. Such a deliberate 'distortion' of the size of the sub-sample may improve the quality of the data if certain strata have an unusually large influence in the situation under investigation and need to be given a more significant role. Here, not every unit has an equal chance of selection, but the chance of selection is still known, thus the laws of probability still rule and appropriate weighting(s) can be used when calculating the results.

The method's major drawback is in finding stratifiers relevant to the research situation.

Cluster sampling

This is similar to stratified sampling in that the total population is divided into strata, but it differs in that instead of sampling from *each* subgroup, a *sample* of the strata is taken, with simple random sampling then taking place inside each of the selected groups. Thus, while in stratified sampling each stratum represents a particular subset of the population, in cluster sampling each stratum should be a miniature representation of the full population. It is a method particularly useful in cases where the population is dispersed over wide geographical areas.

A particular form of cluster sampling is called *multistage sampling* and involves more than the single stage of the cluster sampling system. If, after dividing a country into various areas (counties, regions etc.), they are found to have greatly varying sizes of populations, then they are sampled using a system called the probability proportionate to size method. Thus, if a county has five times the population of the other counties, then in the sampling process it should be allocated five times the chance of being selected. The first stage thus results in a number of counties etc. drawn from the population of counties. Then the research will select from these areas a number of, for example, cities, and again they will be selected using the probability proportionate to size method. These stages may be repeated until the research arrives at the desired final sample. The method has the advantage that the process delivers a sample chosen at random, but concentrated in certain geographical areas, useful when the costs of travel and communication can be high. It also means that probability sampling may be used when, at the macro level, there is no sampling frame. When the final stage has been completed, and the research has arrived at the micro level, sampling frames will be available – city maps, electoral rolls etc.

Non-probability sampling techniques

The researcher does not know the chances of a unit's selection if non-probability sampling techniques are employed. Therefore, the ability to generalize about a population, using the laws of probability, is much reduced and it is not possible to calculate the degree of confidence in the results. The sample is chosen at the convenience of the consultant or to fulfil the demands of some predetermined purpose.

Convenience sampling

Here the sample is chosen for the convenience of the research worker. A street interviewer who needs to sample 50 people, for example, might question the first 50 people who walk past the street corner where the interviewer is standing. It is a quick method and carries the minimum cost. It is a method useful in exploratory research.

Judgement sampling

This makes an attempt to ensure a more representative sample than that gathered using convenience techniques. Research consultants use their expertise, or consult an expert, to evaluate populations and to make recommendations as to which particular units should be sampled. With small populations, accurate assessments and guidance as to a unit's selection, judgement sampling can render samples with less variable error than might result with a sample chosen using a simple random technique, though this cannot be conclusively proved.

Purposive sampling

This does not usually aim for representativeness. Here the choice of the sample is made such that it should meet certain preconditions deemed appropriate to the fulfilment of the objects of the research. Thus, a project might stipulate that the top 50 Professors of French be interviewed as part of the project, so there is no true 'sampling', merely the need to contact those units the research has already delineated.

Quota sampling

This attempts to reflect the characteristics of the population in the chosen sample, and in the same proportions. From national statistics, researchers gather the percentages for such 'stratifiers' as age groupings, income levels etc. and use them to construct 'cells'. This results in statements such as '23 per cent of the population is female, aged between 30 and 40 and earning £12 000–15 000 per annum'. The sample would then be collected, and 23 per cent of it would have to fulfil those demands. Quota controls must be available, easy to use and current. Quota 'stratifiers' shouldn't be used merely because they are available – they must be relevant to the project. This method may be cheaper to operate than a probability-based method, it is quick to use and relatively simple to administrate – it does not require a sampling frame. However, there is the possibility that the interviewer shows bias in the way the individual units are selected and in the difficulty that may arise in uncovering relevant and available quota controls.

Probability versus non-probability sampling techniques

Tull and Hawkins (1993) provide the following list of factors that are worthy of consideration when choosing a sampling method:

1   Are proportions and/or averages required or are projectable totals needed?
2   Are highly accurate estimations of population values necessary?
3   How large might non-sampling error be? What size of error due to frame choice, non-response, measurement and population specifications is likely?
4   Will the population be homogeneous or heterogeneous with respect to the characteristic of interest?
5   What will be the cost if the results are above/below the required error tolerance?

They say that '... the need for projectable totals, low allowable errors, high population heterogeneity, small non-sampling errors and high expected costs of error favour the use of probability sampling'.

Size of sample

The size of a sample depends, in the main, upon the required degree of accuracy that the research objectives demand. This will depend upon:

1   The degree of variability in the population – the more heterogeneous that population, the larger the sample size required.
2   The presence of population subgroups – the sample must be large enough to allow for a valid analysis of these.

Sample size estimation depends upon:

- *Judgement* – rests on the experience of the research consultant. But research workers should beware of making an arbitrary choice, ignoring such factors as cost, value and the required level of accuracy – this is the method of last resort.
- *What can be afforded* – though commonly used, this method ignores the value of the information to be collected, only looking at the cost. For example, a small sample may be more useful, though of a higher cost per unit, than a larger sample if the collected information is of a high value.
- *Required size per cell* – used in quota and stratified sampling techniques. It is usual to accept, as a minimum, 30 units per cell before any statistical analysis can proceed. Thus, if there are two age groups and five geographical areas to be sampled, 10 cells will result, hence a sample of 300 units is required.
- *Statistical methods* – sample sizes may be calculated using the formula:

$$\frac{\sigma}{N} = \frac{\text{Required level of accuracy}}{\text{Level of confidence}}$$

where σ = standard deviation and N = size of sample.

Analysis of the results

The researcher will now be in possession of data from both primary and secondary sources; it must now be processed such that it is possible to draw appropriate conclusions.

In commencing the analysis, two questions need to be answered:

- With reference to the research objectives, what meanings should be obtained?
- What statistical methods should be employed to obtain those meanings given the way in which the data were collected?

Luck and Rubin (1987) define statistical analysis as '. . . the refinement and manipulation of data that prepares them for the application of logical reference'.

After the statistical analysis stage, comes that of interpretation – where data are transformed or refined into a state which will highlight their meaning; inductive and deductive processes are utilized.

Beveridge (1957) says that in inductive reasoning one starts from the position of the observed data and then proceeds to develop a generalization that explains the observed interaction/situation. Deductive reasoning, on the other hand, moves from the general to the specific, by applying a theory to a particular case. Data interpretation should be concluded as objectively as possible. To ensure this, the following points are important:

1 Honest/objective interpretations are aided by not exaggerating or distorting the findings.
2 Interpreters should remember that a small sample will limit the opportunity to generalize about a large population.
3 One should not try to reach a particular conclusion.
4 The validity and reliability of the data must be ensured before interpreting the results, and there should be no confusion between facts and opinion.

Thus, the steps in the analysis of data are as follows:

1 *Put the data in order*
Raw data generated by primary and secondary research are not in a suitable state for immediate interpretation; they need to be transformed.

Editing involves, for example, checking the questionnaire to ensure that all the questions have been answered and that the respondent has given unambiguous answers. If answers are missing or ambiguous, then steps should be taken to either fill them in, or respondents questioned to resolve areas of confusion.

Coding involves the assignation of a number, usually to each particular response for each question; questionnaires which are pre-coded will save a great deal of time at this stage. Open-ended questions also require coding, and this is usually carried out by expert analysts, who review a representative sample of all the questionnaires and devise appropriate categories to which individual answers can be assigned.

Tabulation involves arranging the data such that their significance may be appreciated; data are placed into appropriate categories which are relevant to the research objectives. Tabulation may be carried out manually, mechanically or electronically. Such tables are very well suited to variables measured by ordinal or nominal scales, because of the limited number of response categories. Cross-tabulation is a more developed form of the one-way tabulation described above, and the system allows an investigation into the relationship between two or more key variables by counting the number of responses that occur in each of the categories.

2 *Make a survey of the data*
Unprocessed data need to be transformed. The most common way to compress data is to calculate the data's central tendency: mean, median or mode. Other, more complicated, measures of central tendency include such measures of dispersion or range, variance and standard deviation, and, if two or more distribution dispersions are being compared, the coefficient of variation. The results of the analysis do not need to be presented in purely mathematical forms; graphical display is a very useful method of showing, for example, the frequency differences between different categories. Histograms, line and scatter graphs and pie charts have all been found to be better at communicating results than bald tables of numbers.

3 *Select an appropriate method of analysis*
If the research objectives cannot be reached by survey and/or cross-tabulation of the data and

more sophisticated methods of analysis are required, then consideration should be given as to which particular analytical techniques will provide the appropriate information. However, there is a vast array of available techniques, so some thought needs to be given to the way in which the most appropriate method(s) is (are) selected.

Luck and Rubin (1987) offer the following scheme:

1 What is the technique required to show?
   • A common request is to show whether the results are significant, i.e. are there significant differences between various groups or could the results have occurred by chance because only a sample of the population was under investigation, not the entire population.
2 What scale was used to measure variables?
   • Only certain arithmetic manipulations are allowed on certain types of scale – it depends upon what level of measurement was reached.
   • Non-metric scales, where the data were qualitative rather than quantitative, include nominal and ordinal scales.
   • Metric scales work in real number systems and include ratio and interval scales.
3 Parametric and non-parametric data.
   • Parametric data are those which are distributed around a mean/central value in a symmetrical manner, as in a normal distribution, and have been collected, at least, using an interval scale and may be analysed using probabilistic tests of statistical significance.
   • Non-parametric data have a distribution profile which does not conform to the normal curve of probability and appropriate tests assume that the variables have been measured using nominal or ordinal scales.

4 *Number of variables to be analysed*

Univariate analysis: where a single variable is analysed in isolation.

Bivariate analysis: occurs where some form of association is measured between two variables simultaneously.

Multivariate analysis: this investigates the simultaneous relationships between three or more variables.

5 *Dependence and independence*
Analysis may involve an investigation into the relationship between variables. By relationships is meant that changes in two or more variables are associated with each other. It may be important to be able to calculate by how much the independent variables are responsible for variations in the dependent variable.

6 *How many samples are involved?*
The choice of an appropriate statistical test depends upon whether the data are being tested to measure (a) the significant differences between one sample and a nominated population, (b) the significant differences between two related or independent samples, (c) the significant differences amongst three related or independent groups, or (d) correlation and their significance tests.

Presentation of the final report

Research reports should say what they are supposed to say and do so in a style appropriate to the intended readership. Those which are intended for a technically educated readership may be written using specialist terms and may discuss, in detail, the complex issues of the research process. Those reports intended for a more general readership should not be used as an opportunity to impress with an overt display of technical language/jargon and subject matter. General readers are interested in the results, not in the way they were reached, though, of course, the appropriate amount of background to the project will need to be provided.

Conclusion

Marketing research should not be carried out merely for its own sake; it is a business technique to be used as a service, not as a means of providing employment for marketing researchers! But the process does need to be managed by senior management. It may be thought of as the equivalent of a taxi-cab service and its relationship with the passengers. The taxi-driver (marketing researcher) must be able to drive and know how to reach a certain intended destination. The passenger (client) must know where they wish to go and have the ability to pay the fare. Close co-operation between the parties will result in a mutually beneficial contract; as Zaltman (1998) notes: 'Researchers must engage managers and customers more actively in the research undertaking by enabling them to represent fully their thinking'.

References

Aaker, D. A., Kumar, V. and Day, G. S. (2001) *Marketing Research*, 7th edn, John Wiley, New York.

American Marketing Association (1988) in Bennet, P. D. (ed.), *The Dictionary of Marketing Terms*, American Marketing Association, Chicago, IL.

Bagozzi, R. P. (1975) Marketing as Exchange, *Journal of Marketing*, **39**, 32–39.

Baker, M. J. (1991) *Research for Marketing*, Macmillan, London.

Beveridge, W. I. B. (1957) *The Art of Scientific Investigation*, 3rd edn, William Heinemann, London, pp. 84–85.

Brown, S., Bell, J. and Carson, D. (1998) *Marketing Apocalypse*, Routledge, London.

Carson, D., Gilmore, A., Chad, P. and Gronhaug, K. (2001) *Qualitative Marketing Research*, Sage, London.

Cook, S. W. and Sellitz, C. (1964) A Multiple-indicator Approach to Attitude Measurement, *Psychological Bulletin*, **62**, 36–55.

Crouch, S. and Housden, M. (1996) *Marketing Research for Managers*, The Marketing Series, Butterworth-Heinemann, Oxford.

Dickson, J. and Albaum, G. (1977) A Method for Developing Tailormade Semantic Differentials for Specific Marketing Content Areas, *Journal of Marketing Research*, February, 87–91.

Flick, U. (1998) *An Introduction to Qualitative Marketing Research*, Sage, London.

Gordon, W. and Langmaid, R. (1988) *Qualitative Marketing Research*, Gower, London.

Green, P. A., Tull, D. S. and Albaum, G. (1988) *Research for Marketing Decisions*, Prentice-Hall International, London.

Kahan, H. (1990) One to ones should sparkle like the gems they are, *Marketing News*, 3 September, pp. 8–9.

Kidder, L. H. (1981) *Sellitz, Wrightsman and Cook's Research Methods in Social Relations*, 4th edn, Holt, Rinehart and Winston.

Kinnear, T. C. and Taylor, J. R. (1996) *Marketing Research; An Applied Approach*, 5th edn. McGraw-Hill, New York.

Kumar, V., Aaker, D. and Day, G. S. (1999) *Essentials of Marketing Research*, John Wiley, New York.

Luck, D. J. and Rubin, D. S. (1987) *Marketing Research*, 7th edn, Prentice-Hall International, London.

Malhotra, N. K. (1999) *Marketing Research: An Applied Orientation*, 3rd edn, Prentice-Hall International, London.

Malo, K. and Marone, M. (2002) *Marketing News*, 21 January, Chicago, IL.

Newsom-Smith, N. (1988) Desk Research, in Worcester, R. and Downham, J. (eds), *Consumer Market Research Handbook*, 3rd edn, McGraw-Hill, London.

Osgood, C. E., Suci, G. J. and Tannenbaum, P. H. (1957) *The Measurement of Marketing*, University of Illinois, Urbana, IL.

Piotrowski, C. and Keller J. W. (1993) Projective Techniques; an International Perspective, *Psychological Reports*, **72**.

Proctor, T (1997) *Essentials of Marketing Research*, Pitman, London.

Radas, S. and Shugan, S. M. (1998) Seasonal Marketing and Timing in New Product Introduction, *Journal of Marketing Research*, **35**, August, 296–315.

Rickards, T. (1974) *Problem Solving Through Creative Analysis*, Gower, Aldershot.

Schlegelmilch, B. B. and Sinkovics, R. (1998) Viewpoint: Marketing in the Information Age – Can We Plan for the Unpredictable?, *International Marketing Review*, **15**(2, 3), 162–171.

Sellitz, C., Jahoda, M., Deutsch, M. and Cook, S. W. (1959) *Research Methods in Social Relations*, Methuen, London.

Smith, D. (1998) Designing Market Research Studies, in *ESOMAR Handbook of Market and Opinion Research*, 4th edn, ESOMAR, Amsterdam.

Southern, J. (1988) *Marketing Research*, University of Strathclyde, Distance Learning Unit, M.Com.

Torgerson, W. S. (1958) *Theory and Methods of Scaling*, John Wiley, New York.

Tull, D. S. and Hawkins, D. I. (1993) *Marketing Research: Measurement and Method*, 6th edn, Macmillan, London.

Walters, G. P. (2001) Research at the 'Margin': Challenges for Scholars Working Out of the 'American–European' Domain, *International Marketing Review*, **18**(5), June, 468–474.

Webb, J. R. (2000) Questionnaires and their Design, *The Marketing Review*, **1**, 197–218.

Webb, J. R. (2002) *Understanding and Designing Marketing Research*, 2nd edn, Thomson Learning, London.

Weiers, R. M. (1988) *Marketing Research*, 2nd edn, Prentice-Hall International, London.

Zaltman, G. (1998) Rethinking Marketing Research: Putting People Back In, *Journal of Marketing Research*, **34**, November, 424–437.

CHAPTER 9

Quantitative methods in marketing

LUIZ MOUTINHO and ARTHUR MEIDAN

Introduction

Marketing was one of the last of the major functional areas of management activity to be entered by quantitative methods and techniques in a systematic way, and only in the last four decades or so was any significant progress achieved. This relative lag of quantitative methods progress in marketing was attributed to a number of factors:

1 *The complexity of marketing phenomena.* This is due to the fact that when stimuli are applied to the environment, the responses tend to be non-linear, to exhibit threshold effects (a minimum level of stimulus needs to be applied before response occurs), to have carry-over effects (for example, response to this period of advertising will occur in future) and to decay with time in the absence of further stimulations.

2 *Interaction effects of marketing variables.* This means that the impact of a single controllable marketing variable is difficult to determine due to interactions of the variable with the environment and also with other marketing variables. Indeed, most of the variables in marketing are interdependent and interrelated.

3 *Measurement problems in marketing.* It is often difficult to measure directly the response of consumers to certain stimuli and therefore indirect techniques are often used. An example is the use of recall measures to ascertain the effectiveness of advertisements.

4 *Instability of marketing relationships.* The relationship between marketing responses and marketing decision variables tends to be unstable due to changes in taste, attitude, expectations, and many others. These factors make continuous market measurements and revision of decisions crucial to marketing.

There are several ways in which quantitative methods can be used in marketing. One of these is through the classification of marketing into decision areas which confront the marketing manager and which include product development, pricing, physical distribution, salesforce, advertising and consumer behaviour. However, it is thought to be more appropriate first to classify the techniques which are used in marketing and to fit in the situations where these models are used most frequently.

In this way, most of the models and techniques can be analysed. Their validity can be judged from their usage, how accurately they represent the problem environment, their predictive power, and the consistency and realism of their assumptions.

In selecting an appropriate method of analysis, two major factors should be taken into consideration: first, whether the variables analysed are dependent or interdependent and, second, whether the input data are of a metric or non-metric form. Metric data are measured by interval or ratio scales, while non-metric data are only ordinal scaled. The dependent variables are those which can be explained by other variables, while interdependent variables are those which cannot be explained solely by each other.

Marketing variables are usually interdependent. For example, a firm's objectives are usually interdependent with marketing mix variables; profits usually depend on sales; market share depends on sales; firms' growth depends on profits and sales and vice versa, etc. Also, firms' marketing mix variables, such as price, promotion, distribution and product, are interdependent.

Since marketing research is very often a multivariate analysis involving either dependent or interdependent variables, the major groups of techniques that can be used are as shown in Figure 9.1.

1 *Multivariable methods*. So called because the various techniques attempt to investigate the relationships and patterns of marketing decisions that emerge as a result of the interaction and interdependence among main variables at the same time.

2 *Regression, correlation and forecasting techniques*. **Regression and correlations** are methods that can be employed in inferring the relationships among a set of variables in marketing. **Forecasting methods** are mainly applied in forecasting sales and market demand. Sales forecasting methods are a function of an aggregation of non-controllable environmental variables and

marketing effort factors, which have to be taken into consideration.

3 *Simulation methods* are a group of techniques which are appropriate to use when the variables affecting the marketing situation (such as competition) require complex modelling and are not amenable to analytical solutions. The importance of the simulation technique in marketing is that it offers a form of laboratory experimentation by permitting the researcher to change selected individual variables in turn and holding all the others constant.

4 *Fuzzy sets* could be used for modelling consumer behaviour, marketing planning, new product testing, etc., by determining the rank and size of the possible outcomes.

5 *Artificial intelligence (AI) techniques* are relatively very recent tools for simulating human logic. There are two main models in this set of techniques: expert system – requiring user intervention to accommodate changes within the model; and neural network – less 'rigid' than expert system, facilitating 'retraining' (mainly via addition of new input and output data).

6 *Statistical decision theory or stochastic methods* represent stochastic or random responses of consumers, which allow a multitude of factors that might affect consumer behaviour to be included in the analysis. This means that market responses can be regarded as outcomes of some probabilistic process. Essentially, there are two main uses of these methods: to test structural hypotheses and to make conditional predictions.

7 *Deterministic operational research methods* are OR techniques looking for solutions in cases where there are many interdependent variables and the research is trying to optimize the situation. A classical example of such a situation in marketing is when a company producing various products (or parts) is selling them through two different channels which vary with respect to selling costs, typical order sizes, credit policies, profit margins, etc. Usually in such cases the

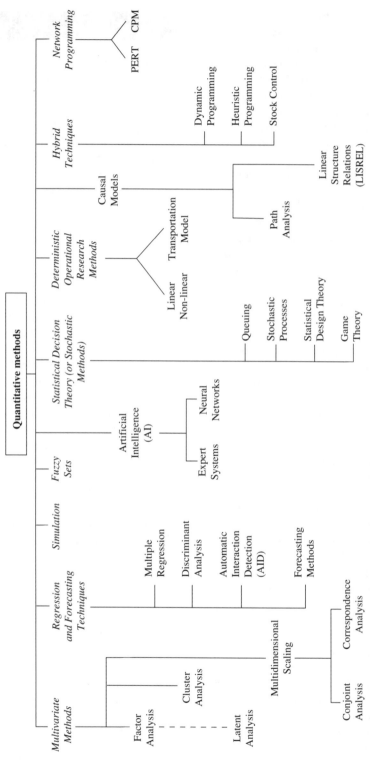

Figure 9.1   The main quantitative methods in marketing – a taxonomy

company's major objective is to maximize total profits by establishing optimal sales target volumes and marketing mixes for the two channels (or customer segments) subject to the existing limiting constraints.

8 *Causal model* consists of two main analytical models for *testing* causal hypotheses (path analysis and LISREL). **Path analysis** is used on those occasions when some of the variables are unobservable or have modest reliabilities. (This tool should not be confused with the critical path method (CPM), which is one of the networking programming models discussed below.) LISREL is of paramount importance in marketing situations, when we want to investigate both measurement and cause, i.e. structural components, of a system (e.g. in a consumer behaviour study).

9 *Hybrid models* are methods that combine deterministic and probabilistic (stochastic) properties (e.g. dynamic programming, heuristic programming and stock control). These models are particularly useful in handling distribution problems, as explained below.

10 *Networking programming models* are generally used for planning, scheduling and controlling complex projects. There are two fundamental analytical techniques: the critical path method (CPM), and the performance evaluation and review technique (PERT). The differences between the two are, first, that the PERT acknowledges uncertainty in the times to complete the activities, while the CPM does not. Second, the PERT restricts its attention to the time variable while the CPM includes time–cost trade-offs. These two together are also called critical path analysis (CPA) techniques.

The ten sets of methods above in no way exhaust the quantitative methods in marketing. The selection of techniques presented in this chapter is based either on their particular current relevance of handling many marketing problems or/and because of their potential in marketing research and analysis.

The multivariate methods in marketing are probably the predominant techniques of the last two decades, not only because of the wide variety of flexible techniques available in this category, but mainly because they answer the most pressing need of marketing research, which is to obtain the ability to analyse complex, often interrelated and interdependent data. There are six main multivariate sets of methods: factor analysis; latent analysis; cluster analysis; multidimensional scaling; conjoint analysis; and correspondence analysis.

Factor analysis

Factor analysis (FA) is primarily a tool to reduce a large number of variables to a few interpretable constructs. The method is used for exploration and detection of patterns in the data with the view to obtaining data reduction, or summarization, which could be more amenable for reaching decisions and taking marketing management actions. The software for FA is readily available and is standard in any SPSS (Statistical Package for Social Science) package. The input data are collected from respondents and the main limitations are how many factors to extract and the labelling of the emerging factors. Factor analysis could be used for analysing consumer behaviour, market segmentation, product/service attributes, company images, etc.

Latent analysis

Latent structure analysis (LA) is a statistical technique somewhat related to factor analysis, which can be used as a framework for investigating causal systems involving both manifest variables and latent factors having discrete components. Latent structure analysis shares the objective of factor analysis, i.e. first, to extract important factors and express relationships of variables with these factors and, second, to classify respondents into typologies.

The latent class model treats the manifest categorical variables as imperfect indicators of underlying traits, which are themselves inherently unobservable. The latent class model treats the observable (manifest) categorical variables as imperfect indicators of underlying traits, which are themselves inherently unobservable (latent). This technique is appropriate for the analysis of data with discrete components.

Essentially, LA attempts to 'explain' the observed association between the manifest variables by introducing one (or more) other variables. Thus, the basic motivation behind latent analysis is the belief that the observed association between two or more manifest categorical variables is due to the mixing of heterogeneous groups. In this sense, latent analysis can be viewed as a data-unmixing procedure. This assumption of conditional independence is directly analogous to the assumption in the factor-analytic model.

The main advantage of latent analysis is that it could be used for investigating causal systems involving latent variables. A very flexible computer program for maximum likelihood latent structure analysis, called MLLSA, is available to marketing researchers. Latent class models have great potential and no doubt will be used more frequently in marketing investigations in the future.

One of the major limitations related to LA concerns the estimation problem, which previously made this class of models largely inaccessible to most marketing researchers. This problem was later solved by formulating latent class models in the same way as in the general framework of log-linear models. Latent structure analysis models have been used in segmentation research, consumer behaviour analysis, advertising research and market structure analysis.

One of the best papers in this field is by Dillon and Mulani (1989). A number of latent structure models have been developed

(DeSarbo, 1993) for problems associated with traditional customer response modelling (for example, for more regression, conjoint analysis, structural equation models, multidimensional scaling, limited dependent variables, etc.). Such latent structure models simultaneously estimate market segment membership and respective model coefficients by market segment, to optimize a common objective function.

Cluster analysis

Cluster analysis is a generic label applied to a set of techniques in order to identify 'similar' entities from the characteristics possessed by these entities. The clusters should have high homogeneity within clusters and high heterogeneity between clusters, and geometrically the points within a cluster should be close together, while different clusters should be far apart.

Cluster analysis is, in a sense, similar to factor analysis and to multidimensional scaling in that all three are used for reduced-space analysis. That is, all three methods could facilitate the presentation of the output data in a graphical two-dimensional format that is easier to comprehend and analyse. Cluster analysis is primarily used for segmentation and for decisions on marketing strategies towards different segments and markets (Saunders, 1994), or in situations which involve grouping products, brands, consumers, cities, distributors, etc. The main limitations of this technique are that there are no defensible procedures for testing the statistical significance of the emerging clusters and often various clustering methods yield differing results. There are several types of clustering procedures. In Figure 9.2 a hierarchical clustering of variables associated with a marketing strategy for hotels is presented (Meidan, 1983). The diagram presents the (level of) aggregation (or clusters) of variables that are product (i.e. hotels) characteristics of a strategy, as defined by the suppliers (i.e. hotel managers). Cluster 2 strategy includes variables that indicate that hotels adopting this strategy are more 'aggressive'

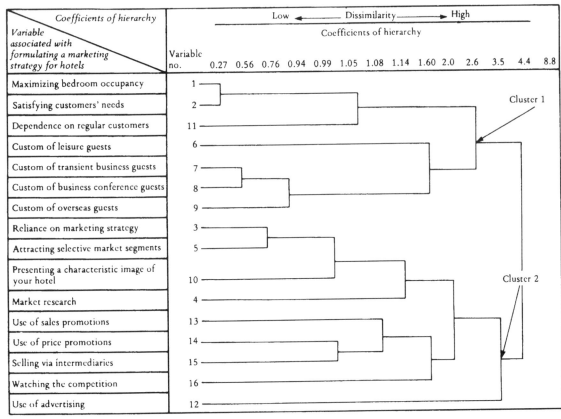

Figure 9.2 Hierarchical clustering of variables associated with a marketing strategy for hotels
Source: Meidan (1983).

using, to a larger extent, marketing tools and techniques, while cluster 1 strategy is more 'passive'. Low coefficients of hierarchy (or low dissimilarity) indicate high relationships or high similarity. For example, variables 1 and 2 are highly correlated, that is, they aggregate early, at a coefficient of 0.27. In contrast, variable 12 (use of advertising) is highly dissimilar to other variables and associates with the remaining coefficients in cluster 2 only at the 3.5 level. A possible explanation of this could be that hotels adopting the marketing strategy indicated by cluster 2 use an alternative communication mix and/or other marketing tools (e.g. variables 13, 14, 15, 4, 5, 10, etc.).

Multidimensional scaling

Multidimensional scaling (MS) is a measurement technique concerned mainly with the representation of relationship, differences, dissimilarities (or similarities), substitutability, interaction, etc. among behavioural data such as perceptions, preferences and attitudes. The input data on various objects (variables) which are to be analysed are collected from the subjects (respondents) by a number of direct or indirect questions. The questions can be either of Likert type (i.e. a five-point scale questionnaire indicating the level of agreement or disagreement to statements) or, alternatively, asking each of the respondents to rank the variables to be investigated (for example, products, brands, characteristics, etc.). When the number of variables investigated is n, the number of all possible relationships among these variables (along k dimensions) is $n(n-1)/2$. In order to visualize and quantify the overall attitudinal data of these respondents with regard to the n variables investigated along (k) dimensions, the data should be inputted onto one of the available software packages.

The solution (output) of the MS computer program is of a metric nature, consisting of a geometric configuration, usually in two or three dimensions. The distances between the variables (objects) and/or respondents (subjects) investigated, which are presented as points in the configuration, represent the (dis) similarity, substitutability, relationship, etc. Multidimensional scaling is used particularly in its non-metric version, non-metric multidimensional scaling (NMS). The advantage of NMS in relation to, say, factor or cluster analyses is the ability to see the entire structure of variables together and to obtain metric output from attitudinal (non-metric) input data. In addition, NMS enables easy comprehension of the results, since the decision maker can visualize and assess the relationships among the variables.

Multidimensional scaling and non-metric multidimensional scaling in particular have been successfully applied in investigating various marketing problems (for example, market research, sales and market share, market segmentation, determination of marketing mix, consumer buyer behaviour, brand positioning, branch preference, export marketing, etc.). An introduction to multidimensional scaling is presented by Diamantopoulos and Schlegelmilch (1997). Discussion on when to use NMS techniques in marketing research is offered by Coates *et al.* (1994).

Conjoint analysis

This technique is concerned with the joint effects of two or more independent variables

on the ordering of a dependent variable. Conjoint analysis, like multidimensional scaling, is concerned with the measurement of psychological judgements, such as consumer preferences. Products are essentially bundles of attributes, such as price and colour. For example, conjoint analysis software generates a deck of cards, each of which combines levels of these product attributes. Respondents are asked to sort the cards generated into an order of preference. Conjoint analysis then assigns a value to each level and produces a 'ready-reckoner' to calculate the preference for each chosen combination. The preference logic of conjoint analysis is as follows. The respondent had to base his or her overall ranking of the versions on an evaluation of the attributes presented. The values that the individual implicitly assigns each attribute associated with the most preferred brand must, in total, sum to a greater value than those associated with the second most-preferred brand. The same relationship must hold for the second and third most-preferred brands, the third and fourth most-preferred brands and so forth. The computation task then is to find a set of values that will meet these requirements.

Potential areas of application for conjoint analysis include product design, new product concept descriptions and testing, price–value relationships, attitude measurement, promotional congruence testing, the study of functional versus symbolic product characteristics, and to rank a hypothetical product against existing competitors already in the market and suggest modifications to existing products which would help to strengthen a product's performance.

The limitations of conjoint analysis are quite clear when, for example, we are using this technique to predict trial rate. These include:

1 Utility measurement rather than actual purchase behaviour is used as the predictor.
2 The configuration of elements used in the concepts may not be complete.

3 In the case of a new product that differs substantially from its principal competitors, the same elements cannot be used for aggregating utilities.

4 The effects of promotion and distribution effort on competitive reaction are not considered.

5 Perceptions from a concept statement and those from the actual product may differ.

6 New products may take several years to reach the market, during which time customer preferences and competitive products may have undergone substantial changes. Conjoint analysis has been applied widely on consumer research (Vriens, 1994), in advertising evaluation (Stanton and Reese, 1983) and other commercial uses (Cattin and Wittink, 1982).

Correspondence analysis

Correspondence analysis (CA) is a visual or graphical technique for representing multi-

dimensional tables. It can often be impossible to identify any relationships in a table and very difficult to account for what is happening. Correspondence analysis unravels the table and presents data in an easy-to-understand chart. One approach for generating maps uses cross-classification data (e.g. brands rated as having or not having a set of attributes) as a basis (Hoffman and Franke, 1986). In this approach both brands and attributes are simultaneously portrayed in a single space. This technique is particularly useful to identify market segments, track brand image, position a product against its competition, and determine who non-respondents in a survey most closely resemble. Correspondence analysis shows the relationships between rows and columns of a correspondence or a cross-tabulation table. This method can be used for analysing binary, discrete or/and continuous data. CA belongs to the family of multidimensional scaling techniques and could be employed to scale a matrix of non-negative data to represent points

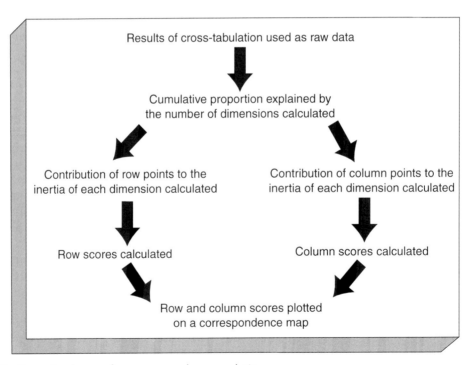

Figure 9.3   Procedural steps for correspondence analysis

(described by rows or columns) in a lower dimensional space. It facilitates both within- and between-set squared distance comparisons (Carroll *et al.*, 1986), and the results can be represented graphically and used as such in marketing investigations.

Figure 9.3 shows the different stages of correspondence analysis. The results of a cross-tabulation are used as raw data in a correspondence analysis. The specific mathematics involved in correspondence analysis can be found in Greenacre (1984).

Figure 9.4 presents the output of a study that maps out how bank branch personnel in various roles see themselves (internal perceptions) and what are their colleagues' (external) perceptions with regard to the 27 selling bank branch functions identified (Meidan and Lim, 1993). The figure represents the output of a study where respondents were asked who they felt were mainly responsible for the

selling function of 'Identifying customers' needs' in a bank. The responses of various function holders are indicated by the triangular signs on the map (e.g. counsellor, manager, business development officer, etc.). The respondents themselves were grouped into three categories indicated by the circles (e.g. lower grades (cashier, statements clerk), middle grades (counsellors, officers), managerial grades (branch managers, etc.)).

The interpretation of data output is fairly straightforward, although not all dimensions could be labelled. The closer two points are on the map, the closer the relationship. For example:

1   Lower grades tend to believe that the enquiries clerk and receptionist are mainly responsible for identifying customer needs.
2   Middle grades, however, are more inclined to see this as mainly the counsellor's

Figure 9.4 External perceptions of the different grade levels on the issue of identifying customer needs
Source: Meidan and Lim (1993).

responsibility. Some middle grades also tend to consider it the responsibility of cashiers, investment officers or everyone (all).

3 Managerial grades believe that this function is mainly their own responsibility. These beliefs of various role players within the branch are, of course, of paramount importance, as it might lead to under-training for certain function(s) at grade levels, where customer contact is higher. Therefore, this kind of study could focus the training efforts and needs for specific selling functions and certain grade levels/roles.

The six multivariate methods described above are summarized in Table 9.1.

Regression and forecasting techniques

Multiple regression

Regression analysis attempts to investigate the nature (and strength) of relationships, if any, between two or more variables in marketing phenomena. It can be used, for example, to establish the nature and form of association between sales and, say, the number of customers, the nature of competitive activity, the amount of resources spent on advertising, etc. The association between Y (sales) – which is the dependent variable – and the independent variables affecting sales are usually expressed in a mathematical function of the type:

$$Y = f(\chi_1, \chi_2, \chi_3, \ldots, \chi_n)$$

The purpose of regression is to make predictions about scores on the dependent variable based upon knowledge of independent variable scores (Speed, 1994).

Regression provides measures of association, not causation; yet regression (and correlation analysis) could assist marketing managers in better understanding the implicit relationships among various independent and dependent variables (for example, age, income, educa-

tion and amount of credit card usage, or various forms of salespeople's incentives and their sales calls, or the number of new orders obtained, etc.).

Generalized linear models

Generalized linear models (GLMs) have a number of advantages over more traditional 'hypothesis testing' statistics:

- They are constituents of a unified theory of data analysis (this makes the whole process of choosing a test and understanding the analyses easier).
- They model rather than hypothesis test (they can therefore be used for both description and prediction).
- They provide significant advantages over the more traditional bivariate tests and in many cases can replace them.
- GLMs can be used to analyse most of the data we are likely to collect in the social sciences.

It is these advantages which make GLMs perhaps the most important set of statistical tests in the social sciences.

What are GLMs?

Basically, they are methods which model data using linear relationships. Linear relationships are important due to the ease with which they can be described mathematically. However, not all relationships between variables are linear and able to be adequately described in this way. In such cases we can still take advantage of linear methods by modelling the relationship between variables using a linear model, but including transformations which approximate non-linear relationships to linear ones.

The techniques that fall under the GLM umbrella include a number of popular techniques:

- Ordinary least-squares (OLS) regression.
- Logistic regression.
- Log-linear modelling.

Table 9.1   Main multivariate methods and their marketing applications

Method	Based on	Marketing applications	Main advantages	Main limitations
Factor analysis	Identification of relationships among variables and establishing the 'weight' (factor loadings) for these variables	Determine corporate marketing images, consumer behaviour and attitudes	Data reduction, identification of the main constructs (factors that underline the data characteristics)	Applicable only to interval-scaled data
Latent analysis	Investigation of both manifest and latent factors by estimating these latent parameters	Segmentation research, market structure analysis (Dillon and Mulani, 1989)	Could be used for investigating causal systems involving latent variables	Difficulties in estimating the latent variables
Cluster analysis	Developing similarity or dissimilarity measures (coefficients), or distance measures, to establish clusters association	Primarily for segmentation studies and strategy (Saunders, 1994)	Enables classification of brands, products, customers, distributors, etc.	Different clustering methods could generate different clusters
Multidimensional scaling	Calculating the proximity (or, alternatively, of dominance) among attributes/variables and respondents	Market research, market share analysis (Coates *et al.*, 1994), market segmentation, brand positioning, etc.	Presents the entire structure of variables, making it easier to visualize and interpret relationship/similarities among data	Different software packages required for different types of data input
Conjoint analysis	Measurement of psychological judgements by measuring the joint effect of two or more independent variables on the ordering of a dependent variable	Consumer research (Vriens, 1994), advertising evaluations (Stanton and Reese, 1983)	Enables calculation of preferences. Suitable for product design and attitude measurement	Measures first utility rather than behaviour
Correspondence analysis	Graphical technique for representing multidimensional tables. For procedure, see Figure 9.3	Selling functions in bank branches (Meidan and Lim, 1993), market segments, track brand images	Can be used for analysing binary, discrete and/or continuous data. Facilitates both within- and between-set squared distance comparison. Fast, easy to interpret	Limited applications in marketing because of lack of suitable software

By way of an introduction we will begin with OLS regression, a technique which is very common and fairly easy to understand.

Ordinary least-squares regression

Simple OLS regression

Simple OLS regression attempts to represent the relationship between two variables using a line. This line is computed using the least-squares method and provides a line of best fit. For two variables, the OLS regression equation is equivalent to $Y = \alpha + \beta X + \varepsilon$ (Figure 9.5).

Using this graph, we are able to define the relationship between the two variables Y and X, and also how strong the relationship is.

The important thing to note from this demonstration is that GLMs can be used to model non-linear relationships even though they are linear techniques. This makes the techniques particularly useful in the social sciences, where relationships are rarely linear.

Multivariate OLS regression

OLS regression can also be used when there are more than two variables. It is important to be able to include a number of variables into a model, as more than one source of information is often required to account for a particular variable.

Take, for example, a situation where a particular company employs on the basis of educational achievement and not on the basis of gender. If this company recruits in a region where males and females do not have equal access to education, it is likely that a simple regression model that predicts wages from gender will show a significant relationship between the two. On the basis of this relationship, it would appear that the company is breaking the law, as it is paying different rates to males and females. This conclusion might be unjust in this case, as it is possible that it is a bias in the provision of education that has resulted in males being more highly educated and, consequently, better paid. In this case, the relationship between gender and wage is a consequence of the relationship between gender and education. To adequately model wages, both pieces of information need to be included in a model. Such a model can be represented in the form of a Venn diagram (Figure 9.6).

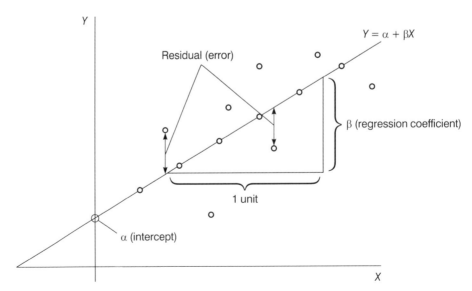

Figure 9.5   Plot of the OLS regression equation

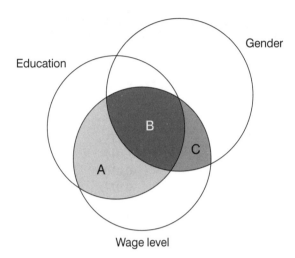

Single regressions:
Wage level
= $a + \beta$ Education
Area = $A + B$: $R^2 = 0.76$

Wage level = $a + \beta$ Gender
Area = $B + C$: $R^2 = 0.47$

Multivariate regression:
Wage level
= $a + \beta_1$ Education = β_2 Gender
Area = $A + B + C$: $R^2 = 0.79$

Figure 9.6 Venn diagram representing multivariate OLS regression

Many variables can be added to a regression analysis. We merely add more terms into the model. A multiple OLS regression model with k variables can be represented by the equation:

$$Y = \alpha + \beta_1 X_1 + \beta_2 X_2 + \beta_3 X_3 + \beta_4 X_4$$
$$+ \ldots + \beta_k X_k + \varepsilon$$

In the above equation, the variable Y is predicted using information from all of the X variables. This could be wages predicted by gender, education, type of work, location, experience, etc. The effect that each variable has on wage is assessed whilst controlling for all other variables. The output from an OLS regression is given in Tables 9.2 and 9.3, and shows how such a model can be interpreted.

Which data can be used in OLS regression?

OLS regression can be used to model response variables (Y variables) which are recorded on at least an interval scale (i.e. continuous variables such as age, output and wages). Explanatory variables (the X variables) can be continuous or ordered and unordered categorical data provided that they are coded appropriately). In short, OLS regression is used to model continuous data from all other types of data.

Conclusions

- OLS regression uses linear equations, as these are relatively easy to formulate and work with.
- Non-linear relationships can be modelled using linear equations if transformations are applied to the data.

Table 9.2 ANOVA[a]

Model		Sum of squares	df	Mean square	F	Sig.
I	Regression	123.581	8	15.448	9.919	0.000[b]
	Residual	722.617	464	1.557		
	Total	846.199	472			

[a] Dependent Variable: SSAT.
[b] Predictors (Constant): SH_TESC, REGR factor score 3 for analysis I, REGR factor score 2 for analysis I, SH_SOLO, SH_ASDA, REGR factor score 4 for analysis I, REGR factor score I for analysis I, SH_SAINS.

Table 9.3 Coefficients[a]

Model	Unstandardized coefficients		Standardized Coefficients	t	Sig.
	B	Std. Error	Beta		
1 (Constant)	4.888	0.102		48.115	0.000
Quality	0.308	0.061	0.234	5.017	0.000
Other Services	−3.06E-03	0.062	−0.002	−0.050	0.961
Value brands	4.524E-03	0.059	0.003	0.077	0.939
Car facilities	−3.44E-02	0.064	−0.026	−0.534	0.594
SH_ASDA	0.851	0.277	0.142	3.076	0.002
SH_SAINS	0.795	0.214	0.178	3.710	0.000
SH_SOLO	9.928E-02	0.253	0.018	0.393	0.694
SH_TESC	0.725	0.137	0.270	5.297	0.000

[a] Dependent Variable: SSAT.

- When there are a number of factors affecting the variable we wish to model, a multiple regression can be used.
- Response variables need to be interval, but with appropriate coding, any explanatory variables can be included.

Logistic regression

Quite often we may wish to model a binary variable, such as male–female, etc. For such analyses, it is not appropriate to use OLS regression as the data are not linear – we have to use logistic regression.

Similar to OLS regression, a whole range of useful statistics can be computed, including standard errors, confidence and prediction intervals. We are not limited by the traditional statistics which can only provide group comparisons.

The logistic regression model

As with OLS regression, we can use any number of explanatory variables, variables which can be interval or categorical. The same considerations apply to the data as with multiple OLS regression. All the power that is available in traditional OLS regression is also available in logistic regression – there should be no need to ever compute a test which assesses group differences (t-test, Mann–Whitney, Wilcoxon, ANOVA, etc.).

The basic form of the model is identical to OLS regression. The only difference is in the interpretation of the parameters. A logistic regression can be represented as:

$$Y = \alpha + \beta_1 X_1 + \beta_2 X_2 + \beta_3 X_3 + \beta_4 X_4 + \ldots + \beta_k X_k + \varepsilon$$

An example of a logistic regression

The data in Tables 9.4–9.6 are taken from a recent study into consumer behaviour. The variables have been selected for the purpose of demonstration and not to provide a 'good' model.

Conclusions

- Binary response variables have a non-linear S-shaped distribution.

Table 9.4 Model, block and step data

	Chi-square	df	Significance
Model	41.781	7	0.0000
Block	41.781	7	0.0000
Step	41.781	7	0.0000

Table 9.5 Classification table for SH_TESC (the cut value is 0.50)

			Predicted			Per cent correct
			0.00 0		1.00 1	
Observed						
0.00	0		174		90	65.91
1.00	1		97		120	55.30
					Overall	61.12

Table 9.6 Variables in the equation

Variable	B	S.E.	Wald	df	Sig.	R	Exp (B)
F1_QUAL	0.3573	0.1099	10.5612	1	0.0012	0.1137	1.4294
F2_OTHER	−0.0296	0.1018	0.0844	1	0.7715	0.0000	0.9709
F3_CHOIC	−0.2022	0.0989	4.1801	1	0.0409	−0.0574	0.8169
F4_CAR	0.2799	0.1018	7.5586	1	0.0060	0.0916	1.3231
DIS_CAT			7.6330	3	0.0542	0.0497	
DIS_CAT(1)	0.6929	0.8451	0.6722	1	0.4123	0.0000	1.9996
DIS_CAT(2)	1.2199	0.8257	2.1825	1	0.1396	0.0166	3.3869
DIS_CAT(3)	1.5018	0.9169	2.6824	1	0.1015	0.0321	4.4896
Constant	−1.3027	0.8175	2.5393	1	0.1110		

- This distribution can be modelled using a linear equation once it has been transformed.
- The model-building approach of the logistic regression provides much more detailed analysis of data than can be obtained using a *t*-test, ANOVA, Mann–Whitney or Kruskal–Wallis.
- The linear component of the model is the same as that used for the OLS regression.

Log-linear analysis

GLMs can also be used to model categorical data (i.e. data in the form of contingency tables). The traditional method of analysing such data is to interpret bar charts and to use the chi-square statistic as part of the cross-tabs procedure. These methods have severe limitations as they can only deal with two variables and cannot model the data to provide predictions. The same considerations apply to contingency table data as applied to OLS regression regarding the problems of interaction variables (e.g. wages, education and gender).

A log-linear analysis enables much more information to be obtained from the data and also enables statistics to assess the overall fit of the model. As the log-linear name suggests, it is a technique which makes use of the linear model and a transformation involving the natural log. Similar to OLS and logistic regression, the form of model is a linear combination:

$$\ln(\text{cell count}) = \alpha + \beta_1 X_1 + \beta_2 X_2 + \beta_3 X_3 + \beta_k X_k$$

The form of the log-linear model is very similar to the previous models discussed – the only difference is that we are now modelling cell counts. In effect, all of the terms in the model have been moved to the right-hand side of the equation. Parameters from the model are similar to the other models, but are interpreted slightly differently.

Conclusions

- The log-linear model is very similar to the OLS and logistic regression models.
- All of the advantages of OLS regression, such as being able to compute model fits, make predictions and investigate complex interactions, also apply to log-linear.
- It enables analysis of multi-category, multi-group data – something not possible using chi-square.

Discriminant analysis

Like regression analysis, discriminant analysis (DA) uses a linear equation to predict the dependent variable (say, sales). However, while in regression analysis the parameters (coefficients) are used to minimize the sum of squares, in discriminant analysis the parameters are selected in such a way as to maximize the ratio:

$$\frac{\text{Variance between group means}}{\text{Variance within groups}}$$

Discriminant analysis is used in marketing for predicting brand loyalty and buying or attempting to predict consumer behaviour in general; this classification method can be used when the data (the independent variables) are interval scales.

Automatic interaction detection (AID)

The regression analysis mentioned above attempts to identify association between the dependent and the independent variables, one at a time. In addition, the assumption is that the data are measured on interval scales. In many other marketing research situations we need a method able to handle nominal *or* ordinal data and to identify *all* the significant relationships between the dependent and the independent variables. Automatic interaction detection (AID) is a computer-based method for inter-actively selecting the independent variables in order to be able to predict the dependent variables. It splits the sample of observations into two groups on a sequential routine, trying to keep the subgroups that emerge as homogeneous as possible, relative to the dependent variable. The homogeneity is measured by minimizing the sum-of-square deviations of each subgroup member from its subgroup mean. AID is used in marketing for market segments analysis, analysing the effect of advertising levels on retail sales, predicting consumption/sales and brand loyalty.

The method is not as powerful as regression analysis and, since the minimum subgroup size should be no less than 30, the original sample of objects required must be fairly large (1000 or more).

Three of the regression and forecasting techniques described above are summarized in Table 9.7.

Forecasting methods

Forecasting methods are mainly applied in forecasting sales and market demand. Chambers *et al.* (1979) classify them into three categories: qualitative techniques, time-series analysis, and causal models. In each category there is a series of models; some are suitable for forecasting initial sales and others for forecasting repeat purchases. Consequently, one should make clear the differentiation between diffusion and adoption models, although, unfortunately, the space available here is not sufficient for a detailed presentation.

Probably the most well-known forecasting techniques are the time-series methods. These rely on historical data and, by definition, are of limited application to the forecasting of new product sales.

In order to select a forecasting technique for new products, the first principle is to match the methodology with the situation. The degree of newness of the product, for example, is crucial, as are product and market characteristics, the forecaster's ability, the cost, the urgency and the purpose for which the forecast is needed.

The second principle is that at least two methods should be used and one of these should always be the subjective judgement of the forecaster, who must override the formal technique decision when information coming from outside the model clearly shows that the technique's forecast may be at fault. There are powerful arguments for combining forecasts by different techniques. Methods are selective in the information they use, so that a combination of methods would incorporate more information and improve accuracy. Doyle and Fenwick (1976) advocate this and produce evidence of improved accuracy.

Simulation methods

The cost, the time involved and other problems associated with field experimentation often preclude a method as a source of information for particular situations. In such instances it is often desirable to construct a model of an operational situation and obtain relevant information through the manipulation of this model. This manipulation, called simulation, describes the act of creating a complex model to resemble a real process or system and experimenting with this model in the hope of learning something about the real system.

Simulations represent a general technique which is useful for studying marketing systems and is one of the most flexible methods in terms of application. Simulation models have been formulated to serve two management functions:

1 Planning.
2 Monitoring and controlling operations.

Marketing simulations can be conveniently divided into three classes (Doyle and Fenwick, 1976). The first deals with computer models of the behaviour of marketing system components, the second with computer models on the effect of different marketing instruments on demand, and the third with marketing games.

Table 9.7	Regression, automatic interaction detection and discriminant analysis – a comparison			
Method	*Based on*	*Marketing applications*	*Main advantages*	*Main limitations*
Regression analysis	Developing a function expressing the association (or relationship) between dependent and independent variables	For segmentation, consumer behaviour analysis, sales forecasting (Speed, 1994)	Enables predictions about a dependent variable (say, sales figures). Provides measures of association between independent variables and certain important marketing dependent variables	Requires fitting a regression line and determining the parameters. This could be quite complex and lead to certain errors
Automatic interaction detection	A computer-based sequential routine attempting to classify objects into groups as possible, by minimizing the within-group sum of squares	For market segments analysis, assess the effects of advertising on retail sales, predict brand loyalty sales prediction, etc.	Suitable for identifying the different variables affecting market segments; determining the importance of each independent variable and the form in which it affects the dependent variable	Less powerful than regression. Minimum group size should be no less than 30, and the original sample size should be quite large
Discriminant analysis	Maximize the ratio of variance between group means, not within-group variance	Predicting brand loyalty, consumer innovators, like/dislike of a service (or product), etc.	Enables predictions of dependent variables	Identifying the statistical significance of the discriminant function; multiple discriminant analysis requires a computer program

A firm wanting to adopt a simulation model would have to take into account the market characteristics of the environment it operates in and model on this basis.

Fuzzy sets

The fuzzy set theory is a relatively new approach that has been growing steadily since its inception in the mid-1960s. In the fuzzy set theory, an abstract concept such as a sunny day can be considered as a fuzzy set and defined mathematically by assigning to each individual in the universe of discourse, a value representing its grade of membership in the fuzzy set. This grade corresponds to the degree to which that individual is similar or compatible with the concept represented by the fuzzy set. Thus, individuals may belong in the fuzzy set to a greater or lesser degree as indicated by a larger or smaller membership grade. These membership grades are very often represented by real member values ranging in the closed interval between 0 and 1. Thus, a fuzzy set representing our concept of sunniness might assign a degree of membership 1 to a cloud cover of 0 per cent, 0.8 to a cloud cover of 20 per cent, 0.4 to a cloud cover of 30 per cent and 0 to a cloud cover of 75 per cent. These grades signify the degree to which each percentage of cloud cover approximates our subjective concept of sunniness, and the set itself models the semantic flexibility inherent in such a common linguistic term. Vagueness in describing many consumer behaviour constructs is intrinsic, not the result of a lack of knowledge about the available rating. That is why a great variety of definitions in marketing exist and most of them cannot describe the fuzzy concepts completely. So long as the semantic assessment facets in the construct can be quantified and explicitly defined by corresponding membership functions, the initial steps of the mathematical definition of marketing constructs are achieved. Recognizing the difficulty of accurate quantification of the semantic assessment facets like product interest, hedonic value and others, some

> **Example: Definition – 'consumer involvement'**
>
> Consumer involvement can be construed as a fuzzy set. It is a family of pairs $(A_i, \mu_{Ai}(y))$, where for each i in the index set is a fuzzy set ϑ, A_i is a fuzzy set of assessment facet and μ_{Ai} is a membership function from A_i to the unit interval $[0,1]$ which describes the behaviour of the fuzzy set A_i, $\mu_{Ai}(y)$ is the membership function of the assessment facet that takes value on $[0,1]$ for all y in A_i, i.e.
>
> Consumer involvement = $\{(A_i \, \mu_{Ai} \, (Y))|\mu A_i;$
> $A_i \rightarrow [0,1]_3 \mu_{Ai}(Y)[0,1]yA_i\}$
>
> and i, ϑ, A_i is a fuzzy set of assessment facet.

researchers utilize the fuzzy mathematical method (Klir and Yuan, 1995; Zimmerman, 1991) to quantify the assessment facets by membership functions so that the results obtained are more accurate than the traditional statistical methods and more suitable for the semantically modified assessment facets.

The benefits of using fuzzy sets are:

1 The membership function is deliberately designed in fuzzy set theory to treat the vagueness caused by natural language. Therefore, using membership functions to assess the semantically defined measuring facets is more reliable and accurate than using the traditional statistical methods – score points or scatter plot.

2 The membership function standardizes the semantic meaning of assessment facets so that we can compare the degree of the definition of marketing constructs regardless of the differences of timing, situation, consumer and so on.

3 The membership functions are continuous functions which are more accurate in measuring the assessment facets than the traditional discrete methods.

4 The fuzzy mathematical method is easier to perform than the traditional method, once the membership of assessment facets is defined.

Some of the main characteristics, advantages, limitations and applications of simulation and fuzzy sets in marketing are presented in Table 9.8.

Fuzzy decision trees

Inductive decision trees were first introduced in 1963 with the Concept Learning System Framework. Since then, they have continued to be developed and applied. The structure of a decision tree starts with a root decision node, from which all branches originate. A branch is a series of nodes where decisions are made at each node, enabling progression through (down) the tree. A progression stops at a leaf node, where a decision classification is given.

As with many data analysis techniques (e.g. traditional regression models), decision trees have been developed within a fuzzy environment. For example, the well-known decision tree method ID3 was developed to include fuzzy entropy measures. The fuzzy decision tree method was introduced by Yuan and Shaw (1995) to take account of cognitive uncertainty, i.e. vagueness and ambiguity.

Central to any method within a fuzzy environment is the defining of the required membership functions. Incorporating a fuzzy aspect (using membership functions) enables the judgements to be made with linguistic scales.

Summary of fuzzy decision tree method

In this section a brief description of the functions used in the fuzzy decision tree method are exposited. A fuzzy set A in a universe of discourse U is characterized by a membership function μ_A, which take values in the interval $[0, 1]$. For all $\mu \in U$, the intersection $A \cap B$ of two fuzzy sets is given by $\mu_{A \cap B} = \min(\mu_A(u), \mu_A(u))$.

A membership function $\mu(x)$ of a fuzzy variable Y defined on X can be viewed as a possibility distribution of Y on X, i.e. $\pi(x) = \mu(x)$, for all $x \in X$. The possibilistic measure of ambiguity – $E_\alpha(Y)$ – is defined as:

$$E_\alpha(Y) = g(\pi) = \sum_{i=1}^{n} (\pi^*_i - \pi^*_{i+1}) \, 1n[i],$$

where $\pi^* = \{\pi^*_1, \pi^*_2, \ldots, \pi^*_n\}$ is the permutation of the possibility distribution $\pi = \{\pi(x_1), \pi(x_2), \ldots, \pi(x_n)\}$, sorted so that $\pi^*_i \geq \pi^*_{i+1}$ for $i = 1, \ldots, n$, and $\pi^*_{n+1} = 0$.

The ambiguity of attribute A is then:

$$E_\alpha(A) = \frac{1}{m} \sum_{i=1}^{m} E_\alpha(A(u_i)),$$

where $E_\alpha(A(u_i)) = g(\mu_{Ts}(u_i) / \max_{15j5s}(\mu_{Tj}(u_i)))$, with T_j the linguistic scales used within an attribute.

The fuzzy subsethood $S(A, B)$ measures the degree to which A is a subset of B (see Kosko, 1986) and is given by:

$$S(A, B) = \frac{\sum_{u \in U} \min(\mu_A(u), \mu_B(u))}{\sum_{u \in U} \mu_A(u)}$$

Given fuzzy evidence E, the possibility of classifying an object to Class C_i can be defined as:

$$\pi = (C_i|E) = \frac{S(E, C_i)}{\max_j S(E, C_j)}$$

where $S(E, C_i)$ represents the degree of truth for the classification rule. Knowing a single piece of evidence (i.e. a fuzzy value from an attribute), the classification ambiguity based on this fuzzy evidence is defined as:

$$G(E) = g(\pi(C|E))$$

The classification ambiguity with fuzzy partitioning $P = \{E_1, \ldots, E_k\}$ on the fuzzy evidence F, denoted as $G(P|F)$, is the weighted average of

Table 9.8 Uses of simulation and fuzzy sets in marketing (the method, advantages, limitations and when recommended to use)

Method	Based on	Marketing applications	Main advantages	Main limitations
Simulation	Conducting experiments using a model to simulate working conditions of the real system	(a) Marketing planning (b) Monitoring and controlling (Kotler and Schultz, 1970), marketing operations (c) Distribution, consumer behaviour, retailing, staffing, advertising (d) Marketing training (Kotler and Schultz, 1970)	(a) A very felxible and simple method easily understood by managers (b) Saves time and resources (c) Simulation has found wide applications in the field of marketing	(a) Tedious arithmetical calculations (b) Rather costly in computer time
Fuzzy sets	The technique is essentially a factual modelling process that attempts to fine tune the expression of knowledge. It does this by using a linguistic scale describing the characteristics under each of the main dimensions of the model to form fuzzy sets; a hierarchical aggregation of information based on fuzzy aggregation operators; and a conceptual hypercube to determine the rank and ranking size of the outcomes. Includes the concept of membership function (between 0 and 1)	Modelling consumer behaviour, marketing planning, new product testing, perceived price testing, marketing communication effects research (Zimmerman, 1991)	Flexibility which accommodates a degree of uncertainty or fuzziness, in diagnosis. This fuzziness is indeed lauded as realistic in expressing human judgement	Difficult measurement scaling and estimation of the bipolar descriptors. Linguistic scale for characteristics description. Description of the values for the parameters of the model

classification ambiguity with each subset of partition:

$$G(P|F) = \sum_{i=1}^{k} W(E_i|F)G(E_i \cap F),$$

where $G(E_i \cap F)$ is the classification ambiguity with fuzzy evidence $E_i \cap F$, $w(E_i|F)$ is the weight which represents the relative size of subset $E_i \cap F$ in F:

$$W(E_i|F) = \frac{\displaystyle\sum_{u \in U} \min(\mu_{E_i}(u), \mu_F(u))}{\displaystyle\sum_{j=1}^{k} \left[\sum_{u \in U} \min(\mu_{E_j}(u), \mu_F(u)) \right]}$$

The fuzzy decision tree method considered here utilizes these functions. In summary, attributes are assigned to nodes based on the lowest level of ambiguity. A node becomes a leaf node if the level of subsethood (based on the conjunction (intersection) of the branches from the root) is higher than some truth value β assigned to the whole of the decision tree. The classification from the leaf node is to the decision class with the largest subsethood value.

The results of the decision tree are classification rules, each with an associated degree of truth in their classification. These rules are relatively simple to read and apply.

Artificial intelligence

Artificial intelligence (AI) models have emerged in the last few years as a follow-up to simulation, attempting to portray, comprehend and analyse the reasoning in a range of situations. Although the two methods of artificial intelligence (expert systems and neural networks) are, in a certain sense, 'simulations', because of the importance and the potential of these methods, we have introduced them under a separate stand-alone heading.

Expert systems

Simply defined, an expert system is a computer program which contains human knowledge or expertise which it can use to generate reasoned

advice or instructions. The knowledge base is usually represented internally in the machine as a set of IF . . . THEN rules and the 'inference engine' of the expert system matches together appropriate combinations of rules in order to generate conclusions.

In determining whether a particular marketing domain is suited for this methodology the following checklist is useful:

- Are the key relationships in the domain logical rather than computational? In practical terms, the answer requires an assessment of whether the decision area is knowledge-intensive (e.g. generating new product areas) or data-intensive (e.g. allocating an advertising budget across media).
- Is the problem domain semi-structured rather than structured or unstructured? If the problem is well structured, a traditional approach using sequential procedures will be more efficient than an expert system approach. This would be true, for example, when the entire problem-solving sequence can be enumerated in advance.
- Is knowledge in the domain incomplete? If the problem is well structured, a traditional approach using sequential procedures will be more efficient than an expert system approach. This would be true, for example, when the entire problem-solving sequence can be enumerated in advance. Moreover, for highly unstructured domains, expert system performance may be disappointing because the available problem-solving strategies may be inadequate.
- Is knowledge in the domain incomplete? In other words, is it difficult to identify all the important variables or to specify fully their interrelationships? Expert systems are particularly applicable in domains with incomplete knowledge.
- Will problem solving in the domain require a direct interface between the manager and the computer system? A direct interface may be necessary in situations calling for on-line decision support. Such situations are generally

characterized by a high level of decision urgency (e.g. buying and selling stocks) or complexity (e.g. retail site selection). Expert systems are particularly useful in these contexts because of their flexible and 'friendly' user interaction facilities, coupled with their ability to explain their reasoning (Rangaswamy *et al.*, 1989). A number of expert systems in marketing have been developed over the years, in particular focusing on the following domains: marketing research, test marketing, pricing, generation of advertising appeals, choice of promotional technique, selection of effective sales techniques, negotiation strategies, site selection, allocation of marketing budget, promotion evaluation, strategic positioning, strategic marketing, assessment of sales territories, brand management, marketing planning, international marketing, bank marketing, tourism marketing and industrial marketing (see Curry and Moutinho, 1991).

The greatest single problem with regard to the effectiveness and applicability of expert system models in the marketing context concerns the construction and validation of the knowledge base.

Neural networks

Neural networks are designed to offer the end-user the capability to bypass the rigidity of expert systems and to develop 'fuzzy logic' decision-making tools. Several authors claim that neural networks provide the user with the ability to design a decision-support tool in less time and with less effort than can be accomplished with other decision-support system tools. Neural networks have been successfully applied in the following marketing areas: consumer behaviour analysis (Curry and Moutinho, 1993), market segmentation, pricing modelling (Ellis *et al.*, 1991), copy strategy and media planning (Kennedy, 1991).

Neural networks use structured input and output data to develop patterns that mimic human decision making. Input data are com-

pared to relative output data for many data points. The relationships between the input data and output data are used to develop a pattern that represents the decision-making style of the user. The development of patterns from data points eliminates the need to build rules that support decision making. Unlike expert systems, which require user intervention to accommodate variable changes within the model, the neural network is capable of retraining, which is accomplished through the addition of new input and output data.

An important strength of this method is its ability to bring together psychometric and econometric analyses, so that the best features of both can be exploited. Whereas expert systems are good at organizing masses of information, neural networks may prove capable of duplicating the kind of intuitive, trial-and-error thinking marketing managers typically require. The accuracy of the neural network is not as high as of other methods, yet it has the ability to learn from increased input/output facts and the ability to address data that other decision-support systems cannot handle logically.

Table 9.9 presents the main applications, advantages and limitations of expert systems and neural networks.

Statistical decision theory or stochastic methods

In this category there are a number of methods, all of which are useful in solving marketing problems.

Queuing

This method is of importance to large retailing institutions such as supermarkets, petrol stations, airline ticket offices, seaports, airports and other areas where services are available through queuing. A notable problem in retailing institutions is that of making salesforce

Table 9.9   Applications of artificial intelligence methods in marketing (basic content, advantages, limitations and when recommended to use)

Method	Content	Marketing applications	Advantages	Limitations
Artificial intelligence	A computer program to express the reasoning process by modelling relationships among various variables (see checklist in text)	Marketing research, test marketing, pricing, site selection, tourism marketing and international marketing (Curry and Moutinho, 1991)	Flexible, able to explain reasoning of interactions	Difficulties in construction of the expert system model
Neural networks	Use of structured input and output data to develop patterns that mimic human decision making. Employs a statistically based procedure of iteratively adjusting the weights	Consumer behaviour (Curry and Moutinho, 1993), price modelling (Ellis *et al.*, 1991), media planning (Kennedy, 1991) and market segmentation	Capable of retraining. Able to bring together psychometric and econometric analyses	Low accuracy. More difficult to interpret than the expert systems above

decisions, the reason being the high cost incurred in hiring sales clerks whose services are almost irreplaceable. Since these sales clerks work in situations which can be systematically regulated and accurately observed, techniques can be used to provide management with information so that the optimal size of the salesforce can be ascertained. A queuing model to determine the optimum number of sales clerks to be assigned to a floor in a department store so as to maximize profitability can be determined. Attention should be focused on five main variables:

1 The number of potential customers arriving and requesting service per unit time.
2 The amount of time required by a sales clerk to wait on a customer.
3 The number of items purchased per customer per transaction.
4 The incremental value to the retail establishment of each item sold (i.e. profits).
5 The amount of time the customer is willing to wait for service.

Most research articles state that the use of queuing theory is mainly concentrated on solving problems in retailing institutions, where the model helps management to decide on the size of their salesforce. Perhaps it was the successful application of this technique in this area of marketing that has contributed to its vast improvements and wide applications. There are, however, limitations to this technique, one of which is that queuing systems must be operated over a sufficiently long period to achieve a steady-state solution, and it is often difficult to predict the length of time required to achieve this.

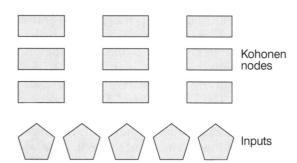

Figure 9.7 A self-organizing map. Connections operate between all inputs and all Kohonen nodes

Self-organizing maps (SOMs)

The Kohonen self-organizing map

Following Gurney (1997), for example, we define a neural network (NN) as a collection of interrelated nodes. Definitions of this nature remove the need to rely on analogies of the brain and take us into more general domains, in which the nodes amount to what are known more familiarly as variables. Neural network techniques have become an accepted part of the 'toolkit' available to researchers in numerous fields. There are other less well-known NN techniques which also hold much potential, and perhaps the most notable of these is the Kohonen SOM. Neelakanta (1999) described self-organization as the 'progressive formation within the system of sequential, ordered relationships between the interacting dynamic variables'. One might also describe the phenomenon as 'adaptation'. The SOM provides, quite literally, a picture or map of a set of data, but it does so in an adaptive or 'intelligent' way. On the other hand, NNs in general, including those which apply supervised learning, are also self-organizing in a similar sense: e.g. the hidden nodes in perceptron models provide approximations to an underlying function and can act to filter the data.

The SOM amounts to a relationship between a set of input nodes and a set of nodes connected to these inputs which perform the operations of transformation and grouping.

There is no output node serving the role of predicted or target value and hence in NN terminology we have 'unsupervised learning'. Specifically, these 'Kohonen' nodes are arranged in a two-dimensional grid, with each node being connected to each of the inputs, as shown in Figure 9.7.

Interestingly, the actual spacing of the Kohonen nodes has no meaning: what is important is their grouping together. This is because each node is regarded as a 'prototype', a set of cognate values of the attributes of the input data. An equivalent term is 'reference vector'. These values are the weights of the node. As discussed below, each vector of observed values, which may be continuous, discrete or categorical, will be closest in terms of Euclidean distance to one particular prototype node. The latter nodes serve to classify or cluster inputs, but the proximity of each node to its neighbours in the grid is a key element, which distinguishes the SOM from conventional statistical clustering techniques. Whereas cluster analysis (CA) operates in the space of actual data values, the SOM operates within its own two-dimensional grid. Standard methods of CA are almost invariably designed to produce non-overlapping clusters (Everitt, 1993), but the prototypes of the SOM are not mutually exclusive. This means that the final feature map, instead of showing several distinct clusters with differing characteristics, shows neighbouring nodes which have many similar characteristics but differ perhaps on one or two, or in the degree of intensity of characteristics.

In the terminology of the SOM, the grid preserves the 'topological structure' of the data or alternatively may help us *uncover* such structure. The *Concise Oxford Dictionary* (1999) defines topology as 'the study of geometrical properties and spatial relations left unchanged by the continuous change of shape or size of the figure'. The topological structure emerges as a 'feature map' in which the prototypes are related and subject to potential overlaps. Topology preservation implies that input vectors close together in input space map to close nodes in the grid. Thus, not only are the prototypes intended to reflect 'typical' values of the inputs in their respective neighbourhoods, but their grid positions reflect the relative positioning and density of the original data. No such ordering exists for the clusters which emerge from CA.

We have noted how, once 'trained', the network classifies a data point by identifying the nearest Kohonen node. As regards the training process, a similar principle is adopted. As is common in NN operation, data points are presented randomly to the network, and at each stage the nearest Kohonen node is identified. This is referred to as the 'winning' node and the learning mechanism itself as 'competitive learning' or 'winner takes all learning'. The weights of the winning node are adjusted so as to move towards the current data point, in which case the training process involves allowing the weights of each node to reflect or describe the data. The topological structure of the data is preserved because not only is the winning node updated, but also its neighbouring nodes. The shape of the neighbourhood may take various forms, such as square or diamond. It is also possible to model the proximity of nodes by a Gaussian decay function.

More formally, we denote the input data by an $m \times n$ matrix $\mathbf{X}$, each row of which contains a data point comprising observed values of the n inputs. Each node k in the SOM grid is characterized by a $1 \times n$ vector $\mathbf{w}^{(k)}$ of

weights. The Euclidean distance between the kth node and the jth input vector is then given by:

$$D = \sum_i (W_i^{(k)} - X_{ji})^2$$

where the observed values of the attributes of each data vector are indexed by i.

During training, the winning node is that with the smallest distance from the current data vector. The distance is in fact modified to allow for the frequency with which nodes have previously been 'winners', a so-called 'conscience mechanism' through which an additional egality is inserted. The adjusted distance is given by:

$$D^* = D - \gamma(NF_k - 1)$$

where N is the number of Kohonen nodes, F_k is the relative frequency with which the kth of these nodes has been the winning node, and γ is a constant between zero and unity. For nodes whose frequency is the average for all nodes, i.e. $1/N$, the adjustment is zero. Nodes winning with higher or lower frequencies have the distances adjusted downwards or upwards respectively. The frequency values are estimates adjusted at each iteration.

The weight adjustment process involves finding the node nearest to the data vector in terms of adjusted distance D^*, and this node, p say, has its weights updated. The actual adjustment used is such that the change in each weight of the prototype is proportional to the Euclidean distance between the current weights and the current input vector. The adjustment proportion λ is referred to as the learning constant. Hence we have:

$$W(p)^*_i = W(p)_i + \lambda(X_{ji} - W(p)_i)$$

where $W(p)^*_i$ and $W(p)_i$ respectively denote new and old weight values.

An interesting presentation of this learning rule is given by Kohonen (1995) and Ritter *et al.*

(1992), who make an analogy with data compression techniques, in which the primary aim is subsequent reconstruction of the data with minimal error. They show that the SOM has a similar interpretation, whereby the learning procedure amounts to a search for a set of weights to minimize the expected reconstruction error. The learning rule embodies the principle of gradient descent and there is therefore an element of similarity with back-propagation. Also, as well as being an independent statistical procedure in its own right, the SOM may be used as a pre-filter to other forms of NN, for instance to a standard multiplayer perceptron using back-propagation.

Business applications

SOMs have been shown to be useful in different types of business applications. Mazanec (1995) analysed positioning issues related to luxury hotels, using SOMs based on the discrete-value neighbourhood technique. Using data on perceptions of hotels and customer satisfaction, he showed that the non-parametric nature of this analysis allowed for compression of binary profile data.

Cottrell *et al.* (1998) applied the SOM in a forecasting context, with the nodes in the Kohonen layer used to store profiles describing the shapes of various trends, as opposed to relying solely on traditional parameters such as mean and standard deviation.

Serrano Cimca (1998) examined strategic groupings among Spanish savings banks, using a combination of SOMs and CA. The idea of the strategic group is often used to explain relationships between firms in the same sector, but here the groups were identified using only data from published financial information, thus giving groups of firms that followed similar financial strategies, with similar levels of profitability, cost structures, etc. The methodology allowed the visualization of similarities between firms in an intuitive manner, and showed up profound regional differences between Spanish savings banks.

The Kohonen SOM is a form of NN, which shares with other networks an origin in models of neural processing. As with other NNs, applications of such methods tend to take us into the realm of statistics, with the SOM operating as a new and interesting variant on CA. The aim is to provide a 'topology preserving' data transformation onto a two-dimensional grid, in which the location of the nodes *vis-à-vis* each other is important.

The SOM has some similarities with CA, in the sense that both involve 'unsupervised learning', where there is no dependent variable. Most clustering techniques involve attempts to find non-overlapping groups, so that each data point belongs uniquely. In the SOM, however, each data point is associated with the nearest prototype, but this does not exclude an association with others. Indeed, the fact that Kohonen nodes are spatially related in defined 'neighbourhoods' is an important feature of the approach. Clustering and SOMs tend to show us different aspects of the data. Clustering, by its concentration on differences, points out the observations that do not conform, while SOMs concentrate on similarities and gradual changes in the data. The relationships between prototypes are a key part of the model. One may navigate between them, and important attributes of the data set may be found in groups of prototypes.

It is also possible to employ the SOM in a predictive format, involving supervised learning. It can be used in this way as a pre-filter to a predictive NN using methods such as back-propagation. The model first of all derives a Kohonen map, and then applies supervised learning as a second step.

Stochastic processes

A stochastic process is a random experiment which occurs over time, the outcome of which is determined by chance. From these random experiments some attributes of interest are observed and numerical values can be given to these attributes according to the probability law. The stochastic process method is commonly used in building brand-choice models of consumers. In all, there are three basic types of stochastic process methods – the zero-order, Markovian and learning models – and each has its own set of assumptions.

The zero-order model assumes that past brand choice has no effect on future brand choice. There are studies on the existence of brand or store loyalties using the zero-order model approach which have defined brand loyalty as a proportion of total purchases within a product class that a household devotes to its favourite or most frequently purchased brand.

The Markov model assumes that only the most recent purchases affect the brand-choice decisions. Using the Markovian model, one can measure the expected number of periods before an individual would try a particular brand. Markov models should be used for dynamic market predictions such as equilibrium market shares, average time to trial, which is a measure of the attractive power of the brand, and for evaluating the success of new product introduction. One other area where Markovian analysis has been employed in marketing is in making personal selling decisions, where it is used in the modelling of sales-effort allocation to customers.

The third of the stochastic process methods is the learning model, which postulates that brand choice is dependent upon a complete history of past brand purchases, as the effect of purchasing a brand is cumulative. Therefore, when applied in the brand-switching complex, this will mean that purchase of a brand will ultimately increase the probability of purchasing the same brand again. This model may be used in monitoring consumer behaviour.

Statistical decision theory

Decision theory is often used to evaluate the alternative outcomes of different decisions and to find the best possible decision. Associated with the statistical decision theory is the deci-

sion tree diagram, which portrays the various alternative decisions and their consequences. Game theory, discussed below, is commonly regarded as an analytical approach to decision making involving two or more conflicting individuals, each trying to minimize the maximum loss (minimax criterion).

One other application of game theory is for formulating advertising budget decisions. In statistical decision theory, probabilities of each outcome are based upon either past data or subjective estimates. Pricing decisions in advertising are another area where decision theory can be applied. The main disadvantage of this method is the subjective estimation of the probability for each decision.

Decision trees can also be used to decide whether or not to test-market a new product before launching it. Cadbury-Schweppes Ltd used this technique to help in deciding the feasibility of test-marketing a new chocolate product. By carrying out a test-market programme of the new chocolate, the earnings obtained exceeded those of embarking on a national launch without prior test-marketing. This method has been used for making merchandising decisions, such as finding the optimum mix of sizes and widths of fashion shoes to be ordered, especially when the possible alternative choices were numerous and carried high costs.

Game theory

Game theory, when compared with decision theory, has found limited applications in marketing. Nevertheless, it has been applied to retailing institutions in making product decisions. Game theory helps management to decide on its advertising budgets without any prior knowledge of competitors' budgeting decisions.

In pricing advertisements, Higgins (1973) used game theory to provide solutions. The total reward for all the firms included in the pricing decision study was considered fixed, the decision resting on which product price to

Table 9.10   Applications of statistical decision theory or stochastic methods in marketing (approaches, advantages, limitations and when recommended to use)

Method	Based on	Marketing applications	Advantages	Limitations
Queuing	Probability distribution analysis of data (empirically gathered on how the major factors/variables will affect the situation-problem under analysis). It is an analysis of queuing systems attempting to determine service levels/performance	(a) Optimize: salesforce (Paul, 1972), number of checkouts, number of attendants, etc. (b) Minimize inventory-carrying costs; suitable and widely used by chain stores, supermarkets, department stores, petrol stations, airline ticket offices, ports, airports, etc.	(a) Predicts how different marketing systems will operate (b) Gives explicit expression relating the design of a system to the length and frequency of queues, waiting time, etc.	(a) Must be operated a sufficient length of time to achieve a steady-state solution (b) Manager's reluctance to have confidence in this method
Stochastic process	A random experiment which occurs over time and whose outcome is determined by chance. This is an analysis of systems with variable/uncertain components	(a) For building choice, models checking on customers' loyalty (b) Predict buying decisions and future purchasing probabilities	Might predict flow of customers and future purchase probabilities	Suitable for short-run predictions only
Statistical decision theory	This is an analysis of decision-making processes where outcomes are uncertain. Probability of each outcome – based upon past data or subjective estimates – is given adequate weight and is taken into consideration for decision-making	For decision-making on: budgeting, advertising, pricing, test-marketing, new product development, merchandising, optimum mix, etc.	Simplifies the level of analysis and suggests a number of possible outcomes	Subjective estimation of the probability for each decision might affect the results' validity

	Table 9.10	Continued		
Method	Based on	Marketing applications	Advantages	Limitations
Game theory	Constant sum game solution, use of a maximum criterion to determine, for example, budget/ resources allocation. Theoretical analysis of competition/ collusion between organizations	For decision making by retailing firms, mainly on: pricing (Higgins, 1973), product stock determination and advertising, budget allocations, also for better decision on negotiation processes	(a) Aids management in decision making (b) Suggests a useful analytical approach to competitive problems, such as: pricing, advertising outlay and product decisions	Does not have much predictive power compared with other quantitative techniques

lower to generate more sales so as to minimize the maximum loss.

A summary of the major stochastic methods, their possible applications in marketing (with some references), advantages and limitations is presented in Table 9.10.

Deterministic operational research methods

Deterministic techniques are those in which chance plays no part and solutions are determined by sets of exact relationships.

Rough set theory

Rough set theory (RST) is a fairly new approach to decision making in the presence of uncertainty and vagueness (Pawlak, 1997). Rough set theory was first introduced by Zdzislaw Pawlak in the early 1980s, as a new mathematical tool to deal with vagueness and uncertainty. This approach seems to be of fundamental importance to artificial intelligence (AI) and cognitive sciences, especially in the areas of machine learning, knowledge discovery from databases, expert systems, decision-support systems, inductive reasoning and pattern recognition. One of the main advantages of RST is that it does not need any preliminary additional information about data, such as probability distributions or basic probability assignments, which means RST has numerous real-world applications (Pawlak *et al.*, 1995).

The main concept of RST is an indiscernibilty relation normally associated with a set of attributes. The key problem in this description is the informal term 'normally associated'. In real life, such an association does not exist until additional assumptions are made. The subjectivity issue is more complicated than in other methods for managing uncertainty, therefore RST is potentially an important tool in the analysis of data with important applications in data mining and knowledge discovery. However, claims of its superiority (objectivity) over other approaches remains to be substantiated by scientific evidence (Koczkodaj *et al.*, 1998). The results of RST are a set of 'if . . . then' rules which enable prediction of classification of objects.

The critical issues of data mining were examined by Lingras and Yao (1998), who used the theory of rough sets, which is a recent proposal for generalizing classical set theory. The Pawlak rough set model is based on the concept of an equivalence relation. Research has shown that a generalized rough set model need not be based on equivalence relations axions. Lingras and Yao (1998) demonstrated that a generalized rough set model could be used for generating rules from incomplete databases. These rules are based on plausibility functions. These authors also emphasized the importance of rule extraction from incomplete databases in data mining.

An RST approach was used by Dimitras *et al.* (1999) to provide a set of rules able to discriminate between healthy and failing firms in order to predict business failure. The evaluation of its predictive ability was the main objective of the study. The results were very encouraging, compared with those from discriminate and logit analyses, and proved the usefulness of the method. The rough set approach discovers relevant subsets of characteristics and represents in these terms all important relationships between the key constructs. The method analyses only facts hidden in the input data and communicates with the decision maker in the material language of rules derived from his or her experience.

A recent development in RST is the variable precision rough set (VPRS) model, by Ziarko (1993a, b). Unlike RST, which constructs deterministic rules (i.e. 100 per cent in correct classification by a rule), the VPRS model enables a level of confidence in correct classification by a rule. That is, they are probabilistic rules.

Dissatisfied customers pose numerous potential problems for any organization – for example, negative word of mouth, reduced change of repeat lower brand loyalty. All of these problems will negatively affect the measurements of any business, e.g. profits and market shares. Therefore, assessing customer satisfaction level and more importantly why they are dissatisfied has great benefits to any company. This is particularly true in high competitive globalized markets, where search costs are low and the cost of switching supplier negligible.

Variable precision rough sets (VPRS)

A further RST innovation has been the development by Ziarko (1993a, b) of a variable precision rough sets (VPRS) model, which incorporates probabilistic decision rules. This is an important extension since, as noted by Kattan and Cooper (1998), when discussing computer-based decision techniques in a corporate failure setting, 'In real world decision making, the patterns of classes often overlap, suggesting that predictor information may be incomplete ... This lack of information results in probabilistic decision making, where perfect prediction accuracy is not expected.'

An *et al.* (1996) applied VPRS (which they termed 'enhanced RST') to generating probabilistic rules to predict the demand for water. Relative to the traditional rough set approach, VPRS has the additional desirable property of allowing for partial classification compared to the complete classification required by RST. More specifically, when an object is classified using RST it is assumed that there is complete certainty that it is a correct classification. In contrast, VPRS facilitates a degree of confidence in classification, invoking a more informed analysis of the data, which is achieved through the use of a *majority inclusion* relation.

This paper extends previous work by providing an empirical exposition of VPRS, where we present the results of an experiment which applies VPRS rules to the corporate failure decision. In addition, we mitigate the impact of using the subjective views of an expert (as employed in previous studies) to discretize the data, by utilizing the sophisticated FUSINTER discretization technique, which is applied to a selection of attributes (variables) relating to companies' financial and non-financial characteristics. The discretized data, in conjunction with other nominal attributes, are then used in this new VPRS framework to identify rules to classify companies in a failure setting.

To facilitate a comparison of our experimental VPRS results with those of existing

Table 9.11 Example of a decision table							
Objects	Condition attributes (C)						Decision attribute D
	c_1	c_2	c_3	c_4	c_5	c_6	d
o_1	I	0	I	I	0	I	L
o_2	I	0	0	0	0	0	L
o_3	0	0	I	0	0	0	L
o_4	I	0	I	I	0	I	H
o_5	0	0	0	0	I	I	H
o_6	I	0	I	I	0	I	H
o_7	0	0	0	0	I	0	H

techniques, we present the predictive ability of classical statistical methods – logit analysis and MDA – together with two more closely related non-parametric decision tree methods, RPA and the Elysee method, which utilizes ordinal discriminant analysis.

An overview of VPRS

VPRS (as with RST) operates on what may be described as a decision table or *information system*. As is illustrated in Table 9.11, a set of objects $U(o_1, \ldots, o_7)$ are contained in the rows of the table. The columns denote *condition attributes* $C(c_1, \ldots, c_6)$ of these objects and a related *decision attribute* $D(d)$. A value denoting the nature of an attribute to an object is called a *descriptor*. As noted above, a VPRS data requirement is that it must be in discrete or categorical form. Table 9.11 shows that, with this particular example, the condition attribute descriptors comprise zeros and ones (for example, denoting yes and no answers), and the decision attribute values are L and H (for example, denoting low and high). The table shows that the objects have been classified into one of these decision values, which are also referred to as *concepts*.

For the condition attributes in this example, all of the objects (U) can be placed in five

groups: $X_1 = \{o_1, o_4, o_6\}$, $X_2 = \{o_2\}$, $X_3 = \{o_3\}$, $X_4 = \{o_5\}$ and $X_5 = \{o_7\}$. The objects within a group are indiscernible to each other, so that objects o_1, o_4 and o_6 in X_1 have the same descriptor values for each of the condition attributes. These groups of objects are referred to as *equivalence classes* or *conditional classes* for the specific attributes. The equivalence classes for the decision attribute are: $Y_L = \{o_1, o_2, o_3\}$ and $Y_H = \{o_4, o_5, o_6, o_7\}$. The abbreviation of the set of equivalence classes for the conditional attributes C is denoted by $E(C) = \{X_1, X_2, X_3, X_4, X_5\}$ and for the decision attribute it is defined $E(D) = \{Y_L, Y_H\}$.

VPRS measurement is based on ratios of elements contained in various sets. A case in point is the conditional probability of a concept given a particular set of objects (a condition class). For example:

$$Pr(Y_L|X_1) = Pr(\{o_1, o_2, o_3\}|\{o_1, o_4, o_6\})$$
$$= \frac{|\{o_1, o_2, o_3\} \cap \{o_1, o_4, o_6\}|}{|\{o_1, o_4, o_6\}|}$$
$$= 0.333$$

It follows that this measures the accuracy of the allocation of the conditional class X_1 to the decision class Y_L. Hence for a given probability value β, the β-positive region corresponding to a concept is delineated as the set of objects with conditional probabilities of allocation at least equal to β. More formally:

β-positive *region of the set* $\mathbf{Z} \subseteq \mathbf{U} : POS_P^{\beta} (\mathbf{Z})$

$$= \bigcup_{Pr(Z|X_i) \geq \beta,} \{\mathbf{X}_i \in \mathbf{E}(\mathbf{P})\} \text{ with } \mathbf{P} \subseteq \mathbf{C}.$$

Following An *et al.* (1996), β is defined to lie between 0.5 and 1. Hence for the current example, the condition equivalence class $\mathbf{X}_1 = \{o_1, o_4, o_6\}$ have a majority inclusion (with at least 60 per cent majority needed, i.e. β = 0.6) in $\mathbf{Y}_H$, in that most objects (two out of three) in $\mathbf{X}_1$ belong in $\mathbf{Y}_H$. Hence $\mathbf{X}_1$ is in $POS_C^{0.6} (\mathbf{Y}_H)$. It follows $POS_C^{0.6} (\mathbf{Y}_H) = \{o_1, o_4, o_5, o_6, o_7\}$.

Corresponding expressions for the β-boundary and β-negative regions are given by Ziarko (1993a) as follows:

β-boundary *region of the set* $\mathbf{Z} \subseteq \mathbf{U} : BND_P^{\beta} (\mathbf{Z})$

$$= \bigcup_{1-\beta \langle Pr(Z|X_i) \rangle \langle \beta} \{\mathbf{X}_i \in \mathbf{E}(\mathbf{P})\} \text{ with } \mathbf{P} \subseteq \mathbf{C},$$

β-negative *region of the set* $\mathbf{Z} \subseteq \mathbf{U} : NEG_P^{\beta} (\mathbf{Z})$

$$= \bigcup_{Pr(Z|X_i) \leq 1-\beta,} \{\mathbf{X}_i \in \mathbf{E}(\mathbf{P})\} \text{ with } \mathbf{P} \subseteq \mathbf{C}.$$

Using **P** and **Z** from the previous example, with β = 0.6, then $BND_C^{0.6} (\mathbf{Y}_H) = 0$ (empty set) and $NEG_C^{0.6} (\mathbf{Y}_H) = \{o_2, o_3\}$. Similarly, for the decision class $\mathbf{Y}_L$ it follows that $POS_C^{0.6} (\mathbf{Y}_L) \{o_2, o_3\}$, $BND_C^{0.6} (\mathbf{Y}_L) = 0$ and $NEG_C^{0.6} (\mathbf{Y}_L) = \{o_1, o_4, o_5, o_6, o_7\}$.

VPRS applies these concepts by firstly seeking subsets of the attributes, which are capable (via construction of decision rules) of explaining allocations given by the whole set of condition attributes. These subsets of attributes are termed β-*reducts* or *approximate reducts*. Ziarko (1993a) states that a β-reduct, a subset **P** of the set of conditional attributes **C** with respect to a set of decision attributes **D**, must satisfy the following conditions: (i) that the subset **P** offers the same quality of classification (subject to the same β value) as the whole set of condition attributes **C**; and (ii) that no attribute can be eliminated from the subset **P** without affecting the quality of the classification (subject to the same β value).

The quality of the classification is defined as the proportion of the objects made up of the union of the β-positive regions of all the decision equivalence classes based on the condition equivalence classes for a subset **P** of the condition attributes **C**.

As with decision tree techniques, *ceteris paribus*, a clear benefit to users of VPRS is the ability to interpret individual rules in a decision-making context (as opposed to interpreting coefficients in conventional statistical models). Hence VPRS-generated rules are relatively simple, comprehensible and are directly interpretable with reference to the decision domain. For example, users are not required to possess the technical knowledge and expertise associated with interpreting classical models. These VPRS characteristics are particularly useful to decision makers, who are interested in interpreting the rules (based on factual cases) with direct reference to the outcomes they are familiar with.

Dempster–Shafer theory

The Dempster–Shafer theory (DST) of evidence originated in the work of Dempster (1967) on the theory of probabilities with upper and lower bounds. It has since been extended by numerous authors and popularized, but only to a degree, in the literature on artificial intelligence (AI) and expert systems, as a technique for modelling reasoning under uncertainty. In this respect, it can be seen to offer numerous advantages over the more 'traditional' methods of statistics and Bayesian decision theory. Hajek (1994) remarked that real, practical applications of DST methods have been rare, but subsequent to these remarks there has been a marked increase in the applications incorporating the use of DST. Although DST is not in widespread use, it has been applied with some success to such topics as face recognition (Ip and Ng,

1994), statistical classification (Denoeux, 1995) and target identification (Buede and Girardi, 1997). Additional applications are centred around multi-source information, including plan recognition (Bauer, 1996).

Applications in the general areas of business decision making are in fact quite rare. An exception is the paper by Cortes-Rello and Golshani (1990), which although written for a computing science/AI readership, does deal with the 'knowledge domain' of forecasting and marketing planning. The DST approach is as yet very largely unexploited.

Decision analysis relies on a subjectivist view of the use of probability, whereby the probability of an event indicates the degree to which someone believes it, rather than the alternative frequentist approach. The latter approach is based only on the number of times an event is observed to occur. Bayesian statisticians may agree that their goal is to estimate objective probabilities from frequency data, but they advocate using subjective prior probabilities to improve the estimates.

Shafer and Pearl (1990) noted that the three defining attributes of the Bayesian approach are:

1   Reliance on a complete probabilistic model of the domain or 'frame of discernment'.
2   Willingness to accept subjective judgements as an expedient substitute for empirical data.
3   The use of Bayes' theorem (conditionality) as the primary mechanism for updating beliefs in light of new information.

However, the Bayesian technique is not without its critics, including among others Walley (1987), as well as Caselton and Luo (1992), who discussed the difficulty arising when conventional Bayesian analysis is presented only with weak information sources. In such cases, we have the 'Bayesian dogma of precision', whereby the information concerning uncertain statistical parameters, no matter how vague, must be represented by conventional, exactly specified, probability distributions.

Some of the difficulties can be understood through the 'Principle of Insufficient Reason', as illustrated by Wilson (1992). Suppose we are given a random device that randomly generates integer numbers between 1 and 6 (its 'frame of discernment'), but with unknown chances. What is our belief in '1' being the next number? A Bayesian will use a symmetry argument, or the Principle of Insufficient Reason, to say that the Bayesian belief in a '1' being the next number, say $P(1)$, should be $1/6$. In general, in a situation of ignorance, a Bayesian is forced to use this principle to evenly allocate subjective (additive) probabilities over the frame of discernment.

To further understand the Bayesian approach, especially with regard to the representation of ignorance, consider the following example, similar to that in Wilson (1992). Let a be a proposition that:

'I live in Byres Road, Glasgow'.

How could one construct $P(a)$, a Bayesian belief in a? First, we must choose a frame of discernment, denoted by Θ and a subset A of Θ representing the proposition a; we would then need to use the Principle of Insufficient Reason to arrive at a Bayesian belief. The problem is there are a number of possible frames of discernment Θ that we could choose, depending effectively on how many Glasgow roads can be enumerated. If only two such streets are identifiable, then $\Theta = \{x_1, x_2\}$, $A = \{x_1\}$. The Principle of Insufficient Reason then gives $P(A)$ to be 0.5, through evenly allocating subjective probabilities over the frame of discernment. If it is estimated that there are about 1000 roads in Glasgow, then $\Theta = \{x_1, x_2, \ldots, x_{1000}\}$ with again $A = \{x_1\}$ and the other x values representing the other roads. In this case, the 'theory of insufficient reason' gives $P(A) = 0.001$.

Either of these frames may be reasonable, but the probability assigned to A is crucially dependent upon the frame chosen. Hence one's Bayesian belief is a function not only of the information given and one's background knowledge, but also of a sometimes arbitrary choice of frame of discernment. To put the point another way, we need to distinguish between uncertainty and ignorance. Similar arguments hold where we are discussing not probabilities *per se* but weights which measure subjective assessments of relative importance. This issue arises in decision-support models such as the analytic hierarchy process (AHP), which requires that certain weights on a given level of the decision tree sum to unity (see Saaty, 1980).

The origins of Dempster–Shafer theory go back to the work by A. P. Dempster (1967, 1968), who developed a system of upper and lower probabilities. Following this, his student, G. Shafer, in his 1976 book *A Mathematical Theory of Evidence*, added to Dempster's work, including a more thorough explanation of belief functions. Even though DST was not created specifically in relation to AI, the name Dempster–Shafer theory was coined by J. A. Barnett (1981) in an article which marked the entry of the belief functions into the AI literature. In summary, it is a numerical method for evidential reasoning (a term often used to denote the body of techniques specifically designed for manipulation of reasoning from evidence, based upon the DST of belief functions; see Lowrance *et al.*, 1986).

Following on from the example concerning Glasgow roads in the previous section, one of the primary features of the DST model is that we are relieved of the need to force our probability or belief measures to sum to unity. There is no requirement that belief not committed to a given proposition should be committed to its negation. The total allocation of belief can vary to suit the extent of our knowledge.

The second basic idea of DST is that numerical measures of uncertainty may be assigned to overlapping sets and subsets of hypotheses, events or propositions, as well as to individual hypotheses. To illustrate, consider the following expression of knowledge concerning murderer identification adapted from Parsons (1994).

Mr Jones has been murdered, and we know that the murderer was one of three notorious assassins, Peter, Paul and Mary, so we have a set of hypotheses, i.e. frame of discernment, Θ = {Peter, Paul, Mary}. The only evidence we have is that the person who saw the killer leaving is 80 per cent sure that it was a man, i.e. $P(\text{man})$ = 0.8. The measures of uncertainty, taken collectively, are known in DST terminology as a 'basic probability assignment' (*bpa*). Hence we have a *bpa*, say m_1 of 0.8, given to the focal element {Peter, Paul}, i.e. $m_1(\{\text{Peter, Paul}\})$ = 0.8; since we know nothing about the remaining probability, it is allocated to the whole of the frame of the discernment, i.e. $m_1(\{\text{Peter, Paul, Mary}\})$ = 0.2.

The key point to note is that assignments to 'singleton' sets may operate at the same time as assignments to sets made up of a number of propositions. Such a situation is simply not permitted in a conventional Bayesian framework, although it is possible to have a Bayesian assignment of prior probabilities for groups of propositions (since conventional probability theory can cope with joint probabilities). As pointed out by Schubert (1994), DST is in this sense a generalization of the Bayesian theory. It avoids the problem of having to assign non-available prior probabilities and makes no assumptions about non-available probabilities.

The DS/AHP method allows opinions on sets of decision alternatives and addresses some of the concerns inherent within the 'standard' AHP:

- The number of comparisons and opinions are at the decision maker's discretion.
- There is no need for consistency checks at the decision alternative level.
- There is an allowance for ignorance/uncertainty in our judgements.

We remind the reader that the direction of this method is not necessarily towards obtaining the most highest ranked decision alternative, but towards reducing the number of serious contenders.

Linear programming

Linear programming (LP) is a mathematical technique for solving specific problems in which an objective function must be maximized or minimized, considering a set of definite restrictions and limited resources. The word 'programming' stands for computing or calculating some unknowns of a set of equations and/or inequalities, under specific conditions, mathematically expressed.

Before the LP technique can be employed in the solution of a marketing problem, five basic requirements must be considered (Meidan, 1981):

1 *Definition of the objective.* A well-defined objective is the target of the solution and the answer to the problem must satisfy the requirements. Objectives such as reduced costs, increased profits, matching of salesforce effort to customer potential or improved media selection can be handled.
2 *Quantitative measurement of problem elements.* A quantitative measurement is needed for each of the elements described in the problem, which is an essential condition for applying mathematical models such as hours, pounds (£), etc.
3 *Alternative choice.* It must be possible to make a selection for reaching a solution which satisfies the objective function.
4 *Linearity.* The term 'linearity' describes the problem and its restrictions. Equations and inequalities must describe the problem in a linear form.
5 *Mathematical formulation.* Information must be compiled in such a manner that it is possible to translate the relationships among variables into a mathematical formulation capable of describing the problem and all the relations among variables.

A number of techniques are available for solving a formulated linear programme. A graphical solution is possible when there are three variables only. An example showing the use of LP in determining the best allocation and mix of marketing effort is presented in detail by Meidan (1981).

One is faced with four kinds of difficulties in using linear programming models:

1 The first difficulty is in describing the problem mathematically. In an industrial situation one must know exactly how much one can use the production resources, such as manpower, raw materials, time, etc.
2 The second problem lies in the interpretation and proper use of the objectively obtained optimum solution. One may need to analyse additional business considerations, over and above the ones used in describing and formulating the problem.
3 Even if the problem has been correctly stated and formulated, technical limitations may exist, such as the amount of data a computer can handle or that no solution exists (for example, the number of constraints and/or variables may be too large).
4 A further limitation lies in the reliability of the proposed solution. This could arise when a linear assumption is taken for real non-linear behaviour of the component.

Physical distribution

Designing an optimal physical distribution system is dependent on choosing those levels of services that minimize the total cost of physical distribution, whose objective function might read: $C = T + F + I + L$, where C = total distribution cost, T = total freight cost, F = total fixed warehouse cost, I = total inventory cost and L = total cost of lost sales.

Given the objective function, one seeks to find the number of warehouses, inventory levels and modes of transportation that will minimize it, subject to at least three constraints:

1 Customer demand must be satisfied.
2 Factory capacity limits must not be exceeded.
3 Warehouse capacity cannot be exceeded.

The linear programming model has been used in solving distribution problems, particularly in the transportation of finished goods to warehouses. The aims were to minimize transport costs subject to certain constraints, such as warehouse costs (Kotler, 1972). Other uses of LP models in marketing include site location, physical distributions and blending products.

Warehouse location

Chentnick (1975) discusses the various methods of locating warehousing systems which are of interest as their usefulness is indicated, thus suggesting the advantage of linear programming in comparison to other methods. Broadly, the function of a warehouse can be broken down into five areas:

1 Storage.
2 Assembling of customer orders.
3 Service of customers.
4 Economies of scale by bulk buying and delivery.
5 Processing and final packaging.

There are two definable sets which characterize the two methods of solution to the warehouse location problem (Meidan, 1978):

1 The infinite set assumes that the warehouse can be positioned anywhere on the map – obvious slight adjustments can be made later to allow for rivers, mountains, etc. A main assumption is that transport costs are directly proportional to distance (as the crow flies), and this is questionable in many situations.
2 The feasible set assumes a finite number of possible locations, and both costs of buildings and haulage can be calculated with a high degree of precision.

Media selection

One area in marketing where linear programming models have been extensively used is in advertising decisions, especially in media mix decisions in a market segment. Higgins (1973),

for example, proposed the use of this model for deciding on the optimum paging schedule for colour supplements of newspapers.

Marketing mix decisions and budget allocations

The marketing mix refers to the amounts and kinds of marketing variables the firm is using at a particular time, and includes price, advertising costs and distribution expenditures, each of which could be subdivided into further variables.

Product mix and the multi-product marketing strategy problem

The problem of product mix, i.e. variety and quantity of products produced, is commonly encountered by almost all multi-product firms during the planning period. Here the objective is to maximize current profits subject to the various constraints, such as capacity, demand levels and quality. Such problems necessitate the use of linear programming.

Other marketing management applications for LP

Wilson (1975) cites a number of potential applications of LP, including new product decisions, resolving conflict in market segmentation and the choice of a new market from a set of possible alternatives, and gives an example of its use in allocating a salesforce to new products. Goal programming, on the other hand, may be used when a minimum knowledge of the situation and realistic objectives are available. Here the subjective constraints placed on the model give direction to an objective and hence an area of solutions, i.e. constraints become goals.

The transportation model

The transportation model is a specialized class of linear programming model. Like the linear programming models, its aim is to optimize the

Table 9.12 Some major deterministic operational research techniques applicable in marketing (the methods, advantages, limitations and when recommended to use)

Method	Based on	Marketing applications	Main advantages	Major limitations
Linear programming	Objective and constraint linear functions	(a) Advertising (Higgins, 1973), space, optimal media mix allocations (b) Distribution problems, site location (Kotler, 1972) (c) Budget allocation, new product decision (Wilson, 1975) (d) Blending product mixes (e) Marketing mix decisions	(a) Maximizes profitability of allocations, subject to constraints (b) Minimizes costs (c) Aids management in decision making	(a) Difficult to obtain and formulate the various functions (b) Constraints must be altered as soon as external and/or internal factors change
Transportation model	Transportation/ allocation matrix ascertaining the minimum costs, routes, quantities supplied, etc.	To allocate resources, supply etc. by reducing transportation costs. Suitable particularly for department stores, truck rental firms, transport companies	Very suitable for managerial decision making	Inaccurate in the longer run as a result of changes in costs
Non-linear programming	Non-linear objective functions and non-linear constraint relationships	To find the maximum return to a new product search, subject to budget constraint	(a) When the relationships are non-linear (b) When the objective function is non-linear while the constraints are non-linear	Difficult to establish non-linear relationships

use of resources, with the exception that it requires separate computational techniques not normally used in other models.

The transportation model seems to have limited application, and the area of marketing where it has been used is in making distribution decisions. This limited usage is the result of the way in which the model is formulated. The major deterministic operational research techniques and their marketing applications, limitations and advantages are summarized in Table 9.12.

Causal models

Under this heading we have two main techniques: path analysis and linear structure relations (LISREL). Both these methods are relatively new to marketing. Of the two, LISREL is more widely applied because of its versatility.

Path analysis

Path analysis (PA) is a method for studying patterns of causation among a set of variables, which was popularized in the sociological literature (Hise, 1975). Though path diagrams are not essential for numerical analysis, they are useful for displaying graphically the pattern of causal relationships among sets of observable and unobservable variables. Path analysis provides means for studying the direct and indirect effects of variables. PA is intended not to accomplish the impossible task of deducing causal relations from the values of the correlation coefficients, but to combine the quantitative information given by the correlations with such qualitative information as may be at hand on causal relations, to give quantitative information.

Path analytic models assume that the relationships among the variables are linear and additive. Path coefficients are equivalent to regression weights. Direct effects are indicated by path coefficients. Indirect effects refer to the situation where an independent variable affects a dependent variable through a third variable, which itself directly or indirectly affects the dependent variables. The indirect effect is given by the product of the respective path coefficients.

In a recent example, developed for a tourism marketing study (McDonagh et al., 1992), PA was used to measure the effects of three major environmental factors (exogenous variables) – preservation of local landscape, preservation of architectural values, and overcrowding – as a direct causal impact on two critical endogenous variables: (1) concern towards a policy of global conservation and (2) preservation of cultural values.

LISREL

LISREL (linear structural relations) is a method of structural equation modelling that allows the researcher to decompose relations among variables and to test causal models that involve both observable (manifest) and unobservable (latent) variables. Path analysis and LISREL models are two important analytical approaches for testing causal hypotheses. Essentially, the analyst wants the reproduced correlations to be close to the original correlations. The LISREL model allows the researcher to simultaneously evaluate both the measurement and causal (i.e. structural) components of a system.

LISREL allows for a holistic, more realistic conception of social and behavioural phenomena. It recognizes that measures are imperfect, errors of measurement may be correlated, residuals may be correlated and that reciprocal causation is a possibility. *A priori* theory is absolutely necessary for covariance structure analysis. An important strength of structural equation modelling is its ability to bring together psychometric and econometric analyses.

Many applications of LISREL modelling can be seen in such areas as consumer behaviour, personal selling, new product adoption, marketing strategy, organizational decision making, distribution channels, advertising

Table 9.13   Applications of causal models in marketing (the techniques, advantages, limitations and when recommended to use)

Model	Content	Marketing applications	Advantages	Limitations
Path analysis	Provides the means for studying the direct and indirect effects of variables, by offering quantitative information on the basis of qualitative data on causal relations	Tourism marketing (McDonagh *et al.*, 1992), other applications (Wasserman, 1989)	Displays graphically the pattern of causal relationships	Assumes relationships among variables are linear
LISREL (linear structural relations)	A structural equation modelling, that enables one to decompose relations among variables and test causal models that involve both observable and unobservable variables	Consumer behaviour, personal selling, marketing strategy, international marketing (Moutinho and Meidan, 1989)	Provides an integral approach to data analysis *and* theory construction. The method easily handles errors in measurement. Ability to bring together psychometric and econometric analyses	Requires an *a priori* theory for structure analysis

research and international marketing. For a detailed example of an application of LISREL, see Moutinho and Meidan (1989). Table 9.13 summarizes the applications of the two causal models in marketing.

Hybrid models

Under this category there are three different types of methods used in solving marketing problems: dynamic programming; heuristic programming; and stock control models.

Dynamic programming

As stated by Budnick *et al.* (1977), dynamic programming is a recursive approach to optimization problems which works on a step-by-step basis utilizing information from the preceding steps. The model has been used to aid decision making in areas such as distribution (i.e. the minimization of transportation costs), the distribution of salespeople to various territories (in such a way that maximum profits will be obtained), and determining the best combination of advertising media and frequency under a budgetary constraint.

Heuristic programming

Heuristics is commonly defined as the use of rule of thumb for solving problems. Therefore, heuristic programming techniques are based on an orderly search procedure guided by these rules of thumb and are mainly applied to problems when mathematical programming techniques are either too expensive or complicated. However, they do not guarantee optimal solutions. In the past, heuristic programming has been applied fairly extensively in certain areas of marketing.

Taylor (1963) devised a graphical heuristic procedure to derive solutions to the problems of media scheduling that suggested the optimal number of advertisements to be placed in each medium and the size of each insertion. The number of insertions was determined by graphical methods, which attempted to find the point where the marginal returns to the last insertion equalled the marginal cost of the advertisements for each medium.

A summary of the main characteristics, advantages, limitations and applications of dynamic and heuristic models in marketing is presented in Table 9.14.

Stock control models

The distribution side of marketing has been successfully modelled using quantitative methods for a number of years. The objective of the distribution system is to get the right goods to the right places at the right time for the least cost, and involves decisions on such problems as the number, location and size of warehouses, transportation policies and inventories. In this section the inventory decision will be discussed, but it must be realized that inventory represents only one part of the local distribution network, a complete analysis of which is outside the scope of this chapter. The inventory decision has two parts to it: when to order (order point) and how much to order (order quantity). These are not independent and can be deduced from a stock control model. The ordering of goods involves costs, such as transportation and handling, which increase the number of orders placed.

On the other hand, the storage of goods also involves costs such as storage space charges, insurance costs, capital costs and depreciation costs. The first two decrease and the last two types of costs increase with the order quantity.

The simplest model assumes that demand is constant, shortages are not allowed (no stockouts), immediate replacements of stocks and a regular order cycle. If C = cost of holding of one unit of stock/unit time, C_o = cost of placing an order, d = demand rate (units/unit time), q = order quantity in units and t = order cycle time (order point), mathematical analysis shows that the total costs (ordering plus stock-holdings) are minimized when the following order quantity is used:

$$q^* = dt^* = \sqrt{\frac{C_o\, d}{C}}$$

q^* = is often referred to as the economic order quantity (EOQ). The simplest model can be improved by relaxing some of the assumptions.

Network programming models

Network programming models are the methods usually used for planning and controlling complex marketing management projects. There are two basic methods: the critical path method (CPM) and the performance evaluation and review technique (PERT). The two methods together are also called critical path analysis (CPA) techniques.

Critical path analysis

Critical path analysis, in its various forms, is one of the techniques developed in recent years to cope with the increased need for planning,

Table 9.14 Applications of dynamic, heuristic and network programming in marketing (the methods, advantages, limitations and when recommended to use)

Model	Based on	Marketing applications	Advantages	Limitations
Dynamic programming	Recursive optimization procedure; optimizing on a step-by-step basis	Solving media selection problems; distribution (minimization of transportation costs; distribution of salespeople to various sales territories)	(a) Maximizes the objective over the planning period (b) Introduces new factors, e.g. 'forgetting time', 'accumulation or intersections' (c) Wide potential application in industry	The programming procedure is rather complex; computational difficulties
Heuristic programming	Orderly search procedure guided by the use of rule of thumb. Based on 'marginal approach' or trial and error	Media selection and scheduling; warehouse location; salesforce allocation; decision on the number of items in a product line; suitable for making product promotion decisions	(a) Good, flexible, simple and inexpensive method (b) Combines the analysis into the style of decision making and the reasoning used by managers	Does not guarantee optimal solution
Network programming (PERT and CPM)	Presents the wide range of critical activities that must be carried out and co-ordinated. PERT acknowledges uncertainty in the times required to complete activities while CPM does not. PERT deals only with the time factor. CPM refers to the time-cost trade-offs as well	Planning, scheduling and controlling complex marketing projects (Bird *et al.*, 1973), e.g. building new stores, new product development (Robertson, 1970), product commercialization, advertising–sales relationships (Johansson and Redinger, 1979), distribution planning (LaLonde and Headon, 1973)	(a) Sequences and times of activities are considered, responsibilities allocated and co-ordinated in large/complex marketing projects (b) Project time can be forecast and completion time may be shortened	(a) Difficulties in estimating costs and times accurately, particularly for new projects (b) Of use only when functions and activities can, in fact, be separated

scheduling and controlling in all functions of management. For a number of reasons, this technique is particularly applicable for use in marketing management. First, marketing management, by definition, involves the co-ordination of many other functions and activities: advertising; distribution; selling; market research; product research and development. Second, much of the work in marketing can be of a project nature (for example, new product launch, organization of a sales promotion, setting up of a new distribution system).

CPA is based on the assumption that some of the activities of a marketing project are in a concurrent relationship and take place simultaneously. The advantages to be gained from CPA in marketing are similar to those obtained in other functions, except that the centrality of the marketing function, particularly in some consumer goods firms, increases its desirability.

There are a large number of possible applications of PERT and CPM: for new product launch (Robertson, 1970); distribution; planning (LaLonde and Headon, 1973); sales negotiations; and purchasing (Bird *et al.*, 1973); launching a marketing company/project/ department; sales promotions; conference organization; advertising campaigns; new store openings; realigning sales territories, etc.

Budnick *et al.* (1977) proposed using network planning for product development, while others suggest the use of the CPM to co-ordinate and plan the hundreds of activities which must be carried out prior to commercialization of a new product. Johansson and Redinger (1979) used path analysis to formulate an advertising–sales relationship of a hairspray product.

Chaos theory

Chaos theory has the potential to contribute valuable insights into the nature of complex systems in the business world. As is often the case with the introduction of a new management metaphor, 'chaos' is now being 'discovered' at all levels of managerial activity (Stacey, 1993).

What is chaos theory?

Chaos theory can be compactly defined as 'the qualitative study of unstable aperiodic behaviour in deterministic non-linear dynamical systems' (Kellert, 1993, p. 2). A researcher can often define a system of interest by representing its important variables and their interrelationships by a set of equations. A system (or, more technically, its equations) is dynamical when the equations are capable of describing changes in the values of system variables from one point in time to another. Non-linear terms involve complicated functions of the system variables such as: $y_t + 1 = x_t y_t$.

Chaos theorists have discovered that even simple non-linear sets of equations can produce complex aperiodic behaviour. The most familiar example is the logistic equation of the form: $x_{t+1} = rx_t(1 - x_t)$, where x lies between 0 and 1. This system is deterministic in the sense that no stochastic or chance elements are involved. Figure 9.8 depicts the behaviour of this system for varying levels of r.

At values of $r < 2$, iterating over the logistic equation will result in the system stabilizing at $x = 0$ (Figure 9.8a). Between $r = 2$ and $r = 3$, the system reaches equilibrium at progressively higher values of x (Figure 9.8b). At around $r = 3$, the system is seen to bifurcate into two values. The steady-state value of x alternates periodically between two values (Figure 9.8c). As r continues to increase, it continues to increase in periodicity, alternating between 2, then 4, 8 and 16 points. When r is approximately 3.7, another qualitative change occurs – the system becomes chaotic. The output ranges over a seemingly infinite (non-repeating) range of x values (Figure 9.8d).

Chaotic systems are also unstable, exhibiting a sensitive dependence on initial conditions.

The Lyapunov exponent is a mathematically precise measure of the degree of sensitive dependence on initial conditions. The Lyapunov exponent takes the one-dimensional form $e^{\lambda t}$. If $\lambda < 0$, then the initial differences will

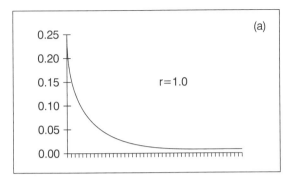

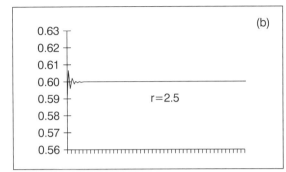

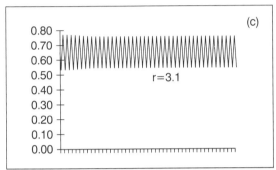

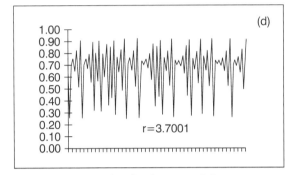

Note: Graphs represent output of the logistic equation: $x_{t+1} = rx_t(1-x_t)$, where $x_0 = 0.5$

Figure 9.8   Output of logistic equation for varying r

converge exponentially. If $\lambda = 0$, then the displacements will remain constant over time, while if $\lambda > 0$, small differences will magnify over time. All chaotic systems have a lambda value that is greater than zero.

Initially, the system of interest would have to be specified in terms of non-linear dynamical equations. Few researchers in the social sciences have attempted to identify non-linear deterministic behaviours in their systems of interest. In the main, quantitative research in the social sciences has tended to be both statistical and linear in nature. Of course, it is possible that the appeal of chaos theory may excite an interest in developing non-linear models.

The researcher would also need to demonstrate that the system was capable of chaotic behaviour over some valid region of its parameters. By running digital simulations of the non-linear systems, researchers would hope to discover regions of chaos in the models that

could be linked with phenomena in the observed world. Ideally, the Lyapunov exponent could then by calculated and found to be greater than zero.

Conclusion

The marketing research literature does not specify which quantitative method is most 'popular'. One can only conclude that the multivariate methods, as well as the stochastic and hybrid techniques and models, are widely used. Correspondence analysis is a method with much potential in marketing, as it displays all the benefits of multidimensional scaling and can be used with a variety of data inputs. The flexibility of both simulation and heuristic programming models mean that they can be applied to almost any situation where other models fail to give satisfactory results. In the last few years, causal models – in particular, LISREL – and artificial intelligence techniques have been widely used. The fuzzy sets technique is a new method that has been applied in marketing only very recently. Expert systems are currently systematically applied in many marketing problem areas. Queuing theory, network planning and transportation models are more restricted in their applications in marketing, as they are formulated to solve problems in specific areas. Regarding deterministic techniques, these are suitable for finding optimum solutions to problems, particularly when set relationships exist between the variables. In summary, the usage of different types of models depends largely on the problem under investigation, as well as on the type of data available and their level of interrelationships.

This chapter has attempted to present the application of the main quantitative methods in marketing. A taxonomic structure was adopted and all the techniques were broadly classified under nine headings: multivariate methods; regression and forecasting techniques; simulation and fuzzy sets methods; operational research techniques; causal models; hybrid techniques; and network programming models. Also discussed were generalized linear models, fuzzy decision trees, self-organizing maps (SOMs), rough set theory (RST), variable precision rough sets (VPRS), Dempster–Shafer theory (DST) and chaos theory. Advantages and limitations in the usage of each of these methods were discussed. However, the use of different types of methods depends largely on the marketing management situation of the problem under consideration.

References

An, A., Shan, N., Chan, C., Cercone, N. and Ziarko, W. (1996) Discovering rules for water demand prediction: an enhanced rough-set approach, *Engineering Applications in Artificial Intelligence*, **9**(6), 645–653.

Barnett, J. A. (1981) Computational methods for a mathematical theory of evidence, *Proceedings of the 7th International Joint Conference on Artificial Intelligence (IJCAI)*, Vancouver, Vol. II, pp. 868–875.

Bauer, M. (1996) A Dempster–Shafer approach to modeling agent preferences for plan recognition, *User Modeling and User-Adapted Interaction*, **5**, 317–348.

Bird, M. M., Clayton, E. R. and Moore, L. J. (1973) Sales negotiation cost planning for corporate level sales, *Journal of Marketing*, **37**(2), April, 7–11.

Budnick, I., Mojena, R. and Vollman, M. (1977) *Principles of OR for Management*, Irwin, Homewood, IL, p. 135.

Buede, D. M. and Girardi, P. (1997) A target identification comparison of Bayesian and Dempster–Shafer multisensor fusion, *IEEE Transaction on Systems, Man and Cybernetics Part A: Systems and Humans*, **27**(5), 569–577.

Carroll, J., Green, E. and Schaffer, M. (1986) Interpoint distance comparisons in correspondence analysis, *Journal of Marketing Research*, **23**, August, 271–290.

Caselton, W. F. and Luo, W. (1992) Decision making with imprecise probabilities: Dempster–Shafer theory and applications, *Water Resources Research*, **28**(12), 3071–3083.

Cattin, P. and Wittink, D. R. (1982) Commercial use of conjoint analysis: a survey, *Journal of Marketing*, Summer, 44–53.

Chambers, J. D., Mullick, S. K. and Smith, D. D. (1979) How to choose the right forecasting technique, *Harvard Business Review*, July–August, 45–74.

Chentnick, C. G. (1975) Fixed facility location technique, *International Journal of Physical Distribution*, **4**(5), 263–275.

Coates, D., Doherty, N. and French, A. (1994) The new multivariate jungle, in Hooley G. J. and Hussey, M. K. (eds), *Quantitative Methods in Marketing*, Academic Press, pp. 20–220.

Concise Oxford Dictionary (1999) Oxford University Press, Oxford.

Cortes-Rello, E. and Golshani, F. (1990) Uncertain reasoning using the Dempster–Shafer method: an application in forecasting and marketing management, *Expert Systems*, **7**(1), 9–17.

Cottrell, M., Girard, B. and Rousset, P. (1998) Forecasting of curves using a Kohonen classification, *Journal of Forecasting*, **17**, 429–439.

Curry, B. and Moutinho, L. (1991) Expert systems and marketing strategy: an application to site location decisions, *Journal of Marketing Channels*, **1**(1), 23–27.

Curry, B. and Moutinho, L. (1993) Neural networks in marketing: modelling consumer responses to advertising stimuli, *European Journal of Marketing*, **27**(7), 5–20.

Dempster, A. P. (1967) Upper and lower probabilities induced by a multi-valued mapping, *Ann. Math. Stat.*, **38**, 325–339.

Dempster, A. P. (1968) A generalization of Bayesian inference (with discussion), *J. Roy. Stat. Soc.*, Series B, **30**(2), 205–247.

Denoeux, T. (1995) A k-nearest neighbour classification rule based on Dempster–Shafer theory, *IEEE Transactions on Systems, Man and Cybernetics*, **25**(5), 804–813.

DeSarbo, W. S. (1993) A lesson in customer response modeling, *Marketing News*, **27**(12), June, H24–H25.

Diamantopoulos, A. and Schlegelmilch, B. B. (1997) *Taking the Fear out of Data Analysis*, Dryden Press, London, pp. 209–218.

Dillon, W. R. and Mulani, N. (1989) LADI: a latent discriminant model for analysing marketing research data, *Journal of Marketing*, **26**, February, 15–29.

Dimitras, A. I. R., Slowinski, R., Susmaga, R. and Zopoundis, C. (1999) Business failure prediction using rough sets, *European Journal of Operational Research*, **11**(4), April, 263–280.

Doyle, P. and Fenwick, I. (1976) Sales forecasting using a combination of approaches, *Long Range Planning*, June, 61–64.

Ellis, R., LeMay, S. and Arnold, D. (1991) A transportation backhaul pricing model: an application of neural network technology, in Johnson, C., Krakay, F. and Laric, M. (eds), *Proceedings of the AMA Microcomputers in the Marketing Education Conference*, San Diego, CA, August, pp. 1–11, 15–17.

Everitt, B. S. (1993) *Cluster Analysis*, Edward Arnold, London.

Greenacre, M. J. (1984) *Theory and Applications of Correspondence Analysis*, Academic Press, New York.

Gurney, G. (1997) *An Introduction to Neural Networks*, University College Press, London.

Hajek, P. (1994) Systems of conditional beliefs in Dempster–Shafer theory and expert systems, *International Journal of General Systems*, **22**, 113–124.

Higgins, J. C. (1973) Some applications of operational research in advertising, *European Journal of Marketing*, **7**(3), 166–175.

Hise, D. R. (1975) *Causal Analysis*, Wiley, New York.

Hoffman, L. and Franke, R. (1986) Correspondence analysis: graphical representation of categorical data in marketing research, *Journal of Marketing Research*, **23**, August, 213–227.

Ip, H. H. S. and Ng, J. M. C. (1994) Human face recognition using Dempster–Shafer theory, *ICIP 1st International Conference on Image Processing*, **2**, 292–295.

Johansson, J. K. and Redinger, R. (1979) Evaluating advertising by path analysis, *Journal of Advertising Research*, 29–35.

Kattan, M. W. and Cooper, R. B. (1998) The predictive accuracy of computer-based classification decision techniques, *A Review and Research Directions OMEGA*, **26**(4), 467–482.

Kellert, S. H. (1993) *In the Wake of Chaos: Unpredictable Order in Dynamical Systems*, University of Chicago Press, Chicago.

Kennedy, M. S. (1991) Artificial intelligence in media planning: an exploration of neural networks, in Gilly, M. C. *et al.* (eds), *Enhancing Knowledge Development in Marketing*, AMA Educators' Summer Conference Proceedings, Vol. 2, San Diego, CA, pp. 390–397.

Klir, J. G. and Yuan, B. (1995) *Fuzzy Sets and Fuzzy Logic: Theory and Application*, Prentice-Hall.

Koczkodaj, W. W., Orlowski, M. and Marek, V. W. (1998) Myths about rough set theory, *Communications of the ACM*, **41**(11), November, 102–103.

Kohonen, T. (1995) *Self Organisation and Associative Memory*, 2nd edn, Springer, New York.

Kosko, B. (1986) Fuzzy entropy and conditioning, *Information Science*, **30**, 165–174.

Kotler, P. (1972) *Marketing Management, Analysis Planning and Control*, Prentice-Hall, Englewood Cliffs, NJ, p. 364.

Kotler, P. and Schultz, R. L. (1970) Marketing simulations: review and prospects, *Journal of Marketing*, July, 237–295.

LaLonde, B. and Headon, R. (1973) Strategic planning for distribution, *Long Range Planning*, December, 23–29.

Lingras, P. J. and Yao, Y. Y. (1998) Data mining using extensions of the rough set model, *Journal of the American Society for Information Science*, **49**(5), April, 415–422.

Lowrance, J. D., Garvey, T. D. and Strat, T. M. (1986) A framework for evidential-reasoning systems, *Proceedings of the 5th National Conference on Artificial Intelligence (AAAI-86)*, Philadelphia, pp. 896–901.

Mazanec, J. A. (1995) Positioning analysis with self-organising maps: an exploratory study on luxury hotels, *Cornell Hotel and Restaurant Administration Quarterly*, **36**, 80–95.

McDonagh, P., Moutinho, E., Evans, M. and Titterington, A. (1992) The effects of environmentalism on the English, Scottish, Welsh and Irish hotel industries, *Journal of Euromarketing*, **1**(3), 51–74.

Meidan, A. (1978) The use of quantitative techniques in warehouse location, *International Journal of Physical Distribution and Materials Management*, **8**(6), 347–358.

Meidan, A. (1981) *Marketing Applications of Operational Research Techniques*, MCB University Press, p. 86.

Meidan, A. (1983) Marketing strategies for hotels – a cluster analysis approach, *Journal of Travel Research*, **21**(4), Spring, 17–22.

Meidan, A. and Lim, I. (1993) The role of bank branch personnel in the sales process – an investigation of internal and external perceptions within the branch, *Proceedings of the 1993 MEG Conference: Emerging Issues in Marketing*, Loughborough Business School, Vol. 2, July, pp. 660–670.

Moutinho, L. and Meidan, A. (1989) Bank customers' perceptions, innovations and new technology, *International Journal of Bank Marketing*, **7**(2), 22–27.

Neelakanta, P. S. (1999) *Information Theoretic Aspects of Neural Networks*, CRC Press, Boca Raton, FL.

Parsons, S. (1994) Some qualitative approaches to applying the Dempster–Shafer theory, *Information and Decision Technologies*, **19**, 321–337.

Paul, R. J. (1972) Retail store as a waiting line model, *Journal of Retailing*, **48**, 3–15.

Pawlak, Z. (1997) Rough set approach to knowledge-based decision support, *European Journal of Operational Research*, **99**(1), May, 48–57.

Pawlak, Z., Grzymala-Busse, J., Slowinski, R. and Ziarko, W. (1995) Rough sets, *Communications of the ACM*, **38**(11), November, 88–95.

Rangaswamy, A., Eliahberg, J. B., Raymond, R. and Wind, J. (1989) Developing marketing expert systems: an application to international negotiations, *Journal of Marketing*, **53**, October, 24–39.

Ritter, H., Martinetz, T. and Schulten, K. (1992) *Neural Computation and Self-Organising Maps*, Addison-Wesley, Reading, MA.

Robertson, A. (1970) Looking out for pitfalls in product innovation, *Business Administration*, June, 39–46.

Saaty, T. L. (1980) *The Analytic Hierarchy Process: Planning, Priority Setting, Resource Allocation*, McGraw-Hill, New York.

Saunders, J. (1994) Cluster analysis, in Hooley, G. J. and Hussey, M. K. (eds), *Quantitative Methods in Marketing*, Academic Press, London, pp. 13–28.

Schubert, J. (1994) *Cluster-Based Specification Techniques in Dempster–Shafer Theory for an*

Evidential Intelligence Analysis of Multiple Target Tracks, Department of Numerical Analysis and Computer Science Royal Institute of Technology, S-100 44 Stockholm, Sweden.

Serrano Cimca, C. (1998) From financial information to strategic groups: a self-organising neural network approach, *Journal of Forecasting*, **17**(5–6), 415–428.

Shafer, G. (1976) *A Mathematical Theory of Evidence*, Princeton University Press, Princeton.

Shafer, G. and Pearl, J. (1990) *Readings in Uncertain Reasoning*, Morgan Kaufman, San Mateo, CA.

Speed, R. (1994) Regression type techniques and small samples, in Hooley, G. J. and Hussey, M. K. (eds), *Quantitative Methods in Marketing*, Academic Press, London, pp. 89–104.

Stacey, R. D. (1993) *Strategic Management and Organisational Dynamics*, Pitman, London.

Stanton, W. W. and Reese, R. M. (1983) Three conjoint segmentation approaches to the evaluation of advertising theme creation, *Journal of Business Research*, June, 201–216.

Taylor, C. J. (1963) Some developments in the theory and applications of media scheduling method, *Operational Research Quarterly*, 291–305.

Vriens, M. (1994) Solving marketing problems with conjoint analysis, in Hooley, G. J. and Hussey, M. K. (eds), *Quantitative Methods in Marketing*, Academic Press, London, pp. 37–56.

Walley, P. (1987) Belief-function representations of statistical evidence, *Ann. Stat.*, **10**, 741–761.

Wasserman, D. (1989) *Neural Computing: Theory and Practice*, Van Nostrand Reinhold, New York.

Wilson, J. M. (1975) The handling of goals in marketing problems, *Management Decision*, **3**(3), 16–23.

Wilson, P. N. (1992) Some theoretical aspects of the Dempster–Shafer theory, PhD Thesis, Oxford Polytechnic.

Yuan, Y. and Shaw, M. J. (1995) Induction of fuzzy decision trees, *Fuzzy Sets and Systems*, 125–139.

Ziarko, W. (1993a) Variable precision rough set model, *Journal of Computer and System Sciences*, **46**, 39–59.

Ziarko, W. (1993b) Analysis of uncertain information in the framework of variable precision rough sets, *Foundations of Computing and Decision Sciences*, **18**, 381–396.

Zimmerman, H. J. (1991) *Fuzzy Set Theory and its Applications*, 2nd edn, Kluwer Academic.

Further reading

Diamantopoulos, A. and Schlegelmilch, B. B. (1997) *Taking the Fear Out of Data Analysis*, Dryden Press, London. This is an excellent text, easy to read, refreshing and amusing, yet introducing a very robust content.

Finerty, J. J. (1971) Product pricing and investment analysis, *Management Accounting*, December, 21–37.

Hooley, G. J. and Hussey, M. K. (1994) *Quantitative Methods in Marketing*, Academic Press, London. This is a good book, introducing a collection of different quantitative research methods ranging from LISREL to neural networks. A new edition was published in 1999.

Kane, G., Richardson, F. and Meade, N. (1998) Rank transformation and the prediction of corporate failure, *Contemporary Accounting Research*, **15**(2), 145–166.

Kinnear, T. C. and Taylor, J. R. (1996) *Marketing Research: An Applied Approach*, 5th edn, McGraw-Hill, New York. An excellent textbook for introductory marketing research.

Lillien, G. L. and Rangaswamy, A. (1998) *Marketing Engineering – Computer-Assisted Marketing Analysis and Planning*, Addison-Wesley, Harlow, UK. Excellent new text on quantitative and computer modelling techniques with CD-ROM included. Techniques range from cluster analysis and conjoint analysis to AHP and neural networks.

Mazanec, J. A. (1994) *A priori* and *a posteriori* segmentation: heading for unification with neural network modelling, in Chias, J. and Sureda, J. (eds), *Marketing for the New Europe: Dealing with Complexity*, 22nd European Marketing Academy Conference Proceedings, Vol. I, Barcelona, Spain, 25–28 May, pp. 889–917.

Meidan, A. (1981) Optimising the number of salesmen, in Baker, M. J. (ed.), *New Directions in Marketing and Research*, University of Strathclyde, Glasgow, pp. 173–197.

Moutinho, L. and Curry, B. (1994) Consumer perceptions of ATMs: an application of neural networks, *Journal of Marketing Management*, **10**(1), 191–206.

Moutinho, L., Goode, M. H. and Fiona Davies, F. (1998) *Quantitative Analysis in Marketing Management*, Wiley, Chichester. This is a very recent text which includes chapters on statistical analysis, forecasting, decision theory and new quantitative methods, among others.

Sharma, S. (1996) *Applied Multivariate Techniques*, Wiley, Chichester. Very good book on the topic. Issues covered range from factor analysis, cluster analysis and discriminant analysis to logistic regression, MANOVA and covariance structure models.

Walters, D. (1975) Applying the Monte Carlo simulation, *Retail and Distribution Management*, February, 50–54.

Zimmerman, H. J. (1991) *Fuzzy Set Theory and its Applications*, 2nd edn, Kluwer Academic. This is probably the best and most up-to-date text on fuzzy sets theory and applications.

CHAPTER 10

Market segmentation

MARTIN EVANS

Chapter objectives

1   To show that, whereas the tradition of grouping individuals together as far as possible within relatively homogeneous segments has been one of the major cornerstones of marketing, that this paradigm has been changing to more personalized and (attempted) relational and one-to-one targeting.
2   To explore implications of the 'the new marketing' and its collection, analysis and use of personalized customer data, for segmentation and targeting of markets.
3   To examine relevant dimensions of segmenting and targeting, such as demographics, psychographics and geodemographics.
4   To explore the fusion of personalized data from a variety of sources which leads to biographical segmentation.
5   To demonstrate the differences involved with segmenting a 'cold' market and a current customer base.
6   To explore aspects of targeting and positioning within the segmentation, targeting, positioning process.

Introduction

Over recent years, many marketers have been party to and have certainly been witness to some of the most dramatic changes in their world. These changes have been in the area of segmenting and targeting markets. This chapter explores these developments along with some of the reasons for them, and how they have been manifested in new segmenting and targeting practices.

The basic principle of market segmentation is that markets are not homogeneous and that it makes commercial sense to differentiate marketing offerings for different customer groups. The days when customers could buy a car ' in any colour as long as it was black' are long gone. Markets have fragmented and technology provides for greater variation in production. Marketing itself can more easily identify more and smaller market segments, and indeed it can target selected segments more effectively. In this respect, developments in the collection, analysis and use of personalized customer data have been a major driver of many of the developments in the 'new marketing', and these issues are discussed in this chapter.

In terms of structure, the chapter initially provides a brief historical perspective on the development of market segmentation, then explores some traditional and conventional criteria, categorization of and bases for segmenting markets. This is then followed by coverage of the new data-driven segmentation and targeting approach. Here, the use of data technology and 'marketing metrics' are demonstrated in terms of how existing customer bases are being segmented in less conventional ways in order to differentially target segments according to their likely contribution to sales and profits. Other strategic targeting issues are then examined, together with the next stage of the process, positioning the marketing offering.

Historical perspective

The famous saying in the car industry by Henry Ford, concerning the model T, that customers could have any colour as long as it was black, was a reflection of the mass marketing of the time. Great economies of scale were achieved through the long production runs of mass producing standardized products for an apparently homogeneous market. In a classic paper by Wendell Smith, who was one of the originators of segmentation thinking, the development of segmentation is explored (Smith, 1956). As mass production and consumption continued, many organizations attempted to gain some competitive advantage and developed the strategy of product differentiation. As Smith stated: 'Product differentiation is concerned with the bending of demand to the will of supply.' In this way, a variety was offered to buyers.

This is the key to product differentiation because, although the result might in some cases look very similar to segmentation, differences in product, image, distribution and/or promotion are offered to the market. Perhaps such differences do indeed appeal to different groups within the overall market, but if they do it is mainly due to coincidence. True segmentation starts with identifying the requirements and behaviour of segments, and varying marketing mixes accordingly in order to more deliberately match marketing offerings with customer behaviour.

Product differentiation clearly represents a product-orientated approach in that it is an 'inside out' management attitude to marketing planning. Market orientation starts with understanding of the market and identification of

market needs and behaviour. In this sense, it is an 'outside in' planning approach. This is the segmentation approach and declares that marketing offerings cannot generally hope to be all things to all people, and that differences between groups and similarities within groups may be analysed for marketing planning purposes. In this way, customers are grouped together as far as it is meaningful for them to be targeted with distinct marketing mixes.

It is not always the case that for each segment a different product must be developed. This might be the case, but equally there might be different prices charged in different segments for the same product or service (e.g. gas, electricity and train travel), or for different segments based on levels of repeat purchase and loyalty. Similarly, there could be differences in promotion – Levi's, for example, advertise on television for a fairly wide market, but the same product lines are also promoted with quite different images and themes in the 'style' press, targeted at the 15- to 19-year-old fashion opinion leaders (Edmonson, 1993); the concept of opinion leadership in segmentation is explored later. There again, there are examples of where distribution might be the main mix difference between segments, and so on.

There is always a danger, however, of segmenting 'too far'. Market 'fragmentation' or 'oversegmenting' may create too small and unprofitable segments, and thus becomes less efficient – the baffling array of shampoo products is, perhaps, an example, as might be the plethora of different rail prices depending on day, time, advance booking, type of rail card, and so on. However, individualized (custom) segmentation or mass customization is the legitimate polar opposite and is the direction in which marketing is certainly taking the segmentation issue, as will be seen later.

Strategic aims to shift the marketing paradigm from a transaction-based one to being more relational, together with practical attempts to operationalize this, have real implications for segmentation and targeting. Developments over the last couple of decades (especially) have meant that marketers are more able to analyse customer behaviour at an individual level, and they increasingly aim to be able to cultivate long-term relationships with those customers who contribute most to the financial position of the organization. In this way, there has been much attention devoted to concepts of relationship marketing, customer relationship management (CRM) and one-to-one marketing. It has to be said that much of this is rhetoric rather than reality, as is discussed later.

The next section outlines what are suggested as being the main criteria for segmentation to be effective.

Segmentation criteria and categories

Segmentation involves identifying homogeneous buying behaviour within a segment (and heterogeneous buying between segments) such that each segment can be considered as a target for a distinct marketing mix.

Criteria for segmentation

To help with this process, potential segments should satisfy a number of criteria (Frank *et al.*, 1972). The four main and nine sub-criteria are (Van Raaij and Verhallen, 1994):

1 Typifying the segments:
   - *Identification*. Differentiation of segment from other segments.
   - *Measurability*. Identification of segments in terms of differences in individual and household characteristics or other 'measurable' characteristics should be possible.
2 Homogeneity:
   - *Variation*. Heterogeneity between segments in terms of behavioural response (Engel *et al.*, 1972).
   - *Stability*. Although this criterion suggests that segments should be relatively stable over

time and that switching of consumers from one segment to another should not be frequent, the use of data mining tools allows the identification of individuals' changed circumstances or behaviour, such that they can now be switched from one target group to another.
   - *Congruity*. Homogeneity within segments in terms of behavioural responses.
3 Usefulness:
   - *Accessibility*. Segments should be accessible in terms of communications media and distribution outlets. This means that it must be possible to reach the segment. Traditionally, this meant the selection of those advertising media that match the segment's media profile in demographic terms, or selecting appropriate distribution channels, again through a matching of demographic profile with the equivalent profile of those most likely to frequent different types of retail outlets. Increasingly, however, especially since around the start of the 1980s, more sophisticated market profiling and targeting dimensions have been deployed. The date is significant because it reflects the first use of the national census for marketing purposes, as is explained later.
   - *Substantiality*. Segments should be of sufficient size to enable specific marketing actions. This does not mean that segments need to be especially large, but profitable enough to have distinct marketing mixes aimed at them. Again, as we will see later, new 'marketing metrics' have facilitated greater sophistication in calculating not only the most profitable segments, but even the most profitable individual customers.
4 Strategic criteria:
   - *Potential*. The segments should have enough potential for marketing objectives, e.g. profitability.
   - *Attractiveness*. Segments should be structurally attractive to the producer, e.g. create a competitive advantage for the company (Porter, 1979).

One of the relatively recent developments in these respects is the cultivation of the more profitable customers via relational campaigns in order to encourage greater loyalty and retention. Relationship marketing has been a topical issue at the heart of much effort to gain strategic competitive advantage. See also Chapters 3 and 19.

Segmentation categories

Segmentation approaches can be categorized as being objective or subjective. An objective base may be measured unambiguously (e.g. age and gender) or may be taken from registrations of transactions (e.g. checkout scanning data). Subjective bases need to be measured with the respondents themselves and are often 'mental constructs' such as attitudes and intentions.

As suggested later, new metrics for segmenting markets are shifting the balance toward the former category in many segmentation programmes.

Further categorization of segmentation bases can be made as shown in Table 10.1. Here, three 'levels' are proposed. At the general level, segmentation is based on permanent or relatively long-lasting consumer characteristics such as gender, education level occupation, family composition and lifestyle. These characteristics are the same for different products, services and usage situations.

For domain-specific segmentation, there are different product classes and consumption domains, such as breakfast, washing clothes or commuting. When these are taken into account, segmentation is domain-specific.

For specific level segmentation, customers are segmented into, for example, heavy and light users of specific brands. Segmentation of present customers is also at the specific level.

Combining the three levels of segmentation and the distinction of objective and subjective variables is shown in Table 10.1. All segmenting bases can be categorized within this framework.

As mentioned earlier and as will be explored and explained in greater depth later, the 'objective' variables are becoming more dominant for many organizations.

'Traditional' segmentation bases

'Traditional' refers to those approaches that were employed before the advent of the data-driven era. The bases used are still around today and used by many organizations, but for those with access to personalized customer data they are perhaps now used more as

Table 10.1	Classification of segmentation variables	
	Objective	*Subjective*
General level (consumption)	Age, education level, geographic area	Lifestyle, general values, personality
Domain-specific level (product class)	Usage frequency, substitution, complementarity	Perception, attitude, preference, interests, opinions, domain-specific values
Specific level (brand)	Brand loyalty (behaviour), usage frequency	Brand loyalty (attitude), brand preference, purchase intention

supporting characteristics rather than as the main segmentation base. We start by exploring some demographic characteristics within the applied context of a hypothetical case study.

Demographics

A drinks company has researched potential markets for its new drink, a cross between an alcopop and 'mixer'. The product might appeal to the youth market as a stronger 'soft' drink and to older markets as a sweet mixer for spirit-based drinks. The company discovered that several market reports such as MINTEL, KEY-NOTE and Market Assessment have conducted some research into the usage of alcopops and spirits. The company also conducted its own survey and qualitative group discussion research amongst consumers, and discovered that those most likely to be interested in their product are 16–24, females from C1 households either as dependent children or in a first household of their own. The next most likely segment was found to be 50–60, males from AB households in which children have grown up and left home.

These are demographic characteristics but respondents to this form of market research are (and should be to comply with the Market Research Society's Code of Conduct) anonymous and not added to any database for, for example, mailing list creation.

The value of these characteristics depends upon the extent to which they satisfy the above criteria for segmentation.

For instance, in terms of estimating market size within the substantial criterion, it would be usual for the demographic profile to be used to estimate the size of this segment in the population as a whole – based on the incidence of their demographic characteristics in the total population. For the accessible criterion it has been traditional for a demographic market profile to be matched with media profiles in order to select appropriate advertising media to reach the selected segment. Similar demographic profiles exist for those frequenting different

retail outlets and therefore selection of channel can be based on demographics as well.

As for understanding why segments behave as they do, demographics are less clear. If there is a relationship between an age group, or gender or social grade and purchasing behaviour, is this a causal relationship or mere coincidence?

Age

Age is still a valid base for many markets. The drinks company here has identified 'young adult' and 'teenage' segments, for example. In general terms, these have become important spenders, for example, demanding their own products and searching for their own identity. A complicating factor is that this group has been found to be especially individualistic and sceptical of marketing activity. This doesn't make them difficult to reach, but it is proving harder to influence them. A decade ago they were labelled as 'Generation X', and Coupland (1991) and Ritchie (1995) have analysed their behaviour and attitudes; these have been further reported by Bashford (2000). It is possible that marketing can provide some of what Generation X might be looking for – greater interactivity and participation in marketing communications. The current 16–24s have been termed Generation Y or the Millennial Generation (Adam Smith Institute, 1998). Many in this category have been found to be materialists, brand orientated, risk takers, keen on business, hedonism, illegal drugs and have a disrespect for politics. The Future Foundation (2000) extended this research and found them to be more accepting of multinationals and less interested in protesting.

Further analysis of Generation Y has been conducted by Shepherdson (2000) and Gofton (2002).

If this group were targeted, this profile could provide useful clues as to the sort of message and media to use and reach them.

The older potential segment for the drinks company is composed of those in their fifties –

these are the 'baby boomers', those born in the years following the Second World War – who have become a very important target for marketers. They were involved in a massive social revolution which changed music, fashions, political thought and social attitudes forever. They were the generation to grow up in the 1960s, when the term 'teenager' hadn't been used previously. They were not 'small adults' who, in previous generations, had worn similar clothes to their parents. The new generation, however, wanted their own culture, their own fashions, music and their own social attitudes which rejected the values of their parents. Coupled with this desire for ownership of their thoughts and lives, the baby boomer generation was the most affluent (generally) of any 'youth market' until their era, so they were able to engage in the consumer market, and marketers responded with a fashion and music explosion of which we had previously never seen the like.

Such a consumerism-literate market should be extremely attractive. Indeed, in the USA, a baby boomer turned 50 every 6.8 seconds in 2001! Not all the over-50s are baby boomers, of course, those in their 60s and 70s, and indeed the over-70s are from other generations with lifestyles and attitudes of their own. Overall, the over-50s have been termed the 'third age'. They represent about a third of the population (in the late 1990s) and are some 18 million strong in the UK. By 2020, they will represent about half of the UK population. In general terms, the ageing baby boomer generation is the most wealthy, in terms of inheritance from their parents. That previous generation was 'blessed' with low house prices when they bought and a lifestyle which was much less materialistic. As a result, their estates have often (but clearly not always) been cascading down to the new over-50 market.

Research amongst the over-50s has revealed several characteristics. They don't like to be portrayed as 'old' but at the same time would see through attempts to portray them as 'young', so caution is needed.

There are differences between those in their 50s, 60s and above. Those in their 60s generally prefer to use cash and are rather cautious consumers. Those over 70 are perhaps even further along this continuum. There has certainly been an explosion of magazine titles aimed at various over-50 groups, demonstrating that the market is not homogeneous and that the various groups can be reached. The profiling in this sector is not merely on the basis of age, however; social grade and geodemographics are also being used, and there is a trend toward overlaying this with attitudinal research. An example of this comes from the analysis of the TGI in 1993 (Cummins, 1994), which found, based on shopping attitudes and behaviour, that there are 'astute cosmopolitans', constituting about 19 per cent of the 50–75s and who are discerning consumers. There are also the 'temperate xenophobes' (20 per cent of 50–75s) who are less likely to go abroad or eat 'foreign food'. The 'thrifty traditionalists' make up 20 per cent and a further 19 per cent are 'outgoing funlovers'! The largest group is the 'apathetic spenders' (21 per cent), who use credit cards to extend their purchasing power beyond what they can really afford (Cummins, 1994).

So, it is important not to generalize when targeting the over-50s and to take into account the very real differences between the subgroups. These are issues which marketers should clearly bear in mind when designing the tactics of marketing campaigns. The drinks company would certainly find useful clues in this analysis for how to target that segment.

Gender

Turning now to gender, the drinks company sees both sexes as potential targets, but how might this affect their marketing? Gender stereotyping has been used extensively over many decades, but it hasn't always escaped criticism. Reliance on 'mother' or 'mistress' or 'career woman' images of women in advertising sometimes attracts complaints on sexist or offensive grounds, as have some more recent demeaning images of men. Increases in the divorce rate and the 'singles' market have added to the more general changes in sex roles, with women becoming more individualistic through their own careers rather than being housewives *per se*. Marketing to women, however, may still be in need of updating. There are new female roles such as the independent assertive woman, independent passive woman and independent sexual woman. Some of these clearly relate to what in popular culture has been termed 'girl power'. As female roles change, so inevitably do those of men. We have seen a variety of male stereotypes such as the 'caring sharing new man', the 'family' man, the 'yob lad', 'modelling' man, 'househusband' man, as well as gay images.

Another implication of gender differences is information processing style between men and women. In a major research project it was found that men and women react differently to certain features of written communication. Women respond well to bright colours, photographs and images, and men respond well to bold headlines, bullet points and graphs (Evans *et al.*, 2000). So, again, an apparently straightforward demographic characteristic hides a multitude of implications for the marketer.

Earlier, the gay market was briefly mentioned. Indeed, it is worth commenting that marketing is increasingly interested in this segment. Gay men, for example, spend twice as much on clothing and four times as much on grooming as straights. They are often relatively more affluent, with few dependants. In terms of satisfying the accessible criterion, these segments are easier to reach nowadays because there are more gay magazines and TV programmes, and they are able to be reached via the Internet and sponsorship of gay events (for example, by Smirnoff, Levi's and Virgin). Many in the gay market have also been found to be more responsive to new products and might be a good target in the early stages in the life of new products and services. This is explored further in a later section.

Social grade

The drinks company also identified occupational grouping. The AB groups would be composed of senior and middle management and professional people, and C1s would be more likely to be clerks, secretaries, junior administrators or full-time students. The traditional justification for the continued use of social grade is basically twofold. It is simple to research. All that is required is for data to be analysed according to the occupation of the 'chief income earner in the household', and from this everyone can be positioned within the A, B, C1, C2, D, E categories. Second, social grade appears to have been a reasonably good discriminator of buying behaviour. However, during the 1980s in particular, a number of significant criticisms of social grade were made. It was also shown that, of 400 respondents to earlier surveys who were reinterviewed to confirm their social grade, 41 per cent had been allocated to the wrong group and this is an indication of instability of the system (O'Brien and Ford, 1988).

Another problem concerning social grade is that although there might be some correlations between social grade and purchase, how can this be used? Certainly, it is relevant for selecting appropriate advertising media based on the matching of segment social grade with the social grade profiles for different media. But there could be dangers in inferring values and attitudes of those in each social grade in order to create marketing communications messages. These more affective dimensions might not be caused by one's occupation.

Family

The drinks company also identified the family life cycle concept. The younger segment was in its 'dependent/first household' stage and the older segment was the 'empty nesters'. This approach shows how the family unit's interests and buying behaviour change over time. A simple model is the progression from the single bachelor stage, to newly married, married with children, empty nester who is married with children who no longer live in the parental home, and finally to the solitary survivor stage. Buying needs, values and behaviour clearly differ for the various stages. A recent promotional campaign by Barclays Bank depicted the life stages through which their customers go, by picturing a young single man, then a couple with a family and an older couple whose children had left home and suggesting that the Bank has financial service products to suit not just each stage 'now', but each individual as they progress through these stages of the life cycle. The Prudential even used a caterpillar to reflect how we metamorphose through life stages – promising equally evolutionary financial products to match each stage. So our drinks company has an opportunity to use this framework since it has identified one potential segment composed of those in the early stages of the life cycle and another in a later one. Again, message styles would be quite different, as the above suggests.

A related factor to consider is one that combines family and age influence, namely the influence of children within the household. The 'pester power' (Carter, 1994) is highly observable. It is possible that the 16- to 17-year-olds for the drinks company exhibit this, to 'try' alcohol in what might be seen as an acceptable form within the home. But it is also likely that these same children will be reacting to peer group pressure to consume (more) alcohol outside the home. There will be ethical issues for the drinks company marketing manager here.

What some marketers do is to target their advertising at a slightly older age group, so that the 'trickle down' theory operates – younger kids see the product being used by their elders and want to follow their lead. By the time it has trickled down to them, the older ones have been enticed to the next craze.

The concept of a 'brand' is probably just beginning to be understood by children when they reach 5 or 6. Parents are targeted with a 'sensible' message and kids with a more per-suasive one. With children of about 7 or 8, parental influence is less constraining and the children themselves develop a repertoire of acceptable brands, TV advertising and observation of older children being the main influences. Parents might be motivated to buy their children those products which help their development, but often they are persuaded to buy things which add to their children's street credibility – the 'right' brand.

When children are of primary school age it is often school friends who become more important product influencers than parents. Observation and word of mouth are then very important in developing children's preferences.

Many marketers have really taken this on board, and have started to get into schools with various sponsorship and 'educational' ventures. Schools need the help to ease financial hardship associated with their budgets, but some teachers are uncomfortable with this way of targeting the children's market.

Any viewing of TV at 'children's' viewing times will confirm saturation by commercials aimed at children. Younger children may merely watch these as entertainment but, as they grow, the brand and image become important and salient in children's' minds as a result of associative learning processes and vicarious learning (seeing others using the product). Personalities and cartoon characters are also heavily used to target children.

As well as child-related consumption, we are also concerned here with the role of children in determining more adult purchases. That is, which car the parents will buy, where to go on holiday, and so on. Parents have succumbed to a youth culture and look to their children for what is 'hip' to buy! In one survey (BBC, 1997) it was found that 72 per cent of parents admitted to £20 of their weekly spending being influenced by their children, 22 per cent of parents thought that up to £50 of weekly spending to be a result of pester power, and even 4 per cent thought that up to £100 of their weekly spending was based on this! This would amount to £5 billion per year if averaged across the UK.

Clearly there are ethical issues here. Children have not fully matured, by definition, yet they are being heavily targeted, sometimes in subtle ways by marketers who want them to develop brand preferences. Some retailers even have loyalty schemes for babies! The Royal Bank of Scotland obtained details of children from subscriptions to the Disney Book Club and sent them offers for a credit card. Children as young as 5 received the mailing offering a 9.9 per cent APR! (Anon, 1997).

Overall, then, we have had a brief look through some of the more prominent demographic characteristics. If you consider the implications of these for the drinks company's two main potential segments (using age, gender, social grade and family life cycle), then you would probably be able to devise a useful targeting strategy for each. Indeed, if we then integrate the above demographic variables rather than just consider each independently, an even more effective strategy should emerge, but that's something you can do for your next assignment or seminar!

Psychographics

This name covers lifestyle, personality and self-image. The last two can be discovered in the previous edition of this book (Evans, 1999) but lifestyle is worth some discussion, especially because it is important to differentiate traditional from contemporary lifestyle segmentation. The latter is covered in a later section, but the following is an analysis of how lifestyle segmentation was originally conceived.

Lifestyle

Lifestyle is based typically on the presentation to respondents of a series of statements (Likert scales). Table 10.2 reproduces a short selection of the (246) lifestyle statements used in the Target Group Index annual research programme (BMRB, 1988).

Table 10.2   Examples of lifestyle statements
I buy clothes for comfort, not for style
Once I find a brand I like, I tend to stick to it
I always buy British whenever I can
I dress to please myself
My family rarely sits down to a meal together at home
I enjoy eating foreign food
I like to do a lot when I am on holiday

Respondents are presented with these statements and asked to give their degree of agreement with each. An example will demonstrate the approach. In the 1980s, Levi Strauss in the USA went through a new product development programme concerning a range of up-market men's suits. The market research programme revolved around an attempt to discover 'lifestyles'. This is concerned with investigating activities, interests and opinions, sometimes referred to as AIO analysis. Such lifestyle data are then cluster analysed to produce groupings of respondents which are relatively homogeneous and at the same time heterogeneous *between* clusters in terms of their activities, interests and opinions. Each cluster would then be allocated a somewhat glib title. In the lifestyle research programme, Levi Strauss labelled the resulting segments: 'classic independent', the 'mainstream traditionalist', the 'price shopper', the 'trendy casual', and so on (BBC, 1984). This sort of profile will help determine appropriate product/service features and will help to arrive at an advertising message which is congruent with the segment's lifestyle.

A UK lifestyle typology was named Taylor Nelson's Applied Futures (McNulty and McNulty, 1987) and identified the following segments, including: The Belonger, the Survivor, the Experimentalist, the Conspicuous Consumer, the Social Resistor, the Self-Explorer and the Aimless. The Self-Explorer group was the fastest growing and further reinforces one of the propositions of this chapter, namely that some markets have become more orientated to self-expression and individualism. Note that the Levi example above also identified the 'classic independent' segment. This is a point taken up later, when data-driven segmentation is explored. This traditional form of lifestyle (AIO) segmentation provides useful insight into what makes people 'tick'. It is based upon traditional market research: administering Likert-scaled statements concerned with activities, interests and opinions to a sample of consumers. The data are anonymized and the resulting profiles are very useful for determining the style and mood of promotional messages.

If the drinks company, for example, had extended its demographic profiling of the market for its new alcopop product, it might have presented respondents with a series of statements concerning drinking and socializing. The results might have produced potential lifestyle segments such as: 'Boozy Kids' – eager to break away from parents, keen to have the approbation of their peer group, like going to parties and dance clubs. Another segment might be the 'Cardigans and Slippers' segment that likes to stay at home, entertain at home and watch television with a whisky and soda. These lifestyle profiles would be very useful for the drinks company in creating the right sort of message to communicate to these potential segments.

Segmentation over time

Earlier, it was suggested that marketers often found more innovative consumers in the gay market. This concept of innovativeness is a useful one for segmentation. It suggests that, over the life of a product, marketing activity might need to change because different seg-

ments of adopting customers are salient at different points in time. The characteristics of each adopter category and the importance of two step flows of communication via opinion leaders can be found in more detail elsewhere (Evans *et al.*, 1996), but the following will provide a useful indication of how these concepts can provide a framework for targeting different adopting segments.

Consider a sports shoe manufacturer wanting to introduce a new up-market trainer. Different adopter categories have their own profiles in terms of demographics, interest in newness and the sources of information they tend to use. The sports company might therefore target each adopter category as a distinct market segment. The Innovators could be targeted via editorial coverage in scientific magazines such as *New Scientist*, i.e. not at this stage in the specialist sports magazines. The style of message would probably be highly technical, with cross-section drawings and weight/drag coefficient tables. Perhaps the product could be exposed on TV's *Tomorrow's World* in a similar way.

For the early adopters, this segment might be targeted via personal selling to the leaders of sports and health clubs. Direct mail shots to these leaders could reinforce the personal selling, and it is likely that the approach would again be technical and the personal selling of a 'two professionals together' nature. More personal selling could be targeted to specialist shoe retailers, and the club leaders and retailers might be invited to an 'event' such as a conference or seminar arranged on behalf of the company. To reinforce this even further, editorials could be developed for appearance in the sporting and health journals. Overall, there could also be similar treatment for the Sports Coaches and even Sports Councils. It is possible that there could be a fashion market, quite outside the sports market, and if so fashion editors and journalists could be targeted in similar ways with fashion shows and personal presentations and, through these, editorial coverage could be secured in order to influence other adopter categories. Remember the Levi's example earlier, in which the targeting of opinion leaders was deliberate.

The early majority, if the early adopters have been properly identified and reached, would be influenced by a knock-on effect of what was done for the early adopters. There could be a trickle-down effect from club leaders to club members to the more innovative in the mass market outside of these clubs. Perhaps now it would be appropriate to use media advertising with a less technical message appeal, but more of a sporting hero type, using well-known sports personalities. Sponsorship of an event, sport or club could also be advantageous at this stage. The use of hospitality boxes at events where these trainers are worn via sponsorship agreements might also be worthwhile considering.

As for the late majority, the approach would need to change significantly – probably concentrating on media advertising with a very different style, suggesting that the shoes are no longer new and suggesting that there are plenty of ordinary people wearing them (even the simulated opinion leaders in the advertising might be of the unknown 'person next door' type). For this late majority it can be noted that all that was appropriate for earlier adopters now becomes right for this segment, with a consequent danger of turning off the earlier adopting segments.

The laggards are perhaps so difficult to reach and even more difficult to influence that, even if they are targeted, the approach might detract so much from the intended image that the laggards might be worth ignoring.

This demonstrates another of the more traditional approaches to segmentation and extends this into more concrete examples of how these approaches might be converted into practical targeting strategies. The point about targeting opinion leaders in order to speed up the diffusion process is one that is returned to later, in the coverage of data-driven segmentation. But before analysing this, it is worth mentioning a couple of other approaches: first, benefit segmentation and then an extension – person–situation segmentation.

Benefit segmentation

Marketing is concerned with satisfying customer needs and wants as a means to achieving the goals of the organization. However, although the human condition means we all have a similar need structure, the same needs will not be salient to every person at the same point in time. Those with similar salient needs and values may be grouped together to form a market segment if their buying behaviour is seen to be sufficiently homogeneous and, at the same time, different from those of other groups. Marketing then has the task of deciding which segments to target with distinct marketing mixes.

A useful illustration of segmentation is the toothpaste market in terms of the benefits, shown in Table 10.3. What is shown is that, even in such an apparently non-differentiated market, there are different consumer segments that buy in different ways for a variety of reasons and, on this basis, can be targeted with different marketing mixes. This is a fundamental rationale for market segmentation.

As will be explored later, the new data-driven approach can often relegate and ignore these fundamental affective benefit reasons for buying, in favour of the tracking of actual purchase behaviour over time and the projection of this for more relevant and effective targeting. This raises the issue of whether segmentation and targeting might be moving rather too much in the measurement metrics direction at the expense of a truer understanding of customer behaviour.

Person–situation segmentation

This approach is strongly related to benefit segmentation because it is based on the interaction of consumer characteristics, product benefits and occasions of use (Dickson, 1982). People with specific characteristics may want to

Table 10.3 Toothpaste consumer benefit segments

	Sensory segment	Sociable segment	Worrier segment	Independent segment
Main benefit	Flavour, appearance	Bright teeth	Decay prevention	Price
Demographic factors	Children/young people	Teens, families	Large families	Men
Lifestyle factors	Hedonistic	Active	Conservative	Concerned with value
Brands label	Colgate, Stripe	Ultra-Brite, Macleans	Crest	Cheapest own brands on sale

Adapted from Haley (1968).

Table 10.4 Person–situation segmentation

Situations	Young children	Teenagers	Adult women	Adult men	Situation benefits
Beach/boat sunbathing	Combined insect repellent		Summer perfume		Windburn protection Product can stand heat Container floats
Home-poolside sunbathing Sunlamp bathing			Combined moisturizer Combined moisturizer and massage oil		Large pump dispenser Won't stain wood, etc. Designed for type of lamp Artificial tanning
Snow skiing			Winter perfume		Protection from rays Anti-freeze formula
Person benefits	Special protection Non-poisonous		Female perfume	Male perfume	
		Fits in jeans pocket Used by opinion leaders			

Source: Dickson (1982).

use products with specific benefits in specific situations. Table 10.4 provides an example with respect to the suntan lotion market with four situations and four target groups. In principle, four times four products may be designed. Taking skin colour and skin factors into account, even more different product formulas may be marketed.

So far, all of the above segmentation bases have been derived from anonymized market research. Targeting would often be determined by estimating where and how potential segments might be found and reached. A company might have all of these details of its customers in its transactional database, but the discussion so far has tackled these characteristics from the more anonymized perspective. Attention is now turned, however, to data that are more closely linked with specific individuals. It is from this point that the new data-driven marketing, based on emerging marketing metrics and the pressures for marketing to be more accountable, has led to quite different approaches to segmentation and targeting.

Data-driven segmentation

In order to build up a picture of how marketing has increasingly moved to technological targeting, it is necessary to go back a couple of decades, to 1981 to be precise. Indeed, earlier it was implied that 1981 was a watershed year for segmentation and targeting. This was the year that the National Census in the UK was used for the first time in a major and influential manner in marketing.

Geodemographics

It is a proposition of this chapter that the use of the UK Census in 1981 was one of the more significant events in moving from generalized customer profiles to more individualized approaches. From that Census, some 40 census variables were cluster analysed and the emerg-ing clusters of households led to the creation of 39 neighbourhood types in the first geode-mographic system in the UK (ACORN – A Classification Of Residential Neighbourhoods, developed by CACI – Consolidated Analysis Centres Incorporated). Table 10.5 summarizes the ACORN neighbourhood categories that could constitute potential market segments for organizations. 'Me-too' versions are now offered by different companies. For example, what originally was the credit referencing arm of Great Universal Stores (CCN – Consumer Credit Nottingham) produced MOSAIC (which is now owned by Experian). This (and now other geodemographic systems) overlays census data with financial details.

Table 10.6 provides an example of the depth of profiling that is possible for each sub-segment.

Figure 10.1 demonstrates one use of geode-mographics. It is possible to profile a catchment area (for example) for the potential citing of a retail outlet. The MOSAIC (in this case) category overlays of the local map shows where different segments live. If, for example, the retailer is mainly targeting the 'stylish single' segment, the map shows the area of greatest concentration of this segment. Indeed, names and addresses of those in this segment can be purchased in order to target these potential customers personally.

The basic rationale behind geodemograph-ics is that 'birds of a feather flock together', making neighbourhoods relatively homoge-neous. An easy criticism in repost is that 'I am not like my neighbour'. Another major limita-tion of census data relates to the difficulties associated with updating information, partic-ularly because in the UK the Census is only carried out every 10 years. Experian has reallo-cated approximately 7 per cent of postcodes and have six name changes in the MOSAIC typology, both as an update and to improve clarity of meaning. There are suggestions that annual updates might be based on survey research, especially of the 'lifestyle' type, which is discussed in the next section.

Table 10.5   ACORN 'segments'

Category and label	Description	
Category A Group 1	Wealthy Achievers, Suburban Areas	The majority of people in this group live in a large detached house and have access to two or more cars. They are typically well-educated professional people, the corporate managers in their middle-age, enjoying the fruits of their labour. These are the consumers with the money and the space to enjoy very comfortable lifestyles.
Category A Group 2	Affluent Greys, Rural Communities	This group covers Britain's better-off farming communities – residents here are 12 times more likely than average to be involved in agriculture. Many are self-employed and work long hours. The very high incidence of visitors and households which are not the main residence show that these areas also include many holiday homes.
Category A Group 3	Prosperous Pensioners, Retirement Areas	The better-off senior citizens in society are to be found in Group 3. Living in flats, detached houses or bungalows, these are old folk who can enjoy their retirement in pensioned comfort after their professional or executive careers. They are likely to own their home outright, so they have the disposable income to enjoy themselves.
Category B Group 4	Affluent Executives, Family Areas	These are the well-qualified business people, successfully juggling jobs and families. There are lots of working women in this group. With mortgages, young children and often two or more cars to support, these busy people need their incomes but aren't having too hard a time making ends meet. They are likely to have large, modern detached houses and generally enjoy a good standard of living.
Category B Group 5	Well-Off Workers, Family Areas	In a wide range of well-paid occupations, people in Group 5 are likely to be in couples, often with children aged 0–14. Both Mum and Dad are working hard to pay off the mortgage on their detached or, more probably, semi-detached home. While they are not as highly qualified as people in Group 4, they still have an agreeable lifestyle, often with more than two cars per household.
Category C Group 6	Affluent Urbanities, Town and City Areas	These are the young couples or single people starting out in life, a few years and a couple of kids behind the people in Group 4! They tend to live in flats, terraced houses or bedsits. There are quite a number of students in this group. Car ownership is average, reflecting the urban setting.
Category C Group 7	Prosperous Professionals, Metropolitan Areas	People in Group 7 share many characteristics with Group 6. However, they live in more cosmopolitan areas with a high ethnic mix. They take the train or underground to the office each day, working long hours in fairly senior roles and making the most of their high qualifications.
Category C Group 8	Better-Off Executives, Inner City Areas	These are well-qualified people, over a third of whom are single with no dependants. The age profile here is younger than for Groups 6 and 7, and there are many more students and other characteristics of academic centres. This group also has a relatively high proportion of professionals and executives, and shares many of the cosmopolitan features of Group 7.
Category D Group 9	Comfortable Middle Agers, Mature Home Owning Areas	Mr and Mrs Average are to be found in these areas – they are close to the national 'norm' on just about every key characteristic. Living in a detached or semi-detached house with at least one car, likely to be an older married couple, Group 9 represents middle-of-the-road Britain. They are not particularly well-off but have few problems with unemployment or health.

Table 10.5   Continued

Category and label	Description	
Category D Group 10	Skilled Workers, Home Owning Areas	People in this group are likely to be found in manufacturing areas, working in skilled occupations. They tend to live in terraced homes and are more likely to be couples with children aged 0–14. Most are homeowners and the majority are buying with a mortgage. Although not quite as comfortable as Group 9 – car ownership is lower – people in these areas are also around the midpoint on the social ladder.
Category E Group 11	New Home Owners, Mature Communities	These areas are characterized by people who have bought up their semi-detached or terraced council houses. They are likely to be older couples, often pensioners. Those still at work tend to be involved in craft or machine-related occupations. Unemployment is only slightly above the national average.
Category E Group 12	White Collar Workers, Better-Off, Multi-Ethnic Areas	The relatively high incidence of people from diverse ethnic groups – especially Afro-Caribbean and Indian – characterizes these multi-ethnic family areas. Accommodation tends to be either terraced houses or flats. Unemployment is slightly higher than in Group 11, but overall living conditions are reasonable.
Category F Group 13	Older People, Less Prosperous Areas	These are the areas of older couples aged 55+ who find the going quite tough. The incidence of limiting long-term illness is high. The majority do not have a car. People are generally living in small terraced houses or purpose-built flats, typically from housing associations. Those still at work tend to be in manual or unskilled occupations; unemployment is above average.
Category F Group 14	Council Estate Residents, Better-Off Homes	These areas are typified by young couples with young children. Housing tends to be council or housing association terraces, often with cramped living conditions, though families tend to be better off than those in other groups in this category. Unemployment is relatively high and there are many single parents.
Category F Group 15	Council Estate Residents, High Unemployment	Group 15 has a greater ethnic mix and higher unemployment than Group 14. This group has an older age profile and the highest incidence of limiting long-term illness – almost double the national average. People live mainly in purpose-built council flats. Car ownership is lower in these areas than anywhere else.
Category F Group 16	Council Estate Residents, Greatest Hardship	Two key features characterize this group: single parents and unemployment, both of which – at roughly three times the national average – are higher in this group than in any other. Overall, living conditions are extremely tough. There are lots of young and very young children, with large households in small council flats.
Category F Group 17	People in Multi-Ethnic, Low-Income Areas	The greatest ethnic mix in Britain is found in this group, especially of Pakistani and Bangladeshi groups, which account for over 40 per cent of the population. Single parenting and unemployment are very high. Many people are living in extremely cramped conditions in unmodernized terraced housing or council flats. Whilst these areas are relatively poor, there is evidence to suggest small pockets of more affluent residents.

Source: ONS and GRO(S). CACI Ltd.

Table 10.6   Type 8.22 academic centres, students and young professionals

Overview

These are predominantly student areas. In addition to students, there are people who work in higher education and young professionals. They are cosmopolitan areas located near universities. ACORN Type 22 neighbourhoods are found all over Britain, but the highest concentration is in Oxford.

Demographics

These areas have 80 per cent more people than average in the 15–24 age group. There is also an above average level of 25- to 44-year-olds, but below average representation of all other age groups. There are above average proportions of ethnic minorities – twice the national proportion of people from the Afro-Caribbean ethnic group, over three times the national proportion of people from the Asian ethnic group and, within this, over five times the national level of people from the Pakistani ethnic group. In terms of household structure, there are 2.2 times the average proportion of single non-pensioner households.

Socio-Economic Profile

The socio-economic profile of ACORN Type 22 is dominated by education. Almost 47 per cent of the adult population are students based in these neighbourhoods in term time. The non-student population is also highly educated, with three times the average proportion of people with degrees. The proportions of women, both with and without children, who work are below average. The level of professionals is over twice the average.

Housing

The housing structure of ACORN Type 22 is a mix of terraced homes (37 per cent more than average), purpose-built flats (twice the national average proportion), converted flats (2.7 times more than average) and bedsits (5.2 times more than average). The key feature of the tenure profile is the level of furnished rented accommodation – almost seven times more than average. The proportion of households sharing amenities is three times greater than average.

Food and Drink

People living in ACORN Type 22 neighbourhoods are more than twice as likely as average to do their grocery shopping on foot, though less likely than average to do daily food shopping. The typical student diet is reflected in the range of foods purchased regularly. Consumption of frozen ready meals is high, though consumption of other frozen foods such as beefburgers is below average. Other popular products are brown sauce and ketchup, tinned steak, boxed chocolates and fruit juice. Beer consumption is extremely high, especially of bottled lager, but consumption of wines and spirits is only just above average.

Durables

Car ownership levels are low, reflecting the socio-economic profile of the population. Twice as many people as average walk to work. Although car ownership is very low the car profile is biased towards new, large and expensive cars. Company car ownership is 75 per cent lower than average; 66 per cent more people than average are buying home computers and 83 per cent more people are buying tumble dryers. Purchase rates for other household durables are extremely low.

Financial

The average income in these areas is very low, as might be expected given the large numbers of students. Almost a quarter of people earn less than £5000 per annum, and only 3 per cent earn over £30 000 per annum. Almost twice as many people as average are opening new current accounts, but virtually no one is opening new savings accounts. Ownership of all financial products is very low except debit cards, which are owned by 48 per cent more people than average.

Media

The penetration of cable television in these neighbourhoods is 46 per cent higher than average. *The Financial Times*, *The Guardian* and *The Independent* all have much higher than average readership levels. Amongst the Sunday newspapers, *The Observer* and *The Independent on Sunday* are read by two to three times more people here than average. Both ITV viewing and commercial radio listening are very light.

Table 10.6   Continued

Leisure   The proportion of people taking holidays is average, but 82 per cent more people than
average take long holidays, 2.5 times more people than average go camping, and
destinations outside Britain and Europe are 82 per cent more popular than average. There
is a very high propensity to visit pubs regularly. The proportion of people eating out
regularly is slightly above average. Burger bars are popular, as are Chinese, Indian and
Italian restaurants. Sports which have very high participation rates are running and
training, cricket, tennis, cycling, squash, table tennis, skiing and climbing. Attendance at
cinemas, theatres and art galleries is very high.

Attitudes   People here are less likely than average to be happy with their standard of living. They are
much more likely than average to search for the lowest prices when shopping. They are
over twice as likely as average to be vegetarian. They like to take holidays off the beaten
track, but are happy to return to the same holiday destination.

Source: ONS and GRO(S). CACI Ltd.

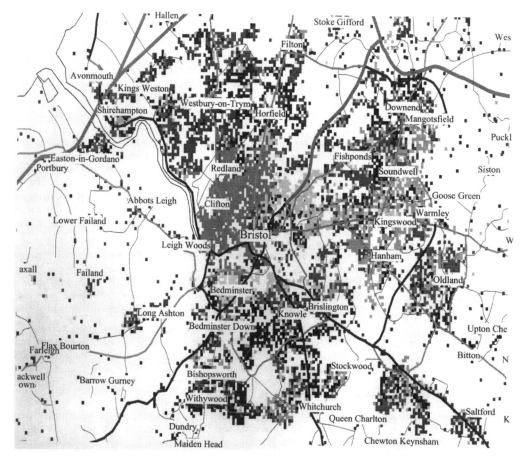

Figure 10.1   The use of geodemographics

Because geodemographics are based on census data, there is the corresponding criticism of those systems. In addition, as sophisticated as geodemographics are – certainly compared with the simplicity of age, gender and occupation (the main variables of the demographic alternative) – the approach is essentially the same, i.e. it 'profiles' people. The method does not in itself explain why people behave as they do and neither does it provide individualized information on what people buy. These issues are, to some extent, addressed by other approaches, outlined in the sections below on 'new' lifestyle segmentation, transactional data and biographic segmentation.

Names and addresses cannot be revealed from the census, but the statistics for enumeration districts can. Census data can be linked with the postcode database (there is one postcode for approximately 15 households) and with the electoral roll (another database); it is possible to identify individual households and their characteristics. One of the current debates (at the time of writing) is between the Information Commissioner's position that the electoral roll was not collected for marketing purposes and should not therefore be used in this way, and on the other hand the marketing industry, which argues for freedom in its use. Although the electoral roll is rarely used as a list in itself, it is used as the base for virtually every targeting tool and geodemographics started this process.

One concern of the Information Commissioner is that some people may disenfranchise themselves by not registering for fear of being over-targeted by marketers. A legal case has already brought this to a head. In November 2001, a member of the public won his case against Wakefield Council after that Council had not been able to confirm that his electoral roll data (name and address) would not be supplied to third parties, such as marketers, without his consent (Acland, 2001).

The full implications of this case were not clear at the time of writing, but if the principle is generally upheld, this could be a significant strait-jacket for data-driven segmentation and targeting. Clearly, without the electoral roll it would be difficult to identify individual households from census data. One study suggests that a ban on using electoral roll data could cost advertisers £55 million per year because 'the cost of not having access to the electoral roll would be five pence per (mail) pack' (Denny, 1999).

Having said this, it is likely that an opt-out option will be added to the electoral roll and this should help to alleviate privacy concerns at the same time as shifting segmentation and targeting in yet another (related) direction – namely based on customer 'permission' to use their personal details. Perhaps the latter will itself become more sophisticated and customers will give permission to specific organizations to use their details for specified purposes.

There have been other developments of the geodemographic principle, as hinted at above, and these are discussed in the following coverage of 'new' lifestyle segmentation, the use of transactional data and the fusion of data to form the new biographics.

'New' lifestyle segmentation

A more recent development in lifestyle research and segmentation is the 'lifestyle survey', which has a somewhat different basis. These surveys essentially ask respondents to 'tick' those responses that apply – Table 10.7 demonstrates some typical questions, some of which will be sponsored by specific companies.

This table reflects just a portion of typical current lifestyle surveys. Many more questions are included, covering claimed buying behaviour across many different product and service categories. Some questions will be sponsored by specific companies – for example, a car insurance company might sponsor a question asking for the month in which the car insurance is renewed. Because these surveys are not anonymized, the data will be filed in a database by name and address of respondent; it is likely that the month prior to that respondent's renewal

Table 10.7 · Contemporary 'lifestyle' research

Please indicate your marital status
(single, married, divorced/separated, widowed)

What is your name and address?

What is your partner's full name?

Holidays:
How much are you likely to spend per person on your next main holiday

up to £500 ☐   £501–£999 ☐   £1000–1499 ☐   £1500–£2000 ☐   £2000 + ☐

In which country are you likely to take your next main holiday?

In which month are you likely to take your main holiday?

date, he or she will receive direct mailings soliciting defection to the sponsoring company.

Although the industry has claimed there is now a lifestyle census, the reality is somewhat different. Admittedly, a large number of individuals (around 20 million in the UK) have responded, but the survey is by definition a self-selected sample and it is known that some respondents do not tell the whole truth in completing the questionnaire (Evans *et al.*, 1997). The difference between the more traditional form of lifestyle segmentation discussed earlier and the current approach is that the former builds psychographic profiles of segments from relatively small data sets and expands these to generalize patterns within the larger population. The latter, however, has the ability to list names and addresses of those who claim to be interested in specific products, brands and services, and it is this, of course, that contributes to more directed segmenting and targeting of markets. It provides data on what respondents claim they buy, but doesn't in itself reveal the same type of *affective* data on opinions and 'outlook on life' that can be derived from traditional AIO analysis.

Table 10.8 shows one segmentation approach, based on the new lifestyle data, for the UK.

What is currently happening, however, is for geodemographic data to be further overlaid with lifestyle data, so the data fusion paradigm continues apace.

Biographic segmentation

A further development, and yet another significant one, is the progression from profile data to *transactional data*. Bar code scanning at point of purchase can match products purchased with details of the customer. A similar story applies to mail, telephone or Internet purchases, because these can match purchases with individuals. For example, an inspection of a resulting retail loyalty scheme database revealed, for a certain Mrs 'Brown', her address and a variety of behavioural information, including: she shops once per week, usually on a Friday, has a baby (because she buys nappies), spends £90 per week on average and usually buys two bottles of gin every week – on Thursdays (Mitchell, 1996). Analysis via data mining software (demonstrated later) can identify purchasing patterns of individuals. By knowing what individual consumers buy, the retailer might be able to target them with relevant offers. For example, special offers relevant to a shopper's child's birthday can be

Table 10.8   People UK

Life stage 1
Silver spoons
Popcorn and pop music
Friends in flats
Urban multicultural

Starting Out
Young people with affluent parents
Singles in low value housing
Young flat sharers
Mixed metropolitan singles

Life stage 2
Legoland families
Caravans and funfairs
Struggling singles

Young with Toddlers
Prosperous marrieds with pre-school children
Young families in mid-value homes
Single parents on low incomes

Life stage 3
On the right track
PC parents
School fetes
Car boot sales
Camping and cottages
Loan-loaded lifestyles
Satellites and scratchcards

Young Families
Up-market executive families
Affluent liberal young families
Aspiring couples with young children
Traditional families with average incomes
Moderate incomes, outdoor pursuits
Low incomes and high loans
Poorer families without bank accounts

Life stage 4
Telebanking townies
Solvent set
On the terraces
Pubs and pool

Singles/Couples No Kids
City flat sharers with affluent active lifestyles
Financially aware middle-aged singles/couples
Blue collar singles
Poorer singles in deprived areas

Life stage 5
Serious money
Affluent intelligentsia
Two-car suburbia
Conventional families
Cross-channel weekenders
Gardens and pets
Neighbourhood watch
Staid at home
Tabloids and TV

Middle Aged Families
Wealthy families in exclusive areas
Cultured well-off couples
Prosperous people with teenage children
Comfortable households with traditional values
Moderately well-off settled families
Established families in country areas
Average incomes, suburban semis
Families with teenage children in low value semis
Lower income families with older children

Life stage 6
Prosperous Empty Nesters
Young at heart
Cautious couples
Radio 2 fans
Urban elderly
Beer and Bookies

Empty Nesters
Older couples living in expensive houses
Older couples with active interests
Modest lifestyles and moderate means
Average incomes and traditional attitudes
Poorer couples in council housing
Low income families with teenage children

Table 10.8 Continued	
Life stage 7	Retired Couples
The golden years	Affluent couples
Cultured living	Retired couples with up market leisure interests
Keeping up appearances	Retirees in bungalows
Put the kettle on	Inactive retirees
Counting the pennies	Elderly couples in low value housing
Just coping	Impoverished elderly couples
Life stage 8	Older Singles
Older affluent urbanites	Older metropolitans in expensive housing
Active pensioners	Older people with active lifestyles
Theatre and travel	Elderly city dwellers with up market interests
Songs of praise	Charitable elderly singles
Grey blues	Pensioners living in very poor areas
Church and bingo	Very old and poor singles
Meals on wheels	Poorest elderly in council flats

Source: CACI: People UK. ONS and GRO(S).

made at the right time and the shopper's new purchases can be added to the bank of information on their previous purchases, and hence the amount and quality of information grows – and so does a potential 'relationship' with individual customers. This would lead to a significant paradigm shift in terms of segmenting and targeting markets, at both the operational and strategic levels. It demonstrates an oft-proclaimed trend toward custom market segmentation, one-to-one marketing and customer relationship management (CRM), and is discussed shortly.

The point is that transactional data become the central focus of segmenters' many databases, and is overlaid with the multitude of profile data discussed earlier. As a result, we have moved into the era of *biographic* segmentation – the fusion of profile and transaction data. Many marketers are able to produce a 'buying biography' of individual customers.

The general point being made here is that markets are being analysed in ever more sophisticated and detailed ways, and this is leading to the identification and targeting of smaller but better-defined (at least in theory) segments.

Segmentation metrics

This section outlines how some of the more popular segmentation metrics operate. For ease of illustration and integration of these metrics through a typical sequence of application, a hypothetical case study is used as a framework. A financial services company markets several financial service products and wants to identify new segments within its existing customer base for a cross-selling strategy. Through the application of data mining/CRM software (this case has been adapted by the author from one provided by SmartFocus; the data mining/CRM software concerned is their VIPER product), the company can easily identify those customers who have already purchased various of the company's products.

Although CRM involves more than a software package, in practice, many organizations either selling or buying CRM 'solutions' tend not to venture much beyond the more narrow IT approach. The chapters on relationship marketing and CRM explore this issue further, but for the sake of our segmentation illustration, the software deployed is described as a CRM solution. As Figure 10.2 shows, the software produces a Venn diagram showing the number of customers who have purchased Account Types A, B and C; 39 426 people have account A only, and their names and addresses are quickly displayed (these are obviously 'scrambled' for this exercise). This is a potential segment for a cross-selling campaign con-cerning another of the company's products, say Account Type B.

The company could target these customers immediately, with a promotional offer for Account B. But this would undervalue customer and transactional data as an asset. In addition, the company would also want the highest return on marketing investment. As we have already mentioned, it is increasingly important to satisfy that strategic criterion for segmentation which is concerned with financial returns.

If the company mailed all 39 426 at, say, £1 per piece, the spend would be £39 426 uniformly across the target, missing the opportunity to 'gravitate' spend towards more profitable groups. So, instead, the company could

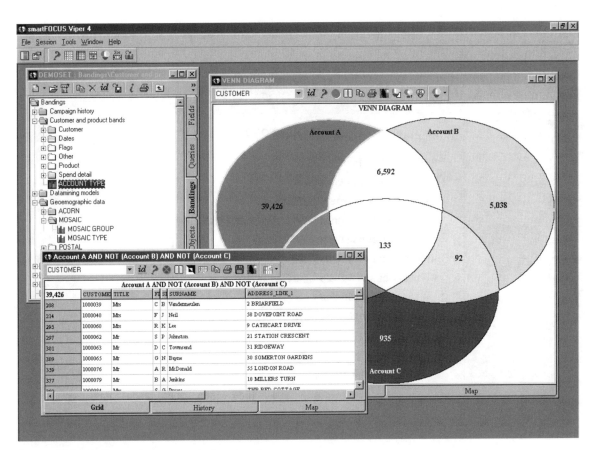

Figure 10.2 Software for segmentation metrics

use the data mining/CRM software to inter-rogate existing customers who have both A and B accounts. Data mining can identify what makes these customers different from others and what makes them more or less likely to take both products.

Taking the overlap area in the middle of the top of the Venn diagram, the data mining/CRM software could be used to overlay geode-mographic profiles for these customers (Figure 10.3).

The results show that the existing A and B account holding customers come mainly from areas classified as Low Rise Council, Council Flats, Town Houses and Flats, Blue Collar Owners. This information could be vital to the

identification of target segments for the cross-sell campaign, to acquire new customers for a different product, but from the company's existing customer base for another product.

The approach can also be valuable for other campaigns, especially acquisition seg-mentation strategies, where customer and transactional data on existing customers can be used to identify the characteristics of existing best customers in order to target others, not currently customers, but who possess similar characteristics. This is the identikit or cloning approach, an example of which is provided in the 'targeting' section.

Figure 10.4 takes the financial services example further. Transactional data can be fused

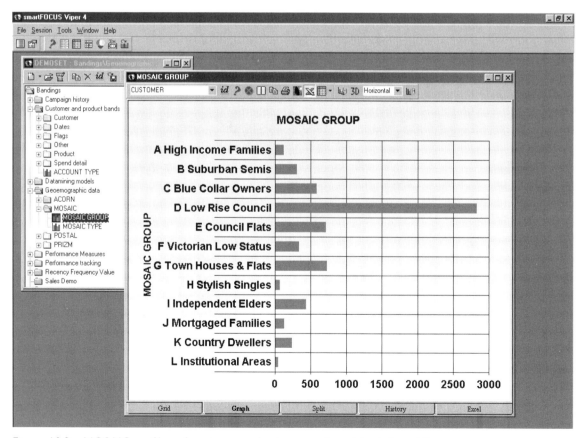

Figure 10.3   MOSAIC profiles of customers who have purchased both A and B

with Experian's MOSAIC geodemographic system and MapInfo's geographical information system (GIS) to show 'hot spots' geographically of where these potentially best target segments might be found. As we have seen, MOSAIC uses postcodes and the data mining/CRM software has spatial analysis capabilities through a dynamic link to MapInfo.

To further hone the characteristics of this 'best prospect' segment, the data mining/CRM software can be used to overlay other customer characteristics onto the map in order to redraw and filter this target segment further. Here, the first map has been filtered using Income over £35 000, Marital Status = Married, and Age in the 45–70 band. These are the characteristics that the same data mining/CRM software identified as being the ones possessed by the 'best' current customers of both Account Types A and B, according to their RFM profile. The data mining/CRM software extracts the names and addresses of customers with these same characteristics who currently have only purchased Account Type A as representing the best prospect segment for the cross-selling campaign for Type B. This is done by merely selecting the 'hot spot zones' from the second map in Figure 10.4. Names and addresses are produced almost instantly, providing a contact list that satisfies the accessible criterion for segmentation. This target segment would presumably have a higher propensity to purchase both products A and B. Although the segment is composed of those who have currently only purchased A, it contains those who possess the characteristics of the best customers who have purchased both products.

There is more that can be done. The fullest benefit from existing customer data comes from looking at all of the attributes together. The easiest way to achieve this is via CHAID, which in this case is an integral component of the data mining/CRM software being used and of most similar packages.

CHAID is a type of cluster analysis in which large samples are broken down into homogeneous subsets. Based on scores on the dependent variable, clusters are formed that differ maximally between clusters on the dependent variable. The approach is very useful for market segmentation and is becoming very popular amongst data-driven marketers.

CHAID will produce a tree-like analysis which identifies different segments based on the variables themselves, but also on the effects of the variables interacting with each other (regression doesn't automatically do this). Where there is no significant difference between some of the variables, CHAID will combine these into a larger 'segment'.

Here, various customer and transactional attributes have been investigated to see which best explain the characteristics of customers who have both A and B. A 'tree' structure represents different 'hot' and 'cold' 'branches' through the data. Each branch represents a different level of importance in explaining who the A and B customers are. Each attribute is assessed and the most important or 'significant' forms the first split. Taking the entire customer base in this instance, 87.37 per cent of all customers have both Accounts A and B (Figure 10.5).

By following the 'hottest branch', the company can understand which characteristics are possessed by those customers who have purchased both Account Types A and B. Figure 10.5 shows these to be: Married and Male. For this group of customers, the percentage with both Accounts A and B rises to 96.12 per cent compared with 87.37 per cent of entire unsegmented base.

Further branches of the CHAID tree might cascade down to even more segments based on whichever variables prove to be significant. Space prevents showing further stages here, but assume the analysis produced 60 target segments. Each of these would have significant and different characteristics. Targeting could be done on a 'test' basis in which a sample from each might be targeted and those with better response rates could then be targeted with the full 'roll-out' campaign. Also, each could be

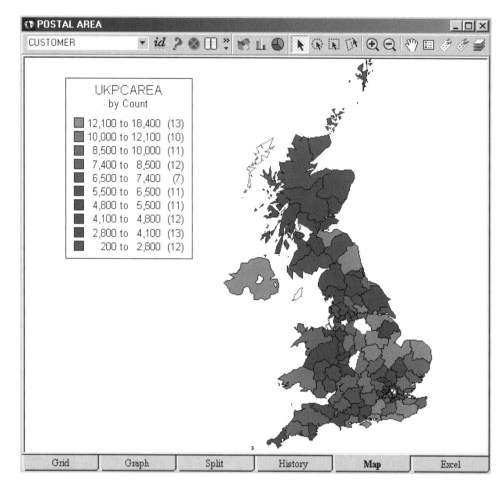

(a)

Figure 10.4 GIS data fusion

targeted with different treatments, according to whatever gender, age, marital status or geodemographic characteristic might underpin the 'creative' (Figure 10.6).

This sort of software incorporates data mining techniques, as shown, but it is worth explaining these a little further. Data mining, in principle, is a 'process of extracting hidden or previously unknown, comprehensible and actionable information from large databases' (Antoniou, 1997). From this there are two approaches that data mining can adopt. The first is *verification driven*: 'extracting information

to validate a hypothesis postulated by a user'. Many organizations will have their own segmentation model. For example, supermarkets, in analysing their loyalty card data, might use a model that incorporates:

- Stage in family life cycle (this is a very popular segmenting base for data-driven marketers).
- Vegetarianism.
- Interest in alcohol.
- Baby products.
- Orientation to predominantly own labels or manufacturer brands, etc.

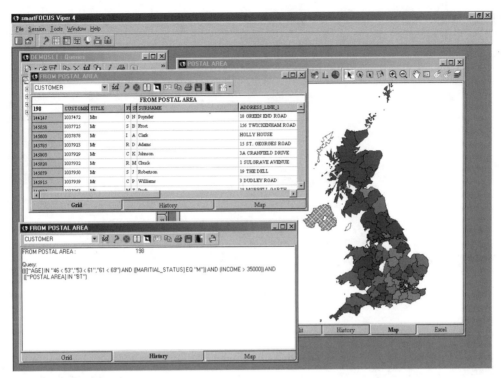

(b)

Figure 10.4   GIS data fusion

All of these can, of course, be identified from the transactional data held in the database for each participating customer.

The second approach refers to the digging around in databases in a relatively unstructured way with the aim of discovering links between customer behaviour and almost any variable that might potentially be useful. This second approach is *discovery driven*: 'identifying and extracting hidden, previously unknown information . . . (to) scour the data for patterns which do not come naturally to the analysts' set of views or ideas' (Antoniou, 1997). Data-driven marketers have tried a variety of unusual or unexpected areas in which to mine. For example, some have examined consumers' individual biorhythms and star signs (Mitchell and Haggett, 1997) as predictors of their purchasing patterns.

At the heart of many data mining packages is CHAID, as shown above. CHAID can use any variable within the data set, so the old rules have been overturned in favour of almost any combination of whatever personal and further overlaid profiling details the organization has on its databases.

It is interesting to compare this with the traditional use of market reports in which entire countries' consumption profiles might be based on samples of just 1000, and profiled in terms of gender, age and occupation. Inferences would have to be made as to why consumption patterns are as identified; profile characteristics *per se* would not necessarily be causal.

By contrast, the new data-driven segmentation and targeting approaches might be based on details of several million customers, each with hundreds of transaction records over

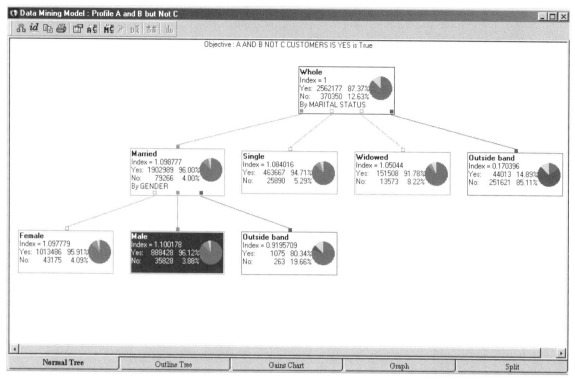

Figure 10.5   Data mining model

several years and which can be further overlaid by geodemographics. Geodemographics itself would be based on the National Census which, in the case of the UK, represents 60 million people and the analysis of up to 80 census variables plus financial and other variables used to cluster neighbourhood groups. This is further overlaid with personalized details of 20 million individuals and the hundreds of product/service interests they have marked on lifestyle surveys.

One-to-one segmentation and CRM

There is some evidence that some segments want to behave more as individuals and therefore perhaps be treated as such by marketers (Evans, 1989), but although the discussion

above probably gives the impression that we have moved to 'segments of one', one-to-one marketing is not the norm and perhaps is more rhetoric than reality. Dibb (2001) explores aspects of this and points out that 'at the heart of segmentation strategy is the notion that customers will allow themselves to be managed'. Indeed, the use of the word 'management' in CRM might signal that 'relationship management' is an oxymoron. It implies power and that that power is one way.

Such data analysis as has been outlined above can lead to individuals being targeted, but not necessarily as individuals. The CHAID example demonstrated that although individual data were processed, the resulting segments are still aggregates even if their constituent members are targeted by name and address, and probably with different styles of offer from

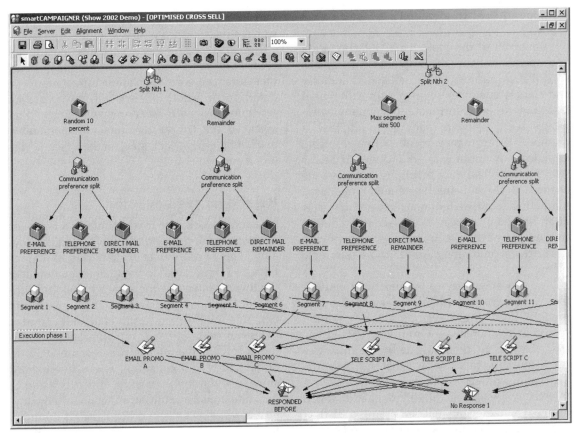

Figure 10.6 Targeted segments and differential treatment according to Offer and Creative, together with Control Groups

those in other segments. Tesco has analysed its loyalty card data and it has been reported (Marsh, 2001) that mining the mountain of transactional data from its 10 million Clubcard users has led to the identification of 100 000 different segments, each targeted with a different set of money-off vouchers via a customer magazine. A similar example is provided by Tower Records. This company has segmented its customer database and e-mails offers to selected targets, but 'out of every 10 000 e-mails sent, no more than three people receive the same offer' (Marsh, 2001).

The 'personalized' approach to relational marketing, however, might experience future flak. Digital printing technology allows personalization to a higher degree. 'You can personalize page by page, its easy to put a name anywhere throughout the copy' (Arnold, 2002). A development of this in the USA was an apparently hand-written mailing targeted at members of a particular health care segment. So convincing was this that over 150 people complained on the basis that it looked like a friend writing to them telling them they needed to lose weight! (Rubach, 2002).

Technology will also facilitate more examples of personalized targeting of segments. It is now possible to target an individualized TV message, analogous to personalized mailing, to a unique address via fibre-optic cable (Channel 4, 1990).

In practice, the most usual interpretation and operationalizing of CRM is essentially this sort of data mining, which is used to identify and classify customer segments for differential targeting. It is unfortunate that many companies see a software package as all that is required. If the management of this resulting knowledge is not integrated and shared across relevant organizational functions, there is little chance of there being sustainable relational marketing. Knowledge management as it is often termed at present is outside the scope of this chapter, but is a framework for moving data-driven marketing to a more strategic plane.

In conceptual terms, relationship marketing is concerned with all activities directed towards attracting, developing and retaining customer relationships. Gronroos (1994, 1996) indicates that there are a number of strategies open to marketers, along what he calls the 'marketing strategy continuum'. At its extreme, *transactional* exchange involves single, short-term exchange events encompassing a distinct beginning and ending. Consumer goods firms with mass markets and little contact with their ultimate customers are most likely to place themselves at this end of the continuum. On the other hand, *relational* exchange involves transactions linked together over an extended time frame.

Rather than treating individual customers according to some rather mechanistic data mining, real relationship marketing should be characterized by more affective factors such as trust, commitment, mutual benefit, adaptation, respect, and regard for privacy (O'Malley *et al.*, 1999). Organizations might want the sort of relationship with customers that results in a continued stream of money from customer to company, but do all customers really see their interaction with companies as a relationship?

Indeed, it is probably more complex in practice because it is not merely a case of whether an individual wants a relationship with a company, but whether the company wants a relationship with that individual (some customers being deselected because they do not contribute sufficiently to profitability). Furthermore, the type of relationship needs to be determined; after all, we all have unique relationships with everyone we know and meet, so the conceptual ideal of relationship marketing might lack pragmatism (see Chapters 3 and 19).

Relational segmentation

One framework that might provide a basis for segmenting along relational lines concerns 'loyalty'. This is more than regular purchasing, as Dick and Basu (1994) in their conceptualizing of the loyalty phenomenon suggest. 'Relative attitudes' are also important. That is, loyalty depends not only on positive attitudes toward the store or brand, but on differentiated attitudes toward the alternatives (Figure 10.7). In other words, if a consumer is positive toward store A, and not very positive towards B and C, then the consumer might indeed develop loyalty toward A. On the other hand, if there are fairly similar positive attitudes toward A, B and C, then there is unlikely to be real loyalty. In this case, the consumer might patronize a particular store regularly, but due to factors such as convenience and familiarity.

This analysis is useful because it is an explanation of why apparent loyalty (at least regular patronage) might not be true loyalty. Conversely, it contributes to our understanding of why some consumers exhibit aspects of real loyalty without holding particularly strong positive attitudes toward that store. In this latter case, the argument would be that a positive but weak attitude toward A might be accentuated by even weaker positive attitudes towards B and C.

Dick and Basu (1994) describe a situation in which relative attitude is low (little to choose between the alternatives) but which is also characterized by high store patronage, and they describe this as 'spurious loyalty'. Where,

Repeat Patronage

	High	Low
High	Loyalty	Latent Loyalty
Low	Spurious Loyalty	No Loyalty

Relative Attitude

Figure 10.7   Loyalty segments
Source: Dick and Basu (1994).

alternatively, there is low patronage but strongly differentiated and positive attitudes toward A, this is 'latent loyalty'. Otherwise, expected high patronage in this case might be inhibited by co-shoppers' preferences, for example (Figure 10.7).

When it comes to real loyalty itself, it is clear by now that they see this as where there is both high patronage and a positive attitude toward the store which is not matched by similarly positive attitudes toward alternative stores. These potential market segments which marketers would want to progress toward are shown in the upper left quadrant of Figure 10.7.

However, the segmentation metrics described above can easily identify those individual customers who are regular purchasers, but cannot, without more affective data being collected, combine this with the 'relative attitude' dimension. This is an important point that is further explored next.

Behavioural vs affective relational segmentation

As discussed, we are seeing moves toward one-to-one targeting in terms of personalized offers based on mining previous buying biographies. However, needs and benefits sought by customers are not always considered to be as important. Some organizations are rejecting the

more affective research in favour of purely behavioural data. For example, the JIGSAW consortium, composed of Unilever, Kimberley Clark and Cadbury Schweppes, has been pooling transactional data on their respective customers in order to grow product categories and to combat the power of intermediary retailers. This consortium has decided not to bother with attitudinal customer data any more and base their segmentation decisions on the massive amount of behavioural transactional data they, collectively, possess.

This is reinforced by Mitchell (2001a), who recently quoted a director of one of the largest retailers in the UK:

> We've given up trying to understand our customers . . . helping us cut a lot of complexity from our business.

The favoured approach by this company, 'sense and respond' (Haeckel, 2001), is to react quickly on the basis of customer contact via call centres, the Internet, interactive digital TV and others. This is understandable in the current context of short-termism. For example, the pressure to achieve short-term profit in order to provide shareholder value, again in the short term, can lead to a subordination of the key components of the marketing concept itself, namely customer satisfaction. The potential (or current?) danger is that the understanding of customer behaviour for segmentation and targeting strategies is not being driven too mechanistically by behavioural data. As Shaw *et al.* (2000) note:

> Market segmentation should be driven by customer needs and wants . . . these techniques are well understood in the academic world but corporate practice seems to be in the dark ages.

This is also reflected in studies into customer relationship marketing. Gofton (2001) reports that Qci found that few organizations distinguish between the satisfaction levels of their most and least valuable segments:

Only 16 per cent (of the 51 blue chip companies interviewed) understand what the main drivers of loyalty are . . . 30 per cent never look at this and only half carry out some research to identify loyalty.

Indeed, a study amongst pharmaceutical companies found that, when asked what the key challenges are for the introduction of CRM, only 6.5 per cent of the issues mentioned related to improving customer satisfaction (Clegg, 2001). So one wonders what happened to the likes of benefit segmentation, for example. Actual behavioural response does not necessarily equate with an understanding of consumers. If responders become the central focus (because they are cheaper to retain than new consumers are to acquire), then aren't we storing up trouble for the future in attending less to why the others are non-responders?

Also, it is clear that the new data-driven segmentation is not always managed by marketers who possess the right skills to cope with the approach or even to talk the same language as those who can. In recent research conducted for the Chartered Institute of Marketing (CIM, 2001a), this was identified as a major skills gap:

Marketers should develop IT/new technology skills (maybe via 'junior mentors' – younger people who are 'IT savvy' and who can educate their senior colleagues). We cannot influence the development and usage of IT within companies unless we know something about it.

Senior manager, financial services multinational (CIM, 2001a)

Indeed, Carson (1999) interviewed a group of leading US marketing practitioners and concluded that analytical skills and statistics topped the list of 'areas in which their education was lacking'. Businesses are demanding more accountability than ever before, making it essential for marketers to 'know how to do the numbers and prove their financial contribution to the bottom line'. Already we are seeing non-marketers taking over some of this ground and losing, for example, control of websites as reported by the CIM in their Marketing Trends Survey (CIM, 2001b).

All in all, then, there are some concerns over the practicalities of CRM as a route for segmentation. It is certainly surely true that the data-driven approach will continue, but will this lead to true organization–customer relationships? Even by 2001, there were signs that the bubble might have burst: 'corporate disillusionment and downright hostility to the whole CRM bandwagon is reaching fever pitch' (Mitchell, 2001b). Perhaps those involved with segmenting and targeting should be more honest – they want to track customer spending in order to target people with what they hope will be offers that are more likely to produce a purchase response. The problem with the 'R' word is that it has too many associations with the human analogy, but organization–customer interaction is not the same.

On this note, the discussion now turns to some of the issues involved with the process of selecting those segments to target.

Targeting

From a marketing strategy point of view, selection of the appropriate target market is paramount to developing successful marketing programmes. Market targeting requires the evaluation and selection of one or more market segments to enter.

With regard to the question of each segment's structural attractiveness, the marketing manager's primary concern is, as has been discussed, accountability and profitability. It may be the case that a segment is both large and growing but that, because of the intensity of competition, the scope for profit is low. Several models for measuring segment attractiveness exist, including Porter's five-force model. This model suggests that segment profitability is affected by five principal factors:

1 Industry competitors and the threat of segment rivalry.
2 Potential entrants to the market and the threat of mobility.
3 The threat of substitute products.
4 Buyers and their relative power.
5 Suppliers and their relative power.

Having measured the size, growth rate and structural attractiveness of each segment, the marketing manager needs to examine each one in turn against the background of the organization's objectives and resources. In doing this, the marketing manager is looking for the degree of compatibility between the segment and the long-term goals of the organization. It is often the case, for example, that a seemingly attractive segment can be dismissed either because it would not move the organization significantly forward towards its goals, or because it would divert organizational energy. Even where there does appear to be a match, consideration needs to be given to whether the organization has the necessary skills, competences, resources and commitment needed to operate effectively. Without these, segment entry is likely to be of little strategic value.

The company has also to decide on how many segments to cover and how to identify the best segments. There are four market coverage alternatives:

1 Undifferentiated marketing (marketing mix for the mass).
2 Differentiated marketing (separate mixes for each segment).
3 Concentrated marketing (separate mix but only for those segments selected).
4 Custom marketing (separate mix for each customer).

Traditional marketers might target all customers within selected segments, but data-driven marketers can choose how many and which customers to target, as indicated in the coverage of segmentation metrics. Data-driven

marketers are increasingly striving to select those segments that are likely to contribute more financially to the organization. This in turn is driven by the need for marketing activity to be more accountable. Some companies, such as a leading electronics retailer in the UK, track the sales of newly launched products, and those customers who purchase within the first few months of launch are then targeted for new complementary products on the basis of the conceptual framework outlined earlier, namely the discussion of early adopters and opinion leadership.

One of the important metrics in data mining which segments to select for targeting purposes is 'RFM analysis'. Here, companies identify the 'recency, frequency and monetary value' of customers; those with the highest rating according to this measure could be selected for targeting and those with poorer RFM scores might be ignored or even deselected (it is interesting to note this development of rejecting customers even if they do not want to be rejected).

Just knowing that a customer has purchased from the organization in the past is important but not sufficient. Marketers are clearly more interested in a customer who has purchased in the last 6 months than a customer who last bought from the organization in 1984. Similarly, a one-off purchase may also make a customer less attractive (depending, of course, on the product-market in which we operate). So knowing how often they buy from the organization is an important measure. The value of orders from the customer hardly requires further explanation, but the combination of these factors clearly could identify the better groups of customers to target.

A simple example of the value of this analysis is afforded by a small mail order wine business. It firstly scored its customers according to RFM criteria and from this identified its 'best' customers. It then approached a geodemographics company and paid for a profiling of these best customers into geodemographic groups. Four groups emerged as representing nearly all of the company's best customers. The company was then able to purchase a list of every citizen who belonged to these groups and who also lived in those geographic areas in which the company wanted to acquire new customers. This is the 'identikit' or 'cloning' approach. It is the process of replicating customer characteristics in non-customers in order to select the best prospects for a marketing programme.

Lifetime value analysis

Another metric of data-driven segmentation is the LTV (lifetime value analysis). Lifetime is perhaps something of an overstatement – it doesn't mean the lifetime of the customer, but rather a designated period of time during which they are a customer of your organization. Depending on the type of products or services on offer, lifetime might be as little as 6 months (as in purchases for baby products) or as long as 10 years (as in the automotive market). Essentially, different sectors have worked out the probable lifetime value of the 'average' customer and calculated accordingly. Whatever period is relevant, however, the concept of what that customer is worth to the organization in sales and profit terms over a period of time is a useful concept that can inform target segment selection.

To take an extreme example, if a car company is only concerned with acquiring customers and does nothing to retain them, there is a fair chance that each customer who buys one of their cars this year will go on to buy another make next time – and the time after that and so on. The value of the sale might be £10 000, but subtracting acquisition costs, production and other costs could mean a net profit of just a few pounds.

With a more dedicated retention programme the company could expect that customer to buy one of their cars every third year for, perhaps, 12 years – not just at £10 000 but as they progress through their life stages they may be able to buy more expensive models. So, with lower costs of retaining a customer than acquiring him/her in the first instance, together with repeat buying and the prospect of up-selling over a period of time, the sales value could be as high as, say, £70 000 (£10k + £12k + £14k + £16k +£18) plus cross-sales of related accessories and servicing. Those segments (analysed as individuals according to their transactional and profile data) would be selected for targeting – and for particular forms of targeting such as loyalty schemes or other retention devices.

Allowable cost for targeting

Furthermore, for those selected target segments, it is then possible to calculate a 'mini' profit and loss account for the 'average' sale. Consider a simple example in which the selling price of a directly distributed computer is £1000, its cost of production is £600, order handling is £40, 'p&p' is £20 and the desired profit is £250. Costs would total £660, so the 'contribution' is £340 (£1000 – £660). The selling price is £1000 and the sum of costs and desired profit for the average sale is £910 (£660 costs + £250 desired profit), so the allowable cost for targeting is £90 (£1000 – £910).

This analysis can be done for different selling prices and different promotional campaigns, and shows how selected segments can be further analysed in order to set allowable costs for targeting them.

Having determined which segments to target – and indeed which customers and/or potential customers to target within these – the next stage is to consider how to position the product or service in the market.

Positioning

The third strand of what is referred to as STP (segmentation, targeting and positioning) involves deciding on the position within the market that the product or service is to occupy. In doing this, the company is stating to customers what the product or service means and how it differs from current and potential competing products or services.

Positioning is therefore the process of designing an image and value so that consumers within the target segment understand what the company or brand stands for in relation to its competitors. In doing this, the organization is sending a message to consumers and trying to establish a competitive advantage that it hopes will appeal to customers in the target segment. In essence, therefore, the marketing mix can be seen as the tactical details of the organization's positioning strategy. Where, for example, the organization is pursuing a high-quality position, this needs to be reflected not just in the quality of the product or service, but in every element of the mix, including price, the pattern of distribution, the style of advertising and the after-sales service. Without this consistency, the believ-

ability of the positioning strategy reduces dramatically.

Multidimensional scaling and correspondence analysis can be used to build perceptual maps. These procedures involve algorithms that start with measures of similarity between pairs of products and try to find a geometric representation of the brands in the product category. These techniques position products that are perceived as similar close to one another and locate dissimilar products far apart. Dimensions of perceptual maps are not named by the multidimensional scaling programmes. Researchers have to interpret the dimensions themselves based on the geometric representation. Additional information may be gathered from consumers to name the dimensions. The attributes that are the most important in consumers' perceptions of a product category can be determined from survey research.

In this way, positioning is not actually something that is done to the product, rather it

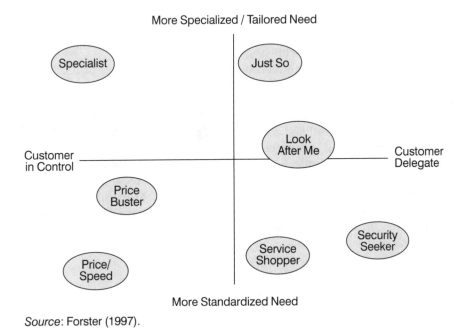

Source: Forster (1997).

Figure 10.8   Travel agencies: service needs

is something that marketers do to the minds of consumers. It relates to how consumers perceive the product in terms of image relative to competing offerings (Reis and Trout, 1986).

Figure 10.8 shows an example of positioning for travel agencies. This suggests that the segments of customers labelled 'specialist', 'price buster' and so on require differing degrees of (a) control over the travel/tour buying process and (b) with the degree of specialized or standardized 'package' the agency provides. Whether this approach would be adopted by travel agencies is debatable, but it could be a significant and worthwhile change in how different known customers are treated in store, perhaps even a good example of the one-to-one segmentation that this chapter has questioned?

Conclusions

It can be said that market segmentation is a real cornerstone of marketing. The very essence of the marketing concept itself leads to an inevitable consideration of market segmentation. If marketing is concerned with satisfying consumer needs and wants as a means to achieving the goals of the organization, it should be recognized that, whereas the human condition means we all have a similar need structure, the same needs will not be salient to every person at the same point in time. Also outlined in the chapter are the stages subsequent to segmentation, such as targeting and positioning.

The chapter has explored some of the traditional approaches to segmenting and targeting markets, and highlighted the value of the more affective ones, in terms of helping to identify salient needs and requirements.

However, the chapter has also submitted the view that data-driven segmentation and targeting is 'taking over' and facilitating greater accountability via the more effective identification of those segments likely to be more profitable. Rather than relying exclusively

on generalized characteristics such as age, social grade and gender, from which buying behaviour is often inferred, the trend is away from profiling and toward using transactional data for targeting. The resulting segmentation data lead to targeting those who are known to buy in that product category on the basis of data fusion to form biographic segmentation.

The new marketing is becoming increasingly reliant upon the metrics of RFM, LTVs, CHAID and data mining. The danger is, perhaps, that these are subverting the role and importance of more affective research that aims to explain why segments behave as they do, rather than just whether and how they behave.

It is interesting to go back in time and remember a prediction from Shubik (1967):

> The computer and modern data processing provide the refinement – the means to treat individuals as individuals rather than parts of a large aggregate . . . the treatment of an individual as an individual will not be an unmixed blessing. Problems concerning the protection of privacy will be large.

This is not a misprint – it was 1967.

The last point is another story – but one not to be ignored.

Review questions

1 If a market is segmented according to age, gender and social grade, what are the contributions of these variables to satisfying the various criteria for segmentation?
2 What are the implications of biographic segmentation for:
   (a) markets
   and
   (b) marketing?
3 How do RFM, LTV and allowable cost metrics help in the segmentation and targeting process?

4 Does increasingly personalized segmentation and targeting inevitably lead to:
(a) one-to-one segmentation
and
(b) relational segmentation?

References

Acland, H. (2001) Ruling Puts DM Industry Firmly on Back Foot, *Marketing Direct*, December, p. 3.

Adam Smith Institute (1998) *The Millennial Generation*, London.

Anon (1997) Taking Advantage of Children, *Sunday Times*, 28 September.

Antoniou, T. (1997) Drilling or Mining? Handling and Analysis of Data Between Now and the Year 2000, *Marketing and Research Today*, May, 115–120.

Arnold, C. (2002) Reported by Rubach, E. (2002) Up Close and Too Personal, *Precision Marketing*, 1 February, p. 12.

Bashford, S. (2000) Generation X Uncovered, *Marketing Direct*, October, 17–19.

BBC (1984) Not By Jeans Alone. Commercial Breaks.

BBC (1997) *Money Programme*, October.

British Market Research Bureau (BMRB) (1988) The Target Group Index.

Carson, C. D. (1999) What It Takes and Where to Get It, Working Paper, University of North Carolina.

Carter, M. (1994) Kids Take Control of the Trolleys, *Marketing Week*, 4 November, pp. 21–22.

Channel 4 (1990) Direct Marketing. *Equinox* Series.

CIM (2001a) The Impact of E-Business on Marketing and Marketers, Chartered Institute of Marketing, October, Cookham (website for CIM direct purchase http://www.connectedinmarketin.co.uk, tel. 44(0)1628 427427)

CIM (2001b) Marketing Trends Survey, library@cim.co.uk

Clegg, A. (2001) Strong Medicine, *Database Marketing*, March, 14–20.

Coupland, D. (1991) *Generation X: Tales for an Accelerated Culture*, Abacus.

Cummins, B. (1994) Time Pundits, *Marketing Week*, 8 April, pp. 29–31.

Denny, N. (1999) Marketing Success is Judged by Cash Criteria, *Marketing*, 13 May, p. 3.

Dibb, S. (2001) New Millennium, New Segments: Moving Towards the Segment of One?, *Journal of Strategic Marketing*, 9(3), 193–214.

Dick, A. S. and Basu, K. (1994) Customer Loyalty: Toward an Integrated Framework, *Journal of the Academy of Marketing Science*, 22(2), 99–113.

Dickson, P. R. (1982) Person–Situation: Segmentation's Missing Link, *Journal of Marketing*, 46(4), 56–64.

di Talamo, cited by Reed (1995), p. 41.

Edmonson, R. (1993) Reported in 'Levi Zips into Youth Market with Hip Ads'. *Marketing*, 17 June.

Engel, J. F., Fiorillo, H. F. and Cayley, M. A. (1972) *Market Segmentation. Concepts and Applications*. Holt, Rinehart & Winston, New York.

Evans, M. J. (1989) Consumer Behaviour Toward Fashion, *European Journal of Marketing*, 23(7).

Evans, M. (1994) Domesday Marketing?, *Journal of Marketing Management*, 10(5), 409–31.

Evans, M. (1999) Chapter 9, in Baker, M. J. (ed.), *The Marketing Book*, 4th edn, Butterworth-Heinemann, Oxford.

Evans, M., Moutinho, L. and Van Raaij, W. F. (1996) *Applied Consumer Behaviour*, Chapter 4, Addison-Wesley.

Evans, M. J., O'Malley, L., Mitchell, S. and Patterson, M. (1997) Consumer Reactions to Data-Based Supermarket Loyalty Schemes, *Journal of Database Marketing*, 4(4).

Evans, M., Nairn, A. and Maltby, A. (2000) The Hidden Sex Life of the Male and Female Shot, *International Journal of Advertising*, 19(1), February, 43–65.

Forster, S. (1997) Direct Marketing in the Travel and Tourism Sector, *IDM Lecture*, UWE, Bristol, May.

Frank, R. E., Massy, W. F. and Wind, Y. (1972) *Market Segmentation*. Prentice-Hall, Englewood Cliffs, NJ.

Future Foundation (2000) *Responding to the Future*, London.

Gofton, K. (2001) Firms Fail to Relate to Customers, *Marketing Direct*, January, 10.

Gofton, K. (2002) In the Heat of the Night Club, *Research*, February, 20–22.

Gronroos, C. (1994) From Marketing Mix to Relationship Marketing, *Management Decision*, **32**(2), 4–20.

Gronroos, C. (1996) Relationship Marketing in Consumer Markets, *Management Decision*, **43**(3), 5–14.

Haeckel, J. (2001) in Mitchell, A. (2001) Playing Cat and Mouse Games with Marketing, *Precision Marketing*, 16 March, p. 14.

Haley, R. I. (1968) Benefit Segmentation: A Decision Oriented Research Tool. *Journal of Marketing*, July, 30–35.

Marsh, H. (2001) Dig Deeper into the Database Goldmine, *Marketing*, 11 January, pp. 29–30.

McNulty, C. and McNulty, R. of Taylor Nelson (1987) Applied Futures, Social Value Groups.

Mitchell, A. (1996) *You and Yours*, Interview transcribed from BBC Radio 4, January.

Mitchell, A. (2001a) Playing Cat and Mouse Games with Marketing, *Precision Marketing*, 16 March, p. 14.

Mitchell, A. (2001b) The End of the Hype, *Marketing Business*, November, 15.

Mitchell, V. W. and Haggett, S. (1997) Sun-Sign Astrology in Market Segmentation: An Empirical Investigation, *Journal of Consumer Marketing*, **14**(2), 113–131.

O'Brien, S. and Ford, R. (1988) Can We At Last Say Goodbye to Social Class?, *Journal of the Market Research Society*, **30**, 289–332.

O'Malley, L., Patterson, M. and Evans, M. (1999) *Exploring Direct Marketing*, Chapter 7. Thomson.

Porter, M. E. (1979) How Competitive Forces Shape Strategy, *Harvard Business Review*, **57**(2), 137–145.

Reis, A. and Trout, J. (1986) *Positioning: The Battle for Your Mind*, McGraw-Hill, New York.

Ritchie, K. (1995) *Marketing to Generation X*, Lexington Books, New York.

Rubach, E. (2002) Up Close and Too Personal, *Precision Marketing*, 1 February, p. 12.

Shaw, R., McDonald, M. and White, C. (2000) Marketing's Black Hole, *Marketing Business*, Jan–Feb, ii–vii.

Shepherdson, N. (2000) Life's a Beach 101, *American Demographics*, May.

Shubik, M. (1996) Information, Rationality and Free Choice in a Future Democratic Society, *Daedalus*, **96**, 771–8.

Smith, W. R. (1956) Product Differentiation and Market Segmentation as Alternative Marketing Strategies, *Journal of Marketing*, 21 July, pp. 3–8.

Tapp, A., Nancarrow, C., Stone, M. and Evans, M. (2001) *Effects of Technology on Marketing and Marketers*, CIM.

Twedt, D. W. (1964) How Important to Marketing Strategy is the Heavy User?, *Journal of Marketing*, **28**(1), 71–72.

Van Raaij, W. F. and Verhallen, T. M. M. (1994) Domain-specific Market Segmentation, *European Journal of Marketing*, **28**(10), 49–66.

Wind, Y. (1978) Issues and Advances in Segmentation Research, *Journal of Marketing*, **42**(3), 317–337.

Further reading

Dibb, S. (2001) New Millennium, New Segments: Moving Towards the Segment of One? *Journal of Strategic Marketing*. This paper provides a view of the trend to one-to-one segmentation.

Frank, R. E., Massey, W. F. and Wind, Y. (1972) *Market Segmentation*, Prentice-Hall, Englewood Cliffs, NJ. A thorough analysis of the benefits, procedures and methods of segmenting markets.

Haley, R. I. (1968) Benefit Segmentation: A Decision Oriented Research Tool, *Journal of Marketing*, July, 30–35. This is the classic paper in which benefit segmentation is clearly expounded, together with useful examples of the application of the approach.

O'Malley, L., Patterson, M. and Evans, M. (1999) *Exploring Direct Marketing*, Thomson. Although this book is concerned with direct marketing, it provides coverage of the new segmenting metrics that are increasingly informing segmentation and targeting programmes.

Smith, W. R. (1956) Product Differentiation and Market Segmentation as Alternative Marketing Strategies, *Journal of Marketing*, July, 3–8. Explains in simple but detailed terms how product differentiation and market segmentation differ and their relative values. The basis of segmentation thought is contained here.

Tynan, A. C. and Drayton, J. (1987) Market Segmentation, *Journal of Marketing Management*, **2**(3), 301–335. A thorough review of market segmentation. The paper also includes a comprehensive list of useful references.

Wells, W. D. (1975) Psychographics: A Critical Review, *Journal of Marketing Research*, May, 196–213. A very readable paper explaining psychographics using straightforward examples to illustrate how psychographics can be applied.

Wind, Y. (1978) Issues and Advances in Segmentation Research, *Journal of Marketing Research*, August, 317–337. Extremely useful paper on segmentation, especially in terms of the research and planning processes involved in segmentation decisions.

Part Three
Managing the Marketing Function

CHAPTER 11

Managing the marketing mix

PETER DOYLE

Introduction

Managing the marketing mix is the central task of marketing professionals. The marketing mix is the set of marketing tools – often summarized as the 'four Ps': the product, its price, promotion and place – that the firm uses to achieve its objectives in its target market (McCarthy, 2001). The key elements in the marketing mix are shown in Figure 11.1. The design of the marketing mix normally forms the core of all marketing courses and the textbooks that support them.

The central assumption is that if marketing professionals make and implement the right decisions about the features of the product, its price, and how it will be promoted and distributed, then the business will be successful. Unfortunately, marketers have ignored the tautological nature of this view. What is the 'right' decision when it comes to making these choices concerning the marketing mix? Most marketing professionals would answer that the right marketing mix is the one that maximizes customer satisfaction and results in the highest sales or market share. But a moment's reflection reveals the fallacy of this approach. Customer satisfaction and sales can always be increased by offering more product features, lower prices than competition, higher promotional budgets and the immediate availability of the product, of outstanding customer service and support.

But inadequate margins and excessive investment requirements would make this strategy a quick route to bankruptcy.

Some writers have tried to get around this problem by stating that the objective is to devise a marketing mix that provides superior customer satisfaction *at a profit* to the company.

Figure 11.1   The marketing mix

But profit is an ambiguous goal. Are managers to aim at short- or long-term profits? Should they seek to maximize profits or achieve some satisficing goal? Each alternative would lead to radically different recommendations for marketing mix decisions. It is fair to conclude that most of the writing on marketing has described the marketing mix but not provided a rational framework for managing it.

In line with the new concept of value-based management, we define the objective of marketing as the development and implementation of a marketing mix that maximizes shareholder value. This definition has two advantages. First, it aligns marketing decision-making to the goals of the board and top management. The board is not interested in sales or market share *per se*, but rather with marketing strategies that will enhance the company's value. Corporate value is determined by the discounted sum of all future free cash flows. Second, shareholder value provides rational and unambiguous criteria for determining the marketing mix. The 'right' marketing mix is the one that maximizes shareholder value.

This chapter focus on marketing mix decisions for private sector firms whose major objective is creating value for shareholders. In non-profit and public sector organizations, the objective is not shareholder value maximization but attracting enough funds to perform their social tasks.

The chapter explains the logic of this new approach to the marketing mix and illustrates its application to typical decisions about product development, pricing, promotion and distribution.

The traditional approach to the marketing mix

Marketing professionals have normally been taught a four-step approach to marketing mix decisions. Step one is to define the product's (or service's) strategic objective. This emerges from an analysis of its strengths, weaknesses, opportunities and threats. Marketers have found the strategic matrices developed by consultants such as the Boston Consulting Group and McKinsey to be useful (for a good summary of these matrices see Grant, 2000, and the comments of Robin Wensley in Chapter 4). Typically, a strategic matrix has market growth or market attractiveness as one dimension and competitive advantage as the other. A product in a highly attractive market with a strong competitive advantage would normally have as its strategic objective rapid sales growth. A product in a poor market with no competitive advantage would be targeted for divesting.

Step two is a detailed analysis of the target market to assess the nature of the opportunity. What is its size and potential? How strong is the competition and how is it likely to evolve in the future. Step three is research into the needs of prospective customers. What is it that customers actually want? Today, this goes beyond merely asking customers what they are looking for, but creatively seeking to discover needs that customers cannot articulate because they are unaware of the possibilities offered by new technologies and the changing environment (see, e.g., Hamel and Prahalad, 1991). To most marketing professionals the marketing mix is designed to meet these customer needs and wants. Each element of the mix is designed to meet a customer need. Lauterborn (1990) articulated this with the concept of the four Cs. Consumers have certain needs, which can be grouped into four Cs – a customer solution, cost, convenience and communication. According to this popular view, the function of the four Ps is to match each of these Cs.

Four Cs	Four Ps
Customer solution	Product
Customer cost	Price
Communication	Promotion
Convenience	Place

An effective marketing mix is then one which offers a product that solves the customer's problem, that is of low cost to the customer, that effectively communicates the benefits, and that can be purchased with the utmost convenience.

The problem with this 'marketing' view of the marketing mix is that it ignores whether the mix makes economic sense for the company. While it maximizes value for customers it can easily minimize value for shareholders. For example, the product that gives the best customer solution is likely to be one individually tailored to a specific customer, incorporating all the features of value to that customer. But for the company, this would require a very broad product line with high manufacturing costs and substantial investment requirements. Unfortunately, what customers also want is low cost, which in most situations will mean offering them low prices. Similarly, the unconstrained pursuit of convenience and communication of the brand's benefits also involves higher costs and investment. The formula of low prices, high operating costs and high investment in promotion and distribution is not one that builds successful businesses.

A striking example of the problems of the marketing-led approach to the marketing mix has been the collapse of the Japanese economic miracle (Porter *et al.*, 2000). Until the early 1980s, the Japanese were held as the paragons of successful marketing (e.g. Ohmae, 1985; Hamel and Prahalad, 1994). Japanese companies such as Nissan, Matsushita, Mitsubishi, Komatsu and Canon appeared set to dominate their markets. Their formulas were similar: an overwhelming focus on investing in market share, and a marketing mix based on fully-featured products, low prices, aggressive promotion and an extensive network of dealers. The strategy did lead to gains in market shares as consumers appreciated the superior value that Japanese companies were offering. But the profit margins and return on investment earned by these companies were very poor. For a time, the support of the Japanese banks disguised their inadequate economic performance. But in the 1980s the bubble burst, investors lost confidence in the ability of Japanese companies to earn an economic return on capital and Japan entered a two-decade recession.

The dot.com 'bust' of 2000 illustrated the same sort of weaknesses. These start-ups made market share their sole priority. Products and services were given away free or below cost. Huge sums were spent on advertising and promotion in the belief that if they achieved a dominant market position in the 'new economy' everything else would fall into place. The result was large number of visitors to their sites, but the companies generated no profit and eventually they ran out of cash. In 2002, Yahoo! counted its global users in millions, but it worked out the average spend per head amounted to less than a cup of coffee annually. It was hardly surprising that, despite its dominant market share and brand leadership, the value of the company collapsed by 90 per cent.

Successful businesses understand that building brands that satisfy consumers is necessary but not sufficient. Without generating an economic return to shareholders, a marketing mix is not sustainable.

The accounting approach to the marketing mix

Faced with poor returns, some companies, especially in the UK, adopted an accounting approach to marketing. The marketing mix was seen not as an instrument for gaining and retaining customers, but rather as a tool for directly increasing the return on investment. Return on investment can be increased in four ways – increasing sales, raising prices, reducing costs or cutting investment. The marketing mix is the central determinant of each of these levers.

For example, cutting back on the number of product variants offered to customers will reduce costs and investment. Raising prices will usually increase profitability in the short term because higher margins will offset the volume loss. Cutting advertising and promotional budgets will also boost short-term profits. Finally, savings on distribution and service will normally have positive effects on profitability, even though customers may suffer some inconvenience.

As illustrated in Figure 11.2, the accounting approach leads to a completely opposite marketing mix to the marketing approach. While the marketing focus, which puts the customer first, normally leads to broader product ranges, lower prices and more spending on promotion and distribution, the accounting one leads to the opposite pressures. The cost of the marketing approach is lower profitability and cash flow, the cost of the accounting approach is the longer-term loss of market share resulting from the lack of customer focus.

Marketers need to be aware that there are other important problems in considering profits as the objective of the business.

- *Short- or long-term profits.* Most managers are conscious of the dangers of focusing on short-term profits. Cutting projects to boost this year's results can lead to permanent erosion of the firm's ability to compete. But emphasizing long-term profits does not help much because they are so ill-defined. Are long-term profits defined over 3, 5 or 20 years? How does one deal with the time value of money?

- *Maximum or acceptable profits.* Should managers be seeking to maximize (short- or long-term) profits or achieving an acceptable level, e.g. the average return in the industry? Each would give quite different recommendations when it comes to the marketing mix. How would shareholders respond to managers consciously accepting sub-optimal returns?

- *Ambiguity of profit measurement.* Unlike cash flow, profits are a matter of judgement. Different, but equally legally acceptable treatments of depreciation, stocks and the costs of restructuring lead to vastly different

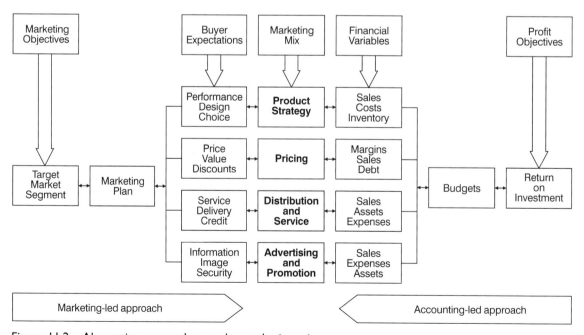

Figure 11.2 Alternative approaches to the marketing mix

reported profits. Profits also fail to incorporate the cost of capital. So a company can be growing profits, but declining in value because it is not achieving a return above its cost of capital on new investment. Finally, profits exclude the added investments in working and fixed capital needed to support the company's growth. So a company can be profitable but rapidly running out of cash.

- *Alternative measures of profitability.* Most companies set objectives not in terms of absolute profits, but express them as a ratio such as return on assets, return on investment, return on equity or earnings per share. All these measures, because they have profits in the numerator, suffer the same problems as outlined above. There are even added problems since measures of assets, investment and equity are equally ambiguous. For example, should assets be valued at cost or replacement value? Should R&D spending be treated as investment or as a cost?

Value-based marketing

A value-based approach to the marketing mix reconciles the marketing and accounting approaches in an optimal manner. The key principle is the optimum marketing mix is that which maximizes shareholder value. The concept of value-based management – that the job of the board and its senior executives is to maximize shareholder value – has become almost universally accepted in major businesses. As a recent *Business Week* (2000) study concluded, 'the fundamental task of today's CEO is simplicity itself: get the stock price up. Period.' Most companies – even those with a strong marketing orientation – now have the goal enshrined in their mission statements; for example:

> We exist to create value for our shareholders on a long term basis ... this is our ultimate commitment.
>
> Coca-Cola Corporation

> Disney's overriding objective is to create shareholder value by ...
>
> Walt Disney Corporation

> Our governing objective is growth in share owner value ...
>
> Cadbury Schweppes plc

Why value-based management?

Value-based management says that decisions have to be made which maximize the wealth of the company's shareholders. Today, these shareholders are not the bloated capitalists of socialist propaganda, but rather the pension funds and insurance companies responsible for managing the savings of ordinary people. It is the financial value of the companies in their portfolios that will determine the future quality of life for most of us.

The key arguments for value-based management are:

1 *Ownership rights.* In a market-based economy, companies are owned by their shareholders. The central responsibility of management is to maximize shareholder value and to do so legally and with integrity. Managers have neither the legitimacy nor the expertise to pursue other social goals. Social objectives are the function of government or other social institutions.
2 *Pressure from capital markets.* Today, chief executives have little choice. Unless shareholders believe top management are pursuing strategies to create shareholder value, executives will not retain their jobs. In recent years, a stream of CEOs from major companies have been ousted for allowing their company's share price to slide. As the *Financial Times* (2000) commented, 'the model of capitalism, which emphasizes shareholder value, is the yardstick on which global capital markets are converging.'
3 *Consistency with other stakeholders' interests.* A company seeking to maximize shareholder value cannot neglect other stakeholders. In

today's knowledge-intensive businesses, satisfying the interests of the knowledge workers is essential for the business' long-run health. No company can ignore the needs of customers if it is interested in retaining long-term cash flows. Conversely, all stakeholders – workers, customers, suppliers and the community – become vulnerable if the business fails to generate shareholder value. Ultimately, the needs of all the stakeholders depend upon the firm's ability to generate sufficient cash to meet them.

4   *Focus on long-term performance.* Marketing people often think of the shareholder value orientation as creating a short-term focus, discouraging long-term investments in brands and market development. Nothing could be further from the truth. As we shall see, short-term movements in profits have little impact on shareholder value. The first 5 years of profits and cash flow rarely account for more than one-third of a company's value. The shareholder value approach encourages a long-term perspective about marketing mix decisions – as long as these investments promise to generate a return above the cost of capital.

5   *Strong intellectual rational.* The key reason why marketing management has failed to develop as an intellectual discipline is its lack of a clear objective. Without a rational goal it is impossible to develop a framework for optimizing marketing mix decisions. As we have noted, maximizing market share or customer satisfaction makes no sense. Nor is a focus on maximizing profits or return on investment any better. Optimizing shareholder value, a framework that lies at the heart of modern finance, offers the basis for redefining marketing in a precise and rational manner. It provides a powerful tool for optimizing the marketing mix.

Key principles

Value-based marketing is based on the belief that management should evaluate marketing mix options in the same way that shareholders do. Shareholders assess companies on their potential to create shareholder value. The company's share price reflects investors' evaluations of how much value management's current strategy will create. We need to review how investors estimate value and evaluate value-creating strategies.

The concept of value is founded on four financial principles. First, *cash flow* is the basis of value – it is the amount left over for shareholders after all the bills have been paid. Without the expectation of free cash flow passing into investors' hands, an asset cannot have value. Most of the dot.com companies founded in the 1990s collapsed because investors could not see how free cash flow was going to be created. The amount being spent looked to permanently exceed the revenues coming in. Next, cash flow has a *time value*: money today is worth more than money coming in the future. This is because investors can earn a return on cash they get today. Typically, £1000 received in 10 years time is 'worth' only about £385 today ($£1000/(1 + r)^{10}$, where r is the discount rate; here r is taken to be 10 per cent). Third, the *opportunity cost of capital* is the return investors could obtain if they invested elsewhere in companies of similar risk. Essentially this means that investors will find risky marketing strategies appealing only if the expected rewards are greater. Finally, the *net present value* concept brings these principles together. It shows that the value of an asset (e.g. a company) is the total of all the future free cash flows that asset generates after discounting these future sums by the appropriate opportunity cost of capital. The task of marketing – and managers generally – is to put in place strategies that maximize the net present value of the business. The optimal marketing mix is that combination of product, price, promotion and distribution that maximizes the net present value.

To calculate the value of an asset, or to assess whether a strategy is likely to create value, management has to forecast the future cash flows that result from their decisions, i.e. net present value (*NPV*):

$$NPV = \sum_{i}^{\infty} \frac{CF_i}{(1 + r)^i} \qquad (11.1)$$

where *CF* is free cash flow and *r* is the discount rate or opportunity cost of capital for shareholders. Clearly, analysts or investors cannot forecast cash flow decades ahead. Instead, the time period is split between a feasible *forecast period*, typically of 5–7 years, and a *continuing value* representing the value of the business at the end of the forecast period (for a comprehensive discussion, see Brearley and Myers, 1999). For a high performing business the forecast period can be called the *differential advantage period*. It is the number of years the business expects to maintain a market advantage over competitors allowing it to earn supernormal profits (i.e. above the cost of capital). However, for virtually all companies, competition, the changing environment and new technologies mean that eventually profitability erodes. It is relatively rare for this differential advantage period to exceed 6 or 7 years (Rappaport and Mauboussin, 2001). After that, companies are fortunate to earn normal profits.

In summary, we can rewrite the value of a company (Equation 11.1) as:

$$NPV = \begin{array}{c} \text{Present value of cash flow during} \\ \text{differential advantage period} \\ + \\ \text{Present value of cash flow after} \\ \text{differential advantage period} \end{array}$$
$$(11.2)$$

There are a number of ways of calculating the latter term representing the continuing value of the business at the end of the forecast period (Copeland *et al.*, 2001, pp. 285–331). The most common one is the perpetuity method that assumes the business just maintains a return on investment equal to its cost of capital.

This is calculated by dividing the company's net operating profit after tax (NOPAT) by the cost of capital:

$$\text{Continuing value} = \frac{\text{NOPAT}}{r} \qquad (11.3)$$

To calculate the present value of the continuing value, this figure has to be discounted back the appropriate number of years. For example, if the net operating profit at the end of a 7-year differential period is £8 million and the cost of capital is 10 per cent, then the continuing value is £80 million and the present value is £80 million divided by $(1 + 0.1)^7$ or £41 million (for a complete discussion, see Doyle, 2000, pp. 32–66).

Uses of value-based marketing

Value-based marketing – the philosophy that the task of marketing management is to maximize the financial value of the business for shareholders – transforms almost every aspect of marketing strategy. Here are some examples of where it can be used:

- *Developing the marketing mix*. A value-based approach leads to quite different decisions about products, price, promotion and distribution. For example, as is illustrated below, the price that maximizes shareholder value is invariably higher than that which maximizes customer satisfaction and lower than that which maximizes short-term profits. A value-based approach offers managers a more rational method of decision-making and one which is more consistent with the goals of the board of directors.
- *Evaluating alternative marketing strategies*. Top managers commonly have to choose between major options. Should they focus on being a premium brand or go for a mass market? Should they diversify the product range or 'stick to the knitting'? Value-based marketing provides a rigorous approach to analysing these alternatives. The right strategy is one

that is most likely to maximize the present value of future cash flows available for shareholders.

- *Justifying marketing budgets.* When companies are under pressure, marketing budgets are usually the first to be cut (IPA, 2000; Doyle, 2001). Boards appear to believe that cuts in marketing spend offer a ready means of boosting short-term profits with limited long-term risks. Marketing directors have lacked the analytical tools for demonstrating the dangers of such a view. Value-based analysis allows marketing managers to demonstrate the positive impact of marketing spending on the company's share price.
- *Valuing brands.* The key difference between today's and yesterday's businesses is that the modern firm's real value lies in its intangible assets – its brands, the knowledge and skills of its people, and its management – rather than its tangible assets – the factories, buildings and equipment that appear on the balance sheet. It is these intangibles that provide the differential advantage and which are difficult for competitors to copy. In marketing, brands are the central assets. Brand names like Coca-Cola, Microsoft and IBM – cultivated by consistent marketing investment – are the foundations of strong share prices. Value-based analysis provides the tools for valuing brands and demonstrating marketing's contribution.
- *Assessing acquisition opportunities.* Acquisitions have proved an appealing avenue for companies seeking growth. They have certain advantages over internal growth: they offer a faster way into new markets; they can be cheaper than costly battles for market share; some strategic assets such as famous brand names and patents simply cannot be achieved internally, and an established business is typically less risky than developing a new one from scratch. Yet the evidence convincingly demonstrates that most acquisitions fail to generate value for the acquirer. They pay too much or fail to achieve the cost and revenue synergies that were anticipated. Again a value-based analysis takes the guesswork out of acquisitions,

providing a clear framework for calculating how much a prospect is worth and what needs to be done to make the acquisition succeed.

The marketing mix and shareholder value

Value-based management is of great importance to marketing because it clarifies the central role of marketing in determining the value of the business. The marketing mix is the key driver of the share price. To understand this we need to look at the determinants of shareholder value. The value of the business and its share price are determined by the discounted sum of future cash flows (Equation 11.1). Examining this equation, we see that there are four ways of creating shareholder value.

Increasing the level of cash flow

This is the most important way of creating shareholder value. A business' free cash flow is cash in less cash out, or specifically in any year i, cash flow is:

$$CF_i = \text{Sales revenue}_i - \text{Operating costs}_i$$
$$- \text{Tax}_i - \text{Investments}_i \quad (11.4)$$

This in turn means there are four ways of increasing the level of cash flow.

Increasing sales

Selling more will create shareholder value as long as the increased sales are not offset by disproportionate increases in costs, taxes or investment. It can be shown (Rappaport, 1998, pp. 51–55) that additional sales increase shareholder value as long as the operating profit margin exceeds a *threshold margin*:

$$\text{Threshold margin} =$$
$$\frac{\text{Incremental investment} \times \text{Cost of capital}}{(1 + \text{Cost of capital})(1 - \text{Tax rate})}$$
$$(11.5)$$

Table 11.1 Baker Company: shareholder value analysis (£ million)						
	Base	*Year*				
		1	*2*	*3*	*4*	*5*
Sales	100.0	105.0	110.3	115.8	121.6	127.6
Operating margin	10.0	10.5	11.0	11.6	12.2	12.8
Tax (30%)	3.0	3.2	3.3	3.5	3.6	3.8
NOPAT	7.0	7.4	7.7	8.1	8.5	8.9
Net investment		2.5	2.6	2.8	2.9	3.0
Cash flow		4.9	5.1	5.3	5.6	5.9
Discount factor (r = 10%)		0.909	0.826	0.751	0.683	0.621
Present value of cash flow		4.4	4.2	4.0	3.8	3.7

Cumulative present value	20.1
PV of continuing value	55.5
Other investments	7.0
Value of debt	25.0
Shareholder value	57.6
Initial shareholder value	52.0
Shareholder value added	5.6
Implied share price (£)	2.88
Initial share price (£)	2.60

For example, if the investment rate is 50 per cent of incremental sales, the cost of capital is 10 per cent and the tax rate is 35 per cent, then the threshold margin is 7 per cent. So if managers expect the long-term operating margin to be above 7 per cent, growth adds value for shareholders.

The marketing mix is the main way management seeks increases in sales. It does this through developing appealing products, competitive prices, and effective promotion and distribution. Value analysis provides the framework for assessing whether these elements are optimized. This is illustrated in Table 11.1 for the Baker Company. Its current sales and net operating profit after tax (NOPAT) are shown in the first column. Assume management put in place a new, modest marketing strategy that will grow sales by 5 per cent annually. To arrive at free cash flow we will have to deduct the investment in working capital and fixed assets that will be needed to support this growth. This is forecast to be 50 per cent of incremental sales. Shareholder value is obtained by discounting the cash flow by the opportunity cost of capital, r, which is taken here to be 10 per cent, and deducting debt. The annual discount factor is $1/(1 + r)^i$, where $i = 1, 2, \ldots$ is the year.

As discussed, the shareholder value calculation divides the estimation of the value created by the strategy into two components. The first is the forecast managers make over a 5-year planning period. Here the present value of the cumulative cash flow is forecast to be £20.1 million. The second component is the continuing value of the business, which is the present value of the cash flow at the end of the planning period. This is estimated by the standard perpetuity method and has a value of £55.5 million. Adding any non-operating investments the firm owns and deducting the market value of any debt leads to the shareholder value of £57.6 million. If there were 20 million shares outstanding, this would produce a predicted share price of £2.88. The 5 per cent sales growth creates additional shareholder value of 5.6 million, just over 10 per cent enhancement in the value of the share price. This could well be an underestimate of the value created, since the calculation assumes a constant operating margin. In practice, overheads might not increase proportionately and other scale economies in costs may occur. For example, if 20 per cent of costs were fixed, the shareholder value added would jump from £5.6 million to £34.4 million as the pre-tax operating profit margin grows from 10 per cent to almost 14 per cent of sales. The difference between £5.6 million and £34.4 million emphasizes the importance of not allowing growth to be at the expense of margin erosion through proportionate cost increases or price erosion.

Higher prices

Higher prices increase the operating profit margin and cash flow, so long as these are not offset by disproportionate losses in volume. Here, in particular, one sees the advantage of value analysis over short-term profitability criteria for evaluating pricing. In the short term, raising prices commonly increases profits because many consumers do not immediately switch. Over the longer term, however, competitive position is often lost, leading to deterioration in cash flow and especially in the continuing value of the business.

The only sure way of achieving price premiums is developing products that offer customers superior value. This may be in terms of greater functional benefits (e.g. Intel, Microsoft) or through offering brands with added psychological values (e.g. Coca-Cola, Nike). If premium brands can be created, the value effects are very substantial. Table 11.1 can be used to simulate a 5 per cent price increase. If sales volume is unchanged, the 5 per cent price increase creates £33 million additional value – i.e. almost six times more than 5 per cent annual volume growth. This is, of course, because a price increase normally incurs no additional operating costs or long-term capital requirement, so that the revenue increase falls straight through into additional free cash flow.

Lower costs

Cutting costs, as long as it does not lead to offsetting declines in customer patronage, increases cash flow and the value of the business. Variable costs can be reduced by better sourcing, fixed costs by taking out overheads, and the development of more efficient sales and marketing channels. There is much evidence that companies with a strong customer franchise need to spend less on marketing and promotion (e.g. Reichheld, 1996).

Table 11.1 can also be used to simulate the effect of a 5 per cent cut in costs. Again they are very significant, adding £31 million to shareholder value. As with a price increase, cost cuts should fall out straight into free cash flow, unlike volume growth, which involves additional capital.

Reducing investment requirements

Though this varies across businesses, typically every £1 million of added sales may demand £500 000 of additional working and fixed capital (Rappaport and Mauboussin, 2001, p. 27). Clearly, cutting investment requirements can have a major impact on the free cash flow generated and consequently the share price. Again, there is increasing recognition that effective customer relationships enhance cash flow by reducing the level of working and fixed investments. The trend towards relationship marketing enables suppliers and customers to link their supply chains to make these economies (e.g. Anderson and Narus, 1996).

If investment requirements are reduced by 5 per cent – from 50 to 47.5 per cent of incremental sales – this would raise the shareholder value added from £5.6 million to £6.1 million. The effects on value creation of these 5 per cent changes can be summarized as follows:

	Shareholder Value Added (£ million)
5 per cent sales increase	5.6–34.4
5 per cent price increase	32.7
5 per cent cost reduction	31.5
5 per cent cut in investment requirements	6.1

Accelerating cash flows

The right marketing mix can accelerate cash flows. This is important because money has a time value: money today is worth more than money tomorrow. If the cost of capital is 10 per cent, £1 million in 5 years time is worth only £621 000, and in 10 years, £1 million is only worth £385 000. The faster acquisition of profitable market share and the consequent cash flows are important means of adding shareholder value.

Many marketing activities are geared to accelerating cash flows, even though marketers never conceptualize their strategies in these financial terms. For example, there is substantial evidence that when consumers have strong, positive attitudes to a brand they are quicker to respond to new products appearing under the brand umbrella. Again, marketers have studied the product life cycle and the characteristics of early adopters with the aim of developing promotional strategies to accelerate the launch and penetration of new products (Robertson, 1993).

Table 11.1 can be used to explore the effect of accelerating cash flow. For example, if year 3

sales were achieved in year 1, year 4 sales in year 2, etc., shareholder value would increase from £57.6 million to £58.4 million, even though final year sales and profits are unchanged. This extra £0.8 million is less than might be anticipated because, while profits are brought forward increasing their present value, so is the investment spending, increasing its real cost. Nevertheless, this may underestimate the effect of accelerated market penetration. Fast penetration can lead to first mover advantages. These include higher prices, greater customer loyalty, access to the best distribution channels and network effects that enable the innovator to become the specification standard. These feed back into both higher sales and higher operating margins.

Reducing business risk

The third factor determining the value of the business is the opportunity cost of capital used to discount future cash flows. This discount rate depends upon market interest rates plus the special risks attached to the specific business unit. The risk attached to a business is determined by the volatility and vulnerability of its cash flows compared to the market average (Brearley and Myers, 1999). Investors expect a higher return to justify investment in risky businesses. Because investors discount risky cash flows with a higher cost of capital, their value is reduced.

Again, there is evidence that an important function of marketing assets is to reduce the risk attached to future cash flows. Strong brands operate by building layers of value that make them less vulnerable to competition. This is a key reason why leading investors rate companies with strong brand portfolios at a premium in their industries (Buffet, 1994). Reichheld (1996) and others have also demonstrated the dramatic effects on the company's net present value of increasing customer loyalty. A major focus of marketing today is on increasing loyalty; shareholder value analysis provides a powerful mechanism for demonstrating the financial contribution of these activities. If the opportunity cost of capital in Table 11.1 is reduced from 10 to 9 per cent, as a result of marketing activities which reduce the vulnerability of cash flows, then shareholder value is boosted by £3.1 million.

Extending the differential advantage period

Shareholder value is made up of two components: the present value of cash flows during the planning period and the present value of the company at the end of the planning period. Not surprisingly, since a company potentially has an infinite life, the continuing value normally greatly exceeds the value of the cash flows over the planning period. In the example of Table 11.1, the continuing value accounts for over two-thirds of the corporate value. This is a typical figure across industry, indeed in high growth industries the continuing value is an even higher proportion of total value.

The problem is valuing the business at the end of the planning period. The most common approach is to use the perpetuity method, as in Table 11.1. This assumes that, at the end of the planning period, the company earns a return on net investment equivalent only to the cost of capital, so that shareholder value remains constant. An alternative assumption is that the business can continue to earn returns that exceed the cost of capital. Another more pessimistic assumption is that after the planning period the cash flows turn negative as competition intensifies. The choice depends upon two factors: the sustainability of the firm's *differential advantage* and the *real options* for growth it has created. Microsoft and Coca-Cola, for example, have very high continuing values because investors perceive them having very long-term brand strengths that can be leveraged to future growth opportunities in new markets or product areas.

Strong marketing assets, such as new product development expertise, brands, customer loyalty and strategic partnerships,

should create competitive advantage and growth options that will often endure beyond the normal period for which a company plans. Because such assets are difficult to copy and create, and offer lasting advantages, they should enhance continual values and so have a marked effect on shareholder value. If in the table the period over which the company earns positive net cash flow is extended by 1 year, from 5 to 6 years, this adds £1 million to shareholder value.

These last three means of creating shareholder value are summarized below. Under the assumptions made, they are substantially less in their impacts than focusing on increasing the level of cash flow through volume and price increases or cuts in costs and investment requirements.

	Shareholder Value Added (£ million)
Accelerated cash flow	0.8
Reducing risk (discount rate)	3.1
Extending the differential period	1.0

Making marketing mix decisions

This section re-examines the four main elements of the marketing mix – product, price, promotion and distribution – from a value-based perspective.

Building valuable brands

Today, marketing professionals prefer to talk about brands rather than products. This reflects the recognition that consumers do not buy just physical attributes, but also the psychological associations associated with a supplier's offers. The concept of the brand also emphasizes that the whole presentation of the offer – design, features, variety, packaging, service and support – have all to be integrated around a common identity (for a comprehensive discussion of brands, see Chapter 15).

	Tangibles (%)	Brands (%)	Other intangibles (%)
Utilities	70	0	30
Industrial	70	5	25
Pharmaceutical	40	10	50
Retail	70	15	15
Info tech	30	20	50
Automotive	50	30	20
Financial services	20	30	50
Food and drink	40	55	5
Luxury goods	25	70	5

Table 11.2 Relative importance of brands and other assets

Source: Interbrand.

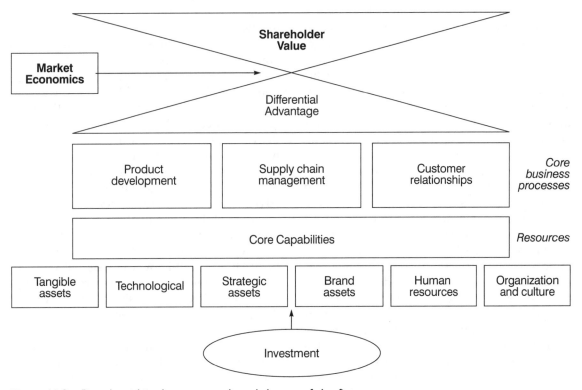

Figure 11.3   Brands within the resource-based theory of the firm

Brands, intangible assets and the firm

In today's firm, it is intangible rather than tangible assets that create value. For many firms, brands are their most important assets, even though these brands rarely appear in published balance sheets (see Table 11.2). The role of brands and intangible assets can be seen in the resource-based theory of the firm (Grant, 2000). Starting from the top of Figure 11.3, the objective of business strategy is to create shareholder value, as measured by rising share prices or dividends. The key to creating shareholder value in competitive markets is possessing a differential advantage – giving customers superior value through offers or relationships that are either higher in quality or lower in cost. Achieving this differential advantage, in turn, depends upon the effectiveness of the firm's business processes. As shown, the core business processes can be grouped into three: (1) the brand development process, which enables a firm to create innovative solutions to customers' problems; (2) the supply chain management process, which acquires inputs and efficiently transforms them into desirable brands; and (3) the customer relationship management process, which identifies customers, understands their needs, builds relationships and shapes consumer perceptions of the organization and its brands.

These core business processes are the drivers of the firm's differential advantage and its ability to create shareholder value. However, these processes themselves are founded on the firm's core capabilities, which derive from the resources or assets it possesses. A firm cannot build superior business processes unless it has access to the right resources and the ability to co-ordinate them effectively. In the past, tangible assets – the firm's factories, raw materials and financial resources – were seen as its key strength. But today it is the intangibles that investors view most highly – its technological skills, the quality of the staff, the business culture and, of course, the strength of its brands. In 2002, tangible assets accounted for less than 20 per cent of the value of the world's top companies. Finally, maintaining an up-to-date resource base, upon which everything else is founded, depends upon continued investment.

How brands enhance business processes

Brands create value by leveraging the firm's business processes – its new product brand development, its supply chain, and especially in building long-term relationships with its customers. An effective brand (B) can be considered as consisting of three components: a good product (P), strong differentiation (D) and added values (AV), or:

$$B = P \times D \times AV \qquad (11.6)$$

Building a successful brand starts with developing an effective product or service. Unfortunately, today, with the speed with which technology travels, it is increasingly difficult to build brands, and certainly to maintain them, on the basis of demonstrable, superior functional benefits. Comparably priced washing powders, cars, computers or auditing firms are usually much alike in the performance they deliver. Consequently, firms must find other ways to differentiate themselves, to create awareness and recall among customers. Hence they turn to design, colour, logos, packaging, advertising and additional services.

But while differentiation creates recognition it does not necessarily create preference. Woolworth's, the Post Office, British Rail and the NHS are well-known brands but they are scarcely admired. To create preference a brand also has to possess positive added values. Added values give customers confidence in the choices they make. Choice today is difficult for customers because of the myriad of competitors seeking patronage, the barrage of communications, and the rapid changes in social mores and technology. Brands aim to simplify the choice process by confirming the functional or emotional associations of the brand. Increasingly, it is the emotional or experience associations that a successful brand promises that creates the consumer value.

The added value successful brands offer usually fall into one of four headings:

- *Confirmation of attributes.* Here the brand's image conveys confidence in its functional claims. For example, Volvo's added values were a belief that it was a safe car to drive. Wal-Mart focused on a brand image confirming it offered the lowest prices. Persil focused on a message that it 'washes whiter'.
- *Satisfying aspirations.* Some brands focus on associations with the rich and famous. They offer customers perceptions of status, recognition and esteem. BMW offers 'the ultimate driving experience'; Rolex is 'the watch the professionals wear'.
- *Shared experiences.* Some brands build added values by offering a vision of shared associations and experiences. Examples are Nike with its 'just do it' attitude; Microsoft suggests the sky's the limit with its 'where do you want to go today?' slogan; Coca-Cola's brand proposition is about sharing the experiences and values of the young, hip generation.
- *Joining causes.* A new trend has been to associate brands with noble social causes, such as fighting Third World poverty, environmental degradation and joining other charitable concerns. In buying a brand, consumers perceive themselves as making a social contribution. Body Shop's championing of action against Third World poverty was a pioneer of this cause-related marketing phenomenon. Pizza Express championed 'Venice in peril', Tesco 'computers for schools', etc.

The above discussion has focused on brands as leveraging the customer relationship business process. But there is much evidence that strong brand names also facilitate the new product development process. New products launched under a strong brand name are more likely to be trusted by consumers and to achieve faster market penetration. Strong brands also contribute to more efficient supply chains. Suppliers are more confident in forging partnerships with established brand names and making the investments to maintain these associations.

Valuing brands

Brands require investment in communications and other resources if they are to achieve recognition and the added values that generate customer preference. But creating customer preference is not enough, brands also have to create value for investors. Managers need to assess whether the brand investment pays off.

As with any other asset, brands create shareholder value if they positively affect the four levers of value – increasing the level of cash flow, accelerating cash flow, extending the differential period, and reducing risk. There is considerable research that brands do have these positive effects (see Doyle, 2000, pp. 229–232).

In recent years, many companies have sought to value their brands to assess their strength and value to investors. The most effective valuation method involves three steps. First, cash flows have to be forecast, as in the standard shareholder value analysis shown in Table 11.1. Second, the fraction of additional earnings due to the brand name has to be calculated. This involves first deducting the return due on tangible assets to arrive at earnings due to intangible assets. Then the percentage of these earnings on intangibles due to the brand name has to be estimated. Finally, a discount rate has to be chosen to discount future cash flows to a present value (for a detailed account, see Doyle, 2000, pp. 248–254).

This approach is illustrated in Table 11.3. The first two rows show the forecast of a brand's sales and its operating profit. Then economic value added is calculated after deducting a charge for the use of tangible

Table 11.3 Valuing the brand (£ million)						
	Base	*Year*				
		1	*2*	*3*	*4*	*5*
Sales	250.0	262.5	275.6	289.4	303.9	319.1
Operating profits (15%)	37.5	39.4	41.3	43.4	45.6	47.9
Tangible capital employed	125.0	131.3	137.8	144.7	151.9	159.5
Charge for capital @ 5%	6.3	6.6	6.9	7.2	7.6	8.0
Economic value added	31.3	32.8	34.5	36.2	38.0	39.9
Brand Value Added @ 70%	21.9	23.0	24.1	25.3	26.6	27.9
Tax (30%)	6.6	6.9	7.2	7.6	8.0	8.4
Post-tax brand earnings	15.3	16.1	16.9	17.7	18.6	19.5
Discount factor (r = 15%)	1.00	0.87	0.76	0.66	0.57	0.50
Discounted cash flow	15.3	14.0	12.8	11.7	10.6	9.7

Cumulative present value	58.8
Present value of residual	64.8
Brand value	123.5

assets. Economic value added is the return on intangible assets. In this example, it is estimated that the brand name accounts for 70 per cent of these residual earnings (for a methodology for estimating this percentage, see Perrier, 1997). The discount factor is estimated at 15 per cent (Haigh, 1998, pp. 20–27). The brand is then valued at £123.5 million. This is the contribution of the brand name to the total value of the business. It demonstrated that past and continuing investments in the brand have created significant shareholder value.

Optimizing price decisions

In many ways price is the most important element of the marketing mix. Price is the only element of the mix that directly produces revenue: all the others produce costs. In addition, small changes in price have bigger effects on both sales and shareholder value than advertising or other marketing mix changes.

There are five key principles that underlie effective pricing:

- The optimum price is that which maximizes shareholder value, not short-term profits or market share.
- Pricing should be based on the value the brand offers customers, not on what it costs to produce.
- Since all customers are different in their needs and the values they attach to a solution, it pays to charge different prices to different customers.
- Pricing has to anticipate competitors' reactions and their objectives in the market.
- Good pricing strategies depend upon effective implementation for results.

Price, profits and value

Accountants frequently recommend price increases to boost short-term profits. The effects are often striking and not appreciated by marketers. For example, consider a company selling 100 million units at a price of £1, with a contribution margin of 50 per cent and an operating margin of 5 per cent. A 5 per cent price increase would double profits if volume remained unchanged. Even if the volume dropped by 50 000 units, profits would still rise by 45 per cent because of the reduction in variable costs. Other ways of increasing profits tend to be less powerful. For example, while a 5 per cent price increase could double profits, a 5 per cent volume increase, or a 5 per cent cut in fixed costs, would have only half that effect.

Effect of a 5 per cent price increase (£ million):

	Now	*Volume unchanged*	*5 per cent volume loss*
Sales	100.00	105.00	99.75
Variable costs	50.00	50.00	47.50
Contribution	50.00	55.00	52.25
Fixed costs	45.00	45.00	45.00
Operating profits	5.00	10.00	7.25

The problem with this approach is that it ignores long-term effects. Over the long term, price elasticity tends to be higher as customers find alternative, cheaper suppliers. Certainly, repeated price increases are likely to lead to continuing erosion of market share, ultimately destroying the value of the business. This can be illustrated by comparing a skimming versus a penetration pricing strategy.

Under skimming pricing, the company introduces a new product with a high price that captures a substantial proportion of the value the innovation offers consumers. As Table 11.4 illustrates, this leads to a big positive cash flow in the early years, but then declines as new competitors enter the market with substantially lower prices. By contrast, under the penetration pricing strategy cash flow is zero in the early years because of the low prices and high capital requirements to support the faster volume growth. But then once a critical market share is achieved, margins and cash flow improve rapidly. Note in the example that the cumulative cash flows over the 7-year planning period are identical. When the cash flows are discounted, the skimming pricing strategy value is £10.2 million greater. Nevertheless, the penetration pricing strategy delivers more than twice the shareholder value of the skimming strategy. The real difference lies in the continuing value of the two strategies: at the end of year 7 the skimmer has lost its market position and is economically worthless; the penetration strategy has a strong market position resulting in a business with a continuing value of £63 million. Confusing short-term profits with long-term value has been disastrous for many businesses. The price that maximizes shareholder value is invariably lower than that which maximizes short-term profits.

Pricing and customer value

Most companies seek to set prices on the basis of various forms of cost plus (see Chapter 13), but this can lead to prices that are too high or too low. What customers are willing to pay depends upon the value to them of the supplier's offer; they do not care what it costs to produce. If customers perceive competitors as making similar offers, their price will determine the upper limit. However, if the company can differentiate its offer and add benefits, then it should determine how customers value these new features in setting its price.

Consider this example from the construction equipment market. The established market leader sells a bulldozer at a price of £50 000. Over the product's economic life, averaging 12 000 operating hours, the customer spends £20 000 on diesel oil and lubricants, £40 000 on servicing and parts, and £20 per hour on labour, making a total lifetime cost of £350 000. A new competitor with advanced technology enters the market and estimates the value of these features as a precursor to setting prices. It envisages launching two models. The basic

Table 11.4   An illustration of skimming vs penetration pricing and shareholder value

	Cash flow (£ million)								PV of cont. value
Year:	1	2	3	4	5	6	7	Cumulative	
Skimming pricing	10	11	12	8	6	3	0	50	
DCF (r = 10%)	9.1	9.1	9.0	5.5	3.7	1.7	0.0	38.1	0
								Shareholder value	38.1
Penetration pricing	0	0	0	4	8	14	24	50	
DCF (r = 10%)	0	0	0.0	2.7	5.0	7.9	12.3	27.9	63.2
								Shareholder value	91.1

model has new digital technology that has the effect of increasing bulldozer productivity by 10 per cent. The advanced model also has finishing technology that produces a higher quality result, which on average should enable the constructor to charge around £50 000 extra over 12 000 hours of work.

Figure 11.4 shows the economic value of the new machines. The basic machine 'saves'

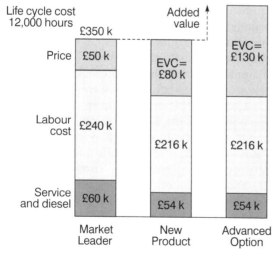

Figure 11.4   Pricing and economic value to the customer

£30 000, implying that its *economic value to the customer* (EVC) is £80 000. The advanced machine has an EVC of £130 000. At any price below the EVC, the customer makes more profit with the new machine, 'other things being equal'. How far the new company can charge the price premium reflected in its EVC depends on the ability of its marketing and sales people to convince customers of its economic benefits. It also depends on persuading them that the support and service that the company offers minimizes the costs and risks in switching from the brand leader.

In consumer markets, emotional added values can be as important as economic, so that value-based pricing needs to estimate the worth of these emotional attributes. Chapter 9 presents some direct and indirect methods for obtaining information from consumers about how much a brand is worth to them.

Customized pricing

Customers always differ greatly in the value they perceive in a particular product or service. If a company charges a uniform price to all customers, it loses two sources of income: one is the revenue lost from customers who find the price too high and do not purchase; the other is

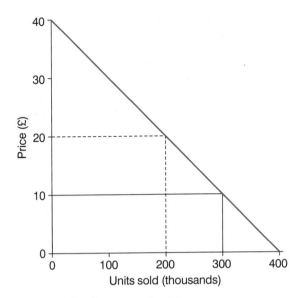

Figure 11.5 Customized pricing

the additional income they could have earned from customers who would have been willing to pay more. A key to effective pricing is customizing pricing to minimize these losses.

This is illustrated in Figure 11.5. A company sets its price at £10 and sells 300 000 units, it has variable costs of £5 per unit and total fixed costs of £1.3 million. It then makes a profit of £200 000. It loses £1 million revenue because some customers find £10 too expensive, and it leaves a consumer surplus of £4.5 million because up to 300 000 could have been sold at higher prices. A more profitable price would be £20; this would have led to a smaller consumer surplus, but a smaller market share, as more potential customers are lost.

The answer is of course charging different prices to different segments of the market or, ideally, to each individual customer. The perfect solution would be a range of prices from £5 (i.e. marginal cost) to £40, which would eliminate the consumer surplus, and any loss of profitable customers. The profit would then be over £3 million.

This type of yield pricing is now becoming common for airlines and hotels, but is ubiqui-

tous in some form in almost all markets. One problem is to keep the segments separate so that high value customers cannot buy at low prices. Another problem is the perceived 'unfairness' of different customers paying different prices. Offering marginally different products is the usual solution. So business class passengers on an airline get better meals or more legroom than economy class. Buyers of expensive credit cards or brands of whisky get them coloured gold! As Figure 11.5 suggests, the gains from such market segmentation and price discrimination can be enormous.

Evaluating competitor reaction

Price competition and price wars can have a devastating effect in destroying shareholder value. We noted earlier a small, 5 per cent price increase can double profits; similarly, small enforced price cuts can eliminate profits altogether.

The importance of considering competitive reactions can be illustrated through *game theory* and, in particular, the famous *Prisoner's Dilemma* game. The game is as follows. Suppose companies A and B are the only producers of a certain product. There is only one customer, who is willing to pay up to £50 per unit for a one-off contract of 10 000 units. The cost of producing the product, including an economic return on the capital employed, is £10 per unit. The company that offers the lowest price wins the contract; if both charge the same prices the contract is shared equally between the two.

Figure 11.6 summarizes the pay-offs of alternative pricing strategies. If both set their prices at £50 and divide the contract, each would make a profit of £200 000. However, this strategy, though attractive, is not individually optimal. If A undercut B and charged £49, then A would win the whole contract, making £390 000 profit, and B would be out of the market. Unfortunately, this strategy is also going to occur to B, who will also seek to maximize its individual profits by cutting price. When price wars like this break out, the price is

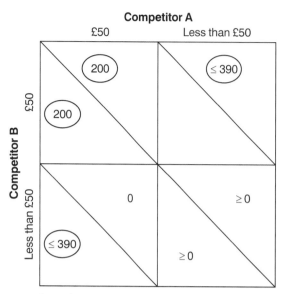

Competitor A

In each quadrant, the top right payoff is for competitor A and the bottom left for B. Circles indicate the payoff that is the best outcome for that player given the strategy of the other.

Figure 11.6   Pricing and the Prisoner's Dilemma.

likely to drop substantially below £49. In fact, at any price higher than £10, the two competitors can improve their individual situation by undercutting the other and obtaining the entire contract.

Only when both competitors are charging £10, and just making the minimum return necessary to stay in the market, is there no incentive for either to undercut the other. In the language of game theory, £10 is the only *Nash equilibrium* of this game – the only price at which neither competitor can individually improve its own situation by reducing prices. But if the two competitors are charging £10, they are both much worse off than they could have been if they had shared the contract at £50.

The Prisoner's Dilemma game is a simplified model of price competition, but it does highlight a conclusion that holds generally. That is, the individual incentive to cut prices can lead to consequences that leave every

competitor worse off. This result, however, does not always occur. The most important oversimplification of the model is that it is a one-off, static decision. In practice, competitors can usually react to each other's price decisions. If a competitor anticipates that his rival will respond, then he may not engage in price competition. Take a simple example of a town with two petrol stations next to each other and customers purely interested in getting the cheapest petrol. To begin with, assume that both are charging the monopoly price – that price which maximizes the joint profits of the two stations. What happens if competitor A lowers its price by 1p a litre? Competitor B, knowing that a price disadvantage will drive his market share to zero, is bound to immediately follow A's price down. Anticipating that this will happen, station A should not lower its price in the first place. The outcome of anticipating a competitive reaction is the exact opposite of the Prisoner's Dilemma – monopoly pricing, rather than competitive pricing.

Note that it is easy to predict a co-operative rather than a competitive price outcome in the petrol station example, because of the assumptions that were made. These include: price starts at the monopoly level; both competitors implicitly agree what this level is; information about prices is available immediately and without cost to both competitors and consumers; there are only two competitors and no substitutes for the commodity. However, most markets have more complex features than the petrol station example, making predictions about prices more difficult. The key to anticipating competitive pricing behaviour is to look at the characteristics of the industry.

Implementing pricing strategy

Just as accountants tend to be biased in favour of high prices, marketers tend to favour low prices. The latter is in part due to their focus on customer satisfaction and market share. It is also often due to the incentive structures that reward marketers for achieving volume rather than profit or shareholder value goals. Volume, market share and customer satisfaction are always increased by lower prices, but this is often at the expense of profit and shareholder value.

Strategies to implement higher prices can be seen in terms of a trade-off between timing and feasibility (Figure 11.7). On the one hand, there are some techniques to improve prices that management can try immediately, but their feasibility is uncertain. On the other hand, there are some very straightforward ways of obtaining higher prices, but their deployment can take many years. The only sure way of achieving higher prices is by finding ways to deliver greater value to customers. This may be via operational excellence, customization, new marketing concepts or innovative products. For example, if a company can develop a new battery that will enable electric cars to operate with the flexibility of petrol-engine ones, or if a pharmaceutical company can develop a cure for cancer, then there will be no problem about attaining a price premium. Superior performance and innovation are the only sustainable means of obtaining better prices. The techniques for implementing price increases are listed in order of their immediacy.

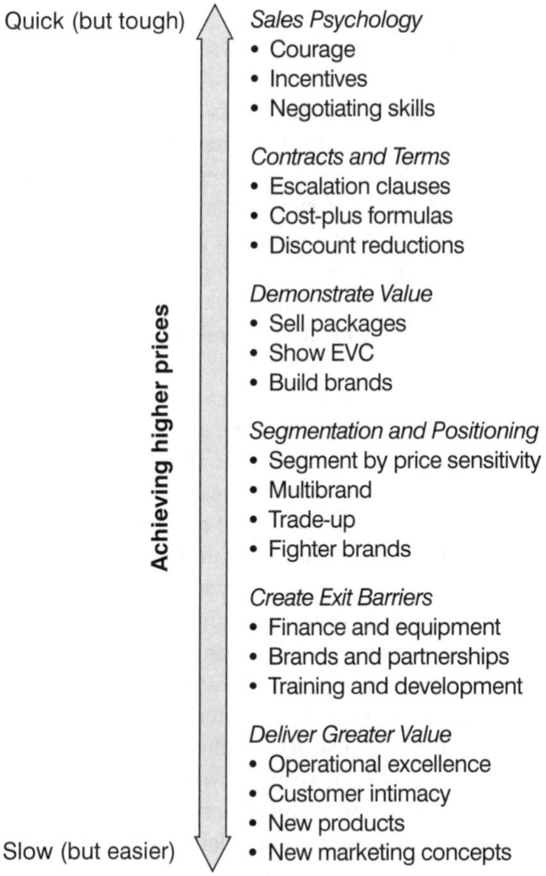

- *Sales psychology.* The reluctance of marketing and salespeople to push for better prices can be offset by clearer direction, shifting incentives away from a purely volume focus, and better training in price negotiations.
- *Contracts and terms.* Contracts can be reviewed to include cost escalation terms, cost-plus formulas and discount reductions.
- *Demonstrating value.* Salespeople often fail to optimize prices because they focus on the features of their product rather than demonstrating its value to the customer. They need to emphasize the added values of the brand, the full range of support services on offer, and the economic value to the customer.
- *Segmentation and positioning.* Key is the recognition that some customers are more price sensitive than others. Some customers will accept price increases, others will not – they need to be treated differently. Multibrands, such as American Express' blue, green, gold and platinum credit cards, and Mercedes A, C, E and S classes of cars, are one way of effectively discriminating on price. Over time, customers who start with cheaper options can often be traded up to premium variants. Fighter brands targeted at emerging price-sensitive segments are another way of holding market share without bringing down prices generally. For example, in 2002 BMI, the British airline, launched BMIBaby, a discount airline positioned at the growing economy segment.
- *Creating exit barriers.* Companies can create barriers to make it difficult to switch to cheap

Quick (but tough)

Sales Psychology
- Courage
- Incentives
- Negotiating skills

Contracts and Terms
- Escalation clauses
- Cost-plus formulas
- Discount reductions

Demonstrate Value
- Sell packages
- Show EVC
- Build brands

Segmentation and Positioning
- Segment by price sensitivity
- Multibrand
- Trade-up
- Fighter brands

Create Exit Barriers
- Finance and equipment
- Brands and partnerships
- Training and development

Deliver Greater Value
- Operational excellence
- Customer intimacy
- New products
- New marketing concepts

Slow (but easier)

Achieving higher prices

Figure 11.7   How to obtain higher prices

competitors. These include: the provision of specialized equipment or finance; training on the company's products and systems; loyalty programmes and long-term development partnerships.

- *Delivering greater value*. In the long run, offering customers added value is the only way to obtain consistently higher prices than competitors. All the other routes are one-off or limited opportunities that eventually erode market share and shareholder value. Without innovation, competitors and new formats inevitably commoditize a company's products and services. Added value strategies can be grouped into five types:

    - *Operational excellence*. Serving the customer more efficiently by cutting costs, increasing reliability, reducing hassle, inconvenience or the need to carry safety stocks (e.g. Wal-Mart, Federal Express).

    - *Customer intimacy*. Designing solutions for customers on a one-to-one basis. Customers will perceive added value when suppliers communicate directly with them and offer solutions tailored precisely to their individual needs rather than being communicated and produced for a mass market (e.g. Dell, American Express).

    - *New products and services*. The most obvious way of obtaining a premium is developing innovative products that meet unmet customer needs, so offering them superior economic, functional or psychological value (e.g. Sony, Merck).

    - *New marketing concepts*. While new products require new technology, new marketing concepts add value by changing the way existing products are presented and marketed. This means finding new markets or new market segments (e.g. Diet Pepsi, Lastminute.com).

    - *New distribution channels*. The Internet, in particular, has stimulated new ways of delivering existing products that offer superior convenience or service to customers (e.g. Amazon, Tesco.com).

Optimizing promotional spending

Promotions – perhaps more effectively termed marketing communications – cover a large and growing array of tools, including direct selling, advertising, sales promotion, public relations and direct response. One of the problems is achieving *integrated communications* – deciding how the communications budget should be optimally divided amongst these alternatives and integrating their messages to achieve a synergistic approach overall. This is made particularly difficult because most companies use different outside specialist agencies to champion and design the individual components.

Developing a communications strategy

Developing a strategy requires five steps:

1 *Understanding the market*. As always, the process starts with understanding the market. This involves assessing the economic potential of the brand, the strength and weaknesses of its current communications profile, and researching customers' needs and buying processes with the objective of learning what messages and media are likely to be most effective.

2 *Setting communications objectives*. Objectives are necessary to align the different communications techniques to a common goal and to judge the effectiveness of the campaign. Ultimately, the *primary goal* of a campaign is to increase, or at least maintain, long-term sales and operating margins. Unfortunately, it is normally difficult to disentangle the effects of a communications vehicle from the array of other factors affecting current sales and margins. As a result, communications objectives are usually specified in terms of *intermediate goals* such as awareness and attitudes to the brand. Considerable judgement is required to determine which are the most relevant measures and what are reasonable targets.

3   *Designing the message.* Once the primary and intermediate goals have been set, then communications messages have to be developed to achieve them. Given the enormous volume of products competing for the consumer's attention, messages have to have impact, to capture attention and to suggest benefits that are desirable, exclusive and meaningful. Chapters 15–18 describe the principles of how message content and presentation are developed to match these requirements.

4   *Deciding the communications budget.* With spending on communications routinely representing 15 per cent or more of sales – or double a company's operating profits – getting the spend right is very important. But few managers have an idea of how to approach the budgeting decision. Most companies use rules of thumb such as setting the spend as a percentage of sales, or what competitors are spending. But the only rational way is to estimate the amount that maximizes the net present value of the brand's cash flow. This is the amount that maximizes shareholder value (for a summary of this approach, see Doyle, 2000, pp. 308–310).

5   *Allocating across communications channels.* The budget has then to be allocated across the various communications vehicles – sales promotion, advertising, public relations, direct response and the sales force. Companies, even within the same market, can employ very different strategies. Each of the channels has its own comparative strengths and weaknesses; they need to be carefully integrated to get the best out of the communications strategy.

Valuing investments in communications

Accounting-led companies invariably underestimate the value of investing in communications. This is especially the case for brands operating in mature markets, when little growth can be expected. One problem is that it is difficult to disentangle the effects of commu-nications spending with the time lags involved and the array of other factors affecting sales. So, cuts in spending often do not appear to be followed by losses in market share. A second problem is that managers misunderstand the baseline to judge communications' effectiveness. Managers tend to assume that if they do not invest in communications, sales will stay at their current level. But in mature markets, the function of communications is often not to increase sales, but rather to maintain them and the price premium a strong brand normally attracts.

Communications create shareholder value if the present value of the brand's cash flow is greater with the investment than without it. Table 11.5 illustrates how the case for advertising can be made, using an example of a leading brand in a recessionary market. The top half forecasts cash flows when the client maintains the £2 million ad budget. The recession is predicted to cut sales by 5 per cent to £20 million in the next 2 years, after which sales are forecast to return to the previous level and then grow with the market at 1 per cent annually. The effective tax rate is taken to be 30 per cent, the cost of capital 10 per cent, and net investment is 40 per cent of sales. Over the 5 years the brand is forecast to generate cash flows with a present value of £3.9 million. The value of the business under this strategy of a maintained ad budget is £10.8 million.

The lower part of the table shows what happens if advertising is cut from £2 million to £1 million. The short-term advertising elasticity is assumed to be 0.2 (typical of a strong brand) and there are diminishing lagged effects over future periods as the brand loses saliency in the minds of consumers. Sales decline steadily over the forecast period, by 14 per cent in the first year, 5 per cent in the second, and almost 3 per cent in the third year. After the first year, profits and then cash flow follow downwards. While the immediate effect of the ad cut is indeed to increase profits by £200 000, the real effect is a major decline in shareholder value by £2.8 million, or 26 per cent. If this were an inde-

Table 11.5 The effect of cutting the advertising budget

	Year				
	1	2	3	4	5
Shareholder value – maintaining budgets (£ million)					
Sales	20.000	20.000	21.000	21.210	21.422
Gross margin	8.000	8.000	8.400	8.484	8.569
Fixed costs	5.000	5.000	5.000	5.000	5.000
Advertising	2.000	2.000	2.000	2.000	2.000
Profit after tax	0.700	0.700	0.980	1.039	1.098
Investment	0	0	0.400	0.084	0.085
Cash flow	0.700	0.700	0.580	0.955	1.013
Present value	0.636	0.579	0.436	0.652	0.629
		PV of forecast cash flows			3.948
		PV of continuing value			6.819
		Corporate value			**10.767**
Shareholder value – cutting budgets (£ million)					
Sales	18.000	17.100	16.670	16.649	16.639
Advertising	1.000	1.000	1.000	1.000	1.000
Profit after tax	0.840	0.588	0.468	0.462	0.459
Investment	0	–0.36	–0.172	–0.008	–0.004
Cash flow	0.840	0.948	0.640	0.470	0.463
		PV of forecast cash flows			3.361
		PV of continuing value			4.589
		Corporate value			**7.950**
		Value loss			**2.817**

pendent company, it would lead to the expectation of an equivalent fall in the share price.

As the example shows, even in a recession, effective communications are not just covering costs, but bolstering the share price in a clear and measurable way. They do this, not so much by increasing sales, but by reinforcing the ability of a strong brand to generate continuing, long-term cash flow.

Distribution strategies

Today, innovation in distribution is becoming one of the most significant ways firms can create competitive advantage. The triggers have been the desire of consumers for greater convenience, global competition forcing companies to search for new ways to cut costs and capital employed, and facilitating technologies, notably information technology and the Internet. New distribution strategies are offering consumers greater benefits in terms of convenience, speed, accessibility and lower costs that are offering pioneering companies opportunities to leapfrog competitors. Besides market advantages, these companies can often significantly reduce their operating costs and investment.

A good example is Dell Computer Corporation. In 1994, Dell was a minor player in the US PC market with a share of 4 per cent; in 2002, it had become the dominant player with a market share of 25 per cent, twice as large as its nearest competitor, Compaq. Furthermore, it was the only PC manufacturer making a profit; in fact, during the 1990s Dell had created the greatest total returns for shareholders of all US companies, with a share price increasing by 85 per cent annually. The basis of Dell's success was its initiative in changing the traditional distribution model. Dell cut out the retailer and sold direct to customers. Instead of holding stock, its PCs were made to order. Dell got paid weeks before it paid suppliers. Dell illustrates how changes in this element of the marketing mix create value first for consumers and then for shareholders:

For consumers:

1 *Convenience*. Customers can order 7 days a week, 24 hours a day.
2 *Lower prices*. By cutting out the retailer, Dell took 25 per cent out of the cost of selling a PC; half of this saving was passed on to the customer.
3 *Customization*. Customers could design the specification of the PC to meet their needs.
4 *Customer relationships*. Dell built a one-to-one relationship with customers, providing the basis for continuing support and new business.

For the supplier:

1 *Higher prices*. By eliminating the middleman's margin, Dell created the virtuous circle of being able to charge customers about 15 per cent less but receive 13 per cent more revenue per unit.
2 *Lower costs*. The company was able to save millions of dollars by replacing brochures, sales and support staff with on-line help.
3 *Minimal investment*. Its build-to-order model meant that it held no inventories.
4 *Reduced investment risk*. Traditional suppliers could have PCs languishing in the retail chain,

often for months. With rapid technological change, stock had often to be discounted to clear, resulting in costly profit write-offs. This reduced vulnerability acts to reduce Dell's cost of capital.
5 *24-cash cycle*. Customers paid for the machines before Dell paid its suppliers, eliminating the need to finance working capital.
6 *Brand protection*. Because the customer relationship was with Dell rather than the retailer, it had greater control over the presentation and positioning of the brand.

These features – higher operating margins, lower investment requirements, faster growth and a lower cost of capital – translate directly into additional shareholder value:

	Traditional PC Co.	Dell
Price to consumer (£)	1000	850
Retailer margin (£)	250	–
Price received (£)	750	850
Operating costs (£)	730	700
Profit (£)	20	150

Selling 10 million PCs a year, this amounts to an *additional* pre-tax cash flow, over traditional suppliers such as Compaq or Apple, with a present value of £13 billion – approximately the value of Dell's value premium.

Summary

1 The marketing mix is at the core of marketing. The marketing mix consists of the key decisions where marketing managers should exhibit their greatest expertise and professionalism. It has become common to summarize the elements of the marketing mix in the four Ps – product, price, promotion and place. Some writers have suggested adding a fifth P – people – to highlight the service element in marketing.

2 However, there is a crucial weakness in the way marketing authors and managers themselves have approached the marketing mix. It has never been clear in marketing theory or practice what the objective is in determining the mix. Without a clear goal it is impossible to design an optimal marketing mix.

3 Marketing professionals have tended to assume the objective was to design a mix that meets purely marketing criteria – notably customer satisfaction or market share. But setting prices, communications budgets or designing products that maximize sales or customer satisfaction is a sure route to financial disaster, because it invariably results in negative cash flow and a failure to cover the cost of capital. Consumers will always perceive value in lower prices, more features and high customer support investments.

4 Equally fallacious is the view of many accountants that the marketing mix should be used to increase profits. This short-termism will usually produce immediate profit improvements but the cost, as many firms have discovered, is a long-term erosion in their market shares and the value investors place on the company.

5 In the private sector, the right marketing mix is the one that maximizes shareholder value. Shareholder value as an objective avoids the short-termism of the accountancy focus because it leads managers to take into account all future cash flows. Long-term performance is almost always a much more important determinant of shareholder value than the profits earned in the next few years. It also avoids the fallacy of the market-led approach by emphasizing that the purpose of the firm is not market share but to create long-term financial value.

6 While applying the shareholder value approach has, of course, many problems associated with forecasting future sales and cash flows (e.g. Day and Fahey, 1988, pp. 55–56; Doyle, 2000, pp. 64–66), it does provide a clear, rational direction for research and decision making.

7 Finally, shareholder value provides the vehicle for marketing professionals to have an increasing impact in the boardroom. In the past, senior managers have often discounted the recommendations of their marketing teams because the marketing mix and strategies for investment have lacked a rational goal. Marketers have not had the framework for translating marketing strategies into what counts for today's top executives – maximizing shareholder value. Value-based marketing provides the tools for optimizing the marketing mix.

References

Anderson, J. C. and Narus, J. A. (1996) Rethinking Distribution: Adaptive Channels, *Harvard Business Review*, **74**, July–August, 112–122.

Brearley, R. A. and Myers, S. C. (1999) *Principles of Corporate Finance*, 6th edn, McGraw-Hill, New York.

Buffet, W. (1994) Letter to Shareholders, *Berkshire Hathaway Annual Report*.

Business Week (2000) The CEO Trap, 11 December, pp. 48–59.

Copeland, T., Koller, T. and Murrin, J. (2001) *Valuation: Measuring and Managing the Value of Companies*, Wiley, New York.

Day, G. and Fahey, L. (1988) Valuing Market Strategies, *Journal of Marketing*, **52**, July, 45–57.

Doyle, P. (2000) *Value-based Marketing: Marketing Strategies for Corporate Growth and Shareholder Value*, Wiley, Chichester.

Doyle, P. (2001) The Case for Advertising in a Recession, *Campaign*, 19 October.

Financial Times (2000) The Convergence of Capitalism, 21 December, p. 9.

Grant, R. M. (2000) *Contemporary Strategy Analysis*, 4th edn. Blackwell, Oxford.

Haigh, D. (1998) Brand Valuation Methodology, in Butterfield, L. and Haigh, D. (eds), *Understanding the Financial Value of Brands*, IPA, London.

Hamel, G. and Prahalad C. K. (1991) Corporate Imagination and Expeditionary Marketing, *Harvard Business Review*, **69**, July–August, 81–92.

Hamel, G. and Prahalad, C. K. (1994) Strategic Intent, *Harvard Business Review*, **73**, May–June, 67–76.

IPA (2000) *Finance Directors Survey 2000*, IPA, London.

Lauterborn, R. (1990) New Marketing Litany: C-Words Take Over, *Advertising Age*, October 1, p. 26.

McCarthy, E. J. (2001) *Basic Marketing: A Managerial Approach*, 13th edn, Irwin, Homewood.

Ohmae, K. (1985) *Triad Power*, Free Press, New York.

Perrier, R. (1997) *Brand Valuation*, Premier Books, London.

Porter, M. E., Takeuchi, H. and Sakakibara, M. (2000) *Can Japan Compete?*, Free Press, New York.

Rappaport, A. (1998) *Creating Shareholder Value*, 2nd edn, Free Press, New York.

Rappaport, A. and Mauboussin, M. J. (2001) *Expectations Investing*, Harvard Business School Press, Boston.

Reichheld, F. F. (1996) *The Loyalty Effect*, Harvard Business School Press, Boston.

Robertson, T. S. (1993) How to Reduce Market Penetration Cycle Times, *Sloan Management Review*, **35**, Fall, 87–96.

Further reading

The standard marketing approach to the marketing mix can be found in most textbooks. Particularly influential are:

Kotler, P. (2000) *Marketing Management*, 10th edn, Prentice-Hall, Englewood Cliffs, NJ.

McCarthy, E. J. (2001) *Basic Marketing: A Managerial Approach*, 13th edn, Irwin, Homewood.

The movement towards value management – that management should orientate the business towards maximizing shareholder value – began to be sharply articulated in the 1980s, though its origins go back much further. Most of the academics that developed these ideas had major impacts on the business community through consultancies they founded or worked for – notably Alcor, MARAKON and McKinsey. All these works have a strong financial orientation and were not well integrated with developments in marketing or business strategy.

Brearley, R. A. and Myers, S. C. (1999) *Principles of Corporate Finance*, 6th edn, McGraw-Hill, New York. Provides a comprehensive treatment of the financial theory on which value-based management is founded.

Copeland, T., Koller, T. and Murrin, J. (2001) *Valuation: Measuring and Managing the Value of Companies*, 3rd edn, Wiley, New York. An influential text developed by McKinsey consultants.

McTaggart, J. M., Kontes, P. W. and Mankins, M. C. (1994) *The Value Imperative*, Free Press, New York. Developed by MARAKON Associates, the market leader in this area of consulting. This book is more successful in linking shareholder value to strategy.

Rappaport, A. (1998) *Creating Shareholder Value*, 2nd edn, Free Press, New York. This was the first major presentation of the theory of value management.

So far, the only text that interprets marketing in value-based terms is:

Doyle, P. (2000) *Value-based Marketing: Marketing Strategies for Corporate Growth and Shareholder Value*, Wiley, Chichester.

A number of journal articles also cover some of the aspects in broad terms, particularly:

Day, G. and Fahey, L. (1988) Valuing Market Strategies, *Journal of Marketing*, **52**, July, 45–57.

Srivastava, R. K., Shervani, T. A. and Fahey, L. (1998) Market-Based Assets and Shareholder Value: A Framework for Analysis, *Journal of Marketing*, **62**, January, 2–18.

CHAPTER 12

New product development

SUSAN HART

Introduction

The need to create customer-relevant business processes is a recurrent theme in marketing evidenced in the underlying themes of previous chapters – particularly those dealing with the nature of marketing, competitiveness and strategies. Today's successful firms learn and re-learn how to deal with the dynamics of consumers, competitors and technologies, all of which require companies to review and reconstitute the products and services they offer to the market. This, in turn, requires the development of new products and services to replace current ones, a notion inherent in the discussion of Levitt's (1960) 'Marketing Myopia'. A recent report into Best New Product Practice in the UK showed that, across a broad range of industry sectors, the average number of new products launched in the previous 5 years was 22, accounting for an average 36 per cent of sales and 37 per cent of profits (Tzokas, 2000). The most recent PDMA Best Practice Survey noted an average number of 38.5 new products in the previous 5 years, contributing to 32.4 per cent of sales and 30.6 per cent of profits (Griffin, 1997).

This chapter is concerned with what is required to bring new products and services to market, often encompassed by the framework known as the new product development (NPD) process.

Of the many factors associated with successful NPD, processes and structures which are customer-focused recur (Cooper, 1979; Maidique and Zirger, 1984; Craig and Hart, 1992). A customer focus may be manifested in NPD in numerous ways, spawning much research into the nature of new product activities: their nature, their sequence and their organization (Mahajan and Wind, 1992; Griffin, 1997). In this chapter, the activities, their sequence and organization required to develop new products are discussed in the light of an extensive body of research into what distinguishes successful from unsuccessful new products. The chapter starts with an overview of the commonly used NPD process model before going on to a general discussion of the usefulness of models in the NPD context. It then develops an integrating model of NPD and, finally, issues identified in current research regarding organizational structures for NPD are considered.

The process of developing new products

Considering some well-known successful innovations of the past 20 years, one might be tempted to think that they are all good ideas: the Walkman, laser printers, Automatic Teller

Machines, mobile phones. And so they are, but does that mean that they could not have failed? What were the basic ideas? The Walkman: portable, personal audio entertainment. The laser printer: fast, accurate, flexible, high-quality reproduction. Automatic Teller Machines: 24-hour cash availability from machines. As ideas, these might have been transformed into products in numerous ways, perhaps less successfully than the products we now find so familiar and convenient.

Imagine the alternative forms for personal audio entertainment: a bulkier headset which contains the tape-playing mechanism and earphones; a small hand-held player, complete with carrying handle, attached to earphones via a cord; a 'backpack' style player with earphones. All of these ideas would have delivered to the idea of 'portable, personal audio entertainment', but which if any of these would have enjoyed the same success as the Walkman? And the Automatic Teller Machines? These might have been developed as stand-alone units, much like bottle banks, requiring the identification of ideal locations, planning permission and consumer confidence to enter them. Would they have been as widespread as the hole-in-the-wall? Finally, the mobile phone: these might have developed with any number of constraining factors, including price, reach, size, weight and functionality.

Think of another 'good idea' – the lightweight, low-pollution, low-cost, easily-parked town car. Now imagine one realization of the idea: three-wheeled, battery-run (with 80 km worth of charge only), and, for the British weather, an *optional* roof. This realization is, of course, the widely-quoted failure, the C5. Yet the *idea* remains a good one.

The issue at stake here is that good ideas do not automatically translate into workable, appealing products. The idea has to be given a physical reality which performs the function of the idea, which potential customers find an attractive alternative for which they are prepared to pay the asking price. This task requires NPD to be managed actively, working though a set of activities which ensure that the eventual product is makeable, affordable, reliable and attractive to customers.

The activities carried out during the process of developing new products are well summarized in various NPD models. These are templates or maps which can be used to describe and guide those activities required to bring a new product from an idea or opportunity, through to a successful market launch. NPD models take numerous forms.

One of the most recognized NPD models is that developed by the consultants, Booz Allen Hamilton (BAH, 1982) and this process continues to be associated with successful outcomes (Griffin, 1997; Tzokas, 2000). This model is shown in Figure 12.1.

This model has been reformulated and shaped over several decades, with the influential derivative from Cooper and Kleinschmidt (1990) known as the Stage–Gate™ process (Figure 12.2). In the US, the Best Practice Study (1997) showed that 60 per cent of firms used some form of Stage–Gate process, whilst the study in the UK by Tzokas (2000) reported only 8 per cent of firms not having some specified form of process.

This and other developments of the BAH model are considered later in the chapter; below is a brief description of the tasks necessary to complete the development and launch of a new product. Each of the stages is described below in turn.

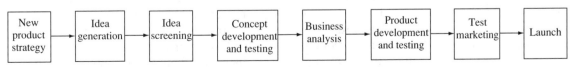

Figure 12.1   The Booz Allen Hamilton model of new product development

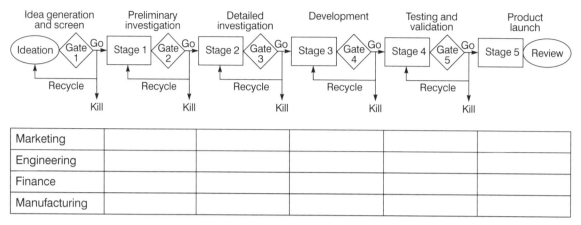

Figure 12.2   The Stage–Gate™ process

The stages of the new product development process

New product strategy

A specific new product strategy explicitly places NPD at the heart of an organization's priorities, sets out the competitive requirements of the company's new products and is effectively the first 'stage' of the development process. It comprises an explicit view of where a new programme of development sits in relation to the technologies that are employed by the company and the markets which these technologies will serve. In addition, this view must be communicated throughout the organization and the extent to which this happens is very much the responsibility of top management. In fact, much research attention has focused on the role of top management in the eventual success of NPD. While Maidique and Zirger (1984) found new product successes to be characterized by a high level of top management support, Cooper and Kleinschmidt (1987) found less proof of top management influence, discovering that many new product failures often have as much top management support. More recently, Dougherty and Hardy (1996) found that although lip-service was given to the importance of innovation, it often takes a backseat compared to other initiatives such as cost-cutting and downsizing, especially where there is less of a history of success in developing new products. And yet, one of the most important roles which top management have to fill is that of incorporating NPD as a meaningful component of an organization's strategy and culture.

In some cases it is necessary for the firm to change its philosophy on NPD, in turn causing a change in the whole culture. Nike's NPD process has changed dramatically over the last 15 years. Previously, they believed that every new product started in the lab and the product was the most important thing. Now, they believe it is the consumer who leads innovation and the specific reason for innovation comes from the marketplace. The reason for this change is the fierce competition that has developed in recent years within the athletic shoe industry, so that product innovation no longer led to sustained competitive advantage and manufacturers could no longer presume that if Mike Jordan chooses a certain shoe everyone else in America will follow. More emphasis was then put on marketing research and targeting smaller groups of individual customers, with the emphasis changing from push to pull NPD. The distinction between technology push and market pull is covered a little later in this chapter; however, it is worth noting that the initial change in philosophy from push to pull has been reinforced by the practice of using the retail setting to encourage 'genuine product innovations instead of inappropriate line extensions'.

While NPD is central to long-term success for companies, it is both expensive and risky, and a majority of 'new' products and services are not entirely 'new'. The new product strategy specifies how innovative the firm intends to be in its NPD and how many new product projects should be resourced at any one time. The seminal work of Booz Allen Hamilton in 1968 and in 1982 revealed the importance of this specification. In their 1968 study, an average of 58 new product ideas were required to produce one successful new product. By 1982, a new study showed this ratio had been reduced to seven to one. The reason forwarded for this change was the addition of a preliminary stage: the development of an explicit, new product strategy that identified the strategic business requirements new products should satisfy. Effective benchmarks were set up so that ideas and concepts were generated to meet strategic objectives. Seventy-seven per cent of the companies studied had initiated this procedure with remarkable success. Reporting 'from experience', Riek (2001) emphasizes clear planning for NPD, including the development of stages and the criteria for each stage being thought out at the initial planning stages of the development programme.

When ideas were generated in line with strategic objectives, an extremely effective 'elimination' of ideas, which in the past cluttered and protracted the NPD process, occurred. Although written in the early 1980s, the lessons to be learned from the work of BAH are still relevant. For example, research by Griffin (1997) showed that 'Best Practice' firms (those which were above average in the relative success of their NPD programmes, in the top third for NPD in their industry and above average in their financial success for NPD) derive their NPD activities through explicit

attention to strategy, thereby becoming more efficient as they require, on average, only 3.5 ideas for one success. The less proficient firms in NPD terms (referred to in the Best Practice Report as The Rest) need 8.4 ideas on average to produce one success, 'because they carefully consider strategy first, they only initiate projects which are more closely aligned to strategy and thus have a much higher probability of success' (p. 11). In a similar study carried out amongst UK firms, Tzokas (2000) found that more top-performing firms include strategy development for NPD, which delineates the target market, determines market need and the attractiveness of the product or service for the target market.

A consultant with PRTM, Mike Anthony, describes a company manning 22 projects, when it had capacity for only nine, and typically would only turn out three new products which would make money. Clearly an agenda – strategy – for cutting down on the effort going into 22 projects would give rise to the opportunity to increase the resources channelled into the remaining projects (*Industry Week*, 1996, p. 45). Setting a clear strategy for NPD also sets up the key criteria against which all projects can be managed through to the market launch. New product strategy, which has also been called the 'product innovation charter' and 'new product protocol' (Crawford, 1984; Cooper, 1993), has been shown to enhance the success rates of the eventual market launch (Hultink *et al.*, 1997, 2000).

The PDMA survey showed that the average ratio of idea:success for the 'best' developers was 3.5, since only projects realizing ideas that are aligned to strategy in the first place are initiated (Griffin, 1997). These in turn have a higher probability of success.

While it is often argued that NPD should be guided by a new product strategy, it is important that the strategy is not so prescriptive as to restrict, or stifle, the creativity necessary for NPD. In addition to stating the level of newness, a new product strategy should encompass the balance between technology and marketing, the level and nature of new product advantage, and the desired levels of synergy and risk acceptance. Each of these is discussed below:

- *Technology and marketing.* One of the most prevalent themes running throughout the contributions on strategic orientations is the merging of the technical and marketing strategic thrust. This is also seen as a dichotomy between allowing the market to 'pull' new products from companies and companies 'pushing' new technologies onto markets. The advantage of the former is that new products, being derived from customers, are more likely to meet their need, while the advantage of the latter is that the new technology will meet needs more effectively than its incumbent and will be harder for competitors to emulate, leading to greater sales, profit and competitive advantage for longer periods of time. However, each has disadvantages. With new products developed through market pull, there is a greater tendency for the new products to be only marginally better than existing products on the market, leading to product proliferation, possible cannibalization of brands and an 'advantage' over competitors that is short-lived, as it is based on technologies with which most of the market players are familiar. With technology-push new products, there is the risk that the new technology is not, in fact, relevant for customers and is rejected by them (Christensen, 1997). As ever, the emphasis should be on achieving a balance between the two: there should be a *fusion* between technology-led and market-led innovations at the strategic level (Johne and Snelson, 1988; Dougherty, 1992). Both Sony and Canon employ 'strategic training' for their engineering and R&D staff, which includes professional training in marketing (Harryson, 1997).
- *Product advantage.* The literature refers to new product strategies which emphasize the search for a differential advantage through the product itself (Cooper, 1984). Product advantage is of course a subjective and multifaceted term, but may be seen as comprising the following elements: technical superiority, product quality, product uniqueness and novelty (Cooper, 1979), product attractiveness (Link, 1987) and high performance to cost ratio (Maidique and Zirger, 1984). The 'war' between Lever Brothers' Persil Power and Ariel Future shows how these companies are competing, strategically, on a platform of technologically-based product advantage. In the battle for cleaning power, Lever Brothers technological advantage was systematically discredited by the competitors and shown to damage clothes, thereby destroying any potential advantages to customers. In the financial service sector, Avlonitis *et al.* (2001) showed that both extremely innovative and minor alterations were the success hallmarks of new developments. On the one hand, the most innovative new products make an impact on the non-financial performance, for example, by enhancing company image and the least innovative ones make a big impact on financial performance. Clearly, then, there are different roles for development projects of various levels of innovation and not all will contribute to firms in the same way.
- *Synergy.* A further strategic consideration discussed here is the relationship between the NPD and existing activities, known as the synergy with existing activities. High levels of synergy are typically less risky, because a company will have more experience and expertise, although perhaps this contradicts the notion of pursuing product differentiation.
- *Risk acceptance.* Finally, the creation of an internal orientation or climate which accepts risk is highlighted as a major role for the new product strategy. Although synergy might help avoid risk associated with lack of knowledge, the pursuit of product advantage must entail acceptance that some projects will fail. An atmosphere that refuses to recognize this tends to stifle activity and the willingness to pursue something new.

Once the general direction for NPD has been set, the process of developing new ideas, discussed below, can become more focused.

Idea generation

This is a misleading term because, in many companies, ideas do not have to be 'generated'. They do, however, need to be managed. This involves identifying sources of ideas and developing means by which these sources can be activated to bring new ideas for products and services to the fore. The aim of this stage in the process is to develop a bank of ideas that fall within the parameters set by 'new product strategy'. Sources of new product ideas exist both within and outside the firm. Inside the company, technical departments such as research and development, design and engineering work on developing applications and technologies which will be translated into new product ideas. Equally, commercial functions such as sales and marketing will be exposed to ideas from customers and competitors. Otherwise, many company employees may have useful ideas: service mechanics, customer relations, manufacturing and warehouse employees are continually exposed to 'product problems' which can be translated into new product ideas. Outside the company, competitors, customers, distributors, inventors and universities are fertile repositories of information from which new product ideas come. Both sources, however, may have to be organized in such a way as to extract ideas. In short, the sources have to be *activated*. A myriad of techniques may be used to activate sources of new ideas, including brainstorming, morphological analysis, perceptual mapping and scenario planning.

Once a bank of ideas has been built, work can begin on selecting those that are most promising for further development.

Screening

The next stage in the product development process involves an initial assessment of the extent of demand for the ideas generated and of the capability the company has to make the product. At this, the first of several evaluative stages, only a rough assessment can be made of an idea, which will not yet be expressed in terms of design, materials, features or price. Internal company opinion will be canvassed from R&D, sales, marketing, finance and production to assess whether the idea has potential, is practical, would fit a market demand, could be produced by existing plants, and to estimate the payback period. The net result of this stage is a body of ideas which are acceptable for further development. Checklists and forms have been devised to facilitate this process, requiring managers to make 'guestimates' regarding potential market size, probable competition, and likely product costs, prices and revenues. However, as at this stage of the process managers are still dealing with ideas, it is unrealistic to imagine that these 'guestimates' can be accurate. The 'newer' the new product, the more guesswork there will be in these screening checks. It is not until the idea is developed into a concept (see below) that more accurate data on market potential and makeability can be assembled.

Concept development and testing

Once screened, an idea is turned into a more clearly specified concept, and testing this concept begins for its fit with company capability and its fulfilment of customer expectations. Developing the concept from the idea requires that a decision be made on the content and form of the idea.

This, however, is easier said than done; the process of turning a new product idea into a fully worked out new product concept is not simply one of semantic labelling. Montoya-Weiss and O'Driscoll (2000) explain that 'an idea is defined as the initial, most embryonic form of new product or service idea – typically a one-line description accompanied by a high-level technical diagram. A concept, on the other hand, is defined as a form, technology plus a

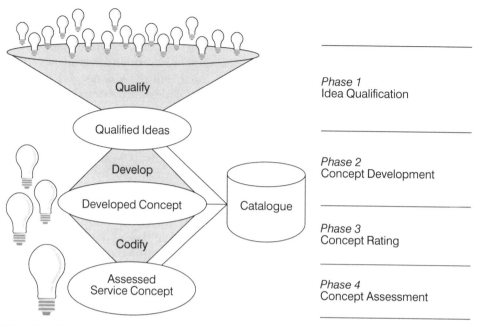

Figure 12.3   The Galileo process

clear statement of customer benefit' (p. 145). They go on to describe a formalized process implemented at Nortel, the large US telecommunications equipment manufacturer, which was developed to assist the transition of idea to concept. The project name for the development of this process was 'Galileo', as the intention was to develop a mechanism (process), which, like the telescope, could aid the identification of 'stars'. The process is shown in Figure 12.3.

Internally, the development team needs to know which varieties are most compatible with the current production plant, which require plant acquisition, which require new supplies, and this needs to be matched externally, in relation to which versions are more attractive to customers. The latter involves direct customer research to identify the appeal of the product concept, or alternative concepts to the customer. Concept testing is worth spending time and effort on, collecting sufficient data to provide adequate information upon which the full business analysis will be made.

Business analysis

At this stage, the major 'go'/'no-go' decision will be made. The company needs to be sure that the venture is potentially worthwhile, as expenditure will increase dramatically after this stage. The analysis is based on the fullest information available to the company thus far. It encompasses:

1   A market analysis detailing potential total market, estimated market share within specific time horizon, competing products, likely price, break-even volume, identification of early adopters and specific market segments.
2   Explicit statement of technical aspects, costs, production implications, supplier management and further R&D.
3   Explanation of how the project fits with corporate objectives.

The sources of information for this stage are both internal and external, incorporating any market or technical research carried out thus far. The output of this stage will be a development plan with budget and an initial marketing plan.

Product development and testing

This is the stage where prototypes are physically made. Several tasks are related to this development. First, the finished product will be assessed regarding its level of functional performance. This is sometimes known as 'alpha testing'. Until now, the product has only existed in theoretical form or mock-up. It is only when component parts are brought together in a functional form that the validity of the theoretical product can be definitively established. Second, it is the first physical step in the manufacturing chain. It is not until the prototype is developed that alterations to the specification or to manufacturing configurations can be designed and put into place. Third, the product has to be tested with potential customers to assess the overall impression of the test product.

The topic of concept testing has been much aided by the development of the Internet, for a number of reasons. The cost of 'building' and 'testing' prototypes virtually is, of course, a fraction of that required by physical prototypes. This is turn means that the market research costs are lower, or that more concepts can be tested by potential customers than is the case with physical products, resulting in a final design which is more attuned to the voice of the customer. In addition, more end customers can be sampled more efficiently via the Internet, although the risk of population deterioration is increased, as is the likelihood of bias, since not all potential customers selected will be willing to 'test' the product virtually. A paper by Dahan and Srinivasan (2000) reported that 'virtual parallel prototyping and testing on the Internet provides a close match to the results generated in person using costlier physical prototypes ...' (p. 108).

Some categories of product are more amenable to customer testing than others. Capital equipment, for example, is difficult to have assessed by potential customers in the same way as a chocolate bar can be taste-tested, or a dishwasher evaluated by an in-house trial. One evolving technique in industrial marketing, however, is called 'beta testing', practised informally by many industrial product developers. The Best Practices research showed that beta site testing was used to a significantly greater degree by the better performing companies (Griffin, 1997).

Test marketing

The penultimate phase in the development cycle, test marketing, consists of small-scale tests with customers. Until now, the idea, the concept and the product have been 'tested' or 'evaluated' in a somewhat artificial context. Although several of these evaluations may well have compared the new product to competitive offerings, other elements of the marketing mix have not been tested, nor the likely marketing reaction by competitors. At this stage the appeal of the product is tested amidst the mix of activities comprising the market launch: salesmanship, advertising, sales promotion, distributor incentives and public relations.

Test marketing is not always feasible, or desirable. Management must decide whether the industrial costs of test marketing can be justified by the additional information that will be gathered. Furthermore, not all products are suitable for a small-scale test launch: passenger cars, for example, have market testing completed before the launch, while other products, once launched on a small scale, cannot be withdrawn, as with personal insurance. Finally, the delay involved in getting a new product to market may be advantageous to the competition, who can use the opportunity to be 'first-to-market'. Competitors may also wait until a company's test market results are known and use the information to help their own launch, or can distort the test results using their own tactics. Problems such as these have encouraged the development and use of computer-based market simulation models, which use basic models of consumer buying as inputs. Information on consumer awareness, trial and repeat purchases, collected via limited surveys or store data, is used to predict adoption of the new product.

That said, there is a discernible trend towards market research tools over the whole process which emphasize in-depth understanding of customer needs rather than quantitative prediction and forecasting. Moreover, this more qualitative understanding is pursued through research methods which privilege continuous, longitudinal dialogue with fewer customers as opposed to snapshot, one-off feedback surveys (Griffin, 1997; Tzokas, 2000).

Commercialization or launch

This is the final stage of the initial development process and is very costly. Decisions such as when to launch the product, where to launch it, how to launch it and to whom will be based on information collected throughout the development process. Table 12.1 summarizes the decisions required to complete the launch of a new product.

Location will, for some companies, entail the number of countries into which the product will be launched, whether national launches will be simultaneous, or roll out from one country to another (Chryssochoidis and Wong, 1998).

Launch strategy also includes any advertising and trade promotions necessary. Space must be booked, copy and visual material prepared, both for the launch proper and the pre-sales into the distribution pipeline. The sales force may require extra training in order to sell the new product effectively.

The final target segments should not, at this stage, be a major decision for companies who have developed a product with the market in mind and who have executed the various testing stages. This should have been identified through the various concept and product testing phases of the development. Attention should be more focused on identifying the

likely early adopters of the product and focusing communications on them. In industrial markets, early adopters tend to be innovators in their own markets. The major concern of the launch should be the development of a strong, unified message to promote to the market, which reinforces the nature of the new product, its benefits over competitive products and its availability to customers. Recent research by Hultink *et al.* (2000) has shown the importance of having the tactics of the launch consistent with the level of innovation in the new product. In other words, the commercialization of the new product cannot successfully make claims for it that are dubious. The most successful launches they studied were innovations aimed at carefully selected niche markets, supported by exclusive distribution and pricing.

This explanation of the new product development process has used the model forwarded by Booz Allen Hamilton as an example; there are numerous other models, which are similar in their representation of a series of activities necessary to bring new products to market. The next section of the chapter considers the usefulness of these models.

Usefulness of models

The usefulness of the process models, such as that by BAH, lies in the way in which they provide an indication of the 'total' number of tasks that might be required in order to develop and launch a new product. The whole procedure has been described as one of information processing (de Meyer, 1985; Allen, 1985), so it is of value if those executing the task of developing new products are given guidance regarding what information is required, where it might reside and to what use it might be put. A recent article by Ottum and Moore (1997) showed that, in particular, the processing of market information (defined as market size and customer needs and wants) is associated with superior new product performance. Table 12.2

Table 12.1 Launch strategy decisions

Variables	Previous study
STRATEGIC LAUNCH VARIABLES	
Firm strategy	
Innovation strategy	2–5,8,9,11,12,17,19
Degree of forward and backward integration	1,4,7
Size of production scale entry	1,4
Product strategy	
Product innovativeness	1,10
Relative product newness	1,10,19
Quality	1,4
Market strategy	
Breadth of segments served	1,4
Stage of the product on its PLC	1,12,19
Target market growth	13,19
Number of competitors	12,19
TACTICAL LAUNCH VARIABLES	
Product	
Breadth of the product line	1,4
Direct manufacturing costs	4
Services	1,4
Price	
Pricing strategy: skim or penetrate?	1,4,12,14,16–18
Promotion	
Advertising	14–18
Promotion	14–17
Distribution	
Distribution intensity	1,4,12,15–18
Sales force effort	14,15,17

1	Biggadike (1979)	11	Urban et al. (1986)
2	Glazer (1985)	12	Choffray and Lilien (1984)
3	Green and Ryans (1990)	13	Cooper (1984)
4	Lambkin (1988)	14	Cooper (1993)
5	Lieberman and Montgomery (1988)	15	Crawford (1984)
6	MacMillan and Day (1987)	16	Little (1975)
7	Roberts and Berry (1985)	17	Urban and Hauser (1991)
8	Robinson and Fornell (1985)	18	Wind (1982)
9	Ryans (1988)	19	Yoon and Lilien (1985)
10	Schmalensee (1982)		

Source: Hultink *et al.* (1997, p. 246).

Table 12.2   Analysis of the NPD process based on Booz Allen Hamilton (1982)

Stage of development	Decision to be taken	Information needed for stage; nature of information	Sources of information
1. Explicit statement of new product strategy, budget allocation	Identification of *market* (NB not product) opportunities to be exploited by new products	Preliminary market and technical analysis; company objectives	Generated as part of continuous MIS and corporate planning
2. Idea generation (or gathering)	Body of initially acceptable ideas	Customer needs and technical developments in *previously* identified markets	Inside company: salesmen, technical functions Outside company: customers, competitors, inventors, etc.
3. Screening ideas: finding those with most potential	Ideas which are acceptable for further development	Assessment of whether there is a *market* for this type of product, and whether the company can make it. Assessment of financial implications: market potential and costs. Knowledge of company goals and assessment of fit	Main internal functions: – R&D – Sales – Marketing – Finance – Production
4. Concept development: turning an idea into a recognizable product concept, with attributed and market position identified	Identification of: key attributes that need to be incorporated in the product, major technical costs, target markets and potential	*Explicit* assessment of customer needs to appraise market potential *Explicit* assessment of technical requirements	Initial research with customer(s). Input from marketing and technical functions
5. Business analysis: full analysis of the proposal in terms of its business potential	Major go/no go decision: company needs to be sure the venture is worthwhile as expenditure dramatically increases after this stage Initial marketing plan Development plan and budget specification	Fullest information thus far: – detailed market analysis – explicit technical feasibility and costs – production implications – corporate objective	Main internal functions Customers
6. Product development: crystallizing the product into semi-finalized shape	Explicit marketing plan	Customer research with product. Production information to check 'makeability'	Customers Production
7. Test marketing: small-scale tests with customers	Final go/no go for launch	Profile of new product performance in light of competition, promotion and marketing mix variables	Market research; production, sales, marketing, technical people
8. Commercialization	Incremental changes to test launch Full-scale launch	Test market results and report	As for test market

shows the decisions required at each stage of the NPD process, together with an indication of the information needed to take that decision and its likely source.

Tzokas identifies six types of uncertainty pervading the NPD process, namely market, technological, competitive, resource, product policy and organizationally-based uncertainties. These can be illustrated and slotted into the NPD process as shown in Table 12.3.

The models of NPD processes as described above tend to be idealized and for this reason may be quite far removed from a specific, real instance of NPD.

A number of authors have researched to what extent the prescriptive activities of the NPD process are undertaken in companies. Cooper and Kleinschmidt (1986) used a 'skeleton' of the process taken from a variety of normative and empirically based prescriptive processes developed by other authors, and found that there is a greater probability of commercial success if all of the process activities are completed. This finding is confirmed in another study, which replicates the investigation in Australian companies (Dwyer and Mellor, 1991). Recent research by Page (1993) showed that a majority of American companies' studies do carry out these main activity stages.

In the Best Practice research studies on both sides of the Atlantic, however, the better-performing firms did tend to use cross functional, third generation processes (those with 'fuzzy and flexible' decision points) and, in the UK survey, the better-performing companies also executed, on average, a higher number of the possible steps in the process (Tzokas, 2000). This echoes the advice 'from experience' of Riek (2001), who said that 'skipping development steps to increase speed to market is the road to disaster' (p. 311).

A further study of NPD practices in the UK and the Netherlands has shown that companies do carry out the activities prescribed by the BAH model, but that the emphasis of every stage is on ascertaining the extent to which the product under development is acceptable to the market (Hart et al., 1998). This is not surprising, since the process of developing a new product is inherently risky, plagued as it is by uncertainty at every stage. Over the process, the uncertainty is reduced – be it regarding technology, makeability or potential customer response.

The conundrum, of course, is that the greatest level of uncertainty exists at the outset of the process – when trying to make decisions regarding these three elements – but until some development of concept begins, the information that can be collected to reduce uncertainty is less reliable than later on, when a clearer picture emerges of the type of product, its features and their likely cost. And yet, despite the warning reported above about the risks involved in missing steps, there is still the persistent view that missing out marketing research steps in the process may not harm, and even improve, the entire NPD process. The well-known and oft-touted example of the Sony Walkman is proffered by those claiming that market research tools are redundant in NPD, and process activities that are research related simply slow the pace of development.

While it may be desirable to have a complete process of NPD, each additional activity extends the overall development time and may lead to late market introduction. There can be a price to pay for late market introduction. For example, Evans (1990) has quantified the consequence of extending the development time: delaying launch by 6 months can equal a loss of 33 per cent in profits over 5 years. Therefore, a trade-off has to be made between completing all the suggested activities in the NPD process and the time which these activities take.

In the case of true innovations, the role of traditional marketing and market research may be less useful. This does not, however, remove the importance of marketing's role in NPD. The PDMA Best Practice research showed that the best companies used significantly more market research tools, including the above-mentioned

| Table 12.3   Types of uncertainty ||||

Types of uncertainty	Stages in process		
	Idea-Concept	Dev.	Launch
Market-based			
Is there customer need for the product?	X		
How stable is the need in the long term?	X		X
How strongly is the need felt?	X		X
Is the market big enough?	X		
Do we have access to distribution?	X		
Do we have experience in this market?	X		
Do customers perceive value in use?	X	X	X
Technology-based			
Can the chosen technology deliver the benefit?		X	
Will the technology become the standard?	X		
Do we have knowledge of the chosen technology?	X		
Do we have manufacturing capability for the chosen technology?		X	
Which OEMs/suppliers do we collaborate with?	X		
Competitive-based			
What would be the reaction of our immediate competitors?			X
What would be the new competitive products?			X
What is the threat of technologies from other industries?		X	
Resource-based			
Do we have the resources to complete NPD on time?		X	
Do we have the resources to support the product in the market?			X
Product policy-based			
What would be the effects on other products of the firm?		X	
What would be the effects on resources for other NPD projects?	X		
Organizational-based			
Do we have the support of top management			
Are there any interdepartmental conflicts?		X	
Is there integration among the departments involved?		X	

Source: Adapted from Tzokas (2000).

beta site test, voice of the customer systems, concept test and customer site visits. Moreover, Tzokas (2000) reported that better-performing companies make more frequent use of all the market research tools studied by the research, including customer site visits, depth interviews with customers, beta site testing, field test markets, creativity sessions for idea generation, concept tests, lead user analysis, concept engineering, conjoint analysis focus group interviews, information acceleration and test market simulations.

The models can provide a useful framework on which to build a complete picture of the development, particularly with regard to the potential advantage of the product viewed from the customers' perspectives. They have been evolving for years and now the BAH model of the 1980s may still serve as the core of what is the Stage–Gate™ model developed by Cooper, but even that has evolved further into what is referred to as 'third generation' processes. These so-called third generation process models, which are characterized by 'fuzzy and flexible gates', have evolved due to a number of limitations on the earlier versions. These are described briefly below.

Related strands of development

These related strands of development refer to marketing, technical (design) and production tasks or decisions that occur as the process unwinds. Each strand of development gives rise to problems and opportunities within the other two. For example, if, at the product development stage, production people have a problem which pushes production costs up, this could affect market potential. The marketing and technical assumptions need to be reworked in the light of this new information. A new design may be considered, or a new approach to the marketplace may be attempted. Whatever the nature of the final solution, it has to be based on the interplay of technical, marketing and manufacturing development issues, meaning that product development

activity is iterative, not only between stages, but also within stages. Indeed, since many of the linear models do not adequately communicate the horizontal dimensions of the NPD process, several 'new generation' models have been developed. Although Cooper's Stage–Gate™ model is one of these (see Figure 12.2), others include the 'fifth generation innovation process' of Rothwell (1994) and the 'blocked' model of Saren (1994). These new generations of process models touch on the idea of 'parallel processing', which acknowledges the iterations between and within stages, categorizing them along functional configurations. The idea of parallel processing is prescriptive: it advises that major functions should be involved from the early stages of the NPD process to its conclusion. This, it is claimed, allows problems to be detected and solved much earlier than in the classic task-by-task, function-by function models. In turn, the entire process is much speedier, which is now recognized to be an important element in new product success. Hence, these are presented as solutions to the dilemma raised earlier, that the execution of the activities is required but not at the expense of speed in the process. Other related techniques which allow firms to accelerate their NPD include quality function deployment (QFD), increasing rewards for R&D performance, relying on external sources of technology and improving the interface among the relevant functional areas (Calantone *et al.*, 1997). So important is the last of these methods that we revisit the substantial amount of research it has attracted towards the end of this chapter.

Idiosyncrasy

The NPD process is idiosyncratic to each individual firm and to the new product project in question. Its shape and sequence depends on the type of new product being developed and its relationship with the firm's current activities (Cooper, 1988; Johne and Snelson, 1988). In addition to the need to adapt the process to individual instances, in real situations there is no clear beginning, middle and end to the NPD process. For example, from one idea, several product concept variants may be developed, each of which might be pursued. Also, as an idea crystallizes, the developers may assess the nature of the market need more easily, and the technical and production costs become more readily identified and evaluated.

Iteration

The iterative nature of the NPD process results from the fact that each stage or phase of development can produce numerous outputs which implicate both previous development work and future development progress. Using the model provided by Booz Allen Hamilton, if a new product concept fails the concept test, then there is no guidance as to what might happen next. In reality, different outcomes may result from a failed concept test, as discussed below:

- *A new idea*. It is possible that, although the original concept is faulty, a better one is found through the concept tests; it would then re-enter the development process at the screening stage.
- *A new customer*. Alternatively, a new customer may be identified through the concept testing

stage, since the objective of concept testing is to be alert to customer needs when formulating a new product. Any new customers would then feed into the idea generation and screening process. Figure 12.4 shows these and other possibilities and illustrates how, viewed as linear or sequential, the BAH model is inadequate, particularly regarding up-front activities.

The inclusion of third parties in the process

Another criticism of the 'traditional' process model forwarded by BAH and others is that it fails to show the importance of parties external to the firm who can have a decided impact on the success of NPD. Research by Littler *et al.* (1995) showed that 'collaborative' product development, which may include suppliers, customers and even, in some instances, competitors, were common in industries such as telecommunications, and Eisenhardt and Tabrizi (1994), studying the computing industry, revealed that developments which involved suppliers could help accelerate development time. In the Discovery example cited above, 'outside' parties such as suppliers were brought

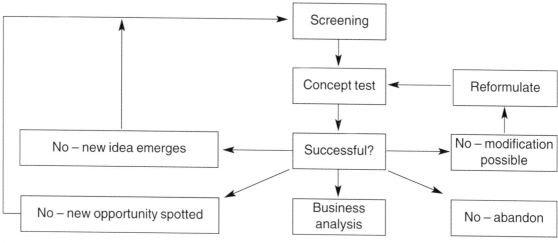

Figure 12.4   Iteration in the NPD process

in at an early stage. Similarly, Intel's development of Pentium departed from its traditional models of development and involved both major customers and software suppliers in the design of the new product.

These shortcomings emphasize that the management of the NPD process is more than simply the number and sequencing of its activities. The extent to which the activities can or cannot be effectively carried out demands attention to the *people, or functions*, within the process. It is to these issues that we now turn our attention.

People involved in the NPD process and the way in which these people are organized are critical factors in the outcome of new product developments. In order to combine technical and marketing expertise, a number of company functions have to be involved: R&D, manufacturing, engineering, marketing and sales. As the development of a new product may be the only purpose for which these people meet professionally, it is important that the NPD process adopted ensures that they work well and effectively together. Linked to this is also the need for the voice of the customer to be heard, as well as that of suppliers, where changes to supply may be required or advantageous.

The Stanford Innovation Project (Maidique and Zirger, 1984) identified functional co-ordination as a critical factor contributing to the development of *successful* new products. Support for the importance of functional co-ordination is to be found in numerous studies, including Pinto and Pinto (1990), who found that the higher the level of cross-functional co-operation, the more successful the outcome of NPD. The benefits of a close relationship between functional co-ordination and an integrated set of NPD activities have already been highlighted, including the reduction of the development cycle time, cost savings and closer communication, so that potential problems are detected very early on in the process (Larson, 1988). Although integration of all the relevant functional specialisms into the NPD process is necessary, one particular interface has been

given more attention in research studies: the R&D/marketing interface, due to the impact of this interface on the success with which a technological development can be made to match customer need.

Although a host of issues pertain to the integration of the R&D and marketing functions, one of the most powerful is that of how information is handled throughout the NPD process.

Information

The role which information can play in facilitating an efficient NPD *process* and achieving *functional co-ordination* is implicit in the literature on success in NPD. The notion of reducing uncertainty as the main objective of the project development activities is reiterated throughout the literature: project activities *'can be considered as discrete information processing activities aimed at reducing uncertainty ...'* (Monaert and Souder, 1990, p. 92). These activities include gathering and disseminating information and making decisions based upon this information, which must include evaluations of *both the market and technical aspects* of the development project. Indeed, it is ultimately this information which is evaluated during the NPD process review through the 'gates'.

In order to reduce uncertainty, it is not sufficient that information be processed, it also has to be transferred between different functions (Monaert and Souder, 1990). In this way, the uncertainty perceived by particular functions can be reduced. At the same time, the efficient transfer of quality information between different functions encourages their co-ordination (Monaert and Souder, 1990).

As well as reducing uncertainty, the transfer of information between the two functions is perceived by both sides to be a key area for establishing *credibility* as a necessary input to the integration described in the previous section. The research by Workman (1993) showed, for example, that in Zytech, lack of credibility between functions inhibited integration.

Table 12.4 The role of market information in achieving critical success factors

Success factor	Studies citing importance	Operationalization of success factors	Expected market information elements
		STRATEGIC SUCCESS FACTORS	
Product advantage	Cooper, 1990; Cooper and Kleinschmidt, 1987, 1990.	Excellent relative product quality in comparison to competitive offerings; good value for money (perceived by the customer); excellence in meeting customer needs; inclusion of benefits perceived by the customer as useful; benefits which are obvious to the customer; superior price/performance characteristics; unique attributes	Customer perceptions of competitive offerings; technological dimensions of competitive offerings; customer perceptions of new product's attributes and benefits; Feedback from customers after trial; feedback on customer understanding of the message; perceptual maps – based on customer data; technical specifications, product design information; attributes and features specifications
Well specified protocol	As above: Rothwell 1972; Rothwell et al., 1974; Rubenstein et al., 1976.	Firm's knowledge and understanding, prior to development, of: the target market; customer needs, wants, preferences; The product concept; product specifications and requirements	Research information detailing market demographics/psycographics; customer needs, wants and preferences; technical specifications, product design information, attributes and features specifications (prior to development)
Market attractiveness	Maidique and Zirger, 1984; de Brentani, 1991.	High growth rates, high market need for product type; stability of demand; relative price insensitivity; high trial of new products	Economic market data; economic trends; level of employment; income levels; inflation rates
Top management support	Ramanujam and Mensch, McDonough, 1986.	Levels of risk aversion; aspects of corporate culture	Risk involved; identification of product champions; power and influence distribution among managers
Synergy/ familiarity	Maidique and Zirger, 1984; Rothwell et al., 1972, 1974.	Knowledge of technology; relevance to other projects; access to scientific institutes and laboratories	Extent of new knowledge involved; technology centres where knowledge resides; key scientists; technological networks of firms
		DEVELOPMENT PROCESS ISSUES	
Proficiency of pre-development activities	Cooper & Cooper and Kleinschmidt as above, Rubenstein et al., 1976;Voss, 1985.	Proficiency of concept screening; preliminary market and technical assessment; preliminary business analysis; preliminary technical assessment	Research on customer perceptions, gap analysis, needs analysis, concept tests; market size potential, market segments; technical feasibility, preliminary costs; market size, likely price, profit, break-even etc.
Proficiency of marketing activities	Roberts and Burke, 1974; Rothwell et al., 1972, 1974; Cooper, 1979, 1980; Maidique and Zirger, 1984; Link, 1987	Proficiency of concept, product and market tests, service, advertising, distribution and elements of market launch	Market information for the acceptance of alternative product concepts or designs, customer preference data; market profile information, information concerning the distribution channels of interest
Proficiency of technological activities	Rothwell et al., 1972, 1974; Maidique and Zirger, 1984.	Proficiency in physical product development; in-house and in-use test iterations; trial production runs; technology acquisition	Technical solutions to functional and marketing problems; technical information on test performance; information on production costs and problems; information on suppliers' developments and adjacent technologies
Integration of R&D and marketing	Maidique and Zirger, 1984; Takeuchi and Nonaka, 1986; Rubenstein et al., 1976; Gupta and Wilemon, 1990; Rochford and Rudelius, 1992.	Amount of information shared; agreement on decision-making authority; functional involvement at each stage	Relevance, novelty, credibility, comprehensibility of information Timeliness of information provision
Speed in development	Takeuchi and Nonaka, 1986; Dumaine, 1992; Cooper and Kleinschmidt, 1994.	Time-to-market; product launched on schedule; no. of competitors on market at time of launch	Timeliness of information exchange; competitive information

Information, therefore, is a base currency of the NPD process; evaluative information is crucial and must be efficiently disseminated to facilitate communication. It is even possible to analyse the various factors which have been shown to correlate with NPD success in such a way as to reveal the information needs of the process for greater success. An example of the information elements implied by the numerous studies into success and failure is given in Table 12.4.

Research by Maltz (2000) has shown that the way in which information is communicated has a profound effect on its perceived quality and therefore use. Specifically, his study showed that, across functions involved in NPD, the frequency of communications needs to be above a threshold level before information is absorbed. Moreover, routine e-mail, contributing as it does to the often unnecessary buzz and obscuring the substantive, is unlikely to be viewed as quality information. Scheduled telephone calls were shown to be of greater value, and impromptu face-to-face conversations are associated with higher levels of perceived information quality.

The foregoing discussion of the usefulness of existing models shows that, while it is useful to have a checklist of the crucial tasks needed to ensure that new products meet customer needs, any useful framework must allow for numerous inputs from a variety of functions both within and outside the company, and must allow for both vertical and horizontal flows of market and technical information across these functions throughout the NPD project. Below, an alternative framework for NPD is discussed, called the multiple convergent approach.

The multiple convergent approach

In suggesting a way forward in NPD research which builds on process models but which also takes account of the lessons to be learned from studies of success and failure in NPD, the multiple convergent process attempts to break down research-discipline boundaries, which has direct and explicit consequences for people. This model is conceptually derived from the idea of parallel processing, and is shown in Figure 12.5.

Although models based on parallel processing were an improvement on earlier versions, there was an inherent problem in their parallelism. Definitions of 'parallel' refer to 'separated by an equal distance at every point' or 'never touching or intersecting', and while there are references to simultaneity, it is a somewhat troublesome notion that suggests functional separation, when all the performance indicators in NPD point to the need for functional integration. On the other hand, 'to converge' is defined as 'to move or cause to move towards the same point' or to 'tend towards a common conclusion or result', and is therefore a more precise indicator of what is required of NPD management.

Realizing, however, that there are still functionally distinct tasks which must be carried out at specific points throughout the NPD process, it is clear that the tasks will be carried out simultaneously at some juncture and that the results must *converge*. Due to the iterations in the process, this convergence is likely to happen several times, culminating at the time of product launch. As previously mentioned, the process is a series of information gathering and evaluating activities, and as the new product develops from idea to concept to prototype and so on, the information gathered becomes more precise and reliable, and the decisions are made with greater certainty. Therefore, as the development project progresses, there are a number of natural points of evaluation and a number of types of evaluation (market, functional) which need to be carried out in an integrated fashion. These convergent points can be set around decision outputs required to further the process.

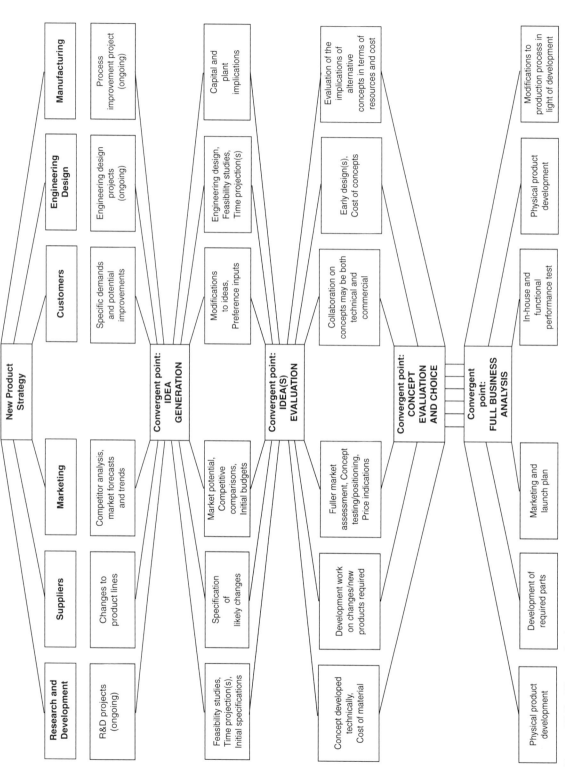

Figure 12.5   The multiple convergent process

The advantages of viewing the process this way are as follows:

1 Iterations among participants within stages are allowed for.
2 The framework can easily accommodate third parties.
3 Mechanisms for integration throughout the process among different functions are set in the convergent points.
4 The model can fit into the most appropriate NPD structures for the company.

Iterations within stages

As the relevant functions are viewed in terms of their contribution to each stage in the process by their specialist contribution, the cross-functional linkages between stages are incorporated. The extent of involvement of different bodies or outside parties will be determined by the specific needs of each development in each firm. Thus, within-stage iteration can benefit from both task specialization, which will increase the quality of inputs, and integration of functions via information sharing and decision making.

Accommodation of third parties

Several studies have shown the importance of involving users in the NPD process to increase success rates (Von Hippel, 1978; Biemans, 1992). Equally, there is growing interest in the need for supplier involvement, in order to benefit from the advantages of supplier innovation and JIT (Ragatz *et al.*, 1997).

Mechanisms for integration

Although the need for cross-functional integration has been widely claimed, there is some evidence to suggest that, in practice, this is not easy to achieve. In Biemans' study, most of the companies showed an understanding of the need to integrate R&D and marketing activities, although the desirability of this is not con-

sidered to be automatic, based on the evidence of the companies surveyed. A key element in integration is the amount of information sharing, and the multiple convergent process offers the opportunity for information sharing which is neglected by other models. Clearly, a host of other factors are likely to influence the amount of cross-functional information sharing, including organizational climate and structure. This said, the multiple convergent model carries within it the impetus for information sharing through the convergent points that can be located liberally throughout the process.

However, studies stress that the appropriate level of integration must be decided upon, and that this level is dependent upon organizational strategies, environmental uncertainty, organizational factors and individual factors. This requires attention, not only to the process of developing new products, but also to the mechanisms used to manage the people responsible for bringing new products and services to the market.

Managing the people in NPD

The process of developing successful new products needs to match technological competence with market relevance. Based on our discussions thus far, numerous inputs are required to achieve these twin goals. Much research has been carried out into various aspects of 'co-ordination' and 'integration' of the perspectives of different disciplines in NPD. This research is confusing, however, not only because of the sheer number of aspects of functional co-ordination which have been investigated, but also because of the variety of terms used to refer to what this article calls 'functional co-ordination'. Pinto and Pinto (1990, p. 203) make an informative summary of the different terms which have been used. Whatever the precise definition, it is important for companies to institute NPD processes and design structures which promote integration and co-ordination, at the same time as preserving the efficiencies and expertise within functional speciality. A recent article by Olsen *et al.* (1995) identified seven types of new product structure, or co-ordination mechanisms, which they describe in terms of four structural attributes: complexity, distribution of authority, formalization and unit autonomy. These are shown in Table 12.5 and discussed briefly below.

- *Bureaucratic control.* This is the most formalized and centralized, and the least participative mechanism, where a high level general manager co-ordinates activities across functions and is the arbiter of conflicts among functions. Each functional development operates with relative

autonomy within the constraints imposed by hierarchical directives, and therefore most information flows vertically within each department. In such a mechanism, the different functional activities work sequentially on the developing product.

- *Individual liaisons.* Individuals within one functional department have to communicate directly with their counterparts in other departments. Therefore, they supplement the vertical communication found in bureaucracies.

- *Integrating managers.* In this co-ordination structure, an additional manager is added to the functional structure, responsible for co-ordinating the efforts of the different functional departments, but without the authority to impose decisions on those

Table 12.5 Attributes of interfunctional co-ordination mechanisms

Types of co-ordination mechanisms

Structural and process variables	Bureaucratic control	Individual liaisons	Temporary task forces	Integrating managers	Matrix structures	Design teams	Design centres
Structural attributes							
Complexity	Simple structures	⟶				Complex structures	
Distribution of authority	Centralized	⟶				Decentralized	
Formalization	High; more reliance on rules and standard procedures	⟶				Low: fewer rules and standard procedures	
Unit autonomy	Low	⟶				High	

Source: Olsen *et al.* (1995).

departments. Thus, such integrating managers have to rely on persuasion and on their ability to encourage group decision making and compromise to achieve successful results.

- *Matrix structures.* Whereas all the previous mechanisms maintain the primacy of the functional departmental structure, a matrix organization structures activities not only according to product or market focus, but also by function. Thus, individuals are responsible to both a functional manager and a new product manager.

According to this research, two newer structural forms have appeared in order to improve the timeliness and the effectiveness of the product development efforts within rapidly changing environments. These forms are:

- *Design teams.* Like the matrix structure, design teams are composed of a set of functional specialists who work together on a specific NPD product. The difference is that such teams tend to be more self-governing and have greater authority to choose their own internal leader(s), who have more autonomy to establish their own operating procedures and to resolve internal conflicts.
- *Design centres.* These centres have many of the same characteristics as a design team. However, such a centre is a permanent addition to an organization's structure, and members of the centre are involved in multiple development projects over time.

As one moves from bureaucratic control toward more organic and participative structures, the structural complexity of the mechanisms increases. Authority becomes more decentralized, rules and procedures less formalized and less rigidly enforced, and the individual units tend to have more autonomy. Consequently, members of relatively organic structures are more likely to share information across functional boundaries and to undertake interdependent tasks concurrently rather than sequentially.

In other words, as we move from left to right, structures become less 'mechanistic' and

more 'organic' (Burns and Stalker, 1961). Relatively organic mechanisms such as design teams have some important potential advantages for co-ordinating product development. Indeed, the participative decision making, consensual conflict resolution and open communication processes of such a structure can help reduce barriers between individuals and functional groups. Such participative structures can also create an atmosphere where innovative ideas are proposed, criticized and refined with a minimum of financial and social risk. Besides, by facilitating the open exchange of creative ideas across multiple functions, the likelihood of producing innovative products that successfully address the market desires, as well as technical and operational requirements, is increased.

Finally, reduced functional barriers help ensure that unanticipated problems that appear during the development process can be tackled directly by the people concerned. This reduces the possibility that vital information may be delayed, lost or altered.

On the other hand, more participative structures also have some potential disadvantages, especially in terms of costs and temporal efficiency. Creating and supporting several development teams can lead to overabundance in personnel and facilities. The main reason for this is that employees have less relevant experience when developing innovative product concepts and then depend more heavily on other functional specialists for the expertise, information and other resources needed to achieve a creative and successful product. And these flows of information and resources are facilitated by less formal participative co-ordination structures. Thus, there is potential for stagnation in the process if the focus of control is unclear.

In the light of this discussion, let us now look at what kinds of structures are used for NPD.

Structures used by industry

In the PDMA Best Practices study, the best companies were more likely to use multifunctional teams, while in the UK, the Best Practice firms used new product teams and NPD permanent staff (Tzokas, 2000). It should be noted, however, that much of the research in NPD into what separates success from failure has concluded that there is no one best way to organize for NPD, as shown in Figure 12.6.

These studies and others tend to show that multiple structures are used for organizing the NPD effort within a firm, depending upon the factors driving the innovation (i.e. its strategy) and the level of innovation of the development. For example, Page's (1993) research shows that the most common mechanism used for NPD is

that of a 'multidisciplinary team', but this was used in combination with other mechanisms, such as product manager, new product manager and new product departments.

Structures used by companies may exist either within or outside what might be termed 'existing line functions' (such as marketing, R&D or engineering), although this is rarely made explicit. Those which exist outside existing line structures are venture teams and NPD departments.

Venture teams

These tend to be a permanent 'maverick' group, with high status, separate budgets and report to the MD. Their responsibilities can vary, but include opportunity identification and feasibility studies, through to management of the new product development.

The advantages are that, freed from the 'humdrum' of current business, creativity can be encouraged and the development has high level support. On the other hand, they can turn into acquisition hunters, may be prone to get into unrelated areas and can be seen as a waste of time if they acquire such information from inside the company, which might occur if they get involved with the development of existing products.

New product departments or divisions

These have the same status as functional divisions and are essentially outside the 'mainstream' of business. They are usually staffed by a combination of functions. They may be used in different ways: as idea hunters, where ideas are passed to the 'mainstream' for development, or as developers, who manage the new product from idea through to the market launch. In the latter instance, the 'handover' of the product will take place at the launch, which may engender feelings of 'not invented here'. However, the rationale for the complete segregation of new

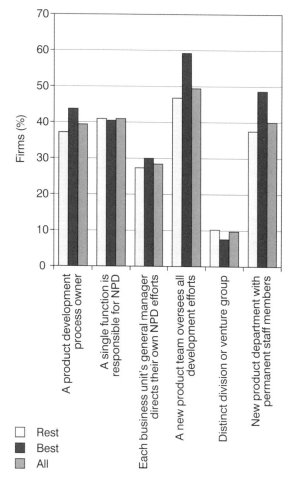

Figure 12.6 NPD structure

product activity is to encourage new ideas for products not contaminated by the vested interests of those managing the account business. If, however, new product activity does need to draw on experience of current technologies in current markets, then some linkage with those managing the current business is clearly beneficial.

Multidisciplinary teams, new products' committees, new product teams, product managers and new product managers are all linked – some more directly than others – to the existing line structures. Indeed Page's (1993) study showed that the line functions most involved in NPD were marketing, R&D and engineering. The various teams, committees or individuals may be given 'part-time' responsibility for NPD.

There is an inevitable tension between the need for integration and existing authority and responsibility lines. Due to this tension, many firms will locate responsibility for NPD in one function, and bring others in as and when required. This, of course, raises problems in that development work may be in conflict with the management of current business. This would be manifested in time pressures, whereby development work is squeezed by existing product management, stifled creativity, due to procedures in place for existing products, and, finally, fresh business perspectives may be lacking in people who are expert in managing the current business.

Alternatively, a post of new products manager may be created in marketing or technical departments. The part-time option can suffer from time pressures and conflict of roles as besets much matrix structures and, worse, NPD can become something of a secondary goal. In addition, the individual new product manager tends not to be interdisciplinary, which forces negotiation with other departments as opposed to collaboration. As a result, there tends to be a 'pass-the-parcel' approach to the development project, which gets shunted around from one department to the next. Finally, this mechanism tends to be low level with little leverage for important resource decisions, leading to an incremental approach to NPD and a new product committee. This is made up of senior managers from salient functions, and has the purpose of encouraging cross-functional co-operation at the appropriate senior level. However, these mechanisms may suffer from a remote perspective, as the line managers are not really carrying out the task.

Location of new product activity inside our outside existing functions requires a trade-off. Since autonomous structures are designed to allow the unfettered development of new ideas, products with greater levels of advantage, without much reliance on the existing business, it follows logically that this type of development is precisely what they should carry out.

Once these autonomous units become involved with what Johne and Snelson (1988) call 'old product development', their inevitable reliance on those within the line function may cause a conflict. In any case, perhaps the efficiency of an autonomous unit to redevelop current lines is questionable. Indeed, the research by Olsen et al. (1995) showed that 'organic, decentralized participative co-ordination mechanisms *are* associated with better development performance...*but only* when used on projects involving innovative or new to the world concepts with which the company has little experience on which to draw' (p. 61).

A number of companies' stories highlight this finding in practice. Guinness' new business unit and the development of Chrysler's Neon, a 'sub-compact', use what they call 'platform teams', which are autonomous groups consisting of all the professionals required to design and produce a new car, or 'platform'.

This section has introduced some of the complexities involved in designing mechanisms which provide the appropriate balance between creativity and innovation on the one hand, and building on the expertise accumulated with regard to technologies and markets on the other.

Although much research points to the need for cross-functional teams, the extent to which these should be autonomous will depend, among other things, on the type of NPD being pursued. In addition, it is noteworthy that in Griffin's latest study, 'structure does not contribute materially to differentiating the Best from the Rest' (p. 443). It seems, then, that research is still some way from explaining how companies can best organize their NPD efforts in order to achieve the cross-functional integration and information sharing that seems so central to successful NPD.

Summary

This chapter has focused exclusively on how new products are developed. Starting with the proposition that it takes more than a good idea to make a successful new product, it has described the main activities needed to bring a new product to market successfully. In so doing, the main critical success factors for NPD which have been revealed through research have been woven into the discussion of the process models commonly exhorted as the blueprints for success. This discussion has, in turn, highlighted the importance of market information to the successful completion of NPD projects, but it has also shown that blind adherence to a model for NPD cannot be productive, as the whole business needs to be characterized by flexibility and open to creativity from various sources within and outside companies. The argument has presented information as a central thread of successful NPD. The NPD process is one of uncertainty reduction, which requires information, constant evaluation of options, which requires information, and integration of various functional perspectives, also requiring the sharing of information.

References

Allen, T. J. (1985) *Managing the Flow of Technology*, MIT Press, Cambridge, MA.

Avlonitis, G., Papastathopoulou, P. G. and Gounaris, S. P. (2001) An empirically-based typology of product innovativeness for new financial services: success and failure scenarios, *Journal of Product Innovation Management*, **18**(5), 324–342.

Biemans, W. (1992) *Managing Innovations Within Networks*, Routledge, London.

Booz Allen Hamilton (1968) *Management of New Products*, Booz Allen Hamilton, Chicago.

Booz Allen Hamilton (1982) *New Products Management for the 1980s*, Booz Allen Hamilton, New York.

Bruce, M. (1992) The black box of design management, Marketing Working Paper Series, UMIST.

Burns, T. and Stalker, G. M. (1961) *The Management of Innovation*, Tavistock, London.

Calantone, R. J., Schmidt, J. B. and di Benedetto, A. (1997) New product activities and performance: The moderating role of environmental hostility, *Journal of Product Innovation Management*, **14**(3), May, 179–189.

Christensen, X. (1997) *The Innovator's Dilemma*, Harvard Business School, Boston.

Chryssochoidis, G. M. and Wong, V. (1998) Rolling out new products across country markets: an empirical study of the causes of delays, *Journal of Product Innovation Management*, **15**(1), 16–41.

Cooper, R. G. (1979) The dimensions of new industrial product success and failure, *Journal of Marketing*, **43**(1), 93–103.

Cooper, R. G. (1984) How new product strategies impact on performance, *Journal of Product Innovation Management*, **1**, 5–18.

Cooper, R. G. (1988) The new product process: a decision guide for management, *Journal of Marketing Management*, **3**(3), 238–255.

Cooper, R. G. (1993) *Winning at New Products;*

Accelerating the Process from Idea to Launch, Addison-Wesley, Reading, MA.

Cooper, R. G. and Kleinschmidt, E. J. (1986) An investigation into the new product process; steps, deficiencies and impact, *Journal of Product Innovation Management*, **3**, 71–85.

Cooper, R. G. and Kleinschmidt, E. J. (1987) New products; what separates winners from losers?, *Journal of Product Innovation Management*, **4**, 169–184.

Cooper, R. G. and Kleinschmidt, E. J. (1990) New product success factors; a comparison of 'kills' versus successes and failures, *R&D Management*, **20**(1), 169–184.

Craig, A. and Hart, S. (1992) Where to now in new product development research?, *European Journal of Marketing*, **26**, 1–49.

Crawford, C. M. (1984) Protocol: new tool for product innovation, *Journal of Product Innovation Management*, **2**, 85–91.

Dahan, E. and Srinivasan, V. (2000) The predictive power of internet-based concept testing using visual depiction and animation, *Journal of Product Innovation Management*, **17**(2), 99–109.

de Meyer, A. (1985) The flow of technological innovation in an R&D department, *Research Policy*, **14**, 315–328.

Dougherty, D. (1992) A practice-centred model of organisational renewal through product innovation, *Strategic Management Journal*, **13**, 77–92.

Dougherty, D. and Hardy, C. (1996) Sustained product innovation in large, mature organizations: overcoming innovation-to-organization problems. *Academy of Management Journal*, **39**(5), 1120–1153.

Dwyer, L. M. and Mellor, R. (1991) Organization environment, new product process activities and project outcomes, *Journal of Product Innovation Management*, **8**(1), March, 39–48.

Eisenhardt, K. M. and Tabrizi, B. N. (1994) Accelerating adaptive processes: product innovation in the global computer industry, *Administrative Science Quarterly*, **40**(1), March, 84–110.

Evans, S. (1990) Implementation framework for integrated design teams, *Journal of Engineering Design*, **1**(4), 355–363.

Griffin, A. (1997) *Drivers of NPD Success: The 1997 PDMA Report*, PDMA, Chicago.

Gupta, A. K. and Wilemon, D. (1988) The credibility–co-operation connection at the R&D marketing interface, *Journal of Product Innovation Management*, **5**, 20–31.

Gupta, A. K., Raj, S. P. and Wilemon, D. (1985) The marketing–R&D interface in high-tech firms, *Journal of Product Innovation Management*, **2**, 12–24.

Harryson, S. J. (1997) How Canon and Sony drive product innovation through networking and application-focused R&D, *Journal of Product Innovation Management*, **14**(3), 288–295.

Hart, S. J. and Baker, M. J. (1994) The multiple convergent process of new product development, *International Marketing Review*, **11**(1), 77–92.

Hart, S. J. and Service, L. M. (1988) The effects of managerial attitudes to design on company performance, *Journal of Marketing Management*, **4**(2), 217–229.

Hart, Tzokas, Hultink and Commandeur (1998) How companies steer the new product development process, *Proceedings of the Annual Conference of the Product Development Management Association*, Atlanta, GA.

Hill, P. (1988) The market research contribution to new product failure and success, *Journal of Marketing Management*, **3**(3), 269–277.

Hultink, E. J., Griffin, A., Hart, S. and Robben, H. S. J. (1997) Industrial new product launch strategies and product development performance, *Journal of Product Innovation Management*, **14**, 246.

Hultink, E. J., Hart, S., Robben, S. J. and Griffin, A. (2000) Launch decisions and new product success: an empirical comparison of consumer and industrial products, *Journal of Product Innovation Management*, **17**(1), 5–23.

Industry Week (1996) 16 December, p. 45.

Johne, A. F. and Snelson, P. (1988) Marketing's role in new product development, *Journal of Marketing Management*, **3**, 256–268.

Larson, C. (1988) Team tactics can cut development costs, *Journal of Business Strategy*, **9**(5), September/October, 22–25.

Levitt, T. (1960) Marketing myopia, *Harvard Business Review*, July–August, 45–56.

Link, P. L. (1987) Keys to new product success and failure, *Industrial Marketing Management*, **16**, 109–118.

Littler, D., Leverick, F. and Bruce, M. (1995) Factors affecting the process of collaborative product development: a study of UK manufacturers of information and communications technology products, *Journal of Product Innovation Management*, **12**(1), 16–23.

Mahajan, V. and Wind, J. (1992) New product models: practice, shortcomings and desired improvements, *Journal of Product Innovation Management*, **9**, 128–139.

Maidique, M. A. and Zirger, B. J. (1984) A study of success and failure in product innovation: the case of the US electronics industry, *IEEE Transactions on Engineering Management*, **31**, 192–203.

Maltz, E. (2000) Is all communication created equal?: an investigation into the effects of communication mode on perceived information quality, *Journal of Product Innovation Management*, **17**(2), 110–127.

Monaert, R. K. and Souder, W. E. (1990) An information transfer model for integrating marketing and R&D personnel in NPD projects, *Journal of Product Innovation Management*, **7**(2), 91–107.

Montoya-Weiss, M. and O'Driscoll, T. (2000) Applying performance support technology in the fuzzy front end, *Journal of Product Innovation Management*, **17**(2), 143–161.

Morita, A., Reingold, M. and Shimomura, I. (1987) *Made in Japan*, Penguin, London.

Nauman, E. and Shannon, P. (1992) 'What is customer-driven marketing?, *Business Horizons*, November–December, 44–52.

O'Connor, G. C. and Veryzer, R. W. (2001) The nature of market visioning for technology-based radical innovation, *Journal of Product Innovation Management*, **18**(4), 231–246.

Olsen, Walker and Ruekert (1995) Organizing for effective new product development: the moderating influence of product innovativeness, *Journal of Marketing*, **59**, 48–62.

Ottum, B. D. and Moore, W. L. (1997) Information processing and new product success, *Journal of Product Innovation Management*, **14**, 258–273.

Page, A. L. (1993) Assessing new product development practices and performance: establishing crucial norms, *Journal of Product Innovation Management*, **10**, September, 273–290.

Pinto, M. B. and Pinto, J. K. (1990) Project team communication and cross-functional co-operation in new product development, *Journal of Product Innovation Management*, **7**(3), September, 200–212.

Ragatz, G. L., Handfield, R. B. and Scannell, T. V. (1997) Success factors for integrating suppliers into new product development, *Journal of Product Innovation Management*, **14**(3), 190–202.

Riek, R. F. (2001) Capturing hard-won NPD lessons in checklists, *Journal of Product Innovation Management*, **18**(5), 324–342.

Rothwell, R. (1994) Towards the fifth generation innovation process, *International Marketing Review*, **11**(1), 7–31.

Saren, M. S. (1994) Reframing the process of new product development: from staged models to blocks, *Journal of Marketing Management*, **10**(7), 633–644.

Shocker, A. D. and Hall, W. A. (1986) Pre-market models: a critical evaluation, *Journal of Product Innovation Management*, **3**(2), 86–107.

Tzokas, N. (2000) Critical information and the quest for customer relevant NPD processes, Unpublished report for the EU.

Von Hippel, E. (1978) Successful industrial products from customer ideas – presentation of a new customer-active paradigm with evidence and implications, *Journal of Marketing*, January, 39–49.

Wind, J. and Mahajan, V. (1987) Marketing hype: a new perspective for new product research and introduction, *Journal of Product Innovation Management*, **4**, 43–49.

Workman, J. P. Jr (1993) Marketing's limited role in NPD in one computer systems firm, *Journal of Marketing Research*, **30**, 405–421.

Further reading

Baker, M. J. and Hart, S. (1999) *Product Strategy and Management*, Prentice-Hall, Hemel Hempstead.

Cooper, R. G. (1993) *Winning at New Products; Accelerating the Process from Idea to Launch*, Addison-Wesley, Reading, MA.

Hart, S. (1996) *New Product Development: A Reader*, Dryden Press, London.

Rosenau, M. (1997) *The PDMA Handbook of New Product Development*, PDMA.

CHAPTER 13

Pricing

ADAMANTIOS DIAMANTOPOULOS

For what is a man if he is not a thief who openly charges as much as he can for the goods he sells?

Mahatma Gandhi

Introduction

Pricing is an issue about which academics and practitioners have been at each others' throats for a very long time. While nobody knows exactly when the 'war' was started – or by whom for that matter – Dean's (1947, p. 4) description of company pricing policies as 'the last stronghold of medievalism in modern management' was probably one of the earliest attacks in the literature about the way companies think about and go about making pricing decisions. Over the next 50 years or so, several academics followed in Dean's footsteps by criticizing practitioner approaches to pricing as lacking in rationality and professionalism, failing to understand the proper role of costs, and bypassing profit opportunities as a result of applying routinized pricing formulae (e.g. Backman, 1953; Staudt and Taylor, 1965; Nimer, 1971; Marshall, 1979; Nagle, 1987; Keil *et al.*, 1999). The following quote encapsulates the essence of the criticism: 'many managers do not understand how to price, and are insecure about the adequacy of their current pricing

methods. As a result, they rely on over-simplistic rules of thumb and place an exaggerated emphasis on costs' (Morris and Morris, 1990, pp. xvii–xviii).

For their part, practitioners have responded by largely *ignoring* what academia has to say about pricing. While an enormous literature on pricing has developed over the past half century (for relevant reviews, see Diamanto-poulos, 1991, 1995; Diamantopoulos and Math-ews, 1995), there have been no radical changes in the actual pricing practices of firms; indeed, 'the pricing literature has produced few insights or approaches that would stimulate most businessmen to change their methods of setting prices' (Monroe, 1979, p. 93). For example, a comparison of the adoption of cost-plus pricing methods over a 50-year period concludes that 'in spite of the fact that the intervening years have seen countless references to the fact that cost-plus pricing pays insufficient attention to environmental dynamics, it remains the predominant price-setting methodology' (Seymour, 1989, p. 4). Practitioners have also been quick to criticize academics as being unable to *really* understand what pricing is all about. In the words of one executive, 'company pricing policy is an area where the academic world has long since retreated in despair of ascribing consistency of principles or rationality of practice' (Alfred, 1972, p. 1).

Thus, the field of pricing is characterized by a paradox. On the one hand, 'price theory is one of the most highly developed fields in economics and marketing science' (Simon, 1989, p. ix). On the other, 'there is hardly another business subject area that has had so little reverberation in practice as has price theory' (Diller, 1991, p. 17). Several reasons seem to underlie this paradox.

First, a lot of academic work on pricing has been focusing on pricing *models* of various sorts (for relevant reviews, see Monroe and Della Bitta, 1978; Monroe and Mazudmar, 1988; Nagle, 1984; Rao, 1984, 1993). While these models are characterized by a high degree of rigour and enable the derivation of 'optimal' prices, pricing strategies, discount structures, etc., they 'do not provide *operational* rules for management to follow' (Monroe and Della Bitta, 1978, p. 426, emphasis added). Moreover, such models are typically very 'heavy' mathematically and thus not particularly appetizing for most business executives. Last – but certainly not least – a lot of price modelling has been concerned with 'mathematical elegance, often at the expense of realism' (Diamantopoulos and Mathews, 1995, p. 18) and has ignored the fact that 'pricing in reality follows a much more complex pattern which does not lend itself so readily to mathematical generalization and diagrammatical simplification' (Liebermann, 1969, p. 20). Taken together, these shortcomings go a long way towards explaining 'the minimal contributions of models in the pricing area' (Jeuland and Dolan, 1982, p. 1). This is disappointing, not least because 'if there is any element in the marketing mix that would seem amenable to rational decision making, it is pricing' (Urbany, 2000, p. 3).

Second, the priorities of managers and the research interests of academics in the pricing field have not always (or even mostly) coincided. As Bonoma *et al.* (1988, p. 359) observe: 'it is not that academics cannot solve managerial pricing problems or that they have no interest in solving them. Rather, it seems that academic researchers have not known, or do not focus on, the key pricing concerns of managers in order to conduct rigorous pricing research.' To the extent that the issues deemed important by managers have not been adequately addressed by researchers, it is not surprising that 'pricing theory and pricing research have won little recognition in practice' (Simon, 1982, p. 23). On the positive side, the gap may be closing, as indicated by the increasingly managerial orientation of several pricing texts published in the past few years (e.g. Montgomery, 1988; Seymour, 1989; Morris and Morris, 1990; Monroe, 1990; Nagle and Holden, 1995; Dolan and Simon, 1996).

Third, pricing has always been a 'difficult' area to study empirically, not least because of confidentiality reasons. As Bain (1949, p. 149) observed half a century ago, 'the reluctance of businessmen to confide to economists their methods of price calculation and the character of their associations with rival firms ... has been a serious barrier to close investigation of price policy as seen by the price maker'. In this context, the participation rates of firms in empirical pricing surveys have often been disappointing (Diamantopoulos, 1991), lending credibility to the view that 'it has not been the tradition of management to be "friendly" to the needs of academic researchers in the area of pricing' (Monroe and Mazudmar, 1988, p. 387). While the adoption of process-oriented methodologies which rely on close co-operation with managers (e.g. Howard and Morgenroth, 1968; Capon *et al.*, 1975; Farley *et al.*, 1980; Bonoma *et al.*, 1988; Woodside, 1992; Diamantopoulos and Mathews, 1995) may overcome the shortcomings of survey-based approaches, gaining *initial* access to firms is likely to remain a key obstacle in the empirical study of pricing practices.

Fourth, in the past, many of the recommendations arising from academic research on pricing have been difficult to *implement* by firms because of information processing capability limitations. It is all very nice to suggest that comprehensive price analyses should be undertaken involving estimation of price response functions, assessment of competitive reactions, and calculations of marginal costs (to name but a few) before prices are set. It is quite another thing to actually *do* this effectively if you do not have access to the relevant information and/or lack the capability to analyse whatever information you might be able to get hold of. In fact, there is evidence suggesting that firms *knowingly* operate suboptimal pricing systems because they are convenient and inexpensive (Seymour, 1989) or because they are consistent with previous practice and thus easier to defend (Krishna *et al.*, 2000). However, recent developments in information technology in terms of better and cheaper applications software, decision support systems and web-based platforms should enhance the capability of firms to engage in more sophisticated analyses of pricing parameters. Even such basic applications as spreadsheets can make the life of a price decision maker *much* easier (see, for example, Laric, 1989). The point is that pricing approaches/systems, formerly seen as being 'esoteric', 'slow' or 'expensive' (or all three), are increasingly becoming much more manageable and within the reach of most firms.

Against this background, the rest of this chapter focuses on some key issues relating to the pricing decisions that have direct implications for practitioners. Specifically, insights gained from the theoretical and empirical pricing literature are used to develop a better *understanding* of the price variable, focusing in particular on the role of the *customer* (i.e. the 'demand' side). The intention is *not* to provide an 'off the shelf' recipe for better pricing because 'no known body of doctrine or proven procedures would lead an executive to the best price for his offering' (Oxenfeldt, 1975, p. viii). Rather, the aim of this chapter is to help the reader develop his/her *own* perspective about customer-oriented pricing and, hopefully, apply the insights gained to the specific pricing situation he/she may be facing. Accordingly, no attempt is made to focus the discussion on a particular industry, type of product or set of competitive conditions.

In the next section, the critical importance of price as a decision variable is highlighted and the need to manage it effectively emphasized. This is followed by an examination of the linkages between price, volume, cost and profit, distinguishing between accounting relationships and cause–effect relationships. Finally, specific attention is drawn to the most important 'pillar' of price: customer demand. Due to space restrictions, the other two pillars of price – competition and costs – are only considered to the extent necessary to put demand considerations in context. The reader is urged to follow up on the issues raised here (and many more) by consulting the pricing texts included in the reference list at the end of the chapter. The works of Monroe (1990), Nagle and Holden (1995), and Dolan and Simon (1996) are highly recommended in this respect.

Is price *really* that important?

The most common – and obvious – rationale given for the importance of price is that price is the only element in the marketing mix that generates revenue; all other elements are associated with costs. Such costs are necessarily incurred in *creating* value via product development, promotion and distribution. In contrast, pricing can be seen as a value *extraction* activity (Dolan and Simon, 1996), since it is through pricing that the 'level of reward is set for all the planning, financing designing, productive efficiency, skill, and quality that have gone into the product' (Marshall, 1979, p. 1). However, the unique role of price as a revenue-generating marketing mix element is by no means the *only* characteristic that makes price so important. Consider the following:

- Price has a very strong impact on sales volume and market share; empirical studies (reviewed in Tellis, 1988; and Sethuraman and Tellis, 1991) have shown that, for most products, price elasticity is *substantially* higher than advertising elasticity – up to 20 times higher!

- Not only does price have a strong influence on demand, but such influence is manifested much *faster* than for other marketing mix instruments (e.g. advertising), for which considerable time lags may be involved (e.g. Ehrenberg and England, 1990).

- Compared to the rest of the marketing mix elements, price can be modified relatively *quickly*; the downside is, of course, that this applies equally to the competition as well! Making/responding to price changes can take place within a short time period, whereas initiation of or reactions to changes in product formulation, advertising, etc. can take much longer due to the nature of the preparations involved (e.g. Simon, 1992).

- Competitive reactions to price variations both in terms of *speed* and in terms of *intensity* tend to be much more severe than competitive reactions to changes in other marketing mix variables; for example, it has been estimated that reaction elasticities to price variations are almost twice as high as reaction elasticities to advertising changes (e.g. Lambin, 1976).

- Irrespective of situation, the manipulation of price is *not* associated with an initially negative cash flow (Simon, 1989); in contrast, the manipulation of other marketing mix elements (e.g. promotion, personal selling) typically results in expenses that are only recovered at a later time (as in the case of a new product, where initial investments have to be set against future income streams).

- The 'leverage' effect of price on profit (discussed in detail in the next section) is *much* greater than that of other profit drivers; for example, it has been argued that 'improvements in price typically have three to four times the effect on profitability as proportionate increases in volume' (Marn and Rosiello, 1992, p. 84).

- Price often fulfils two functions simultaneously: it reflects the 'sacrifice' that the buyer must make in order to acquire the product/service involved and it also acts as a signal of the quality of the product (Monroe, 1990); no other element of the marketing mix serves such a dual function.

- Pricing has also been identified as a key factor governing new product success or failure (e.g. Cooper, 1979), a crucial criterion affecting supplier choice in business-to-business markets (e.g. Shipley, 1985), and the most likely aspect of a firm's activity to draw government attention and/or be subjected to regulation (e.g. Reekie, 1981).

In the light of the above, it is perhaps not surprising that price has been described as a 'dangerously explosive variable' (Oxenfeldt, 1973, p. 48) which, if not properly managed, 'can cripple a business, no matter how otherwise efficient it may be' (Marshall, 1979, p. 1). Indeed, 'few (companies) have figured out how much money they are giving up by using lunkheaded pricing strategies' (Coy, 2000, p. 160). The first step towards effective price management is *understanding*: understanding how price interacts with volume and costs to produce a profit (or loss), and understanding how the 'demand side' works. It is to these issues that we now turn.

The drivers of profit: price, volume and cost

Figure 13.1 shows the familiar decomposition of profit into revenue and cost elements. The revenue side is a function of the price level and the sales volume (in units) sold at that price, while the cost side is made up the fixed costs (which are incurred regardless of the volume of sales attained) and the variable costs (which are dependent upon the volume produced and sold). Thus, there are four distinct forces that 'drive' profit: price, volume, variable unit cost and fixed cost (note that sales volume is the only profit driver which operates both on the revenue *and* the cost side; this has important implications, as will become clear shortly).

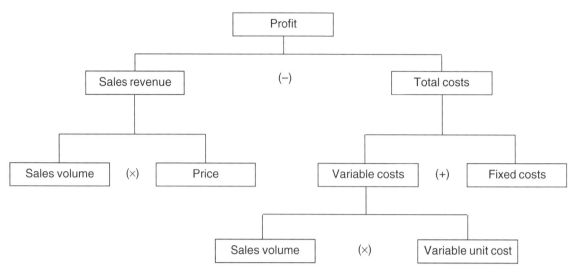

Figure 13.1   The determinants of profit

Given the four drivers of profit, an important question concerns their *relative* importance. In other words, assuming that all other factors remain constant, what is the effect on profit of 'improving' each driver by a certain amount? Clearly, the notion of 'improvement' is different for the revenue and cost sides, i.e. an improvement in price and sales volume refers to an *increase* from existing levels, while an improvement in variable and/or fixed cost refers to a *reduction* from current levels.

Table 13.1 shows the differential impact on profit of a 10 per cent improvement in each

profit driver; it is clear that by far the greatest 'leverage' effect on profit comes from improving price. This is not an accident reflecting either the specific improvement considered (i.e. 10 per cent) or the particular starting values in Table 13.1; experimentation with different figures will not fail to demonstrate that 'price drives profit like no other factor' (Dolan and Simon, 1996, p. 24).

At this stage, the reader may be getting a bit uncomfortable – and rightly so – with the simplifying assumption that 'all other factors remain constant' when the profit impact of a

Table 13.1 Effects on profit of a 10 per cent improvement					
			Profit (£)		Profit improvement (%)
	Before	After	Before	After	
Price (£)	100	110	30 000	40 000	33.3
Sales Volume	1000	1100	30 000	35 000	16.7
Variable Unit Cost (£)	50	45	30 000	35 000	16.7
Fixed Cost (£)	20 000	18 000	30 000	32 000	6.7

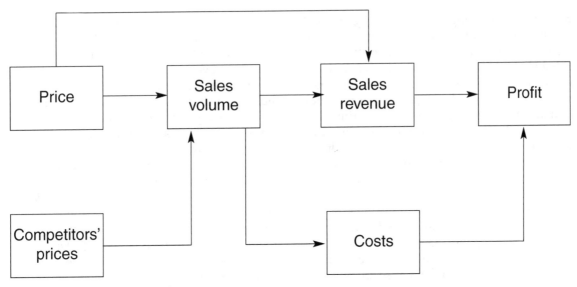

Figure 13.2   The road to profit

particular profit driver is considered.[1] After all, if one 'improves' price by raising it by 10 per cent, surely there will be some reduction in sales volume? And if volume is reduced, there could also be a 'knock-on' effect on variable cost – say, if any scale economies can no longer be realized. Such concerns are well justified and serve to highlight the *definitional* nature of the relationships in Figure 13.1. The decomposition of profit into the four profit drivers highlights what are essentially *accounting* links rather than *causal* relationships; the latter are shown in Figure 13.2, which explicitly considers the

indirect effects of prices on costs (via sales volume) and also introduces competitive considerations as an additional – albeit indirect – influence on profit.

So does Figure 13.2 render Figure 13.1 obsolete? Not at all. The definitional relationships in Figure 13.1 can be used to build scenarios of the following sort: if we were to increase price by X per cent, what would be the acceptable decrease in sales volume to return the *same* profit? Or, if we were to decrease price by Y per cent, what would be the necessary increase in sales volume to maintain the current profit? Or, if we managed to reduce our variable unit costs by Z per cent, what sort of price reduction could we afford without hurting our profitability? Having computed the answers to these questions by reference to Figure 13.1, one can then use Figure 13.2 as a framework for evaluating whether the expected effects are likely to materialize in reality. For example, if a 10 per cent price decrease requires a 25 per cent increase in sales volume to result in the same overall profit level (this would be the case in the example in Table 13.1, where variable costs are 50 per cent of the original price), to what extent is this rise in sales volume

---

[1] Note, however, that in many instances the assumption of all other factors remaining constant is not as far-fetched as it might first seem. For example, empirical research has revealed that companies often face a situation in which manipulation of price *within certain limits* is not accompanied by volume fluctuations (see, for example, Skinner, 1970; Hankinson, 1985; Wied-Nebbeling, 1975, 1985; Diamantopoulos and Mathews, 1993, 1995). Such situations arise because of buyer switching costs (Buckner, 1967), loyalty considerations (Albach, 1979) and/or 'lazy' competitors (Wied-Nebbeling, 1975). Under such conditions there is a clear opportunity to increase profitability by means of (moderate) price increases *without* sacrificing volume; given the leveraging effect of price on profit (see Table 13.1), the resulting gains can be very substantial indeed.

realistic? Will existing customers really buy that much more of our product and/or will sufficient numbers of new customers be attracted to bring about the needed extra volume? And will our competitors sit back and do nothing when we lower our prices by 10 per cent or will they retaliate by matching or even exceeding our price cut? And what about the possibility that the whole thing may backfire if customers *perceive* that the price reduction also reflects a quality reduction and end up buying *less* rather than more? Questions of this nature go a long way towards making the implications of any pricing moves transparent and identifying potential sticky points. Lamentably, such questions are seldom asked in practice; as Urbany (2000, p. 4) points out, 'because of potential ambiguity in estimating demand and profit at alternative prices and predicting competitive reactions, pricing practice in many firms may systematically ignore these two important fundamentals'.

As can be seen in Figure 13.2, sales volume plays a crucial role in the system of relationships between price, cost and profit. As a *dependent* variable, sales volume (q) reflects customer demand and is a function of both the firm's own price (p) than those of competitors (p_j); the specific nature of the relationship between volume and price is captured by the price response function, $q = f(p, p_j)$.[2] As an *independent* variable, sales volume (q) is a determinant of the firm's costs (c), a relationship which is captured by the cost function, $c = g(q)$. Thus, ultimately, cost is a function of price and *not vice versa*[3] or, what amounts to the same thing, any pricing system that uses costs as the

basis of price determination is illogical and bound to result in sub-optimal decisions;[4] as Backman (1953, p. 148) aptly put it a long time ago, 'the graveyard of business is filled with the skeletons of companies that attempted to price their products solely on the basis of costs'.

The above should not be interpreted as implying that costs have no place in pricing decisions. Costs *are* important, but only as *constraints* on the viability or relative attractiveness of different pricing alternatives;[5] they are not important, or even relevant, as *guides* to setting prices, not least because 'the customer does not care about the firm's costs ... only about the *value* he/she is getting' (Diamantopoulos, 1995, p. 187, emphasis in the original). In fact, the most fundamental lesson in pricing is that '*price is a statement of value not a statement of cost*' (Morris and Morris, 1990, p. 2, emphasis in the original); the next section shows why this is the case.

Price from the customer's perspective

The very definition of price as 'the amount of money we must sacrifice to acquire something we desire' (Monroe, 1990, p. 5) provides a clear clue as to the way in which customer considerations impact on pricing. Several points are of importance here.

First, the notion of price as a 'sacrifice' implies that the buyer must give something up. In this context, 'what must be given up

---

[2] It is assumed here that competitive actions directly impact upon the firm's own demand, i.e. there is interdependence among suppliers (oligopolistic market structure). In the case of a single supplier (monopoly) or many suppliers with differentiated products (monopolistic competition), the price response function reduces to $q = f(p)$.

[3] Since $q = f(p, p_j)$ and $c = g(q)$, it follows that $c = h(p, p_j)$; this demonstrates the irrationality of cost-based approaches, according to which 'price is considered a function of cost, whereas the true causal relationship is just the reverse' (Simon, 1989, p. 48).

[4] There are some very special (read: extremely rare) circumstances under which a cost-based approach can lead to optimal (i.e. profit maximizing) prices; for more details, see Simon (1989 or 1992).

[5] For example, variable costs or marginal costs act as short-term price floors (assuming no capacity constraints), while total costs act as long-term price floors; for comprehensive analyses, see Riebel (1972) and Reichmann (1973).

includes not only the monetary price, but also the time and effort that the buyer must invest' (Morris and Morris, 1990, p. 3). Thus, the *purchase* price alone may *not* fully capture the buyer's total sacrifice; things like start-up costs (e.g. transportation and installation) and post-purchase costs (e.g. maintenance and risk of failure) may also be important and should be borne in mind by the price decision maker. Failure to consider the buyer's *life cycle* costs is a common pricing mistake and – particularly in industrial markets – can result in lost opportunities for gaining/keeping customers (see, for example, Forbis and Mehta, 1978; Shapiro and Jackson, 1978; Christopher, 1982).

Second, in incurring a 'sacrifice', the buyer must be *able* to do so. The *ability to pay* is a function of the particular customer's economic circumstances (e.g. disposable income) and can be viewed as a constraining factor on the type and amount of purchases a particular customer can make over a particular period; thus, the ability to pay reflects the 'budget constraint' often mentioned in conventional micro-economic theory. In practice, obstacles relating to the ability to pay may be overcome by changing the time of payment (e.g. providing a period of interest-free credit), the method of payment (e.g. offering an instalment plan) or the form of payment (e.g. providing a trade-in facility).

Third, not only must a potential buyer be able to pay the price, he/she must also be *willing* to do so. *Willingness to pay* is a complex function of a particular buyer's perceived evaluation of the product/service involved, the actual price, competitive offerings, and his/her *reference* price. The latter is 'an internal price to which consumers compare observed prices' (Winer, 1988, p. 35) and represents the amount that the customer regards as fair/appropriate/acceptable for the particular purchase. Reference prices are influenced by such factors as the last price paid, an 'average' price based on historical experience of purchases, the prices of competing products, and expectations about future prices (Kalynaram and Winer, 1995).

Note that it is not necessarily the *actual* prices of previous purchases and/or competing offerings that combine to form a reference price, but prices as *recalled/perceived* by the buyer. Indeed, the price decision maker should appreciate that 'buyers do not have perfect information regarding available products and their prices. Even if such information were available, people are not perfect information processors . . . As a result, buyers are not always very price aware' (Morris and Morris, 1990, p. 60). Obstacles related to the willingness to pay are much more difficult to identify and overcome than obstacles relating to the ability to pay. Not only must the potential buyer be convinced that he/she can *afford* to buy the product, but also that he/she will be making the *right choice*. Thus, non-price instruments (such as advertising and promotion) must be employed to convince the buyer that the product offers superior *value* (see below) and/or to influence the reference price used by the buyer (e.g. as when a 'regular' price is advertised alongside the 'special deal' price at which the product is actually offered).

Fourth, the extent to which a buyer will *decide* to incur the sacrifice implied by the price depends on how he/she will *judge* what he/she will get *in return*. This is the essence of the notion of *value*: a trade-off between the bundle of benefits to be received (as reflected in the product) and what has to be given up (as reflected in the price). In seeking particular benefits, the buyer focuses on a desired set of attributes (which typically differ in their relative importance) and *subjectively* evaluates different products on these attributes (Monroe and Krishnan, 1985). The outcome of this evaluation is then compared to the price of the product and the 'best value' is the one that offers the most benefit (in terms of the customer's desired set of attributes) for the least price. Put simply, 'the customers' goal is to obtain the most value for their money . . . Their concern is to get their money's worth' (Nagle, 1987, p. 2).

Fifth, and related to the previous point, to provide value from a *buyer's perspective*, it is necessary that 'the benefits delivered by the products or services match the benefits wanted by the customers or users ... a product or service is purchased because of its ability to perform a certain function, solve a particular problem, or provide specific pleasures. It is what the product or service does and how well it does it that provides value' (Monroe, 1990, pp. 91–92). This is, of course, a central tenet of marketing; however, its price-specific implications – as reflected in buyer deliberations regarding value – are often forgotten (if ever realized in the first place).

Sixth, given that 'if the customer can select between different competitive products, he will most likely prefer the one which offers the highest net value' (Simon, 1989, p. 1), the aim of the price decision maker *must* be to offer *superior value* (Gale, 1994; Holbrook, 1996). Creating and sustaining superior value lies at the heart of developing (and maintaining) competitive advantage and there only two ways to it: 'either offering customers lower prices than competitors for equivalent benefits or providing unique product benefits that more than compensate customers for paying a higher price' (Morris and Morris, 1990, p. 3). In following the first route, the control of *costs* becomes crucial, as offering a lower price than competitors *while maintaining adequate profit levels* requires 'aggressive construction of efficient-scale facilities, vigorous pursuit of cost reductions from experience, tight cost and overhead control, avoidance of marginal customer accounts, and cost minimization in areas like R&D, service, sales force, advertising, and so on' (Porter, 1980, p. 35). In following the second route, the firm strives for *uniqueness* in some respect, which usually involves 'a trade-off with cost position if the activities required in creating it are inherently costly, such as extensive research, product design, high quality materials, or intensive customer support' (Porter, 1980, p. 38). Note that costs are still important, as any 'premium prices will be nullified by a markedly inferior cost position' (Porter, 1985, p. 14).

Finally, it is important to realize that buyers often have *absolute limits* on what they are prepared to pay for a particular product. The upper limit (known as the *reservation price*) reflects the *maximum* price that a customer is willing to pay (Thaler, 1985) and represents the *marginal* value of the product to the buyer over other consumption alternatives. If the actual price exceeds the reservation price, then no purchase will take place. The lower limit reflects a *minimum* price below which 'quality is regarded as unacceptable' (Simon, 1989, p. 185); if the actual price falls below that limit then – in the absence of any other information – the customer will also not make a purchase. Lower limits are particularly important when price is used – at least partly – as an indicator of quality (see also next section). For a review of the conditions that are likely to encourage such a function of price and the relevant empirical evidence, see Rao and Monroe (1989) and Zeithaml (1988).

From the above, it can be seen that understanding the role of customer considerations in pricing is much more complex than might be initially thought. Of particular importance, in this context, is the fact that customers are likely to be very *heterogeneous* in terms of their knowledge, perceptions of, and reactions to price (Rao, 1993). Differences in the nature, number and relative importance attached to different product attributes, differences in the nature, level and stability of reference prices used, and differences in the magnitude of reservation prices all combine to produce different value perceptions of a particular offer by different buyers (and hence different likelihoods to buy). Thus, one challenge for price management is to capitalize on such differences by *customizing* prices; in this context, 'different customers have different levels of willingness and ability to pay. A common failing in pricing practice is not to adapt prices to these realities, thereby foregoing significant profit opportunities' (Dolan and Simon, 1996, p. 116). Price customization can take place according to customer characteristics, geographic location, transaction size, timing of the purchase and distribution channel (to name but a few). (Good discussions of price customization can be found in Simon, 1992; Nagle and Holden, 1995; and Dolan and Simon, 1996.) However, irrespective of whether price customization or a 'one price policy' is to be pursued by the firm (e.g. see Hoch *et al.*, 1994), the decision maker requires knowledge regarding how customers are likely to respond to prices of different magnitudes; this is the issue of *price sensitivity* and is discussed in the next section.

Understanding price sensitivity

The conventional analysis of price sensitivity stems from economic theory and its analysis of *price elasticity* (ε). This shows the percentage change in quantity demanded (i.e. sales volume) as a result of a percentage change in price:

$$\varepsilon = \text{percentage change in sales volume} \div \text{percentage change in price.}$$

Thus, a price elasticity of –2.0 implies that a 10 per cent *increase* in price would result in a volume *decrease* of 20 per cent (–2.0 × 10 per cent). If $\varepsilon = 0$, then demand is said to be *perfectly inelastic*, as sales volume is completely unresponsive to price changes. If $\varepsilon = -\infty$, demand is said to be *perfectly elastic*, as sales volume goes up from zero to infinity as a result of a price change (a very rare case). If $\varepsilon = -1$, then demand is said to have *unitary elasticity*, i.e. a given percentage change in price is accompanied by exactly the same percentage change in sales volume. If $-1 < \varepsilon < 0$, then demand is said to be *inelastic*, as the proportionate change in sales volume is smaller than the change in price. Finally, if $-\infty < \varepsilon < -1$, then demand is said to be *elastic*, as the proportionate change in sales volume is greater than the change in price. Table 13.2 shows the implications of different elasticity values in terms of their effects on sales revenue.

While the concept of price elasticity is very useful for thinking about the likely effects of price changes on sales volume, a great deal of caution is necessary when applying it. For example, in the light of Table 13.2, one may be tempted to rush into recommendations of the sort: 'if a price elasticity of less than 1 is found, a price increase can be immediately recommended, since this means that the percentage of decrease in sales volume is smaller than the percentage of increase in price' (Dolan and Simon, 1996, p. 30). However, this assumes that (a) the firm is willing to sacrifice *some* sales volume, and (b) the revenue gains are going to be translated into *profit* gains. Neither of these assumptions may be warranted because 'the goal may be to maintain a presence in the market, take customers from competitors, or use the product to help sell other products in the line, even at a revenue loss ... [or] costs

Table 13.2 Impact of price elasticity on sales revenue		
Demand is	*Price increase*	*Price decrease*
Perfectly inelastic	Revenue increases	Revenue decreases
Perfectly elastic	Revenue decreases	Revenue increases
Unitary elasticity	Revenue does not change	Revenue does not change
Inelastic	Revenue increases	Revenue decreases
Elastic	Revenue decreases	Revenue increases

would rise reflecting less efficient use of resources or less economical raw material purchases' (Morris and Morris, 1990, pp. 45 and 101).

In general, the following caveats apply when using the formula for price elasticity:

- The formula is based on a *ceteris paribus* (i.e. 'all other things being equal') assumption, which implies that the *only* variable that affects changes in sales volume is the change in price; prices of competitors, incomes, preferences, etc. are assumed to be constant. This assumption is obviously questionable, particularly in the case of oligopolistic markets, where interdependence among suppliers is likely to lead to reactions when prices are changed (e.g. price wars in the case of price reductions).
- A distinction needs to be made between *market* (or primary) price elasticity (i.e. that relating to the market demand) and *brand* price elasticity (i.e. that relating to the particular brand under consideration). For example, while the demand for an overall product category may be inelastic, demand for particular brands *within* this category may be elastic. Moreover, price elasticity can vary substantially across different product brands within a particular class. For example, 'the sales of small market share brands tend to be more price sensitive than those of brands with larger market shares' (Nagle, 1987, p. 79), while 'price cuts by higher quality tiers are more powerful in pulling customers up from lower tiers, than lower tier price cuts are in pulling customers down from upper tiers; i.e., customers "trade up" more readily than they "trade down"' (Dolan and Simon, 1996, p. 87). What these considerations also imply is that, depending on how broadly one *defines* the market, different elasticity estimates may result.
- From the price elasticity formula, it is not immediately apparent that the value of ε is *not* the same at all prices; for example, an elasticity estimated around a price of, say, £2.00 will not be the same as an elasticity

estimated around a price of, say, £10. A constant elasticity at all prices within a given range is very much the exception rather than the rule. Indeed, a typical mistake that decision makers make is to assume that the price elasticity of demand is equal to the slope of the demand curve (i.e. the price response function); this is *not* the case even when a linear demand function (i.e. of the form $q = a - b \times p$, where a, b > 0) is involved. For more details, as well as a description of the properties of the *isoelastic* (i.e. constant elasticity) price response function, see Simon (1992).

- While also not obvious from the elasticity formula, 'because customers differ in the amount of value they attach to a product or service and in their ability to pay for an item, their elasticities also differ. One customer may respond very little to fairly large changes in price while another reacts strongly to a relatively minor price change for the same product' (Morris and Morris, 1990, p. 46). Indeed, differences in price elasticity are a major basis for segmenting a market with a view of customizing prices (see, for example, Simon, 1989).
- Since individuals tend to be more sensitive to the prospect of a loss than to the prospect of a gain (Kahneman and Tversky, 1979), computations of price elasticity based on price increases of a certain magnitude may produce different results than those based on price decreases of the *same* magnitude.
- Price elasticity does not remain constant over time, since 'the percentage change in a product's sales is usually not the same in the long run as in the short run' (Nagle, 1987, p. 77). Factors such as inventory building, substitute awareness, 'lock-in' contracts, new product introductions and price expectations all combine to introduce differences in the magnitudes of short- versus long-term price elasticities. For a discussion of the dynamics of price elasticity for different types of products, see Simon (1979), Shoemaker (1986), Kucher (1987), Lillien and Yoon (1988), and Parker (1992).

- The conventional analysis of elasticity and the associated revenue implications shown in Table 13.2 are based on the assumption of an *inverse* price–volume relationship (i.e. price and volume move in opposite directions); however, 'if buyers infer quality to the product or service on the basis of price and thereby perceive a higher priced item as more attractive, a positive price–quantity relationship ensues' (Monroe, 1990, pp. 37–38).

- The price elasticity formula provides no clue as to *why* demand may be elastic or inelastic (i.e. the conditions under which buyers are likely to be more or less price sensitive). This is perhaps the greatest shortcoming of the economic analysis of price sensitivity, since it fails to provide the price decision maker with a framework within which the various factors that may influence the degree of price sensitivity can be considered. Indeed, it has been noted that even leading consumer goods companies are confused about the correct interpretation (and use) of the price elasticity concept (Davey *et al.*, 1998).

Bearing the above in mind, what are the key factors that contribute to customers' price sensitivity (or lack of)? Several – often inter-related – factors have been identified in the literature, as summarized below. For more details and illustrative examples, see Morris and Morris (1990), Simon (1992), and Nagle and Holden (1995).

- *Availability of acceptable substitutes*. This is probably the most obvious factor that affects price sensitivity and has long been pointed out as such by economic theory. The fewer the substitutes from which a customer can choose, the lower the price sensitivity for any particular alternative. Conversely, even if market (i.e. primary) demand is inelastic, brand elasticity may still be high because of the availability of alternative products and/or sources of supply.

- *Awareness of available substitutes*. While the existence of many substitutes is a necessary condition for high price sensitivity, it is not a sufficient condition. Customers must be *aware* that such substitutes *do* in fact exist and it cannot be taken for granted that customers will be well informed about substitute availability (or even that they will always *try* to become informed). As Nagle (1987, p. 60) points out: 'the existence of less expensive alternatives of which buyers are unaware cannot affect their purchase behavior'. However, the advent of the Internet has meant that prospective buyers now have much reduced search costs (Bakos, 1997) and are thus much better informed about the range of products available (Lynch and Ariely, 2000).

- *Transparency of prices*. This is a factor contributing to substitute awareness. If price features frequently in advertisements, brochures, etc. of the product in question, then buyers are likely to be more price aware. Moreover, if price comparisons are easy to undertake as a result of similar pricing conventions by different suppliers (e.g. petrol prices), the buyers will be able to determine the true price differences involved. Both these factors are likely to impact positively on the degree of price sensitivity. Again, the availability of online price comparison sites (e.g. ShopSmart, Pricerunner, Kelkoo, DealTime, easyValue, CheckaPrice) has resulted in both greater price transparency and lesser burden on consumers in terms of maintaining their price awareness.

- *Purchase frequency*. This is a factor affecting the amount of information possessed by buyers. For products that are frequently purchased, buyers are more likely to develop a good appreciation of the various product alternatives and range of prices available, and thus become more price sensitive than for infrequent purchases. The ease with which online shopping lists can be stored for future reference suggests that, particularly for grocery shopping (e.g. via sites such as Asda.co.uk and Tesco.com), price awareness and sensitivity are likely to increase.

• *Product uniqueness.* This is an extremely important factor affecting price sensitivity and one that is largely under the firm's control. If the product contains important features that are highly valued by buyers and differentiate the offering from those of competitors, price sensitivity is likely to be low. Not only may customers be willing to pay a price premium to obtain the unique attributes embedded in the product, but they may also view competitive products as less than acceptable substitutes. Note that 'unique attributes' do not refer to physical characteristics only; intangible elements (e.g. a solid reputation for excellent service) may be just as important in creating a 'unique value effect' (Nagle and Holden, 1995) as tangible elements.

• *Ease of product comparison.* This is a factor that is particularly important for industrial purchases and refers to the extent to which the buyer finds it easy to undertake comparisons between alternative products and/or suppliers. When products are difficult to evaluate before the purchase and the cost of failure is high (e.g. mainframe computers), buyers may only consider offers from 'known' or 'approved' suppliers and thus be willing to pay a premium for this 'peace of mind'. In a consumer goods setting (e.g. with food items), while comparison of alternative offers is normally less risky than in industrial contexts, it has to be borne in mind that 'a buyer can compare a new brand with one he regularly buys only if he is willing to risk the cost of an unknown purchase only once' (Nagle, 1987, p. 61). Interactive decision aids such as online product comparison matrices and recommendation agents (Alba *et al.*, 1997; Häubl and Trifts, 2000) can significantly enhance the ease with which product comparisons can be undertaken (e.g. see GoldFishGuide.com), and hence positively impact upon price sensitivity.

• *Importance of purchase.* This refers to both the *absolute* amount of what the price of the item represents and the *relative* importance of the purchase as a proportion of the buyer's

income. As the importance of the purchase increases, so does the degree of price sensitivity. The more, in absolute terms, a buyer spends on a product, the greater the gain from even small reductions in price, and therefore the greater the incentive to shop around (e.g. compare the purchase of a washing machine with that of a new car). Moreover, the greater the significance of the purchase in relation to the buyer's income, the greater the benefit from finding cheaper sources of supply (e.g. wealthy families may spend *more* on food and be *less* price sensitive than lower-income families, since the latter's overall spending on food represents a greater proportion of their income).

• *Shared cost.* This refers to the proportion of the total price *actually* paid by the buyer. In many cases, the buyer does not incur the entire cost associated with a purchase, as part (or even all) of the cost is paid by someone else; obvious examples here are insurance payments, tax deductions (credits) and compensation for business travel. The smaller the proportion of the total price that the buyer must pay himself/herself, the lower the price sensitivity for the purchase under consideration.

• *Switching costs.* This relates to costs that a buyer must incur beyond the purchase price when switching from one product/brand/supplier to another. Sometimes, a product (e.g. a software program) is used with assets bought previously (e.g. a mainframe computer) and which can only be replaced in the long run. In other instances, there are 'sunk' investments in developing relationships with suppliers, learning to use a particular product, and establishing routines to handle transactions efficiently. Under such conditions, the buyer becomes 'locked in' to a particular product and/or supplier, and price sensitivity tends to be low due to the high switching costs involved (at least in the short run). Note that, as a result of the impact of the Internet on substitute awareness, price transparency and ease of product comparisons noted above, a reduction in buyers' switching costs is also likely to be forthcoming (Keeney, 1999).

- *Proportion of product price on total cost.* This factor is particularly important in industrial markets where products are purchased as a direct result of demand for other (final) products. This *derived demand* situation implies that 'the more price sensitive the demand for a company's own product, the more price sensitive that company will be when purchasing supplies' (Nagle, 1987, p. 63). Further, the extent of price sensitivity will depend on the proportion of the *final* product's cost that is accounted for by the price of the raw material or part involved; the greater this proportion, the greater the price sensitivity. In a consumer setting, a similar effect can be observed; for example, when purchasing a new car, the buyer is likely to be less sensitive to the price of, say, a CD player as an add-on extra than would be the case if a separate purchase (i.e. divorced from the car purchase) was contemplated.

- *Inventory considerations.* This influence on price sensitivity applies primarily in the short term and its impact tends to be transitory. If buyers can stock current purchases for future use (e.g. if the product is not perishable) *and* if they expect that future prices are likely to be higher than current prices, then short-term price sensitivity will be higher. Conversely, buyers may run down their inventories if they feel that current prices are likely to be reduced in the future. In assessing the likely impact of inventories on price sensitivity, it is essential to appreciate that it 'depends critically on buyer expectations about future prices ... a price must be judged high or low relative to the prices buyers expect in the future rather than those prices that prevailed in the recent past' (Nagle, 1987, p. 71).

- *Price as indicator of quality.* This refers to the extent to which price acts not only as a measure of sacrifice for acquiring the product, but also as a *signal* about the product's quality. This function of price is typically associated with image products, prestige/exclusive products, and products for which the 'objective' evaluation of their quality is difficult. The more buyers rely on price as a criterion for evaluating quality, the less price sensitive they are likely to be; in fact, 'customers may actually expect the price to be somewhat steep' (Morris and Morris, 1990, p. 44).

A careful analysis of the above factors impacting on price sensitivity will go a long way towards providing price decision makers with a clear picture of the way current and potential buyers are likely to respond to price and of the existence of any market segments with differential price sensitivities. Ideally, such an analysis ought to be followed by more formal research to develop *quantitative* estimates of customers' reactions to price because, ultimately, 'only if we know, in quantitative terms, how customers respond to our own price and to competitive prices can we make a rational price decision' (Dolan and Simon, 1996, p. 45). Unfortunately, despite the existence of a wide variety of different pricing research methodologies,[6] 'companies do not approach demand elasticity in a systematic, strategic fashion ... Qualitative approaches are relied upon more heavily in demand measurement than are quantitative approaches. Firms typically do not maintain detailed price data bases, nor do most regularly make efforts to estimate demand sensitivity' (Morris and Morris, 1990, p. 53; see also Morris and Joyce, 1988). Moreover, because of tradition, convenience and/or inertia, even 'firms that have enough data and expertise to estimate elasticities accurately may have little success in making direct translations from elasticity to recommended price points' (Urbany, 2000, p. 24). This situation contrasts

[6] These range from pricing experiments and customer surveys to conjoint analysis applications and econometric analyses of historic market data; non-technical overviews of the available methodologies can be found in Gabor (1988), Simon (1989), Seymour (1989), Monroe (1990), Nagle and Holden (1995), and Dolan and Simon (1996). For a recent example of estimating price elasticities, as well as references to the (technical) literature, see Danaher and Brodie (2000).

sharply with companies' practices on the cost side, where highly sophisticated costing systems are very much the rule rather than the exception; however, as already argued, it is not cost that determines price: it is the customer and his/her perception of value. A costing system, however refined and sophisticated, can tell us *nothing* about the customer – a demand measurement system, on the other hand, can tell us *a lot*.

Conclusion

Price is probably the most important but least well managed element of the marketing mix. A key reason for this deficiency appears to be a lack of understanding of how customer considerations impact upon pricing, i.e. how the demand side 'works'. This chapter aimed to show how price features in buyers' purchasing decisions and how price sensitivity develops as a result of different influences. The intention was to highlight the key principles of a customer-oriented approach to pricing and provide the reader with sufficient building blocks to enable the construction of his/her own perspective within the particular pricing situation he/she might be facing. It seems appropriate to conclude the chapter with a simple reminder: 'anything that reduces the buyers' cost of evaluating an alternative ... will increase buyers' sensitivity to low-price offers' (Nagle, 1987, p. 62). So, welcome to the wonderful world of price comparison sites, online auctions, interactive bargain hunting, instant information and 'borderless' shopping – hopefully you can survive (in) it!

References

Alba, J., Lynch, J., Weitz, B., Janiszewski, C., Lutz, R., Sawyer, A. and Wood, S. (1997) Interactive home shopping: consumer, retailer, and manufacturer incentives to participate in electronic marketplaces, *Journal of Marketing*, **61**, July, 38–53.

Albach, H. (1979) Market organization and pricing behaviour in oligopolistic firms in the ethical drugs industry: an essay in the measurement of effective competition, *Kyklos*, **32**(3), 523–540.

Alfred, A. M. (1972) *Pricing Decisions*, Scott, Foresman & Co., Glenview, IL.

Backman, J. (1953) *Price Practices and Price Policies*, Ronald Press, New York.

Bain, J. S. (1949) Price and production policies, in Ellis, H. S. (ed.), *A Survey of Contemporary Economics*, Blackiston, Berkeley, CA.

Bakos, J. Y. (1997) Reducing buyer search costs: implications for electronic marketplaces, *Management Science*, **43**(12), December, 1676–1692.

Bonoma, T. V., Crittenden, V. L. and Dolan, R. J. (1988) Can we have rigor and relevance in pricing research?, in Devinney, T. M. (ed.), *Issues in Pricing – Theory and Research*, Lexington Books, Lexington, pp. 333–360.

Buckner, H. (1967) *How British Industry Buys*, Industrial Market Research, London.

Capon, N., Farley, J. U. and Hulbert, J. (1975) Pricing and forecasting in an oligopoly firm, *Journal of Management Studies*, **12**, 133–156.

Christopher, M. (1982) Value-in-use-pricing, *European Journal of Marketing*, **16**(5), 35–47.

Cooper, R. G. (1979) The dimensions of new product failure, *Journal of Marketing*, **43**, 93–103.

Coy, P. (2000) The power of smart pricing, *Business Week*, 10 April, p. 160.

Danaher, P. J. and Brodie, R. J. (2000) Understanding the characteristics of price elasticities for frequently purchased packaged goods, *Journal of Marketing Management*, **16**(8), 917–936.

Davey, K. K. S., Childs, A. and Carlotti, S. J. Jr (1998) Why your price band is wider than it should be, *McKinsey Quarterly*, **1**, Summer, 116–127.

Dean, J. (1947) Research approach to pricing, in *Planning the Price Structure*, Marketing Series

No. 67, American Management Association, New York.

Diamantopoulos, A. (1991) Pricing: theory and evidence – a literature review, in Baker, M. J. (ed.), *Perspectives on Marketing Management*, Wiley, London, Vol. 1, pp. 63–192.

Diamantopoulos, A. (1995) Pricing, in Baker, M. J. (ed.), *Marketing Theory and Practice*, 3rd edn, Macmillan, London.

Diamantopoulos, A. and Mathews, B. P. (1993) Managerial perceptions of the demand curve: evidence from a multi-product firm, *European Journal of Marketing*, **27**(9), 3–16.

Diamantopoulos, A. and Mathews, B. P. (1995) *Making Pricing Decisions: A Study of Managerial Practice*, Chapman & Hall.

Diller, H. (1991) *Preispolitik*, Kohlhammer, Stuttgart.

Dolan, R. J. and Simon, H. (1996) *Power Pricing: How Managing Price Transforms the Bottom Line*, Free Press, New York.

Ehrenberg, A. S. C. and England, L. R. (1990) Generalizing a price effect, *Journal of Industrial Economics*, **39**, 47–68.

Farley, J. U., Hulbert, J. M. and Weinstein, D. (1980) Price setting and volume planning by two European industrial companies: a study and comparison of decision processes, *Journal of Marketing*, **44**, 46–54.

Forbis, J. L. and Mehta, N. T. (1978) Value-based strategies for industrial products, *Business Horizons*, **21**, October, 25–31.

Gabor, A. (1988) *Pricing: Concepts and Methods for Effective Marketing*, Gower, Aldershot.

Gale, B. T. (1994) *Managing Customer Value: Creating Quality and Service That Customers Can See*, Free Press, New York.

Hankinson, A. (1985) Pricing decisions in small engineering firms, *Management Accounting (UK)*, **63**, 36–37.

Häubl, G. and Trifts, V. (2000) Consumer decision making in online shopping environments: the effects of interactive decision aids, *Marketing Science*, **19**(1), Winter, 4–21.

Hoch, S. J., Dreze, X. and Purk, M. E. (1994) EDLP, hi-lo, and margin arithmetic, *Journal of Marketing*, **58**, October, 16–27.

Holbrook, M. (1996) Customer value – a framework for analysis and research, in Corfman, K. P. and Lynch, J. G. Jr (eds), *Advances in Consumer Research*, Association for Consumer Research, Provo, UT, pp. 138–142.

Howard, J. A. and Morgenroth, W. M. (1968) Information processing model of executive decision, *Management Science*, **14**, March, 416–428.

Jeuland, A. and Dolan, R. (1982) An aspect of new product planning: dynamic pricing, in Zoltners, A. (ed.), *TIMS Studies in the Management Sciences*, Special Issue on Marketing Models, North Holland, Amsterdam.

Kahneman, D. and Tversky, A. (1979) Prospect theory: an analysis of decision under risk, *Econometrica*, **47**, March, 263–291.

Kalynaram, G. and Winer, R. S. (1995) Empirical generalizations from reference price research, *Marketing Science*, **14**, 161–169.

Keeney, R. L. (1999) The value of Internet commerce to the customer, *Management Science*, **45**(4), April, 533–542.

Keil, S., Reibstein, D. J. and Wittink, D. R. (1999) The impact of time horizon and objectives on the competitiveness of management behavior, Working Paper, School of Management, Yale University, New Haven, CT.

Krishna, A., Mela, C. F. and Urbany, J. E. (2000) Inertia in pricing, Working Paper, Duke University, Durham, NC.

Kucher, E. (1987) Absatzdynamik nach preisaenderung, *Marketing ZFP*, **3**, August, 177–186.

Lambin, J. J. (1976) *Advertising Competition and Market Conduct in Oligopoly Over Time*, North Holland, Amsterdam.

Laric, M. V. (1989) Pricing analysis using spreadsheets, in Seymour, D. T. (ed.), *The Pricing Decision*, Probus, Chicago, IL.

Liebermann, S. (1969) Has the marginalist–antimarginalist controversy regarding the theory of the firm been settled?, *Schweizerische Zeitschrift fuer Volkswirtschaft*, **105**(4), 535–549.

Lillien, G. L. and Yoon, E. (1988) An exploratory analysis of the dynamic behavior of price elasticity over the product life cycle: an empirical analysis of industrial chemical products, in Devinney, T. M. (ed.), *Issues in Pricing – Theory and Research*, Lexington Books, Lexington, MA.

Lynch, J. G. and Ariely, D. (2000) Wine online: search costs affect competition on price, quality, and distribution, *Marketing Science*, **19**(1), Winter, 83–103.

Marn, M. and Rosiello, R. (1992) Managing price, gaining profit, *Harvard Business Review*, September–October, 84–94.

Marshall, A. (1979) *More Profitable Pricing*, McGraw-Hill, London.

Monroe, K. B. (1979) *Pricing: Making Profitable Decisions*, McGraw-Hill, New York.

Monroe, K. B. (1990) *Pricing: Making Profitable Decisions*, 3rd edn, McGraw-Hill, New York.

Monroe, K. B. and Della Bitta, A. J. (1978) Models for pricing decisions, *Journal of Marketing Research*, **15**, August, 413–428.

Monroe, K. B. and Krishnan, R. (1985) The effect of price on subjective product evaluations, in Jacoby, J. and Olsen, J. (eds), *Perceived Quality: How Consumers View Stores and Merchandise*, Lexington Books, Lexington, MA, pp. 209–232.

Monroe, K. B. and Mazudmar, T. (1988) Pricing-decision models: recent developments and research opportunities, in Devinney, T. M. (ed.), *Issues in Pricing – Theory and Research*, Lexington Books, Lexington, MA, pp. 361–388.

Montgomery, S. L. (1988) *Profitable Pricing Strategies*, McGraw-Hill, New York.

Morris, M. H. and Joyce, M. L. (1988) How marketers evaluate price sensitivity, *Industrial Marketing Management*, **17**, 169–176.

Morris, M. H. and Morris, G. (1990) *Market-Oriented Pricing – Strategies for Management*, Quorum, New York.

Nagle, T. (1984) Economic foundations for pricing, *Journal of Business*, **57**, January, 3–26.

Nagle, T. (1987) *The Strategy and Tactics of Pricing*, Prentice-Hall, Englewood Cliffs, NJ.

Nagle, T. and Holden, R. K. (1995) *The Strategy and Tactics of Pricing*, Prentice-Hall, Englewood Cliffs, NJ.

Nimer, D. A. (1971) There's more to pricing than most companies think, *Innovations*, August. Reprinted in Vernon, I. R. and Lamb, C. W. (eds) (1976), *The Pricing Function*, Lexington Books, D.C. Heath & Co., Lexington, MA, pp. 19–33.

Oxenfeldt, A. R. (1973) A decision making structure for price decisions, *Journal of Marketing*, **37**, 48–53.

Oxenfeldt, A. R. (1975) *Pricing Strategies*, American Management Association, New York.

Parker, P. M. (1992) Price elasticity dynamics over the adoption life cycle, *Journal of Marketing Research*, **29**, August, 358–367.

Porter, M. E. (1980) *Competitive Strategy*, Free Press, New York.

Porter, R. H. (1985) On the incidence and duration of price wars, *Journal of Industrial Economics*, **33**, June, 415–426.

Rao, V. R. (1984) Pricing research in marketing: the state of the art, *Journal of Business*, **57**, 39–60.

Rao, V. R. (1993) Pricing models in marketing, in Eliahsberg, J. and Lilien, G. L. (eds), *Handbooks in OR & MS*, Elsevier, Amsterdam, Vol. 5, pp. 517–552.

Rao, V. R. and Monroe, K. B. (1989) The effect of price, brand name, and store name on buyer's perceptions of product quality: an integrative review, *Journal of Marketing Research*, **26**, August, 351–357.

Reekie, W. D. (1981) Innovation and pricing in the Dutch drug industry, *Managerial and Decision Economics*, **2**(1), 49–56.

Reichmann, T. (1973) *Kosten und Preisgrenzen. Die Bestimmung von Preisuntergrenzen und Preisobergrenzen im Industriebetrieb*, Gabler, Wiesbaden.

Riebel, p. (1972) *Kosten und Preise*, 2nd edn, Opladen, Westdeutscher Verlag.

Sethuraman, A. and Tellis, G. J. (1991) An analysis of the tradeoff between advertising and price discounting, *Journal of Marketing Research*, **28**, May, 160–174.

Seymour, D. T. (ed.) (1989) *The Pricing Decision – A Strategic Planner for Marketing Professionals*, Probus, Chicago, IL.

Shapiro, B. P. and Jackson, B. B. (1978) Industrial pricing to meet consumer needs, *Harvard Business Review*, **56**, November/December, 119–128.

Shipley, D. D. (1985) Resellers' supplier selection criteria for different consumer products, *European Journal of Marketing*, **19**(7), 26–36.

Shoemaker, R. W. (1986) Comment on dynamics of price elasticity and brand life cycles: an empirical study, *Journal of Marketing Research*, **23**, February, 778–782.

Simon, H. (1979) Dynamics of price elasticity and brand life cycles: an empirical study, *Journal of Marketing Research*, **16**, November, 439–452.

Simon, H. (1982) *Preismanagement*, Gabler, Wiesbaden.

Simon, H. (1989) *Price Management*, North Holland, Amsterdam.

Simon, H. (1992) Pricing opportunities – and how to exploit them, *Sloan Management Review*, Winter, 55–65.

Skinner, R. (1970) The determination of selling prices, *Journal of Industrial Economics*, **18**, 201–217.

Staudt, T. A. and Taylor, D. A. (1965) *A Managerial Introduction to Marketing*, Prentice-Hall, Englewood Cliffs, NJ.

Tellis, G. J. (1988) The price elasticity of selective demand: a meta-analysis of econometric models of sales, *Journal of Marketing Research*, **25**, November, 331–341.

Thaler, R. (1985) Mental accounting and customer choice, *Marketing Science*, **4**, 199–214.

Urbany, J. E. (2000) Justifying profitable pricing, Marketing Science Institute, Report Summary 00–117, Cambridge, MA.

Wied-Nebbeling, S. (1975) *Industrielle Preissetzung*, Mohr Siebeck Verlag, Tuebingen.

Wied-Nebbeling, S. (1985) *Das Preisverhalten in der Industrie*, Mohr Siebeck Verlag, Tuebingen.

Winer, R. S. (1988) Behavioral perspectives on pricing: buyers' subjective perceptions of price revisited, in Devinney, T. M. (ed.), *Issues in Pricing: Theory and Research*, Lexington Books, Lexington, MA.

Woodside, A. G. (1992) Ecological research on pricing decisions in manufacturer–distributor channels, *Proceedings of the American Marketing Association Conference*, Summer, 474–480.

Zeithaml, V. A. (1988) Consumer perceptions of price, quality and value: a means-end model and synthesis of evidence, *Journal of Marketing*, **52**, July, 2–22.

CHAPTER 14

Selling and sales management

BILL DONALDSON

Introduction

The role of selling is continuing to change and evolve in response to dramatic moves in the way buyers and sellers interact. Individual knowledge, skills and abilities are still required, perhaps more than ever, but teamwork and technology are also vital ingredients in an effective organizational response to the needs and demands of customers. The salesforce have always been ambassadors for their firm, but in a turbulent business environment the information and persuasion role of salespeople is being absorbed into their relationship role. Salespeople must take responsibility for creating, developing and maintaining profitable relationships with their customers. This being so, the need is paramount to focus on how to win, develop and retain customers to achieve the marketing and sales objectives of the firm. This puts the spotlight once again on the role of selling in the marketing mix and on the management of sales operations. Sales operations are the revenue generation engine of the organization and thus have a direct impact on the success of the firm. In this chapter, we consider how selling is changing and evolving. We examine the new role of salespeople and redefine the sales encounter in different exchange situations. We then address some of the key issues in managing the salesforce as they relate to marketing.

The changing role of salespeople

Consider the following statistics. In 1970, 80 per cent of grocery products were sold to 1656 buying points, the remaining 20 per cent to thousands of smaller units. By 1980, 80 per cent of grocery products were purchased from only 656 buying points. Today, 80 per cent is bought from only five major buying points (Keynote, 1998). Less dramatic but similar trends can be found across industries, and the effects on salespeople and on the efficiency of sales operations has been radical. These changes imply a new perspective for integrating sales and other forms of communication with the operational side of the business. Driven by an urgency arising from more complex supply chains, fewer and larger purchase points, the availability and use of IT in customer contact operations, relative increased costs of labour, and the continuing internationalization of business, sales operations are now different. These factors contribute positively to the need for more efficient exchange and communication systems between firms and their customers, predicated by increases in the costs of acquiring new customers, and the need to retain the existing customer base and stimulate the purchasing power of those customers already on the books.

Personal selling can be defined as the personal contact with one or more purchasers for the purpose of making a sale. To be effective, marketing management needs to integrate personal selling with other promotional elements, with other organizational functions such as distribution and production, and with the customer and competitive structures prevailing in the market. The importance of personal selling is such that expenditure on the salesforce usually exceeds the budget for all other marketing communications activities added together, with the possible exception of advertising in large, fast-moving consumer goods companies or direct marketing organizations.

Personal selling has several interrelated roles within the communications mix. The information role is part of a two-way process whereby information about the company's product or offer needs to be communicated to existing and potential customers and, in the reverse direction, customers' needs are correctly interpreted and understood by management. Salespeople impart knowledge about products or services which provide benefits to customers, and also a range of information on promotional support, finance, technical advice, service and other elements which contribute to customer satisfaction. Salespeople are also the face-to-face contact between purchasers and the company, and for good reason are referred to as 'the eyes and ears of the organization', since senior management's customer contact may be limited.

A second role salespeople must fulfil is persuasion. The importance of correctly identifying customers' needs and market opportunities cannot be overstated. Nevertheless, in competitive markets, prospective customers are usually faced with an abundance of choice. As a result, adoption of the marketing concept can

be no guarantee of competitive advantage. Purchasers will have to be convinced that the company has correctly identified their needs and that the offer provides benefits over any other firm. Salespeople are part of this process through persuasion and service.

A third role is relationship building, and salespeople must initiate, build and develop relationships between the firm and its customers. Owing to their boundary-spanning role, the salesforce of a company has traditionally been a vital link between the firm and its customers, and a prime platform for communicating the firm's marketing message and the voice of the customer to the firm. In the high-tech world, it is easy to overlook the importance of personal relationships and how the interaction with customers has changed, if at all. Salespeople have always realized the importance of relationships, but there is now evidence that salespeople's and customer's understanding of each other may not be accurate (Sharma, 2000). Therefore, the management task is to re-engineer sales practices to maximize the salesforce potential in this new environment.

The nature of the personal selling task is continuing to change in that selling to customers has been replaced by co-operating with customers. The goals and objectives for the salesperson have also changed from achieving or exceeding target, selling X products in Y period and maximizing earnings, to that of building repeat business with the firm's existing and potential customer base. The emphasis has shifted from 'closing' the singular sale to creating the necessary conditions for a long-term relationship between the firm and its customers that breeds successful sales encounters in the long run. This shift renders obsolete many of the currently available sales management practices, and the sales philosophy and culture that has driven the development of the sales management field for decades. It also questions sales performance measures based on individual criteria and sales management practices which reflect recruitment, training and rewards based on sales volumes rather than relationship performance. The role of the salesperson seems to have moved away from traditional aggressive and persuasive selling, to a new role of 'relationship manager' and, in practice, we are witnessing a tendency to change the sales lexicon from salesforce to sales counsellors, professional representatives or sales consultants (Manning and Reece, 1992; DeCormier and Jobber, 1993). Perhaps the change in the title is designed to facilitate the transition of the salesforce's tasks from selling to advising and counselling, from talking to listening and from pushing to helping, as suggested by Pettijohn *et al.* (1995). Recent evidence suggests that often the idea of synergistic relationships and partnerships is slower than hoped for by participants. The expected benefits from developing closer relationships also fail to materialize in the ways expected (Marsh, 2000). This transition is not only a matter of title. The new reality of relationship marketing directs salespeople and sales managers to develop long-lasting relationships with their customers based on mutual trust and commitment (Morgan and Hunt, 1994).

The costs of personal selling

According to a 2001 survey, the average cost of an outside salesperson is in excess of £55 000 per annum (Reward Group/Institute of Sales and Marketing Management, 2001). Yet the time actually spent face to face with customers is typically around 20–30 per cent of working hours. This raises the question of what form of communication is both effective and efficient in today's marketplace. The most significant difference between selling and other elements in the marketing communications mix is the personal contact, but this comes with a relatively high price tag. The need for this personal contact will vary depending on such factors as the scale of risk, size of investment, type of customer, frequency of purchase, newness of

product and many other factors. In some situations the information or persuasion role can be achieved by impersonal means of communication, particularly advertising.

Advertising is impersonal, indirect and aimed at a mass audience, whereas selling is individual, direct and much more adaptable. With advertising the message is more limited, cheaper per contact but unidirectional, relying on a pull approach rather than personal selling, which is two-way, but employs a push strategy and is relatively expensive per contact. Today, yet another dimension needs to be considered. This is the role and position of direct marketing as a form of communications. In Table 14.1, we compare advertising, direct marketing and personal selling.

Therefore, a primary task of management is to be clear on the role of personal selling and what exactly it is we want salespeople to do. Information technology (IT) is the set of technologies related to the processing and communication of information, including computer and electronic databases, advanced telecommunications, CD-ROMs and the Internet. These technologies have led to new and powerful ways to reach customers and are changing the way firms interact.

The use of marketing databases, telemarketing and the Internet is having a significant impact on how sales operations are managed and will continue to do so. For example, the Internet is a powerful tool for providing information and will be an important means of buyer–seller communication. Many traditional intermediaries, particularly those who do not stock a physical product, will find that consumers empower themselves to collect information and make the purchase decision. This changes the information role of salespeople, and travel agencies, car dealerships and financial intermediaries are likely to be most affected by such a process. The demand for secondary sources of information is passing from a number of individual and independent sources to software programs which can browse the Internet and report the findings directly to users

Table 14.1 Choice of communication: comparing advertising, direct marketing and personal selling		
Personal selling	*Direct marketing*	*Advertising*
Individual directionality	Individual directionality	Mass audience directionality
Personal, direct contact	Personal, indirect contact	Impersonal, indirect contact
Highly adaptable	Adaptable but relatively fixed format	Fixed format
Working in-depth	Working on one-to-one	Working in breadth
Two-way	Two-way	One-way
Direct feedback	Indirect feedback	Organized feedback (MIS, market research)
Expensive per contact	Inexpensive per contact	Relatively inexpensive (cost per 1000 criteria)
Push effect	Pull effect	Pull effect

(Autonomy and Melting Pot are examples of this kind of service). Information itself is the market opportunity, and the facilitation between source and consumer the new challenge.

The incredible success of the Internet in terms of access and users has not yet been matched by sales effectiveness. If anything, telephone, e-mail and fax are more essential and powerful at present. In terms of information provision, the Internet is unrivalled. It can reach an audience cheaply with the message you want to convey and allows full interaction – the ultimate in communication. However, unless the website is properly designed and maintained it may prove damaging. To create a website, identify the information you want to communicate and which the users will need, ensure that it is effectively linked to other databases and that as a communication vehicle it conveys the image as well as the content you wish to get across.

Just as telemetry (automatic reordering) and electronic data interchange (bar coding, etc.) have removed many mundane order processing tasks such as stock checking, inventory management and order filling and processing, so the Internet is removing much of the more mundane information role that salespeople perform. The result will be a changing role for salespeople to a more highly skilled, more well informed, computer literate person operating as customer account manager and co-ordinating the difficult interface between customer and company.

What we expect salespeople to do – the sales process

Despite what has been said, the correct approach and technique in selling is still, and always has been, vitally important. While cautioning against the idea of the one best or universal way to sell, nevertheless there are some appropriate guidelines that can be recommended in sales encounters.

Stage 1. Generating leads and identifying prospects

Most salespeople create sales with existing customers and relationship maintenance is a key role. Nevertheless, the job also entails gaining new customers. The first step in achieving this is to identify suitable prospects. Many companies provide leads for salespeople from formal sources (Glenigan is one example from the building industry) or perhaps from response enquiries as a result of trade shows, direct mailing, telemarketing or advertising. Salespeople will also generate their own leads from lists/directories, through personal contacts, newspapers or by telephone prospecting. However, a lead is a suspect that has to be qualified to become a prospect. To qualify a lead, it is important to ensure that the potential customer needs the product or service in question or has a problem to be solved, and that they have the resources and authority to influence or decide on the purchase. Furthermore, that the potential account will be profitable.

Stage 2. Pre-call planning

An old rule of thumb suggests that a good sales process is 40 per cent preparation, 20 per cent presentation and 40 per cent follow-up. Regardless of the accuracy of these percentages, there is no doubt that success can be linked to preparation. All sales calls should have an objective, preferably with a specific outcome or action on the part of the prospect. Pre-call planning involves setting objectives, gathering information about the buyer and their company, deciding what questions to ask and what you intend to say. Remember that situation questions are important in the sales process, but you do not want to ask questions you can and should have known from other sources. Information such as the size of the firm, their products and services, their competitors, names of people in important executive positions, current and previous sales history should be part of pre-call preparation. Further information, such as the customer's buying processes, their current suppliers and their future plans, can be identified in the initial stages of the sales interview. Ways to establish credibility and trust for the salesperson and their company with the buyer should be part of the pre-call preparation.

Stage 3. The approach

Getting an audience with a prospect can often be difficult and indeed harrowing for the inexperienced salesperson. Although the role of selling should not be technique driven, there is a skill in getting to see the right people so that your message can be communicated and understood. Ultimately, it will be on what you do and how you do it that builds long-term customer relationships, but getting there in the first place can be difficult. Experienced salespeople will recommend the importance of getting past the gatekeeper (receptionist, secretary or personal assistant) and building a relationship not only with the buyer, but their gatekeepers and other influencers in the buying process. Making appointments is, in most cases, essential to establishing a professional approach, but letters of introduction and using third party references can also be crucial. Establishing rapport, whether on the basis of similarity or expertise, is necessary before exchange takes place. For larger sales and new products, where the risk for the buyer is greater, establishing credibility is vital. The well-known company has a distinct advantage in this stage and the salesperson from a less well-known company has to work doubly hard to reassure the buyer (Levitt, 1967).

Stage 4. The presentation

As Rackham's (1995) work has shown, the ability to ask questions and the right type of question differentiates successful and less successful salespeople. Nevertheless, too often salespeople overemphasize the oral presentation and ignore the written sales proposal, the quotation or the subsequent follow-up, which technically can also be considered part of the presentation. It is vital to ensure that the buyer's needs have been correctly identified, that the solution offered is as expected and, if possible, that the customer's expectations are exceeded rather than merely satisfied. Furthermore, in the right circumstances the use of visuals can reassure the buyer and instil confidence in the salesperson, their product and their company. Most experienced salespeople rate canned and stylized presentations much less important than the well-organized and individually tailored presentations (Hite and Bellizzi, 1986). Research in manufacturing has also shown that there is a need to segment customers and target your demonstration depending on the type of product. Many demonstrations were too long for the product and customer, in other words overselling (Heiman and Muller, 1996). Industrial buyers are looking for credibility, reliability, responsiveness and the ability to provide answers from salespeople, rather than aggressiveness or persuasiveness (Hayes and Hartley, 1989).

Stage 5. Overcoming objections

It is human nature that a buyer may stall and raise objections to a sales presentation. Again, experienced salespeople will claim that objections are to be welcomed, since they confirm the buyer's interest in the product or service, although the idea of questions is to reveal real needs so that surprises are kept to a minimum. Good salespeople differentiate between types of objections. Some objections are no more than clarifying questions and should be welcomed. However, there are also objections that express real concerns. The advice here is to listen carefully to the problem, clarify that both parties understand the real issue and agree how it can be solved. Listening enhances trust in the

salesperson and leads to anticipation of future interaction (Ramsey and Sohi, 1997). Traditionally, salespeople have put too much emphasis on the ability to overcome resistance by technique instead of by sound solutions that meet the buyers' real needs and provide clear benefits. In other words, salespeople have been overly concerned with a performance orientation rather than a learning orientation, but those who learn, and learn how to adapt, will increase their performance (Sujan *et al.*, 1994). Effective communication is helping the customer learn (Wernerfelt, 1996).

Stage 6. Closing

Since most selling is repeat business to existing and known customers, closing is a bad idea. Nevertheless, the salesperson has set an objective and achievement of this objective is necessary to progress the relationship. Very often, salespeople just simply forget to ask for the order. They are so busy with their presentation that asking for commitment is neglected or forgotten. In some cases, adding on extra features and advantages that the buyer may not be interested in loses the sale by not asking for a decision at the right time. Effective closing means agreeing on the objectives that both parties are trying to meet and which take the relationship forward to further integrated activities.

Stage 7. Follow-up

Vital to the customer-driven business is what happens after the sale. Most buyers object when promises are not delivered and the salesperson doesn't do what was expected. In the modern business this is fatal – where building relationships and the ability to deliver as promised, go the extra mile and delight the customer are at the heart of what a business should be about. The most important question a salesperson can ask is: 'What do I need to do, Mr or Mrs Customer, to get more of your business?'

Sales management issues

Sales management must also adapt to changes in market conditions. The need for closer, more demanding relationships with selected customers brings new problems and opportunities in the organization and deployment of salespeople. Traditional approaches to determining salesforce size, territory deployment and call patterns can be brought into question. As a result, salesforce size may need to be assessed on an estimate of the future revenue stream expected from a customer and the service that customer will require. Call rates, travel patterns and frequency of visits may change. In some cases, companies may have permanent staff on their customers' premises. Marketing orientation would suggest such customer-based sales solutions to be appropriate, but the cost effectiveness of sales operations may need to be even more carefully assessed than in the past.

Similarly, traditional means of setting sales targets on sales volume and revenue may need to be replaced by measures which reflect the new customer relationship job to be done. More appropriate targets are likely to be the retention rate of customers, the contribution these customers make and the satisfaction level they have in doing business with the firm. This is in keeping with a customer-focused, quality-based strategy that leading-edge firms pursue. This has implications for the kind of people to be recruited, who need to be relationship orientated, financially aware, marketing trained, computer literate and skilled negotiators. Individual ability and technique will still be important, but this must be coupled with sound management, particularly in the areas of recruitment, training, leadership, remuneration and control. These issues are considered in the following sections.

Recruitment and selection

Recruiting and selecting suitable applicants is one of the most important and difficult jobs the sales manager can undertake. Formally addressing the recruitment process will help in defining the job, attracting the most suitable applicants, and avoiding unnecessary problems and costs. The time and expense in recruiting is not insignificant, including advertising, selection procedures, and first and second interviews. Add to this other costs, including induction training, the potential cost of lost sales, the costs of dismissal if the wrong applicant is selected and the cost of repeating the process. Recruitment costs can be a major headache for sales managers, as well as for the recruits themselves.

To overcome some of these difficulties, recruitment should be seen as part of a process which includes job analysis, manpower planning, job description, job specification, recruitment, screening and selection. This process should be systematic and thorough, and a planned approach will increase the success rate in selection, build a reputation as a desirable, progressive employer and sharpen the firm's competitive edge, thus improving effectiveness and efficiency in sales operations. The starting point in recruitment is job analysis. Job analysis specifies the tasks involved in a particular job and the factors which affect job performance, including the reporting relationship, the role and tasks necessary to perform effectively, the environment in which the job operates, including policies on sales, distribution and competitors, and company rules and regulations. Sales managers should be careful not to be too intuitive in their job analysis. Of course, the job should reflect corporate ethos, marketing strategy and the specific reporting relationships, but job analysis also requires assessment of what existing salespeople do.

The second stage is manpower planning, which has both qualitative and quantitative dimensions. Initially, an assessment should be made as to how adequate and effective the current salesforce is in meeting sales objectives. What characteristics are considered necessary to do the particular selling job? These are the knowledge, skills and abilities an individual should possess. The second factor is the turnover in personnel. That is, people may be recruited to add to the salesforce, while others will be recruited to replace those who are promoted, leave, retire or are dismissed. A measure of turnover is the number of people who leave per annum divided by the total number in the salesforce.

The next stage is to write a job description for an individual in a sales position, including the integration of the job into a team or organizational unit. The job analysis is the cornerstone on which the job description for the salesperson is based. Therefore, the job description should begin with repeating the main duties, tasks and responsibilities of the job. The key areas can vary, but a job title, the main purpose of the job, key and secondary activities, and performance measures should be included. It is preferable to be specific in the job description about job functions and duties. For example, indications can be given on time allocated to prospecting, travelling, merchandising, servicing, reporting as well as selling time. The approach should cover the most important aspects of the job, essential and preferable criteria, the necessary education, qualifications, experience and other attributes, and an assessment of the validity and reliability of previous methods.

A variety of potential sources can be used to recruit new salespeople. These sources can vary as to their adequacy and consistency in obtaining the best possible candidates for sales positions. Good recruitment policies will take a planned approach to this problem. For example, turnover rates will indicate how many and how often replacements are likely to be required. Furthermore, analysis of previous recruits can indicate more and less productive sources. This analysis can be extended to discriminate between high, average and low performers. There is a need to link sources of recruits in sales to the selling style. For example, recruitment for missionary selling jobs favours employment agencies. For trade selling, sources are primarily from advertisements and educational institutions, while for technical selling, recruiters rely more on personal contacts. The use of different sources is, and should be, related to job- and company-specific criteria, as well as the matching characteristics between buyer and seller.

When the number and type of salespeople has been determined and the various sources have been selected to obtain the necessary applicants, it is then essential to evaluate these in order to recruit the best, i.e. those most suitable to the job and the firm. One possible cause of high turnover in sales personnel is that badly suited applicants are recruited in the first place. Turnover rates (i.e. the number who leave per annum over the number in the salesforce) which are above industry averages or seem to be increasing over previous periods indicate a problem and an unnecessary cost. These turnover rates do vary, being higher in salesforces where the average age is younger, higher in consumer goods than industrial goods companies and significantly higher in the first three years of service. For example, higher turnover rates are found in new, young, consumer goods salespeople. In financial services, 80 per cent of life insurance salespeople leave within two years of joining their company and only 8 per cent had been with their company more than four years (LIMRA, 1992).

Related to the turnover level are the costs of recruiting, selecting, training and supervising new recruits who are poor performers. In addition to these costs, a salesperson leaving the company may well have a negative effect on sales in their territory and, if joining a competitor, business may be lost. The average lost sales multiplied by the number who leave will represent the total cost of lost business.

Commensurate with cost is the time factor. From a decision to recruit or replace through sourcing, interviewing, screening, second or third interviews, checking references, medical, to placing and accepting an offer may take several months.

Training

In addition to recruiting the most appropriate people for the job based on the job specification, every sales manager must try and improve their subordinates' individual effectiveness by appropriate training. Much training is wasted because it covers areas that the person already knows about. For this reason, it is important to separate induction training for new recruits from that suggested for existing staff. Again, planning is important, so the first stage, prior to training, is to conduct some audit of training requirements.

This is stage 1 in the process, determining needs; stage 2 is designing the programme, stage 3 is conducting the training and finally evaluating the results. For example, one of the leading pharmaceutical companies in the USA, Merck, with a salesforce of 3000, have declared that 'training is the key'. To reinforce this, a 1993 study suggested that it is not the amount of money spent on training that counts, but how the money is spent. Higher performers do not outspend lower performers, but they allocate the funds in different ways. High performers have longer induction training, three to nine months, whereas lower performers spend less than three months with new recruits. High performers do less classroom and role playing, but more on-the-job training. Training also has an important role in establishing the values and beliefs that an organization represents in establishing corporate culture within the salesforce.

Leadership and supervision

The ability to get the best from subordinates is a valued characteristic and is referred to as leadership quality. However, leadership is best explained in the context in which it is exercised, and sales managers should assess their leadership style and its appropriateness to the people and circumstances in which it is applied.

In today's organization, where rationalizing, downsizing and restructuring are being implemented, sales managers must encourage their people to adapt and be flexible. Such movers and shakers have been called transformational leaders, who can get their salespeople to perform beyond typical expectations. However, in most situations, sales managers who have not proved themselves by having previously been a successful salesperson will find it hard, if not impossible, to be convincing in this role. Qualities thought to be important in sales managers vary and often extend to a variety of characteristics, usually ending with an ability to walk on water and other superhuman powers.

Perhaps more revealing are studies that reflect how salespeople feel about their boss. The major complaints usually focus on the following:

- Managers do not spend enough time with their salespeople.
- They do not listen to salespeople's concerns.
- They do not take these concerns seriously.
- They do not follow up to resolve problems.

Again, the difficulty may be that many sales managers have not been trained in management or prepared for the new skills and tasks that they are now asked to perform.

Remuneration

Arguably, the most influential factor in the motivational mix is remuneration, which can incorporate basic financial rewards and special incentives. Financial incentives are a popular means used to motivate sales personnel. Sales managers can remunerate salespeople using salary, commission, bonus or a combination of these. Most sales managers, based on their experience, seem to feel that a balance of types of remuneration is most appropriate. A recent study found that most UK companies offer combination remuneration comprising salary and commission or salary and some form of bonus, especially performance-related pay (Donaldson, 1998a). This research also found that a number of salespeople consider job security of higher value than the level of remuneration. Other studies into the effects of pay on the motivation of salespeople have found, for example, that older salespeople with larger families valued financial rewards more, whereas younger, better educated sales staff who had no family valued the so-called higher order rewards, such as recognition, liking and respect, and sense of accomplishment (Churchill and Pecotich, 1982). The variety of payment plans in operation, even within similar industry and sales situations, suggests that management do not fully understand the effect of payment on their employees' motivation. If a company's main objectives were on relationship building and long-term customers, a higher salary and lower incentive component would be recommended. The difficulty with such rules is that, within any one salesforce, there is no one remuneration package that suits everyone and we have to settle for one that best meets the needs of most of our salesforce.

Evaluation and control

Setting targets and quotas for salespeople has a direct effect on their motivation. Targets not only direct sales effort and provide evidence for performance evaluation, but they can also act as an incentive and motivator. It is not only the target and system of control that is important, but the way the target is determined, communicated and applied. For this reason, a system of management by objectives based on the participation and involvement of salespeople themselves is an appropriate option (Donaldson, 1998b).

A problem already identified is that sales tasks and sales effort often can have an indirect rather than a direct effect on sales performance. Missionary or specification selling, such as pharmaceuticals, is particularly prone to this difficulty. For others, organizational complexity or dual effort with intermediaries may confuse the sales process and its effect on performance. Nevertheless, accurate and timely feedback for salespeople has a positive effect on job performance and job satisfaction (Doyle and Shapiro, 1980). At one level evaluation of salespeople is easy – they either make target or they don't! The problem with the link between sales effort and sales response is that it is neither simple nor direct. Most companies do conduct some form of evaluation, but few do this in a formal way that evaluates causes as well as outcomes. Part of the problem with evaluation is that to do it properly, far from being easy, it is time-consuming, costly and downright difficult. At the individual salesperson level evaluation, it is necessary to identify above and below average performers, to identify possible candidates for promotion or dismissal, and to identify areas of weakness in salespeople in carrying out their tasks in meeting sales objectives. For management, evaluation is necessary to assess the efficacy of sales management practices such as territory deployment, recruitment, training, remuneration and so on. Again, our starting point is an audit of current performance.

Conclusion

Personal selling and sales operations are still key to the effective implementation of marketing plans. The role of personal selling is changing as new and different ways such as the telephone, electronic interchange and the Internet can be found to inform and persuade customers. The salesperson must adapt and there is evidence that marketing and sales roles are becoming not only interdependent, but also interchangeable. Positions such as business development manager, customer account manager and category manager reflect that salespeople must be better trained and qualified, able to work in teams and be capable of co-ordinating within their firm and at the boundary between the firm and their customer. The traditional sales process still applies in many exchange situations, but the key role for salespeople is to build, maintain and promote long-term profitable relationships with customers.

This puts an additional burden on management to recruit, train, lead, reward and monitor effective sales performers, since this role is crucial to the prosperity of their business.

References

Churchill, G. A. and Pecotich, A. (1982) A structural equation investigation of the pay satisfaction–valence relationship among salespeople, *Journal of Marketing*, **46**, Fall, 114–124.

DeCormier, R. A. and Jobber, D. (1993) The counsellor selling method: concepts and constructs, *Journal of Personal Selling and Sales Management*, **23**(4), 39–59.

Donaldson, B. (1998a) The importance of financial incentives in motivating industrial salespeople, *Journal of Selling and Major Account Management*, **1**(1), July, 4–16.

Donaldson, B. (1998b) *Sales Management: Theory and Practice*, 2nd edn, Macmillan, Basingstoke.

Doyle, S. X. and Shapiro, B. P. (1980) What counts most in motivating your salesforce?, *Harvard Business Review*, May–June, 134–139.

Hayes, H. M. and Hartley, S. W. (1989) How buyers view industrial salespeople, *Industrial Marketing Management*, **18**, 73–80.

Heiman, A. and Muller, E. (1996) Using demonstration to increase new product acceptance: controlling demonstration time, *Journal of Marketing Research*, **XXXIII**, November, 422–430.

Hite, R. E. and Bellizzi, J. A. (1986) A preferred style of sales management, *Industrial Marketing Management*, **15**(3), 215–223.

Keynote Ltd (1998) *Retailing in the UK*, Keynote Publications, London.

Levitt, T. (1967) Communications and industrial selling, *Journal of Marketing*, **31**, April, 15–21.

LIMRA (1992) *Report on UK Life Insurance*. Life Insurance Marketing and Research Association, London.

Manning, G. L. and Reece, B. L. (1992) *Selling Today: An Extension of the Marketing Concept*, 5th edn, Allyn & Bacon, Boston.

Marsh, L. (2000) Relationship skills for strategic account management, *Journal of Personal Selling and Major Account Management*, **3**(1), Autumn, 53–64.

Morgan, R. M. and Hunt, S. D. (1994) The commitment–trust theory of relationship marketing, *Journal of Marketing*, **58**, July, 20–38.

Pettijohn, C., Pettijohn, L. and Taylor, A. (1995) The relationship between effective counselling and effective behaviors, *Journal of Consumer Marketing*, **12**(1), 5–15.

Rackham, N. (1995) *Spin Selling*, Gower, Aldershot.

Ramsey, R. P. and Sohi, R. S. (1997) Listening to your customers: the impact of perceived salesperson listening behavior on relationship outcomes, *Journal of the Academy of Marketing Science*, **25**(2), 127–137.

Reward Group (2001) Institute of Sales and Marketing Management, Rewards Group/CIM, Stone, Staffordshire, UK.

Sharma, A. (2000) Do salespeople and customers understand each other?, *Journal of Personal Selling and Major Account Management*, **3**(1), Autumn, 29–39.

Sujan, H., Weitz, B. A. and Kumar, N. (1994) Learning orientation, working smart, and effective selling, *Journal of Marketing*, **58**, July, 39–52.

Wernerfelt, B. (1996) Efficient marketing communication: helping the customer learn, *Journal of Marketing Research*, **XXXIII**, May, 239–246.

Further reading

Carlisle, J. A. and Parker, R. C. (1989) *Beyond Negotiation*, Wiley, Chichester.

Cooper, S. (1997) *Selling Principle, Practice and Management*, Pitman, London.

Donaldson, B. (1998) *Sales Management: Theory and Practice*, 2nd edn, Macmillan, Basingstoke.

Donaldson, B. and O'Toole, T. (2001) *Strategic Market Relationships*, John Wiley, Chichester.

Hartley, B. and Starkey, M. W. (1996) *The Management of Sales and Customer Relations*, Thomson Business Press, London.

Jobber, D. (ed.) (1997) *The CIM Handbook of Selling and Sales Strategy*, Butterworth-Heinemann, Oxford.

Rackham, N. (1995) *Spin Selling*, Gower, Aldershot.

Steward, K. (1993) *Marketing Led, Sales Driven*, Butterworth-Heinemann, Oxford.

CHAPTER 15

Brand building

LESLIE de CHERNATONY

Brands are clusters of functional and emotional values which promise stakeholders unique experiences. The functional values are less sustainable than the emotional values. Product or service functionality is now a taken for granted expectation amongst stakeholders. Emotional values represent a source of sustainable competitive advantage. Many organizations recognize that good communications raises stakeholders' expectations about brand promises, yet it is staff who embody the brand. A well co-ordinated, committed group of employees enables an organization to deliver a welcomed difference based on what the customer receives (functional values) and how they receive it (emotional values).

Brands are intangible assets and, because of their ethereal nature, interpretations of a firm's brand can vary between members of the management team. Without surfacing the diverse interpretations of a firm's brand amongst managers, it is likely that different parts of the organization will be 'pulling in different directions', due to diverse views about the firm's brand. This chapter therefore opens with a review of the different meanings of the brand concept.

Historically, brand management solely focused on customers, based on the assumption that efficient production processes could be managed to guarantee the brand's functional capability. Brand managers were responsible for planning and co-ordinating branding activity. In today's competitive environment, where the services sector is far more dominant, there is a realization that attention needs to focus on customers *and* staff. Advertising performs a useful role promoting a brand promise and enrobing a product or service with emotional values, but it is staff who deliver the promise. Without sufficient understanding and commitment, staff may not be delivering the promised benefits. To therefore ensure a co-ordinated, pan-company approach to delivering the brand, there has been a move towards teams of senior managers planning and co-ordinating brand building activity. As a consequence of these issues, this chapter will also look at the importance of internal branding and culture. It will explain a strategic brand building procedure that facilitates a more integrated, pan-company approach which should engender a greater likelihood of brand coherence.

The chapter opens by reviewing the spectrum of brand interpretations. A sequential, iterative process for building and sustaining brands is overviewed. Each block of this process is then explained, showing how a more integrated approach to branding can be enacted.

Spectrum of brand interpretations

A review of the literature and interviews with leading-edge consultants advising clients about their brands showed a variety of interpretations about brands (de Chernatony and Dall'Olmo Riley, 1998). Table 15.1 shows the variety of interpretations encountered which will be considered.

Brand as a logo

One of the more established definitions of a brand was proposed by the American Marketing Association (AMA) in 1960. This stresses the importance of the brand's logo and visual signifiers primarily as a basis for differentiation purposes, i.e.

> A name, term sign, symbol or design, or a combination of them, intended to identify the

Table 15.1   Different interpretations of 'Brand'

Logo
Legal instrument
Company
Shorthand
Risk reducer
Positioning
Personality
Cluster of values
Vision
Adding value
Identity
Image
Relationship

goods or services of one seller or group of sellers and to differentiate them from those of competitors.

The unique shape of Coca-Cola's bottle, the distinctive 'golden arch' of McDonald's, the blue and white roundel of BMW, and the spectrum coloured, part-eaten apple of the Apple Mackintosh are notable examples of brands instantly identifiable through their logos.

While this interpretation represents an important ingredient of brand building, it should not be the primary emphasis. Brand differentiation is more than making a brand distinctive. At its most basic, it is finding an attribute important to customers then seeking to sustain this unique characteristic in a profitable manner. Developing the logo for the brand should be done strategically, rather than tactically. In other words, the vision for what the brand is to become should drive ideas about the core essence of the brand, which should then be used as the brief for designers. Whether the colour or the type of font is appropriate can then be judged against how these will help the brand on its journey.

Brand as legal instrument

One of the simpler interpretations of a brand is that of ensuring a legally enforceable statement of ownership. Branding represents an investment and thus organizations seek legal ownership of title, as protection against imitators. As part of its brand strategy, Absolut Vodka stresses the importance of continually monitoring competitors' brand activity, to quickly stop any firm adopting the name or bottle design. Effective trademark registration offers some legal protection (e.g. Blackett, 1998), but 'look-alike' own labels in retailing exemplify the problem of being over-reliant on legislation as a barrier against competitors (e.g. Lomax *et al.*, 1999). Kapferer (1995) devised an innovative procedure to help evaluate the extent to which a competitor had infringed a brand's equity. Consumers are invited to sit in front of a PC screen and are presented with an unfocused picture of the packaging of the copycat product. They are asked if they want to state what the brand is. Then, in an incremental manner, the picture gradually becomes clearer. At each step of increasing clarity, the consumer is asked if they can state the brand. The measure of confusion is based on the proportion of consumers who stated they had seen the original brand when they actually had the copy.

Brand as company

One way of considering the nature of a brand is to think about the spectrum shown in Figure 15.1.

For a variety of reasons there is a move towards corporate branding, for example the need to curtail the increasing costs of promoting individual line brands, or the prevalence of category management, where priority is given to promoting product sectors to retailers, rather than individual line brands. Mitchell (1997) provides a more complete picture. We have moved from the industrial age, which stressed tangible assets, to the information age, which seeks to exploit intangibles such as ideas, knowledge and information. The new branding model is therefore one which emphasizes value through employees' involvement in relationship building. Internally brand management is becoming culture management and externally it is customer interface management. In the new branding mode corporate branding internally signals messages about the desired culture and externally it reduces the information overload problems from line branding, decreasing customers' information processing costs. Corporate branding facilitates consumers' desires to look deeper into the brand and assess the nature of the corporation. A further reason for corporate branding is that, through building respect and trust with one of the corporation's offerings, consumers are more likely to accept the corporation's promises about other offerings.

Corporate branding thus provides the strategic focus for a clear positioning, facilitates greater cohesion in communication programmes, enables staff to better understand the type of organization they work for, and thus provides inspiration about desired styles of behaviour.

Managing corporate brands needs a different approach to classic line branding. Individual line branding primarily focuses on consumers and distributors, and few staff interact with consumers. By contrast, corporate branding is about multiple stakeholders interacting with many staff from numerous departments, and important objectives are ensuring a consistent message and uniform delivery across all stakeholders' groups. In line branding, consumers mainly assess the brand's values from advertising, packaging, distribution and the people using the brand. Yet, in corporate branding, while values are partly inferred from corporate communication campaigns, stakeholders' interactions with staff are also important.

In the early days of some corporate brands (e.g. Virgin, Body Shop and Hewlett-Packard), strong personality entrepreneurs had a philosophy about their brand making the world a better place and recruited staff with similar values to theirs. With a low number of staff in regular contact with each other, stakeholders were likely to perceive a consistent corporate brand. Success resulted in growth and more staff. The more successful firms communicated their brand philosophy through a culture that rigidly enshrined particular core values, allowing peripheral values and practices to adapt

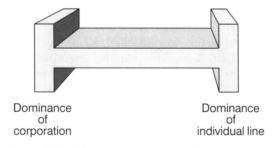

Dominance of corporation

Dominance of individual line

Figure 15.1   Corporate versus line branding

over time. New staff could appreciate from the culture how to contribute as brand builders. In less successful corporations, new managers were uncomfortable with the issues of corporate culture and brand visions, and over time lost sense of their core values. New staff were less confident about the corporation's core values and different styles of behaviour evolved, causing disparate perceptions amongst stakeholders.

In corporate branding, staff are not only critical contributors to the brand's values, but represent evaluative brand cues. As such, the HRM Director should be a key member of the brand's team, since he/she devises policy that impacts on brand building, such as recruitment, induction and training. At Waterstone's, the Marketing Director's view is 'Recruitment is a branding exercise, it's part of the management of the corporate brand' (Ind, 1998, p. 325). For successful corporate branding, staff must understand the brand's vision, be totally committed to delivering it, and more emphasis should be placed on internal communication (e.g. intranets).

In corporate branding, the CEO is responsible for the corporate brand's health and their leadership needs to enable all employees to recognize the importance of the corporation's values. An advantage of focusing everything behind a common name is not only to provide clear direction for staff, but also to achieve a coherent focus for the portfolio and communicate a consistent message to all stakeholders. The disadvantage is that problems with the organization's reputation can taint the image of the whole portfolio.

Brand as shorthand

There are finite limits to our abilities to seek, process and evaluate information. Yet surfing the web, or considering other forms of advertising, quickly makes one aware of the emphasis many organizations place behind the quantity, rather than the quality, of information. To protect their limited cognitive capabilities, peo-

ple have developed methods for processing such large quantities of information. Miller (1956) carried out research into the way the mind encodes information and his research, along with that of Jacoby *et al.* (1977) plus Bettman (1979), helps us to appreciate what happens. If we compare the mind with the way computers work, we can evaluate the quantity of information facing a consumer in terms of the number of 'bits'. All the information on the packaging of a branded grocery item would represent in excess of 100 bits of information. Researchers have shown that, at most, the mind can simultaneously process seven bits of information.

To cope with this deluge of marketing information, the mind aggregates bits of information into larger groups, or 'chunks', which contain more information. An analogy may be useful. Novice yachtsmen learning Morse code initially hear 'dit' and 'dot' as information bits. With experience, they organize these bits of information into chunks (letters), then mentally build these chunks into larger chunks (words). In a similar manner, when first exposed to a new brand of convenience food, the first scanning of the label would reveal an array of wholesome ingredients with few additives. These would be grouped into a chunk interpreted as 'natural ingredients'. Further scanning may show a high price printed on a highly attractive, multicolour label. This would be grouped with the earlier 'natural ingredients' chunk to form a larger chunk, interpreted as 'certainly a high quality offering'. This aggregation of increasingly large chunks would continue until final eye scanning would reveal an unknown brand name but, on seeing that it came from a well-known organization (e.g. Nestlé, Heinz, etc.), the consumer would then aggregate this with the earlier chunks to infer that this was a premium brand: quality contents in a well-presented container, selling at a high price through a reputable retailer, from a respected manufacturer known for quality. Were the consumer not to purchase this new brand of convenience food, but later that day to see an advertisement for the brand, they would be able to recall the brand's attributes rapidly, since the brand name would enable fast accessing of a highly informative chunk in the memory.

The task facing the marketer is to facilitate the way consumers process information about brands, such that ever larger chunks can be built in the memory which, when fully formed, can then be rapidly accessed through associations from brand names. Frequent exposure to advertisements containing a few claims about the brand should help the chunking process. What is important, however, is to reinforce attributes with the brand name rather than continually repeating the brand name without, at the same time, associating the appropriate attributes with it.

Conceiving brands as shorthand devices forces managers to think about the way they emphasize quality of information rather than quantity of information in any brand communication. As our minds cannot cope with more than seven bits of information at once, one test to apply to any brand communication is whether there are more than seven bits of information.

Brand as risk reducer

When people choose between brands they do not always base their decision on choosing the brand which maximizes their utility, as economic theory suggests. Rather, there are situations where consumers perceive risk, for example the perceived risk of friends disapproving of a particular style of clothing. It is not uncommon to find consumers choosing between competing brands according to the extent to which they perceive least risk. Bauer (1960) was one of the early writers to suggest this notion and a stream of research has since evolved showing the importance of perceived risk, i.e. the uncertainty consumers perceive that buying a particular brand will result in a favourable outcome.

Customers perceive risk along several dimensions such as:

- performance risk (will the brand meet the functional specifications?);
- financial risk (will the customer get good value for money from the brand?);
- time risk (will the customer have to spend more time evaluating unknown brands and if the brand proves inappropriate, how much time will have been wasted?);
- social risk (what associations will the customer's peer group link with them as a result of their brand choice and will this enhance or weaken their views about the customer?);
- psychological risk (does the customer feel right with the brand in so far as it matches their self-image?).

Brands are more likely to succeed when time is taken to understand what dimensions of perceived risk customers are most concerned about. From this analysis, a way needs to be found of presenting the brand to minimize customers' perceptions of risk along the dimensions that particularly concern them.

Building trust through brands is a strategy that many firms have followed. Dell's brand investment makes it difficult for new entrants to match the image they have for rapidly and efficiently fulfilling telephone and Internet orders.

To capitalize on the brand as a risk reducer, marketers should segment customers by similar risk perceptions. If any one of the segments has sufficient customers and if the firm is profitably capable of developing the brand as a risk reducer to meet the segment's needs, this strategy should be considered.

Brand as positioning

Another perspective managers adopt when interpreting brands is in terms of positioning, i.e. ensuring customers instantly associate a brand with a particular functional benefit, or a very low number of functional benefits. For example, BMW as performance and Volvo as safety. In the information age people are bombarded with large amounts of data and choice. For example, it has been estimated that the weekend edition of a quality newspaper has more information than someone would have been exposed to in the seventeenth century. In a grocery superstore the customer is faced with over 20 000 lines. To cope with this notable quantity of data, people's perceptual processes take over. In effect, these raise 'barriers' protecting the mind against accepting just any type of data, and perceptual vigilance then focuses attention on particular data which are selectively comprehended and retained in the memory. One of the implications of the perceptual process is that customers may interpret a brand differently from that intended by the organization. For this reason, some managers interpret a brand as a device that enables them to establish a key functional association in the customer's mind.

There are several characteristics of a powerful brand positioning strategy. First, it should be centred ideally around one functional attribute, or if necessary a couple, since the more attributes included the more difficult it is to get these registered in customers' minds. Second, it

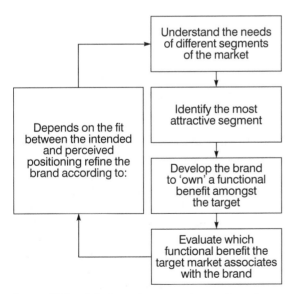

Figure 15.2 A balanced perspective on brand positioning

should be recognized, as Ries and Trout (1986) stressed, that positioning is not what is done to a brand, but rather what results in the customer's mind. In other words, it is myopic to just focus on brand development. Rather, there should be a balanced perspective, evaluating what the customer registers about the brand, then fine-tuning the brand until there is better alignment between the intended positioning and the resultant positioning, as shown in Figure 15.2.

Third, the brand positioning should focus on functional benefits valued by customers, rather than those valued by managers. It is too easy to focus on features which have more to do with reflecting the organization's competencies, rather than taking time to involve the customer in the development process.

Brand as personality

With advancing technology and sufficient investment, competitors can emulate and surpass the functional advantage of a leading brand. One way to sustain a brand's uniqueness is through enrobing it with emotional values, which users sometimes value beyond the brand's functional utility. Customers rarely undertake a thorough review of a brand to identify its emotional values, as can be appreciated from the early discussion about perceptual processes. By using the metaphor of the brand as a personality, manifest sometimes through a celebrity in brand advertisements, customers find it much easier to appreciate the emotional values of the brand.

A brand's emotional values are also inferred from its design and packaging, along with other marketer-controlled clues such as pricing and the type of outlet selling the brand. However, it should be realized that, particularly for conspicuously consumed brands, people form impressions according to the type of people using the brand and this is less easy for the marketer to control. There are some examples of successfully capitalizing on the people consuming a brand, for example the launch of the alcopop drink Hooch in Sweden. One of the emotional values of this brand is a distinctively independent attitude. In its early days, staff from the Swedish importer went to popular holiday skiing slopes and watched young skiers. Those who had a more flamboyant skiing style were approached and asked if they would like to invite friends to a party that evening at a local bar where Hooch was being promoted. This proved to be a successful way of getting the brand associated in its early days with people whose emotional values echoed those of the brand.

This interpretation of the brand has given rise to a considerable amount of research into brands as symbolic devices with personalities that users welcome. When choosing between competing brands, customers assess the fit between the personalities of competing brands and the personality they wish to project, as shown in Figure 15.3.

According to the situation they are in, this may be:

- the self they believe they are (for example, the brands of clothing selected by a manager for daily wear in the office);
- the self they desire to be (for example, the brand of suit worn by a young graduate going for interviews immediately after completing their degree);
- the situational self (for example, the brands of clothing worn by a young man who is to meet for the first time the parents of his fiancée).

When therefore seeking to communicate the emotional values of the brand, it is important to understand the emotional role potential customers expect of the brand.

Brand as a cluster of values

In this interpretation, a brand is considered as a cluster of values. For example, the Virgin brand is a cluster of four values, i.e. quality innovation, value for money, fun and a sense of challenge. Conceiving a brand as a cluster of values

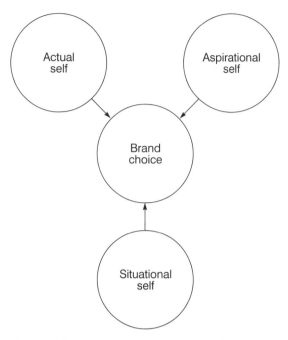

Figure 15.3   Choosing a brand to match self

provides a basis for making the brand different from others. Thus, while there are several brands of off-road four-wheel drive vehicles, Land Rover is distinctive because of its values of individualism, authenticity and freedom.

One of the key reasons for the interest in values is because they influence behaviour, as can be appreciated from Figure 15.4.

As a result of the society and the peer groups people come into regular contact with, so they develop their individual values. These lead to anticipations of particular types of outcomes, albeit varying by situation. For example, someone with the value of honesty may leave their door unlocked because they live in close proximity with neighbours who share the same value, yet when staying in a hotel the door is locked because of uncertainty about the values of other guests. Ultimately though, values affect brand choice.

The challenge managers face when interpreting brands as clusters of values is understanding what values are particularly important

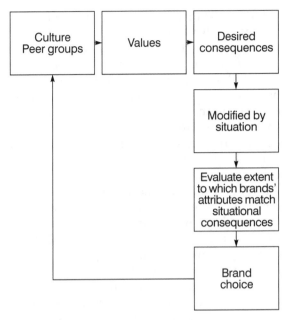

Figure 15.4 How values influence behaviour
Source: Adapted from Gutman, 1982.

to their target market, then ensuring they are able to deliver these. If some staff do not believe in these values, this will show in their behaviour and consumers will change to another brand.

Brand as vision

Another perspective noted about managers' interpretations of brands is akin to a beacon, whose rays provide a clear sense of direction for the traveller. In other words, brands are about a vision senior managers have for making the world a better place. As a result of this vision, a role can be defined for the brand. Within this perspective, brand management is about the senior team taking time to envision a world they want to bring about through their brand. Thus, Apple Mackintosh is about enabling more creativity.

This interpretation is more strategic and takes courage from the brand's team. Gone are incremental extrapolations and instead the team takes time to envision long-term scenarios that they boldly want to bring about through their brand.

Without a well-defined vision, a brand could be in danger of drifting and, when faced with an unforeseen threat, a short-term solution may result which could shift the brand's direction. A good brand vision spurs managers, staff and consumers towards greater things. Nike's consumer advertising campaign, 'You don't win silver. You lose gold', is a good example of the way the brand vision encourages a particular course of action.

Brand as adding value

This perspective on brands is akin to considering the extra benefits over and beyond the basic product or service that are added and which buyers value. These extra benefits could either be functionally based, albeit more difficult to sustain over time, or emotionally based. A functional example is a garage in a commuting town north of London displaying a banner proclaiming, 'We go the extra mile'. They do so through providing an extra service to customers who bring their cars to the garage for maintenance, driving their customers to and from the train station a mile away. By contrast, the Levi jeans owner perceives emotional value in the brand, since wearing these with their peer group, they feel more connected and integrated with the group.

Added value is a relative concept that enables customers to make a purchase on the basis of superiority over competing brands. It can also be judged by customers in terms of how the brand has improved over time, for example the pleasant surprise a car owner experiences when trading in their model for a newer model of the same marque. Interviews with branding consultants (de Chernatony *et al.*, 2000) showed that, unless there has been a breakthrough in technology creating a new market, added values should not be conceived in terms relative to the core commodity form, but rather relative to competition or time.

As a result of the saying 'value is in the eyes of the beholder', if a brand is to thrive, its added values need to be relevant to customers and not just to managers. An engineer may believe they have helped in the branding process by developing a computer chip which repeatedly tells an unbelted car driver 'your belt is not fastened'. Yet to hear of the caravanning enthusiasts saying they would pay to have this removed as it's so irritating when jumping in and out of a car reversing a caravan onto a small pitch at a camp-site provides some indication of its worth to customers!

One way to identify added value opportunities is to accompany customers both on their shopping trip and when they are using the brand. This enables identification of the stages they go through when choosing and using a brand. By then talking with customers about each of the incidents, and getting them to identify what they liked and disliked, how different brands provide different benefits at each of the stages, ideas begin to surface about ways of enhancing the brand.

Brand as identity

Drawing on the International Corporate Identity Group (van Riel and Balmer, 1997), identity is about the ethos, aims and values that present a sense of individuality differentiating a brand. Particularly when the organization brands its offerings with its corporate name, or the brand is strongly endorsed by the corporation, this involves much internal 'soul searching' to understand what the firm stands for and how it can enact the corporate values across all its range. Communication is not directed just at consumers, but also at staff, so that they can appreciate how they must behave to be the embodiment of the brand. For example, the Apple computer company believes in increasing people's productivity through challenging inborn resistance to change. Its corporate identity of the bitten apple epitomizes this – the forbidden fruit with the colours of the rainbow in the wrong order. This perspective of the brand is in sharp contrast to that of the brand as a 'legal instrument' and a 'logo', since the emphasis is on the brand as a holistic entity.

Brand identity can be appreciated from the model shown in Figure 15.5. Central to any brand is its vision, which provides a clear sense of direction about how it is going to bring about a better future. To achieve this stretching future depends on a culture with staff who believe in particular values and managers who have a common mental model about how their market works, and therefore how the brand must be developed. The core thinking behind the brand can now be translated into a positioning strategy, that manifests the brand's functional values and a personality which brings the brand's emotional values to life. Underpinning all of this is a clear understanding amongst staff about the types of relationships they need to have with each other, with customers and other stakeholders to enact the brand's values. If there is a unified form of internal behaviour, the organization can be more confident about presenting the brand to stakeholders with a design and promotional support that differentiates the brand in a manner which stakeholders welcome. Figure 15.5 shows the different interactions between

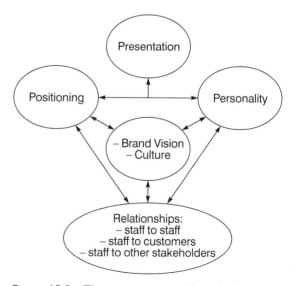

Figure 15.5   The components of brand identity

the five components of a brand's identity and the challenge for managers is to find ways of blending these components to gain maximum internal reinforcement.

This interpretation may help managers reinforce a meaning behind a brand for consumers, and also communicate the essence of the brand to other stakeholders. The concept of brand identity offers the opportunity to develop the brand's positioning better, and encourages a more strategic approach to brand management. A carefully managed identity system also acts as a protective barrier against competitors.

One of the weaknesses of this perspective is that managers focus on the internal aspect of branding, thinking predominantly about the desired positioning. Thought also needs to be given to the way customers perceive the brand, since their perception (brand image) may be different from the intended projection (brand identity). One of the problems with seeking to develop a brand through minimizing the gap between brand identity and brand image is that image refers to a customer's perception at a specific point in time and thus leads to short-term fluctuations. By contrast, reputation relates to perceptions about a brand over time and as a customer-based measure is more stable. Thus, brands could be managed by developing a brand identity, then regularly fine-tuning the brand identity components to minimize the gap with the brand's reputation amongst stakeholders, as shown in Figure 15.6.

Brand as image

People do not react to reality but to what they perceive to be reality. This perspective encourages a more consumer-centred approach to brands as the set of associations perceived by an individual, over time, as a result of direct or indirect experience of a brand. These may be associations with functional qualities, or with individual people or events. It is unlikely for two people to have exactly the same image of a brand (since no two people have the same

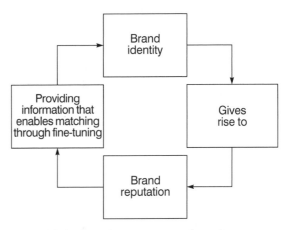

Figure 15.6 Brand management through minimizing gaps

experiences), but their images may have common features. These features constitute, for example, 'the sociable image' of a particular brand of beer.

Adopting an image perspective forces management to face the challenge of consumers' perceptions, i.e. due to their perceptual processes, the sent message is not necessarily understood as was intended. It therefore necessitates checking consumers' perceptions and taking action to encourage favourable perceptions.

Evaluating a brand's image needs to take into consideration customers' levels of involvement with the category (Poiesz, 1989). For those categories where customers are actively involved in spending time and effort seeking out and processing brand information, it has been argued (e.g. Reynolds and Gutman, 1984) that brand image relates to a network of information stored in memory that helps the customer define his or her self. As customers are so involved in the brand selection process it is appropriate to use an involved procedure when measuring brand image, for example means-end chaining. In this approach, customers are first asked what they see as being the difference between the brand in question and a couple of competing brands in the category.

Having elicited a functional attribute, which acts as the anchor point, customers are then asked why such an attribute might be important to them. They are then asked why this reason is important, and through repeatedly probing about why the reason is important, a value emerges. While this takes time to administer, it provides a rich insight into the brand's image.

For low involvement categories, where customers habitually buy the brand, or undertake minimal information searching, brand image is a holistic impression of the brand's position relative to its perceived competitors. To identify the brand's image a low involvement evaluation procedure would be appropriate, for example mental mapping. Customers are asked which brands they believe a particular brand competes against. The brand under attention and the other named brands are then written on cards. These are shuffled and given to the person, who is asked to arrange all the cards on a desk in such a way that those brands perceived to be similar are placed close to each other. After photographing the way the cards were arranged, the respondent is asked to explain their map, and from this insight is provided about the brand's image.

Brand as relationship

The interpretation of a brand as a relationship is a logical extension of the idea of a brand's personality: if brands can be personified, then customers can have relationships with them. Research has shown (e.g. Fournier, 1998) that relationships are purposive and enable both parties to provide meanings. Customers choose brands in part because they seek to understand their self and to communicate aspects of their self to others. Through engaging in a relationship, albeit briefly, customers are able to resolve ideas about their self and, with the brand metaphorically akin to an active member of a dyad, it helps legitimize the customer's thoughts about themselves. Within this perspective managers consider

how the brand's values should give rise to a particular type of relationship.

The interpretation of brands as relationships enables managers to involve staff more in the branding process. Some people find the concept of brand values difficult to understand, but they feel more confident about the idea of describing relationships. One way of getting employees to consider the implications of their brand's values is to use a variant on the party game, 'in the manner of the word'. Members of a department are brought together and someone is asked to leave the room with their manager. That person chooses one of the brand's values and spends a few moments thinking about what this means in terms of the relationship they should be building with their clients to reinforce the brand. They return to the room and in front of their colleagues mime a series of activities. As these are taking place their colleagues shout out the value they think is being enacted and terms to describe the relationship. A facilitator writes on a flip chart what is being shouted and the miming continues until the 'actor' feels someone has correctly mentioned both the value and the relationship implications they are acting. Besides being a fun activity, it surfaces lots of assumptions about the brand's values and relationships. As staff have used their own phrases and their own scenarios, it enables their manager to build on their frames of reference and help them develop more appropriate relationships in their daily working tasks.

When considering what the relationship implications are from the brand's values, it is important to recognize that relationships come about because of reciprocal exchanges between at least two individuals. While the organization may wish to use its brand to develop a close relationship with its customers, they may prefer instead to have a more distant relationship. It is therefore important that, once a relationship has been identified, research be undertaken with customers to evaluate their view about the desired relationship. Through understanding what customers want from a relationship, then revising the

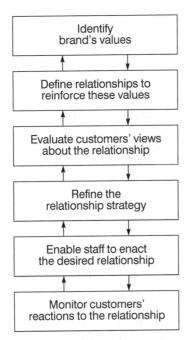

Figure 15.7 The interactive process to develop a relationship which reinforces the brand's values

relationship strategy, there is a greater likelihood of brand success. This process is depicted in Figure 15.7, where a continual process of feedback is used to refine and better develop the brand relationship.

Surface diversity

From the material reviewed in this chapter, it is apparent that there are different interpretations of 'a brand' and if a firm is to ensure its brand thrives, it must encourage members of the brand's team to clarify their assumptions about the nature of their brand. By taking time to surface the taken-for-granted assumptions amongst the brand's team about the nature of their brand, they will be able to appreciate amongst which team members there are conflicting views and then can spend time enabling a consensus to be reached about the nature of the brand. Undertaking this work should contribute to a more coherent branding approach.

A model for strategically building brands

As brand management is a company-wide activity, there may be a lack of integration between different departments. An integrated brand necessitates detailed co-ordination. This can be aided by a planned approach, enabling staff to appreciate the brand objectives and the role they need to play in supporting the brand. Figure 15.8 shows one approach to planning for brand success.

The model is based on an iterative process that forces managers continually to reconsider whether their brand assumptions were appropriate. It is founded on the belief that brand planning should emanate from a multi-disciplinary senior management team. As the

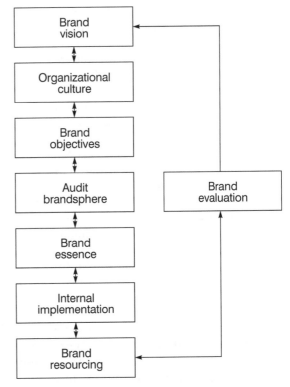

Figure 15.8 The process of building and sustaining brands

management team work through the model, so the emphasis moves from strategy to tactics to implementation. Once a brand has been developed (or an existing brand fine-tuned), instigating a performance monitor ensures that feedback is provided, from which further enhancements can be planned. Each of the blocks in the model will be considered in more detail.

Brand vision

A powerful brand vision indicates the long-term, stretching intent for the brand which must excite staff, encourage their commitment and enable them to interpret how they can contribute to success. Kotter (1996) argues that there are three ways of managing. The first approach is to manage by authoritarian decree, but this gives rise to a fear culture and inhibits staff proposing innovations. The second approach is micro-management, specifying to staff exactly how they should work. This necessitates a notable investment in supervisory staff. The third way is visionary management, which gains staff commitment through everyone believing in the future the firm wants to bring about and people being motivated to find more creative ways of solving problems. This model is based on visionary management.

Developing a brand vision can engender more committed employees if they have been involved in some of the brand visioning workshops. Brand visioning is typically a team-based activity, then involves a process of amending drafts through a combination of analytical thinking and dreaming. It should result in a statement that is simple to understand and can be easily communicated. One of the challenges the senior team have to face when involving staff is that they are raising expectations that staff's views will be incorporated in the final decision. For some cultures, particularly those that are bureaucratic or autocratic, engaging staff in the process may cause senior managers to feel uncomfortable, since they are not used to having their ideas questioned. Some relaxation of control could help these types of organizations to capitalize on staff participation. In an era of greater brand similarity, having a company-wide approach to brand visioning may provide a stronger competitive advantage from staff who are committed to delivering the brand.

There are three components of a brand vision, as Figure 15.9 indicates. The first component, the envisioned future, encourages managers to think about the future environment they would like to bring about 10 years ahead. By saying '10 years ahead', this discourages incremental projections and encourages a more challenging, lateral view about the future. To be appreciated, a brand should bring about *welcomed* change and, by thinking a long way into the future, managers should not consider themselves to be shackled by the current constraints under which they operate. Specifying a long-term horizon encourages managers to think about discontinuities that will result in step changes in the market.

By employing a Delphi technique among the brand's team, different assumptions can be

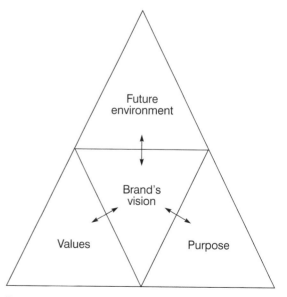

Figure 15.9 The three components of a brand's vision

surfaced about the desired future. Through subsequent workshops, the attractiveness of different futures can be harnessed into a consensus view (Ritchie, 1999). The challenge is to recognize the barrier from managers having entrenched mental models that they are reticent to reassess (Huff, 1990). In this situation, stimulus to change can be helped by drawing on Hamel and Prahalad's (1994) questions:

- Are these managers' ideas based predominantly on information that has circulated within the firm, rather than externally generated information?
- Has their thinking been based predominantly on current and anticipated contracts?

The second component, the brand purpose, considers how the world could be a better place as a consequence of the brand – and will this enthuse and guide staff? A particularly inspirational brand purpose is that of Federal National Mortgage Company, i.e. to strengthen the social fabric of society by democratizing home ownership. A brand purpose must go beyond statements about profitability. Making a profit is taken for granted, just as we must breathe air. The Co-op Bank is a good example of a brand that thinks beyond just making money and seeks to contribute to the world. Nike's purpose is a good example of inspiring staff and customers, i.e. to experience the emotion of competing, winning and crushing competitors.

One way of identifying the brand's purpose is to open a debate within the organization. For example, Oechsle and Henderson (2000) documented how in the early 1990s Shell's CEO encouraged the organization to question the purpose of the Shell brand. This had been around for 100 years, yet had no explicit brand purpose. Thirty-two workshops were undertaken in many countries amongst staff to elicit their views about the brand's purpose. Out of this emerged the purpose of the Shell brand, i.e. helping people build a better world. The intent was to achieve this 'by creating communities of people who relentlessly pursue challenge with

an unwavering commitment to be the best' (p. 76). The route forward became clearer as a result of this exercise. First, the internal programme, 'Count on Shell', was launched to get employees to recognize the need to be able to count on each other. Without a team approach the future would be uncertain and the initiative was strengthened by linking individual and team performance to support behaviours consistent with the brand's purpose. A communication's programme was then devised, which in the first phase was directed at specific publics to inform them of the new campaign. A national campaign was then launched to provoke dialogue on key issues.

Another way of stimulating staff to make explicit their views about the brand's purpose is the 'five whys' method proposed by Collins and Porras (1996). Employees are brought together in a workshop and the facilitator encourages debate around the question: 'We are all involved in producing and delivering this brand. Why is it important?' As each reply is received, and discussed, the facilitator continues to probe 'Why is it important?' After around five rounds of probing, some indication of the brand's purpose should become clear. For example, a market research agency, which had devised a proprietary statistical analysis technique, may argue initially that their brand is important because it provides the best data available. After several rounds of further probing, the purpose of the brand starts to emerge as contributing to customers' success by helping them understand their markets better.

The third component of the brand vision is the brand's values. A particularly clear definition has been advanced by Rokeach (1973), i.e. a value is an enduring belief that a specific mode of conduct or end-state of existence is personally or socially preferable to an opposite or converse mode of conduct or end-state of existence. Values drive staff behaviour as they 'walk the talk', delivering the brand promise. For example, the Red Cross values of humanity, unity and independence motivate staff to go into disaster-stricken areas to help others. They provide the basis for brand differentiation. For example, a different greeting is given by the cabin crew of Virgin Atlantic compared with British Airways, as the first brand relates to fun and the second to being responsible.

Powerful brands are built on a low number of values. One of the reasons for this is that staff find it difficult to remember a large number of values and become unsure about how they should act in particular situations, thereby leading to brand inconsistency. A low number of values also makes it easier for customers to recognize the unique benefits of the brand (Miller, 1956). Alas, regardless of the number of values, some managers espouse values yet act in a contrary manner, reducing staff loyalty (Martin, 1992). Surfacing differences between espoused and enacted values can help ensure greater consistency in brand delivery (Hatch and Schultz, 2001).

As they make explicit their values, some organizations don't differentiate sufficiently between category values and brand values, as depicted in Figure 15.10.

In each market, a brand must have category values as an 'entry price' to compete in that market. To then attract, and repeatedly serve customers, the brand must additionally

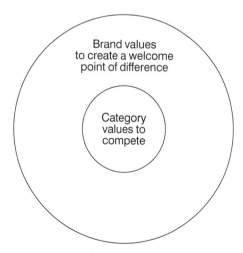

Figure 15.10 The brand as an amalgam of category values and its own unique values

have unique brand values. This may be one of the reasons as to why there are so few successful financial services brands. An examination of financial services advertisements shows many firms majoring on generic category values, such as reliability, security and performance, yet few portray unique brand values.

There are a variety of ways to unearth values. Laddering (Reynolds and Gutman, 1988) is one way and is based on the theory that a brand's attributes have consequences for a person, which in turn reinforce their personal values. It progresses through a facilitator asking an employee to state a key attribute of their firm's brand and, by probing why this is important, a value can be revealed. An alternative is the Mars group method (Collins and Porras, 1996), in which exemplars among staff work together in a group of five people on the challenge of recreating the best of their organization on the planet Mars. By probing to surface their individual beliefs, insights about brand values are revealed.

Organizational culture

One of the components of a powerful vision is the brand's values, and these are recognized as being part of the organization's culture. A clearly understood organizational culture provides a basis for differentiating a brand in a way which is often welcomed by customers. Earlier, it was clarified that a brand can be considered as being a cluster of functional and emotional values. With competitors being able to emulate functional values, a more sustainable route to brand building is through emotional values. In other words, it's not so much *what* the customer receives, but rather *how* they receive it. When two organizations provide similar functional brand benefits, for example Burger King and McDonald's, the discriminator that may influence customers is the way the service is delivered. Organizational cultures are unique and provide a stimulus for staff behaving in ways unique to the organization.

Organizational culture can act as a 'glue' uniting staff in disparate locations to act in a similar manner. It can motivate staff and, through coherence of employees' behaviour, it can help engender a feeling of consistency about a brand. Furthermore, a strong organizational culture can increase the level of trust stakeholders have in a brand, encouraging better brand performance.

Organizational culture can be analysed at three levels (Schein, 1984), as shown in Figure 15.11. The most visible level is to look at the artefacts that reflect an organization's culture. This would include the office layout, manner of dress, the way people talk, any documentation, the firm's technology, etc. While these data are relatively easy to collect, they prove challenging to draw inferences about why a group behaves in a particular way. Seeing an open-plan office layout may indicate the firm's belief in open access to information, but it may also suggest a concern about cutting costs.

A better appreciation of people's behaviour comes through understanding values. However, people can publicly exhort *espoused* values, yet behave in a manner which indicates an additional set of core values. To better understand the concealed reasons for behaviour, there is a need to dig even deeper into the basic assumptions people hold. Individuals have mental maps, or schema (Huff, 1990; Schwenk, 1988), which are the rules they have formed to make sense of their business environment and to

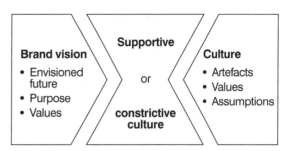

Figure 15.12 Assessing the suitability of the current culture

predict outcomes, given certain factors. For example, some managers might have as their basic assumption that increasing advertising leads to higher levels of awareness and therefore greater sales. By contrast, other managers might have as their basic assumption that advertising works by building a reservoir of goodwill and that all is needed is just to have a continual trickle of expenditure to keep the pressure head of goodwill above a critical level.

By undertaking an audit of the organizational culture, then evaluating this against the brand vision, as shown in Figure 15.12, the appropriateness of the current culture can be assessed and changes identified. One of the problems though is that the shared mental model (cf. assumptions) of managers may engender resistance to change. A period of 'unlearning' (Bettis and Prahalad, 1995) has been suggested by writers, whereby the team is taken away from the office (leaving the incorrectly supporting artefacts) and they work with consultants to recognize the weakness of old assumptions and formulate more appropriate assumptions.

Setting brand objectives

From the brand vision should emerge a sense of direction for the brand. To transform the brand vision into quantified objectives, it may be helpful to think of a two-stage process. A long-term brand objective is set, which is broken down into a series of shorter-term objectives.

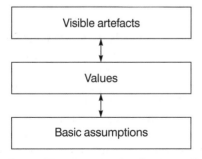

Figure 15.11 The three levels of culture (Schein, 1984)

,hose should sum to the long-term brand objective. For example, British Airways set themselves the long-term brand objective of being the undisputed leader in world travel. They had a series of shorter-term objectives, including delighting customers and having a global network plus a global outlook.

Partly because of organizational bureaucracy, employees' actions become deflected from the central objective and, while a lot of work is done, this makes few strides towards the goal. One way to focus attention on achieving the brand objectives is through catalytic mechanisms (Collins, 1999). These are painful consequences which come into play when an activity is undertaken that does not support the long-term brand objective. For example, Granite Rock had the objective of providing outstanding service. After delivering crushed stones to road building contractors, it presents rather novel invoices. On these are boldly printed a statement that if the customer is not satisfied, they should cross out the sum due, attach a cheque for a lower amount, with a brief note explaining this. Upon receipt of this information, this is rapidly routed to the appropriate managers so they can change matters. To focus everyone's attention on activities critical to achieving the brand objectives, catalytical mechanisms can prove helpful.

Auditing the enhancing/impeding forces

As Figure 15.13 shows, there are five key forces that can enhance or impede a brand. By auditing each of the forces separately, more powerful strategies can be devised which capitalize on the positive forces and circumvent the retarding forces.

Inside the *corporation*, a variety of issues need considering. For example:

- How well are brand building activities being co-ordinated?

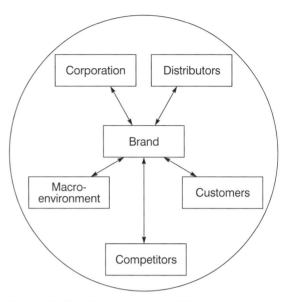

Figure 15.13   The five forces of the brandsphere

- To what extent do employees' values concur with those of the organization and the brand they are working on?
- Do each of the departments' cultures align with the desired organizational culture?
- To what extent do staff understand and feel committed to the brand?
- How appropriate is the brand's heritage in the modern world?
- How strongly do staff identify with the organization and its brands?

Having completed this evaluation of the impact that different corporation factors can have on the brand, the brand's team need to arrive at an overall assessment. After reviewing each of these issues, the team needs to decide whether *overall* they result in the corporation force enhancing or impeding the likelihood of brand success. If it is felt that overall the corporation force enhances the likelihood of brand success, a score of one should be given. However, if this force is thought to impede brand success, it gets a zero score. By forcing this one/zero decision it necessitates the team evaluating whether the *critical issues* overall work for or against the brand.

If a brand goes through *distributors*, some of the following factors need addressing:

- To what extent do the brand's objectives marry with each distributor's objectives?
- Are there some distributors who are using their economic power to demand unreasonably large discounts?
- Does each distributor have a customer profile that matches the desired brand user profile?
- Are all the distributors supporting the brand with the right level of activity?

Once the distributor analysis is completed, a one/zero score needs to be assigned, reflecting whether this force works for or against the brand.

When considering the third force, that of *consumers*, some of the factors to take into consideration include:

- How closely does the brand match consumers' particular needs?
- Does the amount of brand information reflect consumers' involvement in the decision making process?
- To what extent does the brand reduce any perception of risk?
- If there is an expectation of the brand making statements about the consumer, are these the right sorts of associations?

An analysis of the extent to which the consumer force impacts upon the brand enables the brand's team to consider potential changes.

The fourth force that impacts on the well-being of a brand is *competitors*. Some of the issues to assess include:

- the extent to which competitors are differentiated;
- the objectives of competing brands and the impact these might have;
- the strategic direction of competitors;
- the resources backing competitors.

Undertaking an overall assessment, using a zero/one approach, helps appreciate whether or not this force might challenge the brand's growth.

Finally, the macro-environment needs monitoring to appreciate how future political, economic, social and technological changes might impact on the brand.

Brand essence

As the model in Figure 15.8 is followed, analysis becomes combined with creative insights to conceive the core of the brand, ideally summarized in a brief statement about a promise. For example, Hallmark is about caring shared. Creativity and thinking 'out of the box' are critical. For example, while the car breakdown organization, the RAC, used to conceive its brand in terms of providing breakdown services, this was also claimed by the AA, who had a particularly powerful campaign positioning itself as the fourth emergency service. After much analysis, the RAC reconceived itself around managing people's journeys and the brand was repositioned in terms of total mobility and journey management.

One way of deriving the nature of the brand promise is to use the brand pyramid, as shown in Figure 15.14.

When managers devise a new brand, they are initially concerned with finding unexploited gaps in markets, then majoring on their core competencies to devise a brand supported by a novel technology, or process, that delivers unique attributes. However, consumers are less concerned with attributes, e.g. a multifunction remote controller for a video cassette recorder, and more attentive to the benefits from these attributes, e.g. ease of recording a TV programme. With experience, consumers begin to understand the brand better and the benefits lead to emotional rewards. For example, one of the benefits of Emirates Airline, as an early innovator, installing individual TV screens in front of each economy class seat in all their aircraft is in-flight entertainment, leading to the emotional reward of fun during the flight. If the emotional reward is to be appreciated, it must

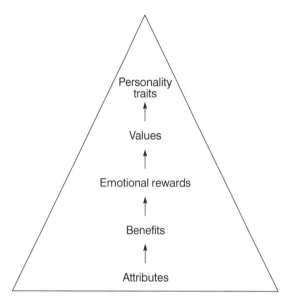

Figure 15.14 Brand pyramid summarizing the nature of the brand promise

lead to a value which is welcomed by consumers. Thus, the emotional reward of fun could lead to the value of autonomy. For these passengers valuing 'what they want to watch when they want to watch', this value of autonomy could be the key reason for some passengers travelling with one airline rather than another. Consumers rarely spend long seeking and interpreting information about brands; therefore, at the top of the pyramid is a personality representing the personality traits associated with the values of the brand. By using a personality who exhibits the traits of the brand to promote the brand, consumers draw inferences that the brand has some of the values of the promoting personality.

One of the benefits of the brand pyramid is simplifying internal communication about the characteristics of the brand. Since consumers' choice decisions are based on a low number of attributes (Miller, 1956), only the three most important attributes are to be included at the base of the pyramid. Once these have been identified from consumer research, the brand's team then need to work together in a workshop

to develop the three 'ladders'. Focusing on the first attribute, the team need to consider what rational benefit this leads to, then what emotional reward arises from this, followed by a debate about which values result and finally what personality traits arise from this value. This laddering is repeated for the other two attributes, resulting in three unique chains. Finally, by then examining the personality traits, the brand's team need to consider which well-known person might represent the elicited personality traits.

There is an advantage of undertaking this work with the brand's team together, rather than as a series of individual exercises. It requires people to 'spark off' each other and a more creative environment results from the team being together, drawing on their diverse backgrounds. Working together as a group, the brand pyramid can stimulate ideas about creatively positioning the brand (from the lower levels of the brand pyramid) and developing the brand's personality (from the upper level of the pyramid).

Internal implementation

To implement the brand essence, a suitable value delivery system is needed to support both the functional and emotional aspects of the brand. By focusing first on the functional aspects of the brand, value chain analysis (Porter, 1985) enables a production flow process to be instigated, and for services brands, a services blueprint (Zeithaml and Bitner, 1996) captures the operational flow process. By referring back to the brand essence, an appropriate balance can be struck between outsourcing some activities and keeping others in-house to strengthen the firm's core competencies (Quinn and Hilmer, 1994).

The emotional values of the brand can be supported by recruiting staff according to the extent to which their personal values align with the brand's values (Kunde, 2000). A further way of engendering employee commitment is to encourage some degree of empowerment, which is increasingly common (Buchanan and

Huczynski, 1997). To decide upon the level of empowerment, consideration must be given to the brand's values, the organization's culture, the business strategy and the types of staff (Bowen and Lawler, 1992).

An outcome from the mechanistic and humanistic components of the value delivery system is that it engenders a unique relationship between customers and the brand. As thinking becomes more refined in the flow model of Figure 15.8, so eventually a genuine relationship of trust and respect should emerge, bonding customers to the brand. Alas, some organizations have become overly attached to the cost savings from IT. There still remains a need for some staff interaction with customers, even just having an empathetic telephone helpline team, otherwise the firm is erecting barriers impeding bonding between consumers and its brands (Pringle and Gordon, 2001).

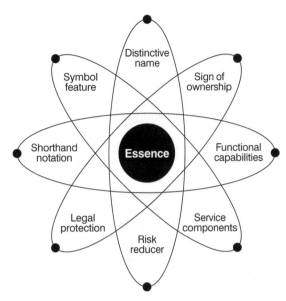

Figure 15.15   The atomic model of the brand

Brand resourcing which characterizes the brand

Just as the marketing mix enables a marketing strategy to be enacted, so the atomic model, shown in Figure 15.15, enables the brand essence to be realized.

There are eight components that can be used to characterize the brand essence. Progressing in a clockwise manner, the first two components relate to brand naming. To what extent is the brand's name going to exhibit the name of the company owning it (sign of ownership) and to what extent will the brand have the freedom to bear its unique name (distinction name)? The functional capability component summarizes the functional advantages of the brand, for example performance, reliability and aesthetics. Provision needs to be made for after-sales service, through the service components. Engendering consumer confidence by allaying particular worries is the task which the risk reducer component addresses. Questions to be resolved here include the extent to which the brand should major on reducing performance risk or time risk, or

social risk, or financial risk. The legal protection component focuses on providing the brand with rights to prosecute counterfeiters. The shorthand notation component forces the brand's team to simplify the brand presentation so there is more emphasis on quality, rather than quantity, of information. Finally, the symbol feature component considers how the brand's values can be brought to life through associations with a personality or lifestyle.

Brand evaluation

By following the flow chart in Figure 15.8, there is a greater likelihood of developing an integrated brand which is respected by all stakeholders. Brands are complex multidimensional entities and thus to use just one measure, e.g. sales, gives a superficial evaluation of brand performance.

Instead, brand metrics are needed that monitor the suitability of the internal supporting systems, along with the external favourability of the brand's essence and the degree of satisfaction generated by the eight components of the brand.

e nature of the brand metric will depend on the ideas that emerged from the model in Figure 15.8, as the nature of the brand emerged. By revisiting the decisions that were made by the brand team as they progressed through the planning process of Figure 15.8, a monitoring system can be developed which addresses issues such as:

Brand vision

● What progress is being made to bring about a welcomed envisioned future?
● To what extent is the brand making its market domain a better place?
● How much do stakeholders recognize and appreciate the brand's values?

Organizational culture

● How well do the artefacts, values and assumptions of the organizational culture support the brand vision?
● Are there any damaging internal counter subcultures?
● How appropriate is the organizational culture for the environment?

Brand objectives

● How aware and committed are staff to achieving the brand's objectives?
● To what extent is the brand under- or over-achieving on its objectives?

Brand essence

● How aware are staff of the elements of the brand pyramid and how committed are they to delivering the inherent brand promise?
● How well do consumers' perceptions of the brand pyramid match the planned pyramid?

Implementation and brand resourcing

● How appropriate is the value delivery system for the brand?

● How aware are stakeholders of the brand?
● What degree of commitment do stakeholders have for the brand?
● Do stakeholders perceive any conflicts between the brand's promise and their experiences with the brand?

Through undertaking regular monitors of a brand's health, the brand's team is better equipped to refine their thinking as they continue the cyclical process around the brand building model shown in Figure 15.8.

Summary

This chapter has sought to provide the reader with knowledge about two critical topics in brand management, i.e. characterizing interpretations about the concept of brands and providing a model which encourages a more integrated approach to brand building. Brands are valuable intangible assets. It is their intangible nature that necessitates all members of the brand's team to be clear about what they understand as being the defining characteristics of their brand. Time spent surfacing individual views about the nature of a team's brand is time well spent, since it enables everyone to not only understand the brand, but also helps them to appreciate how they can better contribute to the success of the brand.

The brand planning model shows how a logical, iterative process can be employed to focus thinking about brand building. Brand management is about understanding consumers and staff. Brand promises are delivered by staff, and unless they understand and are committed to delivering brand benefits, they are unlikely to give the brand the support it demands. Brand building is a pan-company activity and the model enables a greater likelihood of a more coherent brand. By deliberately encouraging managers to adopt a visionary approach, not only do the resulting brands represent a clear sense of direction, but they also can more rapidly refine their supporting strategy when faced with greater competitive challenges.

The material covered in this chapter is addressed in far more detail in the author's book, *From Brand Vision to Brand Evaluation* (2001), published by Butterworth-Heinemann.

References

Bauer, R. (1960) Consumer behaviour as risk taking, in Hanckok, R. (ed.), *Dynamic Marketing for a Changing World*, American Marketing Association, Chicago, pp. 389–398.

Bettis, R. and Prahalad, C. K. (1995) The dominant logic: retrospective and extension, *Strategic Management Journal*, **16**(1), 5–14.

Bettman, J. (1979) *An Information Processing Theory of Consumer Choice*, Addison-Wesley, Reading, MA.

Blackett, T. (1998) *Trademarks*, Macmillan, Basingstoke.

Bowen, D. and Lawler, E. (1992) The empowerment of service workers: what, why, how and when, *Sloan Management Review*, **33**(3), 31–39.

Buchanan, D. and Huczynski, A. (1997) *Organisational Behaviour*, Prentice-Hall, Hemel Hempstead.

Collins, J. (1999) Turning goals into results: the power of catalytic mechanisms, *Harvard Business Review*, July–August, 70–82.

Collins, J. and Porras, J. (1996) Building your company's vision, *Harvard Business Review*, September–October, 65–77.

de Chernatony, L. (2001) *From Brand Vision to Brand Evaluation*, Butterworth-Heinemann, Oxford.

de Chernatony, L. and Dall'Olmo Riley, F. (1998) Defining a 'brand': beyond the literature with experts' interpretations, *Journal of Marketing Management*, **14**(5), 417–443.

de Chernatony, L., Harris, F. and Dall'Olmo Riley, F. (2000) Added value: its nature, roles and sustainability, *European Journal of Marketing*, **34**(1/2).

Fournier, S. (1998) Consumers and their brands: developing relationship theory in consumer research, *Journal of Consumer Research*, **25**(4), 343–373.

Garvin, D. (1987) Competing on the eight dimensions of quality, *Harvard Business Review*, November–December, 101–109.

Gutman, J. (1982) A means–end chain model based on consumer categorization processes, *Journal of Research*, **46** (Spring), 60–72.

Hamel, G. and Prahalad, C. K. (1994) *Competing For The Future*, Harvard Business School Press, Boston.

Hatch, M. J. and Schultz, M. (2001) Are the strategic signs aligned for your corporate brand?, *Harvard Business Review*, February, 1–8.

Huff, A. (1990) *Mapping Strategic Thought*, Wiley, New York.

Ind, N. (1998) An integrated approach to corporate branding, *Journal of Brand Management*, **5**(5), 323–332.

Jacoby, J., Szybillo, G. and Busato-Sehach, J. (1977) Information acquisition behaviour in brand choice situations, *Journal of Consumer Research*, **3**, March, 209–216.

Jacoby, J., Chestnut, R. and Fisher, W. (1978) A behavioural process approach to information acquisition in nondurable purchasing, *Journal of Marketing Research*, **15**(3), 532–544.

Kapferer, J.-N. (1995) Stealing brand equity: measuring perceptual confusion between national brands and 'copycat own labels', *Marketing and Research Today*, **23**, May, 96–103.

Kotter, J. (1996) *Leading Change*, Harvard Business School Press, Boston, Ma.

Kunde, J. (2000) *Corporate Religion*, Pearson Education, Harlow.

Lomax, W., Sherski, E. and Todd, S. (1999) Assessing the risk of consumer confusion: some practical test results, *Journal of Brand Management*, **7**(2), 119–132.

Martin, J. (1992) *Cultures in Organizations: Three Perspectives*, Oxford University Press, Oxford.

Miller, G. (1956) The magic number seven plus

or minus two: some limits on our capacity for processing information, *Psychological Review*, **63**(2), 81–97.

Mitchell, A. (1997) *Brand Strategies in the Information Age*, Financial Times Business, London.

Oechsle, S. and Henderson, T. (2000) Identity: an exploration into purpose and principles at Shell, *Corporate Reputation Review*, **3**(1), 75–77.

Parasuraman, A., Zeithaml, V. and Berry, L. (1988) SERVQUAL: a multiple item scale for measuring consumer perceptions of service quality, *Journal of Retailing*, **64**(1), 12–40.

Poiesz, T. (1989) The image concept: its place in consumer psychology, *Journal of Economic Psychology*, **10**, 457–472.

Porter, M. (1985) *Competitive Advantage*, Free Press, New York.

Pringle, H. and Gordon, W. (2001) *Brand Manners*, Wiley, Chichester.

Quinn, J. and Hilmer, F. (1994) Strategic outsourcing, *Sloan Management Review*, **35**(4), 43–55.

Reynolds, T. and Gutman, J. (1984) Advertising is image management, *Journal of Advertising Research*, **24**, 27–37.

Reynolds, T. and Gutman, J. (1988) Laddering theory, method, analysis and interpretation, *Journal of Advertising Research*, **28**, February–March, 11–31.

Ries, A. and Trout, J. (1986) *Positioning: The Battle for Your Mind*, McGraw-Hill, New York.

Ritchie, J. (1999) Crafting a value-driven vision for a national treasure, *Tourism Marketing*, **20**(3), 273–82.

Rokeach, M. (1973) *The Nature of Human Values*, Free Press, New York.

Schein, E. (1984) Coming to a new awareness of organisational culture, *Sloan Management Review*, Winter, 3–16.

Schlesinger, L. and Heskett, J. (1991) Enfranchisement of service workers, *California Management Review*, Summer, 83–100.

Schultz, M., Hatch, M. J. and Larsen, M. (eds) (2000) *The Expressive Organization*, Oxford University Press, Oxford.

Schwenk, C. (1988) *The Essence of Strategic Decision Making*, Lexington Books, Lexington.

van Riel, C. and Balmer, J. (1997) Corporate identity: the concept, its measure and management, *European Journal of Marketing*, **31**(5/6), 340–355.

Zeithaml, V. and Bitner, M. (1996) *Services Marketing*, McGraw-Hill, New York.

Further reading

de Chernatony, L. (2001) *From Brand Vision to Brand Evaluation*, Butterworth-Heinemann, Oxford.

de Chernatony, L. and McDonald, M. (1998) *Creating Powerful Brands*, Butterworth-Heinemann, Oxford.

Ind, N. (2001) *Living the Brand*, Kogan Page, London.

Jones, R. (2001) *The Big Idea*, Harper Collins Business, London.

Kunde, J. (2000) *Corporate Religion*, Pearson Education, Harlow.

Pringle, H. and Gordon, W. (2001) *Brand Manners*, Wiley, Chichester.

CHAPTER 16

The integration of marketing communications

TONY YESHIN

Recent years have seen significant changes in the way that marketing communications campaigns have been developed and implemented. In the 1960s and 1970s, the primary source for the development of all forms of marketing communications activity was the advertising agency. At that time, separate departments within the agency provided their clients with advice in all of the appropriate areas.

Since then, two strands of change have taken place. First, the wider appreciation of the techniques themselves and the need for specialist personnel to develop them have both resulted in the creation of specialist companies which deal with specific areas of marketing communications. The consequence has been a progressive fragmentation of provisions within the area. Initially, there was an emergence of specialists in each of the major fields of marketing communications, in areas such as sales promotion, public relations, direct marketing and so on.

Today, that specialism has been taken even further. Companies which deal with e-marketing, product placement, the organization of trade and consumer events, sponsorship activities and so on now abound. Individual specialist companies can now provide clients with inputs in areas such as the design and production of point-of-sale materials, the creation of trade and consumer incentives, pack design and guerrilla marketing techniques, amongst many others. Even in the mainstream areas, agencies have become specialized in terms of youth or grey marketing, FMCG or retail marketing communications, dealing with pharmaceutical products or travel and tourism. And the specialisms continue.

Second, and in contradiction, there has been an increasing tendency for this wide variety of specialists to provide inputs which encompass a range of executional devices. Today, several different companies will have the ability and expertise to develop campaigns utilizing a wide range of marketing communications formats. Moreover, few marketing communications campaigns utilize a single component or element. Rather, marketers will tend to employ several different devices which, previously, were the domain of dedicated and specialist companies.

The consequence has been a distinct blurring of the divisions between previous specialist practitioner areas.

Discipline overlap is blurring long standing distinctions. It's becoming increasingly difficult to categorize work as sales promotion or direct marketing. Most direct marketing offers contain some form of sales promotion or vice versa. And with the growth of direct response press and TV advertising, direct marketing is moving closer to conventional advertising.

(Cook, 1994)

of customers as individuals in order to appreciate their perceptions, expectations, needs and wants. The increasing availability of tools to enable the marketer to achieve this deeper understanding of the consumer similarly demands the re-evaluation of the ways in which the tools employed to communicate with those consumers are used.

The strategic challenges facing organizations

Marketing and, for that matter, marketing communications are being readdressed by major corporations to determine the values which they derive from the adoption of their principles. Indeed, the very nature of these principles is being challenged and re-evaluated to determine their relevance to the challenges being faced by companies at the start of the new millennium.

Nilson (1992) suggested that marketing had 'lost its way'. Despite employing high-quality management, organizations have in many instances seemed unable to face the challenges which they face in the broader environment. Growth has come more from acquisition than brand development. The consequence of chasing niche markets has been the continued and growing failure of new products to attract substantial and profitable audiences. The continued growth of private label products in a wide variety of market sectors evidences the fact that retailers are often more successful in their identification and satisfaction of consumer needs. New and innovative competitors have stolen share from the large multinational FMCG companies, despite their comparatively smaller scale, which should have precluded their entry into the market.

The essential requirement of the 'new marketing' approach is the development of a close customer focus throughout the organization which, in turn, demands an understanding

Strategic marketing communications

Schultz *et al.* (1992) argue that marketing communications often present the only differentiating feature that can be offered to potential consumers. By recognizing the fact that everything a company does comprises, in some form, part of the communication which takes place between itself and its customers, it becomes aware of the increasingly important role of marketing communications as a strategic tool.

Just as the premise of the 'new marketing' places the consumer at the centre of all activity, so too must marketing communications be considered from the essential perspective of understanding consumer behaviour. This implies a consideration of more than just the content of the message itself. Close attention needs to be paid to the context of the message (the vehicle used to communicate with the target audience), as well as the timing and tone of the message. The underlying imperative is the need for an identification of clear, concise and measurable communications objectives which will enable the selection of the appropriate communications tools to achieve the tasks set.

By developing an understanding of the identity of the consumer, and their particular needs and wants, we can determine the nature of the behaviour which the communications programme will need to reinforce or change. And, in turn, the specific nature of the message which will affect that behaviour, and the means by which we can reach them.

The strategic role that marketing communications can play is increasingly evidenced by the impact of specific campaigns. These not only affect the way in which consumers think about the particular products and services which are offered to them, but the very way in which they consider the categories in which those products and services exist.

The integration of marketing communications

A major contemporary issue in the field of marketing communications is the drive towards integrated activity. There are a number of reasons for this fundamental change of thinking which need to be examined.

The marketing methods businesses used in the 1980s are no longer working and have lost their value as competitive weapons, such as the constant focus on new products, generic competitive strategies, promotional pricing tactics, and so on. Today's marketing environment has been described as an age of 'hyper-competition' in which there exists a vast array of products and services, both new and variations on existing themes. A casual look in the supermarket will confirm this view. Take, for example, the 'cook-in-sauce' sector. The variety available to the consumer is little short of mind blowing, whole fitments devoted to ethnic and other varieties, with each product replicated by several different brands.

Many of the fastest growing markets are rapidly becoming saturated with large numbers of competitors. And each competitor has similar technology. The consequence is that, as Schultz *et al*. (1995) put it, sustainable competitive advantage has been eroded away. In many categories, new products and services are copied in days or weeks rather than years. And, significantly, anything a company can do, someone else can do it cheaper.

Consumers are searching for more than a single element in any transaction. Instead, they seek to buy into the array of relevant experiences which surround the brand. Successful marketing in the 1990s required total consumer orientation. This means communication with the individual, creating long-term relationships, quality driven, and the aim is customer satisfaction, not just volume and share.

Many writers on the subject, most notably Schultz (1999), argue that integrated marketing communications (IMC) is the natural evolution of mass market media advertising towards targeted direct marketing. Schultz sees IMC as a logical and natural progression within the field of marketing communications. As he describes: 'it appears to be the natural evolution of traditional mass-media advertising, which has been changed, adjusted and refined as a result of new technology'. This author concurs with those who believe that IMC is significantly more than 'merely a management fashion' as attested by Cornellisen *et al*. (2000). Many companies strive to achieve total integration of their marketing communications efforts, recognizing the undeniable benefits which derive from the practice, not least of which is the ability to deliver consistency in their messages to their target audiences.

Integration, however, is not a new phenomenon, as the following quote from J. Walter Thompson in 1899 illustrates:

> We make it our business as advertising agents to advise on the best methods of advertising, in whatever form ... as the best combination of work, such as we give, is the cheapest, as it brings the best results.

Defining integrated marketing communications

Much debate surrounds the very nature of integrated marketing communications (IMC), with the consequence that several alternative definitions have been proposed. Cornellisen *et al*. (2000) argue that one of the problems with the interpretation of IMC is the lack of a consensus decision as to what the phrase actually means in practice. They point to the fact that various writers have argued about the move away from the traditional distinction between 'above-the-line' and 'below-the-line' to 'through-the-line' and 'zero-based' communications. What they fail to recognize is that the practitioners within the field operate as brands and seek to provide a distinctive offering to their clients. Hence the adoption of a variety of nomenclatures for the practice of IMC.

They argue that the theoretical concept of IMC is ambiguous and 'provides the basis for researchers to adopt whichever interpretation of the term best fits their research agendas at any given time'.

According to Schultz and Kitchen (1997), prior to the study by Caywood *et al.* (1991), there was no formal discussion or even description of what is now called integrated marketing communications. There appears to be a discordancy between academic thinking and practice in the marketplace. They argue that most marketing communications activities in the past have focused on breaking down concepts and activities into even more finite specialisms. Few marketing communications approaches have involved integration or holistic thinking. Whilst it is acknowledged that the pace of change towards the adoption of a holistic approach has been relatively slow, nonetheless many practitioners and clients have moved progressively towards a focus on IMC.

Schultz (in Jones, 1999) defines IMC as 'a planning approach that attempts to co-ordinate, consolidate and bring together all the communications messages, programmes and vehicles that affect customers or prospects for a manufacturer or service organization's brands'.

Jeans (1998) provides greater clarity by proposing that 'IMC is the implementation of all marketing communications in such a way that each project, as well as meeting its specific project objects also

- conforms with the brand platform;
- is synergistic with all other projects related to the brand;

- actively reinforces the agreed brand values in any dialogue with the market;
- and is measured by short- and long-term effects on consumer behaviour.'

However, perhaps the clearest definition of integrated marketing communications is that of the American Association of Advertising Agencies (1993):

 A concept of marketing communications planning that recognizes the added value of a comprehensive plan that evaluates the strategic roles of a variety of communications disciplines and combines them to provide clarity, consistency and maximum communications impact through the seamless integration of discrete messages.

The important dimension of this definition is the recognition of the need for a *comprehensive* plan that considers the strategic aspects of each of the tools of marketing communications in a holistic manner, rather than the development of them as separate elements. This approach represents a substantial shift in the underlying planning process, since it aims to ensure cohesion and the delivery of a single-minded message to the target audience.

Paul Smith (writing in *Admap*, 1996) states:

Integrated marketing communications is a simple concept. It brings together all forms of communication into a seamless solution. At its most basic level, IMC integrates all promotional tools so that they work together in harmony.

Key to the issue is the fact that the consumer does not see advertising, public relations, sales promotion and other marketing communications techniques as separate and divisible components. As the receivers of a variety of messages from an equally wide range of sources, they build up an image of a company, its brands and its services – both favourable and unfavourable. As far as they are concerned, the source of the message is unimportant. What they will be concerned with is the content of the message.

> A surge of interest by marketers in integrated communications strategies, where promotional messages are co-ordinated among advertising, public relations and sales promotion efforts, brings with it the implicit acknowledgement that consumers assimilate data about popular culture from many sources.
>
> (Solomon and Englis, 1994)

Equally, according to Lannon (1994):

> Consumers receive impressions of brands from a whole range of sources – first hand experience, impressions of where it can be bought, of people who use it or people who do not, from its role in cultural mores or rituals, from movies, literature, television, editorial, news, fashion, from its connections with events and activities and finally from paid advertising media.

A parallel consideration is the fact that the communicator desires to achieve a sense of cohesion in the messages which he communicates. If, for example, advertising is saying one thing about a brand and sales promotion something different, a sense of dissonance may be created, with the consumer left in some confusion as to what the brand is really trying to say.

There is little doubt that marketing communications funds spent on a single communications message will achieve a far greater impact than when a series of different or contradictory messages are being sent out by the brand. And, with the pressure on funds, marketers desire to ensure that they are presenting a clear and precise picture of their products and services to the end consumer.

Few companies are specifically concerned with issues of whether to spend their money on advertising, sales promotion, public relations or elsewhere. They are concerned with ensuring that they develop a cohesive marketing communications programme which most effectively communicates their proposition to the end consumer. The particular route of communication is far less important than the impact of the message. And, in budgetary terms, companies need to consider where their expenditure will best achieve their defined objectives. The previous notions of separate and distinct advertising, sales promotion, public relations, and other budgets fails to appreciate that the considerations of the overall marketing communications budget need to be addressed as a matter of priority.

However, at the heart of the debate is the recognition that the consumer must be the focus of all marketing communications activity. If we consider the Chartered Institute of Marketing's definition of marketing, we can see that the primary need is the anticipation and satisfaction of consumer wants and needs. It is the development of an understanding of the consumer and his or her wants and needs that will ensure that marketing communications works effectively to achieve the objectives defined for it. This represents a fundamental change of focus. A shift from the functional activity of creating marketing communications campaigns to an attitudinal focus in which the consumer's needs are at the heart of all marketing communications planning. And, with it, a change from a focus from the product itself to the ultimate satisfaction of the end consumer. Of course, there are functional implications. Above all else, there is an increasing recognition that companies need to identify what position their product or service occupies in the minds of the consumer relative to that of other products or services. Only when they have gained that knowledge can they begin the process of planning marketing communications, either to alter or enhance that position:

> As choice becomes an ever greater factor for consumers, both in the products they use and the way they learn about those products, it is increasingly clear that no marketer can rely on advertising alone to deliver its message. Integration permits us to focus the power of all

messages. It holds the greatest, most exciting promise for the future.

George Schweitzer, Senior Vice President,
Marketing and Communications,
CBE's Broadcast Group

The impact of external factors on marketing communications

External and environmental factors have forced marketers to undertake a fundamental rethink both of marketing strategies and the positioning of products, and this, in turn, must impact on the process of marketing communications.

Information overload

The consumer is continuously bombarded with vast quantities of information. According to Dan O'Donoghue (1997), whereas the average consumer was subjected to about 300 commercial messages a day in 1995, today that figure has risen to around 3000. Whether the information is orchestrated by the marketer or the media in general is less relevant than the fact that there is simply too much information for the average consumer to process effectively. The inevitable consequence is that much of the material is simply screened out and discarded. The result is that the consumer may make purchasing decisions based on limited knowledge, or even a misunderstanding of the real facts. The individual is far less concerned with the average advertising message, which makes the task of ensuring appropriate communications with the target audience an even more daunting prospect.

An important dimension of the screening process is what I have described elsewhere as the 'submarine mentality'. In essence, since none of us can absorb all of the information around us, we establish personal defence mechanisms to screen out unwanted or irrelevant information. The analogy would be that of a submarine which goes underwater and, hence,

avoids the surface bombardment. At periodic intervals, the submarine lifts its periscope to examine particular aspects of the world around it. And when it has finished gathering the new information, it descends again – oblivious to any changes which might be taking place.

As consumers, our awareness of specific advertising messages is treated in a similar way. Some form of trigger mechanism is usually required to encourage us to pay attention to the variety of marketing communications messages. Usually, this is an internal recognition of an unfulfilled need which heightens the levels of awareness of pertinent advertising and other information. The principle can be commonly observed. If, for example, you have recently purchased a new car, your awareness of the marque will be enhanced and you will immediately become aware of similar vehicles all around you.

However, in the process of attempting to find better and more effective ways of communicating, we have also gained a greater appreciation of the nature of marketing communications itself. Much work has been done in the area of model construction and theoretical examination which has helped us to enhance areas of implementation.

The discerning consumer

Recent decades have seen the progressive improvement in levels of education which, in turn, has made consumers both more demanding concerning the information they receive and more discerning in their acceptance of it. Marketing communications propositions developed in the 1950s and 1960s would be treated with disdain by today's more aware consumers. Specious technical claims and pseudo-scientific jargon, which were at the heart of many product claims, are no longer given quite the same credence.

This change is reflected in the comment of Judy Lannon (1994): 'Consumers have changed from being deferential and generalized to personal and selective'. She argues that we need to re-examine the way in which consumers use sources of commercial information. A particular issue to be addressed is, as she describes it, the 'credibility dimension', which involves not only the underlying credibility of the message, but the credibility of the sponsor delivering the message.

A contradiction

The inability to store and process new information, coupled with the demand for a greater focus in marketing communications messages, has resulted in the consumer relying more on perceptual values than on factual information. All consumers build up a set of 'values' which they associate with a company or a brand. Some of these values will be based on personal experience, or the experience of others. Much of it will be based, however, on a set of 'short handed conclusions' based on overheard opinions, the evaluation of third party organizations, even the misinterpretation of information. These two factors combine to create a new dynamic for marketing communications.

However, these thought processes are developed, and however the information is received is less important than the fact that for the individual their views represent the truth. A product which is perceived to be inferior (even though there is factual evidence to contradict this view) is unlikely to be chosen in a normal competitive environment. The imperative, therefore, is to understand the process of perceptual encoding and relate it to the task of marketing communications. A simple example will suffice.

Most consumers are responsive to a 'bargain' proposition. And certain assumptions are made, particularly in relation to well-known and familiar brands. If a potential consumer sees a product on sale in a market environment, there is some expectation that the price will be lower than, say, in the normal retail environment. If the brand name is well established, then it is likely that they will be able to draw from it the confidence and reassurance which

will be necessary to the making of a purchase decision. Indeed, there is considerable evidence that these perceptual factors, influenced by the environment, will for some consumers induce them to make a purchase, even though they might have been able to purchase the same product at a lower price elsewhere.

Many retailers have recognized this situation and have adopted a positioning relative to their competitors of low price. By marking down the prices of a narrow range of products, they encourage the consumer to believe that all products are similarly discounted. The result is that the consumer will decide to make all of his or her purchases at that outlet based on the perceptions derived from a limited comparison of those brands upon which the retailer has focused marketing communications activity. Since few consumers are in a position to make objective comparisons across a wide range of comparable outlets, these perceptions are accepted and become the reality.

The situation is compounded by the fact that price is only one consideration in a purchase decision. Most people have an ideal view of a price and quality combination. Needless to say, such a view is highly personal and subjective, but becomes the basis of making subsequent purchase decisions for that individual. Thus, reputation, both for retailers and brands, will be an important consideration in the purchase selection.

Changes in family composition

Long gone are the notions of the family comprising two adults and 2.4 children.

In all countries, the notion of family itself has different meanings. Some communities perceive the family as a small integrated unit, others adopt a model of the extended family with the elder children having responsibility for ageing members of the family – either parents or grandparents. The increasing levels of divorce and the growing acceptance, by some, that marriage is not a norm to which they wish to comply has resulted in growing numbers of single parent families. In all these situations, their needs and expectations will be substantially different from each other, and effective marketing communications need to recognize and respond to these underlying changes in society.

The ageing population

In many countries, the improved standards of living and better health care have resulted in two parallel changes. On the one hand, in order to sustain living standards, people are deferring having children or are having fewer of them. On the other, life expectancy is improving as medical care is enhanced. These forces have resulted in a progressively ageing population in most developed markets. And with it, a change in the values, needs and wants which consumers exhibit about products and services.

The green imperative

Increasing numbers of consumers are concerned with the environmental impact of the products and services they consume. The abandonment of cfcs, the reduction in the volume of packaging waste, the consumption of scarce and irreplaceable resources, and similar factors have all impacted on the consumer's perceptions of desirable products and services.

No longer is the single focus of their attention the efficacy or otherwise of the products they might buy. They require reassurance that not only do the products perform in the way that they expect, but they also contribute to a better environment.

The changing face of media and the growth of narrow casting

The advent of an increased number of media channels – land based, cable and satellite television, an increasing number of radio networks, and a mammoth explosion in the number of 'specialist' magazine titles – has resulted in a fundamental shift in terms of media planning. Where once the advertiser had to recognize that the use of a chosen medium might, whilst providing excellent coverage of the desired target audience, carry with it a substantial wastage factor, the situation has now changed somewhat. Consumer groups can be targeted with a far higher level of precision. A specific message can be developed to appeal to a subgroup of users accessed by the nature of the television programmes they watch or the magazines they read. And the increasing use of direct marketing techniques has resulted in the possibility of one-to-one marketing – where the proposition can be tailored specifically to respond to the individual needs of the single consumer.

> Mass media advertising dominated marketing communications for decades; however, the nineties have seen companies place a greater emphasis on alternative communications mediums.
>
> (Lannon, 1996)

Most people are aware of the increasing fragmentation of media channels. However, perhaps more importantly, there is a wide variety of new channels of communication which can be used by brand owners to communicate with potential consumers and others – postcards, mobile Internet, till receipts, fuel pumps, hoardings around sports grounds and product placement, to name but a few. Research must be capable of monitoring the impact and ability of all of these communications channels to influence the 'viewer'.

Franz (2000) argues that the proliferation of new media adds complexity to the media landscape, since these new media channels rarely replace old media. Rather, they tend to complement each other. What is significant is the way that media are used. Consumers tend to be more selective in their use of media, both because of time and money. The consequence is that media selection tends to be more specific than ever before.

The growth of global marketing

The changes brought about, substantially, by mass communications have, to some degree, encouraged the movement towards global marketing. With the recognition that national and cultural differences are growing ever fewer, major manufacturers have seized upon the opportunity to 'standardize' their marketing across different markets.

It is now possible to purchase an ostensibly similar product with the same name, same identity and similar product ingredients in many different markets. From the ubiquitous Coca-Cola, now available in almost every different country, to products like the Mars bar, manufacturers are seizing the opportunity to ensure a parity of branding throughout all of the markets they serve, and to extend the territories in which they operate. The latter company has unified its branding of the Marathon bar to Snickers and Opal Fruits to Starburst to achieve international parity. Similarly, Unilever recently consolidated the various names of Jif and Vif into Cif for the same reasons.

There are few markets (although the product contents may well be different) which would not recognize the Nescafé coffee label or what it stands for. The big M means McDonald's in any language, and Gillette run the same copy platform for its series range of male shaving preparations in many different countries.

Non-verbal communications

We have already seen that the emergence of new media has enabled a more precise focus on target groups of consumers. But it has also demanded a new approach to the execution of marketing communications propositions, particularly on television.

Increasingly, satellite channels are unrestricted in their availability. The same programmes can be watched simultaneously in France and Finland, Germany and Greece. And, if that is true of the programming, it is equally true of the advertising contained within. Whilst programmers have the opportunity to overcome language and other barriers to communication within their formats, the same is not so readily true for the advertiser.

The response has been a growth in the recognition that visual communication has a vital role to play in the overall process. Increasing numbers of television commercials are being made with a pan-European or global audience in mind. The emphasis is less on the words being used than the impact of the visual treatments employed.

Currently, a constant visual treatment is being utilized by Gillette to support their Series range of products across diverse markets. Here, the voice-over is modified to verbalize the proposition in each marketplace. In fact, the company has adopted an integrated approach for their six-year-old campaign embracing everything the company does. 'It is a much more single minded strategic platform for the brand,' according to Bruce Cleverly, General Manager for Gillette Northern Europe, 'It is the strategic premise of the entire Gillette grooming business'.

Other companies have gone considerably further. The verbal component of the proposition has been minimized, with the storyline being developed entirely, or almost so, in visual form. Television commercials for Dunlop, Levi's and Perrier are examples of this approach.

Speed of information access

Not only has the growth of information technology meant that information can be processed more rapidly, it has also meant that access to that information can be made far more speedily than at any time in the past. This has significant import for the marketer.

Census information, which was previously tabulated by hand or on comparatively slow computers – and which was substantially out of date by the time it was made available – is now available within a relatively short period of time. Marketers can determine with far greater precision than at any time in the past the likely audience for their propositions, and can more readily segment markets into groups of users, rather than communicating with them as an aggregation.

At the same time, of course, this improved level of communication has a direct impact on the consumer. An increased level of media coverage of consumer-related issues means that any problem with a product or service is almost bound to receive media exposure. News stories about product withdrawals, the focus on product deficiencies within programmes like *Watchdog*, all ensure that large groups of consumers become aware of these issues within days, or even hours of the occurrence.

The driving forces behind the growth of integrated marketing communications

Various studies have focused on the factors which are encouraging the adoption of integrated marketing communications programmes (Yeshin, 1996; Duncan and Everett, 1993; Schultz and Kitchen, 1997; Grein and Ducoffe, 1998; Kitchen and Schultz, 1999).

- *Value for money.* The recession of recent years and increasing global competition have brought about substantial changes in the way that client companies are managed. On the one hand, there has been the impact of shrinking marketing departments, in which fewer people are allocated to the management of the products and services which the company produces. On the other, the pressure on margins has encouraged clients to become tougher negotiators. Companies are keen to gain the maximum value for money and the maximum impact from all relevant disciplines.
- *Increasing pressure on organizations' bottom lines.* The inevitable consequence of the variety of economic pressures has resulted in a close focus on company profitability. As all forms of

cost increase, so companies seek to make compensatory savings throughout all of their activities.

- *Increasing client sophistication.* This is particularly true of areas such as an understanding of retailers, customers and consumers. There has been an increasing confidence in the use of other marketing communication disciplines, especially sales promotion, and the greater ability to take the lead in terms of their strategic direction.
- *A disillusionment with advertising.* This has resulted in clients turning to other disciplines in the search to improve customer relationships and more sales.
- *A disillusionment with agencies.* Advertising agencies, in particular, which were often the primary source of strategic input for the clients with whom they worked, have lost significant ground in this respect. Specialist consultancies and others are now being retained by client companies to advise them of the strategic directions they should be taking, with the agency role becoming progressively smaller in many instances.
- *The fragmentation of media channels.* As we have seen earlier, the changing face of the media scene is demanding the re-evaluation of the contribution that the variety of media channels can make to the delivery of the message. With new ways of communicating with the target audiences, new approaches are necessary to achieve maximum impact from marketing communications budgets.
- *Traditional advertising is too expensive and not cost effective.* There is an increased recognition that, for many companies, the use of traditional forms of advertising no longer provides the means of achieving cost-effective reach of their target audiences. As media costs escalate, many companies are turning to other forms of marketing communications to achieve their objectives.
- *The rapid growth and development of database marketing.* The increasing availability of sophisticated database techniques has enabled manufacturers and service providers alike with

a more precise means of targeting consumers. The move away from traditional mass marketing towards closely focused communications techniques is a reflection of the increasing cost of traditional advertising techniques.

- *Power shift towards retailers.* In most consumer markets, comparatively small numbers of retailers have come to dominate their respective categories. In the grocery field, for example, the major supermarket chains – Tesco, Sainsbury, ASDA and Safeway – account for a substantial part of the retail business. Together, these four companies account for around 40 per cent of retail sales. Inevitably, this has resulted in their taking the initiative in terms of the marketing to consumers. To a large degree, even major manufacturers have to bow to the demands of the retailers or face the prospect of their products being de-listed from their shelves.
- *Escalating price competition.* As brands increasingly converge in what they offer to consumers, companies are striving to overcome the debilitating impact of the downward price spiral. The recognition that marketing communication is often the only differentiating factor between competing brands has led to an increased focus on how the tools can be used to achieve brand distinction.
- *Environmental factors.* Consumers are becoming increasingly concerned with the way in which products impact on the general environment. In turn, companies have been forced to adopt a more environmentally friendly approach or risk consumers rejecting their products in favour of those which they consider to be more responsive to these broader concerns.
- *Emergence of a variety of compensation methods.* Where once agencies were bound by a compensation based on commission (a fixed percentage of the monies spent on advertising), today's marketing communications companies are rewarded in many different ways. The most important impact of this change has been to free them (and the

perception of their income) as being tied to recommendations to increase their clients' spend.

- *Agency mergers and acquisitions.* Responding to the needs of the marketplace and, in particular, to pressures from their clients, agencies are increasing merging to form larger groups. Partly, this has been driven by the need to provide client services across a variety of territories. However, a further dimension has been the desire to provide a comprehensive service to clients across the variety of areas encompassed by marketing communications. The large agency groups exist as holding companies controlling operational companies in all of the relevant communications fields.
- *Increased global competition.* The drive towards globalization has increased the necessity to achieve synergy between all forms of marketing communications. Where once a brand might be sold in a single country, today's mega-brands are available across the globe. Significant savings can be achieved through the implementation of a constant communications campaign across all of the territories in which the product is sold.

The impact on marketing communications

We have already seen that marketing communications need to focus on the end-user rather than on the nature of the product or service provided. But, it is suggested, marketing communications need to respond more rapidly to these underlying changes in the social and environmental framework.

In their important work on IMC, Schultz *et al.* (1992) propose that it is time to abandon the principles of the four Ps for the four Cs:

> Forget **P**roduct. Study **C**onsumer wants and needs. You can no longer sell whatever you make. You can only sell something that someone specifically wants to buy.

Forget Price. Understand the consumer's Cost to satisfy that want or need.

Forget Place. Think Convenience to buy.

Forget Promotions. The word in the 90s is Communications.

If marketing communications are to be effective, it is vitally important that we move from a situation of specialization – in which marketers are experts in one area of marketing communications – to people who are trained in all marketing communications disciplines.

At the same time, as we have already seen, the process of change requires us to look at focused marketing approaches rather than adopt the litany of the 1960s – that of mass marketing. With the recognition that all consumers are different and hence have different needs and wants – even of the same product or service – there is the need to ensure that we are able to communicate with them as individuals rather than as a homogeneous unit. The increasing concern is the desire to communicate with ever small segments of the global market and, in an ideal world, reach a position where we can communicate with them individually. This desire manifests itself in the increasing drive towards direct marketing techniques, the most rapidly growing sector of the marketing communications industry.

There needs to be a clear statement of the desired outcomes of marketing activity as a whole. This requires a totally new approach, since most people working within marketing have been brought up in a disintegrated environment.

Objectives need to be longer term and expressed more strategically than would be the case for the short-term objectives of more individual marketing tactics.

Schultz (1999) argues that as the tools of marketing communications are progressively diffused into a variety of specialisms, there has been a natural inclination for those individual specialists to focus entirely within their own area – often to the detriment of the brand or

communication programme. The consequence has been a natural drift towards less integrated, less co-ordinated, less concentrated marketing communications activities.

The task of IMC is to strategically co-ordinate the various elements of the promotional mix in order to achieve synergies and to ensure that the message reaches and registers with the target audience.

Novak and Phelps (1994) have suggested that there are several important dimensions to the process of integration:

- The creation of a single theme and image.
- The integration of both product image and relevant aspects of consumer behaviour in promotional management, as opposed to a focus on one or the other of these two.
- The co-ordinated management of promotion mix disciplines.

Relationship marketing

A development of the marketing communications process, as it moves through the early 2000s, is the area known as relationship marketing. With the ability to reach consumers on a highly segmented or even one-to-one basis, so too has come the recognition that the process itself can become two-way. Hitherto, marketing communications primarily concerned itself with the process of communicating *to* the end consumer. By encouraging the process of feedback, we can now communicate *with* the consumer.

Increasingly, companies such as Nestlé and Heinz have announced moves into club formats which enable the establishment of a direct relationship between the manufacturer and the consumer. Many loyalty programmes, such as the Frequent Flyer and Frequent Stayer programmes now run by most international airlines and hotel groups, have a similar objective of establishing a relationship with the consumer, to their mutual benefit. The increasing use of customer loyalty programmes within the major retail chains is further evidence of the desire to establish direct contact with the customer base – for long-term advantage. The encouragement of a 'feedback' loop is a facet of marketing communications which is destined to grow apace over the next few years and, as companies perceive the benefits of encouraging a positive relationship with their customers, their consumers, their suppliers and others, so we will witness the growth of developed two-way marketing communications programmes.

It has to be recognized that contemporary marketing is more complex than at any other time in the past. No longer is it sufficient to rely on the traditional marketing mix variables to achieve differentiation between manufacturers. Areas such as product design and development, pricing policies, and distribution in themselves are no longer capable of delivering the long-term differentiation required. With an increasing level of convergent technologies, product innovation may be going on in parallel between rival manufacturers, even without their knowing what the other is doing. And, even where this is not the case, any new feature can rapidly be copied by the competition. Where once a new feature, ingredient or other product attribute would enable a manufacturer to achieve a unique stance for an extended period, today this is no longer the case. One has only to look at the area of the rapid innovation within the soap powder and detergent markets to see just how speedily rival manufacturers catch up with each other.

With the concentration of distribution into relatively few hands, the opportunities for achieving sole distribution of brands is minimized. Indeed, the retailers themselves represent an increasing threat to the manufacturers' brands as their packaging moves ever closer to that of the manufacturers' own.

Pricing, once a major area of differentiation, similarly provides less scope. The pressure on margins brought about by the increasingly competitive nature of retailers' own products has restricted the scope to use price to differentiate effectively. Clearly, this is particularly true of fast-moving consumer goods, where price dissimilarity can only operate over a very narrow range. Other products, such as perfumes and toiletries, and luxury goods ranging from hi-fis to cars, still have more flexibility in the area of price.

We are left, therefore, with only one of the four marketing mix variables which can be utilized to achieve effective brand discrimination – marketing communications. Schultz *et al.* (1992) argue that the area of marketing communications will, increasingly, be the only opportunity of achieving sustainable competitive advantage.

If all other things are equal – or at least more or less so – then it is what people think, feel and believe about a product and its competitors which will be important. Since products in many areas will achieve parity or comparability in purely functional terms, it will be the perceptual differences which consumers will use to discriminate between rival brands. Only through the use of sustained and integrated marketing communications campaigns will manufacturers be able to achieve the differentiation they require.

To appreciate the impact of this statement, it is worth looking at a market which replicates many of the features described above. In the bottled water market, several brands coexist, each with unique positionings in the minds of the consumer. Yet, in repeated blind tastings, few consumers can identify any functional characteristics which could be used as the basis for brand discrimination.

The benefits of integrated marketing communications

Undeniably, the process of integration affords a great number of benefits to the companies which adopt it. Linton and Morley (1995) suggest nine potential benefits of IMC:

1 Creative integrity.
2 Consistent messages.

3 Unbiased marketing recommendations.
4 Better use of media.
5 Greater marketing precision.
6 Operational efficiency.
7 Cost savings.
8 High-calibre consistent service.
9 Easier working relations.

Similarly, the study of Kitchen and Schultz (1999) identified a series of benefits which could be derived from IMC programmes. These included:

1 Increased impact.
2 Creative ideas more effective when IMC is used.
3 Greater communications consistency.
4 Increases importance of one brand personality.
5 Helps eliminate misconceptions.
6 Provides greater client control over communication budget.
7 Provides clients with greater professional expertise.

- *Consistency of message delivery.* By approaching the planning process in a holistic manner, companies can ensure that all components of the communications programme deliver the same message to the target audience. Importantly, this demands the adoption of an overall strategy for the brand, rather than developing individual strategies for the separate tools of marketing communications. The avoidance of potential confusion in the minds of consumers is a paramount consideration in the development of effective communications programmes.
- *Corporate cohesion.* For the company, IMC can be used as a strategic tool in communicating its corporate image and product/service benefits. This has important consequences both on an internal and an external level. As consumers increasingly gravitate towards companies with whom they feel comfortable, it becomes important

to ensure that the overall image projected by the organization is favourably received. This demands, in turn, the development of a cohesive communications programme within the organization – to ensure that all people working for the company fully understand the organization's goals and ambitions – and externally – to present the company in the most favourable light.

- *Client relationships.* For the agency, it provides the opportunity to play a significantly more important role in the development of the communications programme, and to become a more effective partner in the relationship. By participating in the totality of the communications requirements, rather than having responsibility for one or more components, the agency can adopt a more strategic stance. This, in turn, yields significant power and provides important advantages over competitors.
- *Interaction.* IMC ensures better communication between agencies and creates a stronger bond between them and the client company. By providing a more open flow of information, it enables the participants in the communication programme to concentrate on the key areas of strategic development, rather than pursue individual and separate agendas.
- *Motivation.* IMC offers the opportunity to motivate agencies. The combined thinking of a team is better than the sum of the parts (and unleashes everyone's creative potential).
- *Participation.* Everyone owns the final plan, having worked together on the brainstorming and implementation, avoiding any internal politics. Potentially, this can overcome the divisive nature of individual departments 'fighting their own corner'.

Perhaps the most important benefit is the delivery of better measurability of response and accountability for the communications programme.

The process of achieving integration

The task of developing and implementing marketing communications campaigns is becoming increasingly divergent. No longer is the task in one pair of hands. As the specialist functions develop further, the marketer must seek and co-ordinate the input from a number of different sources. Many organizations will retain an advertising agency, a public relations consultancy, a sales promotion company and, perhaps, even a media specialist. Ensuring that all of these contributors work to the same set of objectives and deliver a cohesive message to the consumer is a task which is an increasingly challenging one.

The key requirement is the establishment of a feedback mechanism between all elements of the strategic development process and, importantly, the consideration of all of the tools of marketing communications designed to fulfil the promotional objectives established for the campaign. It is the adoption of a holistic approach to campaign development which is at the heart of integration, a fundamental shift from the practice of developing each of the elements on a piecemeal basis.

> Integrated marketing communications offers strategic and creative integrity across all media.
>
> (Linton and Morley, 1995)

This ensures that the company maintains a constant theme and style of communication which can be followed across all applications. In turn, this provides for a strong and unified visual identity in all areas of communication.

This does not imply that all material should have the same copy and visual execution; however, all items used must serve to tell the same story and to reinforce the overall message to the consumer. This enables each element of a campaign to reinforce the others and to achieve the maximum level of impact on the target audience. The best platforms for integrated campaigns are ideas that can be spread across the whole marketing communications mix, e.g. American Express' 'Membership Has Its Privileges' and Gillette's 'The Best A Man Can Get' will work in any discipline.

Andrex has, for many years, used the image of a Labrador puppy in its advertising to symbolize softness. More recently, however, the device has been extended into other promotional areas. Its 'Puppy Tales' campaign offered a series of books about the adventures of a puppy, which was featured on-pack and in television advertising. The promotion gained editorial coverage both for the promotion itself and by way of reviews of the author, Gerald Durrell. All of these devices reinforced the brand message.

Some companies go further. They produce a visual identity manual to which all items produced on behalf of the company must comply. This establishes a series of specific requirements which may cover the typefaces used, the positioning of the logo and other important visual elements, which provides a high level of commonality in all materials produced. Often, this is associated with a redesign of the corporate image. When the author was working with the Prudential Corporation, Woolf Olins were engaged to redesign the company look and, as part of the package, created a corporate ID manual which covered all of the above areas, and to which all agencies were required to comply.

An essential part of IMC is the process of ensuring that the message conveyed is consistent. Whereas this is achievable in the context of a single agency which produces all of the materials required by its client, in the vast majority of cases, companies will employ several different agencies, often independent of each other. Indeed, some of the material will be produced by the company in-house. In this instance, someone must take overall responsibility for ensuring the consistency of the various items to ensure that there is an overall coherence in what is produced. This means that the person or department must consider not only the obvious items such as advertising, point of sale and direct mail pieces, but everything else which is prepared to support the brand. This may include product leaflets and other literature, presentations and audio-visual material, sales training items, exhibition stands, and so on.

A key area within the requirement of IMC is the need for recommendations which are without structural bias. Historically (and still to a large degree), it was inevitable that agencies promoted their own particular corners. Advertising agencies would often present advertising solutions, promotions companies would offer sales promotion responses, and so on.

The move towards IMC has been hastened by the desire for agencies to become more accountable for their recommendations. Inherently, agencies have to be confident, as far as it is possible to be so, that the recommendations they make are those most likely to achieve the outcome desired by the client company.

To many writers on the topic, the central part of the IMC process is the maintenance of an effective database. Not only does this provide the opportunity to gain a greater understanding of existing customers, but from an examination of their profiles (and using those profiles to identify similar target groups) it is possible to achieve a greater degree of precision in all subsequent communications activity.

At the conceptual level, integration is about capturing a single thought which expresses what we wish the brand to stand for and of ensuring that this thought is expressed, whatever the medium. At the process level, it is about ensuring that the development and implementation of communications live up to that brand thought, and drive forward the relationship between the brand and the consumer.

As John Farrell, then Chief Executive of DMB&B (now D'Arcy), said: 'Unless there is close involvement of senior client personnel who truly have a full communications perspective, it's simply unfair on the agencies

involved to expect them to drive the integration process from the outside.' Clients do not need specialist implementation functions within their businesses; rather, at a conceptual stage there has to be a structure and attitude which actively encourage the agency to recommend the most appropriate media solution to solve the particular problem.

Integration is not just about execution. It is about the single brand thought that expresses the essence of the brand personality and then interpreting that thought for the appropriate audience without changing or denigrating it. Integration extends to the point where the client and agency work together as a single team. The total team across all communications requirements is fully integrated with the customer and brand requirements, and that is what drives the focus of the team.

The position is summarized by the approaches adopted by two different companies. After Bisto's annual marketing communications plan has been developed, it is presented at a meeting with all of the Bisto agencies represented. Paula Ross, a group product manager at RHM, says 'this creates a more open flow of information with all of the agencies focusing on the key objectives, not just their ideas. It motivates all that take part and everybody has ownership in the brand plan. And, most important, the combined thinking of the team is better than the parts.' Similarly, Tetley implements the IMC process by holding quarterly meetings when marketing staff meet with its advertising agency, PR consultancy and sales promotion consultancy.

Organizational approaches to integration

The way in which companies are organized into different departments which reflect the various functions of marketing communications is a key cause of disintegrated communications where different messages are communicated to consumers about the same brand. In the worst case scenario, the messages delivered by marketing communications may actually contradict each other.

> Some writers suggest that the most efficient means of achieving integration is to appoint a single agency which is responsible for all aspects of the campaign, contracting out certain areas. The reality, except for a relatively few number of companies, is that such an approach is generally not possible. The need for specialist services in the wide variety of areas which make up the tools of marketing communications requires staff who are skilled in those specialisms.
>
> (Alanko, 2000)

Research by Gronstedt and Thorson (1996) suggests that integrated approaches are necessary because most work related to communications cuts across different knowledge and skills domains, whilst Schultz *et al.* (1992) argue that IMC results in the creation of communications programmes that are both tonally and visually coherent.

The question of how to organize external communications disciplines has been a continuing source of debate within the arena of marketing communications (Cornellisen *et al.*, 2001). The conundrum is whether the organization should be of a functional nature, i.e. with the various departments merged together to create a single entity which can deal with all communications requirements or whether, as suggested by Gronstedt and Thorson (1996), it is more about integrating the processes of marketing communications. Schultz *et al.* (1992) argue that the different mind-sets of professionals operating within the various disciplines inhibit the level of cross-functional operation and the ways in which the disciplines can contribute to the achievement of the desired objectives.

Gronstedt and Thorson (1996) suggest five possible models for an integrated organizational structure:

1 *The consortium.* One agency performs the role of main contractor to a consortium of specialist agencies. The main agency helps its client to develop a strategy and decides which persuasive tools to use. It typically executes traditional advertising, but subcontracts other tools. The account team at the main agency co-ordinates the specialist agencies to ensure that messages and timing are integrated.

2 *Consortium with a dominant agency.* Agencies that have the capacity to plan an integrated campaign and execute traditional advertising as well as some other communications tools. The main agency has various combinations of in-house services and outside suppliers.

3 *Corporation with autonomous units.* All the specialists are brought in-house as separate and autonomous units. The specialist units are separate profit centres, sometimes with separate names and in separate buildings.

4 *The matrix organization.* Agencies not only have specialists in-house but they are integrated in a matrix structure. The matrix design combines functional division and cross-functional task force teams. The matrix structure requires that professionals work across functions whilst maintaining the functional division.

5 *The integrated organization.* All disciplines are incorporated into the advertising agency structure rather than forming separate units for each persuasive tool. The agency is no longer structured by functional departments, but by accounts. Each person works for a particular client, not for a direct marketing or sales promotion department. Each account group comprises personnel who are capable of handling all communications disciplines.

Duncan and Everett (1993) suggest four agency–client relationships which could foster integration:

- The client and its agencies collectively establish strategies, then each communications function is executed by a different agency.
- The client and its agency establish the strategies, then the 'integrated' agency is

responsible for the executions of all or most of the communications functions.

- The client determines overall strategies and assigns individual functions to individual agencies, but requires that all of these suppliers stay in touch with each other.
- The client alone determines overall strategies, then each communications function is executed by a different agency.

Grein and Gould (1996) identify five factors which, they suggest, impact on the organizational dimensions and affect its effective implementation:

1 Inter-office co-ordination.
2 Co-ordination of promotional disciplines across country offices.
3 The degree of centralization.
4 The frequency of inter-office communication.
5 The use of information technology.

Jeans (1998) argues that the most likely route to achieving IMC is in team building, rather than any hierarchical or matrix method of control. Since the necessary practitioner skills are unlikely to be embodied in any single individual, a team of people will be essential to provide the necessary inputs.

A study by McArthur and Griffin (1997) demonstrated the extent to which marketing organizations perceived integration to have been fulfilled. Almost half of the companies surveyed indicated that all marketing communications activities of their companies were co-ordinated either by a single person or as a result of some reporting relationship. A further quarter co-ordinated the majority of their marketing communications programmes. Interestingly, and confirming the results of other studies, the areas of business which indicated the highest level of co-ordination of activities were retail and business-to-business.

The study identified a series of 'inconsistencies' in the sourcing of activities across the different business types. Their study revealed, for example, that consumer marketers tended to use external suppliers for creative input more extensively than others. The business-to-business sector relied more heavily on their advertising agencies for all communications activities. Retailer marketers were significantly more prone to source activities in-house.

There are sound historical reasons for these differences in practice sometimes, but not always, related to the level of marketing communications expenditures within specific categories. Within the consumer sector, budgets tend to be large and activities more extensive. Inevitably, companies involved with these programmes seek high levels of expertise within the respective fields and source suppliers who, in the main, have a demonstrable track record of being able to deal with the market sector. Elsewhere, where budgets are somewhat lower, companies tend to rely more heavily on a single supplier to achieve economies across the range of activities which they implement. The retail sector, by contrast, inevitably demands a greater speed of response and, hence, is more prone to produce material in-house, where those with the specialist skills can be located.

Interesting differences in the global acceptance and implementation of IMC are seen in various recent works.

A similar study by Kitchen and Schultz (1999) showed significant differences between the five countries surveyed. In response to a question about the amount of time devoted to IMC programmes for client firms, for those indicating more than 50 per cent of their time, the percentages were 50 per cent for the US, 43 per cent for the UK, 32 per cent for New Zealand, 5 per cent for Australia and 0 per cent for India. From the expenditure perspective, respondents were asked to identify the percentage of their overall budgets devoted to IMC activities, with similar results (US 52 per cent; UK 42 per cent; New Zealand 40 per cent; Australia 22 per cent; India 15 per cent).

According to Kitchen and Schultz:

whilst IMC is recognized as offering significant value and importance to clients and agencies alike, the fact that no clear proposal, method or acceptable disposition of measurement and evaluation has been offered and/or found widespread acceptance weakens conceptual application in a global sense.

The barriers to integration

Despite the undeniable advantages afforded by integration, an examination of the market situation suggests that relatively few companies have yet reached the stage of fully integrating their communications campaigns.

Various studies (Mitchell, 1996; Yeshin, 1996; Schultz and Kitchen, 1997; Kitchen and Schultz, 1999) have described the progressive adoption of the philosophy of IMC across many major and sophisticated client companies. Nonetheless, many barriers continue to exist.

These studies indicate that, whilst much has been written on the topic, the subject remains largely misunderstood by many of those responsible for its implementation. This is clearly seen by the diversity of 'definitions' provided for IMC by the respondents:

> Co-ordinating all of the tools of promotion to ensure a consistent message.

> Rolling out a single creative theme across all executions.

> Using a single agency to deliver all requirements.

Clearly, there is considerable confusion as to the nature of IMC, with some respondents regarding it as a process, others perceiving it as a facility for 'one-stop' shopping, whilst for others it was a means whereby cohesion might be achieved between creative executions and strategies, even if provided by a multiplicity of suppliers.

Several factors can be identified as presenting barriers to the integration process, both of an internal and an external nature.

Internally, the lack of management understanding of the benefits of IMC, the short-term outlook adopted towards much of the planning process, the inherent nature of the 'political' battles between departments battling for supremacy, the fear of departmental budget reductions with the consequence of staff reductions, together with the turnover of staff and the fear of losing expertise in specialist areas, were all identified as contributing to the general lack of adoption of IMC within companies. Externally, issues such as agency egos, the agencies' fears of losing control, the lack of expertise in the individual areas of communications, the concern over reductions in the scale of the communications budget, and the problems of the system of remuneration were further restrictions of the progress of integration.

Structurally, few companies are in a position to ensure integration. Often, various functions compete with each other for the responsibility of briefing and implementation of the tools of marketing communications. These include the brand manager, the marketing manager, the marketing director, in a few instances, a communications director, together with a variety of 'specialist' heads of departments covering public relations, sales promotion, and so on. Often, these individuals represent 'vested' interests and are protective of their own sectors to the preclusion of an integrated approach. Most importantly, few companies have truly recognized the issue of responsibility for the custodianship of the brand and the negative implications of divisive communications messages.

> ... In practice, the situation is even worse. Company structures perpetuate this division, giving each 'speciality' a different owner, based on technical skills required to execute, rather than conceptual skills required to plan.
>
> (Lannon, 1994)

Undeniably, there are significant problems for the client in terms of commissioning and managing several different agencies, especially in the context of the reduction in the size of marketing departments. The temptation of the integrated one-shop concept is overwhelmingly appealing for many. The attraction of using several different agencies is the possibility of selecting the best people in each field.

Moreover, there is a general lack of experienced people within the field of marketing communications, who exhibit expertise in the variety of fields which make up the total communications process. The need for individuals with a 'broad perspective' and an understanding of the contribution which each of the marketing communications disciplines can provide is underlined by a study by Cleland (1995).

The study by Kitchen and Schultz (1999) identified a number of barriers, real or perceived, to achieving IMC:

- Requires staff to be more generalist.
- Integrated agencies do not have talent across all marcom areas.
- IMC means staff have to develop new skills.
- IMC gives a few individuals too much control.
- Client staff lack expertise to undertake IMC programmes.
- Client centralization difficulties.
- Client organizational structures constrain IMC.

Lannon (1994) asserts that most company communications policies are rooted in an outmoded past, when competition was less intense and the retailer wasn't anything like the powerful force it is today:

- The discontinuities of the 1980s and into the 1990s have fractured and fragmented not only the conventional media scene, but also the corporate structures and cultures of a more stable past.
- Differing agendas of clients and agencies have eroded productive and trusting relationships between clients and their agencies.

Perhaps the most significant barrier to integration is the approach to communications budgeting. In most cases, budgets are substantially determined on an 'historic' basis – considering what has been spent in the past – rather than against an evaluation of specific objectives.

Often, individual departments are required to argue for budget tenure, or an increase if the situation demands it. In the majority of cases, budgets are considered on a line-by-line basis, rather than holistically.

Despite this, some market sectors are more advanced than others in the adoption of an integrated approach. Two, in particular, stand out as having made significant progress in the integration of their campaigns – the financial sector and retailers. In both cases, there has been a more widespread recognition of the benefits of integration. Campaigns by many of the commercial banks, together with high street retailers such as Safeway, underpin the advantages of integration. Certainly, most companies agree that the process of integration will increase apace, as much because of the need to deal with substantial communications budgets in a more positive manner as from the drive towards global considerations, where the desire for a common communications policy and the obvious financial benefits are of major importance.

The consumer and integrated marketing communications

At the heart of the debate is the undeniable need to ensure the clear and effective communication of brand messages to consumers and others. The process demands a change of focus from share and volume to a detailed understanding of the extent to which the manufacturer can satisfy the needs and wants of consumers. The essential focus has to be on customers, relationships, retention levels and satisfaction.

Several authors have suggested that IMC, as well as benefiting the manufacturers of products and services, also works for the consumer. David Iddiols (2000) suggests that IMC works on three levels for the consumer:

1 It provides short cuts to understanding what a brand stands for.

2 It adds depth and amplification to a particular message or set of brand values.
3 It demonstrates professionalism on the part of the brand owner.

Iddiols identifies three potential mechanics for providing integration across activities:

- The use of some form of mnemonic device, such as the red telephone used by Direct Line, or the Tea Folk by Tetley.
- A consistent proposition reinforced across all communications activities, such as Tesco's 'Every Little Helps'.
- Conveying a consistent set of brand values, as in the examples of Coca-Cola, Guinness or Levi's.

A key contributor to the achievement of effective and integrated marketing communications is the appropriate use of market research – both to gain greater insight and understanding of consumer behaviour, as well as to achieve an understanding of the contributions of the individual tools of marketing communications.

The difficulty, as many writers acknowledge, is changing the focus of market research from a disintegrated mode into a holistic practice. Archer and Hubbard (1996) suggest that the vast bulk of market research carried out continues to reflect the outdated theories and structures of disintegrated marketing communications. They argue that a more holistic approach needs to be adopted to measure the aggregate outcomes of all marketing activity whilst, at the same time, monitoring the specific actions which contribute to that outcome.

The clear advantages of a more holistic approach to research are that it is more comprehensive, embracing all activities and both short- and long-term objectives. It provides greater flexibility and it is more realistic in that it measures the end result of all activities on the target audience.

International dimensions of integrated marketing communications

Recent works reflect the increasing growth and impact of global marketing communications. Grein and Gould (1996) have suggested that the concept of IMC should be broadened and renamed 'global integrated marketing communications'. Since, increasingly, manufacturers seek to implement communications campaigns across national boundaries, IMC requires integration beyond that of disciplines to encompass global management of campaigns. The management of international brands demands that strategic marketing decisions are integrated and co-ordinated across all relevant global markets.

They offer a new definition to incorporate the international dimension:

> A system of active promotional management which strategically co-ordinates global communications in all of its component parts both horizontally in terms of countries and organizations and vertically in terms of promotion disciplines.

A study conducted by Grein and Ducoffe (1998) revealed the extent to which advertising agencies in particular are becoming global enterprises, reflecting the needs of their increasingly global clients. They indicated that clients wish to use more standardized campaigns, which are easier and cheaper to administer, have proven track records in some countries, and result in a unified brand image and position around the world. For many companies, these benefits were considered sufficient to outweigh the less than perfect outcomes in some operating countries.

A direct consequence confirmed by the study is a reduction in the extent of local creativity on international accounts. Once campaigns have been developed, usually in one country, they are implemented with relatively few variations on a worldwide basis.

However, as indicated by the work of Grein and Gould (1996), the level of inter-office communications made the task of effective integration difficult to achieve.

Integrated marketing communications – a summary

Using the analogy of Kitchen and Schultz (1999), who considered the state and acceptance of IMC against the product life cycle, it can be reasonably concluded that IMC is a marketing concept which is still emerging. As such, it might be positioned somewhere between its introduction and growth stage.

A point of issue is the difference between academic understanding of the concept and its role in the context of the practitioner. Kitchen argues that IMC, from the academic standpoint, is just over 10 years old, pointing to the work of Caywood *et al.* (1991) as the starting point for academic study.

In practice, the notion of IMC – albeit not the words – has been around for a considerably longer period. The author of this paper was responsible for the establishment of a marketing communications agency, The Above and Below Group, in 1972, whose existence was founded on the provision of integrated communications activities to its clients.

However, several important dimensions of the practice of IMC can be recognized:

- IMC is an increasingly important facet of the practice of marketing communications.
- An increasing number of client companies and their agencies strive to achieve deeper and better integration of their marketing communications activities.
- It reflects both an underlying conceptual as well as a practical change in the way in which marketing communications programmes are developed and implemented.
- The desire to achieve global presence for their brands drives companies towards the achievement of consistent imagery for their brands, and coherent messages in their communications programmes.
- In contrast to the views of Cornellisen *et al.* (2000), IMC is not a management fad.
- A continued inhibition to the development of IMC remains the internal structure of client companies and the defence of departmental independence.
- IMC will require the emergence of a new breed of communicators who can command a generalistic overview of all the tools of marketing communications from a brand management perspective.
- Whilst it remains true that some brands can still achieve effective communications despite disintegration, 'all of the evidence points to the fact that it will take longer and runs the risk of confusing the very people you wish to sell to along the way' (Iddiols, 2000).

The way forward is summarized in the paper prepared by the American Productivity and Quality Centre Study (1998). The study identifies a series of key best practice issues which focus on the achievement of excellence in terms of brand development and communication. Those companies which most exemplified best practice:

- concentrate on a few key brands and provide streamlined and sophisticated brand support;
- provide the leadership and support of senior management in developing and sustaining successful brands;
- provide the consumer and customer-led informational infrastructure to achieve an all-round view of the brand network;
- define their brands in terms of core values, promise and personality that provide guidance, meaning and focus for all brand-related activities;
- view communication as an opportunity to project a unified image, not just of individual brands, but also of the company itself;
- have started to move towards the financial measurement of brands and related communications activities.

References

Alanko, J. (2000) The Case for Integration in B2B Marketing, *Admap*, September.

American Association of Advertising Agencies (1993) *Marketing News*, 18 January.

American Productivity and Quality Centre (1998) Brand Building and Power Strategies for the 21st Century, International Benchmarking Clearing House.

Archer, J. and Hubbard, T. (1996) Integrated Tracking for Integrated Communications, *Admap*, February.

Caywood, C., Schultz, D. and Wang, P. (1991) *Integrated Marketing Communications: A Survey of National Consumer Goods Advertising*, North Western University Report.

Cleland, K. (1995) A Lot of Talk, Little Action on IMC, *Business Marketing*, March.

Cook, W. (1994) The End of the Line, *Marketing*, 24 February.

Cornellisen, J. P., Lock, A. R. and Gardner, H. (2000) Theoretical Concept or Management Fashion, Examining the Significance of IMC, *Journal of Advertising Research*, **40**(5), September.

Duncan, T. and Everett, S. (1993) Client Perceptions of Integrated Marketing Communications, *Journal of Advertising Research*, May/June.

Franz, G. (2000) Better Media Planning For Integrated Communications, *Admap*, January.

Grein, A. and Ducoffe, R. (1998) Strategic Responses to Market Globalisation Amongst Advertising Agencies, *International Journal of Advertising*, **17**(3).

Grein, A. F. and Gould, S. J. (1996) Globally Integrated Marketing Communications, *Journal of Marketing Communications*, **2**(3).

Gronstedt, A. and Thorson, E. (1996) Five Approaches to Organise an Integrated Marketing Communications Agency, *Journal of Advertising Research*, **36**(2), March/April.

Iddiols, D. (2000) Marketing Superglue. Consumer Perceptions of Integrated Marketing Communications, *Admap*, May.

Jeans, R. (1998) Integrating Marketing Communications, *Admap*, December.

Kitchen, P. J. and Schultz, D. E. (1999) A Multi-Country Comparison of the Drive for IMC, *Journal of Advertising Research*, January/February.

Lannon, J. (1994) What Brands Need Now, *Admap*, September.

Lannon, J. (1996) Integrated Marketing Communications From The Consumer End, *Admap*, February.

Linton, I. and Morley, K. (1995) *Integrated Marketing Communications*, Butterworth-Heinemann.

McArthur, D. N. and Griffin, T. (1997) A Marketing Management View of Integrated Marketing Communications, *Journal of Advertising Research*, **37**(5), September/October.

Mitchell, H. (1996) *Client Perceptions of Integrated Marketing Communications in the UK*, Cranfield University.

Nilson, T. S. (1992) *Value Added Marketing*, McGraw-Hill.

Novak, G. J. and Phelps, J. (1994) Conceptualizing the Integrated Marketing Communications Phenomenon: An Examination of its Impact on Advertising Practices and its Implications for Advertising Research, *Journal of Current Issues and Research in Advertising*, **16**(1).

O'Donoghue, D., writing in Cooper, A. (1997) *How to Plan Advertising*, 2nd edn, Cassell.

Schultz, D. E. writing in Jones, J. P. (1999) *The Advertising Business*, Sage.

Schultz, D. E. and Kitchen, P. J. (1997) Integrated Marketing Communications in US Advertising Agencies: An Exploratory Study, *Journal of Advertising Research*, **37**(5), September/October.

Schultz, D. E. and Kitchen, P. J. (2000) Integrated Marketing Communications in US Advertising Agencies: An Exploratory Study, *Journal of Advertising Research*, **37**(5), September/October.

Schultz, D. E., Tannenbaum, S. I. and Lauterborn, R. F. (1992) *Integrated Marketing Communications: Putting It Together and Making It Work*, NTC Business Books.

Schultz, D. E., Tannebaum, S. I. and Lauterborn, R. F. (1995) *The Marketing Paradigm – Integrated Marketing Communications*, NTC Business Books.

Smith, P. (1996) Benefits and Barriers to Integrated Marketing Communications, *Admap*, February.

Solomon, M. R. and Englis, B. G. (1994) The Big Picture: Product Complementarity and Integrated Communications, *Journal of Advertising Research*, January/February.

Yeshin, T. (1996) The Development and Implications of Integrated Marketing Communications, DMB&B Study.

CHAPTER 17

Promotion

KEITH CROSIER

Introduction

The idea that you can merchandise candidates for high office, like breakfast cereal, is the ultimate indignity of the democratic process.

Adlai Stevenson

Advertisements contain the only truths to be relied on in a newspaper.

Thomas Jefferson

In this chapter we turn to the question of *promoting* a product or service that has already been developed (Chapter 12) and priced (Chapter 13), and will concurrently be sold (Chapter 14) and distributed (Chapter 19). What exactly is involved in the management of this particular element of the marketing mix?

The promotional mix

As Figure 17.1 shows, using McCarthy's useful *'four Ps'* terminology, this chapter is concerned with deploying and controlling a mix within a mix. Following his lead, we call it the *promotional mix*, but many recent textbooks prefer a different description of the activities it embraces: for instance, *Marketing Communications: Principles and Practice* (Kitchen, 1998), *Marketing Communications: An Integrated Approach* (Smith and Taylor, 2001), *Marketing Communications: a Critical Introduction* (Varey, 2001) and *Marketing Communications: Frameworks, Theories and Applications* (Fill, 2002). This rapidly developing fashion for a holistic approach to treatment of the promotional mix, which its advocates call 'integrated marketing communications', may well result in the permanent replacement of 'promotion' as the generic term during the lifetime of this edition of *The Marketing Book*, though McCarthy's legacy is proving to be remarkably robust.

Within the confines of a single chapter, it is impossible to take each of the nine ingredients identified in Figure 17.1 in turn, and discuss their implementation in any real detail. Instead, the following working definitions are proposed, demonstrating the close family similarities among them while emphasizing fundamentally important points of difference.

- Advertising is promotion via an advertisement in a chosen advertising medium, guaranteeing exposure to a general or specific target audience, in return for an advertising rate charged by the media owner plus the cost of producing the advertisement.
- Publicity is promotion via a news release to chosen news media, delivering exposure to a known target audience if newsworthiness earns an editorial mention, in return for the cost of producing and distributing the release.

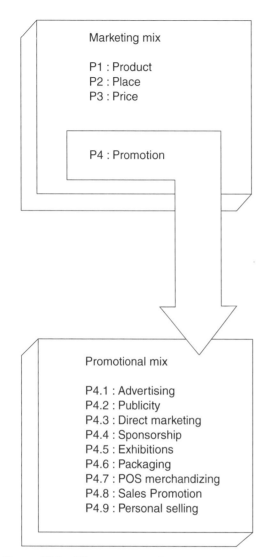

Figure 17.1   The promotional mix

of the sponsor's logo and to a secondary one by means of reference to the sponsor in associated media coverage, in return for the price of a negotiated sponsorship contract plus the cost of producing associated visual identification of the sponsor.

- Exhibitions are promotion via display and the presence of sales representatives on an exhibition stand, delivering exposure to visiting potential customers, in return for the rate charged for the space by the exhibition promoter plus the cost of building, installing and stocking the stand.
- Packaging is promotion via display, guaranteeing exposure to customers at the point of sale, in return for the cost of designing and producing the package.
- Point-of-sale (or 'POS') merchandising is promotion via various forms of display, acting as a reminder to customers of previously noticed promotional messages, in return for the cost of producing the material used.
- Sales promotion is promotion via a diverse range of initiatives not so far defined, delivering exposure to a general target market and in some cases offering an incentive for individuals to respond actively, in return for the cost of producing and distributing the material used.
- Personal selling is promotion via a sales pitch made by a sales representative to a 'prospect' or by a retail sales assistant to a customer, guaranteeing exposure to self-selected members of a target market, in return for the cost of remunerating and training the sales personnel delivering the pitch.

New media

A cursory reading of this definition of 'advertising' may raise the concern that it ignores the so-called 'new media' or 'interactive media' nowadays available to advertisers: in other words, the Internet, the world wide web and wireless telephony. In fact, it is only necessary to abandon the traditional view of 'advertising media' as meaning only press, posters,

- Direct marketing is promotion via any person-to-person communication medium, guaranteeing exposure to identifiable individuals in a chosen target audience in return for the price of disseminating the message plus the cost of producing the associated materials.
- Sponsorship is promotion via association with an entity, event or activity, typically delivering exposure to a primary target audience by means

television, radio and cinema, and to extend the concept 'media owner' to embrace any organization with selling rights to time and space in those new media. Then, a banner advertisement encountered while visiting a website can be thought of as in many ways the cyber-equivalent of a poster glimpsed among the visual clutter of a modern urban environment. They are simply different manifestations of a single ingredient of the mix, in the same way as a telesales call or a 'junk' e-mail message are no more than modern variations on the traditional mail shot as vehicles for direct marketing initiatives.

Percy (2001) concurs that the impact of the Internet is 'unlikely to be as revolutionary as the current climate of excitement would suggest' and expects that 'people will process marketing communication on the Internet much as they process all marketing communications'. The definitive price list for advertising space and time in the UK, *British Rate and Data*, simply lists 'new media' alongside eight other media categories, such as national newspapers and cinema.

Furthermore, because readers of *The Marketing Book* are likely to have more or less unlimited free access to the Internet by virtue of its rapid proliferation in the business and academic communities, they will tend to overestimate the extent of its penetration into several important audiences for promotional messages – for example, the inveterate package-holiday consumers in the 'grey market' or those 'housewives' who fill the supermarket trolley with branded goods. In fact, uptake of the Internet in the UK and the rest of Europe has not yet been as great or as fast as generally predicted in general society, beyond the innovators ('anoraks', 'geeks', 'nerds' and their kin) and early adopters (those working in IT-rich environments). The *NOP Internet User Profile 2000* shows that just over 19 million individuals in the UK had 'tried the Internet' over an unspecified 12-month period, a figure that corresponds to just under a third of the total population (31.9 per cent) and rather less than half of all households (40.9 per cent). The same

survey found that almost 16 million people over the age of 15 had 'used the WorldWide Web' during the four weeks before December 2000. The apparent discrepancy is explained by the fact that dominant use of the Internet is to access e-mail services, not to browse the web. According to the UK government's *Social Trends* survey for 2001, that accounts for a third of all traffic.

The prevailing belief that Internet users are dominantly young and male also requires some qualification. The NOP survey found that the male–female split was 58:42, that 25- to 44-year-olds accounted for roughly half of all usage, and that the number of users aged 45 or over outnumbered those under 25 by the significant margin of 29 per cent to only 23.

Though this combination of innovators and early adopters, whoever they may be, will soon be joined by the early majority, it may take another decade or more for technophobes and traditionalists to become the minority.

Meanwhile, access is by no means the same thing as exposure to the promotional message. Internet-linked computers are often used as nothing more than word processors or record keepers, and the exchange of personal or business e-mail messages accounts for well over half all Internet traffic. Users have to elect to browse the Net before they become part of an advertiser's actual audience. To find and read a marketer's website requires a positive search, among a great deal of competing non-commercial material. Therefore, sensible advertisers seek to counteract the random nature of exposure by including a web address in their media advertising. From the potential customer's point of view, this offers the benefit that pre-purchase information can be obtained anonymously, rather than by requesting literature or being subjected to a sales pitch at the point of sale.

However, there is a counter-productive tendency among many advertisers seeking to harness the potential of the Internet to create over-designed websites which take so long to download on the average PC, or are so difficult to navigate around, that 'visitors' depart elsewhere unless they are very determined to have the information. This seems to be because the design task is routinely delegated either to information technology specialists or to advertising agencies. The former typically have no background in marketing, with predictable communication consequences. As for the latter, a field study in the mid-1990s found them to be staffed by Luddites (Crosier and Abbott, 1996). The researchers believe that the situation has not improved a great deal in the interim, despite the general rate of uptake of the new technology. For clients, the solution may be to switch allegiance to agencies offering 'integrated marketing communications' services, provided those are not simply re-branding themselves while remaining in fact single-discipline specialists. Meanwhile, the initially low price of space on the Internet has begun to catch up with the prevailing cost of advertising in other media. For example, a 'banner ad' on the Teletext and Double-Click networks costs, respectively, £30 and £37 per thousand 'hits'. The price for one at the *Computer Weekly* website is much higher, at £65 per thousand, and the on-line *Financial Times* charges a flat rate of £2000 per month.

Three years ago, the previous edition of this chapter came to the conclusion that 'the new media are passing through the early stages of an awareness explosion but have not yet reached the point at which real understanding of their commercial application is widespread among marketing practitioners'. Typical marketing managers will undoubtedly climb further up the learning curve during the lifetime of this edition, but much has yet to be learnt before the 'new media' are as well understood and effectively used as the 'old'. Nevertheless, annual expenditure on Internet advertising in the UK has increased from £8 million to £155 million in just four years (see Table 17.1).

Personal selling and sales promotion

These last two among the nine ingredients of our promotional mix are sufficiently distinct from the rest to merit chapters in their own right. Consequently, this chapter will restrict itself to the other seven.

Here, *sales promotion* (Chapter 18) is taken to subsume 'promotional literature' (product leaflets, sales brochures, corporate prospectuses, annual reports and the like), which some authors treat separately. Where it is located matters less than the fact that those devices are certainly alternative means of promoting the product or service. Today, cyber-equivalents will typically join the traditional printed manifestations in the sales promotion strategies of forward-looking marketers.

Personal selling (Chapter 14) is the only promotional technique to involve face-to-face communication between seller and buyer, and is normally the focus of an organizational division quite separate from that with responsibility for the rest of the mix.

Public relations

The marketing literature routinely implies that *public relations* is an ingredient of the promotional mix. However, the Institute of Public Relations defines its purpose as 'to establish and maintain goodwill and mutual understanding between an organization and its publics'. Clearly, this activity has a broad and strategic focus, in contrast to the specific tactical aims of the promotional mix. To use an alternative terminology, it is corporate communication rather than marketing communications. It seems likely that colloquial usage is confusing public relations with *publicity*, perhaps simply because the two sound alike but possibly also because media stories generated by news releases and press conferences are the main tools of the trade. In fact, PR campaigns often also involve corporate advertising and sponsorship, not to mention a range of other initiatives beyond the boundaries of the promotional mix. To take account of all this, academic authors have recently begun to distinguish 'marketing public relations' from 'corporate public relations', or MPR from CPR (Kitchen and Schultz,

2001, Chapters 4 and 8). That is a well inten- tioned development, but it would be enough to use existing terminology correctly.

Direct marketing

The definition of the third ingredient of the promotional mix is in fact inaccurate, strictly speaking. 'Direct marketing' should of course encompass not only the delivery of the promo- tional message to the audience, but also the delivery of the goods or services themselves, and more besides. In this context, however, it is normally taken to refer to *direct mail, direct- response advertising* and *mail-order advertising*, via either traditional or new media. It could therefore be argued that it does not deserve a place of its own in the mix, being only a variety of advertising that aims to 'sell off the page', via a variety of response facilities, such as Freepost or (not free) e-mail. However, it figures here in concession to the fact that all the current textbooks of marketing communications cited here include it as a component of their own version of the mix.

'Promotions'

In practice, marketing managers will often describe an individual *sales promotion* initiative as simply a 'promotion', inviting confusion with the broader meaning of the term intended by McCarthy. This is just another reason for looking forward to the day when the fourth of his Ps finally gives way to the altogether more logical 'marketing communications'.

Publicity versus advertising

Here, we turn from largely semantic distinctions to one with important strategic implications. The careful distinction drawn between *advertis- ing* and *publicity* is by no means universally observed in practice, a tendency compounded outside the English-speaking world by the fact that 'advertising' in three major world lan- guages is *publicité, publicidad* and *publicidade.*

Conversely, English speakers routinely describe publicity as 'free' advertising, as distinct from 'paid' advertising. The danger in this usage is that it conceals a fundamental strategic differ- ence: users of publicity spend relatively little in the hope that a third party will relay a version of their message without adding a counter-pro- ductive editorial spin, whereas users of advertis- ing pay relatively heavily for the certainty that it will appear where, when and how they intended. Cost and control are thus traded off against one another.

It is often assumed that favourable pub- licity can be bought by taking advertising space in a newspaper or magazine, but professional etiquette in fact keeps such subterfuges to a minimum. A published comment from the editor of *Cosmopolitan* magazine made this abundantly clear in 1994: 'the marketing man- ager quoted was incorrect in his/her assump- tion that spending a significant amount on advertising gives the right to demand editorial coverage ... [which is] judged purely on its relevance and interest to our magazine's 2.3 million readers'. There is one exception to this rule, the advertisement features, or *advertorials*, which are a familiar feature of many news- papers and magazines. However, the code of practice governing press advertising in the UK requires that:

> Features, announcements or promotions that are disseminated in exchange for a payment or other reciprocal arrangement ... should also be clearly identified as such ... Advertising promotions, sometimes referred to as 'adver- torials', should be designed and presented in such a way that it is clear that they are advertisements.
>
> (Advertising Standards Authority, 1999, clauses 23.2 and 41.1)

The equivalent code regulating television advertising in Britain states explicitly that:

> Close similarity between a programme's con- tent and an advertiser's advertising (or other marketing activity) might constitute grounds

for regarding the programme as having an unacceptable marketing purpose.

(Independent Television Commission, 1998, paragraphs 5 and 17.2)

Where radio advertising is concerned, the relevant code requires that:

Licensees must ensure that the distinction between advertising and programming is not blurred and that listeners are not confused between the two. Legitimate objective coverage of a commercial product or service in editorial is acceptable (but see also ... Product Placement).

(Radio Authority, 2001, Section 2, Rule 1)

Above and below the line

Traditionally, marketing practitioners have distinguished promotional methods as being either 'above the line' or 'below the line'. Advertising lies above and every other ingredient of the promotional mix below – except personal selling, which is not normally assigned to either category. This purely hypothetical boundary, first delineated in 1954 by Procter & Gamble, is based on the fact that advertising agencies are paid for their work in a completely different way from the intermediaries who provide every other form of promotional service. The details follow later in this chapter. The point for the moment is that its relevance to promotional strategy is therefore highly suspect.

Given the semantic loading of 'above' and 'below' in everyday speech, outsiders might be forgiven for assuming that advertising is somehow superior to all the other ingredients of the mix. Indeed, it is easy to observe this lazy assumption being made in practice, the originators of the 'line' themselves, for example, being still massive spenders on media advertising, apparently in preference to other means to the same end. Yet this chapter has already provided ample evidence that advertising is not in fact strategically superior to the rest in any general, systematic way.

Those who perpetuate the dichotomy will argue that advertising is 'remote' from the audience and therefore unlikely to be able to clinch the sale, whereas below-the-line techniques are 'direct' and quite capable of doing so, and will extend the logic to propose that short-term brand-winning can be achieved below the line but long-term brand building demands sustained above-the-line activity. They also argue that the effect of below-the-line campaigns is more easily measured and tracked over time. These are reasonable arguments as far as they go, but have to be qualified by conditions and exclusions in practice. For instance, direct-response advertising (above) is by definition 'direct', but sponsorship (below) is 'remote'. With respect to the measurability criterion, users of sponsorship have so far been notoriously unwilling to make the effort at all, whereas most advertisers (above) at least try, in the face of considerable technical difficulties.

In general, the above/below boundary is being blurred by the rapid growth of Internet advertising, the proliferation of dot.com direct merchants and the arrival of interactive television.

Meanwhile, Table 17.1 shows that advertising continues to dominate the UK promotional mix. A steady, small decline in the amount spent on buying space and time in conventional media has been compensated for over the four-year period by a very steep increase in expenditure in the 'new media', though that remains for the time being a very modest amount in real terms. This share of the mix held by this sole above-the-line ingredient is not far short of half the total UK promotional expenditure, and only seven percentage points less than that held by the two largest below-the-line ingredients in combination. Two of the other three have been losing share, and they collectively represented only just over 5 per cent of the grand total in 2000. There is thus no evidence whatever for the widely held belief that marketers are steadily shifting their money from above to below the line.

Table 17.1 The promotional mix: shares of UK total annual expenditure, 1997–2000			
	1997 (%)	*1998* (%)	*1999* (%)	*2000* (%)
Advertising	43.1	45.6	42.8	43.7
(of which, Internet)	(0.03)	(0.06)	(0.14)	(0.40)
Direct	26.7	26.0	28.0	25.7
Sales promotion	23.4	22.8	23.8	24.9[1]
Exhibitions	3.2	2.7	2.5	2.6[1]
Point-of-purchase	2.2	1.6	1.7[2]	1.9
Sponsorship	1.4	1.3	1.2	1.2
(of which, sport)	(1.19)	(1.12)	(1.04)	(1.02)
(of which, arts)	(0.22)	(0.22)	(0.17)	(0.15)
Base total (£)	26 936 000	31 651 000	36 119 000	39 280 000
Year-on-year change (%)		+17.5	+14.1	+8.9

[1] Estimated from 1999 on the basis of average increase for the other four.
[2] Midpoint between 1998 and 2000 figures.
Dateline: May 2002.
Sources: Advertising Association; Interactive Advertising Bureau; Direct Marketing Association; Institute of Sales Promotion; Association of Exhibition Organizers; Point-of-Purchase Advertising International; Ipsos UK Sponsorship; Arts and Business.

Through the line

A trend which may eventually banish this promotional apartheid has been gaining momentum in recent years.

Throughout the twentieth century, managers responsible for the implementation of promotional strategy either enlisted the services of experts in the separate disciplines individually or turned to an advertising agency for a multidisciplinary solution, accepting that the latter would impartially decide on a promotional mix appropriate to the circumstances. The agencies encouraged that belief by claiming to be able to design and deliver (for example) sales promotion or direct marketing campaigns internally, but in practice often subcontracted the job to independent experts and delivered the outcome to the client at a mark-up. They were *advertising* agencies, staffed by *advertising* people, despite the claimed 'full-service' capability. It would be surprising if they did not exhibit a tendency, putting it no more strongly, to approach promotional strategy from the advertising standpoint and treat the rest of the promotional mix as a selection of possible back-up options. It is only quite recently that specialist 'below-the-line' agencies have prospered in their own right, and most of the largest are in fact quasi-autonomous companies within massive holding companies built up by advertising agencies, such as WPP, Interpublic or Omnicom.

In 1993, what was then the world's largest advertising agency, Saatchi & Saatchi, dropped the word 'advertising' from its title and proclaimed itself a 'through-the-line communications agency'. Five years earlier, the founding partners of a predecessor in Scotland had witnessed the conditioned reflex in favour of an advertising-led strategy while working as a team at a full-service advertising agency handling the promotion of the National Garden Festival. It is abundantly clear in hindsight that the nature of the event demanded a multi-disciplinary strategy, but the agency in fact recommended spending most of limited promotional funds on press and television advertising. The partners were later reported in the business press to have said they were 'frankly, not absolutely convinced that we were right', and the prospectus of their new agency declared: 'We operate with a total disregard for the line. We are neither above-the-line specialists, nor [do we] concentrate on below-the-line activity. Basically, we ignore the line.' This is a clear expression of the 'integrated marketing communications' approach vigorously advocated in such recent British textbooks as Kitchen (1998), Smith and Taylor (2001), Varey (2001), and Fill (2002).

A genuinely integrated, through-the-line promotional strategy must begin with methodical and thorough situational analysis undertaken without prejudice. Consider this hypothetical case in point: you have been briefed by the manufacturer of a material for dental fillings which is white and costs less than either gold or silver amalgam. What key ingredients of such an analysis might form the basis of decisions to allocate promotional effort among the available elements of the mix?

Your answer may perhaps include such factors as: the explicability of the product; its newsworthiness; potential controversy; the accessibility of at least two key audiences; questions of image; budget; controllability of feasible options. Sufficiently detailed explanation of the product to dentists might be thought to demand an *advertisement* in a professional magazine, provided they can be depended on not to ignore it altogether, or a carefully constructed *direct marketing* initiative, if they have not been made resistant by the sheer volume they receive.

Generating the complementary demand-pull among dental patients would seem to require a much less complex but far more emotionally loaded message directed at family decision-making gatekeepers, the delivery of which could perhaps be best accomplished by means of *publicity* targeted at women's magazines. On the other hand, it might be thought desirable to maintain a vaguely mysterious high-technology aura around the product. The product's newsworthiness is self-evident, but the details could contain the germ of a controversy, placing particular emphasis on the issue of control over publicity initiatives. It could be reasoned that consumer *sales promotions* are a feasible option only once the patients have been brought to the point-of-sale by other forces, but dentist incentives could be a fruitful if high-risk ploy.

Whatever the outcome of your personal analysis, a dominantly above-the-line strategy would be hard to justify even if you did happen to be employed by an advertising agency. Likewise one based largely on sales promotion or concentrating heavily on packaging, even if those were your home disciplines. For this particular product, a through-the-line solution seems inescapable.

The promotional budget

Decisions about the allocation of effort above and below the line cannot be made, of course, until it has been established how much money is available to be spent on media buying, the distribution of news releases, telemarketing costs, sponsorship deals, the designing and production of packaging, point-of-sale and sales promotion materials, and so on. This amount is formally defined as the promotional *appropriation*, reflecting the fact that it is *appropriated* from the total funds allocated to the marketing effort. In Britain, but less so in America, it is more likely to be called the 'promotional budget'.

In fact, a budget is not an *amount* of money, as in colloquial usage, but a *plan* for spending it, as in the annual 'budget speech' by the UK Chancellor of the Exchequer. It describes sources and uses of funds over a given future period, normally a year. By demanding forward planning, providing an integrated framework for operational decisions, and establishing quantifiable standards of cost-effective performance, it formalizes *control* over expenditure. If a statement of the promotional appropriation is not accompanied by such a plan for spending it, there is far too much scope for profligate waste of scarce funds in a business that is notoriously image conscious and fashion led. As a noted author from within the business remarks in a book significantly titled *Accountable Advertising*:

> It is no longer enough for the marketing director to determine how much it is right to spend on advertising . . . [he or she] still has to make this decision but must now do more – justify it.
>
> (Broadbent, 1997, p. xv)

The most crucial control mechanism in a promotional budget will be the *cost-effectiveness* criteria it specifies. The tedious but straightforward process of recording all the many costs attributable to a campaign presents no practical difficulties. However, reliable measures of its effectiveness are rarely encountered in practice beyond the direct marketing and advertising disciplines. Even in those two cases, criteria are severely limited. The success or failure of a direct marketing initiative is normally reported in terms of coupon returns, enquiries or off-the-page orders; its communicative efficacy is seldom tested in any way. Advertising effectiveness is typically measured by criteria such as awareness, recall, attitude change and sales movements. Yet there has never been convincing proof that the first three actually increase the probability that the audience will subsequently take appropriate action, while the fourth makes dubious assumptions about

short-term cause and effect. Those arguments will be taken up later in this chapter. Meanwhile, we have to conclude that promotional expenditure may be scrutinized and constrained, but is not controlled in any meaningful sense of the word. Readers interested in pursuing the issue of *budgeting* further should consult Broadbent's excellent 'handbook for managers', cited earlier, mentally converting from advertising to the rest of the promotional mix as necessary. The rest of this section will concern itself with *appropriation setting*.

Almost 30 years ago, Rees (1977) and Dhalla (1977) independently found that, in the UK and the USA respectively, advertising managers and brand managers typically made an initial bid for an adequate appropriation in competition with other claimants on total funds set aside for marketing, but that the ensuing decision process was notably hierarchical. Heads of each major marketing function having negotiated for their slice of the pie, the board of directors would debate the merits of their cases. Vested interests could then result in further bargaining. Almost invariably, the chief executive retained sole authority for final approval, and those decisions were duly transmitted back down the organization to those answerable for using the various appropriations productively.

The generally political nature of this process was confirmed a decade later in Britain by Piercy (1987), and there is no reason to suspect any significant change since then. Nevertheless, textbooks typically imply that the advertising appropriation (the only one they generally consider within 'promotion') is indeed set by those responsible for spending it. The neglected reality that they have no such authority to set their own budget has a crucial impact on strategic planning: a ceiling is imposed on spending which may bear little relationship to promotional objectives or the firm's situation relative to the competition.

Whoever actually decides the amount to be spent on advertising is likely to use one or more of a set of well-known standard methods. Non-standard nomenclature disguises the fact that they can be grouped into the four categories in Table 17.2. The descriptions under each group heading are examples of the general method in question, using the terminology in common use.

The application of *executive judgement* may seem an unacceptably vague and risky approach to such an important decision. However, we shall see that the other methods available to decision makers are themselves illogical, inflexible, based on large assumptions, or all three. Therefore, though the everyday descriptions of this approach to the task hardly inspire confidence, the accumulated wisdom and intuition of experienced practitioners should not be undervalued.

The best known *internal ratio* is advertising-to-sales, which sets the appropriation at a given percentage of either the previous year's figure or the forecast for the coming year. It has the respectability of being an arithmetic formula, but suffers the serious logical flaw that the ratio itself must be decided before the method can be used. In practice, that is normally done by the application of executive judgement or by reference to industry norms, which may not be appropriate to the particular circumstances. Furthermore, it is potentially disastrous to apply this method when sales have been falling. If the purpose of advertising is to help generate sales, then spending a constant ratio of a decreasing amount is a curious way to go about rectifying the situation.

The most familiar *external ratio* is competitive parity, which matches the appropriation to the estimated expenditure of a significant competitor or to the prevailing norm, with the aim of buying a fair share of voice in the general advertising hubbub. The more everyone follows everyone else, the less logical it is to believe that competitors are behaving rationally or the collective wisdom is correct. Furthermore, the method takes no account of the need for a new entrant to a market to take the risk of disproportionately heavy expenditure to gain a foothold.

The reliability of the many proprietary *modelling and experimentation* procedures depends upon the assumptions made and formulae used, and the average practitioner lacks the mathematical sophistication to evaluate those. Using them is in that case rather like

Table 17.2 Methods for determining the promotional appropriation			
Executive judgement	Internal ratios	External ratios	Modelling and experimentation
AYCA = all you can afford	A/S ratio = advertising-to-sales ratio	Competitive parity	Adstock
Affordable approach	Case rate	Dynamic difference	AMTES = area marketing test evaluation systems
Arbitrary method	Historical parity	Market share method	Econometrics
Notional sum	Inertia method	Share of voice	Prescriptive models
	Marginal costing approach		Simulation
	Per-unit allowance		What-if models
	Same as last year		

buying a pig in a poke from a magician. For a dispassionate review of what is available, see Chapter 8 of Broadbent (1997).

Objective-and-task is widely treated as the best option on the grounds that it is more 'logical': starting with objectives and calculating the cost of the tasks required to achieve them, instead of starting with a sum of money and then deciding what to do with it. However, it does not follow that the means of achieving the objectives will be obvious and the costs unequivocal. Practical guides are apt to conclude with the exhortation to 'estimate the required expenditures', a nasty sting in the tail. Nevertheless, this procedure does force decision makers to be more rigorous in their approach to an absolutely crucial task.

A collective weakness of all five methods is their tendency to focus on short-term profit maximization at the expense of long-term goals. Indeed, the very convention of annual budgeting can in practice encourage strategically questionable revision of existing promotional campaigns. The admirable (and evidently effective) thematic continuity of BMW advertising in Britain over a 25-year period, for example, is the exception rather than the rule.

The practical usefulness of this worryingly vague technology can be improved by treating the contents of Table 17.2 as an à la carte menu, rather than table d'hôte. Any and all feasible options can be chosen from it, a variety of 'answers' obtained, and executive judgement applied to the task of deriving the best solution from them. Survey evidence suggests that, on average, two options are combined to arrive at the amount to be spent on advertising. It appears that no equivalent studies relating to other ingredients of the promotional mix have so far been published.

Three of the available appropriation-setting methods have dominated practice over the years. Data from a series of surveys over a 30-year period show that they are executive judgement, the advertising-to-sales ratio and the objective-and-task approach. Until the mid-1980s, that was the rank order of popularity, to

judge by the average of all responses across the surveyed samples. Since then, it has exactly reversed, as a comprehensive transnational survey first found (Synodinos *et al.*, 1989). That might be taken as an improvement, but for the comments made earlier about the pitfalls of applying the objective-and-task method in practice.

It is lastly far from reassuring to report that, in Britain, neither the second edition of a handbook on 'how to plan advertising' (Cooper, 1997) nor a 'guide to best practice' from the Institute of Practitioners in Advertising (Butterfield, 1997) makes any mention at all of appropriation-setting procedures, admirable though both of them otherwise are. Furthermore, there seems to be no readily available published discussion of available approaches to the task in the context of the other elements of the promotional mix.

Deploying the promotional mix

Those responsible for the execution of promotional strategy, faced by the choice of eight broad means to achieve promotional objectives, need a formal framework for deciding which to use and which not, and how much weight to give to each one chosen. An overall constraint on choice will of course be imposed by the funds appropriated for the purpose, the subject of the previous section, and an influence inevitably exerted by the industry-wide trends reported in the one before. Decision makers will furthermore monitor the tactics of their competitors, debating the relative merits of head-to-head assaults versus outflanking manoeuvres. Taking those factors as given, Table 17.3 proposes seven other variables, in the form of a checklist for cost-effective deployment of the promotional mix. To illustrate how this template might be used in practice to include or exclude available options, consider its application to the case of *advertising* a new cinema complex via large

Table 17.3 A promotional mix checklist	
Target:	Can this option reach the right audience?
Message:	Can it deliver this kind of message?
Price:	What will we be charged to use it?
Cost:	What will it cost us produce the material?
Receptivity:	Will the audience accept the message?
Modulation:	Will the vehicle affect their 'reading' of it?
Measurability:	Can we reliably assess effectiveness?

posters in urban locations (what common usage calls 'billboards').

'Outdoor' media of this kind are seen by anybody and everybody: pedestrians, motorists, users of public transport. The proposed campaign therefore could reach the required *target* audience of 18- to 35-year-old couples, but with a great deal of wastage in the process unless particular sites could be identified on the basis of audience profiles provided by an industry-wide programme of continuous research, and bought individually.

The *message* a poster can deliver is self-evidently limited to what can be encapsulated in a short statement in large letters, or conveyed non-verbally. In this case, that is not a disadvantage, for the fact that a brand new, purpose-built, conveniently located multiplex has opened will be enough to encourage trial among potential visitors.

Poster campaigns are normally bought as package deals, at *prices* which are middling in advertising terms but high by comparison with most other ingredients of the promotional mix. For instance, a campaign running on 700 large poster sites around the UK would cost up to £400 000 per month. Buying local sites individually, which this advertiser needs to do, is significantly more expensive than the *pro rata* fraction: perhaps more than half a million for the same coverage of the target audience. The *cost* of producing such a large item of high-quality full-colour print work, in sufficient quantity to allow for periodic

renewal at each site as the weather took its toll, would also be high.

The *receptivity* of typical audiences is much less of a problem than critics of advertising would have us believe. For example, a series of surveys of public attitudes in the UK has consistently found that fewer than one in ten of large and representative samples of the general population 'disliked' or 'did not really like' the posters they encountered in their daily lives (Advertising Association, 2000). Because posters are seen as a rather brash medium, audiences may add subjective interpretations to the objective content of the message. This *modulation* is not as strong as that due to the 'tone of voice' of most newspapers, for example, and could in any case suit the brand image of a cinema complex.

Measurability is a complicated matter. The industry-wide research mentioned earlier can produce likelihood-to-see values for 73 000 poster sites around the country, but that is only a start. There is no easy way to find out how many members of a target audience did see a given site, notice the poster on it, take in the message, or act accordingly. The choice of this option would thus be something of an act of faith. Other promotional options are significantly more measurable, but the assessment of effectiveness is a general problem, and is something that will be taken up later in this chapter.

On balance, poster advertising seems an expensive but potentially effective option for reaching the target audience with the required message in this case. In others, however, conscientious application of the checklist could have quite different outcomes.

If the audience is highly specific, for instance, direct marketing by mail or e-mail has the potential to *target* it more effectively. The mode of *message* delivery permits much more detail than a poster, though it is limited by the recipient's interest and patience. The *price* consists only of postal charges, potentially reduced by volume discounts. However, considerable *cost* is likely to be incurred in producing the kind of mail shot that actually engages the favourable attention of prospective customers. Furthermore, the intrusive reputation of direct mail results in generally low *receptivity*, so the price and cost per converted call can be substantial. Because the verbal message is typically reinforced by visual devices, often in considerable quantity and variety, *modulation* is unavoidable and far from uniform. *Measurability* is self-evidently straightforward.

In another situation, publicity might be chosen as the best way to deliver a simple or detailed *message* to a general or specific *audience*. There is no *price* at all, and the *cost* is very low. Audiences do not generally stop to think whether reportage and editorial comment are spontaneous or the result of a press release, so *receptivity* is a negligible consideration. On the other hand, the potential for *modulation* is highest among all ingredients of the promotional mix, because a third party has been invited to act as interpreter between the originator and the audience. Someone else's agenda can thus determine the form and content of the eventual message. As for *measurability*, the volume of coverage resulting from the initiative can easily be monitored, quantified and classified as productive, neutral or damaging. However, the effect on the target audience will be a matter of pure speculation.

An underlying dimension in all these hypothetical cases is the issue of *controllability*. It is worth reminding ourselves that the marketing mix and its sub-mixes are normally defined as the 'controllable variables' in the marketing equation. The degree of control which can in fact be exerted over the outcome of a promotional initiative is therefore a crucial strategic issue. The three examples above include the two ends of a broad spectrum: advertising is highly controllable, but at a price; publicity is virtually uncontrollable, but cheap. The third may at first seem to occupy a position towards the low end, for authors and commentators generally emphasize the assumed high resistance to its output: mail shots, mail drops, telesales calls and unsolicited promotional messages received by fax or e-mail. On the other hand, prolific use by such sophisticated marketers as *Reader's Digest* and the AA (Automobile Association) suggests that it can yield cost-effective results when applied efficiently.

Among the other techniques in the promotional mix, sponsorship is a relatively new phenomenon, which has been growing rapidly in recent years (see Table 17.1). The strategic aim of sports sponsorship, as one example, is to gain direct real-time exposure, plus secondary exposure through media coverage, plus more general publicity. This poses special controllability problems. For instance, sportswear manufacturers have established formal associations with performers or teams who later generated nothing but negative publicity, an outcome which must have reflected to some extent and in some way on the sponsor. Similarly, event organizers who struck lucrative deals with tobacco companies a decade ago have since inherited a public relations liability, thanks to a sea-change in official and public attitudes to smoking. In 2002, a ban on all tobacco sponsorship of sport was announced, to take effect in 2003. Formula 1 motor racing, much the most prominently linked, was given a reprieve until 2008. Its world organizing body promptly lobbied for Moscow to be added to the list of Grand Prix venues, presumably because such sponsorship is not regulated in Russia, evidence of the faith that major sponsors have in the effectiveness of this ingredient of the mix.

Yet no one has so far proposed any systematic way to measure the positive or negative results of a sponsorship campaign. Meanwhile actual and potential beneficiaries are learning their true value as promotional vehicles, and raising the initially rather modest stakes. Simultaneously, it is becoming very obvious that most wearers of clothing that sports large-scale designer-brand logos are not the kind of people that the companies themselves would presumably choose as endorsers of the brand. For all these reasons, it is very likely that the issue of *controllability* will assume much greater significance in future.

As for the rest of the promotional mix, it might be an interesting intellectual exercise to make a personal judgement about the location of each ingredient in the spectrum, all other things being equal.

Developing the message

Originators of promotional messages normally delegate the task of converting abstract strategy into concrete words and images to a specialist intermediary with expertise in the particular promotional technique concerned, or to a *full-service advertising agency* (see 'Above and below the line'). The generic term 'agency' will be used here. The process is normally described as 'creative planning'.

It starts with a *client brief*, from which the agency distils an internal *creative brief*. Specialists in turn convert that into the *creative executions*, which in due course become finished messages in the form of advertisements, mail shots, promotional packs, or whatever. An authoritative explanation of the processes which produce these transformations is surprisingly elusive. Textbooks and professional monographs focus instead on the executional techniques and outcomes. The framework presented in Figure 17.2 reflects a personal view, drawing upon industry seminars and conversations with practitioners. The sequence of events

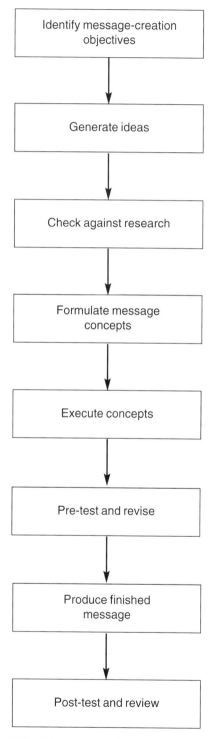

Figure 17.2   The message development process

is by no means invariable, and the process may be altogether less methodical in practice.

Creative planning is a team operation at the agency. It involves *account managers* (see 'Working relationships'), who keep the client involved throughout the process, *account planners*, who bring a research-based understanding of the target audience to the task, *copywriters*, who produce the words to convey the message, and *art directors*, who devise the images to reinforce it. Their collective aim is to meet the objectives in the client brief and outflank the opposition in doing so.

The process begins with the isolation of specifically creative objectives from guidelines in the brief, including a clear statement of the key messages and target audiences. The next stage is likely to be a think-tank session, at which the remit is to 'apply lateral, disruptive thinking to the problem', in the words of a prominent creative director. It was inspiration by such means that redefined the old-fashioned convalescent remedy Lucozade as an energy drink for teenagers and the AA (Automobile Association) as 'the fourth emergency service'. Raw ideas of that kind are next subjected to the discipline of scrutiny against research-based analysis of probable audience responses, and the survivors refined into more precise communication concepts. For example, travelling by Virgin Atlantic emerged from this stage of creative planning as a way to 'get a life', and the Honda HR-V as 'the Joy Machine' in four markets.

Concepts must next be converted into creative executions. The only generally available textbook to provide an expert description of this process was published in 1988, and has long been overtaken by technology. Apple Mac software and ISDN data transmission have seen to it that 'visualizers' no longer produce hand-drawn 'roughs' or 'scamps', to be married up with the output from 'phototypesetting' as 'finished art', and dispatched by messenger to the printer. Next comes a vital precaution against wayward creativity: pre-testing the outcome on a sample of the target audience and

reviewing the strategy in the light of the findings. In practice, agencies and clients will sometimes place their faith in the creative development process and back their own judgement. Once the campaign has run, however, it would be extremely unusual not to conduct a post-test of effectiveness. Findings relevant to creative strategy can be compared with the objectives set at the start of the process, and the conclusions held as an input to the next creative planning cycle.

In contrast to the dearth of published material on creative planning, there is an abundance of literature on its results, which can yield insights into the planning behind them. The most accessible current source is a series of collections of winning submissions for Britain's biennial Creative Planning Awards competition (Account Planning Group, 2002).

Delivering the message

The promotional mix offers a very diverse set of message delivery channels. For example, the gap between originator and audience might be bridged by a team chosen for a sports sponsorship linkage, by telemarketing operators, by the ambience in which packages are displayed or, most obviously, by the media in which publicity and advertising appear. Little has been written formally on the process of selecting specific options within the first four general choices, but a whole sub-industry is devoted to the last. This section will therefore restrict itself to advertisers, and their approach to *media planning*.

As with development of the message, this task is routinely delegated to an external specialist. In the case of advertising, that will be an advertising agency with an in-house media department or a 'media independent', which offers media planning and buying expertise to conventional agencies or their clients, and offers no other service. Over the past 20 years, the latter have expanded steadily at the

expense of the former. In the case of other
ingredients of the marketing mix, the search
will be on for the appropriate expert intermediary. As before, this section will use the
generic term 'agency' for all of these. It will also
by default concentrate on the particularly complex task of allocating available funds among
proliferating advertising media.

Developing the plan for delivering the
message is a team operation. In the advertising
context, it involves *account managers* (see 'Working relationships'), who keep the client
involved throughout the process, in-house or
idependent *media planners*, information technologists with access to a vast array of media
research, and *media buyers*, who bargain with
the *media owners*. Their collective aim is to find
the right targets, outflank the competition, and
do so cost-effectively.

Planning the correct strategy for delivery
of the message starts with the *client brief*, from
which an internal *media brief* is distilled. Specialists apply that to the twin tasks of *media
selection*, choosing the vehicles to deliver the
creative strategy to the target audience, and
media scheduling, fixing the timing of individual
exposures over the duration of the campaign.
The classic British textbook is Broadbent and
Jacobs (1984), to which no equally detailed
successor has yet appeared. Beware, however,
that the media landscape has changed radically
since it was published; the general principles
are all that remain valid. In the absence of a
readily available textbook explanation of the
principles and practices involved, Figure 17.3
offers a procedural framework, based on professional guides and long-term observation of
practitioners in action.

The process begins with the isolation of
objectives in the client brief relevant to such
media-related factors as the 'mood' or 'tone of
voice' of the advertising and the description of
the target audience. The latter must include a
clear psychographic profile, for the sophisticated and comprehensive databases built up by
industry-wide *media research* over many years
can tell planners a great deal about associated

Figure 17.3   The message delivery process

media consumption habits. An essential second step is to establish the *media allocation* within the advertising appropriation, for it places a limit on what is practically possible. The team will next monitor competitors' media usage, in order to find unoccupied ground in the communication landscape. For example, the agency which launched the Häagen-Dazs ice-cream brand in Britain some 10 years ago deliberately avoided the orthodox medium for the product, television, and caught Unilever off guard with a poster campaign that cost less than £500 000. It was a manifestly successful strategy.

These preliminaries completed, media planners can construct a broad-brush *strategic plan*, by matching the objectives in the media brief to the audience delivery capabilities and message modulation propensities of the five so-called 'major media' comprising the UK *media mix*: press, television, radio, cinema and outdoor. This traditional, simplistic categorization is rapidly becoming outmoded in the face of the well-chronicled information explosion, but remains the standard for the time being. The confines of a single chapter do not permit a review of their key characteristics, but thumbnail sketches can be found in an encyclopaedic dictionary of marketing and advertising terms (Baker, 1998), under the five relevant headwords plus 'major media' and 'media share'. No single textbook can be recommended as providing a more comprehensive review that is reasonably up to date.

Once the strategic plan has been debated, refined and agreed, the emphasis shifts to the tactical level. Making choices among the *media options* within each class is in essence a matter of evaluating them with respect to nine key variables. Seven of these have already been identified in Figure 17.3. In addition, media planners need to take into account the *creative scope* offered by an option under consideration: will it place constraints on the execution of the creative strategy being developed simultaneously? They will also be influenced by its *user-friendliness*: the degree of effort required to book and control a campaign. Media buying has

become generally easier during the past decade, but there can still be considerable variation from one case to the next.

With the choices of media made, the planners turn their attention to the building of a *media schedule* capable of delivering the message to the required audience in the right way at the right times. Given that personal viewing, listening and reading habits vary considerably within any audience, frequency and volume of exposure to any schedule can never be uniform. Conceptually difficult discussions in academic and practitioner journals testify to the fact that scheduling is an extremely complex undertaking.

In practice, a first step towards selection and scheduling decisions will be to feed performance requirements into on-line media selection programs or desktop software packages that all media planners now use as a matter of course. Those cannot make decisions by themselves, however, and this highly numerate and technologically sophisticated discipline still depends significantly on the collective experience and wisdom of its practitioners.

By such processes, the strategic plan is in due course transformed into a costed *operational plan*, which is in turn translated into a campaign schedule by *media buyers*. These specialists have the disposition needed to haggle successfully with the hard-nosed representatives of the media sales houses and advertising departments. Bargaining skills are especially important in buying television advertising time, which is effectively auctioned. The complexities of media buying are well explained in Chapter 8 of Brierley (1995). Because the cost of a schedule reflects deals struck with suppliers, it may vary significantly from the forecast in the operational plan, which is consequently reviewed and if necessary revised at intervals. At the end of the campaign, the planning team will assess the cost-effectiveness of their media strategy, and retain the findings in mind as part of the history influencing each future iteration of the planning cycle.

Examples of media planning in practice can be found in the relevant passages of the winning submissions for the biennial IPA Advertising Effectiveness Awards (Institute of Practitioners in Advertising, 2000). If esoteric vocabulary acts as a barrier to understanding the finer points of a particular media strategy, definitions of key terms can be found in Baker (1998). The vital sources of media research are described in detail in Chapter 9 of Brierley (1995).

The medium and the message

Independent observers encountering the twin disciplines of developing and delivering the promotional message inevitably begin to wonder which comes first. In principle, neither should; in practice, it will depend on circumstances. After the *client brief* has been brought to the agency by the *account manager*, the creative and media teams will at first plan independently but in parallel. Once they reach the stages, respectively, of defining key communication concepts and deciding a broad media strategy, each must cross-check the developing plan with the other and, via the account manager, with the client. There is no point in devising a creative strategy which cannot be executed in the media vehicles capable of reaching the target audience, or buying a media vehicle which delivers the right audience at a favourable cost if it cannot offer the required creative scope. Furthermore, we have already seen, in 'Deploying the promotional mix', that the audience's reading of a message can be modulated by their perception of the channel or vehicle which delivers it. This 'vehicle effect' or 'rub-off value' can apply to the team chosen for a sports sponsorship linkage, the regional accents of telemarketing operators, the ambience in which packages are displayed or, most obviously, the media in which publicity and advertising appear.

Nevertheless, popular accounts of the advertising do generally stress the creative aspect. That bias prompted a prominent speaker at an industry seminar to 'explode the myth that media is an add-on service which lies dormant whilst the brand team are developing creative work, and is then called upon to write a plan which delivers the messages to the target audience'. On the contrary, 'a good media brief is as important as a good creative brief. It should excite the planning team into exploring new opportunities to deliver the brand message with impact . . . to be surprised'. In short, the only intellectually proper response to the chicken-and-egg question is neither, however equivocal that may sound.

A mix within a mix: synergy or counter-synergy?

The fact that one of the four Ps, promotion, is explicitly associated with communication conceals another of crucial strategic significance: that the other three also have the potential to convey a message.

The case of the highly successful BMW brand provides a very clear case in point. It was reported in the fourth edition of *The Marketing Book*, and has since been presented elsewhere as a full-length case history (Crosier, 1998a). This analyses the brand's strengths and weaknesses with respect to each of the four Ps of the marketing mix, in turn.

Where *product* is concerned, non-expert observers are likely to speak rather vaguely of 'German engineering' and 'build quality'. Yet the various models in fact sit near the middle of the relevant league tables published by *Which?* magazine. It is a fact, too, that Renault, Honda and Peugeot have recently done just as well on the proving grounds of the Grand Prix racing track and the international rally circuit. Toyota is the brand consistently found to be most reliable in use, and Japanese manufacturers in general dominate those tables. Meanwhile, German brands generally offer equipment that is standard in Japanese models as added-cost extras at considerable cost.

Turning to *price*, and acknowledging the British predilection to associate high price with high value, one finds that BMW dealers are paradoxically likely to emphasize the competitive prices of the entry-level models, and offer deals to fleet buyers and contract hirers that compare directly with the company car workhorses from Ford and Vauxhall. The exclusive cachet promised by the perceived premium price is furthermore threatened in reality by the fact that roughly 50 000 of the marque are sold in Britain every year, giving it a market share almost twice that of Honda and only just below Citroen.

It is not until one considers *place* that the puzzling gap between reality and perception begins to close. BMW dealerships are characteristically dressed in high-technology corporate identity, rigorously controlled from Munich, which gives out the first signals consistent with the brand's evident mystique. Reception areas resemble private hospitals, service managers do not accuse customers of having deviously maltreated their own vehicles, oily overalls are nowhere in sight, and the atmosphere is reverential. However, these facts will normally only be known to those who are already users.

Promotion consists mainly of media advertising, product litetrature and sponsorship. We have already noted the remarkable consistency of BMW advertising in Britain over a quarter of a century. It is heavy on style and low on objective information, but the aim is clearly to predispose the audience to seek out the rest of the story. The literature is another manifestation of centrally controlled corporate identity, coolly understated. The choice of sponsorship associations completes the aspirational message to the target audience.

A key feature of the BMW case is that an admired brand leader is pursuing a promotional strategy which comes dangerously close to placing all its communicative eggs in one basket: the P that is explicitly associated with communication. In so doing, it risks the consequences of ignoring the potential for *synergy* among the elements of the marketing mix – or, more damagingly, *counter-synergy.*

It is arguable that the first two of the four Ps have the potential to convey implicit messages which contradict those explicitly delivered by the fourth, and that the third can only redress the imbalance if something else brings potential customers to the point of sale. This is a knife-edge strategic situation for the future of a brand that has become contradictorily commonplace for something held to be exclusive. If the promotional initiative should be lost for any reason, or if the motorcycles and the eccentric C1 scooter should together challenge the carefully cultivated sporting and executive image of the cars, counter-synergy could threaten to reverse the prevailing synergy. Managers with responsibility for 'promotion' risk a specific form of Levitt's famous 'marketing myopia' if, simply by default, they ignore this interaction within the marketing mix as a system and focus their attention instead on the one element containing the overtly 'communicative' ingredients.

Pulling it all together: the promotional plan

The kind of strategic and tactical decisions discussed so far in this chapter will ideally be formalized into a *promotional plan*, to be disseminated to those charged with the responsibility for translating them into action. Given the obvious importance of such a document, it is surprising that most textbooks and guidebooks for practitioners fall short of the ideal when they focus within the total marketing plan on the sub-plan relating to promotion or communication. An honourable exception is the very detailed treatment in Stapleton and Thomas (1998). For present purposes, Table 17.4 aims to provide a usable template for the construction of a workable plan. It signals its intended use as an action plan by posing questions to be

Table 17.4 Structure and content of the promotional plan

1 INPUTS
What are we offering to whom?
  1.1 Product or service profile
    Specification: what can it do?
    Benefits: what can it offer?
  1.2 Organization profile
    Specification: what do we do?
    Identity: how do we present ourselves?
    Image: how are we seen?
  1.3 Audience profile
    Demographics: who are they, and where?
    Psychographics: what do they want?
  1.4 Market profile
    Structure: what does it look like?
    Competition: who is there with us?
    Dynamics: what is in the future?

2 CONSTRAINTS
What is beyond our control?
  2.1 Marketing mix
    Product policy: what effect on promotion strategy?
    Pricing policy: what effect on promotion strategy?
    Place policy: what effect on promotion strategy?
  2.2 Givens
    Precedents: what is traditional?
    Mandatories: what is compulsory?
    Appropriation: what funds are available?
    Budget: how will efficiency be monitored?

3 OBJECTIVES
What do we need to achieve?
  3.1 Goals: what is the overall, long-term aim?
  3.2 Targets: what are the intermediate aims of this plan?
  3.3 Criteria: how will effectiveness be measured?

4 STRATEGY
How will we achieve campaign objectives?
  4.1 Message: what will it say?
  4.2 Creative: how will it say it?
  4.3 Channel: how will it be delivered?

5 TIMETABLE
How do tactics become a campaign?
  5.1 Timescale: by when must objectives be met?
  5.2 Schedule: what needs to happen when?

6 IMPLEMENTATION
How will the campaign be managed?
  6.1 Authority: who can say yes or no?
  6.2 Responsibility: who will be answerable?
  6.3 Delegation: what will be sub-contracted?
  6.4 Procedures: how will progress be tracked?
  6.5 Evaluation: how will results be measured?

answered. Though those are intended to be more or less self-explanatory, a few further comments are indicated.

Within item 1.1, it will be vital to specify as part of the product or service profile the *benefits* that can be delivered to potential customers in the target audience. In practice, promotional plans are apt to concentrate on the technical specification of the offering, in a production-oriented manner that should be anathema to anyone who has studied marketing. Similarly, the audience profile needs to go beyond mundane geodemographic data if the information is to realize its potential as a key factor in the development of message and delivery strategies. *Acorn Lifestyles* is probably the best known of many target-market classification systems available in Britain, all capable of providing the necessary psychographic and sociographic descriptions: for example, 'LW75: Homesharers in very affluent areas', which is elaborated in a 'neighbourhood overview' and thumbnail personal sketch in the user guide. This is a massive improvement over the typical descriptions in statements of advertising objectives in practice, such as 'ABC1 18- to 34-year-olds in major conurbations'.

Item 2.1 of the plan recalls the issue of interaction within the marketing mix, raised in the preceding section of this chapter. The first two headings in item 2.2 draw attention to the important fact that the execution of promotional strategies may in practice be constrained by precedents set in previous campaigns and by non-negotiable requirements set at a high level in the organizational hierarchy. The power of precedent was illustrated when the St Ivel company, whose product range was natural dairy products, decided to market a wholly synthetic 'yellow-fat spread'. The creative strategy was to preserve their wholesome 'heritage', even when talking to a contemporary audience about a manufactured product. The outcome was a television commercial that combined striking special effects with utterly traditional symbols: a five-barred gate, a milk churn and the rising sun. The importance of so-called 'mandatories' is demonstrated by the house-style guide that enshrines BMW's vital corporate identity. Its agencies and dealers are required, among a number of other injunctions, always to use the standard brand symbol and to ensure that the blue used is the one defined by a given 'Pantone' number. They must also use only the Neue Helvetica typeface for the letters BMW, the name of the dealer or the 'strapline' in an advertisement, and only in black. Though such precedents and mandatories may be a procedural irritant for those who have to observe them, companies have a perfect right to establish them and the writers of promotional plans an obligation to make them explicit to all concerned.

The third ingredient of item 2.2 is a reminder that the whole plan is somewhat hypothetical if the funds available are not specified at the outset, rather than having to be requested at various points along the way. The one following it emphasizes the vital difference between the act of setting a 'budget', as the appropriation will inevitably be described in practice, and the process of budgeting. The term 'efficiency' seeks to distinguish this form of control from measuring the 'effectiveness' of the message in communicating with the audience, against criteria specified at item 3.3. Unfortunately, it is common practice to use 'cost-effectiveness' to sum up the idea intended here by 'efficiency'. These are quite separate criteria, and the effort should be made to keep them distinct in the plan.

The content of section 4 will vary considerably according to the particular pattern of deployment of the promotional mix. The amount of detail in each item will furthermore depend upon decisions about subcontracting the execution of promotional strategy or retaining responsibility in-house, made explicit at item 6.3. Many of the factors governing such choices can be inferred from the explanations and discussions in the next two sections of this chapter.

From the plan to the brief

The completed promotional plan may in turn become the template for construction of a *client brief*, if intermediaries are to be involved in the process of campaign development and implementation. It is a coherent statement of what they are expected to achieve on their client's behalf. The purpose is to provide the necessary guidance, not to give instructions to collaborators who have been employed for their collective experience and expertise. It is a moot point how much detail is needed to discharge that task effectively and efficiently. The only possible answer is the one traditionally given about the length of a piece of string. As the Incorporated Society of British Advertisers puts it in a practical guide: 'A good brief will be as short as possible but as long as is necessary.' This perhaps implies that brevity should be the overriding aim. The recipient can always ask follow-up questions.

The actors in the system

It must already be abundantly clear that the implementation of promotional campaigns is characterized in practice by a variety of working relationships, which can occur in a number of combinations according to circumstances. Figure 17.4 attempts a consolidation of all possible variations in a single system diagram.

Arrow 1 symbolizes the kind of message delivery system in which no intermediary is involved. The most obvious case in point is a sales representative delivering a pitch to a prospect, but personal selling is excluded from our version of the promotional mix. The nearest admissible equivalent would be a direct marketing initiative created, executed and distributed by in-house specialists. Such an uncomplicated arrangement offers two key benefits, the first of which is strong *control* over the content, construction and tone of the message. There is no

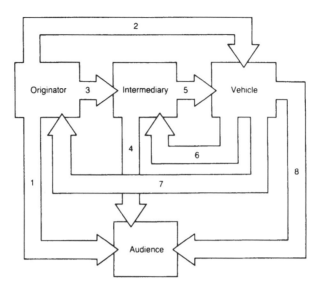

Figure 17.4   The four parties to the advertising transaction

scope for expert outsiders to argue successfully for alternative modes of execution, which may not necessarily achieve any improvement in communication. The second benefit is the lack of scope for *modulation* of the message. Although the two parties are not quite face-to-face and the mail is strictly speaking an intervening vehicle, this system of communication is so much a part of everyday life that perceptions of the transmission medium will have virtually no effect upon interpretation of the message. There may be resistance to the very fact that the initiative is unsolicited, but that is a broader issue. Though this option thus offers a very low level of risk, control of the outcome depends crucially on the originator's own communication *expertise*.

Arrows 2 and 8 together depict a situation in which the promotional message is transmitted to the target audience via some kind of intervening vehicle of communication; for example, when a news release successfully generates editorial comment. Only if the writer of the release is very practised in the craft will the text survive the process more or less intact. If editors do not ignore it altogether, they will treat it as the raw material for their own news item or story, to be given a spin that matches the style of their

publication and the interests of their readers, and decide when the outcome should appear. The originator thereby loses *control* over the outcome, to a largely unpredictable extent. Thereafter, the modified message becomes susceptible to *modulation*, as readers interpret it according to their perception of the publication in question. There is thus a significantly higher risk of ineffective communication than in the situation summed up by *arrow 1*.

Arrow 3 symbolizes the decision to subcontract the job of converting strategies into tactics. The quid pro quo of any such delegation is that the originator must allow the intermediary to argue for its own expert view of the most effective means to the end: the client provides the brief and the agency produces the solution. A degree of *control* is thereby sacrificed as *expertise* is acquired. *Arrow 4* represents the situation in which the intermediary subsequently transmits the message directly to the audience, for example by running a direct marketing campaign. *Arrow 5* applies when a vehicle of communication enters into the transmission, and the loop is closed by *arrow 8*.

That is how about four in every five advertising campaigns are managed in practice.

It is a less common choice for publicity initiatives, but equally possible. The introduction of a vehicle into the process compounds the loss of control in the case of 'free' publicity, as we have just seen, but not in the case of 'paid-for' advertising. In exchange for the price of space or time, the media owner undertakes that advertisements will appear in the booked position at the booked time and in the form in which they are submitted. This option is thus a matter of trading acquired *expertise* and (potentially) lower cost against reduced *control*.

Arrows 6 and 7 refer specifically to professional conventions affecting the working relationship among advertisers, agencies and media owners. Though it is logical to think of advertisers as the sellers in the transaction, because they use advertising to promote their offering to the audience, they are also buyers – of a commodity from media owners and a service from agencies. However, by long-established standard practice explained in more detail later, an advertising agency typically earns roughly two-thirds of its total income by buying the advertising space and time required for a client's campaign from the media owners at one price and claiming reimbursement in due course at another. Consequently, an unwritten code of professional conduct protects the livelihood of agencies by stipulating that media owners do not sell direct to advertisers (*arrow 7*), but make their sales pitch to the advertisers' agencies (*arrow 6*). In practice, they naturally present the case for their medium to both parties – demand-pull to reinforce supply-push – but are careful to observe the correct priority.

Media owners actually play two roles in this system. Their obvious *editorial* function is to deliver news and entertainment to readers, viewers and listeners. But they also allocate a certain portion of their total space or time to advertisers, who subsidize the price of news and entertainment by paying for the opportunity to address those readers, viewers and listeners.

Thus, as *arrow 8* symbolizes, promotional messages are actually transmitted by the media owners. The originators depend on the fact that the target audience will in fact easily 'decode' this familiar social process, and treat them as the source of the message. Except in very unusual situations, this will presumably be the case, which brings us back to the starting point of Figure 17.4, *arrow 1*.

Working relationships

The truism that all service industries are people businesses can in this case be a useful reminder that the system just described in the abstract is in fact a series of relationships between people. The effectiveness of the system depends on their ability to collaborate constructively. From that point of view, the interface between originator and intermediary is critical.

Responsibility for managing the originator's promotional mix will often be one of the responsibilities of a *brand manager* or *marketing manager*, though it will sometimes be devolved to a specialist with a title such as advertising manager or marketing communications co-ordinator. This is the person who delivers the client brief to any intermediary involved in deployment of the mix. The recipient, responsible for interpreting it to the expert specialists within their own organization, is generically described as an *account handler*. The term originated in the advertising business, where 'account' defines a single piece of business awarded to an advertising agency. The more self-explanatory description 'client service' is often applied to the function, but seldom to the person.

It would be logical to assume that the duties are shared more or less equally in such a working partnership, but the fact is that the onus for maintaining a good working relationship rests mainly on the account handler. This function is the classic career ladder in agencies of all kinds, and is characterized by a hierarchy of specific job titles, from junior account executive to group account director.

As in any other kind of service organization, the quality of after-sales customer service is a critical factor in the winning of repeat business, and it is the account handler's job to deliver it. In particular, his or (very often) her role is to minimize the potential for *culture clash* between agency and client. This is crucial because the atmosphere and ethos of typical examples of the former and latter could hardly be more different. Agency creative types do not sit opposite client R&D people at briefing meetings; instead, brand managers report client priorities to account executives, and account executives propose agency solutions to brand managers.

It follows that two skills in particular are essential attributes of effective account executives: *negotiation* and *co-ordination*. The latter is vital because one person is dealing on behalf of a whole organization. Without it, advertising campaigns will suffer the fate of the camel, to be a horse designed by a committee, deadlines will be missed, opportunities lost and much more besides. They also need to be effective co-ordinators and organizers.

Negotiation is not simply a matter of standing between the two parties keeping their respective specialists apart. An essential aspect of the job is to be the *advocate* for the point of view of each side when with the other. Although clearly employed by the agency, account executives have to live in no man's land between agency and client. Certainly, if the relationship is to endure, they must be as conscientious in explaining the client's needs and attitudes to the agency people as they are in advocating the agency's solutions and attitudes to the client – however irritating and petty their colleagues in the agency may find the client's tinkering with creative treatments or media plans. Divided loyalty is part of the *modus operandi* – and a positive one, given that the job remit is in effect after-sales service.

Not all exponents of account handling are conscientious diplomats, negotiators, facilitators, co-ordinators and organizers, however. As a former board director of a large London agency puts it: 'The best account executives are shrewd business operators and perceptive judges of advertising and human nature. The worst are glorified bag carriers, ferrying messages back and forth between agency and client with all the interpretational skills of a yo-yo' (Mayle, 1990).

However effectively or ineffectively client service is delivered in practice, this particular working relationship tends to be shorter lived than the norm in other professions. Several surveys over the years have found that, in the advertising business, the majority last less than 10 years (e.g. Briggs, 1993). The notably consistent and effective advertising for BMW in Britain that emanated over 25 years from a single agency, WCRS, is the exception that proves the rule. Ghosh and Taylor (1990) found that there were five main causes of failed working relationships in New Zealand and Singapore, consistent with those suggested by two earlier studies in the UK and the USA. Those were: poor agency performance (a notably open-ended judgement); changes in agency policy; changes in client policy; changes in agency management; changes in client management. They remark that a few respondents had experienced all five at once.

It is thus clear that not only does the very fact of delegation to an intermediary mean a loss of control over strategy, but also that there is an inherent tendency to instability in such working relationships. In that case, one might justifiably wonder why marketers do not in fact execute their promotional campaigns in-house. There are three key reasons.

First, they often cannot afford to pay the very considerable salaries needed to recruit their own experts in the particular disciplines. Second, because promotional campaigns normally consist of discrete initiatives rather than continuously evolving programmes, originators cannot keep such specialists fully occupied throughout the year. They find themselves paying for substantial periods of 'downtime', to borrow an engineering concept. Lastly, few marketing departments, if any, can offer the degree of stimulation and motivation that agency specialists derive from working for a considerable variety of clients over the course of a typical career. Recruitment would thus be a problem even if the price could be afforded. Therefore, it has become normal practice to buy a share in the collective skills of established service providers, rather than to try developing them in-house. The loss of *control* is offset by the acquisition of affordable *expertise*.

Choosing the collaborator

An obvious way to reduce the probability of a premature rift in the somewhat precarious originator–intermediary working relationships is to take as much care as possible over the selection process that initiates it. Analogies with courtship and marriage characterize the relatively few discussions of this subject in the literature. This is true even of a very recent insider's guide, *Using and Choosing an Advertising Agency* (Ward, 2001), the scope of which is actually rather wider than the title implies. Apart from trivializing an important decision, such vocabulary offers as a template a procedure that is normally far more emotional than rational, and an institution by no means always effective or durable.

Therefore, this section proposes an appropriately systematic approach to the task, based on an excellent pamphlet published by the Incorporated Society of British Advertisers (ISBA), plus the often bitter fruits of personal experience at first and second hand. It assumes that an originator, henceforth 'the client', is setting out to find a suitable intermediary as a working partner, henceforth 'the agency', though the process does occasionally operate in reverse. Figure 17.5 summarizes it as a step-by-step guide.

Step 1, formally defining what will be required of the agency, often falls victim in practice to the false doctrine: 'cut the cackle and get down to business'. To avoid the necessary

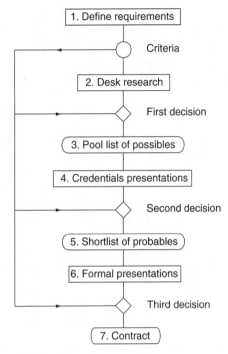

Figure I7.5   Choosing a working partner

intellectual effort would prejudice the outcome at the very outset, for this crucial step is the source of decision criteria needed three times during the process, and avoids the need to reinvent the wheel each time. The requirements should be discussed and agreed by all who have a legitimate interest in the outcome, and then recorded formally.

Step 2 is in effect window shopping. Sources of this preliminary information include the trade press, a range of directories, websites and the informal grapevine within the business. Trade associations such as, in the UK, the Institute of Practitioners in Advertising (IPA), the Institute of Sales Promotion and the Direct Marketing Association will provide a list of suitable agencies, in exchange for a statement of requirements and a company profile. Prospective clients seeking an advertising agency can study video presentations prepared to a standard specification at the premises of the Advertising Agency Register, for a fee, or carry out a keyword search at the free Adforum.com website. At this stage, no agencies need know that a search is in progress. If any clue is given, unsolicited sales pitches will inevitably ensue, muddying the waters and making an eventual objective decision much more difficult.

Step 3 is to draw up a pool list of agencies that seem capable of meeting the criteria defined at Step 1. How many it contains should reflect a pragmatic judgement about the decision makers' span of attention at the next stage. In a recent personal experience, it comprised two incumbents and five others.

At *Step 4*, the client goes public for the first time by inviting credentials presentations from the agencies on the list. Approaches from others can be expected, as the grapevine goes into action and the trade press probably reports the impending move. The terminology of the invitation is crucial. The professional convention is that a 'credentials presentation' does not consist of speculative campaign plans and a full-blown pitch for the business. Instead, presenting agencies should provide a philosophy statement, staff profiles, a client list and case histories plus, depending on the promotional discipline involved, showreels of television and cinema commercials, radio reels, dossiers of print work, and other samples of their work.

It is a moot question whether these presentations should take place at the contenders' premises or on home ground. In the first case, valuable impressions can be gained from non-verbal signals but control over the process is sacrificed; in the second, there is less risk of being overwhelmed by a practised presentation team but no chance to form an opinion about the agency as an organization. Wherever the presentations do happen, they should be seen by a panel, not an individual. *Step 5* can then be the result of informed debate, structured by the criteria defined in Step 1.

Step 6 is to invite survivors on the resulting shortlist to make a formal presentation, which they are likely to describe more graphically as their 'pitch for the business'. It is the client's responsibility to set the ground rules. Each

contender should be given the same brief, including a clear statement of the eventual campaign budget. Ideally, some way should be found to ensure that they all spend the same amount on preparing their presentations, so that like is compared with like. It is important to beware of the specialist pitching team, who will not be the people eventually working on the business if the pitch is successful. The client must take the opportunity to establish who will be, and to raise any key issues that the presentation does not itself address.

A leaflet on best practice in the management of the pitching process, issued jointly by the IPA and ISBA, is adamant about the number of contenders that should be invited to pitch: 'Decide on a list of three agencies – four if the incumbent is involved ... Don't be seduced into lengthening the list.'

At *Step 7*, the choice criteria are consulted for the last time and the decision made. If requirements were never defined in the first place, and formal criteria are therefore unavailable, the ISBA can provide a 13-item checklist and a ranking matrix of 10 attributes to be scored on six-point scales. Although the emphasis is on objective comparison of competing pitches, intuition does have a part to play in making a decision about a long-term working relationship. As the ISBA puts it, 'a clinical and relatively simplistic approach should not be followed too slavishly'. Prudent clients will give themselves time to think after all presentations have been seen, perhaps asking to meet the team that will be allocated to their account, and possibly researching the comparative merits of the competing promotional strategies. However, the ISBA/IPA guide says that the decision should be announced to all the pitching agencies, simultaneously and with reasons, after 'normally not more than one week'.

Until quite recently, *Step 8* was likely to consist of no more than a handshake, imitating the gentlemen's agreements common in the true professions. The transformation of successful advertising agencies from small partnerships into large listed companies has fortunately brought with it more businesslike practices. Advertisers and agencies entering a working relationship today can reduce the likelihood of arguments later by adopting *Some Suggested Provisions for Use in Agency/Client Agreements*, published by the IPA.

Remunerating the working partner

Unless it happens to be an advertising agency, the chosen working partner will be paid for its services by the combination of fees and expenses that is the norm in the professions. In the unique case of advertising, fees paid by clients make the smallest contribution to agencies' total income. The rest is provided by a paradoxical and complicated system of remuneration (American usage prefers 'compensation'), which has its roots in the history of the advertising business. Outsiders have no reason to understand it, insiders often half-understand it, and commentators usually misunderstand it.

A chapter dealing with the whole of the promotional mix is not the place for a detailed explanation of the 'media commission system of advertising agency remuneration' in detail, and the rest of this section will deal only with the essentials. Readers who want to follow up on the details will find them in Crosier (1998b).

In brief, the historical background that explains the idiosyncrasies of the system is as follows. As early as the beginning of the nineteenth century, the proliferation of newspapers, magazines and poster sites was making it very difficult for British advertisers to keep track of the options available, deal efficiently with the profusion of media owners, monitor that their advertisements appeared as booked, and check that they were charged at the correct rates. This situation was fertile ground for entrepreneurial initiatives. Duly, the first *advertising agents* appeared, charging advertisers for expert advice and assistance. They were soon followed by what history has dubbed *space*

brokers, who bought advertising space speculatively and resold it to advertisers at a *mark-up*, accompanied by 'free' advice on campaign planning. By mid-century, the media owners had realized that these intermediaries were in fact the primary customers for their commodity, and were allowing them a routine discount on the price. They were thus transformed into *commission* earning sales agents, whereas the other group remained *fee* earning agents to their clients, the advertisers.

During the second half of the nineteenth century, the whole system became transparent when one space broker in the USA negotiated a fixed-percentage commission discount, and another published a directory of every media owner's pre-discount list prices for space. Brokers took to charging advertisers the list price, and advertisers could check that they were paying exactly what they would if they had booked the space direct. It took nearly a century for the rate of media commission discount to settle to an almost universal 15 per cent, worldwide.

In 1917, English law established that the firms which were by now calling themselves advertising agencies were neither brokers nor agents, but *principals*, making the contract with the media owners in their own right. The result is that present-day advertising agencies must pay for all space and time ordered, even if their client is unwilling or unable to reimburse them. The risk of suffering from bad debts is therefore a constant threat. For this whole system to work properly, media owners must deny the commission discount to advertisers placing orders direct. Outsiders typically find it hard to believe that a media owner could in practice resist a demand for commission from an advertiser with the buying muscle of BT (British Telecom), for example, who spent more than £107 million on advertising in 2000. But advertisers of that type and size invariably use advertising agencies or media independents anyway, so they might as well buy media by that route and benefit from the associated subsidized services and volume discounts. That fact, plus the twin forces of historical precedent and professional etiquette, have so far maintained this feature of the system intact.

It is also essential for the efficient operation of the system that only bona fide agencies receive commission by right. For a long period in the history of the system, the media trade bodies awarded 'recognition' to agencies that met certain criteria. For complex reasons, clearly explained by Brierley (1995, pp. 65–68), this universal and exclusive recognition agreement was eventually abandoned. Nevertheless, media owners' sales contracts still require agencies to meet their own criteria of eligibility for commission.

Crosier (1998b) provides a series of worked examples to illustrate the arithmetic of the commission system in practice. The first of these shows how, in the most straightforward case, an agency or media independent makes a profit by buying space or time from a media owner at list price minus 15 per cent and subsequently charging its client the full amount. It is important to note that, if the media owner's discounted bill is not settled by the due date, which can be as little as two weeks after the first advertisement appears, the terms of the contract provide for the commission rate to reduce progressively. It is therefore in the best interests of the agency or media independent to pay media owners promptly and bill clients immediately. However, normal business practice does not require a client to pay up in turn before 30 days after the invoice is rendered, and most will take anything up to three months to do so. Agencies, reluctant to press for payment too strongly for fear of losing an account, must therefore keep a very close eye on *cash flow* at all times.

So much for the basic commission. The first of many complications now arises. When the system evolved, high production costs were not an issue. Today, advertising campaigns involve large numbers of massive posters printed on vinyl-coated paper, four-colour double-page advertisements in glossy magazines, 60-second mini-epics on television and cinema

screens, and much more besides. As the sophistication of advertising technology increased, agencies struggled to meet escalating production costs out of commission that increased only in line with media price inflation. The media owners could not subsidize the agencies by raising prices further, or they would kill demand for their commodity. The agencies dare not propose unrealistically heavy media schedules, to gain the economies of scale, for fear of losing the business altogether. It soon became clear that agencies with ambitious clients could no longer be expected to survive on media commission alone.

A new convention duly emerged that some consequential costs could be charged direct to the client as top-up *fees*. It is typical of this outwardly dynamic but inwardly conservative business that there is no official, definitive list of what can be included and what not. The IPA's guidelines for agency–client agreements are both vague and ambiguous, while a report on remuneration practices throughout Europe says: 'The range of services provided at no charge will depend on each individual relationship. Where non-commissionable agency services are charged (work done within the agency), this is normally done on the basis of a prior estimate' (European Association of Advertising Agencies, 1994, p. 21).

The increasing sophistication of media production processes also resulted in agencies subcontracting increasing amounts of work. Furthermore, self-proclaimed 'full-service' advertising agencies were routinely carrying out non-advertising assignments for their clients, and commissioning those too from third parties. In all such situations, a second convention arose that a *mark-up* could be added to the agency's buying price to arrive at a selling price which would adequately cover the agency's costs in setting up and managing the extra service. The IPA's guidelines recommend a clause in an agency's contract that the client will pay 'the net cost of all these materials and services bought for you, plus X per cent of such net cost'. The key point about this percentage is that it is in fact standard: a figure which makes the agency's reward for commissioning and co-ordinating the subcontract the same as it would be if the supplier's bill had been discounted by 15 per cent. In other words, it derives absolutely directly from the media commission convention.

Example 2 in Crosier (1998b) illustrates the required arithmetic, and shows that the X per cent referred to in the IPA's guidelines will be 17.65 per cent. This unexpectedly precise figure is confirmed by the European Association of Advertising Agencies (1994, p. 21): 'In addition to the agency retaining 15 per cent on the gross media billings, it is normal practice for all ... outside purchases which are billable to be charged at cost plus 17.65 per cent.'

Thus, the normal pattern of remuneration for a conventional advertising agency is a combination of a 15 per cent *commission* discount allowed by media owners on the price of advertising space and time bought on behalf of its clients, plus top-up *fees* and a 17.56 per cent *mark-up* on subcontracted services, paid by the clients themselves. The first of these has always dominated, in Britain, America and elsewhere. Various industry estimates suggest that it accounts for somewhere between two-thirds and three-quarters of a typical advertising agency's total remuneration. In the case of media independents, the proportion is of course virtually 100 per cent.

Whereas an agency could negotiate the level of a service fee, its earnings in commission and mark-up are limited to a fixed proportion of the amount a client is willing to spend on advertising media and ancillary services. Effectively, agencies can compete for business only on such non-price dimensions as experience and reputation. In practice, however, some will offer *commission rebating* deals as a ploy to win new business or retain a client threatening to move the account elsewhere. Indeed, the impetus may come from a high-spending client expecting to benefit from the economies of scale.

Commentators routinely describe this arrangement in terms that imply an entirely impossible mechanism, reporting that an agency has agreed to 'cut commission' to less than 15 per cent or 'hand back' some of it to the client. Agencies cannot in fact reduce a discount awarded automatically by media owners, and there would in any case be no benefit to the client if they could. Nor can they hand back a sum of money that exists only as a discount, let alone to a third party who did not give it in the first place. Such mistakes are not simply careless, but downright misleading.

Example 3 in Crosier (1998b) explains the mechanism for an agency to allow its client a 3 per cent rebate. What actually happens is that a second discount in the transaction leaves the agency's commission intact but *has the same effect as* reducing it. On the face of it, a 3 per cent discount is hardly generous. Shoppers would not see it as a bargain at the sales, and traders will regularly deduct 5 per cent for cash in hand. However, on a total expenditure of £10 000, the profit is now £1200 instead of £1500. The difference of £300 is exactly a fifth of the unrebated figure, and the agency's concession to its client has reduced its earnings on the transaction by fully 20 per cent. Given that net profit margins are typically around 2 per cent, according to conventional wisdom in the industry, such largesse is clearly unsustainable. At the height of a rebating boom in the 1980s, many rebaters landed themselves in a serious financial predicament, and have had to make up for lost revenue in some way, such as by: cutting corners on creative work for the client; recommending unnecessarily expensive media schedules; proposing extra add-on services; claiming more top-up fees; cutting back on the account-handling service; or cross-subsidizing from other clients. On the other hand, the trade press reported that others had lost multimillion pound accounts by refusing to do so. Yet, clients who demand rebates thus commit themselves to a game of swings and roundabouts, and the long-term outcome can only be damage to the business as a whole. That said, the agency was the only party to suffer financially in Example 3. The media owner's revenue was unchanged, and the client was £300 better off. It is hardly surprising that powerful clients continue to press for rebates.

The implications of rebating are less severe for media independents, who offer no ancillary services to their clients, generally have lower operating overheads, and can earn substantial volume discounts to offset against rebates by virtue of the large sums they spend with the media as a single buying point for a number of separate advertisers.

Clear as the dangers of rebating are, there is a case to be made for it. The crux of the argument is the size of the advertiser's budget. There can be no doubt that a £1 million national television campaign does not incur 10 times the creative and administrative costs of a £100 000 poster campaign, let alone 100 times those for £10 000 worth of regional press advertising. On that basis, it is not unreasonable to expect agencies to be satisfied with remuneration that diminishes *pro rata* as spending increases. If one of them takes the initiative by charging a client less than the actual price of media bought, the argument goes, it has done nothing more than reduce its service charge to an amount that matches the work done.

The debate is likely to continue. Meanwhile, a pan-European research study (European Association of Advertising Agencies, 1994, pp. 5–7) found that 16 per cent of responding agencies had rebated in 1989, and 17 per cent in 1992.

Industry commentators regularly assert that payment by *fee*, the amount being preferably linked to results, is replacing the anachronistic and perennially controversial media commission system. Like their statements about rebating, this claim requires closer inspection. A fee system does have the obvious appeal of reflecting pragmatic reality instead of historical precedent and legal convention, but agencies seeking to implement it have to surmount several practical obstacles. First, they will continue to receive the media commission discount. It does not have to be claimed, and media owners would be unwilling to make special billing arrangements for a few agencies. The discount accumulated therefore has to be calculated for each client periodically, and a credit issued against the fee. A new internal data-handling system will probably be needed to accomplish this. Deciding the amount of the fee poses a second set of problems. Like setting a price, the process demands identification and isolation of the costs to be offset and decisions about the margin required. The calculation will have to be based on past costings, or on forecasts. In either event, the process is notoriously like trying to steer a car by looking in the rear-view mirror. When each fee is renegotiated at the end of a budget period, the client is likely to exert strong downward pressure. That will produce the same consequences as rebating, if the agency gives in. Moreover, other fee-charging agencies are free to start price wars. Lastly, if the fee is to be pegged to results, the agency will face the considerable difficulties involved in measuring them and isolating those attributable to the advertising campaign.

Furthermore, advertisers and media owners both have a vested interest in retention of the commission system. The former have reason to suspect that a fee set on the basis of overheads, salaries, production costs and a reasonable profit margin would be a larger amount than 15 per cent of media bills plus 17.65 per cent mark-up on non-media work plus chargeable costs. The latter value the control that progressive reduction of the commission percentage gives them over their own cash flow, and would much rather deal with a small number of advertising agencies than a large number of advertisers.

It should therefore come as no surprise that a recent survey of 450 advertisers across Europe concluded only that 'the old standard of 15 per cent commission has been replaced by lower commission [meaning rebating], fees and – increasingly – payment by results' (Lace, 2001). In the USA and Japan, too, advertising agencies earn their income from this same combination of three sources, plus the 17.65 mark-up on subcontracted services.

The commission element has survived being declared an anti-competitive business practice by the Sherman Anti-Trust Act in the USA in 1955 and the Restrictive Trade Practices Act in Britain in 1976. Its robust state of health is attributable to considerable practical appeal, for it:

- has a long historical pedigree;
- is generally familiar in the business;
- is easily put into practice;
- requires very little computation;
- involves almost no negotiation;
- suits two of the three parties involved very well.

Measuring campaign effectiveness

In an ideal world, measuring the effectiveness of a promotional initiative would be a simple matter of using a measuring *instrument* to compare actual *performance* with explicit *criteria* derived from predetermined *objectives*. An automotive engineer, for instance, might wish to bench-test an engine for acceptably silent running. That general objective could be translated into a criterion specifying decibel level at a given distance from an engine operating at a given number of revolutions per minute under given laboratory conditions. That criterion would in turn determine the measuring instrument: an audiometer. The readings taken on the instrument would establish that the engine could or could not meet the criterion and that its design therefore was or was not *effective* in that respect. Unfortunately, this straightforward procedure typically fails at the very first stage in the context of assessing promotional effectiveness. The fact is that practitioners typically experience substantial difficulty in articulating objectives that are either achievable or measurable.

For instance, the objective to 'position [the brand] as the ultimate', taken from a published promotional plan for a boxed chocolate selection clearly demonstrates two common tendencies: to mistake aspirations, often grandiose, for realistically achievable objectives; and to charge promotion with the attainment of objectives it could hardly achieve in isolation from other elements of the marketing mix. Another plan, published in the same series of case histories, set this promotional objective for an ice-cream gateau: 'to very quickly establish awareness of a product known to be very interesting to the customer and thereby maximize consumer trial'. Here, we clearly see another common failing: lack of precision and quantification. Awareness of *what* about the product? Among *which* target audience? *How much* awareness, and by *when*? *What* constitutes maximized trial and by *when* is it to be achieved? Precisely *who* are customers?

If criteria are thus unspecified, the tendency is for ready-made tests to substitute for purpose-designed measures. It certainly happens when, as is disturbingly common, objectives have not been formally articulated at all. In a case history intended to demonstrate 'effective' advertising, a world-famous advertising agency states explicitly that 'the advertising had to achieve three things: be quite clear about what [the product] really is; confirm very modern user imagery; confirm the [brand] heritage'. Logically, measurement of effectiveness would certainly be expected to relate to communication, to imagery and to attitudes. In fact, the claimed proof of effectiveness again moved the goalposts: 'within days, sales started to move up ... within a month, ex-factory shipments were more than 60 per cent above previous levels ... housewives do understand more clearly what [the product] is ... and they use it for the whole family, not just slimmers'. The first two achievements are so short term as to be meaningless in the context of a launch and could obviously be attributable to many variables other than advertising. The third does demonstrate achievement of one implied criterion, but is significantly qualified. The last one introduces a completely new criterion, presumably relating to competitive comparisons.

In short, *surrogate* tests are being substituted in practice. Investigation of further case histories would soon lead to the conclusion that they are typically based on a common explanation of how advertising is thought to work, which could equally easily be applied to any other ingredient of the promotional mix. It is unlikely that practitioners themselves are consciously aware that this is happening. As a guide to best practice from the Institute of Practitioners in Advertising puts it, they 'may follow very varied mental models but they too seldom articulate them' (Broadbent, 1995, p. 17).

This particular model is the 'hierarchy of effects', which first appeared in the literature more than 70 years ago. A textbook by a famous American market researcher of the day included a conceptual framework for testing the effectiveness of advertisements, which argued that 'to be effective, an advertisement must be . . . seen, read, believed, remembered, and acted upon' (Starch, 1923). That initiative was closely followed by another for the effective delivery of a sales pitch, which should gain attention, generate interest, create desire and precipitate action (Strong, 1925). Under an acronym derived from the initials of those four required responses, AIDA, it was soon transferred to the formulation of advertising strategy, and has remained popular ever since.

After a considerable interval, the generic description 'hierarchy of effects' was coined by Lavidge and Steiner (1961) to describe a six-step 'model for predictive measurement of advertising effectiveness'. In the same year, a five-step framework for 'defining advertising goals for measured advertising results' was proposed by the Association of National Advertisers in New York (Colley, 1962). It too became known by an acronym, this time derived from the description rather than the steps: 'Dagmar'. The only further progress in the subsequent four decades has been a relatively little noticed article with the telling subtitle 'keeping the hierarchy concept alive' (Preston and Thorson, 1984).

Table 17.5 proposes a consolidation of these five paradigms, and could accommodate other family members not reported here. The left-hand column uses terms from the originals to define the response required from the audience for the initiative to be effective. The right-hand column relates each response to the generic cognitive–affective–conative (C-A-C) pattern of response to stimuli other than advertisements. Since cognitive responses are the outcome of thinking about what is happening, affective responses result from an emotional reaction to the stimulus, and conative responses involve consequent actions, this model is popularly summed up as think–feel–do.

The hierarchy-of-effects hypothesis provides an intuitively reasonable *description* of what is happening, but offers no *explanation* of how or why. It has furthermore been subjected to continuous theoretical criticism over the past 30 years, beginning with a widely reported evaluation of Lavidge and Steiner's model by Palda (1966), who doubted that the accomplishment of one step necessarily increased the probability of the next and called into question their very sequence. Others subsequently demonstrated the existence of do–feel–think, think–do–feel and do–think–feel variations. For each of these, the role of promotion would

Table 17.5 The hierarchy-of-effects model of promotion	
Effectiveness criterion:	*C-A-C equivalent*
Action	Do
Conviction	Feel
Sympathy	Feel
Comprehension	Think
Interest	Think
Attention	Think

logically be rather different, and hence the criteria of effectiveness.

One might expect that these theoretical shortcomings would by now have invalidated the hierarchy of effects as a framework for the measurement of effectiveness, but all the evidence is that they have gone unremarked in practice. Therefore, it is necessary to recognize that AIDA and its kin will remain the implicit conceptual underpinning of present-day practice until marketing academics are able to produce a better model which practitioners can understand and are willing to use. Evidence that this state of affairs remained a pipe dream during the past decade is to be found in two authoritative reviews commissioned by the Advertising Association (McDonald, 1992; Frantzen, 1994).

If there is to be any real progress towards a better, workable model during the next decade, and hence towards more reliable measurement of effectiveness, the impetus will have to come from the 'planning' discipline within advertising agencies. This is the intellectual wing of the business, staffed by people with a lively interest in understanding consumer behaviour and applying its principles to the development of effective communication strategies. Their 'house journal', *Admap*, bridges the gap between academics and practitioners.

Understanding the context

Thoughtful practitioners of any discipline should want to understand the economic, social and cultural context within which they operate. Those with responsibility for deployment of the promotional mix *need* to, for theirs is an overtly persuasive and very public activity. Therefore, this chapter concludes by examining the relevant attitudes of policy formers and opinion leaders in Britain, reporting British public opinion and outlining the domestic regulatory system. Inevitably, the focus will be

on advertising rather than the less high-profile elements of the promotional mix.

To place these external views in a proper context, it will help to bear in mind these relevant characteristics of the social and economic environment in which contemporary promotional initiatives take place:

- A highly developed consumer economy, in which advertising bridges the gap between producers and consumers.
- Well-educated and fairly sophisticated consumers.
- Articulate consumer pressure groups.
- A highly sophisticated promotional business.
- Consumer protection legislation.
- Formal statutory control over broadcast advertising.
- Self-regulatory codes of practice relating to non-broadcast advertising, sales promotion and direct marketing.

Marketing academics and practitioners often find themselves having to defend the *economics* of promotion. As an occasional paper from the Advertising Association comments:

> The normal progression is for someone to suggest the use of advertising exercises an unhealthy influence on some desirable economic function, whereupon defenders cast doubt upon the logic and/or the evidence of the original argument. This usually develops into an increasingly esoteric debate, whose details can be understood by hardly anybody.
>
> (Lind, 1998, p. 18)

The debate in question tends to focus on four charges, typically levelled at advertising in particular: that it is a *cost* that drives up the price of the product; that it sets up *barriers* to the entry of new competitors into the market, and thereby reduces choice; that its *appeals* are emotional, not rational; that it has the *power* to make people want things they don't need, and thereby artificially distorts spending patterns. Defenders respond that: it can stimulate demand and thereby hold price rises in check;

it facilitates competition, rather than inhibiting it; consumers appreciate the added value it can confer on a product; in a generally prosperous economy, 'experts' have no right to tell us what we should or should not want, and ordinary people are in any case quite bright enough to recognize it for what it is, and act accordingly.

It is furthermore highly arbitrary to single out promotional expenditure as the economic culprit. White (1993) points out that: 'When economists say that customers are paying for the advertising when they buy the product, they are guilty of a false analysis – unless they also say that the customer is paying for the sales forces, the delivery vans, the warehouses and the order clerks.'

Likewise, it is not typically promotion that monopolists use to erect barriers against competitors, but rather price wars and saturation of distribution channels. Furthermore, effective advertising is not a matter of simply quantity: quality counts heavily when consumers are sophisticated and know how to play the game.

White puts it well again: 'In fact, the possibility open to new challengers of using media advertising, with its rapid coverage of mass audiences, tends to make monopolies more rather than less vulnerable to attack.' The newspaper circulation wars in the UK in the 1990s are a case in point. *The Times* took on the tabloids by slashing its price, not by spending millions to advertise its intellectual superiority.

The insistence that consumers should want reasons and hard facts, not emotional involvement or intangible satisfactions, reflects the long-standing economic model of 'rational man'. Yet it was a noted economist who remarked, half a century ago, on the 'tremendous spiritual satisfaction in buying a trusted brand of cocoa – not a shovelful of brown powder of uncertain origin'. His choice of the adjective 'trusted' expresses the idea of an intangible added value. The danger of the economists' line of argument is that it denies

legitimate subjective satisfactions. Shoppers do not need to buy the best if the second- or third-best pleases them more. Nor must they always buy the most economical if they trust the promoted brand more. That is why shoppers so often buy Cadbury's drinking chocolate instead of a supermarket's own brand, of course. Readers keen to pursue the economic case for and against advertising will find an excellent review in Lind (1998, pp. 10–33).

Not only economists have strong views about promotion; it is regularly subject to *cultural and ethical* criticism. The main charges in this case are that it 'dumbs down' society – that is, debases cultural values – and controls the news media through their reliance on advertising revenue. These critics also deploy the wants-versus-needs argument.

The first of these rests on the implicit belief that relatively powerful advertisers can manipulate relatively powerless audiences, which in turn hinges on the 'mad scientist' view of advertising people. Those who take this view normally cite the immensely influential book, *The Hidden Persuaders*, first published in 1957 and reissued with an added introduction and epilogue in 1981 (Packard, 1991). They do not always mention that the author was a crusading journalist who wrote a series of trenchant critiques of American business, or that the cases he reports all took place in the 1950s, when times were distinctly different.

If the manipulators of the promotional mix do have special powers, whether based on psychological principles as Packard suggests or derived from whatever else, these remain the most closely guarded of secrets. Even those who work in the business cannot explain what they are.

It is, furthermore, an uncomfortably contradictory fact that, on average, four in every five new products fail in the marketplace despite introductory promotion. Either the hidden persuaders are very bad at making use of their special powers or modern audiences are better than the critics think at resisting the promotional hype.

The charge that promotion debases the culture has been regularly heard from academics and media commentators over the years. Most recently, combined with the accusation that the most heavily promoted worldwide brands can indeed manipulate people into buying products they don't need and can't afford, they have been powerfully levelled by the authors of *No Logo*, a virtual manifesto for counter-insurgency (Klein, 2000), by the authors of the seminar papers collected together in *Buy This Book* (Nava *et al.*, 1997), and by a journalist's updating of Packard in *The Manipulators* (Robinson, 1998).

From the practitioners' point of view, this is alarming sabre-rattling. Such critics seem to detect an organized conspiracy to corrupt society, masterminded on Madison Avenue or in Covent Garden. Supporters of advertising respond that advertisements in fact hold a mirror up to our culture, rather than shaping it, and that the audiences concerned are fully capable of decoding them in their own way and forming their own value judgements. They argue that the critics' view of popular culture, including contemporary advertising, is condescending to the populace.

The proposition that advertisers can control the news media presumes that they will be unwilling to bite the hand that feeds them if it deserves to be bitten in the public interest. There is no evidence that any British advertiser has ever managed to exert such influence; indeed, news has occasionally been made by failed attempts. Nevertheless, observers were concerned that the introduction of programme sponsorship might provide companies with sufficient power to influence editorial comment. In response, the statutory bodies which control commercial broadcasting in Britain have both amended their codes of practice relating to advertising (Independent Television Commission, 1998; Radio Authority, 2001).

Media owners themselves counter-argue that advertising revenue guarantees editorial freedom. Without it, they would need either to charge prices for the product that would guarantee its demise or to ask for a government subsidy. The second solution raises, they point out, the equally dangerous possibility of political control, a familiar obstacle to reporting matters of public concern in too many other countries.

What is not clear about the social criticisms of advertising described is why the critics should assume the worst possible case. There is a strong hint of the polemic in their approach to the issues, which seems unnecessary in the face of a typically British middle-of-the-road approach to the business of producing advertisements. This is not to deny that promotion of all kinds is sometimes misleading, vulgar, full of innuendo or aesthetically disastrous. However, any practitioner consciously setting out to inflict such material on the audience must first deliberately ignore such well-established regulations as the British Codes of Advertising and Sales Promotion, the ITC Code of Advertising Standards and Practice, The Radio Authority Advertising and Sponsorship Code, or the Direct Marketing Association Code of Practice, and secondly face up to the consequences. For further details of these and other forms of control against malpractice, see Baker (1998) under 'advertising control', 'direct mail' and 'sales promotion'. As for manipulation: if the average Western consumer is not in fact sophisticated enough to cope with advertising, then the appropriate counter-measure is *consumer education* rather than more constraints. If people can be taught to recognize and resist political indoctrination, there is no reason to suppose education cannot do the same where promotional initiatives are concerned.

Readers interested in pursuing socio-cultural arguments for and against advertising will find an absorbing textbook-length treatment in Fowles (1996).

Having considered the views of professional observers, we turn now to the attitudes of the ordinary citizens at whom most promotional initiatives are directed. The Advertising Association reports, in the most recent of a series of public opinion surveys dating back to 1961, that only 6 per cent of 1017 respondents chose 'advertising' from among a list of 12 general social topics as one of the 'three or four that you and your friends talk most about'; 5.5 per cent picked it as one of those 'you have the strongest opinions about', and 4.5 per cent as one that 'most needs immediate attention and change'. The first two results are a little lower than in 1996, and the third is exactly the same.

Despite this evidence that advertising is not a salient issue for most people in the UK, respondents were asked for a general opinion on a five-point scale: approve a lot or a little, disapprove a lot or a little, or don't know. Only one in five took the opportunity offered to be critical, though that figure is well up on its equivalent in the 1996 survey (21 versus 16 per cent). They were then asked to express their feelings about the concrete manifestations of the abstract concept, advertisements, on a five-point scale offering the options to like or quite like, dislike or not really like, or be indifferent. Only 17 per cent answered negatively about television commercials, 12 per cent about press advertisements and 10 per cent about posters. There was little change since 1996 in the first two cases, but disliking of posters was up by five percentage points, probably as a result of publicity surrounding high levels of public complaining about Benetton and French Connection campaigns (among others) during the intervening period. Nevertheless, levels of disliking are in general lower than the level of disapproval, and neither is strong enough to suggest any widespread discontent.

In late 2001, the Advertising Standards Authority commissioned a series of 16 focus group discussions with teenagers, 'singles aged between 20 and 24', 'parents of children between 5 and 14', 'empty nesters' and 'greys' (Advertising Standards Authority, 2002). They report that 'the public is more critical of advertising than it has ever been . . . because of a belief that advertising is better than it ever

was', and thus potentially more powerful. Participants defined 'advertising' widely enough to encompass the whole of the promotional mix: it is 'every piece of brand, product or service communication [including] direct mail, door drops, the Internet, branding in store, branded clothing, sponsorship, commercial text messages and even telephone sales . . . simply everything that has a name on it'.

Though disapprovers in the Advertising Association's surveys have always been a minority, it would be interesting to know who they are and what their reasons are. A study of the postcodes of individuals who had made formal complaints about particular advertisements to the Advertising Standards Authority and Independent Television Commission over a five-year period (Crosier *et al.*, 1999) confirmed the obvious stereotype: the incidence reduced steadily across the UK from south-east to north-west, and the majority of complainers lived in strongly middle class areas. Analysis of the nature of their complaints was constrained by the two regulators' own classification systems. Broadly speaking, objections to misleadingness and offensiveness accounted for the great majority of all complaints, the former slightly outnumbering the latter.

The Advertising Standards Authority reports one opinion that notably contradicted the generally tolerant attitude of participants in their study: the prevalence of advertising that does not actually lie but is economical with the truth (Advertising Standards Authority, 2002, p. 8). This is perceived to be especially common in advertising for insurance and financial services. It is felt that the regulation is an effective safeguard in general, but that in this particular respect the regulators should be 'more active, more invasive, more controlling'.

Surprisingly, the Advertising Association has not asked those who expressed disapproval in their surveys about their reasons since 1976, at which time the answer was broadly that advertising drives up prices, is misleading, and creates false needs. Another obvious possibility is that people think there is simply too much of it. In 1983, *Which?* magazine surveyed 1300 subscribers, presumably more likely than average to have critical views of advertising, and found that: 53 per cent thought the volume of advertising they noticed was 'about right', 36 per cent felt there 'should be less' and 11 per cent believed there should be none at all. There has been no increase in the 'minutage' permitted on television or in the number of poster sites around the country since then, so it could be expected that contemporary opinion will be little different.

It is plain that, although advertising affects almost everybody's daily life, it is not something that most find at all salient. Some would argue that they should. Furthermore, the overwhelming majority give it a vote of approval when their attention is directed to the subject, and confess willingly to liking the advertisements they encounter in all media. Fewer than half think they are subjected to too much advertising. We may suspect that the answers would be less favourable if the questioning were about sales promotion or direct marketing, but corresponding figures are hard to find.

Thus, the environment within which British practitioners ply their trade today is undoubtedly benevolent, whatever the critics may say. One can only repeat a warning given by the Advertising Association in the report of its 1996 survey, not to relax the high standards of quality and self-discipline which have allowed such a positive atmosphere to be maintained for more than 30 years.

References

Account Planning Group (2002) *The Awards Book*, The Account Planning Group, London. (Previous volumes were published in 1993, 1995, 1997 and 1999, initially under the title *Creative Planning > Outstanding Advertising*.)

Advertising Association (2000) *Public Attitudes to Advertising 2000*, The Advertising Association, London.

Advertising Standards Authority (1999) *The British Codes of Advertising and Sales Promotion*, The Advertising Standards Authority, London.

Advertising Standards Authority (2002) *The Public's Perception of Advertising in Today's Society: Report on the Findings from a Research Study*, The Advertising Standards Authority, London.

Baker, M. J. (ed.) (1998) *Macmillan Dictionary of Marketing and Advertising*, 3rd edn, Macmillan, London.

Brierley, S. (1995) *The Advertising Handbook*, Routledge, London.

Briggs, M. (1993) Why Ad Agencies Must Change, *Admap*, January, 22.

Broadbent, S. (1995) *Best Practice in Campaign Evaluation*, Institute of Practitioners in Advertising, London.

Broadbent, S. (1997) *Accountable Advertising*, Admap Publications, Henley-on-Thames.

Broadbent, S. and Jacobs, B. (1984) *Spending Advertising Money*, 4th edn, Business Books, London.

Butterfield, L. (ed.) (1997) *Excellence in Advertising: The IPA Guide to Best Practice*, Butterworth-Heinemann, Oxford.

Colley, R. H. (1962) Squeezing the Waste out of Advertising, *Harvard Business Review*, **40**, September/October, 76–88.

Cooper, A. (ed.) (1997) *How to Plan Advertising*, 2nd edn, Cassell in association with The Account Planning Group, London.

Crosier, K. (1998a) Advertising, in Kitchen, P. J. (ed.) *Marketing Communications: Principles and Practice*, International Thompson Business Press, London, Chapter 16.

Crosier, K (1998b) The Argument for Advertising Agency Remuneration, in Kitchen, P. J. (ed.) *Marketing Communications: Principles and Practice*, International Thompson Business Press, London, Chapter 25.

Crosier, K. and Abbott, J. (1996) Net Benefits: Sizing up a Marketing Communications

Vehicle for the Twenty-First Century, *Proceedings of the First International Conference on Corporate and Marketing Communications*, Keele University, April.

Crosier, K., Hernandez, T., Mohabir-Collins, S. and Erdogan, B. Z. (1999) The Risk of Collateral Damage in Advertising Campaigns, *Journal of Marketing Management*, **15**(8), 837–855.

Dhalla, N. K. (1977) How to Set Advertising Budgets, *Journal of Advertising Research*, **17**, October, 11.

European Association of Advertising Agencies (1994) *Client/Advertising Agency Partnerships in the New Europe*, NTC Publications, Henley-on-Thames.

Fill, C. (2002) *Marketing Communications: Frameworks, Theories and Applications*, 3rd edn, Pearson Education, Harlow.

Fowles, J. (1996) *Advertising and Popular Culture*, Sage, Thousand Oaks, CA.

Frantzen, G. (1994) *Advertising Effectiveness: Findings from Empirical Research*, NTC Publications, Henley-on-Thames.

Ghosh, B. C. and Taylor, D. (1990) Switching Advertising Agency – A Cross-Country Analysis, *Marketing Intelligence and Planning*, **17**(3), 140–146.

Independent Television Commission (1998) *The ITC Code of Advertising Standards and Practice*, and *The ITC Code of Programme Sponsorship*, The Independent Television Commission, London.

Institute of Practitioners in Advertising (2000) *Advertising Works*, Volume 11, NTC Publications, Henley-on-Thames. (This is the most recent in a biennial series beginning in 1981.)

Kitchen, P. J. (ed.) (1998) *Marketing Communications: Principle and Practice*, International Thompson Business Press, London.

Kitchen, P. J. and Schultz, D. E. (2001) *Raising the Corporate Umbrella: Corporate Communications in the 21st Century*, Palgrave, Basingstoke.

Klein, N. (2000) *No Logo*, Flamingo, London.

Lace, J. (2001) *Paying for Advertising in Europe*, World Advertising Research Centre, Henley-on-Thames.

Lavidge, R. C. and Steiner, G. A. (1961) A Model for Predictive Measurements of Advertising Effectiveness, *Journal of Marketing*, **25**, October, 59–62.

Lind, H. (ed.) (1998) *Making Sense of Advertising*, Economics Committee of the Advertising Association, London.

Mayle, P. (1990) *Up the Agency*, Pan, London.

McDonald, C. (1992) *How Advertising Works: A Review of Current Thinking*, NTC Publications, Henley-on-Thames.

Nava, M. *et al.* (eds) (1997) *Buy This Book: Studies in Advertising and Consumption*, Routledge, London.

Packard, V. (1991) *The Hidden Persuaders*, Penguin, London.

Palda, K. S. (1966) The Hypothesis of a Hierarchy of Effects: A Partial Evaluation, *Journal of Marketing Research*, **3**, February, 13–24.

Percy, L. (2001) Marketing Communication in Evolution, *Admap*, **36**(2), 30–32.

Piercy, N. (1987) Advertising Budgeting: Process and Structure as Explanatory Variables, *Journal of Advertising*, **16**(2), 59–65.

Preston, I. L. and Thorson, E. (1984) The Expanded Association Model: Keeping the Hierarchy Concept Alive, *Journal of Advertising Research*, **24**(1), February/March, 59–65.

Radio Authority (2001) *The Radio Authority Advertising and Sponsorship Code*, The Radio Authority, London.

Rees, R. D. (1977) *Advertising Budgeting and Appraisal in Practice: Research Study No. 11*, The Advertising Association, London.

Robinson, J. (1998) *The Manipulators: The Conspiracy to Make you Buy*, Simon & Schuster, New York.

Smith, P. R. with Taylor, J. (2001) *Marketing Communications: An Integrated Approach*, Kogan Page, London.

Stapleton, J. and Thomas, M. J. (1998) *How to Prepare a Marketing Plan: A Guide to Reaching the Consumer Market*, 5th edn, Gower, Aldershot, Chapter 9.

Starch, D. (1923) *Principles of Marketing*, A. W. Shaw, Chicago.

Strong, E. K. (1925) *The Psychology of Selling*, McGraw-Hill, New York.

Synodinos, N. E., Keown, C. F. and Jacobs, L. W. (1989) Transnational Advertising Practice: A Survey of Leading Brand Advertisers in Fifteen Countries, *Journal of Advertising Research*, **29**(2), April/May, 43–50.

Varey, R. (2001) *Marketing Communications: A Critical Introduction*, Routledge, Andover.

Ward, J. (2001) *Using and Choosing an Advertising Agency: An Insider's View*, World Advertising Research Centre, Henley-on-Thames.

White, R. (1993) *Advertising: What It Is and How toDo It*, 3rd edn, McGraw-Hill, Maidenhead.

CHAPTER 18

Sales promotion

SUE PEATTIE and KEN PEATTIE

Introduction

In 1697 Jonathon Holder, a London haber-dasher, decided to offer customers spending over a guinea in his shop a free stock and price list. His pioneering decision to offer his custom-ers 'something extra' was not universally wel-comed. The newspapers of the day condemned this sales promotion as 'a dangerous innova-tion' and one which, 'would be destructive to trade, if shopkeepers lavished so much of their capital on printing useless bills'. Over 300 years later, trade still flourishes and so do sales promotions, which now account for more 'capi-tal' than any element of marketing communica-tions except selling. During 2000, promotional expenditure in the USA (excluding discounting programmes) exceeded $100 billion for the first time, according to industry figures. Despite sales promotion's growing importance, some-thing of the scepticism that Mr Holder encoun-tered lives on. In the study and practice of marketing, sales promotion has always been overshadowed by the more glamourous world of advertising. This situation is now changing, with sales promotion beginning to attract the academic study and practitioner scrutiny that its cost and increasingly strategic role surely demands.

Sales promotion defined

Sales promotion is frequently defined in terms of what it is not, typically as those marketing communications activities which do not fall into the categories of advertising, selling or public relations. This is not very helpful, but definitions trying to explain what this encom-passes are often flawed, by failing to embrace all of the marketing tools regarded as sales promotions in practice. We can define sales promotions as 'marketing activities usually specific to a time period, place or customer group, which encourage a direct response from consumers or marketing intermediaries, through the offer of additional benefits'.

The three key elements of this definition are that sales promotions are:

1 *Non-standard.* Promotions are usually temporary, and may be limited to certain customer groups (such as airline frequent flier schemes) or specific to a particular distribution channel (as in 'tailor-made' promotions involving a producer and a single retailer).
2 *Response orientated.* Promotions seek a direct response from customers, or those who deal with customers on the producer's behalf (see Figure 18.1). The direct response sought is not

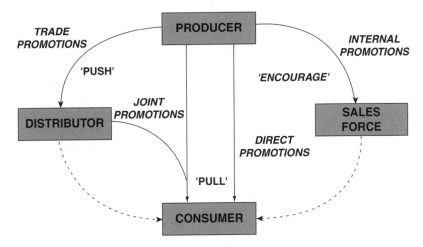

Figure 18.1 Sales promotion targets

necessarily a sale. Promotions may encourage consumers to send for a brochure, visit a dealer or consume a sample. The ultimate aim is always sales, but this is true of marketing generally.

3 *Benefit orientated.* Promotions offer their targets additional benefits, beyond the 'standard' marketing mix. The enhanced mix could include extra product, a reduced price or an added item, service or opportunity.

The everyday vocabulary of marketing promotions is full of inconsistencies. For simplicity and brevity, the word 'promotion' will be used in this chapter to refer to a sales promotion, rather than its broader context of marketing promotion.

Understanding sales promotion – a tale of price and prejudice

Sales promotion is a catch-all term covering a multiplicity of marketing activities. In the past, our understanding of promotions has been hampered by a tendency to bundle all the different types together for study and discussion (Peattie and Peattie, 1993). As Flack (1999),

writing in *Marketing Week*, expressed it, 'the sector suffers largely from a poor definition – a price promotion is not the same as a value-added promotion but the two are often lumped together'. Coupons and discounts are among the most widely used promotions, and research evidence and practical experience from such price-based promotions dominates the literature. This has encouraged:

- A limited view of what promotions can achieve.
- An overly rational–economic view of their effects on consumers.
- A tactical and short-term view of promotion, since economic incentives are only effective while they are on offer.
- A negative perception about the impact that promotions may have on brands and brand positioning.

All of these negative perceptions of sales promotion, and more, were encapsulated in Jones' (1990) *Harvard Business Review* article 'The Double Jeopardy of Sales Promotion'. He concludes that companies, faced with saturated markets, have been misguidedly channelling money away from above-the-line advertising and 'fighting with fury for market share; using promotions (generally a high cost activity) as the main tactical weapon'.

Such indictments, published in leading journals, have helped to prejudice many management academics and some practitioners against promotions. However, it is worth remembering that many of the most outspoken critics (Jones included) are former top advertising practitioners. Advertising Hall of Fame member David Ogilvy's view is that: 'The manufacturer who finds himself up the creek is the short-sighted opportunist who siphons off all his advertising dollars for short-term promotions' (Ogilvy, 1985). It is also worth noting that much of the criticism, including Jones's, is based on an assumption that 'in most circumstances, promotions mean price reductions'.

The reality is that sales promotion needs to be understood for what it is – a diverse and versatile marketing toolkit, in which the majority of tools emphasize creativity over simple economics. The different promotional tools vary in terms of:

1 *Their targets* (see Figure 18.1). 'Push' promotions target marketing intermediaries, supporting the selling effort to get products onto retailers' shelves, while 'pull' promotions target consumers and complement advertising in persuading them to pick products off the shelves again.

2 *Type of benefits offered.* One fundamental distinction is between value-increasing and value-adding promotions. Value-increasing promotions alter the product/price equation by increasing the product quantity or quality, or decreasing its price. Value-adding promotions leave the basic product and price intact, and offer something different in terms of premiums (free or self-liquidating), information or opportunities. The benefits can be instant (scratch-and-win competitions), delayed (postal premiums) or cumulative (loyalty programmes).

3 *Product/market suitability.* While canned beers favour '13 per cent extra free' offers, or on-pack competitions and coupons,

unpackaged draught beers require special price evenings, gamecard competitions and promotional merchandise catalogues. Promotions also vary in their popularity and suitability internationally between countries (Huff and Alden, 1998). In Japan, redeeming coupons at point-of-sale is considered embarrassing, and so competitions are the most popular promotional tool there.

4 *Consumer appeal.* Consumers like extra benefits. In the USA, 70 per cent of consumers now hold at least one retailer loyalty card, and over 80 per cent use coupons. However, different types of promotion appeal to different people. Research by Gallup and numerous sales promotions agencies suggests that our age, sex, nationality, socio-economic grouping and ethnic origin can all influence which promotions we prefer.

5 *Marketing capabilities.* Free samples are obviously useful for encouraging product trial, while a prize draw can provide a mailing list for future promotions.

6 *Implementation priorities.* While printing security is important for gamecards, accurate redemption forecasting is vital for coupons and giveaways, and anticipating competitor reaction is important in price promotions.

Space constraints prevent a detailed discussion of each technique, but Table 18.1 provides examples and notes on some of the most popular forms of consumer promotions.

Academic research to develop a clearer understanding of promotion has taken time to emerge. Between 1965 and 1983 there were only around 40 academic studies published about promotion (Blattberg and Neslin, 1990). This compares to over 200 studies of promotion published between the mid-1980s and the mid-1990s (Chandon, 1995). Despite the increase in the amount of research, nearly all of it has remained focused on value-increasing techniques such as couponing. There have been relatively few studies, such as those by Chandon *et al.* (2000) or Peattie *et al.* (1997), of value-adding promotions.

Perhaps because of the limitations of the research, sales promotion is prone to a number of misconceptions. One frequently overlooked point about promotions, particularly value-adding ones, is that they are not so much a distinct element of the marketing mix as a customization of another mix element. Each mix element offers different benefits to customers (see Figure 18.2). To increase the desirability of the total product offering, sales promotions can:

- Enhance the product offering's utility by enhancing quality, or adding extra tangible benefits.
- Improve affordability by increasing the quantity offered, decreasing the price or easing the payment terms. This element of promotions may make them increasingly important in the near future given the record levels of consumer debt within countries like the UK and USA (Spears, 2001).
- Improve accessibility by gaining access to distribution channels and through extras such as free delivery.
- Support the advertising, sales and PR effort to boost the product's visibility and credibility through eye-catching and newsworthy promotional materials, and by creating subjects for advertising campaigns or discussions with customers.

The sales promotions planning process

Figure 18.3 illustrates a somewhat idealized view of the steps involved in an effectively planned promotion. Amidst the competitive cut and thrust of marketing reality, the practical execution will frequently involve a less orderly decision making process. However, the key issue is the importance of consistency between any promotion and the overall marketing communications effort. This holds good however tactical a particular promotion might be (for further details on the management of trade and consumer promotions, see Shimp, 2000). The process of planning a sales promotion has many similarities to advertising campaigns, including:

- External agencies that frequently play an important role in planning and implementation.
- A choice of media; promotions can be delivered on-pack, on-line or in-store, via direct mail, or in printed media including newspapers and magazines, catalogues and other promotional literature.
- A peculiar jargon, which can be decoded using the *Macmillan Dictionary of Marketing and Advertising* (Baker, 1998).
- Codes of practice, regulatory bodies and complex legal requirements which influence their development. Promotions are bound by the same laws as advertising, and also by more specific legislation such as the Lotteries and Amusements Act 1976, or the Price Marking (Bargain Offers) Order 1979 (for full details, see Circus, 1998).

The major differences in planning for advertising and promotions occur during campaign objective setting and evaluation. In terms of objective setting, promotions present a more complex set of possible alternatives than advertising. In addition to encouraging sales or product trial, promotions are used by marketers to pursue a wide range of other strategic and tactical objectives (Peattie *et al.*, 1997), including:

- Creating awareness or interest.
- Overshadowing a competitor's promotional or other activities.
- Deflecting attention away from price competition.
- Reinforcing advertising themes.
- Developing a relationship with customers.
- Gathering consumer information.

Trade promotions can aim to:

- Encourage or reward sales efforts from intermediaries.

Table 18.1 Major forms of consumer promotions

Promotion	Key user sectors	Notes	Examples
Discount pricing and sales	FMCG firms, retailers	Additional volume must compensate for lost revenue. Can spark price wars. Generally a defensive move	January sales. Retailer campaigns such as 'Asda Price'. Amazon offers a 40% discount on a customer's 'First Anniversary'
Money-off coupons	FMCG grocery retailers	Redemption rates determine costs. Requires retailer co-operation. Allows some differential pricing	Mattel Inc.'s 1988 toy marketing campaign involved 582 million coupons
Refunds	FMCG consumer durables	Avoids problems of reference price changes. Non-redemptions reduce costs compared to discounts	To boost UK sales of its Windows XP operating system, Microsoft offered a £50 cashback deal during the first quarter of 2002
Samples	Foods, toiletries	Expensive. Encourages trial. Effectiveness hard to measure. Can generate market research	Agree shampoo became No. 1 in the US market within 6 months by using 31 million samples
Payment terms	Consumer durables, retailers	Reduces real cost rather than price. Useful for seasonal demand smoothing	Interest-free credit offers. In 2001 brands including Compaq, Microsoft and Mitsubishi used 'Buy now, pay later' promotions
Multipacks and multibuys	Packaged goods, retailers	Best for small, high purchase frequency items	Kodak used a 3-for-2 offer on its Ultra film during 2001 to help boost its share of the crucial winter/festive season market
Special features	Consumer durables	Often packaged as a 'special' or 'limited' edition	The Citroen Xsara West Coast special edition was a major success, offering over £1000 of extras including air conditioning and metallic paint plus a reduced price
Quantity increases	Packaged foods, canned drinks	Relies on ability to customize packaging processes	Canned beers feature regular 500 ml for the price of 400 ml
In-pack premiums	Packaged goods	Items placed in foodstuffs needs care regarding food safety	During 2000 Kelloggs put Sesame Street beanie toys into 25 million cereal boxes
In-mail premiums	Packaged goods	Usually relies on handling houses for redemption	Stonegate Egg's offer of Chicken Run movie tickets, T-shirts and egg cups helped to sell 5.2 million extra eggs during 2000

Type	Product category	Comments	Examples
Piggy-back premiums	Packaged goods	Usually joint promotions. Can generate complementary sales and encourage product trial	'Free Gillette GII with Kleenex For Men' gained Gillette 100 000 trials and KFM 13% extra sales
Competitions	Packaged foods, retailers	Good for creating interest and reinforcing ad campaigns. Needs care with legalities	McDonald's $40m Treasure Hunt. Heinz's 'Win a Car a Day for 100 Days' campaign
Information	Industrial firms, consumer durables, services	Important for reducing perceived risk. Provides consumer benefits of convenience and saved time	Product catalogues. Holiday brochures. Investment guides. CD-ROM catalogues
Valued packaging	Retailers, FMCG firms	Packaging can be useful in itself, or can provide a game, activity, recipe or other information	Sony's regular offer of a free case with cassette and mini-disc multipacks. The enduring Paul Masson wine carafe
Loyalty cards	Retailers	Card applications and usage can be linked to EPOS information to create database marketing and targeted promotion opportunities. Some concerns about level of loyalty achieved	Boots Advantage Card has over 13 million members and over 50% of its sales are card related
Gift coupons	Petrol retailers, draught beers	Useful for non-packaged goods. Helps encourage repeat purchases	Over 3 million users registered on-line for the Pepsi 'Stuff' merchandise collection during 2000
Product trial	Consumer durables	Often twinned with a competition. Needs close sales support	200 000 Apple Macs were 'home tested', 40% led to sales
Guarantees	Consumer durables, retailers	'Pricebeat' promises often back up sales to reduce perceived risk	Supermarket 'Refund and Replace' offers. During 2001 Vodafone and Easyjet used 'Price Promises' of refunding the difference if customers found lower prices elsewhere
Cashback offers	Consumer durables	Costs depend upon redemption rates. Over-redemption can be insured against	Sanyo's 1988 10-year buyback pledge boosted TV sales by 62%
Clubs	Airlines and hotels, children's products	Useful for generating customer loyalty	Marriott Hotels' Rewards scheme has over 15 million members and Burger King's Kids Club has more the 5 million members worldwide

Figure 18.2   Satisfaction chain

- Increase or maintain floor or shelf space for products.
- Encourage stocking up by intermediaries.
- Gain support for special displays or other promotional activities.
- Gain access to new sales outlets.
- Insulate intermediaries from temporary sales downturns or pressure on margins.
- Reinforce communication to, or education of, intermediaries.

In terms of measurability, the direct nature of the consumer response makes their short-term effects easier to measure accurately than those for advertising, particularly with the data available from electronic point-of-sale (EPOS) systems. When running competitions, Heinz use a sophisticated monitoring system using feedback scratch cards, to analyse the effects on behaviour and buying patterns among participants. This allows them to build up an accurate picture of the effect that such promotions can have, and their effectiveness when used through different grocery chains. Similarly, a recent Pepsi promotion, offering four live CDs in return for ring pulls, produced hundreds of thousands of responses. Uniquely numbered mailings allowed response to be measured with pinpoint precision. One drawback of the measurability that direct responses allow is that the less measurable indirect responses relating to brand awareness or image tend to be overlooked. In *Promo* magazine's 2001 survey of US marketing practitioners, only 10 per cent of those running promotions measured their impact on awareness rates compared to around 50 per cent measuring sales volume or redemption rates.

This chapter aims to emphasize the differences between promotions and advertising, which were perhaps best summed up by Hugh Davidson (1975) as follows:

> In general the purpose of advertising is to improve attitudes towards a brand, while the object of promotion is to translate favourable attitudes into actual purchase. Advertising cannot close a sale because its impact is too far from the point of purchase, but promotion can and does.

The comparative ability of promotions to close sales reflects three key differences to advertising,

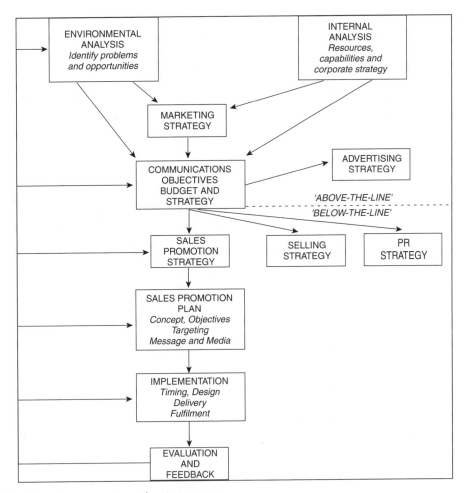

Figure 18.3 The sales promotion planning process

each of which form a theme for the rest of this chapter:

- Communication capabilities.
- Relationship building capabilities.
- Flexibility and manageability.

Sales promotion and advertising – the line and the pendulum

Communications budgets are often spoken of as being invested 'above the line' and 'below the line'. This 'line' originally denoted whether or not communications efforts were channelled through advertising agencies. With sales and PR often classified as separate functions, 'below the line' has become synonymous with sales promotion. The existence of this conceptual divide casts advertising and sales promotion in the role of rivals for the biggest share of a company's marketing communications budget.

During the 1980s and 1990s there was a gradual shift in marketing communications emphasis and expenditure away from traditional 'brand sell' advertising and towards sales promotion. This shift of emphasis reflects growing doubts about the cost effectiveness of advertising in the face of rising prices and increased advertising 'clutter'. A recent consumer survey (Croft, 1999) provided ammunition to those who champion sales promotion. The survey conducted by RSGB on behalf of Mercer Gray revealed that:

> only 16% of people in Britain admitted to paying any attention during commercial breaks. Twice as many say they treat the commercial break as an opportunity to nip out and make a cup of tea. 25% change channels to see if there is anything more interesting on the other side and 17% talk to other people in the room.
>
> Just under a third of respondents (29%) said they bought an item because of a TV ad while more than half (59%) admitted having bought something because it was part of a special offer or promotion such as a two-for-one or a competition.

Developments in broadcasting technology have also eroded television advertisers' confidence in their ability to reach target audiences. Remote controls make channel hopping easy, and where once video recorders could allow the viewer to fast forward through advert breaks, companies like Hitachi are now marketing recorders that edit out advert breaks automatically.

Over time, the emphasis placed on advertising and promotions within markets and firms often resembles a pendulum swinging backwards and forwards across that imaginary line. Each time a blue chip company changes its marketing communication emphasis towards one side of the line, it is interpreted as the beginning of the end for the other. At the start of the 1990s, the swing towards promotion was exemplified by Heinz, who in 1992 cut their US advertising budget and transferred $100 million into (mostly trade) promotions. The result was an immediate 7.3 per cent market share gain for Heinz ketchup alone, reversing a six-month sales decline. However, this proliferation of promotions created concern about 'overkill', and a swing back towards advertising in many markets.

This concern was reflected in the high-profile move away from promotions by one of the world's biggest promotions user, Procter & Gamble, with their 1996 Every Day Low Price (EDLP) campaign. Faced with declining coupon redemption rates and increasing costs, the company decided to test a zero price promotion marketing campaign. As a substitute, they offered 'permanent price reductions aimed at adding extra value and fostering brand loyalty so that the consumer's decision is made to purchase before they even enter the grocery store'. In practice, the EDLP concept was not accepted by consumers. In the UK, P&G's sales and value position dropped, and in the USA the trial was ended four months early in the face of retailer opposition. P&G's couponing policy was not only reinstated, but some consumers and retailers were scheduled to receive compensation from the company for the losses incurred (Gardener and Trivedi, 1998). Ailawadi *et al.* (2001) provide a longitudinal study between 1990 and 1996 of P&G's strategy of decreasing deals and coupons and boosting spending on advertising. Their analysis of customer and competitor reaction to the strategy concludes that: 'The net impact of these consumer and competitor responses is a decrease in market share for the company that institutes sustained decreases in promotion coupled with increases in advertising.'

To some commentators, 1997 was like the beginning of the end for conventional advertising, which came under attack from some of the key brands that sustain it. Dominic Cadbury, Chairman of Cadbury Schweppes, rebuked marketers for their obsession with the 'froth' of advertising. Niall Fitzgerald, Chairman of Unilever, stated that 'I do not find today's advertising agencies being much of a match for tomorrow's marketing opportunities'. Paul Polman, Vice President and General Manager of Procter & Gamble, the world's biggest advertiser, attacked the 47 per cent rise in TV advertising costs between 1992 and 1997 as 'unacceptable'. The decision of Saatchi & Saatchi, a brand synonymous with above-the-line activity, to drop the word 'advertising' from its title as too limiting seemed to be symbolic. These omens of doom were promptly followed by a flood of new money being poured into advertising during the dot-com boom.

Debates about which side of the line is the wisest destination for marketing funds have always been inconclusive, and look increasingly irrelevant. Advertising and sales promotion are both effective techniques, which work best as complementary components of a strategically planned and integrated communications campaign. The trend towards such integration and the blurring of that imaginary line has led to:

- The proliferation of 'integrated communications' (or 'through the line') agencies handling campaigns on both sides of the line.
- An increase in 'Spadspend', advertising expenditure to reinforce promotions. This accounts for an estimated 20 per cent of all advertising. Iceland supermarkets took the top prize for Outstanding Marketing Achievement and the award for Brand Revitalization in the 2000 Marketing Society Awards, for its advertising campaign focused on its 'Feel The Deal' multi-buy promotions.
- More themed promotions aiming to reinforce brand values and advertising messages. Heinz's use of prizes in groups of 57 for their competitions is a simple example of brand theming.
- Some very novel approaches to managing the promotional effort. Sega invited the winners of a promotional competition to form a 'think-tank' with brand managers and advertising agency account managers to help plan their future campaigns.

The growing importance of sales promotion

Measuring total sales promotion expenditure accurately is virtually impossible due to its fragmented nature and the diversity of definitions of what it should include. While some estimates include all direct mail costs, others exclude them. Yet direct mail is actually a medium for sales promotion (and advertising), with approximately 80 per cent of mailshots containing some form of promotion. Discounting is a key promotional activity, but its 'cost' can be calculated in several ways. Although we can only estimate the overall growth in promotions, evidence of it confronts us every time we enter a supermarket. Some of the components of total promotions expenditure can also be measured accurately, even if we cannot agree what constitutes the whole. Coupon distribution in the UK was 5.1 billion in 2000 and a staggering 248 billion in the USA. Table 18.2 shows figures for different elements of promotional expenditure for 2000 in the USA, who lead the world in promotion usage.

There are eight key factors driving the growth in promotions:

1 *Increasing 'respectability'.* Partly through increasing use by market leaders including Heinz, Unilever, McDonald's, Coca-Cola, Pepsi and Cadbury's. Credibility has also been boosted by increasing professionalism among sales promotion agencies.
2 *Increased impulse purchasing.* Purchase decisions are increasingly made in-store, and can therefore be influenced by in-store promotions. Point of Purchase (POP) Institute research sponsored by companies including Procter & Gamble and Anheuser-Busch examined the impact of 60 000 POP displays in 250 US supermarkets. Properly displayed promotions boosted sales between 2 and 65 per cent depending on the product category and the POP display type.
3 *Shortening time horizons.* Time pressure makes the fast responses or sales boosts that promotions can offer attractive. Internet promotions have increased responsiveness further, since companies can rapidly change on-line discounts, coupons and other offers

Table 18.2   Recent trends and expenditure in US sales promotions

Promotion type	2000 expenditure ($ billions)	Comments
Premium incentives	26.9	Split between incentives for the salesforce (33%), dealers (31%), customers (23%) and non-sales employees (13%). Key trends are towards greater use of the Internet, and more distinctive incentives such as adventure trips or Quaker's 102 Dalmatians battery operated 'barking' spoons.
Point of purchase	17	Growth of 18%, much of it from use away from traditional FMCG markets. Fastest growth was in financial services. POP displays linking to a brand's sporting, movie or charity were highly successful, boosting sales by 65% on average.
Ad specialties	16.3	Refers to promotional items (logoed hats, T-shirts, pens, mousemats). Key users are in financial services, information technology and healthcare.
Sponsorship	8.7	Grew 14.5%, dominated by major sporting events and major brands such as Anheuser-Busch GM and Coca-Cola. Music tours and minority sports also attracted sponsorship growth.
Couponing	6.9	Coupon spending in the US dropped around 1% and redemption rates declined by more than 4%. Economic gloom may lift redemption rates. On-line and in-store coupons continue to grow.
Games, competitions and specialty printing	7.6	Competitions saw 9% market growth. Trends towards fewer but larger promotions, and 'cool' and unique prizes such as concert tickets, private parties and celebrity dates. Other promotional printing declined slightly due to growth in Internet promotions.
Promotional licensing	5.8	Continues to grow steadily each year. Dominated by tie-ups between a handful of 'blockbuster' movies and fast food, soft drinks and toys.
Product sampling	1.2	Sampling is increasingly event orientated and active. One million scoops of Ben & Jerry's 'Homemade' were served in 'guerrilla' visits to offices in 13 cities.
Interactive	1.8	Despite the bursting of the dot-com bubble, Internet-based promotion spending rose 40% during 2000. Key trends were greater integration of on-line promotions with overall communications strategy.
In-store services	0.9	32% of US retail market operates a loyalty card scheme and 70% of shoppers belong to at least one. Increasing use of smart cards and purchase kiosks.

to react to consumer uptake and stock availability.

4 *Micro-marketing approaches.* In response to fragmenting markets, where promotions can provide more tailored and targeted communication than mass media. The Kelloggs' 2002 Red Letter Day promotion offered as prizes over 300 different experiential days out, providing something to attract almost everyone.

5 *Declining brand loyalty.* Caused by widening choice, narrowing perceived differences between brands, and the increasing strength of retailer own label products.

6 *A 'snowball' effect.* In some markets, companies increasingly feel obliged to match rivals' sales promotion activity, or risk losing market share and competitive position (Lal, 1990).

7 *Affordability.* National mass media have become prohibitively expensive for many companies, particularly during recessionary squeezes on marketing budgets. Promotions allow national coverage at a lower cost, cost sharing with co-promoters and can even be self-funding.

8 *Interactivity.* With the increase in interactive media like the Internet and interactive TV, there are growing opportunities for sales promotions to play a key role in customer communication. The web surfer is quite likely to 'click through' an on-line advert or may install a program such as *AdWiper* to remove banner ads. An on-line promotion can engage with customers and generate a response through the offer of benefits.

A decision to offer the consumer extra value has some potential drawbacks. Some critics suggest that overuse is training customers to buy products only on promotion (Mela *et al.*, 1997), while others claim that promotional overkill is desensitizing consumers to their benefits. There is also the concern that emphasizing promotions leads marketers to focus on short-term tactical issues instead of longer-term strategy (Strang, 1976).

Consumers and sales promotion

There is general agreement that the marketing mix should be managed as an integrated whole. However, in practice the approach to managing the mix often follows the Product, Price, Place, Promotion sequence, reflecting the perceived importance of each element in winning customers (see Figure 18.4). Once the product is specified, part of the total available market will be lost because the product features (such as colour, size, flavour or facilities) are unsuitable for some potential customers. Further customers will be screened out who desire, but cannot quite afford the product; others will find the channels used inconvenient, and still more will remain untouched by the brand's advertising. The specification of the standard marketing mix therefore creates a customer group for whom the basic product offer is not ideal. These marginal consumers represent a prime target for promotions which, by offering additional benefits, may overcome their reservations about the brand to stimulate a purchase.

The targeting of such marginal consumers is standard practice in political marketing, but has often been neglected by commercial marketers. Cummins (1989) suggests that such non-core, low-loyalty consumers 'tend to be regarded by many companies with the distaste felt for the morally promiscuous'. In fact, the promotional battle to capture and convert marginal consumers can be an important part of marketing strategy because:

- They are very lucrative. Extra sales from marginal consumers, minus variable costs, equals pure profit.
- Those who like the brand may become loyal consumers.
- Each marginal consumer won over deprives a competitor of a potentially lucrative sale.

The good news for marketers needing to win over additional consumers is that promotions

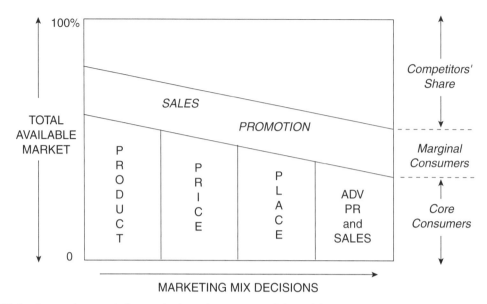

Figure 18.4   Promotions and the marketing mix: a sequential model

are a very effective persuader. In their research into coffee purchasing (a process one might expect to involve a high degree of personal taste and brand loyalty), Fraser and Hite (1990) concluded that: 'The vast majority of consumers are promotion responsive ... Promotional incentives are effective in capturing brand choices, encouraging purchase acceleration and stimulating category demand. Many customers use and expect deals, and many more are induced to alter purchase behaviours by deal offers.'

There are four dimensions of consumer behaviour which determine peoples' response to promotions:

1   *Value consciousness.* Promotions enhance the value of the product offering. Price- and product-based promotions are most directly targeted at consumers' desire for value.
2   *Susceptibility to promotions.* Beyond simple economic rationality, people vary in their responsiveness to promotions (Lichtenstein *et al.*, 1990, 1997). The benefits sought may not reflect only economic rationality, but can also include hedonic benefits such as entertainment,

exploration and self-expression (Chandon *et al.*, 2000). Many people enjoy the sense of being a 'smart shopper', which judicious use of promotions can provide. Susceptibility can vary in relation to the nature of the purchase (Bawa and Shoemaker, 1987), and also to the nature of the shopping trip and retail environment (Chandon, 1995).
3   *Brand loyalty.* Promotions can overcome consumer loyalty to a competitor's brand to encourage brand switching, or they can capitalize on core customer loyalty and encourage increased usage (Ailawadi and Neslin, 1998).
4   *Attitude to risk.* By reducing price, allowing product trial, providing information or improving warranty or payment terms, promotions can overcome consumers' innate conservatism and reduce the perceived risk they associate with purchase.

A promotion does more than provide an opportunity to stimulate a simple response from a consumer. It provides opportunities to change the consumer's whole relationship with a given brand (see Figure 18.5) in three ways:

1 *Conversion.* Promotions are effective as trial incentives, because they reduce perceived risk and can attract non-users through additional benefits rather than relying on the attraction of an unfamiliar product. Consumers who are satisfied with a promoted brand have an increased probability of repeat purchases in future. This is particularly true of previous non-users (Rothschild and Gaidis, 1981). Neilsen Promotion Services found that 55 per cent of consumers who enter competitions will select a brand because of a competition, and that 95 per cent of those will repurchase in future.

2 *Retention.* Providing delayed or cumulative benefits can help to encourage repeat purchases. 'Collect and save' schemes or 'money off next purchase' coupons can help to retain promotion-sensitive brand switchers.

3 *Acceleration.* McDonald's reached a point where awareness levels were becoming difficult to improve through advertising, resulting in declining business potential from new customers. They have therefore switched an increasing proportion of a billion dollar communications budget into promotions aimed at getting more business from existing customers. The 'Happy Meal' promotions provide sets of novelties for children to collect, changed at regular intervals to accelerate visit frequency.

Communicating through sales promotions

Like advertising, promotions seek to connect with the customer to generate awareness, inform, entertain, and generally persuade the customer to change their attitudes and behaviour in the brand's favour. Communicating effectively requires the marketer to develop the right message, select an appropriate medium and accurately target the campaign. When it comes to targeting, promotions are more flexible than advertising, which essentially presents one message at a time to the entire audience (a 'shotgun' approach). By offering a choice of competition prizes, merchandise or

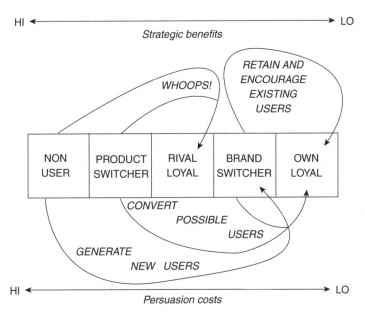

Figure 18.5   The roles of promotion in converting consumers

premiums, promotions can engage and communicate with different customer groups.

Advertising's approach to communication is rooted in the early physical systems-based approaches to human communication developed in the 1940s and 1950s by the likes of Lasswell and Schramm. The message is seen as a 'magic bullet' transferring encoded information from a sender (the advertiser) to be absorbed and decoded, relatively passively, by a receiver (the target audience). Promotions reflect more contemporary theories of human communication, which stress its social context and processes of sharing, response and interaction. Promotions communicate with the aim of encouraging interaction between the producer and the consumer, through a sale, the clipping of a coupon or the testing of a product sample.

In terms of persuasion, promotions' direct response orientation has focused attention on the 'action' phase of the classic AIDA model (see Chapter 17) when discussing their communications capabilities. In fact, promotions work effectively during each phase of this communication process:

1 *Attention.* Promotions are undoubtedly attention grabbing. Words such as 'Extra', 'Free', 'Win' and 'Special' all help promoted products to stand out on the shelves of today's supermarkets. A typical Tesco store will contain around 50 000 different products jostling for the consumer's attention.
2 *Interest.* Promotions can inject novelty and even fun into the most familiar or mundane of products. Financial services companies have found that promotional competitions create considerable interest among customers and staff, which can be important in a price competitive market with an intangible product (Peattie and Peattie, 1994). Barclays 1998 Nest Egg competition encouraged customers to discuss their savings needs with a 'Personal Banker' with the lure of £100 000 in prizes and a free Cadbury's Creme Egg for everyone.
3 *Desire.* Encouraged by the offer of additional benefits. Research by Millward Brown and ASL

into the 1996 Cadbury's Coronation Street interactive on-pack promotion showed that 26 per cent of adults were aware of the promotion and that the lure of the 8 million prizes made 13 per cent feel encouraged to buy more Cadbury's bars.
4 *Action.* Promotions differ from advertising (with the exception of direct response advertising) in seeking a direct response such as replacing a consumer durable or overcoming their previous objections to a brand and sampling it. For the majority of promotions the action sought is a sale, and promotions have been demonstrated as effective in increasing the consumer's sales volume and rate of consumption (Ailawadi and Neslin, 1998).

Promotions can also go beyond prompting action to create interaction and consumer involvement with a product, by requiring them to analyse and rank its attributes, create a recipe around it, test drive it or sum up its virtues in 10 words or less. While advertising is a one-way communication process, promotions can create a dialogue. Competitions, direct mail promotions and sampling programmes are increasingly being used to gather information from consumers, as well as to send messages to them. Guinness used questions on a competition leaflet to help pinpoint more accurately their key competitors in the canned beer market. Beamish Stout capitalized on their sponsorship of the Inspector Morse TV series by sending out a squad of 'policewomen'. They persuaded drinkers to 'help with their enquiries', and combined an effective sampling promotion with a major market research exercise. Kelloggs and Gillette have also used promotions to build up consumer databases and contacts. Kelloggs provided an extra entry into its 2000 *Pokemon Master* competition for each E-card that customers sent onto their friends, and Gillette's *Venus* razor on-line sweepstake offered extra entries to customers in return for their friends' e-mail addresses.

Building relationships through promotions

Because promotions go beyond the 'magic bullet' approach to communication, they create opportunities to build relationships between the promoter and the target. In consumer markets this is often achieved through loyalty schemes. The Boots Advantage Card, for example, has around 13 million members, and over 50 per cent of its sales are linked to the card. Through this loyalty scheme, the company has been able to identify and target its most valuable customers by sending out a free health and beauty magazine to its top-spending 3 million card holders.

Three areas in which relationship building is central are in trade promotions aimed at retailers and distributors, in supporting and encouraging sales activity, and in developing marketing partnerships with other companies. Many products rely heavily on retailer support, and increasing trade promotions reflects their importance in maintaining good channel relationships. Intermediaries have begun to strongly influence the extent and nature of producer promotions, as P&G found when their strategy of reducing reliance on promotions ran into retailer opposition.

Trade promotions are less varied than the consumer promotions in Table 18.1, but operate from similar principles. Intermediaries are offered special discounts or payment terms, gifts, contests, sales information or extra product to gain their enthusiasm and shelf space. Microsoft's promotion for its UK dealers aimed to encourage them to sell branded rather than generic mice, and involved a ceramic musical money box modelled on the Mouse 2.0 in a cheese wedge-shaped box along with a brochure and some cheese wedge sales aids. The number of dealers making Mouse 2.0 sales increased by 55 per cent over a three-month period. Some companies have developed clubs for dealers and intermediaries to try to improve communication and marketing support within supply chains. British Car Auctions in the UK and Rover cars in Germany have both launched on-line clubs to support their dealers.

Promotions also play an important part in supporting the sales efforts of industrial marketers. The negotiation of special deals for key customers, participation at trade fairs, product samples and the provision of product information all play a vital part in reducing the buyers' perception of risk and helping to win contracts. Promotional gifts as humble as calendars, pens and mugs all play a part in communicating, and in keeping the promoter's name at the potential purchaser's fingertips. At the dark end of the spectrum, bribery could qualify as a form of promotion, and in offering intermediaries extra benefits, a producer must always be sensitive to their targets' policies towards the acceptance of promotional gifts.

Salesforce contests are another form of promotion used by around three-quarters of all companies who sell. Their effectiveness is often undermined in practice by overemphasizing financial incentives and by allowing them to become an expected part of salesforce remuneration. More imaginative companies have discovered that effectively designed salesforce promotions can have a major impact. British Car Rentals had a significant problem in the imbalance of business between weekdays and weekends. To stimulate weekend rentals they devised an 'Oscars' competition for their salesforce. Branches were sent movie-themed displays and 'props', and sales staff could win movie merchandise, with a trip to Hollywood for the top performing team. The result was a sales increase of over 450 per cent.

Promotions allow producers to join forces to take advantage of synergies between their products or similarities between their target markets. This can create some unlikely alliances, unthinkable in terms of joint brand–sell advertising. Barclays Bank teamed up with Kelloggs to offer on-pack bank deposit coupons aimed at getting children to eat more cereals and open a bank account. The Clorets breath fresheners brand sought to establish an association of ideas by offering a free curry from The Curry Club. The link between entertainment and refreshments has also led to a wide range of co-promotions, with different fast food and soft drink brands locked in a fierce bidding war for the right to develop promotions based on the latest movie blockbusters. Given that the biggest box office hits for 2001 were *Harry Potter, Shrek* and *Monsters Inc.*, the ultimate value of their combined promotional merchandising and tie-ins should be extraordinary. Recently, there has been a trend towards co-promotions shared between major brands. Kelloggs, for example, has recently shared promotions with Pepsi and McDonald's. An early example of such partnerships occurred when General Motors (GM) teamed up with P&G to give away 750 1988 Cadillacs at a cost of $9 million. This was each company's biggest ever promotion at that time. For P&G, Cadillacs as prizes attracted consumers while reinforcing P&G's quality image, while the seven key P&G brands involved gave GM a direct communication channel into 98 per cent of American homes.

Sales promotion's role in the marketing mix

Promotions which aim to build relationships require a much longer-term approach to promotions management than the 'quick fix' campaign stereotype. Major joint promotions can take years to plan, and loyalty schemes or major mechandising programmes may run for many years. The relationship building capabilities of promotions is just one of several factors causing a re-evaluation of what promotions can achieve for marketers. Awareness of the potential strategic impact of promotions is leading to a more integrated approach to their management and their role within the marketing mix. The intertwining of promotion with the rest of the mix is demonstrated in Figure 18.6. The model's 'nine Ps' are less memorable than the classic four, but they demonstrate the difficulties of isolating promotions within the mix (and it is worth emphasizing that the interactions mentioned are only an illustrative selection). To

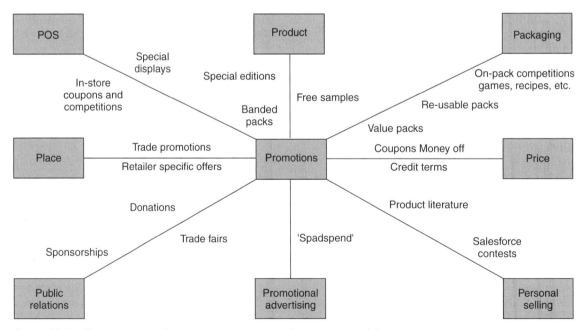

Figure 18.6   Promotions and the marketing mix: an integrated model

take one example, there are now more than 200 promotional magazines published and distributed by companies in the UK; around 20 have a circulation of over a million readers. Many would classify this as public relations activity rather than a sales promotion, and the issue is complicated further by the likes of the Sainsbury's magazine, which is unusual in being sold rather than distributed free.

The entangling of promotions with the rest of the mix account for the problems that occur when people attempt to define or measure sales promotion activity. Quelch (1989) also suggests that, in practice, it is a failure to integrate promotions effectively into the mix that leads to problems and to much of the criticism of promotions. On the positive side, this lack of clear boundaries can be viewed as providing an unrivalled opportunity for marketing managers to find innovative and creative ways of reaching customers. Robinson and Shultz (1982) suggest that the internal boundary spanning nature of promotions make them an ideal 'bridge', providing opportunities to integrate the communications efforts of advertising, selling and PR, which may each be the responsibility of different managers.

Sales promotions – the most manageable P?

Sales promotions appeal to marketing managers because they are flexible and fast acting. They are also more directly controllable than other elements of the marketing mix, because generally speaking:

- Developing new products is a slow process, which often relies on technical specialists.
- Permanent price changes depend on financial management's co-operation internally and customer acceptance or rivals' reactions externally.
- Channel changes involve lengthy negotiations with third parties.

- Advertising campaigns are planned slowly and carefully to nurture the image of the brand.

For the marketer looking to make a mark in a new job, under pressure to respond to competitors or struggling to meet tough sales targets, promotions can offer a speedy solution. Promotions' origins as tactical weapons make them very responsive and manoeuvrable, and well suited to just-in-time approaches to the management of inventories and businesses. This has been taken to extremes by companies such as Mrs Fields' Cookies, with outlets being linked directly to the central information system, so that sales patterns can be analysed and any necessary point-of-sale promotional offers suggested in 'real time'.

There is a wealth of common sense advice available to marketers on how to successfully and strategically manage promotions, mostly covering points such as:

- Look to add value rather than cut prices wherever possible.
- Link the promotion closely to the brand values.
- Theme promotions to reinforce advertising campaigns.
- Develop synergies with sales and PR campaigns.
- Search out cross-promotional opportunities.
- Reward loyal users and encourage repeat purchases.
- Ensure that the promotion is carefully targeted with quantified objectives and overseen by a sufficiently senior executive.
- Constantly monitor and re-evaluate progress.

Sales promotions mismanagement

Sales promotions can achieve many marketing objectives, but they have definite limitations (Shimp, 2000). They will not compensate for fundamental weaknesses in the rest of the marketing mix, they will not revive the fortunes of an outdated brand, and overuse can be counter-productive. Despite their manageability, promotions frequently run into problems. Advertising, with its fixed upfront costs, is often considered to be riskier than sales promotions, whose costs are generally more spread out and related to sales volume. However, while misconceived advertising dents credibility and wastes communications budgets, a bungled promotion can also incur significant 'clean-up' costs. This was graphically illustrated by the legendary Hoover 'Free Flights' promotion, where a drastic underestimate in the redemption rate of a flights giveaway led to losses initially estimated at £20 million, and a great deal of adverse publicity. On-line promotions have opened up many new opportunities for promotions, and also new opportunity for promotion disasters. Vitamins.com, for example, was driven out of business partly through poorly controlled discounts. Their website offered new visitors $25 off purchases of over $25, free delivery and a $15 off next purchase coupon.

The ways in which promotions can go wrong are many and varied, from Pepsi's virtually vowel-free 'Spell Your Surname and Win' contest, won by an unexpectedly large number of people called Ng, to lightning wiping out Bayard Sales' sole copy of its promotional database. Some promotions have even ended in tragedy. In 2000, Burger King had to recall 25 million *Pokemon: The First Movie* premiums after two infants were suffocated by the packaging of the Pokemon trading cards.

There are eight dangers commonly associated with promotions:

1 *Promotional price wars.* These erode margins instead of boosting sales. During 2001, markets including mobile phones, computers and Internet services witnessed promotional price wars among already heavily indebted companies.
2 *Misredemption of coupons.* This presents a major hazard, and although previous estimates of around 20 per cent misredemption seem to

have been an exaggeration, there have been a number of multimillion dollar scams. Three executives from New York's Sloans Supermarket were found to have run a 20-year coupon fraud operation which netted them $3.5 million (Shimp, 2000). Although coupon barcode scanning has provided opportunities to cut fraud, the problem is resurfacing in relation to on-line coupons.

3 *Reference price changes.* A promotional price attracts customers by undercutting the expected 'normal' price. Too long or too frequent price promotions lower customers' 'reference' price, so that they see a return to the original price as an increase (Lattin and Bucklin, 1989).

4 *Printing errors.* Gamecard promotions require careful attention to printing accuracy and security. Esso's Noughts and Crosses game had to be withdrawn after its first two weeks after twenty £100 000 first prize winning tickets emerged when only two should have existed for the entire promotion.

5 *Over-redemption.* Coupons, giveaways and buyback schemes are all based around estimates of the response. A promotion which is unexpectedly successful in attracting customers (as happened to Hoover) can result in disastrous losses. Misjudging the extent or timing of consumer response can also lead to stock-outs and subsequent customer dissatisfaction. One-2-One's offer of free phone calls on Christmas day for purchasers of a mobile phone created demand which virtually seized up their network, preventing many callers getting through to their loved ones.

6 *Quality dissonance.* Reducing prices, or offering low-quality free gifts or competition prizes, risks devaluing an otherwise strong brand in consumers' minds. An unexpected side-effect of P&G's switch from coupons to lower prices was that the price cuts reduced the brand's perceived quality (Gardener and Trivedi, 1998).

7 *Tax.* Several major promoters, including McDonald's, Boots and Sony, have found

themselves in high-profile legal clashes with the Customs and Excise Service over VAT payments on sales promotions.

8 *Fulfilment problems.* Every year, between 200 and 300 promotions result in complaints to the Advertising Standards Authority. Around 90 per cent of these are upheld for breaching the Institute of Sales Promotion (ISP) Code of Practice. About 20 per cent of all such problems are not related to the sponsor, but lie with the handling houses which oversee the logistics of fulfilment.

Promotions encounter such problems because they usually do not enjoy the rigorous planning and control afforded to advertising campaigns. Time pressure and a tendency for the implementation and evaluation of promotions to be delegated too far down the organization contribute to this situation, which was summed up in a classic article by Roger Strang (1976) entitled 'Sales Promotions: Fast Growth, Faulty Management'. Most promotional pitfalls can be avoided by:

- Greater attention to the promotional planning process detailed in Figure 18.3.
- Addressing the type of common sense questions contained in the 'compete using promotions' checklist (Table 18.3) while planning the promotion campaign.
- Adhering to the ISP Code of Practice.

There are also indications that sales promotions are becoming more effectively managed as the industry matures. American companies now spend over $1 billion annually on research related to promotions according to US promotion industry figures.

The future of sales promotion

One golden rule of promotions management is that overuse of any technique will blunt its effectiveness. Innovation and creativity are key success factors, and recent advances in packaging and information technology have provided many exciting new ways to offer customers extra benefits.

1 *High-tech coupons.* These may make coupon clipping a thing of the past. Sinfonia Marketing Systems in France has introduced the Promocarte, a smart card which can hold and automatically redeem coupon information based on previous purchases. Instant Coupon Machines are now being used in branches of Somerfield, Budgens and Safeway, and are claimed by their makers to raise brand sales by an average of 184 per cent.

2 *EPOS systems.* These allow the banding of products in a logical rather than a physical sense. Safeway's 'Linksave' and 'Multisave' promotions involve the EPOS system identifying and refunding the price of the third instance of a 'buy two get one free' product, or automatically refunding a 'piggyback' purchase. This removes much of the repackaging and logistical costs previously associated with product-based promotions.

3 *Packaging innovations.* Increasingly versatile and novel sample packs or encapsulations are now used in letterbox drops or attachments to products and magazine covers. Jacob's 'Fridge 'em to Win' competition used thermochromic ink (which only showed the win/lose message when chilled) on the wrapper of each Club biscuit to encourage users to buy and refrigerate them during the traditionally slow summer period. Initial results showed a 48 per cent increase in sales volume.

4 *Customer database systems.* Marks & Spencer were pioneers in establishing a central marketing database through which all sales promotion campaigns could be managed. This allows the generation of effectively targeted direct mail campaigns, and the accurate measurement of each campaign's results. The US Fairmont Hotel chain's computer network analyses the habits of regular business travellers. This ensures that, wherever travellers stay, their tastes in everything from

Table 18.3   The 'compete using promotions' checklist

Concept	Do we need a promotion? If so, why? Is the promotional effort best aimed at the consumer, the trade or both? Will the promotion be shared with another producer or a retailer? If so, how will costs and responsibilities be divided?
Objectives	What are the marketing communications objectives? What message will it send to consumers and what effect should it produce? Is it only short-term sales uplifts, or are there more long-term objectives such as generating new users or raising product awareness? Should the promotion target all markets and consumers or be more selective?
Mechanics	What types of promotion are feasible, which best suit the product, and which are most likely to meet our objectives? How will it reach consumers? Can a tried and trusted technique be given an innovative and creative edge? What could go wrong logistically and how could it be prevented?
Practical issues	Who will handle the planning and design, in-house or agency? Who will manage the campaign internally? What actions must take place, when, and by whom, to implement the promotion? Will fulfilment be handled internally or by a handling house? Will enough stock be available?
Expenditure	How much of the marketing budget and the time of marketing management should the promotion consume? Should it be supported by 'spadspend'? What level of uptake is expected? How likely and costly could an excessively high level of uptake be? Is sales promotion insurance needed?
Timing	Should the promotion be used to counteract seasonal lows, reinforce seasonal highs or 'spoil' rivals' promotions? Should the duration be long to maximize sales, or short to prevent loss of consumer interest? How long should special packs, coupons or leaflets etc. be available for? Should the benefits be instantly available, delayed or cumulative? What redemption deadline should be set?
Evaluation	How will the effectiveness of the promotion be measured in terms of achieving its objectives? Who should be responsible for evaluation, when and using what measures?

drinks and newspapers to wake-up times can be anticipated.

5   *Customer information systems*. IBM's Ultimedia Touch Activity Centre (a kiosk displaying touch-screen-driven product information) allows customers to view products, product information, prices and availability, and place credit card orders. During in-store tests this proved popular with older consumers, who liked the convenience, detail of information available and the sense of control provided. In industrial markets, companies including Universal Office Supplies, RS Components and SKF are replacing traditional product catalogues with on-line and on-disk catalogues, which include automatic order processing software and in-built key customer discounts.

Perhaps the most significant development for the future of sales promotion is the development of on-line promotions such as 'e-coupons'. These can turn a formerly 'passive' form of sales promotion, the coupon, into something targeted and interactive. Marketers using e-coupons on websites can use registration information and information from tracking consumers' progress through websites to identify consumers' interests. Collected data can then be used to target consumers with future offers more precisely (Bednarz and Bergiel, 2001). Although e-coupons are a reasonably small proportion of the total couponing market, they are growing rapidly and have a far better average redemption rate, of over 56 per cent compared to 1.2 per cent for Sunday paper free standing insert coupons. The Internet allows e-commerce companies like Amazon and CDNow to offer customers regular and customized discount promotions, on-line loyalty schemes, customized e-mail information services based on customer tastes, and numerous information services to reduce perceived purchase risk. Another interesting development is that the Internet is allowing consumers to share information about promotions. A number of websites have been set up to collect and disseminate on-line coupons or offers, and to provide information on competitions and other forms of in-store promotion.

The other major trend in sales promotion is an increase in the levels of creativity being applied to promotions. In competitions, new ways to engage customers are being developed. Unilever launched an on-pack game called 'Wash and Win' on All and Wisk detergents printed using AquaPlay, a device employing a special membrane that reveals information when it gets wet. Consumers threw the game-piece in with their laundry to find out if they won a washer/dryer or a year's supply of detergent. Similarly in promoting an oral hygiene product for dogs, Friskies Petcare used a competition entry which the dog had to lick to reveal whether its owner had won a prize. Sampling programmes today are not just about handing out free samples, but are increasingly interwoven with events, or become events in themselves. Bass tried to improve the positioning of its Worthington beer brand in relation to younger drinkers through a 'mini-drama' acted out at style bars, in which customers who were drawn into the storyline and called the phone number of one of the 'characters' were rewarded with a text message entitling them to two free bottles at the bar.

Summary – the changing concept of sales promotion

For many years a widespread view of promotions was as short-term, tactical tools, often added into the marketing mix of struggling FMCG brands to boost sales. This attitude was summed up in the assertion by Ken Roman of Ogilvy & Mather, that promotions *rent* customers while product benefits (and by implication their communication through advertising) *own* customers.

Much of the early academic research into promotions produced very critical appraisals of their effectiveness (e.g. Dodson *et al.*, 1978; Doob *et al.*, 1969). The implication was that practitioners were foolish to invest so much time and money in them. However, such research was flawed by a concentration on price-based promotions, by ignoring the indirect effects of promotions, and by taking a very narrow view of consumer response. The difficulties experienced by P&G and their strategy of reducing reliance on promotions suggests that it is marketing academics that have the most to learn about promotions and their effectiveness. More recent research into promotions demonstrates that:

- They can boost a brand's sales, awareness levels and image (Aaker, 1991).
- They are effective in encouraging switching between brands, product categories and retailers (Walters, 1991).

- They can overcome significant levels of brand loyalty to 'poach' consumers (McAllister and Totten, 1985).
- They are most effective when backed up by advertising (Bemmaor and Mouchoux, 1991).
- Trade promotions help to secure intermediaries' enthusiasm and support, and can help to build or reduce trade inventories (Hardy, 1986).

Recently, the prejudices against promotions have begun to lessen. A new wisdom is emerging which views them not as a 'bolt-on extra', but as an essential and integral part of the marketing mix, and vital to the process of building and managing successful brands. Marketing practitioners are making it clear that although some promotions are purely tactical, many are central to brand building and marketing strategy. The 2000 *Promo* magazine survey of practitioners found that promotions formed part of an integrated communications plan for over 80 per cent of companies (and for 31 per cent it formed the core of that plan). Academic research is also finding evidence of promotion's increasingly strategic role (Peattie *et al.*, 1997; Ailawadi *et al.*, 2001). The emerging wisdom about sales promotion stresses that:

1 *Top brands promote.* Looking at promotions that have won industry awards in recent years, the client list reads like a selection from the 'Who's Who' of brands and includes Coca-Cola, PepsiCo, Microsoft, Kellogg's, Kraft, Cadbury, Virgin, Budweiser, Southern Comfort, Britvic, Golden Wonder, St Ivel, Bass, Jacob's, Trebor Bassets, Spillers and *The Daily Telegraph.*
2 *Promotions aren't necessarily temporary.* Nor are they of purely short-term value. Airline frequent flier schemes were originally conceived as temporary, but have gone on to represent an industry fixture generating at least $8 billion annually in additional revenues (plus sales from hotel tie-ins and other travel-related products). The Miss Pears Competition ran for over 60 years, and the

2002 *Times* 'Eat Out for £5' described itself as 'not a promotion, but an institution'. The effects of a promotion can also linger far beyond its duration. A promotion communicates to all those consumers who encounter it, not just those who take advantage of it, and can therefore play an important part in brand awareness building. Goodyear's German 'Looking for Winners' promotion increased turnover in participating outlets by 25 per cent and boosted general brand awareness from 12.5 to 30.5 per cent (Toop, 1992).

3 *Promotions have a strategic role.* This complements their more traditional tactical capabilities. Brand strength can overcome adversity, as shown by the example of Tylenol's recovery following poisoning incidents by terrorists and the brand's subsequent withdrawal. Another aspect of this story is the role that promotions can play in the achievement of strategic objectives such as a brand's rehabilitation following disaster. The recovery of Tylenol was a remarkable testament to the brand's robustness, but it was also considerably aided by the 40 million $2.50 coupons issued to reactivate former users.
4 *Promotions suit a wide range of markets.* The stronghold of sales promotion reflects its FMCG origins, and packaged goods in particular, but their use has spread throughout a wide range of markets. Promotions can be found encouraging people to open bank accounts (especially students), donate to charity, test drive cars, purchase shares or submit papers to academic conferences.
5 *Promotions can reinforce brand loyalty.* Promotions, particularly price cutting, have been blamed for the general erosion of brand loyalty (Papatla and Krishnamurthi, 1996). Whether increasing promotion is a symptom or a cause of eroding brand loyalty is open to debate. What is often overlooked is that promotions also build brand loyalty, by providing extra benefits for existing customers and by encouraging repeat purchases through devices such as 'money off next purchase'

coupons, 'one entry per proof-of-purchase' competitions, 'collectable' premiums, or cumulative customer loyalty programmes.

6 *Promotions can strengthen brand positioning.* A 1985 study by Frankel & Co. and Perception Research Services found that, following exposure to adverts featuring promotions for a brand, consumers' opinion of the brand (on issues like quality, value and caring about customers) improved by over 8 percentage points, compared to those exposed to only 'brand sell' adverts.

McKenna (1990) predicted a future renaissance of business based on a marriage of the 'soft skills' and creativity of marketing with the power of new technology. Many might relate to this in terms of advertising, where technology allows us to view spectacular computer-created images which go beyond anything reality has to offer. However, it is in sales promotions that many of the most exciting marriages of technology and creativity are occurring. An example comes from Hiram Walker, who spent $10 million on the *Cutty Sark Virtual Voyage*, a two and a half minute virtual reality experience allowing participants to act as the legendary smuggler William McCoy, fighting high seas, pirates and hostile stowaways to bring the bottles of *Cutty Sark* ashore. Surviving a virtual life-or-death experience to rescue a brand is an experience which is almost bound to cement the participants' relationship with that brand. Another example comes from Hewlett-Packard's MOPy fish, a virtual pet which can be downloaded from the Internet and can act as a computer screensaver. The HP website will also provide items of 'tank' furniture including a plant, rock, bubbles and a thermometer. These can only be downloaded in exchange for MOPy points, and the chief way of accumulating these is to use your HP printer to make 'Multiple Original Printouts'. In exchange for 3200 points you can acquire some aphrodisiac fish food which makes MOPy, who was developed using over 1 million photographs of a

real parrot fish, become so affectionate that it will plant a kiss on the inside of the monitor. Quite what Mr Holder would make of MOPy's antics is hard to imagine, but the general principle of getting extra custom out of people by offering them additional benefits is one that he would recognize and approve of.

The academic view of promotions still suffers from something of a preoccupation with issues of promotional price reduction, coupon redemption, and their effect on consumer behaviour and reference pricing. This is a pity, because it keeps the academic focus on those elements of promotion which are in relative decline, at a time when marketing practice is injecting so much energy and creativity into developing innovative promotions. The implications for marketing management of the boom in promotions is becoming increasingly clear; what sales promotion lacks in glamour compared to advertising, it more than makes up for in flexibility and effectiveness. In today's competitive marketplace, the professional management of sales promotion has become a matter of life and death for an ever growing number of brands.

References

Aaker, D. A. (1991) *Managing Brand Equity*, Free Press.

Ailawadi, K. L. and Neslin, S. A. (1998) The Effect of Promotion on Consumption: Buying More and Consuming It Faster, *Journal of Marketing Research*, **35**, August, 390–398.

Ailawadi, K. L., Lehmann, D. R. and Neslin, S. A. (2001) Market Response to a Major Policy Change in the Marketing Mix: Learning from Procter & Gamble's Value Pricing Strategy, *Journal of Marketing*, **65**(1), 44–61.

Baker, M. J. (1998) *Macmillan Dictionary of Marketing and Advertising*, 3rd edn, Macmillan.

Bawa, K. and Shoemaker, R. W. (1987) The Coupon-Prone Consumer: Some Findings

Based on Purchase Behaviour Across Product Classes, *Journal of Marketing*, **51**(4), 99–100.

Bednarz, M. R. and Bergiel, B. J. (2001) Coupon Clippers Clicking, *Global Competitiveness*, **9**(1), 408–418.

Bemmaor, A. C. and Mouchoux, D. (1991) Measuring the Short-Term Effect of In-Store Promotion and Retail Advertising on Brand Sales: A Factorial Experiment, *Journal of Marketing Research*, **28**(2), 202–214.

Blattberg, R. C. and Neslin, S. A. (1990) *Sales Promotion: Concepts, Methods and Strategies*, Prentice-Hall, Englewood Cliffs, NJ.

Chandon, P. (1995) Consumer Research on Sales Promotion: A State-of-the-Art Literature Review, *Journal of Marketing Management*, **11**(5), 419–441.

Chandon, P., Wansink, B. and Gilles, L. (2000) A Benefit Congruency Framework of Sales Promotion Effectiveness, *Journal of Marketing*, **64**(4), 65–81.

Circus, P. J. (1998) *Sales Promotion and Direct Marketing Law – A Practical Guide*, 3rd edn, Butterworth-Heinemann.

Croft, M. (1999) Viewers Turned Off by TV Ads, *Marketing Week*, **22**(3), 36–37.

Cummins, J. (1989) *Sales Promotion: How to Create and Implement Campaigns that Really Work*, Kogan Page, London.

Davidson, J. H. (1975) *Offensive Marketing*, Pelican, London.

Dodson, J. A., Tybout, A. M. and Sternthal, B. (1978) Impact of Deals and Deal Retractions on Brand Switching, *Journal of Marketing Research*, **15**(1), 72–81.

Doob, A. N., Carlsmith, J. M., Freedman, J. L., Landauer, T. K. and Solong, T. (1969) Effect of Initial Selling Price on Subsequent Sales, *Journal of Personality and Social Psychology*, **2**(4), 345–350.

Flack, J. A. (1999) Measure of Success, *Marketing Week*, **22**(5), 57–60.

Fraser, C. and Hite, R. (1990) Varied Consumer Responses to Promotions: A Case for Response Based Decision Making, *Journal of the Market Research Society*, **32**(3), 349–375.

Gardener, E. and Trivedi, M. (1998) A Commu-

nications Framework to Evaluate Sales Promotion Strategies, *Journal of Advertising Research*, **38**(3), 67–71.

Hardy, K. G. (1986) Key Success Factors for Manufacturers' Sales Promotions in Package Goods, *Journal of Marketing*, **50**(3), 13–23.

Huff, L. and Alden, D. L. (1998) An Investigation of Consumer Response to Sales Promotions in Developing Markets: A Three-Country Analysis, *Journal of Advertising Research*, **38**(3), 47–56.

Jones, J. P. (1990) The Double Jeopardy of Sales Promotion, *Harvard Business Review*, **68**(5), 145–152.

Lal, R. (1990) Manufacturer Trade Deals and Retail Price Promotions, *Journal of Marketing Research*, **27**(6), 428–444.

Lattin, J. M. and Bucklin, R. E. (1989) Reference Effects of Price and Promotion on Brand Choice Behaviour, *Journal of Marketing Research*, **26**(4), 299–310.

Lichtenstein, D. R., Netemeyer, R. G. and Burton, S. (1990) Distinguishing Coupon Proneness From Value Consciousness: An Acquisition–Transaction Utility Theory Perspective, *Journal of Marketing*, **54**(3), 54–67.

Lichtenstein, D. R., Burton, S. and Netemeyer, R. G. (1997) An examination of deal proneness across sales promotion types: a consumer segmentation perspective, *Journal of Retailing*, **73**(2), 283–298.

McAllister, L. and Totten, J. (1985) *Decomposing the Promotional Bump: Switching, Stockpiling and Consumption Increase*, Paper presented at ORSA/TIMS 1985 Joint Meeting.

McKenna, R. (1990) Marketing is Everything, *Harvard Business Review*, **68**(1), 65–79.

Mela, C. F., Gupta, S. and Lehmann, D. R. (1997) The Long Term Impact of Promotion and Advertising on Consumer Brand Choice, *Journal of Marketing Research*, **34**(2), 248–261.

Ogilvy, D. (1985) *Ogilvy on Advertising*, Vintage Books.

Papatla, P. and Krishnamurthi, L. (1996) Measuring the Dynamic Effects of Promotions on Brand Choice, *Journal of Marketing Research*, **33**(1), 20–35.

Peattie, K. and Peattie, S. (1993) Sales Promotions: Playing to Win?, *Journal of Marketing Management*, **9**(3), 255–270.

Peattie, S. and Peattie, K. (1994) Promoting Financial Services with Glittering Prizes, *International Journal of Bank Marketing*, **12**(6), 19–29.

Peattie, K., Peattie, S. and Emafo, E. B. (1997) Promotional Competitions as a Strategic Marketing Weapon, *Journal of Marketing Management*, **13**(8), 777–789.

Quelch, J. A. (1989) *Sales Promotion Management*, Prentice-Hall, Englewood Cliffs, NJ.

Robinson, W. A. and Schultz, D. E. (1982) *Sales Promotion Management*, Crain Books, Chicago.

Rothschild, M. L. and Gaidis, W. C. (1981) Behavioural Learning Theory: Its Relevance to Marketing and Promotions, *Journal of Marketing*, **45**(2), 70–78.

Schultz, D. E. (1987) Above or Below the Line? Growth of Sales Promotion in the United States, *International Journal of Advertising*, **6**, 17–27.

Shimp, T. A. (2000) *Advertising, Promotion and Supplemental Aspects of Integrated Marketing Communications*, 5th edn, Dryden Press, Fort Worth.

Spears, N. (2001) Time Pressure and Information in Sales Promotion Strategy: Conceptual Framework and Content Analysis, *Journal of Advertising*, **30**(1), 67–76.

Strang, R. A. (1976) Sales Promotion: Fast Growth, Faulty Management, *Harvard Business Review*, **54**(1), 115–124.

Toop, A. (1992) *European Sales Promotion: Great Campaigns in Action*, Kogan Page, London.

Walters, R. G. (1991) Assessing the Impact of Retail Price Promotions on Product Substitution, Complementary Purchase, and Interstore Sales Displacement, *Journal of Marketing*, **55**(2), 17–28.

Further reading

Ailawadi, K. L., Lehmann, D. R. and Neslin, S. A. (2001) Market Response to a Major Policy Change in the Marketing Mix: Learning from Procter & Gamble's Value Pricing Strategy, *Journal of Marketing*, **65**(1), 44–61. An unusual study, because it takes a long-term, in-depth and quantitative look at the promotional strategy of one of the world's top marketing organizations. It demonstrates clearly the strategic importance of promotions and the dangers of heeding the conventional academic wisdom that expenditure on promotions is better channelled into brand building advertising.

Chandon, P. (1995) Consumer Research on Sales Promotion: A State-of-the-Art Literature Review, *Journal of Marketing Management*, **11**, 419–441. A thorough and interesting review of the evolution of research into how and why promotions can influence consumers. It reflects the weakness of the discipline in the overemphasis on short-term, rational–economic price effects, but provides some useful criticism of the different research traditions and highlights areas for future research.

Chandon, P., Wansink, B. and Gilles, L. (2000) A Benefit Congruency Framework of Sales Promotion Effectiveness, *Journal of Marketing*, **64**(4), 65–81. Provides some useful quantitative support for the effectiveness of sales promotion, and is interesting for examining a wide range of benefits with a focus on both value-increasing and value-adding promotions.

Gardener, E. and Trivedi, M. (1998) A Communications Framework to Evaluate Sales Promotion Strategies, *Journal of Advertising Research*, **38**(3), 67–71. Takes a communications-orientated view of different types of sales promotion and presents a framework to aid managers in evaluating the success of their campaigns. Provides an accessible and revealing outline of the problems that beset Procter & Gamble when they tried a switch of emphasis away from promotions and towards advertising.

Peattie, K., Peattie, S. and Emafo, E. B. (1997) Promotional Competitions as a Strategic

Marketing Weapon, *Journal of Marketing Management*, **13**(8), 777–789. Demonstrates the use of promotions as a strategic marketing tool through research into the attitudes and practices of promotional competition sponsors. Confirms the versatility of such value-adding promotions in influencing consumer behaviour and meeting a range of marketing objectives.

Quelch, J. A. (1989) *Sales Promotion Management*, Prentice-Hall, Englewood Cliffs, NJ. Uses some very detailed and interesting cases to illustrate perspectives on sales promotion theory, covering different types of markets and targets. Includes a rarity, a vigourous defence of price promotions.

Schultz, D. E., Robinson, W. A. and Petrison, L. A. (1998) *Sales Promotion Essentials: The 10 Basic Sales Promotion Techniques . . . And How to Use Them*, NTC Business Books. A good introduction to the basics of sales promotion for practitioners.

Shimp, T. A. (2000) *Advertising, Promotion and Supplemental Aspects of Integrated Marketing Communications*, 5th edn, Dryden Press, Fort Worth. Although sales promotion is still overshadowed by advertising within this text, its integrated communications perspective highlights the many 'crossover' points between sales promotion and other marketing mix elements, such as direct mail and point-of-purchase promotion. The coverage of consumer behaviour in relation to promotions and promotions planning is excellent. The variety of interesting cases and references provided makes this a particularly helpful book for academics.

Toop, A. (1992) *European Sales Promotion: Great Campaigns in Action*, Kogan Page, London. One of the first books to demonstrate the strategic use of promotions within the marketing mix of leading multinational companies through a series of well-dissected case studies. Helps to capture the creative excitement and fun involved in top-notch promotions, and charts the emergence of the concept of pan-European sales promotions.

CHAPTER 19

Integrating customer relationship management and supply chain management

MARTIN CHRISTOPHER and ADRIAN PAYNE

Introduction

Traditionally, the routes to competitive advantage have typically been based upon strong brands, corporate image, effective advertising and, in some cases, price. These are the classic components of conventional marketing strategies. More recently, however, there have been a number of signs that suggest that the power of the brand – in both consumer and industrial markets – is in decline (Brady and Davis, 1993). For whatever reason, the customer seeks more than 'brand value', as it is sometimes called, and is looking increasingly for *value* in a much wider sense.

In the new paradigm of marketing, the emphasis changes from brand value to customer value. Essentially this means that the supplying organization must focus its efforts upon developing an 'offer' or 'package' that will impact customers' perception of the value they derive through ownership of that offer. This value might either be derived through the delivery of benefits in performance terms and/or in the form of a reduction in the customer's costs. Increasingly, customer relationship man-

agement (CRM) is being viewed as a strategic approach that can help realize improved customer value.

In this chapter we examine CRM with a special focus on its critical linkage with supply chain management (SCM). First, we discuss the decline of the brand. Second, we examine the concept of competing through capabilities and the interlinking roles of CRM and SCM. Third, we outline a strategic framework for understanding the key components of CRM. Fourth, we review the changing nature of customer–supplier relationships and the impact of superior SCM. Next, we examine the role that CRM and SCM have in improving customer service. Finally, we consider the development of market-driven CRM and SCM strategies.

The decline of the brand: the need for integrated CRM and SCM strategies

There is strong evidence from many markets that brand loyalty amongst customers is not what it was. Perhaps because of growing buyer sophistication, or because of a growing similarity in the composition and functionality of competing products, or because of the emphasis on price competition and frequent discounting activity, the power of the brand seems to be in decline (Brady and Davis, 1993). This phenomenon seems to be widespread – from computers to cars.

It is important to distinguish between brand *loyalty* and brand *preference*. Many customers have a preference for a brand or a supplier and will typically express that preference through their purchasing behaviour. However, when the preferred brand is not available, those same customers will quite readily choose an acceptable substitute. This is equally true in industrial markets or consumer markets, for example the choice of suppliers to a just-in-time manufacturer is very much influenced by delivery reliability. Similarly, a retailer in making shelf space allocation decisions will look very carefully at vendors' logistics performance.

The traditional means through which marketers have differentiated their offer from those of competitors, such as advertising and claimed product superiority, need to be augmented by a greater emphasis upon building customer relationships and customer value through service. Today's customer is far more sensitive to service than was previously the case. Survey after survey suggests that perceived quality and service outstrip price as the determining factor in choice of supplier in many markets.

The revised model of marketing effectiveness that is increasingly being recognized is shown as Figure 19.1, which emphasizes that relationships with customers are of equal importance as the relationships we have with consumers, and that both of these need to be underpinned by superior supply chain management.

What is being suggested is that it is no longer sufficient to have a strong franchise with the *consumer* – meaning that because of superior brand values or corporate image the supplier can expect continuing market success. Strong consumer franchises need to be augmented by equally strong relationships with channel intermediaries – the *customer* franchise.

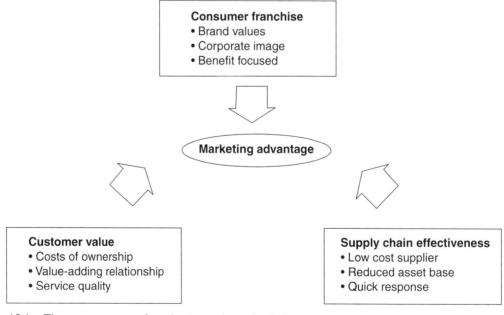

Figure 19.1   The convergence of marketing and supply chain management

Both of these franchises need cost-effective SCM and effective CRM to support them.

Competing through capabilities

As the power of the brand declines, organizations are having to reappraise their traditional definitions of strengths and weaknesses. The view now gathering ground is that the real opportunities for differential advantage come from capabilities or the things we excel at, our 'distinctive competencies'.

Thus, in a market characterized by shortening life cycles, for example, the ability to get new products to market in ever-shorter time frames becomes a source of competitive advantage. Likewise, information systems that can capture demand as it happens and production systems that can respond rapidly are a major strength in a volatile market. Similar advantages accrue to organizations with order fulfilment and logistics systems that enable superior levels of customer service to be achieved.

None of this is to deny the importance of strong brands supported by motivated employees, but they are no longer enough by themselves. Conversely, strong brands and motivated employees supported by best-in-class capabilities will be difficult for competitors to attack. Indeed, wherever enduring leadership in any market is encountered it tends to support this contention – names such as McDonald's, Sony and Disney come to mind.

The more that organizations come to recognize the importance of competing through capabilities, the more they will be forced to accept the need to switch the focus in the business away from managing functions to managing the key activities or processes that create those capabilities. A major change that has taken place in the way in which we think about organizations has been the realization of the importance of processes. Processes are the ways in which firms create value for their customers; they are fundamental and, to a large extent, generic across business types.

Processes are 'horizontal' in that they cut across traditional 'vertical' functions, and by definition they are interdisciplinary and cross-functional. The four 'high-level' business processes that are common to most firms are:

- The market understanding process.
- The innovation management process.
- The supply chain management process.
- The customer relationship management process.

Figure 19.2 illustrates these four 'high-level' business processes. Within these generic processes there will be further processes (or 'sub-processes') which again will need to be managed across functions. Let us now examine each in turn.

The market understanding process

Successful marketing strategies are built around a deep understanding of the marketplace. In particular, the motivations of buyers and the things they value must be the foundation of any marketing strategy. Being in close contact with customers is a prerequisite in fast-changing markets. It is not only the responsibility of the marketing department to have close contact with customers, it is actually important that all parts of the business are informed by customers. It is just as critical that human resources, production management and procurement, to take three examples, are as closely connected to needs of customers as the marketing or sales staff.

Being customer-focused has always been, and always will be, a fundamental foundation of a market-oriented business. However, the requirement today is to be idea-driven and customer-informed, and for the organization to extend its knowledge and to leverage that knowledge in ways which create value for customers. In today's marketplace, *knowledge management* is a critical element of market understanding.

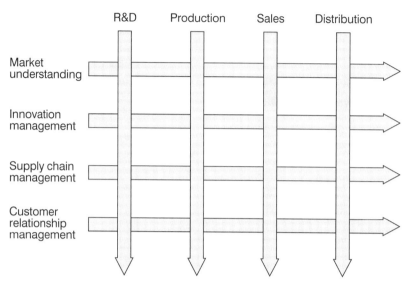

Figure 19.2   Processes cut across conventional functions

Ideas and knowledge exist across the business and beyond it. Thus, there is the need to have processes in place that can capture ideas and knowledge and convert them into marketing opportunities. CRM has a crucial part to play by ensuring that the appropriate systems capture and communicate all relevant information. In a sense, the market understanding process underpins the successful management of all the other business processes.

The innovation process

Businesses need to maintain a continuous flow of successful new product/service introductions into the marketplace. With life cycles becoming shorter and demand more volatile, being able to respond to changes in customer requirements and to exploit new technology-based opportunities has become a key competitive capability.

Innovation is not the sole preserve of any one particular department. It has to be managed cross-functionally. Those companies who have moved towards the cross-functional approach to innovation management have

found that it has paid great dividends. Typically, such companies have formed interdisciplinary teams that bring together a wide range of skills and knowledge bases. These teams are, to a considerable extent, self-managed and autonomous, and are able to take rapid decisions and short-circuit the conventional and time-consuming procedures for taking new products to market.

For example, in the car industry, such teams are now the norm for new product development. As well as drawing their membership from different functions across the business, they will often include representatives from suppliers so that further opportunities for innovative thinking can be exploited.

The supply chain management process

How will demand be fulfilled once it has been generated? This is the role of the supply chain management (SCM) process. In the past, the activity of order fulfilment was not regarded to be of great strategic significance. Whilst it was a necessary activity it was a cost and therefore was something to be managed as efficiently as possible. Today, the emphasis has shifted. The way in which a business satisfies demand and services its customers has become a fundamental basis for successful and enduring relationships.

This process is commonly termed the 'supply chain', but logically the label 'demand chain' describes its central role in demand satisfaction. Whatever the terminology, however, the important principle is that it should be managed as a horizontal business process that connects customers with the organization, extending upstream into the supplier basis. Ideally, we should seek to manage the business as an 'extended enterprise' from the customer's customer back through the internal operations of the firm to the supplier's supplier.

In a sense, these three critical business processes are all subsidiary to, and form the basis of, the fourth key process – the customer relationship management process.

The customer relationship management process

CRM unites the potential of IT and relationship marketing strategies to deliver profitable, long-term relationships. Importantly, CRM provides enhanced opportunities to use data and information both to understand customers and implement relationship marketing strategies better. Customer relationship management, we suggest, builds upon the philosophy of relationship marketing (Christopher *et al.*, 2002) by utilizing information technology to enable a much closer 'fit' to be achieved between the needs and characteristics of the customer and the organization's 'offer'.

The management of customer relationships where those customers are other organizations (i.e. business-to-business) has been the subject of much attention over recent years. It has long been acknowledged that marketing to other organizations requires a deep understanding of those customers' business processes and indeed of their value creation processes.

A major feature of the four high-level processes outlined above is that by definition they are cross-functional and hence they must be managed cross-functionally. This has led to the notion of the 'horizontal organization' (Ostroff and Smith, 1992), which is market facing and market driven – as distinct from the conventional business, which is 'vertical', focused around functions, and is inward looking and budget-driven.

Companies as diverse as Xerox and Unilever are now transforming their organizations to become market-driven and to shift the locus of power from functions to core processes, in effect turning the organization chart through 90°. Figure 19.3 highlights the fundamental change in orientation that such a strategy requires.

The achievement of this transformation must begin with a recognition of the interlinking roles of the CRM and SCM processes. We will shortly examine the CRM process in more detail. However, it is appropriate to first explain why the supply chain is so important in the context of CRM.

The SCM process entails the linking of production plans with materials requirements plans in one direction and distribution requirements plans in the other. The aim of any organization should be to ensure that production produces only what the market requires whilst purchasing supplies production with what it needs to meet its immediate requirements. But how can this fairly obvious idea be converted into reality?

The key lies in the recognition that the *order and its associated information flows* should be at the heart of the business. It may be a truism but the only rationale for any commercial organization is to generate orders and to fulfil those orders. Everything the company does should be directly linked to facilitating this process, and the process must itself be reflected in the organizational design and in its planning and control systems.

Figure 19.4 shows the interlinking roles between CRM and SCM. In the literature on CRM, most of the discussion often focuses on

(a) Vertical organizational focus

Traditional, functional organization

Input-focused, budget-driven

(b) Horizontal organizational focus

Market-driven, Output-focused

Figure 19.3 The shift from functions to processes

the role of information technology, and the linkages between CRM and SCM are not considered sufficiently. We will now examine the CRM process and SCM in greater detail.

A strategic framework for CRM

CRM is a management approach that seeks to create, develop and enhance relationships with

carefully targeted customers. CRM should be viewed as a strategic set of activities that commences with a detailed review of an organization's strategy and concludes with an improvement in shareholder value. The notion that competitive advantage stems from the creation of value for the customer *and* for the company is key to the success of CRM. This demands that responsibility for value delivery is shared across functions and hierarchies. Because CRM is a cross-functional activity, it

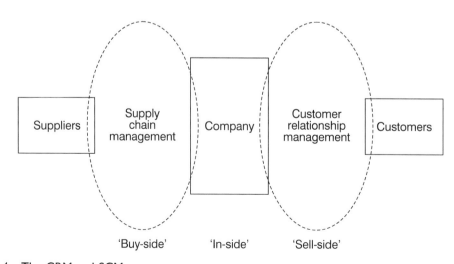

| Suppliers | Supply chain management | Company | Customer relationship management | Customers |

'Buy-side'   'In-side'   'Sell-side'

Figure 19.4 The CRM and SCM processes

can be difficult to achieve without a systematic approach and it needs to be broken down into processes or sub-processes.

The *strategic framework for CRM* presented in Figure 19.5 is based on the interaction of five cross-functional business processes that deal with strategy development, value creation, multichannel integration, information management and performance assessment (Payne, 2002).

These processes, which are discussed below, make a greater contribution to organizational prosperity collectively than they can individually, and must therefore be treated as an integrated set of activities.

The strategy development process

Most companies today recognize that their future depends on the strength of their business

relationships, and most crucially, their relationships with customers. Before turning immediately to a technology solution, managers need to first consider CRM in the context of overall business strategy. CRM must actively reflect and reinforce the wider goals of the business if it is to be successful. The strategy development process therefore demands a dual focus on the organization's business strategy and its customer strategy.

Business strategy

A comprehensive review of the business strategy will provide a realistic platform on which to construct the CRM strategy, as well as generate recommendations for general improvement. The organization needs to fully understand its own competencies within a competitive context in order to be able to

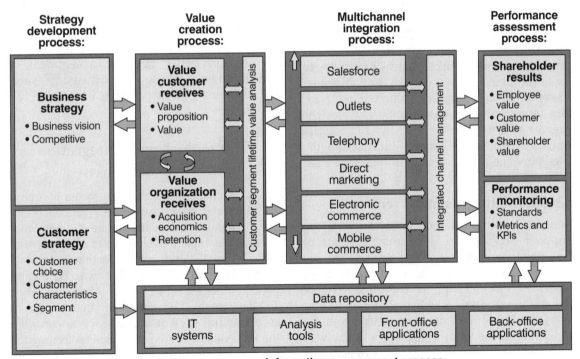

Source: Payne (2002). Used with permission.

Figure 19.5 Strategic framework for CRM

transfer them to the customer as customer value.

Customer strategy

The other half of the strategy equation is deciding which customers the business wants most to attract and to keep, and which customers it would prefer to be without. While the prior review of business strategy will be instrumental in reaching a judgement on broad customer focus, consideration of customer strategy will help to refine customer selection. This will frequently require a reappraisal of the way in which customers are approached and segmented, and the way in which resources are allocated.

The value creation process

The value creation process is concerned with transforming the outputs of the strategy development process into programmes that both *extract and deliver* value. The value creation process consists of three key elements: determining what value the company can provide to its customers (the 'value the customer receives'); determining the value the organization receives from its customers (the 'value the organization receives'); and, by successfully managing this value exchange, maximizing the lifetime value of desirable customer segments.

The value the customer receives

The value the customer receives from the supplier organization is the total package of benefits derived from the 'core' product and the added value that enhances the basic features such as service and support. The aim is to create a value proposition which is superior to and more profitable than those of competitors. To determine if the value proposition is likely to result in a superior customer experience, it is necessary to quantify the relative importance that customers place upon the various attributes of a product. Analytical tools such as trade-off analysis can be applied to discover the importance given to each attribute by the customer.

The value the organization receives

The pursuit of customers must be based on a sound understanding of how acquisition costs vary at both the segment and channel levels. In many instances, customer acquisition can be improved through insights drawn from the value proposition and the value assessment. Research findings have also clearly linked retention to profitability. While the financial implications of emphasizing customer retention to an extent greater than customer acquisition are significant, remarkably few companies have sought to benefit from this knowledge.

Customer segment lifetime value analysis

To decide the relative amount of emphasis that should be placed on customer acquisition and customer retention, it is necessary to understand acquisition and retention economics at segment, or better yet, a micro-segment or individual level. The key metric used to evaluate customers' profit potential is *customer lifetime value*.

The multichannel integration process

The multichannel integration process involves: decisions about the most appropriate combination of channels; how to ensure the customer experiences highly positive interactions within those channels; and, where customers interact with more than one channel, how to create and present a 'single unified view' of the customer. To determine the nature of the business's customer interface, it is necessary to consider: the key issues underlying channel selection; the purpose of multichannel integration; the channel options available; and the importance of integrated channel management in delivering an outstanding customer experience.

Multichannel integration

Faced with the necessity of offering consumers different channel types to meet their changing needs during the sales cycle (pre-sale, during the sale and post-sale), it is imperative to integrate the activities in those different channels to produce the most positive customer experience and to create the maximum value, no matter what channel is being used.

Discussions on channels are usually dominated by those who are involved in making the sale. However, for *strategic* CRM the channels need to be seen in the context of the whole interaction over the life cycle of the customer relationship, not just in terms of the specific sales activity.

A great number of interactions occur between the customer and the organization across different channels. The multichannel integration process should therefore start with the identification of the most appropriate channel options for specific segments. These options fall into six main channel categories, ranging from the physical to the virtual, as shown in the strategic framework. Some will be employed in combination to maximize commercial exposure and return; for example, 'voice-over IP' (voice-over Internet Protocol) integrates both telephony and the Internet.

Integrated channel management

Managing integrated channels relies on the ability to uphold the same high standards *across* multiple, different channels. Having established a set of standards for each channel used, which defines an outstanding customer experience for that channel, the organization can then work to integrate the channels, trying to optimize but not comprise the accepted channel standards. The multichannel service must match the individual (and changing) needs of customers, who may belong to a number of different customer segments simultaneously. To succeed, the company must be able to gather and deploy customer knowledge from the different channels, as well as other sources.

The information management process

The information management process is concerned with the collection and collation of customer information from all customer contact points, and the utilization of this information to construct complete and current customer profiles which can be used to enhance the quality of the customer experience. As companies grow and interact with an increasing number of customers through an increasing diversity of channels, the need for a systematic approach to organizing and employing information becomes ever greater. The key material elements of the information management process are: the data repository and analytical tools; IT systems; and front-office and back-office applications.

Data repository

The *data repository* provides a powerful corporate memory of customers, an integrated enterprise-wide data store capable of relevant data analyses. It consists of *databases* and a *data warehouse*, and where appropriate a collection of related datamarts that ensure the maximum value is extracted from customer information.

IT systems

IT systems refer to the computer hardware and the related software and middleware used within the organization. IT systems must be able to deliver the information needed on customers both now and in the future, and to accomplish other administrative duties. The organization's capacity to scale existing systems or plan for the migration to larger systems without disrupting business operations is critical.

Front-office and back-office applications

Front-office applications are the technologies used to support all those activities that involve direct interface with customers, including salesforce automation and call centre management. These applications are used to increase revenues by improving customer retention and raising sales closure rates. *Back-office applications* support internal administration activities and supplier relationships, involving human resources, procurement, warehouse management, logistics software and some financial processes. The overriding concern about front- and back-office systems is that they are sufficiently connected and co-ordinated to optimize customer relations and workflow.

The performance assessment process

The performance assessment process ensures that the organization's strategic aims in terms of CRM are being delivered to an appropriate and acceptable standard, and that a basis for future improvement is established. Shareholder results provide a 'macro' view of the overall relationships that drive performance, while performance monitoring gives a more detailed 'micro' view of metrics and key performance indicators.

Shareholder results

To achieve the ultimate objective of CRM – the delivery of shareholder results through an increase in shareholder value – the organization must understand the three key drivers of shareholder results: building employee value; building customer value; and reducing end-to-end supply chain costs.

Recent research on the relationship between employees, customers and shareholders has highlighted the need to adopt a more informed and integrated approach to exploiting the linkages between them. For example, the 'service profit chain' research conducted at Harvard illustrates the connection between good leadership and management behaviour, improved employee attitudes, consistent customer satisfaction and increased sales, profits and shareholder results (Heskett *et al.*, 1994).

Two means of cost reduction are also relevant to CRM: deploying electronic systems, such as automated telephony services, which lower costs by enabling reductions in staff and overheads; and utilizing new channels, such as on-line self-service facilities, which lower the costs of customer acquisition, transaction and servicing.

Performance monitoring

Despite the increasing focus on customer-facing activities, there is growing concern that metrics generally used by companies for CRM are not nearly as advanced as they should be. In particular, more detailed standards, measures and key performance indicators are needed to ensure CRM activities are planned and practised effectively, and that a feedback loop exists to maximize performance improvement and organizational learning.

Traditional performance measurement and monitoring systems, which tend to be functionally driven, are inappropriate for the cross-functional and holistic management approach of CRM. Metrics and key perfomance indicators (KPIs) for CRM must adequately reflect the performance standards across the five major CRM processes.

Much of the emphasis on CRM has been placed on the activities necessary to create enduring *consumer* relationships. However, rather less attention has been paid to the issue of building *customer* franchises and achieving superior supply chain performance, at least in the marketing literature. Paradoxically, most organizations market to other organizations. Hence a major opportunity exists to apply the concepts and tools of CRM to building long-term relationships in a business-to-business (B2B) context.

Supply chain management

In many industries there has long been a tradition of adversarial relationships between suppliers and their customers – whether those customers be distributors or manufacturing intermediaries. This hostility has been mutual and there has been little attempt to co-operate and to seek win–win solutions. Now, however, there are increasing signs in many industries that this is changing. There is a recognition by suppliers that intermediaries and distributors often hold the key to the marketplace. Similarly, customers are realizing that closer relations with suppliers can lead to quality improvements, innovation sharing and cost reduction.

The trend is increasingly towards 'single sourcing', meaning placing all of the purchase requirements for an item with just one supplier. This is the reverse of the conventional notion that purchases should be spread between competing suppliers to avoid placing 'all of the eggs in one basket'. Companies like Rover Group in the automobile industry a few years ago had over 2000 suppliers; it is now down to nearer 500. Nissan, in the UK, by contrast, starting their operations with a 'clean sheet of paper', have only 200 suppliers. The advantage of developing closer relations with a limited number of suppliers is that opportunities for mutual benefit through a partnership approach become a

reality. Instead of win–lose it is possible to move to win–win. Many companies have adopted just-in-time (JIT) manufacturing strategies, but have done so by pushing the responsibility for inventory holding upstream to their suppliers. In such cases there will probably have been no overall cost reduction in the distribution channel, only a transfer of costs. Indeed, sometimes the total costs may increase because of the need for the supplier to make more frequent deliveries of small quantities to the JIT customer. In contrast, companies working in partnership seek to identify opportunities to reduce or eliminate costs, not to simply play an industrial version of 'pass the parcel'.

In retailing, as in other forms of distribution, there is also now a growing recognition that co-operation, rather than conflict, in the marketing channel can build competitive advantage. Major suppliers to the retail trade such as Unilever and Nestlé are putting as much effort into 'trade marketing', as it is called, as they expend on traditional brand marketing. There is a strong desire by such companies to broaden the relationship with their customers away from the fairly limited connection shown in Figure 19.6(a), in which

(a) Traditional Buyer / Supplier Interface

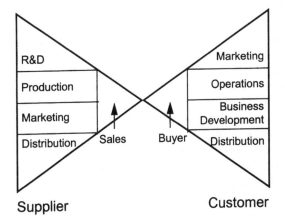

(b) Building Stronger Partnerships Through Multiple Linkages

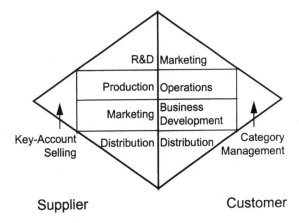

Figure 19.6   The move towards trade marketing

the main point of contact was between a salesperson from the supplier and a buyer from the retailer. Figure 19.6(b) depicts the alternative approach where multiple contacts are established, e.g. the supplier's R&D team with the customer's marketing team, the supplier's logistics team with the customer's operations team and so on.

Such a relationship should prove to be more enduring because it is built upon the search for mutual advantage – not just narrow self-interest. In this scheme of things, the role of the key-account manager is to manage a team-based approach to relationship building with the customer. Whilst this approach has been adopted with success by an increasing number of suppliers to the retail trade, it is equally powerful in any type of business-to-business marketing.

The impact of superior SCM performance

As customer service comes to be recognized as a highly effective way to differentiate the offer – even in a commodity type market – then the challenge becomes one of how to structure and manage supply chain systems capable of meeting customer requirements consistently and efficiently.

Effective supply chain systems can both enable a supplier to achieve lower costs and at the same time enhance the impact it has upon the customer's performance. A prime objective of any business should be constantly to seek out ways of reducing the customer's *total costs of ownership* whilst lowering their own costs.

The concept of total costs of ownership is quite simple. Essentially, any transaction will involve the customer in a number of costs – not just the price that is charged. These costs might include inventory carrying costs, warehousing and handling costs, ordering costs, quality inspection costs and even stock-out costs, for example. Anything that the supplier can do to

reduce or eliminate these costs will enhance its attractiveness to the supplier. On occasion, because total costs of ownership are lowered through superior supplier logistics, it may even be possible to justify a higher price.

One way in which customer ownership costs can be lowered is by the establishment of 'quick response' logistics systems. In quick response logistics, the aim is to capture information on product usage as far down the supply chain as possible and to translate that information rapidly into physical replenishment. The key to making quick response work is shared information.

One chemical company, for example, has installed remote monitoring equipment in the storage tanks of its major customers for bulk liquid chemicals. It can monitor, through telemetry, the actual level of product in the tanks, and with that information it can schedule production optimally and consolidate deliveries with other customers to achieve transport economies. The benefit to the customer is that they no longer need to manage their own inventory and issue purchase orders, but only pay for what they use, and their inventory carrying costs are eliminated, yet they never go out of stock! To the supplier, the benefit is that they can now manage their materials flow optimally and not be taken by surprise by 'rush' emergency orders.

In North America, major retailers such as Wal-Mart have linked the laser scanners at their checkout counters direct to suppliers such as Procter & Gamble. In real time, Procter & Gamble can monitor off-take of their products store by store and, on the basis of that information, plan production and delivery to optimize their own costs, as well as reducing the amount of stock that Wal-Mart needs to carry. The change that these types of SCM and CRM developments have brought about in buyer–supplier relationships is radical. The idea is now one of 'vendor managed inventory', where the supplier becomes responsible for managing the customer's inventory to the benefit of both parties. For example, at Wal-Mart there are fewer stock-outs and higher stock-turns, which has encouraged them to devote more shelf space to those products. In the first year of this partnership between Wal-Mart and Procter & Gamble, it was reported that Procter & Gamble's business with Wal-Mart grew by $200 million, or 40 per cent.

The integration of logistics and the related CRM information flows both upstream and downstream in the marketing channel has come to be known as supply chain management. It reflects an understanding that managing the interfaces between organizations is just as important as managing processes within the organizations themselves. It is at the interfaces that inventories are created, delays occur and service failures are most typically encountered. In many markets there is an observable correlation between successful companies and the extent to which they seek to manage the supply chain as an 'end-to-end' system. These companies understand that supply chains compete – not individual companies.

CRM and SCM: their role in improving customer service

Much of the recent focus on customer service has been towards what might be termed 'the people dimension'. It is often not difficult for competitors to imitate technologies, product features, emotional appeals and conventional marketing strategies. What they cannot imitate is the inherent corporate culture, shared values and knowledge management which distinguish the customer service-oriented business. Thus, a crucial element of the new paradigm of marketing is the focus upon developing attitudes and beliefs within the company that create a 'climate'

in which customer satisfaction is the *raison d'être* of the organization. However, whilst it is clearly paramount that every business has motivated employees who share common values about the importance of customer satisfaction, it is also essential to have in place the systems that can ensure the consistent reliable 'delivery' of the service package. Thus, both CRM and SCM systems must themselves be capable of providing the flexible response that individual customers require if they are to be a true source of differentiation. The idea is to create enduring relationships with customers not just through superior products, but also through superior service. This twin focus on total quality and service as a source of customer satisfaction has come to be called 'relationship marketing' (Christopher *et al.*, 2002).

The impact of customer service and total quality improvement can be enduring, leading to longer-term relationships with customers, improved retention rates and, hence, greater profitability. The connection between SCM performance, CRM and profitability is summarized in Figure 19.7.

The proposition, and one that is supported by a growing body of evidence, is that superior service helps build relationships with customers, which then leads to improved rates of customer retention. The work of Reichheld and Sasser (1990) and others has highlighted the impact that customer retention has on profitability. The first critical finding emerging from these studies is that the longer customers stay with us, the more profitable they become. When this relationship is linked to the customer retention rate, a powerful profit multiplier emerges. The logic is quite simple:

- Customer retention relates directly to the average 'life' of a customer, e.g. a 90 per cent

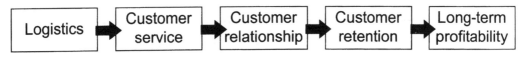

Figure 19.7 SCM and CRM: the linkages

retention rate means that we lose 10 per cent of our customer base each year; thus, on average we turn our customer base over every 10 years. With a 95 per cent retention rate the lifetime doubles to 20 years.

- The longer a customer stays with us, the more they are likely to see us as a preferred supplier, even single sourcing on us. The evidence also suggests that the costs to service these customers reduce as we establish closer relationships and linkages in the supply chain; similarly, the cost of selling to these loyal customers diminishes.
- The combined effect of a high retention rate and the enhanced profitability of loyal customers can lead not only to higher profit, but to a better 'quality of earnings', as the customer base is less volatile. A company with lower market share but high customer retention can often be more profitable than a company with the reverse characteristics.

Figure 19.8 shows the relationship between retention rates, customer lifetime and profitability.

Customer satisfaction at a profit is the goal of any CRM programme and the role of the SCM system is to achieve defined service goals in the most cost-effective way. The establishment of these service goals is a prerequisite for the development of appropriate logistics strategies and structures. There is now widespread acceptance that customer service requirements can only be accurately determined through research and competitive benchmarking. Research amongst customers may also reveal the presence of significant differences in service preferences between customers, thus pointing towards alternative bases for market segmentation based upon service needs. Knowing more about customers' service requirements and how they differ can provide a powerful basis for the development of strategies geared specifically towards improving customer retention.

Time-based competition

Organizations that are responsive to customer needs also tend to focus on 'time' as a source of competitive advantage (Stalk and Hout, 1990). There are a number of key time-related dimensions in marketing, e.g. time to market, time to manufacture, time to replenish and so on. Clearly, the faster we can complete processes then the more quickly we can respond to customer requirements and to market changes.

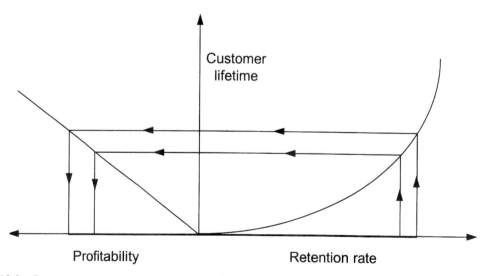

Figure 19.8 Better customer retention impacts long-term profitability

However, the importance of time extends beyond this; simply put, the shorter the time it takes to do things, the more flexible we can be in our response.

One of the main reasons why companies rely on forecasting and hence on inventory is because they have long lead-times to source, manufacture and deliver. The longer the response time, the greater the reliance upon the forecast, hence the more inventory that is required. Conversely, the shorter the response time, the less the reliance on the forecast and the less the need to cover uncertainty with inventory. At the same time, shorter lead-times mean we can offer greater variety. If in one factory it takes several hours to change from making one product to another (set-up time) but a competitor's factory can make the same change in seconds, then very clearly the competitor can offer greater variety to customers.

When we talk about lead-times we mean not only the time it takes to make something, but also the time it takes to gather material from suppliers, to process customer orders and to deliver the product to the customer. By focusing upon lead-time reduction the firm can achieve a substantial improvement in customer service.

Benetton, the Italian fashion manufacturer, has achieved its strong position worldwide not just through its innovative styles and its strong brand, but through the speed with which it can respond to changes in the market. Even though trends in styles and colours will differ from one corner of the globe to another and even though fashion life cycles are short and fickle, Benetton can usually match the market requirement through its advanced logistics systems. By capturing information at the point of sale and swiftly transferring details of what is selling back to the point of production, whole weeks are taken out of the total response time.

Combined with the flexibility in manufacturing for which Benetton are renowned and with state-of-the-art, computerized, global distribution systems, this gives Benetton the ability to get a product into the retail store within weeks of the order being placed. Traditionally, in that industry, it will take months to meet a replenishment order, if indeed it can be achieved at all.

Focusing on time reduction also has the benefit of making the company less reliant upon forecasts. If the lead-time for response to customer requirements is, say, 10 weeks, then clearly we have to forecast 10 weeks ahead and carry 10 weeks of inventory. If that lead-time can be reduced to five weeks, then the forecast horizon is halved, reducing the forecast error, and the need for inventory is also substantially reduced. The closer lead-times of response get towards zero, then the greater the ability of the organization to meet CRM requirements at less cost, yet paradoxically, with the ability to be much more flexible in meeting the demands of the marketplace.

Developing market-driven CRM and SCM strategies

It is a fundamental tenet of market-oriented companies that they seek to focus all their actions towards the goal of customer satisfaction. To support this goal, it is imperative that the CRM and SCM strategies of the organization be designed to support its marketing strategy.

The successful creation of market-driven strategies must inevitably begin with a clear understanding of the service needs of the market. To be more precise, it requires a definition of the *value preferences* that discriminate one market segment from another. A superior value proposition, a key component of the value creation process shown earlier in Figure 19.5, aims to tailor as closely as possible appropriate value packages to all the key value segments.

The starting point, as always, is the market understanding process referred to earlier. Research into customers' service and value preferences is an essential foundation for developing innovative and competitive logistics strategies. Because customer needs and value preferences differ, there is a requirement to engineer flexibility into the organization's CRM and SCM processes.

To highlight this principle, the case of Dell Computers is worth studying.

For a company that only began life in 1984, Dell has achieved amazing success, to the point where is it one of the most profitable companies in the personal computer (PC) market. Its success is not so much due to its products – they embody the same technology as their competitors – but rather the way in which they have developed a supply chain to support an innovative channel management and CRM strategy.

To quote Michael Dell, the founder:

> Our net income grew faster than sales as we continue to improve costs and to capture economies of scale. They stem from a decade of developing and implementing strategies designed to maximize the inherent strengths of the Dell direct business model. We believe our business model will remain the engine of our growth because it provides us with a number of competitive advantages:
>
> - First, we bypass computer dealers and avoid related price mark-ups. This became a dramatic advantage as competition in the indirect channel drove up the cost of dealer incentives.
> - Second, we build each system to a specific customer order, which eliminates inventories of finished goods to resellers and enables us to move new technologies and lower-cost components into our product lines faster.
> - Third, our direct contacts with thousands of customers every day enable us to tailor our support offerings to target markets and to control the consistency of customer service around the world.
> - Fourth, we leverage our relationships with key technology partners and with our customers to incorporate the most relevant new technologies into our products rapidly.
> - Finally, our low inventory and low fixed-asset model gives us one of the highest returns on invested capital in our industry.
>
> (Dell Annual Report, 1998)

By following a strategy of direct distribution, Dell is able to achieve a higher level of customization than many of its competitors whilst operating a low cost supply chain. The results have been impressive. Within a relatively short time, the company had overtaken IBM to become the world's number one manufacturer of PCs and the most profitable.

Dell has recognized that it can gain a significant competitive advantage through its exploitation of a non-traditional distribution channel. Dell also has impressive CRM systems that make great use of its direct customer contact to research needs and to gain feedback. Its pioneering use of the Internet has further strengthened its ability to provide tailored solutions to individual customers' specific needs through a sophisticated software-driven SCM process.

In many respects, the way in which Dell has combined a direct distribution strategy with the technology of the Internet presents a possible model for the future. The trend towards direct distribution can only be accelerated by the widespread use of the Internet and electronic commerce generally. The role of the traditional intermediary in the distribution channel is under threat. Unless such intermediaries can find new ways to add value for customers, then their future may be limited.

The challenge increasingly will be to seek out new ways in which customer demand can be captured and satisfied more cost-effectively. At the same time, customers in every market are seeking tailored solutions to their buying needs, calling for radically different channel strategies and operations capabilities. As we enter the era of 'mass customization' (Pine, 1993), the focus on integrated CRM and SCM strategies will inevitably increase.

Figure 19.9 highlights the fundamental change that is taking place in the marketplace as CRM and supply chain capabilities enable radically different channel strategies to be implemented and supported.

Being in the top left-hand quadrant of the model shown in Figure 19.9 can bring many

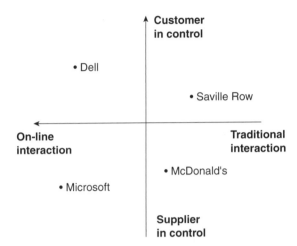

Figure 19.9   Customers take control in an on-line world
Source: Adapted from Steve Bowbrick, Web Media.

advantages, both in terms of customer focus as well as cost reduction. The challenge to those organizations who find themselves stuck with traditional distribution channels is to find new ways to create value for their customers by making better use of their traditional distribution channels. Distributors will increasingly need to take on additional value-creating roles if they are to survive in the future. Innovative approaches to channel strategy, combined with appropriate use of information technology and supply chain capability, will increasingly be fundamental to marketplace success.

Summary: changing the marketing focus

A central theme of this chapter has been the need for a change in the traditional focus of marketing which, in the past at least, has been primarily on winning customers and building market share. The new focus, it is suggested, should be as much upon the retention of existing customers as it is upon the gaining of new ones. The challenge now becomes one of how to develop marketing strategies that will do both these things. CRM is emerging as a new paradigm that recognizes the need to build long-term relationships with customers built upon service and quality. It represents an approach to relationship marketing that is enabled though information technology.

Our experience suggests that there is considerable confusion today about the exact nature of CRM. Breaking CRM down into several manageable processes, as shown in the strategic framework for CRM in Figure 19.5, helps to explain and communicate its strategic role, and to demonstrate the interdependence and cross-functionality of CRM activities. However, for CRM activities to be successful the interlinking role with the SCM process must be managed in an integrated manner. It is for this reason that SCM is now seen by many companies as a critical component of their marketing strategy. SCM focuses upon the physical satisfaction of demand and it provides the key to meeting the ever-growing demand for quick and reliable response.

It is becoming evident that to compete and survive in today's volatile marketplace requires both CRM and SCM processes capable of providing high levels of product availability and variety, yet which are low cost and reliable, and with high levels of customer service. Whilst these goals might appear incompatible, an increasing number of companies are proving otherwise. By asking fundamental questions about the way they do things and with a willingness to re-engineer their business processes, these companies are emerging as the leaders in their markets.

The purpose of managing CRM and SCM in an integrated manner is to enable the organization to become more 'agile' in its response to demand. Agility is an increasingly important competitive capability. As demand becomes more volatile and less predictable, the ability to move quickly, to change direction and to meet changed customer requirements in shorter time frames is critical. Agility is not a single company concept, it requires the closest connections upstream with customers and downstream with suppliers, particularly through the sharing of information on demand.

References

Brady, J. and Davis, I. (1993) Marketing's Mid-Life Crisis, *McKinsey Quarterly*, No. 2, 17–28.

Christopher, M., Payne, A. and Ballantyne, D. (2002) *Relationship Marketing*, 2nd edn, Butterworth-Heinemann.

Heskett, J. L., Jones, T. O., Loveman, G. W., Sasser, E. W., Jr and Schlesinger, L. A. (1994) Putting the Service–Profit Chain to Work, *Harvard Business Review*, March–April, 164–174.

Ostroff, F. and Smith, D. (1992) The Horizontal Organization, *McKinsey Quarterly*, No. 1, 148–168.

Payne, A. (2002) A Strategic Framework for CRM, Cranfield School of Management Working Paper.

Pine, J. (1993) *Mass Customisation*, Harvard Business School Press.

Reichheld, F. and Sasser, E. (1990) Zero Defections: Quality Comes to Services, *Harvard Business Review*, September–October, 105–116.

Stalk, G. and Hout, T. (1990) *Competing Against Time*, Free Press.

Further reading

Christopher, M. (1998) *Logistics and Supply Chain Management*, 2nd edn, Pitman. The goal of supply chain management is to link the marketplace, the distribution network, the manufacturing process and the procurement strategy in such a way that customers are serviced at higher levels yet at lower total cost. This book highlights the role of logistics in achieving these goals.

Christopher, M., Payne, A. and Ballantyne, D. (2002) *Relationship Marketing*, 2nd edn, Butterworth-Heinemann. The strategic emphasis of relationship marketing is as much on keeping customers as it is on getting them in the first place. The aim is to provide unique value in chosen markets, sustainable over time, which brings customers back for more. This new edition of an earlier book focuses on the creation of stakeholder value and emphasizes how quality and customer service are critical foundations for long-term customer relationships.

McDonald, M., Christopher, M., Knox, S. and. Payne, A. (2000) *Creating a Company For Customers*, Financial Times/Prentice-Hall. This book takes a cross-functional or pan-company approach to marketing. It focuses in detail on the key cross-functional processes that need to be managed in order to build a customer-centric organization. It addresses this topic from a board-level perspective.

Peppers, D., Rogers, M. and Dorf, B. (1999) *One to One Fieldbook*, Doubleday. This book, the third by Peppers and Rogers, provides an excellent overview of the role of CRM, especially in the context of an 'on-line' environment. It also deals with the importance of dialogue and privacy issues, as well as likely future developments in CRM.

Reichheld, F. F. (1996) *The Loyalty Effect*, Harvard Business School Press. Reichheld, a partner at US strategy consulting firm Bain & Co., provides the best treatment of customer retention based on exhaustive research undertaken at Bain & Co. A further strength of this book is its treatment of employee and shareholder retention.

Schonberger, R. (1990) *Building a Chain of Customers*, Free Press. This book provides a practical framework for linking the final marketplace with the operations and supply processes of the business. Every organization has internal and external customers, and the challenge is to link them together in such a way through seamless and responsive processes that are superior to those of competitors, both in terms of costs and service.

Sheth, J. N. and Parvatiyar, A. (2000) *The Handbook of Relationship Marketing*, Sage. An excellent academic treatment of the topic of relationship marketing. The editors have obtained contributions from virtually all the leading figures in the relationship marketing arena – a total of 23 contributions from leading scholars.

Swift, R. S. (2001) *Accelerating Customer Relationships: Using CRM and Relationship Technologies*, Prentice-Hall. Swift's book provides an excellent introduction to CRM from a technological viewpoint. Of special value is its treatment of data warehousing and relationship technologies, as well as specific studies of implementations.

CHAPTER 20

Controlling marketing and the measurement of marketing effectiveness

KEITH WARD

Introduction: scope and content of the chapter

Controlling both the 'effectiveness and efficiency' of marketing requires an integrated partnership between finance and marketing managers. Financial control can only be exercised in advance of financial commitment and this necessitates a rigorous financial evaluation of *proposed* marketing expenditure, as well as the application of effective financial controls as the expenditure actually takes place.

Marketing activities are normally absolutely critical to the most common long-term financial objective of commercially oriented organizations, which is creating shareholder value. The best way to create shareholder value in the long term is to develop and then exploit a sustainable competitive advantage. This enables the business to generate a rate of return substantially in excess of that required by its investors, i.e. a super profit.

However, developing a sustainable competitive advantage normally involves significant upfront expenditures by the business. These expenditures are high-risk, long-term investments and should be rigorously evaluated

and controlled, even though any resulting competitive advantage may be intangible (such as a brand). The best financial evaluation techniques for such long-term investments use discounted cash flows to take account of the timing differences between the expenditures and the resulting cash inflows.

If these long-term marketing investments are successful then the business has created a marketing asset, which may continue to produce high returns for many years to come. This will only be true if the marketing asset is properly maintained after it has been successfully developed. A sensible approach to controlling marketing, therefore, is to distinguish between development marketing expenditure and maintenance marketing expenditure, as their objectives are significantly different.

The objective of *development marketing expenditure* is to create a valuable long-term asset, and hence the returns from this type of investment will be received over the economic life of the asset. Conversely, *maintenance marketing expenditure* is designed to keep the existing marketing assets in their present valuable condition, and the returns are much more short term. Indeed, it can be argued that the failure to spend adequately on maintenance is often reflected very rapidly in declining sales revenues and profit streams.

These different objectives and time-scales mean that different financial evaluation and control techniques should be applied to development and maintenance activities. The control process must be tailored to the needs of the business.

This tailoring process is particularly important in designing the appropriate financial planning and control system for the organization. There are widely differing competitive strategies which can be implemented, even in the same industry at the same time, and these differing strategies require suitably tailored control processes and performance measures. There is a need for a hierarchy of both economic and managerial performance measures for all businesses, but it is critical that some of these performance measures incorporate indications of how well the business is doing in terms of its long-term objectives.

It is particularly important that the performance measures are tailored to the key strategic thrusts of the business; if these change, the financial control process may need to be changed as well. One common strategic marketing thrust is to develop strong brands as a source of sustainable competitive advantage. A branded strategy requires a good brand evaluation process if the high brand expenditures are to be properly financially evaluated and controlled. Brands can be based on either products or customers, but other types of marketing strategy can also be customer led or product based.

In a customer-led strategy, the long-term customer relationship should be regarded as a critical asset of the business; thus, development expenditure is invested to win the customer and maintenance expenditure is needed to retain the relationship for its full potential economic life. Life cycle customer account profitability analysis is therefore important in such a relationship marketing-oriented business.

Similar issues occur with product-based strategies and a suitably tailored response is required. Product life cycle costing is quite a well-developed technique in some industries. It uses the concept of the experience curve to establish the long-term decline in real per-unit costs over time as cumulative volume increases. This declining cost analysis can be used to develop a marketing strategy where current pricing is based on anticipated long-term costs rather than the current much higher short-term costs. Resulting short-term losses can be regarded as an investment in developing a sustainable competitive advantage based on the faster progress down the experience curve, which could lead to a sustainably lower cost position in the long term.

The need for closely integrated involvement of finance and marketing managers creates the opportunity for a marketing finance manager to work in the marketing area. Such a role can help immensely with the important financial evaluation of marketing expenditures and their subsequent control. It can also act as the focus for co-ordinating the important strategic competitor analyses which require inputs from many parts of the business.

Potential for conflict

In many businesses, the marketing function and the finance function can often find themselves in apparent direct conflict, due to the lack of the kind of close working relationship which finance has developed with other areas of the business, such as operations or production. Indeed, it can be the case, in some companies, that marketing managers feel that their finance colleagues' main interest in marketing is to try to stop them spending money. Conversely, it can appear to these same finance managers that the principal objective of their marketing colleagues is to spend as much money as possible on increasingly esoteric advertisements, very expensive trade and consumer promotions, higher customer discounts, etc.

Clearly, if the business is to achieve its long-term objectives, it is essential that its marketing expenditures are well directed and effectively controlled. Such effective control can only be exercised if the marketing and finance areas work together in an integrated partnership. A significant challenge facing the finance function in many businesses, therefore, involves changing their perceived involvement in marketing activities from that of a cost-adding constraint to that of a value-adding, enabling, participative role. The organizational structure implications of this change are considered towards the end of this chapter, but 'controlling marketing' requires involvement in two closely related but distinct aspects of marketing activities.

Prior to the actual *commitment* by the organization to spend money, a rigorous financial evaluation should be carried out. This is because true financial control can only be exercised in advance of any legally binding, financial commitment; once committed, the business will incur cancellation charges, or even still have to pay the full cost, if it changes its mind. This financial evaluation compares the proposed expenditure against the potential benefits, taking into account the risks involved in the particular activity. This evaluation should include any other potential ways of achieving the same benefits.

The financial evaluation process should also indicate how the success/failure of the expenditure can be assessed and how quickly this assessment can be made. It may also be possible to improve the overall probability of success before committing the majority of the expenditure; this may be achieved by marketing research activity. This risk-reducing type of marketing expenditure should itself be evaluated financially and any early warning indicators of success/failure should be identified. Any marketing activities where such early indicators can be identified are significantly lower risk than those where 'success' can only be assessed after all the expenditure has been incurred. If the initial expenditure has clearly failed, then the business can avoid incurring the rest of the expenditure if early and effective financial controls have been identified.

'Controlling marketing' can therefore be regarded as two interrelated processes of financial evaluation and financial control. As discussed in depth during this chapter, much of the challenge relates to putting financial values to marketing activities and objectives. Within the marketing area, many specific control measures have been developed to evaluate and control a wide range of marketing activities. Indeed, as discussed in other areas of the book, different marketing objectives are achieved by very specifically aimed marketing techniques. Unfortunately, far too often these very different marketing approaches are financially controlled using a single financial measure, which is consequently often inappropriate. This is exacerbated because the most common financial control measures consider the efficiency with which the activity has been carried out, rather than the effectiveness with which it has achieved its predetermined objectives.

An example using advertising expenditure may make this clearer. The 'efficiency' of purchasing media advertising (whether TV airtime or newspaper space, etc.) can be measured in terms of the cost per thousand customers reached by the campaign. However, such an efficiency-based measure says very little about how 'effective' the advertising expenditure was in terms of achieving its predetermined objectives. These marketing objectives could range from creating brand awareness, through changing the attitudes of potential customers or stimulating trial by new customers, to increasing the rate of usage by existing customers – each of which would probably use a different style of advertisement.

In marketing terms, the achievement of these objectives should be measurable, e.g. any increase in brand awareness can be measured by testing what brand awareness there was before the advertising campaign and re-testing afterwards. Thus, marketing can normally 'prove' whether it has achieved its marketing objective, but the key financial *evaluation* question is whether achieving this objective was financially worthwhile. The company may plan to spend £5 million on a national advertising campaign which is designed to increase brand awareness from 30 to 40 per cent within the target market group of consumers. The brand awareness both before and after the campaign could be tested in order to see if the marketing objective was achieved and the efficiency with which the £5 million expenditure was spent could be monitored. However, the money has not necessarily been effectively spent, unless the benefit of increasing awareness by 10 per cent has been financially evaluated as being significantly greater than the £5 million cost which is to be incurred. Clearly, to be of any value as a financial control, this financial evaluation must be undertaken prior to the expenditure being committed, i.e. the advertising being booked. Even more clearly, such an evaluation, which relies on estimates of the increased future sales revenues which are expected to result ultimately from increased brand awareness, cannot be conducted by the finance function in isolation. It requires an integrated approach from both marketing and finance, as does the ongoing control as the expenditure is committed. This is necessary as it may be possible to reduce the related risk by phasing the advertising expenditure in order to check that it is generating the increased awareness required (e.g. by doing a regional test first).

Against this backdrop of an integrated, co-ordinated approach to trying to control marketing effectiveness rather than just efficiency, this chapter considers a range of marketing strategies and the consequences for the required financial control system.

A market-focused mission

The most common financial objective of commercially oriented organizations is to create shareholder value. Consequently, the differentiating elements within mission statements and long-term corporate objectives relate to the ways (i.e. the 'hows') in which this shareholder value is to be created on a sustainable basis.

Shareholder value is only created when shareholders achieve a total return (which can only be generated by dividend yield and/or an increase in the value of their investment) which is greater than the return which they require from that investment. This definition emphasizes that shareholder value is not automatically created when a company makes a profit. The level of this profit must be placed in the context of the rate of return required by the shareholders, and this required rate of return is determined by the level of risk perceived by the shareholders with regard to this investment.

As shown in Figure 20.1, shareholders naturally dislike risk in that they demand increasing rates of return for increasing risk perceptions. However, what is often forgotten, even by finance professionals, is that the upward sloping 'risk-adjusted required rate of return line' in Figure 20.1 is, in reality, the shareholders' indifference line. In other words, moving from one point on the line to any other point on the line merely compensates the investor for a change in their risk perception; it does not create shareholder value.

Shareholder value is only created when total returns are greater than required returns, and this relationship should be used by the company to assess any investment proposal. Investment decisions will only create real shareholder value when the expected return from the investment is greater than the shareholders' required rate of return. This is encapsulated in Table 20.1 and should be applied to all marketing investments, as is discussed in the next sections of this chapter.

This relationship can also be explained by reference to our risk/return graph (Figure 20.2). As previously stated, moving along the shareholders' risk/return line neither creates nor destroys shareholder value. Shareholder value is only created by implementing a strategy which enables the business to move 'above the line', as shown in Figure 20.2.

As can be seen from the diagram, the company can move in one of three possible

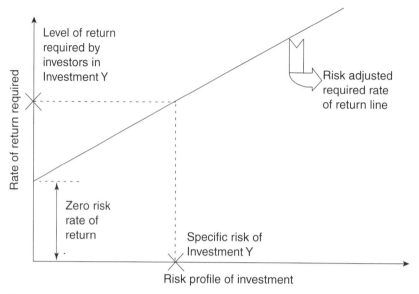

Figure 20.1   Risk-adjusted required rate of return

'value-adding' directions. It can decide to try to increase return, even though it accepts that such a strategy will increase its risk profile as well; the shareholder value created comes from increasing the expected return proportionately more than the risk perception increases. Many marketing-led growth strategies could fall into this category, including launching existing products into new markets, developing new products for existing customers and, particularly, trying to increase market share in a mature, non-growing, highly competitive, existing market. It is vitally important that the financial evaluation, which is carried out prior to these marketing initiatives, considers not only the projected increased future returns, but also the increases in the risk profile of the business. (These issues are considered in detail later in the chapter.)

A second value-creating option is deliberately to reduce the expected rate of return in the future, but to do so in a way which will reduce the associated risk to an even greater extent. This more than proportionate reduction in risk perception makes the slightly lower expected return more valuable to the shareholders than the previous higher, but more risky, rate of return. There are several marketing strategies which seek to create shareholder value through this route, and these include long-term discount arrangements designed to create customer loyalty. These more loyal customers should generate more consistent, less volatile rates of return in the future and volatility in the level of financial return is a key indicator of risk.

However, the most attractive value-adding, strategic direction is obviously to increase the expected rate of return while, at the same time, reducing the risk perception. This reducing risk perception can result in a reduction in the required rate of return, so that the shareholder

Table 20.1	Shareholder value creation
Real shareholder value creation requires that:	
Expected/actual returns	**>** Required returns

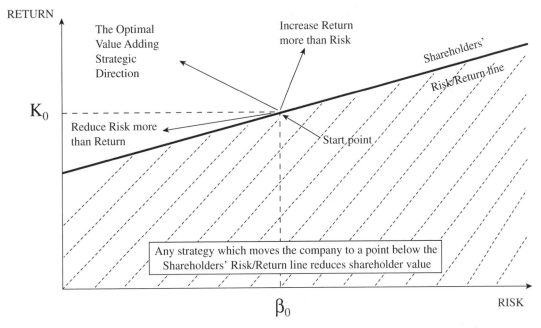

Figure 20.2   Economic value-adding strategies – utilizing a strong sustainable competitive advantage

value-creating gap between expected and required rates of return can be substantial. Not surprisingly, because it is the attractive strategic direction to take, it is also the most difficult to achieve. In order to generate increased future rates of return with reduced levels of risk, the business must have developed a strong 'sustainable competitive advantage', which is, of course, the main objective of modern corporate and competitive strategies. A strong sustainable competitive advantage should enable a company to increase its future rates of return to levels well above both its required rate of return and the rates of return of its competitors.

However, its sustainable competitive advantage could also mean that, even in the event of a downturn in the market, its rates of return are less volatile in the future than those of its competitors. If this is the case, the company's risk profile will be lower than its competition, which could result in a lower required rate of return.

This introduces the key concept, which will be utilized through the chapter, of *a 'super profit'*, which is the excess return achieved by a business due to the development and maintenance of a *sustainable* competitive advantage. The 'excess' return represents the surplus expected or actual return over the rate of return required by investors.

A sustainable competitive advantage

A key aspect of a competitive advantage in terms of its ability to create shareholder value is its sustainability. If competitors can match the competitive advantage immediately, or even relatively quickly, the company will be unable to exploit it to achieve a super profit. This actually highlights an important but simple way of considering any sustainable competitive advantage; it should act as an effective *entry barrier* which stops competitors from coming into the attractive market created by the business. This is shown diagrammatically in Figure 20.3. When any company is achieving a super profit in a particular market, the market is financially attractive to lots of other companies. If these other companies were all able to enter this market, they would rapidly drive down the rate of return for *all* companies in the market to the required rate, thus removing the super profit of the original company and ending the creation of shareholder value. This is what would happen under the economic definition of perfect competition; thus, another way of thinking about *sustainable* competitive advantages is that they can only exist under conditions of imperfect competition.

The possible entry barriers shown in Figure 20.3 are not meant to be totally comprehensive, but they illustrate a number of important issues relating to sustainable competitive advantages and their financial control. It is clear that some potential entry barriers are the direct result of marketing activities, e.g. branding and control of the channel of distribution, but several more can only be fully exploited through the implementation of the appropriate marketing strategy (such as low unit costs, technology barriers, etc.). However, all these entry barriers are normally only developed by substantial investment (i.e. upfront) expenditures and this investment must be regarded as very high risk. If the entry barrier does not work, e.g. if competitors can find a way around it or through it, the company will be unable to generate a return on its expenditure designed to develop the competitive advantage.

It should also be clear from the illustrations of entry barriers that they have a finite life cycle (the best example of this is a patent which expires at the end of 20 years). The company may be able to extend the economic life of some entry barriers by carefully managing the sustainable competitive advantage (e.g. as has

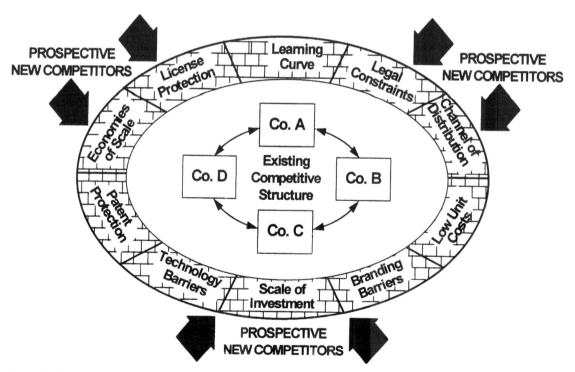

Figure 20.3   Use of entry barriers

been done by certain brands, such as Coca-Cola and Marlboro), but this will normally require additional expenditure on maintaining the entry barrier. Alternatively, the business may decide to reinvest part of its initial super profits in developing a replacement sustainable competitive advantage for when the initial advantage ceases to be effective. Examples of this are pharmaceutical companies which often invest heavily in branding their patented drugs during the patent period. This actually reduces the level of super profit during this period, as they are then effectively a monopoly supplier, but it can create strong customer loyalty, which can work as a very effective competitive advantage once the patent has expired.

These development, maintenance and reinvestment activities must be subjected to the rigorous financial evaluation already discussed, and this is considered in detail below. However, these entry barriers are the really important sources of shareholder value creation and should therefore be managed as the key *assets* of the business. Unfortunately, apparently because many of them are intangible and somewhat nebulous to most finance managers, many companies still regard their fixed assets (factories, offices, plant and machinery, etc.) as the only real assets of the business. Without any intangible marketing assets to exploit, these tangible assets would probably generate, at most, the shareholders' required rate of return.

All of these sustainable competitive advantages are, by definition, really relative statements in that they refer to things which the business does better, cheaper, faster, etc., than anyone else. They also need to be considered in the context of the customers who are willing to continue to pay a price for the good or service which enables the supplier to generate a super profit. In other words, the customers must still perceive themselves as getting good value for money, even in the absence of direct, effective viable competition. This means that the financial evaluation and control process must also have an external focus in that it must include an analysis of competitors and customers. This

competitor analysis must not be limited only to obvious existing competitors, as new potential competitors may be attracted to any industry or sector which is generating significant super profits. Indeed, existing customers and even suppliers may be tempted to become competitors through vertical integration if the potential returns are high enough. It is essential that the company's current position is protected as far as possible by investing in creating strong entry barriers to deter all the identified potential competitors. Once again, finance managers are most unlikely to identify, on their own, all the potential novel marketing strategies which competitors may initiate to try to break through an existing entry barrier. Competitor analysis therefore needs to be done as a co-ordinated effort, utilizing all the knowledge and skills available within the business.

Investing in developing a sustainable competitive advantage

As stated above, many marketing activities should be evaluated and controlled as strategic investment decisions, irrespective of how they are treated for financial accounting purposes. Any financial investment involves spending money now in the expectation that, in the future, returns will be generated to more than recover the initial expenditure. Where the period over which these expected returns will be received is likely to be much longer than the current financial year, it is important that a proper financial evaluation is carried out. This is particularly vital where these investment expenditures are regarded as high risk, due to the volatility associated with the potential outcomes. If the success of these investments is also critical to the achievement of the organization's long-term objectives and overall mission, the need for a sound financial evaluation and control process is absolutely paramount.

In very many businesses, these factors are most obviously present in the key marketing investments which are being made in developing brands, entering new markets, launching new products and developing new potential channels of distribution such as the Internet, etc. Thus, it is vital that these high-risk, long-term investments are financially evaluated using the most sophisticated techniques available. Many companies would automatically calculate a full discounted cash flow for even the simplest, relatively small investment on labour-saving machinery in their factory or their operations areas. Yet these same companies often do not carry out such a long-term financial evaluation of much larger expenditures in the marketing area. Indeed, it is still not uncommon to find almost no *financial* justification supporting many significant marketing initiatives; the rationale for the decision is based on the fact that the initiative is 'strategically important' or that 'it has to be done'.

There appear to be many reasons for the lack of sound financial controls in this area. Almost all marketing expenditure is charged (i.e. written off) to the profit and loss account in the year in which it is spent, irrespective of the time-frame over which the returns may be generated. This is in accordance with the 'prudent' view underlying financial accounting, because the returns from these marketing expenditures cannot be guaranteed. However, there is no way that any new brand launch, new market entry or major new product development is financially justifiable by considering only the returns generated in the first year. All investment decisions must be financially evaluated by comparing the expenditures needed against the future expected returns. Where these returns are only expected well in the future, they should be included as their present value equivalent so that the comparison is validly based (the details of this technique, which is the discounted cash flow referred to above, are outside the scope of this chapter, but are covered in any good finance text). The actual accounting treatment is irrelevant to

this decision evaluation process, as economic business decisions should be based on the future differential cash flows arising from the decision.

Another apparent justification for not applying financial rigour to major marketing investment decisions is that it is very difficult to estimate accurately the future cash flows which may arise quite some time into the future from such expenditures. This is, of course, true but it is also true of many major investments in more tangible assets, where these same companies still try to prepare full financial evaluations. Indeed, most of these companies would find it unacceptable to consider any major tangible asset investment which was not supported by a full cash flow projection into the future.

It can be, and it often is, argued that the cash flows from many marketing investments are even more difficult to project, as they can be dramatically affected by competitor responses or unexpected shifts in the market. This merely indicates the high-risk nature of many marketing investments. A major focus of the financial evaluation should therefore be on highlighting the key risks, how they can be quantified and, wherever possible, how they can be removed or minimized. This is the very essence of good financial control and may indicate a need for extensive marketing research or more thorough competitor analysis before committing the majority of the expenditure.

Marketing investments cannot be left out of the financial evaluation and control process as they are, for most businesses, the major source of long-term shareholder value. As indicated in Figure 20.3, there are several entry barriers that do not directly depend on marketing, but most of these are normally short-lived advantages due to competitor responses. Product innovations are a good example of this unless they are protected by a patent or other restriction on competitive copying. Once the innovation is launched, competitors will attempt to copy the new product, or even improve on it. In many industries the time lag before these competitors can launch their own versions is now very short; e.g. in retail financial services this time lag can normally be measured in weeks not years. Thus, the product innovation does not, of itself, create a long-term sustainable competitive advantage but, if allied to the appropriate marketing strategy, the business may be able to exploit it to create considerable shareholder value. Each individual innovation could be exploited very rapidly as long as marketing creates very strong immediate awareness and instant access to the product (e.g. in retail financial services, mass advertising linked with a telephone- or Internet-based sales system). This strategy increases the associated risk because all the marketing expenditure is required upfront; doing extensive marketing research could easily give away to competitors the product innovation and hence enable them to launch their versions nationally at exactly the same time.

An alternative strategy could be to build a brand around the innovations developed by the company, so that it develops a reputation as the leading innovator in the industry. This branded reputation may attract a substantial loyal group of customers and this could create the ability to earn a super profit; each new product innovation therefore reinforces the brand attributes rather than having to earn a super profit itself.

Marketing assets: development and maintenance expenditures

It has already been argued that the most valuable real assets possessed by most businesses are in the marketing area. The proper definition of an asset is anything which will generate future net cash inflows into the business; this clearly includes brands, trademarks, customers, channels of distribution, products, etc. Thus, assets are by no means limited to the normal tangible items which appear on the balance sheet of the company. This more general attitude to marketing assets has important implications for the control of marketing.

Many businesses still persist with the classification of marketing expenditures between 'above the line' (meaning mainly media advertising) and 'below the line' (meaning promotions for both trade and end customers, etc.). This distinction literally refers to where the expenditures tend to be shown in the profit and loss account but, in today's marketing environment, they have almost no relevance at all. The increasing power of many channels of distribution (such as supermarket retailers) and even consumers, let alone industrial customers, together with an increasing fragmentation in mass advertising media (e.g. TV channels), has led to a significant increase in the proportion of many marketing budgets which is spent 'below the line', i.e. directly to channels and end customers. If this is a more effective means of achieving the marketing objectives of the business, it is extremely sensible to do this; the change in classification is irrelevant.

A much more important way of analysing marketing expenditure has unfortunately been ignored by many companies. Creating any valuable long-term asset requires the investment of substantial funds, as has already been discussed. This is also true of marketing assets, which require significant expenditure during their developing periods. This development expenditure creates the attributes of the asset (e.g. brand awareness, distribution access, customer loyalty), which will generate the super profit returns of the future.

Once the marketing asset has been developed to its full potential, as with any asset, it must be properly maintained or it will decline in value very rapidly. A feature of many marketing assets (such as brands) is that some of their attributes can decline very quickly (such as brand awareness) if they are not properly maintained. Thus, another component of the marketing budget is maintenance expenditure. Development expenditure is designed to increase the long-term value of the marketing asset by improving specific attributes of the asset, while maintenance expenditure aims to keep these attributes at their existing levels.

It has already been stated that really valuable assets (i.e. those that represent a sustainable competitive advantage) have a finite economic life and this is equally true for marketing assets. Thus, the mix of development and maintenance marketing expenditure will change over the life cycle. During the initial launch period all the marketing expenditure will be development activity, as it is aimed at building the value of the asset; also, there are no attributes to be maintained. Once the asset starts to be established, the existing attributes need some level of maintenance expenditure, but the majority of marketing effort still goes to developing the asset to its optimum level. Once this is reached there is no longer a financial justification for more development expenditure, and all the current marketing activity (which may be considerably lower than during the development phase) should be targeted at maintaining the asset's current position and strengths.

Eventually the marketing asset will approach the end of its economic life and, at this time, the business may reduce the marketing expenditure below the full level required properly to maintain the asset. In other words, the decline stage is managed so as to maximize the cash flows received by the business. Indeed, this is the critical financial performance measure for any marketing asset; the objective is to maximize the super profits earned over the economic life of the asset. Due to the long life cycle of many of these assets, this has to be expressed in terms of the net present values of the cash flows expected to be generated over this economic life.

Also, because the economic life can, in certain cases, be extended, some marketing expenditure may be targeted at extending the economic life of the asset. An alternative strategy may be to transfer the existing strong asset attributes (such as from a brand) from a declining product to a new growing product. Even though doing so will accelerate the decline of the current product, it may extend the economic life of the 'brand' asset by associating it with another appropriate product.

This distinction between development and maintenance expenditure is very important because the timing of the returns from each type is very different. Development expenditure represents a long-term investment and the returns may not be received until several years later. Thus, the expenditure is incurred now but the financial benefit is not felt this year. The impact of maintenance expenditure is likely to be much quicker because, as the attributes decline, there is likely to be a corresponding fall-off in sales revenues and profits. This timing difference means that different financial evaluation and control processes must be used for each type of expenditure.

In many companies, the marketing budget represents a very significant proportion of total expenditure. When the company comes under short-term profit pressure it is therefore very common for the financial director to look to marketing to make a substantial contribution to any required reduction. Under the traditional classification system, it is easy to predict where most of these cuts in marketing expenditure are likely to fall: on the long-term development expenditures. This is because reducing these development activities will have no negative impacts on sales revenues in the short term, whereas cutting maintenance activities would probably reduce sales this year.

Unfortunately, the impact of reducing development marketing expenditure will be felt in the future because the asset will not be as fully developed. At least by segmenting marketing expenditure the consequences of this short-term action will be more clearly highlighted and the future expectations for the business can be appropriately modified. However, the best way of really focusing on these issues is through a well-designed financial planning and control process.

The financial planning and control process

The main objectives of any financial planning and control process are to enable the organization to develop, implement and control a strategy which seeks to achieve its long-term objectives and overall mission. A good control process would indicate when modifications were needed in the overall strategy through short-term feedback loops and appropriate performance measures. Thus, as indicated in Figure 20.4, the long-term objectives must be consistent with the short-term budgets actually used by the company on a regular basis.

It is an obvious but important statement that this year's budget must be the first year of the long-term plan but, in many companies, this does not stay the reality as the year unfolds. No plan is ever implemented without significant modifications, not least because there are always unforeseen changes in the external environment. Hence, during the year, the tactics and even the strategy may need to be changed. It is important that these required changes are, as far as possible, still consistent

with the long-term objectives of the business. At least these long-term objectives should be taken into account as the possible modifications to the strategy are being considered. Unfortunately, in many cases, changes are made during the year which enable the short-term budget to be achieved *at the expense* of these long-term objectives.

This can happen because the performance measures in use within most businesses focus almost exclusively on the short-term budget period (i.e. this year). This would not necessarily matter as long as these performance measures include clear indicators of how the business was doing in terms of its long-term objectives. In most cases these longer-term performance indicators are missing. Hence, as discussed in the previous section, it is quite common for the main performance measures to focus on sales revenues and profits this year, even though the long-term strategy may be based on the business developing new sustainable competitive advantages. This concentration on short-term performance increases the pressure on managers to compromise on longer-term investments in order to deliver the required performance now. Marketing expenditure is the major target area for this due to the expensing, in accounting terms writing off all expenditure in the current year, including long-term development activities; few people would consider it completely sensible to stop halfway through building a new factory in order to try to boost profits this year, yet companies often curtail marketing development spending on brands, etc. to achieve the same thing.

It is therefore very important that businesses develop an appropriate set of performance measurements, which are both closely integrated with their long-term objectives and provide early indications when things are going wrong. A business actually needs performance measures at three different levels if it is really to stay in control of its long-term performance.

The highest level of performance measure relates to the overall economic performance of

Figure 20.4   Very simple business model

the company, as this is of fundamental interest to its shareholders. In other words, is the business operating in attractive markets and industries where shareholder value can be created? If not, the long-term strategy should be either to change the competitive environment in order to make it more attractive (e.g. rationalize the industry or develop a new form of sustainable competitive environment) or to exit from this industry in order to invest in more attractive areas.

This top level of performance measure says very little about the relative performance of the business and its managers. In certain very financially attractive industries, the relatively few companies involved may all earn super profits and hence create shareholder value. Equally, in an extremely over-supplied, very unattractive industry, the best management team in the world should lose less money than all the others, but they will find it impossible to create shareholder value. Thus, the second tier of performance measure is needed to put the absolute level of economic performance into an appropriate relative context; a 40 per cent p.a. return on assets looks less impressive if all competitors are achieving over 60 per cent!

This introduces a key issue for performance measures. Some performance measures are designed to reflect the economic performance of the total business or of a particular part, while others focus on the managerial performance of the people running the business or parts of it. Few performance measures work successfully in both areas because, while economic performance measures must take into account all the factors affecting the business, managerial performance measures should only include elements where the manager can exert a degree of control. It is unfair, and extremely demotivating, to hold managers accountable for something over which they can exercise no control.

At the very top of an organization (e.g. the main board of directors in a publicly quoted group of companies) there may be very little need to distinguish between economic and managerial performance measures. If the cur-

rent areas of activity become unattractive, the board can reorganize the group to focus on more attractive areas and could even exit from the now unattractive businesses. At lower levels within the business, managers have increasingly less freedom of action or managerial discretion. Hence different managerial performance measures must be used for different levels. The challenge is to ensure that each level of performance measure is consistent with the overall objectives of the total business. This concept, which is generally known as goal congruence, is based on the simple maxim of 'what you measure is what you get', i.e. people tend to try to achieve the objectives they are set. If, by achieving their objectives, they move the business away from its long-term objectives and strategy, it is the fault of the people setting the objectives, not the people doing the achieving!

Salesforce performance measures can provide two examples of these problems. Any sales manager with responsibility for a normal field salesforce has, in reality, relatively little discretion in terms of the cost of that salesforce. Salesforce total costs are made up of a large number of different items, as illustrated in Table 20.2. At first sight, therefore, it appears that the responsible manager can influence the total salesforce costs of £10 million in a number of ways. However, on closer examination it becomes clear that there is only one real cost driver for the field salesforce.

If salaries per employee are reduced to levels below those prevailing in the industry, this is likely to lead to the loss of the best salespeople. Similarly, attempting to reduce petrol or car expenses per head or accommodation and subsistence per salesperson will reduce the effectiveness of the salesforce, if these relationships have been properly established in the past. The separate cost items per salesperson can be defined fairly tightly for most industries, so that the only real controllable variable is actually the number of salespeople employed by the company. The financial evaluation and control process should

Table 20.2 Field salesforce cost structure	
Salaries	X
Other employment costs	X
Commission	X
Recruitment	X
Car expenses	X
Telephones	X
Petrol	X
Accommodation	X
Subsistence	X
Entertaining	X
Samples	X
Consumables	X
Training	X
Support costs	X
	£10 million

At present, 100 salespeople are employed by the company

companies, the freshness of the product is a significant factor in its overall quality, while they incentivize their salesforce to sell as many goods as possible. The potential problem is that the salesforce do not sell direct to the consumer, but to the channel of distribution (e.g. the retailer) which supplies to the consumer. More sales into the channel pipeline do not automatically lead to more purchases out of the channel by these consumers; if this does not occur there is a risk of more retail stocks and consequently less fresh, poorer quality ultimate purchases by the consumers. However, no blame should be allocated to the salesforce, they merely achieved their objective of higher sales! What is needed are performance measures which are completely in line with the long-term objectives of the business.

Thus, the third level of performance measures is very specific to the particular business and its long-term objectives. These measures must be appropriately tailored to the business and the level within the business at which they are being applied. It has already been established that there is a vast range of potentially successful competitive strategies, which are based on a specific mix of sustainable competitive advantages. Several of these different strategies may be being implemented in various segments of the same industry at the same time. The performance measures used should be appropriate to the specific requirements of the competitive strategy, which clearly means that different companies in the same industry may be using very different performance measures. Indeed, the focus of their financial planning and control system should probably have far more in common with a company in a completely different industry but which is implementing a very similar strategy, than with a company in its own industry which is implementing a completely different strategy.

A key issue for a really good financial planning and control system is that it is tailored to the needs of the business. This means that, if the needs of the business change because the strategy has changed, the control system and

consequently focus on justifying the number of salespeople by considering the relative financial contributions from different sized salesforces, and on validating the engineered cost relationship being used by the salesforce (this relationship is itself slightly dynamic as the costs per employee will change if the size of the salesforce changes significantly).

The other performance measure issue for this field salesforce is how the performance of an individual salesperson should be assessed. In many companies this is done by setting sales revenue targets or sales volume targets against which each salesperson is measured. The problem is that an exclusive focus on short-term sales revenues or volumes may be counterproductive to the long-term strategy of the business. For example, many branded fast-moving consumer goods companies consider improving the quality of the product received by the consumer as being very important to their long-term success. For many of these the resulting tailored performance measures should also change. Unfortunately, many companies are struggling to control their marketing activities because they are still using control systems designed for previous competitive strategies.

One way of illustrating this problem uses a development of the Ansoff matrix to highlight the different strategic thrusts which a business can have. The Ansoff matrix has been used for many years as a marketing planning tool, as it indicates the way in which a business can try to fill the gap between the simple extrapolation of its current level of performance and the performance required to achieve its long-term objectives. The beauty of the matrix is that it describes these strategic options in very clear terms, i.e. increase the share of existing markets with existing products, sell new products to existing customers, sell existing products to new customers, or sell new products to new customers.

The Ansoff matrix illustrated in Figure 20.5 has only been modified in terms of descriptions applied to the boxes for selling new products to existing customers and selling existing products to new customers. Before considering these, the other two possibilities will be briefly examined from a financial control perspective.

The implications of growing the business by selling more existing products to existing customers has been researched extensively over many years, with some very unsurprising results. Strategies to increase market share have been shown to create shareholder value most clearly when the market is growing strongly. This is because, if the market is static or declining, any increase in volume by the company has to be generated at the direct expense of competitors. They are likely to respond aggressively, possibly via a price war, which could reduce the total profitability of the industry and all the players in it. Thus, the strategy may be successful in gaining market share but it will not necessarily generate super profits. If the total industry is growing strongly, there is less chance of such aggressive competitive reaction, as their own sales volumes and revenues may still be increasing despite them losing market share.

As a result, companies are increasingly using games theory-based strategic analyses in order to predict both competitive responses to their marketing initiatives and likely marketing initiatives by competition. From the financial perspective, shareholder value can be separated into two phases: creating value and capturing value.

Creating value refers to marketing strategies which seek to increase the total value

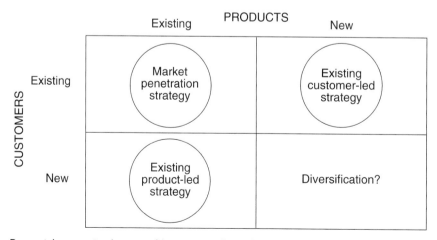

Figure 20.5   Potential strategic thrusts of businesses (based on the Ansoff matrix)

generated by the industry, e.g. increasing the total size of the market, adding value to existing products. Thus, it is possible for all competitors in the industry to benefit from 'creating value' strategies, although they will not all necessarily benefit equally. However, strategies aimed at creating value for the industry should result in less aggressive competitive responses; they can even be described as being 'co-operative' ways of competing.

Capturing value is all about gaining a greater share of the total value available within the industry. As a result, it tends to be a 'win–lose' game, and this can result in much more aggressive competitive reactions. In some disastrous examples these reactions resulted in dramatic price wars, which left everyone much worse off financially.

The financial planning and control process should therefore identify the type of shareholder value creation which should result from the proposed marketing strategy. This will help in predicting the likely competitor response.

Selling new products to new customers has also been quite well researched and the shareholder value creation is also disappointing. Many companies seem to adopt this strategy as a risk-reducing strategy but a 'new, new' strategic thrust is really an increase in risk, because it is not normally built on any

existing competitive advantage, as shown in Figure 20.6.

This introduces the modifications to the Ansoff matrix shown in Figure 20.5 because the key strategic thrust relates to the existing source of competitive advantage on which the growth strategy is based. In the case of selling new products to existing customers, this should be the loyal base of existing customers for whom new products are to be developed or acquired. Correspondingly, the strategy of finding new customer groups, markets or segments in which to sell existing products should be built on an existing successful product which is capable of generating a super profit in its existing market.

These strategic thrusts are examined in more detail in the following sections, which deal respectively with brand-led, customer-led and product-led strategies.

Brand-led strategies

Brands can be based either around products (e.g. Coca-Cola, Marlboro, Microsoft, Intel) or around customers (e.g. Marks & Spencer, Tesco, Virgin). They are therefore considered before either customer-led strategies or product-led

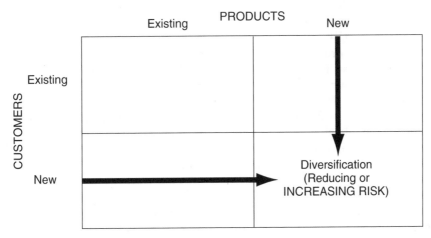

Figure 20.6   Diversification using the Ansoff matrix

strategies, as a number of common issues can be more simply dealt with.

The nature of brands has been dealt with separately in Chapter 15 and so this section focuses on the financial control issues in a brand-led strategy. If a competitive strategy which is based on brands is to be successful, the brand must enable the business to earn a super profit on its more tangible assets, i.e. the brand becomes an intangible asset of the business. However, brand assets can achieve this super profit in different ways, and these different ways require appropriately tailored control processes and performance measures.

A strong brand may enable the branded 'product' to be sold at a higher price than its unbranded equivalent. Alternatively, an equally strong brand could be sold at the same price as other products, but command a significantly greater share of the market on a consistent basis. A third branding positioning would be to combine a slightly higher price together with a higher market share. It is important that the control process understands and focuses on the specific brand strategy.

There are a number of stages involved in developing, and then maintaining, a brand as an asset. Some success, although not necessarily uniform success, must be achieved at each stage if the brand is to have a sustainable super profit earning capability. As discussed earlier and elsewhere in the book, marketing has developed specific effectiveness measures for each element in the brand building process (e.g. awareness creation, propensity to purchase, ability to purchase such as distribution, trial rates, repeat purchase incidence, and levels of regular usage).

The financial control challenge is to develop a financial model which can incorporate these non-financial effectiveness measures into a comprehensive brand evaluation process. Several companies are now using such overall brand evaluation models as key elements in evaluating and controlling their brand marketing expenditures. These models are based on the discounted cash flows which are predicted to be generated by the brand and an assessment of the strength of the brand, which is used to determine the discount rate applied to the cash flows (the stronger the brand, the lower the discount rate applied). It is clear that many judgements must be used to arrive at the brand value, but this is not the point. This is a broad evaluation process, and therefore it is the movements and trend in the brand attributes (the true brand strength indicators) and hence in the value which is important, rather than the absolute value at any point in time.

This type of model can be used to evaluate proposed incremental development expenditure on the brand and to ascertain the required level of maintenance expenditure (that level which should keep the brand strength score at its current level). However, these evaluations are still not simple because the relationship between marketing expenditure and its effectiveness is by no means linear. As can be seen from Figure 20.7, there is a level of marketing expenditure which produces very effective returns but, if the company spends significantly more or less than this amount, the financial return can be dramatically reduced.

If too little marketing support is provided (area 1 in Figure 20.7), this low level of marketing expenditure is likely to be wasted. The effectiveness may be very low due to the relatively higher level of competitive expenditure or other general marketing activity which drowns out the company's specific marketing message (sometimes referred to as 'noise' in the system). Thus, this adds a further complication in that the effectiveness of one company's marketing expenditure is affected by the marketing activities of its competitors. Consequently, marketing expenditure planning must be done against assumptions and expectations regarding the expenditures of competitors, as is discussed below.

At the other end of Figure 20.7, marketing expenditure is also likely to be unproductive, but this time it is because the law of diminishing returns has set in. If the level of marketing expenditure was reduced slightly, the overall

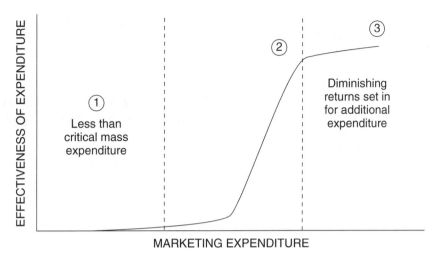

Figure 20.7   Relationship of marketing expenditure and effectiveness

effectiveness would be largely unaffected but the financial return could be improved significantly.

As already mentioned, the required level of marketing expenditure must be assessed by reference to competitive levels of activity. One quite simple and increasingly common relationship can give assistance here, although it does not provide a complete solution to what is a complex area. The relationship is between the proportionate share of the total marketing expenditure spent by the company's brand (i.e. its share of voice, SOV) compared with the relative share of market achieved by the brand (i.e. its value market share, SOM). As shown in Table 20.3, the ratio of SOV/SOM can be greater than 1, equal to 1, or less than 1.

If a brand is proportionately outspending its share of market (i.e. SOV/SOM > 1), then the company is investing in developing the attributes of the brand. This investment should have been rigorously financially evaluated before commitment and should be controlled by monitoring changes in the brand attributes. Once the brand has been fully developed, the marketing support should be

Table 20.3 Share of voice (SOV) compared to share of market (SOM)				
$\dfrac{SOV}{SOM}$	>	1	⇨	A development/investment strategy
$\dfrac{SOV}{SOM}$	=	1	⇨	A maintenance/holding strategy
$\dfrac{SOV}{SOM}$	<	1	⇨	Normally a cash/profit extracting strategy

designed to maintain the brand at its current position. The required level of maintenance marketing expenditure should still be assessed by reference to competitive levels of expenditure; the objective may well be to achieve an SOV/SOM ratio of 1. However, this required expenditure must still be financially justified by evaluating the sustainable level of cash inflows which can be generated by maintaining the brand.

There is potentially one brand in any market which may be able to sustain its current market share while spending proportionately less on marketing support than its share of market (i.e. having an SOV/SOM ratio < 1). This is the brand with the dominant market share, because such a brand often achieves economies of scale in its marketing expenditure which are not available to its smaller competitors. Thus, due to its dominant market share, it can still significantly outspend, in absolute terms, all of its competitors, while spending proportionately below its market share. If it actually spent at its proportionate rate it would find itself in area 3 of Figure 20.7, i.e. in the area of rapidly diminishing returns.

Notwithstanding this powerful sustainable competitive advantage, in most cases, an SOV/SOM ratio below 1 indicates that the brand is not being properly maintained and will, in the long term, decline in strength. This may be the appropriate strategy if the brand and/or the market are coming to the end of their life cycles. However, one particular strength of brands is that it is often possible to transfer the brand attributes to another product before the decline of the original product has irretrievably damaged the brand attributes. If the brand is successfully transferred to another product, the economic life of the brand has clearly been extended. This transfer of brand attributes should be financially compared with the alternative strategy of developing a new brand specifically designed for the new product. Similar financial justifications should be done for all brand umbrella and brand extension strategies, as they involve significant risks

which must be taken into account, as well as reducing the brand investment needed for developing a new independent brand.

Customer-led strategies

As stated above, brands can be built around products or customers, but a customer-based brand is designed to encourage existing loyal customers to try new products which are launched under the same brand (e.g. retailer brands such as St Michael, Tesco and Sainsbury).

Thus, any customer-led strategy is, by definition, built around the existing customers of the business. A critical question for evaluating such a growth strategy is therefore 'which customers should form the basis for future growth?'. If the organization has an overall objective of creating shareholder value, the obvious answer is to base the strategy around those customer groups from which the company can generate sustainable super profits.

This requires a strategically oriented, long-term customer account profitability (CAP) analysis to be carried out. This CAP analysis should indicate the relative profitability of different groups of customers, but it should not be used as an attempt to apportion the net profit of the business among the different customers. Indeed, apportioning (or 'spreading') costs among customers can destroy the main benefits from the CAP analysis. The analysis should support important strategic decisions regarding which customer segments should be invested in, etc. Thus, the resulting information must be relevant to these decisions and this is not achieved if a large proportion of indirect costs are apportioned to these customers.

The key phrase is direct attributable costing, where the real cost drivers for each major customer-related cost are identified. These cost drivers are what causes the cost to be incurred by the business and what makes the level of the cost change. If they are identified, this will

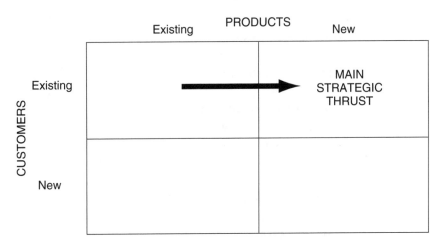

Figure 20.8   Customer-led strategies: maximizing the value of existing customers

indicate how customers should be grouped together. The idea is to group together customers who are treated very similarly and to separate groups where there are significant differences in the costs incurred and, hence, potentially in the rates of financial return achieved. This sort of CAP analysis is illustrated in Figure 20.9, and shows that only customer-specific elements should be included.

As the customer segmentation becomes greater (i.e. the customer groups get smaller and smaller, with the greatest segmentation being to individual customers), it is clear that less and less costs are directly attributable to each group of customers. Hence, for different levels of resource allocation decision, different levels of segmentation will be needed, and the CAP analysis system must be able to cope with this requirement for hierarchical segmentations.

Many companies now operate quite sophisticated CAP systems of this sort but, if the strategy is to be based around customers, the analysis needs to be done on a long-term basis. Such long-term CAP analyses are less common. The idea is to evaluate which types of customer are worth investing in because, over their economic life cycle, the business expects to be able to generate a positive net present value from the investment. This type of marketing strategy is commonly referred to as relationship marketing (and this is considered in detail in Chapter 3) because the business tries to develop (i.e. invests in) a long-term relationship with the customer. If this type of marketing strategy is in use, the business needs to tailor its management accounting system to treat these customer relationships as a long-term asset of the business. Thus, development and maintenance expenditures are as relevant here as in the earlier discussion on brands.

Indeed, in a relationship marketing-based strategy, attention shifts towards customer retention rather than the more common customer acquisition. The key priority is retaining the most valuable long-term customers, who will repay the required marketing expenditure. However, in order to attract and retain these valuable long-term customers, the company must create *more value* for these customers than the competition; any sustainable long-term relationship must be mutually benficial.

Customer value can be defined as the perceived benefit obtained by the customer less the price paid and any other 'costs' (e.g. time, inconvenience) incurred in order to own the good or service. Customers who do not perceive that they are getting value from a relationship are likely to defect. If this happens, the

		£
Gross Sales by Customer		X
Less Sales Discounts & Allowances		X
Net Sales by Customer		X
Less Direct Cost of Sales		X
Gross Customer Contribution		X
Less Customer Specific Marketing Expenses	X	
Direct Sales Support Costs	X	X
		X
Less Customer Specific Direct Transaction Costs		
Order Processing	X	
W/Housing & Distribution	X	
Invoice Processing	X	
Inventory Financing	X	
A/Cs Receivable Processing & Financing	X	
Specific Sales Support	X	X
		X
Less Customer Attributable Overheads		X
Net Customer Contribution		X

Figure 20.9 Customer account profitability analyses: illustrative example for an FMCG company selling through retailers

original marketing investment in acquiring the customer has failed to create shareholder value.

Companies are now trying to assess customer lifetime value and are using increasingly sophisticated tools to do so. Data warehouses and data mining tools assist organizations in measuring the economic value of customers. Predictive modelling techniques can be used to predict the remaining lifetime of the relationship with the customer and the likely resultant future stream of profits and cash flows. The economic lifetime value of the customer is the present value of the *net* cash flows expected to be generated from the customer.

True relationship marketing suggests, however, that even this direct lifetime economic value does not necessarily reflect the total value of the customer to the company. There may be other relationship benefits, which seem to be of

four types. Referrals (word of mouth) and referencability can reduce the cost of acquiring other customers; product innovation for, and learning from, these customers may benefit the whole company. These indirect relationship effects can mean that certain customer relationships do create shareholder value, even though the *direct* financial returns generated do not indicate a positive net present value.

However, because these indirect relationships are more contingent upon the continuing strength of the relationship, different valuation techniques need to be adopted. Three techniques are particularly useful for financially evaluating and controlling these types of customer relationships: conditional probability, simulation, and real options. Real options are particularly fascinating, as there is some evidence to suggest that options thinking explains some significant marketing decisions in this field. Space does not permit any detailed discussions of these approaches, but appropriate references are provided at the end of the chapter for interested readers.

If the main strategic thrust of the business is based on customers, it is also important that these customers form an important element in the performance measures used for the various areas within the business. If this is not done, many of the business support areas will focus on achieving their own performance measures, often to the detriment of the long-term development of these critical customer-based assets.

This CAP analysis is complicated even further when the business sells through an indirect channel of distribution to the ultimate user of the product, e.g. as is done by many consumer goods businesses which sell directly to wholesalers, distributors or retailers, which then sell on to the consumers. Increasingly, this type of business wants to have sound financial analysis on both its direct customers and its ultimate but indirect consumers. Thus, many fast-moving consumer goods companies, particularly in the USA, have invested very large sums of money in developing very extensive *consumer* databases. This enables them to know much more about who eventually uses their product, even though they bought it indirectly. Clearly, if the strategy is to develop new products (which will appeal to these same consumers), this knowledge is critical. However, it also illustrates a significant potential competitive advantage for the indirect channel of distribution (e.g. the retailer), because they can gain even more detailed customer information much more cost effectively. This is being used very proactively by major retailers with their significant investments in both customer loyalty programmes (such as store cards, etc.) and retailer branding, which enable them to develop appropriately designed and tailored new products.

Product-based strategies

An alternative, but possibly equally attractive, strategic thrust is to base future growth around existing products (Figure 20.10). These products may also be strongly branded, but the critical element in the strategy is that the growth opportunities are based on finding new markets, new segments or new customer groups to which to sell these products.

Not surprisingly, this strategic thrust should be built on those products which can achieve a sustainable level of super profit in their existing markets. Hence, a key financial

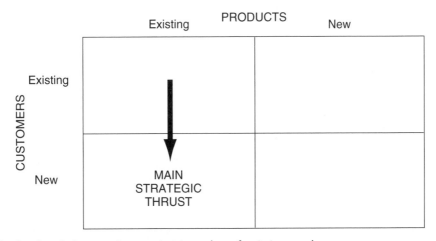

Figure 20.10 Product-led strategies: maximizing value of existing products

analysis for such strategies is a soundly based, decision-focused, long-term direct product profitability (DPP) analysis. As with the customer profitability analysis, the objective of DPP is to indicate the relative profit contributions from the different product groups. Therefore, apportioning indirect costs in an attempt to arrive at a 'net profit' for each product can destroy the validity of the analysis and lead to disastrous decisions being taken.

As shown in Figure 20.11, the allocation of product-specific costs to appropriately grouped products can highlight significant differences in the relative profit contributions from these differing products. Once again, if this analysis is to be used to support long-term strategic decisions (such as to identify those products

which should be launched internationally), the analysis must consider the long-term sustainable profitability of the products.

In some industries this can be done by using product life cycle costing techniques which have been developed over many years. It is now well established that the costs of producing many products (both goods and services) decline, in real terms, over time due to a number of factors. These include learning by employees which makes them more efficient, the introduction of new technologies and economies of scale and scope. These are combined together in the 'experience curve' concept, which enables businesses to predict the rate of decline of their real production costs per unit as cumulative volume increases.

		£
Gross Sales by Product		x
Less Product-Specific Discounts & Rebates		x
Net Sales by Product		x
Less Direct Costs of Product		x
Gross Product Contribution		x
Less Product-Based Marketing Expenses	x	
Product-Specific Direct Sales Support Costs	x	x
		x
Less Product-Specific Direct Transaction Costs		
Sourcing Costs	x	
Operations Support	x	
Fixed Assets Financing	x	
Warehousing & Distribution	x	
Inventory Financing	x	
Order, Invoice & Collection Processing	x	x
		x
Less Product Attributable Overheads		x
Direct Profit Profitability		x

Figure 20.11   Direct product profitability analyses: illustrative example of a manufacturing company's DPP analysis

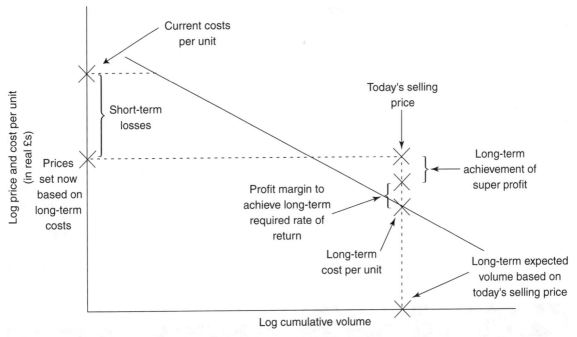

Figure 20.12   Life cycle costing techniques: strategic use of experience curves in setting prices. The short-term loss per unit, if successful, is really an investment in developing a long-term sustainable cost advantage

This predictive knowledge can be used in the marketing strategy because the business could set its prices today based on its long-term costs rather than its current costs; this is diagrammatically illustrated in Figure 20.12.

This pricing strategy would probably result in the business making a loss on its current sales, but these sales should increase rapidly as the low prices stimulated demand. These increasing sales volumes should propel the business rapidly down its experience curve – towards its long-term cost level, at which it should achieve a super profit. If it can gain a sustainable long-term cost advantage over its competitors by this strategy, it should regard the initial losses as an investment in creating a sustainable competitive advantage.

The idea of having a sustainable cost advantage also indicates another important aspect of product-based strategies. The management accounting needs of a low-cost-based strategy are fundamentally different to those of

product-based strategies built on differentiated or value-added products. As was discussed early in the chapter, any sustainable competitive advantage is a relative concept which must be evaluated and controlled by reference to an appropriate set of competitors.

Thus, the required competitor analysis focuses on the source of relative competitive advantage or disadvantage. Where the main basis of competition is on price, because there is no customer-perceived difference among competing products, the relevant competitor analysis should concentrate on cost benchmarking. In this commodity-based, price-conscious environment, the lowest-cost supplier will normally win and relatively small cost differences can be critical.

However, if the basis of competition is differentiation rather than price, an excessive emphasis on external cost comparisons or even internal cost reductions can be very counterproductive. A cost difference no longer necessarily indicates a competitive advantage or disadvantage because it may be the source of the customer-perceived differentiation, which in reality creates the super profit. For these businesses, the focus needs to be on the value-added elements rather than on the costs. This forces finance managers to become involved in the assessment of 'perceived use values' (where the perception is by the customers) of the differences between competing products. The perceived added value is then compared to the incremental cost incurred in achieving the difference, with any resulting positive value gap being evaluated for sustainability.

This type of involvement raises several issues for the way marketing and finance need to work together.

Organizational structures: marketing finance managers

If the integrated and tailored approach to controlling marketing which has been set out in this chapter is to be achieved, marketing and finance managers need to work very closely together at all stages of the marketing process. The rigorous financial evaluation of strategic marketing decisions requires a close involvement of finance managers at the earliest stage possible. Yet this close involvement must continue during the implementation of the strategy if proper control is to be exercised and the necessary amendments to the strategy are to be made in a timely manner.

This continuous close involvement can only really be achieved if finance has a substantive presence within the marketing area. Increasingly, this is being achieved by the creation of the roles of marketing finance managers, who are physically located in the marketing area and are seen as part of the marketing management team. As such, they are automatically involved in the development of the marketing strategy, its implementation, modification and control. Indeed, in some

businesses they now share some managerial performance measures with their marketing colleagues, yet they have a clear financial responsibility to remain objective in their financial evaluations.

The marketing finance manager can also act as a co-ordinator and facilitator for the many inputs which are needed for the strategic competitor analysis which has been advocated during the chapter. In some companies this analysis has been supplemented by customer profitability analyses and even supplier profitability analyses; where well done, these enable a complete picture of the industry value chain to be developed. This can aid the strategy development process immensely, as it can indicate future opportunities and threats at different levels in the total supply chain.

Summary

Controlling marketing involves far more than recording and analysing the accounting transactions which result from marketing activities. It should be regarded as a two-stage process involving the pre-commitment financial evaluation of proposed marketing expenditures, as well as the ongoing control over these expenditures as they take place.

The objectives of these different marketing activities are very diverse, but marketing has itself developed appropriately tailored evaluation processes and non-financial effective measures. The challenge for finance is to find equally tailored and value-added ways of controlling marketing expenditures, which link these activities to the overall objectives of the organization.

This requires a high degree of integration between marketing and finance, and a substantial level of tailoring in the marketing accounting system and resulting performance measures. Ideally, if the marketing strategy changes significantly, this should lead to a corresponding change in the tailored marketing accounting system. If such a change is not made, it is quite likely that the business will be using inappropriate performance measures, which may motivate marketing managers to act against the long-term best interests of the overall business. Another potential risk is that the management information system does not provide adequate timely decision support information for the new, key strategic decisions which the business faces as a result of the change in strategy. Many businesses are taking critical marketing decisions with very little strategic financial evaluation, because they do not have suitably tailored marketing accounting systems. In such businesses there is no real 'strategic control over marketing'.

This chapter has tried to indicate how such strategic control over marketing can be achieved. Many of the areas considered in the chapter require complete books to deal with them in depth. Obviously, restrictions of space have necessitated a very brief overview of these areas; however, there are references and recommendations for further reading which should enable those interested to examine particular areas in significantly greater depth.

References

A market-focused mission

Barwise, P., Marsh, P. R. and Wensley, R. (1989) Must Finance and Strategy Clash?, *Harvard Business Review*, September–October.

Rappaport, A. (1981) Selecting Strategies That Create Shareholder Value, *Harvard Business Review*, May–June.

Ward, K. and Grundy, A. (1996) The Strategic Management of Corporate Value, *European Management Journal*, **14**.

A sustainable competitive advantage

Porter, M. E. (1987) From Competitive Advantage to Corporate Strategy, *Harvard Business Review*, May–June.

Prahalad, C. K. and Hamel, G. (1994) Competing for the Future, *Harvard Business Review*, July–August.

Ward, K. (1997) Competitor Analysis, *ICAEW Good Practice Guidelines*, April.

The financial planning and control process

Bowman, C. and Ambrosini, V. (2000) Value Creation Versus Value Capture, *British Journal of Management*.

Hamel, G. (1997) Killer Strategies That Make Shareholders Rich, *Fortune*, 23 June.

Kaplan, R. S. and Norton, D. P. (1992) The Balanced Scorecard – Measures That Drive Performance, *Harvard Business Review*, January–February.

Kaplan, R. S. and Norton, D. P. (1993) Putting the Balance Scorecard to Work, *Harvard Business Review*, September–October.

Customer-led strategies

Luehrman, T. A. (1998) Investment Opportunities as Real Options: Getting Started on the Numbers, *Harvard Business Review*, July–August.

Ward, K. and Ryals, L. (2001) Latest Thinking on Attaching a Financial Value to Market Strategy: Through Brands to Valuing Relationships, *Journal of Targeting, Measurement and Analysis for Marketing*, **9**(4).

Further reading

A market-focused mission

Rappaport, A. (1986) *Creating Shareholder Value*, Free Press, New York.

Thakor, A. V. (2000) *Becoming a Better Value Creator*, Jossey-Bass, San Francisco.

A sustainable competitive advantage

Hamel, G. and Prahalad, C. K. (1994) *Competing for the Future*, HBS Press.

Porter, M. E. (1980) *Competitive Strategy*, Free Press, New York.
Porter, M. E. (1985) *Competitive Advantage*, Free Press, New York.

Investing in developing a sustainable competitive advantage

Ward, K. (1992) *Strategic Management Accounting*, Butterworth-Heinemann, Oxford.

Marketing assets: development and maintenance expenditures

Maklan, S. and Knox, S. (1998) *Competing on Value*, FT Pitman, London.
Murphy, J. (ed.) (1989) *Brand Valuation*, Hutchinson, London.

The financial planning and control process

Goold, M. and Campbell, A. (1987) *Strategies and Styles*, Blackwell, Oxford.
Kaplan, R. S. and Norton, D. P. (1996) *The Balanced Scorecard*, HBS Press.
Mintzberg, H. (1994) *The Rise and Fall of Strategic Planning*, Prentice-Hall, Englewood Cliffs, NJ.

Brand-led strategies

See relevant chapters elsewhere in this book.

Customer-led strategies

Amram, M. and Kulatilaka, N. (1999) *Real Options*, Harvard Business School Press, Cambridge, MA.
Burnett, K. (1992) *Strategic Customer Alliances*, FT Pitman, London.
Christopher, M., Payne, A. and Ballantyne, D. (1993) *Relationship Marketing*, Butterworth-Heinemann, Oxford.
Hallberg, G. (1995) *All Consumers Are Not Created Equal*, Wiley.
Nalebuff, B. and Brandenburger, A. (1997) *Co-opetition*, Harper Collins, London.

Product-based strategies

Day, G. S. (1986) *Analysis for Strategic Market Decisions*, West.
Johnson, H. T. (1992) *Relevance Regained*, Free Press, New York.
Johnson, H. T. and Kaplan, R. S. (1987) *Relevance Lost: The Rise and Fall of Management Accounting*, Free Press, New York.
Shank, J. K. and Govindarajan, V. (1993) *Strategic Cost Management*, Free Press, New York.

Organizational structures: marketing finance managers

Price Waterhouse (1997) *CFO – Architect of the Corporation's Future*, Wiley.

CHAPTER 21

Marketing implementation, organizational change and internal marketing strategy

NIGEL F. PIERCY

Introduction

Marketing executives in the twenty-first century face complex and turbulent markets, with ever-more demanding and sophisticated customers, new types of competition emerging from multiple sources, multiple channels reflecting the impact of Internet marketing, new technologies impacting on product obsolescence, urgent globalization imperatives, and radical shifts in the type of buyer–seller relationships required to deliver value to the customer. While developing and planning effective and innovative marketing strategies to prosper in these fiercely competitive conditions is a major challenge, it remains unavoidably true that the capability to execute strategies effectively is a critical requirement. Now more than ever before, the successful companies are those who get things done to deliver superior value to customers. For example, Dell Computers is widely admired for its direct business model and sophisticated Internet marketing. One of Dell's hidden capabilities is rapid and effective response to customer needs – when

the US military complex at the Pentagon was attacked by terrorists on 11 September 2001, many computers and servers were damaged, yet Dell had replaced all damaged equipment at the Pentagon within 48 hours of the loss. The most central point to be made in this chapter is that one of the most significant challenges for marketing is *implementation*, but also, by implication, the *organizational changes* that are required to achieve the effective implementation of marketing strategies and programmes.

Perhaps the most central issue here is the manager's pragmatic question: 'We know what marketing *is*, but how do we do it?' In his now classic treatment of the implementation issue in marketing, Tom Bonoma (1985) summarized the problem in the following way:

> Marketing for a number of years has been long on advice about *what to do* in a given competitive or market situation and short on useful recommendations for *how to do it* within company, competitor and customer constraints . . . experiences with both managers and students argue strongly that these parties and customer constraints are often strategy-sophisticated and implementation-bound.

To underline the need for an active and effective approach to implementation in marketing, we adopt an internal market perspective and focus on the underlying problem of the strategy formulation–implementation dichotomy – the all too common situation where we ignore implementation capabilities in developing strategy, and then stand back in amazement when we find the strategy never gets executed effectively, or at all.

An internal market perspective

One useful and practical approach to understanding the significance of organizational change and development to marketing strategy implementation is through an internal market perspective (Piercy, 1995, 1998a). The importance of this internal market perspective in developing coherent marketing implementation strategies can be underlined as follows:

- Much contemporary thinking and practice in strategic marketing is concerned with *managing relationships*: with the customer, with those who influence customers' decisions, with competitors, and with partners in strategic alliances. However, a further aspect of relationship management and relationship marketing is the relationship with the employees and managers, upon whose skills, commitment and performance the success of a marketing strategy unavoidably relies. This is the internal market inside the company. The logic being followed by an increasing number of companies is that building effective relationships with customers and alliance partners will depend in part (and possibly in large part) on the strengths and types of relationships built with employees and managers inside the organization. Much of the competitive strength of firms as diverse as Kwik-Fit, Rosenbluth International and Asda can be traced to those companies' ability to win the hearts and minds of their employees and managers (Piercy, 2002).

- Many companies emphasize the critical need for *competitive differentiation* to build market position. Yet truly exploiting a company's potential competitiveness and its capabilities in reality is often in the hands of what Evert Gummesson (1991) has called the 'part-time marketers', i.e. the people who run the business and provide the real scope for competitive differentiation. Indeed, in some situations, the employees of a company may be the most important resource that provides differentiation – Avis achieves high customer satisfaction and customer retention through its superior employee skills and attitudes, not because the cars it rents out are any different from those of its competitors (Piercy, 2002).

- In a similar way, the growing emphasis on competing through superior *service quality* relies ultimately on the behaviour and effectiveness of the people who deliver the service, rather than the people who design the strategy. Appositely, in considering the issue of intellectual capital, Thomas Stewart (1998) writes: 'Many jobs still require big, expensive machines. But in an age of intellectual capital, the most valuable parts of those jobs are the human tasks: sensing, judging, creating and building relationships.'

- Indeed, increasingly it is recognized that one of the greatest barriers to effectiveness in strategic marketing lies not in a company's ability to conceive and design innovative marketing strategies or to produce sophisticated marketing plans, but in its ability to gain the effective and enduring *implementation* of those strategies. One route to planning and operationalizing implementation in strategic marketing is 'strategic internal marketing' – applying the tools and techniques of marketing to the internal as well as the external marketplace.

We will examine the implementation question in marketing and then introduce strategic internal marketing as a managerial approach to dealing with the organizational problems uncovered by our analysis.

The strategy formulation–implementation dichotomy

However, many difficulties arise in dealing with the implementation issue, not simply because implementation itself is problematic, but because conventional approaches to marketing planning and the generation of marketing strategies have generally adopted the view that strategy formulation and implementation are distinct and sequential activities – a characteristic styled the 'formulation–implementation dichotomy' by Cespedes and Piercy (1996). Where it exists, this 'dichotomy' is fraught with dangers:

- It ignores, or underestimates, the potential synergy between the process of marketing strategy formulation and a company's implementation capabilities (Bonoma, 1985).
- It reduces the ability of an organization to establish competitive advantage, which draws on its unique distinguishing characteristics, i.e. what it is good at or best at in the marketplace (Hamel and Prahalad, 1989).
- It risks divorcing the strategies and plans produced from the realities of the organization (Hutt *et al.*, 1988).
- It takes no account of the need for marketing to span not merely the *external* market boundaries recognized in conventional models of marketing, but also the *internal* boundaries with other functional and organizational interest groups (Aldrich and Herker, 1977; Spekman, 1979; Ruekert and Walker, 1987).
- It underestimates the significance of the political and negotiating infrastructure of the organization, as it impacts on the support of key managers for strategies, and on the process of gaining the commitment of organizational members at all levels (Pfeffer, 1981; Piercy, 1985).

Given the high priority managers place on developing new ways of more effectively handling the implementation problem in marketing, and the dangers of not doing so, the goal of this chapter is to approach the marketing implementation issue by asking five important questions:

1 Can we relate our marketing plans and strategies to the real organizational context for marketing in a particular company, by evaluating the degree of *organizational stretch* for which we are asking?
2 To what extent does the *marketing organization* itself create implementation problems, and how can these problems be avoided or resolved?
3 Can we identify the most important *sources of implementation problems* in an organization by evaluating the existence of strategic gaps?
4 Can we then look at the problems faced in having these strategic gaps addressed, and the *barriers* to this process of change in the organization?
5 Can we use *internal marketing* techniques to develop implementation strategies (or at least to provide better guidance as to which marketing strategies *not* to pursue, because the hidden implementation barriers and costs are too great)?

The underlying rationale for this approach is that it is organizational context that links strategy formulation and implementation in marketing, and it is working on this context that provides us with a way to overcome the dichotomy discussed above (Walker and Ruekert, 1987; Piercy, 1990, 2002). However, this link is potentially complex, since the strategy formulation or planning process is itself inextricably part of the organizational context in which managers work. Understanding the gap between the generation of marketing strategies and their implementation may be improved by: examining the formal organizational positioning and structuring of marketing, including the information and intelligence systems, and the operation of key decision-making processes like budgeting and planning – and using that understanding to build an explicit implementation framework of internal marketing to provide a parallel to more conventional external marketing strategy.

Organizational stretch and implementation capabilities

Implementation capabilities

Perhaps the greatest single danger in underestimating the marketing implementation issue is that we assume it away – we believe that any company can implement any strategy, if we simply 'manage' properly. Traditional approaches to implementation are particularly susceptible to this trap. In conventional approaches, if we think about implementation at all, then we see it as the logistics of getting things 'organized':

- We focus on developing the organizational arrangements needed for the new strategy – allocating responsibilities across departments and units, and possibly creating new organizational structures where necessary.
- We allocate resources in the form of budgets and headcount to support the activities underpinning the strategy to the appropriate part of the organization.
- We produce 'action lists' and 'action plans', and do presentations to tell people the way things are going to be done.
- We develop control systems to monitor outcome performance in sales, market share, profit and so on, to evaluate the success of the strategy, and to take remedial action if things are not turning out how we wanted them.

There are very substantial problems in approaching implementation in this way. First, it is illogical to plan strategies that are not firmly rooted in the organization's capabilities, and yet we seem to set up planning systems to do precisely this. Second, organizational arrangements and resource allocation are important, but on their own they are very weak, and usually very slow, approaches to the organizational change inherent in many new strategies. Third, outcomes likes sales, market share and profit are what we want to achieve, but the driver of these outcomes is likely to be the behaviour of people in the organization who impact on what the customer receives in service and quality, which suggests we should manage the behaviour, not just the outcomes.

It is all too easy to underestimate how serious the consequences may be of designing robust and well-researched innovative market strategies that are a poor fit with our capabilities, systems and policies. We have described in some detail elsewhere the failure of a market segmentation strategy in a commercial bank (Piercy and Morgan, 1993). This failure was because an innovative, new segmentation scheme based on customer benefits was incompatible with the organizational structure, information systems and culture of the company. Reading through this case example may provide some new insights into the problems with new market strategies.

In fact, a starting point in taking organizational and behavioural realities seriously may be to recognize that implementation capabilities are a corporate resource of some importance – but one which is not generally well understood. In fact, a company's implementation capabilities may be:

- *time specific*, in the sense that a company may gain or lose the competencies on which a strategy relies for execution, so implementation capabilities change;
- *culture specific*, where components of a strategy assume understanding and abilities that do not exist in other cultures, perhaps exemplified best by the belief that different countries have equal access to employees able and willing to deliver high levels of customer service;
- *partial*, since a company may be well equipped, for example, to launch a product and provide

technical service but be unable to provide other components of the strategy like customer service;

- *latent*, in the sense that a company may actually possess the technical and human resources required by a marketing strategy but lack the ability to deploy those resources through lack of learning or management experience;
- *internally inconsistent*, since some parts of a company may be better suited to execute a strategy than others;
- *strategy specific*, because there may be specific skills and competencies highly suited to a particular strategy but not the flexibility to change to meet new strategic imperatives; and even
- *person specific*, in the sense that implementation capabilities may rely on a specific manager, who exerts the abilities and influence needed to achieve effective implementation (Piercy, 1998b).

These characteristics pose severe difficulties in understanding and evaluating implementation capabilities as part of marketing strategy models, and more immediately for practitioners in managing the execution of strategy.

Organizational stretch

A simple diagnostic may assist in addressing the question of marketing strategy implementation capabilities with a company, using the model of organizational stretch shown in Figure 21.1.

In this approach, *conventional strategies* are a continuation of the past – the company continues an old strategy that it is good at implementing, while the *obsolete strategy* is one where previous execution capacity no longer exists (e.g. key personnel have left, resources become unavailable). Perhaps the most important distinction, however, is the difference between *synergistic strategy* (a marketing strategy that we assume the company will be good at executing) and the *stretch strategy* (a new strategy requiring substantial new capabilities in execution). The challenge to executives is to adopt a process and organizational perspective to better distinguish between synergy and stretch characteristics of new marketing strategies.

For example, the major grocery retailers Tesco and Sainsbury successfully pursued growth by moving into petrol retailing, which closely matched the skills and capabilities they

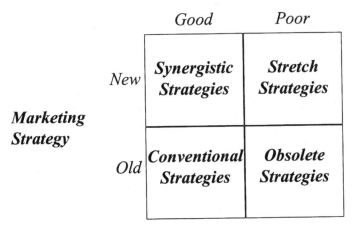

Figure 21.1   Organizational stretch and implementation capabilities

exploited to become market leaders. The same retail companies have started to operate retail banks. They are finding the processing and service requirements for banking somewhat different to those needed in grocery retail, and more important, customer expectations of a bank appear greatly more demanding than those placed on a grocery chain. What appears in rational/analytic terms to be a synergistic strategy may in reality be a stretch strategy.

This model can be used to assist executives in confronting the underlying implementation realities in new marketing strategies. For example, it has been suggested that it is easy to underestimate the degree and type of organizational stretch that is needed to implement relationship marketing strategy effectively – a 'paradigm shift' in marketing strategy suggests the need for a parallel and equal shift in important organizational characteristics (Piercy, 1998a). We need to understand that implementation capabilities may be closely related to the organizational positioning of marketing, and the way that positioning is changing in many major organizations.

Marketing organization and implementation capabilities

Recognizing the importance of implementation capabilities as a resource makes it clearer also that effective strategy implementation relies on more covert aspects of the marketing organization than is commonly recognized. Effective strategy implementation rests not simply on techniques of action planning, budgeting and resource allocation, as well as administrative systems design; it rests on the underlying beliefs and attitudes of organizational participants, and over and above this on the dominating management interests and culture in the organization.

The importance of this, possibly self-evident, statement is that what can be observed

in many international organizations is the loss of the formal organizational position of the marketing function, and even more significantly the weakening of management belief in marketing as a strategic force. The combination of such forces amounts to the weakening of the marketing paradigm, which is becoming a major influence on the marketing strategy implementation capabilities of organizations (Piercy, 1998b).

Reforming the traditional marketing organization

Conventionally, marketing organization has been concerned with the formation and internal structuring of marketing departments. In fact, the strategic significance of organizational issues in marketing and strategy implementation in particular is gaining new attention:

> Had we been contemplating the future of marketing a decade ago, organizational issues would have been at the periphery ... As we approach the millennium, organizational issues are rising to the top of the agenda on the future of marketing.
>
> (Day, 1997)

However, predictions of the future for the marketing organization suggest radical, unfamiliar and revolutionary change to effectively implement the strategies organizations will have to pursue to survive and prosper. Webster (1997) describes this new organizational reality for the future in the following terms:

- Successful organizations will be customer focused not product or technology focused, supported by a market information competence that links the voice of the customer to all the firm's value-delivery processes.
- Customer relationships will be seen as the critical strategic assets of the business, which will be reflected in organizational arrangements with key customers and reseller partners to

integrate marketing competencies around customers and markets.

- Strategies and organizational arrangements will be linked by customer-driven value-delivery processes that are flexible and evolve in response to market change.
- The most serious competitive threats will be from competitors who fundamentally redesign their marketing organizations and systems for going to market, not just their products, because customers will increasingly buy the firm's value-delivery system, not just products.
- Successful marketing organizations will have the skills necessary to manage multiple strategic marketing processes, many of which have not traditionally been seen as in the domain of marketing (e.g. supply chain management, customer linking, product offering development).

To this, add the growing evidence that many companies will go to market through networks held together by a variety of contracts, alliances, partnerships, joint ventures and other links – i.e. as virtual or hollow organizations (e.g. see Cravens *et al.*, 1996). It is unsurprising that commentators point to the 'reinvented organization' needed to compete on capabilities, offer superior customer value and implement complex relationship strategies (Cravens *et al.*, 1997).

However, what remains hidden within these new organizational forms and networks is the question of how organizations can establish, maintain and sustain strategy implementation capabilities. For example, in the airline industry, as companies move towards hollow structures (the airline as brand and booking system employing only core service and operational staff), it is becoming apparent that in devolved network organizations, partner organizations may not be committed to the service quality and excellence needed to sustain the airline's brand. This suggests that new organizational forms will bring a whole new agenda of problems associated with implementation capabilities.

Turning from this scenario of future revolution to the present status quo of the marketing organization also indicates more immediate issues of implementation capabilities. It is almost two decades since it was suggested that the formal organizational positioning and structuring of the marketing function appeared to be subject to an underlying life cycle (Piercy, 1985). Since then, it has been shown, for example, that the organization of marketing in British companies has frequently fallen very short of the integrated models familiar in the prescriptive literature (Piercy, 1986). We found, for example, stereotypical marketing organizations in British manufacturing firms to include limited/staff role forms, responsible for limited areas like market research and some sales promotion; strategy/services forms, with planning responsibilities and little line responsibility; and selling-oriented forms, involved almost wholly in field sales operations. The significance of these observations lies primarily in the symbolism of structure rather than the administrative substance. Tokenism in formal organizational arrangements for marketing was taken as indicative of a lack of resource control and strategic influence for marketing in British companies (Piercy, 1986).

More recently, the organization of marketing in Britain has been characterized by the downsizing and closure of conventional marketing departments, reinforced by the impact of category management and trade marketing strategies, and the resurgence of the power of sales departments and key account management structures in managing customer relationships in business-to-business markets (Piercy, 2002).

Correspondingly, many popular approaches address marketing as an issue of process not function – for example, as the 'process of going to market', which cuts across traditional functional and organizational boundaries (see Figure 21.2). The implications of such marketing process models for the redundancy of traditional functional structures may be extreme, with the unintended side-effect of further weakening the marketing paradigm in organizations.

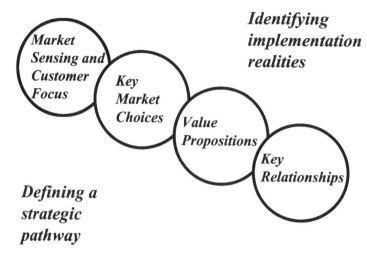

Figure 21.2   The process of going to market
Source: Piercy (2002).

The impact of process models on marketing

As noted above, part of the new organizational design concept is the trend to organize around process instead of function, and the development of new organizational forms like hollow or network organizations.

For example, one view of the new marketing organization is shown in the model of value processes in Figure 21.3. A process perspective appears useful, although as yet largely undeveloped, in building insight into issues like implementation in an organizational context. However, there are various ways of understanding process for these purposes. Most commonly, process is understood in terms of its substantive *content* – the new product development process, the planning process, for example. In addition, processes may be usefully conceived in terms of their *purposes* – value-defining, value-developing and value-delivering processes, for instance (Webster, 1997).

Understanding a process perspective may be critical to identifying and managing strategy implementation capabilities in new organizational forms. For example, a number of studies of key marketing decision-making processes

have proposed that such processes should be analysed in terms of their organizational dimensions. Studies of marketing budgeting and resource allocation (Piercy, 1987), marketing planning (Piercy and Morgan, 1994) and marketing control (Piercy and Morgan, 1996) have shared a model that suggests that many decision-making processes can usefully be analysed in terms of analytic/technical dimensions. We might, for example, consider value processes in the way shown in Figure 21.3. This suggests that to understand the capability of value processes to deliver value, or to implement a value-based marketing strategy, it is useful to examine not simply the analytic/technical aspects of the process (the information gathered, the operations systems, and the logistics for value delivery), but also the behavioural aspects of the process (in terms of the abilities of individuals to interpret information and develop market understanding, and their motivation, commitment and behaviour in developing and delivering value to customers) and the organizational or contextual aspects of the process (the learning capabilities and responsiveness of the organization, and its management's strategic orientation). An important issue is the consistency

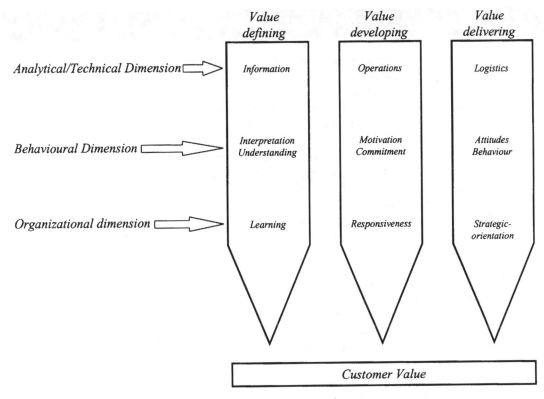

Figure 21.3   Value processes in marketing replacing marketing departments

between the analytic, behavioural and organizational dimensions of process, although this is frequently covert. Consistency between the dimensions of a process is likely to have a substantial impact on implementation capabilities.

For example, while value defining may be driven by the abilities of the organization to collect and disseminate information, 'market sensing' that leads to effective implementation of value-based strategy is likely also to be a function of the interpretative abilities and inclinations of individuals, and the organization's learning capabilities.

While value developing relies on operations capabilities, it is also shaped by the organization's responsiveness to market-based change, the motivation and commitment of individuals to implementing change, and the

motivation and commitment of individuals to implementing change. Value delivering involves supply chain capabilities and logistics, but also the attitudes and behaviours of service personnel, salespeople, distributors and other participants, as well as the priorities communicated by the strategic orientation of management. The danger lies in equating capabilities in the analytic/technical dimension of process with corresponding capabilities in the behavioural and orga...

challenge is to ev...

sistency in the p...

adapting and resh...

fit better with the...

tion capabilities.

While this m...

trative, it serves t...

implementation is...

Table 21.1   Customer relationship management at IBM

- Most of IBM's marketing activities are now embedded in a global initiative called customer relationship management (CRM).
- CRM works through core processes:
  - Market management – to identify and select key market segments
  - Relationship management – handles interaction between IBM and the customer with established customers
  - Opportunity management – as soon as a sales opportunity is identified, the opportunity manager has the role of finding the right 'opportunity owner' who can offer the right type of expertise and the right level of interaction (e.g. mass customization versus one-of-a-kind), drawing on the next processes
  - Offering information – keeping track of every product or solution developed by the company or its business partners, so no-one in IBM has to waste time re-inventing the wheel
  - Skills management – a worldwide database of IBM personnel's skills, graded on scales from levels 1 to 5
  - Solution, design and delivery – each offer and bid is tracked to check the result
  - Customer satisfaction management – handling customer feedback and complaints
  - Message management – handling communications
- The goal is co-ordination of customer relationships through managing business processes that cut across boundaries to achieve maximum effectiveness.

Source: Piercy (2002).

then implementation capabilities are a function of the individual behaviours and motivation of individuals in the organization, and the underlying organizational context in which the process operates. If implementation is viewed in these terms, the question of the strength of the marketing paradigm becomes critical to evaluating true implementation capabilities. At its simplest, if the people in an organization do not believe in marketing and customer imperatives, and management priorities are focused elsewhere than the customer marketplace, the marketing strategy implementation capabilities are likely to be low.

How seriously major firms are taking the management of marketing processes in these structures is well illustrated by the radical customer relationship management initiative at IBM. The main characteristics of this are summarized in Table 21.1.

Interfunctional relationships

One important implication of a process perspective for implementation capabilities is the need for seamless integration of all the activities in the organization that impact on the value offering to the customer – when many of these activities are controlled by other parts of the company, or are located in partner organizations. For example, one way of using the model of value processes in Figure 21.3 is to use the structure to model the 'ownership' of critical parts of value processes by different parts of the organization, and then examine how well integration is achieved. The quest for total integration or organizational processes around customer value promises to be one of the major challenges facing marketing, because in the type of markets we now face:

... integration of the entire organization becomes critical. Everything must work together, fit together, and appear together for the customer ... increasingly it is viewed as a way to develop and implement the critical customer's view of the organization. An organization can no longer consist of a group of unrelated activities and work groups because customers just won't accept that.

(Schultz, 1997)

One part of understanding an organization's marketing strategy implementation capabilities lies in evaluating the skills of marketing in working with other key functions and business units – finance, operations and supply chain management, R&D, human resource management, sales, customer relationship management – to identify the traditional barriers and to exploit the synergies that can be built (Hulbert *et al.*, 2003). The skills of leadership, cross-functional working, superior interfunctional communications and effective co-ordination are likely to be critical to marketing implementation in the process-driven organization of the future.

The competitive power of unleashing new capabilities based on superior interfunctional relationships may be huge. Contrast, for example, the outstanding performance of fashion retailer Zara with its competitors. Zara leverages its supply chain with its design and marketing capabilities to get fashion clothing from the catwalk to the store in a matter of weeks instead of the months taken by its competitors, and at very competitive prices, reflecting the efficiency of its integrated processes. It is difficult for traditional, bureaucratic organizations to compete with this model.

The impact of network organizations on marketing

One of the most important responses by companies to new competitive and market conditions has been the emergence of strategies of collaboration and partnership with other organizations as a key element of the process of going to market – these have variously been termed marketing partnership, strategic alliances and marketing networks (Piercy and Cravens, 1995). These new collaborative organizations are distinctive and different. They are:

characterized by flexibility, specialization, and an emphasis on relationship management instead of market transactions ... to respond quickly and flexibly to accelerating change in technology, competition and customer preferences.

(Webster, 1992)

The emergence of networks of collaborating organizations linked by various forms of alliance and partnership has already become a dominant strategic development in many industries. For example:

- It was estimated in 2001 that the top 500 global businesses had an average of 60 major strategic alliances each.
- Consulting firm Accenture estimates that US companies with at least $2 billion in sales each formed an average of 138 alliances from 1996 to 1999.
- In 1993, when Lou Gerstner took over as CEO, only 5 per cent of IBM's sales outside personal computers were derived from alliances. By 2001, IBM was managing almost 100 000 alliances which contribute over one-third of its income. The company expects these partnerships to boost sales by $10 billion by 2003.
- A survey of global alliances by Accenture Consulting in 1999 found that:
  - Eighty-two per cent of executives surveyed believed that alliances will be the prime vehicle for growth.
  - Alliances account for an average of 26 per cent of Fortune 500 companies' revenues – up from 11 per cent five years earlier.
  - Alliances account for 6–15 per cent of the market value of companies surveyed, and this is expected to increase to 16–25 per cent of the average company's market value within five years.

– Senior management at 25 per cent of companies surveyed expects alliances to contribute more than 40 per cent of their company's value within five years (Cravens and Piercy, 2002).

For these reasons, it is important that our thinking about the implementation of strategy, and also our understanding of the emerging forms of competition we face in the market, should embrace the strategic alliance and the resulting growth of networks of organizations linked to various forms of collaborative relationship.

However, when we think about implementation capabilities in these new types of networked organizations major questions remain unresolved. The role of marketing in network organizations is unclear. In some models, like the 'marketing exchange company', the hub of the network is the marketing facility (Achrol, 1991). Others suggest that the critical role for marketing in the alliance-based network is applying relationship marketing skills to managing the links between partners in the network (Webster, 1992). Certainly, there is a compelling argument that the concepts and processes of relationship marketing are pivotal to the management of value through mutual co-operation and interdependence (Sheth, 1994), and we have seen that co-operation and interdependence are central features of network organizations.

New approaches to marketing organization

Faced with these challenges, many organizations are developing new ways to organize marketing to achieve effective strategy implementation. These approaches include the following:

Restructuring vertically for more effective change

Many organizations throughout the world are restructuring around vertical customer groups as a way of responding better and faster to customer needs than traditional organizational arrangements permitted. For example, since 1999, the Procter & Gamble Co. (P&G) has been implementing major global organizational changes, as part of its 'Organization 2005' plan, at a total cost estimated to approach $2 billion. P&G is widely recognized for its powerful marketing capabilities, but faces intense competition throughout the world and loss of position in several key product markets. By 1999, only half its brands were building market share, and the company has struggled to maintain sales and earnings growth. Previously organized into four business units covering the regions of the world, in 1998 seven new executives reporting to the CEO were given profit responsibility for global product units such as baby care, beauty, and fabric and home care (Global Business Units). Several of the Global Business Units are headquartered overseas. The new design concept also includes eight Market Development Units intended to tackle local market issues (e.g. supermarket retailing in South America), as well as Global Business Services and corporate functions. Key objectives were to increase the speed of decision making and move new products into commercialization faster, and to manage the business on a global basis. 'Change agents' have been appointed to work across the Global Business Units to lead cultural and business change by helping teams to work together more effectively through using real-time collaboration tools. Virtual innovation teams are linked by intranets, which can be accessed by senior executives to keep up with developments. The programme involves considerable downsizing in personnel numbers, and substantial change – 25 per cent of P&G brand managers left the company in 18 months. The sales organization is being revised to focus salesperson attention more specifically on individual brands. P&G's 'Organization 2005' programme underlines the nature of the fundamental changes facing many companies in realigning their structures and processes with the requirements of a turbulent and intensely competitive environment.

Customer-based management structures

One interesting suggestion is that, in organizations of the future, traditional product management structure will evolve into customer-based structures, where several customer portfolios replace products as the 'pillars' of the organization, and product managers will provide services to each customer portfolio group (as will functional specialists) (Berthon *et al.*, 1997).

Venture marketing organization (VMO)

More radically, the VMO is a fluid approach to identifying new opportunities and concentrating resources on the best. It adopts the principles of venture capitalism to fund fluid teams of managers and partner organizations to progress an innovation bypassing the traditional organizational routes. For example, Starbucks has a VMO-style approach to innovation. Starbucks approaches new opportunities by assembling teams whose leaders often come from the functional marketing areas most critical to success. The originator of the idea may take the lead role only if qualified. If teams need skills that are not available internally they look outside. To lead the 'Store of the Future' project, Starbucks hired a top executive with retail experience away from Universal Studios, and to develop its lunch service concept, it chose a manager from Marriott. After the new product is launched, some team members may stay to manage the venture, while others are redeployed to new opportunity teams or return to line management. Success on a team is vital for promotion or a bigger role on another project. Teamwork extends to partner organizations. When pursuing a new ice cream project, Starbucks quickly realized they lacked the in-house packaging and channel management skills to move quickly. Teaming up with Dreyer's Grand Ice Cream got the product to market in half the normal time, and within four months it was the top selling brand of coffee ice cream. Starbucks emphasizes the importance of identifying new opportunities throughout its organization. Anyone in the company with a new idea for an opportunity uses a one-page form to pass it to a senior executive team. If the company pursues the idea, the originator, regardless of tenure or title, is usually invited onto the launch team as a full-time member. In its first year, Starbucks' Frappuccino, a cold coffee drink, contributed 11 per cent of company sales. The idea originated with a front-line manager in May 1994, gaining high priority status from a five-person senior executive team in June. The new team developed marketing, packaging and channel approaches in July. A joint venture arrangement with PepsiCo was in place by August. The first wave of roll-out was in October 1994, with national launch in May 1995. A high-level steering committee meets every two weeks to rate new opportunities against two simple criteria: impact on company revenue growth and effects on the complexity of the retail store. The committee uses a one-page template to assess each idea, relying on a full-time process manager to ensure the information is presented consistently.

It is too early to reach conclusions about the role that marketing can and will take generally in these new organizational and network forms, although it is highly likely that there will be some redefinition of its role which may be radical and which will directly influence strategy implementation capabilities.

Identifying implementation problems in marketing

This more complex organizational setting and its impact on strategy implementation capabilities underlines the importance of adopting practical approaches to the implementation issue. A first step in confronting the marketing implementation issue is to build a picture of the ways in which a company's marketing plans and strategies fail to reach the marketplace.

One method for achieving this is the analysis of 'strategic gaps': the gaps between 'strategic intent' and 'strategic reality'.

Marketing intentions and marketing realities

The analysis of strategic gaps involves evaluating the differences which exist between the marketing strategies which planners have formulated inside the organization and the delivery of these promises in the customer marketplace. This has been stylized elsewhere as the contrast between 'intended' and 'realized' strategies (Mintzberg, 1988). For present purposes this can be reduced to something very simple:

- *intended strategy or strategic intent* – what management and planners inside the organization think the business is about in the marketplace; and
- *perceived strategy or strategic reality* – what the business is actually about in the marketplace,

as it is seen and understood by salespeople, distributors and customers.

The approach illustrated in Figure 21.4 leads to some of the most significant practical questions to be confronted in dealing with the implementation issue.

The technique is straightforward and easily applied, but can be exceptionally productive in isolating the existence and underlying reasons for implementation problems in marketing. The procedure is as follows:

1 *Identify the market in question and the marketing strategy* which is being (or will be) pursued. This is frequently where we encounter the first difficulties – when executives struggle to aptly describe their market, or to encapsulate in a few words the strategy for that market, then we may have found the first source of implementation barriers. If we truly understand our marketing strategy, we should be able to

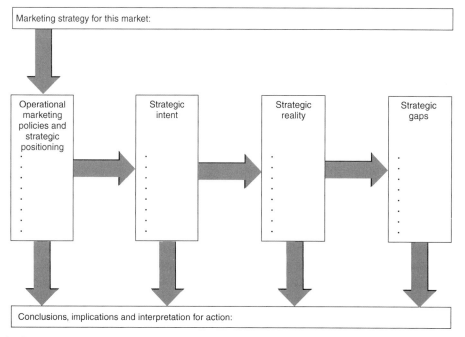

Figure 21.4 **Strategic intent versus strategic reality**

articulate it in a few key points. If we cannot do this, it raises the question of whether we really have a strategy for this market.

2   *Translate the marketing strategy into the practicalities of operational marketing policies*, and what this is intended to achieve in strategic position in the market in question. This should be done in each area of the marketing programme. The question to address is: For our marketing strategy to be effectively implemented in this market, what do we have to achieve with:

- Our *products and services*, in terms of such issues as quality compared to our competitors, fullness of range, image and brand identity compared to alternatives, design attributes, functional features and 'extras', reliability of service, and so on.
- Our *pricing and value*, in terms of the real position in price level against the competitors and alternatives, and how we are seen in 'value for money' compared to others in the market.
- Our *marketing communications*, in terms of the quality and role of our selling efforts and coverage of the market, the image and awareness created by advertising, the effectiveness of our sales promotions, and so on, all as compared to the competition.
- Our *distribution*, in terms of the availability of the product in the marketplace, the quality of the service provided in customer waiting time, service provision, maintenance, and so on; and
- Our *strategic positioning*, in terms of the stage of the product life cycle reached, the strength of our market position, our success in achieving differentiation in the customers' eyes and what we have achieved in customer satisfaction levels compared to the competition.

This analysis defines the *strategic intent* – what our marketing strategy has to achieve in practical terms to become a reality in the marketplace. The goal is to reduce this intent to a few major points under each heading.

1   *Evaluate the strategic reality* – address each of above questions again, but now in terms of what we have *actually* achieved on each issue of marketing programme and strategic position. This is normally quite a lot different from the strategic intent. The richness and insight produced here is also greatly enhanced by asking a new and different group of people for their perceptions. If the strategic intent is defined by the marketing planners or marketing and general management, then the strategic reality may be best identified by the salesforce, by the distributors or even by customers themselves.

2   *Identify the strategic gaps* – at this stage we are simply comparing the strategic intent and the strategic reality, and noting or summarizing the differences as strategic gaps.

3   *Interpret the strategic gaps* – the most important stage of this technique is where we stand back from the analysis of intent and reality and the differences between them, and see what insights we have gained into the real problems of marketing implementation in the situation we are studying. To see what conclusions we can draw, we may address the following types of questions:

- How serious are the gaps we have found between the marketing strategy and the real marketplace situation (and how confident are we that we have genuinely uncovered that reality)?
- Why do the strategic gaps exist – what could be done to move the reality closer to the intent, but would this be possible, and would it be economical?
- Are some of the strategic gaps actually impossible to close on any sensible basis; for example, is the marketing strategy hopelessly out of line with the resources and capabilities of this company at this time?
- Where (if anywhere) have management and the marketing planners confronted the strategic reality in this marketplace, as it is described to us by the salesforce, the distributors and the customers?

- Is the problem one of reformulating the strategy (i.e. moving the intent closer to the reality) or an issue for managerial action (i.e. attempting to bring the reality closer to the intent)?

Figure 21.5 shows an example of how this approach was adopted with one organization – a computer manufacturer – in which top management had difficulty in understanding why their marketing strategy for recovering market share

Company: XYZ Computers Ltd		Market: Financial departmental systems	
Strategy: Regain lost market share (get back to 20% from present 10%) by positioning as a specialist, high-quality systems supplier marketing total business solutions			
Operational marketing policies	Strategic intent	Strategic reality	Strategic gaps
Products and services	• Technical superiority • Maximum service content • Specialist supplier	• The product is difficult to use • We are seen as a computer specialist	• Systems/solutions versus computers
Pricing and value	• High price but high value • Flexibility	• Expensive and over-priced • Intractable	• Value/quality perception problem • Real flexibility?
Communications: • Selling • Advertising • Promotion	• Advertising to reinforce positioning • Regular sales coverage of all accounts • Industry/sector based promotion and training events	• Our advertising is computers, not customer 'business solutions' • We have less sales coverage than the competition • We are seen as computer trainers not hardware suppliers	• Positioning problem? • Market coverage
Distribution: • Channels • Logistics • Service	• Use direct channels • Offer rapid installation • Provides 7-day servicing • Provide technical consultancy • Emphasize personal relationships	• Customers go to traders, not direct • We ignore advisers and recommenders • We talk to users not decision makers • Customers do not trust us	• Understanding of the customer decision-making units? • The real service needs? • Demand for hardware versus demand for services
Strategic positioning • Product/market life cycle • Strategic position • Competitive differentiation • Customer satisfaction	• Rapid market growth for next 5 years • We take a dominant position through technological superiority • Focus on customer visits, social events, etc.	• The market is already mature • We can take a tenable position at best • Our position is likely to weaken • Everyone visits and entertains – mostly better than we do	• Market assumptions? • Customer perceptions? • Real competitive strengths?

Conclusions, implications, actions
- The major product/value issue is 'technical' (our company) versus 'customer-oriented' (the competitors)
- We urgently need to reassess the market in terms of the important customer decision-making units and priorities/needs to different players
- We need to investigate further our real position in the market
- We need to study the growth prospects here (if any)

Figure 21.5 Analysing strategic gaps

in a critical market was floundering. In this example, the information is laid out in a worksheet format as discussed elsewhere (Piercy, 2002), but the important point of the case is the great contrast between the strategic intent as defined by senior managers and the perception of the real marketplace situation, or strategic reality, held by key members of the salesforce. This disparity was true in each area of the marketing programme, as well as in the resulting strategic position in this market. The barriers to implementation of the marketing strategy were fundamental, representing very real gaps: in understanding the customer's view of the product and the value of the company's total offering to the market; in attacking the real drivers in the critical customer decision-making units; in the company's real strength in communications and distribution coverage; and in the real future for the company in this market. As can be seen, this analysis provided a very different agenda to be addressed in implementing the marketing strategy in question and, it should be noted, not the agenda that management was expecting to identify. Their view had moved from blaming the salesforce for underperforming to reconsidering the assumptions they had made in building their marketing strategy, and questioning the attractiveness of this market as a continuing target.

The point of this exercise is that it can produce useful insights into the marketing implementation problem in a company in two ways. First, it can uncover how well the company translates its marketing strategies into the practicalities of integrated operational marketing programmes and plans of action. Second, this analysis forces management to look at the business from the point of view of operational personnel and paying customers, which can be very revealing in its own right, and frequently uncovers yet more of the underlying reasons why marketing strategies do not reach the marketplace level of the business.

Generally, this type of analysis is likely to uncover strategic gaps which may be explained for the following types of reasons:

- Because there are too many internal barriers and obstacles, reflecting both open issues like resource and skills shortages, but also more covert questions like political resistance to change.
- Because line management simply does not accept the validity of the strategic intent, i.e. they have no commitment of 'buy-in' to the marketing strategy.
- Because the strategic intent is out of line with real corporate capabilities, i.e. what the organization is really capable of doing, as opposed to top management's idealized view of how things should be in their company.
- Because when marketing plans and strategies have been constructed, the implementation issue has not been addressed in an explicit and detailed way – simply expecting things to happen because a plan has been written is often ineffective.
- Because line managers do not understand or take seriously the strategic intent represented by the marketing plans and strategy.

Each of these possible conclusions may lead us to different aspects of the implementation issue in marketing. This is recommended as a starting point which leads us quickly towards specific issues, rather than just the general question of implementation. Attention now turns to how we may be able to address the strategic gaps we have identified and their underlying causes, and the possible barriers to this process of change.

Implementation barriers in marketing

It should be borne in mind that frequently it is not enough simply to locate and identify implementation problems in a company. To cope with those problems is likely to require somewhat more effort. Indeed, there is an underlying danger that marketing executives tend to underestimate the degree and type of change that are required in their organizations, if their marketing strategies are to be successfully implemented. In many ways, it is understanding this issue that is the key to the paradox that while marketing implementation problems may often come down to very simple and obvious factors, actually solving such implementation problems may be extremely difficult. These hidden dimensions of the marketing implementation problem may reduce to such issues as:

- The separation of planning from management, leading to an absence of management involvement and commitment.
- Unrealistic optimism about markets, competition and a company's capabilities because planners are separated from the problems of actually running the business.
- The implementation issue is recognized too late in the process, so managers are left trying to gain implementation through coercion, and ignore the underlying costs of organizational change (see below).
- The existence of implementation problems is simply denied by management, who cannot believe that their decisions will not be put into effect.

Do we have an implementation problem in marketing?

Perhaps the most basic reason the marketing implementation issue is ignored when marketing plans and strategies are formulated is that executives do not believe that they have a marketing problem or that they need to change anything to get their strategies implemented. One observation (Piercy, 2002) is that companies, and in fact different units within the same organization, differ significantly in two important respects:

1 The perception that there is a marketing problem in the organization, which should be taken seriously.
2 The willingness to try something new to solve the problem.

A first step in working with a company to get to grips with the marketing implementation issue may be to ask which of the following best describes the situation we face in implementing our marketing strategy?

- *Closed minds* – people do not believe there is any significant marketing problem, and therefore see no reason to change the way they do things.
- *Worried stayers and frightened rabbits* – where people know that they have major marketing problems, but are either unwilling to change the way things are done in their company or simply do not know how to change.
- *Blissful ignorance* – situations where people believe they are always open to new ideas and change, but they do not really need to do anything differently, because they do not really believe that they have any problems.
- *Ready to go* – the only situation where we can reasonably expect new marketing solutions to be implemented is where people are willing to change and adopt new ways of doing things, and they accept that there are important marketing problems to be solved.

The chances are that it is only with the 'Ready to go' case that we can expect implementation of new marketing strategies to happen, and it is also likely that in many cases this is not the situation we will find. The conclusion is that we may need to think of different implementation strategies depending on the type of barrier we face: pressure to maintain the status quo, lack of perception or understanding of marketing problems to be solved, or both of these.

It is often suggested that while resistance to change is a well-known organizational phenomenon (e.g. Darling and Taylor, 1989), it is surprising that we should suggest that executives do not see or recognize that there are marketing problems. Bonoma and Clark (1990) offer some insight into this issue with their 'marketing performance assessment' framework. Their underlying arguments are that:

- Management satisfaction with marketing performance (and thus whether management think there are marketing problems or not) depends in large degree on what management *expected* to achieve in the first place. In short, the argument is that, regardless of the real potentials in the market, satisfaction or dissatisfaction will be predicted by management's high or low expectations.
- How much marketing effort we have to make to get a given result depends on our skills, competencies and structures. We may get good results with small effort, or bad results after massive expenditures of effort, depending on the match between our capabilities and market characteristics. This enormously complicates the problem of seeing whether we have a marketing problem or if one is on the way.
- Results depend not least on the environment – market trends and changes, competitive actions, and so on. Our results may look good or bad because of factors totally outside our control or ability to predict. We may do well because we are in the right place at the right time, and this may further obscure the need for marketing changes for the future and make it difficult to isolate marketing implementation problems.

The underlying point is the need to think of *implementation strategies* which address both issues of inertia and understanding of the real marketing problems. We have argued elsewhere (Piercy, 2002) that building such approaches to marketing implementation may involve us in operating on the underlying decision-making processes of the organization and its 'inner workings', rather than in just writing implementation strategies. For example, to illuminate the marketing problem may involve having executives and key players in the organization work on environmental scanning or participate in marketing planning itself, so they discover and address the real issues, rather than being told what they are. Similarly, overcoming a reluctance to change may be addressed through our internal marketing techniques (see below), but we need to seek a genuine understanding of *why* people in an organization cling to the familiar and established way of doing things. Argyris (1985), for instance, speaks of the 'defensive routines' that people build to protect themselves from the discomfort and disruption of having to change – the 'designed error' in implementation processes, such that we know things are going wrong but choose to do nothing about it.

Testing the strategy

However, as a start, the framework in Figure 21.6 suggests a number of critical questions that should be asked of the marketing strategy or plan, before we assume that marketing failures are due to a company's low execution or implementation skills. These questions involve challenging:

1 The completeness and coherence of the strategy – if it is vague and missing important details, then how can we expect it to be implemented?
2 If the strategy is innovative and brilliant, but beyond the company's capabilities, then the most we can expect is lip-service. Bonoma (1985) outlines some of the common problems created here as: (a) *management by assumption* – we assume 'someone' will get the detailed work done so, in practice, no-one does it; (b) *structural contradictions* – we create marketing strategies that conflict with our systems and structures and just expect people to cope; (c) *empty promises marketing* – we build marketing strategies and plans that rely on abilities and resources that we have not got and cannot get; or (d) *bunny marketing* – we have no clear marketing strategy, so we create a profusion of plans instead (Bonoma's analogy is the man with lots of rabbits who needed an ox, but no matter how much he bred the rabbits, he never seemed to end up with an ox).
3 If we have not made the effort to communicate and to win support for the plans

and strategies with key players inside the organization, then it is likely that non-acceptance and counter-implementation will follow, rather than the 'ownership' and commitment that is needed to gain implementation.

However, while the first stage in our thinking about implementation problems should be to ask such questions about the strategy itself, the fact remains that there may also be problems that genuinely do reflect a company's capabilities and resistance to unwelcome change.

If our analysis of strategic gaps (Figure 21.4), internal perceptions of marketing problems and willingness to change, sources of marketing implementation barriers, and the robustness of our marketing strategy (Figure 21.6) leads us to the conclusion that there are significant marketing implementation problems, then we may need a framework for planning and building a marketing implementation strategy. Although it is far from the perfect answer, one approach to this is to use internal marketing as the structure for our implementation strategy, and the direct counterpart to our conventional external marketing strategy.

Marketing implementation and internal marketing strategy

If we reach the stage where we wish to build an explicit implementation strategy for our

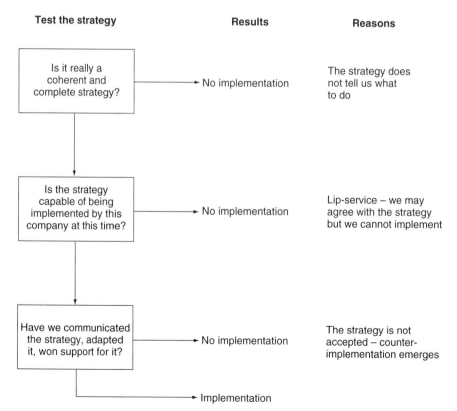

Figure 21.6   Testing marketing strategies
Source: Adapted from Piercy (2002).

marketing plans, then the conventional literature offers little other than action plans and schedules. One method which has proved useful in coping with the implementation issue is to use strategic internal marketing. Internal marketing can encompass many different issues relevant to strategy implementation. In different circumstances, the internal marketing process might include the following types of activity and programme:

- Gaining the *support* of key decision-makers for our plans – but also all that those plans imply in terms of the need to acquire personnel and financial resources, possibly in conflict with established company 'policies', and to get what is needed from other functions like operations and finance departments to implement a marketing strategy effectively.
- Changing some of the *attitudes and behaviour* of employees and managers, who are working at the key interfaces with customers and distributors, to those required to make plans work effectively (but also reinforcing effective attitudes and behaviour as well).
- Winning *commitment* to making the plan work and 'ownership' of the key problem-solving tasks from those units and individuals in the firm whose working support is needed.
- Ultimately, managing incremental *changes in the culture* from 'the way we always do things' to 'the way we need to do things to be successful' and to make the marketing strategy work.
- Building *key internal alliances*, for example with human resource management, to influence employee skills and behaviour, or with the sales organization to link marketing imperatives to salesperson behaviour.

In fact, it follows from the emergence of the internal marketing paradigm from diverse conceptual sources that the practice of internal marketing and its potential contribution to marketing strategy are similarly varied. It is possible to consider the following 'types' of internal marketing, although they are probably not equal in importance:

- internal marketing that focuses on the development and delivery of high standards of *service quality* and customer satisfaction;
- internal marketing that is concerned primarily with developing *internal communications programmes* to provide employees with information and to win their support;
- internal marketing which is used as a systematic approach to managing the *adoption of innovations* within an organization;
- internal marketing concerned with providing products and services to users *inside the organization*; and
- internal marketing as the *implementation strategy* for our marketing plans.

Here we are concerned mainly with the last of these.

The purpose of this approach is to capture our ideas about what has to be done to close the strategic gaps we have found, or to gain the effective implementation of our external marketing plans and strategies. The attraction of the framework is that it utilizes the same structure and analytical tools as external marketing planning, and directly parallels this familiar process throughout. The specific goals of the internal marketing strategy are taken directly from the requirements of the external marketing strategy.

One way of presenting this to a company is shown in Figure 21.7. This model suggests that internal marketing sits alongside external marketing and can be put into exactly the same structure. Internal marketing is taken as the output from the conventional external marketing programme – it simply asks for each element of the external marketing strategy and programme, what will be required inside the company: who will have to change what they do, learn new ways of doing things, give up existing practices, free resources and time, and so on. However, internal marketing analysis is also an *input* to the conventional planning process, in identifying both the constraints and barriers in the internal marketplace, as well as important capabilities which

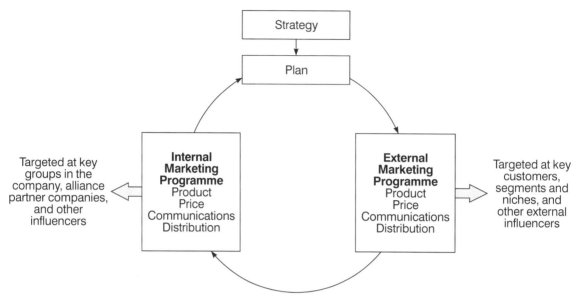

Figure 21.7 Internal and external marketing strategy

should be considered in building external marketing strategies (this is one way of coping with the strategy formulation–implementation dichotomy we considered earlier).

The structure of the internal marketing programme can be put into exactly the same terms as the conventional external marketing programme:

- *The market.* These are the individuals and groups inside the organization who are our internal customers, because without their acceptance and commitment to the external marketing strategy, it will not work.
- *The product.* At its simplest level, the 'product' is the external marketing plan and strategy. However, at a deeper level the product for the internal market is all the changes and innovations that are needed to make the external strategy work, including changes in peoples' attitudes and behaviour.
- *The price.* This is not our costs, but what we are asking our internal customers to give up in order for our external strategy to be effectively implemented. The price may be the

opportunity cost of other projects given up, or the costs to people of adjusting to change.
- *The marketing communications.* The most tangible aspect of internal marketing is the communications media and messages used to inform and persuade the internal customers. This may start with written communications and presentations, but may end up as being more about listening to the problems people perceive with the new strategy, and adapting is necessary. Ultimately, communication is a two-way process – we know this in our external marketing, and should not forget it in our internal marketing.
- *Distribution.* This is concerned with all the ways we have to deliver the 'product' and the 'message' to the internal customer. It may start with meetings, workshops, committees, internal communications vehicles and the like, but may end up as far more concerned with the internal processes of the organization. For example, Ulrich (1989) has described the practices of major US organizations like General Electric, Marriott, DEC, the Ford Motor Company, Honeywell and others in

working for the real customer commitment they need from their employees if their service-based external marketing strategies are to work. Their practices involve giving external customers a significant role in such internal processes as: staff recruitment and selection decisions; staff promotion and development choices; staff appraisal, right from setting the standards to measuring the performance; operating staff reward systems, both financial and non-financial; organizational design strategies; and internal communications programmes. This suggests that the most potent distribution channel for internal marketing may also be more to do with process and culture than simply holding meetings or sending out written communications.

- *Market research.* As with external marketing, we need to remember the role of research and analysis techniques in identifying the internal market characteristics and changes which are significant to the implementation of our external strategies.

It will be apparent from the way the internal marketing structure has been described above that we are concerned with far more than simply producing 'glossies' to persuade people in the organization to support our marketing strategy (although this may be one of the things that we have to do in some situations). We may end up more concerned with the underlying process and culture of the organization, and thus its real capabilities to implement a marketing strategy. This again directly parallels the way we look at the external customer – at different levels.

For example, Tables 21.2 and 21.3 summarize two company cases, where the internal marketing framework is used at different levels to understand the real implementation problems and to develop appropriate responses, i.e. effective implementation responses. To make the levels clearer, the tabulated cases suggest that we look at internal marketing first at a *formal* level, where the concern is with open

and rational presentation issues, second at an *informal* level, where the issues are about the 'inner workings' of the company, and third at a *processual* level, where we confront the underlying processes of change in the organization and the cultural barriers we may face.

The case summarized in Table 21.2 describes the problems faced in a financial services organization in implementing a strategy of key customer focus, developed by a central team of planners, but relying on branch management co-operation and commitment – as well as requiring the collaboration of two traditionally separate and competing field divisions – for effective implementation. The desirability of this strategy was well known in the company, and it had frequently been included in the group marketing plan, but with little or no success in implementation. The analysis in Table 21.2 suggests that while there were practical barriers to implementing the strategy at tactical level – threats to commission earnings, the need for better market information, and so on – there were far more substantial, but covert, blockages to implementation hidden in the culture of the organization. As a result, it can be seen that simply issuing written plans and instructions achieved little, and neither did 'sabre-rattling' by the chief executive. In fact, although attractive in attacking the external market, it was also true that the new strategy would have a considerable and unwelcome impact on the power and freedom of decentralized managers, compared to the planners at the centre, and would substantially change their evaluation and earnings prospects. More intractable still were the political barriers represented by the costs to the managers concerned with collaborating with counterparts in another division, who had historically been perceived at best as competitors – a cultural divide made worse by ethnic and educational background differences between the divisions. Implementation of the strategy was only achieved after operating on the process and culture of the company by building joint planning and problem-solving teams from the two divisions on a regional basis.

Table 21.2 Internal marketing in a financial services organization

Internal marketing	Internal marketing levels		
	Formal	Informal	Processual
Product	Integration of selling efforts around key customers, as a key marketing strategy	Head-office group-based planning and resource allocation with greater central control	Change in the individual manager's role from independent branch 'entrepreneur' to group-based collaborator
Price	Branch profit/commission from independent selling to smaller customers, to be sacrificed to build long-term relationships with key accounts	Loss of freedom/independence of action in the marketplace. Potential loss of commission-earning power	Time, effort and psychological 'pain' of collaborating with former 'competitors' with different ethnic/ educational/professional backgrounds – the 'banker versus the hire-purchase salesman'
			Fear that the other side would damage existing customer relationships
Distribution	Written strategic marketing plans. Sales conferences	Written communications. Informal discussion of chief executive's 'attitude'. Redesign of commission and incentives systems in both companies	Joint planning/problem-solving teams for each region – built around central definition of target market segments
			Combining/integrating management information systems, and changing its structure to reflect new segments
Communications	Formal presentation by chief executive at conferences. Written support from chief executive. Redesign market information systems to be more up to date	Sponsorship by chief executive – 'the train is now leaving the station, you are either on it or ...' (written memo sent to all branches)	Social events Joint training courses Redefinition of markets and target segments
Internal market targets		(1) Branch managers of retail banks and finance company offices (2) Divisional chief executives for the banks and the finance company	

Source: adapted from Piercy and Morgan (1991).

Table 21.3 Internal marketing in a computer company

Internal marketing	Internal marketing levels		
	Formal	Informal	Processual
Product	Marketing plan to attack at small industry as a special vertical market, rather than grouping it with many other industries as at present, with specialized products and advertising	Separation of resources and control of this market from the existing business unit	Change from technology-oriented management to recognition of differences in buyer needs in different industries – the clash between technology and customer orientation
Price	Costs of developing specialized 'badged' or branded products for this industry	Loss of control for existing business units	Fear of 'fragmentation' of markets leading to internal structural and status changes
Distribution	Written plan. Presentations to key groups	Support for key plan by key board members gained by pre-presentation 'softening-up' by planners	Action planning team formed, including original planners, but also key players from business unit and product group – rediscovering the wheel to gain 'ownership'. Advertising the new strategy in trade press read by company technologists and managers
Communications	Business Unit Board meeting Product Group Board meeting Main board meeting Salesforce conference	Informal meetings	Joint seminars in applying IT to this industry, involving business unit managers and key customers. Joint charity events for the industry's benevolent fund
Internal market targets	(1) Business unit management (2) Product group management (3) Salesforce		

Source: adapted from Piercy (2002).

This was exceptionally expensive, and some would argue that if the company had been able to see these hidden costs of organizational change at the outset they would have been well advised to abandon the apparently 'attractive' marketing strategy. However, while the process of change is continuing in this organization, managers do now speak of the 'cultural change' in the organization and there are tangible operating changes in how the two divisions work together. This suggests that the process of internal marketing and organizational change described above may have had the effect of creating new implementation capabilities for the future in this company, and this may be the primary long-term benefit created.

While the financial services example above is primarily 'top-down', the case in Table 21.3 concerns a computer company, where the marketing strategy was to adopt a vertical marketing approach to a small industry, where market share had been lost. This case is primarily concerned with the 'bottom-up' pressure by a group of managers in a large organization to pioneer and introduce a market-focused strategic plan for a particular customer's industry. This was seen as part of a more general need to move the whole of the organization from a technology orientation where the prime purpose was to sell 'boxes' (i.e. computers) to a customer orientation with a main purpose of producing customer business problem 'solutions'. Again, the internal marketing starts with formal presentations, but continues to informal communications and ways of dealing with the hostile reaction of the established business units to the weakening of their control over resources. Ultimately, implementation of the external vertical marketing strategy relied on building teams to take 'ownership' of the new strategy and to collaborate with key customers in a cultural transition from technology orientation to customer orientation (which is what the vertical marketing strategy was really about). One critical element of this was a programme of customer events, where a major objective was simply to expose senior company managers to

customers and their views! Again, the strategy was put in place with some limited degree of success, but at some substantial costs. It is still relatively early days with this strategy, but there has been some success – some market share has been regained at a difficult time for the industry; the industry-specific marketing activities have succeeded. However, far less has been achieved in the related issue of industry-specific products.

This suggests that in our present study of the marketing implementation issue, strategic internal marketing offers us three possible advantages:

1. It provides an operational framework for analysing the internal changes necessary to put the external marketing strategy into effect and for building an internal programme to achieve this.
2. As a framework it directly parallels conventional external marketing – in analysing the customers and building a marketing strategy and programme around them – and can be used at both an overt and relatively superficial level, but can also go deeper into the issues of process and culture in the organization, if this is necessary to get to the real implementation barriers and obstacles.
3. The strategic internal marketing framework offers us a way of evaluating the costs of implementation and organizational change early enough that we can decide whether or not to pursue the external strategy in question.

Conclusions

There can be little doubt that one of the major challenges facing marketing analysts in an era of market turbulence and reinvented organizations is the construction and development of better approaches to the implementation of marketing plans and strategies. We saw initially that this area is not simply problematic in its own right, but that it is further complicated by the tendency of planners and analysts to separate the implementation issue from the process of generating exciting and innovative marketing strategies. It is this dichotomy between strategy formulation and implementation issues which lies at the heart of many of the implementation failures that marketing executives describe. The simple fact is that implementation *is* strategy, and no marketing plan or strategy which does not explicitly, realistically and in detail address the implementation issue can possibly be regarded as satisfactorily completed. However, it is equally important that the way we address implementation issues should go beyond the simple issuing of instructions and building of detailed action plans (although that may follow). What we are seeking is the development of convincing and operational implementation strategies in marketing.

We introduced the notions of implementation capabilities and 'organizational stretch' to describe the issues that managers must confront in building strategy implementation approaches. These issues highlight the importance of understanding the organizational context in which marketing must be implemented. We saw that the organizational positioning of marketing may be weak (probably leading to weak strategy implementation capabilities). However, the future of the marketing organization in the process-based organization and the hollow or network organization is even more uncertain. We argued that radical organizational changes will place even higher priorities on understanding and sustaining implementation capabilities.

The price of ignoring the implementation issue, or treating it as simply tactical, may be considerable in terms of the costs of failed plans and strategies, missed opportunities to exploit competitive advantages, and the damage caused by ignoring the real workings of the infrastructure of the organization which we hope will put our marketing strategies into effect. These are not easy issues to resolve, but we described several ways in which progress may be made:

- By recognizing the degree of organizational stretch that a new strategy represents.
- By putting implementation into the context of the organizational realities of a weaker marketing paradigm, process-based management and new types of structure.
- By focusing attention on the issues with highest priority through the evaluation of strategic gaps.
- By examining the reasons for those strategic gaps in terms of implementation barriers and the match between our strategies and the characteristics of the company.
- By using the strategic internal marketing framework as an operational method for dealing with these issues realistically.

The evaluation of strategic gaps asked us to identify the marketing strategy we are pursuing (or wish to pursue) in a given market, and to identify what we have to achieve in marketing programme elements and strategic position for that strategy to become real. This strategic intent is then contrasted with strategic reality (i.e. what we have actually achieved in practical marketing and positioning) to identify strategic gaps. The most revealing part of the exercise is in attempting to identify the reasons for the strategic gaps we have identified – the strategy, its translation into practical operational marketing terms, or the ability of the organization to successfully deliver that strategic intent into the real marketplace.

Pursuing that latter questioning into the underlying reasons for implementation barriers raises further issues, such as:

- The acceptance by key people of the existence of marketing problems that need to be solved, compared to their willingness to change and learn new ways of doing business, suggesting the need for different implementation approaches.
- Comparing the marketing strategy and the company's execution skills as relative contributors to implementation problems – and testing the key attributes of the strategy.

None of these are complete or universal approaches to the implementation issue, but all are capable of generating insights and a better understanding of what is necessary for marketing strategies to be effectively implemented.

This leads finally to the consideration of internal marketing strategy as a framework for building and applying a marketing implementation strategy. The attraction of this framework is that it mirrors and parallels the conventional external marketing strategy, and allows us to use the same terms and analytical methods with the critical internal customers that we are accustomed to use with the conventional external customers. However, we noted that the source of the internal marketing model is in the services field, where internal marketing is largely concerned with improving the performance of operational employees at the point of sale. In this present context, internal marketing is a different and strategic issue, which is concerned with identifying and acting on those things and people which have to change inside the company for the external strategy to be effectively implemented. We examined some cases of internal marketing strategy in companies to make the further point that there are different organizational levels at which internal marketing may operate. While it may be easiest to see internal marketing operating at the formal level – where the product is the plan or strategy, the price is the cost of change, and communication and distribution are about formal communications – it is perhaps even more important to see internal marketing operating at the deeper level of the decision-making processes and cultural attributes of the organization. It is only in this way that we can get beyond the production of simple action plans and directives, and confront the underlying pressures towards maintaining the status quo, organizational inertia and 'defensive routines' to avoid change – i.e. the real implementation issues in our organizations.

There are no simple and easy-to-apply methods to deal with the implementation issue in marketing. It is hoped that the approaches suggested here may be useful at the operational level. Nonetheless, the implementation issue remains one of the greatest practical and theoretical challenges for the marketing analyst, consultant, teacher and practitioner for the future.

References

Achrol, R. S. (1991) Evolution of the marketing organization: new forms for turbulent environments, *Journal of Marketing*, **55**(4), 77–94.

Aldrich, H. and Herker, D. (1977) Boundary spanning roles and organizational structure, *Academy of Management Review*, **2**, April, 217–230.

Argyris, C. (1985) *Strategy, Change and Defensive Routines*, Harper & Row, New York.

Berthon, P., Hulbert, J. M. and Pitt, L. F. (1997) *Brands, Brand Managers, and the Management of Brands*, Marketing Science Institute, Boston, MA, Report No. 97–122.

Bonoma, T. V. (1985) *The Marketing Edge: Making Strategies Work*, Free Press, New York.

Bonoma, T. V. and Clark, B. (1990) Assessing marketing performance, in Bonoma, T. V. and Kosnik, T. J. (eds), *Marketing Management: Text and Cases*, Irwin, Homewood, IL.

Cespedes, F. V. and Piercy, N. F. (1996) Implementing marketing strategy, *Journal of Marketing Management*, **12**, 135–160.

Cravens, D. W and Piercy, N. F. (2002) *Strategic Marketing*, 7th edn, Irwin/McGraw-Hill, New York.

Cravens, D. W., Piercy, N. F. and Shipp, S. H. (1996) New organizational forms for competing in highly dynamic environments: the network paradigm, *British Journal of Management*, **7**, 203–218.

Cravens, D. W., Greenley, G., Piercy, N. F. and Slater, S. (1997) Integrating contemporary strategic management perspectives, *Long Range Planning*, **30**, 493–506.

Darling, J. R. and Taylor, R. E. (1989) A model for reducing internal resistance to change in a firm's international marketing strategy, *European Journal of Marketing*, **23**(7), 34–41.

Day, G. S. (1997) Aligning the organization to the market, in Lehman, D. R. and Jocz, K. E. (eds), *Reflections on the Futures of Marketing*, Marketing Science Institute, Cambridge, MA, pp. 67–98.

Gummesson, E. (1991) Marketing-orientation revisited: the crucial role of the part-time marketer, *European Journal of Marketing*, **25**(2), 60–75.

Hamel, G. and Prahalad, C. K. (1989) Strategic intent, *Harvard Business Review*, May/June, 63–76.

Hulbert, J. M., Capon, N. and Piercy, N. F. (2003) *Total Integrated Marketing*, Free Press, New York, forthcoming.

Hutt, M. D., Reingen, P. H. and Ronchetto, J. R. (1988) Tracing emergent processes in marketing strategy formation, *Journal of Marketing*, **52**(1), 4–19.

Mintzberg, H. (1988) Opening up the definition of strategy, in Quinn, J. B., Mintzberg, H. and James, R. M. (eds), *The Strategy Process*, Prentice-Hall International, London.

Morgan, N. and Piercy, N. F. (1996) Competitive advantage, quality strategy and the role of marketing, *British Journal of Management*, **7**, 231–245.

Pfeffer, J. (1981) *Power in Organizations*, Pitman, Marshfield, MA.

Piercy, N. F. (1985) *Marketing Organisation: An Analysis of Information Processing, Power and Politics*, Allen & Unwin, London.

Piercy, N. F. (1986) The role and function of the chief marketing executive and the marketing department, *Journal of Marketing Management*, **1**(3), 265–289.

Piercy, N. F. (1987) The marketing budgeting process, *Journal of Marketing*, **51**, January, 45–59.

Piercy, N. F. (1990) Marketing concepts and actions: implementing marketing-led strategic change, *European Journal of Marketing*, **24**(2), 24–42.

Piercy, N. F. (1995) Customer satisfaction and the internal market: marketing our customers to our employees, *Journal of Marketing Practice: Applied Marketing Science*, **1**(1), 22–44.

Piercy, N. F. (1998a) Barriers to implementing relationship marketing: analysing the internal marketplace, *Journal of Strategic Marketing*, **6**(3), 209–222.

Piercy, N. F. (1998b) Marketing implementation: the implications of marketing paradigm weakness for the strategy execution process, *Journal of the Academy of Marketing Science*, **26**(3), 222–236.

Piercy, N. F. (2002) *Market-Led Strategic Change: A Guide To Transforming the Process of Going To Market*, 3rd edn, Butterworth-Heinemann, Oxford.

Piercy, N. F. and Cravens, D. W. (1995) The network paradigm and the marketing organization, *European Journal of Marketing*, **29**(3), 7–34.

Piercy, N. and Morgan, N. (1990) Internal marketing strategy: leverage for managing marketing-led strategic change, *Irish Marketing Review*, **4**(3), 11–28.

Piercy N. and Morgan, N. (1991) Internal marketing – the missing half of the marketing programme, *Long Range Planning*, **24**(2), 82–93.

Piercy, N. F. and Morgan, N. (1993) Strategic and operational market segmentation – a managerial analysis, *Journal of Strategic Marketing*, **1**, 123–140.

Piercy, N. F. and Morgan, N. (1994) The marketing planning process: behavioral problems compared to analytical techniques in explaining marketing plan credibility, *Journal of Business Research*, **29**, 167–178.

Piercy, N. F. and Morgan, N. (1996) Customer satisfaction measurement and management: a processual analysis, *Journal of Marketing Management*, **11**, 817–834.

Ruekert, R. W. and Walker, O. (1987) Marketing's interaction with other function units: a conceptual framework and empirical evidence, *Journal of Marketing*, **51**(1), 1–19.

Schultz, D. E. (1997) Integration is critical for success in the 21st century, *Marketing News*, 15 September, pp. 26.

Sheth, J. N. (1994) Relationship marketing: a customer perspective, Relationship Marketing Conference, Emory University, Atlanta, June.

Spekman, R. E. (1979) Influence and information: an exploratory investigation of the boundary person's basis of power, *Academy of Management Journal*, **22**(1), 104–117.

Stewart, T. (1998) *Intellectual Capital*, Bantam Books, New York.

Ulrich, D. (1989) Tie the corporate knot: gaining complete customer commitment, *Sloan Management Review*, Summer, 19–27.

Walker, O. C. and Ruekert, R. W. (1987) Marketing's role in the implementation of business strategies: a critical review and conceptual framework, *Journal of Marketing*, **51**, July, 15–33.

Webster, F. E. (1992) The changing role of marketing in the corporation, *Journal of Marketing*, **56**, October, 1–17.

Webster, F. E. (1997) The future role of marketing in the organization, in Lehman, D. R. and Jocz, K. E. (eds), *Reflections on the Futures of Marketing*, Marketing Science Institute, Cambridge, MA, pp. 39–66.

Further reading

Bonoma, T. V. (1985) *The Marketing Edge: Making Strategies Work*, Free Press, New York. This is now almost the classic treatise on the marketing implementation issue. Based on executive company case and interview research, it contains many insights and frameworks for analysing the implementation issue in marketing.

Cespedes, F. V. (1991) *Organizing and Implementing the Marketing Effort*, Addison-Wesley, Reading, MA. This is an excellent attempt to relate organizational context to the problems of making marketing effective, with a wealth of case material in support. It also provides some valuable literature reviews on a broad base, concerned with marketing implementation and organizational change.

Cespedes, F. V. and Piercy, N. F. (1996) Implementing marketing strategy, *Journal of Marketing Management*, **12**, 135–160. A theoretical review of the underlying organizational problems in implementation, going deeper into certain of these issues.

Cespedes, F. V. and Piercy, N. F. (1996) Implementation of strategy, in Warner, M. (ed.), *International Encyclopaedia of Business and Management*, Routledge, London. A more detailed and broader review of strategy implementation which has many implications for marketing in the context of strategic management.

Cravens, D. W., Piercy, N. F. and Shipp, S. H. (1996) New organizational forms for competing in highly dynamic environments: the network paradigm, *British Journal of Management*, **7**, 203–218. This article discusses the emergence of new alliance and network-based organizational forms to cope with new marketing environments, and reflects on the implications for strategy implementation.

Cravens, D. W., Greenley, G., Piercy, N. F. and Slater, S. (1997) Integrating contemporary strategic management perspectives, *Long Range Planning*, **30**, 493–506. This article reviews the sources of market-based strategic management and the reinvented organizations emerging in diverse markets.

Giles, W. D. (1991) Making strategy work, *Long Range Planning*, **24**(5), 75–91. This is an excellent summary of the conclusions reached by Giles as a result of many years' practical experience as a marketing manager and consultant, and confronts the underlying implementation issue through re-examining the characteristics of marketing planning as a process.

Möller, K. and Rajala, A. (1999) Organizing marketing in industrial high-tech firms: the role of internal marketing relationships, *Industrial Marketing Management*, **28**, 521–535. An insightful study into the dismantling of traditional marketing departments in favour of a relatively large number of marketing-related units and structures. The development of these internal marketing units and co-ordinating them poses a management challenge for the future.

Piercy, N. (1994) Marketing implementation: analysing structure, information and process, in Saunders, J. (ed.), *The Marketing Initiative*, Prentice-Hall, Hemel Hempstead. This is an attempt to integrate the theoretical and empirical sources of the author's approach to the implementation question, examining research works on the organization of marketing in the UK, information and intelligence systems characteristics, and the operation of budgeting and planning processes in marketing, leading to central questions about achieving the implementation of marketing strategies and the potential role of internal marketing.

Piercy, N. (1998) Marketing implementation: the implications of marketing paradigm weakness for the strategy execution process, *Journal of the Academy of Marketing Science*, **26**(3), 222–236. A study of the implementation issue as it is developing in modern organizations, where the marketing concept competes for management attention with other conflicting paradigms like the lean enterprise, from an increasingly weak organizational position. Concludes that marketing in the future must focus on organizational stretch and acquire a new vocabulary to enumerate and defend marketing capabilities.

Piercy, N. (2002) *Market-Led Strategic Change: A Guide To Transforming the Process of Going to Market*. This book, in its third edition in 2002, represents an attempt to put marketing into this context of the process of going to market, rather than a marketing department. This places the issue of strategy implementation and strategic change in marketing with the new context of cross-functional and intra-organizational value-creating processes, which underpin the achievement of customer focus and developing superior customer value. The book describes a strategic pathway comprising: market sensing and customer focus, key market choices, the development of a value proposition, and the management of a network of key relationships (with customers, collaborators, competitors and co-workers). Accompanying material to the book provides worksheets and diagnosis for managers and students to use in confronting the implementation and change problems that the companies face. The material is supported by an extensive Tutor's Manual.

Walker, O. C. and Ruekert, R. W. (1987) Marketing's role in the implementation of business strategies: a critical review and conceptual framework, *Journal of Marketing*, **51**, July, 15–33. An important, if somewhat theoretical, treatment of the implementation issue in marketing, which emphasizes different perspectives on the problem and develops propositions about the organizational structures and processes best suited for implementing different types of strategy.

Part Four
The Application of Marketing

CHAPTER 22

What are direct marketing and interactive marketing?

GRAEME McCORKELL

Introduction

More than 30 years after Lester Wunderman first called it 'direct marketing', experienced marketing people still argue about what direct marketing is. Some even prefer to give it another name, such as 'relationship marketing'.

In this chapter, we attempt to set the record straight and discuss the essential similarities and differences between direct and interactive marketing.

We look at the origins of direct marketing as a method of distribution, its adoption by multichannel users and how its disciplines underpin interactive marketing. We discuss the four basic principles of direct marketing: *targeting*, *interaction*, *control* and *continuity*.

Finally, we introduce the direct and interactive marketer's information system, establishing its context within the company-wide information system.

Selling direct to the end customer

From its humble beginnings in the mail order business, computer power helped direct marketing to become a sophisticated method of distribution, combining economies of scale with an ability to track the purchase and payment behaviour of customers on a one-to-one basis. As recently as the 1980s Stan Rapp, the US pioneer, defined direct marketing as a *method of distribution*, although it is now defined more broadly.

> Direct marketing is a method of distribution . . . in which the transactions are completed between buyer and seller . . . without the intervention of a sales person or retail outlet.
> Stan Rapp, when CEO of Rapp & Collins

The term 'direct marketing' was first used in 1961. It was the brainchild of another American pioneer, Lester Wunderman. This term caught on because it was more inclusive than 'mail order'. It included a new method of ordering – by telephone – and marketing methods, such as magazine subscription and continuity publishing (book and music series), that did not readily come to mind under the heading of mail order.

Many would agree that direct distribution remains direct marketing's most important function. However, the lessons learned from direct distribution experience have enabled the principles of direct marketing to be applied to every kind of business.

To understand direct marketing, it is crucial to recognize that its beginnings were in mail order, not in direct mail.

Direct mail is simply one (very important) marketing communications medium used by direct marketers. Confusion between direct marketing and direct mail has been caused by their close relationship and by the similarity of the terms. In attempts to avoid confusion, direct marketing practitioners have invented or borrowed a variety of alternative names for direct marketing, including *database marketing*, *data-driven marketing* and *relationship marketing*. Nevertheless, Wunderman's 'direct marketing' remains the most popular name.

Looking again at Stan Rapp's definition of direct marketing, could it be applied to e-commerce?

Well, why not? The definition does not specify any particular choice of medium to replace the salesperson or shop. It could be a printed catalogue, a website, an e-mail, a press advertisement or a radio commercial.

Furthermore, successful practitioners agree that the same principles and disciplines apply. Nearly eight years before his company *jungle.com* went live in August 1999, Steve Bennett had founded Software Warehouse, a major *direct marketer* of computer software. Steve says (*Internet Business*, January 2001):

> The Internet is just a new front end. Everything at the back end, like delivery and logistics, is as it was before.
> Steve Bennett, founder of jungle.com

In September 2000, GUS bought jungle.com, a £75 million turnover software, music and video business, for £37 million. GUS was Britain's largest *direct marketing group*. 'It has half a dozen great catalogue brands and was always the business we tried to learn from,' said Steve Bennett.

In 1994, the year Michael Dell launched his first website, the Dell Direct call centre was already receiving nearly 50 000 calls from customers daily. Even then, Dell was the world's largest *direct marketer* of computers.

Firms that deal direct

Like First Direct and easyJet, Dell is a pure direct marketer, dealing with its customers through its websites and call centres. Home shopping companies, like La Redoute, provide another example.

The logic for dealing direct is based on efficiency – stripping out overheads or unproductive running costs. Such costs can include bricks-and-mortar outlets, salesforces, dealer margins, large stockholdings and so on. The direct model works for both business-to-consumer (B2C) and business-to-business (B2B) applications. In fact, Dell's customers range from large corporations, such as Barclays Bank, to individuals ordering from home. A particular advantage of the direct model is that it can reduce the cost of international expansion (Table 22.1).

A point to note is that it is not only producers of goods or services that conform to the direct model. First Direct, easyJet and Dell are all producers. But La Redoute is a pure retailer, not making any of the clothes or other items that it sells. The insurance company, Direct Line, is a producer. But direct insurance brokers, sourcing policies from a large number of insurers, are not producers.

Furthermore, Dell may sell software and peripherals that it does not produce. In fact, Dell's chief production job is to assemble components made elsewhere. Thus, the direct model can work for retailers providing that it increases retailing efficiency or makes buying easier or more attractive.

Interest in the direct model has been given a huge boost by the Internet, fostering the development of new types of direct business, including:

- *Virtual exchanges* – for example, Covisint, the world's largest B2B automotive marketplace.
- *On-line auctions* and *reverse auctions*, such as priceline.com.
- *Infomediaries*, *search services* and *buying clubs*.

Table 22.1	The direct model	
Features	*Benefits*	*Examples*
On-line, fax, telephone and mail transactions	Lower overheads	First Direct
Catalogues and websites	Cuts out middlemen	easyJet
	Faster stock turn	Dell
	Facilitates exporting	La Redoute

These entirely new types of organization are not controlled by sellers. They are either neutral or working for buyers.

The Internet has the potential to increase the efficiency of the direct model exponentially through a reduction in transaction costs and materials sourcing costs, superior supply chain management and a greatly enhanced ability to tailor the product to the buyer's specification. In principle, it is immaterial whether access is achieved through a PC, iTV or a mobile phone. In practice, the 'front end' can affect the quantity and quality of the information that can be exchanged.

To the customer, the direct model is not always the answer. Many people prefer to go to the shops or send for a sales representative. In fact, our channel preferences are likely to depend on what we are buying. Many companies find multichannel marketing pays.

Multichannel marketing

Multichannel marketers also use direct marketing. Earlier we referred to GUS, the buyers of jungle.com. GUS is a multichannel retailer selling through catalogues, websites and its Argos stores.

Tesco is a multichannel retailer, although its website sales are dwarfed by its store-based sales. Producers, too, may use multiple sales channels. GM (Vauxhall) and Ford sell (a few) cars directly to private motorists on the web. IBM sells direct and through dealers. British Airways sells direct and through agents. Magazine publishers, such as *The Economist* and *Reader's Digest*, sell both through newsagents and through direct subscription. Charities raise funds through direct mail, through charity shops, through events and through street collections.

Some companies have spawned direct brands. Prudential insurance launched Egg as a direct brand. First Direct is, of course, a subsidiary of HSBC. Direct Line is owned by the Royal Bank of Scotland.

Home shopping catalogues have diversified both to website trading and to high street retailing. Lakeland and Past Times are examples. Next is an example of a high street retailer spawning a home shopping business.

For most of these companies, the logic of stripping out costs by conforming exclusively to a direct model does not work. They do better by offering customers a wider choice of ways to deal with them. In a few cases differential pricing may be used, magazine subscription being a prime example, but in most cases the pricing is the same and the inventory is much the same.

Next believes that its catalogue and website assist shop sales and vice versa. By offering customers the widest possible choice of ways to browse and buy, they maximize the return on their marketing investment.

Direct marketing is more than selling direct

All of the companies we have named use direct marketing and not just when they are selling through their mailings, catalogues and websites. Direct marketing has come to mean more than just selling direct.

Any company that uses direct response advertising, on-line or off-line, and maintains a customer database, is using direct marketing.

Tesco would remain a major direct marketer if it scrapped its website tomorrow. Tesco maintains a huge customer database (Clubcard) and tailors offers to its customers, through personalized direct mail, based on their past purchasing behaviour (Table 22.2).

Magnetic-strip cards like Clubcard enable retailers to link customer identities with purchases and use the data to offer the customer rewards, offers, events and service which, to all intents and purposes, are tailored to the customer's needs and preferences. Although more than 10 million people receive quarterly Clubcard mailings, there are many thousands of variations to these mailings, reflecting customers' different shopping patterns.

Even though the vast majority of Clubcard members visit Tesco to do their shopping, this is still termed direct marketing because the programme is based on the collection of shop visit and purchase data, and careful analysis of individual customer preferences. The activity may also be termed relationship marketing or even loyalty marketing. Of these terms, direct marketing is the most meaningful, being capable of precise definition.

Table 22.2   Tesco Clubcard

History, operation and scale

Tested October 1993, launched nationally February 1995.
Card applications in-store, communications in-store and direct mail.
Over 200 million product purchases a day by over 10 million customers.

Customer information and applications

Customer data:

Visit patterns	Spend levels
Departmental usage	Types of purchases
Coupon users/non-users	Profile/geographic data

Broad customer typologies:

Loyalists	Infrequent customers
Regulars	New customers

Applications include:

Recruitment	Lapsed and win back
Clubcard Plus (savings card)	Helpline
Local marketing	

Direct marketing: a new definition

For a more recent definition than Stan Rapp's, we turn to my book *Direct and Database Marketing* (1997):

> Direct marketing is the process in which individual customers' responses and transactions are recorded ... and the data used to inform the targeting, execution and control of actions ... that are designed to start, develop and prolong profitable customer relationships.

This definition is at once broader and narrower than that of Stan Rapp. It is broader in the sense that it applies to any kind of business capable of recognizing individual transactions with its customers. It is narrower to the extent that it is confined to a specific business process.

Could this more recent definition also be applied to e-commerce? Let's take it apart to see.

> Direct marketing is the process in which individual customers' responses and transactions are recorded.

As with Rapp's definition, mine does not specify the media through which customers' responses and transactions are invited or received. In fact, a customer might spot a bargain on a website, make further enquiries by telephone and complete the transaction at a dealership. If the item purchased were a second-hand car, such a scenario would be very likely.

In the definition, *customers' responses are recorded*. If the car dealership did not bother to do this, then the process would not qualify as direct marketing. On the other hand, the form of response is not specified – for example, the data could include clickstream data as readily as phone calls or posted coupons.

> ... and the data used to inform the targeting, execution and control of actions ...

Note that the definition does not specify any interval between recording the data and using

them. It may often apply to data stored on a customer database and used months later (as in the Tesco Clubcard example), but it can equally apply to data used in *real time* during a telephone call or website visit.

In fact, the use of profile, preference and purchase data in real time was pioneered in call centre software before the WorldWide Web was used for marketing. An early example was (and still is) car insurance quotations. The quote given to the caller is driven by the answers to scripted questions. A later example is add-on offers triggered by home shopping orders (e.g. matching accessories). In this case, no questions are asked to prompt the offer – it is driven by the content of the customer's order.

Again, the nature of the actions is not specified – they could include:

- restricting a mailed invitation to the best customers;
- targeting new customers who match the profile of the best-established customers; or
- personalizing a website to make relevant offers to previous visitors.

The purpose of the actions is clearly specified:

> ... that are designed to start, develop and prolong profitable customer relationships.

This part of the definition excludes no business with expectations of success. However, the idea that customer data collection and analysis are the key to success was peculiar to direct marketing – although management consultancies and customer relationship management (CRM) software vendors now also claim ownership of it.

Direct marketing and Pareto's principle

If Thomas Jefferson (... all men are created equal) was the hero of mass marketing, Vilfredo Pareto is the hero of direct marketing. Pareto's principle (of the distribution of incomes) was that 80 per cent would end up in 20 per cent of pockets however society attempted to regulate matters. To Pareto, whether all men are created equal or not, they certainly don't end up that way.

So it is with customers. Every direct marketer knows that some customers are much more valuable than others. Every astute direct marketer knows who the valuable ones are. The really smart direct marketer has a system for forecasting who the valuable ones are going to be.

Why is this so important? Let's consider two examples.

Customers who cost money

Typically, 75 per cent of new customers gained by a home shopping business will have lapsed without providing enough business to recover the cost of recruiting them. All of the profit will be contributed by the remaining 25 per cent.

If the company learns which are the best sources of good customers, it can work to reduce the 75 per cent of loss-making intake. If it fails to learn, the 75 per cent will become 80 or 85 per cent, ensuring that the company loses money.

Again, typically, a bank will lose money on at least 80 per cent of its private customer base at any one time. By devoting special attention to the remaining 20 per cent, it can expect to satisfy more of them and so keep their custom. If it fails to differentiate between its good (and potentially good) customers and its loss-making customers, it is the good customers who are most likely to defect.

Figure 22.1 shows a real life example of segmentation of charity donors based on their response to the last appeal made to them.

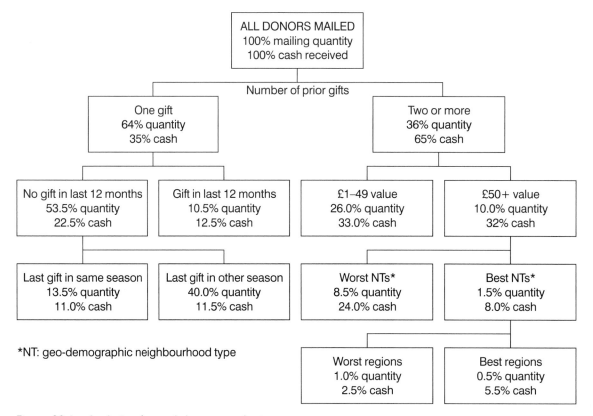

Figure 22.1   Analysis of postal donors to charity

Figure 22.1 displays the result of applying a statistical model called CHAID (CHi-squared Automatic Interaction Detector). This is also sometimes called tree segmentation. Here we are using CHAID to analyse the results of our last mailed appeal. We want CHAID to tell us how to recognize the differences between our most generous donors and our less generous donors. In particular, we would like to know who – if anyone – not to mail next time around.

CHAID splits the mailing base (all donors) into two, by picking out the most important of all the discriminatory variables that distinguish the best donors from the others. This variable turns out to be the number of previous gifts. The 36 per cent who have sent us two or more previous donations contributed 65 per cent of the money. This result is shown near the top of Figure 22.1.

Looking further down, we can see that CHAID keeps on dividing each segment into two, like an amoeba in a Petri dish. Each time it takes the most significant of the remaining discriminatory variables. What CHAID is answering each time is:

> Of all the differences between the more generous and less generous donors in this segment, which is the most important single difference?

Looking at the left-hand side of the model, we see that the least generous 40 per cent of donors contributed only 11.5 per cent of the cash received. The model demonstrates that 88.5 per cent of the cash could have been raised from 60 per cent of the donors by not mailing single gift donors who had been inactive for over 12 months and who last gave at a different time of the year.

If we assume it cost £1 in mailing expense to raise £4 in cash, the overall result from 100 000 donors would be £400 000 raised at a cost of £100 000. However, the least responsive 40 000 would have cost £40 000 to mail and brought in only £46 000 cash. We might decide to send an appeal to these donors only once a year, at Christmas time, when they are most likely to respond. Meanwhile, the other 60 000 donors sent back £354 000 – almost £6 for every £1 of expense.

Sending our appeal to these donors only would improve our income to expense ratio by almost 50 per cent.

The direct marketer looks for solutions by listening to what the data say. As always in direct marketing, actions speak loudest. What people do matters more than their demographic, socio-economic or lifestyle profile.

B2B = Pareto × Pareto

However strongly Pareto's principle applies to B2C marketing, the B2B scene is Pareto squared, one company having 10 000 times the purchasing power of another. So companies differentiate between larger (corporate) customers and smaller customers. Frequently call centres or contact centres (Internet empowered call centres able to deal with telephone and e-mail queries and orders from website visitors) deal with smaller business customers while field sales teams deal with larger customers.

Dell prefers to deal with all customers through its websites but differentiates by offering restricted (extranet) *PremierPages* extending many extra tailored informational services to large corporate customers on a one-to-one basis (see Chaffey *et al.*, 2000, p. 156).

Principles of direct marketing

Direct marketing and its information systems focus on what the customer or prospect does. To put it another way, information about past behaviour is used to predict future behaviour. This information is processed on an individual basis and can be analysed and acted upon on an individual basis, even if the number of customers reaches millions. This does not render marketing research obsolete but, if we can rely only on marketing research information, we are forced to make assumptions about customer behaviour which may be generally right but may be wrong in an individual case.

Successful direct marketing practice depends on four elements. These are: targeting, interaction, control and continuity.

Targeting, interaction, control and continuity (TICC)

As can be seen in Figure 22.2, the four elements of successful direct marketing can be looked at either as four triangles or alternatively as one triangle inside another. Interaction is in the centre. Interaction includes the stimuli we marketers create in the hope of producing a response from the people in our target market. Their response is also included in the inter-action triangle. In all cases we will attempt to attribute a response to the correct stimulus. Thus, the results of our activities form the core of our information system and enable us to become progressively more efficient at targeting, control and continuity. That is because we are learning by experience.

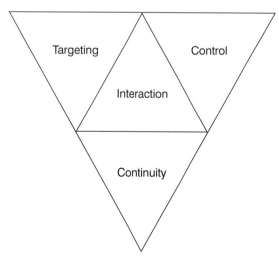

Figure 22.2   Targeting, interaction, control and continuity (TICC)

Interaction takes centre stage in direct marketing's information system.

Targeting refers to our decisions on who will receive our message and includes our media selection: TV, banner ads, print advertising, direct mail, telemarketing, e-mail and so on. We may be targeting our established customers, identified prospects or a much larger audience of 'suspects'. In all of these cases our targeting decisions will generally outweigh in importance decisions about what to offer and how to frame our message. By examining the results of our previous attempts to target correctly, we can keep on refining our future targeting.

Control is the management of our marketing. It includes setting objectives, planning at the strategic and operational levels, budgeting and assessment of results. The process is cyclical, future planning being informed by past results.

Interaction is at the heart of direct marketing. The completeness and accuracy of our data within the interaction triangle will be crucial to the exercise of control. Interaction quantifies the *effects* of our marketing.

Continuity is about retaining customers, cross-selling other products to them and uptrading them. In the vast majority of business enterprises, the bulk of profit arises from dealings with established customers.

Our painstaking care in recording inter-actions enables us to communicate with customers, recognizing their interest and showing appreciation of their custom. The special challenge of e-commerce and of contact centre management is to respond to customers in real time.

Customer interactions

These may not just be orders. They may be returns (of unwanted goods), queries, complaints, requests, suggestions, questionnaire responses and so on.

All four of the TICC elements are critical. Direct marketing is not direct marketing unless they are all in place. Sometimes it is not possible to data capture the identity of every customer and sometimes it is necessary to record the transactions of a sample of customers only. These conditions apply in FMCG (fast moving consumer goods) markets. Nevertheless, if the four TICC elements are in place, it is possible to employ direct marketing methods in these markets.

What is interactive marketing?

Interactive marketing is direct marketing through new media. The intention of direct marketing has always been interaction, if only in soliciting and receiving enquiries and orders by post and fulfilling these requests. Indeed, we have just discussed interaction as one of the four essential elements of direct marketing.

So why refer to new media direct marketing as anything but direct marketing? There are two reasons. Firstly, interactive marketing has already developed a language of its own because most of its pioneers never connected what they were doing with direct marketing. The thinking went, 'Here is a new medium, so we must invent a new way of marketing for it.' Most of those who did are no longer in business, whereas those who applied direct marketing principles and expertise to the new media have done much better. Remember the words of Steve Bennett?

> The Internet is just a new front end. Everything at the back end, like delivery and logistics, is as it was before.

A new front end

To work effectively, the new front requires the same disciplines that work in all direct marketing.

- The advertising agency creative asks, 'How can I make this brand famous?'

- The direct marketer asks, 'How can I make my next offer irresistible?'

There's no need to guess who will pull most customers in. We know from the results.

If you can remember them still, contrast the big dotcom spenders from 1998 and 1999 with the 1995 vintage cash burner, Amazon. The later entrants enriched the TV companies in senseless bids to make their names famous with ill-targeted and fatuous advertising that suggested no good reason to visit their websites.

Now what do you remember about Amazon? Here's a guess:

- Any book or CD you want.
- Fast delivery.
- Forty per cent off.

What you remember is what Amazon offers. And what more could you want? Well, if you are really demanding, Amazon also gives you reviews, an easy site to negotiate, personalized (tailor-made) suggestions on what you might like to read next, easy ordering, etc.

Like the 'make my brand famous' dotcoms who blew millions on untargeted TV, Amazon's high spending days are behind it. With a still growing business but a huge debt burden to carry, Amazon relies primarily on its affiliate marketing network to pull in new customers. You can visit amazon.co.uk to find out how to become an affiliate.

Affiliate marketing programmes

Affiliates place links on their websites to drive traffic to the merchant. They are rewarded by commission payments – usually a percentage of sales. Premium affiliate sites (including portals such as MSN) demand a tenancy fee as well as commission.

A similar idea was pioneered in direct marketing under the name of affinity group marketing. Direct marketers also pioneered PPI (payment per inquiry) deals with media owners many years ago.

The affiliate marketing programme is all on-line, so less audience wastage. Even now, many TV viewers lack access to the Internet. Furthermore, it is payment by results.

Many dotcoms have learned to their backers' cost that buying brand awareness on TV is not an affordable way to drive prospective customers to their websites. Accurate targeting is one of the four elements of successful direct marketing.

The case of buy.com

Buy.com launched on TV in the UK with a massive TV campaign. But before being bought by The John Lewis Partnership, buy.com was already using on-line promotion only; buy.com reported that customer acquisition costs had fallen to £40.

Thirty-eight per cent of site traffic (October 2000) was from buy.com's affiliate marketing programme. The cost of acquiring customers from the volume affiliate programme (i.e. the part of the programme in which no tenancy fees are paid) was only £5.

(Data from e.Business, February 2001)

The lessons learned by buy.com from costly experience illustrate the importance of interaction, the second TICC element, as the chief supplier of actionable marketing information. The classic direct marketing method is to buy this experience quickly and cheaply through testing the most sensible-looking alternatives. It is only because direct marketers record and analyse the results of interaction that low cost testing is possible.

After its expensive TV experience, buy.com started to exercise rigorous Control of its customer acquisition costs. Control is the third TICC element.

At this time the company may not yet know how much it can afford to pay to acquire a new customer. The return on its new customer investment will be learned through continuity

(the fourth TICC element) of customers' business. Forty pounds may be a reasonable price to pay for a new customer but it may well be too high. A lot may depend on how successful buy.com is in satisfying customers and encouraging them to come back for more.

The experienced direct marketer begins by making a calculation of how much he or she can afford to pay to acquire a new customer and this sets the target acquisition cost. The direct marketer then tracks the newly acquired customers to see if they are contributing the same amount of business as expected. The forecast of their lifetime value (LTV) will be adjusted on the basis of their first and second purchases.

Lifetime value (LTV)

The lifetime value of a new customer is the net present value of all future contributions to profit and overhead from that customer.

Is buy.com paying too much and, if so, can it reduce its costs? Time will tell.

If only 38 per cent of buy.com site visitors have clicked through from affiliate sites, where have the others come from? Some will have come through recommendation or idle surfing. Many may have come from banners, intersticials, site registrations or keywords. All these terms are strictly new media and describe opportunities that are exclusive to on-line marketing.

You will remember that one reason why interactive marketing is distinguished from other direct marketing is that it has developed its own vocabulary, being generally regarded as an activity that is quite distinct from direct marketing.

The second reason why interactive marketing deserves its own title is that the new media scene is technologically far more advanced, and offers the marketer challenges and opportunities that are without parallel. The impact of these changes is likely to transform marketing completely.

Ten ways in which interactive marketing is different

1 *The challenge of 24/7.* A trading website is always open. There is no downtime to restock, correct programming errors or repair broken links to other business systems.
2 *Marketing in real time.* A website deals with customers in real time, raising expectations of instant query resolution, immediate response to requests and even faster delivery. Furthermore, customer interaction data are being gathered continuously.
3 *Personalization.* Personalization of a website is very different from personalized print. It must be based on a variety of data sources (e.g. clickstream, personal data and previous purchases) and used within a single site visit if appropriate.
4 *Data volumes and integration.* A website can collect much higher volumes of data of different types than can be collected from other reception points. This poses a systems integration problem and a potentially crippling data volume problem.
5 *Many-to-many communications.* Customers do not phone call centres just for a chat. But the Internet is different. It is open, democratic and even revolutionary. The plus side may be *viral marketing.* The downside could be *flaming* (abusive replies).
6 *Comparison shopping.* Never was comparison shopping so easy. The pricing policy may need to be changed for interactive marketing. A new brand?
7 *Global reach.* The reach of the website may be wide but logistical or legal constraints may apply. It may be necessary to restrict orders geographically.
8 *Keeping in touch.* Unlike direct mail, e-mail can be time-sensitive, especially when sent to a business address. But, because e-mailing is so cheap, it is tempting to overuse it. It is easy to measure the response but not so easy to measure customers lost through irrelevant e-mailing (*spam*, the equivalent of *junk mail*).
9 *Low transaction costs.* The cost of handling on-line orders and information requests is much lower. This may permit lower ticket or lower margin transactions. However, credit card payment queries will be high and delivery costs will remain the same.
10 *A website is more like a shop than a catalogue.* Unlike a catalogue, a website cannot be sent to a list of prospective customers. Like a shop, it must wait for them to call in. Unlike a high street shop, it is not visible to passers-by. It needs promotion.

Can you think of any other ways in which a website is more like a shop than a catalogue? Here are two ideas:

1 Out-of-stock items (stockouts) cannot be deleted from a printed catalogue. They continue to occupy selling space and disappoint customers who try to order them. On the other hand, stockouts can be deleted from websites almost as readily as they disappear from stores.
2 The direct marketer can measure the sales performance of each page and position in the catalogue. But the lessons cannot be applied until the next printing. Furthermore, the cataloguer cannot follow the customer's route through the catalogue, making it harder to explain the sales performance of individual items.

The website designer can use clickstream data to track customers' journeys through the site and can relate these patterns to sales. Then the site layout can be altered to optimize performance. The store can make similar adjustments, although the data will rarely be so accurate or so complete.

Lands' End – the cyber model

A home shopping company for nearly 30 years and the world's most experienced Internet clothing retailer, Lands' End has found another way to make its US website more like a shop. You can have your own personal cyber model try on the garments that interest you to ensure they will fit.

Lands' End will mail you its catalogue even if you buy from their website. Some people prefer to browse in a printed catalogue and shop on-line, others enjoy the interactive website but order by phone. See point 10 under 'Ten ways in which interactive marketing is different'.

A last word about jargon

Viral marketing is the turbocharged Internet version of the direct marketers' referral programme or MGM (member-get-member) scheme. As customers congregate in newsgroups or chat by e-mail, recommendations can spread like a forest fire.

Personalization has a similar meaning in both direct and interactive marketing, but the possibilities are more exciting in a dynamic environment than in print.

Cookies are the small text files stored on your computer to enable the website to recognize it when you call again and record your clickstream. This enables personalization. However, unless you register separately, the website will think that all users of your computer are the same person.

Permission marketing is what direct marketers refer to as an 'opt-in' or positive option programme as opposed to an 'opt-out' or negative option programme.

The interactive success formula

At the Institute of Direct Marketing Symposium 2000, two case history presentations – both

success stories – appeared to point to opposite ways to make money from the web.

Dell showed success following from superior customer service and complete personalization, allowing customers to 'design' their own computers. The Internet and supporting extranets enabled superior customer service, making it unnecessary to compete on a pure price basis.

easyJet used the Internet's low transaction costs to offer a completely standardized product (low cost flights) at a lower than ever cost. Surely Dell and easyJet could not both be right? Yet each was highly successful.

The two companies, both successful direct marketers before trading on the Internet, are past masters of stripping out costs that do not add value. Dell has cut stockholdings to nearly zero by releasing sales data through the extranet to suppliers in real time, so that they can produce parts to order. Meanwhile, customers do all the work of specifying the computer and tracking its progress from assembly to delivery.

easyJet, using its own yield management system to maximize income from each flight, has eliminated wastage by promoting and releasing its schedule on-line only. easyJet has spun-off synergistic businesses, such as easy-Rentacar, at low marketing expense. Even the aircraft, bearing the website address, are travelling direct response ads. Compare and contrast with British Airways' disastrous £60 million adventure in 'masterbrand repositioning'.

Both Dell and easyJet are lean and mean marketers, a direct marketing characteristic.

The direct and interactive marketer's information system

It is essential that the direct and interactive marketing information system includes customer history data. The minimum history required is a history of the customer's transactions. Often this will be summarized, showing us little more than the value of each transaction, the product or the merchandise category and when it occurred.

Without this minimum amount of information, we cannot practise efficient direct marketing because:

> Direct marketing is the process in which … individual customers' responses and transactions are recorded … and the data used to inform the targeting, execution and control of actions … that are designed to start, develop and prolong profitable customer relationships.

Figure 22.3 makes the point graphically.

The components of response, measurement and continuity are common to all good direct marketing activity:

- *Response.* A response is needed to acquire a customer and to begin compiling data relating to that customer. It is very unusual to hear of a direct marketing initiative that does not have response as a key stage in the communication programme.

...Customers' responses are recorded

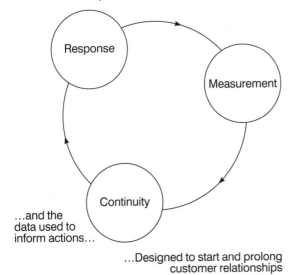

...and the data used to inform actions...

...Designed to start and prolong customer relationships

Figure 22.3 The process of direct marketing

- *Measurement.* This has always been central to direct marketing. Before cheap computing power became available, it was already possible to record and measure the immediate results of marketing expenditures. Reply coupons and telephone numbers included codes to identify the source of responses. Cost per response (CPR) and cost per sale (CPS) were and still are useful measures. Now measurement is extended to individual customers' activity. Because each customer is identified, their buying behaviour can be tracked over time. This enables the eventual return on marketing investments to be measured and forecasting to be improved.
- *Continuity.* This is the aim of every competent direct marketer who seeks to maximize the gearing on the customer acquisition investment by doing more business with the customer for a longer period.

The customer marketing database

An electronic library is needed to receive fresh data, keep them and make them accessible to maintain the continuous learning loop that characterizes direct marketing.

This is the customer marketing database system (Figure 22.4). It brings together information from a variety of sources and links the information to customers.

The database enables marketing costs to be reduced. This is achieved through using information derived from:

- the cost, number and value of new customers obtained by source;
- the results of contacts with established customers.

For example, it may cost twice as much to acquire customers from advertising in *The Economist* as in *The Times*. But the database may reveal that *Economist* readers buy more and stay longer, making them more profitable.

More business per customer is achieved through using customer purchase histories, leading to:

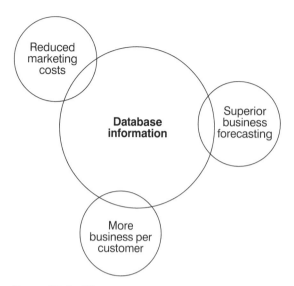

Figure 22.4   The customer marketing database

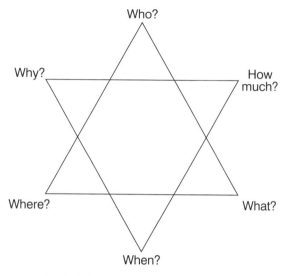

Figure 22.5   The customer marketing database answers six questions

- better identification and segmentation of customers;
- greater personalization and more relevant offers.

For example, customers giving high value orders and paying promptly may receive special treatment. Offers may reflect customers' specific interests.

Superior business forecasting is achieved by analysing campaign and customer history data, using past performance as a guide to future performance. Because the errors in past activities need not be repeated, efficiency should be subject to continuous improvement.

The database answers six questions

At its simplest, the database is the heart of an information system that answers the six simple questions shown in Figure 22.5 every time interaction occurs.

Who?

- name and contact data;
- status (e.g. customer or prospect);

- associations (i.e. same household or company as another customer);
- credit status (if relevant).

What?

- order or enquiry;
- item(s) ordered;
- product category;
- in stock/out of stock.

Where?

- sales channel;
- branch or media code.

The system should allocate a unique reference number (URN) or alphanumeric code to each customer. This enables customer queries to be answered all the more quickly, the URN guiding service and sales staff to the customer record or transaction details.

The system will recognize whether an order is a repeat order from an established customer or a first order from a new customer.

How much?

- the price of each item;
- gross order value;
- less out-of-stocks;
- less returns.

When?

- when last instruction/order received;
- when last instruction/order fulfilled.

Why?

- response/non-response to last promotion;
- identifying code of promotion causing response.

Not every system will contain transactional data because they won't always be available. For example, Lever Brothers would not have full transaction data for every Persil buyer, but would have promotional responses recorded on their database.

Business-to-business customer marketing data are often more extensive and complex. A company may have a number of identities (branches, departments, divisions) and a good many individual buyers or decision makers. A business customer may also use multichannels to secure supplies of different items. Purchases are increasingly likely to be automated, using EDI, Internet exchanges or an extranet.

Real time data

Websites and contact centres can, with the right software, respond to purchase data in real time. When a customer puts a Manchester United Annual in the shopping basket this may trigger the offer of a David Beckham biography.

Opportunistic marketing of this sort will be used in combination with offers or other special treatment that are driven by previously captured data.

Advantages of the database

A database exploiting transactional information tells the marketer everything about customers' purchases updated with each new response (and non-response).

For example, the transactional database:

- includes all customers, not just a sample or cross-section;
- gives customer value data: Recency, Frequency, Monetary value (RFM) of purchases culminating in the lifetime value (LTV) of each customer;
- tells us about new customers: what they responded to and, perhaps, which creative treatment appealed to them;
- tells us about lost, lapsed and inactive customers;
- tells us about who buys which products and/or responds to which types of incentive or message;
- gives continuous information which is automatically updated with each new transaction;
- reports upon, and analyses, marketing campaigns and tactics;
- facilitates controlled tests of alternatives, e.g. product and price comparisons;
- provides back data (historical data) which help the process of predicting the future behaviour of each and every customer.

Correctly used, a transactional customer database gives a running commentary on the marketer's ability to serve the needs of customers, highlighting opportunities to increase efficiency.

At one time car rental advertising was almost untargeted. But the direct marketer differentiates between customers and non-customers, then between casual customers and regular customers, and finally between regular customers and frequent customers. The example of the American car rental market shows why.

The top 25 per cent of customers are those who rent a car more than once. But within this exclusive group, one in 25 of them rent a car 10 times or more in a year. This group, amounting to one in 100 customers (0.2 per cent of adults) is worth 25 times as much as the average customer. These extremely valuable customers provide car rental companies with a quarter of their business.

Pareto and the database – American car rental market

- 20 per cent of American adults rent a car at least once a year.
- Only 5 per cent rent a car more than once.
- 0.2 per cent rent a car 10 or more times.
- This 0.2 per cent represents one in 100 customers.
- One in 100 customers provide car rental companies with one-quarter (25 per cent) of their business.

(Data from Peppers and Rogers, 1993)

It would be cheaper to telephone these customers personally to thank them than it would to reach them all once with a TV commercial.

Recognizing the value of these super-customers, car rental firms offered loyal users free rentals at weekends. But frequent business travellers want time with their families. When this idea failed, National Car Rental came up with a better idea. Targeting the tired, stressed and status-conscious business traveller, their answer was the Emerald Club, having its own aisle in National's car lot at the airport. Members could pick any car in the Emerald Aisle and drive off, pausing only to have their card 'swiped' at the checkout.

National's database enabled them to:

- recognize how much more valuable their best customers were than others;
- discover how much business was at risk if these customers were lost (it would take 33

average new customers to replace one lost top customer);
- recognize the circumstances of these customers, i.e. frequent business travellers;
- send Emerald cards to the right customers.

Notice that the database is used to provide both management information and the means of communicating to customers.

The customer marketing database serves two functions:

1. It provides management information.
2. It facilitates one-to-one customer communications outbound and inbound.

The customer marketing database not only facilitates outbound communications but enables customers to be recognized when they telephone or visit the website. The contact centre agent (operator) can call up the customer's transaction record on screen so that the customer does not have to repeat information that the company should already know.

Data warehousing, CRM and e-CRM

In recent years, many large companies have been dealing with the problem of integrating data from a multiplicity of management information systems. The ideal solution of bringing together all relevant customer information into one Customer Marketing Database System was not available to these companies. The systems they used in different parts of the business were incompatible.

Considering the categories in Figure 22.6 – Accounts, Sales, Marketing, Buying, Distribution, Customer service, Stock control and Credit control – we can see these might all provide information for the marketing database.

Because some of these functions were seen as completely separate in many large businesses, and may have become computerized at different times, their systems are unlikely to be fully compatible. They will certainly not be compatible with e-commerce systems. Old systems are referred to as *legacy* systems.

However, if essential details, such as file formats, are harmonized, it is possible to store data that would otherwise simply be archived in a data warehouse. Now, the data can be processed in such a way that they can be analysed by a competent person, using a PC.

The process of retrieving data for analysis from a data warehouse is called data mining. Data mining is often used in businesses with masses of transactional data, such as banks and airlines.

The idea of the data warehouse is to bring systems together to form an enterprise-wide management information system. In theory, at least, this permits a customer relationship management (CRM) system to be employed. The idea behind CRM is that the whole of a customer's dealings with the company can be put together. Such systems are devised by outside software vendors and may need extensive adaptation.

Figure 22.6 The data warehouse

the data warehouse, but contain only information that is relevant to the departmental interest and are designed to make the data easier to interrogate and analyse.

Integrating e-CRM

When the company's front office is a website, the volume of data being collected, processed and managed is very large. Some data, e.g. DNS (domain name system) and clickstream data, are peculiar to interactive marketing. The latter, particularly, can overwhelm a system unless it is *summarized*. It is not necessary to keep this information for individual customers as long as customer preferences, either declared or implicit through transactional behaviour, are recorded.

The whole customer

As well as having a current account and a savings account, a bank customer may deal with the home loan division, the life and general insurance divisions, the credit card division, and the personal investment management division. Since the average customer holds only 1.2 accounts, such a customer would be very valuable to the bank. Yet, before the creation of an enterprise-wide CRM system, the bank would not have recognized all of these different relationships as being with the same customer.

In practice, company divisions or departments (including marketing) may find their needs better served by data marts. These are fed by

---

When human interaction is by e-mail or chat, there is a full, self-generated digital record of the contact – unlike a phone call or field sales visit. This record may be used to auto-generate e-marketing contacts.

Summary data

The transactional database needs historical data. Otherwise there can be no record of a customer's business relationship with the company. Usually, the data used to portray a customer history (or the results of a promotion) are summarized, so that they don't occupy too much space (memory) in the system.

While this is very sensible, because it saves costs, the problem is that essential details are sometimes lost. Generally speaking, the number, value and dates of a customer's transactions will be retained but the merchandise categories and, certainly, the actual products purchased will often be lost for all except the most recent transaction. Furthermore, companies are usually bad at keeping customer service records. A marketing analyst can waste hours or days looking at customer profiles, seeking an explanation for why some customers are disloyal. The true explanation may lie elsewhere. Perhaps the disloyal customers ordered goods that were out of stock or had to return defective items.

Meanwhile, the sharp reduction in data storage and retrieval costs has encouraged firms to keep more raw data for analysis instead of summarizing them and archiving old data. This is a major benefit of data warehousing.

CRM and database marketing

Although enterprise-wide CRM systems may have grown out of database marketing (some would say call centre operations), they have become distanced from the marketing function.

- CRM systems are essentially operational whereas marketing database systems can exploit data that are downloaded from operational systems without disturbing them. Marketing database needs may be supplied by a data mart within a CRM system.
- The CRM system is generally seen as the software that automates the 'front office'. The front office includes the call or contact centre, the website and any other point of interaction between the company and its customers. Front office functions include service as well as sales.
- The impetus for the adoption of CRM has not necessarily been increased customer knowledge but cost cutting. Cost cutting is achieved by increasing productivity of customer-facing staff and by diverting transactions down completely automated routes.
- The CRM system may work in tandem with an ERP (enterprise resource planning) system that handles the back office functions. The emphasis is on operational efficiency.

CRM and relationship marketing

The very name 'customer relationship management' implies that customers are a resource that can be managed, like the supply chain and sales staff. Although CRM feeds off customer data, it is essentially neutral. It may be customer-focused in a marketing sense or it may be enterprise-focused, being employed to seek ways to save on customer service. It depends who is extracting actionable data and for what purpose. However, the fact that a common information system is being used throughout the organization is clearly advantageous.

The customer as relationship manager

Two features that are apparent in interactive marketing are transparency and customer empowerment. The US software producer, MicroMarketing, has devised software that enables customers to pull information out of data warehouses in order to complete transactions by web or phone. This looks like the way of the future.

CRM should not be confused with *Relationship Marketing*, which is the title of an influential book first published in 1991. Its author was Regis McKenna, a marketing consultant known widely for his work with Apple Computers. McKenna believes that marketing is everything and doing marketing is everyone's job. The key elements of McKenna's notion are:

- Select a specific market segment and dominate through a superior understanding of customers' product and service needs. Integrate customers into the design process.
- Use monitoring, analysis and feedback to maintain 'dynamic positioning' that is always appropriate to the marketing environment.
- Develop partnerships with suppliers, vendors and users to help maintain a competitive edge.

Note that this concept of relationship marketing is also quite distinct from direct marketing, although direct marketers may be ideally placed to exploit it, especially in an e-commerce environment. One example of a direct and interactive marketer apparently following McKenna's strategy to the letter is Dell.

Relationship marketing in action

- Dell set out to develop and dominate the direct distribution segment of the PC market, a segment which (by value) consists primarily of business buyers.
- Dell customers 'build' their own computers on ordering from the Dell website. In practice, Dell believes they 'uptrade themselves' – specifying a higher performance machine than they could be 'sold' by a salesperson. By inviting customers' comments and suggestions and responding accordingly, Dell is also able to keep innovating in a relevant way. For example, DellHost allows customers to rent space for their website from Dell, removing the necessity to buy, monitor and maintain servers. In this way, Dell generates revenue by solving a known problem, not merely by selling hardware.

- Through opening up its order book on the extranet, Dell is able to make suppliers responsible for maintaining just-in-time parts deliveries. Suppliers can also meet on the extranet and collaborate to solve mutual problems. Superior supply chain management has given Dell a competitive edge.

Limitations of the customer information system

The database is inward looking to the extent that it refers only to those customers that a business already has on its books.

Although it is possible to import external data to profile customers and compare them with the market at large, this is not a substitute for marketing research.

The database, however good, remains introspective. It does not admit or report upon external influences. Disturbance to plans and forecasts may result from environmental influences, e.g. the economic situation, environmental concerns or other newsworthy preoccupations which affect purchase behaviour. Worse, it does not report on customers' use of competitors or on the success or otherwise of competitive initiatives. Share of customer (or share of wallet) is a key success measure in direct marketing.

Who is loyal, who is not

The database can often reveal whether a customer's purchase pattern indicates loyal or disloyal purchase behaviour. However, it cannot report directly on customers' use of competitive offerings. This can only be done on a sample basis, using marketing research. N.B. The sample for this research can be taken from the database.

Unless marketers are in a monopolistic situation and have absolutely no competitors (and who is ever in that position?) they still need to be fully alert to competitive influences. Competition and disruption may come not only from direct competitors, but also from indirect competitors.

Quantitative market research is required by all marketers, direct or otherwise. Qualitative research is also needed because the database can only reveal what customers are buying or not buying. It cannot say why, or suggest alternative new product avenues with much confidence. Data analysis relies on back data (customer history) to predict future behaviour. While this is generally the best guide, it is certainly not infallible. Circumstances and attitudes may change, causing sudden shifts in demand.

The database and research – the last word

In their study *The Machine that Changed the World*, Womack, Jones and Roos (1991) made clear how Toyota researched consumer preferences:

> Toyota was determined never to lose a former buyer . . . it could minimize the chance of this happening by using data on its consumer database to predict what Toyota buyers would want next . . . unlike mass-producers who conduct evaluation clinics and other survey research on randomly selected buyers . . . Toyota went directly to its existing customers in planning new products . . . Established customers were treated as members of the Toyota family.

In one generation, Toyota went from small producer to the world's number one in the automotive market.

Clearly, if a manufacturer has 5 per cent of the market and a 70 per cent loyalty rate, it is more sensible for it to learn what its customers want than what other manufacturers' customers want. Yet few of Toyota's competitors accepted this obvious truth.

Toyota's success is a triumph for good marketing, not simply a testament to Japanese technology. While other manufacturers were obsessed with 'conquest sales' (sales made to competitors' customers), Toyota's understanding of the value of customer retention was and is central to the discipline of direct marketing.

A competitor of Toyota estimated that it cost five times as much to make a conquest sale as a repeat sale. Collecting and acting on information like this is the hallmark of successful direct marketing.

References

Chaffey, D., Mayer, R., Johnston, K. and Ellis-Chadwick, F. (2000) *Internet Marketing*, FT Prentice-Hall.

McCorkell, G. (1997) *Direct and Database Marketing*, Kogan Page.

McKenna, R. (1991) *Relationship Marketing*, Century Business.

Peppers, D. and Rogers, M. (1993) *The One-to-One Future*, Currency/Doubleday.

Womack, J. P., Jones, D. T. and Roos, D. (1991) *The Machine that Changed the World*. Harper-Collins, New York.

Further reading

Chaffey, D., Mayer, R., Johnston, K. and Ellis-Chadwick, F. (2000) *Internet Marketing*, FT Prentice-Hall.

Halberg, G. (1995) *All Consumers are NOT Created Equal*, John Wiley.

Hughes, A. M. (1995) *The Complete Database Marketer*, Irwin Professional.

The Institute of Direct Marketing (2002) *The Direct Marketing Guide*.

McCorkell, G. (1997) *Direct and Database Marketing*, Kogan Page.

Nash, E. L. (1999) *Direct Marketing: Strategy, Planning and Execution*, 4th edn, McGraw-Hill.

David Shepard Associates (1999) *The New Direct Marketing*, 3rd edn, McGraw-Hill.

CHAPTER 23

The marketing of services

ADRIAN PALMER

Introduction

Is the marketing of services fundamentally different to the marketing of goods? Or is services marketing just a special case of general marketing theory? This chapter discusses the distinctive characteristics of services and the extent to which these call for a revision to the general principles of marketing. While many of the general principles can be applied to services, there are areas where a new set of tools needs to be developed. Of particular importance are: the effects of service intangibility on buyers' decision-making processes; the effects of producing services 'live' in the presence of the consumer; and the crucial role played by an organization's employees in the total product offer.

There is debate about the significance of services to national economies, and indeed how services should be defined. Before discussing the distinctive marketing needs of services, this chapter offers a contextual background to the service sector. By the end of the chapter, you should be able to judge the extent to which services call for a distinct set of marketing principles, rather than simple adaptation of universal principles of marketing.

The development of the service economy

We have always had service industries, and indeed there are numerous biblical references to services as diverse as inn keeping, money lending and market trading. Over time, the service sector has grown in volume and in the importance ascribed to it.

Early economists saw services as being totally unproductive, adding nothing of value to an economy. Adam Smith included the efforts of intermediaries, doctors, lawyers and the armed forces among those who were 'unproductive of any value' (Smith, 1977) and this remained the dominant attitude towards services until the latter part of the nineteenth century. Economists now recognize that tangible products may not exist at all without a series of services being performed in order to produce them and to make them available to consumers. So an agent distributing agricultural produce performs as valuable a task as the farmer. Without the provision of transport and intermediary services, agricultural products produced in areas of surplus would be of little value.

Services have had a major impact on national economies and many service industries have facilitated improved productivity elsewhere in the manufacturing and agricultural sectors. As an example, transport and distribution services have often had the effect of stimulating economic development at local and national levels (e.g. following the improvement of rail or road services). One reason for many developing countries' inability to fully exploit their natural resources has been the ineffectiveness of their distribution services.

It could even be argued that the economic development which occurred in England during the early part of the nineteenth century was really a services revolution rather than an 'industrial revolution'. Visions of new technologies involving steam power, factory systems and metal production have led to the dominant view that England's development was primarily a result of progress in the manufacturing sector. But could the industrial revolution have happened without the services sector? The period saw the development of many services whose presence was vital to economic development. Without the development of railways, goods could not have been distributed from centralized factories to geographically dispersed consumers and many people would not have been able to get to work. Investment in new factories called for a banking system that could circulate funds at a national rather than a purely local level. A service sector emerged to meet the needs of manufacturing, including intermediaries who were essential to get manufacturers' goods to increasingly dispersed markets. Today, we continue to rely on services to exploit developments in the manufacturing sector.

There is little doubt that the services sector has become a dominant force in developed economies, accounting for about three-quarters of all employment in the USA, UK, Canada and Australia. There appears to be a close correlation between the level of economic development in an economy (expressed by its GDP per capita) and the strength of its service sector.

However, there is the continuing perception among some groups of people that service sector jobs are somehow second rate, often associated with low paid, unskilled and casual employment. It is difficult to generalize on this point, but different cultures at a similar level of economic development may view their service industries quite differently. In the UK and Germany, service is often associated with servitude, while in the USA being of service almost goes to the heart of the national culture.

The academic literature on marketing theory and applications has been dominated by the manufactured goods sector. This is probably not surprising, because marketing in its modern form first took root in those manufacturing sectors that faced the greatest competition from the 1930s onwards. In growing, the services sector has become more competitive and therefore taken on board the principles of marketing. Deregulation of many services and rising expectations of consumers have had a dramatic effect on marketing activities within the sector.

The marketing literature identifies shifts in academics' and practitioners' focal points during the evolution of the discipline. Services marketing emerged when it became insufficient for companies to simply sell a better tangible product. This is consistent with population ecologists' argument that competitive rivalry in a market intensifies as the carrying capacity of the market falls, resulting in new forms of differentiation and value creation (Swaminathan and Delacroix, 1990). With services now being a standard feature of many tangible goods, many have argued that new forms of differentiation have become necessary. The quality of buyer–seller relationships has featured strongly in many companies' marketing strategies from the 1980s. This has been seen in the car industry, for example, where a traditional focus on design features such as reliability, styling and efficiency was supplemented from the 1970s with a focus on added service features. But when these added services, such as extended warranties and financing facilities, became the norm, relationships emerged as a source of competitive advantage. Many car companies introduced relationship-based programmes, which provided customers with ongoing finance, maintenance and renewal facilities.

More recently, some commentators have pointed to *experiences* as a post-service form of differentiation. Pine and Gilmore (1999) used the example of a birthday cake to illustrate how this product has progressed from a tangible collection of ingredients, through ready mixed ingredients, cakes made to order and delivered to the home (service-based differentiation), and ultimately to an outsourced party which provides an experience (e.g. celebration) of which the cake and delivery service have shifted from dominant elements to merely a supporting role.

Services and consumer value

While marketing remained focused on tangible products, value could be assessed with respect to readily observable benchmarks; for example, the value of pure commodity materials such as heating oil, natural gas and coal could be measured by reference to the units of calorific value obtained by the buyer per unit of expenditure. Value could be objectively assessed in the sense that an external observer of a transaction would be able to deduce the existence of a similar level of value.

The introduction of a significant service element to a product offer reduces the power of tangible benchmarks to explain value. There is now a widespread literature which recognizes that services can only be defined in the minds of consumers (e.g. Holbrook, 1995; Oliver, 1999). Considerable research has therefore sought to establish the nature of expectations which consumers develop prior to consumption of a service, and which act as a reference against which service delivery is assessed (Parasuraman *et al.*, 1985).

With the augmentation of services, a link between quality and value becomes more difficult to establish. Quality has been defined as 'conforming to requirements' (Crosby, 1984). This implies that organizations must establish customers' requirements and specifications. Once established, the quality goal of the various functions of an organization is to comply with these specifications. However, the questions remain: whose requirements and whose specifications? A second series of definitions therefore state that quality is all about fitness for use (Juran, 1982), a definition based primarily on satisfying customers' needs. If quality is defined as the extent to which a service meets customers' requirements, the problem remains of identifying just what those requirements are. Service quality is a highly abstract construct. Many analyses of service quality have attempted to distinguish between objective measures of quality and other measures which are based on the more subjective perceptions of customers. Gronroos (1984), for example, identified 'technical' and 'functional' quality respectively as being the two principle components of quality. While tangible products allow consumers to 'see and believe', services require them to 'imagine and believe'. In the buying process for services, quality is much more difficult to assess prior to purchase than is the case for goods.

It was noted earlier that there has been recent comment that 'experience' has supplanted tangible product qualities, service and intangible relationship benefits as a means of adding differential value to a product offer. The centrality of experience to defining value was noted by Holbrook (1999, p. 5), who defined consumer value as an 'interactive, relativistic preference experience'. There has been excited speculation that we are moving to an experience-based economy (Pine and Gilmore, 1999), in which we place increasing value in satisfying higher order needs through experiences. The proliferation of stylish coffee shops and themed restaurants provides some evidence to support this argument. However, evidence of a general movement towards value through experiences is quite patchy, as witnessed by the profitable growth of 'no frills' retailers, hotels and airlines.

What are services?

It can be difficult to define just what is meant by a service because most products we buy contain a mixture of goods elements and service elements. A meal in a restaurant contains a combination of goods elements (the food) and service elements (the manner in which the food is served). Even apparently 'pure' goods such as timber often contain service elements, such as the service required in transporting timber from where it was produced to where a customer requires it.

Modern definitions of services focus on the fact that a service in itself produces no tangible output, although it may be instrumental in producing some tangible output. A contemporary definition is provided by Kotler *et al.* (2001):

> A service is any activity or benefit that one party can offer to another which is essentially intangible and does not result in the ownership of anything.

In a more tongue-in-cheek manner, services have been described as 'anything which cannot be dropped on your foot'.

'Pure' services have a number of distinctive characteristics that differentiate them from goods and have implications for the manner in which they are marketed. These characteristics are often described as intangibility, inseparability, variability, perishability and the inability to own a service.

Intangibility

A pure service cannot be assessed using any of the physical senses – it is an abstraction which cannot be directly examined before it is pur-

chased. A prospective purchaser of most goods is able to examine the goods for physical integrity, aesthetic appearance, taste, smell etc. Many advertising claims relating to these tangible properties can be verified by inspection prior to purchase. On the other hand, pure services have no tangible properties which can be used by consumers to verify advertising claims before the purchase is made. The intangible process characteristics which define services, such as reliability, personal care, attentiveness of staff, their friendliness etc., can only be verified once a service has been purchased and consumed. Goods generally have tangible benchmarks against which quality can be assessed (e.g. durability, reliability, taste). In the case of services, these benchmarks can often only be defined in the minds of consumers. So while there may be little doubt that a car which has leather seats is of better quality than one with cloth seats, the same quality judgement cannot be made between say, a restaurant meal that takes one hour and another that takes two hours. In the latter case, the expectations of diners are crucial to an understanding of their perceptions of service quality, which may not be the same as the judgements of an outside observer.

The level of tangibility present in a service offer derives from three principal sources:

- tangible goods, which are included in the service offer and consumed by the user;
- the physical environment in which the service production/consumption process takes place; and
- tangible evidence of service performance.

Where goods form an important component of a service offer, many of the practices associated with conventional goods marketing can be applied to this part of the service offer. Restaurants represent a mix of tangibles and intangibles, and in respect of the food element few of the particular characteristics of services marketing are encountered. The presence of a tangible component gives customers a visible basis on which to judge quality. While some services (such as restaurants) are rich in such tangible cues, other services provide relatively little tangible evidence (e.g. life insurance).

Intangibility has a number of important marketing implications. The lack of physical evidence which intangibility implies increases the level of uncertainty that a consumer faces when choosing between competing services. An important part of a services marketing programme will therefore involve reducing consumer uncertainty by such means as adding physical evidence and the development of strong brands. It is interesting to note that pure goods and pure services tend to move in opposite directions in terms of their general approach to the issue of tangibility. While service marketers seek to add tangible evidence to their product, pure goods marketers often seek to augment their products by adding intangible elements such as after-sales service and improved distribution services.

Inseparability

The production and consumption of a tangible good are two separate activities. Companies usually produce goods in one central location and then transport them to the place where customers most want to buy them. In this way, manufacturing companies can achieve economies of scale through centralized production and have centralized quality control checks. The manufacturer is also able to make goods at a time which is convenient to itself, then make them available to customers at times which are convenient to customers. Production and consumption are said to be separable. On the other hand, the consumption of a service is said to be inseparable from its means of production. Producer and consumer must interact in order for the benefits of the service to be realized. Both must normally meet at a time and a place which are mutually convenient in order that the producer can directly pass on service benefits. In the extreme case of personal care services, the customer must be present during the entire production process. A surgeon, for example, cannot generally provide a service without the involvement of a patient. For services, marketing becomes a means of facilitating complex producer–consumer interaction, rather than being merely an exchange medium.

Inseparability occurs whether the producer is human – as in the case of health care services – or a machine (e.g. a bank ATM machine). The service of the ATM machine can only be realized if the producer and consumer interact. In some cases, it has been possible to separate service production and consumption, especially where there is a low level of personal contact. This has happened, for example, in the banking sector, where many banks have replaced local branches (where there is face-to-face interaction between producer and consumer) with centralized telephone call centres (where interaction takes place through the medium of the telephone).

Inseparability has a number of important marketing implications for services. First, whereas goods are generally first produced, then offered for sale and finally sold and consumed, inseparability causes this process to be modified for services. They are generally sold first, then produced and consumed simultaneously. Second, while the method of goods production is to a large extent (though by no means always) of little importance to the consumer, production processes are critical to the enjoyment of services.

In the case of goods, the consumer is not a part of the process of production and, in general, so long as the product which they receive meets their expectations, they are satisfied (although there are exceptions, for example where the ethics of production methods cause concern, or where quality can only be assessed with a knowledge of production stages that are hidden from the consumer's view). With services, the active participation of the customer in the production process makes the process as important as the end benefit. In some cases, an apparently slight change in service production methods may totally destroy the value of the service being provided. A person buying a ticket for a concert by Madonna may derive no benefit at all from the concert if it is subsequently produced by Britney Spears instead.

Variability

Most manufactured goods can now be produced with high standards of consistency. However, when asked about the consistency of services such as railway journeys, restaurant meals or legal advice, most people would probably have come across cases of great variability in the standard of service that was delivered. For services, variability impacts upon customers not just in terms of outcomes, but also in terms of processes of production. It is the latter point that causes variability to pose a much greater problem for services, compared to goods. Because the customer is usually involved in the production process for a service at the same time as they consume it, it can be difficult to carry out monitoring and control to ensure consistent standards. The opportunity for pre-delivery inspection and rejection which is open to the goods manufacturer is not normally possible with services. The service must normally be produced in the presence of the customer without the possibility of intervening quality control checks.

Variability in production standards is of greatest concern to services organizations, where customers are highly involved in the production process, especially where production methods make it impractical to monitor service production. This is true of many labour intensive personal services provided in a one-to-one situation, such as personal health care. Some services allow greater scope for quality control checks to be undertaken during the production process, allowing an organization to provide a consistently high level of service. This is especially true of machine-based services; for example, telecommunication services can typically operate with very low failure rates (British Telecom claims that in over 99 per cent of all attempts to obtain service, customers are

able to make a connection to their dialled number at the first attempt).

The tendency today is for equipment-based services to be regarded as less variable than those which involve a high degree of personal intervention in the production process. Many services organizations have sought to reduce variability – and hence to build strong brands – by adopting equipment-based production methods. Replacing human telephone operators with computerized voice systems and the automation of many banking services are typical of this trend. Sometimes reduced personnel variability has been achieved by passing on part of the production process to consumers, in the way that self-service petrol filling stations are no longer dependent on the variability of forecourt serving staff.

Variability can also be considered in terms of the extent to which a service can be deliberately customized to meet the specific needs of individual customers. Because services are created as they are consumed, and because consumers are often a part of the production process, the potential for customization of services is generally greater than for manufactured goods. The extent to which a service can be customized is dependent upon production methods employed. Services that are produced for large numbers of customers simultaneously may offer little scope for individual customization. The production methods of a theatre do not allow individual customers' needs to be met in the way that the simpler production methods of a counsellor may be able to.

The extent to which services can be customized is partly a function of management decisions on the level of authority to be delegated to front-line service personnel. While some service operations seek to give more authority to front-line staff, the tendency is for service firms to 'industrialize' their encounter with customers. This implies following clearly specified standardized procedures in each encounter. While industrialization often reduces the flexibility of producers to meet customers' needs, it also has the effect of reducing variability of processes and outcomes.

The variability of service output can pose problems for brand building in services compared to tangible goods. For the latter it is usually relatively easy to incorporate monitoring and quality control procedures into production processes in order to ensure that a brand stands for a consistency of output. The service sector's attempts to reduce variability concentrate on methods used to select, train, motivate and control personnel. In some cases, service offers have been simplified, jobs have been 'deskilled' and personnel replaced with machines in order to reduce human variability.

Perishability

Services differ from goods in that they cannot be stored. Producers of most manufactured goods who are unable to sell all of their output in the current period can carry forward stocks to sell in a subsequent period. The only significant costs are storage costs, financing costs and the possibility of loss through wastage or obsolescence. By contrast, the producer of a service which cannot sell all of its output produced in the current period gets no chance to carry it forward for sale in a subsequent period. A bus company which offers seats on a bus leaving Manchester for Bury cannot sell any empty seats once the bus has completed its journey. The service offer disappears and spare seats cannot be stored to meet a surge in demand, which may occur at a later time.

Very few services face a constant pattern of demand through time. Many show considerable variation, which could follow a daily pattern (e.g. city centre sandwich bars at lunch time), weekly (the Friday evening peak in demand for railway travel), seasonal (hotels, stores at Christmas time), cyclical (mortgages) or an unpredictable pattern of demand (emergency building repair services following heavy storms).

The perishability of services results in greater attention having to be paid to the management of demand by evening out peaks and troughs in demand and in scheduling service production to follow this pattern as far as possible. It is not good enough to ensure that supply and demand are matched overall in the long term. They must match for each minute and for each place that service is offered. Pricing and promotion are two of the tools commonly adopted to resolve demand and supply imbalances.

Inability to own services

The inability to own a service is related to the characteristics of intangibility and perishability. In purchasing goods, buyers generally acquire title to the goods in question and can subsequently do as they wish with them. On the other hand, when a service is performed, no ownership is transferred from the seller to the buyer. The buyer is merely buying the right to a service process such as the use of a car park or an accountant's time. A distinction should be drawn between the inability to own the service act and the rights which a buyer may acquire to have a service carried out at some time in the future (a theatre gift voucher, for example).

The inability to own a service has implications for the design of distribution channels, so a wholesaler or retailer cannot take title, as is the case with goods. Instead, direct distribution methods are more common and, where intermediaries are used, they generally act as a co-producer with the service provider.

Classification of services

It was noted earlier that the services sector has come to dominate the economies of most western countries. But this dominance has come about through a diverse range of services, so diverse that many have questioned whether the term services is too general to be of any use to marketers.

Many have pointed out that services and goods are very closely intertwined. Theodore

Levitt (1972) argued that services contain many important elements common to goods, thereby making services marketing as a separate discipline obsolete:

> ... there is no such thing as service industries. There are only industries where service components are greater or less than those of other industries.

On the other hand, many have pointed to the distinctiveness of services, which makes the application of traditional marketing principles inappropriate. Examples of early work which sought to define the nature of services are provided by Gronroos (1978), Lovelock (1981), and Shostack (1977).

It can be very difficult to distinguish services from goods, for most products which we buy are a combination of goods and services. In this way, cars have traditionally been considered examples of pure goods. However, today, most cars are sold with considerable service benefits, such as an extended warranty, a maintenance contract or a financing facility. In fact, many car manufacturers now see themselves as service providers in which lease contracts provide all the services necessary to keep a car maintained, insured, financed and replaced. The idea of a manufacturer selling a tangible item (the car) and then not

having any dealings with the customer until they are ready to replace the car is a rapidly disappearing goods approach to the marketing of cars.

Just as many pure goods may in reality be quite service-like, so many apparently pure services contain substantial goods elements. A package holiday may seem like a pure service, but it includes tangible elements in the form of the airplane, the hotel room and transfer coach, for example.

Pure goods and pure services are hypothetical extremes, but which are nevertheless important to note because they help to define the distinctive characteristics of goods and services marketing. In between the extremes is a wide range of products which are a combination of tangible goods elements and intangible service elements. It is therefore common to talk about a goods–service continuum, along which all products can be placed by reference to their service or goods dominance. Rather than talking about the service sector as a homogeneous group of activities, it would be more appropriate to talk about degrees of service orientation. In Figure 23.1, an attempt has been made to place a sample of products on a scale somewhere between being a pure service (no tangible output) and a pure good (no intangible service added to the tangible good).

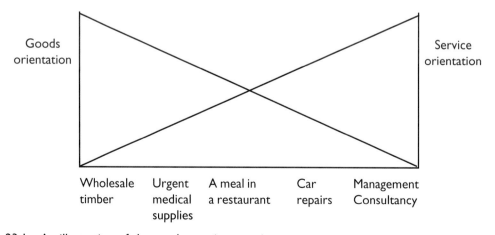

Figure 23.1 An illustration of the goods–services continuum

A further useful approach to understanding the service–goods orientation of any particular product is provided by Shostack's (1977) 'molecular model'. This attempts to analyse the elements of a service in terms of a molecular model of interrelated services and goods components. Thus, an airline offers an essentially intangible service – transport. Yet the total product offer includes tangible elements, such as the airplane, as well as intangible elements, such as the frequency of flights, their reliability and the quality of in-flight services. When many of these intangibles are broken down into their component parts, they too include tangible elements, so that in-flight service includes tangible elements such as food and drink. The principles of services marketing have most relevance where the molecular structure is weighted towards intangible elements. A hypothetical application of the molecular model approach to the analysis of the complex output of a train service is shown in Figure 23.2.

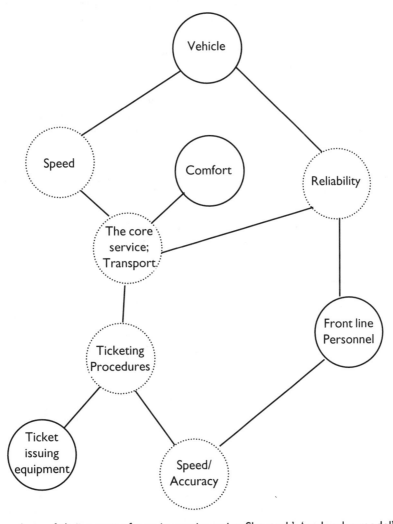

Figure 23.2 An analysis of the output of a train service using Shostack's 'molecular model'. Intangible elements of the service offer are represented by circles with broken lines, tangible elements by solid lines
Source: Shostack (1977).

It was noted above that the five character-istics of intangibility, inseparability, perish-ability, variability and lack of ownership have frequently been described as defining charac-teristics of services. However, many have argued that these characteristics are shared by many manufactured goods. For example, on the subject of variability, there are some non-service industries – such as tropical fruits – that have difficulty in achieving high levels of consistent output, whereas some service indus-tries such as car parks can achieve a consistent standard of service in terms of availability and cleanliness etc. Similarly, many tangible goods share the problem of intangible services in being incapable of full examination before consumption. It is not normally possible, for instance, to judge the taste of a bottle of wine in a supermarket before it has been purchased and (at least partially) consumed.

Services marketers have learnt a lot from the marketing activities in the goods sectors and vice versa. Some of the points of con-vergence are illustrated in Figure 23.3.

It should be clear from the above discus-sion that it is not possible to define a homoge-neous group of products called services. Their diversity raises the question whether it is possible to talk about a body of knowledge known as services marketing which is univer-sally applicable throughout the sector. A small jobbing plumber and a multinational bank both belong to the services sector, but can they share a common body of knowledge about market-ing? Because of the diversity of the services sector, marketing prescriptions will prove to be very weak unless smaller categories of services can be identified and subjected to an analytical framework which is particularly appropriate to that category of service.

The goods sector has traditionally devel-oped classifications to describe the marketing needs of different groups of goods. Terms such as fast moving consumer goods, shopping goods, speciality goods, white goods, brown goods etc. are widely used and convey a lot of information about the marketing requirements of products within a category, for example with respect to buying processes, methods of promo-tion and distribution. The great diversity of services has made attempts to reduce services to a small number of categories difficult to achieve. Instead, many analysts have sought to classify services along a number of continua,

Intangibility:	Services are increasingly augmented with tangible evidence (e.g. brochures, staff uniforms). Goods are increasingly augmented with intangible services (e.g. after-sales warranties).
Inseparability:	Service consumption is increasingly separated from production (e.g. telephone banking). Goods are increasingly produced in the presence of customers (e.g. while-you-wait bespoke tailoring).
Perishability:	Services are becoming better at storing tangible components of a service offer and in managing the pattern of demand (e.g. restaurants).
	Goods are now more likely to be supplied using 'just-in-time' principles (e.g. automo-tive car components).
Variability:	Industrialization of services allows levels of reliability to be achieved that matches those of goods.
Lack of ownership:	Addition of tangibles allows customers to 'own' evidence of service (e.g. a telephone 'calling card'). Goods manufacturers increasingly sell the services which a good pro-vides, rather than passing on ownership (e.g. car leasing agreements).

Figure 23.3   Points of convergence between the goods and services sectors

reflecting the fact that products cannot be classified into dichotomous goods and services categories to begin with.

Traditionally, the most common basis for classifying services has been the type of activity that is performed. Statistics record service activities under headings such as banking, shipping and hotels, based largely on similarity of production methods.

Production-based classification systems are not particularly useful for marketers. A single production sector can cover a very diverse range of activities with quite different marketing needs. Small guest-houses and international hotels may fall within the same sector, but their marketing needs are very different. The marketing needs of a particular production-based sub-sector may share more in common with another unrelated sub-sector rather than other areas within its own sector. Marketers should be more interested in identifying sub-sectors in terms of similarity of marketing requirements. In this way, the provision of banking services may have quite a lot in common with telecommunication services in terms of the processes by which customers make purchase decisions, methods of pricing and promotional strategies, for example.

The following sections identify some of the more commonly used bases for classifying services. It should be noted that many of these bases derive from the five fundamental characteristics of services, which were noted earlier.

Degree of intangibility

Intangibility goes to the heart of most definitions of services. It was noted earlier that intangibility has consequences for the way in which buyers perceive risk in a purchase decision. The task of providing evidence that a service will deliver its promises becomes more difficult where the service is highly intangible. As a classification device, degree of intangibility has many uses and this will be returned to later in the context of the management of the marketing mix.

Producer versus consumer services

Consumer services are provided for individuals who use up the service for their own enjoyment or benefit. No further economic benefit results from the consumption of the service. By contrast, producer services are bought by a business in order that it can produce something else of economic benefit. An industrial cleaning company may sell cleaning services to an airport operator in order that the latter can sell the services of clean terminal buildings to airline operators and their customers.

Many services are provided simultaneously to both consumer and producer markets. Here, the challenge is to adapt the marketing programme to meet the differing needs of each group of users (for example, airlines provide a basically similar service to both consumer and producer markets, but the marketing programme may emphasize low price for the former and greater flexibility for the latter).

The status of the service within the total product offer

Given that most products are a combination of goods and service elements, the service elements can contribute to the total product offer in a number of ways. Many services exist to add value to the total product offer, like a goods manufacturer which augments its core tangible product with additional service benefits, such as after-sales warranties. Sometimes, the service is sold as a separate product that customers purchase to add value to their own goods (for example, a car valeting service is purchased to add to the resale value of a used car). A further group of services may add value to a product more fundamentally by making it available in the first place. Distribution services can facilitate delivery of a tangible good from the point of production to the place where it is required by the consumer. Financial services can provide the means through credit arrangements, which allow tangible goods to be bought (for example, mortgages facilitate house purchase).

Extent of inseparability

Some services can only be provided in the presence of customers, whereas others require them to do little more than initiate the service process. In the first category, the production of personal care services, almost by definition, cannot be separated from their consumption. The involvement of consumers in the production process is often of an interactive nature, like where clients of a hairdresser answer a continuous series of questions about the emerging length and style of their hair. In such circumstances, the quality of service production processes can be just as important as their outcomes. Other services are more able to separate production from consumption; for example, a listener to a radio station does not need to interact with staff of the radio station. Customer involvement in production processes is generally lower where the service is carried out on their possessions, rather than on their mind or body directly. The transport of goods, maintenance of a car or the running of a bank account can generally be separated from the customer, whose main task is to initiate the service and to monitor performance of it.

The marketing of highly inseparable services calls for great attention to the processes of production. Advertising claims about high standards of service will count for little if an organization does not have in place quality management procedures, which are able to ensure consistently high levels of employee performance at the point of consumption. With separable services, there are greater opportunities for 'back-room' quality control checks before service delivery takes place.

The pattern of service delivery

Services differ in the ways that they are typically purchased. At one extreme, some services are purchased only when they are needed as a series of one-off transactions. This is typical of low value, undifferentiated services, which may be bought on impulse or with little conscious search activity (e.g. taxis and snacks in cafés). It can also be true of specialized, high value services that are purchased only as required (e.g. funeral services are generally bought only when needed).

By contrast, other services can be identified where it is impractical to supply the service casually. This can occur where production methods make it difficult to supply a service only when it is needed (for example, it is impractical to provide a telephone line to a house only when it is needed – the line itself is therefore supplied continuously) or where the benefits of a service are required continuously (e.g. insurance policies).

A continuous service supply pattern is often associated with a relationship existing between buyer and seller. A long-term relationship with a supplier can be important to customers in a number of situations: where buyers face a novel purchase situation (here, the existence of a trusted relationship can help to reduce perceived risk); where the production/consumption process takes place over a long period of time (e.g. a programme of medical treatment); and where the benefits will be received only after a long period of time (many financial services). Ongoing relationships can also help to reduce transaction costs (for both buyer and seller) of having to re-order a service every time that it is needed (e.g. a subscription to a car breakdown recovery service avoids the need to find a garage each time that help is required). Increasingly, services organizations are seeking to move the pattern of delivery to customers from one-off and transactional to continuous and relational.

Extent of people orientation

For some services, by far the most important means by which consumers evaluate a service is the quality of the front-line staff who serve them. Service sectors as diverse as hairdressing, accountancy and law can be described as people-intensive. At the other extreme, many services can be delivered with very little human involvement – a pay and display car park involves minimal human input in the form of checking tickets and keeping the car park clean.

The management and marketing of people-based services can be very different from those based on equipment. While equipment can generally be programmed to perform consistently, personnel need to be carefully recruited, trained and monitored. The marketing of people-intensive services cannot be sensibly separated from issues of human resource management. For the marketer, people-based services can usually allow greater customization of services to meet individual customers' needs (although this is changing with the development of computer-based delivery systems).

The significance of the service to the purchaser

Some services are purchased frequently, are of low value, are consumed very rapidly and are likely to be purchased on impulse with very little pre-purchase activity. Such services may represent a very small proportion of the purchaser's total expenditure and correspond to the goods marketer's definition of fast moving consumer goods (FMCGs). The casual purchase of a lottery ticket would fit into this category. At the other end of the scale, long-lasting services may be purchased infrequently and, when they are, the decision-making process takes longer and involves more people. Life insurance and package holidays fit into this category.

Just as the marketing of FMCGs differs from that of consumer durables, so the marketing effort required to sell these two extreme types of services will need to be adapted. For more complex services, care must be taken to identify the decision-making unit and to target it with appropriate messages. Risk is more likely to be perceived as a major issue with this type of service and must be addressed in a company's promotional programme.

Marketable versus unmarketable services

Finally, it should be remembered that many services are still considered by some cultures to be unmarketable. Many government services are provided for the public benefit and no attempt has been made to charge users of the service. This can arise where it is impossible to exclude individuals or groups of individuals from benefiting from a service. For example, it is not possible in practice for a local authority to charge individuals for the use of local footpaths.

A second major group of services which many cultures do not consider to be marketable are those commonly provided within household units, such as the bringing up of children, cooking and cleaning. While many of these services are now commonly marketed within western societies (e.g. child minding services), many societies – and segments within societies – would regard the internal provision of such services as central to the functioning of family units. Attempts by western companies to launch family-based services in cultures with strong family traditions may result in failure because no market exists.

What was considered yesterday by a society to be unmarketable may be an opportunity for tomorrow. Firms who have been quick to seize the opportunities presented have often had to contend with an initially apathetic or hostile public, as has happened in the UK with the emerging market for privatized prison services, public water supply and toll roads.

Multiple classifications

The great diversity of services have now been classified in a way which focuses on their marketing needs rather than their dominant methods of production. It will be apparent that, within any sector, there are likely to be major sub-categories of services which have distinctive marketing needs, and which may share a lot with other sectors. This commonality of marketing needs has provided great opportunities for companies who have extended their product range into services, which are basically similar in their marketing needs if not in their production methods. Many of the UK grocery retailers have considered that the way people open bank savings accounts is similar to the way that they select groceries, so have extended their marketing expertise by applying it to the savings market.

Although a number of bases for classifying services have been presented in isolation, services are, in practice, like goods, classified by a number of criteria simultaneously. There have been a number of attempts to develop multi-dimensional approaches for identifying clusters of similar services (for example, see Solomon and Gould (1991), who researched consumers' perceptions of 16 different personal and household services).

The services marketing mix

The marketing mix is the set of tools available to an organization to shape the nature of its offer to customers. The mix is not based on any theory, but on the need for marketing managers to break down their decision making into a number of identifiable and actionable headings. Goods marketers are familiar with the '4Ps' of product, price, promotion and place. Early analysis by Borden (1965) of marketing mix elements was based on a study of manufacturing industry at a time when the importance of services to the economy was relatively unimportant. More recently, the 4Ps of the marketing mix have been found to be too limited in their application to services. Particular problems which limit their usefulness to services are:

- The intangible nature of services is overlooked in most analyses of the mix – for example, the product mix is frequently analysed in terms of tangible design properties which may not be relevant to a service. Similarly, physical

distribution management may not be an important element of place mix decisions.
- The promotion mix of the traditional 4Ps fails to recognize the promotion of services which takes place at the point of consumption by the production personnel, unlike the situation with most goods which are normally produced away from the consumer and therefore the producer has no direct involvement in promotion to the final consumer. For a bank clerk, hairdresser or singer, the manner in which the service is produced is an essential element of the total promotion of the service.
- The price element overlooks the fact that many services are produced by the public sector without a price being charged to the final consumer.

The basic list of four 'Ps' also fails to recognize a number of key factors which marketing managers in the service sector use to design their service output. Particular problems focus on:

- the importance of people as an element of the service product, both as producers and co-consumers;
- the over-simplification of the elements of distribution which are of relevance to intangible services;
- definition of the concept of quality for intangible services, and identification and measurement of the mix elements that can be managed in order to create a quality service.

These weaknesses have resulted in a number of attempts to redefine the marketing mix in a manner which is more useful for the services sector. While many have sought to refine the marketing mix for general application (e.g. Kent, 1986; Wind, 1986), the expansion by Booms and Bitner (1981) provides a useful framework for the services sector. It should be stressed that these are not empirically proven theories of services marketing, but different authors' interpretations of the decisions that face services marketers in developing services to satisfy customers' needs. In addition to the four traditional elements of the marketing mix, it is common to recognize the importance of people and processes as additional elements. Booms and Bitner also talk about physical evidence making up a seventh 'P'.

Decisions on one element of the extended marketing mix can only be made by reference to other elements of the mix in order to give a sustainable product positioning. The importance attached to each element of the extended marketing mix will vary between services. In a highly automated service such as vending machine dispensing, the people element will be a less important element of the mix than in a people-intensive business such as a restaurant.

A brief overview of the extended services marketing mix ingredients is given below. In the case of the four traditional 'Ps', emphasis will be given to distinguishing their application in a services rather than a goods context.

Products

A product is anything that an organization offers to potential customers, whether it is tangible or intangible. After initial hesitation, most marketing managers are now happy to talk about an intangible service as a product. Thus, bank accounts, insurance policies and holidays are frequently referred to as products, sometimes to the amusement of non-marketers, and pop stars or even politicians are referred to as a product to be marketed.

Marketing mix management must recognize a number of significant differences between goods and services. A number of authors (e.g. Kotler, 1997) have described a model comprising various levels of product definition. The model developed by Kotler starts from the 'core' level (defining the basic needs which are satisfied by the product), through a 'tangible' level (the tangible manifestation of the product), through to an 'augmented' level (the additional services which are added to the product). While this analysis is held to be true of products in general, doubts

have been expressed about whether it can be applied to the service offer. Is it possible to identify a core service representing the essence of a consumer's perceived need that requires satisfying?

If such a core service exists, can it be made available in a form that is 'consumer friendly', and if so, what elements are included in this form? Finally, is there a level of service corresponding to the augmented product that allows a service provider to differentiate its service offer from that of its competitors in the same way as a car manufacturer differentiates its augmented product from that of its competitors?

Most analyses of the service offer recognize that the problems of inseparability and intangibility make application of the three generic levels of product offer less meaningful to the service offer. Instead, the product offer in respect of services can be more usefully analysed in terms of two components:

- the core service, which represents the core benefit; and
- the secondary service, which represents both the tangible and augmented product levels (Figure 23.4).

Sasser *et al.* (1978) described the core service level as the *substantive* service, which is best understood as the essential function of a service. Gronroos (1984) used the term *service concept* to denote the core of a service offering. Gronroos stated that it can be general, such as offering a solution to transport problems (e.g. car hire), or it could be more specific, such as offering Indian cuisine in a restaurant.

The secondary service can be best understood in terms of the manner in which a service is delivered. For example, Little Chef and Brewers Fayre restaurants both satisfy the same basic need for fast, economical, hygienic food, but they do so in differing ways. This is reflected in different procedures for taking and delivering orders, differences in menus and in the ambience of the restaurants.

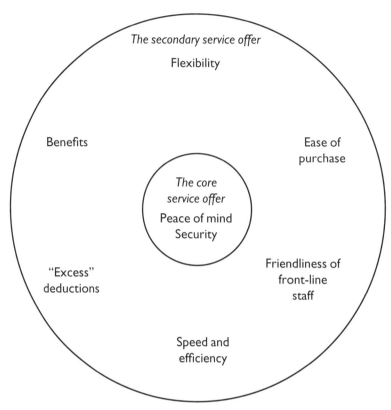

Figure 23.4   An analysis of the product offer of an insurance policy, comprising core and secondary levels of service offer

Services tend to be relatively easy to copy and cannot generally benefit from patent protection, as is often the case with goods. New product development often occurs in an incremental fashion, with many variants of a basic service. The proliferation of mortgage products by a building society, all with slightly differing terms and conditions, but basically similar in their function, is an example of this.

Pricing

Within the services sector, the term price often passes under a number of names, sometimes reflecting the nature of the relationship between customer and provider in which exchanges take place. Professional services companies therefore talk about fees, while other organizations use terms such as fares, tolls, rates, charges and subscriptions. The art of successful pricing is to establish a price level which is sufficiently low that an exchange represents good value to buyers, yet is high enough to allow a service provider to achieve its financial objectives.

In principle, setting prices for services is fundamentally similar to the processes involved in respect of goods. At a strategic level, a price position needs to be established and implemented with respect to the strength of customer demand, the costs of production and the prices that competitors are charging. A number of points of difference with respect to services pricing are noted here: the effects of inseparability; the effects on pricing of cost structures; and the effects of distorted markets for services.

The inseparable nature of services makes the possibilities for price discrimination between different groups of users much greater than is usually the case with manufactured goods. Goods can easily be purchased by one person, stored and sold to another person. If price segmentation allowed one group to buy a manufactured good at a discounted price, it would be possible for this group to buy the item and sell it on to people in higher priced segments, thereby reducing the effectiveness of the segmentation exercise. This point has not been lost on entrepreneurs who buy branded perfumes cheaply in the Far Eastern 'grey market' and import them to the UK, where prices are relatively high. Because services are produced at the point of consumption, it is possible to control the availability of services to different segments. Therefore, a hairdresser who offers a discounted price for the elderly segment is able to ensure that only such people are charged the lower price – the elderly person cannot go into the hairdressers to buy a haircut and sell it on to a younger segment, which would otherwise be charged the full price for the service.

Services organizations frequently charge different prices at different service locations. The inseparability of service production and consumption results in services organizations defining their price segments both on the basis of the point of consumption and the point of production. An example of this is found in hotel chains, who in addition to using price to target particular types of customers, also often charge different prices at different locations. Some retailers with a combination of large superstores and small convenience stores can justify charging higher prices in their convenience stores.

A second major difference between goods and services pricing is based on the high level of fixed costs that many service providers experience. The marginal cost of one additional telephone call, one additional seat on an air-plane or one additional place in a cinema is often very low. This can give service suppliers a lot of scope for charging different prices for what is basically the same product offer. High air fares in the peak period reflect a buoyant level of demand, as well as the amount needed to cover fixed costs at the peak. To encourage additional demand in quieter periods, airlines, like many other service industries, can reduce their prices. This is often referred to as marginal cost pricing. The price that any individual customer is charged is based not on the total unit cost of producing it, but only the additional costs that will result directly from servicing that additional customer. It is used where the bulk of a company's output has been sold at a full price that recovers its fixed costs, but in order to fill remaining capacity, the company brings its prices down to a level that at least covers its variable, or avoidable, costs. Marginal cost pricing is widely used in service industries with low short-term supply elasticity and high fixed costs. It is common in the airline industry, where the perishability of a seat renders it unsaleable after departure. Rather than receive no revenue for an empty seat, an airline may prefer to get some income from a passenger, so long as the transaction provides a contribution by more than covering the cost of additional food and departure taxes.

The final point of difference in managing the price element of the services marketing mix relates to the fact that services are more likely than goods to be made available in distorted markets, or in circumstances where no market exists at all. Public services such as museums and schools that have sought to adopt marketing principles often do not have any control over the price element of the marketing mix. The reward for attracting more visitors to a museum or pupils to a school may be additional centrally derived grants, rather than income received directly from the users of the service.

Services are more likely than goods to be supplied in non-competitive business environments. As an example, the high fixed costs associated with many public utility services means that it is unrealistic to expect two companies to compete. More importantly, much investment in services infrastructure is fixed and cannot be moved to where market opportunities are greatest. While a car manufacturer can quite easily redirect its new cars for sale from a declining market to an expanding one, a railway operator cannot easily transfer its track and stations from one area to another. The immobility of many services can encourage the development of local monopoly power.

Promotion

A well-formulated service offer, distributed through appropriate channels at a price that represents good value to potential customers, places less emphasis on the promotion element of the marketing mix. Nevertheless, few services – especially those provided in competitive markets – can dispense with promotion completely.

Although the principles of communication are similar for goods and services, a number of distinctive promotional needs of services can be identified, deriving from the distinguishing characteristics of services. The following are particularly important:

- The intangible nature of the service offer often results in consumers perceiving a high level of risk in the buying process, which promotion must seek to overcome. A number of methods are commonly used to remedy this, including the development of strong brands, encouragement of word-of-mouth recommendation, promotion of trial usage of a service, and the use of credible message sources in promotion (especially through public relations activity).
- Promotion of a service offer cannot generally be isolated from promotion of the service provider. Customers cannot sensibly evaluate many intangible, high perceived risk services, such as pensions and insurance policies, without knowing the identity of the service provider. In

many cases, the service may be difficult to comprehend in any case (this is true of pensions for most people), so promotion of the service provider becomes far more important than promotion of individual service offers.
- Visible production processes, especially service personnel, become an important element of the promotion effort. Where service production processes are inseparable from their consumption, new opportunities are provided for promoting a service. Front-line staff can become salespeople for an organization. The service outlet can become a billboard which people see as they pass by.
- The intangible nature of services and the heightened possibilities for fraud results in their promotion being generally more constrained by legal and voluntary controls than is the case with goods. Financial services and overseas holidays are two examples of service industries with extensive voluntary and statutory limitations on promotion.

Place

Place decisions refer to the ease of access which potential customers have to a service. For services, it is more appropriate to talk about accessibility as a mix element, rather than place.

The inseparability of services makes the task of passing on service benefits much more complex than is the case with manufactured goods. Inseparability implies that services are consumed at the point of production; in other words, a service cannot be produced by one person in one place and handled by other people to make it available to customers in other places. A service cannot therefore be produced where costs are lowest and sold where demand is greatest – customer accessibility must be designed into the service production system.

While services organizations often have a desire to centralize production in order to achieve economies of scale, consumers usually seek local access to services, often at a time that may not be economic for the producer to cater to. Service location decisions therefore involve a trade-off between the needs of the producer and the needs of the consumer. This is in contrast to goods manufacturers who can manufacture goods in one location where production is most economic, then ship the goods to where they are most needed.

Place decisions can involve physical location decisions (as in deciding where to place a hotel), decisions about which intermediaries to use in making a service accessible to a consumer (e.g. whether a tour operator uses travel agents or sells its holidays direct to customers) and non-locational decisions which are used to make services available (e.g. the use of telephone delivery systems). For pure services, decisions about how to physically move a good are of little strategic relevance. However, most services involve movement of goods of some form. These can either be materials necessary to produce a service (such as travel brochures and fast food packaging material) or the service can have as its whole purpose the movement of goods (e.g. road haulage, plant hire).

People

For most services, people are a vital element of the marketing mix. It can be almost a cliché to say that, for some businesses, the employees are the business – if these are taken away, the organization is left with very few assets with which it can seek to gain competitive advantage in meeting customers' needs.

Where production can be separated from consumption – as is the case with most manufactured goods – management can usually take measures to reduce the direct effects of people on the final output as received by customers. Therefore, the buyer of a car is not concerned whether a production worker dresses untidily, uses bad language at work or turns up for work late, so long as there are quality control measures which reject the results of lax behaviour before they reach the customer. In service industries, everybody is what Gummesson

(1999) has called a 'part-time marketer' in that their actions have a much more direct effect on the output received by customers.

While the importance attached to people management in improving quality within manufacturing companies is increasing (for example, through the development of quality circles), people planning assumes much greater importance within the services sector. This is especially true in those services where staff have a high level of contact with customers. For this reason, it is essential that services organizations clearly specify what is expected from personnel in their interaction with customers. To achieve the specified standard, methods of recruiting, training, motivating and rewarding staff cannot be regarded as purely personnel decisions – they are important marketing mix decisions.

People planning in its widest sense has impacts on a firm's service offer in three main ways:

- Most service production processes require the service organization's own personnel to provide significant inputs to the service production process, both at the front-line point of delivery and in those parts of the production process which are relatively removed from the final consumer. In the case of many one-to-one personal services, the service provider's own personnel constitute by far the most important element of the total service offering.
- Many service processes require the active involvement of consumers of the service and consumers therefore become involved as a co-producer of the service. At its simplest, this can involve the consumers in merely presenting themselves or their objects to the service provider in order for the service to be provided – for example, a customer might deliver their car to the garage rather than have it collected by the garage. In the case of services performed on the body or mind, the consumer must necessarily be designed into the production process.

- Other people who simultaneously consume a mass-produced service can affect the benefits which an individual receives from the service in a number of ways. First, the characteristics of other users of a service can affect the image of the service, in much the same way as owners of certain brands of goods can lend them some degree of 'snob' appeal. In this way, a nightclub can build up an exclusive image on account of the high-spending, high-profile users who patronize it. Second, the presence of other consumers in the service production–delivery process means that the final quality of the service which any customer receives is dependent on the performance of other consumers. In effect, they become co-producers of the service offering. Often, fellow consumers have an important role to play in enhancing the quality of the service offering, such as a full house in a theatre that creates an ambience for all customers to enjoy. On other occasions, fellow consumers can contribute negatively to the service production process, like where rowdy behaviour in a pub or smoking in a restaurant detracts from the enjoyment of an event for other customers.

Processes

Production processes are usually of little concern to consumers of manufactured goods, but can be of critical concern to consumers of 'high contact' services, where the consumer can be seen as a co-producer of the service. A customer of a restaurant is deeply affected by the manner in which staff serve them and the amount of waiting which is involved during the production process. Issues arise as to the boundary between the producer and consumer in terms of the allocation of production functions – for example, a restaurant might require a customer to collect their meal from a counter, or to deposit their own rubbish. With services, a clear distinction cannot be made between marketing and operations management.

Much attention has gone into the study of 'service encounters', defined by Shostack (1985)

as 'a period of time during which a consumer directly interacts with a service'. Among the multiplicity of service encounters, some will be crucial to successful completion of the service delivery process. These are often referred to as critical incidents and have been defined by Bitner *et al.* (1990) as '. . . specific interactions between customers and service firm employees that are especially satisfying or especially dissatisfying'. While their definition focuses on the role of personnel in critical incidents, they can also arise as a result of interaction with the service provider's equipment.

Where service production processes are complex and involve multiple service encounters, it is important for an organization to gain a holistic view of how the elements of the service relate to each other. 'Blueprinting' is a graphical approach proposed by Shostack (1984), designed to overcome problems which occur where a new service is launched without adequate identification of the necessary support functions. A customer blueprint has three main elements:

- All of the principal functions required to make and distribute a service are identified, along with the responsible company unit or personnel.
- Timing and sequencing relationships among the functions are depicted graphically.
- For each function, acceptable tolerances are identified in terms of the variation from standard which can be tolerated without adversely affecting customers' perception of quality.

Services are, in general, very labour intensive and have not witnessed the major productivity increases seen in many manufacturing industries. Sometimes, mechanization can be used to improve the efficiency of the service production process, but for many personal services this remains a difficult possibility. An alternative way to increase the service provider's productivity is to involve the consumer more fully in the production process.

As real labour costs have increased and service markets become more competitive, many service organizations have sought to pass on a greater part of the production process to their customers in order to try and retain price competitiveness. At first, customers' expectations may hinder this process, but productivity savings often result from one segment taking on additional responsibilities in return for lower prices. This then becomes the norm for other follower segments. Examples where the boundary has been redefined to include greater production by the customer are supermarkets who have replaced checkout operators with customer-operated scanners and restaurants which replace waiter service with a self-service buffet.

While service production boundaries have generally been pushed out to involve consumers more fully in the production process, some services organizations have identified segments who are prepared to pay higher prices in order to relieve themselves of parts of their co-production responsibilities. Examples include car repairers who collect and deliver cars to the owner's home, and fast food firms who avoid the need for customers to come to their outlet by offering a delivery service.

Despite handing over parts of the production process to consumers, many services remain complex, offering many opportunities for mistakes to be made. In many service sectors, giving too much judgement to staff results in a level of variability which is incompatible with consistent brand development. The existence of multiple choices in the service offer can make training staff to become familiar with all of the options very expensive. For these reasons, service organizations often seek to simplify their service offerings and to 'de-skill' many of the tasks performed by front-line service staff. By offering a limited range of services at a high standard of consistency, the process follows the pattern of the early development of factory production of goods. The process has sometimes been described as the 'industrialization' of services.

Physical evidence

The intangible nature of a service means that potential customers are unable to judge a service before it is consumed, increasing the risk inherent in a purchase decision. An important element of marketing planning is therefore to reduce this level of risk by offering tangible evidence of the promised service delivery. This evidence can take a number of forms. At its simplest, a brochure can describe and give pictures of important elements of the service product – a holiday brochure gives pictorial evidence of hotels and resorts for this purpose. The appearance of staff can give evidence about the nature of a service – a tidily dressed ticket clerk for an airline gives some evidence that the airline operation as a whole is run with care and attention. Buildings are frequently used to give evidence of service characteristics. Towards the end of the nineteenth century, UK banks outbid each other to produce grand buildings which signified stability and substance to potential investors, who had been frightened by a history of banks disappearing with their savings. Today, a clean, bright environment used in a service outlet can help reassure potential customers at the point where they make a service purchase decision. For this reason, fast food and photo processing outlets often use red and yellow colour schemes to convey an image of speedy service.

Tangibility is further provided by evidence of service production methods. Some services provide many opportunities for customers to see the process of production; indeed, the whole purpose of the service may be to see the production process (e.g. a pop concert). Often, this tangible evidence can be seen before a decision to purchase a service is made, either by direct observation of a service being performed on somebody else (e.g. watching the work of a builder) or indirectly through a description of the service production process (a role played by brochures which specify and illustrate the service production process). On the other hand, some services provide very few tangible clues about the nature of the service production process. Portfolio management services are not only produced largely out of sight of the consumer, it is also difficult to specify in advance in a brochure what the service outcomes will be.

Managing the marketing effort

Services marketing cannot sensibly be separated from issues of services management. The increasing dominance of the services sector has fuelled much of the current debate about the role of marketing within commercial organizations. While epitaphs for the marketing department are probably premature, there is considerable debate about the extent to which marketing should be fully integrated into every employee's job function, rather than left as a specialist function in its own right.

Should a service organization actually have a marketing department? The idea is becoming increasingly popular that the existence of a marketing department in an organization may in fact be a barrier to the development of a true customer-centred marketing orientation. By placing all marketing activity in a marketing department, non-marketing staff may consider themselves to be absolved of responsibility for the development of customer relationships. In service industries where production personnel are in frequent contact with the consumers of their service, a narrow definition of marketing responsibility can be potentially very harmful. On the other hand, a marketing department is usually required in order to co-ordinate and implement those functions that cannot sensibly be delegated to operational personnel – advertising, sales management and pricing decisions, for example.

In marketing-oriented organizations, the customer is at the centre of all of the organization's activities. The customer is not simply the concern of the marketing department, but also all of the production and administrative personnel whose actions may directly or indirectly impinge upon the customers' enjoyment of the service. In a typical service organization, the activities of a number of functional departments impinge on the service outcome received by customers:

- Personnel plans can have a crucial bearing on marketing plans. The selection, training, motivation and control of staff cannot be considered in isolation from marketing objectives and strategies. Possible conflict between the personnel and marketing functions may arise where, for example, marketing demands highly trained and motivated front-line staff, but the personnel function pursues a policy which places cost reduction above all else.
- Production managers may have a different outlook compared to marketing managers. A marketing manager may seek to respond as closely as possible to customers' needs, only to find opposition from production managers who argue that a service of the required standard cannot be achieved. A marketing manager of a railway operating company may seek to segment markets with fares tailored to meet the needs of small groups of customers, only to encounter hostility from operations managers who are responsible for actually issuing and checking travel tickets on a day-to-day basis, and who may have misgivings about the confusion which finely segmented fares might cause.
- The actions of finance managers frequently have direct or indirect impact on marketing plans. Ultimately, finance managers assume responsibility for the allocation of funds which are needed to implement a marketing plan. At a more operational level, finance managers' actions in respect of the level of credit offered to customers, or towards stockholdings where these are an important element of the service offering, can also significantly affect the quality of service and the volume of customers that the organization is able to serve.

Marketing requires all of these departments to 'think customer' and to work together to satisfy customer needs and expectations. There is argument as to what authority the traditional marketing department should have in bringing about this customer orientation. In a truly mature marketing-oriented service company, marketing is an implicit part of everybody's job. In such a scenario, marketing becomes responsible for a narrow range of specialist functions such as advertising and marketing research. Responsibility for the relationship between the organization and its customers is spread more diffusely throughout the organization.

There is some evidence of the possibly harmful effect of placing too much authority in the marketing department of services organizations. In a survey of 219 executives representing public and private sector services organizations in Sweden, Gronroos (1982) tested the idea that a separate marketing department may widen the gap between marketing and operations staff. This idea was put to a sample drawn from marketing as well as other functional positions. The results indicated that respondents in a wide range of service organizations considered there to be dangers in the creation of a marketing department – an average of 66 per cent agreed with the notion, with higher than average agreement being found among non-marketing executives, and those working in the hotel, restaurant, professional services and insurance sectors.

Summary

The services sector is now a dominant part of the economies of most developed countries. However, defining just what is meant by a service has caused some debate and this chapter has reviewed some of the bases for classifying services into categories that are useful for the purposes of marketing management. Pure services are distinguished by the characteristics of intangibility, inseparability, perishability, variability and a lack of ownership. Increasingly, however, goods and services are converging in terms of these characteristics. Buyer–seller relationships and consumer experiences are supplementing services as a basis for competitive differentiation of product offers. Few products can be described as pure goods or pure services – most are a combination of the two. There has been considerable debate about whether a new set of principles of marketing are required to understand services, or whether the established basic principles merely need adapting to the needs of services. The traditional marketing mix of the '4Ps' has been found to be inadequate for managers in the services sector and this chapter has discussed an alternative extended marketing mix of '7Ps', which recognizes the distinctive characteristics of services.

References

Bitner, M. J., Booms, B. H. and Tetreault, M. S. (1990) The Service Encounter: Diagnosing Favorable and Unfavorable Incidents, *Journal of Marketing*, **54**, January, 71–84.

Booms, B. H. and Bitner, M. J. (1981) Marketing Strategies and Organization Structures for Service Firms, in Donnelly, J. H. and George, W. R. (eds), *Marketing of Services*, American Marketing Association, Chicago, IL, pp. 51–67.

Borden, N. H. (1965) The Concept of the Marketing Mix, in Schwartz, G. (ed.), *Science in Marketing*, John Wiley, New York, pp. 386–397.

Crosby, P. B. (1984) *Quality Without Tears*, New American Library, New York.

Gronroos, C. (1978) A Service Oriented Approach to Marketing of Services, *European Journal of Marketing*, **12**(8), 588–601.

Gronroos, C. (1982) *Strategic Management and Marketing in the Service Sector*, Swedish School of Economics and Business Administration, Helsingfors, Finland.

Gronroos, C. (1984) A Service Quality Model and its Marketing Implications, *European Journal of Marketing*, **18**(4), 36–43.

Gummesson, E. (1999) *Total Relationship Marketing*, Butterworth-Heinemann, London.

Holbrook, M. (1995) *Consumer Research: Introspective Essays on the Study of Consumption*, Sage, Thousand Oaks, CA.

Holbrook, M. (ed.) (1999) *Consumer Value. A Framework for Analysis and Research*, Routledge, London.

Juran, J. M. (1982) *Upper Management and Quality*, Juran Institute, New York.

Kent, R. A. (1986) Faith in the Four Ps: An Alternative, *Journal of Marketing Management*, **2**(2), 145–154.

Kotler, p. (1997) *Marketing Management: Analysis, Planning, Implementation and Control*, 9th edn, Prentice-Hall, Englewood Cliffs, NJ.

Kotler, P., Armstrong, G., Saunders, J. and Wong, V. (2001) *Principles of Marketing*, 3rd European edn, Prentice-Hall, London.

Levitt, T. (1972) Production Line Approach to Service, *Harvard Business Review*, **50**, September/October, 41–52.

Lovelock, C. (1981) Why Marketing Needs to be Different for Services, in Donnelly, J. H. and George, W. R. (eds), *Marketing of Services*, American Marketing Association, Chicago, IL.

Oliver, R. (1999) Value as Excellence in the Consumption Experience, in Holbrook, M. (ed.), *Consumer Value. A Framework for Analysis and Research*, Routledge, London, pp. 43–62.

Pine, B. J. II and Gilmore, J. H. (1999) *The Experience Economy: Work is Theatre & Every Business a Stage*, Harvard Business School Press, Boston, MA.

Parasuraman, A., Zeithaml, V. and Berry, L. (1985) A Conceptual Model of Service Quality and its Implications for Future Research, *Journal of Marketing*, **49**(4), 41–50.

Sasser, W. E., Olsen, R. P. and Wyckoff, D. D. (1978) *Management of Service Operations: Texts, Cases, Readings*, Allyn & Bacon, Boston, MA.

Shostack, G. L. (1977) Breaking Free From Product Marketing, *Journal of Marketing*, **41**, April, 73–80.

Shostack, G. L. (1984) Designing Services That Deliver, *Harvard Business Review*, January/February, 133–139.

Shostack, G. L. (1985) Planning the Service Encounter, in Czepiel, J. A., Solomon, M. R. and Suprenant, C. F. (eds), *The Service Encounter*, Lexington Books, Lexington, MA, pp. 243–254.

Smith, A. (1977) *The Wealth of Nations*, Penguin, Middlesex (first published 1776).

Solomon, M. R. and Gould, S. J. (1991) Benefiting From Structural Similarities Among Personal Services, *Journal of Services Marketing*, **5**(2), Spring, 23–32.

Swaminathan, A. and Delacroix, J. (1990) Differentiation within an Organisational Population: Additional Evidence from the Wine Industry, *Academy of Management Journal*, **34**(3), 679–692.

Wind, Y. (1986) Models for Marketing Planning and Decision Making, in Buell, V. P. (ed.), *Handbook of Modern Marketing*, 2nd edn, McGraw-Hill, pp. 49.1–49.12.

Further reading

There are now numerous texts which deal specifically with the marketing of services and the following are among the recent works which provide a comprehensive coverage:

Gabbott, M. and Hogg, G. (1998) *Consumers and Services*, John Wiley, London.

Hoffman, K. D. (1999) *Essentials of Services Marketing*, Thomson Learning.

Kasper, H., De Vries, W. and Van Helsdingen, P. (1999) *Services Marketing Management*, John Wiley, London.

Lovelock, C., Lewis, B. and Vandermerwe, S. (1999) *Services Marketing*, FT Prentice-Hall, London.

Palmer, A. (2001) *Principles of Services Marketing,* 3rd edn, McGraw-Hill, Maidenhead.

Zeithaml, V. and Bitner, M. (2000) *Services Marketing,* 2nd edition, McGraw-Hill, New York.

The literature on services marketing has grown significantly during the past couple of decades, reflecting the growing importance of the services sector. The following article discusses the development of the literature:

Fisk, R. P., Brown, S. W. and Bitner, M. J. (1993) Tracking the Evolution of the Services Marketing Literature, *Journal of Retailing,* **69**(1), 61–103.

A number of articles appeared towards the end of the 1970s seeking to identify the nature of services and their distinctive marketing needs. The articles in the References by Lovelock (1981), Sasser *et al.* (1978), and Shostack (1977) are worth revisiting. In addition, the following are still worth reading because they establish many of the basic principles of services marketing.

Bateson, J. (1977) Do We Need Service Marketing?, *Marketing Consumer Services: New Insights,* Report 77–115, Marketing Science Institute, Boston.

Berry, L. L. (1980) Service Marketing Is Different, *Business,* **30**(3), May/June, 24–29.

Eiglier, P. and Langeard, E. (1977) A New Approach to Service Marketing, *Marketing Consumer Services: New Insights,* Report 77–115, Marketing Science Institute, Boston.

Levitt, T. (1981) Marketing Intangible Products and Product Intangibles, *Harvard Business Review,* **59**, May/June, 95–102.

Zeithaml, V. A. (1981) How Consumers' Evaluation Processes Differ Between Goods and Services, in Donnelly, J. H. and George, W. R. (eds), *Marketing of Services,* American Marketing Association, Chicago, pp. 186–190.

For a good selection of classic articles covering the breadth of services marketing issues, the following is useful:

Gabbott, M. and Hogg, G. (1997) *Contemporary Services Marketing Management: A Reader,* Dryden, London.

CHAPTER 24

International marketing – the issues

STANLEY J. PALIWODA

Overview

This chapter presents a distillation of thought and practice in an area of activity that was once seen only as constituting a different application of marketing but today has come of age. Consolidation is evidenced by the creation of the Special Interest Groups or SIGs now existing for the study and dissemination of international marketing thought and practice amongst marketing educators and researchers within both the American Marketing Association and the Academy of Marketing. Given the way in which this literature has expanded in a number of different lines of enquiry, what is provided here is more of a roadmap with references to specific sources for further information.

This chapter is structured in 11 parts. 'Why market abroad?' is perhaps the most basic of questions but is the starting point of inquiry. Next, situational analysis and the SLEPT framework are discussed, then, as might be expected, the differences between domestic and international marketing are highlighted. Operationalization is the title of the fifth section, reviewing experiential exporter profiles and foreign market entry strategies. Continuing and future challenges are reviewed, as well as ways in which to maintain a sustainable advantage in a highly competitive dynamic market. Conclusions are offered together with some further reading and some useful websites.

Why market abroad? What are the driving forces?

Why should a domestic company consider marketing overseas? The excitement and sense of adventure that previously accompanied this endeavour has been greatly reduced as a result of access to information systems, which appear capable of monitoring each and every action that we take as a consumer within the developed economies (Nancarrow *et al.*, 1997). Store loyalty cards and credit cards track all our expenditures and provide information not only for us but for others as well. Credit rating agencies not only know where we live but how we live. The world has changed greatly. Meanwhile, it also has to be said that the exchange process, which forms the basis of international marketing, is different from that found in the domestic market and involves more than exporting. The motivation for marketing abroad is best defined by contextual characteristics facing the individual firm and this will be discussed in more detail later in terms of the 'drivers' motivating companies.

To export means simply to send or carry abroad, especially for trade or sale. International marketing goes beyond that in introducing the concept of the end-user, moving the orientation away from finding sales for a company's existing products to analysing the market and assessing whether the company is able to produce a product or service (Knight, 1999) for which there is either current or potential demand, assuming that other factors can be controlled, such as price, promotion and distribution. International marketing can be very profitable but it is a serious business, which requires the long-term commitment of resources. It will mean the outlay of a substantial investment in a foreign market, often with a long projected payback. This issue of the planning time horizon is quite crucial. It is important then to differentiate between a short-term sales-oriented approach and a longer-term entry strategy of three to four years, which is aimed at market building.

Change: present and anticipated

Markets are changing demographically, politically and economically, and the techniques of bringing goods to market and arranging financing, as well as the means of financing themselves, are changing. Increasingly, the world over, economies are being subjected to the same social, economic, technological and political forces which shape our own markets. Technological companies are being 'born global' because the nature and specificity of the technological advantage they possess requires them to explore an international rather than a domestic market. Certainly there is a characteristic technological and industry specificity to that phenomenon (Zahra *et al.*, 2000; Zhao and Zou, 2002). Ohmae (1990) put it rather succinctly in identifying three global trends which he felt could not be ignored:

1 Increasing market fragmentation. Today, there are specialist competitors with tailored offerings.

2 Traditional market boundaries are blurring with substitutes from new technologies.
3 The transformation of previously self-contained national markets into linked global markets.

Ohmae combined these three trends then with the four 'I's which he identified with the 'borderless' economy, namely: Industry, Investment, Individuals and Information. All of these are highly mobile resources and so emphasize the dynamism of the international marketplace. This thread can be explored further in the work of Michael Porter, the Harvard economist, whose views are quite different from those of Ohmae. Porter's general work on strategy is discussed in this book by Wensley. Porter saw successful internationalization arising from a successful national competitive advantage. It was necessary to be successful in the home market first. This, however, does not help to explain the more recent phenomenon of the small highly competitive niche company which is 'born global', requiring internationalization to fully exploit its technological niche. Ohmae focused on the need to be an insider within the developed market economies of the Triad of Europe, North America and Japan, comprising a total of more than 600 million consumers with broadly similar spending patterns, tastes and desires, leading then into his thesis of the California-ization of consumers. Porter shares some similarities but is different, however, and sees the macro-environment as being shaped by what he terms currents and cross-currents, as below:

1 *Currents* which drive international competition, as evidenced by:
   a Growing similarity of countries with universal features, large retail chains, and TV advertising and credit cards.
   b Falling tariff barriers.
   c Technological revolutions which reshape industry and create shifts in leadership.
   d Integrating role of technology. Improved communication dismantles geographical barriers to trade and improves information in a world where buyers are increasingly aware of world markets.

e   New global competitors. The Pacific Basin
    countries have become fully-fledged
    competitors to well-established Western
    rivals.

2   *Cross-currents* which make the pattern of
    international competition different from earlier
    decades, evidenced in:
    a   Slowing rates of economic growth.
    b   Changes in the basis of competitive
        advantage. Labour cost natural resources
        and technology access are less important
        than before.
    c   New forms of protectionism, e.g.
        requirements for local content and local
        ownership.
    d   New types of government inducement,
        working between governments to attract
        foreign direct investment.
    e   Joint ventures, proliferating coalitions
        among firms from different countries.
        Broader, deeper collaboration than the
        marketing joint venture and production
        licences of the past.
    f   Growing ability to tailor to local conditions.
        New technologies support globalization but
        allow customized tailored product offerings.
        The need to standardize products
        worldwide is diminishing.

Porter believes that a prerequisite for success
internationally is to be strong domestically. It
is important to add, though, that both Ohmae
and Porter converge on the importance of
'clusters'. These clusters may be economic,
political or geographic groupings of countries
(e.g. the Baltic states) or it may be the effect
of one country economy upon its neighbours,
such as Brazil within South America. The
economic effect of one is still felt by several.
Most recently, Ohmae (2001) has been pro-
pounding the 'invisible continent' as an extension of the 'borderless world', but one in
which we have to embrace the old and the
new in a new dynamic uncharted territory
where finance and communications create as
well as destroy business empires at lightning
speed.

Add to this debate the diverse arguments
now being propounded for relationship marketing, building upon existing networks, and
the overall rationale for international marketing becomes clearer. More than one type of
international strategy can be viable in a given
industry. Johanson and Mattson (1986) put
forward the argument that the internationalization of the firm is affected by the internationalization of its markets. The marketing
mix may still contain the same 4Ps of product,
price, promotion and place of sale, but each P
introduces new variables now that it has been
transposed from a purely domestic setting to an
international marketing environment. The
environment is seen now as dynamic not static
and markets have been reinterpreted here as
networks of relationships between firms.

Figure 24.1 shows four cells, each of
which depicts a company and its environment
at different developmental stages of
internationalization.

1   The *early starter* is the company which has few
    rather unimportant relationships abroad, but is
    no different in this respect from its
    competitors, so this kind of situation is a
    developmental one which, for example, faced
    Europe at the start of this century.
2   The *lonely international* is highly
    internationalized while its market environment
    is not.
3   The *late starter* is indirectly involved with
    foreign markets. This is a specialized company,
    which has to decide whether to adapt or to
    get customers to adapt.
4   The *international among others*. Both the firm
    and its environment are highly
    internationalized.

Aside from the fact that Johanson and Mattson
blow away the whole concept of passive markets where sellers have only the four variables
– product, place, promotion and price – to play
with, they also introduce explanations for
internationalization that are more industry and
company specific. Raw material extraction may

Figure 24.1   Market internationalization
Source: Johanson and Mattson, 1986.

have forced some firms to become multi-national at the turn of the century so as to assure themselves of reliable sourcing. This is the case of the 'early starter', whereas the 'late starter' is one who has realized belatedly that the growth opportunities are all abroad, but so too are the competition. The 'lonely international' is not only more adventurous, but has resource, knowledge and skills to redeploy. It is driving the competition, not being driven by it. The last cell of the 'international among others' is of a company that is competent internationally but does not enjoy any sustainable competitive advantage over its competitors in this regard. Conditions describe a high degree of internationalization of the market and the degree of internationalization of the firm is already high, so here is a company that must hunt with the rest of the pack.

Economic change drivers

Worldwide trends towards regionalization

Worldwide, important trends towards regionalization and the economic free trade areas of ASEAN and NAFTA alongside the EU can be

detected: economic integration and industrial concentration continues apace and the following visible signs are beginning to come into focus:

- Trend to fewer larger groupings evident in food, cars, airlines, telecommunications and financial services.
- Growth of the services sector in all major Western developed economies and the networks that are required to service that international demand (Fisk, 1999).
- Retailers are showing distinct signs of both internationalization and concentration.
- The introduction of the 'Euro' currency on 1 January 2002 created a single currency for 12 of the 15 member states of the EU, when 305 million Europeans learned to use a new currency. The implications for companies considering themselves international are obvious.
- Ten more European nations that were formerly communist states, including Poland, Hungary, Czech Republic, Slovakia, Estonia, Latvia, Lithuania, Slovenia, Bulgaria and Romania, are waiting to join the EU and, together with Cyprus, Malta and Turkey, that could take the EU membership to 28. However, it is more likely that membership will be phased over several years. Even so, it is mooted that Poland, Hungary, Estonia, Czech Republic, Cyprus and Malta could join the EU from 2004.
- Taking into account the Euro and other economic policies of the EU, small and medium-sized European companies which are still anchored in national markets are at risk, since they could be squeezed without the advantage of size or of flexibility.
- A weak Asia with key economies such as Japan and South Korea continuing in recession will have significant effects upon the world economy. The loss of markets in that region will force companies to seek markets elsewhere instead; hence, we can expect a displacement effect and can expect to witness even keener competition in the West as a result.

Where then is theory?

The benefits of international marketing are many and dissipate risk, and provide almost an insurance of a foreign market alongside the domestic market. There are advantages not only in extended sales volume, but also in a possible price premium offered by the foreign market over the domestic market. Access to sought-after commodities or inputs into the production process provide a further rationale, particularly where costs may be lower. Over time, different arguments have been made, and some have lost their relevance as our economies modernize and our national companies integrate with foreign competitors. Michael Thomas pointed to the following as concepts, though, which remain yet to be proved:

- Product life cycle.
- Wheel of retailing.
- Hierarchy of advertising effects.
- The Boston box (BCG matrix).
- Information processing paradigms of consumer behaviour.
- Stages in internationalization process models.

Not all of these will be explored in this chapter, but what emerges is that we are seeking laws, regularity and predictability.

1 Product life cycle effects are often cited but seldom proved. Where a product on the home market enters a mature phase, theory argues that the company concerned may then be able to find new export markets abroad where product markets have not reached the same stage of development. This argument, however, becomes increasingly less relevant with the passage of time as a result of two trends. First, competition today, being international rather than domestic for all goods and services, has reduced the time lag between product research, development and production, leading to the simultaneous appearance of a standardized product in all major world markets, as with Microsoft and the launch of

their XP operating system or Iomega with their zip drives. Second, it is not production in the highly labour-intensive industries that is moving to the low labour cost countries with freeport advantages, such as Taiwan, but the capital-intensive industries, such as electronics, creating the anomalous situation of basing production for high-value, high-technology goods, in the countries least able to afford but best able to produce and export. Competition in a chosen target market may be less intense than at home or there may be the promise of tariff barriers to exclude potential competitors in return for a substantial foreign investment in plant machinery and know-how.

2 Excess capacity utilization. When the domestic market experiences a downturn or reaches saturation, companies may turn to export markets to make good the shortfall. For companies in industries requiring long production runs to ensure commercial viability, foreign orders may make the crucial difference between profit and loss. However, there is no commitment to exporting or to foreign markets at this stage.

3 Another feature which may also appear is that low prices are often quoted to ensure sales success in order to secure long production runs or to sell off high inventory levels. It is indeed possible for a company which has a mature product line to regard its original investment in product research and development to have been long since recouped, and therefore to price on the basis of actual production costs plus overheads. This is profitable exporting, but means that a company will be charging a different price in foreign markets from that which it charges in its own domestic market. This invites charges of 'dumping', which in the case of the USA and also the EU is assessed on two criteria: the basis of injury to local industry and whether the price being charged is lower than the price charged in the producer's own domestic market. This strategy may succeed in the short term, solving the need for near-capacity production runs. Finding foreign customers on

whom to offload production also means that the company does not have to resort to discounting for established customers, thereby protecting its price structure and avoiding the setting of precedents for future price negotiations.

4   Geographical diversification arises where companies find it preferable to remain with the product line which they know and are successful with rather than diversifying into new product lines or product technologies. This is a strategy of finding new markets for existing products.

5   Market potential as assessed by the population and their purchasing power. There are few untapped markets left. Cuba is certainly one, but various economic and political US sanctions are in place to discourage foreign companies considering moving there, although some countries are now doing so, most notably Canada. China is the most populous of the developing countries, but it is not untapped. Your competition is aware of what China has to offer. The capacity to consume or to absorb the product has to be matched with the capacity to pay for it. High levels of indebtedness in the Third World have created financial innovations in the variants of countertrade now available, much to the displeasure of the World Bank and IMF (Paun and Shoham, 1996).

6   Market 'spoiling'. The purpose here is less actively to pursue a market than to register a presence with a competitor, particularly where this also concerns market entry into a rival's domestic market. Timing is on the side of the existing market player who draws revenue from sales while his competitors plan their response. In world markets, it is the case that multinationals scan market segments for the presence of their multinational rivals. Narrowly defined segments in which there is little competition add to their total corporate power structure. A small but significant base in one part of the world may enable a multinational to access other markets in the same region and, at the same time, discourage competitors. Market entry can also be viewed as an offensive strategy, showing that by entering a rival's home market the company is capable of taking occasionally retaliatory action. Entry can then be seen as a warning against a multinational rival of its presence in the rival's home market, and its ability therefore to undercut the rival's home base and therefore the market for its main product.

Marketing arguments: the California-ization of consumers

The world is changing. Developed markets have affluent, knowledgeable consumers who share similar tastes and needs; hence, this growing phenomenon of an international marketplace for goods and services, which knows no frontiers. The term was first coined by Kenichi Ohmae, and refers to the increasing product standardization found across markets and the consequent supposed homogenization of consumers. Ohmae drew two important conclusions from this phenomenon:

1   That this therefore reaches beyond taste to worldview, mindset and thought processes in a mental programming as first described by Hofstede.
2   Teenagers around the world have in common that they have been subjected to a multimedia-rich instant response electronic environment.

Risk can be classified

International marketing differs from domestic marketing in that when the company is dealing with its own domestic market, key variables can be taken as known, such as:

- Political risk.
- Economic/financial risk.
- Commercial risk.
- Taxes and legislation relating to company incorporation.

To a marketer in his or her own country, these are background factors which influence the business climate, but in the international context become unknown factors which could assume important proportions, particularly when combined with historical, cultural and linguistic differences.

Political risk

To illustrate this, the Middle East may perhaps be popularly perceived as an area of political uncertainty, yet many British companies can claim punctual payment for supplies and that expropriation has not taken place in recent years. Instead, the various oil states who were previously only oil producers have engaged in forward vertical integration to control refining, shipping and, to some degree, retail distribution within Europe. On the other hand, a quite different form of political risk emerged in calm, politically stable France, when a socialist government under Mitterand started to create widespread uncertainty when it embarked on a nationalization policy. The greatest risks may not arise from within the most unstable economies.

International trade sanctions and embargoes may be found in place against specific countries. Important also to consider are the Voluntary Export Restraints (VERs) whereby exporting nations, most notably Japan, agree to curb exports to importing nations beyond a certain amount on pain of unspecified sanctions. Another quite different form of government intervention is through a countervailing duty. By introducing a countervailing duty, a government increases the selling price of the cheapest imported good to the level of the cheapest domestic competitor by means of a specific tax. In this way, governments may discriminate against cheap imports and effectively price them out of the market by instantly removing their price competitiveness.

The World Trade Organization (WTO) has now taken over the role of arbiter of free trade from GATT, the General Agreement on Tariffs and Trade, that was created to facilitate free trade in the aftermath of the Second World War. GATT had been created in different times when sovereign nations existed. Today, the move is towards the formation of economic trading blocs and so a new organization had to be created. China is the one major trading country that is not yet a member, but China will have to meet some rather stringent demands relating to freeing controls on its foreign trade before being able to join this organization.

Economic/financial risk

Similarly, there are economic risks where there are difficulties in repatriating capital due to host government exchange controls, high taxation or a rapidly devaluing currency. However, this may be surmounted by resorting to devices such as management fees, royalties and repayments on loans and/or interest, leasing, or intra-corporate transfers, known also as 'transfer pricing'. As it is entirely the responsibility of the individual company to price final goods, intermediate goods, such as assemblies and components, that are transferred within the company also provide an opportunity to move money out of one country into another where levels of taxation may also be lower.

Transfer pricing then may become a political issue when foreign subsidiaries are seen to be exporting but are recording losses. The price at which goods are to be transferred remains at all times a company issue over which the national customs services have no control.

Given a situation where multinational corporations control more than two-thirds of world trade, transfer pricing is viewed by politicians as an ever-constant threat to the nation state. To counter this, many large companies such as Exxon take the trouble to produce a code of ethics in which they publish the basis on which they transfer goods between company subsidiaries. Most commonly, this is found to be 'arms length' pricing, which means setting a market price as though to an outsider. However, the basis of this pricing has never been fully defined to the satisfaction of all.

Other possibilities include 'cost plus' pricing, which means including a proportion such as 10 per cent for overheads, including administration. Transfer pricing could therefore provide a means for a company to close down a plant abroad by showing how unprofitable it was by simply sending imports with a high transfer price. Alternatively, a plant in a low labour cost country with a very favourable tax regime could be seen as even more profitable if benefiting from low transfer prices from the parent company organization. Taxation and politics are important factors in this highly sensitive area of operations.

Commercial risk

The critical factor here is the uncertainty as to whether the company's goods will prove ultimately acceptable to the foreign consumer. However, even small companies are aware today of prevailing international industrial standards for technical equipment, as there are few national markets left. In the pursuit of critical mass and the need for economies of scale in production, domestic markets are rarely large enough to satisfy customers. Consequently, producers have sought every opportunity to standardize their products and make them available to an ever-larger number of markets. The BSI scheme Technical Help for Exporters was created to provide British manufacturers with information on national product standards worldwide. However, even if manufactured to acceptable national standards, there is still the risk that the goods may yet be found to be unacceptable to consumers in the target market, perhaps because of price, design, lack of state-of-the-art technology, inappropriate brand name or inability to provide the package of benefits, including service which customers, particularly in Western developed markets, have come to expect.

The risks of transportation, transhipment, pilferage, damage and loss are risks against which the supplier may obtain insurance, but increasingly this is only available at a high price and against demands that the exporter gives the insurance company all its export business and not just the risky part of the export portfolio or, alternatively, accept perhaps only 30 per cent cover. Insurers are providing less of a service nowadays and are dictating terms, pointing to the bad debt provisions of the major clearing banks and state export insurance agencies. To some degree, improved export packing and product packaging have reduced some of this risk, but certain regions of the world are more risky in this sense than others.

There is an important aspect often overlooked as to the ability of the buyer to pay for the goods ordered. Frequently, the creditworthiness of the nation is confused with the creditworthiness of the individual buyer. This is reflected in insurance practice, where there is often found to be a mistaken assumption that it is less important to have insurance cover for an importer in North America as opposed to South America. This confuses the solvency of the nation with the solvency of an industrial buyer, to say nothing about actual intent to pay. Financial status reports on a buyer should always be obtained whenever there is a shadow of doubt. Insurance is available to an exporter, but the cost increases with the exposure to risk and so the exporter should decide whether to proceed knowing fully the risk and whether he or the buyer is to accept the costs of insurance cover.

Agents are the most common form of going international, but here there may be a conflict of interest where an agent is sharing his time over a portfolio of products for which he receives differential rates of commission. Each supplier is just one of many and there may well be loss of central focus for the brand or product in question. There is an important experiential factor at play here. In a study of marketing know-how transfer, Simonin (1999) found that the effects of cultural distance, asset specificity and prior experience were moderated respectively by the firm's level of collaborative experience, the duration of the alliance and the firm's size.

Ownership may imply but does not mean control in practice. It usually means only that large-scale investment in a sales subsidiary and/or manufacturing plant has taken place, and that there will be a payback period before this investment is able to achieve a significant return. More effective control may be achieved by other means that do not involve equity or ownership, but may be a form of leverage over the foreign partner exercised via the flow of funds, components, technology and know-how by the Western partner. In longer-term agreements, the search for a continuing form of leveraged control over a foreign partner is difficult.

Situational or environmental analysis

Complexity and uncertainty predominate in the international arena, but the risks and the attendant expectations of return are what in turn make it so appealing. It is unwise to skimp on research because it costs too much, is not relevant to what is considered the mainstream domestic market business, is not as accurate as domestic market or because it is felt (but not proved) that the company already knows how to sell. Environmental scanning is wider in scope than traditional market research. There is a need for a comprehensive background report alongside studies of market potential, as these factors could affect market access and the ongoing internal operations of foreign companies in the host country. A simple but useful mnemonic is SLEPT:

- Social.
- Legal.
- Economic.
- Political.
- Technological.

This framework, using a series of questions, can help orient the company towards the most efficient use of its resources.

Where are you now?

Here are some checklist questions, to help with positioning:

- New company or subsidiary following a merger, take-over, joint venture or strategic alliance?
- New products incompatible with existing lines?
- Rethinking marketing strategy to bring a closer fit between product and prospect?
- Is there a mismatch now between your product and the target segment?
- Has the target segment profile changed?
- Has the distribution channel changed due to either new entrants or new and improved competitive offerings?
- Is this a new product in terms of concept and brand that you are trying to introduce to international markets?
- Are you looking abroad because of competition at home or because your domestic competitors are looking abroad also?
- Have you compared growth potential at home versus abroad?
- What flexibility do you have to market your product at home versus abroad?
- How would you describe the current market situation for this product in your home market?
- Does it differ when we look at foreign markets?
- Are there certain economic constraints regarding production runs, or anything else, which would affect either the quality that needs to be manufactured or the quantity that needs to be delivered to any one customer?
- Are there any other problems confronting you now or likely to confront you in the near future which you can foresee?
- Have you undertaken any regular monitoring either of the home market or your target foreign market to foretell the unforeseen?
- Lastly, monitoring performance relative to the marketplace should be an ongoing activity that never ends, although the excuses certainly should.

Where do you want to be?

There are differences between companies as to whether they perceive foreign market entry as:

1 A strategic or tactical option, i.e. whether they see entry into the target market as being of potential value in the medium to long term or whether it is a spoiling tactic undertaken by multinationals as they pursue their global quest for global market share.
2 Whether in terms of motivation and behaviour it is opportunity-seeking or problem-solving behaviour that is being reflected. Foreign market entry may be motivated by a desire to reduce current excess capacity. Alternatively, there may be a genuine desire to continue to service the target market in question. The underlying motivation is an important factor as it determines the company's degree of commitment to foreign markets as well.

What do you need to know?

It has often been said that knowledge is power. Well, no more so than in international markets, where your company is at the disadvantage of competing with local companies which presumably know the market conditions better. Knowing market conditions allows a company to fine-tune a technological advantage and turn it into a marketing advantage. Panasonic became the best known brand in Poland shortly after it became a market economy in 1990 for the simple reason that Panasonic had studied the Polish market situation and saw that voltage surges were common. A high-voltage surge would knock out most equipment, but what Panasonic did was brilliant and yet so basic. They simply incorporated resistors into television sets for Poland and became known as a manufacturer that made television sets especially for the Polish market. The Polish television market had belonged to the Russians and there were many foreign competitors now, but Panasonic's action saw off the competition. Knowledge of market conditions is important.

Today, licensing is seldom found without the sale also of know-how, which may simply be the transferral of production experience and so training or updating to a new licensee of the most modern production methods. However, it is with franchising that we see the sale of marketing know-how embodied in a successful branded product or service and encapsulated in a livery, logo or design so as to make it universally recognizable. In recognition there is market power.

Market research comprises hard and soft facts

The purpose, process and limitations of market research are discussed elsewhere in this book. However, in reviewing environmental scanning, Brownlie (1999) commented on the lack of empiricism and hard science, a point which has to be echoed here, especially with regard to:

• Culture, e.g. language, dress.
• Traditions that are important within the society and have their own rationale.
• Social customs, e.g. forms of communication, addressing hierarchies, perhaps even the need to have a drinking partner on the negotiating team. In some countries, it was the case that you could not do business unless you had been out with the client and got drunk with them. That achieved an important social breakthrough and, after that point, it would be possible to converse on a friendlier basis as you had shared something together. Some companies have actually employed individuals for foreign business and particularly negotiating teams because the most important asset that they could offer was a cast iron liver! The requirement to imbibe in volume remains in certain cultures and it is not just impolite to refuse, to decline means simply that you lose all prospect of doing business there.

Information empowers, but where it is missing, as a study by Birgelen et al. (2000) showed, incomplete information will not be ignored but decision makers will adopt a strategy of inferential, assumption-based reasoning.

The need to identify good potential markets

- Companies want sure-fire winners not theories!
- Measures used for analysis? Usually, per capita GNP or PPP (Purchasing Power Parity)? Just two measures of personal disposable income, both flawed. See a current issue of *The Economist* for a discussion on PPP and international comparisons on this measure, or Paliwoda and Thomas (1998) for a discussion of both GNP and PPP (further explanation of per capita GNP is found below).
- The number of psychologically close countries is increasing for West European markets, with a large number of pending EU membership applications!
- The Internet has changed forever the way in which we access information, which has now become a global commodity.

As an activity, international market research attracts only a small percentage of a company's total market research budget. Many companies do not spend money on foreign market research or entrust an on-the-spot appraisal to one of the most junior members of the firm, often entering into a particular target market for the first time and without any proper briefing or linguistic skills. What results is a 'go/no go' decision based on a poor understanding of the specific market characteristics. This activity should be approached as part of the company's ongoing strategic planning and development. A decision to enter a market should only be taken with proper understanding and appreciation of what is currently happening in the target market, and what is likely to happen.

Market research is possible but less reliable in those markets where market research data are scarce or the data available are not directly comparable due to the different statistical bases being used. Source credibility and comparability of results are the major headaches experienced. Another increasingly important factor is that we approach foreign markets with a self-reference criterion, meaning that we seek to understand foreign markets by comparing them with our own market. While that may be helpful, it is also important to underline that models created for Western markets may not be as effective outside Western markets. Consumer behaviour intention models may not be as effective in the Pacific Basin as they are in North America (Malhotra and McCort, 2001).

To research country markets effectively, governmental sources should be used where they exist. Where these are deficient, there are a number of agencies, including the US Central Intelligence Agency and many specialist companies such as Business International SA and others, which offer best estimates as to probable production and consumption figures. A company that thinks it knows its market should then assess its state of preparation against the Industrial Marketer's Checklist provided free by the Department of Trade and Industry. Identification of national personal disposable income levels may well be meaningless, and one should seek to identify important affluent target segments within a national market with data on lifestyles, educational background, location and spending patterns, all of which are useful indicators for any company seriously considering market entry.

What is important to remember is that GNP per capita as a measure of national wealth is an arithmetic mean, which gives a value for national wealth when calculated on a per capita basis. It does not equate with disposable income actually available to citizens to spend, nor their willingness to spend it. This statistic is fairly meaningless, as it offers no guidance as to the dispersion of wealth across the population or the possible identification of important affluent segments across a nation. Segmentation remains the key marketing tool, and the identification of feasible cross-national segments, the means to international access and profitability, as little product modification will then be required.

What you need to know

- Effects of culture.
- Market research of markets abroad.
- Psychic or psychological distance, also known as socio-cultural distance.
- Segmentation possibilities.
- Modes of market entry.
- More than four simple 'Ps' to worry about!

What is required to succeed in foreign markets

This can be summarized in terms of three main elements, each comprising a number of variables:

- Marketing policy elements:
  - Market selection, pricing, packaging.
- Firm-specific factors:
  - Technology, planning, control.
- External factors:
  - Diplomatic relations; subsidies, market accessibility, market potential.

Evidence of success in foreign markets

- A match between competencies of the firm with opportunities and threats of the marketplace.
- A competitive advantage that is sustainable in the light of probable competitive moves.
- A commitment of time and resources.
- Acculturation, meaning that a knowledge of the culture is as important as a knowledge of the language. In that way, social rituals, including the differences between the French and the British over observance of the lunch break, may be better understood.

Differences between domestic and international marketing

If we have only four Ps to worry about, we exclude much from our consideration. The difference between international and domestic marketing is best highlighted by Kotler (1986) as 'megamarketing' as opposed to simply 'marketing'. It is perhaps easy to oversimplify the vast number of variables to be managed within the marketing function, especially in the international arena, where the marketing manager's own knowledge of the foreign market is limited and so the number of variables on which we need information thereby increases dramatically. It overlooks many of the individual variables in return for making a simple point and providing a mnemonic for marketing managers. Paliwoda (1995) identified a 10-point checklist for approaching international marketing, consisting of:

1. *People* – all stakeholders, internal and external to the firm, employees and customers.
2. *Process* – which is unique to the corporate culture and may include willingness or not to consider a certain form of market entry such as joint venture.
3. *Positioning* – differentiation from rivals.
4. *Power* – market power transferability from home country to host country.
5. *Product/service* – delivering value added through the channel to the foreign consumer.
6. *Promotion and publicity* – what is available, what is allowable, what is free.
7. *Pricing* – an overplayed dimension and the weakest factor with which to lead.
8. *Place of sale/distribution* – delivery. From arrival portside to the final consumer through channels as diverse as the Internet.
9. *Planning and control* – with flexibility. Monitoring is one aspect but another is the ability to plan ahead with room to manoeuvre so as not to forestall strategic alternatives.

10 *Precedents* – learned from market scanning. Through environmental scanning at home and abroad, it is possible to discover strategies that may be borrowed from other companies in other industries or in other countries and applied to your own situation.

Effects of culture

Culture is a composite of many interrelated components – as we shall see shortly – although it is generally accepted that language is the embodiment of a culture. Certain of these other components have been investigated by Manrai *et al.* (2001), who studied style (meaning fashion consciousness and dress conformity) across three East European emerging markets, and these findings indicate chiefly demographic age, income and gender differences. However, let us focus for the moment on language. Language is important to conduct business successfully and here there is a net advantage for the English-speaking countries. Overall, English (with 427 million speakers) is second to Mandarin Chinese (726 million speakers) in terms of the number of people who speak the language. However, in many countries, English is a second language and the first or second language for business. Foreign investors such as the Japanese and South Koreans have established themselves in Britain because they feel comfortable with the language. A further advantage is that foreign students wishing to learn English bring £500 million each year into the British economy. In countries and within multinational corporations, the business language is often just English, and not just internally; English language will be prominent on all products and communications as well. This has an important value that must not be overlooked. Taking this further, the possible expansion of the European Union, whether or not it reaches 27 or 28 member states or even more, augurs well for the increased usage of the English language. Telecommunications have developed in English-speaking countries. This was the case with the telegraph, radio, telephone and now Internet. Countries such as France – and the province of Quebec in Canada – have actively resisted this English invasion and sought to place curbs on the use of certain words so as to outlaw 'franglais', but now even in Russia, the same cry is being heard of the widespread use of the English language on billboards and in general advertising. There will always be resistance to what is seen as foreign encroachment upon the national identity, but an inability to speak English today means an inability to be heard. English will continue to be prominent as it is being learned by the wealthy and well educated in all parts of the world. The question also must arise as to whether, with different levels of fluency and regional variations, not just in dialect but word usage and meaning, people actually mean what they say?

International marketing and the interface with local culture

To understand culture, we have to realize that it is behavioural attitudes, which we as members of a society learn and pass on to others. Whereas exporting is about sending products and services blindly into foreign markets for others to distribute, promote and sell to final customers, the intelligent international marketer recognizes the importance of maintaining control over branded products at the point of sale. Culture for the international marketer is seen to operate at three levels:

1 *Habits and conventions.* Where we may be able to most effectively change behaviour by influencing potential users, possibly by demonstration of a better, more modern, more intelligent way of doing a certain frequently repeated daily task or chore. With habits which rely on automatic responses, if we are able to demonstrate a better way of doing something and that product concept does not ask us to challenge our own value system, then we can usually rely on that idea being successfully adopted. For example,

electronic calculators have been successfully taken up everywhere. No disquiet has been voiced over the demise of the abacus or slide rule.

2 *Mores.* This is a Latin word for 'morals' or 'customs' and is often taken to mean the established religion of a particular society and the norms which it observes. Attempts to challenge the established religion within a country will not meet with success. With regard to international advertising, scantily clad women must not appear in advertising destined for Muslim countries or Muslim regions. Sometimes it is not the fundamentalists or adherents who may raise the problem, but those who do not practise the religion in question but nevertheless feel a certain unease over issues such as shops being open on a Sunday or extensions to the licensed drinking hours for bars and hotels.

3 *Laws.* There is very little international law, and so with the exception of cases such as the Law of the Sea and areas where international treaties are seen to prevail, usually it is then only domestic law which may have extra territorial reach. This is primarily the case with US law, which affects the operations not only of US multinationals, but other Western companies represented in the USA as well. The lack of international law means there is a gap to be filled in the case of international trading disputes. In effect, the various industrial arbitration councils whose establishment is not formally recognized but whose judgements have always been accepted in subsequent actions in civil courts of law often undertake this. Where existing law prohibits the sale of a product, the only strategy may be to try to have that law rescinded. This means lobbying for a change in legislation or even new legislation to enable this new and proposed product or service to be offered to the buying public. This could range from a variation being required in planning permission to allow out-of-hours shopping centres, Sunday opening of shops or settling the ethical questions raised by medical science, such as *in vitro* fertilization of women, human embryo experimentation and storage. As laws reflect a society's attitude towards a certain issue at a given moment in time, and society changes, there is always scope and argument for legal revision. In the USA and Japan, the EU is seen as being an effective legislative agency in its own right, lobbying is becoming more intense, while in a corresponding, separate movement, markets slowly become more similar. New services, such as satellite television, are not national but international in character and require special legal attention for their effective regulation.

Segmentation

Segmentation is a process whereby instead of focusing on the market at large we focus instead on identifying likely buyers for goods and services, and targeting them with information. Success arises from having identified a customer's needs exactly. Buyers differ in terms of their needs, perceptions and buying behaviour, so the intention is to try and get as close as possible to the needs of a segment, provided that segment meets the test of economic feasibility. Segmentation makes economic sense in terms of resource allocation, because it means that all advertising and promotion has to be narrowly defined for a product that has been built with a well-defined customer base in mind. Aside from the youth market, who are the only demographically defined segment internationally, there are many different forms of segment to be found in terms of psychographic segmentation, e.g. the BMW-3 series or shampoos for certain specific types of hair or scalp condition. For different levels of value added and across all product ranges, segmentation proves to be a very useful tool.

Before proceeding further with considerations of product distribution, we have to establish that the product is legal in the country in which it is to be sold and that the resources exist to target the chosen segment effectively. Some companies seek to promote their highly standardized product to essentially the same segment across national frontiers, i.e. a buying public with very similar profiles, as in the case of the major credit cards such as Visa Gold or the travel and entertainment cards of Diners Club and American Express. Essentially, this is an international segment who share many commonalities, including travel.

It may also be possible to sell the same products to different segments in foreign markets. However, to do this successfully may require product or communication strategy modifications. Small companies with a niche product may be able to do this as successfully as their multinational counterpart.

Now, back to the operational 4Ps. . .

Price

This always has a strategic role in terms of positioning the brand. However, it is better to take pricing out of this narrow box and emphasize instead how marketing can create price inelasticity. Pricing is strategically important from export contract pricing to final sale to the ultimate consumer. Garda (1995) discusses how tactical pricing can protect the company's pricing structure by tracking competitive bids made by rivals; timing price increases rather than following competitors can shift customer perceptions. Further confusion can be caused amongst competitors by making price information confidential to each customer, thereby making it difficult for competitors to follow. Customer price sensitivity and switching costs are further keys to tactical pricing.

- The Euro currency introduced by the European Union in 1999 for paper transaction and on 1 January 2002 as a complete replacement for 12 national currencies will usher in a new era where there will be the most transparent situation we have ever experienced to date as regards global pricing amongst 12 of the 15 EU states. Pricing will

become more transparent and more easily comparable across the 12 states of the EU. The strategic implications are far-reaching.
- Marginal pricing is tantamount to 'dumping', which can take three forms: sporadic, predatory or persistent. Each implies a different competitive threat from an aggressive foreign supplier.
- Countertrade (CT) is the precise generic term for barter, which today has many possible variants. It means that an overseas buyer pays partly in cash and partly in goods. The merchantability of the countertrade goods determines whether or not a countertrade specialist is required to offload those goods and realize a cash value for them. The costs of countertrade transactions can escalate dramatically depending upon the goods offered and, even where specialist equipment of high quality is offered, it can have serious supplier displacement effects at home. However, while the total trade in countertrade has declined from 1989 estimates of around 30 per cent of world trade, in the aerospace and computer industries particularly, it would be virtually impossible to conduct business without recourse to such contract alternatives. Paliwoda and Thomas (1998) discuss the countertrade variants at length with examples.
- Transfer pricing, which is intra-corporate pricing, is another important aspect, often because it has political overtones, since it has the potential at least to move money with goods. As a company has the power to decide for itself the price it will charge for transfers within its own organization, transfer pricing has therefore been seen as an insidious threat to governments who stand to lose tax revenue as the corporation moves its highest value added to the countries with the lowest tax regime. To workforces everywhere there is the risk of them being demoralized through unfair pricing of their output, which in turn may provide a reason for closure.
- Price harmonization between country markets is impossible to achieve except within fixed bands, but when this gap widens, it opens up.

The introduction of the Euro in 2002 will be the first time that direct comparisons can be made for the same branded product across markets and in exactly the same currency.

Product

Market research answers the question as to what sort of product or brand is required in terms of:

1　The acceptability of the company's product or service offering at the price which it expects to command (Zou et al., 1997; Palmer, 1997; Ozsomer and Prussia, 2000).
2　Acceptability of country of origin (Clarke et al., 2000).
3　Branding and the degree of local protection.
4　Patent and trademark issues, and again the degree of protection for those intellectual and industrial property rights.
5　Conflicting pressures to standardize or modify for local markets.
6　Packaging for various export markets.
7　Certification of origin, which allows imports right of access.

There may well be some compelling reasons for product modification in view of lower disposable incomes, poor infrastructure, traditional shopping habits etc. Frozen foods will only sell if consumers have freezers and will only sell in bulk if consumers have large chest freezers and the means of transportation to carry these goods home. Entering a market first may well bring 'first mover' advantage, but the cost may well include investing in the infrastructure so as to make your product concept workable. 'Late mover' advantage also needs to be considered. The advantages of first mover or late mover are contextually and industry specific.

International product policy management comprises many key strategic decisions, as discussed in Harrell and Kiefer (1995), so as to arrive at a successful market portfolio. The strategic alternatives facing the multinational have been delineated by Keegan (1969, 1995) and

developed by Saxena (1995), but more recent considerations have arisen out of the ISO standards, which are becoming increasingly important in setting internationally agreed threshold standards where company and brand names are not well established. Quality is important and should be seen as setting minimal acceptable standards for all products and services, not the commonly considered luxury products (Nakhai and Neves, 1995; Orsini, 1994).

Place of sale (or channels of distribution to be employed)

If proof were required that the concept of the 4Ps described only passive markets, then this is a good example. More is required than simply to make a product or service available and much is required of the producer by intermediaries within the channel to measure commercial success. Katsikeas et al. (2000) found that an overseas distributor's use of reward is positively related to its informational, referent, legitimate and expert power sources, and that there was a negative relationship between an importer's use of coercion and its informational base of power over the exporter. Christopher, who is also to be found in this book, writes not of distribution but of customer service and logistics strategy. Cooper (1995) discusses logistics strategies for multinational corporations. Elsewhere, some of the issues arising may be seen to include:

1　Length of distribution channel may be less a function of economic activity than of history, e.g. the Japanese have the longest distribution channels in the world, from producer to consumer. Long channels mean added costs and loss of control over product and intermediary. Learn how to work with local distributors, selection is important, then support for those you have appointed (Merrilees and Tiessen, 1999; Arnold, 2000).
2　Black markets are illegal but exist because of consumer demand for products, which are forbidden or else rationed, or simply in short

supply. Black markets exist to exploit such a market imbalance at a high price for the consumer, but since it is also an illegal activity, there is no redress for the consumer in terms of the quality of goods provided. All the risks are borne by the consumer. The existence of a black market also indicates a market opportunity, often for a legitimate business operation.

3   Grey markets exist where the incidence of parallel exports/imports referred to above is ever increasing, and is threatening manufacturers, but still is being championed by the EU in the name of free trade. This is increasing in pharmaceuticals because of the high value added involved.

4   Freeports now account for more than 9 per cent of world trade. Those freeports of the Pacific Basin which encourage manufacture, assembly and transhipment of goods for export are particularly important, and are now actively competing with each other. However, the costs of building port cargo handling facilities such as those found in Singapore are very high, but Malaysia is or was actively doing so until the advent of the 'Asian 'flu', which curtailed many of the more ambitious infrastructure projects. Freeports are located mainly within the NICs or the Third World and it is difficult to compete with these freeports on price, as their governments have in many cases exempted the freeports not only from taxes and duties which would otherwise be payable, but also from minimum wage controls and health and safety at work legislation which might apply outside the freeport area. This creates a cost advantage but also a legislative anomaly within a jurisdiction. Freeports now exist in all parts of the world, but their operating regulations vary widely. To be successful, they need to have a locational advantage as well as a cost advantage.

Promotion

There are a number of questions here, starting with the degree of similarity with the domestic market and the availability and regulation of suitable types of promotion (Koudelova and Whitelock, 2001), including personal selling as well as availability, regulation and relative cost of suitable advertising media, such as: sales promotion, direct mail (Iyer and Hill, 1996; McDonald, 1999), trade shows and exhibitions, sampling, contest and competitions, merchandising displays and public relations or publicity. There are other sources within this book, such as Crosier, who discuss these aspects. Where similar market conditions and media are found, then the question arises as to whether a successful domestic advertising campaign can be transferred abroad, thus eliminating origination costs. Gruber (1995) is one of the key sources in international campaign transferability. Further possibilities arise with the use of collaborative joint advertising with distributors, wholesalers or major retailers.

Essentially, markets are unlike because the forces that drive them are different or function to a lesser or greater degree compared to home. Most commonly, per capita income is sought as a guide to personal disposable income available for product purchases. This is simply naive in that a company requires a market to have size, measurability, plus the ability and willingness to buy, before it has a market. What is required therefore is knowledge, for, with knowledge, it is possible to plan for products which build upon similarities across countries and therefore maximize the opportunities for standardization and economies of scale. However, it also has to be said that there may also be mandatory requirements for advertising as well as product modification. Beliefs derive from religion, which may not countenance advertising and promotion, seeing in it a force which makes society consume more and more and be less respectful towards the world's finite resources. Religion may find itself at odds with products and services being promoted for sale as well as promotional themes, which may include partial nudity of the female form. Nevertheless, Vardar (1995), an advertising practitioner herself, has explored the uses and practice of advertising within a Muslim economy, namely Turkey.

Operationalization

Experiential research

Experiential research on exporters has identified several phases. From work initially conducted in Sweden by Weidersheim-Paul and replicated later in the USA by Bilkey and Tesar and by Cavusgil, we know of the following behavioural phases of exporters:

1 The company is totally uninterested.
2 The company will fulfil unsolicited orders but no more.
3 The company will undertake market research of that market.
4 The company begins to export to a psychologically close country.
5 The company is now experienced and ready to export to any market.

Of these stages, the most important was the finding relating to psychological closeness. Psychological closeness or as it will be referred to later, psychological distance or socio-cultural distance, is a key to understanding exporter behaviour.

Psychic or psychological distance (also socio-cultural distance)

This affects both supplier and buyer. For a supplier, knowledge of a market takes away the fear and lessens risks, both actual and perceived. For marketers, unlike sociologists or social anthropologists, the aim is to identify that which unites people as a common characteristic or feature, which is to be found with the same degree of frequency across national boundaries. The more we know of a target market and the degree that it approximates to our own, the better placed we are to design an acceptable offering.

In numerous studies, newcomers to exporting have been found to export first to those markets, which were more like extended domestic markets because of similarities of language, customs and institutions. British exporters for long periods were able to find the psychological distance between themselves and Australian, Canadian, Nigerian or Ghanaian buyers much less than that existing with France or another very closely neighbouring European country. Language, history, institutions, currency and familiar standards of size, weight or volume influence greatly the perceived degree of foreignness. The European Union is proceeding apace with harmonization and common measures including a common currency.

Selection of foreign market entry mode

There is a wide selection of entry methods to choose from and no easy solutions. An interesting approach, however, was that taken by Davis *et al.* (2000), taking the host country institutional environment and the internal institutional environment as two sources of isomorphic pressure. Davis *et al.* hypothesized that SBUs would adopt similar organizational forms, structures, policies and practices to conform to behavioural norms within those two environments. They found that SBUs using wholly owned entry modes demonstrated high levels of internal (parent) isomorphism: those using exporting, joint ventures or licensing agreements demonstrated external isomorphism and those using multiple or mixed entry mode demonstrated low levels of isomorphic pressure.

- There is no single 'best' strategy. Adopt a contingency approach.
- Have you considered the needs and desires of the local market?
- Has anyone asked the local natives about their expectations?
- Can you reconcile their expectations with your demands of a new market?
- As socio-cultural distance increases, firms are more likely to choose contractual rather than investment modes.

Three basic choices

The issue of mode of market entry choice ties in with the degree of commitment which the company has to export business generally, as well as to corporate policy which may rule out certain types of overseas association, e.g. joint equity venture or trading with a certain country or political or economic bloc on the basis of human rights record or political repression. There is no single 'best' strategy which may be adopted for market entry. There is no correct answer, only to say that this must be examined within an exclusive situational context. For each market, this may throw up new and exciting but untried alternatives, leading an experienced international marketing firm to be able then to boast of a portfolio of different market entry modes currently in operation internationally. Situational 'fit' is the answer. While the choice of entry mode is wide, the costs of making a mistake are heavy. Selection is best made against a number of criteria, such as the company's estimation of the perceived value of this particular market and their total commitment to it, whether short or long term.

- Export.
- Taking it further:
  - Contractual modes.
  - Investment modes.

Four underlying dimensions

Choice of mode of market entry may be dependent upon the firm's needs with regard to the following (Driscoll and Paliwoda, 1997):

- Control dissemination risk, i.e. authority over operational and strategic decision making.
- Dissemination risk or the extent to which a firm perceives that its firm specific advantages will be expropriated by a contractual partner.
- Resource commitment, namely the financial, physical and human resources that firms commit to enter foreign markets.

- Flexibility or the ability of a firm to change entry modes quickly and with minimal costs in the face of evolving circumstances. This is inversely related to resource commitment.

Seven situational influences

From in-depth interviews conducted by Driscoll and Paliwoda (1997), a number of situational variables emerge which have been classified into two broad groupings of firm-specific (or ownership) advantages and locational advantages:

- Product differentiation.
- Tacit know-how.
- International experience.
- Governmental intervention.
- Market attractiveness.
- Socio-cultural distance.
- Country risk.

However, only one variable – socio-cultural distance – was found to have a statistically significant influence on mode choice. Increasing socio-cultural distance between a firm's home country and its host country makes it more likely that the firm will choose contractual modes of entry over investment modes. One other variable, tacit know-how, approaches significance, suggesting that as know-how becomes more tacit in nature, firms prefer the use of investment entry modes to contractual modes. These findings confirm mode choice as comprising a number of decision dimensions, each of which is influenced by different situational factors. Examining the ability of various mode choice dimensions to differentiate among distinct mode options, it has been shown that resource commitment, control and dissemination risk are the most important aspects of mode choice. Of the three, resource commitment appears to be the most prominent consideration. The results confirm that socio-cultural distance and tacit know-how play an important role in mode choice. This research had indicated that, in making mode choices, international marketers frequently have preferred modes of entry that they may use over and over again irrespective of the entry situation. The dangers of this strategy are two-fold. First, a firm may forfeit a promising market because its institutionally accepted mode is incapable of penetrating the foreign market. Second, although the firm may be able to penetrate the market, its mode of entry may prevent it from fully capitalizing on market opportunities. Being aware of and avoiding the pitfalls inherent in institutionalizing entry modes might lead to more long-term success in international markets. Planning is everything, the plan itself is nothing. Make contingency plans (Chae and Hill, 2000).

Continuing and future challenges

1   Economic integration. The impact of economic integration within the European Union is having a formidable effect in regenerating many West European economies. As indicated earlier, EU membership could easily rise to 28 member states. However, while there is interest worldwide in the European experiment, other trading blocs stop at the economic stage and keep well clear of any permanent political association where, to take the case of the EU again, it officially represents its member states. Clearly, in terms of size and membership, APEC (Asia Pacific Economic Cooperation), spanning two continents, has tremendous potential to influence world trade if ever it chooses to do so, but there are many other large free trade agreements, including NAFTA and ASEAN.
2   Strategic alliances are increasing in all industries across all nations as a preferred means of corporate foreign market entry.
3   Brands are replacing products. Consumers have become increasingly sophisticated and product knowledgeable with the advent of new means of communication and the concentration of suppliers. While this has led

to globalization and product standardization in the main, segmentation and pre-testing are still necessary. Over-standardization in an era of anti-globalization is a sin.
4   Time to market and product differentiation (physical and psychological) are important.
5   Market data are increasingly important, especially for the many relatively new transitional economies. Need for awareness, image and preference data has led to new types of market research.
6   Regulation is important in a world trade order dominated not by trading nations but by economic blocs such as the European Union, which accounts for nearly 40 per cent of world trade. This has led to the establishment of a new organization in the World Trade Organization (WTO).
7   Distribution channel change. Major changes in distribution channels, e.g. concentration in retailing, use of the Internet (Hamill, 1997; Palumbo and Herbig, 1998; Zugelder et al., 2000) and the rise of international retailing. There is the problem of finding exclusive agents and representatives.
8   Consumer price sensitivity. Worldwide, consumers are becoming more price sensitive, so private labels are a response by retailers to ensure margins and customer loyalty.

Maintaining a sustainable advantage

Wensley provides an excellent review in this book of general marketing strategy (Chapter 4). Comments here focus on international marketing strategy.

Traditional marketing theory dictates that by adjusting the 4Ps for the correct marketing mix, companies are able to communicate effectively with their buying public. The marketing mix, reduced to only 4Ps, assumes passive markets while the interaction approach accepts that there are dynamic relationships between buyers and sellers involving product and process adjustments, logistical co-ordination, knowledge about the counterpart, personal confidence and liking, special credit agreements, and long-term contracts. Getting established in a new market involves creating a network new to the firm. It has to build relationships new to itself and its counterparts. This may lead to the breaking of old existing relationships, sometimes adding a new relationship to an existing one. Either the buyer or the seller may take initiatives. Markets then are seen only as networks of relationships between firms. This environment is not static but dynamic. The opportunities exist then for grey markets, for parallel exports and parallel imports, whereby domestic wholesalers effectively disrupt a manufacturer's official channels of distribution in a foreign market with exports designated for the home market. The aim is to take advantage of a higher profit margin in the price differential between home and overseas markets. This trade is not illegal and is encouraged by the European Union in the interest of free trade. It may have been brought about by a particularly favourable foreign rate of exchange, but, given the volatility of exchange rates, this can change suddenly in the opposite direction. For the manufacturer concerned, who is facing hostile distributors abroad, the option is to take the product off the market at home, increase the price on the home market or do nothing and wait for exchange rates to move against the domestic wholesalers who are doing this exporting.

Levels of personal disposable income vary across markets. There are differences in inflation rates, access to personal credit, product prices, specifications and sizes. All this serves to create confusion and to make direct comparisons very difficult. In such circumstances, grey marketers can flourish.

- Will this strategy ward off known threats, exploit opportunities, enhance current advantages and provide new sources of advantages?

- Can this strategy adapt to different foreseeable environments?
- Can competitors match, offset or leapfrog the expected advantages?

Conclusions

International marketing is not to be seen as an esoteric interest or as a standby when the domestic market undergoes an economic downturn. It is increasingly becoming a vital commercial activity for companies of all sizes and commitment. With greater moves towards political and commercial harmonization worldwide, the potential market that a company can reach correspondingly increases. Small companies in high-technology sectors of industry have increasingly to turn not to the domestic market but to international or even the global market for their specialized products and services.

International marketing is different from marketing simply within one's own domestic economy. Variables which can be assessed domestically (for example, political change, rate of inflation, pending political legislation and likely political responses) are known in this domestic context, but unknown when one starts to consider the international marketing arena. There are just too many variables to consider and to amass all that knowledge would require resources input. For large companies it is not a problem but for the smaller companies it is a minefield, although the range and quality of information is rapidly improving through access to new information tools such as the Internet where banks, Dun & Bradstreet and others may be easily contacted for their valued opinion, which may come at little, no or low cost.

Again, markets are not passive but active, even if your company happens to treat the domestic market as passive. Do not assume that your standard marketing mix will work even if successful at home – the examples of truly global brands are few. Coca-Cola and Pepsi-Cola are seen as archetypal global brands, but remember that they are also fast moving consumer goods and that they both satisfy a very basic need, i.e. thirst. IBM as a brand has been less successful in maintaining the stranglehold over personal computers that Microsoft has achieved worldwide but, again, here is a worldwide need for information technology being satisfied by an industry that is internationally concentrated. On the other hand, Gucci has been very successful in opening shops in China, where the per capita disposable income is amongst the lowest in the world, proving the point that there is always a market segment to be found that is willing to pay a premium for prestige, status and quality.

- Markets are constantly changing. Demographically, Western Europe's population is becoming older, while economically it remains affluent. The challenge arrives early in the new millennium around 2006–2016, when the bulk of the population enters retirement or early retirement. Those in employment will have to shoulder the responsibility for all those in retirement. It creates many new marketing opportunities for creative segmentation, as the newly retired and affluent still have the health and the wealth to enjoy themselves. Many new leisure and tourism opportunities are likely to arise.
- Lifestyle changes have arisen over the years as a result of lobbying regarding being environmentally friendly or eating a healthier lower fat diet or using less packaging or avoiding certain products entirely (Polonsky et al., 1997). Consequently, we have fewer one-product companies. Both Coca-Cola and Pepsi-Cola have responded to the consumer demand for new diet products that are low fat, low calorie, sugar free. Elsewhere, affluent consumers have to live with themselves for using disposable nappies, which are not degradable over anything less than 500 years. A demand is there to be met for there is as yet no such supply. Market information is

important to keep abreast of such changes.
- Money is not going out of fashion, but everywhere plastic cards are replacing cash transactions. Elsewhere, financial creativity is required when dealing with markets where there is a willingness to buy, but not the means with which to pay. Credit and leasing terms and countertrade have stepped into this vacuum.
- Internationalization of minimum threshold product and service standards, as embodied in the ISO 9000 and 1400 series of standards, creates a new dynamic for international supplier comparison and partly compensates also for smaller unknown companies, giving them the ability to compete internationally with confidence, almost as a brand. There is certainly a situation developing where asymmetries in information exist and these may prevent firms from supplying goods which consumers are willing to pay for. At the same time, as Vertinsky and Zhou (2000) have pointed out, the move from physical and functional properties as determinants of quality to the domain of social and environmental attributes, where value judgements are dominant, has made the design and management of quality certification systems subject to intensive political processes.
- Competitive conditions are going to become tougher. Competitors should never be underestimated. Market dynamics create constant change. Asian 'flu has affected what has been the powerhouse of international trade. However, the area known as Central and Eastern Europe is now a focus of much economic activity and continuing productivity gains through harmonization within the European Union are making Europe a good place in which to invest once again.
- Internationalization is the only means by which companies can exist in the future. Be proactive rather than reactive.
- Success requires constant market monitoring and performance evaluation so as to read market changes, but before the reader starts to wonder whether he or she can fit in with

this New World trade order, take heed of the advice of Tom Peters for the managers of tomorrow:

> Over the years, we have developed a style of doing business that is detached, calculating, dispassionate, analytical, methodological, dull and hard. My own hypothesis about tomorrow's survivors is that they will be fast, intuitive, opportunistic, hustling, caring, and trusting. Empathising, cheer leading, emotional, mistake making and action taking.

We often make the mistake of assuming that there is an explanation for everything, but as Michael Baker has often stated, marketing is part art and part science. When we are dealing with the buying public, we are dealing with people and so an irrational human element is ever-present. They, as consumers, are the ones who will control our commercial future and survival.

References

Arnold, D. (2000) Seven Rules of International Distribution, *Harvard Business Review*, November–December.

Birgelen, Marcel van, de Ruyter, K. and Wetzels, Martin (2000) The Impact of Incomplete Information on the Use of Marketing Research Intelligence in International Service Settings: An Experimental Study, *Journal of Service Research*, **2**, 372–87.

Brownlie, D. (1999) Environmental Scanning, in Baker, M. J. (ed.), *The Marketing Book*, 4th edn, Butterworth-Heinemann, Oxford, Chapter 4.

Chae, M.-S. and Hill, J. S. (2000) Determinants and Benefits of Global Strategic Marketing Planning Formality, *International Marketing Review*, **17**(6), 538–562.

Clarke, I. III, Owens, M. and Ford, J. B. (2000) Integrating Country of Origin into Global Marketing Strategy: A Review of US Marking Statutes, *International Marketing Review*, **17**(2), 114–126.

Cooper, J. (1995) Logistics Strategies for Global Businesses, in Paliwoda, S. J. and Ryans, J. K. Jr (eds), *International Marketing Reader*, Routledge, London, pp. 217–239.

Davis, P. S., Desai, A. B. and Francis, J. D. (2000) Mode of International Entry: An Isomorphic Perspective, *Journal of International Business Studies*, **31**(2), 239–258.

Driscoll, A. M. and Paliwoda, S. J. (1997) Dimensionalising the International Market Entry Mode, Special Issue on Internationalisation, *Journal of Marketing Management*, **13**(1–3), 57–88.

Fisk, R. P. (1999) Wiring and Growing the Technology of International Services Marketing, *Journal of Services Marketing*, **13**(4/5), 311–318.

Garda, R. A. (1995) Tactical Pricing, in Paliwoda, S. J. and Ryans, J. K. Jr (eds), *International Marketing Reader*, Routledge, London, pp. 257–265.

Gruber, U. (1995) The Role of Multilingual Copy Adaptation in International Advertising, in Stanley J. Paliwoda, John K. Ryans Jr (eds), *International Marketing Reader*, Routledge, London, ch. 14, pp. 202–13.

Hamill, J. (1997) The Internet and International Marketing, *International Marketing Review*, **14**(5), 300–323.

Harrell, G. A. and Kiefer, R. O. (1995) Multinational Market Portfolios in Global Strategy Development, in Paliwoda, S. J. and Ryans, J. K. Jr (eds), *International Marketing Reader*, Routledge, London.

Iyer, R. T. and Hill, J. S. (1996) International Direct Marketing Strategies: A US–European Comparison, *European Journal of Marketing*, **30**(3), 65–83.

Johanson, J. and Mattson, L. G. (1986) International Marketing and Internationalisation Processes – A Network Approach, in Turnbull, P. W. and Paliwoda, S. J. (eds), *Research In International Marketing*, Croom-Helm, London.

Katsikeas, C. S., Goode, M. M. H. and Katsikea, E. (2000) Sources of Power in International Marketing Channels, *Journal of Marketing*

Management, **16**, 185–202.

Keegan, W. J. (1969) Multinational Product Planning: Strategic Alternatives, *Journal of Marketing*, January, 58–62.

Keegan, W. J. (1995) Global Product Management: Strategic Alternatives, in Paliwoda, S. J. and Ryans, J. K. Jr (eds), *International Marketing Reader*, Routledge, London, pp. 105–109.

Knight, G. (1999) International Services Marketing: Review of Research, *Journal of Services Marketing*, **13**(4/5), 347–360.

Kotler, P. (1986) Megamarketing, *Harvard Business Review*, March–April.

Koudelova, R. and Whitelock, J. (2001) A Cross Cultural Analysis of Television Advertising in the UK and Czech Republic, *International Marketing Review*, **18**(3), 286–300.

Malhotra, N. K. and McCort, J. D. (2001) A Cross Cultural Comparison of Behaviour Intention Models, *International Marketing Review*, **18**(3), 235–269.

Manrai, L. A., Lascu, D. N., Manrai, A. K. and Babb, H. W. (2001) A Cross Cultural Comparison of Style in Eastern European Emerging Markets, *International Marketing Review*, **18**(3), 270–285.

McDonald, W. J. (1999) International Direct Marketing in a Rapidly Changing World, *International Direct Marketing*.

Merrilees, B. and Tiessen, J. H. (1999) Building Generalizable SME International Marketing Models Using Case Studies, *International Marketing Review*, **16**(4/5), 326–344.

Nakhai, B. and Neves, J. S. (1995) The Deming, Baldridge and European Quality Awards, *Quality Progress*, **27**,(4), 35–8.

Nancarrow, C., Wright, L. T. and Page, J. (1997) A Study in International Marketing: The Development of a Consumer Database Marketing Capability, *Journal of Marketing Management*, **13**, 625–636.

Ohmae, K. (1990) *The Borderless World*, Harper Business, New York.

Ohmae, K. (2001) *The Invisible Continent*, Nicholas Brealey, London.

Orsini, J. L. (1994) Make Marketing Part of the Quality Effort, *Quality Progress*, **27**(4), 43–7.

Ozsomer, A. and Prussia, G. E. (2000) Competing Perspectives in International Marketing Strategy: Contingency and Process Models, *Journal of International Marketing*, **8**(1), 27–50.

Paliwoda, S. J. (1995) *The Essence of International Marketing*, Prentice-Hall, Hemel Hempstead (also available in Spanish).

Paliwoda, S. J. and Thomas, M. J. (1998) *International Marketing*, 3rd edn, Butterworth-Heinemann, Oxford.

Palmer, A. (1997) Defining Relationship Marketing: An International Perspective, *Management Decision*, **35**(4), 319–321.

Palumbo, F. and Herbig, P. (1998) International Marketing Tool: The Internet, *Industrial Management and Data Systems*, **98**(6), 253–261.

Paun, D. A. and Shoham, A. (1996) Marketing Motives in International Countertrade: An Empirical Examination, *Journal of International Marketing*, **4**(3), 29–47.

Polonsky, M. J., Carlson, L., Grove, S. and Kangun, N. (1997) International Environmental Marketing Claims: Real Changes or Simple Posturing?, *International Marketing Review*, 14(4), 218–232.

Saxena, R. (1995) Generic Product Strategies for the World Market, in Paliwoda, S. J. and Ryans, J. K. Jr (eds), *International Marketing Reader*, Routledge, London.

Simonin, B. L. (1999) Transfer of Marketing Knowhow in International Strategic Alliances: An Empirical Investigation of the Role and Antecedents of Knowledge Ambiguity, *Journal of International Business Studies*, **30**(3), 463–490.

Vardar, N. (1995), Media Burst in a Euroasian Country – A Blessing or a Burden?, in Paliwoda, S. J. and Ryans, J. K. Jr (eds), *International Marketing Reader*, Routledge, London, pp. 177–201.

Vertinsky, I. and Dongsheng Zhou (2000) Product and Process Certification: Systems, Regulations and International Marketing Strategies, *International Marketing Review*, **17**(3), 231–252.

Zahra, S. A., Ireland, R. D. and Hitt, M. A.

(2000) International Expansion by New Venture Firms: International Diversity, Mode of Market Entry, Technological Learning and Performance, *Academy of Management Journal*, **43**(5), 925–950.

Zhao, H. and Zou, S. (2002) The Impact of Industry Concentration and Firm Location on Export Propensity and Intensity: An Empirical Analysis of Chinese Manufacturing Firms, *Journal of International Marketing*, **10**(1), 52–71.

Zou, S., Andrus, D. M. and Norvell, D. W. (1997) Standardisation of International Marketing Strategy by Firms from a Developing Country, *International Marketing Review*, **14**(2), 107–123.

Zugelder, M. T., Flaherty, T. B. and Johnson, J. P. (2000) Legal Issues Associated with International Internet Marketing, *International Marketing Review*, **17**(3), 253–271.

Further reading

Albers-Miller, N. D. (1996) Designing Cross-cultural Advertising Research: A Closer Look at Paired Comparisons, *International Marketing Review*, **13**(5), 59–74.

Bilkey, W. J. and Tesar, G. (1977) The Export Behaviour of Smaller Wisconsin Manufacturing Firms, *Journal of International Business Studies*, **10**(1), 93–98.

Coviello, N. and Munro, H. (1997) Network Relationships and the Internationalisation Process of Small Software Firms, *International Business Review*, **6**(4), 361–386.

Craig, C. S. and Douglas, S. P. (1999) *International Market Research*, 2nd edn, Wiley, Chichester.

Diamantopoulos, A. and Horncastle, S. (1997) Use of Export Marketing Research by Industrial Firms, *International Business Review*, **6**(3), 245–270.

Douglas, S. P. and Craig, C. S. (1992) Advances in International Marketing, *International Journal of Research in Marketing*, **9**, 291–318.

Drucker, P., Ohmae, K., Porter, M. and Peters, T. (1990) *Management Briefings*, Special Report No. 1202, Economist Intelligence Unit, London, April.

Easton, G. and Hakansson, H. (1996) Markets as Networks, *International Journal of Research in Marketing*, Special Issue, **13**(5).

Egan, C. and Shipley, D. (1996) Strategic Orientations towards Countertrade Opportunities in Emerging Markets, *International Marketing Review*, **13**(4), 102–120.

Hayes, M. H. (1995) ISO 9000: The New Strategic Consideration, in Paliwoda, S. J. and Ryans, J. K. Jr (eds), *International Marketing Reader*, Routledge, London, pp. 122–136.

Kashani, K. (1989) Beware the Pitfalls of Global Marketing, *Harvard Business Review*, September–October.

Keng, K. A. and Tan Soo Jiuan (1989) Differences Between Small and Medium Sized Exporting and Non-Exporting Firms: Nature or Nurture, *International Marketing Review*, **6**(4), 27–40.

Kotler, P. (1986) Megamarketing, *Harvard Business Review*, March–April.

Leeflang, P. S. H. and van Raaij, W. F. (guest editors) (1995) Special Issue: The Changing Consumer in the European Union, *International Journal of Research in Marketing*, **12**(5).

Millington, A. I. and Bayliss, B. T. (1997) Instability of Market Penetration Joint Ventures: A Study of UK Joint Ventures in the European Union, *International Business Review*, **6**(1), 1–18.

Morgan, R. E. and Katsikeas, C. S. (1997) Export Stimuli: Export Intention Compared with Export Activity, *International Business Review*, **6**(5), 477–500.

OECD (1997) *Globalisation and Small and Medium Enterprises*, 2 vols, Paris.

Paliwoda, S. J. and Ryans, J. K. Jr (1995) *International Marketing Reader*, Routledge, London.

Paliwoda, S. J. and Thomas, M. J. (1998) *International Marketing*, 3rd edn, Butterworth-Heinemann, Oxford.

Quester, P. G. and Conduit, J. (1996) Standardisation, Centralisation and Marketing in Multinational Companies, *International Business Review*, **5**(4), 395–422.

Roos, J., von Krogh, G. and Yip, G. (1994) An Epistemology of Globalizing Firms, *International Business Review*, **3**(4), 395–410.

Russow, L. C. and Okoroafo, S. C. (1996) On the Way Towards Developing a Global Screening Model, *International Marketing Review*, **13**(1), 46–64.

Shipley, D., Egan, C. and Wong, K. S. (1993) Dimensions of Trade Show Exhibiting Management, *Journal of Marketing Management*, **9**(1), January, 55–64.

Tanzi, V. and Davoodi, H. (1998) Roads to Nowhere: How Corruption in Public Investment Hurts Growth, *Economic Issues*, No. 12, International Monetary Fund, Washington, DC.

Thomas, M. J. (1996) Post Modernism for Dummies, Occasional Paper, Department of Marketing, University of Strathclyde, Glasgow.

Wood, V. R. and Robertson, K. R. (1997) Strategic Orientation and Export Success: An Empirical Study, *International Marketing Review*, **14**(6), 424–444.

Useful international marketing websites

American Demographics: www.marketing-tools.com/Publications/AD/Index.HTM

APEC – Asia Pacific Economic Cooperation (potentially the world's largest economic grouping):

www.apecsec.org.sg/apecpnewg.html

www.iijnet.or.jp/vj/p-asia/g-info/S1-J.html

APEC – Home Page of the Asia Pacific Economic Cooperation Secretariat: www.apecsec.org.sg/apecnet.html

Asia Business Connection: http://asiabiz.com/news.html

Asia Business Daily: http://infomanage.com/~icr/abd

Canada Up Close: http://strategis.ic.gc.ca

CIA World Factbook: www.odci.gov/cia/publications/nsolo//wfb-help/index.htm

Currency Exchange: www.fx4business.com

ExportNet: www.exporttoday.com

International Business Forum: www.ibf.com

Mellinger Global Trade Center: www.tradezone.com/tz

Price Waterhouse: www.i-trade.com/infsrc/pw

Statistical Agencies on the Internet: www.science.gmu.edu/csi779/drope/govstats.html

Statistics UK: www.emap.com\cso

Statistics USA: www.stat-usa.gov

Statistics Canada – reputedly the best governmental statistical reporting service: www.statcan.ca

TradePort – extensive information on international business: www.tradeport.org

Trade Statistics: www.census.gov/ftp/pub/foreign-trade/www/

TradeWave Galaxy – public and commercial information and services: www.einet.net/galaxy.html

Trading Standards Net – consumer legislation and full list of product recalls: www.xodesign.co.uk/tsnet

Transition Brief – Newsletter of CCET (Centre for Cooperation with Economies in Transition), OECD: www.oecd.org/sge/ccet/

UNDP – UN Development Program Human Development Report 1997 discusses world poverty and a six-point strategy for poverty reduction: www.undp.org/undp/hdro/index.htm

US Department of Commerce: www.doc.gov/CommerceHomePage.html

US – Fedworld: www.fedworld.gov

US International Trade Commission (ITC) – weekly updates of new trade dispute filings and press releases: www.usitc.gov

US News and World Report Online: www.usnews.com

US on EU: Country Report on Economic Policy

& Trade Practices, gopher: UMSLVMA.UM-SL.EDU:70/00/library/gophers/CRPT0023

US Trademark Library: www.micropat.com

US WEST features 50 000 suppliers from USA, Mexico, Canada: http://export.uswest.com

US WEST Export Yellow Pages: http://yp.uswest.com

USA – Economic Bulletin Board, gopher://una.hh.lib.umich.edu/11/ebb

US National Trade Databank: www.stat-usa-.gov/BEN/Services/nidbhome.html

UT-LANIC – University of Texas Latin American Network Information Center: http://lanic.utexas.edu/la/region.html

UT-MENIC – University of Texas Middle East Studies: http://menic.utexas.edu/mes.html

Virtual Reference Desk: http://thorplus.lib-.purdue.edu/reference/index.html

Wall Street Journal Interactive Edition: www.update.wsj.com/

Wall Street Net: www.netresource.com/wsn/

Web Page for Global Business: www.seattleu.edu/~parker/homepage.html

Websites for International Information:

http://www.ustr.gov/

http://www.i-trade.com/

http://www.stat-usa.gov/BEN/subject/trade.html

http://www.itaiep.doc.gov/

Western European geography software: http://ourworld.compuserve.com/homepages/torpedo

White House – welcome to the White House: www.whitehouse.gov

World Bank: www.worldbank.gov/

World Health Organization, gopher: gopher.gsfc.nasa.gov

World History Chart: www.hyperhistory.com

World Population Clock: www.census.gov/cgi-bin/ipc/popclockw

WorldWide Web Virtual Library: http://W3.org

World Trade Analyzer – Trade Compass: www.tradecompass.com/trade_analyzer

WTCA On-Line – World Trade Centers Association On-Line: www.wtca.org/etindex.html

WTO (World Trade Organization) – Agreement Establishing the WTO: www.soton.ac.uk/~nukop/data/fullrecs/1660.htm

WTO: www.unicc.org//wto/Welcome.html

WWW Yellow Pages: www.cba.uh.edu/ylowpges/ylowpges.html)

A list of further websites is available at:

http://business.bham.ac.uk/business/page868.htm

CHAPTER 25

E-marketing

DAVE CHAFFEY

Introduction

In a short period of time, e-marketing has become a facet of marketing that cannot be ignored. With some enthusiastic adopters of digital technologies such as Cisco, easyJet and IBM now achieving the majority of their sales and customer service on-line, many organizations are examining how they can best make use of this new medium. However, the medium is perhaps best known for the spectacular 'dot-com' failures such as Boo.com, Peapod, Click-mango etc. Consequently, marketers need to carefully assess the significance of e-marketing and assimilate it, as appropriate, into all aspects of marketing from strategy and planning to marketing research, objectives setting, buyer behaviour, marketing communications and the marketing mix. The key phrase here is 'as appropriate'. The impact of new technologies such as the Internet will vary greatly according to the existing product, market, channel structure and business model of each organization.

This chapter outlines an approach to e-marketing planning, which can be applied to all organizations. The approach is based on careful assessment of the opportunities and threats, clearly defined objectives and strategies, and selection of appropriate e-marketing tactical tools and resources to achieve these strategies.

What is e-marketing?

There are now many terms with the e-prefix, and many different interpretations. Within any organization, developing a common understanding for terms such as e-commerce, e-business and e-marketing, and how they interrelate, is important to enable development of a consistent, coherent strategy. We will now briefly review these terms and how they relate.

Electronic commerce (*e-commerce*) is often thought to simply refer to buying and selling using the Internet; people immediately think of consumer retail purchases from companies such as Amazon. But e-commerce involves much more than electronically mediated financial transactions between organizations and customers. Most commentators now consider e-commerce to refer to *all* electronically mediated transactions between an organization and any third party it deals with. By this definition, all 'moments of truth' involving electronically mediated requests for information and all on-line inbound and outbound marketing communications such as e-mail marketing are also part of e-commerce. Kalakota and Whinston (1997) refer to a range of different perspectives for e-commerce that highlight the type of communications involved:

1   *A communications perspective* – the delivery of information, products/services or payment by electronic means.
2   *A business process perspective* – the application of technology towards the automation of business transactions and workflows.
3   *A service perspective* – enabling cost cutting at the same time as increasing the speed and quality of service delivery.
4   *An on-line perspective* – the buying and selling of products and information on-line.

Similarly, Zwass (1998) uses a broad definition of e-commerce. He refers to it as:

> the sharing of business information, maintaining business relationships, and conducting business transactions by means of telecommunications networks.

When evaluating the impact of e-commerce on an organization, it is instructive to identify opportunities for buy-side and sell-side e-commerce transactions. *Buy-side e-commerce* refers to transactions to procure resources needed by an organization from its suppliers. These business-to-business (B2B) transactions are often neglected in favour of discussion of *Sell-side e-commerce*, which refers to transactions involved with selling products to an organization's customers through distributors as appropriate.

E-business is broader: referring to both buy-side and sell-side e-commerce and the internal use of Internet technologies through an intranet to streamline business processes. Using an intranet to share ideas and market research on a new product development or marketing per-

formance data are examples of e-business marketing applications.

E-marketing can be simply expressed as the use of electronic communications technology to achieve marketing objectives (see, for example, McDonald and Wilson, 1999). The electronic communications technology refers to:

1   The use of Internet-based (TCP/IP) network technology for communications within an organization using an intranet, beyond the organization to partners such as suppliers, distributors and key account customers using password-based access to extranets and the open Internet, where information is accessible by all with Internet access.
2   The use of web servers or websites to enable informational or financial exchanges as e-commerce transactions.
3   The use of other digital access platforms, such as interactive digital TV, wireless or mobile phones and games consoles.
4   The use of electronic mail for managing enquiries (inbound e-mail) and for promotion (outbound e-mail).
5   Integration of the digital access platforms and e-mail with other information systems, such as customer databases and applications for customer relationship management and supply chain management.

To illustrate some of the opportunities of e-marketing, it is useful to reapply the definition of marketing from the Chartered Institute of Marketing:

> E-marketing can identify, anticipate and satisfy customer needs efficiently.

Taking a website as a major part of e-marketing, consider how a website can fulfil these requirements of marketing. It can:

● *Identify* needs from customer comments, enquiries, requests and complaints solicited via e-mail and the website's contact facility, bulletin boards, chat rooms, on-line searches and sales patterns (seeing what's selling and what's not, recorded in the web log, which reveals insights into interests determined by pages visited). On-line surveys ask how to improve the site or products. Finally, there is a proliferation of on-line secondary sources of research, many of which provide free in-depth insights into customer needs.

- *Anticipate* customer needs by asking customers questions and engaging them in a dynamic dialogue built on the trust of opt-in e-mail. Collaborative filtering, as used by Amazon, helps to identify and anticipate what customers might like given that buyers of similar books have similar interests. Profiling techniques allow many companies to perform data mining to discover and anticipate buyer's needs. Cookie-based profiling allows companies to analyse a visitor's interests without even knowing your name – courtesy of a piece of code sent to the visitor's PC. It recognizes your PC and records which types of sites (interests) you have and can serve adverts and offers based on predicted interests.
- *Satisfy* needs with prompt responses, punctual deliveries, order status updates, helpful reminders, after-sales services and added value services, combined with the dynamic dialogue. The dialogue maintains permission to continue communicating and then adds value by delivering useful content in the right context (right time and right amount).
- *Efficiently* means in an automated way (or partially automated) . . . an efficient, yet hopefully not impersonal, way (i.e. it allows tailor-made technology to improve service quality and increase the marketer's memory to help maintain the customer relationship through time).

It is apparent from these applications that e-marketing extends beyond the website to include all use of digital technology to manage the customer relationship. Databases are increasingly used to manage and record all interactions with customers, whether sales transactions, inbound enquiries via phone or e-mail and outbound communications such as a mail shot or e-mail shot.

An alternative perspective on e-marketing is provided by the term 'Internet marketing', which has been described simply as *'the application of the Internet and related digital technologies to achieve marketing objectives'* (Chaffey *et al.*, 2003). In practice, Internet-based marketing is a subset of e-marketing that will include the use of a company website in conjunction with promotional techniques such as banner advertising, direct e-mail and links or services from other websites to acquire new customers and provide services to existing customers that help develop the customer relationship.

Participants in e-marketing

The options for digital communications between a business and its customers are summarized in Figure 25.1. The bulk of Internet business both now and in the forseeable future comes from industrial and commercial markets known as business-to-business (B2B), and not consumer markets known as business-to-consumer (B2C) markets. Most estimates suggest that B2B companies will reap 10 times more revenue than their B2C counterparts. In 2000, Gartner estimated that worldwide B2B transactions will rise from $145 billion in 1999 to $7.3 trillion in the year 2004. These increases are driven by the desire of large organizations to reduce costs and increase supply chain efficiency. For example, in the late 1990s, General Electric made the decision to procure $1 billion worth of purchases on-line in year 1, followed by $3 billion in year 2, followed by total procurement on-line. More recently, Cisco Systems announced that they will no longer do business with suppliers who can't take orders via the web. Ford and General Motors have combined forces through the *B2B marketplace* Covisint (www.covisint.net) and moved their $300 and $500 billion dollar supply chains on-line. Already large-scale trading is occurring. It was reported in May 2001 that the largest auction

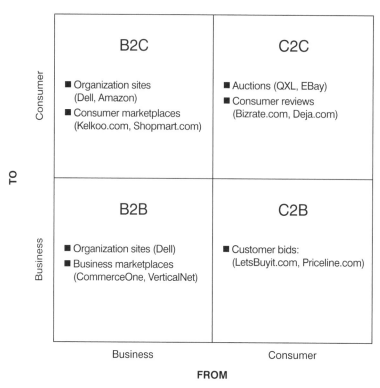

Figure 25.1   Options for on-line communications between an organization and its customers

ever had occurred in which five suppliers participated, 1200 different parts changed hands, with total order volume over 3 billion euros.

The other transaction types shown in Figure 25.1 are less significant in terms of revenue volumes: these are customer-to-customer interactions (C2C; best known as consumer auctions, but can also be achieved as B2C and B2B communities) and customer-to-business (C2B; novel buying models where customers approach the business on their own terms).

New media communications characteristics

Through understanding the key communications characteristics of the digital media, we can exploit these media while guarding against their weaknesses. The six key changes in moving from traditional media to new media are:

1   *From push to pull.* Traditional media such as Print, TV and Radio are push media, a one-way street where information flows are mainly unidirectional, unless direct response elements are built in. In contrast, the web is a pull medium. This is its biggest strength and its biggest weakness. It is a strength since pull means that prospects and customers only visit your site when it enters their head to do so – when they have a defined need. They are proactive and self-selecting. But this is a weakness since on-line pull means we have less control than in traditional communications, where the message is pushed out to a defined audience. What are the e-marketing implications of the pull medium? First, we need to provide the physical stimuli to encourage visits to websites. This may mean traditional

ads, direct mail or physical reminders. Second, we need to ensure our site is optimized for search engines – it is registered and is ranked highly on relevant keyword searches. Third, e-mail is important – this is an on-line push medium, it should be a priority objective of website design to capture customer's e-mail addresses in order that opt-in e-mail can be used to push relevant and timely messages to customers.

2 *From monologue to dialogue.* Creating a dialogue through interactivity is the next important feature of the web and new media. A website, interactive digital TV and even a mobile phone enables us to enter dialogue with customers. These can be short term (perhaps an on-line chat to customer support) or long term (lifelong dialogues discussing product and supply requirements). These dialogues can enhance customer service, deepen relationships and trust, and so build loyalty.

But digital dialogues have a less obvious benefit also – intelligence. Interactive tools for customer self-help can help collect intelligence – clickstream analysis recorded in the web log file can help us build up valuable pictures of customer preferences. If we profile customers, placing them into different segments, then we can build a more detailed picture that is used to refine our products and offers.

3 *From one-to-many to one-to-some and one-to-one.* Traditional push communications are one-to-many. From one company to many customers, often the same message to different segments and often poorly targeted. With new media, 'one-to-some' – reaching a niche becomes more practical – e-marketers can tailor and target their message to different segments through providing different site content for different audiences through mass customization. We can even move to one-to-one communications where personalized messages can be delivered according to customer preferences.

4 *From one-to-many to many-to-many communications.* New media also enable many-to-many communications. Hoffman and

Novak (1996) noted that new media are many-to-many media. Here customers can interact with other customers via your website or in independent communities. The success of on-line auctions such as eBay also shows the power of many-to-many communications. However, on-line discussion groups represent a threat, since it is difficult to control negative communications about a company. For example, one recent post to newsgroup 'uk.food+drink.misc' by a consumer referred to finding a rat's foot in a supermarket product. Since the supermarket was monitoring these groups it was able to attempt to control the situation by explaining that it was 'an irregularly shaped, very thin fragment of vegetable material'. So, the e-marketing actions of many-to-many communications are to consider whether you should set up on-line communities on your site, or whether you can tap into other independent communities on specialist portals.

5 *From 'lean-back' to 'lean-forward'.* New media are also intense media – they are lean-forward media in which the website usually has the visitor's undivided attention. This intensity means that the customer wants to be in control and wants to experience flow and responsiveness to their needs. First impressions are important. If the visitor to your site does not find what they are looking for immediately, whether through poor design or slow speed, they will move on, probably never to return.

6 *Integrated.* Although new media have distinct characteristics compared to traditional media, this does not mean we should necessarily concentrate our communications on new media. Rather, we should combine and integrate new and traditional media according to their strengths. We can then achieve synergy – the sum is greater than their parts. Most of us still spend most of our time in the real world rather than the virtual world, so off-line promotion of the proposition of a website is important. It is also important to support mixed-mode buying. For example, a

customer wanting to buy a computer may see a TV ad for a certain brand which raises awareness of the brand and then sees an advert in a print ad that directs him across to the website for further information. However, the customer does not want to buy on-line, preferring the phone, but the site allows for this by prompting with a phone number at the right time. Here all the different communications channels are mutually supporting each other. Similarly, inbound communications to a company needs to be managed. Consider if the customer needs support for an error with their system. They may start by using the on-site diagnostics, which do not solve the problem. They then ring customer support. This process will be much more effective if support can access the details of the problem as previously typed in by the customer to the diagnostics package.

E-marketing planning

The e-marketing plan should be informed by, and integrate with, the objectives and strategies of the marketing plan. Plans should be integrated such that developing the e-marketing plan may give insights that result in the other plans being updated. Smith and Chaffey (2001) use the SOSTAC® framework to suggest an approach to e-marketing planning, and a similar approach will be adopted here. SOSTAC stands for: Situation, Objectives and Strategy, Tactics, Action and Control. As such, it has a structure that is broadly consistent with other models of the process of strategic marketing planning as described, for example, by McDonald in Chapter 5.

Situation analysis

Situation analysis is the first part of the e-marketing plan. It explains 'where are we now?' This includes analysis internally within the organization and, externally, of the business environment. These traditional analytical areas

should also be assessed from an e-marketing perspective as follows:

- *KPIs* – Key Performance Indicators which identify the business success criteria, results and performance against targets and benchmarks.
- *SWOT analysis* – identifying e-marketing specific internal Strengths, and Weaknesses, as well as external Opportunities and Threats. For instance, are resources adequate, what are the SWOT elements for the current on-line presence compared with competitors?
- *PEST* – Political, Economic, Social and Technological variables that shape your marketplace. Legal constraints on e-marketing are particularly significant in controlling use of customer data for direct marketing, for example through e-mail, and the introduction of new laws should be carefully monitored.
- *Customers* – how many are on-line, how many prefer different platforms such as iTV and mobile or wireless? Are there new channel segments emerging?
- *Competitors* – who are they? What is their on-line proposition? How successful are they on-line? Are there new on-line adversaries?
- *Distributors* – are new, on-line, intermediaries emerging while old off-line distributors are being wiped out (disintermediation)? What are the potential channel conflicts?

External analysis

We will concentrate on the micro-environment factors of customers (demand analysis), competitors and distributors.

Demand analysis

For customers, market research should identify which customers are on-line – what are their profiles in terms of geo-demographics and for B2B their position in the decision-making unit. To build demand estimates, we need to know the proportion of customers in each market and segment who:

1 *Have access to different channels.* Figure 25.2, a curve typical for most western countries, shows that digital TV and mobile phone access are increasingly important for B2C marketing, while in B2B markets Internet access is higher (Figure 25.3).

2 *Are influenced by using which channel or channels?* Although the proportion of e-commerce transactions for all purchases is low, the role of the Internet in influencing purchase is significant for high involvement purchases such as financial services, holidays or cars. For example, it is now estimated that over half the purchasers of new cars in some western countries will research the purchase on-line, even though the proportion purchasing entirely on-line is only in single figures. Understanding the reach of a website and its role in influencing purchase is clearly important in setting e-marketing budgets.

3 *Purchase using which channel or channels?* The propensity to purchase on-line is dependent on different variables over which the marketer has relatively little control. However, factors which affect the propensity to purchase can be estimated for different types of products. De Kare-Silver (2000) suggests factors that should be considered include product characteristics, familiarity and confidence, and consumer attributes. Typical results from the evaluation are: groceries (27/50), mortgages (15/50), travel (31/50) and books (38/50). De Kare-Silver states that any product scoring over 20 has good potential, since the score for consumer attributes is likely to increase through time. Given this, he suggests companies will regularly need to review the score for their products. The effectiveness of this test is now demonstrated by data for on-line purchases in different product categories (Figure 25.4).

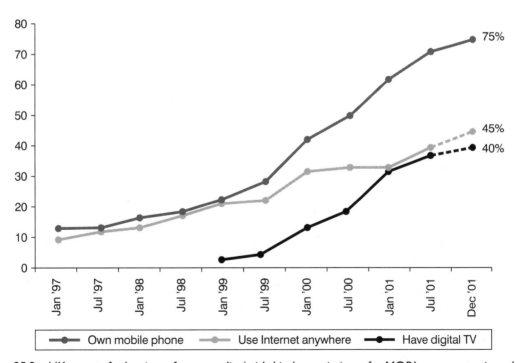

Figure 25.2   UK rates of adoption of new media (with kind permission of e-MORI, www.e-mori.co.uk)

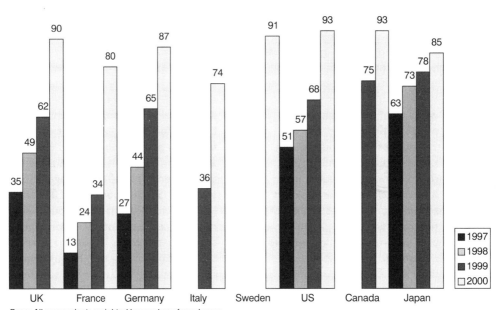

Base: All respondents weighted by number of employees
Source for 1997, 1998, 1999: Spectrum/NOP International Benchmarking Study

Figure 25.3   Proportion of organizations with Internet access
Source: DTI (2000).

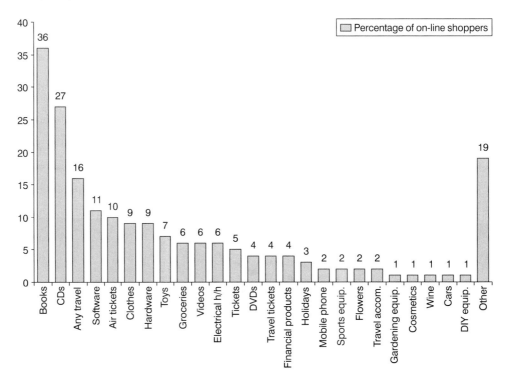

Figure 25.4   Percentage of on-line purchasers in the six months to November 2000 (BMRB, 2001)

It is also important to understand the barriers and motivations that affect the use of digital media by consumers. The reasons, aspirations and expectations can then be reflected in your communications.

Competitor analysis

For competitors, benchmarking will reveal how digital media are being exploited. For e-tailers continuous monitoring is required and services such as that of Gomez.com provide independent scorecards. Criteria include ease of use, customer confidence (e.g. availability, depth and breadth of customer service options, including phone, e-mail and branch locations), on-site resources, relationship services and overall cost. The success of different companies in and out of sector in achieving on-line sales should also be benchmarked (see Table 25.1 and the section on objective setting).

Intermediary analysis

For distributors and intermediaries, a key influence of the Internet is its impact on channel structures. These marketplace phenomena should be assessed and then evaluated as part of strategy:

- *Disintermediation* – the removal of intermediaries such as distributors or brokers that formerly linked a company to its customers. A car manufacturer selling direct to customers rather than through a dealership is an example of this.
- *Reintermediation* – the creation of new intermediaries between customers and suppliers providing services such as supplier search and product evaluation. Many new brokers offering discounted cars have had a significant impact on the car market.
- *Countermediation* – the creation of a new intermediary by an established company. Here an existing player or players form a new intermediary to compete against new intermediaries.

Internal analysis

Internal analysis involves assessment of the current status of e-marketing implementation. Quelch and Klein (1996) developed a five-stage model referring to the development of sell-side e-commerce. For existing companies the stages are: (1) image and product information; (2) information collection; (3) customer support and service; (4) internal support and service; (5) transactions. Considering sell-side e-commerce,

Table 25.1	Variations in on-line revenue contribution		
Organization	*Sector*	*On-line contribution (%)*	*Overall turnover*
Cisco	B2B Networking hardware	90	$19 bn
easyJet	B2C Air travel	85	£264 m
Dell	B2B, B2C Computers	48	$25 bn
Land's End Clothing	B2C Clothing	11	$1.3 bn
Book Club Associates	B2C Books	10	£100 m
Electrocomponents	B2B Electronics	7	£761 m group
Domino's Pizza	B2C Food	3.4	£76 m
Tesco	B2C Grocery	1.4	£18.4 bn
Thomas Cook	B2C Travel	<1	£1.8 bn

Source: Company websites, end 2000.

Chaffey *et al.* (2003) suggest there are six choices for a company deciding on which *marketing services* to offer via an on-line presence.

- *Level 0. No website or presence on the web.*
- *Level 1. Basic web presence.* Company places an entry in a website listing company names such as www.yell.co.uk to make people searching the web aware of the existence of a company or its products. There is no website at this stage.
- *Level 2. Simple static informational website.* Contains basic company and product information, sometimes referred to as brochureware.
- *Level 3. Simple interactive site.* Users are able to search the site and make queries to retrieve information such as product availability and pricing. Queries by e-mail may also be supported.
- *Level 4. Interactive site supporting transactions with users.* The functions offered will vary according to the company. They will usually be limited to on-line buying. Other functions might include an interactive customer service helpdesk which is linked into direct marketing objectives.
- *Level 5. Fully interactive site supporting the whole buying process.* Provides relationship marketing with individual customers and facilitates the full range of marketing exchanges.

Note that such stage models of website development are most appropriate to companies whose products can be sold on-line through transactional e-commerce. Stage models also apply to a range of different types of on-line presence and business models, each with different objectives. Four of the major different types of on-line presence are:

1 *Transactional e-commerce site.* Stage models as described above. Examples: a car manufacturer such as Vauxhall (www.buypower.vauxhall.co.uk) or retailers such as Tesco (www.tesco.com).
2 *Services-oriented relationship building website.* For companies such as professional services companies, on-line transactions are inappropriate. Through time these sites will develop increasing information depth and question and answer facilities. Examples: PricewaterhouseCooper (www.pwcglobal.com), Accenture (www.accenture.com) and Arthur Andersen KnowledgeSpace (www.knowledgespace.com).
3 *Brand building site.* These are intended to support the off-line brand by developing an on-line experience of the brand. They are typical for low-value, high-volume Fast Moving Consumer Goods (FMCG brands). Examples: Tango (www.tango.com), Guinness (www.guinness.com).
4 *Portal site.* Service delivery and links to information services. Examples: Yahoo! (www.yahoo.com) and Vertical Net (www.verticalnet.com).

Similar stage models can also be developed for all aspects of supply chain management which are necessary as part of delivering the marketing concept. Table 25.2 presents a synthesis of stage models for e-business development. Organizations can assess their position on the continuum between stages 1 and 4 for the different aspects of e-business development shown in the column on the left. When companies devise strategies and tactics they may return to the stage models to specify which level of innovation they are looking to achieve at future points in time.

The internal analysis also looks at key performance indicators (KPIs) of e-marketing. Common KPIs used to assess on-line the significance of e-marketing activities include traditional measures such as:

- Enquiries.
- Sales.
- Market share.
- ROI (return on investment).

Other KPIs are specific to e-marketing:

- *On-line revenue contribution* (see section on objective setting).
- *Unique visitors* – the number of separate, individual visitors who visit the site (typically over a month).

Table 25.2 A stage model for e-business development

	1. Web presence	2. E-commerce	3. Integrated e-commerce	4. E-business
Services available	Brochureware or interaction with product catalogues and customer service	Transactional e-commerce on buy-side or sell-side	Buy- and sell-side integrated with ERP or legacy systems. Personalization of services	Full integration between all internal organizational processes and elements of the value network
Organizational scope	Isolated departments, e.g. marketing department	Cross-organizational	Cross-organizational	Across the enterprise and beyond (extraprise)
Transformation	Technological infrastructure	Technology and new responsibilities identified for e-commerce	Internal business processes and company structure	Change to e-business culture, linking of business processes with partners
Strategy	Limited	Sell-side e-commerce strategy, not well integrated with business strategy	E-commerce strategy integrated with business strategy using a value-chain approach	E-business strategy incorporated as part of business strategy

Source: Chaffey (2002).

- Total numbers of *sessions* or *visits* to a website. (Note that '*hits*' are a spurious measure, since when a web page is downloaded to the PC, a number of separate data transfers or hits takes place, usually one for each HTML and graphics file. Marketers should measure *page impressions* because they are a real measure of customer traffic to your site and, for an advertiser, this equates with other familiar measures such as 'opportunities to view'.) Attraction efficiency (Figure 25.5) indicates the proportion of your target audience you attract to the site or its reach.
- *Repeat visits* – average number of visits per individual. Total number of sessions divided by the number of unique visitors. Update your site more often and people come back more often. *Cookies* can help track repeat visits.
- *Duration* – average length of time visitors spend on your site (but remember that for some areas of the site such as on-line sales or customer service you may want to minimize duration). A similar measure is number of pages viewed per visitor.
- *Subscription rates* – numbers of visitors subscribing for services such as opt-in e-mail and newsletters.
- *Conversion rates* – the percentage of visitors converting to subscribers (or becoming customers). This is critical to e-marketing. Let's take an example. Say 2 per cent of 5000 visitors to a site in a month convert to 100

customers who place an order; £10 000 cost divided by 100 conversions = £100 cost per order. Now imagine you can double your conversion rate, or better still quadruple it to 8 per cent; you then get £25 cost per order. The leverage impact caused by improved conversion rates is huge – revenues go up and percentage of marketing costs go down. Figure 25.5 provides a summary of different aspects of conversion from Chaffey (2001), which is adapted from Figure 2 in Berthon *et al.* (1998). It also highlights the importance of measuring return visitors to the site.

- *Attrition rates* through the on-line buying process.
- *Churn rates* – percentage of subscribers withdrawing or unsubscribing.
- *Click-through rates* (CTR) from a banner ad or web link on another site to your own.

E-marketing objectives

Objectives clarify the purpose and direction of e-marketing. Smith and Chaffey (2001) suggest there are five broad benefits, reasons or objectives of e-marketing. These can be summarized as the 5Ss of e-marketing objectives. Marketers will decide whether all or only some will drive e-marketing:

- *Sell.* Grow sales (through wider distribution to customers you can't service off-line or perhaps a wider product range than in local store, or better prices).
- *Serve.* Add value (give customers extra benefits on-line, or product development in response to on-line dialogue).
- *Speak.* Get closer to customers by tracking them, asking them questions, conducting on-line interviews, creating a dialogue, monitoring chat rooms, learning about them.
- *Save.* Save costs – of service, sales transactions and administration, print and post. Can you reduce transaction costs and therefore either make on-line sales more profitable or use cost savings to enable you to cut prices, which in turn could enable you to generate greater market share?
- *Sizzle.* Extend the brand on-line. Reinforce brand values in a totally new medium. The web scores very highly as a medium for creating brand awareness and recognition.

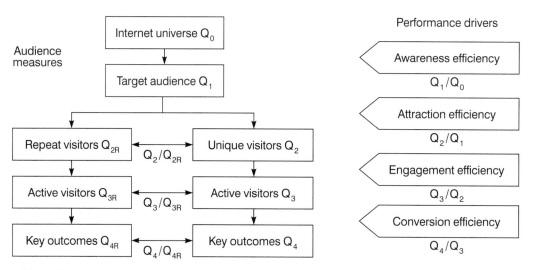

Figure 25.5   Key metrics indicating the efficiency of web marketing in attracting and converting visitors to customers

Specific objectives are created for each. Consider sales – a typical objective might be:

> To grow the business with on-line sales, e.g. to generate at least 10 per cent of sales on-line. Within six months.

Or

> To generate an extra £100 000 worth of sales on-line by December.

These objectives can be further broken down, e.g. to achieve £100 000 of on-line sales means you have to generate 1000 on-line customers spending on average £100 in the time period. If, say, your conversion rate of visitors to customers was a high 10 per cent, then this means you have to generate 10 000 visitors to your site.

Specific targets for the *on-line revenue contribution* for different e-channels should be set for the future, as shown in Figure 25.6. For example, Fisher (2001), in the *Financial Times*, reported a range of variation in on-line revenue contribution for Sandvik Steel. At the time of the article, only a small number of all orders were transacted over the web. Nordic countries are leading the way. Around 20 per cent of all orders from Denmark are on-line and 31 per cent of those from Sweden. The proportion in the US, however, is only 3 per cent, since most business goes through distributors and is conducted by *electronic data interchange* (EDI). Over the next six months, the company hopes to raise the US figure to 40 per cent and, in two years, between 40 and 50 per cent of total orders are planned to come via the web.

Annika Roos, marketing manager at Sandvik Steel, specified Sandvik's objectives as follows: 'by the end of December, 2001, we want a confirmation from at least 80 per cent of key customers that they consider the extranet to be a major reason to deal with Sandvik. Our aim is to have 200 key customers using the extranet at the end of June 2001.'

Objectives should also be set for the percentage of customers who are reached or influenced by each channel (*indirect on-line revenue contribution* or brand awareness in the target market). The on-line revenue contribution should also consider *cannibalization* – are

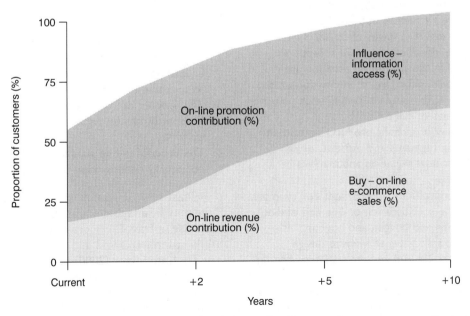

Figure 25.6   An example of objective targets for direct and indirect on-line revenue contribution

on-line sales achieved at the expense of traditional channels? Another major on-line objective might be to consolidate relationships and increase loyalty from 50 to 75 per cent among high-spending customer segments during the year.

Strategies

Strategy summarizes objectives and establishes how they'll be achieved. Many of the key questions that an e-marketing strategy should answer are common to those for a marketing strategy, namely:

- Which *segments*, and selected *target markets* are being targeted.
- *Positioning* (P) is a fundamental part of the overall customer proposition or offering, e.g. what exactly is the product, its price and perceived value in the marketplace.
- Source of differentiation – what is the value proposition?
- Which access platforms should e-marketing be achieved through. For most organizations, websites or e-mail marketing will be appropriate, but are mobile marketing or interactive TV further options? For each platform, different stages of on-line services should be identified for future roll-out, as discussed in the section on situation analysis. For example, what level of interaction on-site – brochure, two-way interactive sales support, on-line sales or full e-CRM?
- Should new or existing products be sold into all existing segments and markets, or can specific or new segments and markets be targeted?
- What resources are appropriate? For example, what is the split between on-line and off-line e-marketing and budget, and how are resources split between website design, website service and website traffic generation.

In this section, some of the key strategic e-marketing options are outlined below based on the discussion in Chaffey (2002).

Decision 1. E-marketing priorities

The e-marketing strategy must be directed according to the priority of different strategic objectives, as discussed above. E-marketing strategy priorities can be summarized as Gulati and Garino (2000) have said by *'Getting the right mix of bricks and clicks'*. 'Bricks and mortar' refers to a traditional organization with limited on-line presence, 'clicks and mortar' to a business combining an on-line and off-line presence, and 'clicks only or Internet pure-play' refers to an organization principally with an on-line presence. In reality, there is a continuum of options from a replacement strategy (Internet pure-play) to complementary strategy (clicks and mortar).

If it is believed that sales through digital channels will primarily replace other channels, then it is important to invest in the technical, human and organizational resources to achieve this. A replace strategy was chosen by airlines such as easyJet and Ryanair, who now sell over 90 per cent of their tickets on-line. Kumar (1999) provides a framework to assess the replace versus complement strategy options. He suggests that replacement is most likely to happen when:

1 Customer access to the Internet is high.
2 The Internet can offer a better value proposition than other media (i.e. propensity to purchase on-line is high).
3 The product can be delivered over the Internet (it can be argued that this is not essential).
4 The product can be standardized (user does not usually need to view to purchase).

If at least two of Kumar's conditions are met there may be a replacement effect. For example, purchase of travel services or insurance on-line fulfils criteria 1, 2 and 4.

De Kare-Silver (2000) suggests that strategic e-commerce alternatives for companies should be selected according to the percentage of the target market using the channel and the commitment of the company, the idea being that the commitment should mirror the readiness of consumers to use the new medium. If the objective is to achieve a high on-line revenue contribution of >70 per cent, then this will require fundamental change for the company to transform to a 'bricks and clicks' or 'clicks only' company.

Decision 2. Restructuring

Closely related to decision 1 is whether the company should restructure in order to achieve the priorities set for e-marketing. Gulati and Garino (2000) identify a range of approaches from integration to separation. The choices are:

1 *In-house division (integration)*. Example: RS Components Internet Trading Channel (www.rswww.com).
2 *Joint venture (mixed)*. The company creates an on-line presence in association with another player.
3 *Strategic partnership (mixed)*. This may also be achieved through purchase of existing dot-coms; for example, in the UK Great Universal Stores acquired e-tailer Jungle.com for its strength in selling technology products and strong brand, while John Lewis purchased Buy.com's UK operations.
4 *Spin-off (separation)*. Example: Egg bank is a spin-off from Prudential financial services company.

Gulati and Garino (2000) give the advantages of the integration approach as being able to leverage existing brands, to be able to share information and achieve economies of scale (e.g. purchasing and distribution efficiencies). They say the spin-off approach gives better focus, more flexibility for innovation and the possibility of funding through flotation. For example, Egg have been able to create a brand distinct from Prudential and has developed new revenue models such as retail sales commission. They say that separation is preferable in situations where:

- A different customer segment or product mix will be offered on-line.
- Differential pricing is required between on-line and off-line.
- If there is a major channel conflict.
- If the Internet threatens the current business model.
- If additional funding or specialist staff need to be attracted.

Additionally, from a technology viewpoint it may be quicker to develop a new infrastructure rather than integrating with an existing one, but again economies of scale are lost.

Decision 3. Business and revenue models

Another aspect of e-marketing strategy formulation is review of opportunities from new business and revenue models, which are a summary of how a company will generate revenue by identifying its product offering, value-added services, revenue sources and target customers.

Timmers (1999) identifies no less than 11 different types of business model that can be facilitated by the web as follows:

1 *E-shop*. Marketing of a company or shop via web.
2 *E-procurement*. Electronic tendering and procurement of goods and services.
3 *E-malls*. A collection of e-shops such as Barclays Square (www.barclays-square.com).
4 *E-auctions*. These can be for B2C, e.g. Ebay (www.ebay.com), or B2C, e.g. QXL (www.qxl.com).
5 *Virtual communities*. These can be B2C communities such as Xoom (www.xoom.com) or B2B communities such as Vertical Net (www.vertical.net). They are important for their potential in e-marketing and are described in the 'Focus on virtual communities' section in Chapter 6.
6 *Collaboration platforms*. These enable collaboration between businesses or individuals, e.g. e-groups (www.egroups.com),

now part of Yahoo! (www.yahoo.com)
services.

7   *Third-party marketplaces.* Marketplaces are
    described in the 'Focus on' section of
    Chapter 9.

8   *Value-chain integrators.* Offer a range of
    services across the value chain.

9   *Value-chain service providers.* Specialize in
    providing functions for a specific part of the
    value chain, such as the logistics company
    UPS (www.ups.com).

10 *Information brokerage.* Providing information
    for consumers and businesses, often to assist
    in making the buying decision or for business
    operations or leisure.

11 *Trust and other services.* Examples of trust
    services include Which Web Trader
    (www.which.net/webtrader) or Truste
    (www.truste.org), which authenticate the
    quality of service provided by companies
    trading on the web.

Evaluating new models is important, since if
companies do not innovate then competitors
and new entrants will and companies will find
it difficult to regain the initiative. Equally, if
inappropriate business or distribution models
are chosen, then companies may make substantial losses.

One example of how companies can
review and revise their business model is
provided by Dell Computers. Dell gained early
mover advantage in the mid-1990s when it
became one of the first companies to offer PCs
for sale on-line. Its sales of PCs and peripherals
grew from the mid-1990s with on-line sales of
$1 million per day to 2000 sales of $50 million
per day. Based on this success, it has looked at
new business models it can use in combination
with its powerful brand to provide new services to its existing customer base and also to
generate revenue through new customers. In
September 2000, Dell announced plans to
become a supplier of IT consulting services
through linking with enterprise resource planning specialists such as software suppliers,
systems integrators and business consulting

firms. This venture will enable the facility of
Dell's Premier Pages to be integrated into the
procurement component of ERP systems such
as SAP and Baan, thus avoiding the need for
rekeying and reducing costs.

In a separate initiative, Dell launched a
B2B marketplace aimed at discounted office
goods and services procurements, including
PCs, peripherals, software, stationery and
travel (www.dellmarketplace.com).

Chaffey (2002) describes three different
perspectives for considering business and revenue models, shown in Figure 25.7. Yahoo!
(marked with Y in the figure) has been one of
the more successful Internet pure-plays, since it
has developed a range of revenue sources
through growth and acquisition.

1   *Marketplace position perspective.* Here Yahoo! is
    both a retailer and a marketplace intermediary.

2   *Revenue model perspective.* Yahoo! has
    commission-based sales through Yahoo!
    shopping and also has advertising as a revenue
    model.

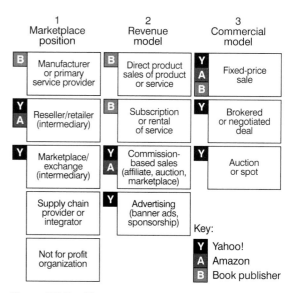

Figure 25.7   Alternative perspectives on business
and revenue models.
Source: Chaffey (2002).

3 *Commercial arrangement perspective.* Yahoo! is involved in all three types of commercial arrangement shown.

Michael Porter (2001) urges caution against overemphasis on new business or revenue models, and attacks those who have suggested that the Internet invalidates his well-known strategy models. He says:

> Many have assumed that the Internet changes everything, rendering all the old rules about companies and competition obsolete. That may be a natural reaction, but it is a dangerous one . . . decisions that have eroded the attractiveness of their industries and undermined their own competitive advantages.

He gives the example of some industries using the Internet to change the basis of competition away from quality, features and service and towards price, making it harder for anyone in their industries to turn a profit. In reviewing industry structure, he reinterprets the well-known five forces model, concluding that many of the effects of the Internet, such as commoditization, are damaging to industry. He also reiterates the importance of six fundamental principles of strategic positioning:

1 The right goal: superior long-term return on investment.
2 A value proposition distinct from those of the competition.
3 A distinctive value chain to achieve competitive advantage.
4 Trade-offs in products or services may be required to achieve distinction.
5 Strategy defines how all elements of what a company does fit together.
6 Strategy involves continuity of direction.

Decision 4. Marketplace restructuring

A related issue to reviewing new business and revenue models is to consider the options created through disintermediation and reintermediation within a marketplace, as discussed in the section on situation analysis. Options can be summarized as:

- Disintermediation (sell direct).
- Create new on-line intermediary (countermediation).
- Partner with new on-line or existing intermediaries.
- Do-nothing!

Prioritizing strategic partnerships as part of the move from a value chain to a value network should also occur as part of this decision.

Decision 5. Market and product development strategies

A further e-marketing strategy decision is whether to use new technologies to expand the scope of the business into new markets and products. As for decision 1 the decision is a balance between fear of the do-nothing option and fear of poor return on investment for strategies that fail. The model of Ansoff (1957) is still useful as a means for marketing managers to discuss market and product development using electronic technologies. Options to be considered in an e-marketing context are:

1 *Market penetration.* Digital channels can be used to sell more existing products into existing markets. On-line channels can help consolidate or increase market share by providing additional promotion and customer service facilities amongst customers in an existing market. The Internet can also be used for customer retention management. This is a relatively conservative use of the Internet.
2 *Market development.* Here on-line channels are used to sell into new markets, taking advantage of the low cost of advertising internationally without the necessity for a supporting sales infrastructure in the customers' country. This is a relatively

conservative use of the Internet, but is a great opportunity for SMEs to increase exports at a low cost, but it does require overcoming the barriers to exporting.

A less evident benefit of the Internet is that as well as selling into new geographical markets, products can also be sold to new market segments or different types of customers. This may happen simply as a by-product of having a website. For example, RS components (www.rswww.com), a supplier of a range of MRO items, found that 10 per cent of the web-based sales were to individual consumers rather than traditional business customers. The UK retailer Argos found the opposite was true, with 10 per cent of website sales from businesses, when their traditional market was consumer based. The Internet may offer further opportunities for selling to market sub-segments that have not been previously targeted. For example, a product sold to large businesses may also appeal to SMEs, or a product targeted at young people could also appeal to some members of an older audience. Target market strategies and positioning are described in Chapter 5.

3 *Product development.* New digital products or services can be developed that can be delivered by the Internet. These are typically information products, for example on-line trade magazine *Construction Weekly* has diversified to a B2B portal *Construction Plus* (www.constructionplus.com), which has new revenue streams. This is innovative use of the Internet.

4 *Diversification.* In this sector, new products are developed which are sold into new markets. For example, *Construction Plus* now has a more international orientation.

Strategy should also exploit your *distinctive competitive advantage*. Play to your strengths. Strategy is also is influenced by both the prioritization of objectives (sell, serve, speak, save and sizzle) and, of course, the amount of resources available.

Decision 6. Positioning and differentiation strategies

Companies can position their products relative to competitor offerings according to four main variables: product quality, service quality, price and fulfilment time. As mentioned earlier, Deise *et al.* (2000) suggest it is useful to review these as an equation of how they combine to influence customer perceptions of value or brand.

$$\text{Customer value (brand perception)} = \frac{\text{Product quality} \times \text{Service quality}}{\text{Price} \times \text{Fulfilment time}}$$

Strategies should review the extent to which increases in product and service quality can be matched by decreases in price and fulfilment time.

Chaston (2000) argues that there are four options for strategic focus to position a company in the on-line marketplace. He says that these should build on existing strengths, but can use the on-line facilities to enhance the positioning as follows:

- *Product performance excellence.* Enhance by providing on-line product customization.
- *Price performance excellence.* Use the facilities of the Internet to offer favourable pricing to loyal customers or to reduce prices where demand is low (for example, British Midland airlines use auctions to sell underused capacity on flights).
- *Transactional excellence.* A software and hardware e-tailer can offer transactional excellence through combining pricing information with dynamic availability information on products listing number in stock, number on order and when expected.
- *Relationship excellence.* For example, personalization features to enable customers to review sales order history and place repeat orders.

Plant (2000) also identifies four different positional e-strategic directions which he refers to as technology leadership, service leadership, market leadership and brand leadership. The author acknowledges that these aren't exclusive. It is interesting that this author does not see price differentiation as important, rather on-line he sees brand and service as important to success.

The differential advantage and positioning of on-line services can be clarified and communicated internally and externally by developing an *on-line value proposition* (OVP) or *Internet value proposition* (IVP). This is similar to a unique selling proposition, but is developed for e-commerce services. In developing an IVP, managers should identify:

- A clear differentiation of the Internet proposition from competitors based on product features or service quality.
- Target market segment(s) that the proposition will appeal to.
- How the proposition will be communicated to site visitors and in all marketing communications. Developing a strap line can help this.
- How the proposition is delivered across different parts of the buying process.
- How the proposition will be delivered and supported by resources. Is the proposition genuine? Will resources be internal or external?

Ideally, the e-commerce site should have an additional value proposition to further differentiate the company's products or services.

Having a clear on-line value proposition has several benefits:

- It helps distinguish an e-commerce site from its competitors (this should be a website design objective).
- It helps provide a focus to marketing efforts and company staff are clear about the purpose of the site.
- If the proposition is clear it can be used for PR and word of mouth recommendations may be made about the company. For example, the

clear proposition of Amazon has used is that prices are discounted and that a wide range of titles are available.
- It can be linked to the normal product propositions of a company or its product.

Tactics

Tactics are the details of strategy. E-marketing tactics define the different e-marketing tools to be used and their sequence or stages. The main tools used to implement the e-marketing tactics are:

1 The website and integrated database.
2 Customer relationship management tools, principally the integrated database.
3 Opt-in e-mail, again linked to the CRM database.
4 On-line communication tools such as banner advertising, sponsorship, links and PR.
5 Traditional off-line communication tools such as advertising and PR.

One approach to defining e-marketing tactics, which we will use here, is to re-examine the options that e-marketing provides through these tools for varying the marketing mix. We will focus on the '4Ps' of product, price, place and promotion, defined around the start of the 1960s by Canadian Jerome McCarthy (1960), together with the extended mix of the American academics, Booms and Bitner (1981). They considered the extra Ps crucial in the delivery of services – people, processes and physical evidence.

Some feel that for interactive marketing the 5Is (Peppers and Rogers, 1997) should replace the 7Ps in the information age. The 5Is do not supplant the 7Ps, but rather are complementary to them, since the 5Is define the process needed, whereas the 7Ps are the variables which the marketer controls.

These are:

- *Identification* – customer specifics.
- *Individualization* – tailored for lifetime purchases.

- *Interaction* – dialogue to learn about customers' needs.
- *Integration* – of knowledge of customers into all parts of the company.
- *Integrity* – develop trust through non-intrusion, as in permission marketing.

Although the mix provides a useful framework for marketers, other factors also need to be considered. Decisions on the mix are not made until marketing strategy first determines target markets and required brand positionings. New marketers also need to know how to manage alliances or partnerships and build customer relationships to build lifetime value through using customer knowledge stored in databases. We will now review the implications of the new media for the different elements of the marketing mix.

Product

The on-line world offers a host of new opportunities and prompts these product-related questions:

- What benefits do you deliver to your customers?
- Can they be delivered on-line?
- What other benefits might your customers like?
- Can these benefits be delivered on-line?
- What is your business? Can it be delivered on-line?

Ghosh (1998) suggested companies should consider how to modify product and add *digital value* to customers. These are huge questions that can reshape your whole business. He urged companies to ask:

- Can I afford additional information on or transaction services to my existing customer base?
- Can I address the needs of new customer segments by repackaging my current information assets or by creating new business propositions using the Internet?

- Can I use my ability to attract customers to generate new sources of revenue such as advertising or sales of complementary products?
- Will my current business be significantly harmed by other companies providing some of the value I currently offer?

He suggests you need to analyse each feature of your product or service and ask how each of these features can be improved or adapted on-line. Developing these on-line services should be customer-led by asking what information the ideal target customers seek. How can a company excel at giving them this on-line? Communities of customers can be tapped into to help answer this question. This is the idea of the 'prosumer' – the proactive consumer. The prosumer concept was introduced in 1980 by futurist Alvin Toffler in his book *The Third Wave*. According to Toffler, the future would once again combine production with consumption. In *The Third Wave*, Toffler saw a world where interconnected users would collaboratively 'create' products. Note that he foresaw this over 10 years before the web was invented!

These changes to products can be substantial – one such example is Hughes Christenson, an oil drilling tool company who discovered they could provide a more lucrative on-line oil drilling advisory service.

The different elements of *extended product* can also be highlighted or delivered on-line. Often, extended product contributes greatly to quality. Think about these aspects of extended product which can be highlighted or delivered on-line:

- Endorsements.
- Awards.
- Testimonies.
- Customer lists.
- Customer comments.
- Warranties.
- Guarantees.
- Money-back offers.
- Customer service (see 'People' and 'Process').

Extended product also includes incorporating tools to help users during their use of the product. For example, engineers can be provided with technical diagrams and updates on regulations to assist them with their work.

Price

The changes to pricing and price models introduced by the advent of the Internet have been significant.

New buying models require new pricing approaches, which have forced marketers to radically rethink their pricing strategies. There have been many experiments, some successful, others less so. Examples include customer unions such as LetsBuyit (www.letsbuyit.com) and 'name your price' services such as Priceline (www.priceline.com), transparent pricing and global sourcing (particularly by giant procurement mergers like Ford and Chrysler).

A growth in competition is caused partly by global suppliers and partly by globalized customers searching via the web to add further pressure on prices. Many on-line companies enjoy lower margins, with more efficient web-enabled databases and processes which cut out the middleman and his margin. These on-line cost savings can be passed to customers to give further downward pressure. Take the car market: at launch, several new on-line car retailers such as Virgin Cars (www.virgincars.com) and Jamjar (www.jamjar.com) promised 30 per cent savings.

Pricing is also under pressure through the trend towards *commoditization*. Once buyers can (a) specify exactly what they want and (b) identify suppliers, they can run *reverse auctions*. *Price transparency* is another factor. As prices are published on the web, buyer comparison of prices is more rapid than ever before. Storing prices digitally in databases also enables shopping bots to find the best price. This customer empowerment creates further downward pressure on prices.

Prices are complex; options for the price package include:

- Basic price.
- Discounts.
- Add-ons and extra products and services.
- Guarantees and warranties.
- Refund policies.
- Order cancellation terms
- Revoke action buttons.

Ironically, the money-rich and time-poor customers in B2C markets may be much slower purchasing on-line than buyers in B2B markets, where transaction values are often higher and savings more significant. B2B marketplaces, known as exchanges or hubs, and auctions will grow in significance. An increasing volume of routine and repetitive buying will be carried out in the B2B exchanges that survive the initial competition. Major corporations are already buying through on-line exchanges and auctions. Healthcare company GlaxoSmithKline started using on-line reverse auctions in 2000 to drive down the price of its supplies. For example, it bought supplies of a basic solvent for a price 15 per cent lower than the day's spot price in the commodity market, and Queree (2000) reported that on other purchases of highly specified solvents and chemicals, SmithKline Beecham is regularly beating its own historic pricing by between 7 and 25 per cent. Clearly, such new forms of buying have major implications for suppliers, requiring them to be able to participate in these exchanges and review the impact on their margin and cost structure.

A final consideration is the move from fixed prices to rental, and leasing prices. Cars, computers, flight simulators and now even music can be hired or leased.

Place

Place involves the place of purchase, distribution and, in some cases, consumption. Some products exploit all three aspects of place on-line, for example digitizable products such as software, media and entertainment. Esther

Dyson has drawn this analogy with the electronic marketspace:

> You put Coke machines in places where you think people might want to drink a Coke. On the Internet you put Amazon buttons in places where there might be people inclined to buy books.

But it's not just digitizable products and services – all products and services can extend themselves on-line by considering their on-line representation for place of purchase and distribution. Other products, such as cars, are partially sold on-line and eventually bought off-line using *mixed-mode buying*, where some activities of the buying process are completed off-line and some on-line.

Off-line marketing communications and on-line marketing communications through the website should integrate with different buying modes, as shown in Figure 25.8. Common buying modes include:

- *On-line purchase.* Some customers want to search, compare and buy on-line. Does your website accommodate all stages of the buying process? Few products can be delivered on-line, so fulfilment is usually off-line.
- *On-line browse and off-line purchase – mixed-mode buying.* This is when customers like to browse, look or research *on-line*, and eventually purchase *off-line* in a real store or in a real meeting. Some of these customers might like to browse on-line but purchase via fax or telephone because of security and privacy issues. Does your site have fax forms and telephone numbers for placing orders or taking further enquiries? Does your site integrate with other communications channels? Some sites also have '*call-back facilities*', which allow visitors to request a telephone call from a salesperson to complete the purchase.

Another tactic related to place is an organization's on-line *representation*. Berryman *et al.* (1998) highlighted the importance of place in e-commerce transactions when they identified the three different locations for on-line B2B purchases shown in Figure 25.9. When com-

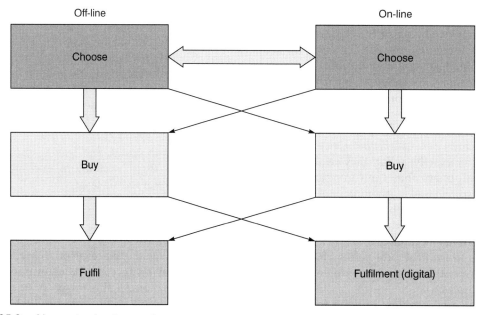

Figure 25.8   Alternative buying modes

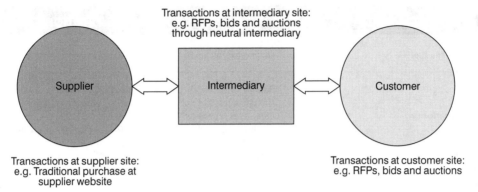

Figure 25.9 Alternative representation locations for on-line purchases

panies think about making their products available on-line, the tendency is to think only in terms of selling direct from their website (a). However, other alternatives for selling products are from a neutral marketplace (b), such as CommerceOne (www.commerceone.net), and also through going direct to the customer (c) – an example of this is a B2B auction such as that described for GlaxoSmithKline in the previous section, where the supplier goes to the customer's site to bid.

A few examples of other concepts of place which have been changed on-line are as follows:

- *Disintermediation*. This is removing the middleman to deal direct with customers instead of through agents, distributors and wholesalers. Note that this can create channel conflict as middlemen feel the squeeze. For example, Hewlett-Packard sell a lot of equipment to hospitals. But when hospitals started going directly to the HP site firstly for information and secondly to place orders, it posed a big question: do we pay commission to the sales representative for this?
- *Re-intermediation*. This is the emergence of new types of middlemen who are brokers, such as Bizrate that unite buyers with sellers.
- *Infomediation*. A related concept where middlemen hold data or information to benefit customers and suppliers.

- *Channel confluence*. This has occurred where distribution channels start to offer the same deal to the end customer.
- *Peer-to-peer services*. Music swapping services such as Napster and Gnutella opened up an entirely new approach to music distribution with both supplier and middleman removed completely providing a great threat, but also opportunity to the music industry.
- *Affiliation*. Affiliate programmes can turn customers into salespeople. Many consider salespeople as part of distribution. Others see them as part of the communications mix.

Excellent distribution requires a deep understanding of when and where customers want products and services. Partnership skills are also required, as much distribution is externally sourced, whether order fulfilment, warehousing, logistics or transport.

Promotion

The Internet can be used to extend and integrate all communications tools, as summarized in Table 25.3.

Although websites can be considered a separate communications tool, they are perhaps best thought of as an integrator of all 10 tools shown in the table.

The following are offered as guidelines for effective promotion tactics (see Table 25.4):

Table 25.3   On-line executions of different communications tools

Communications tool	On-line executions
1 Advertising	Banner ads, search engine registration
2 Selling	Virtual sales staff, affiliate marketing, web rings, links
3 Sales promotion	Incentives, rewards, loyalty schemes
4 PR	On-line editorial, e-zines, newsletters, discussion groups, portals
5 Sponsorship	Sponsoring an on-line event, site or service
6 Direct mail	Opt-in e-mail and web response
7 Exhibitions	Virtual exhibitions
8 Merchandising	Shopping malls, e-tailing, the interface
9 Packaging	Real packaging is displayed on-line
10 Word of mouth	Viral, affiliate marketing, e-mail a friend, web rings, links

Table 25.4   Summary of the strengths and weaknesses of different communications tools for promoting an on-line presence

Promotion technique	Main strengths	Main weaknesses
Search engine registration and advertising	Large on-line reach – used by high proportion of web users. Visitors are self-selecting. Relatively low cost, but increasing.	Works best for specialist products rather than generic products, e.g. insurance. Cost – search engine optimization is continuous as techniques change.
Link-building campaigns	Relatively low cost and good targeting.	Setting up a large number of links can be time consuming.
Affiliate campaigns	Payment is by results (e.g. 10% of sale goes to referring site).	Further payment to affiliate manager required for large-scale campaigns.
Banner	Main intention to achieve visit, i.e. direct response model. Useful role in branding also.	Response rates have declined historically to banner blindness.
Sponsorship	Most effective if low-cost, long-term co-branding arrangement with synergistic site.	May increase mind-share, but does not directly lead to sales.
E-mail marketing	Push medium – can't be ignored in users' in-box. Can be used for direct response link to website.	Requires opt-in list for effectiveness. Better for customer retention than acquisition? Message diluted amongst other e-mails.
Viral marketing	With effective creative marketing, possible to reach a large number at relatively low cost.	Risks damaging brand, since unsolicited messages may be received.
PR	Relatively low cost vehicle for PR. Many alternatives for innovation.	Off-line PR may give higher impact and reach.
Traditional off-line advertising (TV, Print, etc.)	Larger reach than most on-line techniques. Greater creativity possible leading to greater impact. Can use direct response or website.	Targeting arguably less easy than on-line. Typically high cost of acquisition.

1 *Mix.* E-marketers need to mix the promotional mix. This involves looking at the strengths and weaknesses of the promotional tools in the context of an organization and deciding on the optimum mix for different on-line promotional tools.

2 *Integration.* Both on-line and off-line communications must be integrated. All communications should support the overall positioning and *on-line or Internet value proposition* which the e-marketing strategy defines. A single consistent message and a single integrated database are needed – which recognizes and remembers customers' names and needs regardless of which access devices are being used (TV, telephone or PC).

3 *Creativity.* Today's marketer can exploit the creative opportunities presented by the Internet. For example, sending opt-in e-mails that make customers sit up and take notice, developing an on-line virtual exhibition or seminar.

4 *Interaction.* Next comes the extra layer of creativity – interaction. This enhances the experience and deepens the communications impact (and it also collects customer data).

5 *Globalization.* Then of course there are the added complications of a global audience. Websites open your window to the world. When a global audience looks in (to your site) they may not like what they see.

6 *Resourcing.* The on-line communications opportunity is infinite. However, resources to design and maintain the content, interactions and the database are not infinite. Resources are also needed to service customer enquiries whether on-line or off-line.

Figure 25.10 shows two alternatives for balancing these three variables. Figure 25.10(a) is a model where traffic building expenditure exceeds service and design. This is more typical for a dot-com that needs to promote its brand. Figure 25.10(b) is a model where traffic building

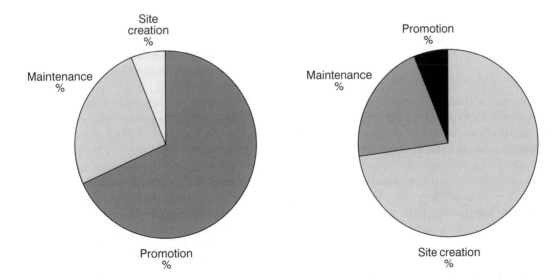

Figure 25.10   Alternatives for balance between expenditure on e-marketing promotion

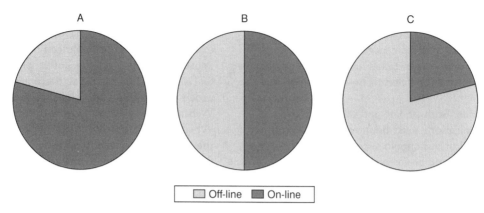

Figure 25.11   Alternative options for investment in on-line and off-line traffic building

expenditure is less than service and design. This is more typical for a traditional bricks and mortar company that already has a brand recognition and an established customer base.

Defining the correct balance between on-line and off-line promotion is another key aspect of resourcing.

Organizations need to decide which of the options in Figure 25.11 is the best balance. Surveys indicate that, for many companies, situation B is most common. However, there is a general trend to higher spend on on-line promotion, possibly because of better targeting and a direct response between advertising and site visits.

People

In services marketing, people, or staff, are considered a crucial element of the marketing mix. As more products add on-line services to enhance their offerings 'people' become more important. In an on-line context, 'people' corresponds to customer service whether delivered through the website as 'customer self-service' or through interaction with staff. Automated self-service options include:

- *Autoresponders.* These automatically generate a response when a company e-mails an organization, or submits an on-line form.

- *E-mail notification.* Automatically generated by a companies systems to update customers on the status of their order; for example, order received, item now in stock, order dispatched.
- *Call-back facility.* Customers fill in their phone number on a form and specify a convenient time to be contacted. Dialling from a representative in the call centre occurs automatically at the appointed time and the company pays, which is popular.
- *Frequently asked questions (FAQ).* For these, the art is in compiling and categorizing the questions so customers can easily find (a) the question and (b) a helpful answer.
- *On-site search engines.* These help customers find what they're looking for quickly and are popular when available. Site maps are a related feature.
- *Virtual assistants.* These come in varying degrees of sophistication and usually help to guide the customer through a maze of choices.

Customer contact strategies also need to be considered – we need to ask whether all customers want to conduct all their interactions on-line. Many companies use an inbound contact strategy of customer choice or *customer preferred channel* – offering customers a range of contact options. But a more cost-effective contact strategy may involve steering customers towards using the web as a contact tool.

Of course, staff need to be trained and motivated whether they man the website, the telephones, the field sales or the reception. What happens if a web transaction fails and the customer calls the centre – can call centre staff access the web database to complete the transaction, or do they have to collect all the details again? A seamless, integrated contact database is required.

Physical evidence

When buying intangible services, customers look for physical evidence to reassure them. In the off-line world this includes buildings, uniforms, logos and more. In the on-line world the evidence is digital – primarily through websites but also through e-mail. In the on-line world, customers look for other cues and clues to reassure themselves about the organization.

So, first, a reassuring sense of order is required. This means websites should be designed with a consistent look and feel that customers feel comfortable with (see 'Site design' chapter in Smith and Chaffey, 2001). But on-site reassurance can extend far beyond this, particularly for an e-tailer, by using:

- Guarantees.
- Refund policies.
- Privacy policies.
- Security icons.
- Trade body memberships.
- Awards.
- Customer lists.
- Customer endorsements.
- Independent reviews.
- News clippings.

Physical evidence can also help integrate the on-line and off-line worlds. Some white goods retailers use coupons printed out on-line which can be redeemed for a discount at a store. This helps conversion-to-sale rates and also tracks how the on-line presence is impacting off-line sales.

Process

Process refers to the internal and sometimes external processes, transactions and internal communications that are required to run a business.

Excellent processes are devised as part of the move towards e-business. Non-integrated e-commerce sites create problems as witnessed by US on-line toy stores, whose websites and associated processes did not link into an information system explaining to customers when stocks were unavailable. A well-managed process integrates into the business processes and systems which, in turn, shave costs and slash inventories.

On-line services and their process of production are not as visible, since many of the processes operate in systems unseen by the customer. Some of the process, or system, is on view, like menus, form filling, shopping baskets, follow-up e-mails and of course the interactions on websites – are all visible. It is on this part of the process and its outputs that customers will judge service.

It seems that many companies have not yet learnt how to optimize these processes – 98 per cent of potential buyers exit before they make their purchase. This suggests ordering is too complicated or confusing, or the system simply doesn't work smoothly.

Optimization also involves minimizing the people involved with responding to each event and providing them with the right information to serve the customer. Minimizing human resources can occur through redesigning the processes and/or automating them through technology. Processes continue beyond the sale with feedback, upselling, cross-selling, product development and improvement built in as part of the processes.

Controlling tactics

Who has control of these tactics and implementation is a big question, and the e-marketer must win the ownership argument. Take the website: is it controlled by marketing or by technical or some other function? Many websites actually damage the brand with their broken links, dead ends, cumbersome downloads, out of date content, impossible navigation and unanswered e-mails. Regular reviews should not be devoted to reviewing the latest technology but, rather, they should be focused on customer reviews.

Actions

According to John Stubbs (executive director, CIM), up to 40 per cent of marketing expenditure is wasted through poor execution. So, the action stage may be the weakest link in the planning process. So tactics break down into actions; in fact, a series of actions, for example to build a website or run an on-line advertising campaign. Each tactic becomes a mini project.

Each tactical e-tool requires careful planning and implementation. Whether building a website, a banner ad, an interactive TV ad, a viral campaign or an opt-in campaign, good project management skills and diligent attention to detail are required.

Typical actions that may be pursued for achieving different website objectives are:

1 *Traffic building actions.* To generate visits and/or traffic to your website or portal or iTV channel, you will probably be using links or banners on other sites, sponsoring other on-line activities, possibly using competitions or creative content ideas to generate interest. You'll need creative input and a budget to buy media space.
2 *Actions to achieve customer response.* To capture user enquiries – thus turning visitors into sales prospects, capturing data, using enquiry data to analyse customer needs, plan development – you'll need a response mechanism for customers to enter their data on-line and a database logging and processing the data as they come in.
3 *Actions to gain sales.* For collecting sales orders, use interactive TV or a website to generate

actual sales, handle money transactions and initiate the order process system.
4 *Fulfilment actions.* Efficient data transfer to warehouse to get products off the shelf and into the box for despatch. Orders might be one-off products or subscription services. More software and hardware solutions to implement here: ideally, dovetail into the parent's existing systems used for mail order and phone order businesses, then you know the processes which are invisible to the customer have been installed, tested and proven already.
5 *e-CRM actions.* To build better relationships by creating dialogue with customers you might be running on-line polls, using rewards and competitions to secure commitment and response; you could also set up and moderate an on-line user group. In this way, you empower customers by means of interactivity – respond to feedback, listen to customer response and visibly act on it.

Success in all these actions requires good implementation. It is possible to have a poor strategy but to mask it with outstanding actions which bring the company success, but the best strategy in the world will achieve nothing if it is not implemented well.

Action, or implementation, also requires an appreciation of what can go wrong from cyber libel to viruses, to mail bombs, hackers and hijackers to cyber squatting and much more; contingency planning is required. What happens when the server goes down or a virus comes to town? What happens if one of the e-tools is not working, or is not generating enough enquiries? Something has to be changed. A risk management approach to e-marketing is useful. This involves:

- Brainstorming a list of all the things that could go wrong.
- Assessing their impact and likelihood.
- Taking actions to minimize the risk of the most highest impact, most probable risk.
- Revising and refining according to lessons learnt.

Control

Without control mechanisms, e-marketing depends on luck. It's a bit like playing darts in the dark. How do you know if you are hitting the target or are just shooting blindly and wildly? How do you know if you're targeting the right customers? Who are they? What do they like and not like? How many of them become repeat customers? Which e-marketing tools work best? How much does each customer actually cost you? Control also includes monitoring your competitors – what they're doing, what they're repeating, what works for them, what they're stopping doing.

To answer these questions, an e-marketing performance measurement system is required. The requirements for this have been summarized by Chaffey (2001). These are:

1 *A performance measurement process.* This defines responsibilities for the different measurement activities, such as objective setting, metrics collection and reporting, analysis, diagnosis and changing e-tactics, or even strategy through corrective action if necessary.
2 *A metrics framework.* You need to determine what data you will look at each day, each week, each month, each quarter. Time has to be made for a regular review of what's working and what's not – performance diagnosis. Performance is measured against detailed targets, based on the objectives and strategy. So you need to measure the KPIs, which were detailed in the section on situation analysis.

So where do you get this information? Many of the metrics concerning visitor behaviour are available from web log file analysers, which summarize the clickstreams of different site visitors. Collection by other information systems or processes is required for key measures such as sales, subscriptions, conversion and attrition rates. Standard practice should ensure data from the different sources is compiled into a monthly or weekly report and is delivered *and* reviewed by the right people. Decide which metrics need to be reviewed daily, weekly or monthly, and by whom. The e-marketer must know which tools are working, that's why 'source of' sales or enquiries is useful – if a particular banner ad doesn't pull customers, drop it and try another until you find one that does.

Remember all forms of measurement, or metrics, cost money – you'll have to factor in budgets and resources for the following mechanisms:

- Monitoring customer awareness.
- Monitoring customer satisfaction.
- Monitoring customer attitudes.

Other forms of control, like sales analysis, require only that you allocate quality time. So how do you know if things are going well? Some objectives are easy to state and easy to measure: existing recording systems in the organization will produce the data to answer the question: so if the objective is to grow sales, well what was the target for growth and the timetable for achieving it, and did you make it?

Chaffey (2001) has suggested that control should consider the effectiveness of e-marketing in the five key areas shown in Figure 25.12. Each e-marketing channel, such as web or interactive TV, should be considered separately against traditional channels using this framework.

Resourcing

A further question is what to outsource. For example, do you design the website or produce content in-house or contract out to an agency? And what balance should you strike between resources allocated to building the site and those required to maintain it on a regular basis and leaving a budget for a complete review and upgrade in three, six or nine months? Other resources to consider include promotion (see Figure 25.11) and telesales (are additional staff required or can the in-house team do it?). Who

1. **Business contribution:**
On-line revenue contribution (direct and indirect), category penetration, costs and profitability.

2. **Marketing outcomes:**
Leads, sales, service contacts, conversion and retention efficiencies.

3. **Customer satisfaction:**
Site usability, performance/availability, contact strategies. Opinions, attitudes and brand impact.

4. **Customer behaviour:**
Profiles, customer orientation (segmentation), usability, clickstreams and site actions.

5. **Site promotion:**
Attraction efficiency. Referrer efficiency, cost of acquisition and reach. Search engine visibility and link building. E-mail marketing. Integration.

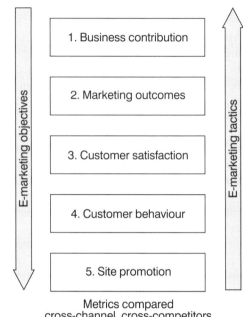

Figure 25.12   Key metrics from the Chaffey (2001) framework for assessing e-marketing effectiveness

will do the e-marketing research? Who is going to analyse the data you get from the customer feedback, and who is going to produce the recommendation? Is it the existing team, or a new position? If customers show there is a need to change procedures, do we have the people to react and respond?

Summary

We have seen that well-established approaches to marketing strategy and planning can be applied to e-marketing. It can be argued that the main challenge of e-marketing is assessing its future significance to an organization and resourcing accordingly. Companies that have business models and products that can be readily migrated to the Internet have already successfully turned the Internet into their main sales, distribution and service channel. However, such organizations are in the minority. For

the majority, the Internet simply represents another channel to market. For these organizations, the difficulty is deciding how to resource it and mastering the new e-tools. Assessment of customer demand for on-line services as measured by the direct and indirect revenue contribution is crucial. Overambitious targets or too much investment in the on-line presence may not yield a return on investment, but conservative targets coupled with insufficient investment or inappropriate use of e-marketing tools may see competitors achieving an advantage which is difficult to overcome. A reading of the short history of on-line book and grocery retailing and B2B exchanges indicates that there may only be room for several major competitors who will be difficult to displace.

A further challenge for e-marketers is finding the staff or agency skills needed to select and deploy new e-marketing tools which may have a short-term future. For example, at the time of writing, viral marketing and e-mail marketing are in vogue, but new legislation and negative consumer reaction may reduce their effectiveness in future. Despite these challenges, the significance of e-marketing seems likely to increase in the future, regardless of industry or sector.

References

Ansoff, H. (1957) Strategies for diversification. *Harvard Business Review*, September–October, 113–124.

Berthon, P., Lane, N., Pitt, L. and Watson, R. (1998) The World Wide Web as an industrial marketing communications tool: models for the identification and assessment of opportunities, *Journal of Marketing Management*, **14**, 691–704.

Berryman, K., Harrington, L., Layton-Rodin, D. and Rerolle, V. (1998) Electronic commerce: three emerging strategies, *The Mckinsey Quarterly*, No. 1, 152–159.

BMRB (2001) International Internet Monitor, February. Published at www.brmb.co.uk.

Booms, B. H. and Bitner, M. J. (1981) Marketing strategies and organizational structures for service firms, in Donnelly, J. and George, W. (eds), *Marketing of Services*, American Marketing Association, Chicago, pp. 477–451.

Chaffey, D. (2001) Optimising e-marketing performance – a review of approaches and tools. In *Proceedings of IBM Workshop on Business Intelligence and E-marketing*, Warwick, 6 December.

Chaffey, D. (2002) *E-business and E-commerce Management. Strategy, Implementation and Practice*, Financial Times/Prentice-Hall, Harlow, UK.

Chaffey, D., Mayer, R., Johnston, K. and Ellis-Chadwick, F. (2003) *Internet Marketing: Strategy, Implementation and Practice*, 2nd edn, Financial Times/Prentice-Hall, Harlow, UK.

Chaston, I. (2000) *E-marketing Strategy*, McGraw-Hill, UK.

Deise, M., Nowikow, C., King, P. and Wright, A. (2000) *Executive's Guide to E-business. From Tactics to Strategy*, John Wiley, New York.

De Kare-Silver, M. (2000) *eShock 2000*, Macmillan, Basingstoke, UK.

DTI (2000) *Business In The Information Age – International Benchmarking Study 2000*, UK Department of Trade and Industry. Based on 6000 phone interviews across businesses of all sizes in eight countries. Statistics update available on-line at: www.ukonlinefor business.gov.uk

Fisher, A. (2001) Sandvik – the challenge of becoming an e-business, *Financial Times*, 4 June.

Ghosh, S. (1998) Making business sense of the Internet, *Harvard Business Review*, March–April, 126–135.

Gulati, R. and Garino, J. (2000) Getting the right mix of bricks and clicks for your company, *Harvard Business Review*, May–June, 107–114.

Hoffman, D. L. and Novak, T. P. (1996) Marketing in hypermedia computer-mediated environments: conceptual foundations, *Journal of Marketing*, **60**, July, 50–68.

Hoffman, D. L. and Novak, T. P. (2000) How to acquire customers on the web, *Harvard Business Review*, May–June, 179–188. Available on-line at: http://ecommerce.vanderbilt.edu/papers.html

Kalakota, R. and Whinston, A. (1997) *Electronic Commerce. A Manager's Guide*, Addison-Wesley, Reading, MA.

Kumar, N. (1999) Internet distribution strategies: dilemmas for the incumbent, *Financial Times Special Issue on Mastering Information Management*, No 7, Electronic Commerce.

McCarthy, J. (1960) *Basic Marketing: A Managerial Approach*, Irwin, Homewood, IL.

McDonald, M. and Wilson, H. (1999) *E-Marketing: Improving Marketing Effectiveness in a Digital World*, Financial Times Management/Pearson Education, Harlow.

Peppers, D. and Rogers, M. (1997) *One to One Future*, 2nd edn, Doubleday, New York.

Porter, M. (2001) Strategy and the Internet, *Harvard Business Review*, March, 62–78.

Plant, R. (2000) *E-commerce Strategy*, Financial Times/Pearson, Harlow, UK.

Quelch, J. and Klein, L. (1996) The Internet and international marketing, *Sloan Management Review*, Spring, 61–75.

Queree, A. (2000) *Financial Times Technology Supplement*, 1 March.

Smith, P. R. and Chaffey, D. (2001) *eMarketing eXcellence: At The Heart of eBusiness*, Butterworth-Heinemann, Oxford.

Timmers, P. (1999) *Electronic Commerce Strategies and Models for Business-to-business Trading*, Series in Information Systems, John Wiley, Chichester, UK.

Toffler, A. (1980) *The Third Wave*, Bantam Books, New York.

Zwass, V. (1998) Structure and macro-level impacts of electronic commerce: from technological infrastructure to electronic marketplaces, in Kendall, K. (ed.), *Emerging Information Technologies*, Sage, Thousand Oaks, CA.

CHAPTER 26

Cause-related marketing: who cares wins

SUE ADKINS

Introduction

Over seven years ago, when the cause-related marketing campaign at Business in the Community[1] was set up, few companies were aware of cause-related marketing or understood it. Fewer still were practising it. Today the situation is very different. The purpose of this chapter is to provide an understanding of cause-related marketing. Cause-related marketing will be defined and set in context, providing an outline of the business case and evidence from the marketing perspective. Case studies will be used to illustrate cause-related marketing and identify some of the critical success factors in developing effective programmes. Finally, guiding principles and processes will

[1] Business in the Community is a unique movement of companies across the UK committed to improving continually their positive impact on society, with a core membership of over 700 companies, including 77 per cent of the FTSE 100. The cause-related marketing campaign was initially set up and funded by Sir Dominic Cadbury and Cadbury Schweppes, and led by Sue Adkins. The purpose of the campaign was to define cause-related marketing, develop the business case and to establish it as a marketing strategy in the UK. For further information, please see www.bitc.org.uk and www.crm.org.uk

be provided to support readers in developing their own strategies and programmes.

Business in the Community, through its cause-related marketing campaign, has been the key provider of research, resource, guidelines and information on cause-related marketing since 1995. This body of work and *Cause Related Marketing: Who Cares Wins* (Adkins, 1999a) are the key resources drawn on for this chapter.

Cause-related marketing defined

Cause-related marketing is not a new concept. Examples exist from as early as the 1890s, for example, when William Heskith Lever introduced schemes on Sunlight Soap and a variety of charities in the USA (Adkins, 1999a, Chapter 2). Although not referred to as cause-related marketing at the time, these early examples demonstrated the commercial link between a charity and a business for mutual benefit. They also identify core components of today's effective cause-related marketing programmes, namely a win for business, a win for the cause or charity and a win for the consumer.

More recent interest in cause-related marketing is generally argued to stem from American Express, who apparently coined the phrase in 1983 and developed a number of cause-related marketing programmes. American Express's support for the Statue of Liberty was the most well-known programme. The concept and the link were straightforward, with approximately $4 million in support, including print, radio and TV advertising. Customers were encouraged to use their American Express card: each time it was used a 1 cent donation was made to the restoration of the Statue of Liberty fund. New customers were encouraged to apply for an American Express card and participate. For every new American Express card account approved, a $1 donation would be made to the fund. American Express also made donations on purchases of other American Express products and services. In the course of this three-month promotion from September to December 1983, it was reported that over $1.7 million was raised for the Restoration of the Statue of Liberty: use of American Express cards rose by 28 per cent in just the first month, compared to the previous year, and new card applications increased by 45 per cent. Since then, American Express has run over 90 programmes in 17 different countries (Adkins, 1999a, Chapter 3).

Cause-related marketing is defined by Business in the Community as 'a commercial activity by which businesses and charities or good causes form a partnership with each other to market an image, product or service for mutual benefit'. This is Business in the Community's definition, developed following extensive consultation amongst consumers and practitioners, both in business and in charities. This definition is now widely used in the UK and abroad. The critical words within the definition are *commercial, partnership, marketing* and *mutual benefit*. Whatever cause-related marketing is, it is certainly not philanthropy, nor is it altruism. Cause-related marketing is a marketing-driven activity. Parties, be they businesses, charities or good causes, enter a cause-related marketing relationship in order to meet their objectives and in order to receive a return on their investment, where that investment may be in cash, time or other resources, or a combination of all.

There is no universal measure to show the extent to which cause-related marketing is being utilized; however, there are measures that look at part of the picture. According to American statistics, cause-related marketing in the USA is worth 9 per cent ($828 million) of the America sponsorship market and has been one of the areas of growth over the last few years (IEG, 2001).

Done well, cause-related marketing provides commercial advantage for all parties involved, where commercial applies equally to the charity, cause or business. Objectives partners may wish to address can cover the full marketing mix. They can range from organizational reputation, brand or image enhancement, increasing loyalty and developing relationships with consumers, building customer traffic or PR, to generating income and resources. Each of these objectives is of course equally relevant to a charity, cause or business. Cause-related marketing is about a win–win–win scenario where the charity or cause and business win, and indeed where the benefits also extend to consumers and other stakeholders.

Cause-related marketing programmes are based on partnerships, mutually agreed objectives and mutual benefit. They should be founded on relationships of equal balance over time, where each partner appreciates the contribution, strengths and weaknesses of the other. Neither side has greater weight, value or importance in the equation, or gains at the expense of the other. Integrity, sincerity, transparency, mutual respect, partnership and mutual benefit form the foundation (Adkins, 1998).

Cause-related marketing is therefore good business, and it is good business for charities and businesses alike. There should be no question that, in the end, cause-related marketing partnerships are entered into because both parties have something to gain.

Cause-related marketing in context

Over the last five years, the context in which cause-related marketing is operating today in terms of the social, legal, economic, political and technological developments has developed enormously. Together, these factors impact on the development of business strategies including marketing.

The symbiotic relationship between business and society is increasingly evident. It has manifested itself in many ways, from local dissatisfaction to global protests. With the public (social) unrest comes business (and economic) unrest. The nature of this symbiotic relationship and shared destiny is brought starkly into focus by the socio-economic and political events of recent years.

Around the world we are witnessing the drawing back of the state and the process of deregulation, trade liberalization and the rapid internationalizing of markets. As state funding reduces across the globe, a gap is developing between society's needs and the government's or the state's ability to provide for them. In such an environment, businesses have become an increasingly powerful force within society and consumers recognize this. With global mergers and acquisitions, their economic power is enormous. The revenue of some companies far exceeds the GDP of many nations (Roddick, 2001):

- The 200 biggest corporations in the world control 28 per cent of the world economic activity but employ less than 0.25 per cent of the global workforce.
- The wealth of the world's 84 richest people is bigger than the GDP of China with 1.3 billion people.
- The world's richest 20 per cent received 82.7 per cent of the total world income compared to the poorest 20 per cent, who received 1.4 per cent. These figures have not changed since 1992.

With such significant economic power and influence in society, business has a profound influence on the lives of individuals and communities around the world. With this role comes responsibilities. These responsibilities are increasingly recognized by consumers and acknowledged by business. This in turn impacts on the marketing of the business.

> Large corporations play an ever increasing role in the global economy and so have a greater impact on global society. People in the dual role as consumers and citizens will expect companies to use their power and influence widely and to meet their needs more effectively. Cause related marketing is one part of the portfolio of ways that companies can use/respond to these demands, enabling the companies to contribute to the development of the societies in which they operate, as well as enabling them to build long term benefits for brands.
>
> Jerry Wright, Senior Strategist, Unilever (Adkins, 1999a, Chapter 4)

From a legislative point of view, the context has also developed considerably and has a knock-on effect on the marketing and communication of a business. The Turnbull Report and the recent pensions act in the UK, for example, both focus business attention on the risks and indeed the rewards associated with effective management of environmental and social issues. This not only serves to change the context for business generally and in turn for marketing, but also serves to build the momentum and interest in these aspects of the business. Social reporting and business ethics are now firmly on the radar screens for every business. They cannot fail to be. This can of course be regarded as a threat or an opportunity. Consumers, after all, have the power of knowledge, the power to purchase, the power to protest and the power to boycott. They also have the potential to be engaged, to believe and to become advocates. Consumers have shown themselves to be increasingly restless and vociferous, and are prepared to demonstrate their displeasure with corporate behaviour. Which came first, the consumer outcry, or corporate recognition of the importance and business benefits of corporate social responsibility, is hard to tell. There is no denying, however, that together they have a significant impact. These factors are impacting on the way businesses conduct themselves in every respect from governance to marketing. Stakeholders generally and consumers particularly are becoming increasingly empowered. With the IT revolution, this power, both positive and negative, is available at the touch of a button.

According to IBM, in 1997, 40 million people surfed the Internet. In 1998, 60 million surfed the net (Adkins, 1999a, Chapter 4). In 2000, 94 million and 157.2 million used the Internet in Europe and North America, respectively (Grayson and Hodges, 2001). The estimated global Internet population is now 400 million (*The Little Internet Factbook*, 2001) and it is said that today's average consumer wears more computing power on their wrist than existed in the entire world before 1961! Today, millions of messages can be sent 24/7 at the touch of a button.

The information, communication and technological revolution means that not only has the speed and access to information increased exponentially, but that information and good practice can be shared faster and faster, facilitating global benchmarking and indeed global boycotting. This has impacts on the way the business manages its business from a reputation, financial and logistical point of view, all of which impacts on marketing and on which marketing can have a profound impact. One of the outcomes is that this forces the pace of change. Innovation and product development can now be copied at a much greater rate and are therefore no longer sustainable areas for differentiation. Differentiation therefore has to be built on additional levels. Communication of reputation, values and vision are becoming more and more important aspects of this matrix, aspects which fall under the marketer's remit. For the marketeer of the twenty-first century, managing reputation, developing

values and communicating them is a critical part of the way business is conducted. Cause-related marketing provides the opportunity for a tangible demonstration of an organization's values. These values are increasingly under scrutiny by a number of stakeholders. These stakeholders include the media and consumers who want to see behind the brands and are prepared to show their dissatisfaction when there is a lack of transparency or when there is perceived to be a lack of values. Evidence of this trend has and is being demonstrated through the social unrest in the UK, across Europe and across the world.

The anti-globalization riots and consumer protests over the last few years, in relation to issues as varied as petrol pricing, human rights, animal rights, supply chain management, the environment and third world debt, have focused consumer attention on business, their values and the role they have to play. They have also focused business attention on the need to develop their relationships and approaches with the various stakeholder groups, in order to be able to face such scrutiny and attention. These demonstrations of unrest have therefore impacted on the development of marketing strategies.

From a business and marketing perspective it may have been convenient, if dangerous, to assume that individuals involved in these actions are simply militant activists. Such an interpretation is naive and short-sighted. The protests around the world have been made up of many groups and represent the tip of the iceberg. Similar passions and heated protests have been demonstrated on the streets and across campuses throughout Europe and around the world. Whatever the venue, whatever the cause, whatever the issue, one thing is certain: stakeholders, publics, consumers, call them what you will, are wanting, needing, expecting and indeed demanding to be heard and taken into account. These are the consumers with whom businesses providing products and services ultimately need to connect and form a relationship.

It is these protests that focus the media and consumer spotlight on brands and the companies behind them, with the result that business and indeed their marketing approaches are very much under the public spotlight. It is these pressures from the social, political, economic and technological points of view that are driving the developments in marketing, where values and trust provide the foundation on which to build relationships amongst stakeholders.

Building successful marketing relationships is dependent upon managing a matrix of internal and external stakeholder relationships (Figure 26.1). The stakeholder model is core to the development of marketing today and is critical to the effectiveness of cause-related marketing. Without consulting with stakeholders on their various levels, the future for brands and marketing looks bleak.

Successful relationship marketing requires a relationship based on commitment and trust, which is underpinned by values including honesty, transparency and integrity. Strategic cause-related marketing can play a role in developing the value proposition and in building and maintaining many of these relationships, both internally and externally. Stakeholder relationships and perceptions of organizations are formed as the result of a whole variety of interactions and interfaces with the business. This can range from broadcast advertising and in-store or on-pack promotional

Figure 26.1   An organization and its stakeholders
Source: Adkins (1999a).

messages, to direct mail and customer care. It is clearly the role of marketing to manage these interfaces, to ensure a consistent delivery of the product promise and the reception of key messages amongst all stakeholder groups, across all markets, over time. These interfaces and opportunities need to be continuously leveraged. There is no doubt that one of the key attributes of strategic cause-related marketing is its ability to connect with stakeholder groups on a number of different levels simultaneously.

As has been suggested, price and functionality are increasingly equal and replicable in this world of fast-paced communication at a touch of a button. Values are increasingly scrutinized by consumers and can indeed be the way forward as a differentiator for the marketing of business in the future. Hence the importance of cause-related marketing as a way of demonstrating these values in a highly visible and tangible way.

Common themes that can be seen in marketing plans include enhancing reputation, building image and brands, creating relationships and loyalty amongst customers and the stakeholders, adding value, generating awareness and PR, driving trial and traffic, providing product and service differentiation, developing emotional engagement with the consumer and other stakeholders, and obviously increasing sales, income and volume. These are all core objectives driving the marketing in business in today's context. Cause-related marketing has been shown to help achieve these objectives and more.

The consumer and other stakeholders have ever higher expectations of business, both in terms of product and service provision and in terms of quality and price, but, as has been argued, they are also increasingly interested in understanding the values behind the products, service and company. Values, and adding value to those values, are not only an increasingly important part of the business proposition but are being seen to be key influences in consumers' buying decisions. The marketing department therefore needs to be attuned to

and aware of this, and develop their marketing strategies accordingly. The evidence demonstrating the concern, expectation of stakeholders and the positive effect of cause-related marketing on consumers, is building. The business case is compelling. Consumers expect businesses to be socially responsible, a responsibility which consumers regard as close to that of government and above that of charities and religious institutions (Adkins, 1999b). Business in the Community research has shown that 81 per cent of consumers agree that, price and quality being equal, linking with a cause would make a difference; consumers would switch brands, change retail outlets and have a much better perception of a company doing something to make the world a better place (Adkins, 1999b). Consumers' demand and expectation for corporates to be social responsible, cannot be underestimated.

Evidence of consumer support is demonstrated through Business in the Community's quantitative and qualitative research, including *The Ultimate Win Win Win*, *Profitable Partnerships* and *The Game Plan*. All these research studies were conducted during the course of Business in the Community's cause-related marketing campaign work as part of a research programme that continues. *The Ultimate Win Win Win*, conducted amongst a representative sample of over 1000 consumers and supported by Research International, indicated not only consumer expectations of business, but also the predicted impact of their behaviour and perceptions based on their understanding of a company's corporate social responsibility and cause-related marketing (Adkins, 1999b):

- 81 per cent of consumers indicated, price and quality being equal, linking with a cause would make a difference.
- 66 per cent would switch brands.
- 57 per cent would change retail outlets.
- 86 per cent had a much better perception of a company trying to do something to make the world a better place.

The sense and reality of the power and empowerment of the vigilante has been evident through the various demonstrations of social unrest, as already mentioned. Whether the consumers have taken to the streets with placards, taken to their desks with pencil and paper or to their bedrooms with the computer and the Internet, the power of consumers to make their voices heard is ever stronger. Whilst the forms of protest may vary, the core message is the same. Consumers are empowered and prepared to take action. Research indicates that over 70 per cent of consumers indicated they were prepared to take action and over half of those aged 55+ agreed. The form and face of vigilantism may not be predictable, but their power is unmistakable.

The evidence for the positive effects of cause-related marketing is compelling. A unique study undertaken by Business in the Community and supported by Research International called *Profitable Partnerships*, conducted amongst over 2000 consumers, aimed to identify the link between cause-related marketing, brand affinity, brand equity, *actual* customer perception, loyalty and buying behaviour (Adkins, 2000). The data speaks for itself:

- Almost nine out of 10 (88 per cent) consumers are aware of a cause-related marketing programme.
- Companies which take part in cause-related marketing are perceived as being more trustworthy and more innovative by consumers, both of which are key drivers of equity.
- At least two-thirds (67 per cent) of consumers have taken part in a cause-related marketing programme.
- 77 per cent of participants were positively influenced at the point of purchase or decision making by the cause-related marketing programme.
- 80 per cent of all consumers who have taken part in a cause-related marketing programme will continue to feel positive about the company.

- 96 per cent of consumers thought it was good for charities and causes.
- 67 per cent of consumers want more companies to be involved in cause-related marketing.

Consumer support for cause-related marketing is reinforced across Europe and around the world. Depending on the country, between 65 and 80 per cent plus indicate that they have a propensity to switch brands based on cause-related marketing (Adkins, 1999a, Chapter 11). The message is clear: consumers are seriously motivated by socially responsible corporate behaviour, when they are aware of it. When it is demonstrated through marketing, consumers are willing to change their buying behaviour and perceptions. These pull factors are increasingly understood by business. Businesses are starting to think creatively about what they can achieve by putting the power of their marketing and brands behind some of the key social issues, to make a positive social difference and at the same time through engaging the consumer and other stakeholders, also benefiting the business.

The trend in marketing seems to be moving away from mass transaction-based marketing towards relationship marketing, with an increased focus on the importance of maintaining and developing these relationships. Corporates continually search for competitive advantage, differentiating themselves by adding perceived value to products and services for their target markets. Evidence suggests that, increasingly, affinity as well as functionality of the brand is driving consumer preference and in some cases can make up 98 per cent of the equity of a brand (Adkins, 1999a, Chapter 11). Cause-related marketing clearly has a role to play in this context, as emotional as well as rational engagement of the consumer becomes more critical. Naturally, building relationships takes time and is based on a clear understanding of the intrinsic values of the brand. It is here in building and communicating the overall value proposition that cause-related marketing has a key role to play.

Models

Increasingly, enlightened companies like Tesco, Centrica, Lever Fabergé (Adkins, 1999a, Chapter 16) and others are getting behind key social issues and linking their brands to charities and good causes, to develop mutually beneficial partnerships. It is easy to see why. As has been explained, cause-related marketing is 'a commercial activity by which businesses and charities or good causes form a partnership with each other to market an image, product or service for mutual benefit'. This is Business in the Community's definition, developed following extensive consultation amongst consumers and practitioners, both in business and in charities. Cause-related marketing is precisely that, marketing related to a cause, where marketing is constantly developing new strategies and techniques. If one accepts that the marketing mix consists of the four 'Ps' of product, price, place (distribution) and promotion or promotional mix, cause-related marketing falls within this promotional mix. The promotional mix is ever growing and therefore so is the scope of cause-related marketing. The promotional mix includes advertising, sales promotion, public relations or publicity, sponsorship, licensing and direct marketing, which includes loyalty and relationship marketing etc. The limits of cause-related marketing are created or defined only by the limitations of one's imagination.

In order to provide a useful framework, cause-related marketing approaches can perhaps be grouped under six broad categories as a minimum. These are advertising, public relations, sponsorship, licensing, direct marketing and sales promotion. A brief explanation for each is provided below, followed by case studies (Adkins, 1999a, Chapter 15).

Advertising

Advertising clearly includes a variety of media, ranging from broadcast, including radio and the Internet, advertising to print and press campaigns. Cause-related marketing advertising therefore can include any or all of these media and more. From a content point of view, advertising-led cause-related marketing may focus for instance on communicating a particular sales promotion, as in the Tesco's Computers for Schools programme (Adkins, 1999a, Chapter 16). Apart from raising awareness, funds and resources for a particular cause or issue, the objectives from the organization's point of view can range from anything from building, reinforcing and demonstrating corporate and brand reputation, to providing differentiation, encouraging relationships and loyalty between the product, service or charity cause, or corporate to driving traffic, trial and sales. Advertising-led cause-related marketing can also refer to the advertising of a particular cause or issue where the business aligns itself to a particular good cause and uses its advertising to communicate that cause's message. An example of this would be Nambarrie and the support of Action Cancer (Adkins, 1999a, Chapter 16).

Public relations

Public relations (PR) is often cited as a key benefit and indeed key objective for a cause-related marketing partnership, and in some cases represents the lead marketing discipline in defining, creating and implementing a programme or strategy. The key to getting PR coverage for the cause-related marketing programme is the same as the key for generating PR for any other activity. Newsworthiness, innovation, excitement and a compelling message are all crucial. There is, however, a significant difference for cause-related marketing. The balance in communication for a cause-related marketing programme must be absolutely appropriate. Essentially, both the media and the public have to be clear that any cause-related marketing partnership is sincere, open, transparent and honest: that the relationship is based upon a partnership of mutual respect and that there is a balanced benefit to be accrued on all sides. It is not appropriate, for instance, for the business or the brand to spend more time and effort publicizing their involvement in the activity than it is investing in it. Consumers are more cynical and sophisticated and, as has been shown, the strength of vigilante consumers is thriving and growing. Messages therefore have to be communicated openly and honestly if the public and the media are going to support the partnerships and help generate maximum benefits for all parties.

Sponsorship

Sponsorship can be the primary focus for realizing a cause-related marketing partnership and may relate to a particular event or activity. What makes it cause-related marketing as opposed to standard sponsorship is the fact that what is being sponsored is a good cause or charity. This relationship is then marketed to meet the mutual objectives of the partnership. In some cases, the sponsorship might be a straight commercial relationship with the cause links interwoven within it, as demonstrated by Coca-Cola's sponsorship of Harry Potter. Essentially this partnership, whilst a straight commercial sponsorship on one level, uses the power of the Coca-Cola brand to support the critical issue of child literacy which is interwoven into the sponsorship. As the communications director of Coca-Cola Great Britain commented:

> [The campaign] brings together the uniqueness of Harry Potter and Coca-Cola in order to benefit young people through the joy of reading. As it develops in the years ahead, it will make a major contribution to Coca-Cola's basic business proposition, to benefit everyone who is touched by our business.
>
> (Adkins, 2002)

Licensing

In a licensing relationship, the corporate pays for the license to use the charity logo or identity on its products or services. The corporate generally wants to use a charity logo, to benefit from the implied endorsement and halo effect of the charity or cause and the positive values that it projects, and to sell more products and services. This is very much a commercial relationship. As with all cause-related marketing partnerships, the parties, be they the charity, cause or business, negotiate the detail with each other and of course decide whether or not to sign up to. As part of that process, parties need to understand and put a value on the opportunity, which will be made up of elements beyond the purely financial. The parties involved will also need to consider the effects on their own brands and reputation as part of this assessment (Adkins, 1999a, Chapter 22).

Licensing can sometimes form part of a much broader strategy where the purchase of the right to use the charities logo is just part of an overall package of activities that together represent the cause-related marketing partnership. It is important to understand that there are important tax and VAT regulations to consider when developing a licensing agreement. Certain aspects of the cause-related marketing relationship, for instance, may fall under different tax rules. Individuals concerned in negotiating such arrangements should ensure that they are clear about these implications and take proper advice.

Direct marketing

Direct marketing is an obvious channel for cause-related marketing messages. Many charities, like businesses, are expert in the field, managing databases of millions of records. Often, access to a charity's database is considered the big prize for the corporate and the cause-related marketing relationship. Clearly, it is very much up to the parties involved whether or not it makes their databases available. If the database is made available, the circumstances have to be agreed and also whether existing or new direct marketing strategies are developed to support, enhance or indeed lead the cause-related marketing partnership. Clearly, relationships with customers or supporters, whether as a charity, cause or business, are crucial and should be guarded with great care.

Affinity credit cards probably represent the largest sector in this aspect of cause-related marketing. To date, more than 1000 organizations have launched affinity or co-branded credit cards in a bid to raise funds, extend their brand awareness, to add value and give something back to their customers, supporters, members or fans. Starting in the UK in 1987, when the Bank of Scotland launched the NSPCC card, 7 per cent of all UK credit cards are now affinity cards. Since 1987, more than £40 million has been generated for various organizations (Adkins, 1999a, Chapter 15).

The basic mechanic for an affinity card is that in signing up for the particular card a donation is made to the charity or cause. In addition, in using the card further donations are made for every £100 or so spent. The charity therefore earns an income dependent on the applications and usage of the card. The credit card company gains access to a new universe of potential users and makes its money in the usual way, donating a percentage of this to the charity or cause. Some cards offer the user a choice of charities to support, whilst others are dedicated to a particular cause (Adkins, 1999a, Chapter 15).

Sales promotion

Sales promotion is such a broad category that it is almost impossible to cover every possible option. In the following paragraphs, therefore, only some of the most frequently used and innovative mechanics are outlined.

Purchase triggered donations

This is probably one of the most familiar mechanisms used for cause-related marketing within this broad category. Donations to causes are triggered by purchase. The range of partnerships using this type of approach is endless

and includes companies, charities and causes of all sizes (Adkins, 1999a, Chapter 15, 2002). Examples range from biscuits, books, bank accounts and bath oils to sauce, soap and soap powder, amongst many other things. They range from local Pizza restaurants wanting to encourage sales by donating a percentage of the sale of wine to local schools, to tens of thousands of pounds raised by Comic Relief through the sale of Persil (Adkins, 1999a, Chapter 15).

Trial triggered donations

Cause-related marketing can also be used to trigger donations through trial, application or signing up to a product or service and through usage. The American Express Restoration of the Statue of Liberty programme, already mentioned, is an example of such a model.

Voucher collection schemes

Voucher collection schemes are a frequently used mechanic for cause-related marketing. Tesco's Computers for Schools programme and the Walkers Books for Schools programmes are exemplary demonstrations, which together have contributed over £100 million of benefit to schools, whilst at the same time building their brands, customer loyalty and sales. There are many others, including a number of retailers in the UK and abroad (Adkins, 1999a, Chapter 15). Further details are provided in the case studies to follow.

Cause-related marketing as an incentive to action

Cause-related marketing has been used effectively as an incentive to promote interest, dialogue, response, action and sales from markets as diverse as banking and insurance to telecommunications. Examples range from organizations wanting to increase the response rate to research surveys where a donation was promised to a charity in return for the survey's completion, to cause-related marketing as an incentive for a mortgage product. Cause-related marketing partnerships have also been used by large department stores as incentives for shopping evenings and by car manufacturers as a mechanism to drive trial.

Pilot tests have been carried out to evaluate the effectiveness of a widget versus a cause-related marketing-based incentive where the charitable donation has proved very successful. The value of the cause-related marketing donation needs to be carefully judged, but when right, it can significantly boost responses and actions. It also provides the potential start of the dialogue with customers or potential customers, and reinforces the organization's values and commitment to their wider community by making a real contribution, a factor that has increasing resonance with many stakeholder groups, including customers (Adkins, 1999a, Chapter 15). An example of cause-related marketing being used in this way would be Toyota using a donation to The Muscular Dystrophy Group to incentivize the return of market research surveys (Adkins, 1999a, Chapter 15).

Competitions, games and draws

Charitable benefits have been incorporated into competitions, games and draws, when the individual not only wins a prize but a donation is made by the business to the charity at the same time. This approach has been used by businesses as diverse as soap and toilet tissue manufacturers to tree growers and high street banks. This enables both the winner and the competition organizer to be seen as heroes, and the consumer and the charity to win, providing a potent proposition (Adkins, 1999a, Chapter 15). Examples included a major high street bank that was trying to encourage the public to review their financial arrangements. In booking to see the financial adviser, the customer received a pack of Christmas cards. Inside each one was the chance to win a financial prize, which the bank matched with a donation to a children's charity (Adkins, 1999a, Chapter 15).

Self-liquidating cause-related marketing promotions

Another means of integrating cause-related marketing into the marketing mix is through the use of self-liquidating promotions, whereby consumers are presented with a special offer, which is available at a small cost. The small price the consumer pays finances the offer and the donation is made to a charity. Examples of this type of application include a savoury snack product in support of Comic Relief in 1999. In this case a promotion was run on the packet, offering consumers the chance to purchase a Comic Relief video. For every video bought, the manufacturer donated £1 to the charity (Adkins, 1999a, Chapter 15).

New for old

Under the sales promotion umbrella 'new for old' is a mechanic often employed for cause-related marketing with the objective of, for instance, encouraging trial, awareness, differentiation or reinforcement of the brand values etc. Basically, consumers are encouraged to trade in their old product for a new one when a donation of cash or the second-hand product is made to the charity or good cause. Examples include the cause-related marketing partnership between a clothes retailer and a homeless charity, and also between an office supplies company and a school, where a number of schemes have been run to supply schools with much needed printers and fax machines (Adkins, 1999a, Chapter 15).

Facilitated giving

Cause-related marketing can also take the form of facilitated giving, whereby the business partner provides a vehicle to facilitate customer donations to the charity. Airline foreign coin collections like BA's 'Change for Good' are classic examples. At its simplest it consists of an in-flight appeal by video, envelopes or in the in-flight magazine, and on-board announcements for customers to donate their unwanted foreign currency. This currency is then donated to a variety of charities, which in BA's case is UNICEF. To date, the BA Change for Good programme has raised over £12 million for needy children around the world, by exposing over 40 million passengers a year to the partnership. There are many other examples using the same mechanic, including utilities, restaurants and hotels, to name but a few (Adkins, 1999a, Chapter 15).

Summary

As has been argued, consumers and other stakeholder groups have high expectations of businesses. Clearly, in an age where information held on consumer's interests and habits is growing at an incredible rate, the opportunity exists to understand what motivates an individual from a charity or cause point of view, and to develop marketing strategies which are in tune with their expectations and interests, and to communicate with them accordingly. Research shows that over 80 per cent of consumers have indicated that, price and quality being equal, linking with a cause would make a difference; they would change brands, switch retail outlets and have a much better perception of a company trying to do something to make the world a better place. The opportunities to build the business whilst making a real positive difference to the wider community are therefore significant, providing a win–win–win (Adkins, 1999b).

Towards excellence

Developing a company's cause-related marketing programme takes time. It also needs to be handled very carefully. There are huge rewards to be gained from cause-related marketing, from the business, charity and good cause, and consumer perspective. There are also huge risks. Brands take decades to build and only moments to destroy. Cause-related marketing is

not a fig leaf to cover fundamental flaws within a business. In order to create an award-winning programme, therefore, it is essential to develop and implement the partnership with sensitivity. There is no substitute for a great creative idea, but that alone will not guarantee success in cause-related marketing. The potential risks and rewards are much greater than a standard marketing activity, as it engages the emotions of the consumer and other stakeholder groups, and emotions must be handled with care. The Business in the Community cause-related marketing guidelines outline the key principles and processes for effective cause-related marketing. These cause-related marketing guidelines were developed through extensive consultation with consumers, practitioners in businesses and charities, as well as agencies and representative bodies. The key principles for cause-related marketing were identified for these guidelines as follows (Adkins, 1998):

- Integrity.
- Transparency.
- Sincerity.
- Mutual respect.
- Partnership.
- Mutual benefit.

If the partnership with a charity or good cause is not based on these key principles, it is not cause-related marketing, and it is likely to flounder. If it is based on these principles, however, and key processes are followed, it is likely that an excellent programme will be developed that provides mutual benefit for all parties. The key processes that were identified through the Business in the Community cause-related marketing guidelines (Adkins, 1998) are:

- Planning and preparation.
- Negotiating the partnership.
- The formal agreement.
- Managing the programme.
- Communicating the programme.
- Monitoring, measuring and evaluating the programme.

This whole area is covered in great detail in Adkins (1998, 1999a). It is only possible to provide an outline in this chapter of some of the key issues to consider when developing cause-related marketing partnerships.

Planning and preparation

The maxim 'failing to plan is planning to fail' is true of cause-related marketing as it is for any other activity. Investing time and effort at the beginning is critical. A clear first stage of this process is to understand what the organization wants to achieve and why. The creators need to be clear on the vision, values and style of their own organization in order that they know what they are looking for in a partner. The next step is to develop a clear brief. And in doing so, it is essential to provide the following types of information (Adkins, 1998, 1999a):

- The background and nature of your organization.
- The organization's vision, values and objectives.
- The specific objectives with regard to this brief, including details of the target market and any known constraints.
- The budgets and timing.
- The selection criteria.
- What is expected by when in way of a response, for example a presentation or report etc.
- The contact name for further information.

The more detail included at this stage the better. With a solid brief in place, the next step is to find a partner. This can be done in a number of ways. Methods range from desk research and a tendering process through to responding to a whim of a senior member of the organization. Clearly, the more solid the foundation the more lasting the structure. There are also important details to consider as part of the selection process, for instance what costs may be incurred and who will meet them. Also, if a tendering process is followed, it is important to adhere to the existing guidelines and protocols (Adkins, 1998, p. 8). Before deciding on a partner or partners, it is critical to fully understand the other organization's objectives and values, in broad terms, and ensure that they fully understand yours. Organizations whose values have no synergy are unlikely to be able to develop an effective partnership. It is important therefore to take time to understand and present these values and culture to all parties in order to appreciate the potential synergies and opportunities. Business and the voluntary sector often work in very different ways from each other, and therefore be sure the following are clearly understood (Adkins, 1998, 1999a):

- The organizational structure.
- The geographical distribution.
- The relationship between the organization and its employees, volunteers, supporters and beneficiaries, as appropriate.
- The work ethos, decision-making processes and levels of authority.
- The planning and investment cycles.

Defining the scope of your partnership

Before any negotiations take place on the details of how the partnership will operate, it is important to be clear who owns the idea and the intended duration of the relationship, including an exit strategy and the likely scale of investment, contributions and rewards. Managing the expectations of all involved at this stage is crucial if the partnership is to be founded on the key principles and is to be a success. Misleading partners about capacity, investment, contribution and commitment etc. is clearly unethical, and will be counter-productive and destructive of any potential partnership(Adkins, 1998, 1999a, Chapter 21).

Gaining commitment to the partnership

To be a success, the commitment of senior executives in the partner organization is essential. Having this level of the organization embrace the partnership is a priority from the outset. The chairman, board, non-executive directors, shareholders and/or trustees are ideal ambassadors for the cause-related marketing partnership, as are employees, volunteers, supporters and beneficiaries. Their backing demonstrates organizational commitment and can bring valuable support and resources to the relationship. Without this support, the partnership may not reach its full potential, or may fail even to get off the ground (Adkins, 1998, pp. 9–10, 1999a, Chapter 21).

Negotiating the partnership

Cause-related marketing partnerships may include one or more partners. When a partner has been identified, the next step is to negotiate and agree the details of the partnership and programme. It is essential that these negotiations be conducted in the spirit of the key principles. If the partners do not share the same ethical assumptions, it is unlikely that a rewarding partnership will develop. All parties should be delighted by the partnership and the benefits it aims to provide; there should be no feelings of exploitation. It is critical as part of this process that the mutual objectives are aligned and that each party is comfortable with these. It is also important to understand how,

should conflict arise, this will be reconciled. Transparency and honesty are crucial here to avoid misunderstandings. SMART objectives are to be recommended. That is, objectives should be Simple, Measurable, Achievable, Realistic and Time limited (Adkins, 1999a, Chapter 22).

As part of negotiating the partnership, 'auditing your assets' (Adkins, 1998, p. 10) is an important part of the process. All organizations, whether commercial or not for profit, have assets that extend beyond financial or brand strength and influence. Financial contributions are key, of course. There are, however, also other contributions or pillars that could be considered in support of the constitution and implementation of the partnership. These include the 7Ps described in Table 26.1.

Key contributions are often those of skills, expertise, know-how and goodwill, which can come from both internal and external sources. Contributions, support and resources should be explored from all potential sources, including other departments, employees or volunteers, suppliers and indeed local authorities, government and European and international bodies (Adkins, 1998, 1999a, Chapter 22).

By auditing all such assets, the potential to combine individual strengths to amplify and leverage the impact of the programme can be

Table 26.1   The 7Ps of cause-related marketing

The pillar	The explanation
Power	The strength of the brand and the organization's reputation
People	The army of employees, volunteers and networks as well as individual expertise
Promotion	Marketing promotion and strategies to leverage support
Purchasing	The purchasing and leverage of the supply chain and organization network
Profit	Cash contribution
Product	Gifts in kind
Premises	Donating or lending facilities and premises in support of the partnership

Source: Adkins (1999a, Chapter 6).

seen. The audit also serves as a useful basis for the later stages of negotiations and programme implementation. Apart from setting SMART objectives, it is important also that the mechanics for programmes are simple and straightforward. The 'KISS' principle of 'Keeping It Simple' is critical in the development of an effective cause-related marketing partnership. When defining the nature of an activity, therefore, the following must be considered (Adkins, 1998):

- The creative idea.
- The balance of benefit between charity or cause, business and consumer.
- The range of products/services involved.
- The mechanics of delivery.
- Whether the goals are achievable.
- Appropriate donation value.
- The communications messages and strategy.
- The exit strategy.

Valuing the opportunity

The value of a potential partnership will be unique to it. There is no formula, but it is clear that 'value' refers to many elements beyond the purely financial. Increased awareness, enhanced reputation, product or service differentiation, developed relationships, loyalty and emotional engagement, added value, increased sales or contributions and an exciting PR story etc. all contribute to the potential value of a partnership for both the business and the charity or cause. When negotiating the details of the partnership, everything that will contribute to this value needs to be considered and will be helped by referring to the results of the 'audit of your assets'. All of these elements have the potential to add value to the relationship and help to achieve common objectives. It is important to remember that consumers support cause-related marketing, and fully accept and indeed expect that there should be benefits to business as well as to the good cause (Adkins, 1997, 1999b).

It is also important to consider in negotiating the partnership what the reaction of the various stakeholders will be to the balance of the final agreement. When negotiations are concluded, all parties should be pleased with the outcome and the potential mutual benefit to be derived from the cause-related marketing partnership.

Assessing the risks

Clearly, there are risks with cause-related marketing. Reputations take years of investment, are fragile and can be destroyed in a moment. Neither side can afford for their reputations to be tarnished. It is important, therefore, to appreciate the potential risks on both sides and, before setting up a cause-related marketing programme, to conduct a full risk assessment independent of the potential partner. Risk assessment covers three key considerations: reputation, logistics and financial risks (Adkins, 1998, 1999a). The risk audit should be done thoroughly as it is critical that partnerships are developed on solid foundations.

The formal agreement

Before drafting any legal document it is important to seek qualified legal advice. In this chapter only a basic outline of the types of issues to be considered is provided. Legal advice needs to be taken in every case. There are a number of basic documents that cause-related marketing practitioners should be aware of, at least when developing a cause-related marketing partnership and programme. These are as follows (Adkins, 1998, p. 12, 1999a, Chapter 23):

- The Charities Act 1992 and 1993.
- The Charitable Institutions (Fundraising) Regulations 1994.
- The British Codes of Advertising and Sales Promotion.
- The Trades Description Act 1968.
- The Control of Misleading Advertisements Regulations 1988.

These are just some of the potential legal instruments that could impact and be relevant to a cause-related marketing programme, but is it important to take qualified legal advice. An overview of the legal issues around cause-related marketing is provided in Adkins (1998, 1999a). These include the requirement for a written agreement, the requirement to make the nature of the partnership clear to customers and that all relevant records must be made available to the beneficiary (Adkins, 1998, p. 12, 1999a, Chapter 23). In developing the formalized contract it is also important to consider minimum guarantees, exclusivity, and the tax and VAT issues.

Managing the programme

Even a perfect partnership and an innovative programme can fail without effective programme management, leaving all involved disappointed. To manage a programme effectively, it is important to be clear about the roles and responsibilities of all parties. Setting out a work plan and communicating regularly throughout the process will help ensure the process works effectively. Essentially, managing a cause-related marketing programme requires the same skills and dedication as any project management exercise. At a basic level, it is important to understand who has responsibility for the activities, set out in the formal agreement (Adkins, 1998, p. 16, 1999a, Chapter 24):

- What are the work and timing plans for the programme?
- Who are the main points of contact?
- Who has decision-making authority?
- What is the decision-making process and time scale?
- Who has responsibility for different aspects of the process in what time frame?
- Who is being paid to carry out what tasks?
- Who is responsible for recording meetings and decisions, and in what time frame?
- What is the approval and sign process, and how long should it take?

- What are the success criteria and have the processes been put in place to measure them?

Communicating the programme

Communication of the cause-related marketing programme is critical, in order for it to maximize its potential for all parties. It must be effective, compelling, based on the key principles and be present throughout the process. Essentially, what is invested in effort and resource is often directly related to what is achieved.

Consideration must be given to what is going to be communicated and how, beyond the legal requirements. Is it more compelling, for instance, to highlight an amount of money or what that money can achieve? Consumer research clearly indicates that what can be achieved is the critical message.

To be effective it is important that the communication is compelling, balanced, based on the key principles, is legal, honest, decent and truthful, and must not mislead stakeholders and partners. The investment and communication must also be considered in relation to the funds being raised, and the balance of costs and mutual benefit must be appropriate. It is important that communication is applied throughout all stages of the programme development, externally and internally. The key phases in the communication process to consider are (Adkins, 1998, 1999a, Chapter 25):

- Preparing the ground.
- Pre-launch publicity.
- Launch.
- Ongoing commitment.
- Post programme.

All of these elements are important for effective cause-related marketing partnerships and in some cases are subject to legal requirements in the British Codes of Advertising and Sales Promotion. Apart from the legal requirements and codes, and the fact that the communication must be legal, decent, honest and truthful, the key concepts that should form the foundations of the communications are (Adkins, 1998, p. 17, 1999a, Chapter 25):

- Communication must give balanced emphasis to the business and the cause.
- Both partners should promote the benefits of the partnership.
- It must not mislead partners or the public; in particular, the benefits to all parties need to be clear.
- It needs to be compelling, sincere and not patronizing.
- The contribution of the consumers needs to be acknowledged.

One aspect that is often forgotten in developing these programmes is the importance of thanking all participants, including the consumers, for their involvement in a cause-related marketing programme. After all, it is only through the consumers attention, action or purchase that the objectives of the cause-related marketing programme, be they from the charity or the business point of view, are achieved.

The 'media test'

A critical aspect of a cause-related marketing programme is to ensure that it resonates with all of the stakeholder groups, both internally and externally. When considering the external audience, a critical group is the media, hence the 'media test'. The exercise here is to take the perspective of an investigative journalist who is negative towards the business sector or organization. Pose the questions they would ask and provide the answers. If the verbal equivalent of small print and sub-clauses and sub-texts is being used by way of explanation, then the programme is wrong. Cause-related marketing programmes, to be most effective, are based on the 'KISS principle' of 'keeping it simple'. These programmes need to be transparent, sincere, honest and truthful. Having gone through this and considered the questions, if the answers are

all positive, simple and compelling, it is likely that a strong programme is being developed. If, on the other hand, the answers are weak, then this sends a strong warning bell to review the preparation and plan. The 'media test' is actually part of the process that runs throughout the duration of the planning of a programme, right from the very start. It has many uses. Apart from refining the detail of the programme as it develops, ensuring that when the programme finally launches it is well received, it also provides a solid Q and A for the board, employees and networks of the partners involved, and the essence of the media brief (Adkins 1999a).

Monitoring, measuring and evaluating the programme

Monitoring, measuring and evaluating programmes and partnerships is a clearly understood discipline, and a requirement of effective business management today. Cause-related marketing is no different. The investment made at the planning and preparation stage and in identifying the key objectives is time well spent. It helps to identify the performance indicators against which the programme or partnership can be monitored, measured and evaluated.

Monitoring the programme makes it possible to refine the details of the partnership; measurement and evaluation provide the evidence for continued investment or not. Effective data makes it possible to judge the success of a programme and are the vital basis for future support, without which the future of the partnership is always potentially in jeopardy.

Monitoring, measuring and evaluating are in the interest of all parties involved; resources should be allocated from the outset. Depending on the agreed performance indicators, the following aspects should be considered for monitoring, measuring and evaluating (Adkins, 1998, p. 18):

- Funds raised.
- Effect on sales, volume and/or customer traffic.

- Media coverage.
- Effect on reputation, image and/or awareness.
- Effect on usage and/or attitude/favourability.
- Customer satisfaction.
- Employee satisfaction.
- Other stakeholder satisfaction.
- Impact on society.

Without measuring these aspects of the cause-related marketing partnership, some of the intrinsic elements of the programme can be overlooked.

What is beyond doubt is that cause-related marketing is becoming too much a part of the marketing armoury to be left to its own devices. It will not be enough to be seen broadly as a 'good thing', and there will be increasing pressure to measure this effectiveness well.

Case studies

Case studies have been provided to illustrate the motivation, mechanics and results of some award-winning examples, each of which have won or been a finalist in the Business in the Community Awards for Excellence in Cause Related Marketing (for further information, please see www.bitc.org.uk).

Tesco Computers for Schools

This cause-related marketing programme is probably the most successful in the UK from both the business and the cause point of view.

Essentially, it was developed as a one-off 10-week loyalty-based sales promotion programme, based on a mechanic seen in the USA. This was refined and developed by the Tesco team and became what is today known as Tesco Computers for Schools. So successful was it when it first launched that it became a core part of Tesco's marketing strategy and has been in the marketplace since about 1991, when Tesco was a very different business than it is today.

Following research, schools were identified as a key cause of concern for parents and

communities and, within that broad category, it was evident that IT equipment was a much needed resource. The mechanic is straightforward, has been refined over the years but has remained essentially the same and has been the inspiration for many other schools-based programmes.

During the spring term, for an eight to ten week period, consumers are encouraged to shop at Tesco and to spend £10. For every £10 spent, customers receive a voucher. Customers donate these vouchers to their chosen school. Schools have to register with Tesco and collect the vouchers, which can then be redeemed against IT and related equipment chosen from an extensive catalogue.

The critical factor throughout the programme is choice. Consumers and schools choose whether or not to participate. Should they decide to participate, then the consumer chooses the school they want to support, and the school chooses the equipment to suit children of all ages and for schools with varying budgets. Special needs equipment is also included.

The objective for the programme from the business point of view has been to build customer loyalty, drive traffic into stores, increase spend and reinforce Tesco's proposition of 'Every Little Helps'.

From the cause point of view, Tesco has been committed to making a real impact on IT literacy in schools. Since 1991, when the programme first began, Tesco has provided £70 million worth of IT-related equipment to schools.

The programme has been thoroughly supported since it began, with TV, press and radio advertising, as well as significant communications in-store and on-pack. Over the years, Tesco suppliers have participated too, by offering special promotional packs, and Tesco has extended the offer to include petrol.

Importantly, this Tesco Computers for Schools programme is very clearly a national strategy, but it is delivered locally. Local stores are the 'face' of Tesco in the community and are, alongside the customer, the 'hero' for the school in the community. The store manager presents the equipment to the schools as it is delivered, often with local MP presence and support. Tesco's support for education has also evolved and has included a number of important elements. This has included, through Xemplar Education, the partner and provider of the equipment, support to schools in doing audits of schools' computer systems, to help schools identify what is needed. Basic training and access to training rooms have also been provided, as have dedicated helplines etc.

To date (2001), over £70 million worth of equipment has gone to schools nationwide, including over 46 200 computers and 394 000 items of additional IT-related equipment. There has also been approximately £100 000 worth of IT training for teachers.

From the business point of view, the benefits have included enhanced reputation, image and profile, as well as reinforcement of the brand values. Tesco is recognized as an innovative retailer and has also increased customer footfall and sales as a result.

> Cause-related marketing makes commercial sense. It can deliver greater benefits per pounds spent than almost anything else a company can do and can achieve a wide range of business, marketing, fundraising, and social benefits.
> Tim Mason, Marketing Director, Tesco plc

A more detailed case study is provided in Adkins (1999a).

Nambarrie Think Pink for Action Cancer

Nambarrie Tea Company Ltd, a 35-person tea company in Northern Ireland, has an ongoing partnership with Action Cancer. The main cause-related marketing focus of this partnership happens in October each year, when Nambarrie support Breast Cancer Awareness month. Nambarrie's target market is women aged 16–60 and sadly so is the target group for breast cancer, where Northern Ireland has the highest incidence anywhere in the world, and this is therefore a prominent social issue.

Looking for an innovative way to develop their marketing approach and build relationships with their customers, the partnership between Nambarrie and Action Cancer was highly complementary. Both organizations were marketing orientated, targeting the same audiences. Nambarrie brought its FMCG marketing expertise to bear on the Action Cancer challenge, which was to increase awareness of the issues, encourage self-examination and fundraise. Action Cancer benefited Nambarrie through the use of their identity and the halo effect of such an association.

The breadth of depth of Nambarrie's support for the cause is exceptional in a number of ways. The holistic support of the company has included donations to the charity from sales of promotional packs of tea, television advertising and website development support, as well as extensive staff involvement, from fundraising activities through to stopping the production line for a day to help the charity pack their pink ribbons. The company has also used its warehousing and distribution networks to store and deliver the charity's fundraising ribbons.

Nambarrie demonstrated through the ongoing cause-related marketing partnership that size of company and number of employees are not necessarily the only or the critical factors in developing an award-winning cause-related marketing strategy. Imagination, creativity and commitment are essential if the programme is to be fully leveraged and have maximum benefit for all concerned.

> ... I particularly urge smaller companies like ourselves to get involved with cause-related marketing because the benefits are absolutely enormous, for the company, for the cause and for the consumers themselves.
> This is the most comprehensive marketing initiative that the company has ever undertaken. The return on investment has been enormous in terms of corporate, brand and

internal communications. Most importantly it has directly benefited our community and our customers, the women in Northern Ireland who buy our tea.

Brian Davis, Managing Director,
Nambarrie Tea Company Ltd.

A more detailed case study is provided in Adkins (1999a, Chapter 16).

Walkers and News International 'Free Books for Schools'

Now in its fourth year, this cause-related marketing partnership, launched in 1998, created a national collecting frenzy amongst consumers, through a promotion that reached 80 per cent of the population. Free Books for Schools tokens were distributed free to consumers via Walkers crisps packets, and in *The Sun*, *The News of the World*, *The Times* and *The Sunday Times*. Consumers were encouraged to collect these tokens and donate them to schools. Schools in turn redeemed the tokens for books, from a catalogue supplied by Walkers and News International, that was compiled with advice from the DfEE (Department for Education and Employment, now called the Department for Education and Skills).

Walkers' market share of the snacks category grew over the promotional period, and *The Sun* saw an increase in sales in an overall declining market, as a result of this partnership. Whilst achieving these business benefits, the partnership is making a tangible positive impact on society. These companies are using the power of their brands to address the very real problem of low literacy levels in schools across the UK, where one in four children aged 11 fail to reach their appropriate level in reading.

Six million free books, worth £30 million, were distributed to schools through Walkers and News International's 'Free Books for Schools' cause-related marketing partnership, with 85 per cent of UK schools taking part. Each school on average received over 174 free books.

As well as providing all the books, 'Free Books for Schools' actively supported the Government's national literacy strategy, providing large-scale leverage to the Government-run National Year of Reading. A brilliant cause-related marketing 'win–win–win' (for more details, please refer to Adkins, 1999a, Chapter 16).

> Literacy is fundamental to News International's business. 'Free Books for Schools' is one way that we have been able to support the Government's literacy targets, tangibly, whilst adding value to our business and giving something back to our readers.
>
> Andy Agar, Promotions Director,
> News Group Newspapers

> We wanted to make a real contribution to the Government's literacy initiative by supporting the National Year of Reading and joining together two everyday brands, Walkers crisps and *The Sun*, to support the cause. Free Books for Schools has proved to be a phenomenal success for News International, Walkers and society.
>
> Martin Glenn, President,
> Walkers Snacks Ltd

Avon Crusade Against Breast Cancer

Avon is a company which reaches around a billion women through 3 million independent sales representatives in 136 countries, and is committed to its mission 'to be the company that best understands and satisfies the product, service and self-fulfilment needs of women globally'. The Crusade Against Breast Cancer is a wonderful demonstration of this commitment. It enables Avon to meet business marketing and communications objectives at the same time as supporting a cause of real concern to their target market.

Breast cancer is the biggest single health concern for women in the UK as one in 11 women will get breast cancer at some point in their life. The Avon Crusade has raised over £8 million for UK breast cancer charities since 1992. This money has helped to fund both the first dedicated research centre in the UK to focus on the causes and treatments of breast cancer, and 15 breast cancer nurses.

Through a strategic partnership with Breakthrough Breast Cancer and Macmillan Cancer Relief, Avon's cause-related marketing strategy has been implemented using a number of different elements of the marketing mix. The Crusade has involved sales of products where a proportion of the price is donated to charity. It has also included sales of charity fundraising products, sponsorship of Fashion Targets Breast Cancer and political lobbying via consumer petitions. Avon has benefited greatly from this association, enhancing their corporate profile, engaging new and existing customers, receiving enormous publicity, fostering feelings of affiliation amongst staff, representatives and customers, bringing the company's vision to life (for more details, please refer to Adkins, 1999a, Chapter 17).

> To assure our future success Avon is committed to high performance in every aspect of our business operation. Through the Avon Breast Cancer Crusade we have raised over $190 million around the world to help the fight against breast cancer, whilst harnessing all elements of our business and making a positive impact on the company's corporate profile and overall image.
>
> Andrea Slater, Vice President Marketing, Avon UK

Breakthrough Breast Cancer and Avon have been partners for more than eight years. At the outset Breakthrough needed a major corporate supporter to help establish us at a time when neither breasts nor cancer were mentioned in the boardroom. Avon have raised more than £8 million which has helped to establish the first dedicated breast cancer research centre in the UK. The Avon Kiss Goodbye to Breast Cancer campaign in 1999 firmly established Avon as one the leaders in cause-related marketing in this country.

> Delyth Morgan, Chief Executive, Breakthrough Breast Cancer

Centrica plc: the British Gas and Help the Aged partnership

British Gas has raised more than £4 million for Help the Aged since the partnership was launched in 1999, through a combination of direct funding, in-kind support and customer fundraising. Already the partnership has delivered benefits to more than 400 000 older people.

British Gas embarked on a long-term cause-related marketing partnership with Help the Aged to reduce the number of unnecessary winter deaths and to make the lives of older people warmer and less isolated. In 1998/99, the deaths of 44 000 older people in the UK could be directly attributed to cold-related diseases. The partnership has developed a solutions-based approach to the issues facing vulnerable older people. It seeks to provide long-term solutions to fuel poverty and isolation to save lives, allied to practical short-term measures for immediate impact.

British Gas has communicated the issues of excess winter deaths and isolation to a national audience through advertising and direct marketing. It has also delivered a combination of traditional sponsorship activity and new, innovative fundraising. It has generated huge employee support, external media coverage and has been particularly beneficial in reinforcing British Gas's brand attributes in a number of competitive product markets (for more details, please refer to Adkins, 1999, Chapter 16).

> The partnership is one of unique strength. Both partners bring to the relationship different skills and expertise, but together it is a union of tremendous potency. The partnership has already helped thousands of vulnerable older people, providing direct help and support to those who need it most. We are literally saving lives – now and in the future.
>
> Mike Lake, Help the Aged Director General

British Gas has sought to address the issue of fuel poverty and excess winter deaths through a holistic partnership that combines the skills of one of Britain's leading charities with British Gas funding, expertise and stakeholder support. Our work with Help the Aged has realised both positive community impact and commercial business benefits.

Simon Waugh, Centrica Group Director of Marketing

Lever Fabergé – Persil 'Say Pants to Poverty' with Comic Relief

Persil raised £300 000 in just six weeks for Comic Relief 2001, bringing the total raised from the two-year cause-related marketing partnership to over £560 000.

Persil's aim was to create an innovative and eye-catching campaign, and make as much 'noise' around Red Nose Day's 2001 theme, 'Say Pants to Poverty'. Special promotional Persil packs, sporting Y-fronts, bloomers and boxer shorts on the front, went on sale from February through to Red Nose Day on 16 March.

A donation went to Comic Relief for each pack sold – the amount of the donation varying according to the size of the pack purchased, from 2p to 16p. The back of Persil packs gave details of how to obtain a Comic Relief information pack, full of fun ideas on how to raise funds for Red Nose Day. Further money was donated as a result of internal fundraising.

Persil extended its support for Comic Relief through awareness raising events, including TV, press and poster advertising, toilet door signage in over 500 pubs, a PR campaign featuring the Persil 'Arty Pants' collection and radio activity. Persil also sponsored Comic Relief's fundraising packs for schools and youth clubs, and the office lottery posters (for more details, please refer to Adkins, 1999a, Chapter 17).

There is an excellent fit between Persil and Comic Relief – both are trusted brands with a strong heritage and caring attributes.

The partnership has clearly demonstrated that both parties can benefit hugely – for Persil it provides an innovative, eye-catching way to communicate with its consumers; for Comic Relief significant funds have been raised for causes in the UK and Africa. It truly is a win–win situation.

John Ballington, Corporate and Consumer Affairs Director, Lever Fabergé

The relationship with Persil has worked very well and been a real pleasure for everyone working with them on Red Nose Day 2001. The relationship has involved many elements because of the different aspects of the campaign and the Persil team has embraced them all with a commitment and determination to make Persil's contribution as effective as possible. Persil and Comic Relief had already worked together as a major partner in 1999 and this has meant that we could both benefit from our experience and maximize the opportunities open to us in 2001. Persil's marketing team have been completely focused on the Comic Relief campaign and have worked tirelessly to make it the biggest and cleanest Red Nose Day ever!

Terry Mills, Corporate Fundraising Manager, Comic Relief

Summary

With the increasing economic power of and pressure on business in society today, consumers and other stakeholders are increasingly demanding of businesses. The context in which organizations are operating has changed dramatically in the last decade. There is a rising tide of expectation across all sectors of society which manifests itself in many ways, from taking to the street with placards to taking to the desk with a pen and paper, to taking to the Internet. Protest, silent or violent, is a factor in today's society, and one which business and marketing within the business have to take into account if they are to continue to thrive. As understanding of the new dynamic develops, so does the appreciation of the potential of cause-related marketing (Adkins, 2001):

- 70 per cent of Chief Executives report that corporate social responsibility is an essential issue to their business.
- 89 per cent of Marketing Directors believe that businesses should be involved in addressing the social issues of the day.
- 96 per cent of Marketing and Community Affairs Directors appreciate the benefits of cause-related marketing in addressing business and social issues.
- 77 per cent of Chief Executives, Marketing Directors and Community Affairs Directors believe that cause-related marketing can enhance corporate or brand reputation.
- 69 per cent of all respondents believe that cause-related marketing will continue to increase in importance over the next two to three years.

The situation, however, is not only entirely threatening and confrontational. When organizations get it right, they have and can earn the respect and belief of their consumer and stakeholder groups. Marketers have increasingly understood that one-off transaction-based marketing is yesterday's world. Today, relationships and loyalty are critical to the marketing and business strategy, and these relationships need to be developed carefully, nurtured and grown on the basis of decent, honest, truthful and values based propositions. The developments in legal codes, socio-economic and political factors, as well as the ICT revolution, ensure that it cannot be otherwise.

Price, quality and functionality are today taken as given. These are no longer sustainable differentiators. With the speed of communication, details of price, quality, functionality and innovation can be broadcast at the touch of a button and replicated in a matter of days or weeks. This has accelerated the need for innovation, and has also made businesses increasingly transparent. It has enabled effective benchmarking and informed debate. 'Bedroom

protest' is now a vibrant and powerful reality. The concept of a silent minority no longer exists. These new realities have driven the push for new platforms for differentiation, which in turn have pushed the focus on values and the truth behind the brand up the agenda.

The symbiotic relationship between business and society has never been more evident. These changes in the way business and society operate are not just a threat, but represent an exciting opportunity for those businesses who have a clear set of principles and values. The drivers of marketing today are about integrity, transparency, sincerity, mutual respect, partnership and mutual benefit. Those organizations that have these principles at their core or are able to develop their values proposition will reap the rewards. This is not, however, about gloss and hype. Values run more than skin deep. Consumers are far too cynical and sophisticated to be fooled by tokenism and exploitation. Consumers are powerful and unforgiving.

In such an environment where honest value-based relationships are the way forward, cause-related marketing is imperative in the marketing tool kit. Where cause-related marketing is implemented well, corporately or with a product or service that is robust in terms of quality, price and functionality; where the partnership is built on the key principles of integrity, transparency, sincerity, mutual respect, partnership and mutual benefit; where the cause has been identified and the partners have a solid affinity; where the partnership has been developed on a solid footing, and there is a creative and compelling proposition, the business and the charity or cause have a potent proposition to present to their stakeholders.

There is no doubt about consumer expectation for corporate responsibility and support for cause-related marketing. Over 80 per cent of consumers clearly indicate that, price and quality being equal, linking with a cause would make a difference; they would switch retail outlets, change brands and have a much better perception of a company trying to make the world a better place (Adkins, 1999b).

Cause-related marketing is one highly effective way of making an organization's corporate social responsibility visible. It is a powerful way of engaging consumers and other stakeholders, not just on the functional level but on the emotional level too. Cause-related marketing does not replace the key requisites of price, quality and function, but with these in place cause-related marketing takes the proposition to another level, the level on which consumers are expecting to be honestly engaged.

Cause-related marketing, however, has to be done well and be based on the key principles. When it is, cause-related marketing has the ability to engage stakeholders, add value to the values of an organization and to the product or service proposition. Cause-related marketing can enhance image and reputation, it can provide differentiation, it can build relationships and loyalty. Cause-related marketing can provide a win for the business, a win for the charity or cause, and a win for the consumer and other stakeholder groups. Ultimately, cause-related marketing can provide a visible, tangible positive impact on the business, the charity or good cause, and the consumer and our wider society.

Done well, cause-related marketing is a powerful and potent tool, but as yet its potential is not fully leveraged. It provides a compelling proposition for consumers and other stakeholders. Despite being a relatively new discipline whose potential as yet remains untapped, the evidence and track record of its effectiveness to date are undeniable. Cause-related marketing has shown itself to benefit the business, the charity or good cause, the consumer and our communities. Cause-related marketing not only offers a core marketing strategy for the future, but can demonstrate business and indeed marketing at its best. It provides marketing with the opportunity to achieve its business objectives whilst at the same time benefiting a charity or good cause and making a positive impact on society. Cause-related marketing provides a rare and compelling combination for business and society.

References

Adkins, S. (1997) *The Game Plan*, Business in the Community Qualitative Research, supported by Research International.

Adkins, S. (1998) *Cause Related Marketing Guidelines: Towards Excellence*, Business in the Community.

Adkins, S. (1999a) *Cause Related Marketing: Who Cares Wins*, Butterworth-Heinemann, Oxford.

Adkins, S. (1999b) *The Ultimate Win Win Win*, Business in the Community Quantitative Consumer Research, supported by Research International

Adkins, S. (2000) *Profitable Partnerships*, Business in the Community Quantitative Research, supported by Research International.

Adkins, S. (2001) *The Corporate Survey III*, Business in the Community, supported by Research International.

Adkins, S. (2002) *Business in the Community Cause Related Marketing News*, Volume 9.

Grayson, D. and Hodges, A. (2001) *Everybody's Business*, Dorling Kindersley/The Financial Times.

IEG (2001) Sponsorship Report, **20**(24), 24 December.

The Little Internet Factbook (2001) Ipsos Reid, www.angusreid.com

Roddick, A. (2001) *Take It Personally*, Section 5, Thorsons.

Further reading

Adkins, S. (1997) *The Game Plan*, Business in the Community, supported by Research International.

Adkins, S. (1998) *The Cause Related Marketing Guidelines: Towards Excellence*, Business in the Community, supported by Research International.

Adkins, S. (1998) *The Corporate Survey II*, Business in the Community, supported by Research International.

Adkins, S. (Winter 1998–Spring 2001) *Cause Related Marketing News*, Business in the Community.

Adkins, S. (1999) *Cause Related Marketing: Who Cares Wins*, Butterworth Heinemann, Oxford. Provides a detailed commentary, business case, models, examples and guidance on how to develop effective cause-related marketing, drawing on UK, European and international examples and research.

Adkins, S. (1999) *The Ultimate Win Win Win*, Business in the Community, supported by Research International.

Adkins, S. (2000) *Profitable Partnerships*, Business in the Community, supported by Research International.

Adkins, S. (2001) *The Corporate Survey III*, Business in the Community, supported by Research International.

Collins, J. C. and Porras, J. I. (1977) *Built to Last: Successful Habits of Visionary Companies*, HarperBusiness.

Grayson, D. and Hodges, A. (2001) *Everybody's Business*, Dorling Kindersley/The Financial Times.

Klein, N. (2001) *No Logo*, Flamingo.

Moss Kanter, R. (1995) *World Class, Thriving in the Global Economy*, Simon & Schuster.

Roddick, A. (2001) *Take it Personally*, Thorsons.

www.bitc.org.uk. With detailed information on the campaigns running under the four impact areas of marketplace (including cause-related marketing), workplace, environment and community, the Business in the Community website provides up to date news on issues surrounding corporate social responsibility, as well as information on events, case studies and the Business in the Community Awards for Excellence 2002.

www.crm.org.uk. The cause-related marketing campaign at Business in the Community's site is dedicated to providing latest cause-related marketing news, case study information, executive summaries of all the research reports and details of forthcoming events.

CHAPTER 27

Social marketing

LYNN MacFADYEN, MARTINE STEAD and GERARD HASTINGS

Introduction

The term social marketing was first coined by Kotler and Zaltman back in 1971 to refer to the application of marketing to the solution of social and health problems. Marketing has been remarkably successful in encouraging people to buy products such as Coca-Cola and Nike trainers, so, the argument runs, it can also encourage people to adopt behaviours that will enhance their own – and their fellow citizens' – lives. In essence, social marketers argue that it is possible, at least to some extent, to sell brotherhood like soap.

This chapter will examine these ideas. It begins by explaining why social marketing is needed and how it has developed. It then examines current definitions of social marketing, before identifying ways in which it differs from its commercial counterpart. The chapter then looks at how these differences impact on the practice of social marketing, focusing on segmentation and the marketing mix.

Why do social marketing?

Efforts to influence and improve the quality of our lives can be traced back through history. Chartists, parliamentary reformers, Luddites, suffragettes, feminists and many others have tried to change the social circumstances of particular groups, as well as society as a whole, with varying degrees of success. Today, health promoters, government agencies and other non-profit organizations use marketing expertise to achieve similar goals. Social marketing is a social change management technology which offers a framework with which to change the unhealthful or unsocial behaviour of others (Kotler and Roberto, 1989).

Many social and health problems have behavioural causes: the spread of AIDS, traffic accidents and unwanted pregnancies are all the result of everyday, voluntary human activity. The most dramatic example of this is tobacco use, which kills one in two smokers (Peto, 1994) – an estimated 6 million people in the UK alone since the health consequences were first established in the early 1950s. Social marketing provides a mechanism for tackling these problems by encouraging people to adopt healthier lifestyles.

However, there are many instances where the individual finds it hard to change his or her behaviour: protecting oneself from HIV is challenging if condoms are difficult to obtain; traffic accidents may result from poor roads as well as bad driving; and the addicted smoker struggles to quit. Health problems have a social, as well as an individual, dimension. This phenomenon is most clearly demonstrated by the epidemiological data which show that poverty is one of the most consistent and basic predictors of ill-health in the UK (Smith, 1997a; Jarvis, 1994; Marsh and MacKay, 1994), Europe (Whitehead and Diderichsen, 1997), the USA (McCord and Freeman, 1990; Pappas *et al.*, 1993) and the southern hemisphere (WHO, 1995). The lack of opportunity, choice and empowerment it generates prevents people from adopting healthy lifestyles.

Social marketing also has a great deal to offer here by influencing the behaviour, not just of the individual citizen, but also of policy makers and influential interest groups. Social marketers might target school governors to get condoms distributed through schools or local councils, and motoring organizations to get roads improved. For example, Case 2, which is discussed later in the chapter, explains how social marketing was used to advance water fluoridation, a measure that greatly improves dental health without any behaviour change at all on the part of the individual citizen.

Social marketing is now widely practised in both the developing (Manoff, 1985; Brieger *et al.*, 1986–87) and the developed world (e.g. Hastings and Elliot, 1993; Fishbein *et al.*, 1997; Hastings and Haywood, 1991).

Social marketing, like generic marketing, is not a theory in itself. Rather, it is a framework or structure that draws from many other bodies of knowledge, such as psychology, sociology, anthropology and communications theory, to understand how to influence people's behaviour (Kotler and Zaltman, 1971). Like generic marketing, social marketing offers a logical planning process involving consumer-oriented research, marketing analysis, market segmentation, objective setting, and the identification of strategies and tactics. It is based on the voluntary exchange of costs and benefits between two or more parties (Kotler and Zaltman, 1971). However, social marketing is more difficult than generic marketing. It involves changing intractable behaviours, in complex economic,

social and political climates, with often very limited resources (Lefebvre and Flora, 1988). Furthermore, while, for generic marketing the ultimate goal is to meet shareholder objectives, for the social marketer the bottom line is to meet society's desire to improve its citizens' quality of life. This is a much more ambitious – and more blurred – bottom line.

The development of social marketing

Social marketing evolved in parallel with commercial marketing. During the late 1950s and early 1960s, marketing academics considered the potential and limitations of applying marketing to new arenas such as the political or social. For example, in 1951–52, Wiebe asked the question: 'Can brotherhood be sold like soap?'. Having evaluated four different social change campaigns, he concluded that the more a social change campaign mimicked that of a commercial marketing campaign, the greater the likelihood of its success.

To many, however, the idea of expanding the application of marketing to social causes was abhorrent. Luck (1974) objected on the grounds that replacing a tangible product with an idea or bundle of values threatened the economic exchange concept. Others feared the power of marketing, misconceiving its potential for social control and propaganda (Laczniak *et al.*, 1979). Despite these concerns, the marketing concept was redefined to include the marketing of ideas and the consideration of its ethical implications.

The expansion of the marketing concept combined with a shift in public health policy towards disease prevention began to pave the way for the development of social marketing. During the 1960s, commercial marketing technologies began to be applied to health education campaigns in developing countries (Ling *et al.*, 1992; Manoff, 1985). In 1971, Kotler and Zaltman published their seminal article in the

Journal of Marketing, 'Social marketing: an approach to planned social change'. This was the first time the term 'social marketing' had been used and is often heralded as its birth. They defined social marketing as:

> the design, implementation and control of programs calculated to influence the acceptability of social ideas and involving considerations of product planning, pricing, communication, distribution and marketing research.
>
> (p. 5)

In practice, social marketing was being explored by a number of people at the same time, including Paul Bloom, Karen Fox, Dick Manoff and Bill Novelli. Early examples of social marketing emerged during the 1960s as part of international development efforts in Third World and developing countries (Manoff, 1985; Walsh *et al.*, 1993). For example, family planning programmes in Sri Lanka moved away from clinical approaches and examined the distribution of contraceptives through pharmacists and small shops (Population Services International, 1977). They began to experiment with marketing techniques such as audience segmentation and mass communication. Similarly, oral rehydration projects in Africa began to take a more consumer-oriented approach to programme development. Important initiatives in the developed world included the Stanford Heart Disease Prevention Program, the National High Blood Pressure Prevention Program, and the Pawtucket Heart Health Program (Farquar *et al.*, 1983; National Heart, Lung and Blood Institute, 1973; Lefebvre *et al.*, 1987). While many of these early programmes were primarily exercises in social communications, they were important for the inception of social marketing.

By the 1980s, academics were no longer asking *if* marketing should be applied to social issues, but rather *how* should this be done? During this period, practitioners shared their experiences and made suggestions for the development of social marketing theory and practice (Ling *et al.*, 1992). Fox and Kotler (1980)

described the evolution of social advertising into social communications. Bloom (1980) explored the evaluation of social marketing projects and found that many studies were poorly designed and conducted. In 1981, Bloom and Novelli reviewed the first 10 years of social marketing and advocated more research to dispel criticism that social marketing lacked rigour or theory. They identified a need for research to examine audience segmentation, choosing media channels and designing appeals, implementing long-term positioning strategies, and organizational and management issues (Bloom and Novelli, 1981).

Lefebvre and Flora (1988) and Hastings and Haywood (1991, 1994) then gave social marketing widespread exposure in the public health field, generating lively debates about its applicability and contribution. While social marketing was being practised in many countries by this time, the publication of these papers was followed by a widespread growth in its popularity (Lefebvre, 1996). Centres of expertise began to emerge, most notably at the College of Public Health at the University of South Florida, the Centre for Social Marketing at Strathclyde University in Scotland, and at Carleton University in Ottawa, Canada.

A number of books have been published on the subject, illustrating the historical evolution of social marketing's definition. Seymour Fine's *The Marketing of Ideas and Social Issues* (1981) viewed social marketing as the marketing of ideas to solve consumer problems. Kotler and Roberto's (1989) *Social Marketing: Strategies for Changing Public Behaviour* characterized social marketing as a social change management technology. Andreasen's (1995) book *Marketing Social Change* makes further refinements, arguing that social marketing should focus on changing behaviour, rather than ideas, and introduces the transtheoretical model to the discipline (see p. 23).

Today, social marketing specialists are relatively clear on its definition, but outwith the discipline, especially in public health and health promotion, confusion is still apparent, with social marketing often being equated with social advertising. Correcting these misapprehensions is a key challenge for the 1990s, and the instigation of two annual conferences, one targeting academics and the other practitioners, and the founding of a peer reviewed journal – *Social Marketing Quarterly* – will help meet it.

Defining social marketing

Kotler and Zaltman's (1971) early definition of social marketing emphasized the marketing mix and the marketing planning process. The authors observed the tendency for 'campaigners' to focus solely on the role of advertising and the mass media. They argued that the role of the mass media had been overestimated, and that more attention should be given to developing the social product, price and distribution, as well as to the role of market research. The authors' emphasis on the 'design, implementation and control of programs' (p. 7) illustrated their belief that social marketing should take the form of long-term programmes rather than short-term campaigns, and that strategic planning was required to manage this.

As social marketing developed, this early conceptualization was criticized for its imprecision (Andreasen, 1994). In particular, Rangun and Karim (1991) noted the potential for the operationalization of this definition to confuse social marketing with societal marketing and socially responsible marketing. *Societal marketing* is concerned with the ethical or societal implications of commercial activity. So, the 'societal marketing concept' encourages firms to 'market goods and services that will satisfy consumers under circumstances that are fair to consumers and that enable them to make intelligent purchase decisions, and counsels firms to avoid marketing practices which have dubious consequences for society' (Schwartz, 1971, p. 32). In short, societal marketing is concerned with ensuring that commercial marketers go about their business properly, without prejudicing either their customers or society as a whole.

Socially responsible marketing harnesses desirable social causes, such as the environment and consumerism, to advance the interests of a commercial organization (Kotler *et al.*, 1996). Public concern about the environment or the social implications of commercial activity can lead to bad publicity for the organization. Some organizations have chosen to act proactively and position themselves as socially responsible or ethical organizations – the Body Shop or ice-cream producers Ben & Jerry's are typical examples. However, this does not constitute social marketing, because, as with other for-profit organizations, the success of the Body Shop or Ben & Jerry's is measured by shareholder value and profitability and not, for example, by improvements to the environment. Similarly, commercial organizations which market ethically sound products, such as condoms, are not engaged in social marketing because their success is measured in terms of commercial goals rather than reductions in the prevalence of sexually transmitted diseases.

To confuse things further, however, it is possible for commercial marketers to do social marketing. Procter & Gamble, for example, have contributed to a major social marketing drugs prevention initiative in the north-east of England (Home Office, 1998). Nonetheless, such activities will always remain marginal compared with the company's main concern of commercial success. Engaging in it does not make them social marketers any more than corporate donations to good causes would make them a charity.

Social marketing should also be differentiated from *non-profit marketing* (Fox and Kotler, 1980), of which it is sometimes considered a subset (Blois, 1994). Non-profit marketers are concerned with the marketing management of institutions or organizations in the non-profit arena: hospitals, cancer charities or educational institutions. As with socially responsible marketing, the difference lies in the objectives of the two activities: non-profit marketers are ultimately concerned with the success and survival of their organization, social marketers with changes in their target population. Again, however, there is a confusing degree of overlap. There are some bodies whose primary business is social marketing, such as the Health Education Authority in England or the Centers for Disease Control in the US, who may also use non-profit marketing to manage their own organization. On the other hand, there are non-profit organizations like the Cancer Research Campaign, whose primary function is to raise money for cancer research, who may sometimes get involved in social marketing activities.

To help clarify matters, a special edition of the *Social Marketing Quarterly* invited key figures in the field to define social marketing, which was then 25 years old (Albrecht, 1996) (see Figure 27.1).

A number of key, common elements arise from these different definitions of social marketing. The first is the focus on voluntary behaviour change. The second is that social marketers try to induce voluntary behaviour change by applying the principle of exchange – the recognition that there must be a clear benefit for the customer if change is to occur. Third, marketing techniques such as consumer-oriented market research, segmentation and the marketing mix should be used.

Andreasen's (1995) definition of social marketing encapsulates these points:

> Social marketing is the application of commercial marketing technologies to the analysis, planning, execution and evaluation of programs designed to influence the voluntary behaviour of target audiences in order to improve their personal welfare and that of society.
>
> (p. 7)

Definitions of Social Marketing:

'*Social marketing is the simultaneous adoption of marketing philosophy and adaptation of marketing technologies to further causes leading to changes in individual behaviours which ultimately, in the view of the campaign's originator, will result in socially beneficial outcomes.*' (Michael Basil)

'*Social marketing is the application of marketing concepts and techniques to exchanges that result in the achievement of socially desirable aims; that is, objectives that benefit society as a whole.*' (Susan Dann)

'*Social marketing is an attempt to influence consumers for the greater good, and as such, always has an ethical aspect; specifically social marketing seeks to induce consumer change that is deemed to be inherently good, as opposed to change that is good merely because it increases profits or non-profit earnings.*' (Rob Donovan)

'*Social marketing is the application of appropriate marketing tools and the systematic analysis, development, implementation, evaluation and integration of a set of comprehensive, scientifically based, ethically formulated and user-relevant program components designed to ultimately influence behaviour change that benefits society.*' (Brian Gibbs)

'*Social marketing is a program planning process which promotes voluntary behaviour change based on building beneficial exchange relationships with a target audience for the benefit of society.*' (Susan Kirby)

'*a large scale program planning process designed to influence the voluntary behaviour of a specific audience segment to achieve a social rather than a financial objective, and based upon offering benefits the audience wants, reducing barriers the audience faces and/or using persuasion to influence the segment's intention to act favourably.*' (Beverly Schwartz)

Figure 27.1   Definitions of social marketing

Case 1   A consumer-driven approach to safer sex

Leading AIDS charity London Lighthouse wanted to produce a consumer-driven guide on safer sex for people with HIV/AIDS, but research with the target audience revealed that they had no need for sex education. After all, most of the respondents had acquired HIV through unsafe sex and were perfectly capable of learning from their own mistakes.

However, at a more subtle level the prospect of a leaflet was welcomed for three reasons. First, it could provide reassurance that people with HIV/AIDS were not alone, that other people were struggling with the same problems. Second, it would bring formal recognition and legitimacy: if you have a leaflet written for you, you at least exist; you are a significant subgroup of society. Third, it would acknowledge that it is acceptable for positive people to think about having sex – a particularly important point, given that most other AIDS messages imply that acquiring HIV is the end of the world.

These perceptions fundamentally changed how Lighthouse viewed the leaflet, and in this way the target audience influenced its context, purpose and very existence.

Source: Hastings (1994).

More recent definitions have begun to discuss the key role of long-term relationships in social marketing (e.g. Hastings *et al.*, 1998b).

Pulling these threads together, for a social change campaign or programme to be defined as social marketing it must contain the following elements: a consumer orientation (Lefebvre and Flora, 1988; Lefebvre, 1992; Andreasen, 1995), an exchange (Lefebvre and Flora, 1988; Lefebvre, 1996; Leathar and Hastings, 1987; Smith, 1997b) and a long-term planning outlook (Andreasen, 1995). Social marketing is often perceived to be concerned only with individual behaviour, but as noted earlier it can also be used to change the behaviour of groups and organizations, and to target broader environmental influences on behaviour (Lefebvre, 1996; Goldberg, 1995). Each of these essential elements of social marketing is now discussed in turn.

A consumer orientation

Consumer orientation is probably the key element of all forms of marketing, distinguishing it from selling, product- and other expert-driven approaches (Kotler *et al.*, 1996). In social marketing, the consumer is assumed to

be an active participant in the change process. The social marketer seeks to build a relationship with target consumers over time, and their input is sought at all stages in the development of a programme through formative, process and evaluative research. Case 1 illustrates how the consumer influenced the purpose, context and very existence of a safer sex initiative.

In short, the consumer-centred approach of social marketing asks not 'What is wrong with these people, why won't they understand?', but 'What is wrong with us? What don't we understand about our target audience?'

An exchange

Social marketing not only shares generic marketing's underlying philosophy of consumer orientation, but also its key mechanism, exchange (Kotler and Zaltman, 1971). While marketing principles can be applied to a new and diverse range of issues – services, education, high technology, political parties, social change – each with their own definitions and theories, the basic principle of exchange is at the core of each (Bagozzi, 1975). Kotler and Zaltman (1971) argue that:

marketing does not occur unless there are two or more parties, each with something to exchange, and both able to carry out communications and distribution.

(p 4)

Exchange is defined as an exchange of resources or values between two or more parties with the expectation of some benefits. The motivation to become involved in an exchange is to satisfy needs (Houston and Gassenheimer, 1987). Exchange is easily understood as the exchange of goods for money, but can also be conceived in a variety of other ways: further education in return for fees; a vote in return for lower taxes; or immunization in return for the peace of mind that one's child is protected from rubella.

Exchange in social marketing puts a key emphasis on *voluntary behaviour*. To facilitate voluntary exchanges, social marketers have to offer people something that they really want. For example, suppose that during the development of a programme to reduce teenage prevalence of sexually transmitted diseases (STDs) by encouraging condom use, research with the target finds that they are more concerned with pregnancy than STDs. The social marketer should consider highlighting the contraceptive benefits of condoms, rather than, or at least as well as, the disease prevention ones. In this way, consumer research can identify the benefits which are associated with a particular behaviour change, thereby facilitating the voluntary exchange process.

Long-term planning approach

Like generic marketing, social marketing should have a long-term outlook based on continuing programmes rather than one-off campaigns. It should be strategic rather than tactical. This is why the marketing planning function has been a consistent theme in social marketing definitions, from Kotler in 1971 to Andreasen in 1995.

The social marketing planning process is the same as in generic marketing. It starts and finishes with research, and research is conducted throughout to inform the development of the strategy. A situational analysis of the internal and external environment and of the consumer is conducted first. This assists in the segmentation of the market and the targeting strategy. Further research is needed to define the problem, to set objectives for the programme and to inform the formulation of the marketing strategy. The elements of the social marketing mix are then developed and pretested, before being implemented. Finally, the relative success of the plan is monitored and the outcome evaluated.

Figure 27.2 shows a social marketing plan produced for a road safety initiative. With minimal changes it could just as easily be applied to baked beans.

Moving beyond the individual consumer

Social marketing is not only concerned with influencing the behaviour of the individual consumer, but also the broader social, cultural, structural and policy influences on health and social behaviour (e.g. Hastings *et al.*, 1994b, 2000; Lawther and Lowry, 1995; Lawther *et al.*, 1997; Murray and Douglas, 1988; Smith, 1998). Defining the role and scope of social marketing in this broader way is important, as the discipline's detractors often misperceive 'marketing' as little more than advertising and persuasion (e.g. Buchanan *et al.*, 1994; Vanden Heede and Pelican, 1995; Wallack *et al.*, 1993). For example, Wallack *et al.* (1993) have criticized social marketing for its inability to intervene at the level of 'the social and political environment in which decisions that affect health are made', and for the assumption that 'power over health status evolves from gaining greater control over individual health behaviours' (Wallack *et al.*, 1993, p. 24). However, when it first emerged, social marketing was conceived to constitute a much broader remit than individual behaviour change. Levy and

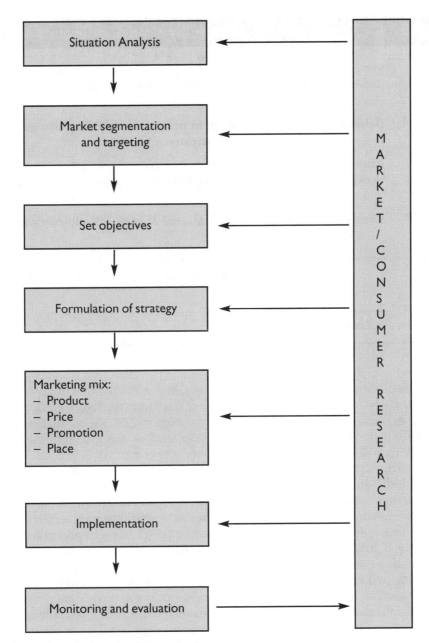

Figure 27.2 A social marketing plan for road safety
Source: Hastings and Elliot, 1993.

Zaltman (1975) suggested a sixfold classification of the types of change sought in social marketing, that incorporate three levels: (i) the micro level (the individual consumer); (ii) the group level (group or organization); and (iii) the macro level (society). This perspective also permitted short- and long-term forms of behaviour change (see Table 27.1).

The importance of moving 'upstream' and tackling the contextual influences on health and

Table 27.1	Types of social change, by time and level of society		
	Micro level (individual consumer)	Group level (group or organization)	Macro level (society)
Short-term change	**Behaviour change**	**Change in norms Administrative change**	**Policy change**
Example:	Attendance at stop-smoking clinic	Removal of tobacco advertising from outside a school	Banning of all forms of tobacco marketing
Long-term change	**Lifestyle change**	**Organizational change**	**'Socio-cultural evolution'**
Example:	Smoking cessation	Deter retailers from selling cigarettes to minors	Eradication of all tobacco-related disease

Adapted from Levy and Zaltman (1975).

social behaviour is illustrated if we examine the known correlates and predictors of health behaviour. For example, if we examine the issue of tobacco smoking, the evidence base demonstrates that smoking initiation is influenced by many factors, of which some may be related to the individual (e.g. gender, age, academic achievements, socio-economic group, personality factors, ethnicity), social factors (e.g. peer group or family) and wider, environmental factors (e.g. price of cigarettes, their availability, media portrayal of smoking, tobacco marketing and cultural representation of smoking). Most of these influences are outside the reach of the individual, and while it is possible to intervene to prevent smoking or to encourage cessation, a comprehensive social marketing strategy should also intervene at these other levels. These other upstream strategic options may be more cost effective and offer a more constructive, less victim-blaming, approach (Hastings *et al.*, 2000).

Therefore, social marketing campaigns need to address behaviour change at the individual level, the immediate environment and the wider social context (see Figure 27.3).

Figure 27.3 shows that social marketing interventions can influence the desired behaviour, either directly (e.g. a smoking prevention campaign aimed at adolescents) or indirectly by either challenging social pressures (e.g. a peer education approach) or by tackling the wider social context (e.g. banning tobacco advertising). In each sphere the same principles of social marketing can be applied. At either the individual, immediate or wider levels, the social marketer's objective is behaviour change, either of the end consumer or some other key stakeholder, such as families, community groups, policy-makers or the media. For example, Case 2 shows how social marketing can be used to encourage local authorities and private water companies to fluoridate the water supply, a measure that would have tremendous dental health benefits.

Finally, social marketers can encourage independent environmental improvements to reach their objectives, which involve no

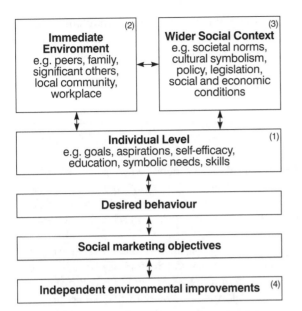

Figure 27.3   Addressing the context of social marketing – four types of social marketing activity

- The products tend to be more complex.
- Demand is more varied.
- Target groups are more challenging to reach.
- Consumer involvement is more intense.
- The competition is more subtle and varied.

These differences have an important impact on the ways in which social marketing plans are implemented. The remainder of this section will look at the differences between social and commercial marketing in more detail. The subsequent sections will then examine the influence they have on the use of the two key marketing tools: segmentation and the marketing mix.

The products are more complex

The marketing product has traditionally been conceived of as something tangible – a physical good which can be exchanged with the target market for a price, and which can be manipulated in terms of characteristics such as packaging, name, physical attributes, positioning and so on. As marketing has extended its scope beyond physical goods, marketers have had to grapple with formulating product strategy for less tangible entities such as services (see Chapter 23 in this volume for a discussion of the characteristics of services; Woodruffe, 1995). In social marketing, the product is extended even further from the tangible to encompass ideas and behaviour change. Figure 27.4 illustrates the different types of social marketing product.

behaviour change. For example, the risk of certain birth defects can be prevented by increased consumption of folic acid during the very early stages of pregnancy. As the defects may occur before the mother has suspected a pregnancy, encouraging increased consumption of folic acid presents a challenging behaviour change problem for the social marketer. One solution is the addition of folic acid to staple foodstuffs, e.g. bread, a measure that would reduce risk without difficult behaviour change.

Departures from commercial marketing

The previous section highlighted the common features of social and commercial marketing, and showed that this leads to broadly similar strategic processes. However, there are also important differences between the two approaches. Specifically, in social marketing:

Under behaviour, Kotler and Roberto (1989) distinguish between adoption of a single act (having a cholesterol check) and adoption of a sustained practice (changing one's diet). A further distinction could be made between adoption of a new behaviour (taking up jogging), desistence from a current behaviour (giving up drinking), and non-adoption of a future behaviour (not taking drugs). In practice, the behavioural objective may be some combination of these. So, for example, a driving safety initiative may seek both to prevent drivers from drink-driving (desistence) and to encourage them to use a designated-driver system (adoption).

Even where the behaviour change being sought by the social marketer involves a tangible object (the third category) such as condoms, Kotler and Roberto point out that the

---

Case 2   Water fluoridation

Water fluoridation involves adjusting the natural level of fluoride in the public water supply so as to produce substantial improvements in the dental health of the population – especially among children and those living in deprived communities. Water fluoridation is a classic example of health promotion – safe, simple, effective – but, in the UK at least, not happening. No new water fluoridation schemes have gone ahead since the necessary legislation was passed in 1985.

Introducing water fluoridation in the UK is a complex process. Local health authorities request (but do not tell) water companies to start adding fluoride to the water once they have formally consulted the public and the relevant local government authorities. Research with the general public found that they were largely supportive of fluoridation and wanted to be kept informed of developments, but confirmed that they had little role to play in actively progressing the initiative. Furthermore, they were quite happy with the state of affairs, seeing it as a job for the health professionals, to whom they were prepared to defer.

Thus, fluoridation is an example of a valuable public health measure which will not be progressed by any behavioural change in the general population. Nonetheless, social marketing has a key role to play: its concepts of consumer orientation, voluntary involvement and mutually beneficial exchange are still very useful. In this case the key consumers are local authorities and water companies, whose co-operation can be encouraged by emphasizing the benefits *to them* of fluoridation. Market research showed these to differ for the two groups.

The local government authorities were not interested in public health, at least for its own sake, and being Labour-dominated, had no love for health authorities or their (Conservative) government-inspired policies. Their main concern was to represent and meet the needs of their constituents. If they were going to 'buy' fluoridation, their interest in and ownership of it would need to be stimulated by emphasizing the benefits that fluoridation would bring to *their* voters and by reminding them that the first UK fluoridation schemes, back in the 1960s, had been introduced by local authorities, not health authorities. In short, if they were going to buy it, fluoridation had to meet their political needs.

Similarly, the private water companies were not interested in public health. They wanted to provide their customers with clean, wholesome water, and their shareholders with a reasonable return. However, they were interested in helping the government carry out its policies, retaining good relationships with public health professionals in their area and positive public relations. At a more practical level, they also needed a fluoridation product that met their technical requirements: that would suit their existing plant and have an acceptable safety standard, for example. They needed more than the basic 'benefit to the public' product that would satisfy the local authorities.

Finally, segmentation and targeting ensured that the correct fluoridation product was marketed to the two customer groups.

Source: adapted from Hastings *et al.* (1998a).

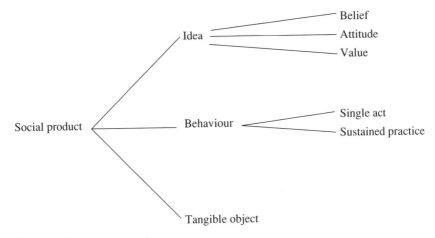

Figure 27.4   The social marketing product
Source: Adapted from Kotler and Roberto (1989).

social marketer is not in the business of selling condoms *per se*, but of selling a change in attitudes (more favourable beliefs about condom use) or behaviour (correct use of condoms) in order to bring about the social or health benefit which condom use can confer – improved reproductive and sexual health and more satisfying relationships. Kotler and Roberto (1989) caution that family planning social marketers 'who say their product is a condom misunderstand their market' (p. 140).

As a partial solution to this difficulty, some commentators suggest conceptualizing a 'core product' such as 'safer driving' (Kotler and Zaltman, 1971, p. 7), which may be accompanied by a range of 'buyable' products and services such as road safety campaigns, driver training and transport policies which contribute to the objective. Fine (1981) suggests a similar conceptualization, in which a 'class of products' – e.g. 'education' – might comprise various product 'forms', such as adult education classes, literacy training and so on.

This complexity makes social marketing products difficult to conceptualize. As a consequence, social marketers have a bigger task in defining exactly what their product is and the benefits associated with its use. This is discussed further in the section on the marketing mix below.

Varied demand

Marketing cannot create needs but commercial marketers do manage to harness needs previously unknown for new product categories such as CDs, catalytic converters and 'new' washing powders. Social marketers must not only uncover new demand, but in addition must frequently deal with *negative demand* when the target group is apathetic about or strongly resistant to a proposed behaviour change. Young recreational drug users, for instance, may see no problems with their current behaviour (Andreasen, 1997). In these situations, social marketers must challenge entrenched attitudes and beliefs. Demarketing approaches may help here (Lawther *et al.*, 1997; Hastings *et al.*, 1998a).

Rangun *et al.* (1996) suggest a typology of the benefits associated with a behaviour change. The benefits may be tangible, intangible, relevant to the individual or relevant to society. Demand is easier to generate where the benefits are both tangible and personally relevant. In those situations where the product benefits are intangible and relevant to society rather than the individual (as with CFCs in aerosols), social marketers must work much harder to generate a need for the product. This, they argue, is the hardest type of behaviour change, as the benefits are difficult to personalize and quantify.

Challenging target groups

Social marketers must often target groups whom commercial marketers tend to ignore: the least accessible, hardest to reach and least likely to change their behaviour. For example, health agencies charged with improving population health status must, if they are to avoid widening health inequalities further in the general population (Whitehead, 1992; Smith, 1997b), target their efforts at those groups with

the poorest health and the most needs (Hastings *et al.*, 1998b). Far from being the most profitable market segments, these groups often constitute the least attractive ones: hardest to reach, most resistant to changing health behaviour, most lacking in the psychological, social and practical resources necessary to make the change, most unresponsive to interventions to influence their behaviour and so on. This poses considerable challenges for segmentation and targeting, as discussed later in the chapter. Case 3 illustrates the problem vividly.

Greater consumer involvement

Marketing traditionally divides products into high and low involvement categories, with the former comprising purchases for items such as cars or mortgages which are 'expensive, bought

---

Case 3   Cervical screening: barriers to segmentation in social marketing

A public health department wishes to encourage women within a certain age range in the health authority area to attend for cervical screening. There are a number of possible ways in which this population can be segmented, including:

- socio-demographic (social class, education, income, employment);
- psychographic (beliefs regarding preventive health, fatalism, attitudes towards health services);
- health behaviour (smokers/non-smokers etc.);
- previous usage behaviour (attendance for screening); and so on.

From available secondary research into the characteristics of attenders and non-attenders for cervical and other screening (e.g. Thorogood *et al.*, 1993; Austoker *et al.*, 1997; Sugg Skinner *et al.*, 1994), the public health department could make certain assumptions about the women most likely to respond positively to the programme: ABC1, well educated, in work, positive beliefs about ability to protect oneself from cancer, favourable attitudes towards health service and so on. If the screening programme were to be run as a profit-making service, this would be the segment to target. The screening agency could develop messages consonant with these women's beliefs, deliver them through workplaces at which the women are most likely to be employed, utilize media most likely to be consumed by them, and so forth. However, the health authority's objective is not to run the most profitable screening service possible, but to make the biggest possible impact on public health by reducing incidence of cervical cancer. To do this, the screening programme needs to reach those groups with the highest risk of cancer – the groups who, the same research shows, are the least likely to attend for screening.

infrequently, risky and highly self-expressive' (Kotler, 1994), and the latter comprising items such as confectionery or cigarettes which are much more habitual. High involvement products typically command careful consideration by the consumer ('central processing') and demand detailed factual information from the marketer. Low involvement products are consumed much more passively, with very limited (or no) search and evaluation ('peripheral processing'), and simple advertising emphasizing 'visual symbols and imagery' (Kotler, 1994) is called for.

Or, as Petty *et al.* (1988) expressed it, for high involvement products consumers are attracted by the tangible attributes of the products, the 'steak', but for low involvement purchases, consumers are more attracted by the intangible qualities or the 'sizzle'.

Both the categorization scheme – high and low – and its marketing implications need to be extended in social marketing. Social marketing frequently deals with products with which the consumer is very highly involved (complex lifestyle changes such as changing one's diet fall into this category). While high involvement can result in a motivated and attentive consumer, higher involvement may be associated with feelings of anxiety, guilt and denial, which inhibit attempts to change. At the other extreme, social marketers might seek to stimulate change where there is very low or no involvement – for example, persuading Scots to save water. Thus, taking the example of smoking, involvement can be divided into at least four levels:

- *Very high, or hyper involvement* – the smoker who can't quit despite deep concern about the consequences of continuing, and is typically in a state of defensive denial.
- *High involvement* – the smoker who is motivated and struggling with some success to quit.
- *Low involvement* – the smoker who knows of the consequences of smoking but does not care enough about them to make the decision to quit.

- *Very low involvement* – the smoker who is unaware of the health risks and has never considered quitting.

In addition, there may be an additional category of *negative involvement* amongst those who see the health risks and forbidden nature of tobacco as part of its attraction.

The type of campaign that will address these categories cannot be determined by simply applying marketing's rubric that 'the greater involvement, the greater the need for factual information'. For example, very low involvement consumers may well respond well to factual information, and hyper involvement consumers to emotional messages offering reassurance and empowerment.

More varied competition

Social marketers, like their commercial counterparts, must be aware of their competition (Andreasen, 1995). The most obvious source of competition in social marketing is the consumer's tendency to continue in his or her current behavioural patterns, especially when addiction is involved. Inertia is a very powerful competitor.

Other sources of competition involve alternative behaviours. For example, time spent donating blood is time which the consumer could spend doing other more enjoyable, more convenient and more personally beneficial activities.

Competitive organizations include other health promoters, educators or government organizations trying to use similar methods to reach their target audiences. For example, the typical doctor's surgery in the UK displays such a plethora of leaflets and posters that any one message or idea stands little chance of being noticed. Social marketers must then be innovative and careful not to overwhelm their target audience.

Finally, one of the most serious forms of competition comes from commercial marketing itself, where this markets unhealthful or unsocial behaviours. The most obvious examples are the tobacco and alcohol industries.

In summary, therefore, social marketing differs in a number of ways from commercial marketing. These differences have a big impact on implementation, and the next two sections look specifically at how this is manifested in segmentation and the use of the marketing mix.

Segmentation in social marketing

The particular characteristics of social marketing create a number of barriers to segmentation and a need for specialized segmentation criteria (see also Chapter 10). These phenomena are discussed in turn.

Barriers to segmentation in social marketing

Despite the importance of segmentation, many social marketing programmes employ 'undifferentiated target marketing' (Andreasen, 1995, p. 174), treating the target group as a relatively homogeneous mass for whom a single strategy is developed, or adopting relatively basic segmentation approaches based on simple demographic variables such as age or gender (see Chapter 10). This limited application of segmentation is attributable to a number of factors:

- *Ambitious objectives.* Social marketing is typically concerned with ambitious objectives (e.g. reducing incidence of dental caries) which involve targeting very large populations (e.g. all parents of children under five).
- *The operating environment.* Social marketing organizations are much more subject to political and policy demands than commercial organizations. A national body may be required by statute to deliver a programme to the whole population, or it may be local public health policy to target an initiative at a whole

population subgroup (for example, in the UK mammography screening programmes are required to target all women over 50). In this environment, it is difficult for a social marketing organization to concentrate resources on specific market segments even where this would increase the likelihood of effectiveness.
- *Culture.* There may be cultural and philosophical resistance to the idea of segmentation (Bloom and Novelli, 1981) – for example, it may be seen as unethical for a health professional, in offering a product to one particular market segment, to withhold it by implication from another. Alternatively, segmentation on the basis of need can lead to accusations of discrimination and stigmatization.
- *Resources.* Finally, social marketing organizations may lack an understanding of the potential of more sophisticated segmentation approaches, the information on which to base such approaches, or the skills and resources to implement them (Andreasen, 1995; Currence, 1997).

Some of these barriers are surmountable, particularly those in the fourth category. Social marketers can acquire better understanding of the potential and uses of segmentation, and as social marketing evolves, lessons learnt will disseminate through the field, as in commercial marketing. Useful segmentation case studies such as the 5-a-Day initiative to promote fruit and vegetable consumption (see Case 4) and the American Cancer Society's campaign to promote mammography screening, which utilized sophisticated database information (Currence, 1997), are already contributing to this.

In addition, social marketers may have access to other valuable – and free – databases themselves. For example, in the UK, health promoters may be able to use the National Health Service patient register, either on its own or combined with additional information of the sort outlined in Case 4.

Case 4 '5-a-Day for Better Health': segmentation in a social marketing programme

This programme in the USA aiming to increase fruit and vegetable consumption was one of the first large applications of marketing database technology to a health promotion initiative (Lefebvre *et al.*, 1995). Quantitative and qualitative research was conducted before programme planning to quantify the nature of the problem, to explore possible messages, and to begin to identify potential segments. This information was then augmented by data collected annually from the Market Research Corporation of America's survey of 2000 representative US households' food consumption, attitudes, interests, lifestyle and media habits. Data from the survey were analysed to profile two population segments, those eating five fruit and vegetables a day and those eating around three a day, in the contemplation stage (i.e. reportedly trying to eat more) (Prochaska and DiClemente, 1983). The latter was the target group.

  To refine this profile further, the intervention planners added a question on previous day's fruit and vegetable consumption to an omnibus survey, the DDB Needham Lifestyle Survey of 4000 individuals. From these two information sources, people in the target group could be identified as impulse buyers who led hectic lives with little spare time. Their media habits were also described. As a result of this profiling, the intervention planners could not only build up a clear 'visual representation of the target' (Lefebvre *et al.*, 1995, p. 233), but could also develop a 'personality' or 'tonality' for the campaign (p. 224), and choose appropriate communication materials and channels.

However, the other barriers to segmentation are more fundamental. For example, as already discussed, because of the nature of their objectives, social marketers have less freedom than commercial marketers to choose target segments.

Ethical considerations may also prevent a social marketer from targeting a particular segment, even where this segment is identifiable, accessible and the most in need. Case 5 illustrates how a government drugs prevention initiative using social marketing principles was unable overtly to target young drug users for fear of stigmatization. In this instance, a partial solution was found by combining blanket targeting with self-selection, whereby young people with particular interests and needs could 'opt in' to certain components, such as peer-led workshops (MacKintosh *et al.*, 2001). The assumption is that small groups with similar interests and experiences regarding drugs will naturally gravitate towards suitably tailored offerings.

Segmentation criteria in social marketing

Commercial marketers typically segment according to three broad criteria: personal characteristics, behavioural characteristics and benefits sought by consumers (Wilkie, 1994), all of which are relevant to social marketers. They are outlined in Table 27.2, along with some additional attributes which are of particular relevance to social marketing.

Personal characteristics

The relevance of *demographic* segmentation to social marketing is widely accepted. As noted at the beginning of the chapter, for many health and social problems, the main predictors of mortality, morbidity, health behaviour and health risk continue to be demographic. The role of poverty has already been highlighted, but ethnicity (Kochanek *et al.*, 1994), gender (for types of cancer and for coronary heart disease)

Case 5   Ethical problems in social marketing segmentation

A government social marketing initiative in the north-east of England is seeking to reduce adolescent drug use and associated harm through a social cognitive schools and media programme (Home Office, 1998; MacKintosh *et al.*, 2001). Drugs prevention literature indicates that current drug use status is an important variable which should be addressed in designing such programmes: the most effective interventions are those which, among other things, target users and non-users separately, with product offerings tailored to their current experiences and attitudes regarding drugs (Bandy and President, 1983; Makkai *et al.*, 1991; Werch and DiClemente, 1994). However, had the programme developed a range of intervention components for young people already using drugs – who could in principle have been identified from extensive baseline data gathered on the target population before the programme began – it would never have secured the necessary co-operation of the schools, communities and parents who understandably would not have wanted their young people to be labelled as drug users (Stead *et al.*, 1997a). Building and managing the relationship with these key gatekeepers and stakeholders was critical to the programme's existence. The only option was to adopt a non-stigmatizing undifferentiated targeting strategy – offering the programme to all young people in all schools in the area.

---

and age (for the prevention of substance and tobacco use) are also very significant. Existing health status may be an additional characteristic addressed in this classification; for example, health promotion programmes may be directed at people with asthma or diabetes (so-called secondary prevention).

Moving beyond basic demographic characteristics, the application of *psychographic* segmentation in social marketing is less well

Table 27.2   Major segmentation approaches

Characteristics		Attributes	Social marketing
Personal	Demographic	Age, Gender, Social class, Ethnicity, Family profile, Income, Employment	+ Health status
	Psychographic	Lifestyle, Personality	+ Health beliefs, motivation, locus of control
	Geodemographic	Geographical area, Neighbourhood type	+ Residence in disadvantaged area
Behavioural		Usage, Loyalty, Response, Attitudes	+ Health behaviour, Stage of Change
Benefits		Benefits sought	+ Barriers

established. However, its relevance is clear. Many of the major causes of mortality and morbidity in the developed world are lifestyle related, and health promoters have in the last 20 years or so reoriented their efforts from a focus on specific disease prevention to a focus on the lifestyle risk factors which impact on a wide range of disease – exercise, nutrition, smoking, drinking, safer sex. Knowing that middle aged C2DE men are at most risk of coronary heart disease is not sufficient: the social marketer needs to understand why some men in this group are motivated to engage in lifestyle behaviours which are protective of their health and why others are not, and to develop product offerings accordingly. Social marketers need to adopt segmentation approaches that acknowledge the complex psychosocial determinants of health behaviour (Slater, 1995).

Information which enables the social marketer to distinguish between targets on the basis of their values, beliefs and norms is also important. Various behaviour change theories, such as the theory of reasoned action (Fishbein and Ajzen, 1975), social learning theory (Bandura, 1977, 1986) and social cognitive theory (Maibach and Cotton, 1995) have posited that traits such as attitudes and norms influence adoption of health and risk behaviours (e.g. Manstead, 1991; Fishbein et al., 1997). Increasingly, these theories are being adopted as the theoretical basis for segmented social marketing interventions (e.g. Fishbein et al., 1997).

Geodemographics

This is the classification of people on the basis of where they live (Sleight, 1995). The geographical distribution of much ill-health (e.g. Whitehead, 1992; Smith, 1997a) and the clustering of health and social problems in certain areas, particularly urban areas of deprivation (e.g. Glasgow City Council, 1998), suggest that this approach can contribute usefully to social marketing. Obvious applications of geodemographics to social marketing are in selecting channels for health advertising, identifying locations for health services, and direct mail.

A number of syndicated geodemographic information systems have been developed in the commercial marketing context (Sleight, 1995). While these are already proving to be useful to social marketers, public health is very often most concerned with geodemographic segments who are of least interest to many commercial marketers – the very poor. Classification systems such as ACORN and MOSAIC provide socio-economic indicators of small areas, and these can be combined with classification systems such as the Carstairs index for Scotland (McLoone, 1991) which provide a measure of affluence or deprivation within postcode sectors. Measures of deprivation, such as housing tenure, telephone and car ownership, and financial status, can also be incorporated to provide accurate targeting data for social marketers.

Behavioural characteristics

In commercial marketing, behavioural characteristics may include volume of product usage – heavy, medium, light users – transactional history (previous usage), readiness to use, responsiveness, and attitudes towards usage (Wilkie, 1994).

Again, these categories are of relevance to social marketing. Social marketers planning an initiative to encourage participation in a health promotion clinic could segment on the basis of current health behaviour, previous usage of health clinics, frequency of GP consultation and so on. Health service records held by GP practices and health authorities provide valuable information on patients' previous transactions with health services as well as on their current health behaviours (e.g. smoking, drinking, use of medicines).

A particularly important behavioural characteristic in social marketing is the concept of readiness to change. The transtheoretical model of behaviour change (Prochaska and DiClemente, 1983) posits that behaviour change is not a discrete event, but a process that occurs through several stages: pre-contemplation, contemplation, preparation, action and maintenance. The model was initially developed to explain smoking cessation behaviour, but has since been applied to smoking, alcohol and drug addiction, weight control and eating disorders, safer sex behaviour, exercise participation, mammography screening, sunscreen use, and other health behaviours (Prochaska *et al.*, 1994). During pre-contemplation, individuals either do not want to change their behaviour or are unaware of its consequences for themselves or others. During contemplation, they begin to think about the costs and benefits of changing their behaviour. In preparation, the individual is motivated to change, and makes initial mental and practical preparations. During the action stage, the individual is in the process of changing, following which he or she may proceed to either maintenance or relapse to an earlier state.

The model is helpful in two ways. First, it emphasizes that behaviour change is complex and multi-staged, and that relapse may occur a number of times. Second, it provides a framework for designing appropriate messages and support interventions (see Figure 27.3). By understanding the target audience's readiness to change, the social marketer can develop strategies appropriate to the group's needs and wants (Werch and DiClemente, 1994). For example, Andreasen (1995) proposes a series of marketing tasks for each stage of change. During pre-contemplation, the marketer must create awareness and interest in the behaviour, and it may be necessary to try and shift value and belief systems. During contemplation, the marketer must persuade and motivate to enhance the benefits of the behaviour (e.g. mobilize social influence) and reduce the costs associated with change (time, effort or money). Andreasen deals with preparation and action stages simultaneously, and proposes that marketers must focus on creating action by, for example, focusing on skills training exercises or confidence building. Finally, to maintain change, social marketers

should consider reducing cognitive dissonance through reinforcement.

Benefit characteristics

Classification by benefit sought is specific to the particular product being marketed; for example, the market for cigarettes could be segmented on the basis of those who seek status (e.g. smokers of exclusive brands of cigarettes and cigars), those who need a cost-effective nicotine fix (e.g. established smokers), and those who seek reassuringly mainstream smokes (e.g. adolescents).

This type of segmentation analysis seems at first glance to have less relevance in social marketing than the preceding three types. Social marketing targets very often do not welcome efforts to ameliorate their health and social circumstances (Levy and Zaltman, 1975), and if they are fundamentally resistant to changing behaviour may see no benefits in the messages and support being offered to them to facilitate this process. However, social marketers still need to think in terms of consumers and the benefits they seek rather than products. For example, Case 6 shows how benefit segmentation enhanced an attempt to influence oral health in Scotland. The target (retailers) was segmented on the basis of function (marketing staff, space planners and buyers) and different product benefits identified for each. This case also illustrates how important segmentation is when targeting not only the final consumer, but those decision makers who can influence their operating environment.

Another example is exercise. A comparative study into younger and older people's perceptions of exercise (Stead *et al.*, 1997b) found that different subgroups perceived different benefits in the product 'physical activity': some, typically younger men, wanted to compete against an opponent, while others aimed to better their own personal targets – to run faster or swim further, for example. A third group was most concerned with body image, and a fourth enjoyed the prospect of meeting

Case 6 The immediate environment: a case of candy

A recent attempt to redress the appalling oral health record of five-year-old children in west, central Scotland examined one immediate environmental influence on confectionery consumption – the availability of candy at supermarket checkouts.

Scotland is renowned for its sweet tooth and Scottish children consume 28 per cent more confectionery than their counterparts in the rest of the UK. Candy is frequently used to reward or pacify children, who come to associate comfort or praise with these sweet and familiar foodstuffs, thereby reinforcing their liking for them. Children often successfully 'pester' their parents for candy in supermarkets and shops. The strategic positioning of candy at the till-points greatly exacerbates this problem.

Research was conducted to inform a policy which would address the problem of confectionery at till-points. An audit of store policy and in-depth interviews with policy makers was conducted. This work identified the group of decision makers within each organization and the criteria for making space allocation decisions.

It was found that space planning decisions were rigorous and predictable: confectionery was placed at the point of sale to maximize profits from the available space. Three broad groups with an interest in confectionery policy were identified – marketers, space planners and buyers – and the barriers to adopting a confectionery policy reflected each party's needs. The research concluded that any initiative must demonstrate customer loyalty (to satisfy marketers), be profitable (to satisfy space planners), and offer long-term profitability for the products and alternative merchandising arrangements (to satisfy buyers). As a result, possible initiatives to reduce confectionery from the immediate environment are being explored, including endorsement schemes, community partnerships and public opinion surveys.

	Marketing staff	*Space planners*	*Buyers*
Exchange	Customer loyalty	Profitability	Supply relationships
Intervention	Endorsement schemes	Economic benefits	Long-term profitability
	Public opinion surveys	Competitive advantage	Alternative merchandising strategies

new people, maintaining friendships and just 'getting out'.

These benefit segments formed the basis of a targeted strategy to encourage physical activity.

The same research also examined perceived and actual *barriers* to participation in exercise. Again, it was possible to differentiate between segments whose lifestyle, health, health beliefs, personal circumstances and awareness prevented their involvement in exercise, to develop appropriate communication and support strategies for each segment. Given the type of 'negative demand' social marketers often face (see 'Departures from commercial marketing' above), *barrier segmentation* is perhaps of particular value to social marketers.

It also suggests that social marketers should go one step further and, despite the potential philosophical problems noted above, segment their markets in terms of need. As well as bringing the standard segmentation benefits, this will ensure that limited resources are used most efficiently.

Need can be classified in a number of ways. Andreasen (1995) suggests that three factors should be considered: problem incidence (rates of need or problem per segment), problem severity (severity of need or problem per segment), and 'population defencelessness', ability per segment to cope with the problem or need (p. 177).

The social marketing mix

The marketing mix (see Chapter 11) also has to be adapted for use in social marketing. This section examines the relevance and application of each element of the mix (see Table 27.3).

Product

As described above, social marketing products are frequently intangible and complex behaviours. This makes it difficult to formulate simple, meaningful product concepts (Bloom and Novelli, 1981). To take an example, 'reducing one's fat intake' is a complex behaviour in a number of ways: it involves a change in food choice, menu design, shopping behaviour, food preparation, personal habits, family routines, wider social norms and so on. Further, it is a behaviour which needs to be practised not just once, but repeated and sustained over a long period of time (Kotler and Roberto, 1989). As a first step towards formulating product concepts, social marketers need to identify and

Table 27.3   The social marketing mix

Tool		Types
Product	The offer made to target adopters	Adoption of idea (belief, attitude, value) Adoption of behaviour (one-off, sustained) Desistence from current behaviour Non-adoption of future behaviour
Price	The costs that target adopters have to bear	Psychological, emotional, cultural, social, behavioural, temporal, practical, physical, financial
Place	The channels by which the change is promoted and places in which the change is supported and encouraged	Media channels Distribution channels Interpersonal channels Physical places Non-physical places (e.g. social and cultural climate)
Promotion	The means by which the change is promoted to the target	Advertising Public relations Media advocacy Direct mail Interpersonal

Adapted from Kotler and Roberto (1989, p. 44).

clarify their product attributes. In commercial marketing, product attributes range on a continuum from the tangible (colour, taste, shape, size, packaging, performance) to the intangible (brand, image, status). Social marketing product attributes are largely situated at the intangible end of this continuum. Some potential classifications of product attributes are suggested below:

- *Trialability* – Can the behaviour be tried out beforehand before permanent or full adoption (e.g. wearing a cycling helmet)?
- *Ease* – How easy or difficult is it to adopt the behaviour (wearing a seat belt versus giving up smoking)?
- *Risks* – What are the risks of adopting the behaviour?
- *Image* – Is the behaviour attractive or unattractive?
- *Acceptability* – Is the behaviour socially acceptable?
- *Duration* – Is the behaviour to be practised once or repeatedly? Is it to be sustained over the short or long term?
- *Cost* – Does the behaviour have a financial cost or not (eating a healthier diet may involve more expense, drinking less alcohol does not)?

Analysing product attributes in this way helps social marketers to formulate meaningful and communicable product concepts. For example, in addressing teen smoking, research may suggest that image is a key issue, rather than the avoidance of health risks. The social marketer can then put particular emphasis on producing non-smoking options that are cool and trendy – such as freedom of choice – rather than ones that major on the health benefits of quitting.

A second major potential problem with the product for social marketers is flexibility. It is commonly argued that social marketers have less flexibility than commercial marketers in shaping their product offerings (Bloom and Novelli, 1981), for a number of reasons. First, the resources, technology and skills to develop alternative products may not be as readily available to the social marketer as they are in commercial marketing, so the range of product innovation options is smaller. Fox and Kotler (1980) note that the anti-smoking social marketer seeking to develop the most attractive substitute product really should invent a safe cigarette, but is constrained by technological, financial and political factors. Second, product offerings may be constrained by political factors outside the social marketer's control. Government policy or local public health strategy may dictate that only one behaviour or way of practising the behaviour should be endorsed. For example, harm minimization, as opposed to abstention, solutions to the problem of drug abuse may be unacceptable in certain political climates.

Third, social marketing's offerings often appear to be 'absolutes' in that the social or health benefit pertains only if the behaviour is adopted wholesale (so partial or temporary adoption is not possible) or is adopted in one particular form (so different forms of the behaviour cannot be marketed to different adopter groups). An example of such an absolute is smoking, where only total abstinence produces meaningful health benefits, as opposed to drinking, where different moderation messages can be promoted. Immunization and fluoridation of the public water supply are also examples of absolutes.

However, many other social marketing offerings are 'relative', in that a health or social benefit accrues even if the behaviour is adopted only in a moderate way. Exercise by elderly people is one example (Stead *et al.*, 1997b). Nutrition is another instance where social marketers can develop a wide range of product offerings for different target segments: the fruit and vegetable consumption programme outlined in Case 4 above is one such example.

Furthermore, even in the case of absolute products, although social marketers may have limited control over the fundamental aspects of their offerings, they do, like commercial marketers, have potential control over how their products are perceived and positioned. For example, in Case 2 above, different water fluoridation products were offered to local councils and water companies.

Price

Only a few of social marketing's products have a monetary price (condoms are an obvious example: see Harvey (1997) and Dahl *et al.* (1997) for discussion of pricing strategy in contraceptive social marketing.

However, there are almost always costs associated with behaviour change which act as obstacles to marketing social change; these may be financial, time, embarrassment, effort, inertia, pain, perceived social exclusion (e.g. Marteau, 1990). However, there should be benefits also. These may be tangible and personal benefits such as a longer life or intangible, societal benefits such as a better environment. Rangun *et al.* (1996) argue that there are four broad types of social marketing initiatives according to this cost-benefit analysis:

1 *Low cost and tangible, personal benefits*, e.g. cervical screening for women. In this case the target perceives clear, direct benefits to themselves. As change is easy, relative to the four other types of initiative, communication and information are key elements of the social marketing strategy.
2 *Low cost and intangible, societal benefits*, e.g. recycling programmes. Here the behavioural change is relatively easy to adopt, but the benefits are not perceived to be as relevant to the individual. The authors argue that convenience is the key to this type of programme, and the ultimate benefit to themselves and to society should be stressed.
3 *High cost and tangible, personal benefits*, e. g. smoking cessation programmes. In this case there is a very clear personal benefit to adopting the suggested behaviour, but the costs associated with doing so are high. It is suggested that the social marketer adopts a strong 'push marketing' approach, supported by

communications campaigns and community level initiatives.
4 *High cost and intangible, societal benefits*, e.g. CFCs in aerosols. This is clearly the hardest type of behaviour change to induce, as the costs are high and the benefits are hard to personalize and quantify. In this case, it may be necessary to adopt de-marketing approaches, use moral persuasion or social influence.

Place

Kotler and Zaltman (1971) suggest that place should be defined in social marketing as encompassing distribution and response channels, and 'clear action outlets for those motivated to acquire the product' (p. 9). Where there is a communications element to a social marketing initiative – for example, television advertising, outdoor advertising, direct mail, health education leaflets – place applies to the media channels through which messages are to be delivered. Place can also apply to distribution channels where a social marketing programme has a tangible product base (e.g. condoms, needle exchanges). In these two instances and in social marketing programmes where a specific service is being offered – for example, an antenatal class or workplace smoking cessation group – place variables such as channel, coverage, cost, timing (Kotler and Roberto, 1989), location, transport (Woodruffe, 1995) and accessibility (Cowell, 1994) are all relevant. For example, an initiative to increase uptake of cervical screening could reduce the costs of attending by manipulating the place variables of distance, time and convenience (offering screening at flexible times and in different locations).

In addition, many social marketing initiatives depend on intermediaries such as health professionals, pharmacists, teachers and community workers to act as distribution channels for media materials or as retailers for a particular behaviour change product – for example, GPs are often given responsibility for changing smoking and drinking behaviour

(Kotler and Roberto, 1989). Where intermediaries are to act primarily as distribution agents for media products, key variables such as accessibility and appropriateness should be considered. When these intermediaries have a more complex role (e.g. youth workers and teachers delivering a sex education curriculum), place variables such as source visibility, credibility, attractiveness and power (Percy, 1983; Hastings and Stead, 1999) should guide the selection of appropriate agents and inform the sort of support and training which is offered to them. For example, the drugs prevention literature has examined the relative merits of teachers, youth workers, police and peers as delivery channels for drugs prevention messages (e.g. Bandy and President, 1983; Shiner and Newburn, 1996).

Social marketers are often dependent on the goodwill and co-operation of intermediaries for access to their end targets. This is particularly the case when dealing with sensitive health issues or with vulnerable groups such as young people, where there is usually a need to communicate not only with young people themselves, but also with key groups such as parents, teachers and politicians. These groups may act as 'gatekeepers', controlling or influencing the distribution of a message to a target group, or as 'stakeholders', taking an interest in and scrutinizing the activities of the prevention agency (McGrath, 1995). If an initiative is to be effective, it needs to satisfy the information and other needs of these two groups, and to maintain their support. Communicating with gatekeepers and stakeholders is therefore just as important as communicating with the direct target group, and it should be approached in the same way in order to be effective (Hastings and Stead, 1999).

In Figure 27.2 above, one category of social marketing objectives is concerned with influencing policy and social norms. Here, 'place' becomes the centres of influence on public opinion and policy. In this context, media advocacy is likely to become particularly important (see below).

Promotion

Of the four marketing mix tools, promotion has received the most attention in social marketing. Indeed, the prominence of social advertising in social marketing practice and literature has contributed to a tendency among non-marketers to perceive the two as synonymous (Stead and Hastings, 1997; Sutton, 1991; Andreasen, 1994). In turn, this perception has given rise to criticisms of social marketing as ineffective because media interventions alone are deemed to be insufficient to change behaviour (Tones, 1994), expensive and difficult to do well (Bloom and Novelli, 1981; Stead and Hastings, 1997), and lacking new insights (Tones, 1994).

Three decades of mass media social advertising campaigns on smoking prevention, smoking cessation, exercise, nutrition, drug use, safer sex and other health issues have refined theoretical and practical understanding of how communication campaigns should be developed, designed, targeted, implemented and evaluated in order to have the best impact on public awareness, opinions and behaviour (e.g. Atkin and Freimuth, 1989; Backer *et al.*, 1992; Flay, 1987; Hastings and Haywood, 1991; Leathar and Hastings, 1987; Maibach and Cotton, 1995; Reid, 1996; Slater, 1995; Solomon, 1989; Worden *et al.*, 1996). The conclusions are broadly in accord with mainstream marketing communication theory, so require no repetition here (see Chapter 17).

However, two aspects of social marketing communication do warrant further examination: branding and media advocacy. The first because it is underdeveloped in the social sector and would benefit from further thought by mainstream marketers, and the second because it is well advanced in social marketing and therefore may provide some useful insights.

Branding

In commercial marketing, branding provides a crucial means of enhancing the product. Brands are deliberately designed to hone the emotional benefits of the product, thereby adding value and encouraging consumption and loyalty (see Chapter 15).

Similar thinking can be applied in social marketing. For example, Lefebvre (1996) argues that all health communications have an emotional dimension – a 'personality' or 'tonality' – whether the health promoter intends it or not. The message, channel and execution all contribute to this. He cautions that health communicators – just like their commercial counterparts – must use research, design and careful targeting to ensure that the tonality matches the needs of their target audience.

Leathar (1980) and Monahan (1995) endorse the notion that health communicators should actively promote positive images about health. For example, Monahan concludes her paper:

> Positive affect can be used to stress the benefits of healthy behaviour, to give individuals a sense of control, and to reduce anxiety or fear. All of these tactics are likely to enhance the success of a communication campaign.

On a more specific level, qualitative research conducted with pregnant women (Bolling and Owen, 1997) also emphasizes the importance of emotional communication, concluding that messages have to be sympathetic, supportive and non-judgemental. The primary need, the research suggested, is to establish a sense of trust.

Taking things a step further, social marketers have also adopted the idea of branding. Case 7 describes an attempt to brand positive health in Scotland during the 1980s. The brand was called 'Be All You Can Be'.

Media advocacy

Another channel by which social marketers seek to influence public opinion and policy makers is via unpaid publicity in the mass media (Wallack *et al.*, 1993; Chapman and Lupton, 1994). This involves negotiating with and satisfying *media gatekeepers*: newspaper editors and journalists, television and radio producers, advertising regulation authorities.

Case 7   Branding in social marketing

During the 1980s, SHEG, the government body responsible for health education in Scotland, were facing three problems with their use of the media. Their campaigns tended to be fragmented, topic based rather than whole person oriented and authoritarian rather than empathetic. Material seemed to be telling people how to run their lives, rather than enabling and encouraging them to make their own informed health decisions.

These problems could not be solved within individual campaigns, however carefully pretested or creatively developed. It was therefore decided to develop an overview or 'umbrella' campaign that could communicate a general lifestyle message of empowerment. In addition, the campaign needed to link the positive imagery to clear solutions to real health problems – that is, provide branded health products. The result was 'Be All You Can Be', a communication campaign which ran in broadcast and print media, promoting a theme of empowerment and positive health. An extensive communication and awareness monitor showed that it became familiar to, and was strongly endorsed by, the Scottish population.

However, there were problems with the campaign. First, the general Be All You Can Be messages left people uncertain as to what they should do next. People needed specific guidance to work out a response. Second, the campaign was restricted to the media, with few links to other delivery modes, again making it appear insubstantial. In essence, the campaign was succeeding in promoting a corporate identity for health, but not offering the branded products that enabled people to buy into it.

Sources: Hastings and Leathar (1987); Leathar (1988).

Health promoters often see the mass media and themselves as having conflicting priorities (e.g. Atkin and Arkin, 1990). However, generating effective unpaid publicity relies not only on producing the 'right' message or story, but on tailoring the message or story so that it meets the priorities and needs of the newspaper, radio or television station for topical, newsworthy, human interest material – on 'thinking like a journalist' (Wallack *et al.*, 1999; Meyer, 1990).

In other words, the media are a target audience in their own right, with their own needs, expectations and opinions. They can be segmented just as the end target audience of young people or the community can – for example, different press releases may be needed for tabloid and broadsheet newspapers. Building up good personal relationships with the media helps the process, as does making available well-trained media spokespersons. Research can also play a crucial role in advancing policy and generating controversy (e.g. Wallack, 1990; Hastings *et al.*, 1994a; Carr-Gregg, 1993; Whitehead, 1998; Stead *et al.*, 2002). Again, effectiveness depends on understanding the media gatekeepers' needs and agenda.

Ethical challenges

The special, and often delicate, nature of social marketing problems necessitates careful consideration of certain moral and ethical dilemmas. Social marketers are in the business of entrenched, taboo or even illegal behaviours, and their resolution may involve the conflicting interests of the social marketer, the consumer and wider society (MacFadyen and Hastings, 2001). Social marketers must decide which behaviour to address, ultimately prioritizing certain issues over others, and, implicit in this, advocating the desirability of certain lifestyles or habits. Furthermore, reaching an exchange ultimately involves some form of compromise, but 'harm reduction' approaches are notoriously controversial. The design of the social marketing mix is no less thorny. The temptation

is the use of strong fear-based appeals, but the over-reliance on threats may be at best ineffective, at worse disempowering, distressing and damaging. While powerful and hard-hitting campaigns can be political successes, the underlying assumption that consumers are awkward, fearless and irrational is not constructive. Finally, social marketing research, while absolutely vital to the development of interventions, can pose its own difficulties. Researchers need to be sensitive not to raise fears about health risks, suggest risky behaviours are normal or cause embarrassment.

Careful consideration needs to be given to the consequences, intended or otherwise, of the development and implementation of social marketing programmes.

Conclusion

Over the last 30 years, social marketing has established itself as a coherent and valuable discipline, taking the principles of commercial marketing and applying them to the resolution of important social problems. It overlaps with commercial marketing, creating strong strategic links between them, but its unique characteristics mean that the resulting strategies are frequently implemented in different ways. This has set up a symbiotic relationship of mutual respect and learning – it is no accident that Philip Kotler is a key figure in the evolution of both fields of endeavour. The inclusion of this chapter in a core marketing text also underlines this connection.

Social marketing faces three main challenges over the next decade. First, it must continue to develop its theoretical base using rigorous research combined with marketing's magpie-like capacity to steal ideas from every other social science discipline. Second, it must establish its credentials more firmly outside the marketing domain, by successfully tackling real social problems. Until now, the vast majority of our effort has focused on health problems, and these are likely to remain central to the discipline. However, other arenas, such as crime prevention, Third World development and the alleviation of poverty, could also benefit from social marketing. There is a need to produce and publish reliable case studies in these areas.

Finally, we need to provide more educational opportunities in social marketing. Only when well-trained social marketers, who can live and breathe the discipline, join the major agencies of social change will its full potential be realized.

References

Albrecht, T. L. (1996) Defining social marketing: 25 years later, *Social Marketing Quarterly*, Special Issue, 21–23.

Andreasen, A. R. (1994) Social marketing: its definition and domain, *Journal of Public Policy and Marketing*, **13**(1), 108–114.

Andreasen, A. R. (1995) *Marketing Social Change: Changing Behaviour to Promote Health, Social Development, and the Environment*, Jossey-Bass, San Francisco.

Andreasen, A. R. (1997) Challenges for the science and practice of social marketing, in Goldberg, M. E., Fishbein, M. and Middlestadt, S. E. (eds), *Social Marketing: Theoretical and Practical Perspectives*, Lawrence Erlbaum Associates, Mahwah, NJ, Chapter 1.

Atkin, C. and Arkin, E. B. (1990) Issues and initiatives in communicating health information to the public, in Atkin, C. K. and Wallack, L. (eds), *Mass Communication and Public Health: Complexities and Conflicts*, Sage, Newbury Park, CA, Chapter 1.

Atkin, C. K. and Freimuth, V. (1989) Formative evaluation research in campaign design., in Rice, R. E. and Atkin, C. K. (eds), *Public Communication Campaigns*, 2nd edn, Sage, Newbury Park, CA, Chapter 6.

Austoker, J., Davey, C. and Jansen, C. (1997) *Improving the Quality of the Written Information Sent to Women About Cervical Screening, NHS Cervical Screening Programme Publication No. 6*, NHSCSP Publications, London.

Backer, T. E., Rogers, E. M. and Sopory, P. (1992) *Designing Health Communication Campaigns: What Works?*, Sage, Newbury Park, CA.

Bagozzi, R. (1975) Marketing and exchange, *Journal of Marketing*, **39**, October, 32–39.

Bandura, A. (1977) *Social Learning Theory*, Prentice-Hall, Englewood Cliffs, NJ.

Bandura, A (1986) *Social Foundations of Thought and Action: A Social Cognitive Approach*, Prentice-Hall, Englewood Cliffs, NJ.

Bandy, P. and President, P. A. (1983) Recent literature on drug abuse prevention and mass media: focusing on youth, parents and the elderly, *Journal of Drug Education*, **13**(3), 255–271.

Blois, K. (1994) Non-profit marketing, in Baker, M. J. (ed.), *The Marketing Book*, 3rd edn, Butterworth-Heinemann, Oxford, Chapter 30.

Bloom, P. N. (1980) Evaluating social marketing programs: problems and prospects, *The 1980 Educators Conference Proceedings*, American Marketing Association, Chicago.

Bloom, P. N. and Novelli, W. D. (1981) Problems and challenges in social marketing, *Journal of Marketing*, **45**, 79–88.

Bolling, K. and Owen, L. (1997) *Smoking and Pregnancy: A Survey of Knowledge, Attitudes and Behaviour*, Health Education Authority, London.

Brieger, W. R., Ramakrishna, J. and Adeniyi, J. D. (1986–87) Community involvement in social marketing: Guineaworm control, *International Quarterly of Community Health Education*, **7**(1), 19–31.

Buchanan, D. R., Reddy, S. and Hossain, H. (1994) Social marketing: a critical appraisal, *Health Promotion International*, **9**(1), 49–57.

Carr-Gregg, M. (1993) Interaction of public policy advocacy and research in the passage of New Zealand's Smoke-free Environments Act 1990, *Addiction*, **88**(Supplement), 35S–41S.

Chapman, S. and Lupton, D. (eds) (1994) *The Fight for Public Health: Principles and Practice of Media Advocacy*, BMJ Publishing, London.

Cowell, D. W. (1994) Marketing of services, in Baker, M. J. (ed.), *The Marketing Book*, 3rd edn, Butterworth-Heinemann, Oxford, Chapter 29.

Currence, C. (1997) Demographic and lifestyle data: a practical application to stimulating compliance with mammography guidelines among poor women, in Goldberg, M. E., Fishbein, M. and Middlestadt, S. E. (eds), *Social Marketing: Theoretical and Practical Perspectives*, Lawrence Erlbaum Associates, Mahwah, NJ, Chapter 8.

Dahl, D. W., Gorn, G. J. and Weinberg, C. B. (1997) Marketing, safer sex and condom acquisition, in Goldberg, M. E., Fishbein, M. and Middlestadt, S. E. (eds), *Social Marketing: Theoretical and Practical Perspectives*. Lawrence Erlbaum Associates, Mahwah, NJ, Chapter 11.

Farquar, J. W., Fortmann, S. P., Maccoby, W., Haskell, W. L., Williams, P. J., Flora, J. P., Taylor, C. B., Brown, B. W. Jr, Solomon, D. S. and Hulley, S. B. (1983) The Stanford Five City Project: design and methods, *American Journal of Epidemiology*, **122**, 323–334.

Fine, S. (1981) *The Marketing of Ideas and Social Issues*, Praeger, New York.

Fishbein, M. and Ajzen, I. (1975) *Belief, Attitude, Intention and Behaviour: An Introduction to Theory and Research*, Addison-Wesley, Reading, MA.

Fishbein, M., Guenther-Grey, C., Johnson, W., Wolitski, R. J., McAlister, A., Rietmeijer, C. A., O'Reilly, K. *et al.* (1997). Using a theory-based intervention to reduce AIDS risk behaviours: the CDC's AIDS Community Demonstration Projects, in Goldberg, M. E., Fishbein, M. and Middlestadt, S. E. (eds), *Social Marketing: Theoretical and Practical Perspectives*, Lawrence Erlbaum Associates, Mahwah, NJ, Chapter 9.

Flay, B. R. (1987) Mass media and smoking cessation: a critical review, *American Journal of Public Health*, **77**, 153–160.

Fox, K. F. A. and Kotler, P. (1980) The marketing of social causes: the first ten years, *Journal of Marketing*, **44**, 24–33.

Glasgow City Council (1998) *Glasgow Figures No. 2: Poverty and Deprivation in Glasgow*, Glasgow City Council, Glasgow.

Goldberg, M. E. (1995) Social marketing: are we fiddling while Rome burns?, *Journal of Consumer Psychology*, **4**(4), 347–370.

Harvey, P. D. (1997) Advertising affordable contraceptives: the social marketing experience, in Goldberg, M. E., Fishbein, M. and Middlestadt, S. E. (eds), *Social Marketing: Theoretical and Practical Perspectives*, Lawrence Erlbaum Associates, Mahwah, NJ, Chapter 10.

Hastings, G. B. (1994) Sex, AIDS and research, *Social Marketing Quarterly*, **III**, 1.

Hastings, G. B. and Elliot, B. (1993) Social marketing in practice in traffic safety, in *Marketing of Traffic Safety*, OECD, Paris, Chapter III, pp. 35–53.

Hastings, G. B. and Haywood, A. J. (1991) Social marketing and communication in health promotion, *Health Promotion International*, **6**(2), 135–145.

Hastings, G. B. and Haywood, A. J. (1994) Social marketing: a critical response, *Health Promotion International*, **9**(1), 59–63.

Hastings, G. B. and Leathar, D. S. (1987) The creative potential of research, *International Journal of Advertising*, **6**, 159–168.

Hastings, G. B. and Stead, M. (1999) *Using the Media in Drugs Prevention. Drugs Prevention Initiative Green Paper*, Home Office Central Drugs Prevention Initiative, London, Paper 19.

Hastings, G. B., Lawther, S., Eadie, D. R., Haywood, A. J., Lowry, R. J. and Evans, D. (1994a) General anaesthesia: who decides and why? *British Dental Journal*, **177**, 332–336.

Hastings, G. B., Smith, C. S. and Lowry, R. J. (1994b) Fluoridation – a time for hope, a time for action, *British Dental Journal*, **177**, May, 273–274.

Hastings, G. B., Hughes, K., Lawther, S. and Lowry, R. J. (1998a) The role of the public in water fluoridation: public health champions or anti-fluoridation freedom fighters?, *British Dental Journal*, **184**, 39–41.

Hastings, G. B., Stead, M., Whitehead, M., Lowry, R., MacFadyen, L., McVey, D., Owen, L. and Tones, K. (1998b) Using the media to tackle the health divide: future directions, *Social Marketing Quarterly*, **IV**(3), 42–67.

Hastings, G. B., MacFadyen, L. and Anderson, S. (2000) Whose behaviour is it anyway? The broader potential of social marketing, *Social Marketing Quarterly*, **VI**(2), June, 46–58.

Home Office (1998) *Managing a Drugs Prevention Programme: The Experience of NE Choices 1996–1998*, Northumbria Drugs Prevention Team, Home Office, Newcastle.

Houston, F. S. and Gassenheimer, J. B. (1987) Marketing and exchange, *Journal of Marketing*, **51**, October, 3–18.

Jarvis, M. J. (1994) A profile of tobacco smoking, *Addiction*, **89**, 1371–1376.

Kochanek, K. D., Maurer, J. D. and Rosenberg, H. M. (1994) Why did black life expectancy decline from 1984 through 1989 in the United States?, *American Journal of Public Health*, **84**, 938–944.

Kotler, P. (1994) Reconceptualizing marketing: an interview with Philip Kotler, *European Management Journal*, **12**(4), 353–361.

Kotler, P. and Roberto, E. L. (1989) *Social Marketing: Strategies for Changing Public Behaviour*, Free Press, New York.

Kotler, P. and Zaltman, G. (1971) Social marketing: an approach to planned social change, *Journal of Marketing*, **35**, 3–12.

Kotler, P., Armstrong, G., Saunders, J. and Wong, V. (1996) *Principles of Marketing*, European edn, Prentice-Hall, London.

Laczniak, G. R., Lusch, R. F. and Murphy, P. E. (1979) Social marketing: its ethical dimensions, *Journal of Marketing*, **43**, Spring, 29–36.

Lawther, S. and Lowry, R. (1995) Social marketing and behaviour change among professionals, *Social Marketing Quarterly*, **II**(1), 10–11.

Lawther, S., Hastings, G. B. and Lowry, R. (1997) De-marketing: putting Kotler and Levy's ideas into practice, *Journal of Marketing Management*, **13**(4), 315–325.

Leathar, D. S. (1980) Images in health education, *Health Education Journal*, **39**(4), 123–128.

Leathar, D. S. (1988) The development and assessment of mass media campaigns: the work of the Advertising Research Unit. Be All You Can Be Case Study – Part 2, *Journal of the Institute of Health Education*, **26**(2), 85–93.

Leathar, D. S. and Hastings, G. B. (1987) Social marketing and health education, *Journal of Services Marketing*, **1**(2), Fall, 49–52.

Lefebvre, R. C. (1992) The social marketing imbroglio in health promotion, *Health Promotion International*, **7**(1), 61–64.

Lefebvre, R. C. (1996) 25 years of social marketing: looking back to the future, *Social Marketing Quarterly*, Special Issue, 51–58.

Lefebvre, R. C. and Flora, J. A. (1988) Social marketing and public health intervention, *Health Education Quarterly*, **15**(3), 299–315.

Lefebvre, R. C., Lancaster, T. M., Carleton, R. A. and Peterson, G. (1987) Theory and delivery of health programming in the community: the Pawtucket Heart Health Program, *Preventative Medicine*, **16**, 80–95.

Lefebvre, R. C., Doner, L., Johnston, C., Loughrey, K., Balch, G. I. and Sutton, S. M. (1995) Use of database marketing and consumer-based health communication in message design: an example from the office of cancer communications' '5 A Day for Better Health' program, in Maibach, E. and Parrott, R. L. (eds), *Designing Health Messages. Approaches From Communication Theory and Public Health Practice*, Sage, Newbury Park, CA, Chapter 12.

Levy, S. J. and Zaltman, G. (1975) *Marketing, Society and Conflict*, Prentice-Hall, Englewood Cliffs, NJ.

Ling, J. C., Franklin, B. A. K., Lindsteadt, J. F. and Gearion, S. A. N. (1992) Social marketing: its place in public health, *Annual Review of Public Health*, **13**, 341–362.

Luck, D. J. (1974) Social marketing: confusion compounded, *Journal of Marketing*, **38**, October, 70–72.

MacFadyen, L. and Hastings, G. B. (2001) First do no harm: the case for ethical considerations in social marketing. Presented at The Academy of Marketing Science 10th Biennial World Marketing Congress – *Global Marketing Issues at the Turn of the Millennium*, jointly organized with Cardiff University, 30 May–2 June.

MacKintosh, A. M., Stead, M., Eadie, D. and Hastings, G. (2001) NE Choices: The Results of a Multi-component Drug Prevention Programme for Adolescents. DPAS Paper 14, Home Office Drugs Prevention Advisory Service, London.

Maibach, E. W. and Cotton, D. (1995) Moving people to behaviour change: a staged social cognitive approach to message design, in Maibach, E. and Parrott, R. L. (eds), *Designing Health Messages. Approaches From Communication Theory and Public Health Practice*, Sage, Newbury Park, CA, Chapter 3, pp. 41–64.

Makkai, T., Moore, R. and McAllister, I. (1991) Health education campaigns and drug use: the 'drug offensive' in Australia, *Health Education Research Theory and Practice*, 6(1), 65–76.

Manoff, R. K. (1985) *Social Marketing: New Imperative for Public Health*, Praeger, New York.

Manstead, A. S. R. (1991) Social psychological aspects of driver behaviour, in *New Aspects of Driver Behaviour*: Proceedings of a conference organized by the Parliamentary Advisory Council for Transport Safety (PACTS), PACTS, London.

Marsh, A. and MacKay, S. (1994) *Poor Smokers*, Policy Studies Institute, London.

Marteau, T. M. (1990) Reducing the psychological costs, *British Medical Journal*, 301, 26–28.

McCord, C. and Freeman, H. P. (1990) Excess mortality in Harlem, *New England Journal of Medicine*, 322, 173–177.

McGrath, J. (1995) The gatekeeping process: the right combinations to unlock the gates, in Maibach, E. and Parrott, R. C. (eds), *Designing Health Messages. Approaches From Communication Theory and Public Health Practice*, Sage, Newbury Park, CA, Chapter 11.

McLoone, P. (1991) *Carstairs Scores for Scottish Postcode Sectors from the 1991 Census*, Public Health Research Unit, University of Glasgow, Glasgow.

Meyer, P. (1990) News media responsiveness to public health, in Atkin, C. K. and Wallack, L. (eds), *Mass Communication and Public Health: Complexities and Conflicts*, Sage, Newbury Park, CA, Chapter 3.

Monahan, J. L. (1995) Thinking positively: using positive affect when designing health messages, in Maibach, E. and Parrott, R. L. (eds), *Designing Health Messages. Approaches From Communication Theory and Public Health Practice*, Sage, Newbury Park, CA, Chapter 5.

Murray, G. G. and Douglas, R. R. (1988) Social marketing in the alcohol policy arena, *British Journal of Addiction*, 83, 505–511.

National Heart, Lung and Blood Institute (1973) *The Public and High Blood Pressure: A Survey – DHED Publication No. 73.736*, National Heart, Lung and Blood Institute, Bethesda, MD.

Pappas, G., Queen, S., Hadden, W. and Fisher, G. (1993) The increasing disparity in mortality between socio-economic groups in the United States, 1960 and 1986, *New England Journal of Medicine*, 329, 103–109.

Percy, L. (1983) A review of the effect of specific advertising elements upon overall communication response, in *Current Issues and Research in Advertising*, University of Michigan.

Peto, D. (1994) Smoking and death: the past 40 years and the next 40, *British Medical Journal*, 309, 937–938.

Petty, R. E., Cacioppo, J. T., Sedikides, C. and Strathman, A. J. (1988) Affect and persuasion: a contemporary perspective, *American Behavioural Scientist*, 32, 355–371.

Population Services International (1977) Preetni Project. Transferred to Sri Lanka FPA, *PSI Newsletter*, November/December, p. 4.

Prochaska, J. O. and DiClemente, C. C. (1983) Stages and processes of self-change of smoking: toward an integrative model of change, *Journal of Consulting and Clinical Psychology*, 51, 390–395.

Prochaska, J. O., Vlicer, W. F., Rossi, J. S., Goldstein, M. G., Marcus, B. H., Rakowksi, W., Fiore, C., Harlow, L. L., Redding, C. A., Rosenbloom, D. and Rossi, S. R. (1994) Stages of change and decisional balance for 12 problem behaviours, *Health Psychology*, 13(1), 39–46.

Rangun, V. K. and Karim, S. (1991) *Teaching Note: Focusing the Concept of Social Marketing*, Harvard Business School, Cambridge, MA.

Rangun, V. K., Karim, S. and Sandberg, S. K. (1996) Do better at doing good, *Harvard Business Review*, May–June, 4–11.

Reid, D. (1996) How effective is health education via mass communications?, *Health Education Journal*, **55**, 332–344.

Schwartz, G. (1971) Marketing: the societal marketing concept, *University of Washington Business Review*, **31**, 31–38.

Shiner, M. and Newburn, T. (1996) *Young People, Drugs and Peer Education: An Evaluation of the Youth Awareness Programme (YAP)*, DPI, Home Office, London.

Slater, M. D. (1995) Choosing audience segmentation strategies and methods for health communication, in Maibach, E. and Parrott, R. L. (eds), *Designing Health Messages. Approaches From Communication Theory and Public Health Practice*, Sage, Newbury Park, CA, Chapter 10.

Sleight, P. (1995) Explaining geodemographics, *Admap*, January, 27–29.

Smith, B. (1998) Forget messages . . . think about structural change first, *Social Marketing Quarterly*, **IV**(3), 13–19.

Smith, R. (1997a) Gap between death rates of rich and poor widens, *British Medical Journal*, **314**, 9.

Smith, W. A. (1997b) Social marketing: moving beyond the nostalgia, in Goldberg, M. E., Fishbein, M. and Middlestadt, S. E. (eds), *Social Marketing: Theoretical and Practical Perspectives*, Lawrence Erlbaum Associates, Mahwah, NJ, Chapter 2.

Solomon, D. S. (1989) A social marketing perspective on communication campaigns, in Rice, R. E. and Atkin, C. K. (eds), *Public Communication Campaigns*, 2nd edn, Sage, Newbury Park, CA, Chapter 4.

Stead, M. and Hastings, G. (1997) Advertising in the social marketing mix: getting the balance right, in Goldberg, M. E., Fishbein, M. and Middlestadt, S. E. (eds), *Social Marketing: Theoretical and Practical Perspectives*, Lawrence Erlbaum Associates, Mahwah, NJ, Chapter 3.

Stead, M., Hastings, G. and Eadie, D. (2002) The Challenge of Evaluating Complex Interventions: A Framework for Evaluating Media Advocacy, *Health Education Research Theory and Practice*, **17**(3), 351–64.

Stead, M., MacKintosh, A. M., Hastings, G., Eadie, D., Young, F. and Regan, T. (1997a) Preventing adolescent drug use: design, implementation and evaluation design of 'new choices', Paper presented at Home Office, DPI Research Conference, Liverpool, 3–5 December.

Stead, M., Wimbush, E., Eadie, D. and Teer, P. (1997b) A qualitative study of older people's perceptions of ageing and exercise: the implications for health promotion, *Health Education Journal*, **56**, 3–16.

Sugg Skinner, C., Strecher, V. J. and Hospers, H. (1994) Physicians' recommendations for mammography: do tailored messages make a difference?, *American Journal of Public Health*, **84**(1), 43–49.

Sutton, S. M. (1991) in AED, *Social Marketing: Views from Inside the Government, 30th Anniversary Seminar Series*, Academy for Educational Development.

Thorogood, M, Coulter, A., Jones, L., Yudkin, P., Muir, J. and Mant, D. (1993) Factors affecting response to an invitation to attend for a health check, *Journal of Epidemiology and Community Health*, **47**, 224–228.

Tones, K. (1994) Marketing and the mass media: theory and myth. Reflections on social marketing theory, *Health Education Research Theory and Practice*, **9**(2), 165–169.

Vanden Heede, F. A. and Pelican, S. (1995) Reflections on marketing as an inappropriate model of nutritional education, *Society for Nutritional Education*, **27**(3), 141–145.

Wallack, L. (1990) Improving health promotion: media advocacy and social marketing approaches, in Atkin, C. and Wallack, L. (eds), *Mass Communication and Public Health: Complexities and Conflicts*, Sage, Newbury Park, CA, Chapter 11, pp. 147–163.

Wallack, L., Dorfman, L., Jernigan, D. and Themba, D. (1993) *Media Advocacy and Public Health*, Sage, Newbury Park, CA.

Wallack, L., Woodruff, K., Dorfman, L. and Diaz, I. (1999) *News for a Change: An Advocate's Guide to Working with the Media*, Sage, Newbury Park, CA.

Walsh, D. C., Rudd, R. E., Moeykens, B. A. and Moloney, T. W. (1993) Social marketing for public health, *Health Affairs*, Summer, 104–119.

Werch, C. E. and DiClemente, C. C. (1994) A multi-component stage model for matching drug prevention strategies and messages to youth stage of use, *Health Education Research, Theory and Practice*, 9(1), 37–46.

Whitehead, M. (1992) The health divide, in Townsend, P., Whitehead, M. and Davidson, N. (eds), *Inequalities in Health: The Black Report and the Health Divide*, 2nd edn, Penguin, London.

Whitehead, M. (1998) Diffusion of ideas on social inequalities in health: a European perspective, *The Milbank Quarterly*, 76(3), 469–492.

Whitehead, M. and Diderichsen, F. (1997) International evidence on social inequalities in health, in Drever, F. and Whitehead, M. (eds), *Health Inequalities: Decennial Supplement. Office for National Statistics Series DS No 15*, The Stationery Office, London.

Wiebe, G. D. (1951–52) Merchandising commodities and citizenship in television, *Public Opinion Quarterly*, 15, Winter, 679–691.

Wilkie, W. L. (1994) *Consumer Behavior*, 3rd edn, Wiley, New York.

Woodruffe, H. (1995) *Services Marketing*, M&E Pitman, London.

Worden, J. K., Flynn, B. S., Solomon, L. J., Secker-Walker, R. H., Badger, G. J. and Carpenter, J. H. (1996) Using mass media to prevent cigarette smoking among adolescent girls, *Health Education Quarterly*, 23(4), 453–468.

World Health Organization (WHO) (1995) *Bridging the Gaps. World Health Report for 1995*, World Health Organization, Geneva.

Further reading

Andreasen, A. R. (1995) *Marketing Social Change: Changing Behaviour to Promote Health, Social, Development, and the Environment*, Jossey-Bass, San Francisco.

Andreasen, A. R. (2001) *Ethics in Social Marketing*, Georgetown University Press, Washington.

Goldberg, M. E., Fishbein, M. and Middlestadt, S. E. (eds) (1997) *Social Marketing: Theoretical and Practical Perspectives*, Lawrence Erlbaum Associates, Mahwah, NJ.

Hastings, G. B. and Haywood, A. J. (1991) Social marketing and communication in health promotion, *Health Promotion International*, 6(2), 135–145.

Hastings, G. B. and Haywood, A. J. (1994) Social marketing: a critical response, *Health Promotion International*, 9(1), 59–63.

Kotler, P. and Roberto, E. L. (1989) *Social Marketing: Strategies for Changing Public Behaviour*, Free Press, New York.

Kotler, P. and Zaltman, G. (1971) Social marketing: an approach to planned social change, *Journal of Marketing*, 35, 3–12.

Maibach, E. and Parrott, R. L. (eds) (1995) *Designing Health Messages: Approaches from Communication Theory and Public Health Practice*, Sage, Newbury Park, CA.

Wallack, L., Dorfman, L., Jernigan, D. and Themba, M. (1993) *Media Advocacy and Public Health: Power for Prevention*, Sage, Newbury Park, CA.

Weinreich, N. K. (1999) *Hands-On Social Marketing: A Step-by-Step Guide*, Sage, Newbury Park, CA.

Websites

The Centre for Social Marketing, University of Strathclyde, Scotland:
  http://www.csm.strath.ac.uk
'The Social Marketing Network', Canada:
  http://www.hc-hc.gc.ca/socialmarketing
Weinreich Communications, on-line resource:
  http://www.social-marketing.com
Academy for Educational Development:
  http://www.aed.org/health_social.html

CHAPTER 28

Green marketing

KEN PEATTIE and MARTIN CHARTER

Introduction

The twentieth century was a time of unparalleled growth. The world's population grew to pass the six billion mark. We witnessed the birth of the mass market and the boom in mass production to satisfy its needs. As markets became more competitive, so formal marketing emerged and became increasingly important as a means by which companies could continue to grow their markets and their market shares. The comfortable assumption was that the all-out pursuit of economic growth was the most beneficial strategy for development, because the wealth generated could be invested to improve the quality of life of those inside and outside the industrialized economies.

At the beginning of the twenty-first century, the social and environmental consequences of the unquestioning pursuit of economic growth have become increasingly clear. Increasing levels of greenhouse gasses in the atmosphere, a hole in the ozone layer caused by CFC releases, widespread destruction of the rain forests, and a growing list of endangered species and ecosystems are just a few of the indicators that all is not well. By 2000, World Bank figures showed that nearly half the world's population live on under $2 per day.

For this half of the world, issues of consumer choice and sovereignty or discretionary spending have little meaning, and promises that the growth in the industrialized economies would lead to a better quality of life for them have generally not been fulfilled.

For the new century, the key challenge for mankind is to find more sustainable and equitable ways to produce, consume and live. Sustainability was once a vision of the future shared by an environmentally-orientated few. The publication of the Brundtland Report 'Our Common Future' in 1987 brought the issue into the mainstream. In the wake of the 1992 Rio Earth Summit, the world's governments and major corporations have increasingly adopted the pursuit of sustainability as a goal. The real challenge lies in turning these good intentions into meaningful progress in the face of powerful vested interests, a deeply entrenched and environmentally-hostile management paradigm, and a global economy with tremendous momentum on a trajectory which aims towards conventional economic growth.

For marketing, the challenge is twofold. In the short term, ecological and social issues have become significant external influences on companies and the markets within which they operate. Companies are having to react to changing customer needs, new regulations and a new social zeitgeist which reflects increasing concern about the socio-environmental impacts of business. In the longer term, the pursuit of sustainability will demand fundamental changes to the management paradigm which underpins marketing and the other business functions (Shrivastava, 1994). This chapter aims to illustrate how the 'green challenge' is exerting an influence on current marketing practice and how its implications will require a more profound shift in the marketing paradigm, if marketers are to continue delivering customer satisfaction at a profit throughout this new millennium.

Green marketing in context

Management theory in general is firmly rooted in an economic and technical systems perspective which concentrates on exchanges, products, production and profits. Over time it has evolved to become more 'human', with the emergence of disciplines like organizational behaviour, human resource management, business ethics and societal marketing. The fact that businesses are physical systems which exist within a finite and vulnerable physical environment has, until recently, largely been ignored as a management and marketing issue. During the 1990s, the marketing discipline began to seriously discuss the physical implications and sustainability of marketing (e.g. O'Hara, 1995; van Dam and Apeldoorn, 1996).

The roots of green marketing can be traced back to the wave of environmental concern of the 1970s which spawned the 'ecological marketing' concept (Hennison and Kinnear, 1976). This was largely concerned with those industries with the most severe environmental impacts, and with developing new technologies to alleviate particular environmental problems. The reaction of many marketing academics and practitioners to the environmental concern which emerged in the late 1980s and early 1990s was therefore a feeling of *déjà vu*. However, there are some important differences between

the environmental movement of the 1970s and the green movement of today, which are summarized in Table 28.1.

The integration of environmental concern into marketing theory and practice is also viewed by some as simply an extension of the societal marketing concept. However, it is more helpful to view the concept of 'green marketing' which has developed as a response to the green movement of today, as something which integrates and expands upon the ideas embedded in the ecological and societal marketing concepts. We can define it as:

> The holistic management process responsible for identifying, anticipating and satisfying the needs of customers and society, in a profitable and sustainable way.

The key differences between the green marketing concept and societal marketing lie in:

- An emphasis on the physical sustainability of the marketing process, as well as its social acceptability.
- A more holistic and interdependent view of the relationship between the economy, society and the environment.
- An open-ended rather than a long-term perspective.
- A treatment of the environment as something with intrinsic value over and above its usefulness to society.
- A focus on global concerns, rather than those of particular societies.

In both the ecological and societal marketing concepts, the emphasis on socio-environmental issues for marketers has mostly been framed in terms of costs and constraints. Another important new dimension that green marketing introduced was an emphasis on socio-environmental issues as a potential source of innovation and opportunity for marketers.

Combining environmental concern (which traditionally involves encouraging conservation), with the discipline of marketing (which aims to stimulate and facilitate consumption)

Table 28.1   The evolution of environmental concern

Factor	1970s environmentalism	1990s green
Emphasis	On 'environmental' problems	On the underlying problems with our social, economic, technical or legal systems
Geographic focus	On local problems (e.g. pollution)	On global issues (e.g. global warming)
Identity	Closely linked to other anti-establishment causes	A separate movement embraced by many elements of 'the establishment'
Source of support	An intellectual elite, and those at the fringes of society	A broad base
Basis of campaigns	Used forecasts of exponential growth to predict future environmental problems (e.g. limits to growth)	Uses evidence of current environmental degradation (e.g. the hole in the ozone layer)
Attitude to businesses	Business is the problem. Generally adversarial	Businesses seen as part of the solution. More partnerships formed
Attitude to growth	Desire for zero growth	Desire for sustainable growth
View of environment/ business interaction	Focused on negative effects of business activity on the environment	Focuses on the dynamic interrelationship between business, society and the environment

can appear somewhat paradoxical. Sustainability is the keystone of the green marketing philosophy, which resolves this apparent paradox. A sustainable approach to consumption and production involves enjoying a material standard of living today, which is not at the expense of the standard of living of future generations. It is a deceptively simple concept comprising two parts:

1 Using natural resources at a rate at which environmental systems or human activity can replenish them (or in the case of non-renewable resources, at a rate at which renewable alternatives can be substituted in).

2 Producing pollution and waste at a rate which can be absorbed by environmental systems without impairing their viability.

Green marketing's key concepts of sustainability and holism are both apparently simple, but can be extremely difficult to translate into action. This is largely because conventional management wisdom emphasizes reductionalism and specialism, and is founded on economic theories which mistakenly treat environmental resources as limitless, free (beyond the cost of extraction) or, for market-less commodities like stratospheric ozone, worthless. Green marketing attempts to relocate marketing theory and practice away from the economic hyperspace it has evolved in, and bring it back down to earth and reality.

Reconceputalizing the marketing environment

Companies benefit from a marketing orientation in many ways, and one of the most important is the external focus on the marketing environment it encourages. However, marketing theory has followed the tradition of mechanistic economic models, which dismiss the ecological contexts in which economic activity occurs (Capra, 1983). So entire books discussing the marketing environment dedicate chapters to the social, cultural, technological, economic and political environments, without discussing the physical environment which underpins them, and on which they all depend. At best, the response to increased environmental concern has been to try to accommodate it within existing models of the environment (of the PEST type) by discussing it as a political pressure, an influence on the economics of business, a social trend or a technological challenge. The reality is that the physical environment is the foundation on which societies and economies are based. Figure 28.1 visualizes the marketing environment

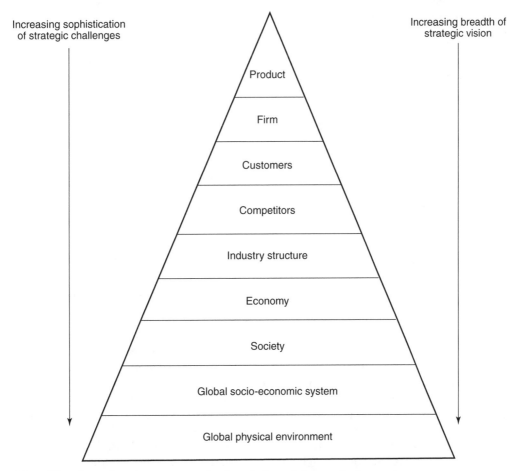

Figure 28.1   The physical environment as the foundation of the marketing environment

as composed of layers of issues and interactions.

The most immediate issues for marketing managers are typically internal ones relating to the product and the company itself, and externally to customers. Beyond this, the analysis of the environment broadens out externally through different, but interwoven, levels of environment. Each level has important implications for marketing, but dealing with the deeper levels of the environment is perhaps a more difficult strategic challenge, due to their increasing breadth and complexity, and their decreasing proximity to the company itself. The physical global biosphere may seem distant to many companies' day-to-day activities, but ultimately all business activity depends upon it, and its continuing stability and viability. Problems in the underlying global physical environment will impact firms, and their products and strategies, through interactions with each layer of the model.

Global physical environment

Measurable deterioration in many different aspects of the biosphere has created a scientific consensus that action is needed to better safeguard it, and its future viability, from the consequences of unsustainable consumption and production (although there is not unanimity, and there is controversy about the extent, causes and implications of many of the issues). At the simplest level, the environment affects businesses because it represents the physical space within which they and their customers exist, and it provides the resources upon which they depend. Climate change, for example, is a serious threat to companies in tourism, agriculture, insurance or those situated on flood plains. For some companies there is a very direct relationship between the health of the environment and their business prospects. The fishing industry's agenda, for example, is dominated by the need to protect stocks from over-fishing.

Although global issues such as climate change and ozone depletion dominate the headlines, the green agenda contains a vast array of issues, each of which creates marketing opportunities and threats for different businesses. For the car and oil companies, concerns about carbon dioxide emissions and global warming constitute a major threat. For companies working in alternative fuels and energy efficiency devices it represents a major opportunity. Some issues, such as over-fishing, are industry specific, while others like global warming have a much wider impact. It is interesting to note that all of the major industries in the world face important environmentally related challenges. In tourism, destinations need to be developed sustainably to prevent them being destroyed by their own success in attracting visitors, and to safeguard the cultures and lifestyles of the local population. The oil industry is under pressure from concerns about global warming and water pollution. For the car industry, air pollution, global warming and the fate of cars at the end of their working lives are key issues. In electronics, the use of CFCs as solvents and the disposal of obsolete equipment are important. For agriculture, forestry and fishing, the threat that unsustainable production poses in terms of loss of biodiversity, deforestation and soil erosion are crucial issues for the future. Even in the apparently abstract world of financial services there is increasing interest in ethical investment policies and concern about environmental instability as a source of risk.

Global socio-economic system

The biosphere is global in nature, since it knows no geopolitical boundaries. Recent decades have also seen a more global social perspective emergence reflected in global companies, markets, technologies and sociocultural trends. The response to the green challenge has also become more global through increasing international environmental legislation (such as the Montreal Protocol to reduce CFC use, or the worldwide ban on commercial whaling) and intergovernmental conferences.

Although issues of social concern vary over time and between countries, survey data reveal that concern about the state of the environment is spread across the planet, and (contrary to many peoples' expectations) is shared by the populations (if not always the governments) of the less-industrialized as well as the industrialized nations. However, the 1997 Kyoto Intergovernmental Conference on Climate Change and subsequent meetings in Marakesh and The Hague have demonstrated the difficulties of progressing and implementing international agreements to tackle common environmental problems.

There is also growing concern about the power, influence and accountability of global corporations. This concern has been expressed in protests such as at the infamous 'Battle of Seattle' during the 1999 World Trade Organization meeting. According to Institute of Policy Studies figures, 51 of the 100 largest economic entities on the planet are now corporations, the remaining 49 being nations. In a world still largely governed through national laws, it is a considerable challenge to ensure that the behaviour of transnational corporations, of which over 60 000 now exist, does not sacrifice the social and environmental interests of citizens in some countries for the benefits of shareholders and consumers in others.

Society

Within societies, concern about the environmental and social impacts of business is generally increasing and is being reflected in a number of ways, including:

- *Changing values and attitudes.* In the last few decades many social values have changed, particularly in relation to the levels of trust placed in companies and other institutions. According to Edelman PR's 2000 international social attitude survey, on issues related to the environment, human rights and health, information from non-governmental organizations (NGOs) was trusted by 60 per cent of people compared to 15 per cent who trusted the government and media, and 10 per cent who trusted major corporations. Social attitudes towards the environment have also changed, so that it is perceived as vulnerable, valuable and in need of protection. This has been reflected in changes in the values associated with products and their features. For Kodak, the 'convenient disposable' camera of the early 1980s metamorphosed into the 'single-use recyclable' camera of the 1990s.

- *Pressure group activity.* The last 20 years have witnessed a considerable increase in the size, budgets and sophistication of pressure groups concerned with the socio-environmental impacts of businesses. Many of their communications campaigns are now produced by the same agencies that work for the major companies. As the experience of companies like Nike and Gap has shown in relation to international labour standards, companies with the most famous brand names are the most likely to be targeted, even though they may not be the worst offenders. There has also been a recent trend towards partnership approaches between pressure groups and companies, such as that between McDonald's and the Environmental Defense Fund.

- *Media interest.* An increasing amount of media output is devoted to nature and environmentally related messages, and examples of poor eco-performance are a favourite target for investigative journalism. As Mulhall (1992) notes: 'The massive impact of instant media in accelerating the message of gross environmental incompetence by our leaders can be summarized in three letters – CNN. It means that a company's reputation can be destroyed globally in one day'. By 2000, CNN was available in 151 million households.

- *Political and legal interest.* The quantity and complexity of social and environmental legislation faced by companies continues to grow. Businesses in Europe are now affected by over 80 EU environmental directives and regulations. Companies that rely on mere compliance risk being left behind by the upward 'ratcheting' of legislation. In the USA, the trend towards forcing the CEOs of polluters to make personal court appearances, and in some cases jailing them, has helped to focus corporate minds.

The economy

Conventional wisdom viewed investments in environmental protection as involving a trade-off with economic growth (Porter and van der Linde, 1995). Recognition is growing that the two are interlinked in many complex ways, and that long-term economic growth will be dependent on better environmental protection. Many business opportunities are now emerging for technologies, goods and services which address environmental problems, or at least make less of a contribution towards them. The European Commission estimates that by 2010 'environmental industries' will be worth $640 billion, and that their growth will provide an additional half million European jobs.

Key areas where environmental concern is influencing economic issues include:

- *Production economics.* Environmental considerations are radically altering the production economics of some front-line industries such as cars, chemicals and power generation. Rising landfill costs and tougher regulations on emissions mean that production costs are increasingly influenced not by what has gone into a product, but by what is discarded when making it. The BSE crisis within the UK beef industry has also demonstrated the economic damage that poor eco-performance can inflict upon an entire industry.
- *Investor pressure.* The Ethical Investment Research Service estimate that the value of investments in the UK held in ethical investment funds passed the £4 billion mark by mid-2001. Although this is a relatively small proportion of total funds, the impact on corporate reputations of being de-listed from a particular ethical fund gives them a disproportionately large influence in public relations terms. Interest in ethical and

environmental investment looks set to intensify, with new initiatives such as the FTSE4Good index of socially responsible companies and changes to legislation requiring institutional investors to focus more on the social and environmental performance of holdings.

- *Green taxes.* A new generation of environmentally related taxes including landfill taxes and climate change levies are being introduced in many countries. There are also product-specific taxes being used to encourage particular changes in consumer behaviour in favour of smaller engined cars, or reusable, rather than disposable, shopping bags.
- *Access to capital.* Environmental performance is seen by lenders and investors as an important influence on risk in many industries. An effective environmental strategy is becoming important to guarantee access to capital and insurance in a number of environmentally sensitive industries.

Industry structure

Industry structures have conventionally been visualized as composed of linear exchanges and value chains. The green challenge is one of many forces encouraging a more relationship-based view of industry structures, particularly through an emphasis on recycling and supply loops. These feature relationships in which the customer returns products or packaging to the manufacturer, and in the process become another form of supplier. Xerox are veterans of recycling, having begun the routine reuse of components in 1968. By 1997, Xerox were reclaiming and reusing about 1 million parts and 150 000 office machines each year. For its 'Eco Series' copier line, the company has achieved recycling rates of up to 75 per cent for components from end-of-life products.

The changes that greening is bringing to industry structures includes:

- *The threat of substitutes.* Products with a relatively poor eco-performance can become targets for new substitutes. Concern about the destruction of peat wetlands has led to a number of products such as ground coconut husks being launched to act as a peat substitute for gardeners. In the future a more radical set of substitutions may emerge, as markets which were traditionally based around purchase and ownership of products move towards greater use of services, hire and leasing (Cooper and Evans, 2000).

- *Supplier relationships.* Greening is forcing many companies to reconsider supplier relationships, since their total environmental impact will be strongly influenced earlier in the supply chain. Tools like 'life cycle analysis' and environmental supplier audits are being used by companies to monitor and often to improve their suppliers' eco-performance. Some major companies such as BT have de-listed the 'greyest' of their suppliers; others such as Boots are collaborating with suppliers to reduce the number scoring poorly on their Environmental Management Index. A key feature of the greening of industries has been the need for partnership approaches between companies and their suppliers (Morton, 1996).

- *Market entry barriers.* Strict national environmental laws can act as an entry barrier for foreign firms. Recent years have witnessed friction between the USA and the EU over the EU's resistance to genetically modified food. The EU's concern about the health and environmental safety of GM crops was interpreted by the USA as a disguised market entry barrier. For some companies, good environmental performance can act as a key to gain entry into a new market. Varta batteries had failed in several attempts to translate their European market strength into penetration of the UK market, but this was achieved very rapidly with the introduction of their innovative mercury-free battery range.

Competitors

Much has been made of the potential of good eco-performance to generate competitive advantage (e.g. Elkington, 1994; Porter and van der Linde, 1995). In a wide range of markets, including detergents, retailing, batteries, white goods, cars, toilet paper and banks, companies have used eco-performance as a basis on which to compete. Global competition and continuous improvement philosophies have narrowed the differences between products to the extent that 'softer' issues such as perceived environmental impact can act as a 'tie-breaker' for the consumer trying to choose brands (Christensen, 1995). The Co-operative Bank, for example, adopted an explicit ethical policy, which it has since used to differentiate itself and encourage customer loyalty, gaining over 200 000 customers as a result (Hedstrom *et al.*, 2000).

Experience shows that environmental disasters such as the *Exxon-Valdez* or *Braer* oil spills, or spills at major chemicals plants, put all players in an industry under increased stakeholder pressure. This suggests that as the green challenge deepens, it may reduce the intensity of competitive rivalry, instead of acting as a new arena for it to be played out in. Many key environmental problems confront entire industries and require industry-wide responses. Alliances are emerging between rivals to address common environmental challenges and to develop greener technologies. In the USA, Ford, Chrysler and GM have collaborated in an effort to develop low-emission vehicles, and also to pool millions of dollars to lobby against stricter greenhouse gas restrictions. The Industrial Coalition for Ozone Layer Protection is a consortium of major US and Japanese electronics companies, collaborating to replace CFCs as electrical solvents.

Customers

The worldwide boycott of CFC-driven aerosols in the late 1980s demonstrated the potential of consumers to unite behind an environmental issue that they understood and could relate to, in a way that enforced rapid change to an entire industry back down the supply chain. Recent UK research by the Co-operative Bank suggested that around one in three Britons make some purchases on the basis of ethics and environment, and that at least 5 per cent consistently search for ethical labelling, recycle, participate in boycotts and discuss green issues in relation to the brands they buy. The identity, characteristics and sincerity of these 'green consumers' has been the dominant theme in discussions about green marketing, but this emphasis may be misplaced. Partly, this is because the conventional concept of the green consumer may be both an oxymoron and poorly conceived. Secondly, the most important impacts that environmental concern are having are often in business-to-business marketing, not in supplying the ultimate consumer (Drumwright, 1994; Morton, 1996).

Firms

As external concern about the socio-environmental impacts grows, so companies large and small are having to respond through changes to a range of organizational dimensions. Environmental management appointments, the introduction of green auditing and reporting systems, and changes to company policies and facilities to reduce waste and pollution are common responses. Corporate strategies and cultures are increasingly seeking to address green issues, often to reflect external stakeholder pressure, but also to reflect the concerns of employees and investors. For marketers, pressure to address the eco-performance of the products that they manage may stem from external customers or regulatory requirements, or it may reflect internal requirements to pursue sustainability as a corporate goal.

Products

Environmental concern is creating demands for new products (such as pollution control equipment), and is causing existing products to be reconsidered and in many cases redesigned, reformulated or produced differently. The impact on products will vary across markets. In some, such as cars, cleaning products or paper products, changes in response to the green

challenge are widespread. In others, such as food, financial services or computers, examples of change are more sporadic. There was a flurry of green product introductions in the late 1980s and early 1990s. In the USA, the proportion of green products among new product introductions rose from 1.1 per cent in 1986 to a high of 13.4 per cent in 1991 (Ottman, 1994). Since that high-water mark, the level of product introductions has decreased, mainly in response to concerns about the validity of some of the green claims involved (Carlson *et al.*, 1993; Mohr *et al.*, 2001), increased levels of media and NGO scrutiny, and mounting consumer scepticism. By 1997, green products accounted for 9.5 per cent of all new US product introductions, with the highest proportion in the 'household products' category, accounting for 29.5 per cent of product introductions (Fuller, 1999).

Environmental concern can also lead to the repositioning of products. In response to concern about exposure to ultraviolet radiation and the risk of skin cancer, sun tan lotions have changed from an emphasis on sun exposure and beauty to an emphasis on skin protection.

The greening of marketing strategy

The evolution of the green challenge has brought about a change in the relationship between marketing and the physical environment (for details, see Menon and Menon, 1997). The environmental concern of the 1970s inspired a raft of legislation and a relatively reactive response among companies. The emphasis was on compliance and bolting-on 'end-of-pipe' technologies to alleviate pollution. The focus was also generally on issues relating to production, rather than on issues relating to the scale and nature of consumption. Therefore, for marketers it was easy to dismiss the challenge as something to concern the production engineers and corporate lawyers. Environmental response was viewed as an additional cost burden and as an operational issue, which concerned a relatively small number of 'front-line' industries such as oil, chemicals and cars.

During the 1980s and 1990s, a more proactive style of corporate response emerged, and the front line broadened to include a much wider range of industries. Companies began to recognize that environmental responsiveness is something that customers, investors and other stakeholders take an interest in, and which can provide opportunities for innovation and competitive advantage. As the environment emerged as an issue of strategic importance, and one with the potential to influence the attitudes and behaviour of consumers, so marketers increasingly began to take an interest. However, much of the early response among marketers was rather superficial, in seeking to connect particular attributes of existing products to the environmental concern being expressed by customers.

Marketers' response to the green agenda is sometimes proactive and sometimes reactive. Reactive strategists tend to emphasize compliance with legislation, and responding to any specific customer pressure for improvements to socio-environmental performance. The dangers of a reactive approach were demonstrated by the controversy stirred up by Shell's decision to dispose of the Brent Spar oil facility by dumping it at sea. This apparently technical and operational issue had been given UK government approval, and Shell believed that it had evidence to demonstrate that their strategy was the optimal solution in environmental and economic terms. Once environmental groups and other North Sea governments learned about the strategy, and decided to oppose it, Shell found itself in a major public relations battle and faced with a forecourt boycott by European consumers. The company learned a rather painful lesson about the need for stakeholder dialogue and consultation, and the ability of NGOs to focus consumer and media attention. Proactive strategists tend to emphasize communication with stakeholders, keeping ahead of legislation and customer demands for improvement, and participation in debates about social and environmental issues.

Competitive advantage and the environment

During the 1990s, the argument that greening can act as a source of competitive advantage emerged, from authors such as Elkington (1994), Azzone and Bertele (1994), and Porter and van der Linde (1995). Obvious examples come from companies such as The Body Shop, who compete on the basis of strong eco-performance and by tapping into customer demand for greener products. Porter and van der Linde's argument is that the search for environmentally superior solutions leads to innovation and the creation of more efficient and effective technologies. Their logic is that tough environmental legislation (often vigourously opposed by companies) sets new challenges for companies, which prompts them to be innovative and secure improvements in competitive, as well as environmental, performance. This is what Varadajan (1992) termed 'enviropreneurial marketing'.

Others have argued that it is difficult in practice to achieve and sustain competitive advantage from good eco-performance (e.g. Walley and Whitehead, 1994; Wong *et al.*, 1996). The issues have often proved complex and costly to address; customers have often proved difficult to convince; greener product offerings have sometimes struggled to compete on technical merits against conventional products; and the media have often proved more critical of those attempting to improve their eco-performance and capitalize on it, than of the most polluting and wasteful companies. Despite this, it is clear that poor eco-performance can put a company at a massive competitive disadvantage. Exxon's combined bill for clean-up costs, fines and legal costs estimated at over $3 billion in the immediate aftermath of the *Exxon-Valdez* disaster, which also left 41 per cent of Americans describing themselves as 'angry enough to boycott Exxon products' (Kirkpatrick, 1990).

For the marketing strategist it is vital to understand the potential impact of the green agenda on their business and its customers. It is important to understand the relative strengths and weaknesses of the company's eco-perform-ance. Good eco-performance is important in many markets because it can provide:

- *New market opportunities.* Through access to growing green markets. In markets such as financial services and tourism, green products represent the fastest growing area for new business.
- *Differentiation opportunities.* AEG increased their sales by 30 per cent within an otherwise static white goods market, following an advertising campaign stressing the relative energy and water efficiency of their products.
- *Opportunities for cost advantages.* Although conventional wisdom associates good eco-performance with investment and increased costs, this is partly a reflection of the 'end-of-pipe' methods used (since adding a catalytic converter onto a car can only increase its costs). Investments using a more radical, clean technology approach are being shown to be capable of reducing material and energy inputs, and cutting inefficient pollution and waste. Among 181 waste reduction projects within 29 chemical industry plants studies by Porter and van der Linde (1995), only one led to a net cost increase and the average annual savings (on the projects where this could be meaningfully measured) was $3.49 per dollar spent.
- *Niche opportunities.* In the short term, greener products such as organic food and cruelty-free cosmetics have succeeded within market niches comprised of the most environmentally aware consumers and marketed at premium prices. However, when such products catch the imagination of the mass market, the niche can rapidly expand to encompass the bulk of

the market. Phosphate-free detergents captured around 80 per cent of the German detergent market within three years of their launch. There is, however, a danger that the success of green niche products could effectively hold back the greening of markets. This would occur if, by satisfying the most environmentally aware consumers, pressure to green the market becomes diluted and the momentum of change falters. In many industries it will require the greening of the mass market to make a substantive contribution to sustainability.

The green consumer

It seems logical for marketers, when faced with a population professing increased environmental concern, to respond by trying to identify 'green consumers' and finding out what motivates purchases of environmentally marketed products. If this can be done, and appropriate market offerings created, then the competitive advantage outlined by Porter and others can be achieved.

Academic researchers and market research agencies have striven to define and understand the relationship between peoples' environmental concern and their purchasing behaviour. Many factors have been proposed as influences on green consumer behaviour such as changing consumer values, demographic factors, knowledge of environmental problems and alternative products, perceived personal relevance, and the ability of the individual to make an effective contribution (for a model which integrates the majority of these, see Dembkowski and Hanmer-Lloyd, 1994). All of these efforts have sought to discover a reliable basis upon which green consumer segments can be defined and targeted. Socio-demographic criteria such as gender, age and income were often used, but as Wagner (1997) comments: 'Socio-demographic attempts to profile the green consumer have not always yielded strongly indicative results, and the results produced in one study have been repeatedly contradicted in another.' Other segmentation attempts have used environmental attitudes, environmental knowledge, level of education, social consciousness or related behaviours. However, once again 'results of these studies were frequently inconclusive and sometimes contradictory' (Kilbourne and Beckmann, 1998).

The difficulties in isolating green consumer behaviour reflect several factors:

- It overlooks the point made by Kardash (1974) that all consumers (barring a few who enjoy contrariness for its own sake) are 'green consumers' in that, faced with a choice between two products that are identical in all respects except that one is superior in terms of its eco-performance, they would differentiate in terms of the environmentally superior product.
- By attempting to relate a consumer's environmental concern to purchases, marketing researchers may be looking in the wrong place. Many of the most significant contributions that consumers can make towards environmental quality come in product use, maintenance and disposal, or in delaying or avoiding a purchase through a 'make do and mend' mentality.
- Environmental improvements in products are often entangled with economic or technical benefits. Therefore, drivers may choose lead-free fuel for environmental or economic reasons, or people may choose organic food for reasons of environmental concern, personal health concern or simply for the taste benefits.
- Different answers are achieved depending on what is defined as constituting green consumer behaviour, and whether the environmental issues that it is linked to are defined in general or specific terms. General environmental concern is often measured by researchers, but it is less easily related to products than specific environmental issues (such as concern for dolphins translating into the purchase of rod-and-line caught tuna fish).

Perhaps the solution to understanding green purchasing behaviour is to try and understand the purchase rather than the purchaser. If we accept Kardash's proposal that, all other things being equal, most customers would differentiate in favour of greener products, then understanding environmental purchasing behaviour (and often the lack of it) is assisted by looking at the extent to which other things are not 'equal'. Many green purchases involve some form of compromise over conventional purchases. The compromise can take a variety of forms, including:

- Paying a green premium. This can be imposed by economic necessity where improving eco-performance increases production costs. Alternatively, it can be created by marketing strategies in which greener products aimed at green market niches are given a premium price irrespective of production costs.
- Accepting a lower level of technical performance in exchange for improved eco-performance (e.g. rechargeable batteries provide less power but are ultimately cheaper and greener).
- Travelling to non-standard distribution outlets (e.g. Ecover detergents were originally marketed through health food shops).

Where there is a compromise involved in making a greener purchase, a key factor which will determine whether or not this is acceptable to customers is the confidence they have in the environmental benefits involved. Customers will need to be confident that:

- the environmental issue(s) involved are real problems;
- the company's market offering has improved eco-performance compared to competitor or previous offerings;
- purchasing the product will make some sort of material difference.

Analysing green purchases in terms of the compromises and confidence involved can help to explain some of the inconsistencies in the research findings into green consumer behaviour. The majority of consumers profess concern for the environment, a desire to buy greener products and a willingness to pay more for them or accept technical performance reductions. The numbers of consumers measurably changing their purchasing behaviour to buy green is much less, and this has generally been interpreted as a failure to back up intentions with purchase and a tendency to over-report social and environmental concerns (Wong *et al.*, 1996). This undoubtedly explains part of the discrepancy, but the missing element is the confidence that customers have in companies' green marketing offerings. A BRMB/Mintel survey found that 71 per cent of UK consumers thought that companies were using green issues as an excuse to charge higher prices.

In trying to relate environmental knowledge to green consumption, researchers are making an assumption that increasing environmental knowledge will lead to an increased desire to purchase green products. The reverse may be true, in that increasing environmental knowledge can actually reduce the consumers' confidence in the effectiveness of market-based solutions for environmental challenges, and it may make them more aware of the shortcomings of products seeking to market themselves on a green platform (Peattie, 2001).

Eco-performance

For proactive companies seeking to gain competitive advantage, and for the more reactive companies seeking to avoid the costs and potential for competitive disadvantage associated with environmental damage, the central issue concerns their 'eco-performance'. This represents the impact that products and businesses have on the human and natural environment within which they exist, but it is not a straightforward concept. A question like 'What

constitutes a green product?' has no simple answer. Is it one that has achieved sustainability? One that is better than its competitors? One that is less harmful than the product it replaces? Or one produced by a company with an environmental management system?

The eco-performance of businesses and products, like the demand of consumers, comprises many different shades of green. Trying to identify a company as either green or 'dirty' is rather misleading, in the same way as trying to classify a company as marketing orientated or not. Such 'black or white' distinctions are inappropriate for a performance continuum, and the relativity of eco-performance is reflected in Charter's (1992) concept of 'greener' rather than 'green' marketing.

The pursuit of sustainability is the underlying principle of green marketing, and a company can justifiably claim green credentials if it is demonstrably and consistently moving towards sustainability. Achieving sustainability is not a prerequisite for a valid claim to be green, just as 100 per cent customer satisfaction is not a prerequisite to claim a marketing orientation. In many markets, economic and technical considerations preclude sustainability as a short-term objective for green companies, even though sustainability can be their ultimate goal.

Measuring and managing the eco-performance of products is made difficult by the variety of factors which can contribute to a good or bad customer perception of eco-performance. Some companies have run into problems by claiming their products as 'green' by focusing simply on the product itself, while ignoring the environmental performance of the means of production or the company as a whole. For example, the £8 million advertising campaign launching Ariel Ultra as a green detergent was somewhat negated by front page news coverage highlighting that it had been tested on animals. Companies whose green strategy is product orientated or one-dimensional, instead of holistic, are prone to exposure by green interest groups, to charges of hypocrisy and green hype, and to a loss of consumer confidence in their green message. Ben & Jerry's ice-cream was an icon among green brands, but came under pressure when the company was accused of a relatively poor social performance on issues such as the treatment of suppliers and workplace health and safety. Developing a more holistic green strategy requires an appreciation of the product itself, what goes into it, and what goes into, and out of, the environment as a result of its production and use. This process is analogous to Porter's 'value chain' approach, as shown in Figure 28.2.

An important new frontier for business academics and practitioners will be to try to develop measures of social and environmental performance to allow comparisons of eco-performance among companies, products and technologies (see, for example, Epstein and Roy, 2001).

Going green – the philosophical challenge

In its underlying quest to satisfy consumers, and in the marketing activities involved, green marketing resembles conventional marketing. Many of the key differences between the two relate to the values and philosophies which underpin the marketing strategy and the ways in which particular elements of marketing are conceptualized (Peattie, 1999). Green marketing seeks to balance the techno-economic market perspective with a broader socio-environmental approach. This will require a re-evaluation of some fundamental marketing assumptions and concepts (Kilbourne *et al.*, 1997). Some important areas to re-evaluate include:

- *Marketing's legitimacy*. Marketing's role in driving forward economic growth by stimulating demand and its role in satisfying customer wants have always legitimized marketing, to the extent that the benefits of ever increasing

consumer choice and economic growth have gone unquestioned. The green challenge has changed this. Mulhern (1992) proposes the need to focus on customer welfare rather than purely on customer wants. Issues such as passive smoking and car safety (which usually equates to driver safety) have highlighted the failure of marketing to address the needs and welfare of non-consumers. During (1992) points out that only one-fifth of the world's population have sufficient disposable wealth to make consumption choices and belong to the 'consumer class'. He also questions the morality of that richest fifth continuing to enjoy a standard of living that the planet cannot sustain, and which the remaining four-fifths can aspire to (encouraged by the images from marketing communications) but are unlikely to attain. The need for sustainability also requires us to question the validity of striving to satisfy all current consumer wants, if they are at the expense of future generations of consumers.

- *Consumers*. Henri Fayol once quipped about sending out for workers, but human beings turning up instead. Similarly, green marketers need to reconsider their approach to consumers. The word 'consumer' epitomizes a view of customers, not as people, but as a means of consumption. Marketing theory tends to deal with a very limited number of customer wants or needs at a time. However, peoples' needs and wants are many, varied and often potentially incompatible. One may yearn to live in an area free from the pollution, congestion and danger posed by cars, and yet be unwilling to give up the benefits of personal mobility that car ownership provides. Just as a product is more accurately analysed as a 'bundle of benefits', a customer should be considered as possessing a 'bundle of wants and needs'. In the face of conflicting desires to consume and conserve, customers may increasingly seek satisfaction through non-purchase decisions (such as repairs). By contributing to reduced environmental degradation, green consumer behaviour

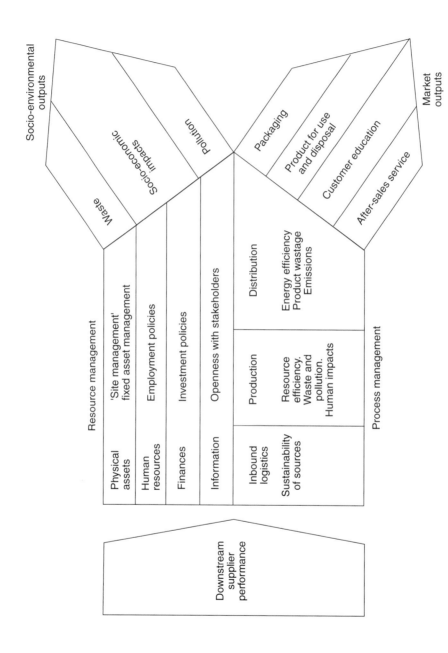

Figure 28.2 Components of environmental performance

addresses an inherent human need for a viable environment, which may sometimes be at the expense of more explicit material wants. Recent years have witnessed an increasing range of conservation-orientated behaviour among consumers, from the recycling of cans and bottles to the boom in returning consumer durables to the supply chain through small ads or car boot fairs.

- *Customer satisfaction.* In the past, customer satisfaction has been judged in terms of the performance of the product at the moment (or during the period) of consumption. A green consumer may reject a product because they become aware of the environmental harm that the product causes in production or disposal. They may also avoid a product because they disapprove of the activities of the producer, its suppliers or investors.

- *The product concept.* If customer satisfaction is increasingly dependent upon the production process and on all the activities of the producer, we are approaching the situation where the company itself is becoming the product consumed. Drucker's (1973) famous concept that 'Marketing is the whole business seen from its final result, that is from the customers' point of view' seems set to become an enforced reality for many businesses, because the green movement means that customers (or those who influence them) are now actively looking at all aspects of their company. As Bernstein (1992) comments: 'The consumer wants to know about the company. Companies won't be able to hide behind their brands. Who makes it will be as important as what goes into it since the former may reassure the customer about the latter.'

- *Producer responsibility.* The responsibilities of the producer were conventionally seen in terms of ensuring that products were fit for purpose, fairly represented, safe and not priced or promoted in a way that exploited customers. Environmental concern has added a new layer of responsibility concerned with the fate of the product at the end of its life-span, an issue which was previously irrelevant to marketers beyond signalling the possibility of a new purchase. For consumer durables such as cars, white goods and consumer electronics, these new responsibilities will have considerable impacts on product design and supply chain management.

- *Criteria for success.* Traditional marketing theory implies that if the traditional four Ps of the mix are right, then success will follow in the form of a fifth P, 'Profits'. Green marketing success involves ensuring that the marketing mix and the company also meet four 'S' criteria (Peattie, 1995):
  - Satisfaction of customer needs.
  - Safety of products and production for consumers, workers, society and the environment.
  - Social acceptability of the products, their production and the other activities of the company.
  - Sustainability of the products, their production and the other activities of the company.

- *Demarketing.* One unavoidable conclusion of green marketing logic is that where a product is being consumed and produced in an unsustainable way, it may have to be demarketed (either voluntarily or forcibly) to reduce consumption. In tourism and energy markets, changes in pricing or access to products have been used to try to reduce the level of consumption.

Companies can embrace environmental and social improvements to their products or production processes in a very pragmatic way that reflects their desire to respond to customer needs and to gain or maintain competitive advantage. However, companies seeking to pursue improved eco-performance often seem to find it difficult if it is not underpinned by a belief in the values and philosophy of greening. This is analogous to total quality management, where the difficulties that many western companies have experienced in implementing it reflects their focus on attempting to apply the management tools and techniques without embracing the underlying philosophy, as their Japanese competitors have done. Evidence suggests that the most successful corporate social and environmental improvement programmes are those which reflect both a belief in the business benefits of such programmes and the underlying values of the company (Weaver *et al.*, 1999).

An example of a company whose corporate philosophy has embraced the pursuit of sustainability is household products manufacturer SC Johnson, famous for brands such as Pledge and Mr. Muscle, and acknowledged as a leader in terms of eco-performance. The following is an excerpt from their statement of values:

> SC Johnson is dedicated to sustaining and protecting the environment. Our vision is to be a world leader in delivering innovative solutions to meet human needs through sustainability principles. Specific, measurable goals to reduce pollution and waste in our products and processes have been part of a decade of continuous progress toward sustainability . . . Through the SC Johnson Fund, Inc. in the US, we donate, on average, 5 per cent of pre-tax profits every year to increase local and global well-being. Our contributions are targeted to advancing the three legs of sustainability: economic vitality, social progress, and a healthy environment.

Going green – the management challenge

Marketers' interest in eco-performance may reflect external drivers of legislation, customer demand and public opinion, or internal drivers relating to top management commitment, corporate strategy or the pursuit of competitive advantage (Bannerjee, 1999). Whatever the motivation, making a commitment to improve or compete on eco-performance can be a major challenge. Even among those companies well known for good eco-performance, greening

programmes have often been prone to hitting what Robert Shelton of Arthur D. Little describes as a 'green wall'. Here the management responsible for environmental improvement, and their strategies, come into conflict with entrenched corporate power balances and values once the 'low-hanging fruit' have been picked (Shelton, 1994). It is clear that, for managers seeking to promote corporate social and environmental improvement, there is a significant internal marketing task to address.

Taking a leadership role

Marketing has an important leadership role to play within firms in relation to the environment. Coddington (1993) recommends that firms engaged in a greening process should set up an environmental task force in which marketers play a leading role. He identifies two sets of strengths that marketers can contribute to the greening process, the marketing perspective and the marketing skill-set. The greening challenge requires creativity, the ability to work effectively across internal organizational boundaries and excellent communication skills. Coddington identifies marketing managers as being often 'superbly qualified' for the task because:

- Marketers are able to identify and analyse the marketing implications of corporate environmental exposures and initiatives.
- Marketers can help to identify new business product and service opportunities that arise out of those same environmental exposures and initiatives (for example, using hazardous waste clean-up obligations as a springboard for entry into the hazardous waste remediation business).
- Marketers can work to ensure that, when corporate environmental policies are developed, the marketing implications are given due consideration.
- As a matter of course, marketers must co-ordinate their activities across multiple departments (R&D, manufacturing, packaging, sales, public relations).

- Marketers are professional communicators. This skill is enormously useful in virtually every aspect of environmental management – on the task force itself, and in such areas as environmental management training, emergency response training, community relations and other domains which put a premium on communications.

B&Q periodically publishes an environmental review, incorporating a detailed environmental policy statement, that defines the responsibilities of different functions, including marketing, finance, personnel, logistics and systems. The second of these, published in 1993, articulated the leadership role that marketing can play in the greening process:

> The marketing director is the main board director responsible for environmental issues and is therefore ultimately responsible for researching the issues, writing the policy and auditing progress. As marketing director he also has responsibility to ensure that the environmental policies and targets of marketing are implemented.
>
> In market development B&Q shall monitor through market research, customers' concerns and perceptions on environmental issues and customers' understanding and appreciation of B&Q's response to them. Market development will also incorporate environmental considerations into the strategic planning in the company and refer to strategic environmental issues in the five year plan.
>
> Marketing services is responsible for most of the purchasing decisions handled by marketing. They shall ensure that 'Point of Sale' material, carrier bags and all their other purchases consider environmental specifications. These include use of recycled post consumer waste, recyclability, and waste minimization. Marketing services will ensure that no misleading environmental statements or claims are made on any POS material or other communications such as press enquiries. Marketing recognizes that some of the products it sells have distinct environmental attributes, for energy efficiency equipment and home composting. We also recognize a need to inform our

customers more about our environmental policies and the environmental performance of all products.

Adopting a holistic perspective

Although the marketing philosophy embraces the entire business, the sphere of influence of marketing and marketers in practice is often more limited. Carson's (1968) observation that, for many companies, marketing is 'the integration, just below senior management level, of those activities related primarily towards customers', unfortunately still holds true today.

As green issues become important within markets, green marketing and the management of eco-performance need to transcend functional boundaries to become pan-organizational management concerns. This mirrors the way that quality slipped its functional bonds to become total quality management (TQM). Indeed, for many companies the most practical way of addressing environmental issues has been through TQM. As social and environmental pressures on business grow, so marketers need to have an appreciation of, and input into, all aspects of a business, its products and its production system. How energy efficient is our production process? Where are raw materials sourced from? Where is spare capital being invested? How well do we treat our workforce and suppliers? Such questions were once not the concern of marketers. Today, they are increasingly likely to influence the perceptions of important stakeholders such as customers.

Addressing these questions, and the demands for answers to them, requires a lot of new information for marketers and new approaches to the management of that information. A range of new auditing services is now available to companies so that their conventional financial, strategic and marketing audits can be complemented by social and environmental audits. Increasing stakeholder demand for information about eco-performance is requiring companies to adopt a new openness and to move away from a view of the production process as a 'black box' into which the customer is not encouraged to peer. This is particularly the case in industrial markets, where it is becoming the norm among leading companies to insist upon environmental auditing and reporting by all suppliers. 'Right to Know' legislation in the USA and the EU is also ensuring that companies have to disclose information relating to issues such as pollution.

Embracing a stakeholder approach

A 'stakeholder approach' is vital for the development of appropriate and holistic green philosophies, strategies and policies (Polonsky and Ottman, 1998). Internally and externally, organizations face an increasing depth of interest in their eco-performance from an increasing range of interested parties. One by-product of the growth in the Internet is that it provides opportunities for customers and interest groups to share information about companies and their behaviour. This has strengthened the ability of interest groups to mobilize customers and interest the media in campaigns relating to particular companies.

Table 28.2 highlights a range of stakeholders and examples of socio-environmental issues that could be associated with the development, manufacture and marketing of a particular product.

The importance of a stakeholder perspective to companies with strong socio-environmental focus is demonstrated by the following statement from the The Body Shop:

> The Body Shop is a stakeholder led company. We believe its success is dependent upon its relationships with all its stakeholders, including its employees, franchisees, customers, communities, suppliers, The Body Shop At Home (formerly The Body Shop Direct) consultants, shareholders and campaigning partners . . . The Body Shop has always believed that business is primarily about human relationships. We believe that the more we listen to our stakeholders and involve them in decision making, the better our business will run.

New management responsibilities

The concept of companies taking greater responsibility for their customers and products has been reflected in the idea of 'brand managers' being replaced by 'brand stewards'. In agrochemicals markets, where difficulties with correct product use often occur in countries with low literacy rates among farmers, some companies are using the concept of brand stewardship to ensure that products are used correctly. Dow Corning, for example, demands that its sales staff:

- inform customers about known hazards relating to the products;
- advise customers to use products in accordance with label recommendations;
- insist that distributors pass on handling, use and disposal information to their customers;
- report and respond vigorously against cases of misuse;
- co-ordinate visits by company staff to customer sites, to ensure safe use and disposal of products.

Changing the marketing time frame

Green marketing focuses on the performance of products before purchase and after use, which requires a new time perspective for marketers. A 'cradle-to-grave' view of products may mean that their performance must be considered over a period of years instead of moments. For consumer durables, the question of actual durability assumes a new importance. Evidence suggests that many products currently exist only as semi-durables and creating more durable products can form an important part of a green strategy. Agfa Gevaert switched from a policy of selling photocopiers to leasing them on a full service basis. This led to a product redesign brief based around durability, and the upgrading of the copy drums from a lifespan of under 3 million to over 100 million copies. For marketers this

Table 28.2   Stakeholder interest in product impacts

Stakeholder	Potential issue	Indicator
Company shareholders and managers	Product safety and acceptability	Prosecutions; inclusion rate in ethical funds
Employees	Harmful processes and substances	Accident rate; time lost due to injury
Customers	Labelling	Customer satisfaction; breaches of government/industry guidelines
Business partners	Product recall handling	Efficiency, speed and success of product recalls
Suppliers	Involvement in research and development	Results of supplier element of life cycle analysis and use of results in the design process
Competitors	Health and safety performance and effect on industry reputation	Performance against industry benchmarks and guidelines
Government and regulators	Product stewardship	Quantity of hazardous non-product output (NPO) returned to process or market by reuse/recycling
NGOs, pressure groups and other influencers	Product safety and socio-environmental impacts	Incidence of NGO/regulatory targeting
Communities	Harmful substances	Releases to air, land and water of NPO

Source: adapted from WBCSD (2000) Corporate Social Responsibility: Making Good Business Sense, Geneva, Switzerland.

can represent a significant departure from previous strategies, since it effectively reduces rates for product replacement, and may require a switch of emphasis in strategy away from purchase and towards leasing or towards the marketing of complementary products and services.

The need to examine the impact of products from cradle to grave is leading towards the concept of re-marketing or even closed-loop (waste free) marketing. Various tools are being developed to aid the green marketer to assess the full environmental impact of products, the best known being life cycle analysis and eco-balance analysis. The greatest difficulty for the marketer is to know how far forward or back, and down how many of the branches of the supply chain, such an analysis should go. An example of a cradle-to-grave life cycle is provided in Figure 28.3.

- Design
- Choice of material
- Extraction of raw materials
- Material manufacture
- Use of recycled materials
- Transport of materials and components
- Manufacture of components
- Washing machine manufacture

- Packaging
- Transport

- Operation
- Durability
- Reliability
- Detergent use
- Water use

- Collection, transport
- Recycling
- Landfill, incineration

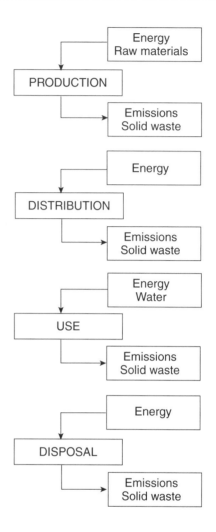

Figure 28.3   A washing machine's life cycle

The practical challenge – greening the marketing mix

Green product management

To create a significantly greener economy, there will need to be a range of new and greener products and technologies. Instead of seeking to ameliorate environmental and social impacts of existing products and technologies through 'end-of-pipe' initiatives, there is a growth in more innovative 'clean technology' solutions.

This is reflected in the inclusion of eco-performance criteria in the new product development processes of many industries through concepts like 'Design for Environment'. Successful development of new green products requires a process characterized by high levels of cross-functional communication and integration, good information, early consideration of green issues, support from top management, and a specific approach to measurement and benchmarking (Pujari *et al.*, 2002).

Measuring and understanding the relative eco-performance of products is important for companies, whether or not they are pursuing a green strategy. Even if a good performance is unlikely to yield competitive advantage in a particular market, poor performance can still represent a strategic vulnerability and lead to a competitive disadvantage. Analysing product eco-performance needs to be multidimensional, since it is influenced by many factors, and it also should be done with reference to competitors' offerings. Guidelines for conducting product-specific marketing audits that summarize the relative socio-environmental impacts of products are now available to help marketers tackle these issues (see, for example, Fuller, 1999).

Green product attributes fall into two general categories. First, there are those relating to the social and environmental impacts of the tangible product (or service encounter) itself. For a car manufacturer, these attributes would include issues like fuel efficiency, longevity and safety during use, and recyclability once the vehicle reaches the end of its working life. A key new dimension of product management and design from a green perspective is the emphasis on the product's fate post-use. Improving the post-use eco-performance of products requires the integration of opportunities for some or all of the 'five Rs' into the product concept:

1 *Repair.* A modular design approach and good after-sales service provision can make repairing products cost effective and extend their useful life.
2 *Reconditioning.* In the automotive market a wide range of reconditioned parts, from tyres to engines, can be purchased.
3 *Reuse.* The average dairy milk bottle is used 12 times.
4 *Recycling.* Products ranging from beer cans to BMWs are now designed to be more recyclable.
5 *Re-manufacture.* Kodak collects over 50 million single-use cameras each year from 20 countries for re-manufacturing.

The second category of attributes is those that relate to the processes by which the product is created and the attributes of the company that produces it. Conventional marketing talks about the core product, the tangible product (which includes packaging and other physical dimensions) and the augmented product (including service dimensions). Since green marketing requires an approach to product management which incorporates how the product is made as a product attribute, it is helpful to think of this as the 'total product' concept (Peattie, 1995).

Creating a total green product: Ecover

The challenge in developing a total green product is to improve eco-performance while producing acceptably comparable levels of functionality and service, at a competitive price. This is not an easy task, but one which has been accomplished by some pioneering green companies such as Ecover within the highly competitive green detergent market. Their approach involves adopting cleaner technologies that design out waste in the manufacturing processes, rather than using 'end-of-pipe' solutions which inevitably represent an added cost.

In October 1992 in Belgium, Ecover launched the world's first ecological factory (Develter, 1992). Their approach was to ensure that all processes, products and philosophies are sufficiently green to meet increasingly close stakeholder scrutiny. Innovations ranged from the use of factory bricks derived from coal slag, to monetary incentives given to employees for the use of company bicycles. Ecover is also championing the concept of a zero-impact business park which produces no, or minimal, environmental pollution, and has energy efficiency and recycling 'built-in'.

Green packaging

Discarded packaging accounts for a large proportion of waste in industrialized economies and a good deal of the environmental impact of many products. Packaging has been an obvious starting point for many companies' green marketing efforts, since packaging can often be safely reduced without expensive changes to core products or production processes and without a risk of disaffecting customers. Varian Medical Systems, a leading manufacturer of medical scanning equipment, redesigned the shipping packaging for its products to enable the multiple boxes used to be easily 'nested' within each other for return and reuse. This simple step produced worthwhile cost savings. As with many dimensions of green marketing, success in practice can be more difficult than some of the prescriptive advice available for marketers suggests. When Sony experimented with reclaiming and reusing packaging materials for its television sets, it led to a customer misconception that the product inside the packaging was also not new. For the reuse and recycling of packaging materials to make a meaningful difference, manufacturers need to ensure that efforts are supported by the infrastructure of collection systems and customer information and education.

Green promotion

Many companies have sought to promote themselves and their products through explicit or implicit association with environmental or social issues. However, promotion has been one of the most controversial areas of the green marketing agenda. Conventional advertising has been criticized for presenting green products as oversimplified solutions to complex environmental problems. Revelations about unfounded and misleading claims have also fuelled concerns about 'greenwashing' and 'green hype' (Carlson *et al.*, 1993). Companies like the Body Shop, for example, have deliberately avoided above-the-line 'brand sell' style advertising, preferring to concentrate on public relations and in-store communications. There is widespread consumer scepticism about environmental advertising, which is being fuelled by initiatives such as Friends of the Earth's 'Green Con of the Year Awards'.

The result of these concerns has been an increasing emphasis on the concept of 'sustainable communications' rather than the more narrowly defined concept of green promotion. Sustainable communications strongly stress a dialogue with stakeholders, particularly customers, aimed at informing and educating those customers, and seeking to establish the social and environmental credentials of the company and its products. Often, this has been addressed through an emphasis on corporate level communication campaigns, and through partnerships and alliances. MORI survey results indicated that 30 per cent of British adults had recently bought a product or service because of the company's link to a charitable organization.

A number of prescriptive and regulatory guidelines have been developed to guide marketers in formulating and using claims about environmental performance. Davis (1993) suggests the following:

- Ensure that the promoted benefit has a real impact, e.g. reduced harmful emissions.
- Identify the product's specific benefit in terms of the product attribute that contributes to improved environmental performance.
- Provide specific data about the benefits, e.g. specifying the proportion and nature of recycled content.
- Provide a context to allow consumers to make meaningful comparisons.
- Define any technical terms used.
- Explain the benefit, since consumers often have limited understanding of environmental issues.

Different communications issues will arise depending upon the nature of the media that marketers use. Advertising brings with it the danger that the company will be accused of green hype or trivializing or exploiting serious social and environmental issues. On-pack promotion appears a useful and effective means to influence consumer decisions, but it can be difficult to explain a complex issue on a package that you are also trying to reduce in size. Direct mail may seem like an effective way to target the most environmentally concerned consumers, but creates the danger of being perceived as 'junk mailers'. Sales promotions or sponsorships linked to social or environmental causes have been shown to be very effective, but they need to be selected carefully to ensure that there is synergy with the product being promoted. Otherwise, customer evaluations of the company can actually deteriorate (Mohr *et al.*, 2001). Personal selling in non-consumer markets is often important, and requires the salesforce to be aware of the environmental implications of the company and its products and processes (Drumwright, 1994). Public relations has also been a key communications channel for companies to put across messages relating to good eco-performance, both in relations to brands and to corporate level communications aimed at building corporate reputation and identity.

Green issues provide good opportunities for both informative and emotive marketing communications. Fort Sterling's green brand Nouvelle captured 3 per cent of the £500 million toilet tissue market in its first year with a modestly funded advertising campaign which used such hard-hitting copy as 'It feels a little uncomfortable using toilet tissue that wipes out forests'.

Integrated communications is increasingly viewed as a key ingredient to marketing success. It is particularly important when companies are attempting to promote themselves, or protect themselves, in relation to social and environmental issues. If one part of a company is attempting to gain competitive advantage on the basis of eco-performance, then competitors, NGOs, the media and regulators will be forming an orderly queue to attack the company if another part of that company is seen to be failing to live up to the image. The key is to understand the concerns of stakeholder audiences and then to communicate effectively and efficiently.

Green pricing

Pricing is, in many ways, the crux of the green marketing challenge. If the external social and environmental costs of production were reflected in the prices that customers pay, then there would be considerable incentives for manufacturers to reduce those costs and become more sustainable. Companies seeking to absorb those costs and pass them onto the consumer are vulnerable both to accusations of exploiting customer interest in green pricing and to undercutting from competitors still effectively subsidized by the environment. The 'win–win' argument for greening proposed by the likes of Porter and van der Linde (1995) suggests that consumer demand for green products can allow for the addition of green price premiums, as applies to free-range eggs and dolphin-friendly (rod-and-line caught) tuna.

Greening strategies can affect the cost structures of a business with a knock-on effect on prices, particularly if pricing is on a 'cost plus' basis. Developing new sustainable raw material sources, complying with legislation, writing off old, 'dirty' technology, capital expenditure on clean technology and the overheads associated with greening the organization can impose a heavy cost burden. However, this can be counterbalanced by the savings made by reducing raw materials and energy inputs, by reducing packaging, cutting waste disposal costs and by finding markets for by-products. If costs are looked at holistically and managed on a portfolio basis, then wider eco-efficiency process benefits, when added to premium demand benefits, can counterbalance the costs of greening to make a positive contribution to profitability. Electrolux's 'Green Range' of white goods, for example, has a lower environmental impact than the company's standard range, and has also achieved a 3.5 per cent higher gross margin.

Progress towards sustainability may be aided if the focus on 'price' within marketing could be reduced in favour of focus on 'cost'. Low-energy light bulbs, for example, have a higher purchase price, but a lower overall running cost for consumers. Buildings are also built to a price, rather than built to deliver a certain level of overall usage costs. A total cost focus would result in buildings which were more expensive to purchase, but which were economical in the long term and which would reduce a significant element of society's environmental impact. Also, better information about the social and environmental costs attached to products would give consumers more complete information and more incentive to change their behaviour. It is quite common for consumers of veal, for example, to enjoy it far less once they discover exactly how it is produced.

Green logistics

The environmental impact of many products is strongly determined by the fuel consumed and materials used in transporting them to customers. The implementation of 'carbon taxes' on fossil fuel consumption would have a significant impact on the economics of distribution. This would encourage industries to replace global production and distribution chains with global networks of operations producing and distributing on a more regional or local scale.

Getting the optimal environmental performance in distribution can be difficult. Reducing package thickness, for example, can reduce the resources consumed and the energy used in distribution, but increase the level of in-channel waste due to the reduced level of protection for the product. Similarly, larger trucks reduce the amount of fuel consumed per product unit moved, but have a greater negative impact on roads and the communities they pass through. The new requirements for companies to take back products and discarded packaging will also require a significant redesign of distribution channels to handle the 'reverse logistics' involved in reusing containers, and reclaiming waste and end-of-life products.

An example of logistics forming a key component of a greening strategy comes from B&Q, whose logistics function has been rewarded with several major awards for environmental excellence. Their 1993 Environmental Review included:

- The development of 'centralized distribution' at B&Q, bringing environmental benefits such as reduced vehicle movements and a reduction in transit packaging.
- The establishment of a policy and targets aimed at reducing vehicle emission impacts.
- The reduction of transit packaging in conjunction with suppliers, aiming for a 30 per cent reduction in the total corrugated board used by UK suppliers within the first year.
- A cost and benefit analysis undertaken into the practicalities of store-based collection and recycling systems for packaging materials.
- Insistence that logistics subcontractors operate an environmental policy consistent with B&Q's and commission their own comprehensive environmental audit.
- The promotion of environmental awareness both within B&Q's logistics department and its subcontractors.

Labelling

Labelling has been a particularly important issue within green marketing, with relevance to both promotion and logistics. As a promotional device, green labels are often important to provide customers with a simple and trustworthy signal of a product's social and environmental credentials. There are long-standing national labelling schemes such as the German 'Blue Angel' scheme which are extensively trusted and used by consumers. There are also more specific schemes which relate to particular industries or products (e.g. Rug-mark carpets made without child labour), or to particular methods of production (e.g. organic certification from the Soil Association) or business conduct (e.g. the Fair Trade mark). In terms of logistics, labelling is important in terms of providing customers with information to support their recycling behaviour. For example, labelling plastic containers to indicate the type of plastic used makes the recycling process simpler.

Labelling programmes vary in terms of whether or not they are mandatory or voluntary within a particular industry, whether they involve single or multiple issues, the level of information they provide, and the level and style of verification that underpins them. Each of these dimensions has provided ample opportunity for controversies about labelling schemes within industries and between companies, regulators and NGOs. The EU eco-labelling scheme, for example, has been mired in political wrangling for much of the last decade, and has had relatively little impact on consumption and consumers within Europe as yet.

The evolving agenda – from green products to sustainable value

The early years of green marketing, much like the early years of industrial growth after the Second World War, have been dominated by a focus on products. Initially, greening centred on specific physical products such as lead-free fuel, recycled paper, organic food or cruelty-free cosmetics. The key difference lay in the emphasis on how the product was made, both as a product attribute and as an influence on consumer demand.

Gradually, the focus in green marketing has broadened to include services such as tourism and financial services. Globally, services account for the majority of economic activity and of economic growth, yet there is little research on the sustainability impacts of services, coupled with a lack of methodologies to pursue sustainable service design and development. Yet some elements of the service economy, such as transport, travel and hospitality, have considerable social and environmental impacts. Typically, services are a combination of intangible elements (services) and physical elements (products) supported by an infrastructure (systems). Viewing the delivery of value to customers holistically as a product service system (PSS) is an increasingly common approach in research communities, but it is an approach which most businesses are, as yet, unfamiliar with.

Taking a holistic PSS-based view is important, because increasingly there is a blurring of the edges as to what exactly represents a 'service'. Also, the extensive use of outsourcing as a service in many industries can obscure the nature and distribution of the socio-environmental impacts of production. To make progress towards sustainability, supply chain management and service design will become increasingly important business processes. It is important for people involved in the design of any product, service or PSS (including marketers, design engineers, industrial designers, procurers, supply chain managers and entrepreneurs) to take account of life cycle impacts to determine environmental and social impacts, and to seek strategies to minimize negative impacts.

The blurring of the distinction between products, services and systems means that, for the future of green marketing, perhaps we should be thinking more in terms of 'sustainable solutions'. Sustainable solutions are products, services or system changes that minimize negative and maximize positive sustainability impacts (economic, environmental, social and ethical) throughout and beyond the life cycle of existing products or solutions, while fulfilling acceptable societal demands and needs. In improving these aggregate impacts, these solutions are delivering 'sustainable value'. These concepts allow us to take a more holistic view of the economy and its outputs, process and goals. Sustainable solutions (whether products, services or PSS), represent the outputs, and green marketing and sustainable design represent the processes which aim to deliver those outputs. However, the ultimate goal should be to deliver higher levels of net sustainable value (that satisfy customers and other stakeholders) through those outputs (Charter and Clark, 2002).

This holistic approach to the way in which marketing delivers the goods and services that we consume takes us far beyond trying to identify green consumers, develop green products, and persuade the former to pay an extra few per cent for the latter. It suggests a much broader research agenda, encompassing:

- sustainable service and PSS impacts;
- sustainable service and PSS methodologies;
- the relationship between sustainable 'solutions development' and supply chain/network or value management;
- cross-functional working practices required to achieve higher net sustainable value through sustainable solutions;
- management approaches required to create higher levels of net sustainable value.

The future of green marketing

Sustainability as a concept can be controversial, open to multiple interpretations, very hard to measure, and difficult to translate into meaningful action amongst the very real political, economic and technological constraints faced by companies and governments. The underlying point, however, is very clear. Any system or activity that is not sustainable ultimately cannot be sustained. Although this can be dismissed as a truism, it is a point that often seems to be missed. The last 50 years have witnessed some extraordinary developments in technologies, products, markets and marketing. They have also witnessed a doubling of world population from around three to around six billion. Without becoming more sustainable, over the next 50 years, marketing will struggle to do more than to deliver an increasingly mixed and short-term set of blessings, to a shrinking proportion of the world's population.

The dangers of unsustainable growth have rarely been more clearly illustrated than during the boom and bust of the 'dotcom'

financial bubble and the subsequent Enron and WorldCom scandals. It demonstrated many simple truths about the need for businesses to deliver real benefits and generate real and sustainable income streams, and also the dangers of profligate spending today on the promise of the wealth that new technologies will deliver tomorrow. These truths also apply to the industrialized economies as a whole. Many of the environmental costs of production and consumption are not being fully reflected (either directly or indirectly via taxation) in the cost structures of companies and the prices paid by their customers. This means that society and the environment are currently subsidizing our consumption and production. Our businesses are environmentally 'over-trading' – a position that cannot be maintained indefinitely. Companies can grow and apparently prosper while running up huge financial debts (as Enron showed). The danger is that the longer the bills go unpaid, and the longer the debt mounts up, the more destructive the crash then becomes. While our businesses continue to consume the Earth's natural capital at an unsustainable rate, the risks grow that this environmental debt will create significant social and environmental consequences. The world cannot maintain its recent trends of growth in consumption and production without future consumers, and the billions living outside the consumer economy, bearing the cost.

The role that marketing can, and should, play in the development of a more sustainable economy has been the subject of some debate. Marketing has often been presented as part of the problem in stimulating unsustainable levels of consumption, and in using public relations and other means of communication to obscure or deny the negative consequences of that consumption. Marketing is also frequently presented as an important part of the solution in the context of market mechanisms being used to encourage more sustainable consumption. It is certainly true that marketing as a tool can be used to help or hinder the sustainability agenda. Some environmentalists have criticized green marketing on the basis that 'Changing our shopping habits will not save the world'. This is true, but if it creates improvement in the eco-performance of businesses, it will buy much needed time in which to understand how to make the more important changes to our economic, technical and political systems, in order to manage our environment in a sustainable way. It is clear that the greening of marketing and market forces will only have real meaning if accompanied by changes to corporate values and strategies, regulations, investment processes, political systems, education and trade.

Another important role that will need to be played by marketing in the future is to promote more sustainable ways to live and consume. In addition to the marketing of new products, technologies and services, we will need the social marketing of many ideas, old and new, in order to make our economies more sustainable. These will include recycling, fair trade, product-service substitutions, composting, frugality, energy efficiency and less materialistic ways of life. The concept of sustainability itself will also need to be marketed. A major piece of social market research commissioned by Lancashire County Council, which examined perceptions of 'quality of life' (MacNaghten *et al.*, 1995), drew two conclusions that have significant implications for the greening of marketing:

> People generally are unfamiliar with the idea of 'sustainability' in its environmental sense. But once they understand it, they appear to identify positively with its values and priorities ... Overall, whilst there is substantial latent public support for the aims and aspirations of sustainability, there is also substantial and pervasive scepticism about the goodwill of government and other corporate interests towards its achievement.

These findings illustrate both the importance and the challenge of making marketing more sustainable. They confirm other research findings showing that most people would like to buy greener products from greener companies. For companies that choose to ignore this customer demand (whether explicit or latent), it is questionable whether they are practising marketing at all. Creating more sustainable marketing strategies will remain an uphill battle while the majority of consumers remain ignorant of what sustainability is all about, and dubious about the ability of companies to contribute to it. Winning this battle will be a key challenge for marketers in this new millennium, and the outcome will have a significant impact on the quality of life of consumers and citizens for generations to come.

References

Azzone, G. and Bertele, U. (1994) Exploiting Green Strategies for Competitive Advantage, *Long Range Planning*, **27**(6), 69–81.

Bannerjee, S. B. (1999) Corporate Environmentalism and the Greening of Marketing: Implications for Theory and Practice, in Charter, M. J. and Polonsky, M. J. (eds), *Greener Marketing*, 2nd edn, Greenleaf, Sheffield.

Bernstein, D. (1992) *In The Company of Green: Corporate Communication for the New Environment*, ISBA, London.

Capra, F. (1983) *The Turning Point*, Bantam.

Carlson, L., Grove, S. J. and Kangun, N. (1993) A Content Analysis of Environmental Advertising Claims: A Matrix Method Approach, *Journal of Advertising*, **22**(3), 27–39.

Carson, D. (1968) Marketing Organisation in British Manufacturing Firms, *Journal of Marketing*, **32**, 268–325.

Charter, M. (1992) Emerging Concepts in a Greener World, in Charter, M. (ed.), *Greener Marketing*, Greenleaf, Sheffield.

Charter M. and Clark, T. (2002) *Sustainable Value*, Greenleaf, Sheffield.

Christensen, P. D. (1995) The Environment: It's Not Time to Relax, *McKinsey Quarterly*, **4**, 146–154.

Coddington, W. (1993) *Environmental Marketing*, McGraw-Hill.

Cooper, T. and Evans, S. (2000), *Products to Services*, Friends of the Earth, London.

Davis, J. J. (1993) Strategies for Environmental Advertising, *Journal of Consumer Marketing*, **10**(2), 19–36.

Dembkowski, S. and Hanmer-Lloyd, S. (1994), The Environmental-Value-Attitude-System Model: A Framework to Guide the Understanding of Environmentally Conscious Consumer Behaviour, *Journal of Marketing Management*, **10**(7), 593–603.

Develter, D. (1992) *Ecover – The Ecological Factory Manual*, Ecover Publications.

Drucker, P. F. (1973) *Top Management*, Heinemann, London.

Drumwright, M. (1994) Socially Responsible Organizational Buying: Environmental Concern as a Noneconomic Buying Criterion, *Journal of Marketing*, **58**(3), 1–19.

Durning, A. T. (1992) *How Much is Enough?*, Earthscan, London.

Elkington, J. (1994) Toward the Sustainable Corporation: Win–Win–Win Business Strategies for Sustainable Development, *California Management Review*, **36**(2), 90–100.

Epstein, M. J. and Roy, M. J. (2001) Sustainability in Action: Identifying and Measuring the Key Performance Drivers, *Long Range Planning*, **34**(5), 585–604.

Fuller, D. A. (1999), *Sustainable Marketing*, Sage, Thousand Oaks, CA.

Hedstrom, G., Shopley, J. and LeDuc, C. (2000) *Realising the Sustainable Development Premium*, Arthur D. Little.

Hennison, K. and Kinnear, T. (1976) *Ecological Marketing*, Prentice-Hall, Englewood Cliffs, NJ.

Kardash, W. J. (1974) Corporate Responsibility and the Quality of Life: Developing the Ecologically Concerned Consumer, in Henion and Kinner (eds), *Ecological Marketing*, American Marketing Association.

Kilbourne, W. E. and Beckmann, S. C. (1998) Review and Critical Assessment of Research on Marketing and the Environment, *Journal of Marketing Management*, **14**(6), 513–532.

Kilbourne, W. E., McDonagh, P. and Prothero, A. (1997) Sustainable Consumption and the Quality of Life: A Macromarketing Challenge to the Dominant Social Paradigm, *Journal of Macromarketing*, **17**(1), 4–24.

Kirkpatrick, D. (1990) Environmentalism: The New Crusade, *Fortune*, 12 February, 44–52.

MacNaghten, P. *et al.* (1995) *Public Perceptions and Sustainability in Lancashire: Indicators, Institutions, Participation*, Lancashire County Council and Lancaster University Centre for the Study of Environmental Change.

Menon, A. and Menon, A. (1997) Enviropreneurial Marketing Strategy: The Emergence of Corporate Environmentalism as Market Strategy, *Journal of Marketing*, **61**(1), 51–67.

Mohr, L. A., Webb, K. J. and Harris, K. E. (2001) Do Consumers Expect Companies to be Socially Responsible? The Impact of Corporate Social Responsibility on Buying Behavior, *Journal of Consumer Affairs*, **35**(1), 45.

Morton, B. (1996) The Role of Purchasing and Supply Management in Environmental Improvement, in *Proceedings of the 1996 Business Strategy and the Environment Conference*, ERP Environment, Leeds, pp. 136–141.

Mulhall, D. (1992), Environmental Management: The Relationship Between Pressure Groups and Industry – a Radical Redesign, in Koechlin, D. and Muller, K. (eds), *Green Business Opportunities*, Pitman, London.

Mulhern, F. J. (1992) Consumer Wants and Consumer Welfare, in Allen, T. C. *et al.* (eds), *Marketing Theory and Applications*, Proceedings of the 1992 AMA Winter Educators' Conference, pp. 407–412.

O'Hara, S. U. (1995), The Baby is Sick/The Baby is Well: A Test of Environmental Communication Appeals, *Journal of Advertising*, **24**(2), 55–70.

Ottman, J. A. (1994) *Green Marketing: Challenges & Opportunities*, NTC Business Books, Lincolnwood, IL.

Peattie, K. (1995) *Environmental Marketing Management: Meeting the Green Challenge*, Pitman, London.

Peattie, K. (1999) Trappings Versus Substance in the Greening of Marketing Planning, *Journal of Strategic Marketing*, **7**, 131–148.

Peattie, K. (2001) Golden Goose or Wild Goose? The Hunt for the Green Consumer, *Business Strategy and the Environment*, **10**(4), 187–199.

Polonsky, M. and Ottman, J. (1998) Stakeholders in Green Product Development Process, *Journal of Marketing Management*, **14**, 533–557.

Porter, M. E. and van der Linde, C. (1995) Green and Competitive: Ending the Stalemate, *Harvard Business Review*, September–October, 120–133.

Pujari, D., Wright, G. and Peattie, K. (2002) Green and Competitive: Influences on Environmental New Product Development (ENPD) Performance, *Journal of Business Research*, forthcoming.

Shelton, R. D. (1994) Hitting the Green Wall: Why Corporate Programs Get Stalled, *Corporate Environmental Strategy*, **2**(2), 5–11.

Shrivastava, P. (1994) 'CASTRATED Environment: GREENING Organizational Studies, *Organization Studies*, **15**(5), 705–726.

van Dam, Y. K. and Apeldoorn, P. A. C. (1996) Sustainable Marketing, *Journal of Macromarketing*, **16**(2), 45–56.

Varadajan, P. R. (1992) Marketing's Contribution to Strategy: The View From a Different Looking Glass, *Journal of the Academy of Marketing Science*, **20**, 323–343.

Wagner, S. A. (1997) *Understanding Green Consumer Behaviour*, Routledge, London.

Walley, N. and Whitehead, B. (1994) It's Not Easy Being Green, *Harvard Business Review*, **72**(3), 46–52.

Weaver, G. R., Trevino, L. K. and Cochran, P. L. (1999) Corporate Ethics Practices in the Mid 1990s: An Empirical Study of the Fortune 1000, *Journal of Business Ethics*, **18**(3), 283–294.

Wong, V., Turner, W. and Stoneman, P. (1996), Marketing Strategies and Market Prospects for Environmentally-friendly Consumer Products, *British Journal of Management*, **7**, 263–281.

Further reading

Charter, M. and Polonsky, M. J. (1999) *Greener Marketing*, 2nd edn, Greenleaf, Sheffield. An edited collection which provides detailed coverage of the strategic implications of the greening of marketing, and the implications of this for the management of an extended marketing mix. The themes of the text are reinforced through a collection of detailed case studies covering a wide range of organizations.

Develter, D. (1992) *Ecover Manual*, 2nd edn, Ecover Publications, Oostemalle, Belgium. A comprehensive manual covering Ecover's experience in developing the world's first ecological factory. Demonstrates the wealth of detail that must be dealt with to ensure that the means of production, as well as the product itself, are environmentally sound.

Durning, A. T. (1992) *How Much is Enough?*, Earthscan, London. A scathing and thought-provoking indictment of over-consumption. Provides a stimulating challenge to many of the fundamental assumptions about marketing, its legitimacy, and the way it is practised.

Fuller, D. A. (1999) *Sustainable Marketing*, Sage, Thousand Oaks, CA. An excellent exploration of marketing from a physical systems and sustainability perspective. For anyone who suspects that green marketing is in some way 'woolly', this book provides a very specific and factual guide to the forces promoting the greening of marketing and the processes by which it can be achieved.

Journal of Marketing Management, Special Issue on Contemporary Issues in Green Marketing, **14**(6). This issue pulled together eight papers from leading experts in the field of green marketing, covering theoretical contributions, a critical review of research in the field, and papers relating to product development, recycling, sustainable communications and green alliances. An invaluable starting point for anyone seeking to understand green marketing from an academic perspective.

McDonagh, P. and Prothero, A. (1997) *Green Management: A Reader*, Dryden Press, London. An excellent edited collection of papers combining the deeply philosophical with the highly practical. The practical papers have a strong marketing bias, and the entire collection is invaluable for putting marketing and the environment clearly in its organizational, social and global context.

Menon, A. and Menon, A. (1997) Enviropreneurial Marketing Strategy: The Emergence of Corporate Environmentalism as Market Strategy, *Journal of Marketing*, **61**(1), 51–67. Analyses the evolution of the relationship between marketing and the environment, and in particular the emergence of 'enviropreneurial marketing'. Provides a useful discussion of the driving forces behind the greening of marketing, the opportunities that it provides, and the relationship with corporate strategy.

Peattie, K. (1995) *Environmental Marketing Management: Meeting the Green Challenge*, Financial Times/Pitman, London. A book which attempts to pull together much of what was written about marketing and the environment in the late 1980s and early 1990s to develop a comprehensive picture of what the green challenge means for marketing. Discusses the environment as a philosophical, strategic and practical challenge for marketing management, and illustrates the issues with short case studies at the end of most chapters.

Shrivastava, P. (1994) CASTRATED Environment: GREENING Organizational Studies, *Organization Studies*, **15**(5), 705–726. An astonishing article which deconstructs the existing management paradigm to detail exactly how and why it is inherently incompatible with the physical environment within which it exists. Outlines a new environmental management paradigm and points the way forward towards a more sustainable way of managing businesses.

CHAPTER 29

Marketing for small-to-medium enterprises

DAVID CARSON

Introduction

What is 'marketing for SMEs' and why should it be treated as a separate topic? There are two strong reasons why it is important to view marketing as being different in this context. One is the recognition that SMEs (small to medium sized enterprises), are not simply little big business. By a definition of size they are certainly small to medium sized in relation to large corporations; however, as a consequence of its size an SME has unique characteristics which make it distinctly different, not only to large corporations but also to many or all other enterprises. A significant second factor is the relative number of SME enterprises to large corporations; in any market or region the vast majority of enterprises will be SMEs with only a few large corporations. A consequence of this is that most people who work in marketing are likely to work in SMEs. Of course, many high profile marketing jobs will belong in large organizations but most marketing and related jobs are to be found in SMEs. Further support for this argument can be found by recognizing the growing size of the service sector of any economy and acknowledging that most service firms are inherently marketing orientated and also SMEs.

There are a number of implications arising from the above which this chapter attempts to address. Consideration is given to the unique characteristics of SMEs and how these characteristics impact upon the activities of SMEs. Recognition is also given to the influence of the entrepreneur/owner/manager and his/her strengths and weaknesses. A significant realization arising out of this is the incompatibility of SME capabilities and activities and much of marketing theory. This is illustrated in this chapter by comparing textbook marketing theory and SME marketing in practice. Following this an examination is made of the nature of SME marketing which allows a framework to be devised for effective SME marketing based upon the inherent strengths of such enterprises. This framework is presented as a model of SME marketing.

At the conclusion of this chapter the reader can expect to have gleaned an understanding of SMEs' marketing practices and a realization that this marketing is different to conventional descriptions and practices as preached in the textbook literature. The reader is not required to decide whether one or the other is better, but it is hoped that s/he will have an appreciation that there is some sort of difference which needs to be acknowledged. The reader can expect to know how an SME entrepreneur can improve his/her marketing activity within the resource constraints inherent in such enterprises.

The origins of this chapter lie in many years of involvement with SMEs from a variety of perspectives, as owner and partner in several enterprises and as consultant, trainer, educator and researcher of SMEs. In all of these activities, there is the firm belief that every SME is unique and as a consequence, the marketing activity is also uniquely different. Of course, it is possible to generalize but in doing so it is also important to remember the unique individuality of SMEs.

Characteristics of SMEs

There is purposefully no attempt in this chapter to define the term SME. There are many definitions incorporating some or all of aspects covering number of employees, revenue and turnover, size and range of products and markets, and so on. Suffice to acknowledge here, the term SME as definition in itself, that is, 'small-to-medium-size-enterprise'. SMEs are just this, they are small to medium sized relative to large corporations. A significant differentiator between SMEs and large corporations is that of resources. All enterprises have limitations as to what they can or wish to do. Any managerial activity will be inhibited by lack of finance, people and expertise. However, the larger an organization, the more scope it has to generate funding for projects, moving people around according to where they're needed most and if necessary, buying in expertise where and when it is needed. In the case of SMEs few if any of these options are available.

A distinctive characteristic of SMEs is a lack of finance. True some SMEs may begin life as cash rich and perhaps some will grow into cash rich enterprises, but for the vast majority of SMEs lack of cash and financial resources impose severe limitations upon activities. The reasons for this may be many. For example, when an enterprise is established it invariably soaks up all available capital resources in structuring the business and seeding initial market development. Thus, at the start-up stage most enterprises will experience financial limitations. Most enterprises after start up are reliant upon income generation to fund the initial investment and gain a surplus. Such surpluses will fund future growth which in turn requires further returns. Since just about every SME needs to grow in order to sustain and strengthen the business base, then just about every SME experiences financial limitations throughout the growing years. Until certain thresholds are reached, financial constraints tend to dominate decision making. Indeed, as an enterprise expands so does the complexity of its financial requirements and commitments.

Partly as a consequence of financial limitations, SMEs also have human resource limitations. Most people employed in SMEs work in a logistical process/delivery capacity. An SME tends to have few management decision makers, indeed, much of the meaningful decision making is undertaken by the owner/ manager or the entrepreneur. SMEs tend not to have specialist experts whose job is to do one task only. Instead, managers in an SME are 'generalists' who carry out a wide variety of tasks and decision making. As a consequence, decision makers' attention is often distracted away from a specific function which can often be to the detrimental inefficiency of a given functions performance.

Both of the limitations of lack of finance and lack of specialist expertise serve as severe constraints upon marketing ability and activity (Carson *et al.*, 1995). Small firms will often have very limited funds available for marketing purposes and what is more, limited marketing expertise in carrying out marketing decisions and activities. Therefore, that marketing which is performed may be undermined by simply not having enough money to spend with the added danger that even this limited spend may be used incorrectly or inefficiently. Even if marketing money is spent wisely, the nature of an SME, in that it is 'small' relative to its market place and position within that market, means that its marketing will invariably have a limited impact upon the market. The old metaphors of 'small fish in a large pond' and 'a drop in the ocean' serve to illustrate this significant limitation. Of course, the consequence of such limited impact upon the market is that SMEs must adapt and focus any marketing practice to suit the individual and unique characteristics of the enterprise.

Characteristics of entrepreneurs/owners/managers

One of the major influences upon an SME's marketing practice is that of the lead entrepreneur/owner/manager. Indeed, it is probably this individual's influence which most characterizes the style and nature of marketing performed by an SME. There is a large literature which is devoted to defining the characteristics of entrepreneurs (Timmons, 1978; Meredith *et al.*, 1982; Hofer and Bygrave, 1992). Typically they are perceived to be risk takers and in being so, to be opportunistic and visionary; innovative and creative; adaptive and change oriented. Perhaps two further characteristics are the most influential with regards to marketing, the perception that entrepreneurs are individualistic and highly focused upon the enterprise's well being.

Individualistic can of course mean a variety of things, however in the case of entrepreneurial behaviour it is often manifest as the nature of an individual's personality and how this impacts upon his/her decision making. The issue is not whether an individual is aggressive, persuasive, assertive, placid, or some other personality trait, it is in terms of how the 'individualistic' characteristic impacts upon marketing decision making. Bearing in mind the SME limitations discussed above and in consideration of how these can impact upon 'individualistic' decision making, such decision making will invariably be simplistic because of

the limited expertise with regards to marketing. It will be haphazard and unstructured because it is reactive to events and intuitively individualistic. All of these characteristics can lead to apparently irrational decision making which has a predominately short-term focus.

The highly focused nature of entrepreneurial decision making is centred around the enterprise's well being. The entrepreneur is continuously concerned with ensuring the survival and safety of the enterprise. While it can be argued that SMEs are highly customer oriented, the dominating preoccupation of the entrepreneur is to maintain positive revenue and cash flows towards profit. This assertion would suggest that the lack of finance limitation is dominant within the entrepreneur's thought process. Whatever, the highly focused nature of entrepreneurs can sometimes manifest itself as being obsessively self-centred about the enterprise and its well being.

Acknowledging that the influence of the entrepreneur has a huge significance upon the character and style of SME decision making, it is not to say that such influence is detrimental to decision making effectiveness or business success. Established entrepreneurial SMEs benefit hugely from the influence of the lead entrepreneur. Whilst the limitations of SMEs may represent inherent weaknesses, the entrepreneur will counteract these weaknesses by bringing inherent strengths to the SME. These strengths are centred around the entrepreneurial network and his/her competencies for doing business. Both these phenomena are described and discussed later in this chapter.

In summary, we can say that most enterprises can be categorized as SME and that these enterprises have distinctive characteristics which differentiate them, not only from large corporations but also from most other enterprises. It is recognized that SMEs have several severe limitations represented by lack of finance, lack of expertise and lack of market impact. Within this limiting framework the influence of the entrepreneur/owner/manager is acknowledged, particularly in relation to the distinctive style and focus of decision making. In compensating for much of the limitations it is recognized that entrepreneurs will possess or develop counteractive capabilities for decision making specifically refined to exploit the opportunities best suited for an SME.

Incompatibility of marketing theory to SMEs

It is clear from the previous section that the inherent characteristics and style and influence of entrepreneurs will impact substantially, perhaps even completely upon the type and nature of marketing in SMEs. An interesting question is to ask, 'What is the type and nature of marketing in SMEs'? Simply by asking such a question suggests that somehow SME marketing may be different to marketing elsewhere. In which case how and in what way might it be different? Perhaps more fundamentally, do SMEs perform marketing according to textbook frameworks and if so, then what are the differences? Alternatively, if SMEs do not do marketing according to textbook frameworks then why not and what is the type and nature of such marketing if it does not conform to textbook frameworks?

In considering some of these issues it is perhaps useful to examine the inherent characteristics of some textbook marketing approaches. The rest of this section considers these characteristics in relation to marketing planning and market research and also by way of example, textbook issues of segmentation and niche marketing, market share and pricing.

Marketing planning

This is a much vaunted tool of good professional marketing which has many clear and precise descriptions in the textbook literature. There is no doubt that it has substantial benefits when used comprehensively. The literature is in general agreement that it is a valued tool of marketing. Consider for a moment, the inherent characteristics of marketing planning. It is fundamentally sequential in that it follows a careful and logical process from appraisal through to evaluation and analysis before devising carefully considered and alternative courses of action for implementation. It is also formal and structured in its frameworks. By its very nature it carries comprehensive time scales covering short-, medium-and long-term dimensions.

The prior debate on entrepreneurial characteristics contended that decision making is inherently simplistic and haphazard, undisciplined and spontaneous, unstructured and irrational and invariably short-term in time scales. In comparison to the inherent characteristics of marketing planning outlined above, there is a clear incompatibility between this textbook technique and the way entrepreneurial decision making is naturally performed. Indeed, it would be very unnatural, if not impossible, for an SME entrepreneur/owner/manager to plan marketing according to textbook frameworks. SMEs, because of their relative smallness and therefore their lack of market or industry dominance, must be very flexible and reactive to changes in market circumstances; a formal marketing planning procedure would inhibit such flexibility and reactiveness.

Market research

Textbook market research frameworks can be traced back to the rigour and validity requirements of social science research. Again such rigour requires formality, sequentiality, validity and correct application of one best method for research. As with the incompatibility of marketing planning, SME's inherent limitations make it virtually impossible for such enterprises to carry out market research according to textbook principles. Lack of money and expertise combined with short time scales would make it unlikely that SMEs entrepreneurs/owner/managers would do textbook market research. Instead, the inherent characteristics of the entrepreneur mean that a much more casual and natural approach to market research is done. In fact, it is unlikely even to be recognized as market research; instead it is more about 'gathering information' which may occur by any method or means. Correctness and rigour are not considerations. Intuitive judgement is the basis of evaluation.

Segmentation, niche marketing and market share

These are well recognized marketing strategy tools in the textbook literature, indeed, much of the support literature for SME development advocates that such enterprises follow these strategies. However, in practice, whilst many SMEs may in fact attempt to implement such strategies, the relative smallness of SMEs and their vulnerability to market forces means that they will often 'fall-into' market niches which previously had not been considered. Equally, whilst a market segmentation strategy may be advocated, the opportunistic nature of the entrepreneur will often take an SME outside such segments to an extent they become meaningless.

Market share is of little consequence to SMEs. The resources needed to measure market share would far outweigh any benefits, especially when the outcome is likely to be a percentage figure which is so small as to be meaningless. Even if market share is known, it is unlikely an SME can do much to increase it since it has neither the resources nor the ability to make significant impact upon the market. For most SMEs, the strive for increased revenues and the subsequent positive effect on the enterprise's well being are much more important than knowing whether or not market share has grown.

Pricing strategies

The textbook literature advocates elaborate alternatives on pricing strategies which have an implied aspect of control over the consumer's decision making perception. However, because of SMEs' relative smallness, such control is almost impossible without substantial differentiation which most firms do not enjoy. An option advocated by the textbook literature is to use price discounting as a sales stimulation, however, given the limitation of finance and the implications for adverse cash flow and the innate survival and enterprise protection instinct of the entrepreneur, this is neither an attractive or natural option.

These are just a few examples of the incompatibility of marketing theory in the context of SMEs. Of course, there are those who will argue that any marketing theory can be applied in any context, and taken in the most general sense this would be a fair argument. However, SMEs do not function at a 'general' level, they operate at the 'situation specific' level – a circumstance which is uniquely individualistic. In applying general marketing principles to a 'situation specific' SME, another well known analogy comes to mind – 'putting round pegs into square holes' with enough forced manipulation they can be made to fit, but not perfectly.

So, if marketing theory is incompatible with SME marketing characteristics, what is the alternative? A useful start point is to consider which aspects of marketing that fit closest to SME characteristics and which can be performed by entrepreneurs/owners/managers as *they* 'do business'. Thus, let us consider the nature of SME marketing.

Nature of SME marketing

In the general sense, the basic principles and concepts of marketing are as relevant to SMEs as to any other domain. However, as illustrated by the examples in the previous section, some theories, tools and techniques of marketing are not as relevant or useful to SMEs. The nature of SME marketing is that of a concept which is dominated by the inherent characteristics of the entrepreneur/owner/manager and the SME itself. Thus, the inherent limitations of SMEs and the resultant characteristics that they create, coupled with the way entrepreneurs/ owners/managers take decisions will determine, indeed dictate, the nature of SME marketing. These underlying factors are taken into account later in this chapter; at this point let us consider some other aspects of influence and consequence in relation to the nature of SME marketing.

The life cycle stage of SMEs

SMEs will perform marketing differently according to their stage of life. A start-up SME's marketing will likely be characterized, indeed dominated, by reactive marketing practices, in terms of reacting to customer enquiries and market changes. As the business develops, much of the marketing will be characterized by experimenting or tinkering with a variety of marketing techniques, for example, the creation of a brochure or a visit to an exhibition. As the enterprise becomes established over a number of years it will have developed its own marketing style and practice which it has learned and shaped along the way. The enterprise will know what works for it and what does not. It is unlikely to accommodate wider or new marketing perspectives until it encounters a significant change of some kind, for example, a new market venture. In moving through the various life cycle phases, an SME will progress from what is sometimes an uncontrollable marketing circumstance to one in which it feels that every aspect of marketing it performs is controlled. Again because of the inherent characteristics, this 'controlled' marketing is likely to be quite conservative and restricted to the tried and trusted methods refined over the years. Thus, whilst marketing activity is established, comfortable, affordable and apparently working, it is also potentially complacent, dull, unimaginative and perhaps inefficient. However, it feels safe, after the traumas probably experienced at various times in the tinkering period,

nothing too radical or different is tried; caution and conformity prevail.

Conformity with industry norms

Generally, SMEs must 'conform' to established norms in order to do business, primarily because they are small and cannot hope to 'buck' established practices. What are the established norms? Any industry or market will exist within certain customs and practices outside of which it is difficult to find acceptance. Examine any industry and these 'norms' can de identified. For example, in the way products are presented, where and to whom, the way and when they are distributed, the degree of service that is expected and provided, the price parameters, margins and mark-up that exist, the hierarchical infrastructures, the traditions and histories, the precedents and rules that exist and which must be adhered to. These established norms are so strong in most markets/ industries that they create their own distinctive characteristics which determine how business is done. The most striking illustration of these established norms comes sharply into focus in two areas. When an enterprise enters a new export market, an emphasis is placed upon understanding the culture of a region in general and the culture of doing business in particular. Of course this cultural understanding involves much more than just sociological issues, it also involves understanding of a variety of expectations and practices. A depth of understanding is required before a business can expect to successfully exploit opportunities previously identified. Another, less common area is where someone launches a new business in a market area in which they have no prior experience. Most of the initial period is taken up with finding out how to do things, who to contact and rely upon, what will please and offend, what is expected as a minimum, what levels of service, price, delivery, quality are expected and how these all interrelate.

Such industry norms will require an SME to use established and existing distribution channels, to price within certain known and expected parameters, to provide certain expected levels of quality and service, and so on. To step too far away from any of these norms will require the SME to have some significant differentiation in some aspect of its business. Such circumstances are rare in the extreme. Most SMEs can only hope to attain some marginal differentiation to exploit and because of this must conform to the industry customs and practices in presenting this differentiation. Take a few examples by way of illustration, if normal distribution channels rely on intermediaries such as trade distributors, an SME which by-passes these will meet with a variety of resistance unless it achieves differentiation. Retailers or end users will be wary of doing business for fear of upsetting the wider industry supply channels. Consider also, price/profit mark-up and margins. An SME failing to offer prices that fall within expected parameters, either positive or negative variance, will meet with query and resistance. Too low a price margin/mark-up and interest is spurned, too high margin/mark-up and suspicion and credibility doubts arise.

There are only a few circumstances where industry norms may not apply. One is where a large dominant player within a close knit market community decides to 'break-the-mould' by some act of marketing variance, others will be forced to follow. Such an option is not open to an SME unless it possesses a huge differentiation in relation to product or technological innovation, a rare circumstance in normal everyday trading, although history will record many examples. Another circumstance is where a market enters a period of dynamic change, such as technological developments or consumer attitudinal shifts. In such circumstances opportunities will exist to break and create new industry/market practices. Such dynamic change occurs only occasionally but when it does occur it is significant. For example, in the tourist industry when the advent of cheap air travel created a huge new market expansion and many new entrants, and currently in the financial services industry where

de-regulations and greater consumer awareness and spending power allow many new ways of doing business, such as 'service direct' concepts. In both of these circumstances SMEs can actually be more dynamic and effective than large established organizations who can sometimes find it difficult to break away from their long established and traditional practices.

In summarizing the nature of SME marketing, we have acknowledged the inherent influence of SME characteristics and the entrepreneur/owner/manager. In addition we have highlighted two other factors of significance, the SME stage of life cycle and the industry/market norms by which most SMEs must conform, except in an few exceptional circumstances. A model of 'situation specific' marketing serves to illustrate and integrate this discussion (see Figure 29.1).

Marketing principles, concepts and theories at the most general level can apply to SMEs as much as in any other domain. However, to actually perform marketing certain factors must be taken into account, perhaps to 'filter' and 'refine' marketing towards the unique and individualistic character of an individual SME. Some marketing theories can contribute to this process, for example, the theories and principles behind goods/services marketing or industrial/consumer marketing. Taking account of the inherent characteristics of any of these contexts will automatically guide marketing frameworks. Obvious illustrations are provided by services marketing being characterized by aspects of intangibility and industrial marketing being characterized by aspects of relationship.

In a similar way, (discussed earlier), any firm's marketing will be influenced and characterized by the nature of the industry or market it exists within. Although service firms or industrial firms may have inherent characteristics of influence dictated by the characteristics of services and industrial marketing, they will also be characterized by the nature of their industry or market. So, for example, service firms in a particular food sector will all behave in a similar fashion which is dictated by the industry/

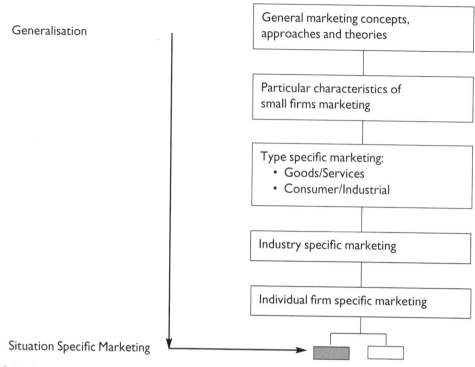

Figure 29.1   Situation specific marketing
Source: Adapted from K. J. Blois (1974) 'The Marketing of Services: An Approach', *European Journal of Marketing*, **8**, 137–149.

market customs and practices. Any variation or innovation will most probably occur within the normal expected parameters of doing business which have evolved and become established over time.

The variation and innovations are of course what makes any enterprise unique. For example, two service firms situated side by side, as is often the case with two SME restaurants, will still have differentiations which make them unique. Their names will be different and these names will conjure a difference of perception. Their interior design and atmosphere will create further differentiation. The attitude and appearance of staff will create further difference, the variety and quality of the menu clearly will also have an influence. A whole host of influences will create a specific situation which is unique to the individual firm. It is the collective combina-

tion of all these factors which forms the basis of an enterprise's marketing activity and message. Thus, while both such enterprises are influenced by the same inherent characteristics of both their marketing domain and their industry/market, the decisions of the entrepreneur/owner/manager will create a differentiation which is unique.

This issue of the influence of the entrepreneur/owner/manager upon the decision making of an SME is worthy of further consideration, in terms of how an entrepreneur can not only create differentiation but also how s/he can improve the impact and efficiency of marketing decisions and activities of the SME. Such impact and efficiency will undoubtedly build upon inherent and learned strengths that best reflect the constraints and resources of an SME.

SME marketing based on strengths

A number of approaches are described here, which both reflect and contribute to SME marketing based upon strengths. In this section the following are considered:

- adaptation of standard textbook marketing frameworks
- marketing in 'context' (situation specific marketing)
- 'alternative' SME marketing
- competency marketing
- network marketing
- scope of 'innovative' marketing

It needs to be recognized that while each of these approaches are about marketing, in practice none of these are likely to be performed as marketing. Instead, they will be performed as part of 'doing business' and taking decisions. As an illustration of this notion, consider the marketing activity of *pricing*. Decisions on pricing will probably be driven by considerations with regards to cost or cash flow, as much as any specific pricing policy. Of course, such decisions will impact upon pricing and an entrepreneur will be intuitively aware of this in the same way s/he will be aware of a price change because of competitive pressure and how this will impact upon bottom line costs and cash flows within the business. Thus, although the following descriptions focus upon marketing aspects, they must be considered in the wider context of overall business decision making as much as marketing decision making.

Adaptation of standard textbook marketing frameworks

In most SMEs marketing will be performed in some form or other. Marketing is inherently and intuitively performed in SMEs. Since most SMEs will have a *product* or *service* which they will offer at a *price* and they will *promote* this through some kind of medium that reaches their market *place*, it can be easily determined that SMEs marketing can be described under the frameworks of the 'four Ps'. Again, at the general level, this is undoubtedly true, however, in just about every circumstance an entrepreneur will 'adapt' this concept to suit the situation specific of his/her firm. Since this situation specific will be structured around the functions and activities of the firm itself, the marketing activity will be closely allied to this. Therefore, if image and personal service are important features of an enterprise's standing, these will be an integral part of its marketing mix. Often the product *is* the firm, so this too will be an integral part of its mix. Such an SME's marketing mix therefore, may be nothing more than this. Of course, many of the 4P aspects will be inherent in the SMEs activities, for example, communication and delivery will be inherent aspects of image and personal service. Clearly, the concept of the '4Ps' will be adapted to suit the SME. An entrepreneur may find it sufficient to describe a marketing mix as product, image and personal service.

For an SME practitioner to accept a concept such as the '4P's' it must have relevance, therefore, if a simple '4Ps' description is not relevant to an entrepreneur it will not be used. There is a significant point here, that is, marketing activities in SMEs will always by pragmatic, practical and relevant to the individual SME; anything which does not meet these conditions is academically theoretical and of little value.

An illustration of 'pragmatic, practical and relevant' adaptation is provided by the marketing planning process. This was highlighted earlier as being of little relevance to SMEs because of its logical foundations which are incompatible with the inherent characteristics of SMEs and entrepreneurial decision making practices. However, some aspects of the marketing planning process may be performed in a pragmatic, practical and relevant sense. Take as a point in example, the notion of market feasibility analysis incorporating external and internal analysis over a wide range of issues. The textbook descriptions of this aspect of the process will outline a comprehensive list of aspects for consideration in a 'complete' market analysis, thus external issues may be outlined as covering market environment; marketing information; market knowledge; market segmentation; market opportunities; competition, and so on. Similarly, internal issues may be outlined as covering internal environment; marketing variables; marketing organization; marketing systems; marketing strategies and plans, and so on. The entrepreneurial adaptation of this is simply an intuitive consideration of those issues concerned with all/any aspect outside of the firm's influence and control (external) and those issues that are within the firm's control (internal). This is the market feasibility analysis process in practice, but it will bear no relationship, either conceptually or descriptively, with any textbook description.

Thus, SMEs will pragmatically adapt any marketing theory to make it relevant to the way they do business. Whether this looks like or meets the criteria of good textbook marketing has no consideration with an entrepreneur, it is the intuitive performance in practice which is the prime consideration.

Marketing in 'context'

It has been argued above that in practice any marketing in SMEs is intuitively performed and that this marketing practice will be set in the situation specific of the firm (Figure 29.1). Some indication of how this marketing is determined is given in relation to incorporating a number of factors of influence which must be taken into account when determining what or how to do marketing in SMEs. Some mention was made to the 'context' of marketing and how certain marketing characteristics will impact upon the type and style of marketing that will be carried out by an SME. Taking this logic a little further it is possible to construct a 'marketing in context picture' for

any SME by taking account of a number of factors of significance.

While marketing activity and environment can be and are complex, it is still possible to identify the essential key factors which determine and dictate the type and style of marketing that can and should be performed. Firstly, consider the key marketing characteristics that stem from the relevant domains of marketing. There may be many but they are easily clustered within a common grouping, for example, services marketing will generate its own list of services characteristics which belong in some form or other to any services context. Similar lists of characteristics can be generated for any domain of marketing. Any student or practitioner of marketing will be able to generate such lists of characteristics simply by thinking of the definitional context of the groupings. So as for services, consumer marketing has distinctive characteristics; similarly industrial marketing; and so on. Of course, since we are concerned with SME marketing, then the inherent characteristics of SMEs can be generated. In most marketing in context situations there will be two or three key groupings of characteristics which impact upon the marketing activity performed. Not all characteristics will impact upon the marketing in the same way or with the same degree of influence. Neither should the groupings be considered in isolation, in fact it is how they interact together that determines the significance of influence. By visually overlapping the identified groupings it is possible to determine with some degree of accuracy the *common* characteristics and their linkages between groupings and to evaluate the *most significant*; these therefore, represent the inherent *features* and *factors* of influence. Figure 29.2 offers a simple illustration of this process. Each circle may represent known characteristics belonging to a given domain of marketing. By considering a number of these domains of marketing together, rather than in isolation, it is possible to arrive at those characteristics which are common and which therefore, are most significant in a given marketing context.

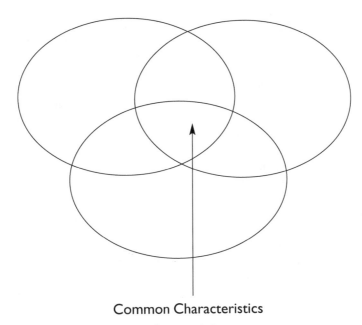

Common Characteristics

Figure 29.2   Marketing in context – common characteristics

This process will allow an assessment of 'key marketing issues' which belong to any firm in a given context. These key marketing issues are those aspects of marketing which any firm in a given context will simply have to perform; it cannot ignore these if it is to do business. How well it performs these key marketing issues will determine how successful it is.

This process is applied to an example of an SME hotel in tourism marketing. The inherent characteristics of tourism marketing are that it is a service and that it has a predominately consumer-based marketing orientation. Issues of domestic or international may or may not have significance. Of greater significance is the SME dimension. Thus an illustration of marketing in this context would be something like Figure 29.3.

Common characteristics are easy to identify. Service marketing characteristics of intangibility and service delivery are closely related to SME characteristics of personal/unique service and lack of resources for any tangible and impersonal service. Similarly, consumer

marketing characteristics of retail location and communication are uniquely influenced by SME characteristics and limitations. Thus, the key marketing issues which arise out of these and other common characteristics are image/reputation; personal service; and location/communication. The intuitive logic for these three key marketing issues is as follows:

- *Image/reputation* – That any SME hotel will seek to emphasize its smallness as differentiation from large corporate chains. It will build competitive advantage by establishing a reputation for 'homeliness', 'family orientation', 'friendliness', 'intimacy', etc. The reputation will serve to 'promote' the SME by word of mouth communication and publicity.
- *Personal service* – Further enhancement of the image and reputation will come from attention to providing a personal service which is focused upon individual customers needs. Strong emphasis will be given to developing 'regular' customers who are known by name.
- *Location/communication* – This is emphasized because an SME hotel will need to draw on

the marketing aspects of its local environment and infrastructure and it will use appropriate literature to communicate this. It cannot hope to promote this message itself to a wider market, instead it will rely upon the local tourist industry to do this.

Of course, there will undoubtedly be other aspects of marketing that an SME hotel may wish to engage, however, it simply cannot ignore these key marketing issues. These key marketing issues are almost imposed upon the context because of the underlying inherent characteristics. An SME hotel may want to do mass media communication to reflect mass consumer marketing, but it simply cannot hope to do such even if the outcomes were desirable or controllable. It will of course employ a variety of industry marketing activities as part

of its ongoing revenue generation. For example, functions and events built around themes of interest to its local community as well as the transient market.

Thus, the message from 'marketing in context' is that because of certain inherent characteristics which will impact upon an SME in its given context, it cannot ignore these and indeed, they will determine and perhaps dictate the type and style of marketing that an SME can perform.

Competency marketing

Competency marketing is a term which means using inherent and learned skills (competencies) to do marketing. To do marketing means anything which impacts upon, or which influences marketing, as well as actually performing

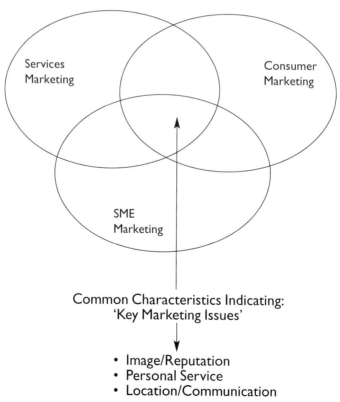

Figure 29.3   Marketing in context – SME hotel marketing

marketing activity. This is in recognition that marketing decisions are often inseparable from any other decisions in an SME. Many entrepreneurs/owners/managers will perceive themselves to have limited marketing ability, primarily because their prior interests and background mean that they are unlikely to bring meaningful marketing experience and skills to a business. Many will bring a 'technical' competency to the enterprise. Many will learn new competencies as the business develops. Primary amongst these learned competencies is that of 'doing business', which is the manifestation of a range of competencies coming together as contributors to decision making. Again, much has been written about management and decision making competencies; as many as several hundred have been identified (Mintzberg, 1973; Boyatzis, 1982; Koontz *et al.*, 1984; Kotter, 1990; Tichy and Charan, 1991).

Obviously, since marketing is derived from management, many of the known management competencies could be relevant to marketing in some way. Consideration of what the marketing job entails will group marketing into two categories, those competencies which are analytical and those which are creative. However, in once again taking account of the hugely strong influential characteristics of SMEs and entrepreneurs/owner/managers, such competency groupings need to be adapted and refined to suit these inherent characteristics. Taking account also of the interactive relatedness of SME decision making it is important that competency marketing in SMEs is compatible with this dimension.

Most entrepreneurs will learn their marketing skills by experience and practice. However, it is not uncommon to hear entrepreneurs describe marketing as 'just common sense', or 'I don't know anything about marketing' whilst demonstrably performing marketing activity. Indeed, entrepreneurial characteristics/competencies/skills can be closely aligned to marketing characteristics, for example, both have characteristics of *vision* and *creativity*; *communication* is inherent to both; *adaptability* and *flexibility* also; *opportunism* is another common competency factor. On this latter factor entrepreneurs will often perceive themselves to be opportunistic to the point of enthusiasm; recently for example, an entrepreneur, in responding to the notion of problems experienced stated, 'I don't see problems, I see opportunities'.

Taking cognisance of the above dimensions and focusing upon the one most significant core competency concept for SMEs it is that of *experiential knowledge*. This contains four significant marketing competencies which are entirely compatible with the entrepreneurial way of doing business. One competency component is knowledge itself; such knowledge will cover a range of aspects, particularly about how to do business and what is needed to do it successfully. Knowledge is a significant competency, in a variety of ways; it can relate to technical expertise, business acumen, including knowledge of the market environment, etc. A second competency component is experience derived from accumulated knowledge of doing business and which is evolved and developed by accumulation of experience over time, learning from successes and failures. It is obvious how these two competency components are integral to experiential knowledge; however, there are two further competency components which contribute significantly to experiential knowledge, one is communication competency which reflects both the marketing and entrepreneurial focus of SME decision making. Communication competency is a reflection of an ability to communicate to and with all interactive parties. It is a competency which can be improved through the development of knowledge and experience competencies. A final competency, the level of which is clearly derived from the accumulation of the others, is that of judgement ability which clearly impacts upon the quality and timing of decision making.

From a marketing in SME perspective, these four competencies can be considered together, because of their clear interaction and inter-connection. Thus, we can describe marketing competency in SMEs to be that of experiential knowledge, that is, knowledge acquired through experience and developed as an accumulation of knowledge and experience built upon and from communication and judgement. Such experiential knowledge represents a powerful SME marketing tool that can significantly compensate for the inherent SME limitations, particularly with regards to marketing activity.

Experiential knowledge is something which every entrepreneur/owner/manager will acquire over time. It will develop intuitively as the enterprise becomes established and customs and practices emerge and evolve. The point here is that it will develop naturally, the question though is whether the level and quality of experiential knowledge is of the best possible or whether it is just mediocre. For an entrepreneur/owner/manager who can utilize experiential knowledge proactively and in an accelerated way, by concentrating on developing experiential knowledge and therefore competency marketing, this will substantially strengthen his/hers and the SME's marketing effectiveness.

Network marketing

Networks and networking have been debated for sometime in the literature (Aldrich and Zimmer, 1986; Johannisson, 1986; Andersson and Soderlund, 1988; Dubini and Aldrich, 1991; Anderson *et al.*, 1994; Hansen, 1995). Much of the discussion has been focused on identifying specific types of networks and how they are used and why they exist. Fundamental definitions of networks include personal contact networks (PCNs); social networks; trade and business networks. Such networks can exist in isolation or more often they will be interactive and overlapping. The type of network or variety of networks is not a concern here. Neither is it important to precisely define the concept of networks other than a description which acknowledges that 'a network is a

collection of individuals who may be known or not known to each other and who, in some way contribute something to the entrepreneur/ owner/manager, either passively, reactively or proactively, whether specifically elicited or not'.

What is the value of networks and networking to SMEs? Networking is both a natural and an acquired skill or competency of the entrepreneur. Entrepreneurs may not be aware that they have a 'network' as such, since the way they perform networking is a process which is haphazard, disjointed, spontaneous and opportunistic, and consists of one-to-one interactions with a few or a variety of individuals. Sometimes entrepreneurs will consciously seek out information from certain individuals believed to have a contribution to make, on other occasions information will be gleaned sub-consciously as part of naturally doing business or as part of an informal conversation. Networking can be both proactive and passive depending upon the issue at hand. Indeed, on the same issue it can be proactive with some individuals in the network and passive with others. Similarly, it can be both overt and covert depending on the closeness or otherwise of individuals to the entrepreneur. Timescales within networking can vary enormously, some individuals may be networked continuously and frequently, whilst others may only be contacted infrequently and occasionally. Sometimes, the entrepreneur will have a clear issue in mind and will raise this issue with individuals in a way which is deemed to be appropriate for that individual to respond with meaningful feedback. On other occasions, knowledge or information will be acquired as part of other apparently unrelated conversation or observation. Some individuals may receive a flurry of contact at a particular time and then find that no contact is made for some time before contact is re-established. It is unlikely that any one aspect of networking will lead to decisive decision making by the SME entrepreneur, instead networking will represent an array of assessments which all contribute towards a final decision. The point here is that normally, entrepreneurial networking has no fixed or standard mechanism in operation, there is seldom an agenda or objective because there is no demonstrative 'process' in operation. Networking can be likened to a cloud; when observed it can be seen but it is difficult to make tangible contact with all its dimensions. It will appear to be in constant flux but at the same time it is always recognizable.

Similar to the importance of competency development for SMEs, networks and networking are hugely important to SMEs. Indeed, it might be argued that SMEs would find it extremely difficult to become established without networking and that networking is an integral part of the continued existence and survival. It is safe to say that entrepreneurs/owners/managers in SMEs intuitively build a network of contacts around themselves that serve a multiplicity of purposes. Indeed, one might go further and argue that networking is an inherent and significant characteristic of entrepreneurship. The fact is that where there are entrepreneurs there are networks.

Networking is very useful to SME entrepreneurs/owners/managers, mainly because it is integral to doing business, it does not have to be constructed and contrived, it is not a task to be completed, it is simply part of everyday business activity and therefore happens anyway. All entrepreneurs do networking in some form or other; indeed, like in any aspect of life, some will be better at networking than others. Whatever, because networking is such an intuitively natural dimension of entrepreneurial SME activity, it represents a significant strength for marketing purposes. Since SMEs are invariably 'close' to their customers, aspects of marketing such as relationship and communication are important. Networking is precisely the mechanism by which SMEs can meaningfully achieve such aspects of marketing and in a way that is compatible with their resource constraints.

Accepting that networking happens intuitively and naturally, is it possible to 'improve'

networking competency? Here lies a key, networking is indeed a competency skill and therefore it can certainly be developed and improved. Similar to the notion of accumulation of experiential knowledge through a conscious accelerated development, networking competency can be accelerated by a consciously proactive approach. Such an approach simply requires an entrepreneur to address an issue or problem of marketing around a two-part construct. First, loosely define the issue or problem, then make a list of people who might offer an opinion on the issue. These people are likely to be regular contacts of the entrepreneur, although with a little concentration some lesser contacts may emerge. The entrepreneur is now in a position to trawl his/her newly defined network. Nothing much has changed except that the trawling process may accelerate because it has been consciously defined and the trawl is now proactive and not simply naturally occurring. The entrepreneur will intuitively know what information is good, through the dimension of experiential knowledge, and will be able to make a judgemental assessment of the issue and a decision on how to address it.

Indeed, the two dimensions of networking and competencies together can represent the core essence of SME marketing which impacts upon the nature, type and style of SME marketing activity. These dimensions represent significant strengths which can be utilized effectively for successful SME marketing.

The importance of these strengths can be seen when the SME business environment is considered. The vast majority of SMEs operate in two main sectors in any economy. Many operate in a 'business-to-business' environment whereby they deal with other business, both large and small. The essence of such business relates closely to the SME strengths discussed above, in that it allows SMEs to utilize networking amongst a relatively close-knit and familiar environment and to exploit experiential knowledge of an industry or market. A second major area for SMEs is that of services, both consumer and industrial services. This area allows SMEs to exploit the well recognized 'closeness' to the customer and consequent customer orientation of SMEs. Of course, taken in the broadest sense, these two areas or sectors can represent all sectors of enterprise and since most sectors are populated by a majority of SMEs in terms of numbers of businesses, then this can be deemed to be true.

Clearly, the dimension of network marketing is inexplicably linked with competency marketing and both will be set within the domain of marketing in context and all of this will result in some form of adaptation of marketing tools and techniques to suit the unique characteristics of SMEs. One further piece of the 'jigsaw' of SME marketing remains to be set in place.

Innovative marketing

Like much of the emphasis in textbook marketing literature, which is essentially inappropriate for SMEs because they are concerned with 'how to do' more than 'how to construct', the literature on innovation is often inappropriate or of marginal value. A large portion of entrepreneurial and SME literature is devoted to innovation in recognition that a distinctive characteristic of SMEs is creativity and innovation. The problem is that the vast majority of literature on innovation is focused on 'product innovation' on the assumption that this is where most SMEs are innovative. It may be true to say that SMEs display a high degree of product innovation since many new SME enterprises will be founded upon a new and innovative product or service, and such innovations are easily identified as fact. However, in most cases, the vast majority of SMEs develop products which are only marginally differentiated from others and much of the product innovation is in response or reaction to customer demand. Fair enough, SMEs' entrepreneurial flexibility will meet the demands of

customers and the outcomes can be construed as product innovation.

Whether the above reasoning is accepted or not, it is contented here that innovative marketing in SMEs is much wider than simple product innovation, indeed, much research in the area recognizes this wider spectrum (UIC/AMA Marketing/Entrepreneurship Interface Symposium Proceedings, 1987–1997). Of course, many writers have already acknowledged this but much of their insight has been lost behind the higher profile of product innovation in SMEs. Innovative marketing covers the full spectrum of marketing related activity in an SME. The concepts addressed above, networking, adaptation, etc., are clear demonstrations of innovative marketing. It is useful to reflect on why these concepts and indeed innovative marketing exists within SMEs. It can be deemed to stem from the immensely strong and influential inherent characteristics of SMEs and entrepreneurs/owners/managers. It is also useful to acknowledge that as a result of this influence, the focus of perception or need is to '*do things*' that achieve results which serve the survival and development objectives of an enterprise. Therefore innovative marketing is profoundly pragmatic in achieving objectives. Some manifestations of innovative marketing are:

- aspects of added value which are designed to enhance the product or service;
- personal selling which is built around an intuitive assessment of the personality of the customer/buyer, including adapting to the mood of the buyer;
- distribution, delivery and customer service, which are largely reactive to requirements.

The point to emphasize here is that innovative marketing is not simply focused on product innovation, instead it covers the whole spectrum of marketing activity within an SME; consequently, there is likely to be more innovation in other aspects of marketing activity than there will be around the product or service.

Conclusion: a model of SME marketing

This chapter has been framed around a pragmatic model of SME marketing. This model is illustrated in Figure 29.4. It incorporates the dimensions of adaptation of marketing techniques, competency marketing, networking marketing, and innovative marketing. These approaches are centred around the notion that all SME marketing is done in a unique context and that cognisance of this context must be carefully taken into account.

The unique context of SME marketing is built upon recognition of the huge influence of the inherent characteristics of SMEs, particularly the limitations of resources, and the inherent characteristics of the entrepreneur/owner/manager upon marketing and related decision making.

This model is not intended as an alternative theory of marketing which inherently rejects other established theories trusted and recognized by the marketing establishment. Instead, it should be viewed as a model of marketing 'application' in SMEs. The model requires students of marketing to adopt an 'experienced', 'real-world' perspective of marketing. It represents 'how-to-do-marketing' rather than 'what-marketing-is', and as such is highly compatible with SME entrepreneurs/owners/managers' way of thinking, indeed, way of 'doing business'.

Such a model construct will be in a constant state of flux. It will change shape and emphasis according to the requirements of the market environment, and the aims and desires of the entrepreneur/owner/manager and the SME. Whatever, can we speculate about how marketing for SMEs will look in the future?

It is easy to ride the bandwagon of technological change and development, especially since such developments are happening with increasing rapidity and increasingly impacting upon SMEs way of doing business and marketing. Is this technological development a threat or opportunity to SMEs and to what extent will

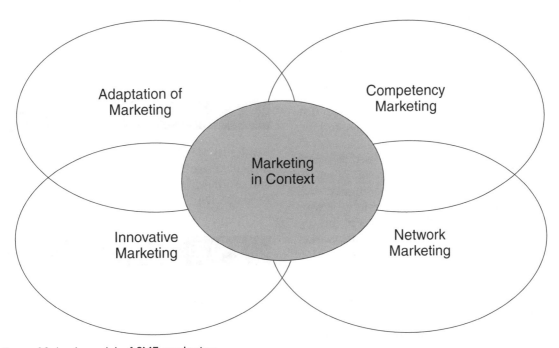

Figure 29.4   A model of SME marketing

it impact upon Marketing for SMEs? The true answer lies somewhere in the future, however, we can accept that technological development *will* impact upon Marketing for SMEs, but in what way and how?

Much is currently written about the World Wide Web, the Internet and E-Marketing, etc. Undoubtedly, such phenomena are being absorbed into SME Marketing. To date though and probably for several years hence, it does not dominate marketing activity in *most* SMEs as much as champions of the WWW would have us believe. Certainly, many SMEs have incorporated the 'Internet', but in what capacity? Most SMEs using the Internet do so as an additional means of communication and information source, both from the market environment and to their customers and potential customers.

Many advocates of the Internet argue that it will replace existing practices. Perhaps, but most unlikely. How can we make such an assertion? Examine for a moment the inherent and fundamental characteristics and components of marketing and SMEs entrepreneurs/owners/managers. Fundamental to marketing are people, either as the recipient of communication or as provider of communication. Similarly, inherent and fundamental to an SME is the decision making of a single 'person', the entrepreneur/owner/manager. This individual has built and accumulated experience over time by dealing with people of importance to him/her.

The point of this reflection is that people *need* to interact in some form or other. Of course, whilst interactions can be singular most people prefer to interact in a variety of ways rather than one way only. If we accept this and the above argument, then future SME marketing will still be people centred, but will of course embrace new technologies in whatever form they develop into the future. Future SME Marketing will need to compatibly combine the personal contact dimension inherent in the model construct presented above and the future technology, whether WEB based or other

new electronic and technological forms of communication.

New *technology* in whatever form it develops will increasingly influence marketing infrastructures and performance to the point of being fully integral to marketing per se. As technology develops so too in tandem will marketing competency and skill, based on a foundation of knowledge and expertise. However, regardless of the nature and influence of technology, there will remain one overriding factor of main influence over any perspective of marketing, that is, the dimension that we are all *Human Beings*. As *Human Beings* we will continue to need to interact with each other in a variety of forms, but most importantly as individuals and personally. As *Human Beings* we will maintain all of our senses and use these together in our interactions. We need to *see* each other, to *smell* each other, to *touch* each other, to *hear* each other. Technology may find ways to provide some semblance of these senses but will always be a poorer substitute for the real thing. It is argued that *personal human interaction* will prevail over and beyond any technological developments in the foreseeable future. This personal interaction, inherent in the model, is the essence of marketing for Small-to-Medium Enterprises.

Acknowledgements

Reader in Marketing, Dr Audrey Gilmore, and former research assistants, Darryl Cummins and Aodheen O'Donnell, the SME Marketing Research Unit, University of Ulster.

References

Aldrich, H. and Zimmer, C. (1986) Entrepreneurship Through Social Networks, in D. Sexton and R. W. Smilor (eds) *Art and Science of Entrepreneurship*, Ballinger Publishing Company, pp. 3–23.

Anderson, J. C., Hakansson, H. and Johanson, J. (1994) Dyadic Business Relationships Within a Business Network Context, *Journal of Marketing*, **58**(4), 1–15.

Andersson, P. and Soderlund, M. (1988) The Network Approach to Marketing, *Irish Marketing Review*, **3**, 63–68.

Blois, K. J. (1974) The Marketing of Services: An Approach, *European Journal of Marketing*, **8**, 137–149.

Boyatzis, R. E. (1982) *The Competent Manager: A Model for Effective Performance*, John Wiley & Sons, New York, NY.

Carson, D., Cromie, S., McGowan, P. and Hill, J. (1995) *Marketing and Entrepreneurship in SMEs: An Innovative Approach*, Prentice-Hall, UK.

Dubini, P. and Aldrich, H. (1991) Personal and Extended Networks are Central to the Entrepreneurial Process, *Journal of Business Venturing*, **6**, 305–313.

Hansen, E. L. (1995) Entrepreneurial Networks and New Organization Growth, *Entrepreneurial Theory and Practice*, **19**(4), 7–20.

Hofer, C. W. and Bygrave, W. D. (1992) Researching Entrepreneurship, *Entrepreneurial Theory and Practice*, Spring, 91–100.

Johannisson, B. (1986) Network Strategies: Management Technology for Entrepreneurship and Change, *International Small Business Journal*, **5**, 19–30.

Koontz, H., O'Donnell, C. and Weinrich, H. (1984) *Management*, McGraw-Hill, New York, NY.

Kotter, J. P. (1990) What Leaders Really Do? *Harvard Business Review*, May/June.

Meredith, G. G., Nelson, R. E. and Neck, P. A. (1982) *The Practice of Entrepreneurship*, International Labour Office, Geneva.

Mintzberg, H. (1973) *The Nature of Managerial Work*, Harper and Row, New York, NY.

Tichy, N. and Charan, R. (1991) Speed, Simplicity and Self-confidence: An Interview with Jack Welsh, *Harvard Business Review Classic*

from Managers as Leaders, Harvard Business School Press, Boston.

Timmons, J. A. (1978) Characteristics and Role Demands of Entrepreneurship, *American Journal of Small Business*, **3**, 5–17.

UIC/AMA *Marketing/Entrepreneurship Interface Symposium Proceedings 1987–2000*, available from University of Illinois at Chicago, Department of Entrepreneurship Studies.

Further reading

The following is useful further reading which covers the broad basis of the issues discussed in this chapter.

Carson, D., Cromie, S. McGowan, P. and Hill, J. (1995) *Marketing and Entrepreneurship in SMEs: An Innovative Approach*, Prentice-Hall, UK.

Chaston, I. (2000) *Entrepreneurial Marketing: Competing by Challenging Convention*, Palgrave Macmillan, Basingstoke.

Hisrich, R. D. and Peters, M. P. (1995) *Entrepreneurship: Starting, Developing and Managing a New Enterprise*, 3rd edn, Irwin, Holmewood, Ill.

Levinson, J. C. (1984) *Guerrilla Marketing: Secrets for Making Big Profits from your Small Business*, Houghton Mifflin, Boston.

Lodish, L. M., Morgan, H. L. and Kallianpur, A. (2001), *Entrepreneurial Marketing*, John Wiley, New York.

Prushan, V. H. (1997) *No-Nonsense Marketing: 101 Practical Ways to Win and Keep Customers*, Wiley and Sons, USA.

Smith, J. (1996) *Guide to Integrated Marketing*, Entrepreneur Magazine Series, Wiley and Sons, USA.

UIC/AMA *Marketing/Entrepreneurship Interface Symposium Proceedings 1987–2000*, available from the University of Illinois at Chicago, Department of Entrepreneurship Studies.

CHAPTER 30

Retailing

PETER J. McGOLDRICK

Introduction

Originally defined as 'the sale of goods in small quantities', a better working definition of retailing is:

> the sale of goods and services to consumers for their own use.

This distinguishes retailing from the supply of goods, in quantities large or small, to industrial buyers. It also recognizes the adoption of retailing terms and concepts by a wide range of services providers. For example, banks and other financial services providers use the term 'retail' to differentiate their consumer and their corporate activities (McGoldrick and Greenland, 1994). As the marketing of services is considered elsewhere, the focus of this chapter is upon the sale of goods to consumers.

There is nothing very new about the basic principles of retailing. It is still all about the identification and satisfaction of consumer needs and wants, at a profit. What has developed quite dramatically in recent years is the way in which retailers pursue these basic principles. Progressively, the folklore and rules of thumb that guided many decisions have been replaced by rigorous analysis and scientific modelling. While creativity and flair are still important, it is fair to say that the science of retailing has now been born.

In part, this new sophistication in retailing can be ascribed to the growth in size and power of major retailers. Much of the 'received wisdom' on marketing, imported from the United States, still tends to relegate the role of the retailer to that of a channel of distribution for manufacturers' goods. This is a dangerously myopic view, in a world in which it is equally appropriate to view manufacturers as channels of supply for powerful retailers. As retailers extend this power across national frontiers, they are joining the ranks of oil companies, car makers and computer manufacturers as the world's largest companies.

With this size comes the ability to invest in the best equipment, the latest techniques and, most importantly, the most able management. This is reflected by the increased interest in retailing courses and careers amongst our best undergraduate and graduate students. Retailing has indeed come of age as a worthwhile area of study and as a rewarding and highly professional area of management.

This brief tour of retailing considers first how retailing has evolved, and some of the theories that attempt to explain retail change. Attention then turns to the structure of retailing, examining first the different types of retail organization, then the various types of outlet.

Retail strategy is then considered briefly, stressing the importance of customer focus. The specific functions of retailing are then examined, representing an extended 'retail marketing mix'. Given the emphasis in recent years upon retail internationalization, additional attention is given to that element of retail strategy. The chapter concludes by looking at non-store retailing, notably the progress and prospects of e-tailing.

Evolution of retailing

The growth of power

Retailing has always been a major component of economic activity. In Great Britian, over £200 billion in consumer spending passes through retailers, some 35.6 per cent of all expenditure, and the sector employs 2.5 million people, 10.5 per cent of all employees (Nielsen, 2001; National Statistics, 2001). In the European Union as a whole, over 14 million are employed in retail, around 20 million in the United States (Euromonitor, 2000). Such expressions of scale cannot alone capture the major changes that have taken place, as retailing has switched from a more passive to a highly proactive role within the overall marketing process.

Many of the revered concepts of marketing, including the marketing mix, originated in a period when the manufacturer was truly 'king'. Post-war product shortages focused attention upon production, which gave way to an emphasis upon branding as shortages diminished. Inevitably, retailing tended to be depicted as just part of the marketing channels, largely controlled by manufacturers. Recent decades have seen retailers grow in size and sophistication, often exceeding that of their largest suppliers.

Figure 30.1 depicts in outline the growth cycle of powerful retailers. Growth enhances buying power and helps in the achievement of other economies of scale. The improved margins thus gained may be used to achieve further

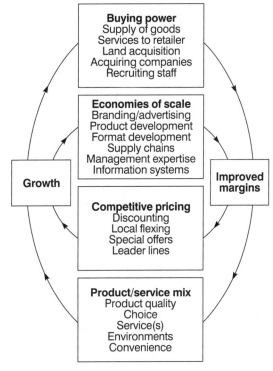

Figure 30.1 The retail growth cycle

growth, through competitive pricing and/or a product–service mix which offers superior value to customers. As the growth cycle continues, major retailers have invested in better management and superior information systems. Their power has been increased further by the development of retailer brands, extensive advertising and sophisticated trading environments.

Many large retailers have subsumed the roles traditionally ascribed to wholesalers, increasing further their dominance of the marketing channel. It is now equally appropriate to present a view of consumer goods marketing that is retailer driven (McGoldrick, 2002). Within this alternative view, manufacturers may be depicted as part of the 'channels of supply', with only limited power to influence the marketing strategies of major retailers. Large-scale retailers have truly evolved from shopkeeping to strategic marketing.

Theories of retail change

Given the dynamic nature of retailing, several theories have developed to explain aspects of evolution and change. Two of the most influential are the 'wheel of retailing' and the 'retail life cycle'. These and other theories of retail change are discussed in detail by Brown (1987).

The wheel of retailing suggests that new types of retailers tend to enter as low-price, low-margin, low-status operators. Over time, they acquire more elaborate facilities, incur higher operating costs and cease to be as price competitive. Eventually, they mature as higher-cost, higher-price retailers, vulnerable to newer types who enter at the first phase of 'the wheel'. Many examples can be found of retail types and individual companies that have evolved in this way, including department stores and supermarkets. The process has been ascribed to various influences, including a shift away from the aggressive management style of the founders, the attraction of the up-market segments, a preference amongst leading retailers for non-price forms of competition, and possible 'misguidance' by suppliers of elaborate equipment and fitments. It is also possible that the boom–recession cycles within most advanced economies contribute to the process, encouraging trading-up during the boom years and encouraging new forms of price competition during recessions.

The retail life cycle concept derives from the better known product life cycle. Retail institutions and formats appear to be moving from innovation to maturity with increasing speed. Davidson *et al.* (1976) estimated that the city centre department store took some 80 years to mature, whereas the home improvement centre in the USA took only 15 years. More recently, Burns *et al.* (1997) observed retail concepts that had peaked after just eight years. Figure 30.2 illustrates the four phases of the life cycle, with examples of formats generally regarded as being at each stage. Clearly, there are many exceptions to these generalizations, as well as international differences (Eurostat, 1997).

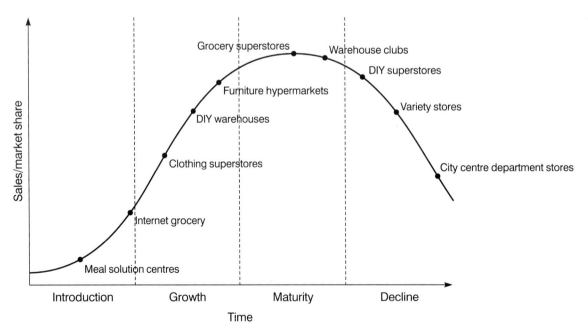

Figure 30.2   The retail life cycle

Types of retail organization

The growth of retailer power and influence has stemmed largely from the concentration of trade into the hands of fewer, larger enterprises. This section looks first at this process of concentration, involving the shift of trade from independent to multiple retailers. Consideration is then given to symbol retailing, franchises and co-operatives.

Independents and multiples

The term 'multiple' signifies more than one outlet, but different data sources use different definitions, e.g. at least two, five or 10 outlets. In Great Britain, nearly 70 per cent of retail trade is accounted for by multiples with 10 or more outlets. The concentration of trade is especially marked in the grocery sector, where the multiples' share grew from 20 to 84 per cent between 1950 and 2000 (Nielsen, 2001). Table 30.1 estimates the shares held by the top three multiples in six retail sectors, showing the power of leading players in grocery, electricals and DIY.

Retail concentration levels differ markedly between countries, as Table 30.2 illustrates, and the UK is by no means unique in experiencing the growth of retail power. In Australia, Coles Myer and Woolworth hold 19.0 and 15.5 per cent respectively of retail trade. In New Zealand, the Foodstuffs Group and Progressive Enterprises hold respective shares of 19.1 and 10.7 per cent (Euromonitor, 2000). The Canadian and US retail sectors have also seen rapid growth of chain store shares (Management Horizons, 2000). In Eastern Europe, concentration is increasing rapidly: in the Czech Republic, all of the top five retailers, which include Tesco, are international.

Voluntary groups

One response of independent retailers and wholesalers to the growth of the multiples has been the formation of 'voluntary', 'symbol' or 'affiliation' groups. Within this form of contractual chain, a group name is utilized and the retailers are normally required to buy a given proportion of their merchandise through the group. The organization typically provides buying and other marketing services, including special promotions, advertising and frequently own brands. The group is therefore able to achieve some of the buying power and economies of scale characteristic of major multiples.

Table 30.3 gives examples of voluntary groups in four sectors. The original Spar group was founded in the Netherlands in the 1930s, emulating voluntary group practices then observed in the USA. It has grown to become a

Table 30.1   Share held by top three multiples

Sector	Leading retailers	Share %
Womenswear	Marks & Spencer, Arcadia, Next	29.5
Menswear	Marks & Spencer, Arcadia, Next	23.9
Grocery	Tesco, Sainsbury, Asda	36.3
Furniture	MFI, GUS/Argos, IKEA	16.6
Electricals	Dixon Group, Comet, Argos	40.1
DIY	B&Q, Focus, Homebase	73.7

Data are based on IGD and Verdict Research estimates.

Table 30.2 Concentration of retail trade

Country	Per cent trade by top		Country	Per cent trade by top	
	Five	*Ten*		*Five*	*Ten*
Australia	43.1	49.3	Indonesia	4.7	6.4
Argentina	9.0	11.9	Japan	5.1	7.6
Belgium	24.2	28.8	Ireland	36.2	46.7
Brazil	8.5	11.8	Italy	10.0	15.7
Canada	23.9	38.3	Malaysia	8.2	11.8
Czech Rep.	8.1	10.7	Mexico	13.5	16.4
China	0.4	0.8	Netherlands	63.5	77.5
Denmark	31.1	36.7	New Zealand	45.0	53.4
Finland	43.2	49.8	Portugal	24.3	26.5
France	28.4	41.6	Spain	18.9	27.4
Germany	25.9	34.8	Sweden	51.0	63.5
Greece	9.4	13.2	Switzerland	35.2	40.2
Hungary	19.2	26.7	United Kingdom	23.5	33.3
India	0.6	0.8	United States	17.2	25.0

Source: Euromonitor (2000).

Table 30.3 Examples of voluntary (symbol) groups

Sector	Group	Outlets
Grocery	Spar Convenience Stores	2800
	Happy Shopper	2000
	Londis	1800
Chemists	Vantage	1500
	Newmark	1385
Florists	Interflora	2400
Electrical	Euronics	1500

Data are based on Nielsen's (2001) estimates.

truly international brand, being represented across five contintents, with 19 000 stores in 28 countries. Spar is the largest of the UK symbol groups, but the Nisa/Today buying group actually serves more outlets, 3500 in all. Although some carry the 'Nisa' name, scope to become a fully branded store group is limited, as Nisa buys for other groups and small multiples, including Booths, Jacksons and Londis.

Franchises

Franchising, in various forms, has a long history both in Europe and the USA. Only from the 1980s, however, has it emerged as a major element of retail structure in the UK. The number of franchised units grew from around 2600 in 1980 to 38 000 in 1998 (Key Note, 2000a). France has proved especially conducive to franchised retailing, with 40 per cent of Europe's franchised businesses. By 1998, in the USA, there were around half a million franchised businesses, capturing between one-third and two-thirds of sales in many retail and service sectors. Franchising can take many different forms, notably the following:

1 The manufacturer–retailer franchise, common in the sale of cars and petrol.
2 The manufacturer–wholesaler franchise, e.g. franchises to bottle Coca-Cola or Pepsi-Cola.
3 The wholesaler–retailer franchise, which includes some voluntary groups, discussed above.
4 The business format franchise, typical in fast food or car hire.

The benefits of franchising can flow from achieving the best of both worlds in business, combining the power, sophistication and reputation of a large organization with the energy, motivation and commitment of the independent owner-manager. For well-conceived and well-managed business formats, franchising has proved to be a powerful vehicle for expansion, as in the cases of Body Shop, Benetton and Seven-Eleven Japan (Sparks, in McGoldrick, 1994).

Co-operative societies

There is essentially one co-operative movement in the UK, but its retail activities have been fragmented into a large number of relatively autonomous societies. This fragmentation has been a major reason for the decline in the share of retail trade held by the co-operatives, in spite of the potential for buying power and economies of scale within the movement as a whole. The Co-op share of UK grocery sales fell from 15 per cent in 1970 to 4.5 per cent by 1998 (Euromonitor, 2000). In 2000, two of the largest societies finally merged to form the Co-operative Group (CWS); by then, the Co-operative Retail Trading Group (CRTG) was also co-ordinating the buying of 27 societies, representing nearly 2000 outlets.

The co-operatives have also been under severe pressure in Europe, Japan and elsewhere; by 1990, they had all but disappeared in Belgium and the Netherlands. However, they retain pockets of strength, as Table 30.4 illustrates. Migros in Switzerland, FDB in Denmark and Co-op Italia are leaders in their respective markets. If co-operative societies had earlier combined internationally, they could have been Europe's largest retail organization.

Table 30.4 Co-operatives' share of food trade

Country	Share of food trade	
	1998 (%)	2003(f) (%)
Switzerland	59.2	57.2
Denmark	21.5	21.5
Sweden	19.7	20.4
Hungary	16.6	6.0
Poland	13.5	11.7
Norway	9.5	9.4
Italy	6.2	8.4
United Kingdom	4.5	4.3

Source: Euromonitor (2000).

Major retail formats

The type of organization that owns or manages a store is not always obvious to the consumer. Other, more striking characteristics of shops serve to differentiate one format from another in the minds of shoppers. A retail format can be defined along a number of different dimensions, including:

single store	↔	group of stores
in-town	↔	out-of-town
large	↔	small
innovative	↔	mature
food	↔	non-food
specialized	↔	generalized
niche	↔	commodity
high added value	↔	discounter

This section examines briefly shopping centres, retail parks, superstores, hypermarkets, department stores, variety stores and a number of formats that use the term 'discounter'.

Shopping centres and retail parks

The term 'shopping centre' is normally applied to a coherent, planned and controlled group of retail establishments, as distinct from the more random grouping of a 'shopping district'. In Europe, the most typical location for shopping centres is still within existing town centres. Whereas out-of-town centres developed from the 1920s in the USA, some 50 years elapsed before they started to make an impact in Europe. The differences between the USA and European development patterns can be ascribed in part to differences of economics, geography and demography. Most of all, the more restrictive planning regulations within most European countries have served to restrict developments out-of-town. The planning debates revolve around a range of economic, environmental and social issues (McGoldrick and Thompson, 1992).

The move out of town has been described as three 'waves' of development (Schiller, in McGoldrick and Thompson, 1992). The first comprised the superstores, selling mostly food and limited ranges of non-food items. The second wave of decentralization involved bulky goods, such as DIY, carpets, furniture, large electrical items and garden centres. The third wave involved clothing and other comparison shopping, representing the most direct threat to existing town centres. The Metro Centre on Tyneside was an early example of this 'third wave', joined more recently by the Trafford Centre near Manchester and Bluewater in Kent. However, as suburban areas have become besieged by sprawl and traffic, there has been a policy shift in many governments towards urban containment and public transport (Ibrahim and McGoldrick, 2002). Town centre management schemes have been another response by some older shopping districts, trying to emulate features of the newer, planned centres.

Table 30.5 illustrates again the enormous diversity of retailing within Europe. In France, Denmark and the UK, shopping centre development was well under way by the early 1970s, whereas Italy, Spain, Finland and Sweden started rapid growth in the mid-1980s. Portugal saw a surge of development in the mid-1990s, followed by Hungary in the late 1990s.

Table 30.5   Shopping centre space in Europe

Country	m^2 per 1000 population	Country	m^2 per 1000 population
Austria	160.6	Ireland	213.6
Belgium	66.4	Italy	80.7
Denmark	206.4	Netherlands	120.6
Finland	145.0	Portugal	100.0
France	211.9	Spain	139.5
Germany	51.2	Switzerland	97.7
Greece	13.3	Turkey	5.4
Hungary	37.5	United Kingdom	228.9

Sources: Advertising Association (2001) and others.

Retail parks are more utilitarian groupings of 'retail sheds' and are also termed 'retail warehouse parks'. They offer convenient access and car parking arrangements but lack the indoor malls and many of the other comforts of the major, out-of-town shopping centres. The first such scheme opened in the UK in 1982; by 2000, there were 537 in operation. They involve far lower development costs than the major, full service shopping centres, which typically include extensive leisure and catering facilities. The trading format of the retail park has proved fairly resilient to varying economic conditions and they have continued to evolve, some adding cinemas, bowling alleys, fitness centres and pubs/restaurants to their mix. A parallel development in the USA, albeit typically based on larger units, is the 'power centre', defined by Hahn (2000) as 'an agglomeration of big box retailers'.

Factory outlet centres increased their presence in the UK in the 1990s and, by 2001, 34 were trading, with another 18 in the planning/ development pipeline. One of the largest, Cheshire Oaks, includes 300 000 sq. ft of retail area and 120 factory outlets. Designer names such as Calvin Klein, Ted Baker, Nike and Reebok tend to predominate with their discount outlets, but high street names are also there in force, such as Principles, Marks & Spencer, Diesel and Next (Key Note, 2000b).

Department and variety stores

In most new shopping centres, developers seek to ensure that they attract key 'anchor tenants' in the form of major department and variety stores. Ironically, the market shares of both these retail formats have tended towards decline in most European countries. According to the International Association of Department Stores, a department store must have at least 2500 m^2 of space (26 900 sq. ft). Furthermore, it must offer a product range that is both wide and deep in several product categories.

Table 30.6 estimates the shares of non-food sales of department stores in various countries.

Table 30.6 Department and variety stores

Country	Share of non-food sales (%)	
	Department stores	Variety stores
Australia	8.8	7.5
Austria	6.9	3.8
Canada	16.1	6.7
Denmark	6.7	11.3
France	2.9	0.8
Germany	5.9	0.7
Hungary	5.9	26.2
Ireland	13.4	–
Netherlands	9.7	3.4
Russia	36.8	–
Spain	8.0	–
Sweden	2.5	1.4
UK	3.6	18.4
USA	8.6	10.2

Source: Euromonitor (2000).

In the USA, traditional, full-line department stores continue to decline in number, although the leading-edge operators, such as Federated, May & Co. and Dillard's, have made gains through acquisitions and more focused strategies. In the UK, John Lewis and Debenhams lead among the traditional department stores, Marks & Spencer holding the largest share of the variety store category.

Many European variety stores were founded in the 1930s by department store operators, in order to offer a lower priced, lower service and lower assortment format. Examples include Prisunic by Printemps and Priminime by Bon Marche. In the UK, there are few such links between the department and variety store sectors, and variety stores hold a relatively strong 18.4 per cent of non-food sales. Many variety stores have traded up and diversified; on the other hand, department stores have tended to withdraw from some product ranges in the face of specialist, lower-priced competition. Accordingly, the distinction between the department and variety formats has become blurred.

Superstores and hypermarkets

Whereas the supermarket format has reached maturity in most countries, the superstore and hypermarket formats have been claiming increased share. Being situated mostly outside traditional shopping centres, they tend to enjoy greater accessibility by car, greater economies of scale and the benefits of being purpose built. Superstores form the 'anchor stores' of retail warehouse parks and of many partnership schemes, such as the Marks & Spencer–Tesco partnership at Handforth, Cheshire.

In Britain, a superstore is defined as having at least 25 000 sq. ft of selling space, while a hypermarket has at least 50 000 sq. ft. Some sources use the near equivalent metric measures of 2500 and 5000 m² respectively. Comparisons between countries encounter great difficulties, as these thresholds vary considerably. In some cases, the terms imply large stores selling primarily groceries; in others, the terms are used with more flexibility to describe any large-scale,

---

Table 30.7
Superstore/hypermarket shares of food sales

Country	%	Country	%
Australia	40.0	Ireland	25.0
Belgium	11.0	Netherlands	2.4
Denmark	17.4	Portugal	37.2
France	43.0	Spain	24.0
Germany	19.1	UK	38.1
Italy	11.0	USA	18.9

Sources: Euromonitor (2000) and others.

---

specialist format, offering a strong depth of assortment, trading on one level and providing ample car parking. Having noted these caveats, Table 30.7 offers an indication of importance within 12 countries. As noted earlier, the UK is now adopting a more restrictive approach to out-of-town developments; large store developments have also become tightly regulated in France, Germany, Italy, the Netherlands and Spain.

Discounters

Like so many of the descriptive terms in retailing, 'discounter' is regrettably imprecise. As the wheel of retailing concept suggests, many new concepts have entered by offering prices at levels below existing competition, i.e. by discounting. Accordingly, the term 'hard discounter' has been adopted in some countries to distinguish between deep discount formats and other, more mild manifestations of price competition.

In the context of food retailing, Tordjman (1993) distinguished between the key financial and operational characteristics of discounters and hypermarkets, as shown in Table 30.8. This demonstrates the ability of the format to produce reasonable net margins through the strict control of operating costs. Estimates of discounters' 2003 shares of food markets show the highest penetration in Germany, Denmark and Austria, at 26.5, 17.5 and 12.3 per cent respectively. In the UK, they hold a more modest 6.0 per cent (Euromonitor, 2000).

The concept of the warehouse club represented an addition to hard discounting in Europe in the 1990s. These clubs started to develop from 1982 in the USA; the first such unit opened in the UK in 1993, after strong opposition from major supermarket chains. A wide range of mostly packaged foods and non-foods is offered, usually in large or multiple packs, in sparse surroundings of 100 000 sq. ft or over. However, this format achieved minimal impact in the UK and is considered to be in decline already in the USA (Management Horizons, 2000).

Table 30.8 Discounters and hypermarkets: financial models

Typical key indices	Discount supermarket	Hypermarket
Store size (m²)	600	6000
Number of lines	1000	35,000
Stockturns per year	40	22
Gross margin % of sales	14.5	16.0
As % of sales:		
Labour	5	7
Distribution	2	3
Property	1	2
Other costs	3	2
Net margin as % of sales	3.5	2.0
Asset turnover (times)	7	9
Return on investment (%)	24.5	18.0

Source: derived from Tordjman (1993).

While food discounters attracted most interest in the 1990s, attention has now shifted to discounting in non-food sectors. In their decision to exit the UK market in 2001, C&A cited the growth of clothing discounters, including Matalan, which had rapidly overtaken C&A in the menswear sector shares. International discounters have also entered the clothing market, including the US chain TK Maxx and Dublin-based Primark (Key Note, 2000b).

Retailing strategy

Each element of the value chain can serve to increase value, real or perceived. Most elements incur costs but can contribute to the process of differentiation. For comprehensive discussions of strategic planning in retailing, see Johnson (1987) or Walters and Hanrahan (2000).

Understanding needs and wants

Fundamental to the formulation of retail marketing strategy is a clear understanding of customer needs, motives and patronage decision processes. Without this, there is a tendency for strategy formulation to dwell upon the range of existing solutions, rather than developing formats to satisfy specific sets of consumer requirements.

The constant and widespread interface between retailers and their customers can easily lead to an illusion of empathy. In some large organizations, however, the key decision makers have become remote and largely isolated from their customers. It then becomes all too easy to impose their own values and preferences, in the sincere belief that these reflect those of the customers: this is somewhat improbable. Sophisticated retail marketers have had to develop new ways of hearing and understanding their customers, and their non-customers.

The research industry has responded with a range of information services, including tracking studies of customer attitudes/opinions and large panels of shoppers, whose purchase and patronage decisions are monitored in considerable detail. These data are, however, in the public domain, albeit to the exclusive club of competitors that can afford to purchase. In-house focus groups can also help to keep decision makers attuned to customer needs; however busy the diary or crowded the in-tray, some marketing managers insist on taking time out to attend these discussions, or simply to watch and talk to shoppers using their stores.

Complaints/suggestions should also be welcomed positively, rather than seen as a nuisance to be handled. There are few more cost-effective approaches to diagnosing dissatisfaction, often before it becomes fatal, or of identifying new ways of satisfying customers. In the words of Jeremy Mitchell (1978):

> When the complaints stop coming … it will mean the business is dying. The consumers will have made the ultimate protest. They will have gone elsewhere.

Image and brand equity

The accumulation of customer perceptions relating to an organization comprise that seemingly nebulous commodity: image. Having been convinced of the strong relationship between good image and good financial performance, retailers and researchers have invested extensively in the techniques to measure, compare and track images.

The study of images has been given further impetus through the development of the concept of brand equity (Aaker, 1991). This forges a clear link between the psychological domain of perceptions and images, and the financial domain of assets and equity. Image is taken out of the nebulous role of 'soft data' and moved centre stage as a key measure of company performance, where it matters most, in the mind of the consumer. This shift is also reflec-

ted in the concept of the balanced scorecard, which recognizes the importance of customer perceptions when evaluating company or unit performance (Kaplan and Norton, 1996).

Early work on image monitoring tended to dwell upon the more tangible attributes, such as perceptions of locations, prices, etc. Although these attributes are of no less importance today, the battle for effective differentiation has extended the concept of image towards the values that the 'retail brand' represents for consumers. For example, shopping in a discount store such as Aldi reinforces for some the need to be seen by friends and family as thrifty, or the need to beat the marketing embellishments of the superstores. If the growth of discounters in Europe were ascribed simply to economic motives, limited insight would be yielded into the best ways of harnessing, or of combating, the format.

The intricacy and multidimensionality of retail images is summarized in Figure 30.3. Retail image comprises a bundle of perceptions of attribute strengths/weaknesses, plus beliefs about the inner and outer directed values to which the retailer contributes. The importance of measuring perceptions of clienteles has also been recognized: a major reason why stores are

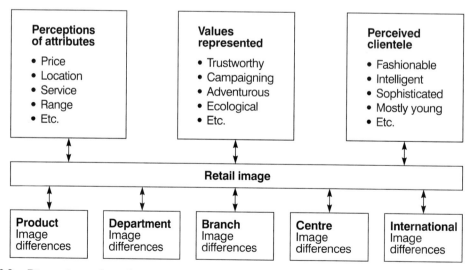

Figure 30.3 Dimensions of retail image

excluded from a shopper's list of alternatives is because other shoppers are too affluent/poor, trendy/conservative, etc. The bases of these beliefs, however, are also multifaceted. Perceptions are based upon individual stores, centres in which they are located, departments and product ranges, which can of course vary within a chain.

The critical role of image in the formulation and evaluation of retail strategy has also been realized in the international setting. A strong image in the home market may have little or no brand equity in the new market, unless that market comprises many tourists or expatriates from the home market. In most cases, the image has to be created, providing an opportunity to monitor the birth and development of an image.

Based upon studies of retailers' images in a number of international markets, Figure 30.4

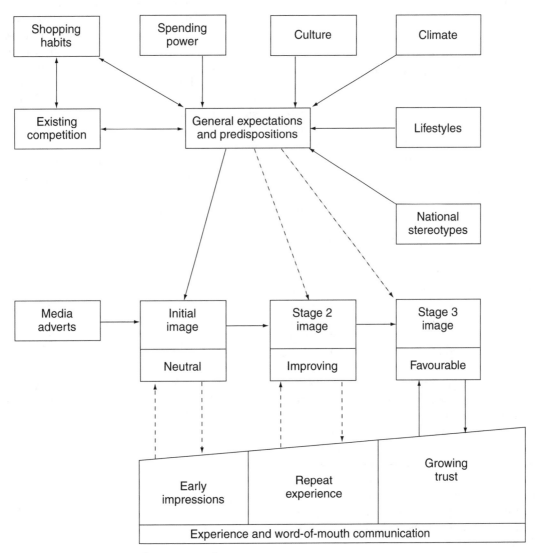

Figure 30.4 Determinants of international image
Source: McGoldrick (1998).

summarizes the development of image. Initial images are heavily influenced by advertising and by general predispositions, including national stereotypes. Initial experience or word-of-mouth communication tends to lead fairly quickly to images of such attributes as prices and fashion. It takes longer for beliefs to develop about some of the values which are part of the core proposition within the home market, such as beliefs about trust and the integrity of the retailer.

Positioning and the value proposition

As the attributes, values and dimensions of image monitoring become ever more intricate, the opportunities to differentiate through positioning abound. Until relatively recently, positioning was typically defined in highly tangible terms, such as price levels and the age range of the target shoppers. Thus, using a simple, two-dimensional chart, a shoe retailer could identify gaps in the market, for example, for more expensive shoes for shoppers under 30, or for budget shoppers in their 40s.

These early approaches to positioning were appealing in that they focused upon easily defined market segments. However, they tended to lead to mob positioning, with most retailers chasing the (seemingly) most profitable target markets. They also offered little scope for more creative approaches to identifying viable and profitable targets. There are numerous examples of retailers with similar price levels, similar product ranges, similar age targets, yet most dissimilar levels of customer appeal. While these stores may be close on the retailers' positioning maps, they are clearly differentiated in the customers' mental maps. Yet another reason emerges to use the best available techniques to explore perceptions, beliefs and values represented by retailers (e.g. Supphellan, 2000).

Another development in retail marketing has been the emergence of store positions not

previously considered attractive, or even viable. For example, the combination of wide assortments and low prices was not considered to be an attractive financial proposition, however attractive it may be for the consumer. The advent of the 'category killer', sometimes ascribed the alternative title 'power retailer', has changed the rules (Rogers, 1996). For many people, Toys'R'Us symbolizes this format, with a combination of wide choice, reasonable prices, efficient systems and easy access.

The category killer format has proved attractive for relatively infrequent, comparison purchases, where a large/vast choice adds significant value for the consumer. DIY would appear vulnerable/attractive to this format: why drive between several, modest sized DIY stores to compare similar, restricted ranges, when a single, longer drive reaches a genuinely expanded range? Thus, the development of the B&Q warehouse format, IKEA and Olympus Sportsworld are other examples of the format.

Positioning is therefore a multidimensional exploration of mindspace, to identify gaps in consumer preference maps. However, the

Figure 30.5   The value equation

identification of gaps does not alone ensure their attractiveness. A sophisticated blend of financial and psychological modelling is required to predict the viability of the new market position. Neither is simple, but the prediction of consumer preferences is undoubtedly the greater challenge. It requires an understanding of the complex systems of trade-offs that consumers make when choosing a store.

Figure 30.5 offers a simple but useful summary of this difficult area of analysis. At the core of retail marketing strategy there must be a focus upon value, as perceived by the target customer. In general, they seek more of the positive attributes, less of the negative attributes, such as cost, risk, time effort and stress. A better understanding of the response patterns and trade-offs within the 'value equation' is, without doubt, a worthwhile area of investigation in the new science of retailing.

Loyalty: schemes or strategies?

It is appropriate to conclude this section with comments on one of the major preoccupations of retail strategy in recent years: loyalty schemes. It is hard to deny that there have been distinct waves of emphasis in retail strategy over the last 30 years, as illustrated in Figure 30.6. We can all argue exactly when each phase started and ended; more difficult to argue is the fact that these emphases, for a short period of time, become obsessions, if not fixations. This leads us to a sad conclusion: *most retail strategies have been formed in someone else's head office!*

One beneficial difference between this 'wave' and previous ones is that it focused upon the consumer, rather than upon a specific aspect of the mix. Loyalty schemes are driven by the philosophy that it is cheaper to retain a customer than it is to attract a new one, or to recover a lost one. They come in many different shapes and

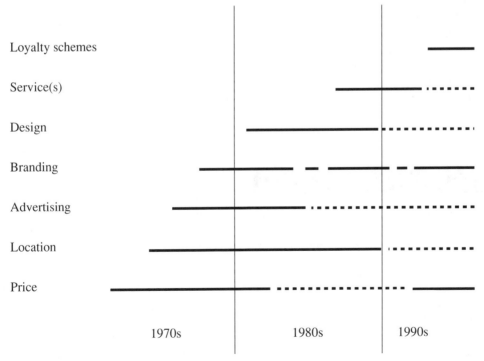

Figure 30.6   Waves of emphasis in retail strategy
Source: McGoldrick and Andre (1997).

forms: a review of these is provided by Mintel (1999). Some schemes have proved prohibitively expensive, necessitating their reduction or withdrawal. Others have produced loyalty to the loyalty scheme, rather than to retailers, giving them a status similar to trading stamps, largely abandoned in the 1970s.

In theory, a loyalty scheme which is well thought out, rather than hastily bought in, can yield considerable information benefits. To that mass of EPoS data can be added information about the income, family, age, etc. of the purchaser. For the first time since the corner shop, where most customers were known by name, retailers have the potential to practice elements of one-to-one micromarketing.

However, as many retailers are still grappling to harness the full information benefits of EPoS data, they can only scratch the surface of this potential. While the concept of a 'segment of one' makes obvious sense in business-to-business marketing, retail marketing involves a vast number of (relatively) small accounts. Computers can be programmed to tailor incentives, offers and communications to (assumed) customer types, but mistakes will inevitably occur. As loyalty schemes become imitated and institutionalized, the challenge is to maintain customer interest through innovations and added value, while strictly controlling the costs of the scheme.

Retail functions

Given the enormous breadth of activities that comprise retailing, it is possible here to provide only a glimpse of its major functions. A more comprehensive treatment is provided in the chapters of McGoldrick (2002). The emphasis here is to:

1 Indicate the role of each function within the overall process of marketing consumer goods.
2 Outline the significance of each function within the strategic mix and within the value chain of retailers.

Location

Store location decisions are probably the single most crucial elements of retail marketing strategy. They represent long-term investment decisions which, if incorrect, are very difficult to change. While good locations cannot alone compensate for a weak overall strategy, a poor location is a very difficult deficit to overcome. Bad location decisions also undermine the asset value of the retail organization; such stores are difficult to sell.

The retail location decisions must address macro and micro issues; they are often depicted in three stages (Brown, 1992):

1 *Search* – identifying geographical areas that may have market potential.
2 *Viability* – evaluating the turnover potential of the best available sites.
3 *Micro* – examining the detailed features of the short-listed sites.

Clearly, not all location decisions pass through this sequence, and a great deal of intuition and executive judgement are still applied. A number of more systematic techniques are available to assist decision makers:

1 *Checklists.* Very detailed lists of factors relevant to location evaluations have been evolved and are widely used. The factors include many aspects of the population within the catchment area, competition (existing and potential), accessibility by car and by foot, and the specific costs of developing a store on that site.
2 *Geographic information systems* (GIS). These can provide detailed analysis of many checklist factors, such as income, employment and expenditure profiles, within specified localities.
3 *Analogue methods.* These extrapolate the performance of a site under consideration, based upon analogous sites already in operation.
4 *Regression models.* These help to forecast turnover by modelling the influence of location factors which contribute to, or detract from, the turnover of existing stores.

Although no self-respecting retailer would set aside the checklist, or the need to experience the 'look-feel' of a potential site, GIS offers immediate answers to many 'what if?' questions. These questions are not restricted to new sites but can be extended to the evaluation of branch performance, set against an objective model of potential. The knowledge of neighbourhood characteristics provided by GIS can also guide decisions about product ranges, price levels and promotion at the branch level.

Product selection and buying

The buying function represents the main interface between retailers and other members of the supply chain. Accordingly, many suppliers create specialist sales teams to serve key retail accounts, developing a close knowledge of the organization and the individuals involved. In some retail organizations, individual buyers have extensive autonomy within their specific product category; in others, the buying team is the norm, which typically includes selectors, merchandisers, technologists and quality controllers.

In selecting products and suppliers, numerous criteria must be considered by retail buyers, not least of which are the projections of sales and profitability. Product selection is a key element of differentiation and buyers are becoming increasingly proactive in sourcing items that will help to provide a competitive edge. Buyers must also consider the capabilities of the supplier, in terms of volume, flexibility and reliability.

Nowhere is the shift of power from manufacturers to retailers more directly manifest than in the buying offices of major retailers. The 'table banging' style of buying, characteristic of the early days of retailer power, has indeed given way to more sophisticated and, sometimes, longer-term forms of retailer–manufacturer relationship. Talk of 'relationship marketing' can, however, obscure the considerable power of the retail buyers within that

relationship. To their economic buying power, retailers have now added more focus, expertise and information, increasing further their overall power.

Although large retailers clearly hold the balance of power, the development of category management practices has increased the involvement of some large suppliers in product category decisions. Category management is defined as:

> a retailer/supplier process of managing categories as strategic business units, producing enhanced business results by focussing on delivering consumer value.
>
> (IGD, 1999)

Category management has, in some cases, opened up much broader information exchanges between major suppliers and retailers, as experts within both firms deal more directly with each other. Figure 30.7 illustrates these typical linkages, which seek to overcome the 'information bottleneck' that can be created within the traditional buying model. In the case of Procter & Gamble and Wal-Mart, many of the supplier's executives were moved to the retailer's headquarters in Arkansas, running some categories on behalf of Wal-Mart, to agreed performance targets (Management Horizons, 1999).

While category management may have increased the influence of the supplier chosen as 'category captain', it may have the reverse effect for other suppliers. The Competition Commission in the UK, and its predecessor the Monopolies and Mergers Commission, have been monitoring over many years the effects of retailer power. Both stopped short of advocating legislation to limit the scope of retail buyers to extract better terms, purely on account of their buying power (such as the Robinson Patman Acts in the USA). However, the Commission noted concerns about some possible effects of category management, which could act as a barrier to others wishing to enter the market (Competitition Commission, 2000).

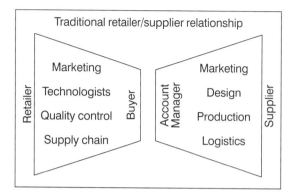

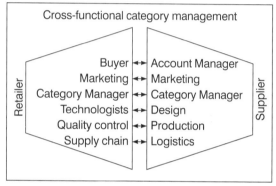

Adapted from Management Horizons (1999)

Figure 30.7   Widening the retailer–supplier interface

Retail brand products

A significant manifestation of retailer power has been the ability of major retailers to develop their own brand product ranges. An 'own brand' has been defined as a brand name owned by the retailer (or a wholesaler) for a line or variety of items under exclusive or controlled distribution (Koskinen, 1999). The name may be that of the retailer, for example Tesco, or a name closely linked with the company, such as Marks & Spencer's St Michael brand. From time to time, grocery retailers have also launched ranges of 'generics', a low-priced, plain label variant upon the own brand concept.

Retailer brands have been especially important within grocery retailing. The three leading grocers in the UK, Tesco, J. Sainsbury and Asda (Wal-Mart) derived 55, 61 and 58 per cent of their turnover respectively from their own brands (KPMG, 2000). Table 30.9 compares own brand shares in the food sectors of eight countries: as own brand prices are usually lower than those of manufacturer brands, volume shares are greater than shares of sales. Such brands are not restricted to grocery sectors; with 100 per cent own brands, Marks & Spencer has been described as 'a manufacturer without factories'. This company is very closely involved in the specification, design and quality control processes.

The primary driver of own-brand development has been to produce better margins, often around 10 per cent better, while simultaneously increasing pressure upon manufacturers. As retailers have become more accomplished and confident in their brand building, other motives have played an increasing role. The potential contribution of own brands to store image and maintaining store loyalty has been recognized, as own brands have evolved from 'copycat' to differentiation status. Indeed, retailers such as Marks & Spencer and the Body Shop can claim impressive records of product innovation, to the extent that own brands can trade in a

Table 30.9   Retailer brand shares in Europe

Country	Shares of food sector (%)	
	Volume	Sales
Switzerland	59.6	50.7
UK	42.0	34.0
Belgium	34.5	23.9
The Netherlands	25.3	20.9
Spain	24.1	17.9
France	20.0	16.5
Germany	18.5	12.2
Finland	9.7	8.0

Source: KPMG (2000), based on Nielsen data.

premium position. For fashion and other design-led retailers, the ability to co-ordinate aspects of product and store design is another significant motive.

The implications for manufacturers, however, have been serious, with retailers able to switch sources of own brands, if prices or specifications cannot be agreed. Some manufacturers have learnt to coexist as largely anonymous suppliers of major retailers, freed of most marketing expenditures but with extreme dependence upon the retailer(s). Some major brand manufacturers such as Heinz, along with Kellogg's, held out for many years against producing retailers' own brands; however, Heinz now adopts a 'mixed branding' policy. This has the advantages of maximizing plant utilization and maintaining influence, if not control, over product differentiation. The old adage 'if you can't beat them, join them' also holds true.

The evolution of own brands has demanded the development of skills in design and product testing, previously in the domain of the manufacturer. Leading grocers now employ large teams of food scientists to help develop, specify and test product characteristics. Consumer tests are also of critical importance, to ensure that the effect on image is the right direction. Retailers must also monitor possible consumer resistance to own brands, if their predominance in displays is creating the impression of a restriction of choice.

Retail pricing

One of the most complex areas of retail decision making is that of pricing. Whereas a manufacturer may have 50–100 items to price, a superstore or department store retailer may be responsible for 1000 times more SKUs (stock-keeping units). Added to this complexity is the fact that chain store retailers operate in many different geographical markets. Figure 30.8 summarizes the main dimensions of retail pricing: developments within each are considered briefly.

The 'comparative dimension' represents the many differences in price between those of the retailer and those of direct and indirect, local and national competitors. This comprises a vast number of price comparisons, far more than can be collected to inform each pricing decision. The information industry has responded with a range of pricing data, some comprising a pooling of retailers' own scanner data, others deriving information from the purchase records of large panels of consumers. In some sectors, such as clothing retailing, much comparative data on prices and markdowns are still obtained by auditors visiting a sample of stores at regular intervals. Many retailers price different parts of their range to compete for different market segments, so the positioning may vary according to the product prices that are compared.

The 'geographical dimension' reflects the fact that all retailing is local retailing, for chain stores and independents alike. Many chains that initially charged uniform prices in all their locations have shifted progressively towards greater local adaptation, reflecting better the local market conditions. Some use relatively crude stratifications of locations, others now try to tailor more precisely their product/price mix to each locality. Again, the external information from GIS, combined with internal EPoS data at store level, provide the basis for cost-effective local pricing, referred to as 'price flexing' by the Competition Commission (2000).

The 'assortment' dimension of retail pricing concerns the thousands of decisions between prices of categories and items within the range. Decisions based upon crude mark-up rules are giving way to more intricate approaches, information again being the catalyst. EPoS provides great scope to experiment with price, controlling the inputs (prices) and monitoring the outputs (sales) precisely. Assortment pricing decisions should also be informed by research into consumers' awareness of items prices (McGoldrick *et al.*, 2000). Through this type of research, the 'leader line' pricing technique was evolved. Within this approach, the

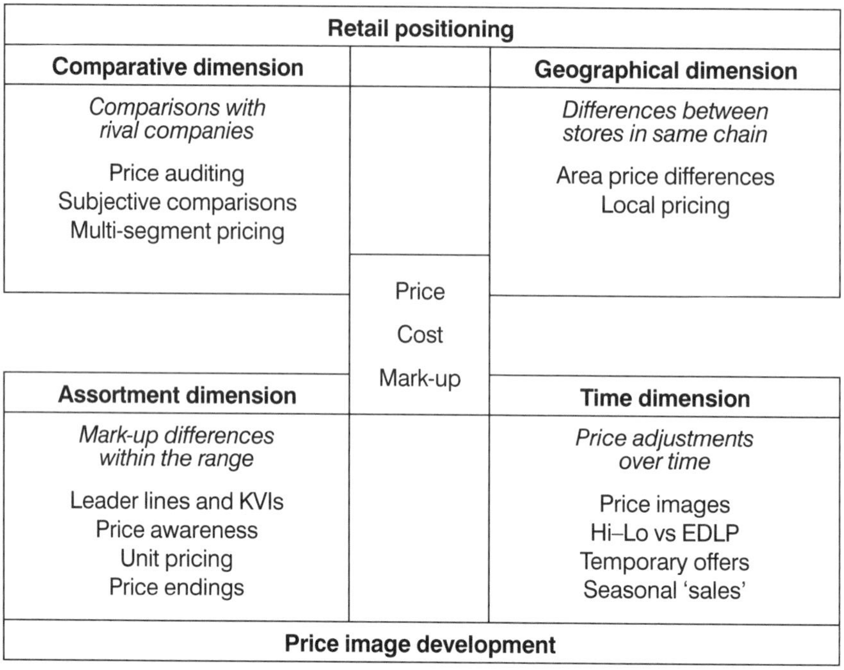

Retail positioning		
Comparative dimension		**Geographical dimension**
Comparisons with rival companies Price auditing Subjective comparisons Multi-segment pricing	Price Cost Mark-up	*Differences between stores in same chain* Area price differences Local pricing
Assortment dimension		**Time dimension**
Mark-up differences within the range Leader lines and KVIs Price awareness Unit pricing Price endings		*Price adjustments over time* Price images Hi–Lo vs EDLP Temporary offers Seasonal 'sales'
Price image development		

Figure 30.8   The dimensions of retail pricing
Source: McGoldrick (2002).

prices of (say) 500 grocery prices on 'known value items' (KVIs) are held at low levels, creating a beneficial image of prices across the whole assortment.

Time is also a critical dimension of retail pricing, and an area of great concern in recent years. Some years ago, the major grocers were advised to reduce their dependence upon short-term special offers, in favour of more stable pricing arrangements. Other sectors have tried to limit their use of seasonal sales, which at one stage were seriously eroding margins in clothing and other sectors. While seasonal sales can help to clear stock and also generate some excitement, their overuse can devalue hard-won retail images. Table 30.10 summarizes the relative benefits of high–low (Hi-Lo) and everyday low pricing (EDLP).

Advertising and sales promotion

While much has been written about the alleged 'death of advertising', expenditure by UK retailers continues to grow apace. Expenditure by UK retailers grew from £423 million in 1991 to £1034 million in 2000 (Nielsen, 2001). Table 30.11 shows a few of the major spenders, although it should be recognized that some of this expenditure is subsidized by manufacturers, in the form of 'co-operative advertising' deals. Neither do the figures take full account of discounts available to shrewd media buyers. In spite of these important caveats, which apply to both time periods, the data show a strong commitment by retailers to building their brands through advertising.

Indeed, there is a virtuous circle in the brand advertising of large retailers. As they increase their penetration within trading/advertising areas, the cost-effectiveness of media advertising improves. As own-brand development continues, the advertising builds both aspects of the brand: the store and the product. As store formats and ranges develop, the spread of the advertising benefit increases still further.

Table 30.10 EDLP vs high–low pricing

Everyday low pricing	High–low pricing
Reduced price wars	Price discrimination: merchandise appeals to multiple market segments
Reduced promotional advertising	Creates excitement
More efficient use of store personnel	All merchandise can be sold eventually
Improved inventory management	Price confusion reduces awareness of prices
Increased profit margins	High initial prices guide customers' judgements of product and store quality
The retailer can concentrate on being a seller, rather than a deal buyer	EDLP can be extremely difficult to maintain
Less buyer time spent managing 'sale' events and more time merchandising the entire line	
More consumer appeal: price perceived as more honest	

Source: McGoldrick *et al.* (2000).

Table 30.11 Major retail advertisers

Retailer	1996 (£ thousands)	2000 (£ thousands)
J. Sainsbury	20 669	33 293
B&Q	12 073	29 374
PC World	15 850	27 860
Currys	24 073	27 239
DFS Northern Upholstery	14 666	26 279
Homebase	6100	25 074
Comet	19 334	20 066
Tesco	15 006	19 532
Asda	14 253	17 787
Dixons	13 527	15 266
Iceland	10 680	14 784
Woolworths	9483	13 550
Boots the Chemists	8271	12 483

Source: Nielsen (2001).

Retailers have many ways of communicating with their own regular customers, both in store and by mailings sent to account or loyalty/store card holders. Major objectives of media advertising are therefore to attract new customers, or to increase the visit frequency/ expenditure of more marginal customers. Some retailers also make use of sponsorship as a promotional vehicle, which can avoid much of the 'clutter' in conventional media advertising. Retailers have become increasingly sophisticated in their public relations (PR) activities, which are directed not only to consumers but also to shareholders, government, suppliers, employees and unions.

Numeric and visual merchandising

Many innovations have occurred in the ways in which store space is designed and allocated. The store environment fulfils a number of objectives, seeking to achieve a balance between maximizing unplanned purchasing, offering a wide assortment of goods, holding adequate stock, and offering a convenient, safe and pleasant place to shop. In pursuit of these aims, the store has become an excellent laboratory for the development and refinement of merchandising techniques.

At the most detailed level, models have been developed to allocate display space between categories and individual lines. Whereas some items are 'space elastic', with sales increasing in response to higher allocations of space, others are not. It makes sense therefore to study the response functions, which are rarely simple or linear, and allocate space to yield the best returns. To the equation, however, should be added measures of direct product profitability and estimates of shelf replenishment frequencies/costs; an overall view must also be taken of the impact of revised allocations upon images of the store.

In its earlier incarnations, the science of 'numeric' merchandising gave little impression of the 'look' of the displays. Improvements in computer graphics have facilitated the development of 'visual' merchandising, by which the calculated allocations can be vividly portrayed, such that the colours, sizes, shapes, etc. of individual items can be arranged both effectively and aesthetically. Visual merchandising also helps to convey the intended appearance of the displays to the individual stores.

Camera-based techniques, used by advertising agencies to track eye movements in response to advertising images, are now being used to examine responses to displays. Cameras are also used to track customer movements within the store as a whole, leading to major improvements in layout effectiveness. They pinpoint areas of high, possibly dysfunctional density, and 'cold' areas visited by few shoppers. They record where people stop to look and where they tend to ignore the displays. Sometimes, the store security system can provide sufficient detail: for more detailed analyses, tiny cameras can be built into the displays.

Retail atmospherics

At the broader level of store design, a blend of science and artistic creativity is also being achieved. The lack of success of some expensive refurbishments has given great impetus to the quest to establish sound principles to govern the choice of design components. The new science of 'atmospherics' is gaining momentum, as researchers seek to understand better the effects of environmental cues upon feelings and behaviours.

Research has investigated in some detail the effects upon behaviour of different music levels and types, giving retailers various options to influence mood states, speed of movement through the store and general impressions of the store. The effects of colours have also been researched, from their use on individual packages and displays, to the decor of the store as a whole. More recently, the use of scents has been tested by researchers, to understand better the influence of another factor that often operates at the subconscious level.

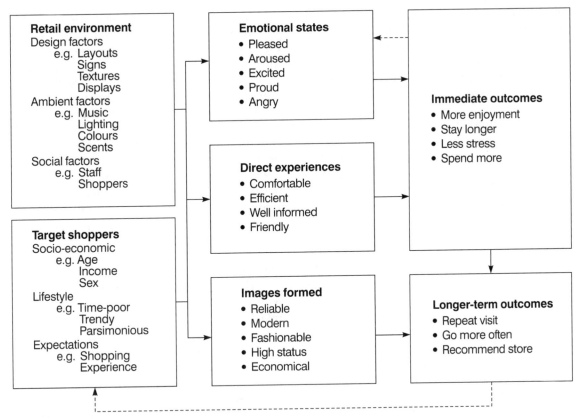

Figure 30.9   Influences of retail environments
Source: McGoldrick (2002).

Models developed in the broader field of environmental psychology have been applied extensively to the retail environment, measuring for example the effects of atmospherics upon the customer's level of pleasure and arousal. Figure 30.9 illustrates how some of the environmental elements influence the emotions, experiences and images formed. These, in turn, can influence the immediate and long-term outcomes, in terms of the loyalty of target customers.

Service and customer care

In spite of all that has been written and preached about retail service in recent years, the concept remains ill-defined and, accordingly, difficult to measure. Part of the problem

lies in the word itself, retailing involving service(s) at various different levels:

1   Retailing as a service industry, along with banking, catering, travel, etc.
2   Retailing as a service, bringing a combination of products together in a convenient location, within a pleasant environment, open long hours.
3   Services that retailers may or may not offer, such as free carriers, bag packing, credit/debit card payments, etc.
4   Quality of service provided, i.e. doing it well, reliability, etc.

At the second level of definition, retailers have sought to enhance temporal accessibility, as well as geographical accessibility. Following the changes to the Sunday Trading Act, most large stores in England and Wales now open for six hours on Sundays, usually longer in Scotland. On other days, some stores in busy urban areas now open for 24 hours a day, including many Tesco superstores (Morgan Stanley Dean Witter, 2001).

At the third level, services have proliferated but competitive advantage is usually short-lived if the service is easily copied. The problem is that expectations shift rapidly as services lose their novelty and become institutionalized. Consequently, the acceptance of debit and credit cards spread very rapidly in most sectors, now being anticipated. Marks & Spencer and John Lewis were reluctant to offer credit services, other than their own, but eventually gave in to the pressure of consumer expectations.

At the fourth level, retailers and shopping centres have instituted pledges and guarantees that they will 'do it well'. The law imposes liability for defective products but the returns policies of retailers such as Marks & Spencer go far beyond the requirement of the law. This removes much of the risk from the negative side of the value equation, discussed earlier. Centres such as Meadowhall near Sheffield have issued various detailed guarantees of service levels, for customers in general, for motorists, for families and for disabled shoppers.

Various scales have been applied to the measurement of retail service quality, including SERVQUAL and the more specific Retail Service Quality scale (Dabholkar *et al.*, 1996). However, retailers have been warned against excessive reliance upon satisfaction scores, which can become an end in themselves. Some make use of 'mystery shoppers' to visit their stores and to provide relatively objective assessments of their service encounters.

Human resources

With around 14 million people employed in retailing in Europe (Eurostat, 1997) and 2.5 million in Great Britain, it is clear that retailing is a 'people business'. Retailers also face the challenge that their lowest paid staff interface directly with their customers. Imagine how images of cars or chocolates would change if customers dealt directly with assembly line workers, rather than receiving these images through carefully crafted advertisements.

In retailing, the shelf packers, cleaners and checkout operators all represent key components of the service experience. This highlights the need for careful selection and training; overall, the need for an effective human resource function (see Marchington, in McGoldrick, 1994). Large retail chains also have the challenge of communicating their mission, values and expectations to a large and geographically dispersed staff.

There are of course some retail contexts within which staff hold highly creative selling roles. In the retailing of fashion goods, cars or other major durables, the sales staff are expected to combine extensive product knowledge with the skills of personal selling. Here, in particular, the value of effective training is most manifest: as Figure 30.10 illustrates, training can contribute to profitability through reduced costs, higher sales, better service and improved customer relationships.

Information and logistics

The logistics role is largely unseen by most customers, becoming more apparent when it fails to maintain stock levels. Out-of-stock conditions may cause not only the immediate loss of item sales, but also undermine customer loyalty by increasing the need to shop elsewhere. The efficient management of the supply chain is therefore a key strategic function.

The benefits of checkout scanning equipment to supply chain management are starting to be fully realized. 'Efficient consumer response' (ECR) developments include the sharing of live data with some major suppliers, with the effect of increasing stock availability, improving choice for customers, reducing stock levels and improving stockturns. At

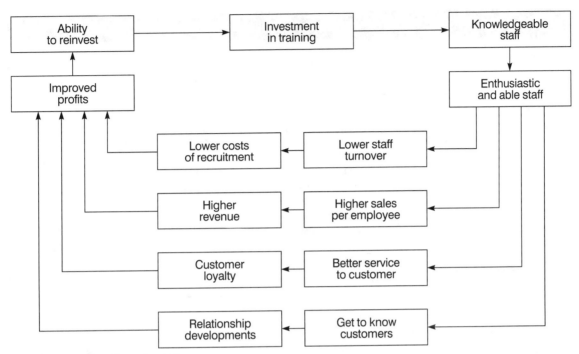

Figure 30.10 Benefits of training
Source: Adapted from Uncles (1995).

Asda, for example, the average rate of stock-turn per year improved from 15 to 23 in just five years. Using just-in-time (JIT) delivery principles, retailers can minimize the space devoted to stockholding and reduce the proportion of older stock. To an extent, this may push stockholding costs back up the supply chain, but it does provide better product availability and space utilization for the retailer.

Such systems require a high proportion of scanner equipped stores: by the year 2000, 91.4 per cent of grocery volume in the UK was scanned (Nielsen, 2001). This also offers direct benefits to customers in terms of faster service and itemized receipts. Further service enhancement is provided by the integration of electronic payment systems, accepting credit or debit payments and, in the latter case, offering customers the facility to request cash back. The same systems also capture individual customer purchase data, via the 50 million loyalty cards estimated to be in use in the UK.

Internationalization of retailing

In spite of the power and sophistication of large-scale retailers, the process of internationalization has been slow and painful. In addition to the legal, linguistic and logistical problems, it is difficult to export even the most successful of retail concepts into other markets. As noted earlier, competitive structures differ greatly and there are still major differences in consumer tastes and preferences (McGoldrick and Davies, 1995).

Difficult or not, the internationalization of retailing is gaining pace. A view of internationalization should also recognize the flow of know-how and the import/export of retail concepts. International product sourcing has a long history in some companies but is becoming more widespread; for some retailers, it has also facilitated the development of branches abroad (Liu and McGoldrick, 1996). International buying groups and alliances are another major facet

Table 30.12   Major retailers with international involvement

Company	Domestic base	Main activity	Sales (million Euro)	Number of countries	Foreign sales (%)
Wal-Mart	USA	Discount stores	194 290.2	9	17.2
Carrefour	France	Hypermarkets/grocery	65 609.8	27	47.5
Ahold	The Netherlands	Supermarkets	49 170.4	24	80.8
Home Depot	USA	DIY	49 154.2	4	5.5
Metro	Germany	Diversified	47 489.9	22	42.1
Sears, Roebuck	USA	Department stores	39 573.3	2	11.6
ITM Enterprises	France	Supermarkets	36 272.1	8	36.0
Safeway	USA	Supermarkets	34 365.3	3	10.8
Costco	USA	Warehouse clubs	33 982.5	7	18.7
Tesco	UK	Supermarkets	33 680.3	10	12.5

Source: PricewaterhouseCoopers (2001).

of the internationalization process, such as the EMD alliance, with a turnover across 13 countries of over 100 billion Euros.

Table 30.12 compares the scale and extent of international participation by 10 of the world's largest retailers. This helps to explain why a retailer which leads at home, such as Tesco, is motivated to expand abroad in pursuit of growth.

Motives for internationalization

The pressures towards/reasons for internationalization are diverse, but may be summarized as 'push', 'pull' or 'facilitating' factors:

1 'Push' factors, including the maturity or saturation of home markets, domestic trading restrictions, unfavourable economic conditions, rising costs, adverse demographic changes and imitation of trading styles.
2 'Pull' factors, including more enlightened corporate philosophies, perceptions of growth opportunities abroad (niche or underdeveloped markets), established bridgeheads in other countries and imitative 'bandwagon' effects.

3 'Facilitating' factors, including the lowering of political, economic and perceived barriers between countries, the broader vision of senior management, an accumulation of expertise, the ability to assess other retailers' international moves and the improvement of communication technologies.

The particular mix of these factors often determines the most appropriate route to internationalization. Also relevant are the availability of capital, the level of understanding of market needs within other countries, and the compatibility of the domestic trading format(s) with those needs. It is clear that retailers have sometimes adopted the wrong approach to internationalization. There are several examples of leading retailers in domestic markets running into difficulties abroad.

Entry strategies

A number of alternative approaches are available, including the following:

1 Self-start entry, the chain being built up from scratch, or developed through organic growth

from a very modest initial acquisition. Examples include Woolworths in the UK and Laura Ashley in the USA.

2 Acquisition, providing a quick entry route but at a cost, not least because companies available for acquisition may well be in financial difficulty. The approach has been used by many UK retailers, including Marks & Spencer's North American acquisitions, which the company subsequently disposed of.

3 Franchising, avoiding much of the risk and demands upon capital; especially appropriate where a retailing concept can be readily exported. Notable examples include Italian manufacturer/franchiser Benetton, with over 6000 outlets in over 80 countries.

4 Joint venture, reducing time, cost and risk of entry by working with a partner already familiar with the market. In spite of their benefits at the outset, many joint ventures/partnerships have been terminated, having not met expectations.

5 Concessions (shops in shops), a relatively low cost/risk approach to exploring new markets, used for example by Burton in Spain and elsewhere.

The internationalization of retailing has produced very diverse styles of operation, ranging from global to multinational. Global retailers such as Benetton vary their format very little across national boundaries, achieving the greatest economies of scale but showing the least local responsiveness. Multinationals, on the other hand, tend to develop or acquire a diversity of formats internationally, usually achieving rather lower benefits from integration. A middle course may be termed 'transnational' retailing, whereby the company seeks to achieve global efficiency while responding to national needs, opportunities and constraints. This approach may be seen as more closely aligned with the trend towards greater localization within domestic markets.

The experiences of many international retailers illustrate that formats that work well at home do not always work well in foreign markets. Sometimes, the increased complexity over-extends the company's financial and managerial resources, making it less reactive to local conditions. Figure 30.11 illustrates how retail internationalization can result in either a vicious or a virtuous spiral of events.

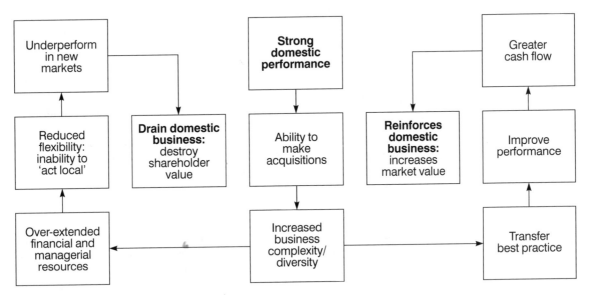

Figure 30.11 Vicious or virtuous spirals
Source: Adapted from IGD (1999).

Non-store retailing

In that telephone and Internet ordering has largely replaced the posting of orders, the term 'home shopping' has largely replaced 'mail order'. In spite of numerous predictions that home shoppping would take over a large share of retail trade, its role in most countries is still fairly modest. As Table 30.13 illustrates, home shopping was estimated to account for 10 per cent of non-food sales in the USA by 2003, rather less in European countries.

Table 30.13 Home shopping shares of non-food sales

Country	%	Country	%
Austria	7.5	Japan	3.1
Canada	2.8	Netherlands	4.6
Denmark	5.6	Norway	6.3
France	5.4	Sweden	4.2
Germany	7.0	Switzerland	4.4
Ireland	0.8	UK	7.5
Italy	0.6	USA	10.0

Source: Euromonitor (2000) estimates for 2003.

Catalogue home shopping

In both the UK and the USA, the history of 'mail order' can be traced back to the nineteenth century. In the UK, networks of agents sold through catalogues to 'clubs' of friends, neighbours and fellow workers, as well as collecting their payments. Their customers were mainly urban working class and the major attraction was the credit terms offered. In the USA, the rural markets were the main focus, these being inadequately served by other forms of retailing.

By 1970, home shopping in the UK accounted for under 5 per cent of all retail trade,

reaching the end of the century at almost the same level. However, much changed during that 30-year period, with traditional 'big book' mail order and agency networks declining. The entry of Next Directory breathed new life into the sector, appealing directly to a much more up-market clientele. More recently, other retailers' catalogues, television shopping channels and Internet retailers have brought new impetus to the sector.

Unlike most retail sectors, home shopping is actually becoming less concentrated in the UK, as some of the largest players continue to lose share. As recently as 1990, GUS (Great Universal Stores), which includes Kays and many other catalogue names, held over 30 per cent of the home shopping market: this had fallen to under 20 per cent by the end of the decade. Littlewoods also lost share during that period, its second place challenged by Otto Versand of Germany, which acquired both Grattan and Freemans.

Next Directory, on the other hand, continues to grow, benefiting from the branding, buying and logistical synergies of this multi-channel retailer. GUS also looked to a multi-channel solution to arrest its decline, through the acquisition of catalogue showroom trader Argos. A major advantage of the catalogue showroom format is that goods can be selected at home, stock availability checked by telephone, goods then being collected (and inspected) at one of the showrooms, without having to wait for home delivery. The combination of GUS and Argos took the latter into mainstream home shopping, with the option of home deliveries, an expanded catalogue and a presence on digital television.

E-tailing

Electronic retailing has been a long time coming. Commentators were predicting its arrival 35 years ago and, in 1980, Rosenberg and Hirschman presented vivid scenarios of retailing without stores. However, there have been many false dawns for e-tailing, numerous

Figure 30.12 Driving forces and impacts of e-shopping
Source: McGoldrick (2000).

experiments and services having been withdrawn, or failing to meet expectations. The dotcom boom of the late 1990s was followed by harsh re-evaluation of technology stocks from 2000. Porter (2001) concluded that the 'new economy' is in fact the old economy, but with access to new technology: the fundamentals of competition remain the same.

Figure 30.11 summarizes the driving forces behind e-tailing developments, in terms of technology cost/availability, competition factors, consumer demand and regulations upon conventional shops and shopping patterns. Developments are also facilitated by increased acceptance of, and familiarity with, home-based technologies, plus an increased use of remote payment systems. There are, however, some major obstacles, notably concerns about privacy and security, perceived risks in using e-tailers and problems with home deliveries. Figure 30.12 also points to potential areas of social, individual, environmental and commerical impact, if e-shopping becomes very widespread.

However, while the dotcom boom was fuelled largely by 'pure Internet' companies, much of the development that followed was by existing retailers, adopting hybrid channels of marketing and distribution. Thus, Tesco became the world's largest Internet grocer, also exporting its expertise in cost-effective e-tailing to the United States. John Lewis acquired the loss-making UK operations of the US e-tailer buy.com, after which new customers were added at the rate of 3000 per week. Unlike some Internet start-up companies, these well-known retail brands are able to overcome many of the perceived risks associated with e-shopping.

It seems that consumers too are developing hybrid search and shopping behaviours. A US survey of 5000 consumers showed that 34 per cent of store shoppers looked for or purchased something in-store that they had seen on the retailers' website. Likewise, 27 per cent looked for or bought something on-line that they had seen in the store (NRF, 2000). Consequently, while e-tailing may reduce the

utilization of physical stores, it seems unlikely to replace them in most sectors. For most shoppers, 'clicks and bricks' will play complementary roles in helping to fulfil their shopping needs.

References

Aaker, D. A. (1991) *Managing Brand Equity*, Free Press, New York.

Advertising Association (2001) *Lifestyle Pocket Book 2001*, NTC Publications, Henley-on-Thames.

Brown, S. (1987) Institutional change in retailing: a review and synthesis, *European Journal of Marketing*, **21**(6), 5–36.

Brown, S. (1992) *Retail Location: a Micro-Scale Perspective*, Avebury, Aldershot.

Burns, K., Enright, E., Hayes, J., McLaughlin, K. and Shi, C. (1997) The art and science of retail renewal, *McKinsey Quarterly*, **2**, 100–113.

Chain Store Age Executive (1994) Retailing in the 21st Century, *Chain Store Age Executive*, **69**, 12 (Special Edition).

Competition Commission (2000) *Supermarkets: A Report on the Supply of Groceries from Multiple Stores in the United Kingdom*, The Stationery Office, London.

Dabholkar, P. A., Thorpe, D. I. and Rentz, J. O. (1996) A measure of service quality for retail stores: scale development and validation, *Journal of the Academy of Marketing Science*, **24**(1), 3–16.

Davidson, W. R., Bates, A. D. and Bass, S. J. (1976) The retail life cycle, *Harvard Business Review*, **54**(6), 89–96.

Euromonitor (2000) *Retail Trade International*, Euromonitor, London.

Eurostat (1997) *Retailing in the European Economic Area 1996*, Statistical Office of the European Communities, Brussels.

Hahn, B. (2000) Power centres: a new retail format in the United States of America, *Journal of Retailing and Consumer Services*, **7**(4), 223–231.

Ibrahim, M. F. and McGoldrick, P. J. (2002) *Shopping Choices with Public Transport Options: An Agenda for the 21st Century*, Ashgate, Aldershot.

IGD (1999) *Category Management in Action*, Institute of Grocery Distribution, Watford.

Johnson, G. (1987) *Business Strategy and Retailing*, John Wiley, Chichester.

Kaplan, R. S. and Norton, D. P. (1996) Using the balanced scorecard as a strategic management system, *Harvard Business Review*, **74**(1), 75–85.

Key Note (2000a) *Franchising*, Key Note, London.

Key Note (2000b) *Discount Retailing*, Key Note, London.

Koskinen, S. (1999) UK private label: European brand leader?, *European Retail Digest*, **21**, 5–8.

KPMG (2000) *Customer Loyalty & Private Label Products*, KPMG, London.

Liu, H. and McGoldrick, P. J. (1996) International retail sourcing: trend, nature and process, *Journal of International Marketing*, **4**(4), 9–33.

Management Horizons (1999) *Profit from Category Management*, Management Horizons, London.

Management Horizons (2000) *American Dream: High Performance US Retailing*, Management Horizons Europe, London.

McGoldrick, P. J. (1994) *Retail Management Cases*, London.

McGoldrick, P. J. (1998) Spatial and temporal shifts in the development of international retail images, *Journal of Business Research*, **42**, June, 189–196.

McGoldrick, P. J. (2000) The driving forces and impacts of e-tailing, in *Personal Perspectives on 2010*, DTI Foresight, London, pp. 34–38.

McGoldrick, P. J. (2002) *Retail Marketing*, McGraw-Hill, London.

McGoldrick, P. J. and Andre, E. (1997) Consumer misbehaviour: promiscuity or loyalty in grocery shopping, *Journal of Retail and Consumer Services*, **4**(2), 73–81.

McGoldrick, P. J. and Davies, G. (1995) *International Retailing: Trends and Strategies*, Pitman, London.

McGoldrick, P. J. and Greenland, S. J. (1994) *The Retailing of Financial Services*, McGraw-Hill, London.

McGoldrick, P. J. and Thompson, M. G. (1992) *Regional Shopping Centres*, Avebury, Aldershot.

McGoldrick, P. J., Betts, E. and Keeling, K. (2000) High–low pricing: audit evidence and consumer preferences, *Pricing Strategy and Practice*, **9**(5), 316–324.

Michael, S. C. (1999) Do franchised chains advertise enough?, *Journal of Retailing*, **75**(4), 461–478.

Mintel (1999) *Customer Loyalty in Retailing*, Mintel, London.

Mitchell, J. (1978) *Marketing and the Consumer Movement*, McGraw-Hill, London.

Morgan Stanley Dean Witter (2001) *Tesco: We Have Lift Off?* MSDW, London.

National Statistics (2001) *Social Trends*, The Stationery Office, London.

Nielsen (2001) *The Retail Pocket Book*, NTC Publications, Henley-on-Thames.

NRF (2000) *Channel Surfing: Measuring Multi-Channel Shopping*, National Retail Federation, New York.

Porter, M. E. (2001) Strategy and the Internet, *Harvard Business Review*, **79**(3), 63–78.

PricewaterhouseCoopers (2001) Food for thought, *Retail and Consumer Worlds*, **38**(2), special insert.

Rogers, D. (1996) Power retailers in Europe, *European Retail Digest*, **10**, 13–16.

Supphellan, M. (2000) Understanding core brand equity: guidelines for in-depth elicitation of brand associations, *International Journal of Market Research*, **42**(3), 319–338.

Tordjman, A. (1993) *Evolution of Retailing Formats in the EC*, Groupe HEC, Jouy-en-Josas.

Uncles, M. (1995) Securing competitive advantage through progressive staffing policies, *International Journal of Retail & Distribution Management*, **23**(7), 4–6.

Walters, D. and Hanrahan, J. (2000) *Retail Strategy: Planning and Control*, Macmillan, Basingstoke.

Index

Marketing titles from Butterworth-Heinemann

Student List

Creating Powerful Brands (second edition), Leslie de Chernatony and Malcolm McDonald

Direct Marketing in Practice, Brian Thomas and Matthew Housden

eMarketing eXcellence, PR Smith and Dave Chaffey

Fashion Marketing, Margaret Bruce and Tony Hines

Innovation in Marketing, Peter Doyle and Susan Bridgewater

Integrated Marketing Communications, Tony Yeshin

Internal Marketing, Pervaiz Ahmed and Mohammed Rafiq

International Marketing (third edition), Stanley J. Paliwoda and Michael J. Thomas

Key Customers, Malcolm McDonald, Beth Rogers and Diana Woodburn

Marketing Briefs, Sally Dibb and Lyndon Simkin

Marketing in Travel and Tourism (third edition), Victor T. C. Middleton with Jackie R. Clarke

Marketing Plans (fifth edition), Malcolm McDonald

Marketing: the One Semester Introduction, Geoff Lancaster and Paul Reynolds

Market-Led Strategic Change (third edition), Nigel Piercy

Relationship Marketing (second edition), Martin Christopher, Adrian Payne and David Ballantyne

Relationship Marketing for Competitive Advantage, Adrian Payne, Martin Christopher, Moira Clark and Helen Peck

Relationship Marketing: Strategy & Implementation, Helen Peck, Adrian Payne, Martin Christopher and Moira Clark

Strategic Marketing Management (second edition), Richard M. S. Wilson and Colin Gilligan

Strategic Marketing: Planning and Control (second edition), Graeme Drummond and John Ensor

Successful Marketing Communications, Cathy Ace

Tales from the Market Place, Nigel Piercy

The CIM Handbook of Export Marketing, Chris Noonan

The Fundamentals of Advertising (second edition), John Wilmshurst and Adrian Mackay

The Fundamentals and Practice of Marketing (fourth edition), John Wilmshurst and Adrian Mackay

The Marketing Book (fifth edition), Michael J. Baker (ed.)

The New Marketing, Malcolm McDonald and Hugh Wilson

Total Relationship Marketing (second edition), Evert Gummesson

Forthcoming
Marketing Logistics (second edition), Martin Christopher and Helen Peck
Marketing Research for Managers (third edition), Sunny Crouch and Matthew Housden
Marketing Strategy (third edition), Paul Fifield
Political Marketing, Phil Harris and Dominic Wring

Professional List
Cause Related Marketing, Sue Adkins
Creating Value, Shiv S. Mathur and Alfred Kenyon
Cybermarketing (second edition), Pauline Bickerton and Matthew Bickerton
Cyberstrategy, Pauline Bickerton, Matthew Bickerton and Kate Simpson-Holley
Direct Marketing in Practice, Brian Thomas and Matthew Housden
e-Business, J. A. Matthewson
Effective Promotional Practice for eBusiness, Cathy Ace
Essential Law for Marketers, Ardi Kolah
Excellence in Advertising (second edition), Leslie Butterfield
Fashion Marketing, Margaret Bruce and Tony Hines
Financial Services and the Multimedia Revolution, Paul Lucas, Rachel Kinniburgh and Donna Terp
From Brand Vision to Brand Evaluation, Leslie de Chernatony
Go to Market Strategy, Lawrence Friedman
Internal Marketing, Pervaiz Ahmed and Mohammed Rafiq
Marketing Made Simple, Geoff Lancaster and Paul Reynolds
Marketing Professional Services, Michael Roe
Marketing Strategy (second edition), Paul Fifield
Market-Led Strategic Change (third edition), Nigel Piercy
The Channel Advantage, Lawrence Friedman, Tim Furey
The CIM Handbook of Export Marketing, Chris Noonan
The Committed Enterprise, Hugh Davidson
The Fundamentals of Corporate Communications, Richard Dolphin
The Marketing Plan in Colour, Malcolm McDonald and Peter Morris
The New Marketing, Malcolm McDonald and Hugh Wilson

Forthcoming
Marketing Logistics (second edition), Martin Christopher and Helen Peck
Marketing Research for Managers (third edition), Sunny Crouch and Matthew Housden
Marketing Strategy (third edition), Paul Fifield
Political Marketing, Phil Harris and Dominic Wring

For more information on all these titles, as well as the ability to buy online, please visit
www.bh.com/marketing